Saunders College Publishing

Harcourt Brace Jovanovich College Publishers

Fort Worth   Philadelphia   San Diego
New York   Orlando   Austin   San Antonio
Toronto   Montreal   London   Sydney   Tokyo

Jonathan Turk   Amos Turk

Darby, Montana

City College of the City
University of New York

Environmental Science

Fourth Edition

Text Typeface: 10/12 ITC Cheltenham Light
Compositor: The Clarinda Company
Acquisitions Editor: John Vondeling
Project Editor: Becca Gruliow
Copy Editor: Ann Blum
Art Director: Carol Bleistine
Art Assistant: Doris Roessner
Text Designer: Tracy Baldwin
Cover Designer: Lawrence R. Didona
Text Artwork: Tasa Graphic Arts, Inc.
Layout Artist: Copperfield Graphics: Jim Gross
Production Manager: Harry Dean

Cover Credit: Winter whooper swans, © Teiji Saga/Photo Researchers

Printed in the United States of America

ENVIRONMENTAL SCIENCE

ISBN 0-03-016657-8

Library of Congress Catalog Card Number: 87-27524

2   039   987654

Preface

The beginning of the modern environmental movement can be dated from Earth Day, in April of 1970. However, widespread public awareness of environmental issues goes back to much earlier times—to the urban stenches of pre-industrial Europe, the coal smoke of England, and the air pollution episodes of the post World War II era such as those in Donora, Pennsylvania (1948), Poza Rica, Mexico (1950), and the smogs of London and Los Angeles.

Courses and textbooks on environmental science became standard college fare starting in the 1970s; our own first book was published in 1972. Since those years, textbooks as well as the environmental movement have gone through various phases and expressed various viewpoints. Some environmentalists have emphasized the "space-ship Earth" concept, which leads to a "limits to growth" approach. According to this view, control of population and of the exploitation of resources is the key to environmental protection and to the development of a sustainable society. Others disagree, contending that solar energy, the major driving force of the Earth's ecosystems, is sufficiently abundant for present and future human needs and that improvements in the human condition will occur most rapidly if changes are made in political and economic systems.

What approach, then, should a modern text on environmental science take? On this we have a firm viewpoint, which underlies all we write about in this text. Our view is that the central objective is the elucidation of principles, not the advocacy of political policy.

Our major strategy in writing a principles-oriented text is to introduce several major themes in the first two chapters and then apply them throughout the book. Some of these themes include the Tragedy of the Commons, the interplay between social and technical solutions, the role played by the legal system in environmental management, cost/benefit analysis, risk assessment, and natural constraints such as those imposed by the law of conservation of matter and the laws of thermodynamics.

Following the development of these fundamental concepts, the book introduces various types of environmental problems and discusses different possible solutions based on the central themes. The principles are illuminated by a limited number of significant examples that are discussed in some depth. We believe that these examples are sufficiently interesting to "fix" the principles in the students' minds and to motivate them to pursue studies of other topics of regional or personal interest.

We have always attempted to be realistic in discussing the true complexity of the world in which we live without oversimplifying or providing simplistic solutions that really don't work.

In a field as all-encompassing and complex as environmental science, there are many independent topics. In this edition, we have rearranged the book significantly to provide what we feel is the best possible pedagogic sequence. However, individual instructors may choose to alter the order of topics somewhat. For this reason we have organized the book into individually self-contained units, as shown on the following page:

Unit 1   Environmental Science: An Overview

This unit introduces environmental science and its relation to the human condition, discusses the classification of environmental problems, shows how environmental improvement is tied to economic and legal concerns, and discusses how the laws of nature limit our response to environmental challenges.

Unit 2   The Ecological Background

This unit provides a comprehensive look at the biology of natural ecosystems, changes in populations, successional changes, speciation, and an overview of the biosphere.

Unit 3   The Crowding of the Earth

This unit discusses the growth of the human population, problems related to food production and world hunger, the growth of urban centers, rural land use, timber reserves, and the extinction of species.

Unit 4   Resources

This unit discusses problems related to possible depletion of nonagricultural resources: energy, minerals, and water.

Unit 5   Chemicals in the Environment

This unit discusses the environment and human health in relation to hazardous wastes, pesticides and herbicides, water pollution, air pollution, and solid waste disposal.

Special Features of the Fourth Edition

In writing the fourth edition, we have expanded the amount of material incorporated into the book. Although the book is physically larger than the previous edition, we have maintained a similar conceptual level. Only minimal science background is required by the student, and no mathematics is needed to comprehend the concepts presented.

Enrichment Material   The supplementary material has been expanded by the inclusion of numerous additional special topics and boxes, which are set in different type size and interspersed throughout the text. These are presented, for the most part, because they are interesting. Many offer a human outlook that is not necessarily conveyed by a purely didactic approach. However, they are not required for an understanding of the chapter and can be assigned or omitted at the discretion of the instructor.

Chapter Summaries   These summaries highlight the principles of each chapter and can be used for review.

Questions   End-of-chapter questions function in two ways. First, they help students review important points covered in the chapter. Second, they present real-world problems that challenge students to apply what they have learned to the analysis of situations not presented in the text.

Suggested Readings   The references at the end of each chapter are selected to include classic sources, readings at introductory and more advanced levels, and some recent contributions to the field. They are not intended to be exhaustive in scope.

Appendix   The appendix is a reference section on units, various physical concepts, chemical formulas, and calculations of growth rates and of decibel levels.

Glossary   An extensive glossary of terms used in the text is provided at the end of the book.

Take-home Experiments   The various "take home experiments" that appeared in the previous edition, as well as new ones, have been gathered into a supplementary laboratory manual that is provided, free, with the text. These experiments require no more, or very little more, equipment and supplies than are commonly available in a grocery, hobby, or hardware store. Some of the experiments can be used in classroom projects or can serve as springboards for class discussion.

Supplements   Three supplementary items are available to adopters of ENVIRONMENTAL SCIENCE. An instructor's manual provides answers to the questions and two multiple choice tests for each chapter. A set of overhead transparencies containing about 100 illustrations from the text is also available. An environmental computer simulation provides an additional teaching aid.

Acknowledgments

The following reviewers read the manuscript and offered many valuable and incisive suggestions. We benefited from their expertise and are deeply grateful for their help.

John Adams, *University of Texas at San Antonio*
Dudley J. Burton, *Baylor University*
Sanat Dhungel, *Department of National Parks and Wildlife: Nepal*
David Johnson, *Michigan State University*
Frederick Kakis, *Chapman College*
Seymour Katcoff, *Brookhaven National Laboratory*
Stanley Mehlman, *State University of New York*
Richard Meyer, *University of Arkansas*
Gary Miller, *University of North Carolina*
Chris Norment, *Westover School*
Jonas Richmond, *University of California, Berkeley*
Frank Schiavo, *San Jose State University*
Janet Wittes, *National Institute of Health*
Joe Yelderman, *Baylor University*

Pearl Turk and Christine Seashore helped by gathering, editing, and classifying source material and photographs.

The editorial and production staff at Saunders College Publishing did their usual superlative work: John Vondeling, Associate Publisher; Kate Pachuta, Assistant Editor; Becca Gruliow, Project Editor; Carol Bleistine, Art Director.

Jonathan Turk
Amos Turk

Contents Overview

Contents

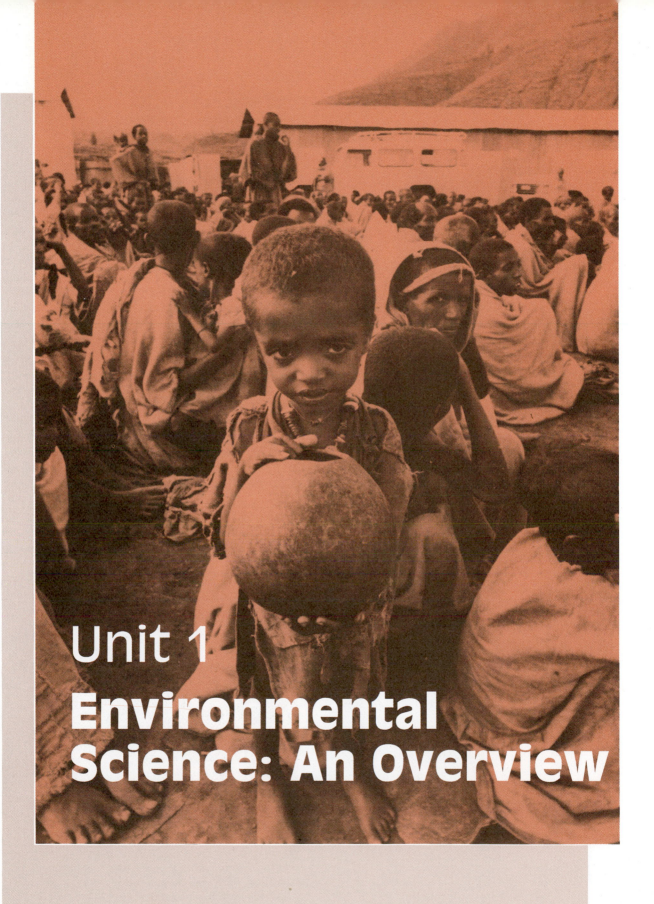

Unit 1
Environmental Science: An Overview

A hungry boy begging in a refugee camp in Ethiopia. (Steve Reynolds, World Vision Communications)

1

Studying the Environment

1.1
Introduction

Almost everyone will agree that our environment is not as pristine or as unspoiled as we would like it to be. You look out the window and note that a haze generated by too much air pollution obscures your view; the noise from a bus or an early morning garbage collection disturbs your peace of mind; the water that you drink has an unsavory taste. Our society is not the first to face environmental problems. Throughout history, people have encountered difficulties related to depletion of resources, pollution, and regional overpopulation. For example, in ancient Greece, the Athenians logged the hills surrounding their cities. The trees were cut to supply the city with firewood, building material, masts for ships, and various other amenities of civilization. After the forests were destroyed, the grasslands were overgrazed by sheep and goats, and, soon thereafter, the rich loamy soils were eroded, leaving behind barren rocky hillsides. Rocky surfaces do not retain water nearly as well as does soil, so the sparse rainfall flowed rapidly downhill. Reservoirs of underground water became depleted, and many natural springs dried up. Thus, the cool, pleasant, productive forests were replaced by zones of dry, barren, unproductive, brush-covered hillsides (Fig. 1–1).

Figure 1–1
The rocky plateau of the ancient Acropolis overlooks modern Athens. The Parthenon *(center),* temple of the goddess Athena, dates from the fifth century B.C. The bare rocky hills lying beyond the city were once forested. (Greek National Tourist Office Photo)

Box 1.1
Ozymandias

I met a traveller from an antique land
Who said: Two vast and trunkless legs of stone
Stand in the desert . . . Near them, on the sand,
Half sunk, a shattered visage lies, whose frown,
And wrinkled lip, and sneer of cold command,
Tell that its sculptor well those passions read
Which yet survive, stamped on these lifeless things,
The hand that mocked them, and the heart that fed:
And on the pedestal these words appear:
"My name is Ozymandias, king of kings:
Look on my works, ye Mighty, and despair!"
Nothing beside remains. Round the decay
Of that colossal wreck, boundless and bare
The lone and level sands stretch far away.
P.B. Shelley (1817)

The desert to which Shelley referred was the Sahara.

in the neighborhood turn brown and die. Residents complain that the smelter is responsible. Yet these complaints, valid as they may be, do not prove cause and effect. The environmental scientist would identify the wastes that are emitted from the smelter and then determine how these wastes affect natural systems.

(3) *Search for scientific solutions to problems that exist.* Once a problem is identified, solutions must be sought. In the example given above, envi-

Box 1.2

Plato, who lived during the height of the period of the deforestation of the Athenian hills, wrote his observations, as quoted below:

"What now remains compared with what then existed is like the skeleton of a sick man, all the fat and soft earth having wasted away, and only the bare framework of the land being left. But at that epoch the country was unimpaired, and for its mountains it had high arable hills, and in place of the "moorlands," as they are now called, it contained plains full of rich soil; and it had much forest-land in its mountains, of which there are visible signs even to this day; for there are some mountains which now have nothing but food for bees, but they had trees not very long ago, and the rafters from those felled there to roof the largest buildings are still sound. And besides, there were many lofty trees of cultivated species; and it produced boundless pasturage for flocks. Moreover, it was enriched by the yearly rains from Zeus, which were not lost to it, as now, by flowing from the bare land into the sea; but the soil it had was deep, and therein it received the water, storing it up in the retentive loamy soil; and by drawing off into the hollows from the heights the water that was there absorbed, it provided all the various districts with abundant supplies of springwaters and streams, whereof the shrines which still remain even now, at the spots where the fountains formerly existed, are signs which testify that our present description of the land is true."

Although ecological disasters such as the deforestation of the Athenian hills were understood by the naturalists of the ancient world, environmental science, as it is practiced today, is a much more complex discipline. The activities of environmental scientists can be divided into four categories.

(1) *Understand the natural world.* The first step is to understand how natural systems operate and maintain themselves. As an example, typical questions that are asked, and must be answered, would include: "Why does a forest grow in one region and a prairie in another?" or "What geological processes have led to the formation of silver deposits, and are these processes likely to repeat themselves in the near future?"

(2) *Identify problems that arise from human interaction with the environment.* A smelter is built at the edge of a city and soon thereafter the trees

ronmental chemists and engineers would examine different types of measures to control the pollution caused by the smelter.

(4) *Implement these solutions.* Theoretical solutions, by themselves, do not improve environmental quality. Continuing the example of the smelter, pollution control measures must actually be built and installed. This final step cannot be completed by the scientists and engineers alone. Because human behavior is governed by political, legal, economic, and social factors as well as by scientific ones, these social sciences are also important to our study.

1.2
The Human Condition

In past eras, life was difficult and short for most people. Then, at the beginning of the twentieth century, rapid progress in medicine, agriculture, and industrial techniques seemed to promise that everyone might soon be able to enjoy long life, decent food, satisfying employment, and adequate housing. This promise has not been realized. In 1987, there were about 5 billion people on Earth. One quarter of them lived in the wealthy, *developed countries,* had a greater life expectancy, and lived in greater luxury than anyone a hundred years ago would have believed possible. At the same time, the remaining three quarters of all people live in poorer regions. The poorest of these are called the *less-developed countries.* Regions that are intermediate between the two extremes are called the *developing countries.* (See Special Topic A.) Within the less-developed countries and even in the developing countries, many people have just enough of the necessities of life to maintain their health. Millions of others live even below this level. According to a study by the World Bank, at least 800 million people—one person in six throughout the world— have a diet that is so limited that they do not have sufficient energy to conduct normal physical activ-

Special Topic A

Developed and Less-Developed Countries

The **developed countries** are considered to be those in which technology is well developed and the standard of living is generally high. Examples include the United States, Canada, Australia, New Zealand, Japan, and all of western Europe. The **less-developed countries** are poorer nations that have not yet fully benefited from the technological advancements of the twentieth century. In these regions, people are often poor and underfed, life ex-pectancy is short, and infant mortality is high. Some examples include Niger in Africa, Bolivia in South America, and Bhutan in Asia. A third class, called the **developing nations** includes those countries that have made a significant start toward modernization but have not yet achieved full success. Mexico is a developing country because many regions are industrialized. However, in the squalid slums of Mexico City and in many impoverished rural regions, extreme poverty is still commonplace.

Country Group	Average Per Capita GNP ($)	Infant Mortality Rate (per 1000 live births)	Life Expectancy (years)	Population with Access to Safe Water (%)	Adult Literacy Rate (%)	Per Capita Public Expense in Health ($)
Less-developed countries	170	160	45	31	28	1.70
Developing countries	525	94	60	41	55	6.50
Developed countries	6,230	19	72	100	98	244

ities. Perhaps more alarming, the World Health Organization estimates that in some of the poorer countries in Africa, Latin America, and Asia, 70 to 80 percent of the children in the population, some 300 million total, have suffered such extreme damage from malnutrition that they will never be able to realize their full genetic potential (Fig. 1–2). With so many people living on the very edge of starvation, it should be no surprise that periodic famines have brought death to millions. In the 1984 to 1985 drought in north Africa, between 2 and 3 million people died of starvation. According to a report by UNICEF (United Nations International Children's Emergency Fund), every day more than 40,000 children die of malnutrition or diseases caused by malnutrition.

Most of the people who starve to death live in poverty-stricken, less-developed nations. But now, at the end of the twentieth century, even the wealthiest nations face serious environmental problems. There is concern about the continued availability of a variety of resources such as oil, timber, soil, pure drinking water, and some minerals. Pollutants contaminate cities, towns, and even rural environments. Sewage or toxic wastes in waterways, smog-laden air, pesticides in the groundwater, and garbage in streets or parks lower the standard of living for everyone, no matter how wealthy.

Our vast and swiftly growing population consumes the Earth's resources of agricultural land, minerals, and fuel faster than natural processes can replace them. This is a serious problem in it-

A

B

Figure 1–2

A, A woman holds her starving child in the Sahel region of North Africa. Today, many people starve to death every year and many more are permanently crippled by malnutrition. (Photo courtesy of Agency for International Development) *B,* A hungry girl searches through a pile of garbage for something to eat in a slum in New Delhi.

Steam and air pollutants from an electrical generating station. (Courtesy of EPA)

Figure 1–3
This house, found in a small village on the Yucatan Peninsula of Mexico, is built out of local materials such as stone, sticks, and grass thatch. Yet the television antenna rising out of the roof provides a positive link with the rest of the world.

self. But global conditions are further endangered because these resources are not distributed evenly. One quarter of the population, those who live in the developed nations, use nearly 80 percent of the resources consumed by humankind in any 1 year. The other three quarters of the population must survive on the remaining 20 percent. People in the United States alone, although they constitute only 5 percent of the Earth's population, use about 35 percent of all raw materials. The gap between the haves and the have-nots is growing wider. Today, when transistor radios are to be found even in the most remote African villages, the world's poor know how underprivileged they are (Fig. 1–3). This knowledge produces political instability. Years ago, political upheaval in one nation meant little to the rest of the world. But times have changed, because modern technology ensures that nearly all nations possess weapons that can wreak havoc far beyond their own borders. As a result, no nation can afford to ignore the problems of another.

1.3
Classifying Environmental Problems

Environmental problems are always interrelated. Sometimes a solution to one problem actually creates another problem. For example, when people are sick and dying from disease, it is natural to want to improve human health. When health is im-

proved and infant mortality is reduced, a population explosion may result. To feed this growing population, natural habitats are often converted into farmland. In turn, the destruction of natural habitats eliminates the native wild plants, predatory animals, and parasites. But, when natural predators and parasites are killed, outbreaks of insect pests become more common. When farmers use pesticides to control the pests and protect the crops, they also pollute the environment. The development of this entire cycle in itself consumes irreplaceable fossil fuel supplies, and, when fuels are burned, air pollutants are generated.

How does a person begin to study such a network of interlocking problems? To make the task a bit more manageable, we will divide environmental disruptions into five main types.

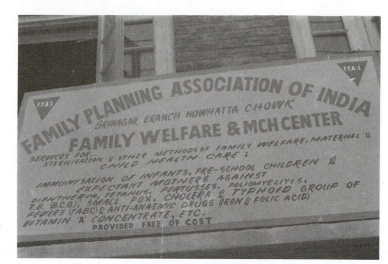

Some densely populated nations view over-population as one of their most devastating problems and encourage small families. This sign appears above a family planning clinic in northern India.

(1) Overpopulation The human population has risen very rapidly in recent years (Fig. 1–4). This increase has led people to ask whether the Earth has become overpopulated. **Overpopulation** may be defined as the presence in a given area of more people than can be supported adequately by the resources available in that area. Many people argue that the population explosion that has taken place in the twentieth century is now

the most important problem we face. It is important first because overpopulation is a major cause of all other environmental problems. Fewer people would need less food, chop down fewer trees, burn less oil, and discharge less sewage into rivers. Second, remedies for overpopulation and the starvation that accompanies it are generally higher on our list of priorities than are other environmental concerns. It is hard to argue that an area should be

Two million years of population growth

Population

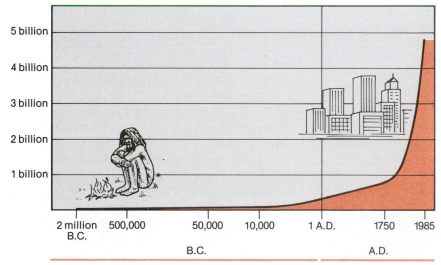

Time line is based on altered logarithmic scale.

Figure 1–4
The growth of the human population. (The time line is based on a logarithmic scale.)

set aside as parkland to preserve a vanishing forest or savanna when that land might be used to raise crops that would prevent fellow human beings from starving to death.

(2) Pollution **Pollution** is a reduction in the quality of the environment by the introduction of impurities.

There are two distinctly different types of pollution.

a. Concentration of Natural Wastes All living organisms produce waste products as an integral part of the act of living. Upon death, the entire organism becomes a waste product. Before modern civilization, most organic wastes did not accumulate in the environment, because they were dispersed sufficiently so that decay organisms could consume and recycle them. Thus, the quality of the environment was not impaired.

In modern times, the organic wastes are often produced in such a concentrated manner that natural decomposition cannot cleanse the environment rapidly enough. For example, a city may house several million people in a small area of land. Organic wastes from such a city are not spread evenly about the countryside but instead are concentrated in a few locations. Sewage that is dumped into a river decays naturally, but the process takes time. If the volume or the concentration of sewage is high, the water may not become purified by the time it reaches the next site downstream where pure drinking water is needed. If several cities line the river and each city discharges its wastes, the river cannot cleanse itself. The result is a loss of many plants and animals that depend on the river and are beneficial to people. Organisms that take their place are often less useful to humans or may even carry disease.

Natural wastes can be inorganic as well as organic. Inorganic wastes would include compounds of elements such as lead, cadmium, and arsenic. These elements exist naturally in the soil and rock all around us and are also present in small concentrations in our bodies. As trace elements, some are harmless, and many are even essential to bodily functions. However, even moderate doses of most inorganic compounds are poisonous. Such substances are often concentrated during mining and smelting operations. For example, many copper deposits contain small amounts of arsenic and other toxic elements. In a natural system, the deposits are usually buried deep underground where they do not enter into biological systems. When they are mined and brought to the surface, the situation changes. The raw materials are crushed, concentrated, and purified. Any mineral that is abundant enough to be extracted profitably is removed, converted to the metal, and sold. The others, which have been inadvertently concentrated to some extent by the entire process, are discarded. These wastes can pollute streams, groundwater supplies, the soil, and the atmosphere. Thus, a natural material that was harmless in its original state can become a pollutant if it is transported and concentrated.

BOX 1.3

For many years, the word **pollute** has meant "to impair the purity of," either morally* or physically.† The terms **air pollution** and **water pollution** refer to the impairment of the normal compositions of air and water by the addition of foreign matter, such as sulfuric acid. Within the past few years, two new expressions, "thermal pollution" and "noise pollution," have become common. Neither of these refers to the impairment of purity by the addition of foreign matter. **Thermal pollution** is the impairment of the quality of environmental air or water by raising its temperature. The relative intensity of thermal pollution cannot be assessed with a thermometer, because what is pleasantly warm water for a man can be death to a trout. Thermal pollution must therefore be appraised by observing the effect of a rise in temperature. Similarly, noise pollution has nothing to do with purity: Foul air can be quiet, and pure air can be noisy. **Noise pollution** (to be discussed in Chapter 18) is the impairment of the environmental quality of air by noise.

*(1857) Buckle, *Civilization*, I, viii, p. 526: "The Clergy . . . urging him to exterminate the heretics, whose presence they thought polluted France."

†(1585) T. Washington. Trans. *Nicholay's Voyage*, IV, ii, p. 115: "No drop of the bloud should fall into the water, least the same should thereby be polluted."

b. Introduction of Synthetic Chemicals into the Environment Everything is made of chemicals, including people, eagles, trees, lakes, and plastics. Although many natural chemical compounds have existed for billions of years, people have recently learned to make new chemical compounds, called **synthetic chemicals.** In 1985, 70,000 different synthetic chemicals were produced in quantity for common use, and about 2000 new compounds have been entering the environment every year since then. They are present in paints, dyes, food additives, drugs, pesticides, fertilizers, fire retardants, building materials, clothes, cleaning supplies, cosmetics, plastics, and so on. Just before the beginning of World War II, production of synthetic chemicals in the United States totaled less than 0.5 billion kg per year. By 1985, that annual total had jumped to over 80 billion kg.

Synthetic chemicals are noted for the variety of their properties. Some of them are drugs that save millions of lives every year, and others are poisons. But because most of them are new to the environment, the traditional patterns of decay and recycling do not necessarily apply. Some synthetic chemicals break down rapidly in the environment by the action of sunlight, air, water, or soil, and some are eaten by living organisms. Such processes may take place over a span of minutes, hours, or days. A material that decomposes in the environment as a result of biological action is said to be **biodegradable.**

Most natural organic wastes are biodegradable while many synthetic chemicals are not. For example, plastics remain in the environment for a long time because organisms that feed on them and break them down are rare. (Scientists have bred bacteria that do decompose a few plastics.) Plastic shampoo bottles may produce unsightly litter, but they are not biologically active. However, many other chemical compounds not only are persistent but also are poisonous and, therefore, represent a significant threat to the environment.

(3) Depletion of Resources A **resource** is any source of raw materials. Fuels, minerals, water, soil, and timber are all resources. A material is depleted, or used up, as it becomes less available for its intended function. Material resources can become depleted in three different ways.

First, a substance can be **destroyed,** that is, converted into something else. Fuels are destroyed when they are used: Coal is converted to ashes and gas; uranium is converted to radioactive waste products. The ashes or waste products are no longer fuels.

Second, a substance can be lost by being **diluted,** or by being **displaced** to some location from which it cannot easily be recovered. If you open a helium-filled balloon, the gas escapes to the atmosphere. Not one atom of helium is destroyed, but the gas is lost because it would be impossible, as a practical matter, to recover it. The same concept of loss by dilution applies to minerals. Today, iron becomes profitable to mine when the rock and soil contain about 40 percent iron. However, iron is also widely dispersed throughout the crust of the Earth and even in the ocean, where its concentration is about one millionth of 1 percent. These sources of iron are useless as minerals because it would take far too much energy and equipment to recover them. When products containing iron, such as automobiles or paper clips, are thrown away, the metal rusts. The rust is iron oxide, which could be reprocessed to produce iron again. The iron atoms are never lost or destroyed.* However, some of the old automobile hulks (and almost all of the paper clips) are scattered so widely over the countryside that it is uneconomical to find and collect them. It is in this way that our reserves of iron are being depleted.

Third, a substance can be rendered unfit for use by being **polluted.** In this way, pollution and depletion are related to each other. If industrial or agricultural wastes are discharged into a stream or if they percolate down through soil and porous rock to reach a supply of groundwater, these water resources become less fit for drinking or, in the case of the stream, for recreation or for the support of aquatic life.

(4) Changes in the Global Condition
a. Climate The environment of the Earth has fluctuated throughout geologic time. The global climate has changed on numerous occasions, mountains have risen and fallen, even the chemical composition of the atmosphere itself has changed radically. However, over the past 150 years or so— a mere instant in geological time—humans have

---

*Atoms are not destroyed or transformed in chemical reactions. Nuclear reactions are quite different.

Special Topic B

Depletion of Resources

Seven crucial areas of resource depletion are briefly summarized in the following paragraphs. The problems are discussed in more detail in appropriate sections throughout the text.

Soil.   Soil erosion is currently exceeding soil formation on 35 percent of the world's cropland. The global loss amounts to an estimated 7 percent of the total topsoil per decade. Soil erosion is most severe in Africa, where 40 percent of the population lives in regions where land productivity is lower than it was a generation ago.

Forests.   The world's tropical forests are disappearing at a rate of 2 percent per year. The depletion rate is far faster in West Africa and southeast Asia, where many forests will be virtually destroyed by the end of the century if current trends continue. In the temperate regions, forests are succumbing to the effects of various types of air pollution, specifically acid rain.

Grasslands.   The destruction of grasslands is closely related to the loss of forests and soils. Economic pressures lead to overexploitation of the resource and to eventual destruction. In some regions of North Africa, in particular, entire herds are dying or being killed because it is impossible to feed them.

Fisheries.   During the 1950s and 1960s, there was a rapid increase in global fish harvest per person (called the **per capita harvest**). However, overfishing has led to the depletion of many fisheries. Per capita catch declined 15 percent between 1970 and 1986.

Water.   The demand for water is exceeding sustainable supplies in many locations. As a result, there has been a recent widespread trend toward utilizing essentially nonrenewable reserves of groundwater, often called **fossil water.**

Oil.   The price and availability of petroleum have fluctuated widely over the past few decades. These fluctuations are based on immediate political and economic factors. However, the physical reality remains: Petroleum reserves are nonrenewable and are being consumed at a rapid rate.

Minerals.   The immediate availability of mineral reserves, like the availability of oil, is linked with global economics and politics. However, once again, the resources are being consumed. In the case of minerals, after the richest mines are depleted, there are large reserves of low-grade ores that can be extracted if we have the energy and are willing to pay the price.

Note: Many of the statistics given in this special section are global averages and do not account for large regional differences in performance (see Section 1.6).

---

significantly altered the chemistry of our environment. Today, many scientists believe that these changes might affect the life support systems of the Earth. For example, when fossil fuels are burned, carbon dioxide is released. In turn, the excess atmospheric carbon dioxide could possibly cause a general warming of the entire Earth. Many other types of human activities might also affect climate. Deforestation could affect global rates of photosynthesis and, therefore, the composition of the atmosphere; industrial dust may contribute to a global warming; and aerosol sprays and aircraft exhaust may be destroying the ozone layer in the atmosphere that filters out ultraviolet radiation.

b. Extinction of Species   Throughout much of the world, forests, shrublands, and other natural systems are being converted to farmland. When habitats are destroyed, many organisms cannot survive. Therefore hundreds of thousands of species of plants and animals are faced with extinction. People often do not know precisely what has been lost when a species becomes extinct. Scientists are convinced that endangered species of plants or animals should be saved to preserve the genetic diversity of our planet. Some of these species are especially important, because they may produce life-saving drugs or may be essential in breeding valuable crops or domestic animals.

(5) War   In many ways, war is a combination of all environmental problems rather than a separate category. In modern times, war and the preparation

A hydrogen bomb explosion. Nuclear war has the potential to be the ultimate ecological disaster. (Photograph by H. Armstrong Roberts)

for war have led to pollution and depletion of resources far more extreme than any single peacetime activity. The devastation caused by outright hostilities is obvious. People are killed, cities and farms are ruined, and forested regions are destroyed. But even in the absence of actual conflict, the cost of maintaining armaments and standing armies is enormous (Fig. 1–5).

Finally, the potential for a nuclear war places the global systems of the Earth, human civilization, and even the human species itself at risk.

1.4
The Tragedy of the Commons

The Sahel is a broad band of semidesert extending across North Africa just south of the Sahara desert. It is a zone of sparse grasslands inhabited traditionally by nomadic herders and their livestock. In modern times, the populations of both humans and animals have risen significantly, and, as a result, the region has suffered severe ecological disruption. Pasturelands have been overgrazed, and, as

Figure 1–5
Military expenditures in the United States.

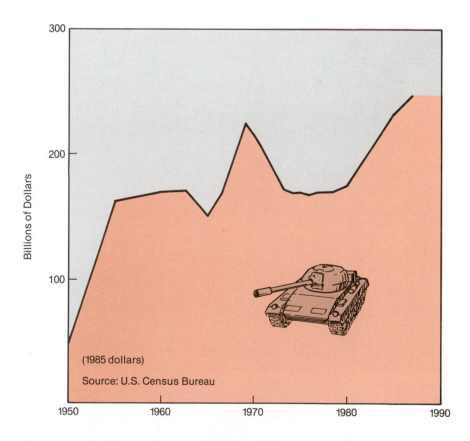

Billions of Dollars

(1985 dollars)

Source: U.S. Census Bureau

the plant cover has been removed, the land has dried up and summer winds have blown the meager topsoil away. Thus, in many areas, semidesert pasture has been converted into true desert. In turn, the destruction of the land has led to human tragedy: Extreme poverty and starvation have become commonplace in the Sahel (Fig. 1–6).

The sequence of events just described is a classic example of a biological catastrophe that was caused by social factors. Any pasture has an intrinsic ability to support a certain number of animals. The number of animals that can live on a sustained basis in a given region is called the **carrying capacity.** If the population of animals remains below the carrying capacity, the grasses will grow faster than they are being eaten and the pasture will remain healthy, whereas if the carrying capacity is exceeded, the grasslands will be destroyed.

Most of the Sahel is a commons, a community grazing land open, without restriction, to all. In these regions, there is very little private ownership of land. Now, imagine that you are a herder in the

Sahel at a time when the total population of livestock has just reached the carrying capacity of the land. Suppose, further, that you have an opportunity to buy five more animals. Let us also assume that you are aware of the concept of carrying capacity and understand the dangers of overgrazing. You ask yourself, should you or should you not add five more animals to your herd? Since the additional animals would be five beyond the total carrying capacity, your entire herd would have just a little less food to eat. But this loss would be trivial compared with the net gain of the additional animals. The reason for this favorable balance is that the gain would be all yours, but the loss would be shared by all the herders. Balancing *your* gain against *your* loss, you decide to take on the additional animals. This is a selfish decision, to be sure, but economically it is the most profitable choice, and it is the path that many people actually take.

A problem arises, however, because every other herder is likely to make the same decision. The net result is that if each person tries to maxi-

Figure 1–6
The effects of overgrazing and drought in the Sahel region of North Africa.
(Courtesy of Alain Nogues, Sygma)

mize his or her personal profit, the pasture becomes overgrazed and all the cattle starve—everyone loses. Garrett Hardin has called this sequence of events "The Tragedy of the Commons."*

In the early 1970s, at the height of a recent drought, satellite photographs showed a large green area in the middle of the brownish sands. This region was a private ranch encompassing a quarter of a million acres. The boundary was fenced, and, within the ranch itself, the grazing land was divided into five sections. The total number of cattle was regulated, and they were moved from one section to another to allow the grasses to regenerate. As a result of this careful control, the farm not only survived, but prospered. The point here is that a person who will suffer the direct consequences of an irresponsible act is likely to practice conservation. On the other hand, a person who can pass most of the consequences of an irresponsible act onto others is less likely to act in the best interests of society as a whole.

While the concept of a commons was originally defined in terms of grazing lands, the example is general; our air, our water, and our resources can also be considered to be commons. Although there are certainly some persons or groups of people who will voluntarily sacrifice personal gain for the good of society, this type of behavior has not been the rule over the broad range of human activ-

*See Garrett Hardin and John Baden, *Managing the Commons,* listed in the bibliography.

Its takes time and effort to bring cans to a recycling center, and so most people don't do it. If one pays consumers even a small amount to return cans, this enormously increases the number of cans that are recycled.

ity. Thus, for example, the owner of a smoky factory might be reluctant to install expensive air pollution control equipment. Then the entire society must pay for the degradation of the environment. The owner also pays a share of this environmental loss, but this cost is trivial compared with the amount of money saved by operating a polluting factory. Of course, if everyone acts in the same manner, an ecological catastrophe, analogous to the destruction of the Sahel, will occur. This dilemma, and possible solutions to it, will be discussed further in Chapter 2.

1.5
Frontier Economics or a Sustainable Society

Think for a moment of how the early pioneers felt as they pushed westward into the wilderness of North and South America. The continents were just so large, the forests so dense, and the prairies so bountiful that it seemed as though people could take whatever they wanted, whenever they wanted, and however they wanted, without destroying or diminishing the productivity of the land. This feeling gave rise to what has been called **frontier economics,** which is, in effect, the economics of limitless, uncontrolled consumption.

As long as the human population is small in relation to the available land and as long as the technology of resource extraction is relatively inefficient, frontier economics is a rational and productive way to obtain the necessities of life. The situation is analogous to a situation in which a person had access to an unlimited bank account. A rational person with an infinite bank account would withdraw money without bothering to compute the sums. However, the Earth's resources are limited, not infinite, and, when populations grow and technology improves, the frontier mentality can lead to disaster.

The Numbers Game

Humans or humanoid beings have been on the Earth for roughly 3 or 4 million years. However, it was not until about the year 1800 that the human population reached 1 billion. One hundred thirty years later, in 1930, the population had doubled to 2 billion, and, only 45 years after that, by 1975, the next doubling to 4 billion had occurred. Thus, the

Table 1–1
What Would Happen if the Human Population Continued to Increase as Rapidly as it Had Between 1930 and 1975?

Year	Population	Number of Years Required for Doubling (assuming that every doubling occurs in 1/3 the time in which the last doubling occurred)	
1800	1 billion		
		130	
1930	2 billion		1/3
		45 (approx)	
1975	4 billion		1/3
		15	
1990	8 billion		1/3
		5	
1995	16 billion		1/3
		1.7	
1996.7	32 billion		1/3
		0.5	
1997.2	64 billion		1/3
		0.2	
1997.4	128 billion		1/3
		0.06	
1997.5	256 billion		
July 1997	More than one person per square meter over the entire surface of the Earth		

last doubling occurred in roughly one third the time as the previous one. Now, for the sake of argument, let's make the assumption that this historical trend will continue. In other words, each future doubling will require one third the time required for the previous doubling. In order to simplify the arithmetic, let us start at January 1, 1975, with a population of 4 billion. Following our projections, we find that the population would be 8 billion by January 1, 1990 (1975 + 15), 16 billion by 1995, and more than 32 billion by January 1, 1997 (see Table 1–1). By about July 1 of 1997, there would be more than one person per square meter over the entire surface of the Earth (including the oceans and Antarctica).

Consider another calculation. The annual consumption of petroleum in the United States doubled between 1948 and 1970. If energy consumption were to continue to double every 22 years, 660 years from now, the people in the world would consume as much petroleum every year as there is water in all the world's oceans.

Are these calculations absurd? Well, yes and no. Obviously the Earth cannot support one person per square meter, and obviously fuel consumption cannot continue to grow at such rates of increase, so, in one sense, the projections just outlined are absurd. But the point of the argument is that current trends of consumption and growth cannot continue for long. Some change must occur. The change may occur sooner or later, peacefully or violently, gradually or catastrophically, but change is inevitable.

If human societies are to exist for long periods of time, the frontier mentality must eventually be replaced by the ethics of a **sustainable society.** In a sustainable society, goods are used only as fast as they can be replenished. As a result,

**Box 1.4
A Riddle**

Riddle: Assume that the area covered by lily plants in a lake doubles in size every day. If allowed to grow freely, the plants would cover the entire surface of the pond in 30 days. As an individual, you decide to ignore the problem until the pond is half covered. Then you will take actions to reduce the plant cover so that the lake isn't entirely choked off. On what day will the pond be half covered, and how much time will you have to avert disaster?

Answer: The pond will be half covered in 29 days and you have only 1 day to act.

there is no net impoverishment of the land. Returning to our analogy of money in the bank, such a society would live off the interest, not the principal.

1.6
Predicting the Future: Uncertainty and Controversy

The argument illustrated by the calculations performed in the previous section is not new. In 1789, Thomas Robert Malthus, an English clergyman and economist, published an *Essay on the Principle of Population.* In this essay, he argued that populations, which can grow exponentially, tend to grow faster than food supplies, which can grow only arithmetically. Therefore, he predicted, any uncontrolled population would eventually outstrip its food supply. (See Appendix E for a discussion of arithmetic and geometric growth rates.)

Malthus predicted that change would be accompanied by "misery and vice." He wrote:

By that law of our nature which makes food necessary to the life of man, the effects of these two unequal powers must be kept equal.

This implies a strong and constantly operating check on population from the difficulty of subsistence. This difficulty must fall somewhere and must necessarily be severely felt by a large portion of mankind.

. . . The race of plants and the race of animals shrink under this great restrictive law. And the race of man cannot, by any efforts of reason, escape

from it. Among plants and animals its effects are waste of seed, sickness, and premature death. Among mankind, misery and vice.

Malthus' pessimistic predictions have not been realized as yet, because technical advancements have increased agricultural productivity faster than he had thought possible. Yet the core of his premise cannot be ignored.

Almost 200 years later, in 1980, a committee appointed by President Carter published the *Global 2000 Report.* This document was largely a warning. The following excerpts are taken from the introduction:

If present trends continue, the world in 2000 will be more crowded, more polluted, less stable ecologically, and more vulnerable to disruption than the world we live in now. Serious stresses involving population, resources, and environment are clearly visible ahead. Despite greater material output, the world's people will be poorer in many ways than they are today.

. . . Regional water shortages will become more severe.

. . . Significant losses of world forests will continue over the next 20 years as demand for forest products and fuelwood increases. . . .The world's forests are now disappearing at the rate of 18 to 20 million hectares a year (an area half the size of California), with most of the loss occurring in the humid tropical forests of Africa, Asia, and South America.

Serious deterioration of agricultural soils will occur worldwide, due to erosion, loss of organic matter, desertification, salinization, alkalinization, and waterlogging. Already, an area of cropland and grassland approximately the size of Maine is becoming barren wasteland each year. . . .

Atmospheric concentrations of carbon dioxide and ozone-depleting chemicals are expected to increase at rates that could alter the world's climate and upper atmosphere significantly by 2050. Acid rain from increased combustion of fossil fuels (especially coal) threatens damage to lakes, soils, and crops. Radioactive and other hazardous materials present health and safety problems in increasing numbers of countries.

Extinctions of plant and animal species will increase dramatically. Hundreds of thousands of species—perhaps as many as 20 percent of all species on earth—will be irretrievably lost as their habitats vanish, especially in tropical forests.

The final paragraph, which follows, echoes the "misery and vice" predicted by Malthus:

Vigorous, determined new initiatives are needed if worsening poverty and human suffering, environmental degradation, and international tension and conflicts are to be prevented. There are no quick fixes.

Is there any way out? Reread the first phrase of the first sentence of the report carefully. It states, "If present trends continue . . . "

The previous calculations ensure that present trends cannot possibly continue indefinitely. But the key question remains unanswered, "Will human society change in an orderly manner, or will it fail to adapt until it is faced with a major calamity?" Another way to phrase the same question is, "Are we living along a smooth continuum of adaptation and change where minor disruptions are balanced by development and innovation? Or, alternatively, is the twentieth century a turning point, an era of crisis where human actions are threatening our very existence?"

Some people believe that we are rapidly approaching a crisis. They argue that today the human population is so much larger than it has ever been and that the technological potential to change the Earth is so many orders of magnitude greater than ever before that a very real disaster is possible, or even probable.

The other argument is that there have always been environmental problems and that solutions have always been found. According to this viewpoint, human ingenuity and adaptation should not be underestimated. As an example, consider the availability of fuel resources over the past few hundred years. In the seventeenth and eighteenth centuries, charcoal made from wood was the fuel used for the smelting of iron. Consequently, large tracts of forests were cut to supply the charcoal industry. Coal was available, but raw coal cannot be used to reduce iron ores. As the industrial revolution began to intensify, the specter of timber depletion became a serious consideration. However, before an energy crisis became acute, a process was discovered whereby coal can be converted to a fuel called **coke,** which is ideal for refining iron. Thus, calamity was temporarily averted through substitution of one fuel for another. However, a second crisis arose shortly after the use of coke became commonplace. Although Britain had abundant coal deposits, many lay deep underground. When miners attempted to extract this coal, the pits would fill with water and the hand-operated pumps avail-

able at the time could not drain the water fast enough. Again the threat of scarcity arose. However, in 1712, the steam pump was invented, and suddenly it became possible to mine many new coal deposits. Thus, once again, technology came to the rescue.

In the twentieth century, petroleum has replaced coal for many uses. Note from Figure 1–7 that the price of oil has declined dramatically over the past 50 years, despite some small fluctuations in the curve. This decline has resulted from a long series of technological advancements that have led to increased efficiency in the drilling and refining of petroleum.

The Global Possible

Which viewpoint is correct? Are we facing an unprecedented global crisis, or, alternatively, will human ingenuity solve the problems that we face before a monumental disruption to society occurs? In a book entitled *The Global Possible* edited by Robert Repetto (see bibliography), the author writes, "There are ample grounds in experience for both optimistic and pessimistic assumptions." He goes on to say that global statistics represent an average of the most and the least successful strategies. Thus, the numbers can hide the true complexity of the issues. He writes, "The gap between the best performance and failure is enormous." If we study the successes, we have reason to hope. If we pro-

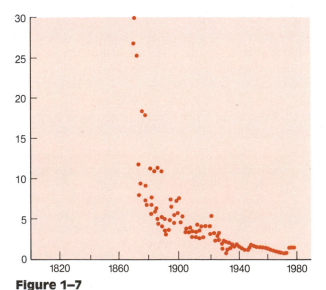

Figure 1–7

The price of oil relative to wages. (Julian Simon)

ject continuation of the failures, we can predict doom. For example, in the less-developed countries, excluding China, human population is now growing at a rate of 2 percent per year. Predictions based on a continuation of that trend are liable to be pessimistic. On the other hand, consider the case of Cuba. Even though Cuba is still primarily an agricultural society, the growth rate dropped from 2.5 percent in 1960 to 1.0 percent in 1985. During that time, birthrates dropped so dramatically that the population is stabilizing.

In the less-developed countries, per capita food production rose by a modest 10 percent between 1960 and 1985, and the rate of growth is declining. Once again, the overall trend can lead to pessimism. But during the same time period, India and China have become self reliant in cereal pro-

duction. In Sri-Lanka, per capita food production increased 54 percent. The global averages are so low, because many regions in Africa have shown a decline in the last few decades.

Repetto goes on to say ". . . examples of success demonstrate how much better the record would be if the policies and actions underlying those successes were followed more universally. The failures are reminders of the probable consequences if wrong policies are pursued."

There are no quick answers to the issues raised here, but surely the first step forward is to understand the technological, economic, social, and political components of our environmental problems. A more complete education is certainly an essential foundation for any intelligent action.

Summary

Although many people are better off today than ever before in human history, many others are so poor that they cannot live healthy lives, and others are dying of starvation or starvation- related diseases.

The major environmental problems can be divided into five main categories: (1) **overpopulation,** which causes human suffering directly and amplifies all other environmental problems; (2) **pollution,** which makes vital resources less useful and reduces the quality of life; (3) **depletion of resources,** which makes things that are vital to human existence more expensive or impossible to obtain; (4) **global changes,** which result from human activities and may permanently alter the Earth in unpredictable ways; (5) **war,** which may be caused by or may cause all other environmental problems—modern warfare threatens the survival of the human species.

Individuals act in ways that promote their own short-term welfare, which often conflicts directly with the long-term environmental interests of present and future generations. This "tragedy of the commons" is the main factor that limits the effectiveness of voluntary action as a solution to environmental problems.

We are assured that the trends that have been observed over the past 50 years cannot continue for the next 50 years. However, there is considerable disagreement about what the future will bring.

Questions

An Overview of Environmental Problems

1. List three types of environmental disruptions that have the potential for long-range degradation of the environment.

2. Identify an environmental problem that is current in your neighborhood. Discuss, very briefly, the nature of the problem, the potential damage done, and the types of actions that could be taken to reverse the degradation.

3. The five major types of environmental disruptions were listed as a series of isolated topics. Explain how each one of them may be related to one or more of the other four in certain circumstances.

4. Consider the following definition of the word **pollution.** Pollution is the introduction of waste products into the environment. Compare this definition with the one in the text. Give an example of an action that would be pollution according to the definition given here but that would not be considered to be pollution according to the definition given in the text. Discuss the differences.

5. Today, people talk about the depletion of soil and timber resources. What is meant by the word **depletion** is these two contexts?

6. Which class of environmental problems is represented by each of the following examples: (a) An aluminum beer can is thrown in the garbage; (b) the ash from a volcanic eruption rises into the upper atmosphere, blocks sunlight, and cools the Earth; (c) emergency food donations that were shipped to a famine-stricken area are intercepted by a local dictator, and, as a result, many people in the relief camps starve to death; (d) pesticides are sprayed onto a forest to control the spruce budworm, a pest that kills spruce trees. Some of the pesticides are ingested by bald eagles, whose reproductive rates decline sharply.

7. Which substance would be least likely to be degraded in natural systems: human sewage, agricultural wastes such as manure and rotten straw, cotton clothes, or a chemical herbicide used to control the growth of weeds?

Tragedy of the Commons

8. Suggest one action that you personally might take to help preserve the environment. How do you assess the importance of your own action? How would you estimate the number of people who would have to join you before the action would have a significant environmental impact?

9. Apply the "tragedy of the commons" principle to one of the environmental problems introduced in this chapter.

10. In the United States, about 54 percent of the aluminum beverage cans are recycled. On the scrap market, aluminum was worth $.20 per pound in 1987. Make an estimate of the number of aluminum cans that would be recycled if the scrap value were: zero, $.50 per pound, $1.00 per pound, $5.00 per pound. Discuss your estimates with your classmates.

11. In the United States today, many farmers are losing considerable quantities of soil to erosion. Yet, agricultural yields remain high because the losses can be balanced by increased application of fertilizers. Is this an example of the "tragedy of the commons?" If your answer is no, defend your reasoning. If your answer is yes, what is the commons, and how is this situation similar to that of the overgrazing of the Sahel?

Looking into the Future

12. Prepare a class debate, with one side arguing the "doomsday" forecast, that the human condition will be much worse in the year 2000 than it is today, and the other side taking the opposite view, that conditions on Earth will improve.

Suggested Readings

A discussion of ecological disruptions in Mediterranean civilizations is given in:

J. Donald Hughes: *Ecology in Ancient Civilizations.* Albuquerque, University of New Mexico Press, 1975. 181 pp.

Several books that offer an overview of the human condition at the present time are:

John Allen (ed.): *Environment 85/86.* Guilford, CT, Dushkin Publishing Group, 1985. 241 pp.

"Ambio, Journal of the Human Environment." Vol. XII:2 1983. Stockholm, Pergamon Press, 1983. 137 pp.

Lester R. Brown, Christopher Flavin, Cynthia Pollock, Sandra Postel, Linda Starke, and Edward C. Wolf: *State of the World 1986.* New York, W. W. Norton Company Ltd., 1986. 263 pp.

Lynton Keith Caldwell: *International Environmental Policy, Emergence and Dimensions.* Durham, North Carolina, Duke University Press, 1984.

W. C. Clark and R. E. Munn: *Sustainable Development of the Biosphere.* New York, Cambridge University Press, 1986.

John Harte: *Consider a Spherical Cow . . . Concepts in Environmental Problem Solving.* Los Altos, CA, William Kaufmann, Inc., 1985. 304 pp.

OECD (Organization for Economic Co-operation and Development): *The State of the Environment 1985.* Paris, 1985. 271 pp.

William Ophuls: *Ecology and the Politics of Scarcity.* San Francisco, W. H. Freeman and Company, 1977. 303 pp.

Langdon Winner: *The Whale and the Reactor: A Search for Limits in an Age of High Technology.* Chicago, University of Chicago Press, 1986.

The thought-provoking argument that the environmentally ethical individual is doomed is introduced and discussed in the following works:

G. Hardin: The tragedy of the commons. *Science,* 162:1243, 1968.

Garrett Hardin: "Crisis on the Commons" from *Filters Against Folly: How to Survive Despite Economists, Ecologists, and the Merely Eloquent.* New York, Viking Press, 1986.

Garrett Hardin and John Baden (eds.): *Managing the Commons.* San Francisco, W. H. Freeman, 1977. 294 pp.

One interesting book that introduces both sides of several environmental controversies is:

Theodore D. Goldfarb: *Taking Sides: Clashing Views on Controversial Environmental Issues.* 2nd ed. Guilford, CT, Dushkin Publishing Group, 1987. 323 pp.

The Global 2000 report can be found in:

Gerald O. Barney (director): *The Global 2000 Report.* New York, Pergamon Press, 1980. (Vol. I, *Summary Report;* Vol. II, *Technical Report;* Vol. III, *Government Global Model*). 360 pp.

The argument that human adaptation and change will avert disaster is given in:

Julian L. Simon: *The Ultimate Resource.* Princeton, NJ, Princeton University Press, 1981. 415 pp.

Julian Simon and Herman Kahn: *The Resourceful Earth.* Oxford, Basil Blackwell Ltd., 1984. 585 pp.

A book that discusses historical trends in the interplay between technology and environmental problems:

Antoni Maczak and William N. Parker (eds.): *Natural Resources in European History.* Washington, D.C., Resources for the Future, 1978.

Many books predict future trends in environmental issues. A few of these are:

Robert Cahn (ed.): *An Environmental Agenda for the Future.* Washington, D.C., Island Press, 1985. 155 pp.

Robert Repetto (ed.): *The Global Possible Resources, Development, and the New Century.* New Haven, CT, Yale University Press, 1985. 583 pp.

Robert Repetto: *World Enough and Time.* New Haven, CT, Yale University Press, 1986. 147 pp.

Francis R. Thibodeau and Hermann H. Field (eds.): *Sustaining Tomorrow a Strategy for World Conservation and Development.* Hanover, University Press of New England, 1984.

2

Environmental Improvement: An Interplay of Social and Technological Problems

2.1
There Are No Easy Answers
In the Less-Developed Countries

Nepal is one of the poorer countries of the world, with an average per capita income of only about $125 per year. Yet it is a peaceful country and incredibly beautiful and varied. The geography ranges from hot tropical forests inhabited by rhinoceroses and tigers to the high peaks of the Himalayan range. Altogether, more than three fourths of the country is mountainous. Even in the foothills, the terrain is steep, and very little level land is available. One of the major problems in Nepal stems from a shortage of fuel. In general, village farmers are too poor to purchase fossil fuels such as kerosene, so almost all of them rely on wood or animal dung as a primary source of energy. In recent years, the demand for firewood has become so high that forests are being cut faster than they are being replenished. As a result, many hillsides have been stripped of their vegetation and therefore exposed to erosion during the severe summer monsoons.*

Now let us focus our attention on an individual Nepali family living in one of the lower elevation foothills. Typically, the house will be built of adobe (dried mud), or sticks, depending on the location, and topped with a thatched roof made of grass. If you entered at dinner time, you would find the family squatting around an open fire in the middle of the central room. There would be no chimney, and the entire room might easily be smoky enough to make your eyes water.

A few years ago, Peace Corps workers from the United States noted that the open fires are not only unhealthy but also inefficient. If a simple cook stove were built, wood consumption could be reduced by one third, and use of a chimney would eliminate the smoke problem. Villagers were educated, materials were collected, and stoves were built. However, within a year, an unforeseen disaster occurred. People's roofs began to fall apart. The reason: In the wet, tropical monsoon environment, there are a host of decay organisms present that are capable of consuming the dry grass of the roof thatch. In the old system, the smoke from the fires filtered up through the thatch and repelled the de-

*Forests are also being cut to provide new areas for cultivation. This subject will be discussed further in Chapter 8.

The mountains of Nepal are the highest in the world and attract many climbers and tourists. However, the steep hillsides are difficult to farm and prone to erosion. When forests are cut for fuel wood, the monsoon rains frequently wash entire hillsides away.

cay organisms, thus preserving the roof. With the advent of chimneys and the effective channeling of the smoke, decay was rapid and the roofs collapsed.

In the Developed Countries

Whereas most environmental problems in the less-developed countries originate out of difficulties in meeting the needs of survival, in the developed countries, problems often arise from too much wealth. In the United States, people are affluent enough to produce goods that are used for a short period of time and then thrown away. The problem is, where do you put the trash? In New York City, for example, 25,000 tonnes of refuse are collected every day, more than 8 million tonnes a year (see Box 2.1 for a definition of a tonne). The simplest solution is to bury the trash on land, but landfills require large areas of vacant ground that lie conveniently close to metropolitan centers. These requirements are not easy to fulfill, because property is scarce and expensive in the New York City area. A few alternatives are available and are being studied. One alternative is to burn the trash and use the energy to produce electricity. An incineration system of this type could conceivably reduce a solid waste problem, save money, and conserve fossil fuel supplies, all at the same time. Therefore, planning is under way for the construction of five incinerators that will burn about half the city's trash. If

A small village in the mountains of Nepal.

Box 2.1

One tonne means 1 metric ton, or 1000 kg, and equals about 2205 lb, which is larger than the short ton (2000 lb) usually referred to in the British system of units. Metric units are used throughout this book and are reviewed in Appendix A.

all of these incinerators were operating to full capacity, they would produce 30 percent of the total electricity needed for commercial buildings in New York.

Without studying the system in detail, it might appear that trash incinerators would benefit everyone. Yet many environmentalists object to the projects. Why? All municipal garbage contains large quantities of various types of plastics. When plastics are burned in air, the original materials are destroyed. The heat breaks the large molecules apart, and the molecular fragments then recombine to form new, smaller, more stable molecules. Many of these compounds are benign, such as carbon dioxide and water. On the other hand, there are other waste products that are real troublemakers. One of these is **dioxin,** an acute poison, as well as a suspected carcinogen (see Chapter 18). Air pollution control equipment used for incinerator exhausts can remove most of the dioxin, but not all of it. Planning problems arise because (1) no one can predict exactly how much dioxin will be released by the New York incinerators, which are now only in the planning stage, and (2) no one really knows how harmful low level dioxin contamination really is. So the question remains, how do you get rid of the garbage? Do you accept some dioxin contamination in return for the benefits of the incinerators, or do you look for some other solution?

We tell these stories to emphasize an important point in environmental science. Many systems are much more complex than they appear to be after a casual analysis. Global environments are complex. Sometimes a solution to one problem creates new problems that didn't exist in the first place. It is often desirable to implement change, but it is not always possible to change any one part of the system without affecting the whole. There are no simple answers.

2.2
Social and Technical Approaches—An Overview

We are all aware of the need to improve the quality of our environment, but this realization is only a first step. How are specific problems actually solved? Solutions to environmental problems can be divided into two general categories: **social** and **technical.** A **social solution** is one that is implemented when people make a conscious choice to alter their habits. Sometimes, but not always, this choice generates a certain amount of inconvenience or personal sacrifice in exchange for the benefits of a cleaner environment. On the other hand, a **technical solution** is realized when the design of goods or machinery is improved so that a given task can be performed with less impact on environmental systems. To illustrate the difference between the two approaches, let us use petroleum consumption as an example. Today, petroleum reserves are being depleted to provide fuel for automobiles. One social solution to the problem would be to encourage people to drive less. With fewer cars on the road, there would be less demand for gasoline. On the other hand, a technical solution would be to design automobiles to burn fuel more efficiently so that a car could go further on a liter of gasoline.

Although both types of solutions are helpful, each has its limitations. In a country such as the United States, it is reasonable to expect that people can drive less and still maintain a high standard of

A sanitary landfill in New York City. Available dumping sites are rapidly filling up, and large cities in the United States are searching for other means of disposing of their garbage.

living. Transportation patterns did, in fact, change during the fuel crisis of the late 1970s, contributing to the decline in gasoline consumption during the first half of the 1980s. No one expects, however, that the entire population will abandon the automobile in favor of buses, bicycles, walking, or riding horses to work. Thus, this social answer is only a partial solution to the problem.

Technical solutions are also powerful and are also limited. In the 1970s, large inefficient "gas-hogs" were popular in the United States. The average car traveled only 13.6 miles per gallon (5.8 km per liter) of gasoline. When the price of fuel rose and the threat of shortages became apparent, there was a rapid trend toward lighter vehicles with smaller, more efficient engines. By 1985, the total efficiency of the entire United States fleet increased to 17.3 miles per gallon (7.4 km per liter) (see Fig. 2–1). Thus, the average American car traveled 32 percent farther on a gallon of gasoline in 1985 than in 1973. Moreover, the average performance of the cars sold in 1985 was 26.9 miles per gallon (11.4 km per liter), indicating that there is significant room for further improvement. Thus, considerable

This experimental car can travel at 50 miles per hour with a 2.1-horsepower engine. If a shell of this type were mounted on a conventional mid-sized car, it would reduce air drag sufficiently to place the highway mileage at about 65 miles per gallon. (General Motors Corporation)

quantities of fuel are being saved by the implementation of advanced design and engineering.

Throughout this book, both social and technological approaches to environmental problems will be examined. But remember that the two are not separate, isolated, entities. Engineers can build

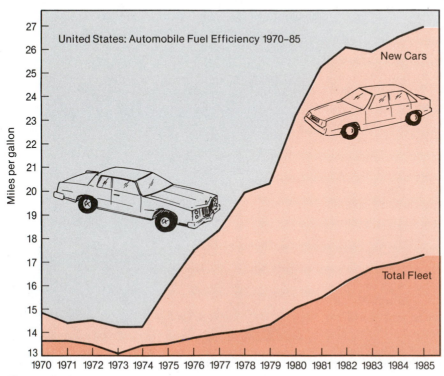

Figure 2–1
Efficiency of automobiles in the United States.

better cars or safe, efficient mass transit systems, but they do no good unless people decide to use them.

2.3
Environmental Degradation and the Law

In many situations, environmental degradation results from one form of the "tragedy of the commons." Recall from Chapter 1 that it is generally profitable for an individual herder to graze as many cattle as possible on a common pasture, but if all the herders follow suit, the pasture becomes overgrazed and all the cattle starve. Similarly, it is generally more profitable for one person or corporation to pollute the environment than not to pollute it. The reason for this is straightforward. The cost of pollution control equipment is borne directly by the manufacturing operation. However, the negative effects of pollution, the dirty air and water, are shared by the population at large. If everyone released pollutants and there were no controls, our environment would become foul and unhealthy. Crops would fail, materials would corrode, people would sicken and die, and everyone would suffer. Therefore, a legitimate role of governments is to regulate pollution. Legal systems of government have always recognized the need to prevent one individual from harming another. Criminal statutes punish direct assaults on the well-being of others such as robbery or murder. A second type of wrongful act, called a **tort,** is a noncriminal action that results in personal injury or damage to property.

Legal Actions in Tort Law

1. Nuisance In legal usage, a nuisance is the "substantial, unreasonable interference with the reasonable use and enjoyment of property." In an early form of environmental legislation, the Romans interpreted pollution as a form of nuisance, and anyone caught polluting the city aqueduct system was subject to severe penalties. Today, air pollution, water pollution, and excess noise are also considered nuisances and therefore belong in the jurisdiction of legal concern.

However, the legal issues are not always simple or straightforward. Jet planes are noisy, and, as a consequence, some of the people who live near

Figure 2–2
Jet planes use the most power and make the most noise during take-off. (Photo by David F. Hall; courtesy of the Connecticut Lung Association)

Kennedy International Airport in New York City filed suit claiming that the airport was a nuisance and should be closed permanently (Fig. 2–2). The courts recognized that such a closure would disrupt the economy of the city of New York and provide a dangerous precedent for other airport closures. In addition, defense lawyers pointed out that many of the people who had filed the suit had moved to the area after the airport had been in operation for many years. They argued that it is unreasonable for a person to move to an industrial area and then claim at a later date that his or her personal rights have been infringed. In cases such as this one, the court is forced to balance competing interests. The airport agreed to adopt certain noise control procedures, and the local residents agreed to drop the suit.

2. Trespass Medieval English law was strict in prohibiting people from intruding upon or invading other people's property. It was illegal for peasants to hunt in a forest belonging to a noble, and one of the first illegal acts committed by the legendary figure Robin Hood and his followers was simple trespass. Trespass has become important in environmental law because it has been recognized that an object, as well as a person, can trespass. For example, if the pollutants from a factory fall on a forest and kill the trees, the intrusion of pollutants on another person's property is a form of trespass.

Box 2.2

There are many references in English literature to the fact that trespass was considered to be a serious crime. In Shakespeare's play, *King Lear,* one of Lear's servants is punished for abusing another servant. The punishment is considered to be so excessive that the Earl of Gloucester argues . . .

"your purposed low correction
Is such as basest and contemned'st wretches
For pilferings and most common trespasses
Are punish'd with: the king must take it ill.

3. Negligence   An act carelessly performed or carelessly omitted when it should have been performed is called **negligence.** For example, imagine that an automobile is designed in such a way that some component fails, leading to an accident that causes injury or death. If it can be proved that the car was designed or built in a careless manner and that reasonable safety precautions were not followed, the manufacturers may be liable and proved guilty of negligence. Similarly, a factory manager who fails to maintain an air pollution control system is also considered to be negligent. Many lawsuits, some amounting to millions of dollars, have been successfully prosecuted on these grounds.

General Types of Legal Actions for Environmental Improvement

Within the broad philosophy outlined by our legal structure, several general types of legal actions are commonly used.

1. Restriction   Some pollutants are so poisonous that even small concentrations can kill wildlife, domestic animals, agricultural crops, or even people. Here the government has the power to restrict or abolish the harmful practices. For example, in the United States, the use of several pesticides, including DDT, has been banned (see Chapter 19). In some cases, violators are subject to criminal prosecution.

In one extreme case, plant managers were actually convicted of murder for maintaining an un-

safe environment in the workplace. The company involved, called Film Recovery Systems, used a cyanide solution to recover silver from exposed x-ray film. Cyanide is an acute poison. The conditions in the plant were, in the words of Cook County Judge Ronald Banks, "totally unsafe. There was inadequate safety equipment on the premises. There were no safety instructions given to the workers. The workers were not properly warned of the hazards and dangers of working with cyanide." On February 10, 1983, one of the workers died of cyanide poisoning. Two years later, three of the plant managers were convicted of murder. The final decision stated that the "employers who knowingly expose their workers to dangerous conditions leading to infection or even death can be held criminally responsible."

2. Qualified Restriction   Many pollutants are not acute poisons. For example, sulfur dioxide is an air pollutant released in various concentrations whenever fossil fuels are burned. It is harmful in many ways, but a small dose is not lethal. In addition, it would be economically impractical to prohibit the release of all sulfur dioxide. One approach to such a problem is to permit each factory to release a specific quantity of the gas. If more than the legal limit is released, fines can be levied. For example, under the Clean Air Act, a company can be fined up to $25,000 *per day* for violation of air pollution standards. If violations continue or are particularly flagrant, the system of fines can be replaced by outright restriction, plants can be shut down, and, as explained previously, managers can even be charged with criminal actions.

3. Subsidies   Regulations that simply prohibit pollution ignore the resulting hardships that are imposed on individual companies or communities. An alternative approach is to offer economic incentives that will persuade polluters not to despoil the environment. One common type of subsidy is given in the form of **tax deductions** for environmentally favorable practices. In the late 1970s and early 1980s, tax deductions were allotted for adding insulation, solar heating, or other energy conservation devices to older homes and businesses.

4. Pollution Tax or Residual Charge   Another approach is the so-called **pollution tax,** or **residual charge.** Each polluter is charged an amount proportional to the quantity of pollutant emitted. Such a scheme would encourage environmentally sound manufacturing because it penalizes processes that pollute. Ideally, residual charges present the polluter with a choice—either dump the waste and pay the fine, or deal with the waste in some other way—treat it, recycle it, store it, or minimize it in manufacturing. If the residual charge is too low, there will be little economic incentive to prevent waste, and pollutants will continue to be discharged into the environment.

Pollution taxes can be charged either to the manufacturer of an item or directly to the consumer. For example, an electric generating utility could be charged for the sulfur dioxide emitted, or, alternatively, people could be encouraged to use less by imposing taxes on their consumption. One suggestion is a steeply increasing tax. The tax should allow a reasonable amount of usage at very low rates, so the poor are not charged exorbitantly for necessities. Then, according to this system, heavy users would be taxed severely.

5. Rationing   Rationing is a form of control of a limited resource. For example, if fuel is rationed, every person is allotted a certain amount and no more. Rationing was used during World War II, but it would be very unpopular at the present time.

2.4
Environmental Law in the United States
Legislation

Implicitly the United States Constitution gives the federal government the power to regulate environmental issues. However the Constitution, by itself, only outlines the powers and the limitations of the government; it says nothing specific about environmental legislation. It is the job of Congress to identify specific problems and write laws to address them. Prior to 1970, there was little environmental legislation. However, this situation was changed by the environmental awareness that started to bloom in the 1960s. During the decade between 1970 and 1980, approximately 25 separate pieces of legislation were passed to regulate environmental quality. Some of these laws are listed in Table 2–1. It is important to understand that when a law is written, it is intended to outline the broad intent of Con-

Special Topic A
The Constitutional Justification for Environmental Law in the United States

The fundamental source of federal jurisdiction over environmental matters is derived from the United States Constitution, which empowers congress "to regulate commerce . . . among the several states . . ." How is environmental degradation related to commerce? As an example, imagine that an industry buries hazardous wastes in an uncontrolled dump. The dumping operation occurs in one state, and actions that do not involve interstate commerce are out of the sphere of federal control. But the consequences of the actions do involve more than one state. If the hazardous wastes leak into the groundwater, wells and rivers in adjacent areas may be polluted, disrupting the commercial activity of people living there. One might argue that a small dumpsite in one state has trivial consequences on the entire spectrum of interstate commerce. That argument was answered by a 1942 Supreme Court decision. In that case, a small farmer was cited for growing more wheat on his farm than was allowed under the quota system that was in effect at that time. The farmer argued that the amount of wheat involved was so small that it was insignificant on a national level. The court disagreed and argued that the farmer's "contribution to the demand for wheat may be trivial by itself . . . his contribution, taken with that of many others similarly situated, is far from trivial."

gress, and, in general, environmental laws do *not* set specific guidelines for action. For example, consider the wording of one section of the Federal Insecticide, Fungicide, and Rodenticide Act. The law reads that the government will allow a pesticide to be sold and distributed only if "When used in accordance with widespread and commonly recognized practice, it (the pesticide) will not generally cause unreasonable effects on the environment." (This topic will be discussed further in Chapter 19.)

The law states very clearly that it is the intent of the government to regulate the dispersal of pesticides that may be harmful to the environment.

Table 2–1
Major Environmental Legislation in the United States

Law	Purpose of Law	See Following Chapters
National Environmental Policy Act (NEPA)	(a) To "use all practicable means, consistent with other essential considerations of national policy, to . . . fulfill the responsibilities of each generation as a trustee of the environment for succeeding generations." (b) Any person or corporation planning to engage in any act that affects the environment must file an "Environmental Impact Statement."	
Wilderness Act	To designate various undeveloped areas as wilderness areas to be protected and preserved in their original character.	11
Alaskan Land-Use Bill	To designate and protect additional wilderness land in Alaska.	11
Wild and Scenic River Act	To designate certain rivers to be protected from development based on primitive natural characteristics.	11
National Coastal Zone Management Act	To provide federal aid to 35 coastal states and territories to develop programs for protecting and managing coastlines.	11
Forest Reserves Management Act	To mandate the Forest Service to manage according to principles of sustained yield.	11
National Forest Management Act	To allow clear-cutting on National Forest only under specific circumstances.	11
Multiple Use Sustained Yield Act	To require the Forest Service and Bureau of Land Management to attempt to balance outdoor recreation, timber, rangeland, watershed, fish and wildlife habitats, mineral extraction, and other uses to provide optimal value to the nation as a whole.	11
Endangered Species Act	To authorize appropriate agencies to identify all plant and animal species endangered or threatened in the U.S. and abroad, and to conduct programs to protect, recover, or conserve them. It also prohibits the commercial trade of these species.	12
Marine Protection, Research, and Sanctuaries Act	To authorize appropriate agencies to identify and list marine species that are endangered or threatened.	12
National Energy Act	To establish the Department of Energy, to be in charge of taking measures to promote energy efficiency, such as setting a national speed limit and deregulating the price of domestic oil.	13, 15
Surface Mining Control and Reclamation Act	To ensure reclamation and restoration of mined land to former use; to prohibit mining on prime agricultural land; to protect watersheds and water quality; and to establish a restoration fund under the direction of the Department of Interior.	15, 16
Resource Conservation and Recovery Act (RCRA)	To initiate a federal role in overseeing solid wastes, hazardous wastes, and resource recovery.	18

Table 2–1
Major Environmental Legislation in the United States *continued*

Law	Purpose of Law	See Following Chapters
Comprehensive Environmental Response, Compensation and Liabilities Act (CERLA) (commonly known as the the Superfund Law)	To provide for liability, compensation, cleanup, and emergency response for hazardous substances released into the environment and the cleanup of inactive hazardous waste disposal sites.	18
Federal Insecticide, Fungicide, and Rodenticide Control Act (FIFRA)	To regulate poisonous agricultural chemicals.	18, 19
Quiet Communities Act	To authorize the EPA to develop programs to help state and local government to combat excessive noise.	18, 19
Noise Control Act	To protect all Americans from "noise that jeopardizes their health and welfare."	18, 19
Toxic Substances Control Act (TSCA)	To regulate toxic substances that are not under the jurisdiction of the Federal Drug Administration (FDA) or FIFRA.	18, 19
Ocean Dumping Act	To regulate the amount of industrial waste allowed to be dumped into U.S. ocean waters.	20
Federal Water Pollution Control Act	To regulate the discharge of toxic pollutants into the natural waterways.	20
Safe Drinking Water Act	To establish safe drinking water standards for the U.S.	20
Clean Water Act	To protect and enhance water quality by requiring states to submit water quality reports to congress.	20
Clean Air Act	To protect and enhance air quality in order to ensure public health and welfare.	21
Solid Waste Disposal Act	To prevent contamination of water supplies by regulating the operation of sanitary landfills.	22

But, on the other hand, phrases such as "widespread and commonly recognized practice" and "unreasonable adverse effects" are exceedingly vague. There is nothing specific in this statement, per se, that would give a chemist technical information on which compounds may or may not be produced and distributed.

The Environmental Protection Agency

The ambiguity in environmental legislation is intentional, because Congress cannot possibly review every new pesticide or keep abreast with the changing technology of pollution emission and control. In 1970, President Richard Nixon created the Environmental Protection Agency (EPA). Its purpose was to establish an environmental policy within the guidelines set by federal laws and to coordinate other agencies involved in environmental issues. There are several steps in this process (Fig. 2–3).

1. Research The first step is to study the technical aspects of any given environmental problem. For example, if a chemical such as a pesticide or an air pollutant is being introduced into the environment, it is essential to study the toxicity of the

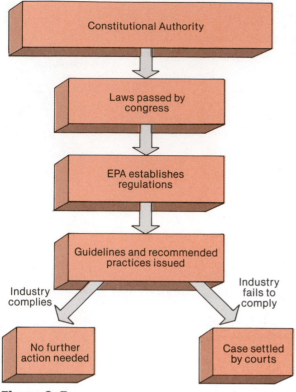

Figure 2–3
The legal process for environmental improvement in the United States.

compound both to humans and to other organisms.

2. Establishment of Regulation Once the technical aspects of a problem are understood, the EPA then establishes regulations consistent with the law. This process can be quite complex. Suppose, for example, that a factory is emitting a harmful chemical into the air or water. Suppose further that EPA officials decide that the emissions should be reduced. In turn, the company may take the position that there is no way to attain the required goal. The EPA must then consider whether the company's allegation is true, and, if it is, whether new technology can be developed to achieve the goal. EPA officials may then decide whether to prohibit the manufacturing process or to make the regulations less stringent. Before regulations are established, public hearings are held to resolve such questions. In such instances, the EPA must identify the "Best Conventional Technology" (BCT), the "Best Available Technology" (BAT), and the "Best

Practicable Technology" (BPT). These terms are interpreted as follows:

- BCT: The best pollution control that companies actually use.
- BAT: The best technology that has been or is capable of being achieved.
- BPT: The average of the best existing performance by well-operated plants.

The EPA can take the least controversial position that its regulations should be consistent with the BPT. But what if such control is considered by scientists to be insufficient for protecting human health? If Congress appropriates enough money, the EPA can conduct or sponsor research to reach a higher level of the BAT. However, what if a company takes the position that the BAT or BCT is too expensive for its process and would put it out of business if the regulations were enforced? Such a position is usually a prediction, not an actual statement of experience. If forced to a higher level of pollution control, a company may elect to upgrade its operations throughout its manufacturing process and may surprise itself by becoming more profitable, not less. The EPA is often compelled to carry out its own analysis to arrive at a conclusion in such difficult and complex issues.

3. Enforcement Once regulations are made, the EPA issues **guidelines** and **recommended practices,** often in the form of technical booklets. What happens if the guidelines are not obeyed? In the last section, we discussed types of penalties that are available under western law. However, these penalties are effective only if they are enforced. If an administration wishes to relax pollution standards, it is not necessary to change laws or regulations. A simpler and easier method is to reduce the money available for enforcement. If motorists know that there are very few traffic police, more cars will exceed the speed limit. Similarly, if there are few smoke inspectors, there will be more smoke.

4. Pollution Problems and the Courts In many cases, disputes between the EPA and a polluter cannot be solved amicably. If a stalemate occurs, the issue must be resolved in court. The Anglo-American legal system has developed judicial rules and procedures governing controversies in which one party, the **plaintiff,** alleges that he has been harmed by another party, the **defendant.** If

Can valleys and mountains, like corporations, have legal standing? (Photo of Mt. Temple in the Canadian Rockies)

the court judges that harm has indeed occurred, the defendant is often ordered to pay the plaintiff money to offset the damage. In some situations, a plaintiff might not want money but rather an **injunction,** which is a legal order that requires the defendant to stop doing the wrongful act. The EPA has the authority to become a plaintiff in environmental cases and therefore pursue its enforcement through the legal system.

Imagine for a moment that a factory in your neighborhood is polluting the air and water around you so badly that the odor makes your life unpleasant and the emissions cause the paint on your house to peel and the tires on your car to crack. What can you do as an individual? Perhaps the first step would be to discuss the problem with local EPA officials. However, as stated previously, the EPA is responsive to the policies of the current administration. During the period of the Reagan administration, for example, many environmentalists believed that enforcement of environmental laws was lax. As an alternative, an individual may bypass the EPA and file suit directly. In order to take a case to court, an individual must have what is called **legal standing.** Legal standing for damage suits is granted only if an individual's harm is distinguishable from that of the public in general or, as the United States Supreme Court* has stated,

*Flast vs. Cohen. 392 U.S. 83(1968)

one is required to have a "personal stake in the outcome of the controversy." The question of standing has rendered the courts inaccessible to many environmental suits. For example, an individual could not sue a drilling company for the effects of an oil spill to compensate for personal anguish over the killing of birds and the fouling of beaches. However, a person who owns waterfront land near the spill could sue for property damage. Similarly an individual could not sue the Department of Interior for destroying a wilderness area by commercializing it, even though that person believes that his or her tax money is being wasted for needless development. A single taxpayer lacks standing, because the individual's harm cannot be distinguished from that of the public in general.

Sometimes a group is granted standing when an individual is not. For example, a city or town can file a case representing all its citizens. Thus, a factory spewing noxious gases into the atmosphere might be sued by a town and legally be declared a "public nuisance." One pivotal decision on legal standing concerned a proposed hydroelectric plant at Storm King Mountain on the Hudson River. In that case, a citizens' group, the Scenic Hudson Preservation Conference, sued to stop construction of the project on environmental grounds. The electric company first argued that the case should be dismissed because the group did not have legal standing. The court disagreed, stating that an organization did have the right to represent all of its members. Although the group eventually lost the case, the decision on standing opened an important avenue for environmental litigation that has, in turn, led to environmental victories in a number of more recent cases.

It is not easy or cheap to solve environmental problems through court battles. Litigation is very slow and expensive. Another disadvantage is that lawsuits may be addressed to a very small issue. In addition, a given decision is not necessarily binding on future offenders. Each violation may require a new case. Environmentalist groups may be pitted against an array of giant corporations and govern-

ment agencies, and an individual case may cost as much as a million dollars or more.

Has the net effect of all this effort been progress in environmental protection by the law and progress in environmental quality? As far as the law is concerned, the answer is yes. If our sets of environmental laws were repealed and polluters did not regulate themselves, the results would be catastrophic. It is true that progress in legal protection has sometimes been slowed by deferments of environmental goals and by cutbacks in support for research and enforcement, but the overall trend has certainly been an improvement. However, the larger question, "Has environmental quality improved over the last few decades?" is more difficult to answer. It is clear that most of us would not benefit by a return to what some call the "good old days." The filth and stench of many cities through the nineteenth century would be intolerable to modern sensitivities. At the same time, however, new environmental hazards are being introduced. Thousands of new synthetic chemicals are introduced every year, unprecedented radiation sources are being created, and the global population continues to grow at a rapid rate.

Special Topic B
Should an Ecosystem Have Legal Standing?

Sierra Club vs. Morton. Supreme Court of the United States 405 U.S. 727 (1972). Dissent by Justice Douglas:

"Inanimate objects are sometimes parties in litigation. A ship has legal personality, a fiction found useful for maritime purpose. The corporation sole—a creature of ecclesiastical law—is an acceptable adversary and large fortunes ride on its cases. The ordinary corporation is a "person" for purposes of the adjudicatory processes, whether it represents proprietary, spiritual, aesthetic, or charitable causes.

So it should be as respects valleys, alpine meadows, rivers, lakes, estuaries, beaches, ridges, groves of trees, swampland, or even air that feels the destructive pressures of modern technology and modern life. The river, for example, is the living symbol of all the life it sustains or nourishes—fish, aquatic insects, water ouzels, otter, fish, deer, elk, bear, and all other animals, including man, who are dependent on it or who enjoy it for its sight, its sound, or its life. The river as plaintiff speaks for the ecological unit of life that is part of it. Those people who have a meaningful relation to that body of water—whether it be a fisherman, a canoeist, a zoologist, or a logger—must be able to speak for the values which the river represents and which are threatened with destruction."

2.5

Environmental Degradation and the Economy
Cost/Benefit Analysis

Nearly everyone agrees that the government has both the fundamental right and the responsibility to regulate environmental quality. But there is significant disagreement about how much regulation is desirable.

Pollution control is not a yes-no, on-off affair. Imagine that a factory with no pollution control devices releases a certain quantity of sulfur dioxide into the air every month. Equipment can be designed to remove any portion of the pollutant, from a minor amount to practically all of it. In general, the more pollution that is removed, the more expensive the process becomes.

A rough general rule is that the cost of pollution control is constant for each reduction of pollution by 50 percent. That means that if it costs $1 million per year to remove 50 percent of a given pollutant, it will cost another $1 million to remove 50 percent of the remaining pollution. Therefore,

$2 million will accomplish a 75 percent (50 percent + 25 percent) removal, $3 million will achieve 87.5 percent, and so on. Thus, limited pollution control can be relatively inexpensive, but an essentially pollution-free environment is very costly.

How much pollution control can be justified? Some people suggest that pollution control measures should be applied only when it can be shown that there is a positive economic return on the investment. This approach, known as **cost/benefit analysis**, balances the cost of pollution control against the price that society must pay to live in a polluted environment.

Let us consider both of these factors. The cost of pollution control is relatively easy to quantify. It is the sum total of all the capital and operating expenses of all the control equipment and strategies. It would include the cost of such items as a sewage treatment plant, a scrubber to remove air pollutants, and an incinerator to burn solid wastes. It would also include the cost of rerouting a pipeline around a wildlife preserve, or of performing toxicity tests on a pesticide before releasing it for sale.

On the other hand, what are the costs of living in a polluted environment? These expenses are not paid for by manufacturers. They are therefore separate or outside the direct cost of manufacturing and are called external costs, or **externalities.** Externalities are generally not so obvious or easy to quantify as direct, internal manufacturing costs, but they are nevertheless quite real (Fig. 2–4). For example, pollution can affect human health. Consider medical bills, loss of work because of illness, decreased productivity, and death of a wage earner at an early age. In addition, if the smoke from manufacturing (or from disposal) darkens nearby houses and soils the clothes of local residents, the costs of more frequent repainting and laundering are also externalities. Many pollutants are reactive chemicals, such as corrosive acids. Some of these acids collect in the atmosphere, dissolve in water droplets, and fall to the Earth in the form of acid rain that corrodes buildings, destroys forests, kills fish, and slows the growth of agricultural crops. All of these losses are also part of the cost that society pays for manufactured goods. In many areas, severe pollution has resulted in loss of tourist trade. In these instances, factory and smelter owners may gain by ignoring the expense of pollution control devices, but motel and restaurant owners and many other local businesses must bear the cost. Note that external costs are not always borne by those who benefit from an industrial process. For example, when coal is mined and electricity is generated in Arizona, some local ranchers suffer eco-

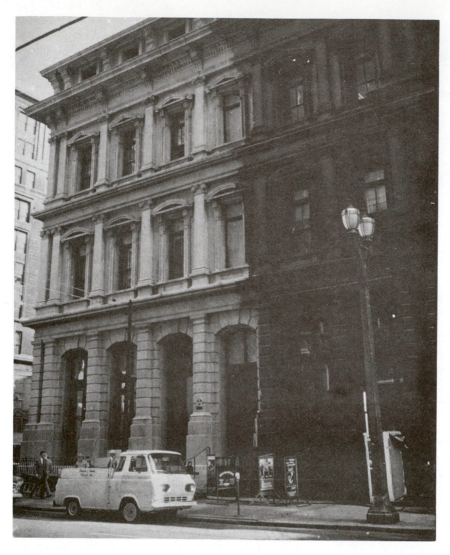

Figure 2–4
An example of an economic externality. The cost of cleaning buildings dirtied by air pollution is generally not paid for by the manufacturers that pollute the air. (Courtesy of H. Neff Jenkins. From Stern: *Air Pollution.* 2nd ed. New York, Academic Press, 1968.)

nomic losses from the resultant environmental degradation (see Section 15.4). However, much of the electricity (and therefore the benefits) is transmitted to California. Note also that externalities include only factors that can be measured in monetary terms. Human pain or suffering cannot be valued in this manner and is therefore not accounted for in this type of analysis (Fig. 2–5).

The principle of cost/benefit analysis recognizes that society as a whole must pay for both the manufacturing costs and the external costs (Fig. 2–6). Therefore, an argument is made that the government should set pollution standards so that the total cost to the consumer will be minimized. To understand this concept, suppose that some modest pollution control devices are installed in a factory.

At first a moderate outlay of money will reduce the pollution by a significant amount. The small increased cost of manufacturing will eventually be passed on to the consumer who will have to pay a little more for various goods. But at the same time, the consumer will save a lot more money because the cost of the externalities will decline dramatically. This level of pollution control is economically beneficial. Examine Figure 2–7 and note the two solid curves that show the relationship between pollution control costs and externalities. Imagine that more and more money is spent on pollution control. At first, a small amount of money causes a large drop in external costs (left side of the graph). As complete pollution control is approached, a large increase of manufacturing expen-

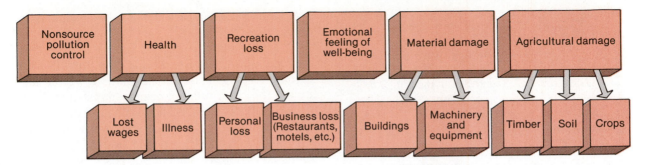

Figure 2–5
Some external and human costs of pollution.

diture yields only a small decrease in the cost of externalities (right side of the graph). The dotted line in Figure 2–7 is the sum total of all costs to an individual consumer who must pay both manufacturing costs and external costs. This line is roughly U-shaped, and the low point in the curve represents the level of pollution control at which the total cost to an individual is at a minimum. Proponents of cost/benefit analysis argue that pollution control should be regulated only to this point.

In accordance with this principle, estimates have been made of the costs and benefits of pollution control. A few of these are summarized in the following paragraphs. In all cases, remember that the numbers have been obtained by making many approximations.

- In 1984, the total cost of all pollution controls in the United States was about $70 billion. According to the Council on Environmental

Quality, the benefit of all pollution control in 1985 was also about $70 billion. Thus, control measures really did pay for themselves.

- In 1984, the federal ambient air quality standards were being constantly exceeded in the greater Los Angeles area, and air quality was often rated as "fair" or "poor." The cost of bringing the region into compliance would be $600 million to $1 billion per year. The benefits of the cleaner air that would result were estimated at $1.5 to $3 billion.*

- The estimated cost of making a 50 per cent reduction in sulfur dioxide emissions by util-

*Source: Allen V. Kneese. *Measuring the Benefits of Clean Air and Water.* Washington, DC, Resources for the Future, Inc, 1984. p. 159.

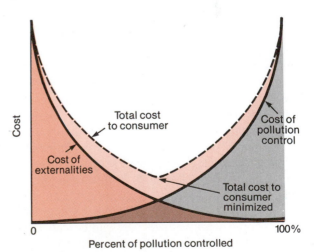

Figure 2–7
Schematic graph showing the relationship between the cost of pollution control and the cost of externalities. The actual numbers will vary with the situation.

Pollution control equipment and maintenance

Medical bills
Cleaning, painting
Damage to materials
Damage to crops, livestock
Loss of tourist trade
Long-term effects

Figure 2–6
The principle of cost/benefit analysis. This accounting system does not recognize psychological trauma, pain of illness, or emotional needs for a clean environment.

BOX 2.3

Americans spent approximately $70 billion for pollution control and abatement in 1985. Does that sound like a small or a large sum? Assuming a population of 228 million, that amounts to an average of $307 per person for the privilege of living in a healthier, cleaner environment.

ities in the United States is $2 to $4 billion. The estimated gain of such a reduction is $4 to $5 billion.*

There are several objections to the principle of cost/benefit analysis. One objection is, How do you place a dollar value on the price of externalities? How is it possible, for example, to evaluate accurately what portion of human illness has been caused by pollutants? Or as another example, what is the value of a human life that ends too soon? Is it simply the future potential earning power of that person? If so, what is the value of an unemployed person? Is it zero?

Another objection is raised because some people believe that economic balances are not the only indicators of human welfare. How can a dollar value be placed on the annoyance of a vile odor, or of unclear air, or of industrial noise? Such annoyance involves not the destruction of property but the deterioration of the quality of human life. What about recreational opportunities? One hundred years ago, for instance, most rivers in the United States were relatively unpolluted. People fished, boated, swam, and explored along the shores and marshes. Today, swimming is dangerous to human health in many parts of the country, the number of tasty game fish has declined dramatically, and many of the wild secluded marshes have disappeared. Alternative recreational opportunities are now available. Swimmers can find swimming pools, children can play in approved parks, people who want to see wildlife can drive to a zoo or watch educational programs on television. For many, these recreational changes involve

*Source: T. Crocker and J. Regis: *Environmental Science and Technology* 19(2):112, 1985.

poignant losses, but their dollar value is difficult to assess (Fig. 2–8).

This ethical argument is supported by a 1981 Supreme Court decision. In that case, the EPA was arguing for stricter health standards in textile factories. The court ruled in favor of the standards. In the majority decision, Justice William Brenner concluded that the health of the employees outweighs "all other considerations." He added, "any standards based on a balancing of costs and benefits would be inconsistent with the law." (Note that the Supreme Court decision just cited was specific to a given case and cannot be generalized to all environmental litigation.)

The issue remains unresolved at the present time, and the legal interpretation varies from case to case. However, in general, if a pollutant is highly toxic, it is often banned, regardless of the cost. This is the principle of restriction discussed in the previous section. On the other hand, if a pollutant is considered to be harmful but not an acute poison, the principle of cost/benefit analysis is likely to be applied, and the pollutant will be regulated but not prohibited.

Pollution Control and Jobs

Many people argue that pollution control laws raise the cost of manufacturing so severely that many companies are put out of business. When factories shut down, people lose their jobs. The argument continues that this loss of employment is too high

Pollution control creates jobs. (Photo courtesy of E. D. Switala, Owens-Corning Corp.)

Figure 2–8
Swimming in a pool is different from swimming in a natural environment. Who can place a dollar value on such differences?

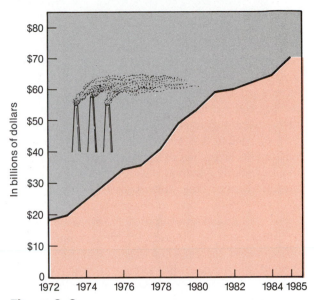

Figure 2–9
The annual spending by the U.S. pollution control industry from 1972 to 1985.

a human price to pay for a clean environment. The rebuttal to this argument is that although it is true that some jobs are lost through environmental legislation, many more new jobs are created by the pollution control and abatement industry itself. For example, in 1985, approximately 2.2 million people were employed to build, install, maintain, and operate pollution control equipment. With a total budget of $70 billion, the pollution control industry was in itself a major source of employment in the United States* (Fig. 2–9). A recent study reported by the Conservation Foundation found that the environmental laws have not blocked construction of new oil refineries, steel mills, and other industrial plants. Moreover, there is no evidence that environmental and land-use laws have caused a major movement of industry from states perceived to be environmentally strict to those that are thought to be more permissive. The most important factors that determine locations of plants are still the traditional ones: access to markets, to labor, and to raw materials. If these factors are favorable, the strictness of environmental regulations is not a handicap.

Yet, on the other hand, think of a single individual. What happens if a smelter is shut down to comply with regional air pollution emission standards? The smelter worker who loses a job is not automatically offered another job in a factory that manufactures pollution control equipment. This is a real problem for which there is no easy answer.

*Source: U.S. Dept of Commerce

2.6
Risk Assessment

In many cases, cost/benefit analysis leads to a fairly well-defined economic balance sheet that can serve as a guideline for choices in personal and public policies. For example, if sewage is dumped into a river, the river *will* become polluted. If the level of pollution is known, it is possible to make reasonable estimates of various costs, such as the loss of fisheries or the added expense of purifying drinking water further downstream. In other cases, however, the relationship between cause and effect is not so clear. For example, if certain chemicals are introduced into the environment, some people will develop cancer, but others will remain unharmed. In this case, the foreign chemical poses a **risk,** but not a certainty, that a cancer will develop. This element of probability has made the assessment of risks a significant and often controversial issue in public policy.

It is impossible to live without risk. People drown in their bathtubs, are swept away by tornados, or are killed or injured by any of a variety of calamities. However, each one of us makes personal decisions on the magnitude of the risks that we, as individuals, choose to accept. Some people live cautiously and seldom leave their homes, others climb rock cliffs or ski avalanche-prone mountains, and still others elect cosmetic surgery, despite the fact that any surgery involves risks of injury or even death. Other risks are imposed on us by society. Nuclear power plants, the threat of nuclear war, and the existence of synthetic chemicals in the environment are imposed on society as a whole.

What factors should be considered when making decisions on how much risk to accept? First, the magnitude of the risk must be determined, and the danger must then be balanced against the perceived benefits that are realized by taking the risk. Two significant factors involved in determining the magnitude are (1) the probability that the effect will occur and (2) the severity of the effect if it does occur.

If you go out to pick blackberries, you will almost certainly get scratched by a thorn, but berry picking is not considered to be a high-risk activity, because the effect is not severe. You could walk outdoors and be hit by a meteorite, which would be very severe, but this event is extremely unlikely, so going for a walk is not risky either. Driving fast on a hilly, icy road when you are drunk, however, is very risky, because the probability of an accident is high and the consequences could be disastrous.

If a risky activity is chanced, we ask ourselves, "What are the benefits that we gain by exposing ourselves to the danger?" If you were very sick, near death, and someone offered you a drug that had a 1 in 1000 chance of causing cancer, but a 999 in 1000 chance of curing you, you would probably decide to take it. But, on the other hand, if a chemical coloring agent that was used in soda pop had a 1 in 1000 chance of causing cancer, you might choose to drink another brand instead. Two examples of choices people make are listed below:

- **Nuclear Power Plants** If everything went wrong, the consequences of a major disaster at a nuclear power plant could be severe, but industry and government officials assure us that the probability of such an event is so low that the magnitude of the risk is low. Furthermore, nuclear power provides us with electricity and reduces our dependence on foreign fuels. Therefore, society as a whole accepts the risk, and nuclear power plants continue to operate. However, not everyone agrees with the evaluation of the risk, so considerable controversy remains (see Chapter 14).

- **Smoking** Compared with nonsmokers, smokers have a very high probability of dying prematurely from a variety of different diseases. One might logically assume that people would avoid a risk of such magnitude, but about one third of the adult population in the United States smokes anyway.

The decisions about risks, by their very nature, are subjective. First of all, some people are willing to take more chances than others. Second, as in the case of nuclear power plants just discussed, the judgments are sometimes based on assumptions that may or may not be correct. Nonetheless, decisions must be made, and, in making decisions there are some widely believed fallacies that one should learn to avoid:

- **The "Law of Averages" Fallacy** You are thinking about moving into an area where the average time between floods is said to be 100 years. There was a flood last year, so you are told that you are safe for another 99 years. The statement really means that *in any 1 year* the chance of a flood is 1 in 100, regardless of the past history of floods. There could be a flood next year, or even tomorrow.

- **The "Russian Roulette" Fallacy** In this deadly game, the player inserts a bullet in one of six chambers, spins the cylinder, points the gun at his head, and pulls the trigger. The chance of dying is 1 of 6. The player in the movie *The Deer Hunter* survived a nightly game for many months—it seems as though the chance of escaping (5 of 6) persists for a long time. People who drive dangerously or who smoke and survive begin to feel lucky after a period of time. It is not true; the chances get cumulatively worse. (For Russian roulette, the chance of surviving 10 plays

is about 1 in 6; the chance of surviving 100 plays is about 1 in a hundred million.)

- **The Fallacy of Believing That the "Experts (or Computers) Know Best"** Most laboratory procedures for estimating risks use conditions that are designed to achieve the same results as those that would happen in real life. But samples are small, tests are accelerated to save time, and methods are simplified. Therefore, many of the scientific conclusions based on these tests are open to question and there is often considerable disagreement among experts. These problems are discussed in more detail in Chapters 14 and 18.

Unfortunately, when economic interests are involved, there is often bias and sometimes even fraud. Consider the following example: As shown in Figure 2–10*A*, geologists have divided the United States into different

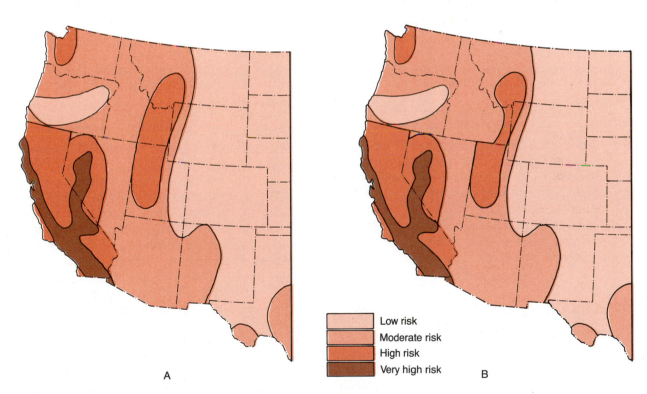

Low risk
Moderate risk
High risk
Very high risk

A   B

Figure 2–10
A, Earthquake zones in the western United States as reported in 1976. *B*, Earthquake zones in the western United States as reported in 1985. Note that in the 1985 report, a large chunk has been removed from the high-risk zone in southeastern Idaho. Risk is an estimation of the probability of danger, and, as such, there is room for human interpretation. We ask ourselves, "Do we always trust the judgments of the experts?"

zones, each with its own probability of experiencing an earthquake. As shown in the figure, in 1976 most of southeastern Idaho was originally classified as zone 3, a high-risk area. According to the Uniform Building Code of the United States, a structure that is built in zone 3 must contain twice as much steel as one that is built in zone 2, a low-risk area. Several important military research installations are located in southeastern Idaho. In 1985, the earthquake risk zones were re-evaluated, and new lines were drawn as shown in Figure 2–10*B*. Under the new zoning, the military installations are now located in a relatively low-risk earthquake area, and new structures can be built cheaply, with less steel. If one were to believe the officials, one might have a feeling of safety that the earthquake danger has diminished. But many people, including professional geologists, question the new zoning. They point out that there is no significant new geological data to warrant the change, and they ask why the earthquake zone should follow the state line so precisely and neatly exclude the military complex.

- **The Fallacy That "Your Own Gut Feeling Is Best"** Many of us are afraid of natural dangers such as snakes, spiders, and lightning, while we give little thought to much greater dangers such as highway traffic and household poisons. Some biologists believe that these fears were genetically programmed in early human evolution. Whatever the reason, intuitive feelings are not always reliable estimates of risk.

2.7
Legal and Economic Issues in Practice: A Case History

Reserve Mining Company was one of the largest iron mining and processing corporations in the world. When their mines were in full production, they dug nearly 50,000 tonnes of ore per day (Fig. 2–11). This ore contained iron mixed with less valuable minerals and rocks. Of the 50,000 tonnes mined, about 15,000 tonnes of concentrated iron ore pellets were produced, and 35,000 tonnes of solid waste were thrown away. In the 1950s, 60s,

Figure 2–11
The iron ore processed at Silver Bay, Minnesota, is mined with the aid of huge power shovels. Each shovel removes more than 10 tonnes of ore in a single scoop. (Photo courtesy of Reserve Mining Company)

and 70s, the company was dumping these wastes along the shores and into the waters of Lake Superior (Fig. 2–12).

The Reserve Mining operations were economically important to regions of northern Minnesota as well as to the country in general. The company employed 3000 people and once supplied over 15 percent of the iron ore used in the United States.

The waste that was dumped into Lake Superior destroyed wildlife habitats and silted streams and waterways. One of the waste products is a fibrous material called **chrysotile,** which is a type of **asbestos.** Some of these fibers float along the lake to Duluth, Minnesota, and to Superior, Wisconsin, and enter the drinking water in these cities. It is known that asbestos fibers in the air cause cancer in humans. Experts believe that it is likely that chrysotile fibers in water also cause cancer, but no one is sure. Since there is a strong possibility that Reserve Mining is endangering the health of local residents, various government agencies have tried to force the company to stop the pollution. The legal battle was long and complex.

In 1969, the federal government recommended that Reserve Mining stop polluting Lake Superior. Nothing was done. Two years later, the EPA ordered the company to develop a water pol-

Figure 2–12
Aerial view of the Reserve Mining Company plant at Silver Bay, Minnesota. The white area in the photograph consists of taconite tailings poured into Lake Superior. (Wide World Photos)

lution control program within 6 months. Reserve Mining submitted a plan that was unacceptable, so the EPA took the company to court. The first court battle lasted 2 years. On April 20, 1974, a district judge ruled that the air and water pollution endangered the health of the people living in the area. He ordered the plant to shut down. Rather than clean up their operations, Reserve Mining immediately appealed the legal case to a higher court. Two days later, a court of appeals judge overruled the district judge and said that more time was needed to review the case. The plant was allowed to resume operations immediately. The company continued to dump 35,000 tonnes of waste into Lake Superior every day. One year later, the higher court ruled that Reserve Mining must stop water pollution "within a reasonable time." Nothing was done. In 1976, the court ordered that all water pollution must cease by July 7, 1977, unless "circumstances in the case had changed before that time."

By now, 7 years had gone by since the United States government had demanded that the pollution stop. During that 7 years, the mining had continued without any change in operation. After 1976, the company finally agreed to start construction of a water pollution control facility. This agreement was considered to be a "change in circumstances." In May, 1977, the court stated that as long as construction of the water pollution control facilities

was proceeding normally, the company would be allowed to continue to pollute until April 15, 1980.

The company completed construction of a waste disposal facility, and in April 1982 Reserve Mining agreed pay $1.84 million to Duluth, Minnesota, and three smaller communities for the costs of filtering their drinking water. However, problems continued because various infractions of pollution control ordinances were recorded in 1985. In the summer of 1986, Reserve Mining went bankrupt owing to the fact that taconite mining was no longer economical. The bankruptcy and the subsequent closure of the mine suddenly opened a host of new environmental questions. The major one is, "Who would be responsible for the stabilization of the tailings and the maintenance of the filtration system needed to purify runoff water from the abandoned mine sites?"

This example illustrates the fact that the legal system, powerful as it is, is slow and cumbersome. From 1969, when the case first went to court, to 1980, when the pollution control facilities were finally installed, people lived in a polluted and perhaps poisonous environment for 11 years. But perhaps an even more disturbing fact is that pollution continued after the case was officially resolved. In the spring of 1987, when this book was being written, no final settlement had yet been reached.

2.8
Environmental Problems and Laws of Nature
The Law of Conservation of Matter

In Section 2.2, we introduced the idea that solutions to environmental problems can be divided into two general categories: social and technical. While each of these approaches is powerful, each has its limitations. As noted previously, people in a developed country such as the United States have been persuaded to adopt social measures to conserve fuel, but they could not be persuaded to abandon the automobile entirely. By the same token, technical solutions are bound by certain inexorable physical laws. One of the most fundamental of these is the **Law of Conservation of Matter.** This law simply states:

> In ordinary physical or chemical changes matter cannot be created or destroyed.

During physical and chemical changes, materials are routinely converted from one form to another, but matter is never lost or gained.

There are two practical consequences to this law:

1. *We can never find something for nothing.* For all practical purposes, very little matter is exchanged between Earth and the rest of the Universe. Therefore, there is a fixed quantity of fundamental resources available to us. For example, there is a certain amount of iron on the surface of the Earth. While some of it exists as the pure metal, most of it is bonded with other elements into any of a variety of compounds such as rust or other forms of iron oxide, and some is dissolved in lakes, rivers, and oceans. Metallic iron can react to form iron oxides, which, in turn, can be reduced to metallic iron. During these chemical conversions, iron atoms can be made to be more or less available or useful for our purposes, but the total quantity of iron will neither increase nor decrease.

2. *Everything must go somewhere.* When a liter of gasoline burns, the liquid fuel seems to disappear. Actually, the molecules of gasoline break apart and then recombine to form various gases and larger particles of smoke and soot. If gasoline is burned in an open flame, large quantities of noxious smoke and smelly fumes will be released, whereas, in an efficient engine, the products will be mostly carbon dioxide and water. One might ask, "Is it possible to design an engine that is so efficient that it burns gasoline so completely that no waste products are produced at all?" The answer is no. The Law of Conservation of Matter assures us that matter must always be conserved. Any chemical reaction generates some product or products that will then enter our environment.

2.9
Natural Laws and the Utilization of Energy— Thermodynamics

Let us return to Section 2.2 again. Recall that recent changes in engineering and design have improved the efficiency of the automobile fleet in the United States. Now we ask, "How much more improvement is possible?" Prototype commuter cars have been built that drive over 100 miles per gallon (42 km per liter), and experimental vehicles have topped 1500 miles per gallon (637 km per liter). But the laws of physics eventually impose limits on what is possible. Some energy is required to transport a person or a cargo from one place to another. We are assured that no one will ever be able to drive to the grocery store or to haul a load of bricks up a hill for free.

The science that describes the relationships between heat and work and the limits of the efficiency of engines is called **thermodynamics.** Before introducing thermodynamics, however, we must first learn a few definitions.

In every-day, nontechnical conversation, the term **work** is used loosely to describe any physical or mental effort. To the physicist, however, work has a very definite meaning:

> Work is done on a body when the body is forced to move (Fig. 2–13).

More specifically, the mechanical work performed on an object is equal to the force exerted on it times the distance the body is forced to move. Merely holding a heavy weight requires the application of force, but it is not work because the weight is not being moved. Lifting a weight, however, is work. Climbing a mountain or a flight of stairs is work, as is stretching a spring or compressing the gas in a cylinder or in a balloon, because all these activities force something to move.

A   B

Figure 2–13
Work = force × distance. *A*, The little girl is pulling on the rope, but since
she cannot move the car, *d* = 0, and no work is performed on the car. *B*, The
little girl can move the toy cart, so she is performing work in this situation.

In turn, energy is defined in terms of work.

Energy is the capacity to perform work.

There are various types of energy. If a freight train is coasting along a level track, it is not performing any work at the moment, but if it strikes something in its path, it will force it to move. Therefore, the train, or any other moving object—large or small—has the capacity to perform work. This energy of motion is called **kinetic energy.** (We assume here that the freight train is operating in an ideal system, where there is no wind resistance or friction. In a real system, work is being performed by the engine to overcome these forces.)

Now imagine that you see an object lying on the ground. Does it have energy? If it can perform work, the answer is yes. If it is a rock lying on the edge of a cliff, you could nudge it with your toe and it would tumble down, doing work by hitting other objects during its descent and forcing them into motion. Therefore, the rock must have had energy by virtue of the **potential to do work** that was inherent in its cliffside position. This type of potential is called **gravitational potential energy.**

What about a lump of coal, a piece of wood, or a liter of gasoline? We all know that fuels can be burned in the boiler of a steam engine or in the engine of a car, and work can be performed. A fuel has potential energy, in this case called **chemical potential.**

When a fuel is burned, the temperature of the immediate region rises. On a molecular level, the atoms and molecules in the fuel and the surrounding gases start to move rapidly. The collective energy of motion of all of the particles is known as **thermal energy** commonly called heat. Thus, all other factors being equal, hot objects have more thermal energy than do cold objects. In turn, thermal energy can be converted to mechanical work in an engine.

In the examples just given, we have shown that energy can be converted from one form to an-

A moving race car has kinetic energy. (Peterson Publishing Co.)

This pile of coal can burn to produce heat. It has chemical potential energy.

This campfire is producing thermal energy.

other. Thus, chemical potential can be converted to work in an automobile engine. Or, as another example, a turbine located at the bottom of a waterfall converts the gravitational potential energy of the water to mechanical work. It is obviously important to learn more about the efficiency of energy transfers. Thus, engineers would like to know how much mechanical work can be derived from a liter of gasoline, or how much electricity can be generated by a given amount of falling water.

The First Law of Thermodynamics

Since the beginning of civilization, people have been faced with the problem of how to lift heavy loads. Buildings have been traditionally built of wood or stone, and engineers have had to move these heavy items from the ground onto the walls and roofs. In the early days, we can imagine that people worked together to lift stones and timbers. Later, clever inventors developed simple machines,

such as the lever, the wheel, and the inclined plane. A person who can lift 50 kg unaided can lift hundreds of kilograms with a lever and even more with a well-designed system of gears or pulleys. In the early days, engineers believed that machines actually reduced the amount of work required to lift an object. Scientists now understand that such devices do not actually reduce the amount of work. Instead, they spread it out over a longer period of time and smooth out the effort. However, this difference can easily be overlooked, and a device such as a lever can be mistakenly thought of as a "work-saver." Since many "work-savers" had been invented, people reasoned that if you were clever enough, you could build a machine that would do all the work for free. They called this imaginary device a **perpetual motion machine.**

Table 2–2
Energy: What It Can Do

Source	Heat a Body Above the Surrounding Temperature	Work
Apple	Eating it helps you to maintain your body temperature at 37° C (98.6° F) even when you are surrounded by air at 20° C (68° F).	Eating it helps you to be able to pull a loaded wagon up a hill.
Coal	Burning it keeps the inside of the house warm in winter.	Burning it produces heat that boils water that makes steam that drives a turbine that turns a wheel that pulls a freight train up a hill.

If you owned a perpetual motion machine, you could turn it on and it would lift all the boulders you wanted while you sat and watched. It may be difficult for the modern reader to appreciate that the search for the perpetual motion machine seemed entirely reasonable. Many very clever people looked for a solution. However, all attempts failed. The failures have been so consistent that we are now convinced that the effort is hopeless. We believe that it is a fundamental law of nature that it is impossible to build a perpetual motion machine. This conclusion is one statement of the First Law of Thermodynamics.

The First Law can be stated in another way:

Energy cannot be created or destroyed.

The perpetual motion machine fails because it cannot create the energy needed to keep itself running forever. A real machine or engine works because energy is constantly being supplied to it.

When that energy is used up (converted to another form), the machine or engine stops. When your gasoline tank is empty, your engine can't run and your car won't move. All the energy in the gasoline has been converted by the engine into other forms of energy, such as the motion of the car.

Don't ask for a formal proof of the First Law; there is none. Its truth comes from a broad range of experience. Careful experiments repeated again and again support the truth of the First Law.

It is immediately obvious that the First Law limits technical solutions to environmental problems. If a person must move from a home in the suburbs to a job in the city, some form of energy is required. The energy may be in the form of gasoline to drive a car. It may be coal to produce electricity to operate an electric trolley or potatoes and apples to provide the muscle energy to ride a bicycle, but some form of energy is absolutely essential. There is no magic way to perform work without a supply of energy.

The Second Law of Thermodynamics

If energy cannot be found for free, you may say, at least let's not waste any. But, unfortunately, this, too, is impossible. Whenever thermal energy is transformed to work, some energy must always be wasted. Thus, any engine such as a steam turbine or a gasoline engine is necessarily inefficient. The inability to convert all the thermal energy into useful work is another fundamental law of nature and is called the Second Law of Thermodynamics.

The Second Law, like the First Law, arose out of a long series of observations. If a hot iron bar is placed on a cold one, the hot bar always cools, while the cold one becomes warmer, until both pieces of metal are at the same temperature. No one has ever observed any other behavior. Similarly, if a small quantity of blue ink is dropped into a glass of water, the ink will disperse until the solution becomes uniformly light blue. The ink does not stay concentrated in one section of the clear water (Fig. 2–14).

Thus, there appears to be a natural drive toward sameness or disorder. If we have two blocks of iron at different temperatures in a system, or a drop of ink in a glass of water, there is a differentiation of physical properties. Such differentiation results from some kind of *orderly* arrangement among the individual parts of the system. This is a

Drawing by Pieter Pourbus the Elder of a man-powered crane in use in the sixteenth century. The development of clever machines led some early inventors to believe that it would be possible to build a perpetual-motion machine. However, we are now certain that this is impossible.

Figure 2–14

The Second Law of Thermodynamics states that any undisturbed system will naturally tend toward maximal disorder. If a drop of ink is placed in a glass of water, the ink will eventually disperse until it is evenly distributed.

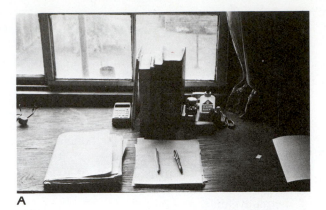

A

B

Figure 2–15

A desk when it is *(A)* neat and *(B)* messy. Unless work is performed to clean the desk, it will tend to stay messy, because the entropy of the messy desk is higher than that of the desk when it is orderly.

subtle but important point. In your experience, how is *order* different from *disorder?* The answer is that *order* is characterized by repeated *separations.* Your room is orderly if all the books are separated from your socks; books on the shelves, socks in the drawer. It is disorderly if books and socks are all mixed up in both places. Similarly, if a small spot of blue ink is *separated* from clear water, the system is *orderly.* In all cases, disordered systems are more natural (that is, more probable) than ordered systems. In your own common experience, you know that if you neglect your room, it naturally becomes disorderly. The reason is that there are always more ways to be disorderly than to be orderly. Therefore, any isolated system,* if left alone, will tend toward disorder. **Entropy** is a thermody-

---

*An isolated system is one that exchanges no matter or energy with the rest of the Universe. Thus, no matter or heat flows into or out of the system and no external work is done on it or by it.

namic measure of disorder. It has been observed that:

> The entropy of an undisturbed isolated system always increases during any spontaneous process;

that is, the degree of disorder always increases. Thus, if you drop a spot of ink in water, the ink will eventually spread out evenly throughout the liquid. It will become disorderly. If you don't clean your room regularly, it will become messy (Fig. 2–15).

Superficially, living organisms also appear to run counter to the Second Law by creating order out of disorder. Consider a flower developing from a tiny seed. The seedling builds large, highly ordered molecules and structures from smaller building blocks such as carbon dioxide and water. However, living things are not really exempt from the Second Law of Thermodynamics. They are not isolated systems, and they must use an outside supply of energy—food—to move substances around and to combat the universal tendency toward increasing disorganization, as well as for the actual matter required to synthesize the molecules.

What does entropy and the study of order and disorder have to do with steam engines and automobiles? To understand the connection, it is first necessary to understand how a heat engine works. Imagine you have a box, and one side of the box is filled with hot air and the other side is filled with cold air. If left undisturbed, this system will spontaneously become disorderly, that is, heat will be exchanged until the temperature is uniform throughout the box. But now imagine that energy is continuously added to the system. Suppose that a flame is placed under one side of the box, as shown in Figure 2–16. The flame will heat the air above it, and, in turn, the hot air will rise. This process creates order, hot air in one corner and cold air in the other. Cold air will then flow along the bottom of the box as shown in the figure. This moving air has kinetic energy and has the capacity to perform work. If a well-balanced toy windmill is placed in the box, it will rotate. Thus, the heat of the flame is converted to work. This is not a perpetual motion machine and is not in violation of the First Law, because thermal energy from the candle is constantly being added to the system.

The amount of work performed on the windmill is related to the velocity of the moving air. In turn, the air will move most rapidly if the temperature difference between the hot air and the cold air is greatest. Think of it in this way. If you have very hot air and very cold air, the difference in density between them will be great, and the hot air will rise rapidly. In turn, this rapidly rising air will initiate a rapid convection current, and the windmill will be forced to rotate rapidly. Conversely, if the hot air is only slightly warmer than the cold air, it will rise slowly, and the convection current will move slowly. The weak convection current transmits little force, and only little work will be performed.

This reasoning leads to one statement of the Second Law of Thermodynamics:

The quantity of work performed by a heat engine depends on the temperature difference between the hot reservoir and the cold reservoir.

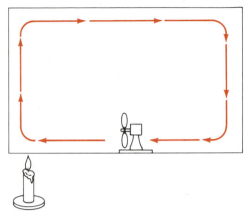

Figure 2–16
A simple heat engine. The flame sustains a convection current, and the moving air turns the blades of the toy windmill.

Heat energy can be converted efficiently into work only if large differences in temperature are available.

Suppose that a mass of coal is burned in a steam locomotive. The heat is converted to useful work, and the engine travels from Paris to Amsterdam (Fig. 2–17). When the engine arrives in Amsterdam, the coal is gone. What happened to the energy? Could you somehow find it, save it, and use it to drive the train back to Paris? The answer is no. The heat from the coal was spread out into the environment. The air between Paris and Amsterdam was warmed slightly. But the locomotive cannot extract enough energy from the warm air to drive back to Paris. Thus, the energy from the coal cannot be recycled. This observation is a general one and explains why energy, once used, cannot be reused to perform work efficiently. In brief, materials can be recycled but energy cannot. The energy that was dissipated into the environment has not been destroyed—it still exists somewhere—but it is lost in the sense that it is no longer available to do work. Ingenious scientists have tried to invent heat engines that can convert *all* the energy of a fuel into work, but they have always failed. It was found, instead, that a heat engine could be made to work *only* by the following two sets of processes: (1) Heat must be absorbed by the working parts from some hot source. The hot source is generally provided when some substance such as water or air (called the "working substance") is heated by the energy obtained from a fuel, such as

Figure 2–17
Energy lost to the environment through the exhaust system of a locomotive (or any heat engine) cannot be recycled to drive the locomotive back to Paris.

wood, coal, oil, or uranium. (2) Waste heat must be rejected to an external reservoir at a lower temperature.

There are three important practical consequences of the Second Law:

1. The energy in a fuel can never be completely converted to work.

2. Useful energy cannot be recycled. If a lump of coal is burned, some of its capacity to do work is lost forever. It can never be reused.

3. Highly ordered systems are more difficult to maintain than are less-ordered systems. This is an important point. Imagine that you have two brand new cars with identical engines. One car has automatic transmission and air conditioning. It also has electrically powered windows, door locks, radio antenna, and seat adjustments—the works. The other car, built with the same quality craftsmanship, has manually operated transmission and accessories. Which car will break down more often? Of course, there are more things to go wrong with the fully equipped model; it is more orderly. More effort must be spent maintaining that order. All other things being equal, it will spend more time in the repair shop.

Figure 2–18
Many modern systems, like this vegetable farm, are highly ordered. Large inputs of energy are required to maintain this order.

The same situation also arises in many other instances. Consider agricultural systems. In a natural prairie, grains, weeds, and scrub bushes all grow together and intermingle with each other. These plants are consumed by insects, rodents, birds, large grazers, and other animals. In a modern agricultural system, on the other hand, the farmer separates weeds from the grain and cultivates only the grains (Fig. 2–18). Likewise, cattle are separated from rodents and insects, and the unwanted species are removed. This type of system produces more food for human consumption than a natural prairie. But it is more orderly and, hence, more vulnerable. Work must be constantly expended to maintain the order. This subject will be discussed further in Chapters 8 and 9. For now, the important point is this. A technical response to a problem—such as the need to grow more food—often results in creation of a more ordered system, but additional energy inputs are needed to maintain these ordered systems. And remember, ordered systems are always more susceptible to breakdown than are less-ordered systems. It is a law of nature.

Summary

This chapter opened with a discussion of the complexity of environmental problems. Solutions to environmental problems can be either technical, social, or some combination of the two.

Three actions used in environmental law are nuisance, trespass, and negligence. Legal approaches to pollution control can assume the form of: (1) restrictions, (2) a system of qualified restrictions and penalties, (3) subsidies, (4) pollution tax, or (5) rationing.

Once environmental legislation is passed by Congress, the EPA is responsible for administering the law and prosecuting offenders. Private individuals, local communities, and citizens' groups can also take environmental cases to court if they have **legal standing.**

The costs that are not accounted for by the manufacturer of a product but are borne by some other sector of the society are external costs, or **externalities.** In recent years, the cost of pollution control in the United States has been more than offset by the savings in external costs. **Cost/benefit analysis** is an attempt to balance the cost of pollution control against the cost of externalities in order to minimize the total impact of the cost on individuals.

Risk assessment is an attempt to evaluate a danger by estimating the probability that an event will occur and the consequences of that event. The magnitude of the risk is then weighed against the benefits realized by a given event.

Technical solutions to environmental problems are limited by the physical laws that govern the behavior of all matter. **The Law of Conservation of Matter** states that matter is never created or destroyed. **The First Law of Thermodynamics** states that energy cannot be created or destroyed. **The Second Law of Thermodynamics** states that when thermal energy is transformed to mechanical work, some energy is lost in the sense that it cannot be used to perform work. As a consequence of this law, useful energy cannot be recycled, because some of it is lost forever whenever it is used to do work. As a result, the supply of certain fuels is inexorably running out.

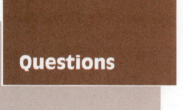

Questions

Social and Technical Approaches

1. Given the table listed below, which of the following scenarios involve social and which involve technical solutions?

Problem	Solution
Overpopulation	Encourage women to bear fewer children
Acid rain from sulfur dioxide emissions from electric power plants	Design pollution control equipment to remove the sulfur dioxide from the smokestack
Proliferation of poisonous pesticides	Develop nontoxic pest control systems

In each of the examples just given, if you chose social as your answer, show how technical solutions are part of the social remedy; if you chose technical as your answer, show how the technology would not be effective without social cooperation.

2. Discuss the differences between social and technical solutions to (a) fuel consumption for automobiles, (b) wood consumption for paper production.

Legal Aspects

3. Imagine that you were a lawyer. In each of the following cases, which type of tort—nuisance, trespass, or negligence—would you use to argue each of the following cases? In some cases would you use more than one? (a) Pesticides applied to a field spill into a river that is the drinking water supply for a town downstream. You are representing the town that is suing the farmer. (b) A company is drilling for oil at the mouth of a river in a rich salmon fishing ground. A pipe breaks, spilling oil into the river and killing the fish. You are representing the owners of fishing boats in their suit against the drilling company. (c) A rendering plant has installed insufficient air pollution control. As a result, the odor is vile. You are representing a citizen's group opposing the rendering plant.

4. Five types of legal approaches to environmental improvement were given in this chapter. If you were a legislator, which approach would you use in each of the following situations: (a) Rainwater that washes through the town dump carries toxic substances into the groundwater. (b) Sulfur dioxide emission from power plants leads to acid rain, which in turn causes significant environmental damage. (c) A new pesticide has just been discovered. It is effective against a broad range of insects, but, even in very low doses, it causes cancer in humans.

5. In 1973 and again in 1978, gasoline shortages led to widespread fear that further shortages would disrupt the economy. Therefore, many people advocated some form of government action. Rationing and gasoline taxes were proposed. What groups of people would be most affected by these two approaches? Can you think of other types of legal approaches to the problem of gasoline shortages? Discuss your proposals with your classmates.

6. For each of the following cases, list an individual or group that would have legal standing and one that would not. (a) The Forest Service sprays pesticides on a national forest to control the spruce budworm, a pest that kills spruce trees. (b) A pipeline breaks, spilling crude oil into the local river. (c) A power company proposes to build a dam that will cover a scenic canyon.

7. Identify a source of pollution or environmental degradation in your community. Discuss various types of government action that might alleviate the problem. Describe the benefits provided by each action and the problems that might arise.

8. Some legislative approaches for reducing water consumption include (a) Tax all water usage at a constant rate per liter. (b) Tax water usage at a progressive rate, that is, allow the tax to rise with increasing use. (c) Shut off all water from 2 P.M. to 4 P.M. (d) Shut off all water from 2 A.M. to 4 A.M. (e) Ration water at some reasonable level. How would each measure accomplish the purpose? What are the side effects? Can you propose better legislation?

9. Argue for or against the proposition that noise can be a form of trespass.

Cost/Benefit Analysis

10. The Natural Resources Defense Council (NRDC) is a private organization that protects environmental quality by filing lawsuits against companies or individuals allegedly causing excess pollution. Former EPA administrator William Ruckelshaus has criticized the NRDC for failing to account for the costs of regulation that their suits have mandated. In response, D. Doniger, a lawyer for the NRDC replied "We take the view that there are rights involved here . . . rights to be protected from threats to your health regardless of the cost involved." Prepare a class debate. Have one side argue Mr. Ruckelshaus' position and the other argue Mr. Doniger's position.

11. On February 26, 1972, heavy rains destroyed a dam across Buffalo Creek in Logan County, West Virginia. The resulting flood killed 75 people and rendered 5000 homeless. The dam was built from unstable coal mine refuse or "spoil." A United States Geological Survey had warned of the instability of many dams in Logan County, especially the one at Buffalo Creek. Soil stabilization and reclamation programs directed at mine spoil dams would have added to the cost of producing coal. After the flood, the Bureau of Mines denied responsibility for corrective action, contending that although mine spoil is within the Bureau's jurisdiction, dams are not. (a) How would you relate the concept of economic externalities to this tragedy? (b) Suggest legislation designed to prevent future Appalachian dam disasters. (c) How will your legislation affect the price of coal and its competitive position in the fuel market?

12. Explain why the control of pollution may result in a net increase in the number of jobs. Give examples.

13. If you were the mayor of a small town, and a prosperous factory, the largest single employer in the town, were illegally dumping untreated wastes into a stream, what action would you recommend? What if the factory were barely profitable?

14. If the burden of environmental control falls heavily on some particular segments of society, do you think it would be fair to provide compensation? Would you favor granting such compensation to workers who lose their jobs? To companies whose costs for environmental cleanup are high? To stockholders whose equities are reduced in value? For each of these segments, what kinds of abuses are possible? What benefits to the environment would such compensations provide?

15. Suppose that you were a reporter assigned to compare the cost of stopping the pollution of the local river with the economic cost of the pollution. What sources of information would you seek out? Which category of costs would be more difficult to estimate? Defend your answer.

Risk Assessment

16. Some risks such as smoking or engaging in dangerous sports are self-imposed. Prepare a class debate. Have one side argue that self-imposed risks involve individual choice and should not come under government jurisdiction, while the other side opposes.

17. Do you think that it would be reasonable to eliminate all risks generated by technology? Defend your answer.

Thermodynamics

18. An engineer designed and built the roller coaster shown in Figure 2–19. He was fired. Why?

19. Suppose that a refrigerator is placed in the middle of a room, turned on, and the door left open. Will the temperature of the room rise, fall, or remain the same? Explain.

20. Mountain ranges slowly erode and crumble, ultimately weathering down to flat land. Is entropy increasing or decreasing during this process? Explain.

21. The food-growing capacity of the world could be increased if salt were removed from seawater to provide fresh water to irrigate deserts that lie close to the sea. However, all seawater purification plants built

Figure 2–19

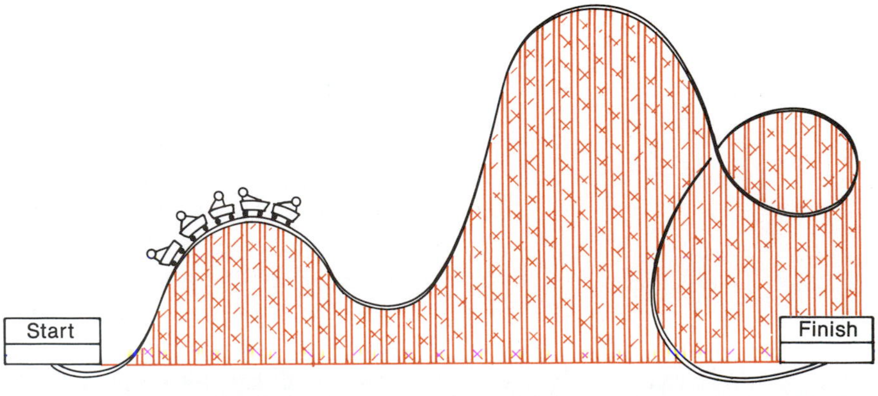

to date consume large quantities of energy. Explain why energy is needed for the separation. Do you think that someone may invent a process whereby salt water could be purified without the input of auxiliary energy? Explain.

22. Referring to the difficulty in recovering dispersed minerals from the ocean, a scientist commented, "The Second Law of Thermodynamics comes in with a vengeance. . . ." Explain what the remark meant.

23. Energy from the sun, wind, and tides is considered to be "renewable," whereas energy from fossil fuels is not. Is this evaluation true in a theoretical sense or in a practical sense? Discuss.

24. Explain, in terms of the Second Law, why a complex establishment such as a nuclear power plant has many different potential modes of failure.

Suggested Readings

A good introduction to environmental economics is given by:

Paul Burrows: *The Economic Theory of Pollution Control.* Cambridge, MA, MIT Press, 1980. 192 pp.

John A. Butlin (ed): *The Economics of Environmental and Natural Resources Policy.* Boulder, CO, Westview Press, 1981. 206 pp.

Allen V. Kneese: *Measuring the Benefits of Clean Air and Water.* Washington, D.C., Resources for the Future, Inc., 1984. 159 pp.

Timothy O'Riordan: *An Annotated Reader in Environmental Planning and Management.* New York, Pergamon Press, 1983. 460 pp.

Henry M. Peskin, Paul R. Portney, and Allen V. Kneese (eds.): *Environmental Regulation and the U. S. Economy.* Washington D.C., Resources for the Future, 1981. 163 pp.

Tom Tietenberg: *Environmental and Natural Resource Economics.* Glenview, IL, Scott Foresman and Company, 1984.

Two periodical articles outlining cost/benefit analysis and the cost of pollution controls include:

Gordon L. Brady and Blair T. Bower: Benefit-cost analysis in air quality management. *Environmental Science and Technology, 15*(3):256, 1981.

Conservation Foundation: Cost-benefit analysis, a tricky game. *Conservation Foundation Letter,* December 1980.

A treatment of the Reserve Mining episode is:

Robert V. Bartlett: *The Reserve Mining Controversy Science, Technology and Environmental Quality.* Indiana University Press, 1982. 293 pp.

United States environmental law is discussed in:

J. Gordon Arbuckle, et al.: *Environmental Law Handbook* 8th ed. Rockville, MD, Government Institutes, Inc., 1985. 586 pp.

David B. Firestone and Dr. Frank C. Reed: *Environmental Law For Non-Lawyers.* Ann Arbor, MI, Ann Arbor Science Publishers, 1983. 282 pp.

Government Institutes: *Environmental Statutes.* Washington, D.C., Government Institutes, 1985. 731 pp.

D.R. Greenwood et al.: *A Handbook of Key Federal Regulations and Criteria for Multimedia Environmental Control.* Environmental Protection Agency, EPA-600/7-79-175, 1979. 277 pp.

R. Shep Melnick: Regulation and the Courts: *The Case of the Clean Air Act.* Washington D.C., The Brookings Institution, 1983. 404 pp.

Risk assessment is summarized in:

Robert W. Crandall and Lester B. Lave: *The Scientific Basis of Health and Safety Regulation.* Washington, D.C., The Brookings Institution, 1981. 309 pp.

Pascal J. Imperato and Greg Mitchell: *Acceptable Risk.* New York, NY, Viking Penguin, 1985. 286 pp.

Lester B. Lave (ed.): *Quantitative Risk Assessment in Regulation.* Washington D.C., The Brookings Institution, 1982. 264 pp.

You will find further discussion of heat engines and the Second Law of Thermodynamics in:

Jonathan Turk and Amos Turk: *Physical Science.* 3rd ed. Philadelphia, Saunders College Publishing, 1987. 642 pp.

An interesting book that relates thermodynamics to world planning is:

J. Rifkin: *Entropy: A New World View.* New York, Viking Press, 1980.

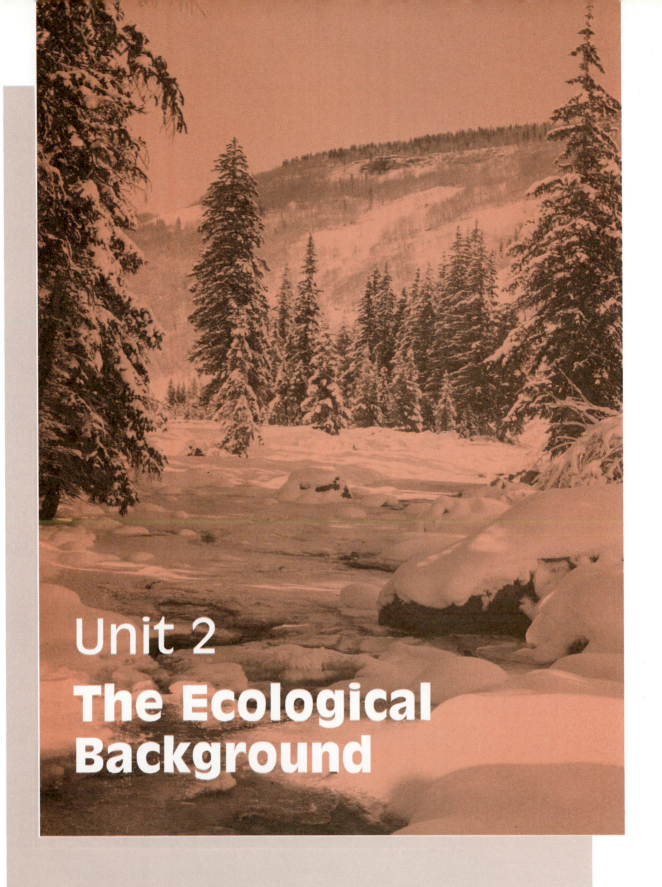

Unit 2
The Ecological Background

3.1
Ecosystems

If you look around a forest, or a city park, or your own backyard, you may wonder why animals and plants live the way they do. Grass grows in the open but not under that tree. What does grass need in the way of soil, sunshine, water, or minerals that it finds in one place but not in another? A single housefly may lay several thousand eggs every year. What happened to all the offspring? Why haven't they overpopulated the Earth? Another question may come to mind: "If this forest is cut down, could crops be grown on the land or would the soil and climate be unsuitable in some way?"

All these questions are about **ecology,** the branch of biology that examines the interactions between living organisms and their environments. All living things, including people, can survive only in appropriate environments. These statements generate still more questions: "What constitutes an appropriate environment?" "When are environments being endangered?"

Ecologists have discovered that there are certain rules about organisms and their environments that can be used to answer these and other questions. In this and the following three chapters, these general principles of ecology will be considered, with an emphasis on systems that do not include people.

Ecosystems

What Is a System?

We hear the word **system** used in a variety of contexts. People speak of a digestive system, a cooling system, a system of government, or an ecosystem. The four examples given here are all quite different from one another, yet they all share a common concept:

> A system is a collection of objects bonded together in some way so that the collection is more than an independent assemblage of the parts.

Thus, a digestive system is more than a random assembly of stomach, liver, intestines, pancreas, and other organs; the individual parts work together in an integrated manner. If one of the components is removed or damaged, the entire system malfunctions.

Very often, the size and complexity of a system depends mainly on what we choose to study

A high, semidesert ecosystem in Bolivia.

at any one time. For example, a national government that is made up of many people working together can be considered to be a system. However, an individual human body is also a system. Looking at a human being from another perspective, the body is composed of smaller units such as the digestive system and the circulatory system.

What Is an Ecosystem?

This book is a study of our environment. Although the natural environment consists of the entire Earth and the atmosphere that surrounds it, this complete system is much too complex to study at one time. Even a single forest may cover thousands of square kilometers and contain thousands of different types of plants and animals living together. In order to separate these large systems into smaller areas that can be studied more precisely, ecologists work with manageable units such as a hillside, a forested valley, a lake, or a field. In 1887, Stephen Forbes, a biologist for the Illinois Natural History Survey, wrote:

> A lake . . . forms a little world within itself—a microcosm within which all the elemental forces are at work and the play of life goes on in full, but on so small a scale as to bring it easily within the mental grasp. . . .
> If one wishes to become acquainted with the black bass, for example, he will learn but little if he limits himself to that species. He must evidently study also the species upon which it depends for

its existence and the various conditions upon which these depend.

Today we would call Forbes's lake, or any other manageably small unit with more or less distinct boundaries, an **ecosystem** (Fig. 3–1). Forbes's com-

Figure 3–1
A lake forms a partly isolated ecosystem enclosed by its banks.

ments point out the other characteristics of an ecosystem: It consists of all the different organisms living in an area, along with their physical environment.

One of the most important concepts to understand about an ecosystem is that it is nearly self-contained. In an extreme case, think of an island in the middle of the ocean. Plants grow, die, and decay. Animals eat and in turn are eaten. Yet there is very little exchange of life or raw materials with other islands, or other ecosystems. The system survives largely in biological isolation. Similarly, think of a valley in the mountains. Although seeds occasionally blow from one valley to another, and some animals such as birds and migratory mammals roam far from their birthplace, most of the exchanges occur within the system. On the other hand, no system functions in a truly independent manner. Sunlight is absorbed and atmospheric gases are exchanged; thus, each tiny ecosystem is just one part of the Earth.

Combining what we have learned about ecosystems we can arrive at a definition:

An ecosystem is a system formed by the interactions of a variety of individual organisms with each other and with their physical environment. Ecosystems are nearly self-contained so that the exchange of nutrients within the system is much greater than exchanges with other systems.

Not all ecosystems are natural. A farm may be considered an ecosystem, because, in order to manage the farm effectively, all the interactions between crop plants, fertilizers, soil, climate, and the natural animal and plant life of the area must be recognized. Similarly, space stations and aquaria are all artificial ecosystems.

3.2
The Biotic and Abiotic Components of Ecosystems

An ecosystem is not entirely a biological entity. Any complete description of an ecosystem must include the physical environment as well as the biological components, and the interactions between the two.

The biological, or **biotic,** components of an ecosystem include both living organisms and products of these organisms. Thus all bacteria, fungi, plants, and animals are included, as well as waste products of these organisms such as fallen leaves

and branches from plants and feces and urine from animals. In addition, when an organism dies, it generally remains within the ecosystem, and the body or stalk or trunk remains as a part of the system.

The nonbiological, or physical portions, of an ecosystem are called the **abiotic** components. The biological world lives within and depends on the abiotic environment. In fact, as we shall see, the interrelationships between the biotic and abiotic are so intimate that living and nonliving systems must be studied simultaneously.

Sunlight

Recall from the Chapter 2 that the laws of thermodynamics assure us that energy cannot be recycled. If coal is burned in the boiler of a steam locomotive and the train drives from Paris to Amsterdam, that energy is lost in the sense that it can never be reused to perform mechanical work. If you wish to ride back to Paris, you must buy more coal or find some other type of fuel. Organisms are also bound by the constraints of thermodynamics and need a continuous supply of energy to survive. The source of energy in nearly all ecosystems is the Sun. Some of the energy in sunlight is absorbed within the green leaves of plants and used in the biomanufacture of complex, energy-rich materials such as sugars. In turn, sugars and other related compounds are used as a primary fuel source by the plants and animals that eat them. The Sun also provides the energy to warm the Earth. Without the Sun, temperatures would approach absolute zero, there would be few gases or liquids, and there would not be enough thermal energy to initiate the complex chemical reactions necessary for life.

Nutrients

Organisms are made up of matter and need a constant supply of chemical nutrients to grow, to reproduce, and to regulate bodily functions. The main components of living tissues are carbon, hydrogen, oxygen, nitrogen, phosphorus, and sulfur, but a large variety of other nutrients are also required. Nutrients are found in the air, soil, and water.

Air

The atmosphere is composed mainly of molecules of nitrogen and oxygen, with smaller concentrations of carbon dioxide, water vapor, and other gases. Most of the gases that exist in our atmosphere exist in the atmospheres of other planets and have also been detected far out in space, drifting about between the stars and collected in large masses around the core of the Milky Way galaxy. Therefore, the existence of an atmosphere on Earth and the presence of specific gases can be explained by abiological laws. However, the composition of the Earth's atmosphere is not easily explained by abiological laws alone. Therefore, many scientists believe that living organisms may have been active agents in the evolution of the modern atmosphere. This subject will be discussed further in Chapter 6.

Soil

Soil is composed partly of finely ground rock and minerals, so it might be considered to be a physical material. But the pulverized rock that is found on Mars is called dust, not soil. True soil contains minerals mixed with large quantities of partially decayed plant and animal matter. The organic material serves many functions. It provides nutrients that can be reused and recycled by plants. Organic matter also changes the physical nature of ground rock so that it retains moisture more effectively. In addition, the roots of living plants hold the soil together and prevent erosion during spring rains and summer wind storms. A single kilogram of fertile soil in a temperate ecosystem may house 2 trillion bacteria, 400 million fungi, 50 million algae, and 30 million protozoa as well as thousands of worms, insects, and mites. All these organisms are an integral part of the process of decay and recycling that are essential to the growth of the plants and animals that live on the surface.

Water

Water is formed by a great number of different kinds of chemical reactions and is found throughout our galaxy and all the planets in our Solar System. On Earth, water was present long before life evolved, and today much of the water transport is initiated by nonliving influences. Sunlight causes water to evaporate; water vapor then condenses and falls to the earth as rain or snow. Eventually, liquid water is pulled by gravity back toward the sea. Yet living organisms, too, play an important part in the water cycle. Plants withdraw water from the soil, and much of this eventually moves through and evaporates from the surface of leaves or needles by the process of **evapotranspiration.** In recent years, humans have become an important factor in the water cycle by damming rivers and pumping groundwater. The water cycle (hydrological cycle) will be discussed in more detail in Chapter 17.

Climate

The combinations of temperature and moisture in an area are the important factors that establish the climate, the yearly cycle of weather patterns. Obviously, climate, in turn, affects the characteristics of an ecosystem; polar bears do not live in the desert, and desert cacti cannot live in a tropical rain forest.

Many other factors combine to create the abiotic environment. Thus, the salinity of a bay where rivers and ocean meet, the turbulence of water at a seashore, or the amount of wind on a mountaintop all contribute to the physical environment to which organisms must adapt.

3.3
Photosynthesis and Respiration
Photosynthesis

Since the Second Law of Thermodynamics assures us that useful energy cannot be recycled, ecosystems need a continuous supply of energy to survive. Almost all the energy available to us on Earth comes from the Sun. Sunlight evaporates water that later falls as rain. The Sun heats the Earth unevenly, causing winds to blow. Plants are fundamental to all life on Earth because they have the ability to trap some of the solar energy that strikes their leaves and needles and to use this energy to build living tissues. This process, known as **photosynthesis,** is expressed by the following equation:

$$\text{carbon dioxide} + \text{water} \xrightarrow[\text{of sunlight}]{\text{gives, in the presence}} \text{sugar} + \text{oxygen}$$

$$6CO_2 + 6H_2O \xrightarrow{\text{sunlight}} C_6H_{12}O_6 + 6O_2$$

During photosynthesis, the inorganic energy-poor molecules, carbon dioxide and water, are converted into organic energy-rich food molecules such as sugars. ("Organic" and "inorganic" are defined in Special Topic A.) Since plants do not need to feed on other organisms, they are called **autotrophs,** meaning "self-nourishers." Animals cannot use the Sun in this manner; they are therefore dependent on plants, directly or indirectly, as their fundamental source of food.

To better understand the process of photosynthesis, think of the following experiment. Take a small seed, say a pumpkin seed, and plant it in a pot of dry soil. Weigh the soil and the seed together. Then water the plant and allow it to grow. Huge vines spread, and large orange pumpkins appear at the ends of the vines. But the soil does not disappear. If you dry the grown plant with the soil and weigh the entire system, you will find that it is

Special Topic A
Minerals and Nutrients: Vocabulary

An **element** is a substance that consists of only one kind of atom. Carbon consists of only carbon atoms, oxygen of oxygen atoms, and hydrogen of hydrogen atoms. Therefore, carbon, oxygen, and hydrogen are **elements**. Water is not an element because it consists of groups of hydrogen and oxygen atoms bonded together (H_2O). Groups of bonded atoms are **molecules,** and a substance consisting of molecules containing more than one element is a **compound.** Under terrestrial conditions, most elements exist as molecules rather than as single, isolated atoms. For instance, nitrogen gas consists of molecules containing two atoms each, N_2; oxygen is O_2; and hydrogen is H_2. Solid elements, such as carbon and iron, consist of networks of many atoms bonded together.

One particular group of substances has always been considered unique and very important. It consists of substances found mainly in living organisms. Many of these substances, such as proteins and cellulose (in plant cell walls), are very complex and cannot be represented by simple formulas. For many years, chemists thought that these substances could be produced only by living organisms. Hence, they came to be called **organic** compounds. All these compounds contain carbon atoms bonded to hydrogen atoms or to other carbon atoms. After it was shown in a series of discoveries from 1828 to 1845 that some components of these substances could be synthesized from nonliving sources, "organic" came to refer to compounds containing C–C or C–H bonds, with or without other atoms. (Marble, $CaCO_3$, is not considered organic, because, although it contains carbon, the carbon atom is not bonded to carbon or hydrogen.)

By this definition, substances such as proteins, carbohydrates, and fats are organic, but synthetic plastics also qualify. Their molecules contain long chains of carbon atoms. Plastics are generally synthesized from oil or coal, organic molecules produced by living organisms millions of years ago. However, plastics could be made from inorganic carbon dioxide and water, and they would still be organic compounds.

Having defined "organic," we can define "inorganic' simply by exclusion. An **inorganic** substance is any substance that is not organic. Or, any substance that does not contain carbon atoms bonded to other carbon atoms or to hydrogen atoms is inorganic.

Nutrients are substances that organisms must take in from outside themselves, as part of their diet. They may be organic or inorganic. In the human diet, proteins, carbohydrates, and vitamins are organic. Iron and calcium are inorganic nutrients. **Minerals** are inorganic solids that occur naturally in the Earth. Each usually has a specific composition and characteristic structure. Thus, the mineral quartz is composed of silicon dioxide (SiO_2) arranged in a particular crystalline structure. **Water,** which is also vital to all living organisms, is inorganic but not a mineral because it is a liquid.

much heavier than the original soil. The question is, "Where did the additional matter come from?" The green leaves of the pumpkin combined carbon dioxide from the air and water from the soil to form sugar and other plant tissues.

Respiration

The energy trapped by the plant during photosynthesis is not lost. If a pumpkin is burned, it will produce light and heat, which is a way of releasing the stored chemical energy (Fig. 3–2). Carbon dioxide and water are low-energy compounds; they cannot be burned to produce heat. Sugar, the product of photosynthesis, contains stored chemical energy and can be burned to produce heat. Carbon dioxide and water are released as byproducts:

$$\text{sugar} + \text{oxygen} \xrightarrow[\text{produce}]{\text{burns to}} \begin{array}{c}\text{carbon}\\\text{dioxide}\end{array} + \text{water} + \text{energy}$$

$$C_6H_{12}O_6 + 6O_2 \longrightarrow 6CO_2 + 6H_2O + \text{energy}$$

A fire is a rapid form of oxidation. Sugar also combines with oxygen inside living cells to produce the same products (carbon dioxide, water, and energy) in the same proportions. The difference is that in a living organism, the oxidation proceeds at a slower and more controlled rate. This process, **respiration,** releases the energy stored in complex molecules for use in maintaining cell functions.

Think of respiration as a slow, controlled burning. In fact, the equation describing this process is the same as the equation for a fire:

$$\text{sugar} + \text{oxygen} \xrightarrow{\text{respiration}} \begin{array}{c}\text{carbon}\\\text{dioxide}\end{array} + \text{water} + \text{energy}$$

$$C_6H_{12}O_6 + 6O_2 \longrightarrow 6CO_2 + 6H_2O + \text{energy}$$

Plants engage in both photosynthesis and respiration. Sugars are produced by photosynthesis. These sugars are then used as a source of chemical energy, which is released during respiration within the leaf tissues. The energy is then used to build other complex molecules and to maintain cell functions. Animals cannot make their own food but must eat other organisms to obtain energy-rich molecules needed for survival. Therefore, they are consumers. Consumers are called **heterotrophs,** referring to organisms that are nourished from other sources.

3.4
Production and Consumption in Ecosystems

Heterotrophs can be further divided into two large categories. **Herbivores** are animals that eat plants. **Carnivores** are animals that eat the flesh of other animals. Carnivores can be large, like a tiger, or small, like a ladybug, or even tiny, like a microscopic amoeba.

A few insect-catching plants are both producers and consumers, and many animals, such as pigs, bears, rats, and humans, are **omnivores,** animals that eat both plants and animals.

Scavengers are animals that eat dead plant and animal matter. Thus, a vulture is a scavenger because it eats dead animals, and a termite is part of the same classification because it feeds on dead and decaying wood. The distinction between a scavenger and a herbivore or a carnivore is not always clear in nature. Thus, an arctic fox is generally considered to be a carnivore because it hunts and consumes a wide variety of small animals. But in the winter, when game is scarce, foxes follow polar bears and scavenge the remains of seals and other large marine animals killed by the bear.

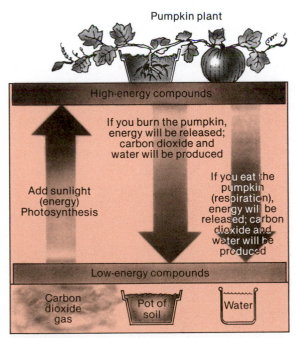

Figure 3–2
Some energy relationships of a pumpkin plant.

A reindeer in the tundra. All animals must obtain their food by eating plants or other animals. (Photography by Eric Hosking, National Audubon Society)

Decomposers

Because plants can manufacture their own food, it would seem at first glance that an ecosystem could survive indefinitely if it contained only plants. But this is not the case. Plants remove minerals from the soil, and soil minerals are replaced only very slowly from the rock beneath. In an agricultural system, nutrients are often replaced artificially by fertilization. In a natural system, if plants just went on living and growing and dying, eventually all the minerals in the ecosystem would be absorbed into the bodies of plants. Then there would be huge piles of dead plants containing minerals but no more minerals in the soil, and plant growth would stop. Therefore, every ecosystem needs, and contains, **decomposers** (Fig. 3–3).

Heterotrophic organisms that feed solely on dead organic matter are called **saprophytes.** The bulk of the saprophytic decomposition is carried out by bacteria, fungi, and protozoans. Imagine that a piece of organic litter falls to the floor of a forest. In a typical sequence, microscopic bacteria or fungi will excrete chemicals, called **enzymes,** that break down the complex chemical compounds in the object. Some of the breakdown products are absorbed as food, whereas others are left behind. These serve as a food supply for other organisms that carry the decomposition one step further. Eventually, the waste products of the final line of decomposers are energy-poor mineral nutrients that are reabsorbed, and thus recycled, by plants.

Trophic Levels

The **trophic level** to which an organism belongs describes how far the organism is removed from plants in its level of nourishment. Green plants make up the first trophic level, herbivores make up the second trophic level, and the higher trophic levels are composed of the carnivores. For example, a grasshopper that eats grass belongs to the second trophic level, a shrew that eats the grasshopper belongs to the third, an owl that eats the shrew belongs to the fourth, and so on (Fig. 3–4). In another commonly used set of terms, plants are said to be **producers,** herbivores are **primary consumers,** and carnivores are **secondary, tertiary,** and **quaternary consumers,** depending on what they eat. Omnivores, which eat both consumers and producers, may belong to many trophic levels (Fig. 3–5 and Table 3–1).

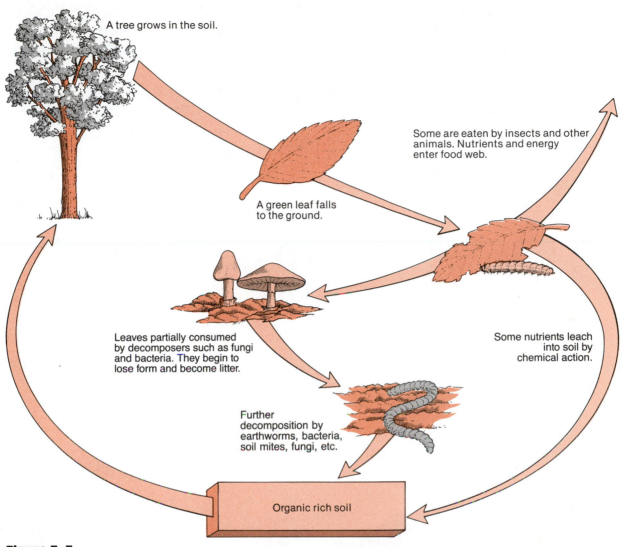

A tree grows in the soil.

A green leaf falls to the ground.

Some are eaten by insects and other animals. Nutrients and energy enter food web.

Leaves partially consumed by decomposers such as fungi and bacteria. They begin to lose form and become litter.

Some nutrients leach into soil by chemical action.

Further decomposition by earthworms, bacteria, soil mites, fungi, etc.

Organic rich soil

Figure 3–3
The decomposition cycle.

Table 3–1
Ecological Classification of Organisms Based on What They Eat

Ecological Classification	Trophic Level	Level of Consumption	Examples
Autotroph	First	Nonconsumer	Trees, grass
Heterotroph	Second	Primary consumer	Grasshopper, field mouse, cow
	Third	Secondary consumer	Praying mantis, owl, wolf
	Fourth	Tertiary consumer	Shrew, owl

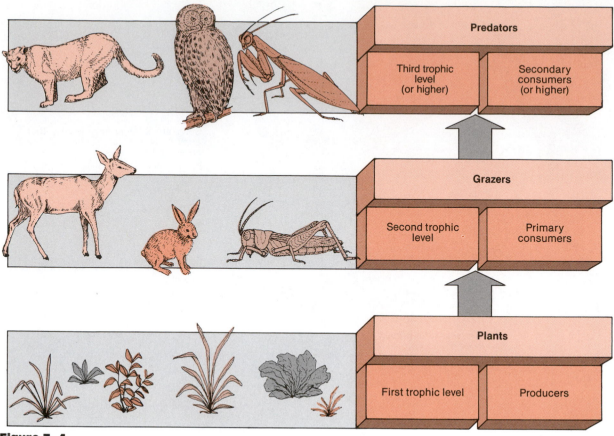

Figure 3–4
A simplified representation of the trophic levels in a temperate forest ecosystem.

Figure 3–5
The bear, an omnivore, consumes organisms from various trophic levels in the food chain, acting as a primary, secondary, tertiary, and quaternary consumer.

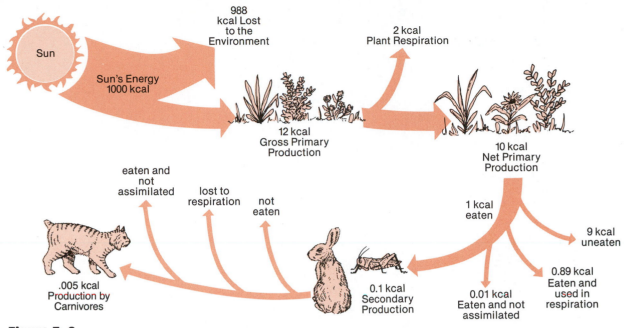

Figure 3–6
Energy relationships in an ecosystem. This diagram illustrates average values
for energy transfers; actual values will vary from system to system.

3.5
Productivity and Energy Flow

During the process of production and consumption, energy is passed along, or flows, from one organism to another. For example, solar energy is converted to chemical energy within the leaves of green plants. The leaves can then be eaten by some herbivore, and the herbivore may in turn be eaten by a carnivore.

Consider a hypothetical ecosystem that receives 1000 kilocalories (kcal) of light energy in a given day (Fig. 3–6). Most of this energy is not absorbed at all. Some is simply reflected back into space. Of the energy that is absorbed, most is stored as heat or used for evaporation of water. A small amount is assimilated by plants.

The **gross primary productivity** of an ecosystem is the rate at which organic matter is produced during photosynthesis. Gross primary productivity is often expressed in terms of kilocalories of chemical energy stored per square meter per year (kcal/m^2/yr). Alternatively, productivity can be expressed in terms of grams of material produced per square meter per year (g/m^2/yr). Only about half of the gross productivity accumulates as new

plant matter, because the rest of the chemical energy is metabolized by the plant's own respiration and released to the environment as heat. The net gain in plant matter is called the **net primary productivity.** The net primary productivity appears as plant growth and is available for consumption by heterotrophs.

Net primary productivity =
Gross primary productivity − plant respiration

Productivity depends on a variety of factors such as sunlight, temperature, rainfall, and the availability of nutrients. As shown in Table 3–2, the net productivity of a tropical rain forest is orders of magnitude greater than that in a desert.

Some of the plant matter produced is consumed by animals or decomposers, and some accumulates in the environment. The total quantity of organic matter present at any one time in an ecosystem is called the **biomass.** The biomass equals the total organic matter gained through net productivity over a period of time minus the quantity of material that is consumed and lost during respiration by animals.

Let us return to the hypothetical ecosystem that receives 1000 kcal of sunlight. Although the ef-

Table 3–2
Net Primary Productivity of Major Ecosystems*

Type of Ecosystem	Net Primary Productivity, g/(m² year)	
	Normal Range	Mean
Tropical rain forest	1000–3500	2200
Tropical seasonal forest	1000–2500	1600
Temperate evergreen forest	600–2500	1300
Temperate deciduous forest	600–2500	1200
Boreal forest (taiga)	400–2000	800
Woodland and shrubland	250–1200	700
Savanna	200–2000	900
Temperate grassland	200–1500	600
Tundra and alpine	10–400	140
Desert and semidesert scrub	10–250	90
Extreme desert, rock, sand, and ice	0–10	3
Cultivated land	100–3500	650
Swamp and marsh	800–3500	2000
Lake and stream	100–1500	250
Open ocean	2–400	125
Upwelling zones	400–1000	500
Continental shelf	200–600	360
Algal beds and reefs	500–4000	2500
Estuaries	200–3500	1500

*From R. H. Whittaker: *Communities and Ecosystems,* 2nd ed. New York, Macmillan, 1975.

ficiency of energy transfer varies from ecosystem to ecosystem, as an average value, of the 1000 kcal absorbed, only about 12 kcal are utilized during photosynthesis. Of these 12 kcal 2 are used for plant respiration and about 10 kcal are stored in the plant tissue as energy-rich material, which animals can use for food. What happened to the 990 kcal that is not stored in plant tissue? Where did they go? They are dispersed into the air in unusable forms, just as the energy from a liter of gasoline that drives an automobile is dispersed and unavailable to power the car again.

$$
\begin{array}{lll}
1000\ \text{kcal} \longrightarrow & 990\ \text{kcal} & +\ 10\ \text{kcal stored} \\
\text{of sunlight} & \text{lost to the} & \text{as plant tissue} \\
& \text{environment} &
\end{array}
$$

Secondary productivity is defined as the rate of formation of new organic matter by heterotrophs. Of the net primary productivity available in a northern forest, herbivores (e.g., caterpillars, deer, most insects) eat only about 1 to 3 percent.

In other communities on land, as much as 15 percent of the vegetation may be eaten. In the oceans, this figure is much higher; for example, in some systems, 80 percent of the net primary productivity is consumed by herbivores.

Very little of the plant matter that is consumed is actually converted to animal tissue. In terms of energy content, the conversion is only about 10 percent. This energy loss is shown in Figure 3–6 where a rabbit gains 0.1 kcal of secondary production for every 1 kcal of food eaten. What happens to the other 90 percent? Figure 3–6 shows that most of this difference is used in respiration to power the animal's movements and maintain its body functions. A small amount is not assimilated at all and is therefore excreted in the feces. Thus, relatively little energy is left over for the production of new body tissue. To put this concept on a familiar level, consider an adult human. A person eats daily, yet a healthy adult doesn't gain any weight at all.

To summarize, although there are large variations from ecosystem to ecosystem, as a generalization, for every 10 kcal of plant tissue available to herbivores, about 1 kcal will be eaten, and only about 0.1 kcal will be stored in the form of body weight.

Carnivores that eat herbivores are likewise inefficient in converting food to body weight, so the energy available to the carnivore is even less. It is obvious, then, that the amount of usable energy *decreases* as it is transferred from sunlight to plants to animals. Therefore, animals have *less* useful energy available to them than do plants. For example, even if the organisms at each trophic level were able to find, capture, and eat all the net productivity from the previous trophic level, the tertiary consumers would receive only about one tenth times one tenth times one tenth (or one thousandth) of the energy present in the original producers in their food web.

Thus, we see that there is a decreasing quantity of energy available at each trophic level. As a consequence, there will be a decreasing mass of organisms at each level. This relationship can be shown pictorially in a graph called a **food pyramid** (Fig. 3–7).

Owing to the structure of food pyramids, there are seldom more than 5 trophic levels in an ecosystem. For example, a deer, which is a primary consumer, travels only a few kilometers a day as it grazes, whereas a wolf, which is a secondary or tertiary consumer, may have to travel 30 km a day to find enough to eat. A hypothetical animal that feeds on wolves or tigers would have to cover an extremely large hunting area to find enough of its widely scattered prey. It is not energetically feasible to try to harvest the small amount of food energy available in the highest trophic levels. This is one reason why humans eat herbivores, such as cows and sheep, rather than carnivores, such as hawks and lions.

It is also clear that in times of food scarcity, omnivores, including humans, can avoid the energy losses at one tropic level and use the Earth's resources more efficiently by adopting a vegetarian diet. For example, suppose that a farmer wishes to plant a crop of soybeans and corn. The farmer can either eat the vegetables directly or feed them to a cow and then eat the cow. Figure 3–8 shows that the Sun's energy is used most effectively if people eat plants. If vegetable crops such as soybeans and

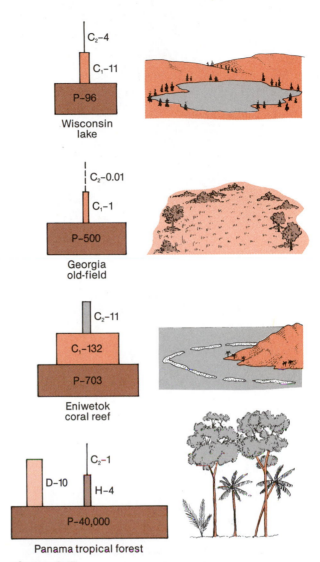

Figure 3–7
Pyramids of biomass in some typical ecosystems. Values in grams of dry weight per square meter. (From Krebs, *Basic Ecology*)

corn are eaten directly, 1350 kg of harvest can support about 22 people. If the plants are fed to cattle first and the meat is then eaten, only one person can be supported. (This topic will be discussed further in Chapter 9.)

3.6
Food Webs

From the discussion in the previous section, we can envision that the flow of food energy in an ecosystem progresses through a **food chain** in which

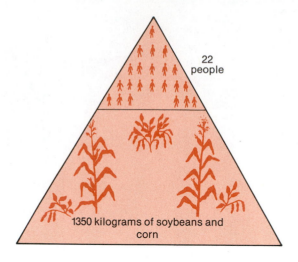

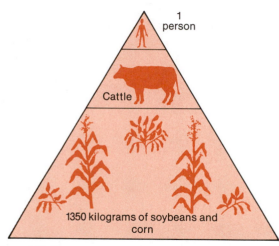

Figure 3–8
The relative efficiencies of vegetarian and carnivorous diets for humans. *A,* In a vegetarian diet, 1350 kg of plant matter can support 22 people for the same length of time that *B,* 1350 kg of plant matter, can support only one person who eats only meat.

one step follows another: Primary consumers eat producers, secondary consumers eat primary consumers, and so on.

However, natural systems are rarely so orderly and linear. Many organisms occupy several trophic levels simultaneously. For example, a raven can be a primary consumer when it eats corn, a secondary consumer when it eats grasshoppers, and a tertiary consumer if it manages to catch a shrew or small snake. In addition, ravens will eat dead animals and are therefore also scavengers. In nearly all natural ecosystems, the patterns of con-

A gecko climbing up a glass window. Note the padlike toes that enable this animal to climb on vertical surfaces. (Gordon Smith, National Audubon Society)

sumption are so complicated that the term **food web** is more descriptive because there are many cross-links connecting the various organisms. Figure 3–9 is a greatly simplified food web because it shows none of the decomposers in the systems.

In Chapter 2, we introduced the concept that environmental systems are often so complex that seemingly obvious solutions disturb the system in unpredicted ways. This generalization frequently applies to food webs. Ecologist Lamont Cole investigated one such situation in the 1950s. The World Health Organization tried to eliminate malaria from Borneo by spraying the environment with the insecticide DDT. The spray killed the mosquitoes that carry malaria, but unforeseen problems arose. Quantities of DDT were consumed by cockroaches. These insects, which are larger than mosquitoes and more resistant to DDT, did not die immediatley. Geckos (insect-eating lizards), which ate the cockroaches, ingested the insecticide in turn and suffered nerve damage from it. Their reflexes became slower, and many more of them than usual

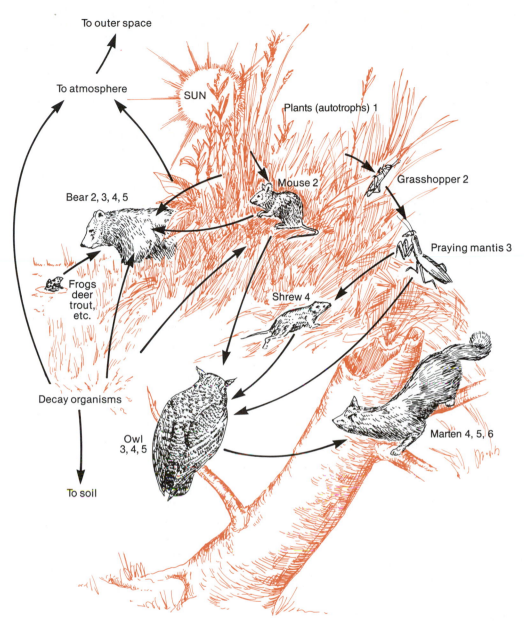

Figure 3–9
Simplified land-based food web. Arrows are in the direction of progressive loss
of energy available for life processes. Numerals refer to levels of consumption.

were caught and eaten by cats. Because most of their gecko predators were now dead, caterpillars eating the thatched roofs of local houses multiplied unchecked, and the roofs started to collapse. In addition, the cats were soon dying of DDT poisoning from eating the geckos, rats moved in from the forest, and with them came rat fleas carrying the bacteria that cause plague. If untreated, plague is more immediately fatal than malaria. Thus, the problem escalated, and, as a consequence, the World Health Organization stopped spraying DDT and, in an attempt to remedy the damage already done, parachuted a large number of cats into the jungle. The whole experience was an expensive lesson on the importance of understanding a food web before trying to alter or improve a complex system.

by Plato—or by any other person in history you care to choose (Fig. 3–10).

Special Topic C
Two Unusual Food Webs

A Simple Food Web   Most food webs are extraordinarily complex, with hundreds or even thousands of species involved. Perhaps the simplest food web on record is found in lakes on the Palau islands in the South Pacific. There is one species of autotrophs, a type of one-celled algae. These are eaten by one species of small crustaceans, *Oithona nana,* about the size of a pinhead. There are no carnivores—a two-species ecosystem. Biologists are studying these systems to try to understand why they remain stable. In most other systems, if the carnivores are removed, ecosystem stability is destroyed.

Ecosystems Without Sunlight or Producers Some ecosystems contain no sunlight and therefore have no producers. Consider the depths of the ocean or a stream in a dense forest where little light reaches the ground. These ecosystems depend on producers growing in sunnier areas to supply their food. Animal life in a forest stream feeds on leaves and twigs falling from the trees above; likewise, for nourishment many organisms in the deep ocean depend on dead bodies sinking from the upper layers of water where photosynthesis occurs. Ultimately, the source of energy for these ecosystems is still the Sun. A few species of bacteria can use energy from chemical reactions rather than from sunlight to produce their food. These producers, however, account for an insignificant fraction of the total energy trapped by living organisms on Earth. If the Sun were snuffed out tomorrow, life as we know it would rapidly grind to a halt.

3.7
Cycling of Nutrients

As discussed in the previous sections, energy cannot be recycled; the total quantity of *useful* energy decreases in any series of transfers. On the other hand, elements never get "tired" or "used up." They can be recycled again and again indefinitely. For example, on the average, every breath you inhale contains several million atoms once inhaled

During all nutrient cycles, there is a continuous exchange of materials between the pool of organic compounds and the pool of inorganic compounds. Thus, during photosynthesis, carbon dioxide and water (inorganic) are converted to sugar (organic) and oxygen (inorganic), and the reverse process occurs during respiration.

Living organisms require six elements in relatively large quantities: carbon, hydrogen, oxygen, nitrogen, phosphorus, and sulfur. These elements are available to organisms in the form of a variety of different chemical compounds. For example, nitrogen, as N_2, carbon, as CO_2, and oxygen, as O_2 are present in the atmosphere. Water (H_2O) is present throughout the biosphere in its liquid, solid, or vapor form. Compounds of phosphorus, sulfur, and other elements are incorporated into the chemical structure of various rocks. Under the proper conditions, they are released by weathering into soil, rivers, lakes, and oceans. The movements of nutrient elements through an ecosystem are called **biogeochemical cycles.**

Nutrients are sometimes recycled rapidly through ecosystems, as in grasslands, where the aboveground vegetation dies back each year and its nutrients are made available again the following season. In other cases, nutrients may spend many years or millennia away from the activities of the biological world. For example, coal and oil deposits were formed from partially decayed organic matter that has been isolated from the biosphere for millions of years. Every nutrient element has a somewhat different fate, depending on its physical and chemical properties and its role in living organisms.

3.8
The Carbon Cycle

The carbon cycle is complicated by the fact that carbon can exist in a wide variety of different types of compounds occurring in plants, animals, rocks, liquid solutions, and air. The most important compounds and some of their reactions are listed below.

1. Carbon dioxide, (CO_2)   A molecule of carbon dioxide consists of one atom of carbon

Figure 3–10
The general pattern by which minerals pass through an ecosystem.

bonded to two atoms of oxygen as shown below.

$$O = C = O$$

At the temperature and pressure found on the surface of the Earth, carbon dioxide is a gas and comprises approximately 0.03 percent by volume of the atmosphere.

2. Organic matter The complex molecules of all living organisms are chemically composed of a framework made of carbon atoms. As discussed in Section 3.3, during the process of photosynthesis, carbon dioxide gas reacts with water to form sugars. Sugars are the ultimate raw materials for the construction of more complex organic molecules and tissues. Respiration is the reverse process whereby organic matter is broken down to form carbon dioxide and water, with the release of energy.

3. Carbonates, such as calcium carbonate (CaCO₃) Carbon dioxide dissolves in water to form a solution that is mildly acidic. The acidity is just enough to give the solution a slightly tart taste. The sequence of reactions may be represented as follows (see also Fig. 3–11).

$$\text{CO}_2 + \text{H}_2\text{O} \longrightarrow \underset{\text{carbonic acid}}{\overset{\text{about 1\%}}{\text{H}_2\text{CO}_3}} \longrightarrow$$

$$\underset{\text{bicarbonate ion}}{\overset{\text{much less than 1\%}}{\text{H}^+ + \text{HCO}_3^-}} \longrightarrow \underset{\text{carbonate ion}}{\overset{\text{still less}}{\text{H}^+ + \text{CO}_3^{2-}}}$$

Hydrogen ions responsible for acidity

Note that about 99 percent of the carbon dioxide in water remains as dissolved carbon dioxide molecules, and only a very small portion is converted to carbonate (CO_3^{2-}) ions.

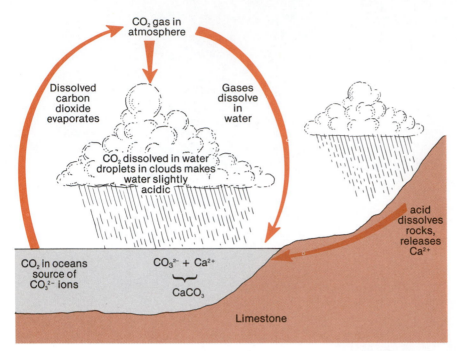

Figure 3–11
Inorganic reactions of carbon on the Earth.

Atmospheric carbon dioxide not only dissolves in surface water, but it dissolves in rainwater as well, making it slightly acidic. Note that this acidity is *not* what is called "acid rain." The acidity caused by pollutants that lead to acid rain is many orders of magnitude stronger than that resulting from carbon dioxide, and it is this stronger acidity that leads to environmental problems.

The greatest quantity of global carbon dioxide is that which is dissolved in the oceans; today, there is 70 times as much carbon in the oceans as there is gaseous carbon in the atmosphere.

When dissolved carbonates react with certain minerals, such as calcium, they form insoluble compounds such as calcium carbonate ($CaCO_3$).

$$Ca^{2+} + CO_3^{2-} \longrightarrow CaCO_3$$

When calcium carbonate mineralizes, it forms limestone. Most of the limestone formation occurs in the sea. Two processes are important. One is strictly geological. Certain types of rocks found on land are slowly dissolved by flowing water. The water then carries its load of dissolved minerals into the sea. In turn, the minerals may react with the carbonates dissolved in the sea and precipitate out as limestone.

Limestone can also be formed by biological processes. Some types of aquatic animals absorb

A cliff made of limestone, a mineralized form of calcium carbonate. (Christine Seashore)

carbon dioxide and convert it to insoluble calcium carbonate, which is then used to construct hard protective shells. When the animals die, the seashells accumulate as bottom sediments, which may eventually turn into sedimentary rocks such as limestone and dolomite.

Because of the variety of different reactions of carbon, the carbon cycle involves biotic and abiotic components, and the rates of transfer vary from a matter of hours to periods of millions of years.

1. Daily cycles In many situations, the cycling of carbon can occur quite rapidly, completing itself in a matter of hours. During daylight, plants assimilate large quantities of gaseous carbon dioxide, and the local atmospheric concentration declines dramatically (Fig. 3–12). During the nighttime, when there is no sunlight available for photosynthesis, respiration predominates, with the conse-

quent release of carbon dioxide. Therefore, the carbon dioxide concentration in the atmosphere fluctuates on a daily basis.

2. Cycles requiring years, decades, or centuries Although plants fix carbon and release some on a daily basis, large quantities are converted into plant tissues such as leaves, branches, or woody matter. This material may remain as part of the living organism for a period of a season in the case of annual flowers or grasses, or for a few centuries in the case of trees. When plants die, the material is eventually decomposed, and the complex tissues are broken down to simple compounds such as carbon dioxide and water.

3. Cycles of 100,000 years or more Only a small percentage of the total carbon budget of the Earth is involved in the relatively rapid cycling be-

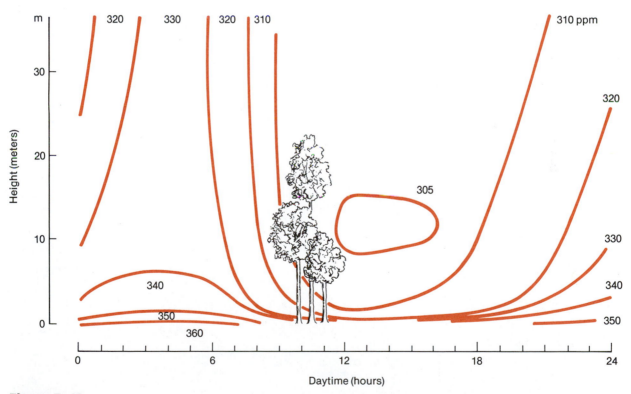

Figure 3–12

Daily fluctuations of the atmospheric carbon dioxide concentration near the ground level. Note that the carbon dioxide concentration declines dramatically during the day, when carbon is assimilated during photosynthesis. The concentration rises during the nighttime, when carbon is released during respiration.

tween living organisms and the atmosphere. Much larger quantities are involved in geochemical cycling. Looking at Figure 3–13, you can see that the largest quantity of carbon (71%) is dissolved in the oceans. This material exchanges slowly with the atmosphere. A given carbon atom in the oceans will move into the atmosphere on the average of once every 100,000 years.

4. Cycles involving millions of years   There are two long-term carbon cycles, one involving organic carbon compounds, and the other involving inorganic material such as carbonate rocks.

a. Organic matter   As just mentioned, much of the growth and decay of organic matter occurs in a matter of weeks, years, or centuries, but, occasionally, decay is incomplete and organic matter accumulates. This type of circumstance occurs in the peaty layers of bogs and moorlands, or on the ocean floor. Such carbon has entered a cycle of longer duration, and it may be thousands or even millions of years before it is released. For example, deposits of coal, oil, and natural gas are part of the primary productivity of a bygone era. These fossil fuels are organic compounds that were buried before they could decompose and were subsequently transformed by time and geological processes. When they are burned, their carbon is finally released back into the atmosphere, largely as carbon dioxide.

b. Cycling of carbonate rocks   As previously mentioned, carbon-containing rocks are formed in the ocean. By any short-term reckoning, this is essentially a one-way process, whereby carbon is removed from the biological components of the carbon cycle. If the process continued in this manner without any recycling, eventually enough carbon would be removed so that life as we know it on Earth could not exist. Fortunately for us, however, long-range recycling does occur. The interior of the Earth is hot and active, and huge masses of semifluid rock move about slowly. This movement carries the continents and sea floor basins with it, so that the surface of the Earth is segmented into discreet units, called **plates,** which move about and crash into each other. This activity is called **plate tectonics.** During tectonic movement, some bottom sediments may be pushed upward to the surface where they are exposed to the air. Some carbon may then be released by chemical reactions. Alternatively, as the tectonic plates move, the edges of the ocean floors are continuously pushed down into the interior and remelted. The molten material remains buried for long periods of time. Eventually, some of it is forced back to the surface through giant fissures that lie mainly in the center of the major ocean basins. Smaller amounts are injected back into the atmosphere during volcanic eruptions. Thus, there is a geological recycling of minerals (Fig. 3–14).

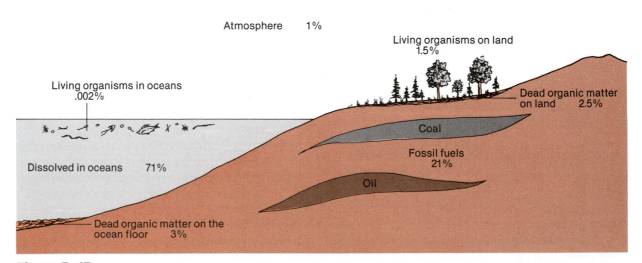

Figure 3–13
Percentages of the total quantity of global carbon in different portions of the Earth.

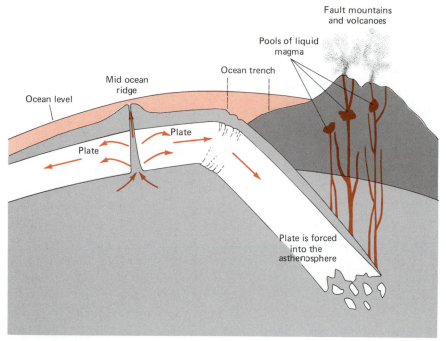

Figure 3–14
Geological cycling of carbon. Limestone that is deposited on the ocean floor is pushed under the continents by tectonic forces. Eventually, the rock is melted and carbon compounds are reinjected back to the surface of the Earth.

Industrial Activity and the Carbon Cycle

In modern times, human activities are making a significant impact on the global carbon cycle. When fossil fuels are burned, geological reserves of carbon are converted into carbon dioxide and released into the atmosphere. Additional carbon is released when forests are cut. Large quantities of plant matter then decompose or are burned, and again carbon dioxide is released as a product. In addition, decomposition of material in the forest floor is accelerated when the dead plant matter is stirred up and exposed by heavy machinery. Today, the release of carbon dioxide or discharge of carbon dioxide into the atmosphere is steadily increasing, owing both to the burning of fossil fuels and to the destruction of forests. However, the concentration of carbon dioxide in the atmosphere is increasing at less than half the rate that would be expected from these human activities. The remainder is dissolved in the oceans, which act as a global carbon dioxide sink. This important topic will be discussed further in Chapter 21. The various components of the carbon cycle are consolidated in Figure 3–15.

3.9
The Nitrogen Cycle

Even though our atmosphere is mostly nitrogen (about 78 percent by volume), the growth of many organisms is limited by a shortage of nitrogen. This shortage occurs because very few organisms can utilize the atmospheric nitrogen (N_2) directly. Most plants can absorb this vital nutrient only when it is in the form of nitrites (NO_2^-), nitrates NO_3^-), or ammonium ions (NH_4^+). The nitrogen cycle must therefore provide various bridges between the atmospheric reservoirs and the biological communities. In natural systems, atmospheric nitrogen is fixed (converted to usable form) by various bacteria. Plants can absorb available nitrogen compounds either directly from nitrogen-fixing bacteria or indirectly from the pool of inorganic compounds

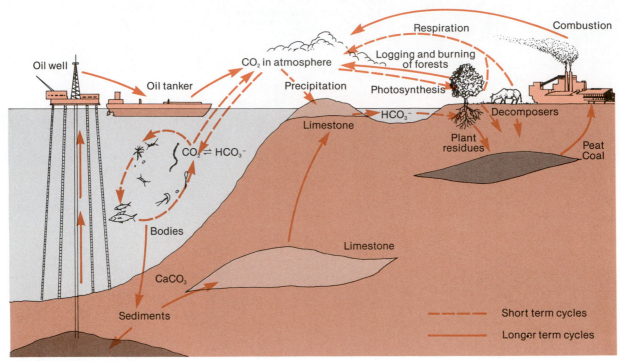

Figure 3–15

A simplified carbon cycle. Carbon passes through the processes indicated by dashed arrows much more rapidly than through those indicated by solid arrows.

that the bacteria excrete into the soil, water, rivers, lakes, and oceans (Fig. 3–16). Available nitrogen is also added to an ecosystem by various other means. One of these is lightning, which makes atmospheric nitrogen react with oxygen and converts it, in a series of steps, into nitrates. Other means include the erosion of rocks rich in nitrates and the decomposition of organic matter. When an organism dies, the nitrogen that it contains in organic molecules is converted back into inorganic forms by steps carried out by a series of different decay organisms. Most of the usable nitrogen that is found in a natural ecosystem is made available by this biological recycling.

Nitrogen is returned to the atmosphere when it is once more released as a gas by **denitrifying** bacteria that break up organic molecules for their own food. These bacteria live in anaerobic (without oxygen) conditions in the mud at the bottom of some lakes, in bogs and estuaries, and in parts of the sea floor.

All terrestrial ecosystems continuously lose some nitrogen when nitrates and organic matter are washed, or **leached,** out of the soil into groundwater and streams. In most cases, the nutrients are then eventually carried into the oceans. In a few places on Earth, leached nutrients have collected in natural geological deposits. For example, certain streams flowing out of the Andes Mountains in Chile travel across one of the driest deserts in the world. Much of this water evaporates before it completes its journey to the sea, leaving behind deposits of nitrate.

Today, large quantities of fixed nitrogen are artificially added to agricultural soils in the form of fertilizers. The production of nitrogen fertilizers is accomplished by combining nitrogen and hydrogen in the presence of heat and pressure. This process, discussed in more detail in Chapter 8, has increased the fertility of agricultural systems but consumes large quantities of energy.

3.10
The Phosphorus Cycle

Phosphorus is a major constituent of biological membranes. Many animals also need large quantities of this element to make shells, bones, and

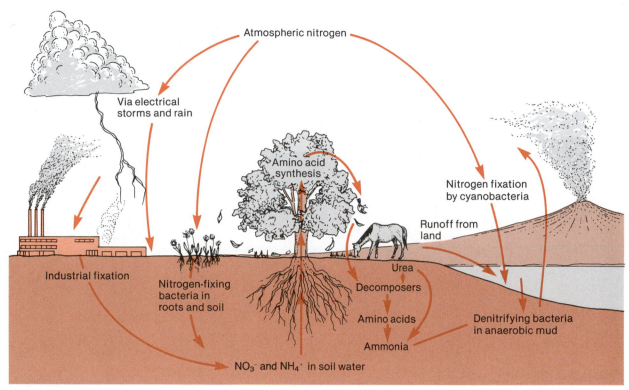

Figure 3–16
A simplified nitrogen cycle.

teeth. Since phosphorus does not occur naturally as a gas, its cycle, unlike those of carbon and nitrogen, is a **sedimentary cycle** (Fig. 3–17). Many rocks contain phosphorus, usually in the form of phosphates (PO_4^{3-}) that are bound into the mineral structure. When rocks are weathered, minute amounts of these phosphates dissolve and become available to plants. Animals then absorb this element when they eat plants or other animals.

Much of the phosphorus excreted by animals is also in the form of phosphate, which plants can reuse immediately. Thus, on land, phosphate cycles round and round from plants to animals and back again. Land ecosystems preserve phosphorus efficiently, since both organic and inorganic soil particles absorb phosphates, providing a local reservoir of this element.

In an undisturbed ecosystem, the intake and loss of phosphorus are small compared with the amounts of phosphorus that are internally recycled in the day-to-day exchange among plants and animals. Some phosphorus is inevitably lost by leaching and erosion of the soil into streams and rivers.

When an ecosystem is disturbed, as by mining or farming, erosion can become so significant that large quantities of phosphorus and other nutrients are washed away. When phosphate reaches the ocean, it encounters other minerals in the water and reacts with some of them. Since most phosphates are very insoluble in water, they eventually settle to the ocean floor. One reason for the infertility of open oceans is their low phosphorus content.

In the short term, the movement of phosphorus from ecosystems on land to the bottom of the ocean is a one-way flow. Trivial amounts of phosphorus are returned to land from the droppings of ocean birds or from fish when caught by terrestrial animals and brought onto the shore. Other than that, the only way for phosphorus to return to land is by way of extremely slow geological processes such as those discussed in reference to the carbon cycle. Soil erosion robs an ecosystem of its phosphorus, and it may take thousands or tens of thousands of years to recoup this loss through the weathering of rocks. Phosphate is much in demand

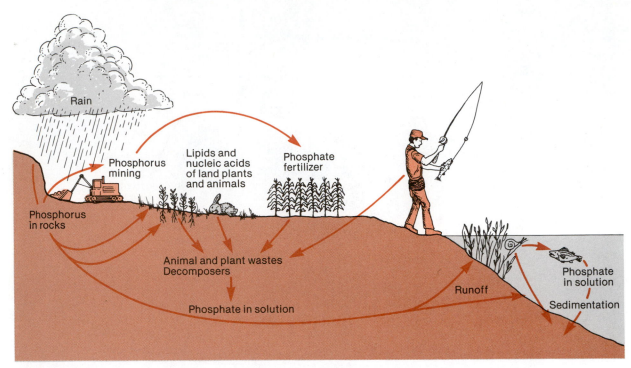

Figure 3–17
The phosphorus cycle.

as a fertilizer, but the richest and most easily mined deposits of phosphate are being depleted rapidly. The environmental problems associated with the depletion of mineral resources such as phosphorus are discussed in Chapter 16.

3.11
An Experimental Ecosystem

One important question is how human activities affect nutrient cycles in natural ecosystems. To answer this question, scientists first observe cycling rates and efficiency in an undisturbed system, then disturb the system in some way, and again measure the movement of nutrients. One experimental ecosystem is the Hubbard Brook Experimental Forest in the White Mountains of central New Hampshire, which has been studied over a period of many years. This system is ideal for such a study because it consists of a series of small valleys each with a creek running down the middle. The soil and rock structure prevents seepage of water from one system to another, so each valley is isolated

from the others. Researchers built concrete dams across the creeks at the bottom of each valley. The dams were anchored in bedrock so that all the water leaving the forest, except the amount that evaporated into the atmosphere, had to cross the dams (Fig. 3–18). Thus, the rate of flow and the nutrient content of the streams could easily be measured. Precipitation gauges throughout the valleys were used to measure the amount of water that fell as rain or snow and the nutrients that it contained.

The first project at Hubbard Brook was to measure the amounts of water and nutrients that entered and left an undisturbed forest. The results of this study showed that the forest is extremely efficient at retaining nutrients. Nutrients that left the ecosystem by way of the creek approximately balanced the quantity of nutrients that entered the system as solutions in water or snow. However, the quantities that entered and left the ecosystem were very small compared with the total amounts of nutrients present. Most nutrients cycled many times within the biological community before they left the system.

Figure 3–18
V-shaped dam at the lower end of a valley in the Hubbard Brook Experimental Forest. The rate of water runoff from the watershed is measured by the height of water in the V (very low when this photograph was taken). (Photograph by Peter Marks)

Figure 3–19
An aerial view of part of Hubbard Brook in winter, showing the deforested valley (unbroken white snow) and parts of two adjacent valleys. On the left is a watershed in which trees have been cut down in horizontal strips. (Photograph by Robert Pierce, U.S. Forest Service)

The next experiment was to disturb the system and observe any changes that occurred. One winter, the investigators cut down all the trees and shrubs in one valley, leaving them where they fell. The area was then sprayed with herbicides to prevent regrowth (Fig. 3–19). With no plants to absorb water from the soil, most of the rainwater ran over the surface of the ground and into the stream, and stream flow increased by 40 percent. More important, whereas the stream in an undisturbed system was clear, the stream in the denuded valley was muddy. As the excess water ran rapidly over the surface of the ground, it eroded the soil and carried nutrients out of the ecosystem. Overall, the loss of mineral nutrients in the cut forest was six to eight times greater than the loss in the undisturbed forest (Fig. 3–20).

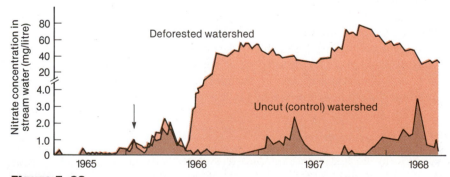

Figure 3–20
Accelerated loss of nitrate in stream water in one of the watersheds at Hubbard Brook after it was deforested. The date the forest was clearcut is shown by the arrow. (Note the change of scale on the *y*-axis, needed to keep the lines for control and clearcut watersheds on the same graph.)

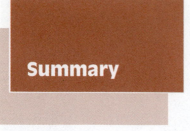

Summary

An **ecosystem** is a group of plants and animals occurring together plus that part of the physical environment with which they interact. An ecosystem is defined to be nearly self-contained, so that the matter which flows into and out of it is small compared with that which is internally recycled in a continuous exchange of the essentials of life.

Ecosystems contain biotic components that include all living organisms or remains of organisms and abiotic components such as sunlight, nutrients, air, water, soil, and climate. There are many interactions between the biotic and the abiotic components of ecosystems.

Photosynthesis can be summarized by the equation:

$$\text{carbon dioxide} + \text{water} \xrightarrow{\text{sunlight}} \text{sugar} + \text{oxygen}$$

The equation for respiration is:

$$\text{sugar} + \text{oxygen} \longrightarrow \text{carbon dioxide} + \text{water} + \text{energy}$$

Plants are the main autotrophic producers of an ecosystem because they can perform photosynthesis, using the energy of sunlight to convert energy-poor inorganic carbon dioxide and water into energy-rich organic food molecules. If an ecosystem is to survive indefinitely, it must contain at least some autotrophs, some decomposers, and the water, air, light, and minerals that these organisms need to survive. Most ecosystems also contain heterotrophic consumers, which feed on producers or on each other. The trophic level to which an organism belongs describes how far the organism is removed from plants in its level of nourishment.

The **productivity** of an ecosystem is defined as the amount of material produced in a given area. Energy passes from one trophic level to the next. Approximately 90 percent of the energy is lost at each transfer. Therefore, the biomass that an ecosystem can support at each trophic level declines rapidly, and energy flow through the system is, for all intents and purposes, one way.

The patterns of consumption in an ecosystem are complex and are described in a **food web.**

Nutrients cycle continuously through an ecosystem. They are taken in by organisms as inorganic substances and may remain as minerals or be incorporated into organic molecules. Nutrients may pass through the food web for a period of time, but, eventually, they are once again released into the environment as inorganic substances. An ecosystem may be very efficient at conserving and recycling nutrients.

Key nutrient cycles are the carbon cycle, the nitrogen cycle, and mineral cycles, as exemplified by the phosphorus cycle.

Questions

Ecosystems

1. In the text, four examples of systems were given: a digestive system, a cooling system, a system of government, and an ecosystem. Show how each example fits the definition of a system. Would the Solar System be considered to be a system under this definition? Why or why not?

2. Which of the following would be considered to be an ecosystem? (a) a drop of pond water; (b) an entire pond; (c) a valley in the mountains with a pond in it; (d) an entire forest with many valleys and ponds; (e) a continent. Defend your answer in each case.

3. What is missing from the following statement? An ecosystem consists of all the different organisms living in a given area.

The Components of Ecosystems

4. Explain how water, soil, and air are abiotic but are not really isolated from biological systems.

5. Explain why every ecosystem must have some continuous supply of energy to survive but can do quite well without a continuous influx of nutrients.

6. Certain essentials of life are abundant in some ecosystems but rare in others. Give examples of situations in which each of the following is abundant and in which each is rare: (a) water; (b) oxygen; (c) light; (d) space; (e) nitrogen.

Energy Relationships

7. For each of the processes given in the list below, which are more similar in energy flow to respiration, and which are more similar to photosynthesis: (a) the building of a house; (b) the burning of gasoline in an automobile engine; (c) the process by which vitamin D is manufactured on a person's skin when it is exposed to sunlight; (d) the manufacture of vitamins in a chemical factory; (e) the crumbling and decay of buildings? Defend your answers.

8. List five substances that are energy-rich, and five that are energy-poor.

9. Plants are called autotrophs, meaning self-nourishers. Does this statement apply to energy, nutrients, or both? Discuss.

10. Name two organisms that occupy the first trophic level, two that occupy the second, and two that occupy the third.

11. Pick an animal that you are familiar with and show how it can occupy several different trophic levels.

12. In many areas of the world, available habitats for wild animals have become smaller and smaller. Using an energy flow argument, explain why this shrinkage would affect animals in the highest trophic levels more severely than those in lower levels.

13. Which of the following ecosystems could be self-contained and which could not? One that had: (a) autotrophs but no heterotrophs or decomposers; (b) heterotrophs and decomposers, but no autotrophs; (c) autotrophs and decomposers, but no heterotrophs; (d) autotrophs and heterotrophs, but no decomposers. Defend your answers.

Productivity

14. Assume that a plant uses 1 percent of the light energy it receives from the Sun for growth, and that an animal uses 10 percent of the energy of its food for the synthesis of body tissue. Starting with 10,000 kcal of light energy, how much energy is available to a person who eats (a) corn, (b) beef, and (c) frogs that eat insects that eat leaves?

15. Explain the difference between gross primary productivity and net primary productivity.

16. Productivity can be expressed in terms of kcal/m²/yr or g/m²/yr. Discuss the differences and the similarities between these two definitions. How do both of these terms differ from secondary productivity?

17. A human continues to eat throughout his or her entire adult life, yet may gain no weight at all over a period of many decades. Explain this observation.

18. More energy from the Sun is used to nourish a human who eats meat than a human who eats vegetables. Is this fact, by itself, an argument for or against vegetarianism? Take into account the following questions: Does the choice of human diet affect the total energy flow through the food web? Does it affect the total biomass of plant matter on Earth? Does the choice between the alternatives of a large human population living largely on vegetable food or a smaller human population living largely on meat and fish significantly affect the total biomass of animal matter on Earth?

19. It is desired to establish a large but isolated area with an adequate supply of plant food, equal numbers of lion and antelope, and no other large animals. The antelope eat only plant matter, the lions, only antelope. Is it possible for the population of the two species to remain approximately equal if we start with equal numbers of each and then leave the system alone? Would you expect the final population ratio to be any different if we started with twice as many antelope? Twice as many lions?

20. How is the flow of energy in an ecosystem linked to the flow of nutrients? How do energy and nutrient flow differ?

21. An experiment has shown that the total weight of the consumers in the English Channel is five times the total weight of the plants. Does this information agree with the food pyramid shown in Figure 3–7? Can you offer some reasonable explanations for the findings?

Food Webs

22. Is there one or more than one food web in any ecosystem?

23. Consider the food web in the Figure 3–21. Arrow number 15 can be explained by the relationship: Mountain lion eats deer. Write similar statements for each of the other 27 arrows.

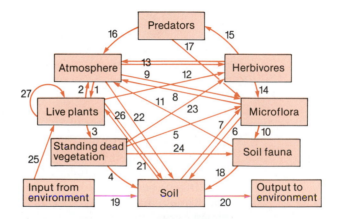

Figure 3–21

Nutrient Cycles

24. Give three examples supporting the observation that nutrient cycling hasn't been 100 percent effective over geological time.

25. Trace a carbon atom through a cycle that takes (a) days, (b) weeks, (c) years, (d) millions of years.

26. Why don't farmers need to buy carbon at the fertilizer store? Why do they need to buy nitrogen?

27. Describe three pathways whereby atmospheric nitrogen is converted to fixed forms that are usable by plants, and three pathways whereby fixed nitrogen is returned to the atmosphere.

28. Loggers can harvest timber either by clearcutting (removing all the trees from an area) or by selective cutting (removing only the most desirable trees). Explain why clearcutting is an ecologically unsound practice in most woodlands.

Suggested Readings

For further reading on subjects in basic ecology, refer to any of the excellent basic textbooks on the subject. Five recommended books are:

Begon, Harper, and Townsend: *Ecology of Individuals, Populations, and Communities.* Sunderland, MA, Sinauer Associates. 1986. 876 pp.

Charles J. Krebs: *Ecology,* 3rd ed. New York, Harper & Row, 1985. 800 pp.

Eugene P. Odum: *Basic Ecology.* Philadelphia, Saunders College Publishing, 1983. 613 pp.

Peter W. Price, C. N. Slobodchikoff, and William S. Gaud, eds.: *A New Ecology, Novel Approaches to Interactive System.* Somerset, NJ, John Wiley & Sons, 1984. 515 pp.

Robert Leo Smith: *Elements of Ecology,* 2nd ed. New York, Harper & Row, 1986. 677 pp.

Biogeochemical cycles and food webs are discussed in:

Robert B. Cook. Man and the biogeochemical cycles, interacting with the elements. *Environment 26:7,* September 1984.

G. E. Likens: *Some Perspectives of the Major Biogeochemical Cycles, Scope 17.* New York, John Wiley & Sons, 1981.

Stuart L. Pimm: *Population and Community Biology.* New York, Methuen, 1982. 219 pp.

A classic study of ecology and conservation as seen through the eyes of a naturalist is:

A. Leopold: *A Sand County Almanac.* New York, Sierra Club/Ballantine Books, 1966. 296 pp.

A complete account of the Hubbard Brook watershed study of nutrient cycles is given in:

F. H. Bormann and G. E. Likens: *Patterns and Process in a Forested Ecosystem: Distribution, Development, and the Steady State Based on the Hubbard Brook Ecosystem Study.* New York, Springer-Verlag, 1984.

A description of the nonphotosynthetic ecosystem discovered in the ocean depths is found in:

J. B. Corliss and R. D. Ballard. Oases of life in the cold abyss. *National Geographic,* October 1977.

4

Populations of Organisms

Recall from Chapter 3 that an ecosystem was defined as a system formed by the interactions of organisms in a community with each other and with their physical environment. In that chapter, the components of ecosystems and the basic processes of production, consumption, and nutrient cycling were introduced. However, study of these broad concepts is only a first step toward an understanding of the structure and the functions of ecosystems. As stated in the definition above, the ecologist studies the mechanisms by which individual organisms interact to produce an integrated community. Thus, a measurement of the primary productivity of a prairie is but one piece of the puzzle. The ecologist must probe further and ask how the growth of grasses is related to the lives of herbivores and carnivores and ultimately how the whole system is tied together to become a recognizable whole. In this chapter, we will introduce the role of individuals and the dynamics of populations, and proceed toward a look at community interactions and ecosystem stability.

4.1
What is a Species?

No two individual organisms are exactly alike. You are different from your best friend, your brother, your sister, and even your "identical twin." But there are groups of organisms that have common characteristics. Plants are basically different from animals. Animals can be divided into many subgroups. For example, animals with backbones form one broad classification. In turn, these animals can be further divided into classes such as reptiles, birds, and mammals. To continue, any given class, such as mammals, can be subdivided into separate orders. Rodents (mice, rats, squirrels), cretacea (whales, dolphins, porpoises), and primates (monkeys, apes, people) are all orders of mammals. How far is a classification scheme useful?

Individual plants or animals breed only with plants and animals that are quite similar. Therefore, it is convenient to classify organisms that breed together into discrete groups.

A species is defined as a group of plants or animals that can breed together to produce viable, fertile offspring but that cannot do so with members outside the group.

One look tells us that all elephants are alike in many ways. But Indian elephants are slightly different from African elephants. These two groups of animals do not mate with each other. Therefore, they form separate species.

When organisms mate, many of the characteristics of the parents are often passed on to the infants. Tall people tend to bear tall children. Swift antelopes have a high probability of giving birth to swift baby antelopes. Character traits are mixed within a species because members of the species breed together. But traits cannot be passed from one species to another because members of different species do not mate, or, if they do, their offspring are not fertile. Therefore, each species forms a unique group. If a species is destroyed, it can never be recreated.

Groups of organisms that make up a species may be reproductively isolated from other species in many different ways. In some cases, mating between different species is physically impossible because the reproductive organs are incompatible. Alternatively, closely related species often have different mating seasons or spawning grounds so that males and females of the two species never meet when both are in breeding condition. Members of one species will not recognize or respond to the courtship behavior of another species. If mating between species does occur, the egg may not be fertilized or, if it is fertilized, it may die before many cell divisions take place. An egg may even develop into an adult organism, but one with greatly reduced fertility, as in the case with the mule (which is a cross between a horse and a donkey). All these mechanisms operate in nature on various groups, singly or in combination, to ensure their identities as separate species.

Although distinctions between species are usually clearcut, many ambiguities do exist. For instance, a lion and a tiger in a zoo may mate and produce a healthy offspring. Does this mean that lions and tigers belong to the same species? As another example, many plants never reproduce sexually. Scientists cannot say that they breed with each other and not with members of other species because they never breed at all. Some of these arguments are resolved by consensus by biologists (lions and tigers are generally considered to be separate species), and others remain arguable, but the few uncertainties that do exist do not destroy the usefulness of the general concept.

Populations

Although any member of a species can, in theory, breed with any other member, studies have shown that an organism usually finds a mate from within a much smaller group. A **population** is the breeding group to which an organism belongs in practice. Many populations are surprisingly small, consisting of fewer than 100 individuals. Organisms usually breed only within their own populations for purely practical reasons. The mice on one island off the coast of Maine or in one particular wheatfield never meet the mice from another island or wheatfield and so cannot breed with them. When organisms interbreed, genes from both parents are passed to the offspring, so there are genetic similarities between the members of a population just as there are between members of a family. (Genes are defined in Box 4.1.) For example, skin color tells us whether a person comes from a human population that originated in Africa, Asia, or Europe, even though all people belong to the same species, **homo sapiens.** As people travel and interbreed more than they used to, the genetic differences between human populations are steadily disappearing. The more interbreeding there is between two populations, the more similar their members will be.

4.2
The Ecological Niche

To date, about one and a half million different species of plants and animals have been identified and categorized. However, biologists estimate that

> **Box 4.1**
> **Genes**
>
> **Genes** are the physical entities passed from parent to offspring that determine many, but not all, of the characteristics of an organism. They determine various aspects of the biochemistry, structure, and behavior of organisms. Genes are composed of DNA (deoxyribonucleic acid), which exists in enormously long molecules in almost every cell.

Special Topic A
Kingdoms of Organisms

In many ecological studies, it is convenient to classify organisms by their **function** rather than by the shape, size, or other characteristics of their bodies. Thus, a cow and a grasshopper are both herbivores and thus serve the same ecological function, even though they are biologically quite different from each other. In other biological studies, it is often more convenient to classify organisms by their anatomy, evolutionary development, and the chemistry of their cellular functions. The five kingdoms of organisms are listed below:

1. *Plants.* Plants are fundamental to all life on Earth because they have the ability to trap energy from the Sun and use that energy to build living tissue. All plants have rigid cell walls, and most are multicellular.

2. *Animals.* Members of the animal kingdom are heterotrophs and must eat other organisms to survive. Animals differ from plants in that animals do not have rigid cell walls. Most are mobile.

3. *Fungi.* Fungi are plant-like organisms that have rigid cell walls. However, fungi are not able to conduct photosynthesis, and thus, they are heterotrophs. Fungi are extremely important because of their role as decomposers. Some common examples are mushrooms, molds, and yeasts.

4. *Monera.* The kingdom of monera contains non-photosynthetic bacteria and blue-green bacteria, sometimes called blue-green algae, that are able to conduct photosynthesis. All monera consist of one-celled organisms whose cells are different from those of other forms of life. The genetic material (DNA) in a monera is not surrounded by a membrane as it is in all other organisms. Some monera are capable of photosynthesis, which means that they are autotrophic producers, providing food for heterotrophs. Most of them, however, are saprophytic decomposers, like the fungi. The main difference between fungal and bacterial decomposers is that many bacteria can survive without oxygen, whereas most fungi cannot. Deep layers of soil or mud, where little oxygen exists, are populated by bacteria rather than by fungi. There is almost no natural organic substance that some bacterium cannot use for food, which makes bacteria very versatile decomposers.

5. *Protista.* This kingdom is made up of all those one-celled organisms that are not monera. It includes *Amoeba, Paramecium,* and most of the one-celled **algae** that float near the surfaces of oceans and lakes. Some protists are heterotrophs, feeding on smaller protists or on bacteria, or they exist as parasites feeding on animals. Others, such as the one-celled floating algae, are photosynthetic. These protists are important ecologically as the main producers in aquatic ecosystems such as lakes, rivers, and oceans.

many more exist. There may be as many as five to ten million different species throughout the world. Each species performs unique functions and occupies specific habitats. An organism's **habitat** is its address, the place where it lives. The **ecological niche** is a description of an organism's habitat—its physical location within an ecosystem—plus its function in the patterns of energy flow and nutrient cycling. Thus, a niche can be considered to be analogous to a human profession, the way in which an organism makes a living. A niche includes all of an organism's interactions with the physical environment and with other organisms that share its habitat. To describe a niche, one would first have to describe all physical characteristics of a species' home. One might start with specifying the gross location (for example, the Rocky Mountains or the central floor of the Atlantic Ocean) and the type of living quarters (e.g., a burrow under the roots of trees). For plants and the less mobile animals, one would describe the preferred microenvironment, such as the water salinity for species living at the interfaces of rivers and oceans, the soil acidity for plants, or the necessary turbulence for stream dwellers. An animal's trophic level and a description of the organisms that it feeds upon are also part of its niche. Similarly, the predators and competitors that an organism must

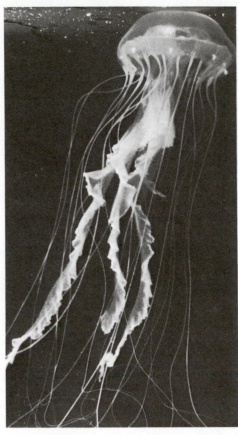

The sea nettle, *Crysaora quinquecirrha,* a common jellyfish along the Atlantic coast. (William H. Amos)

contend with are part of its place and function in an ecosystem. Mobile animals generally have a more or less clearly defined food-gathering territory, or **home range,** which is another factor in establishing the physical niche.

A niche is not an inherent property of a species, because it is governed by factors other than genetic ones. Social and environmental factors also play a part in establishing the niche. For example, a certain population of tropical jellyfish, *Aurelia aurita,* swims fastest in water that is at a temperature of 29°C. Of course, it would be unreasonable to expect all the jellyfish of this population to be living in waters of exactly 29°C all the time. The weather changes, cold and warm spells occur, yet organisms survive. Imagine a situation in which a warm, sunny, sheltered bay provided an optimal physical environment for jellyfish but exposed them to a high concentration of enemies. Since the conditions in the bay would not be optimal, many individuals might migrate to a less favorable physical environment to find more favorable biotic surroundings. Thus, the observed niches of these jellyfish are different from the theoretical optimal niche. The niche of a given species in a given ecosystem is not a set of conditions that would be best suited to the genetic makeup of the organism, but rather, it is the set of conditions in which it actually survives.

4.3
Population Growth

The size of a population of mice in a field or of violets in a wood lot seems at first sight to vary little from year to year. Yet, a violet produces several dozen seeds each year, and a mouse may give birth to 10 offspring every few weeks. Surely, these organisms produce so many offspring that their populations could increase greatly from one year to the next. Why then is the actual population so constant? What determines how many violets or mice live in the wood lot at any one time? A study of other ecosystems leads to still more questions. How does the population of a rare species become so reduced that it is in danger of extinction? If we introduce an animal that eats Japanese beetles, will it exterminate this pest or merely reduce the beetle population, or will it have no effect?

The answers to these and other related questions constitute the subject of population ecology. Since humans are an animal species living on this planet, many of the basics of population ecology apply to us. On the other hand, the dynamics of human population are different enough from those of any other species to warrant a separate chapter (see Chapter 7).

Individuals are added to a population by birth and by immigration. They leave a population by death and by emigration. The size of a population at any given time, therefore, depends on the balance between these processes. Ecologists talk about the **rates** at which births, deaths, or migrations occur. A rate is a measure of one quantity expressed in relation to another. A type of rate that is familiar to all of us is the speed of an automobile, which can be expressed in terms of kilometers (one quantity) divided by hours (a different quantity), or, more simply, km/hr. A rate of birth is computed as the number of births in a population divided by the size of the population as a whole.

Special Topic B
Exponential Growth

A population is said to change exponentially if it increases, or decreases, at a rate proportional to its size (Fig. 4–1). Exponential growth commonly refers to an increase. Think of it this way: Assume that there is one bacterium at time zero, that each individual splits into two offspring in 20 minutes, and that no bacteria die. Then there will be two bacteria in 20 minutes, and 20 minutes after that, each

will have split again, so there will be four. After another 20 minutes, there will be eight, and so on, as shown below. (The general equations are given in Appendix E.)

At the end of 1 1/2 days, the single bacterium would have multiplied into 10^{33} individuals, enough to cover the entire surface of the Earth to a uniform depth of 30 cm!

Time	Generation	Population
0	0	$1 \times 2^0 = 1$
20 min	1	$1 \times 2^1 = 2$
40 min	2	$1 \times 2^2 = 4$
60 min (1 hr)	3	$1 \times 2^3 = 8$
.	.	.
.	.	.
.	.	.
1 1/2 days	108	$1 \times 2^{108} = 10^{33}$

This ratio is often multiplied by 100 to arrive at a percent.

$$\text{rate of birth (\%)} = \frac{\text{number of births}}{\text{size of population}} \times 100$$

Death rates and migration rates are expressed in the same manner. If the rate of birth and immigration in any period of time exceeds the rate of death and emigration, the population will grow. If the reverse is true, the population will decrease, and if the rates are the same, the population will remain constant.

Now we ask the question, "How would a population grow if nothing impeded its growth?" The Russian ecologist G.F. Gause examined this problem by studying the growth of experimental populations of the freshwater protist *Paramecium caudatum.* Every few hours, a well-nourished paramecium divides to form two new individuals. Gause set up tubes containing plenty of bacteria for food and introduced one paramecium into each tube. He then followed the growth of the *Paramecium* populations. If nothing checks its growth, each population grows **exponentially;** that is, it

grows at a rate proportional to its size. Thus, the number of individuals added in each increment of time keeps increasing by a constant multiple (see Special Topic B and Appendix E). If exponential growth is plotted on a graph, it forms a curve that grows steeper and steeper, sometimes rather inaccurately called a "J" curve (Fig. 4–1).

Gause found that no matter how much food, space, light, and warmth he gave them, there was a limit to the rate at which the *Paramecium* populations grew. This maximal rate, called the **biotic potential,** is determined by the reproductive capacity of the organism. The biotic potential of *Paramecium* is quite high, one generation every few hours. In contrast, polar bears give birth to one or two infants once every 3 or 4 years, so their potential growth rate is considerably lower.

Many factors affect the biotic potential of a population, and values differ widely from species to species. The factors with the most direct influence are (1) the age at which the organism first reproduces, (2) the frequency of the reproductive cycle, (3) the total number of times each organism reproduces in its life span, and (4) the number of

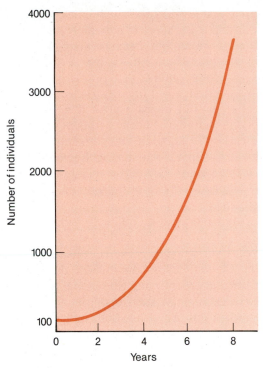

Figure 4–1
A graphic representation of exponential growth.

offspring produced each time an organism reproduces.

All these factors are important and are related to each other, but the influence of the first factor (the age of first reproduction) is especially noteworthy. For example, a paramecium does not produce many offspring each time it reproduces nor does it have a long reproductive life. On the other hand, an oak tree produces hundreds of seeds every year and lives for many years. Yet a paramecium can reproduce within an hour of being formed, whereas an oak tree must be more than 10 years old before it can reproduce for the first time. As a result, *Paramecium* populations can grow many orders of times faster than populations of oak trees.

No natural population can grow at its biotic potential for long; because, if it did, the population would increase so rapidly that vital resources such as food or water would become exhausted. Therefore, some combination of environmental pressures must act to inhibit the rate of population growth of every species. The sum of all the environmental interactions that collectively inhibit the growth of a population is known as the **environmental resistance.**

The growth rate of populations is controlled in two different ways. These factors are considered in the following two sections.

4.4
Reduction of Birth Rates

Many adults do not reproduce at their maximal possible rate, and some do not reproduce at all, even though they are biologically capable of reproduction. Internal regulation of populations may be triggered in various ways when an individual, a family, or a group spontaneously restricts its birth rate. A human female may choose to bear one or two or even no children at all, even though she has enough money to feed, clothe, and shelter many more and is biologically capable of bearing a larger family. Alternatively, she may delay having her children for years, or even decades, past the time when she reaches sexual maturity. Birth control is observed in many other animal species as well. Many birds in desert areas suppress their breeding, often for years, in periods of drought. After prolonged rainfall, however, such birds may breed more than once, producing several broods of young. The availability of food may also trigger breeding. Tropical grass warblers (birds) of the genus *Cisticola* normally breed in the wet season when the grass is growing. In areas of banana plantations, however, the birds breed whenever plantation owners flood the bananas, causing grass to grow, regardless of the season.

Many social animals, such as hippopotamuses, rats, honey bees, and wolves control their reproduction. For example, a wolf pack typically consists of a dominant male (the leader), his mate (the dominant female), and a number of subordinate males and females. The dominant pair mate every year, but other members of the pack generally do not copulate, even though they are sexually mature. In one study of a wolf pack kept in a large fenced enclosure, the dominant male became aroused and tried to mate with a subordinate female, but she would not allow it, and, with tail between her legs, she cowered and avoided his advances. This birth control is beneficial to a family of wolves in the wild; otherwise, the wolves, who have few natural enemies, would overpopulate their range and face starvation.

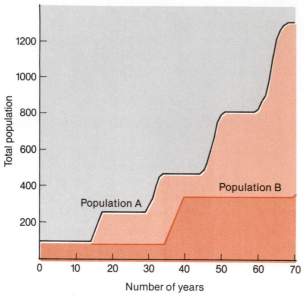

Figure 4–2
The growth of two hypothetical populations. In this example, both populations start with 100 newborn infants, 50 girls and 50 boys, and no individuals die before the age of 70. In population A, all women bear a total of three children. The first child is born when each woman is 15 years old, and the next two are born at ages 16 and 17. In population B, all women bear 5 children, 1 each year, but starting at age 35. Although real populations behave in a more complex manner than is depicted here, this graph illustrates the fact that populations grow rapidly when females bear young at an early age.

The choice of when to bear young also affects population growth rates. Consider, for example, two hypothetical human populations. In the first one, all women bear a total of three children. The first child is born when each woman is 15 years old, and the next two are born at ages 16 and 17. In the second population, all women bear 5 children, 1 each year, but starting at age 35. As shown in Figure 4–2, the first population will grow at a much faster rate than the second!

4.5
Mortality and Survivorship

In all populations, many individuals die before they grow up, mature, and reproduce. Thus, in any natural ecosystem, the biotic potential of all species is counterbalanced by mortality factors. The patterns of mortality differ widely from species to species. At one extreme, parents may produce many

offspring and provide each with little or no parental care. In this case, there is extremely high mortality among the young, but, because there are so many, there is a good chance that a few of them will survive to become parents of the next generation. At the other extreme, an organism may produce very few offspring but invest a great deal of energy in each one before it becomes independent of the parents. In this situation, the parental care encourages a high survival rate among the young, but, because there were only a few infants to start with, only a limited number of individuals will grow up to reproduce.

The patterns of mortality of each species can be shown by a type of graph called a **survivorship curve.** A survivorship curve is constructed by following the fate of young individuals throughout their lives, in order to describe mortality at different ages. To construct a survivorship curve, ecologists start with a **cohort** of newborn individuals. A cohort (or **birth cohort)** is a group of individuals born in a given period of time, such as in a particular year. The members of the cohort are then followed to determine the age at which each of them dies. If the number of survivors is plotted against ages (Fig. 4–3), the curve can be used to predict the probability that a newborn individual will reach any particular age. In this way, the life expectancy can be determined for any population.

Survivorship curves take various forms, depending on the characteristics of the particular population (Fig. 4–4). A Type I survivorship curve is usually associated with a reproductive strategy in which the parents devote considerable care and energy to each offspring. In this situation, most infants survive to maturity, and the older members of the population live for a long time, finally dying as a result of diseases of old age. A "perfect" Type I curve never occurs because some individuals always die early in life. In all populations, some newborn organisms are genetically defective or suffer accidents during the process of birth. Thus, even in Type I populations, the death rate for the embryo and the newborn is higher than the population experiences at any other time until the onset of old age. The Type I survivorship curve is characteristic of prosperous human populations and of other animals such as some large birds and mammals, for example, eagles, polar bears, elephants, and whales, which produce few offspring but devote considerable care to their development.

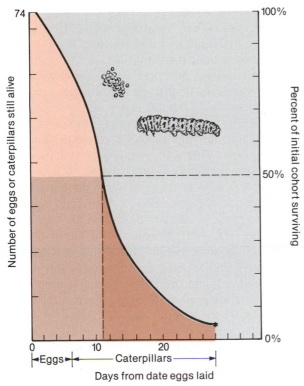

Figure 4–3

Survivorship curve for eggs and caterpillars of the black swallowtail butterfly *(Papilio glaucus)* on wild carrot plants in a New York hayfield. The initial cohort of 74 eggs was found by following butterflies and marking where they laid their eggs. These were then visited daily as they hatched into caterpillars. Fifty percent of the insects had died by day 11; that is, an egg laid on day 1 had only a 50 percent chance of surviving to day 11. Most of the deaths are due to predation by spiders and mites. (Data courtesy of Paul Fenny)

In a Type III survivorship curve, most individuals die at an early age. This type of survivorship is associated with a reproductive strategy in which large numbers of offspring are produced but receive little parental care. It is characteristic of many species of invertebrates, fish, plants, and fungi.

The Type II curve falls between those of Types I and III. There is again an initial period of high mortality due to genetic defects or accidents during development, birth, or hatching. Once past this critical period, however, a smaller but constant number of individuals die at any subsequent age. This curve is typical of several bird species and of humans exposed to poor nutrition and hygiene. With this curve, reproductive strategy lies some-

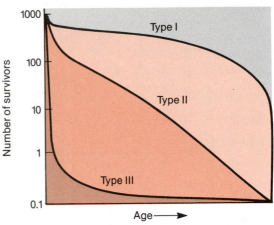

Figure 4–4

The main types of hypothetical survivorship curves.

where between the other two. Parents usually produce more offspring than do members of Type I populations, a situation selected for by the higher mortality rate of offspring.

4.6
Population Growth Curves

Imagine a population that is initially very small. The very fact that it is small places it in danger of extinction because it may not be able to recover from such setbacks as epidemics, famine, or poor breeding. Even if such factors do not totally destroy the population, they will generally limit its growth rate, and, therefore, the population will increase only slowly at first. However, once the population is established, its size will grow more rapidly as long as there are adequate food sources, relatively few predators and favorable living conditions. When the population becomes very large with respect to its food supply, availability of shelter, and vulnerability to predators and becomes so dense that disease spreads rapidly, the mortality increases and the growth rate decreases. The entire curve of growth looks like an S and is said to be **sigmoid** or S-like, as shown in Figure 4–5. (These functions are also called **logistic** functions in some ecology texts.) The rate of growth shown by the upper right portion of the sigmoid curve is nearly zero. A zero growth rate does not mean that there are no births and no deaths. It simply means that the total number of births plus immigrations equals the total number of deaths plus emigrations.

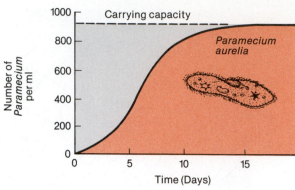

Figure 4–5

Carrying capacity for one of Gause's *Paramecium* populations. Carrying capacity is the maximal population that the environment can sustain indefinitely. A single individual is introduced into a tube. The experimenter supplies food at some constant rate. At first, the population grows exponentially, but, when it becomes sufficiently dense, competition for food sets in. The population finally stabilizes at the carrying capacity, which, in this case, is determined by the rate at which food is supplied.

When this equilibrium is reached, the biotic potential is balanced by the environmental resistance. The magnitude of the upper, stable population level in an ecosystem is called the **carrying capacity,** the maximal number of individuals of a given species that can be supported indefinitely by a particular environment.

When the carrying capacity has been reached, the system cannot continue to support any more individuals of that species. The carrying capacity is not constant from region to region; for example, a wheat field has an inherent ability to support more locusts than can a short-grass prairie.

In any stable natural ecosystem, the populations of most species have already reached a level close to the carrying capacity. However, fluctuations do occur owing to a variety of factors, such as changes in weather, immigration of new species, or any of a number of other perturbations. Therefore, most growth curves of existing populations are most accurately described by a slightly wavy line (Fig. 4–6). However, if a population is decimated by some natural disaster, or if a species is imported into a new environment where food, water, and sunlight are plentiful and natural enemies or competitors are absent, exponential rates are observed for a short period of time. Dandelions, starlings, and house sparrows that were introduced into the United States underwent dramatic population explosions. Exponential growth is common within a small area, as, for example, when bacteria invade the intestinal tract of a newborn animal or when decomposers invade an animal or plant that has recently died. Inevitably, however, every population must stabilize in some manner.

Although most populations exhibit relatively smooth growth curves, natural systems are not always predictable, nor are they universally harmo-

Figure 4–6

Changes in size of a natural population. The number of breeding pairs of gray herons in part of northwest England fluctuated little over 25 years. The population recovered rapidly from the decline caused by the severe winter of 1947. We deduce that the carrying capacity of the environment is about 250 breeding pairs. Fluctuations around the carrying capacity are small compared with the heron's biotic potential, which is about 3 new birds per pair per year. (After Lack, 1966)

nious. In the early 1900s, reindeer were introduced onto several islands on the Bering Sea, off the west coast of Alaska. In all cases, the environment was favorable, vegetation was lush, and there were no predators. On one island, St. George, the reindeer population increased moderately from an initial group of 6 animals to a peak of 222, and then decreased to a stable herd of 40 to 60. This behavior is reasonably close to the sigmoid-type growth function. However, the herd on nearby St. Paul Island grew exponentially for several years (Fig. 4–7). Even after the sustained carrying capacity was surpassed, vegetation was still available, and reindeer continued to multiply until the population numbered 2000. Then, quite suddenly, almost all the food was gone. The island became barren, and mass starvation and death occurred, until only 8 animals remained alive. No one can explain why the population behaved so differently on two islands that are otherwise similar ecologically.

In some systems, populations oscillate in a more or less cyclic pattern. North of the Canadian forest lies the arctic tundra, and one common rodent of the tundra is the lemming. Lemmings exhibit predictable 3- or 4-year population cycles. One summer, the population is extremely high; the next year, the population rapidly declines, or crashes. For another year or two, the population recovers slowly, then it skyrockets for a season, and the cyclic pattern repeats itself.

Lemming abundance is associated with forage cycles (Fig. 4–8). During an abundant lemming year, the tundra plants are plentiful and healthy. Most of the available nutrients exist in plant tissue, and there is little stored in the soil reservoir. In the

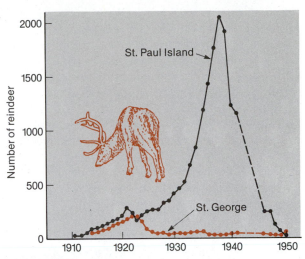

Figure 4–7
Growth function for reindeer on two similar islands. (From C. J. Krebs: *Ecology.* New York, Harper & Row Publishers, 1972.)

spring, following the overabundance of lemmings, the heavily overgrazed plants become scarce, and most of the nutrients in the ecosystem are locked in the dead and dying lemmings. The process of decay and return to the soil requires another year or two, during which time the population and health of both plants and rodents increase.

Unfortunately, recognition of the relationship between lemmings and forage cycles does not prove either that forage cycles cause rodent cycles or vice versa.* Some researchers argue that per-

*Judith H. Meyers and Charles J. Krebs: Population cycles in rodents. *Scientific American,* June, 1974, p. 38.

Figure 4–8
Lemming population cycles at Point Barrow, Alaska, from 1946 to 1966.

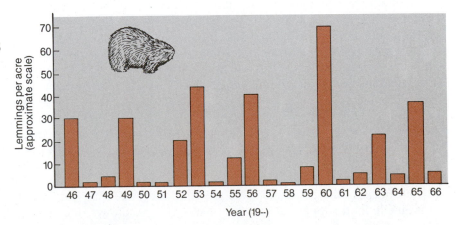

haps internal genetic factors may be responsible for the cycles in some rodent populations.

Erratic **population blooms** occur even in old, seemingly stable systems. Since recorded history, a species of a red microorganism has often been observed to enter a period of rapid growth in coastal areas. There seems to be no predictable cyclic pattern associated with this phenomenon; instead, plankton grow very rapidly at unexpected times—seemingly in response to a new influx of nutrients. Traditionally, these "red tides" were often observed after flood waters washed large quantities of soil nutrients into the sea. This influx created a plentiful food source. The red-colored plants were best able to take advantage of it. Unfortunately, these organisms discharge toxic substances into the sea, killing fish and aquatic mammals, and are, therefore, considered a great hazard. Recently, a series of red tides apparently unrelated to natural phenomena has been tentatively attributed to the nutrient content of pollutants discharged into the sea.

In contrast to the large fluctuations in population that occur from time to time, a noteworthy feature of most large ecosystems is that the size of most of the populations changes relatively little over the years—certainly less than one might expect from their biotic potential (refer back to Fig. 4–6).

4.7
Mortality Factors

In the discussion of population growth curves, we have seen that if a few individuals are introduced into a previously uninhabited area and if conditions are favorable, the population may increase exponentially. Eventually, the population becomes so dense that death rates increase dramatically, and the population levels off or stabilizes. One reason that populations behave in this manner is that certain environmental pressures are more severe when a population is dense than when it is less dense. Population pressures that act in this manner are called **density-dependent mortality factors** (Fig. 4–9.)

One density-dependent factor is simply the availability of nutrients. Recall the massive death of reindeer on St. Paul Island. These animals starved to death because the population was too large for the available food supply.

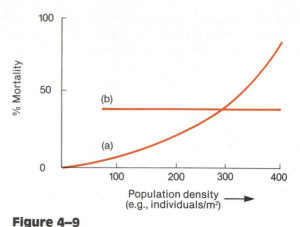

Figure 4–9
Hypothetical curves describing the actions of *(a)* density-dependent mortality factors—an increasing fraction of the population is killed as the population density increases; *(b)* density-independent mortality—the same fraction of the population is killed regardless of the population density (although higher *numbers* of individuals are killed at higher densities).

Another density-dependent factor is competition for resources. When the population is dense, a higher proportion of individuals will perish if they lose out in competition for food or nest spaces than in a population that is less dense. In an extreme case, if there is one nest site per square kilometer and one breeding pair in the same area, no individual will die or be prevented from breeding by lack of a nest site. But if many individuals must compete for a limited number of nest sites, some must be displaced.

A third type of density-dependent mortality is attack by various predators, parasites, and disease organisms. In most all cases, members of a dense population are more vulnerable to their enemies than are individuals in a sparse population. Competition and predation will be discussed in greater detail in Section 4.9.

Alternatively, other causes of death, called **density-independent mortality factors,** kill a constant proportion of the population regardless of its density. A frequently cited density-independent mortality factor is bad weather. A hurricane, a severe winter, or a drought may kill all the individuals in a population, no matter what the population density (Fig. 4–10). The action of weather is not always independent of density, however, since

Figure 4–10
A weather-beaten tree growing on a mountaintop. The state of the tree and the absence of other trees suggest that the size of the tree population here is controlled by density-independent factors such as the very high winds, which few trees can withstand.

some individuals may be able to find shelter from bad weather. If the number of shelters is limited, all the members of a small population can find shelter, whereas only a fraction of a more dense population will be protected.

4.8
Environmental Resistance—Physical Factors

An organism can thrive only if *all* the essentials of life are available. For example, a plant may have adequate supplies of space, light, moisture, and most nutrients, but, if one essential mineral is lacking, the organism will not survive.

The **Law of Limiting Factors** states that the growth of a species is limited by the resource that is *least* available in the ecosystem.

Limiting factors can take many different forms, physical or biological.

Shortage of Nutrients, Light, and Space

If you study the growth of microscopic floating plants that live in the surface layers of the central oceans, you will find that although there is a lot of light, there are relatively few organisms. There is, of course, enough water; why, then, isn't there more life? The answer is that many nutrients are scarce in these regions. The motion of nutrients from the land toward the central oceans is slow, and many of these materials fall to the bottom of the sea, where they are unavailable to the plants and animals that live near the surface. Thus, the biological productivity of the oceans is limited by a shortage of a few nutrients, even though there is plenty of water, light, and many mineral salts.

In some regions, such as in certain deserts, many nutrients are relatively plentiful, but water limits the growth of plants and animals. In rainforests, plants are crowded together so densely that light and space become limiting. In general, the population growth will be slow if any of the essentials of life are scarce.

Climatic Factors

Temperature, wind, and wave action are other factors that limit population growth. Trees cannot grow on high windswept ridges in the mountains or in the arctic regions where winters are particularly severe. Many ocean plants and animals do not live where wave action is intense. Polar bears do not migrate to the sunny south.

Disasters

In addition to the normal characteristics of the physical environment, natural disasters such as fire, flood, or storm can occasionally reduce population size or even destroy a local population completely.

4.9
Environmental Resistance—Biological Factors

An encounter between two individuals can be beneficial, harmful, or neutral to either or both of them. Likewise, the sum of *many* encounters between individuals can be beneficial, harmful, or neutral to the populations to which the individuals belong. The effects on the individuals are not necessarily the same as they are on the populations; if a coyote eats a mouse, it is the end for that mouse, but not for mice. Ecology deals mainly with the effects of the sum of individual encounters on the total community.

The important encounters between any two individuals, A and B, are those that are potentially beneficial to at least one of them. These interactions are described in the following paragraphs.

Competition

Competition is an interaction in which two or more individuals try to gain control of the same resource. There are many different ways that organisms can compete with each other in nature.

Scramble competition occurs when a number of organisms share a limited resource in such a way that no individuals have a particular advantage; therefore, all the individuals suffer. A human example of scramble competition would be a situation in which a number of people live in a refugee camp. If there is sufficient food to go around, everyone has enough to eat, and there is no competition. Now imagine that food supplies are severely limited. If the food were divided equally among all the individuals, everyone would starve.

Contest competition occurs when one organism harms another in an effort to gain control over a resource. It is easy to observe contest competition. Simply set up a bird feeder and watch it for a few days. Invariably, a small bird will come to eat, and a larger one will chase it away. In most cases, there is no physical contact between the birds. The larger animal harms the smaller one by chasing it away from its meal, not by physically injuring it.

Notice that in scramble competition, there is an equal distribution of resources, and all the individuals suffer. If the competition is severe enough, the entire population may perish. On the other hand, in contest competition, there is an unequal distribution of resources, and only certain organisms suffer. The successful ones flourish.

Intraspecific competition occurs between members of the same species and is therefore very common. Members of the same species generally need the same resources and thus are bound to compete for them except when they are colonizing a new habitat or when the population is very small in relation to the available resources.

In order to illustrate intraspecific scramble competition, ecologists planted two plots of white clover, *Trifolium repens,* at two different densities. Half the plants in each plot were watered throughout the experiment, but the other half were watered only until they germinated. Among the seedlings that were watered continuously, competition was minimal because the resources were never limiting. Therefore, mortality was low regardless of the density of the seedlings. Among the plants deprived of water, however, serious desiccation of all the plants was observed. In the high-density plot, mortality was 300 percent greater than it was in the low-density plot. This density-dependent mortality was presumably caused by competition for the limited supply of water (Fig. 4–11).

Intraspecific contest competition encompasses a wide variety of different types of behavior. In

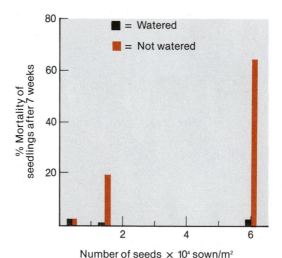

Figure 4–11
The effect of seed density on the survival of white clover seedlings. Unshaded bars represent the mortality of seedlings that were not watered after day 18. (After J. L. Harper, *Society for Experimental Biology Symposium,* 15:1, 1961, Cambridge University Press.)

some situations, animals may not compete directly for a specific resource, but indirectly for a social status or for territories. **Territories** are areas of land that an individual will defend against invaders. The possession of a territory guarantees access to certain resources, such as food, shelter, nesting sites, or a mate. Similarly, most social animals have "pecking orders." These are social hierarchies in which low-ranking members defer to those of higher rank. Individuals of low status get out of the way when a higher ranking member of the group demands access to a resource such as food or a mate. Humans and many other species of primates are among those animals that compete for social status and, so, indirectly, for any scarce resources that such status might bring.

Competition for territories that guarantee their owners access to shelter and food is common among higher animals. Ecologists studied the muskrat population of an Iowa marsh for 25 years. During this time, the marsh always contained almost exactly 400 muskrats. The researchers found that the remarkable stability of the muskrat population occurred because the carrying capacity of the marsh was extremely density-dependent. Males compete for territories where they find food, hide from predators, and build nests to protect their young. The marsh always contained the same number of territories and therefore the same number of muskrat families. Males who failed to secure territories were forced to breed in less-than-ideal conditions outside the marsh. In these home sites,

food was scarce, and shelter from enemies was poor. As a result, the parents and offspring suffered enormous mortality. Thus, the carrying capacity of the marsh was dictated primarily by the physical characteristics of the marsh. Even a flood that killed off most of the population of the marsh in one year did not affect the population size for long. Muskrats have a high biotic potential and rapidly repopulated the marsh to its previous density. This kind of situation is common in the many animal species that hold territories. The population size is very constant, because only those animals that possess territories breed successfully.

Interspecific competition is competition between members of two or more different species for the same resource. One ecological theory states that two different species living in a single ecosystem cannot have identical niches. In other words, if individuals of two species compete intensely for the same resource, one species will always be the more successful. The loser will then be eliminated from the ecosystem or will be forced to change its niche requirements in some way. Many biologists believe that the changes resulting from interspecific competition are a powerful force in evolution. This topic will be discussed in Chapter 6.

It often looks as though several species co-exist while competing strongly for the same resource. For example, several species of warblers (birds) often feed on the same species of insects in the same part of a forest. However when the feeding habits of the warblers were examined in

BLACKBURNIAN WARBLER   BAY-BREASTED WARBLER   MYRTLE WARBLER

Figure 4–12
Several species of warbler in the genus *Dendroica* hunt for insects in coniferous trees in the same New England forest. Each usually forages in a different part of the tree (shaded), thus reducing the competition for food.

detail, researchers found that different species of birds foraged for insects in different parts of the trees, thereby reducing competition between them (Fig. 4–12). Many ecologists believe that this observation can be generalized and that, in all ecosystems, the different species will invariably partition the resources between them to reduce direct competition.

It is therefore reasonable to ask whether or not two species of plants living side by side with their roots in the same soil and their tops touching are not in fact in direct competition. Where these situations have been studied, investigators have found that if there is not a difference in nutrient requirements or root depth, there usually is a difference in timing of the life cycles. Of two species of clover that coexist, one was observed to grow faster and spread its leaves sooner than the other. The second species ultimately grows taller than the first. Thus, each has its period of peak sunlight, and they are both able to survive.

Interspecific competition often restricts the abundance and distribution of natural populations. An example is competition between two species of barnacles, *Balanus* and *Chthamalus* (pronounced "thamalus") on the rocky coast of western Scotland (Fig. 4–13). *Chthamalus* occupies the upper part of the intertidal zone, and *Balanus* the lower, with little overlap between them. The larvae of both species settle on rocks in both zones. However, *Balanus* cannot survive in the upper zone, because it dries out and dies during low tide. What goes on in the lower zone? The scientist who studied them removed *Balanus* larvae from the lower zone and found that *Chthamalus* soon filled the lower zone. Obviously, only competition from *Balanus* usually keeps *Chthamalus* out of the lower zone. Because *Balanus* grows faster than *Chthamalus, Balanus* grows over *Chthamalus* and crowds it out when the two occur together in the lower zone.

Populations limited by this sort of competition are very common in nature. If a species did not face competition, it could survive in many areas where it is not found. A species is *actually* found only in areas where it is capable of fighting off the competition. Gardens are full of examples. Exotic flowers and vegetables may grow successfully in gardens where they are protected from competition for light, water, and space. But they would rapidly succumb to competition from native plants if they were planted in untended fields or woods.

In almost all cases, competition between two species reduces the population of both competitors; therefore, it is tempting to say that one species would be "better off" if its competitors were eliminated. This is not always the case, however. In one section of the shoreline in the state of Washington, barnacles and sea anemones competed for suitable living space in the intertidal regions. When all the barnacles were removed during an experiment, the anemone population grew rapidly, as

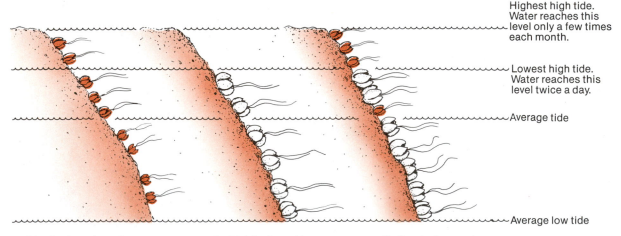

Highest high tide. Water reaches this level only a few times each month.

Lowest high tide. Water reaches this level twice a day.

Average tide

Average low tide

A. Distribution of smaller barnacle *(Chthamalus)* in the absence of competition from larger species

B. Distribution of larger barnacle *(Balanus)* in the absence of competition from smaller species.

C. In actual ecosystems predators limit growth of *Chthamalus* below lowest high tide; dessication limits growth of *Balanus* above lowest high tide.

Figure 4–13
Competition between two species of barnacles on the Scottish coast.

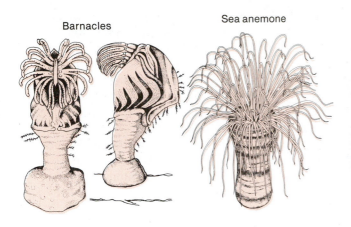

Barnacles   Sea anemone

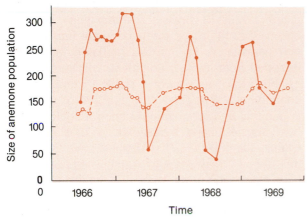

Figure 4–14

Effect of removal of barnacles from intertidal region. Solid circles indicate anemone population in an area where barnacles were removed. Open circles indicate control; anemone population in an undisturbed area. (From P. K. Kayton: *Ecological Monographs.* 41*(4)*:373, 1972. Reprinted with permission of author.)

one might have expected, but this bloom was followed by a rapid decline, as shown in Figure 4–14. The decline did not result from a food shortage; rather, it was found that the anemones died of desiccation. In an undisturbed system, anemones grow close to their competitors, the barnacles, thereby finding shelter from the hot summer wind.

Predation

Predation is an interaction in which certain individuals eat others. Since all heterotrophs must eat to survive, predation is an integral part of any ecosystem. Examples include a mountain lion eating a deer, a frog eating a fly, and a paramecium eating a bacterium. What about a cow; is it a pred-

Several species of barnacles and mussels compete for space in this intertidal zone in northern California.

ator of grass? Because the action of eating another organism, regardless of how savage the act is, depletes the population of the prey organism, all consumers—herbivores and carnivores alike—can be considered to be predators. Predation is a major cause of mortality to most natural populations. But recall that ecology does not emphasize the effect of a single event on a single individual. Rather, it is primarily concerned with the effects of a series of events on an entire community. In many systems, it has been shown that predatory pressures either improve the health and vitality of a community of prey animals or increase the number of species of prey in a system. Studies of moose killed by wolves have shown that the old, the crippled, the sick, and the very young are killed in disproportionately high numbers. Only rarely does a wolf or a wolf pack kill a healthy adult moose. Predation helps to select for a healthy breeding population of prey by eliminating individuals weakened by genetic disorders or susceptibility to disease.

Even though predators kill individuals, predation may *increase* the number of prey species in an ecosystem. For example, in a series of experiments performed in intertidal communities on the Pacific coast, a typical section of shoreline harbored 15 resident species. There were several predators in the community, one of which was a type of starfish. When the starfish were removed from

An Alaskan brown bear with a salmon it has just caught. (Leonard Lee Rue, National Audubon Society)

land. In the early spring, the grasses grew faster and denser than the grasses in nearby areas that were subject to grazing. When the summer drought arrived, the ungrazed grasses lost so much moisture through their extensive leaf systems that many plants yellowed, and, by the end of the season, the ungrazed plot was less healthy than the natural one.

Parasitism is a special case of predation in which the predator is much smaller than the victim and obtains nourishment by consuming the tissue or food supply of a living organism known as a **host.** Just as predator–prey interactions are balanced in healthy ecosystems, parasite–host relationships have also become part of the balance of nature. It must be stressed that this type of balance observed in the old systems does not imply that a new parasite (or an invading predator), artificially imported from another continent, will immediately establish itself as part of a stable system. On the contrary, a new species may find that competition is minimal and food supplies are abundant or that host species have inadequate natural defenses against the invaders. If conditions are favorable, this species may increase unchecked until, perhaps many years later, food supplies decline or another species migrates, is introduced, or evolves to control the rampant one.

Commensalism

Commensalism is a relationship in which one species benefits from an unaffected host. Several species of fish, clams, worms, and crabs live in the burrows of large sea worms and shrimp. They gain shelter and often eat their host's excess food or waste products but do not seem to affect their benefactors.

an experimental area, the community was altered drastically. Interspecific competition for space and food became intense. Of the 15 original species, 7 were eliminated. Apparently the niches of many of the organisms were quite similar. In spite of this similarity, however, competitive displacement did not occur in the undisturbed system, because starfish are general rather than specific predators. They put the greatest hunting pressure on the most common species, thereby controlling overpopulation by any one type of organism.

In yet another ecosystem, ecologists removed all the grazers from a section of a western range

A coyote chasing a mouse. When predators are killed by humans, their prey, such as mice and rabbits, multiply. (Photo by Jen and Des Bartlett, courtesy of National Audubon Society; Photo Researchers, Inc.)

Special Topic C
Prey Switching in a Simple Ecosystem

In 1956, a study was initiated to determine the cause of a rapid decline in the caribou population in Newfoundland, an island off the northeast coast of Canada. After observing the ecosystem carefully, biologists determined that one of the prime factors that led to the decline of the caribou was the importation of snowshoe hares in the late 1800s. The connection between the hares and the caribou is an interesting one and illustrates the complex interactions that can occur within an ecosystem.

In the early 1800s, the caribou population on Newfoundland was high and relatively stable. Birth was approximately equal to death, which was caused mainly by predation from wolves. Because Newfoundland is an island, there was very little migration to or from the area. There were some lynx on the island, but, as near as can be determined from trappers' reports, the lynx population was low.

In 1880, snowshoe hares were imported to the island to serve as a food source for fishermen and their families. The environment was favorable to the hares, and the population bloomed (see Fig 4–19). The abundant hares provided a new food source for the lynx, and the lynx population bloomed in response. In about 1915, the hares were faced with heavy pressure owing to overgrazing of the food supply and the mortality caused by heavy predation. Therefore, the population declined dramatically. The lynx, faced with loss of their primary food source, began to prey heavily on caribou calves, leading to a decline in the size of the caribou herd. Eventually, when the populations of both prey species declined, the number of lynx also declined (Fig. 4–19). In turn, when the lynx declined, the hares and the caribou were relieved of pressure and the populations of these species increased once again. The pattern established a cycle that continued throughout the 25-year span of the study.

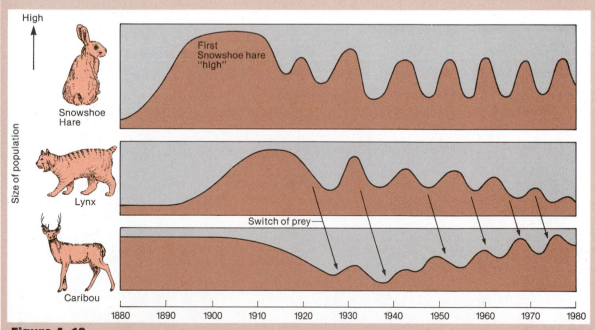

Figure 4–19
Changes in the population of lynx, hare, and caribou in Newfoundland between 1880 and 1980.

Mutualism or Cooperation

Mutualism, or **cooperation**, is a relationship that is favorable and sometimes necessary to both species. For example, crabs often carry certain sessile marine animals on their backs. The transported animals cannot move on their own power and depend on the crabs to move them from one rich feeding ground to another. In turn, the crabs benefit from the camouflage and protective stingers of their guests.

Another example of a mutualistic interaction can be found within our own bodies. Millions of bacteria live in the digestive tracts of every person. These organisms depend on their host for food but, in return, aid in the digestive process and are essential to our survival.

An interesting mutualistic system of defense has been observed between a certain species of ants and the acacia tree. The ants live in the hollow thorns of the tree and feed on its leaves and flowers. They are uniquely adapted to survive only in that very specific environment. But in exchange for food and shelter, the ants defend the acacia by stinging other herbivores and clearing competitive plants from the ground beneath the tree. When the ants were experimentally removed from a collection of trees, the growth rates of the trees were reduced to about one sixth of their values, and mortality doubled. Thus, each species needs the other to survive.

4.10
Community Interactions

Most of the examples used thus far in this chapter have involved interactions between two organisms or two different species. Moose eat willows, wolves eat moose. Yet studies of interactions between two species, important as they are, represent only a part of the understanding of ecology. Recall that the community energy exchange in an ecosystem is described by a complex, interwoven food web, not by a simple, linear, food chain. In many instances, the complexity provides feedback mechanisms that help stabilize population levels.

Figure 4–15
Grazers in Elk Island National Park. *A,* moose; *B,* elk; *C,* American bison.

Many examples can be found to support this statement. In the last section, we discussed an intertidal community that contained 15 resident species. When one of the predators was removed, seven other species disappeared from the community.

Or, as another example, there are three species of large herbivores in Elk Island National Park in Canada—moose, elk, and bison (Fig. 4–15). Moose eat saplings and small bushes. With brush growth held in check, grasses find room to grow. Bison eat grass. Elk eat either leaves or grasses. In this way, the community of herbivores acts on the community of plants. If one species were eliminated, the balance would be disrupted.

A natural prairie contains many different species of plants (Fig. 4–16). Bushes and perennial grasses do not die in winter but live for many years. They grow deep roots that collect water and nutrients from lower layers in the soil. On the other hand, annual plants sprout from seed every spring. They grow quickly, produce seeds, and then die in the fall. Annuals generally have shallow roots that lie near the surface. During dry years, there is so little water that many of the annuals die. However, the perennials, which use water from deep under-

ground, are able to live. These living plants hold the soil and protect it from blowing away with the dry summer winds. In years of high rainfall, the annuals sprout quickly. Their extensive root systems spread rapidly and prevent soil erosion and water run-off. Thus, the soil is maintained in both dry and wet years.

Many opposing forces operate within a natural ecosystem. Animals eat and in turn are eaten. Fertility rates vary. Migration is common. Weather varies and climates change. Moisture and nutrients travel into and out of the soil. The net effect of all these events happening together is that, in general, most systems do not change rapidly unless affected by some major calamity. If an ecosystem is disrupted at some time, the system usually tends to regain balance. Such a tendency is called the "balance of nature," or more formally, **ecosystem homeostasis.** For example, when there is a drought in a grassland, plants do not grow well. The meadow mice that eat the grass become malnourished. When this happens, their fertility rate drops, and their birth rate decreases. The hungry mice retreat to their burrows and sleep. They need less food and are less exposed to predators while they sleep, so their death rate decreases. Their behavior

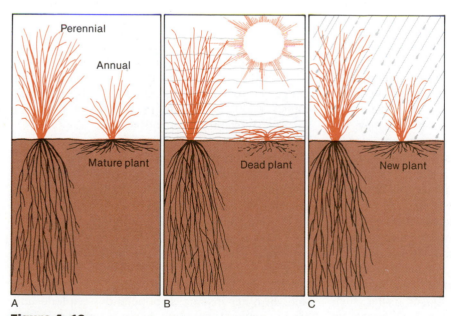

A   B   C

Figure 4–16
Root systems of prairie plants. *A,* Both annual and perennial plants grow in a prairie. *B,* In a dry year, the annuals die but the perennials hold the soil. *C,* In years of high rainfall, annuals sprout quickly and hold the soil.

The south-facing slope of this ridge is covered with grasses, cacti, and a few pine trees, whereas the north slope is densely wooded. This type of diversity is characteristic of many stable ecosystems.

protects their own population balance as well as that of the grasses, which are not consumed by hibernating mice.

Stable ecosystems, if examined superficially, do not seem to go out of balance at all. Actually, their homeostatic mechanisms work so well that slight imbalances are corrected before they become severe. If severe imbalances are prevented, it is likely that the system will last for a long time.

A wonderful example of a stable system is a redwood forest. To the hiker entering the redwood forest on a hot summer day, two characteristics of the environment are immediately obvious. It is cool, and there is a thick floor of spongy matter. The coolness, caused by the extensive shade of the tall trees, reduces the water loss caused by evaporation. The spongy floor is formed by a large bed of decomposed or partly decomposed matter, such as fallen needles and rotting wood. This material holds the rainwater and thus serves as a reservoir for water and nutrients. Thus, a mild drought does not kill the trees. In addition, a large amount of

organic matter ensures a steady functioning of the recycling system. The coolness of the forest offers still another advantage. Clouds passing over a cool air mass are likely to condense into droplets and collect as fog or fall as rain. Thus, the redwood forests tend to cause rain, restrict evaporation, and retain a substantial supply of water.

Redwood forests also protect themselves from fire. During the long life span of a redwood grove, intermittent fires are inevitable. However, because the bark and the wood of the redwood tree are fire-resistant, the big trees are scarred but not killed, and the ecosystem is not destroyed.

The concept of ecosystem homeostasis does *not* imply that all systems are in harmonious balance all the time. Disasters occur in natural systems. Sometimes fires do destroy the landscape, and, in other instances, populations explode and famines occur. In extreme cases, entire species are driven to extinction. The entire question of ecosystem stability is an important one and will be discussed further throughout this book.

Temperate rain forest: a redwood forest in California.

The eastern slope of the Colorado Rockies has a relatively dry climate compared with that of other forest systems. Only abut 45 cm (18 inches) of rain falls annually, and the dry air and the hot sun of the region encourage rapid evaporation. Small cacti and yuccas grow on exposed hillsides. The trees tend to thrive best in gullies or shaded areas where water is more plentiful and the summer sun is less intense. About 100 years ago, before gold and silver miners settled in large numbers in these regions, there were only a few trees on the mountainsides. The Colorado gold rush brought many settlers to the area. These miners cut nearly all the trees that existed, and they used the wood to build cabins and to timber mines (Fig. 4–18). Within a few years, the hillsides were virtually stripped. Only the low-lying brush, grasses, and cacti remained.

Of course, many pine cones must have lain on the ground. As the seeds sprouted, the young

4.11
Case History: The Pine Beetle Epidemic on the Eastern Slope of the Colorado Rockies

The pine beetle *(Dendroctonus ponderosae)* is a natural parasite of the ponderosa pine. It bores holes into healthy trees, sucks the sap, and lays its eggs in the tunnels, thereby disrupting the flow of water from the roots to the needles. Certain species of fungi infect the beetle holes and further upset the tree's life support system. If enough beetles attack a given tree, the tree will die.

During the late 1970s, a heavy infestation of pine beetles destroyed many stands of ponderosa in several Rocky Mountain regions. On certain hillsides near Boulder, Colorado, the epidemic was so severe that all the mature trees were killed (Fig. 4–17). The pine beetle is not new to these hills. It has been a part of the ecosystem for many years. Why, then, did this epidemic occur only recently?

Figure 4–17
A woman cutting dead timber from a stand of ponderosa pine killed by pine beetles.

Figure 4–18
Miners cut trees to build cabins and provide timbers for mine supports. (Courtesy of State Historical Society of Colorado)

A healthy ponderosa pine.

trees started to grow in a favorable environment. With the large trees gone, there was initially little competition for space, sunlight, and water. Therefore, the saplings were healthy, and new forests began to grow quickly. Since several young trees require less space and water than are needed by one large tree, these new forests grew to be much denser than the original system. By the 1960s, many of the young trees had grown to substantial size, and the ecosystem appeared to be healthy. Yet, since the new forests were much denser than the original ones, competition for vital nutrients, especially water, was much keener. The available moisture was now distributed among many more trees, so all the trees suffered from lack of water.

If a beetle attacks a strong, well-watered tree, the tree will produce enough sap to force the beetle out of its burrow. Thus, a healthy tree can repel a beetle attack, just as a healthy person can avoid infection even if there are many disease organisms in the environment. On the other hand, a weak tree, living with inadequate supplies of water, cannot produce excess quantities of sap. Therefore, it is more likely to be infected by beetles. In the dense weakened forests of the 1960s, there were large areas in which there were no trees healthy enough to repel a beetle attack. The beetles bored successfully into the wood of these trees and destroyed the forests.

What will happen in the future? Of course, no one can predict with certainty. In some regions, all the trees have died, leaving a grassland similar to that left by the miners and loggers a hundred years ago. In that case, the cycle may repeat itself. A new dense forest may grow, only to be killed by beetles a century from now. In such a situation, true ecological balance will not be achieved. Instead, there would be a cycle of rapid growth followed by death. In other regions however, a few of the strongest trees survived. With the death of the weaker trees, the remaining ones face reduced competition for water, and, it is hoped, a stable for-est system might regenerate. There is yet a third possibility for the future of the forest. Individual landowners and government agencies, having realized the nature of the problem, are actively managing the forests by thinning weak trees, planting beetle-resistant species, and spraying to reduce the existing beetle population. Thus, a natural system is being converted into a managed one. The management process itself raises a host of questions, which will be discussed further in future chapters.

Summary

A **species** is defined as a group of organisms of related individuals that resemble each other and are able to breed with one another but not with members of other species. A **population** is the breeding group to which an organism belongs in practice.

A **niche** is a description of an organism's physical location within an ecosystem and its function in the patterns of energy flow and nutrient cycling.

Given ideal environmental conditions, the number of individuals in a population increases exponentially at the population's **biotic potential.** This potential is determined by various factors, including the age of the female parent at first reproduction, the number of offspring produced at each reproduction, the frequency of reproduction, and the parents' reproductive life span. A population seldom, if ever, reproduces as fast as its biotic potential would permit, even when the population is growing exponentially.

The size of a population is limited by the **environmental resistance.** Components of the environmental resistance include reduction of birth rates and mortality factors. Survivorship curves for members of a population reflect the population's reproductive strategy. At the two extremes, the members of a population may produce many small offspring to which they give no parental assistance toward their subsequent survival, or they may produce a few large offspring that are nourished and trained by the parents. A classic growth curve is represented by a **sigmoid** (sometimes called a logistic) function. The magnitude of the largest stable population of a species is called the **carrying capacity.** Many populations are remarkably stable, but others oscillate sharply.

Factors that limit population growth may be density-dependent, for example, predation or competition for resources; or they may be density-independent, for example, bad weather.

Encounters between two individuals can be classified on the basis of their potential benefit or harm to one or both of them. **Competition,** in which two or more individuals try to gain control of the same resource, benefits the victor. **Predation,** in which some individuals eat others, also benefits only the predator, but it can help to select for a healthy breeding population of prey by eliminating weak individuals. **Parasitism** is a special form of predation by a small organism against a much larger host. Other interactions include **commensalism,** in which one individual benefits from an unaffected host, and **mutualism,** or **cooperation,** in which both organisms benefit.

Studies of encounters between two individuals are only a first step towards understanding how many interactions among many individuals affect the community as a whole. **Ecosystem homeostasis,** often called the balance of nature, is the tendency of ecosystems to adjust to change and to regain balance when disturbed.

Questions

Species

1. Although intermarriage between different ethnic groups is relatively rare in human societies, many such unions do occur. Are specific ethnic groups separate species? If your answer is no, are they likely to become separate species in the future? Explain.

2. Explain the difference between a species and a population. Give examples.

Niche

3. Choose an organism that you are familiar with and describe its niche as completely as you can.

4. Again, using an organism that you are familiar with, show that in a real situation, the niche is the set of conditions that an organism adapts to, not the optimal conditions for life.

5. Design an experiment (you do not have to perform it) to illustrate the statement in problem 4.

Growth of Populations

6. Imagine that the population of a given species quadrupled (increased by multiples of four) every 10 years. If there were 10 individuals in 1950, how many would there be in 1960, 1970, 1980, 2000? Draw a graph showing the number of individuals as a function of time. (Plot time on the horizontal, or X, axis, and population on the vertical, or Y, axis.)

7. Describe a real or imaginary organism whose biotic potential depends mostly on (a) the age at first reproduction and the frequency of the reproductive cycle; (b) the total number of times it reproduces in its lifetime.

8. Describe the kinds of organisms that exhibit (a) a Type I survival curve; (b) a Type II survival curve; (c) a Type III survival curve.

9. If a new species is introduced into an established ecosystem and if conditions are favorable and there are no significant predators or disease organisms, the species may exhibit an extremely rapid growth rate for a short period of time. Under these conditions, would an organism belonging to a Type I, Type II, or Type III survivorship curve be likely to increase most rapidly? Explain.

10. The worldwide human population has been increasing continuously for the past few hundred years. Can this trend continue indefinitely? Are human populations subject to the constraints of a worldwide carrying capacity? Explain.

11. Give an example of a situation in which a population may exist (a) above the carrying capacity and (b) below the carrying capacity of an ecosystem.

12. It is mentioned in the text that lemming populations vary on a 3- to 4-year cycle. Do you think that the populations of other species in the ecosystem would also cycle? Discuss.

Environmental Resistance

13. Select a wild plant or animal with which you are familiar and discuss the primary components of the environmental resistance that affect it.

14. Does the carrying capacity of an environment for a given species change (a) if the environmental resistance changes; (b) if there is an accident, such as a hurricane, that kills off half the population of the species? Defend your answers.

15. The physical components of the environmental resistance (e.g., shortage of inorganic nutrients, adverse climate) are sometimes closely associated with the biological components (e.g., predation, competition). Discuss this statement and give examples to support it.

16. Classify each of the following mortality factors as density-dependent or density-independent: (a) competition for food; (b) competition for nest sites; (c) precipitation of hot ashes from a major volcanic eruption. Defend your answers.

Species Interactions

17. An organism may compete with another organism of the same species or with organisms of other species. Explain and give two examples of each.

18. Categorize each of the following as either scramble or contest competition: (a) There was a massive mortality of reindeer on St. Paul Island after the population greatly exceeded the carrying capacity (see Section 4.6). (b) Two male lions fight for hunting territories for their families. (c) Entire forests of pine trees succumbed to a beetle infestation in the Colorado Rockies (see Section 4.11). (d) In Yellowstone National Park, where hunting is illegal, the elk population is much greater than that of deer, whereas in many nearby areas where hunting is permitted, there are generally more deer than elk.

19. Give one example not offered in the text of scramble competition and one of contest competition.

20. Explain how competition and predation are interconnected in their role in regulating populations in an ecosystem.

21. Describe the mechanisms that reduce the harm that (a) interspecific competitors and (b) intraspecific competitors can do to each other.

22. One ecologist stated that predators live on capital, whereas parasites live on interest. Explain. Is this true from an individual or from a community standpoint? Defend your answer.

23. Is there any way in which predation can benefit (a) the individual prey organism; (b) the community of prey organisms? Explain your answers.

24. Imagine that you observed that two species always lived in close proximity throughout their range. Design a generalized experiment to show whether the relationship between the two can be described as commensalism or mutualism.

Natural Systems

25. What is meant by the term "ecosystem homeostasis?" Give an example of a homeostatic mechanism. Give an example of a situation in which homeostatic mechanisms break down.

26. Which do you expect to be better able to survive a drought, a cornfield or a natural prairie? Explain.

Suggested Readings

Refer to references in Chapter 3. In addition, specific books relating to this chapter include:

J. G. Blower, et al.: *Estimating the Size of Animal Populations.* Winchester, MA, George Allen & Unwin, 1981. 96 pp.

Jared Diamond and Ted Case (eds.): *Community Ecology.* New York, Harper & Row, 1985. 665 pp.

Gerald Elseth and Candy Baumgardner: *Population Biology.* New York, Van Nostrand, 1980.

Paul R. Erlich and Jonathan R. Roughgarden: *The Science of Ecology.* New York, Macmillan, 1987.

George A. Seber: *The Estimation of Animal Abundance and Related Parameters.* New York, Macmillan, 1982. 672 pp.

Lawrence B. Slobodkin: *Growth and Regulation of Animal Populations.* New York, Dover Press, 1980.

Robert J. Taylor: *Predation.* New York, Chapman and Hall, 1984. 166 pp.

A variety of articles that explore some of the topics in this chapter in greater depth are:

Vernon Ahmandjian: The nature of lichens. *Natural History 91*:2, March 1982.

Robert Lewin: Finches show competition in ecology. *Science, 219*:1411, 1983.

Robert Lewin: Plant communities resist climatic change. *Science, 228*:165, 1985.

Robert Lewin: Predators and hurricanes change ecology. *Science, 221*:737, 1983.

Robert M. May: Parasitic infections as regulators of animal populations. *American Scientist, 71*:36, 1983.

Janice Moore: Parasites that change the behavior of their host. *Smithsonian,* May 1984, p. 108.

Douglass H. Moore: Milkweeds and their visitors. *Scientific American,* July 1985, p. 112.

Kenneth P. Sebens: The ecology of the rocky subtidal zone. *American Scientist, 73*:548, 1985.

John A. Wiens: Competition or peaceful coexistence? *Natural History,* March 1983, p.30.

An article discussing the role of competition in community structure is:

Robert Lewin: Santa Rosalia was a goat. *Science, 221*:636, 1983.

Special Topic B was taken from:

Arthur T. Begerud: Prey switching in a simple ecosystem. *Scientific American,* December 1983, pp. 130–141.

5

The Biosphere

5.1
Introduction

When European explorers and naturalists started to travel over the Earth in the 1600s, 1700s, and 1800s, they began to study and categorize its ecosystems. As an exotic array of diverse landforms and different species was discovered, people began to appreciate the richness and diversity of life on our planet. Yet, as studies became more systematic, scientists learned that there are really only a dozen or so basic types of ecosystems. A tropical forest in South America contains tall trees with large leaves and fruits, draped with colorful butterflies and birds flying through the gloomy shade. A tropical forest thousands of miles away in Africa looks very much the same, although the particular species of trees and vines, and of butterflies and birds, would be different. Other types of ecosystems—desert, shrubland, grassland, or tundra—also look much the same wherever in the world they occur.

5.2
Climate and Vegetation

Even the most casual observer of natural systems notices that there are several different types of ecosystems on Earth. Deserts, jungles, forests, and grasslands are all noticeably different from each other. It is also apparent that the character of each ecosystem is dependent on the climate—the yearly patterns of sunlight, temperature, humidity, precipitation, and winds.

The most important factor that affects climate is the amount of sunlight in an area, which influences temperature and less directly affects air motion and rainfall. Near the Equator, the Sun's rays strike the Earth almost vertically, thus giving tropical plants large amounts of the Sun's energy. Outside the tropics, the Sun's rays strike obliquely (Fig. 5–1); plants outside the tropics, therefore, receive less of the Sun's energy. Because of the tilt of the Earth on its axis, in nontropical areas the seasons change with the time of year, whereas in the tropics, there is little seasonal difference in day length and temperature. Tropical climates, therefore, have fairly steady high temperatures. In the temperate regions, there are distinct winter and summer seasons, and growth rates vary dramatically with the changes in light and temperature.

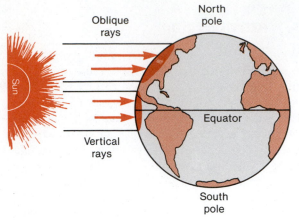

Figure 5–1
A beam of sunlight striking the Earth at high latitudes is spread over a wider area and is, therefore, less intense at any one point than a similar beam striking near the Equator.

In the Southern Hemisphere, there is no land between 56° south latitude and the ice-covered continent of Antarctica. In the Northern Hemisphere, however, land continues into the high Arc-

tic. In this zone, the Sun never sets at all for several months during the summer, and, alternately, in the winter, the Sun never rises. Air temperatures vary from −60° C in the winter to +20° C or even higher in the summer. This area, called the **Arctic zone,** has its own specific and uniquely adapted set of ecosystems.

The amount of sunlight incident on a certain area is one factor that determines the movement of masses of air. At the Equator, air is heated and rises vertically upward. This vertical movement produces only intermittent wind on the surface of the Earth. At sea, the region is known as the **doldrums** (Fig. 5–2). The rising air cools as it mounts higher into the atmosphere and releases some of its moisture as it does so. Therefore, many areas near the Equator receive large amounts of rain. Examples include the steamy tropical jungles of the Congo River Basin in Africa and of the Amazon Basin in South America.

The air that rises at the Equator moves both north and south at high altitudes. When the air masses reach latitudes of about 30° north and south, they have cooled enough to sink to Earth

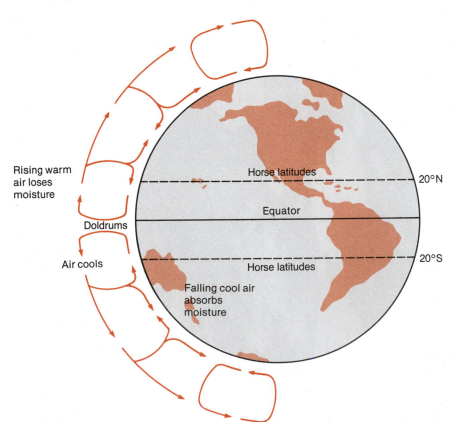

Figure 5–2
Vegetation changes with latitude and altitude. Temperature, which affects vegetation, falls as one travels up a mountain or away from the Equator, so that, if there is plenty of moisture, vegetation is similar at high altitudes and at high latitudes as shown here.

again. Falling air warms up and absorbs moisture. Thus, these latitudes are among the driest on Earth. The world's great deserts, such as the Sahara in North Africa and the coastal desert in Chile, are found here. At sea, these regions are called the "horse latitudes." This name was given because sailing ships were often becalmed for long periods in these latitudes, and horses transported as cargo often died of thirst and hunger.

Still further north and south, in the temperate latitudes that include most of the United States, Europe, and central Asia, swirling winds pull masses of air, sometimes from warm tropical areas and sometimes from frigid polar regions. When masses of warm air and cold air collide with each other, the warm air rises. This condition of rising air often generates storm systems and precipitation. The world's most productive agricultural land lies in the temperate zone.

5.3
The Biosphere

As mentioned earlier, life on Earth requires water, a source of energy (usually light from the Sun), and various nutrients found in the soil, water, and air. Suitable combinations of these essentials cannot be found high in the upper atmosphere or deep underground. They exist only in a narrow layer near the surface of the Earth. This layer is called the **biosphere** because it is, as far as we know, the only place where life can exist. The biosphere extends over most of the surface of the Earth. It includes the upper layers of the Earth's crust and the thin layer of soil that supports plant life. This zone of life also extends about 8 km up into the atmosphere (where insects and the spores of bacteria and fungi are to be found), and as much as 8 km down into the depths of the sea. Living organisms are not distributed uniformly through the biosphere: Few organisms live on polar ice caps and glaciers, whereas many live in tropical rainforests.

Within the biosphere, there are several major regions containing specific types of ecosystems. These major regions are called **biomes.** Biomes are recognized by the types of dominant vegetation. Some typical examples include tropical rainforests, temperate forests, prairies, deserts, and arctic tundra. Each biome is further subdivided into its specific ecosystems (Fig. 5–3).

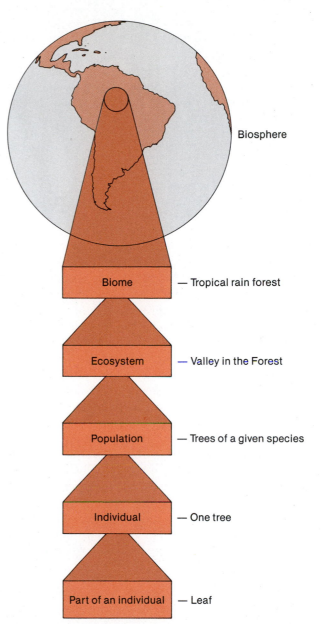

Figure 5–3
Any particular biological study can focus on a minute part of an individual or on the entire biosphere. The type of information that is obtained from the study is naturally related to the breadth of the study.

Imagine for a moment that you have the time, the resources, and the energy to take a grand tour of the Earth, and, being a naturalist, you set out to observe, in a general way, the biomes of our planet. Let us start our journey on a sheet of ice floating about in the vicinity of the North Pole. The sea ice is a cold, barren, lifeless place. There are no patches of land, no plants, and very few living creatures of any kind in the area. If you arrived on a summer day, the Sun would never set; on a winter day, there would be 24 hours of unbroken darkness. Walking south for several hundred miles over the treacherous terrain, you would eventually reach a region where sea and land meet. This is the arctic tundra, the northernmost biome on the planet.

5.4
Tundra

Your first impression of the tundra might be that there are no trees; the predominant plants are grasses, mosses, sedges, lichens, and scattered woody bushes lying low to the ground. Despite the lack of trees, animal life can be found on the land, in the air, in the nearby ocean, and on the ice (Fig. 5–4). In the summer, you might see huge herds of caribou, flocks of waterfowl, or unbelievable swarms of mosquitoes. Even though there are a great number of living creatures in the Arctic, there are relatively few different species. For example, of the 3200 species of mammals on the Earth, only 23 survive in the Arctic. Some of the most common of the North American arctic mammals are caribou, musk ox, grizzly bears, and polar bears. Smaller mammals include foxes, wolves, wolverines, weasels, mink, and hares. Similarly, of the 8600 or so species of birds living on the planet, only 6 or 7— raven, snowy owl, rock ptarmigan, hoary redpole, gyrfalcon, Ross's gull, and ivory gull—live in the Arctic year round. Another 70 species come north to breed. These include many types of waterfowl— ducks, geese, and swans—that breed in such num-

bers that the tundra appears to be quite lush during the brief nesting period in the summer.

Several years ago, I (Jon), was traveling in the Arctic along the north coast of Canada. I was speaking to an old man who had lived in the region all his life, and he told me, "Up here, the ice is king." Indeed, with short summers and long ice-bound winters, the climate is a ruling force in the high latitudes. For example, trees cannot live in the Arctic because they cannot survive the intensely cold winters. In most areas, a permanent layer of ice or frozen soil, called **permafrost,** lies beneath the layer of true soil (Fig. 5–5). Many regions have poor drainage because ice blocks the flow of groundwater, and as a result, bogs and marshes are common.

One important characteristic of tundra soils is that decomposition occurs very slowly, because the ground is so cold for most of the time. Thus, bits of leaves, tiny sticks, and dead flowers may lie on the ground for years before they rot. Owing to the low rate of decomposition, the shallow soil, and the short growing season, there are few nutrients available, and soils are generally poor. Plants grow slowly, and the tundra takes a long time to recover when it is disrupted.

Tundra does not occur in the southern hemisphere because continents do not extend far enough south. Antarctica harbors only a very scanty population of organisms around its edges. In Antarctica, as in the northern parts of the Arctic, life on the land (or, more often, on the ice) depends largely on the productivity of the sea. Many birds and mammals, though they breed on land, live on fish. These animals may die on land or

Figure 5–4
Caribou in flight in shallow water on the northern coast of Canada. Note the thin layer of ice and the flat tundra horizon in the background.

Figure 5–5
A profile of soil in the Arctic. Note that the grasses and sedges are growing on a thin layer of soil that, in turn, lies over a layer of ice.

leave feces that supply the main nutrients for the few land plants that survive in areas of almost constant ice.

Although the arctic tundra occurs only at high latitudes, small sections of **alpine tundra** and **al-**

Figure 5–6
Alpine tundra in early spring in the Rocky Mountains in Colorado.

pine grasslands are found on mountains even at the equator. Alpine tundra exists between the **timberline** (the greatest height at which trees can grow) and higher regions where few life forms survive (Fig. 5–6). Alpine tundra resembles arctic tundra in many ways, although nights are cool throughout the year in alpine areas, whereas they are warm during the brief arctic summer. In northern temperate mountains, alpine meadows cover extensive areas. These meadows are dominated by sedges and grasses, interspersed with dwarf willows, heaths, and other shrubs. Alpine meadows in North America are inhabited by mountain sheep, mountain goats, grizzly bears, and marmots. Many of the larger animals migrate to lower elevations during the winter, and all organisms are adapted to take advantage of the short growing season.

5.5
Taiga

If you travel southward from the arctic tundra you will observe a gradual onset of trees followed by an expansive forest system farther south. This region is called the **taiga,** a word derived from a Russian root meaning "primeval forest." The taiga, or **boreal forest,** as it is sometimes called, is dominated by subarctic needle-leafed forests, consisting mainly of conifers (mostly spruces, with a few pines and firs) that can survive extremely cold winters (Fig. 5–7). This biome stretches in almost unending monotony in a giant circle through Canada, Alaska, and Siberia. The monotony is due to the low diversity of tree species, which is occa-

Figure 5–7
A dogsled crossing a frozen swamp in the northern forest, or taiga. (Christine Seashore)

sionally interrupted by extensive areas of bog or "muskeg."

Much of the precipitation in the taiga falls as snow, and, in the winter, many of the resident animals grow fur or plumage that blends in with the white background. Animals characteristic of the North American taiga include moose, wolverine, wolves, lynx, spruce grouse, gray jays, crossbills, and (in summer) many different species of migratory birds.

5.6
Temperate Biomes

Continuing southward past the taiga, you would reach the world's temperate regions, so-called because on the average they experience moderate temperatures. However, this moderation represents an average temperature over the entire year; some parts of the temperate zones are hotter in the summer than the tropics and nearly as cold as the Arctic in winter.

The temperate regions are generally the most productive agricultural areas of the Earth. Part of this productivity arises from the structure of the soil. Recall that the tundra soils are nutrient-poor because decomposition is slow. In the next section, we will learn that tropical soils are nutrient-poor because decomposition is rapid. In the temperate zone, decomposition and decay occur at a controlled pace. If you examine a temperate forest or prairie floor, you will note the presence of undecomposed plant matter on the surface. A few centimeters below this layer you will find material that has rotted enough to exhibit a change in color and form, yet the decomposition is incomplete, so the individual pieces of twigs or leaves are still recognizable. The intact and partially decayed material is called **litter.** Below the layer of litter lies a layer of organic material called **humus,** which has been decomposed to the point where the origin of the individual pieces is obscure. This layering develops as material gradually decays and is buried by newly fallen plant matter. Because the rate of decay and recycling is balanced to the rate at which the new material falls, fertile soil is established. The temperate regions are so productive that most of the original forest and prairie lands have been converted to farmland, and the original biomes that remain are found mostly on hillsides or in semiarid regions.

Temperate forest biomes occur in temperate regions with abundant rainfall. The composition of temperate forests and the proportions of different varieties of trees and their spacing and height depend largely on the seasonal distribution of precipitation, the severity of the winters, the nature of the soil, and the frequency of fires. Three major categories of temperate forest can be distinguished: deciduous forest, evergreen forest, and rainforest.

Temperate deciduous forests occur in moderately humid climates where precipitation occurs throughout the year, but where winters are cold, restricting plant growth to warm summers. Most of the trees are deciduous and drop their leaves in the winter. Thus, they lose little water by evapotranspiration (evaporation through the leaves) in the winter when their roots could not replace it from the frozen soil. Broad-leaved deciduous trees, such as beeches, hickories, and maples dominate this kind of forest; there is also a well-developed understory of shrubs and herbaceous plants on the forest floor (Fig. 5–8).

Mammals typical of North American deciduous forests include white-tailed deer, chipmunks, squirrels, opossums, raccoons, and foxes. Wolves, bears, bobcats, and mountain lions roamed widely until they were largely eliminated by human activities. As winter draws near, up to three quarters of the birds migrate south, and many of the mammals hibernate. In the spring, herbaceous plants such as skunk cabbage, violets, Solomon's seal, and *Trillium* produce their leaves and flowers before the tree canopy has leafed out and cut off most of the light from the forest floor.

Temperate evergreen forests occur over wide areas where conditions favor needle-leafed conifers or broad-leafed evergreens over deciduous

Figure 5–8
Young temperate deciduous forest in the Northeastern United States. (Paul Feeny)

trees. These conditions include poor soils and a high frequency of droughts and forest fires. Various species of pine can grow in poor soils and have specialized adaptations for surviving fire. In some pines, for example, the cones open and their seeds germinate only when exposed to temperatures of several hundred degrees. The seeds thus germinate in areas that have just been burned. In the western United States, temperate evergreen forests include impressive stands of ponderosa pine, spruces, and firs. Extensive pine forests are also found in the southern states. Today, these forests are carefully managed for timber production, and much of the original variety has been lost.

Temperate rainforests occur in cool climates near the sea with abundant winter rainfall and summer cloudiness or fog. They include the forests of giant trees along the Pacific coast of North America, stretching from the Sitka spruce forest of the Alaskan and British Columbian coast, to the mixed coniferous forest of the Olympic Peninsula of Washington, and southward to the coastal redwood forests of northern California. The heights of these forests may reach 60 to 90 m, and they include some of the tallest trees in the world. Although there is little rainfall in California in summer, the foliage of redwoods can absorb water from the frequent fogs. Other temperate rainforests exist in New Zealand and Chile and in various places at higher elevations on tropical mountains.

The **temperate shrubland** biome is best represented by the **chaparral** communities that occur in all five regions of the world with a Mediterranean climate: coastal California and Chile, the Mediterranean coast, southern Australia, and the southern tip of Africa (Fig. 5–9). These areas have moderately dry climates with little or no summer rain. Most of the shrubs have leathery leaves and range in height from about 1 to 5 m. They are often distinctly aromatic, with volatile and flammable compounds in their leaves. Fires are frequent and are part of the natural cycles. After fires, the dominant shrubs regrow from surviving tissues near the ground. In modern times, many chaparral regions have become heavily populated, and the fires pose a constant threat to the local residents. Disastrous chaparral fires occur on a regular basis in many parts of Southern California.

Temperate grassland, known variously as prairie (North America), steppe (Asia), pampas (South America), or veldt (South Africa), covers ex-

Figure 5–9
A chaparral ecosystem in southern California. (Visuals Unlimited)

Figure 5–10
Temperate grassland (prairie) in central North America. Grassland in the Red Rock Lakes National Wildlife Refuge, Montana, with a herd of pronghorn antelopes. (From Odum, *Fundamentals of Ecology.* 3rd ed. Philadelphia, W.B. Saunders Co., 1971)

tensive areas in the interiors of continents where there is not enough moisture to support forest or woodland (Fig. 5–10). There is a wide variety of different types of grassland, depending on moisture. In regions where rainfall is scarce, short-grass prairie predominates, and some of the earlier pioneers of the American West reported that they could "see the horizon under the bellies of millions of bison." When the grasses of these semiarid grasslands are overgrazed, water loss owing to evaporation from the leaves ceases, leaving enough water in the soil to support woody plants such as mesquite, which has invaded overgrazed grassland in the southwestern United States. Tall grass prairie in North America once stood more than 2 m high, but very little of this ecosystem remains unfarmed today.

Although grassland vegetation forms only a single layer, many plant species may be present. Mammals of North American prairies include small burrowing species, such as prairie dogs and ground squirrels. Most of the large mammals of the

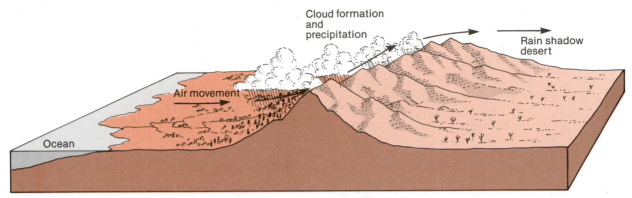

Figure 5–11
Rain shadow deserts form on the leeward side of coastal mountain ranges.

virgin prairie, such as bison, elk, grizzly bears, and wolves, have been driven into isolated preserves or mountainous regions as the prairie habitat has been destroyed.

5.7
Desert

If you choose your tour carefully, you could travel across the temperate zone without encountering any deserts. However, if you had the curiosity of an explorer-naturalist, you could find regions lying between mountains and grasslands that are too dry to support much life. These are called **deserts** and generally experience rainfall of less than about 20 cm per year. Temperate deserts are generally found in what is called the **rain shadow** of major mountain ranges. When moisture-laden air blows across the high mountain peaks, the air necessarily rises, creating a low pressure area where precipitation is common. Thus, the windward side of these mountain ranges receive large quantities of rain and snow. On the lee side of these mountains, the air that has risen then falls. Falling air is compressed and warmed, generating high-pressure conditions that lead to a dry desert environment (Fig. 5–11).

Regardless of what you saw in the temperate regions, if you continue to travel toward the Equator, you will encounter desert when you approach 20° to 30° north or south latitudes. Recall that these are the horse latitudes, where equatorial air is falling from the upper atmosphere, creating a zone of high pressure.

The driest deserts, such as the Sahara, receive less than 2 cm of rain per year and support

little life of any kind. Less extreme areas, including parts of the Sahara, have highly specialized plants, many of them annuals that grow, bloom, and develop seeds in the few days every year when water is available.

Many desert perennials, such as the American cactuses, are **succulents,** plants that store water in their tissues, or small woody shrubs that shed their leaves during the dry season (Fig. 5–12). Desert animals have adaptations that restrict loss of water through their skins and lungs and in their urine and feces. Many are nocturnal, avoiding the desiccating

Figure 5–12
Cacti and succulents in a desert in Arizona.

Special Topic A
Why Are There So Many More Species in the Tropics Than in the Arctic?

Biologists have observed that there are many more species in the Tropics than in the Arctic. Why has this relationship evolved? Several theories have been proposed, but none is completely satisfactory.

1. Climate *Theory:* The climate is so harsh in the Arctic that organisms must evolve special adaptations to survive there. These adaptations have proved elusive, and relatively few organisms have been able to make the necessary changes. *Objections:* Other environments in temperate and tropical regions are also harsh, such as semiarid or desert regions, yet many of these ecosystems harbor more species than does the Arctic.

2. Productivity *Theory:* The productivity is so high in the tropics that there are a great number of individual organisms. A positive feedback mechanism develops whereby the large number of plants has led to a large number of different species. In turn, the variety of plants provides many habitats for animals, and community grazing by the animals reinforces the cycle by establishing more niches for plants. In addition, there are so many organisms of all types that even a rare species with a specific, narrow niche can find sufficient food and shelter to survive. *Objections:* A number of examples can be found whereby increased productivity leads to a decrease in the number of resident species. For example, if a stream is polluted, the productivity will increase, but the number of species will decrease dramatically.

3. Historical Reasons *Theory:* The Tropics have been undisturbed by major climatic changes for many millennia. Therefore, there has been ample time for many species to evolve. In contrast, the Arctic regions have been covered with ice periodically over the last few hundred thousand years, and the last Ice Age ended only about 15,000 to 10,000 years ago. Therefore, there simply hasn't been enough time for more organisms to evolve to survive in the Arctic. *Objections:* There are no significant objections to oppose this theory, and most ecologists believe that this circumstance is an important part of the explanation. However, the other theories should not be entirely discounted.

heat of the day by burrowing into the cooler soil. Desert soil is often fertile enough to support agriculture if enough water can be supplied. Many desert areas throughout the world have been converted into productive farmland through irrigation. However, there is not enough fresh water available to cultivate the largest desert areas, and these cannot be counted on to feed the human population (see Chapters 8 and 9).

5.8
Tropical Biomes

As you continue your journey toward the Equator, the climate will become increasingly hot, and the annual change in the seasons will decrease until you can no longer distinguish winter from summer. The equatorial regions abound with life, and thousands upon thousands of different species can be seen, but no particular species predominates. In fact, as a broad generalization, it has been observed that at high latitudes (toward the poles), there are only a few different species, but there are many individuals of each species, whereas at lower latitudes, there are generally a multitude of different species, with proportionally few individuals in each. More specifically, 70 percent of the total number of species on Earth live in the Tropics. There are several different types of tropical biomes (Fig. 5–13).

Tropical rainforests occur in areas where high, fairly constant rainfall and temperatures permit plants to grow rapidly throughout the year. In such areas, a month with less than 10 cm of rain is considered dry, and annual precipitation may exceed 400 cm (Fig. 5–14). Tropical rainforests cover only about 7 percent of the Earth's surface, yet they are so incredibly lush and varied that they house approximately 40 percent of all plant and animal species.

A tropical rainforest is both familiar and strange to a visitor from a temperate area. It is familiar because so many of the plants grown in our homes and offices come from this biome. The dark, leathery leaves of familiar houseplants abound, although a plant that is less than a meter tall in your living room may soar as high as a house in a forest. The dominant plants here are tall trees with slender trunks that branch only near the top, covering the forest with a dense **canopy** of leathery evergreen leaves. The canopy blocks out most of the light. Plants that can survive in the permanent twilight under the canopy can also survive

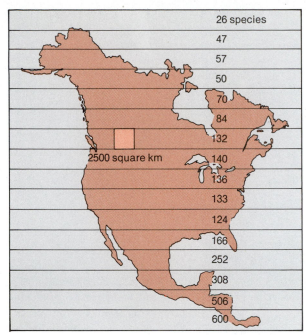

	26 species
	47
	57
	50
	70
	84
	132
2500 square km	140
	136
	133
	124
	166
	252
	308
	506
	600

Figure 5–13
Average number of bird species per 2500 sq km of land area as a function of latitude. The species in the Arctic include migratory birds; if only residents are considered the number will be less.

Figure 5–14
A tropical rainforest in New Guinea. (Carl Frank, National Audubon Society)

at the low-light levels that exist in buildings (although tropical forests are more humid). The dense canopy prevents as much as 99.9 percent of the sunlight from reaching the forest floor. Since only a few types of plants can grow in this permanent twilight, the lower levels of a tropical rainforest are fairly open and easy to walk through. The kind of impenetrable "jungle" for which a person would need a machete occurs only in open areas, along river banks, or in clearings created by fallen trees, where sunlight can reach the ground.

The ground in a tropical forest is soggy, the tree trunks are wet, and water drips down everywhere. The canopy overhead is so dense that a person could not tell whether it is actually raining or if this is just water dripping down from the treetops. Whatever the time of year, some of the trees are in flower and some are in fruit. There are no definite seasons in the forest.

Many plants are not rooted in the soil, but rather on the surfaces of other plants in the canopy overhead. These plants are called **epiphytes.** The epiphytes include a wide variety of orchids, largest of all plant families, as well as bromeliads, cactuses, and ferns. Many of these plants collect their own soil high in the air by acting as traps for dust and organic matter. The organic matter trapped by epiphytes may amount to several tonnes per hectare. In addition to conserving moisture for the roots of epiphytes, this organic matter provides a habitat for many other plants and animals. Because most of their plant food is in the canopy, most of the animals live there, too. Another type of plant found in the canopy is vines, or **lianas,** which have their roots in the soil but are supported by the giant trees. There are few animals on the forest floor, but huge colorful butterflies and beetles fly about in the canopy. The chatter of monkeys and the call of many species of birds and frogs can be heard.

Productivity is high in a tropical rainforest but, paradoxically, much of the soil is poor. As explained in the last section, fertile temperate soil contains large quantities of litter and humus. In a rainforest, temperature and moisture are so ideal for decomposer organisms that organic matter falling to the forest floor is quickly decomposed. The minerals released by the decomposers are rapidly taken up again by the plants, and as a result, al-

Tropical grasslands vary in height. In semidesert regions the grasses are short, but in regions with high rainfall they can be taller than an elephant.

most the entire nutrient pool of the forest is locked within the bodies of living organisms. So efficient are these systems that very little organic matter remains in the soil; therefore, soil quality is quite poor.

Sadly, most of us will never see the incredible beauty of a tropical rainforest. These forests are rapidly being cut down. (Tropical soils will be discussed in further detail in Chapter 8 and the destruction of tropical rainforests will be discussed in Chapter 11.)

Tropical savanna consists of grassland dotted with scattered small trees and shrubs. It extends over large areas, often in the interiors of continents, where rainfall is insufficient to support forests, or where the development of forests is prevented by recurrent fires. Some savannas are entirely grassland, whereas others contain many trees (Fig. 5–15).

The proportion of trees in a savanna reflects competition between trees and grasses for water. Where rainfall is light, grass roots lying close to the surface absorb nearly all the water during the dry season. As a result, woody plants, which have deeper roots, cannot obtain enough moisture to survive. Where rainfall is greater, the grasses are unable to absorb all of it, leaving water available for scattered trees. In regions where rainfall is suf-

ficient to support a woodland, the canopy shade inhibits the development of grasses, resulting in a tropical forest (Fig. 5–16).

Savannas are most extensive in Africa, where they support a rich fauna of grazing mammals such

Figure 5–15

A herd of impala and gazelles migrating across the savannah in Kenya. (C. A. Spinage)

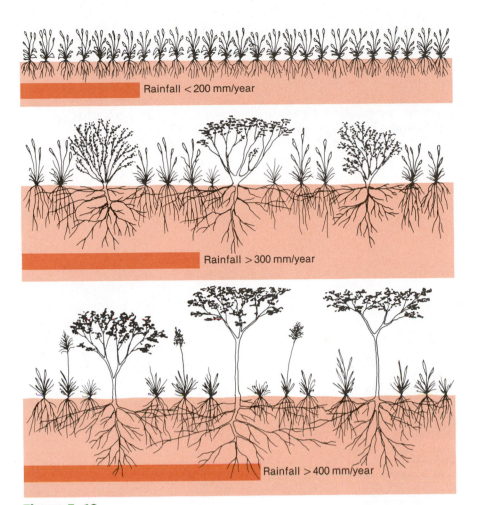

Figure 5–16

Relative proportions of trees and grasses in a savanna are influenced by rainfall (black bars). In *(A)*, where annual rainfall is 200 mm or less, the roots of grasses use up all the water available during the rainy season. If annual rainfall reaches 300 mm or more *(B)*, not all the water is used up by grasses and some is available to permit scattered trees and shrubs to survive the dry season. At annual rainfalls above 400 mm *(C)*, trees come to predominate, forming tree savanna or (at higher rainfall levels) tropical woodland. (After H. Walter: *Vegetation of the Earth*. New York, Springer-Verlag, 1973)

as zebras, wildebeest, and gazelles. The spectacular migrations of some of these species are related to shifting patterns of local rainfall that permit the growth of the young, nutritious foliage of grasses.

5.9
Marine Communities

Very often, ecologists use the term biome to refer to communities on land. However, there is a great array of aquatic communities, both marine and freshwater, which, like biomes, exhibit similarities wherever in the world they occur.

Like the land, the ocean can be divided into various zones, based on the prevailing physical conditions and the different types of organisms that these conditions support (Fig. 5–18; see p. 126). As on land, temperature and the intensity of sunlight determine what grows where. Lack of water is not a problem in the sea, but there are large areas where a shortage of dissolved nutrients limits ocean life.

Special Topic B
The Major Terrestrial Biomes—A Summary

The relationships between climate and the major terrestrial biomes are illustrated in Figure 5–17 and summarized in Table 5–1.

While this classification scheme is certainly useful and is universally recognized by biologists, it is important to note that the boundaries between biomes and the distinctions between major types

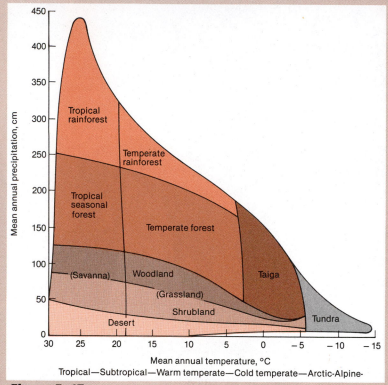

Figure 5–17
Simplified scheme of the major terrestrial biomes, showing the changes that occur with latitude and moisture.

Along the seacoasts, many kinds of plants and animals thrive in the **intertidal zone,** the area between high and low water marks. This zone is submerged for part of the day and exposed to the air for the remainder. The organisms in the intertidal zone must be adapted to withstand desiccation when the tide is out. Adaptation techniques are varied; some organisms have a waterproof covering, whereas others hide or burrow in moist places or retire into a tube or shell. Many different types of organisms live in an intertidal zone, de-

pending on the type of ground surface available. Muddy regions provide a habitat for numerous types of algae, mollusks, worms, and crustaceans. Firmly anchored species, such as specialized algae and animals such as barnacles, live in rocky zones exposed to wave action.

Coastal bays, river mouths, and tidal marshes are all physically contiguous to the open ocean and are also close to fresh water and to land (Fig. 5–19). These areas, known as **estuaries,** have (1) easy access to the deep sea, (2) less salinity than

of vegetation are not always as sharp in nature as they are drawn on a graph. An area that otherwise might support a woodland might be maintained as grassland by repeated fires. In many instances, the quality of the soil can shift the balance among woodlands, shrublands, and grasslands. In all systems, the region along the boundaries between two biomes will contain species of both systems. For example, along the southern zone edge of the arctic tundra, small spruce trees thrive in protected areas close to streams or on the southern or lee slopes of hillsides. This zone is also the northern limit of the taiga, and, in between, it is difficult to classify a given region as one or the other. These transitional zones are called **ecotones** and often contain a greater diversity of species than either biome alone.

Table 5–1
Major Biomes

Domain (Temperature)	Biome	Rainfall	Vegetation
Polar(−5° C to −15° C)	Tundra	Water deficiency during winter	Moss, sedges, some grasses, and small shrubs
Subpolar (−5° C to +3° C)	Taiga	Water deficiency during winter	Forests, muskeg
Temperate (+3° C to 18° C)	Temperate rainforest	Heavy throughout year	Forests, often coniferous
	Temperate forest	100–225 cm/yr	Forests, (variable)
	Prairie	75 cm/yr; precipitation throughout year	Grasses, parkland
	Chaparral	50 cm/yr; dry summers, wet winters	Evergreen woodlands, and shrubs
	Desert	Very dry in all seasons	Cactus, sparse grasses
Tropical (18° C to 30° C)	Savannah	50–125 cm/yr; dry and wet seasons	Grasses in dry zones with grass and scattered woodlands in wetter areas
	Tropical rainforest	Heavy rain throughout year; 6 cm/month minimum	Dense forests with canopy; open spaces at ground level

the open ocean, (3) a high concentration and retention of nutrients originating from land and sea, (4) protective shelter, and (5) rooted or attached plants supported in shallow water. As a result of these factors, estuaries are very productive areas. They provide nurseries for many deep-water fish that could not produce viable young in the harsher environment of the open sea.

The **neritic zone,** found below the low tide mark, is a region that is shallow enough to support plants that are rooted to the sea floor. Extending outward from the neritic zone, most seacoasts have a **continental shelf** that extends to a depth of about 200 meters. In this region, waters are deep enough to support large fish and other aquatic animals. In addition, mineral nutrients are readily available, washed from the land by rivers. These areas support many of the world's great fisheries. Even the productivity of coastal oceans, however, has its limits. Almost everywhere in the world, the combined effects of extensive fishing and pollution have reduced the commercial fishing

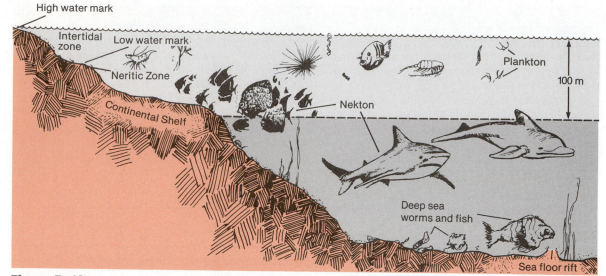

Figure 5–18
The major types of different habitats to be found in the oceans (not to scale).

catch. (These topics will be discussed in Chapters 9 and 11.)

Coral reefs are found only in the Tropics. They are restricted to warm oceans where the water temperature seldom falls below 21°C. Corals are small animals related to jellyfish that live in association with photosynthetic protists. The reef itself is made up of calcareous (calcium-containing) material, secreted by the coral animals and by green and red algae. Since photosynthetic organisms are so important to their formation, coral reefs are found only in clear, shallow water (less than 100 m deep) where there is enough light for photosynthesis. The reef acts physically like a rocky shore in providing anchorage for algae and sessile animals, those that live their lives attached to some immobile object. Since most of the reef is usually under water, the water movement is usually less than that on a rocky shore, and a wide variety of fish and swimming vertebrates can find shelter

Figure 5–19
Mudflats and marsh in an estuary.

Coral reefs are rich aquatic zones that contain a wide variety of different species. (Ron Church, National Audubon Society)

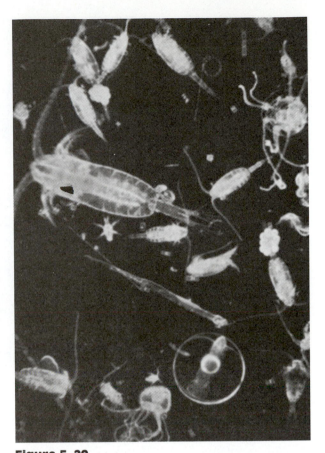

Figure 5–20
Living zooplankton magnified 16 times. Various shrimp-like crustaceans and two tiny jellyfish are visible. These types of animals are the main consumers in the oceans. (From A. Hardy: *The Open Sea.* London, William Collins Sons, 1966)

within the crevices of the reef. Coral reefs are extremely productive ecosystems. Coral is easily destroyed, however, and regrows very slowly, so that reefs must be carefully preserved if they are to survive.

The **open ocean** can be divided into two main regions: the top 100 m or so, where sufficient light penetrates for photosynthesis to occur; and the ocean depths. Small organisms in the surface waters make up the **plankton,** consisting of protists, plants, and animals not powerful enough to swim against the ocean currents. Plankton can be subdivided into the autotrophs, called **phytoplankton,** and the consumers, called **zooplankton** (Fig. 5–20). Zooplankton range in size from roughly 0.2 mm to 20 mm in diameter and consist both of permanent zooplankton and larvae of larger forms of life. Most of the production and respiration in the ocean is carried out by plankton. The larger and more familiar animals such as fish, sharks, and marine mammals such as whales and dolphins have a relatively small role in the energy balance. These animals are collectively called **nekton,** creatures that can swim in any direction. Nektonic organisms feed mainly on plankton and on each other, so their presence in an area depends

largely on whether the water contains enough mineral nutrients to support a large population of phytoplankton.

The productivity of the central oceans is limited by the fact that light is available only at the surface, whereas gravity tends to pull nutrients downward toward the sea floor. As a result, key nutrients, especially nitrates and phosphates, are scarce in the photosynthetic zone in many parts of the ocean, and productivity is so low that these regions have been likened to a great desert.

Biologically productive marine environments are limited to nutrient-rich zones. These fall into three categories: (1) the coastal zones (discussed previously) that are fertilized by run-off from land and are shallow enough so that wave and current action cause rapid vertical mixing of nutrients; (2) certain regions where rifts and volcanic action on

Figure 5–21
Deep sea fish attack a piece of bait.
(Richard A. Schwartzlose, Scripps In-
stitute of Oceanography)

the ocean floor lead to movement of minerals to the surface; and (3) other regions where deep water ocean currents rise vertically to the surface. This phenomenon is called **upwelling** and produces nutrient-rich, highly productive deep-water ocean systems. Upwelling zones are found along the coast of Peru and in regions near Antarctica.

Seventy-five percent of the oceans' water lies more than 1,000 m deep. For many years, people assumed that there was little life in the depths of the ocean because it was too dark for photosyn-

thesis. Improved diving techniques that permit sampling at depths of more than 6,000 m have, however, revealed fascinating communities on the ocean floor, and many divers have turned up hitherto unknown organisms. It is now clear that the ocean floor, at all depths, supports populations of both large animals and of decomposer bacteria. The food chain for these organisms depends on the carcasses of dead plants and animals or on feces falling from the surface layers above them (Fig. 5–21).

Summary

Near the equator, the Sun's rays strike the Earth almost vertically. Air is heated and rises vertically upward. This heated air moves toward higher latitudes at high elevations and then falls again at about 20° to 30° north and south latitudes. Climates are caused by the heat of the Sun combined with the movement of large masses of air.

The northernmost biome is the **tundra,** which is dominated by low-lying, cold-resistant mosses, sedges, and grasses, with a few woody shrubs. Decomposition is slow, and soil fertility is poor. There are relatively few species, with a great number of individuals of each species. Below the tundra lies the boreal forest, or **taiga,** a biome dominated by coniferous trees adapted to growing in sparse soil and to resisting extreme cold and water loss during the winter.

In temperate regions, the soil is much richer in nutrients than it is in the Arctic, because decomposition occurs at a controlled rate, not too rapidly or too slowly. Therefore, layers of **litter** and **humus** develop, and nutrient retention and recycling are efficient. **Deciduous forest** is an important biome of North America, Europe, and Asia in areas with warm, moist summers and cold winters. Where the soil is poor or fires are frequent, **temperate evergreen forest** replaces temperate deciduous forest. **Temperate rainforest** is found in temperate regions with abundant rainfall.

Grasslands receive more rain than deserts and less than forests. Grassland occurs in the dry interiors of continents in the Americas, Asia, and Australia. Shrubs and trees may be scattered among the tall grasses.

Deserts have hot days, cold nights, and very little rainfall. Their plant life is mainly annuals with very short growing seasons and succulent perennials adapted to the low rainfall.

The biome with the greatest number of species is a **tropical rainforest,** where high temperature and rainfall permit plants to grow throughout the year. Most of the plant and animal life is found in the canopy among the broad evergreen leaves of tall trees. Decomposition is rapid, and the soil is usually poor. At any one time, most of the nutrients in the forest are locked in the bodies of organisms.

The distribution of marine organisms is determined by water temperature and the availability of light and nutrients. The **intertidal** and **neritic zones** are well supplied with both light and nutrients and support dense communities of life. **Coral reefs** are specialized communities found only in tropical waters. In the open ocean, the availability of light for photosynthesis restricts plankton to the upper layers of the water, but scarcity of nutrients in these layers usually limits the numbers of organisms. Larger nektonic organisms are found mainly where plankton is abundant. Dead organisms from the surface layers of the ocean supply food for a community of organisms that live on the deep-sea floor.

Questions

Climate

1. Which of the following is most likely to experience the greatest difference in weather between summer and winter: the Arctic, the temperate zones, the Tropics? Explain.

2. The 30° north latitude line runs through the moist regions of southern Louisiana and northern Florida as well as through desert country in Mexico and Texas. What does this information tell us about the relationship between latitude and the character of the biomes in an area?

3. Study a map of the world and answer the following questions. (a) Why does the temperate zone in the northern hemisphere produce more food for humans than the temperate zone in the southern hemisphere? (b) Compare the latitude of the Sahara Desert (North Africa) with that of the desert in central Chile (north of Santiago). What conclusions can you draw? (c) Compare the latitude of New York City with that of Rome. What do you know about the climates of these two regions? Is latitude the only factor that determines the temperature and rainfall of a region?

Biomes

4. What biome do you live in?

5. Many arctic regions receive little precipitation, yet bogs are common in the tundra. Explain.

6. Discuss the relationship between rates of decomposition and fertility of the soil in the tundra, the temperate regions, and the Tropics.

7. Discuss similarities and differences between the tundra and temperate grasslands.

8. List the following temperate biomes in order of increasing moisture (arrange from the driest to the wettest): grassland, chaparral, deciduous forest, rainforest, desert.

9. Which of the biomes listed below cannot be categorized according to latitude? List the remaining biomes in order of increasing latitude: taiga, desert, alpine tundra, arctic tundra, savannah, temperate evergreen forest.

10. Discuss the trends in soil quality and number of different species as you travel from the polar regions to the Equator.

11. Name the biome that would be found in each of the following regions: (a) a tropical region with a moderate amount of rainfall; (b) a temperate region with poor soil and a moderate amount of rainfall; (c) a temperate region with dry summers and a moderate amount of rainfall during the winter; (d) a high latitude region with a moderate amount of rainfall.

Marine Communities

12. The North Sea, the Bering Sea, and the Grand Banks are all rich fisheries and are all ecologically similar. Without any more information, make an educated guess about the nature of these seas. (Are they deep? shallow? close to land? in the central oceans? and so on.) Defend your assumptions.

13. Discuss similarities and differences in the food chain of terrestrial ecosystems and marine ecosystems.

14. Do you think that it would be economically advantageous to fertilize the central oceans with nitrates or phosphates to improve the world's fisheries? Discuss.

Suggested Readings

Two references that explain the climate systems of the Earth are:

John G. Navarra: *Atmosphere, Weather and Climate: An Introduction to Meteorology.* Philadelphia, Saunders College Publishing, 1979. 519 pp.

Turk and Turk: *Physical Science. 3rd edition.* Philadelphia, Saunders College Publishing, 1987. 629 pp.

Despite its formidable title, this book is short and readable, and is an excellent account of world vegetation zones and the conditions that determine what biome occurs where:

H. Walter: *Vegetation of the Earth in Relation to Climate and the Eco-Physio-logical Conditions.* Translated from 2nd German edition by Joy Weiser. London, The English Universities Press Ltd.; New York, Heidelberg, Berlin, Springer-Verlag, 1973.

Wildlife in the Earth's Biomes is described in:

International Wildlife Series: This Fragile Earth.
Part I: Doomed jungles? by Peter Gwynne. July–August 1976.
Part II: The island dilemma, by Mariana Gosnell. September–October 1976.
Part III: Mountains besieged, by Edward R. Ricciuti. November-December 1976.
Part IV: Shifting sands, by Frederick Golden. January–February 1977.
Part V: Margin of life, by Robert Allen. March–April 1977.
Part VI: The living sea, by Arthur Fisher. May–June 1977.

The microbiology of deep ecosystems in the ocean is described in:

H. W. Jannasch and C.O. Wirsen: Microbial life in the deep sea. *Scientific American,* June 1977.

A beautifully written description of the arctic is given in:

Barry Lopez: *Arctic Dreams, Imagination and Desire in a Northern Landscape.* New York, Charles Scribner's Sons, 1986. 464 pp.

6

Changes in Ecosystems

6.1
Succession

If you made several casual visits to any of the biomes discussed in the previous chapter you would probably observe very little change from year to year. A more careful study of a particular ecosystem might show shifts in the population levels of one species or another. Thus, in a desert community, an unusually wet spring would provide conditions favorable to growth of many annual plants, whereas in a dry year, many species would suffer. Also, as noted in Chapter 4 (Special Topic C), populations of predators and prey do fluctuate in certain circumstances. But these fluctuations do not change the fundamental character of a biome; the overwhelming image is one of stability and constancy. A community that forms in an undisturbed environment and that perpetuates itself as long as no major disturbance occurs is called the **climax community.** Each of the biomes of the Earth represents one type of climax community.

On the other hand, many areas do not contain the climax community expected from their resources and climates. They have been disturbed either by natural processes such as floods, fire, or volcanic eruptions, or by human activities. When a climax community is disturbed, it begins to return to its original state. **Succession** is a progressive series of changes that drives a natural ecosystem toward the re-establishment of a climax community. The onset of succession can be seen even in an urban environment. Mosses and weeds establish themselves in cracks in the sidewalk, quite large plants may grow in a corner where leaf litter and dirt have been deposited by a rain gutter, and moss invades a roof that needs repair.

Primary Succession

Primary succession occurs when the terrain is initially lifeless or almost so, when a new island rises out of the sea, when a volcano erupts and lava or ashes blanket the countryside, when a glacier retreats, or when any event occurs that destroys both the vegetation and the soil in a region (Fig. 6–1). Primary succession is usually quite slow, because it starts without any soil. Consider an area of barren lava created by a recent volcanic eruption. A variety of processes contribute to the formation of soil. Water seeping into cracks in the

Special Topic A
Succession on Mt. St. Helens

On May 18, 1980, the volcanic core of Mt. St. Helens in western Washington erupted, spewing millions of tonnes of ash into the air and destroying many square kilometers of once-lush vegetation. In the most highly devastated regions, the ash completely blanketed the existing soil, and the heat vaporized soil particles and nutrients. Four months after the eruption, biologist Roger del Moral found an active ant nest *(Formica subnuda)* high on the mountain and far from any visible vegetation. Presumably, these ants were at the top of a subterranean food chain. The lower levels of this micro food chain probably survived on decomposing organic matter buried by the ash. The following spring, a mushroom was found in the original blast zone, growing in the ash and the slowly decomposing organic matter present. Within a year after the eruption, many different types of pioneer plants were colonizing the less severely disturbed areas. Migrating deer and elk passed over the ash, and their footprints formed small indentations that provided shelter and pockets of moisture favorable for the germination of seeds blown in the wind or transported by birds. In border areas between the devastated zone and places where vegetation had survived, pocket gophers are burrowing into the ash and breaking up the impermeable layers. Full succession to a stable climax system will take many years, but the process has already begun.

rock may freeze, expanding and breaking the rock into chunks. The surface of the rock is also weathered by the beating of wind and rain. The acid solution formed when atmospheric carbon dioxide dissolves in water helps to dissolve minerals in the rock fragments, providing nutrients. Certain plant communities such as lichens are adapted to live in exposed conditions. (Lichens appear to be a single organism, but, in reality, they consist as fungi and algae growing together.) Lichens live on rock surfaces and produce organic acids, which further dissolve the rock. Dead lichens also contribute or-

Figure 6–1

Primary succession. During the past million years, volcanic activity has deposited several layers of lava over large portions in southeastern Idaho. Over the years, soil and organic matter have blown into the region from nearby areas and new soil has been created by biological and physical activity. Today, vegetation is growing out of cracks in the lava. However, many more centuries must pass before a climax ecosystem will exist on this hillside.

ganic matter to form soil, and mosses may gain a hold in even a thin layer of lichen litter and rock dust. As the mosses continue to break up the rock and add their own dead bodies to the pile, the seeds of small rooted plants can germinate and grow. At the same time that soil is formed from natural decomposition of rock, additional soil and organic matter are carried into the area by winds. As these processes continue, progressively more soil is formed and progressively larger plants move in, until the climax community becomes established. This development is quite slow; it may take up to thousands of years for the soil and the climax vegetation to develop fully.

Primary succession also occurs when a lake or pond fills up with silt and fallen leaves and the shoreline creeps toward the center of the lake (Fig. 6–2). Gradually the lake turns into a marsh and then into dry land, eventually colonized by plants of climax species from surrounding ecosystems.

As succession proceeds, both the number and types of species in the area change. The number of species present depends on the number of different niches available. As discussed previously, two species with identical niches cannot survive together in the same area. One species will inevitably be better at capturing some resource than the other, and the poorer competitor will die for lack of this resource. During succession, the number of

niches available changes with time, so the number of species also changes. Bare rock provides only a few simple niches and will support only a few different species. When the rock has been colonized by lichens, mosses, and a few larger plants, however, niches exist for insects that eat each of the plants, for parasites and predators of these insects, and for animals and plants that may live in the developing soil. As grasses, bushes, and, in some cases, trees start to grow, even more niches become available. The trend may reverse itself, because many climax systems are simpler than their successional precursors, and the number of species may fall again when the climax is reached.

Secondary Succession

Secondary succession is the series of community changes that takes place in disturbed areas that have not been totally stripped of their soil and vegetation. Although it may take a hundred years or more for the climax stage to return during secondary succession, the process is nevertheless much faster than primary succession because soil already exists.

A familiar example of secondary succession in the New England area is "old field succession," by which abandoned farms return to the climax forest (Fig. 6–3). When a farmer stops cultivating the

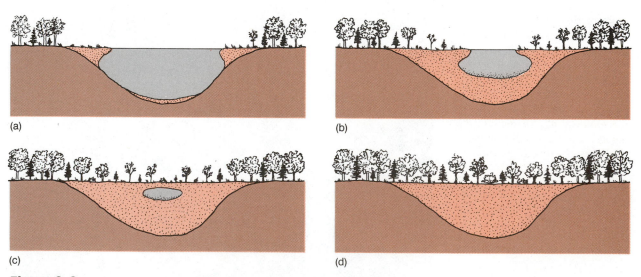

(a)

(b)

(c)

(d)

Figure 6–2

Succession as a lake turns into a bog and then a forest. A floating mat of vegetation extends progressively out from the shore, eventually covering the open water. After thousands of years, the former lake will be covered with forest.

Figure 6–3

Old field (secondary) succession. Shrubs are starting to grow in the field on the right. Small trees, such as the aspens and pin cherries on the left, will soon invade.

land, a wide variety of wild plants quickly move in and displace many of the domestic ones. Many of these invading species, called **pioneers,** are colorful wildflowers such as dandelions and black-eyed susans. Pioneers produce seeds that can spread over appreciable distances, carried by wind or by animals, and, thus, they are quick to colonize an new area. In addition, the seeds of many pioneer plants are adapted to live for long periods in a dormant state, germinating when a disturbance provides the proper conditions, such as increased light. Soon, plants that are taller than the pioneers, such as tall grasses and woody bushes, move in. Because these newcomers shade the ground and their long root systems monopolize the soil water, it is difficult for seedlings of the pioneer species to survive. But even as these taller species choke out the sun-loving pioneers, they are in turn shaded and deprived of water by the seedlings of certain trees, such as pin cherries, dogwoods, sumac, and birch, which take longer (5 to 10 years) to become established but command most of the resources once they reach a respectable size. Succession is still not complete, because the first trees that grow in an area are not usually members of the species that make up the mature climax forest. After 10 to 30 years, slower-growing oak, maple, beech, elm, and hickory trees will move in and take over, shading out the saplings of the tree species that preceded them. After a century or two, the land is covered with mature climax forest.

TABLE 6–1
Some Comparisons Between Early Successional Stages and Climax Systems

Characteristic	Early Successional Stage	Climax System
Total organic matter	Small	Large
Inorganic nutrients	Mostly found in physical environment	Large amounts locked in organic matter
Diversity of species	Low	Considerably higher
Food chains	Predominantly linear	More complex, weblike
Net productivity of organic matter	High	Low

*The *net* productivity is the total productivity minus the total consumption, or the *gain* in biomass of an ecosystem. A climax system has reached a steady state in which productivity and consumption are balanced, so the net gain approaches zero. Therefore it is not profitable to try to farm a climax system. On the other hand, an early successional stage has a high net productivity. In fact, farms are systems that are artificially maintained in an early successional stage. Such maintenance requires energy, as will be discussed in Chapter 8.

One of the reasons that succession occurs is that many species, especially those characteristic of early successional systems, change the environment in which they live in ways that make it less favorable for themselves and more favorable for others. For example, a corn plant removes the nitrogen it needs from the soil, leaving soil in which corn cannot grow again (unless fertilizer is added), but in which alfalfa, which needs no nitrogen from the soil, can flourish. Similarly, in the Rocky Mountain region, when the leaves and branches of aspen trees decompose, the soil chemistry is changed, making the land less fit for aspen, but quite fertile for pine, spruce, and fir.

Some of our agricultural pest problems stem from the fact that many crop plants originated as pioneer species. In nature, these plants depend on their sparse distribution and their nomadic habits (never in the same place for many seasons in a row) to protect them from their insect predators. By planting fields exclusively to one crop year after year, farmers create a paradise for animals that eat these species, such as cabbage worms and cucumber beetles, which no longer have to spend energy to find food and have nothing to do but eat and multiply.

Fire-Maintained Communities

Fires set by lightning storms or human carelessness occasionally sweep through large areas of forest, destroying whole communities of animals and plants (Fig. 6–4). Burned areas undergo secondary succession. In the spruce–fir forests of the Rocky Mountains, for example, burned areas are rapidly colonized by wind-borne seeds of fireweed, which grows and clothes the slopes with its purple flowers in summer, until it is displaced by aspen, after which the spruce–fir system eventually becomes re-established.

Figure 6–4
This forest fire burns along the ground and does not destroy mature trees.
(H. Armstrong Roberts)

In many communities, fires do not often recur in the same place and thus do not prevent the system from reaching the normal climax pattern. In others, fire is sufficiently frequent to determine the nature of the climax vegetation. For example, before Europeans colonized the area, parts of central Wisconsin were characterized by a climax grassland system that traditionally caught fire and burned on a regular basis. When farms were established in the area and range fires were controlled, untilled land started to be succeeded by forest. This growth showed that the climate and the soil in the region were favorable for the growth of trees. In the natural system, however, the saplings were repeatedly destroyed by frequent fires, and the fast-growing grasses dominated.

Many pines are adapted to survive, and even to exploit, fires. The seedlings of longleaf pine *(Pinus palustris)* in the southern United States, for example, remain as grassy tufts for approximately the first 6 years of their lives. Meanwhile, they accumulate large food reserves in their roots, with the result that during about their seventh year, they can grow extremely rapidly. Fires in the southern forests are usually light ground fires, very different from the intense crown fires that often occur in northern forests. The longleaf pine saplings can survive ground fires both when they are in their young "grass" stage and when they are more than about 6 m tall (Fig. 6–5). Their peculiar growth habit permits them to go through the middle stage, when they are most vulnerable to fire, in a very short time. In the Rocky Mountains and other regions, lodgepole pine *(Pinus contorta)* cones are adapted to germinate rapidly after they have been heated by a fire.

If fires are prevented in a fire-adapted pine forest, deciduous trees may become established. In addition, dead wood and litter build up on the ground; so, when fire eventually does occur, it is more severe than usual, destroying not only any deciduous trees but also the original pines. Odd though it may seem at first, frequent burning is essential for the preservation of many natural communities. Some pine barrens, such as those of New Jersey and around Albany, New York, are slowly dying because human interference prevents fires in those areas. The pitch pine *(Pinus rigida)* of the pine barrens live on poor sandy soil. They can survive only in open areas where they do not have to compete with shrubs. When fires are prevented,

Figure 6–5
Longleaf pine forest in Texas. A ground fire swept through this area only months before this photograph was taken. It killed most shrubs, but these longleaf pines of various ages were unscathed because their growing points were above the fire. (Paul Feeny)

shrubs grow under the pine trees, competing for moisture and eventually killing the pines.

6.2
Evolution—Long-Range Change in Ecosystems

The apparent constancy of an ecosystem is only a function of the time span of our observation. Over the course of the broad expanses of geologic time, many different types of change occur. For example, climates change; the semi-desert of the southwestern United States was once covered with humid swamplands, and the land that now supports fertile wheat fields of Canada once lay beneath icy glaciers. As shown in Figure 6–6, species exhibit a variety of different responses to environmental change. Some species survive quite well without appreciable modification. This situation is called **stasis,** one of no change. Others cannot adapt and

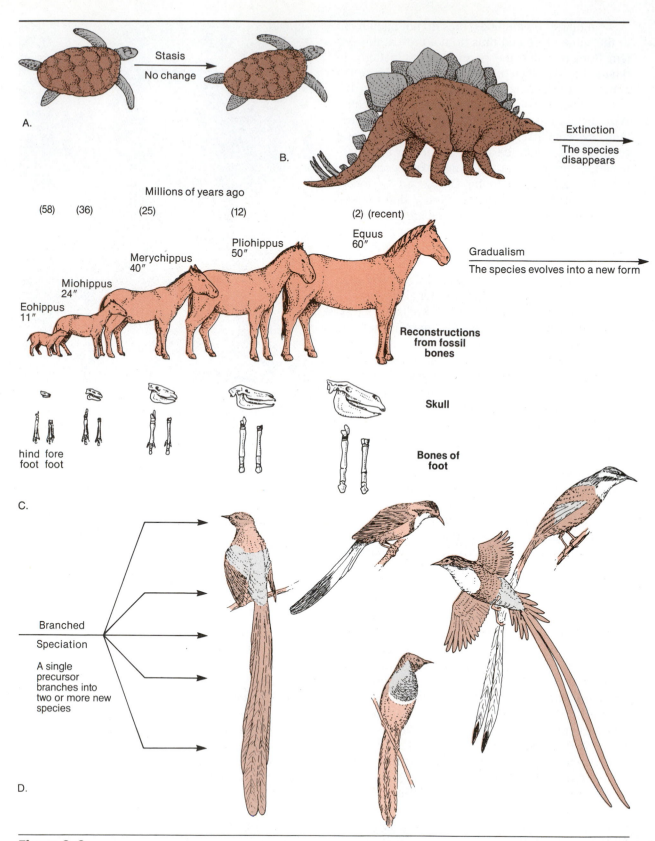

A.

Stasis
No change

B.

Extinction
The species disappears

Millions of years ago

(58) (36)   (25)   (12)   (2) (recent)

Eohippus
11″

Miohippus
24″

Merychippus
40″

Pliohippus
50″

Equus
60″

Gradualism
The species evolves into a new form

**Reconstructions
from fossil
bones**

Skull

hind fore
foot foot

**Bones of
foot**

C.

Branched

Speciation

A single
precursor
branches into
two or more new
species

D.

Figure 6–6

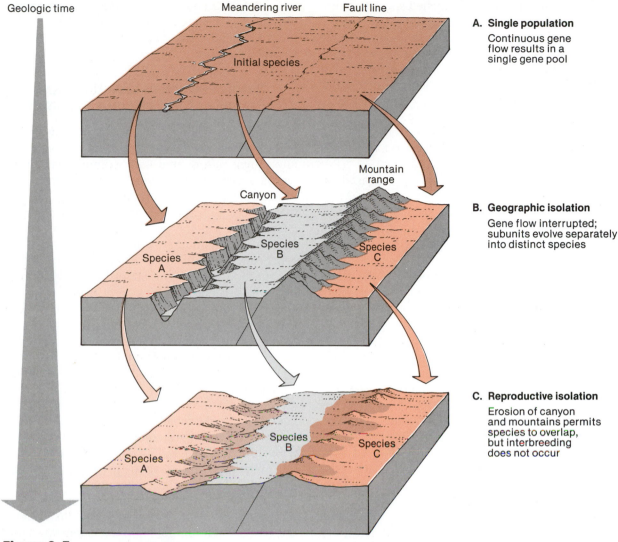

Geologic time

Meandering river   Fault line

Initial species

A. Single population
Continuous gene
flow results in a
single gene pool

Mountain
range

Canyon

Species
A

Species
B

Species
C

B. Geographic isolation
Gene flow interrupted;
subunits evolve separately
into distinct species

Species
B

Species
A

Species
C

C. Reproductive isolation
Erosion of canyon
and mountains permits
species to overlap,
but interbreeding
does not occur

Figure 6–7
Stages by which three new species might evolve from one species. In *B*, geo-
graphical boundaries form that split the initial species into three populations.
A new species evolves from each. (From Mary E. Clark: *Contemporary Biology*.
Philadelphia. W. B. Saunders Co., 1973)

◄**Figure 6–6**
(Left) A species can respond to environmental change
in a variety of ways. *A*, Often, an organism can survive
in a changing environment with very little adaptation.
Turtles have existed virtually unchanged for millennia.
B, Some organisms, such as dinosaurs, have not been
able to adjust and have become extinct. *C*, Others
evolve gradually. A common example of gradualism is
the evolution of the horse. *D*, A fourth response is
branched speciation. This drawing shows five different
species of birds of paradise that have evolved from a
common precursor on the island of New Guinea.

become **extinct** and disappear forever. Many species adapt to a changing environment by changing
genetically with time, a process known as **evolution.** Evolution can proceed by a variety of different mechanisms. **Gradualism** is a process
whereby a species changes in small increments
(gradually). A familiar example of this is the horse,
as shown in the Figure 6–6. An alternate response
to environmental change is **branched speciation.**
In this situation, a single species will branch to
form two or more new independent species (Fig.

6–7). Gradual change and branched speciation represent long-term change or evolution.

The theory of evolution was brought to the public attention by Charles Darwin in 1858. Darwin was an advocate of gradualism and believed that evolution occurs in a gradual sequence of steps, each step endowing an organism with some particular, small, advantage over others that have not made the change. The process whereby small genetic advantages become dominant in a species is called **natural selection.**

The theory of natural selection is based on three observations.

- First, as can readily be seen by comparing one dog or one human with another, different individuals of a species differ from one another.
- Second, some, although not all, of the differences between individuals are inherited, which means that they are genetically determined.
- Third, more organisms are born than live to grow up and reproduce; many organisms die as embryos, seedlings, nestlings, larvae, infants, or even adults of reproductive age.

The logical conclusion from these three observations is that some of the inherited characteristics of an organism must increase its chances of living to grow up and reproduce, compared with the chances of organisms with other characteristics. Inherited characteristics that improve an organism's chance of living and reproducing will be more common in the next generation than those that decrease the chance of reproducing. Thus, the various genes will be naturally selected for or against, from one generation to the next, depending on how they affect reproductive potential. In this manner, genetic characteristics will change or evolve with time.

There are many different ways that a given character trait can be selected for. A predator that is strong and powerful or a prey organism that is quick and alert may be more likely to survive and reproduce. But strength and speed are only two characteristics that improve the chance of successful reproduction. A tree that produces a lot of seeds, a mosquito that is resistant to pesticides, a desert lizard that preserves water efficiently, or a moth with coloration that camouflages it from predators are all more likely to pass their genes on to the next generation than are those organisms

that are not so endowed. *Anything* that determines that some genes are passed to the next generation more frequently than others constitutes a natural selective pressure.

Natural Selection in Action—An Example of Intraspecific Evolution

In nineteenth-century England, a popular hobby was to collect moths and butterflies. Collectors avidly sought rare or unusually colored individuals, just as stamp collectors seek unusual stamps. One such rare specimen was the black form of the normally gray, British-peppered moth *(Biston betularia).* Black and gray are two genetic forms of this species, just as blue eyes and brown eyes are two genetically different forms of humans. By looking at collections made from about 1850 to 1950, biologists found that the black form of the moth became more and more common during the century, and the gray form became scarcer, particularly near industrial cities. Why had this change occurred?

To answer this question, biologists first investigated the habits of the moths. They noted that the peppered moth flies and feeds at night and rests on tree trunks throughout the day. During this rest period, it is vulnerable to predators, and its main defense system is its coloration, which provides protective camouflage (Fig. 6–8).

With this information in hand, scientists asked "What environmental parameters changed to account for the observed success of the black moths and the decline of the gray moths?" Someone noted that as air pollution levels increased during the late 1800s and early 1900s, many of the trees near major cities were blackened, and the lichens that grew on them were killed. The gray moths were no longer camouflaged against this dark smooth background, and they became more vulnerable to predation. On the other hand, the black variants were harder to see and thus better adapted to survival in the new environment.

Bernard Kettlewell, an Oxford ecologist, recognized that this was an opportunity to study natural selection experimentally. He raised large numbers of both black and gray forms of the moth in the laboratory, marked them, and released them in two places. One group was released in an unpolluted rural area where the black form was more visible, while the other group was released in a polluted industrial area where the gray form was

Figure 6–8
The two forms of the peppered moth. *a,* On a lichen-covered tree trunk in an unpolluted area. The gray form is so well camouflaged that it is almost invisible, below and to the right of the black moth. *b,* On a soot-covered tree trunk. The gray form is much more obvious than the black. (Bernard Kettlewell)

A

B

easier to see against the blackened tree trunks. Kettlewell then recaptured as many of the marked moths as he could. In the industrial area, the percentage of black moths recovered was twice that of gray moths, but, in the unpolluted countryside the situation was reversed, and twice as many gray moths as black ones were recovered (Table 6–2). This agreed with the prediction that the black moths were more likely to survive near the cities, whereas the opposite was true in rural areas.

It is clear that, in a polluted area, many more of the black than of the gray moths will live long enough to reproduce. Since the color of these moths is inherited, the next generation will contain proportionally more black moths than the last gen-

eration. In other words, in a polluted area, the proportion of genes for black color increases in the population with time—and that is evolution.

Thus, natural selection produces populations of moths that are well adapted to survive in their environments—populations whose characteristics change as the environment changes.

Following this logic, one would predict that if pollution were reduced, black moths would become rarer and gray forms more common. In fact, the Clean Air Act of 1952 has reduced air pollution in England. Collection of the peppered moth from industrial Manchester in the years since 1952 reveals a dramatic increase in the ratio of gray to black individuals in the moth population. This find-

TABLE 6–2
Numbers of Gray and Black Peppered Moths Recaptured After the Release of Marked Individuals in Two Areas

Location	Percent Recaptured	
	Gray	Black
Dorset (unpolluted) 1953	13.2%	6.3%
Birmingham (polluted) 1953	13.1%	27.5%
Birmingham (polluted) 1955	25.0%	53.5%

ing is impressive evidence that the populations of moths will indeed evolve under the influence of natural selection as Kettlewell suggested.

Speciation and Punctuated Evolution

The theory of gradualism is satisfactory in many ways, but it also leaves certain questions unanswered. Think, for example, of the evolution of wings. Flight gives an organism obvious evolutionary advantages. According to Darwin's theory, wings developed gradually, over the course of many generations. But now we ask, what possible advantage could a mini-wing or a proto wing offer to an individual? If an animal developed a small wing-like appendage, it would not gain the advantages of flight, so why would such an organism be selected for? Darwin was aware of this argument and countered that proto wings were not inadequate wings but well adapted something-elses. Perhaps they were used as sexual attractants, or as stabilizers in running. In later years scientists have suggested that they were used to regulate body temperature. When folded close to the chest, the proto wings retained heat and when extended they allowed heat to escape. Over the centuries, these organs grew until they became large enough to be used for gliding and eventually for flight.

One problem with this argument is that there is very little firm, direct evidence for such functional shifts. Therefore, some scientists speculate that evolution might occur, instead, in a series of rapid steps broken by long periods of little or no change. This concept is called **punctuated equilibria** (Fig. 6–9).

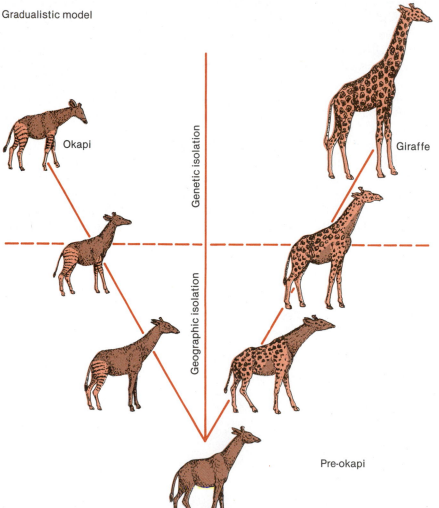

Gradualistic model

Okapi

Giraffe

Genetic isolation

Geographic isolation

Pre-okapi

A.

Figure 6–9
Two possible scenarios for the evolutionary processes that led to the development of the okapi and the giraffe. *A*, Gradualistic model; *B*, punctuated model. The best evidence indicates that the actual evolution was partly gradualistic and partly punctuated. Remember that real systems are often much more complicated than our easy-to-visualize models.

Punctuated model

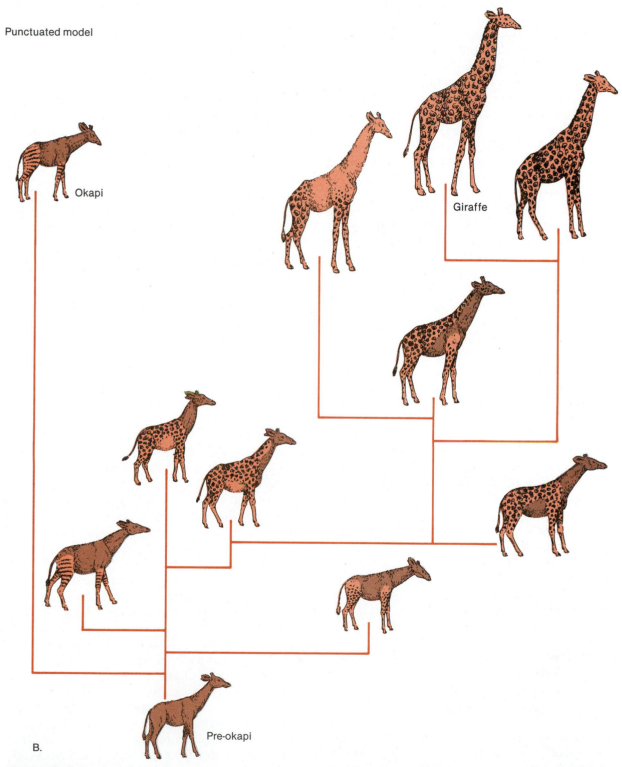

Okapi

Giraffe

Pre-okapi

B.

Figure 6–9 *Continued*

Today, there is significant debate between proponents of these two theories: Gradualism and punctuated equilibria. One approach that scientists have used to search for a choice between the two mechanisms is to examine the fossil record. To date, studies of fossils indicate that many species have remained remarkably unchanged over long periods of time, even when environments and climates are changing. Then, within a very short period of geologic time, perhaps only thousands or even hundreds of years, a particular species disappears and is replaced by a newly evolved descendant. This type of evidence suggests that gradual change in species is less common than Darwin had postulated. Instead, development may, in fact, occur in rapid steps. Imagine that a small population were isolated from the other members of a species. Imagine further that a rare but radical genetic change occurred. If the change is favorable, it may spread rapidly through the small population by natural selection, thereby creating a new species. The two species may then coexist, or, alternatively, the new one may migrate into traditional areas and displace the old.

Several examples of punctuated equilibria have been observed in modern times. Many cases are known among flowering plants, where the number of genes in a plant doubles in one step. Plants with double the normal number of genes cannot breed with their normal relatives, but must breed with each other to form a new species that is reproductively isolated from the parent species. New species of animals may occasionally arise through a doubling of the normal number of genes. (Several grasshopper species are thought to have arisen in this way.)

The debate on the mechanisms of evolution continues, and many interesting and subtle points are argued on both sides. It is probable that both mechanisms operate; gradualism is the driving process in some instances, and punctuated equilibria predominates in others.

6.3
Long-Range Stability of Ecosystems

What Do We Mean by Ecosystem Stability?

Recall from our discussion in Chapter 4 that ecosystems tend to maintain balance through opposition of vital rates. In a year of high rainfall, annual plants will grow rapidly and absorb some of the excess moisture. In time of drought, the growth of plants and the fertility rates of many animals are reduced. This balance of nature is called **ecosystem homeostasis.** However, stability is not universal—ecosystems are disrupted and catastrophic change does occur. An important question to ask is, "When does an ecological disruption become an ecological catastrophe?" In other words, "When does a particular stress become so severe that the homeostatic mechanisms of the system are unable to counter it, leading to a breakdown of the system as a whole?"

It is impossible to answer this question in a general way. Sometimes ecosystems are amazingly resistant to change and continue to function more or less normally despite severe stress. In other situations, systems seem to be excessively fragile and are disrupted by a seemingly small perturbation. Even though a simple, definitive answer is not possible, we can approach this question by examining the nature of ecosystem stability in more detail.

A **stable object** is one that does not change or move with time. A building is stable if it doesn't move, change, or fall down. But a **stable ecosystem** is different; there must be cycles and change if it is to survive. Thus, the essence of continuity of an ecosystem involves change: birth, death, decay, and rebirth. A system can change and maintain stability at the same time if the composition, or makeup, of the entire system remains constant even though the individual components are being altered. The constancy results from the fact that the changing processes balance each other, that is, they proceed at the same rate, but one process opposes the other, resulting in no net change. There are fundamentally two different ways in which opposing processes can maintain a stable system.

In a **steady state,** some things are entering the system and others are leaving, so that the system is not isolated from its surroundings. Balance is achieved because the inflow equals the outflow. As an example of a steady state, imagine a bathtub with the drain open and the water faucet turned on. If the inflow and the outflow are equal, the level of water in the tub will remain constant even though individual water molecules come and go (Fig. 6–10*B*). In biology, an example of a steady state system might be a population in which the rates of birth and immigration balance those of death and emigration, so that the number of individuals in the population remains constant.

A

B

C

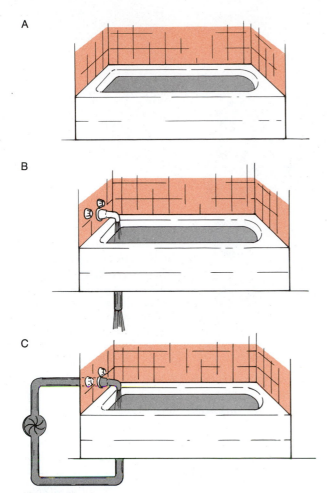

Figure 6–10

A, A static system: a bathtub full of water. Even though such systems appear not to change, they are often more vulnerable than dynamic systems. For example, water loss due to evaporation will not be replaced, and, after some time, the tub will be empty. *B,* A steady-state condition where the rate of inflow of water through the faucet equals the rate of outflow through the drain. Under these circumstances, the level of water in the tub will remain constant. A steady state can adjust itself to outside perturbations. For example, if some water evaporates, the flow through the drain will decrease, and the original level will be re-established. *C,* An equilibrium condition in which the drain water is recycled back through the faucet. This system is analogous to an ecosystem. Most of the materials are replenished by the recycling processes, but, if the system is to continue, small losses owing to evaporation must be replaced.

An alternative way of maintaining stability is through **dynamic equilibrium.** In a dynamic equilibrium, nothing enters or leaves the system, so the balancing processes are all internal. Referring back to our bathtub analogy, an equilibrium system

would be one in which the drained water from the tub is pumped back into the faucet, as shown in Figure 6–10*C*. Thus, the level of water in the tub is maintained at a constant level by continuous recycling. Even though there is a continuous exchange of water, no material enters or leaves the system, and the level in the tub remains constant.

An ecosystem behaves much like a system at equilibrium. Although there is always a continuous influx of new material into an ecosystem, and some matter is always flowing out, a characteristic of all ecosystems is that *most* of the matter and nutrients remain within the system and are continuously recycled by the processes of growth, consumption, and decay. As long as these processes oppose each other equally, the system remains unchanged. There is some argument against this analogy, because, in a true equilibrium, the opposing processes proceed at exactly identical rates all the time, whereas in an ecosystem, balance is often disrupted temporarily, to be regained at a later time. Thus, if the population of hares increases during one year, the lynx population will rise the next spring, and so on. Despite these objections, it is useful to maintain the image of equilibrium when thinking about ecosystems.

Now let us return to the question previously posed, "What types of perturbations are likely to lead to a catastrophic disruption of an ecosystem?" A dynamic equilibrium is disrupted either when it is no longer isolated so that something begins to enter or leave the system, or when some factor changes the rates of the internal processes. Examples include the immigration of new species into a previously stable ecosystem, or a change in the rates of decay caused by some factor such as the poisoning of the soil. Ecosystems have internal mechanisms to compensate for such disruptions to some extent, but, if the disruption is excessive, the system may be overburdened and no longer able to compensate.

The concept of stability can be illustrated by analyzing two different types of perturbations that might occur to a forest system on a hillside in the Rocky Motains. Imagine, first, that an avalanche sweeps down a slope, snapping off trees in its path. The avalanche destroys timber and deposits logs and branches in an unsightly mess at the bottom of the slope. In an instant, the death of many species of plants has suddenly exceeded their rates of growth. But what happens to the system as time goes on? In general, an avalanche will not uproot

An avalanche path in the Canadian Rockies. When avalanches sweep down from the high peaks they kill the large trees that grow in their path. However, the ground surfaces are not disturbed, and the ecosystems suffer no permanent damage.

low-lying plants such as grasses and bushes, nor will it destroy young flexible trees that can bend with the flow. The organisms that live in the soil are also largely unaffected. The following spring there will be a definite shift in the numbers and types of organisms living in the area as pioneer species establish themselves, but the processes of growth and decay will continue, and the system will regenerate itself.

Now consider what will happen if a nearby hillside is logged in a careless manner without regard for environmental consequences. Trees are removed, just as in the example of an avalanche. But there is a major difference between the two situations. During the commercial cutting and harvesting of the timber, heavy machinery such as bulldozers and skidders drive up and down the slopes, disrupting the surface vegetation and exposing the

An area that has been logged intensively. As roads are built and machinery disturbs the natural vegetation, the soil is exposed to erosion, and serious ecological damage can result.

soil to erosion. In addition, roads are cut across the region to provide access for trucks, and the roadcuts are always barren and devoid of plant cover. As a result, spring rains wash tonnes of topsoil into the streams below. The erosion of the soil removes the reservoir of nutrients that is essential to the health of the system. In addition, when the surface vegetation is uprooted and the litter is exposed to oxidation, the soil loses much of its ability to hold water and retain the nutrients that remain. Thus, the cycle of growth and decay is upset, and, if the disruption is severe enough, the long-term health and stability of the system may be threatened.

Ecosystem Stability and Diversity of Species

Another important question in ecology is, "What is the relationship, if any, between the number of species in an ecosystem and the stability of the system?" Mathematical models imply that very simple systems are likely to be unstable. Imagine, as an extreme case, that there is one species of large herbivores in a area and one major predator. If a disease microorganism decimated the herbivore population, the predator population would crash as well. Then, continuing our hypothetical scenario, if the herbivores recovered from the disease epidemic, the population could rise precipitously and then crash when the forage was overgrazed (Fig. 6–11). Such widely fluctuating cycles are indicative of instability. Several observations support the reasoning that complex systems are more stable than simple systems.

- Many experimentalists have tried to construct artificial ecosystems with just two, three, or four species, but most of these simple systems have been unstable.
- When a natural ecosystem such as a forest or a prairie is converted to an apple orchard or a cornfield, the overall effect is the replacement of a complex ecosystem by a simple one. In general, cultivated ecosystems are less stable than natural ones.
- Similarly, when complex natural insect food webs are destroyed by spraying farms with indiscriminate pesticides such as DDT, unstable situations are often created. The result, in many cases, has been the population explosions of undesirable species.

- Small, ecologically simple islands are particularly vulnerable to invasion and are easily disrupted.

On the other hand, not all ecologists are convinced that stability is always directly related to diversity.

Some very major ecological disruptions have occurred when foreign species have been *added* to an existing ecosystem. Thus, even though the addition of a species increases the total diversity, if the new species has no natural enemies, its population may increase dramatically and cause fluctuations in other populations.

As discussed in Chapter 5, there are generally fewer species in the Arctic than in the tropical rainforests. Consequently, if a relationship does exist between diversity and stability, the tropical rainforest should be more stable. What are the facts? It is difficult to say. There are many more radical population fluctuations in the Arctic than in the Tropics; thus, if population fluctuations are the main indicator of stability, the rainforest is more stable than the tundra. But perhaps the primary criterion for stability is that the potential for adaptation and growth remain intact. A population fluctuation does not necessarily destroy the system. If a section of tundra is disrupted by a bulldozer, it will regenerate very slowly, but it will regenerate. However, when certain tropical rainforests are cut, the nutrient-poor clayey soils harden, and the forest cannot be re-established. In this sense, the long-term stability of the tundra may be greater than that of the tropical forest.

Ecosystem Stability and Human Intervention

Throughout the remainder of this text, the relationship between ecosystem stability and human intervention will explored in detail. As should be obvious by now, the problems are complex, and accurate predictions are often elusive. However, two factors are fundamental and should be emphasized.

1. Any activity that disrupts natural cycles or causes populations to fluctuate threatens stability.

2. Any activity that alters the numbers and types of organisms in an area, by adding new species or by destroying existing species, can also be considered a potential threat to environmental stability.

A

B

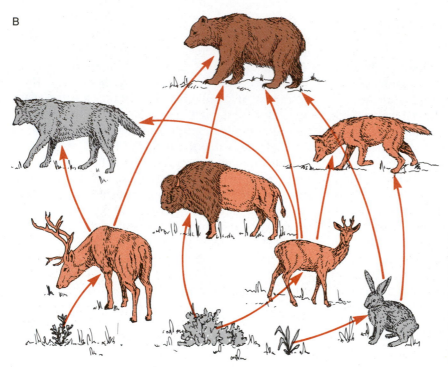

Figure 6–11

A, There are no cross-links in the food chain of a three-species system, so the system is vulnerable to disruption. *B,* In a multispecies system, there are many cross-links, so if one pathway is disrupted, the system can readjust.

6.4
The Stability of the Atmosphere

The study of environmental science involves an understanding of both small areas and systems, often called **microcosms,** and large areas and systems, called **macrocosms.** Both are important. A farmer is dependent on the balance of organisms that live within the soil in one particular field, but, at the same time, changes in the global climate also affect the condition of crops.

In the last section, we considered the stability of an individual ecosystem. Now let's consider the stability of the entire biosphere—the life support zone of the planet Earth. Is the biosphere stable, or is it vulnerable to change? One interesting perspective to this question concerns the structure of the atmosphere.

The story of the evolution of the modern atmosphere starts with the formation of the Earth itself, some 4.6 billion years ago. Today, most scientists are in agreement in the belief that the entire Solar System was formed from a single cloud of dust and gas, spiraling slowly in space. According to this theory, the original cloud gradually coalesced into distinct spheres, which further evolved into the Sun, the nine planets, their moons, and other objects currently found in the Solar System (Fig. 6–12). Let's think, for a moment, about the Earth and its two closest planets, Venus and Mars. These three planets were originally formed from the same cloud of dust, they are roughly the same size, and the differences in their distances from the Sun are not that great. Therefore, if no additional information were available, one might assume that the environments on all three planets should be reasonably similar. In fact, just a few decades ago, before spacecraft had been used to provide a more detailed look at the Solar System, many scientists believed that life might exist in our neighborhood

in space. We now know that this is not true and that the environments on Venus and Mars are not at all hospitable. The surface on Venus is about as hot as the inside of a self-cleaning oven, about 450°C (850°F). The atmospheric pressure is so great that to find an equivalent pressure on Earth, one would have to dive one km under the sea. Overhead, clouds composed partially of sulfuric acid are blown about, sparking lightning storms and raining deadly acids. On the other hand, Mars has a frigid environment. Today, polar Martian temperatures plummet to −123°C, cold enough to freeze carbon dioxide and form an "ice cap" of dry ice. The temperatures recorded at the equator on Mars are comparable to those found in the polar regions on Earth. Eons ago, liquid water existed on the planet, and spacecraft have photographed dry

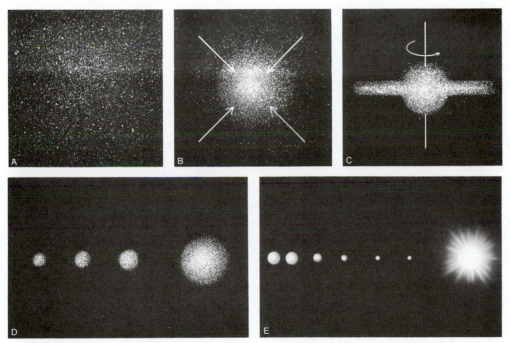

Figure 6–12

Formation of the Solar System. *A,* The Solar System was originally a diffuse cloud of dust and gas. *B,* This dust and gas began to coalesce under its internal gravitation. *C,* The shrinking mass began to rotate and was distorted. *D,* The mass broke up into a discrete protosun orbited by large planets composed primarily of hydrogen and helium. *E,* The sun heated up until fusion temperatures were reached. The heat from the Sun then drove most of the hydrogen and helium away from the closest planets, leaving small, solid cores behind. The massive outer planets remain mostly composed of hydrogen and helium. (From Jay M. Pasachoff: *Contempoarry Astronomy.* 2nd ed. Philadelphia, Saunders College Publishing, 1981)

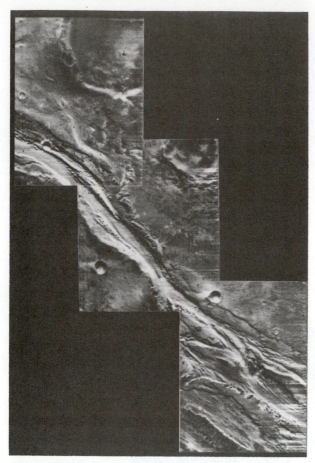

Figure 6–13
Close-up of Mars taken by Mariner 9 spacecraft, showing a deep canyon. This channel is thought to have been formed by running water in Mars' geological past.

riverbeds and canyons (Fig. 6–13), but now, almost all the water is frozen, and scientists believe that most of it is located in underground reservoirs of ice. Today, the planet is drier than any desert found on Earth.

Meanwhile, on Earth, a temperate climate predominates, flowers bloom, and animals, including humans, wander from place to place. One might ask, how did the Earth inherit such a favorable environment? Why are we so different?

The answer seems to be twofold. First, the evidence indicates that hospitality for life requires rather narrow ranges of many conditions. This means simply that we were lucky. The geology of the Earth and its distance from the Sun were simply fortuitous for the development of favorable conditions for the evolution of living organisms. Second,

the best evidence indicates that the modern atmosphere and life evolved together. Thus, the geological and biological environments are intimately interconnected and integrated. There is a mutual interdependence between life and the gases that sustain life.

Scientists believe that the precursor to the modern atmosphere, which formed about 3.8 billion years ago, contained primarily carbon dioxide and nitrogen, with smaller quantities of water and other compounds. Carbon dioxide is an important determinant of climate because of its heat-absorbing properties. Energy is transmitted from the Sun to the Earth in the form of electromagnetic radiation. There are many types of electromagnetic radiation; some familiar examples include radio waves, infrared, visible light, ultraviolet, and x-rays. Most of the energy that we receive from the Sun comes in the form of visible or ultraviolet light. After this radiation is absorbed by the surface of the Earth, it is re-emitted back out toward space. However, the re-emitted energy is mainly in the form of infrared radiation. Any atmospheric gas that absorbs infrared traps this energy before it escapes into space and, therefore, acts as a type of insulating layer. Two important compounds that absorb infrared are carbon dioxide and water.

Carbon dioxide is central to our story because it is available from many sources in many different places. Recall from Chapter 3 that carbon dioxide reacts with water to form carbonates, and, in turn, the carbonates can react with calcium ions to form insoluble calcium carbonate, which makes up limestone.

If this were the end of the story, there would be a one-way removal of atmospheric carbon dioxide. If such a process had occurred, the insulating blanket would have been slowly reduced over the millennia. Eventually, the temperature would have dropped below freezing, and the water in the atmosphere would have turned to ice, further reducing the infrared absorbing capacity of the environment. After a period of time, the planet would have grown so cold that life as we know it could not have survived. This is what is believed to have occurred on Mars, contributing to the evolution of a frozen, lifeless, desert.

One major difference between the Earth and Mars is that the Earth is just a little bit larger than its neighboring planet. To understand the importance of this difference, let us return once more to the original formation of the planet. As stated earlier, all the planets were formed from a diffuse cloud of dust and gas that coalesced into discrete spheres. Think of the dust particles coming together. They were pulled inward by gravitation, and, as they fell together, they speeded up and smashed into each other. These energetic collisions caused the temperature of the particles to rise. This thermal energy, combined with the heat released by naturally radioactive minerals, was great enough to melt each of the planets. But Mars, being smaller than the Earth, cooled more rapidly, so, today, its interior is mostly solid. In contrast, the interior of the Earth has remained hot, liquid, and active.

Recall also from Chapter 3 that because the Earth is geologically active, limestone sediments are forced into the interior where they are melted, and, eventually, the carbon dioxide is reinjected back into the atmosphere by a variety of processes. Thus, the Earth hasn't lost its insulating layer and hasn't frozen.

To appreciate the delicacy of the cycle, let us turn our attention briefly to the planet Venus. Venus is just a little closer to the Sun, and, therefore, was originally just a little warmer than the Earth. This added warmth speeded up the evaporation of the surface water. In turn, the gaseous water warmed the planet still further (recall that water also absorbs infrared). As temperatures slowly spiraled upward, some of the carbon-containing rocks became hot enough to decompose, thereby releasing excess carbon dioxide into the atmosphere. Conditions continued to escalate until, today, Venus is much too hot to support life.

The study of the geology of the Earth can explain why we inherited such a fortuitous temperature, but the explanation still leaves us with an atmosphere almost devoid of oxygen. Where did the oxygen come from? Some scientists believe that it was formed by abiotic processes, such as the decomposition of water by the action of sunlight:

$$2H_2O \rightarrow 2H_2 + O_2$$
Water gives hydrogen plus oxygen

However, the best evidence seems to indicate that abiotic processes could not account for the high concentration of oxygen in the modern atmosphere.

No one knows how or where the first living organisms appeared. Perhaps they were formed by the action of sunlight and lightning on molecules found in the atmosphere and dissolved in the surface water of the primordial ocean. Other scientists believe that they evolved in the vicinity of underwater volcanic vents where carbon, nitrogen, and sulfur compounds were more concentrated. Yet another theory postulates that the earliest forms of life evolved on the surface of certain clay minerals.

In any case, it is fairly certain that shortly after their first appearance, living creatures must have lived in water. Because there was little oxygen, they could not have metabolized their food as most organisms do today, but must have lived by some **anaerobic** (without oxygen) process. Up to this point, one theory contends, there was little free oxygen in the atmosphere, and the organisms required none. The next evolutionary step was a crucial one. Some types of one-celled plants evolved and acquired the ability to conduct photosynthesis. During photosynthesis, carbon dioxide and water are combined in the presence of sunlight to form glucose (a sugar) and oxygen.

Most scientists believe that the excess oxygen released by the first plants accumulated slowly over the millennia until its concentration reached about 0.6 percent of the atmosphere. Most multicellular organisms require oxygen to survive and could have evolved only at this point. The emergence of various multicelled organisms about one billion years ago triggered an accelerated biological production of oxygen. The present oxygen level of 21 percent of the atmosphere was reached about 450 million years ago. Although the concentration has not been precisely constant since that time, an overall oxygen balance has always been maintained. This scenario is illustrated schematically in Figure 6–14.

If the oxygen concentration in the atmosphere were to increase even by a few percent, fires would burn uncontrollably across the planet; if it were to decrease appreciably, complex plants and animals could not survive. If the carbon dioxide concentration were to increase by a small amount, the average temperature of the Earth would rise. However, conditions on Earth have remained relatively constant for hundreds of millions of years. Therefore, atmospheric gases must have remained balanced to the needs of living organisms during the long

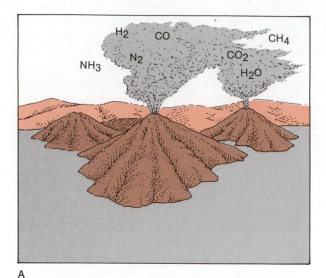

A

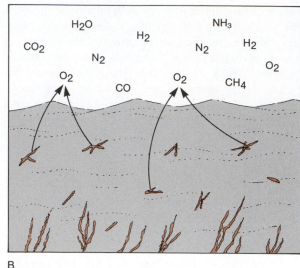

B

Figure 6–14

Evolution of the atmosphere. *A,* The primitive atmosphere contained carbon dioxide, nitrogen, and other gases. *B,* As plants evolved, the composition of the atmosphere began to change. Oxygen, released during photosynthesis, began to accumulate. *C,* The modern atmosphere is composed mainly of nitrogen and oxygen, with smaller concentrations of carbon dioxide, water, and other gases. The ratio of oxygen to carbon dioxide is maintained by dynamic exchange among plants and animals.

C

span of life on Earth. By what mechanism has this gaseous atmospheric balance been maintained? Today, many scientists believe that it is maintained by the living systems themselves. According to this theory, not only is the delicate oxygen-carbon dioxide balance biologically maintained, but the very presence of oxygen in our atmosphere can be explained only by biological activity. If all life on Earth were to cease and the chemistry of our planet were to depend solely on inorganic processes, oxygen would once again become a trace gas, and the atmosphere would revert to its primitive condition and be poisonous to any complex plants and animals that were reintroduced.

If it is true that the required atmospheric oxygen concentration and perhaps even the Earth's climate is maintained by biological processes, the atmosphere is not in danger of disastrous changes as long as living species survive. However, a large ecological catastrophe, such as the death of the oceans or the destruction of the rain forests in the Amazon Basin, could cause reverberations throughout our world that might eventually create an inhospitable environment for life on Earth. An important lesson from our study of planetary science is that seemingly small differences in planetary chemistry may initiate a series of chain reactions that eventually lead to large changes in final conditions.

Summary

Although the climate mainly determines the **climax community** of an area, ecosystems or parts of ecosystems are often disturbed by natural events or human intervention. **Succession** is a progressive series of changes that occur after a disturbance. The sum of these changes drives the system toward re-establishment of the climax community. **Primary succession** occurs when the terrain is initially lifeless or nearly lifeless, and **secondary succession** occurs in areas that have been disturbed but that have not been totally stripped of their soil or vegetation.

The **theory of evolution** states that species are not unchangeable, but arise by descent and modification from pre-existing species. Individuals in any population differ from one another, and some of these differences are inherited. **Natural selection** is any force that makes individuals with some genes produce more offspring than individuals with other genes. It leads to evolution, a change in the proportions of different genes in a population from one generation to the next.

Evolution can occur by gradual change or by **punctuated equilibria.**

An ecosystem is stable if the cycles of decay, consumption, and growth continue in a balanced manner. In a stable system, nutrients are retained and recycled, and the potential for adaptation and growth remains intact. Diverse systems are often considered to be more stable than simple ones, but the relationship between stability and diversity is sometimes ambiguous. Humans can disrupt ecosystem stability by interfering with natural cycles or by altering the numbers and types of organisms in an area.

Carbon dioxide is removed from the atmosphere by reactions that lead to the formation of limestone and other minerals. Eventually this material is recycled back into the atmosphere by geologic activity. This geological recycling is responsible for maintaining a favorable carbon dioxide concentration in the atmosphere, which, in turn, has led to favorable climate. One of the interesting theories for the formation of the modern atmosphere states that living organisms are responsible for the generation and maintenance of almost all the gaseous oxygen observed today. The ratio of oxygen to carbon dioxide is also maintained by biological systems.

Questions

Succession

1. During the past 100 years, the large glaciers in Glacier Bay, Alaska, have receded approximately 65 km. Describe the types of vegetation you would expect to find in this 65 km zone.

2. Explain why a farmer's field must be maintained as an early successional system. Why is energy needed to maintain it?

3. Imagine that a new volcanic island were formed in the middle of the ocean out of hardened lava. Outline a possible successional sequence for the island, and give the time periods for each stage of development.

4. When a tree blows down in a forest, a small open area is produced that is quickly populated with pioneer species. Would you describe this change as primary or secondary succession, or neither? Defend your answer.

5. Imagine two volcanic areas, both the same size. In both areas, a fresh lava flow has spread newly formed rock over the land. One area is an island, far from land, and the entire island has been covered with lava. The second area exists in the middle of a large continent. Would succession occur faster on the island or on the continent, or would the two be the same? Defend your answer.

Fitness

6. In primitive societies, in which physical strength and stamina may have counted for more than they do today, physical fitness may have endowed its possessors with Darwinian fitness. Can you imagine a type of social organization in which the best physical specimens were actually at a reproductive *disadvantage* with respect to others? Describe such a hypothetical situation.

7. A disease that infects individuals before they are old enough to reproduce or during the reproductive years will necessarily have a selective effect on a population. Suggest a way in which a disease that occurs principally in the *post*-reproductive period could have a selective effect on a population.

8. Would evolutionary change be more likely to occur rapidly in a small population or a large population? Defend your answer.

9. Describe the difference between gradualism and punctuated equilibria.

10. Explain why a great deal of fossil data are needed to distinguish between gradualism and punctuated equilibria.

Stability of Ecosystems

11. Discuss the relationship between the number of species in an ecosystem and the stability of the system.

12. Explain why the extinction of species is a serious threat to ecosystem stability.

13. Which of the following activities would be likely to threaten the stability of an entire ecosystem? Which would be unlikely to threaten overall stability? (a) A careless hiker leaves messy trash and dirty fire rings around a campsite. (b) Pollutants from a city fall on a lake and kill the resident phytoplankton. (c) A swamp is drained. (d) A fire, started by humans, sweeps through a Ponderosa pine forest on a mountainside in the Rocky Mountains.

The Evolution of the Atmosphere

14. Of the three planets, Venus, Earth, and Mars, Venus is the closest to the Sun, Earth is next, and Mars is the farthest from the Sun. Does this factor, by itself, explain the temperature differences observed on the three planets? Defend your answer.

15. Explain the relationship between the movement of tectonic plates and the climate of the Earth.

16. Astronomers believe that in a few billion years, the thermal output of the Sun will increase for some time. Discuss some changes that may occur on Venus, Earth, and Mars.

17. Discuss the role of living organisms on the structure of the modern atmosphere.

Suggested Readings

An article discussing fire-maintained communities in the chaparral is:

Donald Perry and Sylvia Merschel: In the chaparral, life begins and ends in a big blaze. *Smithsonian,* 13:132–136, Oct 82.

Accounts of succession that have occurred in the aftermath of major volcanic eruptions are given in:

Dieter and Mary Plage: In the shadow of Krakatau, return of Java's wildlife. National Geographic Magazine, June 1985, p. 750.

Michael Tennesen: Rising from the ashes. National Wildlife, 24:34–39, Sept 86.

Several works outlining the modern theories of evolution are:

David Briggs and S. M. Walters: *Plant Variation and Evolution,* Second Edition. New York, Cambridge University Press, 1984. 412 pp.

John A. Endler: *Natural Selection in the Wild.* Princeton, Princeton University Press, 1986. 337 pp.

Stephen Jay Gould: Darwinism and the expansion of evolutionary theory. *Science,* April 23, 1982, p. 380.

Stephen Jay Gould: Not necessarily a wing, which came first the function or the form? *Natural History.* Oct. 1985.

H. B. D. Kettlewell: The phenomenon of industrial melanism in the lepidoptera. *Annual Review of Entomology,* 6:245, 1961.

Laurene M. Ratcliffe and Peter T. Boag (eds.): *Darwin's Finches, the late David Lack.* New York, Cambridge University Press, 1983. 208 pp.

G. Ledyard Stebbins and Francisco J. Ayala: The evolution of Darwinism. *Scientific American,* July, 1985, p 72.

E. S. Vrba (ed.): *Species and Speciation.* Pretoria, South Africa, Transvaal Museum Monograph, 1985. 176 pp.

The subject of stability and diversity of species is discussed in a variety of books and articles:

Stephen Jay Gould: *The Panda's Thumb, More Reflections in Natural History.* New York, W. W. Norton & Co., 1980. 343 pp.

Robert H. MacArthur: *Geographical Ecology—Patterns in the Distribution of Species.* New York, Harper & Row, 1972. 269 pp.

Robert H. MacArthur and E. O. Wilson: *The Theory of Island Biogeography.* Princeton, NJ, Princeton University Press, 1967.

Robert M. May: *Stability and Complexity in Model Ecosystems.* Princeton, NJ, Princeton University Press, 1973. 235 pp.

Knut Schmidt-Nielsen: *Scaling: Why is Animal Size so Important?* New York, Cambridge University Press, 1984. 241 pp.

Michael E. Soule (ed.): *Conservation Biology: The Science of Scarcity and Diversity.* Sunderland, MA, Sinauer Associates, 1986.

Two books that discuss the evolution of the atmosphere are:

J. E. Lovelock: *Gaia A New Look at Life on Earth.* Oxford, Oxford University Press, 1979. 157 pp.

Stephen H. Schneider and Randi Londer: *The Coevolution of Climate and Life.* San Francisco, Sierra Club Books, 1984. 563 pp.

Several recent articles that discuss the evolution of the atmosphere of the Earth and its neighbors are:

A. G Cairns-Smith: The first organisms. *Scientific American,* June 1985. pp. 90–100.

James P. Ferris: The chemistry of life's origin. *Chemical and Engineering News,* August 27, 1984. pp. 22–35.

Stephen L. Gillett: The rise and fall of the early reducing atmosphere. *Astronomy,* July 1985. pp. 66–71.

Robert M. Haberle: The climate of Mars. *Scientific American,* May 1986. pp. 54–62.

Harold Morowitz: Two views of life. *Science 83,* January/February 1983. pp. 21–25.

Owen B. Toon and Steve Olson: The warm earth. *Science 85,* October, 1985.

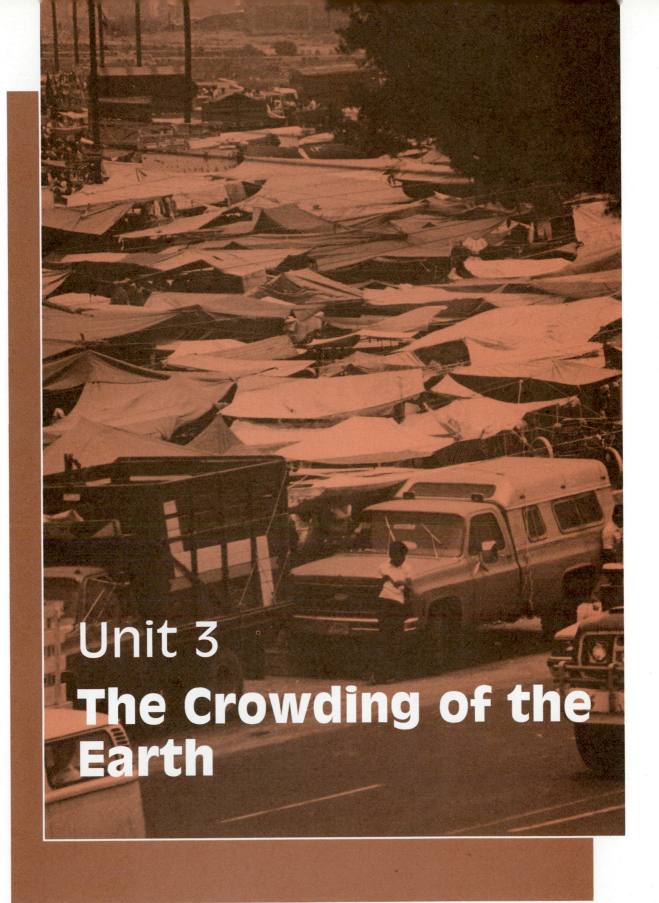

Unit 3
The Crowding of the Earth

In Mexico City many people live in tents along the roadside with inadequate access to clean water, sewage, or waste disposal facilities. (Tonio Turok)

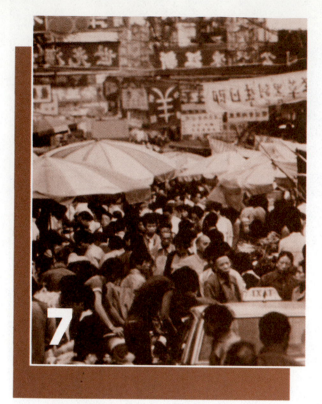

7

Human Populations

The Human Population

Although estimates vary considerably, it is generally believed that hominoid species have existed for approximately three to four million years, and *Homo sapiens* have been living on this planet for about 100 thousand years. For more than 99 percent of this time span on Earth, humans have lived in small families or tribes and have survived by hunting and gathering. In this capacity, the ecological impact of humans was small, and the human population was stable over long periods of time.

Studies of skeletal remains of early humans and studies of hunter–gatherer societies that have lived in modern times indicate that the average life expectancy of people in these primitive cultures was about 20 to 30 years. By comparison, life expectancy in India between 1910 and 1920 was 20 years, and life expectancy in the United States in 1900 was 33.8 years. Yet in hunter–gatherer societies, the population was constant over a great many millennia, whereas in the United States and India at the turn of the century, the population was

A Kalahari bushman beside a partly constructed hut in the family camp. Until a few years ago, most of these people lived a life of hunting and gathering. Hunter-gatherer societies are usually characterized by low birth and relatively high death rates, leading to a stable population.

increasing rapidly. Because the life expectancies in the two eras were reasonably similar but the overall rate of population growth was much greater in the early 1900s than in prehistoric times, demographers have concluded that primitive cultures experienced a low birth rate.

About ten to twelve thousand years ago, humans in several different regions learned how to domesticate plants and animals. This technological advancement marked the start of a major global environmental change. For the first time, a single species began to exert very significant control over growth and development of many other species. As agriculture became increasingly efficient, women began to bear more children, and the human population increased. Why did the birth rate increase with the advent of agriculture? First, it is possible to obtain much more food in a given area of land by farming than by hunting and gathering. Second, hunter–gatherers are usually nomadic, following the migrations of their prey, and infants are a severe liability to travelers, whereas in a stationary, domestic, agricultural society, babies are not so much trouble. Third, children are not very effective as hunters until they are nearly adults, but they can help around the farm when they are much younger. Therefore, the population increase between 10,000 B.C. and about 1800 A.D. (Fig. 7–1) was largely a result of the increasing birth rates that coincided with the development of agriculture.

After 1800, a second and more dramatic increase in the rate of population growth occurred. This increase coincided with the second major development of the human race, the industrial revolution. As cities grew, goods and services became more readily available, and as medical science progressed, death rates declined drastically, and the human population increased exponentially.

The past is relatively easy to study. But what will happen in the future? What kind of world will our children and grandchildren inherit? Of course, the future is always shrouded in considerable mystery and uncertainty. In this chapter, we will examine human populations and study the methods for projecting the changes that may occur during the next generation or two.

7.2
Extrapolation of Population Growth Curves

The most obvious method for predicting population growth is to construct a graph that plots past population size against time and then guess how the curve will continue. Guessing points on a curve

Two million years of population growth

Population

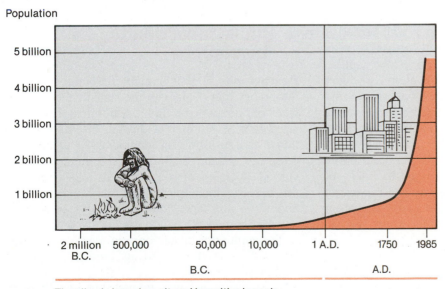

Time line is based on altered logarithmic scale.

Figure 7–1
Growth of world population from emergence of *Homo hablis*, the first tool-maker, to 1985.

Farmers in Peru harvesting wheat. In most primitive agricultural societies, birth and death rates are high, but birth rates are higher, leading to a rapid rate of population increase.

outside the range of observation is called **extrapolation.** Extrapolation is a subtle art. Refer to Figure 7–1 again. Even a casual glance at the curve shows that world population growth has become more and more rapid in recent years. If an extrapolation is made by drawing the curve to continue its ever increasing rate, one may well be led to panic. As discussed in Chapter 1, an ever-increasing population would rapidly outstrip food supplies and eventually lead to mass starvation and death. However, our study of ecology has shown that plant and animal populations exhibit a wide variety of different growth functions. Figure 7–2A shows the shape of arithmetic and exponential growth functions (see Appendix E). Recall that populations of paramecium exhibit a rapid increase, followed by a leveling when the carrying capacity is reached (Fig. 7–2B). Other populations oscillate in size (Fig. 7–2C) or even become extinct (Fig. 7–2D).

Again, let us return to the question, "What will happen to the human population?" We know that it cannot continue to increase at current rates for long, but, without any additional information, a more precise prediction is difficult. However, there are a variety of techniques that can be used to analyze population growth rates more accurately. These procedures will be discussed in the following sections.

7.3
An Introduction to Demography

Demography is that branch of sociology or anthropology that deals with the statistical characteristics of human populations, with reference to total size, density, number of deaths, diseases, migrations, and so forth. The demographer attempts to construct a numerical profile of the population viewed as groups of people, not as individuals. For this purpose, the demographer needs to know facts about the size and composition of populations, such as the number of females alive at a given time or the number of infants born in a given year. This information is then used to predict population change with time.

The simplest way to measure growth is by subtracting the population at an earlier date from that at a later time. The following example does

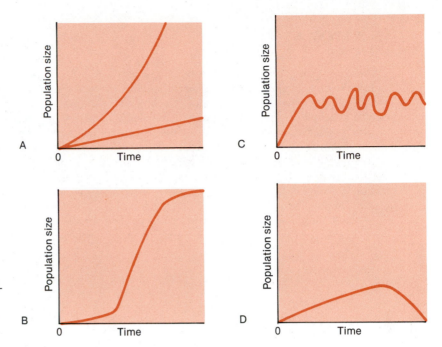

Figure 7–2
Schematic growth curves. *A,* Arithmetic (straight-line) and geometric (curved-line) patterns of growth. *B,* Sigmoid curve of growth. *C,* Oscillating population curve. *D,* Growth curve of a population that becomes extinct.

this for the populations of India and the United States during the 36-year period from 1950 to 1986.

Populations (millions)

	India	U.S.
1986	785	241
1950	360	152
Increase	425	89

These differences show that the United States, with many times the wealth of India and about three times the land area, had less than one quarter the population increase.

Unfortunately, these population differences give little indication about how fast a country is growing in relation to its population. More useful are **rates of growth.** The average annual rate of growth is calculated as follows:

$$
\begin{aligned}
&\text{Average annual} \\
&\quad \text{growth rate} = \\
&\quad (\text{percent})
\end{aligned}
$$

$$
\frac{\text{population in final year} - \text{population in initial year}}{\text{population in initial year} \times \text{number of years}} \times 100\%
$$

For India, the average annual rate of growth from 1950 through 1980 was approximately:

$$
\begin{aligned}
&\text{Average annual} \\
&\quad \text{growth rate} = \\
&(\text{India, }1950{-}1986)
\end{aligned}
$$

$$
\frac{(785 \times 10^6 \text{ persons} - 360 \times 10^6 \text{ persons}) \times 100\%}{360 \times 10^6 \text{ persons} \times 36 \text{ years}}
$$

$$
= 3.3\%/\text{yr}
$$

For the United States in the same period the average growth rate was:

$$
\begin{aligned}
&\text{Average annual} \\
&\quad \text{growth rate} = \\
&(\text{U.S., }1950{-}1986)
\end{aligned}
$$

$$
\frac{(241 \times 10^6 \text{ persons} - 152 \times 10^6 \text{ persons}) \times 100\%}{152 \times 10^6 \text{ persons} \times 36 \text{ years}}
$$

$$
= 1.6\%/\text{yr}
$$

Average rates of growth represent only the crudest form of demographic data. They tell us how fast a population has been growing but provide few clues that can be used to base predictions about the future. A more thorough demographic analysis must be based on much more data.

Special Topic A
Migration

There are three mechanisms that can cause populations to change: birth, death, and migration. Birth and death occur in every population and are discussed at length in the text. Migration is negligible in some societies, but important in others. For example, between 1980 and 1984, about 2.8 million people immigrated legally to the United States. During that period, the population increased by 15.6 million, so immigration accounted for about 18 percent of the total increase.

Often, migration can have a greater impact on populations than is indicated by simply counting the total number of people who have moved from one place to another. In many cases, there is a disproportionately high number of young males in a migrating group. This happens because young men are most likely to face the adventure of moving in exchange for the chance that they might find greater opportunities in a new place. If a numerically significant number of men in the reproductive age group leave an area, many of the women who were left behind will not be able to find husbands and will remain childless. Therefore, migration can lead to a reduction in birth rates in the remaining population.

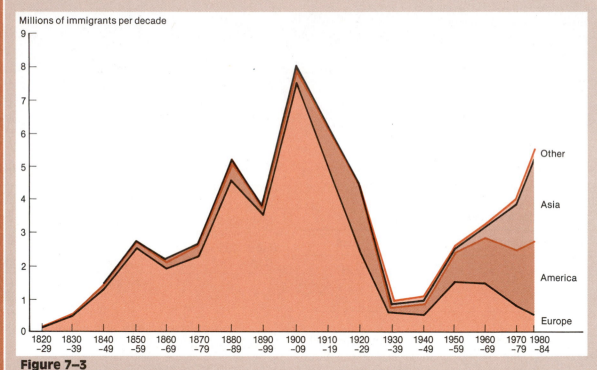

Figure 7–3

Immigration into the United States from 1820 to 1984. (Note that the last entry is for a five-year period, not a ten-year period. As an approximation, the number of immigrants in five years was doubled to keep the graph to scale.) (Source: U.S. Dept. of Immigration and Naturalization)

A demographer is interested in the number of **vital events**—births, deaths, marriages, and migrations—that occur in a given period of time. Two very basic measures of population growth are the **birth rate** and the **death rate.** The difference between these two rates is the **rate of natural increase.** For any geographical area or ethnic group being studied, these rates are computed as follows:

(a) Birth rate in year X =

$$\frac{\text{Number of live children born in year X}}{\text{Midyear population in year X}} \times 100\%$$

(b) Death rate in year X =

$$\frac{\text{Number of deaths in year X}}{\text{Midyear population in year X}} \times 100\%$$

(c) Rate of natural increase in year X =

Birth rate − death rate

Stated in words, the birth rates and death rates are the number of births and deaths as a percentage of the population as a whole (counting the population size at the midpoint of the year).

Vital rates are concise expressions of long-term historical trends. However, even more information is needed to predict future population trends accurately. To understand how populations grow, it will be helpful first to review the principles of geometric or exponential growth (see Special Topic B in Chapter 4 and Appendix E) and then to see how the growth of populations differs from, say, the growth of money in a bank.

Let us start with money. Imagine you decided to deposit $100 in a bank that offered 5 percent interest per year. Suppose you started walking to the bank carrying a collection of change and bills of various denominations for a total of $100. If you deposited the entire $100, you would expect to have $105 at the end of the year. But on the way to the bank you bought an irresistible ice cream sundae for $1. You then had only $99 to deposit when you arrived at the bank. No matter how you paid for your sundae, whether you used coins, a dollar bill, or a bill of higher denomination and received change, your $99 would grow at a rate of 5 percent. In 1 year, you would have $99 + ($99 × 0.05) = $103.95.

How different a population is! Imagine a population of 100 people—3 infants, 7 children, 50 adults under 65 years of age, and 40 people at least 65 years of age. Suppose that during an entire year, no one moved in or out of the population, 7 of the women younger than 65 had babies, and 2 of the people older than 65 died. These were the only vital events. At the end of the year, the population would be 100 + 7 − 2 = 105, for an annual rate of growth of 5 percent.

Now suppose that the population had contained only 99 people at the beginning of the year.

What would the rate of increase have been? If the population grew in the same way that money in the bank grows, the rate of growth would be 5 percent no matter which person in the original population was no longer there. People, however, are not interchangeable like dollar bills. If the population had been missing an infant, there still would have been 7 births and 2 deaths. There would have been 99 + 7 − 2 = 104 persons at the end of the year. The annual rate of growth would have been:

$$\frac{104 - 99}{99} \times 100\% = 5.05\%$$

On the other hand, if the population had been missing one of the women who had a child, only 6 births would have occurred, and the rate of growth would have been:

$$\frac{103 - 99}{99} \times 100\% = 4.04\%$$

If one of the elderly persons who died had been missing from the population, the population would be 99 + 7 − 1 = 105 persons at the end of a year, for an annual growth rate of:

$$\frac{105 - 99}{99} \times 100\% = 6.06\%$$

This very simple example indicates some of the difficulties confronting the student of population size, but it also leads to an important insight that is necessary for an effective approach to the investigation of growth. Since the probability of dying or of giving birth within any given year varies with age and sex, the **age–sex composition,** or **distribution,** of the population has a profound effect upon a country's birth rate, its death rate, and, hence, its growth rate. A graph of an age–sex distribution can be made by plotting the number of males and females in each age group in a population. Alternatively, age–sex distributions are also drawn by plotting the percentage of the population of each sex in each group.

Figure 7–4 shows a hypothetical age–sex distribution for an imaginary population. In this situation, each age group has the same number of males and females. In particular, there are 500 boys and 500 girls younger than 10 years of age, and 50 men and 50 women between 90 and 100 years of age. Furthermore, there are exactly 50 fewer men and 50 fewer women at each succeeding age decade. Thus, there are 450 males and fe-

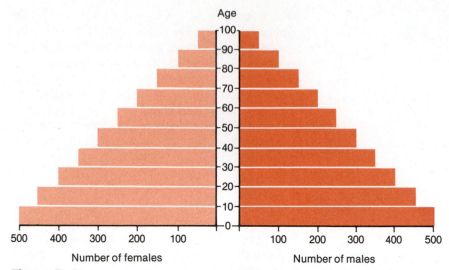

Age

Number of females

Number of males

Figure 7–4

Age and sex distribution of an imaginary population. In this population, the same number of boys and girls are born every year, and the probability of dying is a constant throughout a person's lifetime. In reality, these conditions are never encountered.

males between the ages of 10 and 20, 400 between the ages of 20 and 30, and so on. This graph can be used to predict future population growth. It shows that there are more babies than teen-agers, more teen-agers than young adults, and more young adults than older people. Women in the age group 17 to 40 years are most likely to bear children. In 5 years, the large population of young teen-agers will become adults and bear children. In 10 years, the even larger population of children will grow up and bear more children. Therefore, the graph in Figure 7–4 indicates that the population will increase rapidly in the near future.

Most human age–sex distributions don't look like Figure 7–4. Figure 7–4 would represent a population in which (1) boys and girls were born with equal frequency; (2) the same number of persons were born every year for more than a century; (3) everyone died by the age of 100; and (4) an equal number of people in each age group died every year. However, in real human populations, on the average, about 106 boys are born for every 100 girls. In addition, the probability of dying varies in a regular way throughout one's life span. Thus, a relatively large proportion of people die when they are very young, comparatively few die between the ages of 10 and 50, and the proportion of people dying each year after 50 increases rapidly. In addi-

tion, there are marked sex differences in mortality. Women have a higher probability of surviving from one year to the next throughout their life span except during the childbearing years in areas without modern medical care.

Consider the effects of realistic patterns of vital events on a group of people born in the same 5-year period. The greater survivorship of women over men means that even though more boys are born than girls, the ratio of women to men increases as the group grows older. By the time that the group is elderly, there are considerably more women than men. Also, data are usually collected in such a way that we know only the total population of each sex over 70, 80, or 85 years. Therefore, the graphs can be only approximate for the very old age groups. Figure 7–5 presents an age–sex distribution that more nearly reflects these demographic characteristics.

Even though Figure 7–5 is more realistic than Figure 7–4, it still does not portray all human populations accurately. The discrepancies arise because Figure 7–5 assumes that birth rates and death rates will remain constant over the years. In fact, this assumption is not always correct.

Figure 7–6 shows the age–sex distribution for three nations, India, France, and West Germany. Note that the curves are very different from one an-

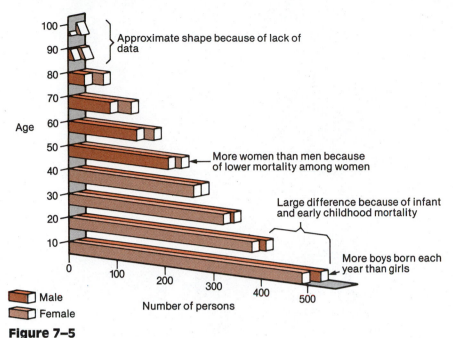

Figure 7–5

A typical age–sex distribution.

other. The distribution for India has a very broad base. This broad base tells us that birth rates have been high in the recent past. It also tells us that there are many young children in the population. If no catastrophes occur, these children will reach reproductive age in the near future and the population can be expected to expand rapidly during the next generation. In France, birth rates have declined so that today there is approximately an equal number of people in each age group between 0 and 35 years of age. Ten years from now, there will be about the same number of men and women in the reproductive age group as there are now. The population will probably remain fairly constant in the near future. In West Germany, birth rates have been quite low in the past few decades, so that at the present time, there are *fewer* infants and children than young adults. Ten years from now, there will be fewer people in the reproductive age group than there are at present. Therefore, if current trends continue, the population will eventually decline.

The change in population distribution over time has been likened to the digestion of a mouse by a snake. A snake swallows a mouse whole and thereby gets a big lump in its throat. The body of the mouse then moves slowly through the digestive system of the snake. The bump in the snake gets smaller and smaller as the mouse is slowly digested. The movement from head to tail can be considered analogous to the aging of a generation, and digestion to its gradual dying. The problem with guessing what a snake will look like tomorrow is that the observer doesn't know when, or what, the snake will eat next. Once a mouse is in the snake's body, it is easy to predict what will happen to the shape of the snake. So it is with population distributions. Once a generation has been born, demographers can predict quite accurately how that generation will change. However, accurate prediction of the size of the next generation is extremely difficult. The size of the generation of childbearing age gives clues but not definitive information. For example, Figure 7–7 shows that the distribution for Sweden had a broad base in 1910. Not knowing anything about changes in vital rates, one would predict a similar shape in 1930. However, in 1930, the base of the age distribution was pinched. This pinch occurred as a result of the social and economic effects of World War I. With fewer eligible males in the population, there were fewer marriages and thus fewer births. A demographer would have had to predict World War I as well as its profound economic and social effects on all of Europe

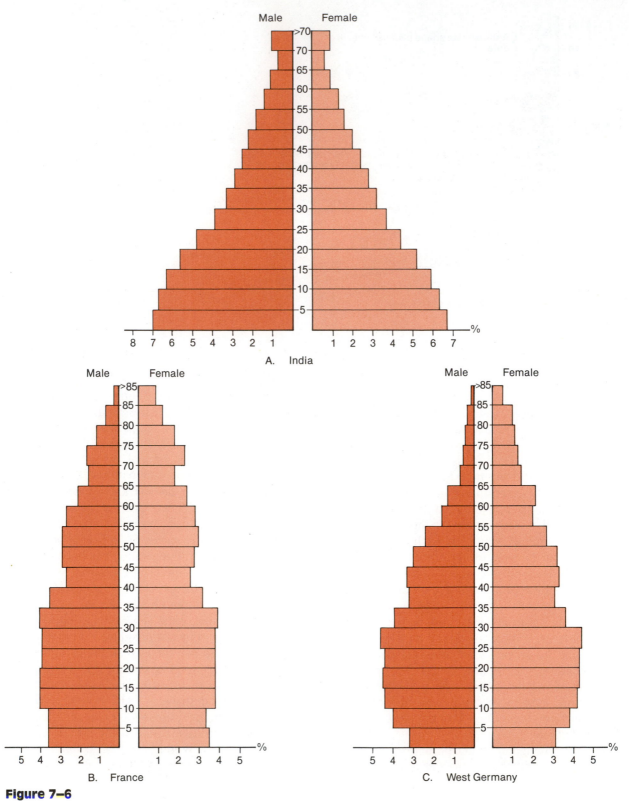

Figure 7–6
Age–sex distributions for three nations. *A,* India, a rapidly expanding population. *B,* France, a stable population. *C,* West Germany, a declining population. (From *U.N. Demographic Yearbook,* 1984)

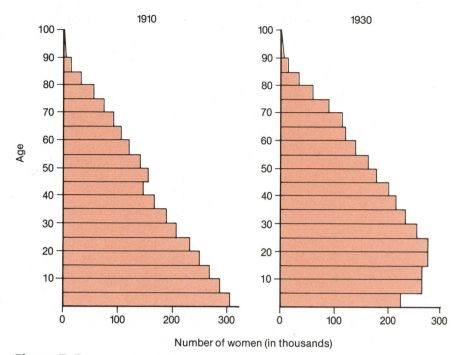

Figure 7–7
Female age distribution in Sweden in 1910 and 1930.

to have accurately projected the population of Sweden from 1910 to 1930.

The discussion thus far has shown some of the techniques used in making demographic predictions and also some of the uncertainties involved. Additional indicators are available that are helpful in foreseeing future changes.

As previously stated, the death rate is computed by dividing the total number of deaths by the total population. But the death of a person in the reproductive or prereproductive age group will have a greater impact on the rate of population growth than the death of a grandparent. Therefore, the rate of **infant mortality** is often used in conjunction with death rates. Infant mortality can be expressed as:

$$\text{Infant mortality (\%)} = \frac{\text{number of infant deaths}}{\text{number of live births}} \times 100\%$$

Similarly, the birth rate tells us how many births are occurring in the population as a whole but gives us no indication of current fertility patterns. The **total fertility rate (TFR)** is the total number of children a woman in a given population can be expected to bear during the course of her life if birth rates remain constant for at least one generation. The **replacement level** is the value of the TFR that corresponds to a population exactly replacing itself. In the developed countries, where hygiene and medical attention are superior, the replacement level is 2.1, whereas in the less-developed world, the insufficiency of medical services has led to high infant mortality, and the replacement level is about 2.7. There is considerable variability in TFRs. In 1985, Kenya had the fastest growing population in the world, with a TFR of 8.1, leading to a rate of natural increase of 4.1 percent per year. On the other hand, in Sweden, the TFR was 1.55, well below the replacement level. Therefore, if current trends continue and if immigration is kept low, the population will actually decrease.

If a demographer knows how many females of reproductive age there are in a population from the age-sex distribution and the average number of births per female from the TFR, and *if birth rates do not change*, it is relatively easy to predict the population in the next generation. In reality, vital rates do change through changing patterns of social behavior. They are also influenced by external factors such as war, migration, famine, or changes in hygiene or the availability of medical attention. If the TFR changes unpredictably, the demographic prediction will be wrong.

7.4
Current Worldwide Population Trends

In the beginning of this chapter, we looked at a graph of the size of the human population throughout history and asked ourselves how we could extrapolate the curve to predict future trends. However, Figure 7–1 by itself does not provide enough information on which to base a reliable extrapolation. To illustrate how demographic data provide a more detailed profile of trends in population growth, look at Figure 7–8 and compare it with Figure 7–1. Figure 7–8 shows the global rate of growth of the human population. You can see that the rate of growth peaked at 2.06 percent in 1970, and then declined to 1.7 percent in 1986. This decline was caused by declining birth rates in many regions of the world.

You may ask, "If the rate of growth is declining, why does the population continue to increase?" This question can be answered in two parts: 1. Any positive rate of growth will lead to an increase in the population. If the rate of growth declines but still remains positive, the increase will be less than it would have been if the rate of growth had been constant or had increased, but the population will continue to grow (Fig. 7–9). 2.

In recent years, even though the rate of growth has declined, the number of newborn infants has increased every year. This increase has occurred because the base population is increasing. For example, when the population of the world was 3.8 billion, the rate of growth was about 2 percent, leading to 3,800,000,000 × 0.02 = 76 million new infants annually. In 1986, the rate of growth had decreased to 1.7 percent, but the population had increased to 5 billion, leading to 5,000,000,000 × 0.017 = 85 million new infants.

On the one hand, these data are alarming. Population continues to increase. There are 85 million new mouths to feed every year, about 2.7 new babies every second. On the other hand, the decline in the rate of growth gives reason for hope, because, if this trend continues, the population will eventually stabilize.

Look again at Figure 7–6. As you can see, the age–sex distribution for India, a less-developed country, is quite different from that of France and West Germany, two developed countries. Because this observation is a general one, demographers often study the developed and the less-developed nations separately.

In general, the wealthier, industrialized, developed nations are experiencing low birth rates and a low rate of growth, leading to a slow in-

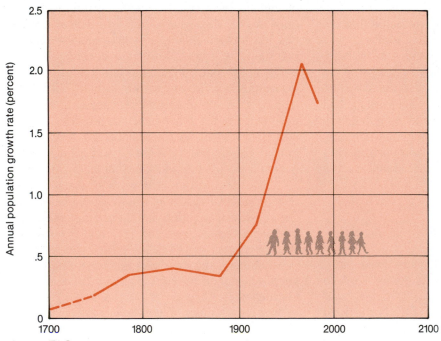

Figure 7–8
The rate of growth of the world population from 1700 to 1985.

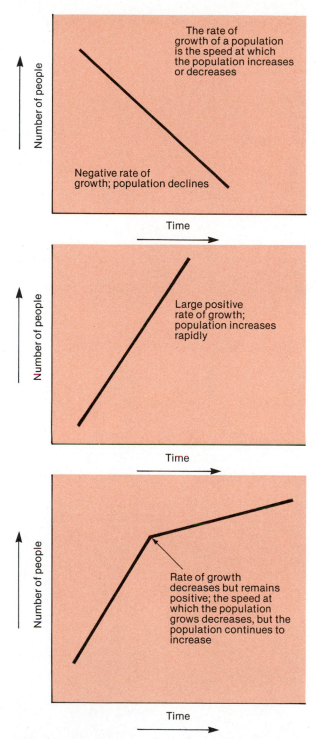

Figure 7–9

The relationship between rates of growth and increases in population. Note that as long as the rate of growth is positive, the population will increase. Thus, although the rate of population growth has slowed in recent years, it is still positive (see Fig. 7–8). The global population is still increasing rapidly, although not as rapidly as it would have if the rate had continued to increase.

crease in population. On the other hand, the rate of growth in most of the poor, primarily agrarian, less-developed countries is still increasing rapidly, because birth rates are high. The differences between the two regions are summarized in Table 7–1. Notice that the growth rate in the less-developed countries is 2 percent, whereas in the developed countries it is only 0.6 percent.

If the growth rate is available, it is relatively easy to calculate the doubling time, the time required for the population to double in size. The formula for doubling time is derived in Appendix E. As as approximation, doubling time can be calculated according to the following relationship:

$$\text{doubling time} = \frac{0.70}{\text{growth rate}}$$

Thus, in the less-developed countries, the population is expected to double in 0.70/0.02 = 35 years, whereas the doubling time in the developed countries is 122 years. Doubling times by region are shown graphically in Figure 7–10. As you can see, in Africa, where many millions of people are already underfed or even starving, underclothed, and living without adequate hygiene or shelter, the population is expected to double every 24 years. In contrast, the average doubling time in European countries is 248 years! Think of it in this way. If current trends continue, in 100 years, a group of one million Africans will double in number approximately four times and increase to 16 million, whereas in the same time period, an initial population of one million Europeans would increase to less than 1.5 million.

7.5
Populations in the Less-Developed Countries—The Demographic Transition

Recall from Section 7–1 that when the social structure of a society or its level of technology changes, the birth rates and/or the death rates of its population will also change. A simplified explanation for the patterns of change in the vital rates that have occurred in many human populations is given below:

When nutrition is poor, water is unclean, and infectious disease is common, relatively few people live to adulthood. Many children are born, but many die. In some societies, half of all live-born

Table 7–1
Comparisons of Developed and Less-Developed Countries*

Feature	Developed	Less-Developed
Wealth (per capita income in U.S. dollars)	High	Low
Industrialization	High	Low
Energy use per capita	High	Low
Illiteracy rate	Low (1%–4%)	High (75%)
Per capita food intake	High (3100–3500 cal/day)	Low (1500–2700 cal/day)
Crude birthrate	Low (1.6%)	High (3.1%)
Crude death rate	Lower (1.0%)	Higher (1.1%)
Rate of natural increase	Low (0.6%)	High (2.0%)
Infant mortality	Low (1.7%)	High (11%)
Total fertility rate	Low (1.9)	High (4.2)
Life expectancy at birth	High (73 yr)	Lower (50 yr)
Population under age 15	Lower (23%)	High (39%)
Doubling time	High (117 yr)	Low (35 yr)
Population projected to 2020 in millions	1,417	9,028

*Population Reference Bureau

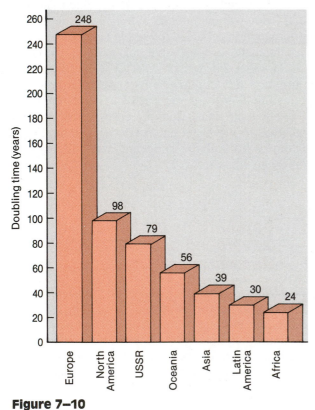

Figure 7–10
The doubling time for various regions. The doubling time is time (in years) required for the population to double in size.

In many cases, overpopulation leads to poverty. Here, homeless people sleep on the streets of New Delhi.

Birth and death rates: Sweden, 1751–1984, and
Mexico, 1895/99–1980/85

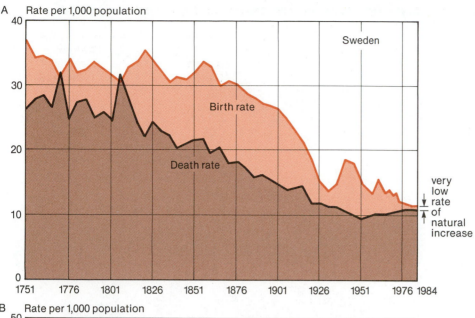

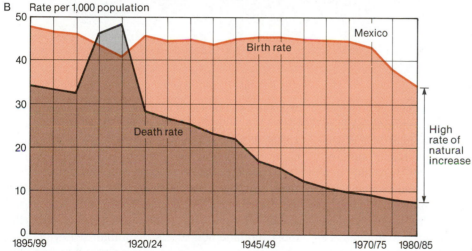

Figure 7–11

Historic trends in birth and death rates in: *A,* Sweden, a developed country,
and *B,* Mexico, a developing country. Note that the high population growth in
Mexico is due to the fact that death rates have declined faster than birth rates.
Rapid oscillations in the curves have been caused by wars, epidemics, and
periodic "baby booms."

infants do not reach their fifth birthday. As modern
principles of health care are introduced into a society, death rates start to decline.

In the developed countries, death rates have
been dropping steadily for more than a century.
During the past one hundred years, clean water has
become increasingly available, milk has been pas-
teurized, and new drugs have reduced death from
disease. In addition, improved agriculture and

more equitable distribution of food have continued
to aid in improving children's health. Therefore,
death rates have declined gradually. During this
time, people have come to understand that it is
possible to raise a family without having many babies. Consequently, the birth rate has been gradually declining for almost a century. Since birthrates
and death rates have *both* declined, the populations have remained relatively stable (Fig. 7–11).

Table 7–2
Some Typical Birth Rates and Death Rates Before, During, and After a Demographic Transition*

Representative Countries	Birth Rate (%)	Death Rate (%)	Rate of Natural Growth (%)
Very high birthrates and death rates:			
Niger	5.1	2.3	2.8
Uganda	5.0	1.7	3.4
High birthrate, moderate death rate:			
India	3.5	1.3	2.3
Bolivia	4.3	1.5	2.8
Moderate birthrate, low death rate:			
Iceland	1.8	0.9	0.9
Canada	1.5	0.7	0.8
Low birthrate, low death rate:			
Sweden	1.1	1.1	0.0
West Germany	1.0	1.1	−0.1

*Population Reference Bureau, 1986

Poor countries of the world have not experienced such gradual change. For centuries, women bore large families, and in some over half of the children died. Then, in the twentieth century, modern medicine arrived suddenly from the rich nations. Health care improved dramatically in a relatively few years. Death rates dropped very quickly. People's patterns of behavior in the less-developed nations have not had time to adjust. Birth rates are still high. With high birth rates and lower death rates, population has increased rapidly (Table 7–2).

Demographers summarize the population change of a country in the following way. Societies with primitive medical care are characterized by both high birth rates and high death rates. Since the difference is small, there is little or no growth. When modern medicine is introduced, death rates among children decline. Birth rates, however, remain relatively constant. The combined effect of these two trends—falling death rates and constant birth rates—causes the population to grow rapidly.

A rational Western observer might ask, "In many less-developed countries, poverty is endemic

and even starvation is common, so why would couples choose to have large families?" By the mid 1980s, family planning centers had made contraceptives available in many regions of the world, even in some of the poorest villages. Therefore, large families are a result of conscious choice, not mere accident. The answer to the question posed above—if there is an answer—reaches into the most fundamental levels of human behavior. One contributing factor is the relationship between children and security. This viewpoint is summed up in a recent article in *Natural History* magazine entitled "One Son is No Sons." The opening paragraph is quoted in full below:*

Devi and her five children were sitting in their village home in north India watching "Star Trek" on television. Caught up in the adventure, the children struggled to understand the English words. Their mother, meanwhile, was explaining why she was not interested in the government's program of birth control. Noting that her first four children

* Stanley A. Freed and Ruth S. Freed: One son is no sons. *Natural History*, January 1985.

High infant mortality in Bolivia is reflected by this casket shop in La Paz.

Children working in a grinding shop in New Delhi, India, to add to the family income.

were girls, Devi said, "I would have gotten sterilized if I had had sons instead of daughters in the beginning. My six-year-old son is very weak physically, which is why I want to have one more son. Girls get married and leave the village to live with their husbands; they are no longer your own. A son in the family is necessary."

The article goes on to explain that there is no government-sponsored system of social security in India, and very few people have any sort of private pension plan. Therefore, parents count on their children, especially their sons, to provide support in their old age. Furthermore, since infant and child death rates remain quite high, there is always a significant probability that any one child might die before growing to adulthood. Therefore, a popular saying in India is "One eye is no eyes, one son is no sons."

Is there any solution? Any way out? One proposal is to institute a government-operated system

of social security. According to this argument, if people could trust the government to care for them when they were elderly, they might limit their family when they were young. Unfortunately, the governments in less-developed countries don't have the resources to institute social security, and, even if they did, most people believe that governments and policies change too frequently to be trustworthy in the long run.

Many population experts believe that population growth will decline if medical attention becomes more readily available and more effective than it is today. This argument proceeds as follows:

In the short run, medical attention leads to an increase in the population by lowering the infant mortality. However, in the long run, if people become convinced that their children will survive, they might consider having smaller families. Unfortunately, modern medical attention is also too expensive for most less-developed countries, and, even if it were available immediately, a generation would probably pass before people would become convinced that infant and child mortality were being lowered. In the meantime, population continues to expand at a rapid rate, and many people continue to starve. There are no easy answers.

7.6
Population Changes in the Developed World—Example: The United States

The demographic history of the United States is largely the history of rapidly changing patterns of fertility (Fig. 7–12); by contrast, mortality has remained relatively constant. Fertility reflects social and economic events: In the 1920s, a period of economic boom and the Great Gatsby, fertility was quite high. The TFR was then about 3.2. The TFR fell sharply throughout the years of the Great Depression. It reached a low of about 2.2 in 1936. During World War II, in spite of the fact that many men were overseas, the fertility rate increased steadily. In 1946, the year after the war ended, the TFR was about 2.5. At that time, demographers and social scientists believed that the trend was due to

the return of war veterans. They predicted that fertility would soon decrease. Instead, it rose rapidly to a peak of 3.7 in the late 1950s. Analysts then attributed the rise to economic and social well-being. Businesses that specialized in baby products flourished; the middle class began in earnest its flight from the cities to provide its children with "fresh air" and places to play. Schools became overcrowded; communities couldn't build schools fast enough to keep pace with the growing numbers of children. Experts predicted a continued pattern of high births. Then, suddenly and inexplicably, the TFR began to drop quite rapidly. In 1971, it fell below the replacement level of 2.1 and continued to fall until 1976. Fluctuations occurred between 1976 and 1986 when the TFR reached a new low of 1.7.

Although few experts were able to predict the decline in TFR, explanations are offered in retrospect. During the 1970s, many women attained high levels of education and sought challenging career opportunities. In many instances, women chose to delay childbearing until later in life, to have only one or two children, or even to forego

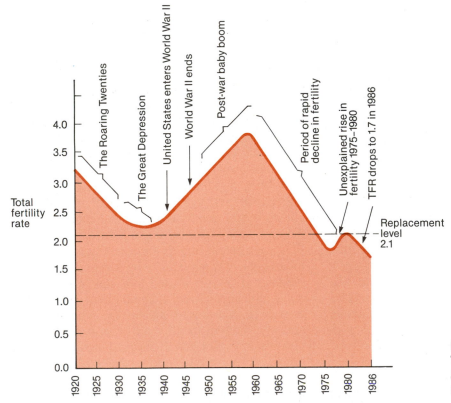

Figure 7–12

Total fertility rate for the United States 1925–1986. (From U.S. Bureau of the Census)

bearing children altogether in exchange for alter-native pursuits. As the decade progressed, a general change in attitude about family size developed. Whereas in prior generations many couples felt satisfied and proud if they raised a large family, in the 1970s many couples opted for the personal, materialistic, and economic advantages of a small family. These choices were facilitated by the easy access to effective means of birth control.

During the first half of the 1980s, the TFR rose above the 1976 low, and then dropped again. When the TFR is below replacement level, the population may continue to grow for awhile if there is a disproportionate number of young persons. To understand this concept, look at the age–sex distribution for the United States in 1980 (Fig. 7–13B). Note the bulge formed by the age group between 25 and 35

In developed countries many recreational and career opportunities are available for women. As a result, many women make a conscious choice to delay childbirth, to raise small families, or to have no children at all.

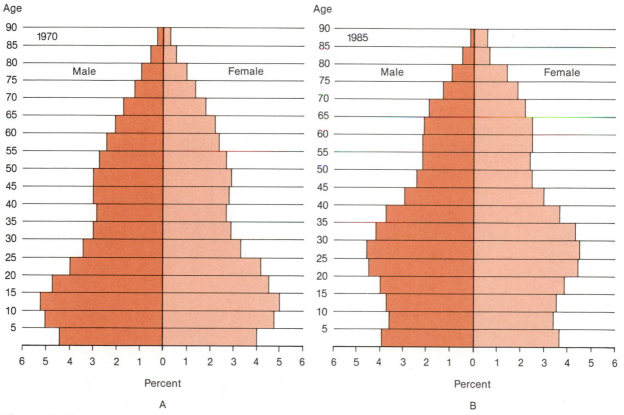

Figure 7–13
The age distribution in the United States, 1970 and 1985. *A,* Note that in 1970, the postwar baby boom children were between 5 and 15 years old. *B,* Fifteen years later, this group was between 20 and 30 years old and had entered the reproductive age group. Therefore, we can expect an increase in population, even if women bear children at the replacement level.

U.S. Population, as of July 1, 1985, was 239.3 Million People		
If	Then The Population Will	And Will
1. The TFR rises to 2.1 and immigration (legal and illegal) is 800,000 per year,	be 337 million by the year 2025	continue to increase indefinitely.
2. The TFR stabilizes at 1.8 and immigration stabilizes at 400,000 per year,	reach 270 million by the year 2035,	stabilize at that level.
3. The TFR decreases to 1.6 by 1987 and immigration decreases to 150,000 per year,	reach 241 million by the year 2007,	stabilize at that level.

years. These adults were the baby boom infants born in the late 1950s and early 1960s. Today, this large group of people is in the reproductive age group. Even if all the women in this group bear children at less than the replacement level, the population will increase.

Once again we come to the question of how to predict the future. As stated earlier, population curves can be extrapolated accurately if we know the TFR and the age–sex distribution and *if current trends continue.* But current trends change, and the experts are often fooled. Subtle changes in social attitude can lead to drastic change in TFR, which in turn leads to significant changes in growth rates. The Census Bureau has attempted to predict the U.S. population into the early part of the twenty-first century. There are two major uncertainties in formulating this prediction: (1) How will the TFR change in the future, and (2) what will the level of immigration be? Since these factors cannot be predicted with certainty, three different scenarios are proposed.

The Aging of a Population

Look back at Figure 7–13A and *B.* Note that between 1970 and 1985, the baby boom bulge in the population distribution moved steadily upward. (Remember the snake digesting the mouse.) This trend will continue, so that by the year 2000 the average age of the population will be significantly older than it is today. Also contributing to the same effect is the fact that people can expect to live longer now than they used to.

As a result, there will be a higher proportion of old people in the future population than in the present one. This change in the age distribution has profound effects on the economy. Old people are often retired, and are therefore not direct wage earners. Today, many are supported by pensions or by Social Security. The Social Security system was established on a pay-as-you-go basis. Thus, the money that an individual pays in this year is not saved for his or her pension but is used directly for paying the pension of an older person alive today. The system was established under the premise that the ratio of workers to retired persons would remain high. In 1950, there were 16 workers for every retiree. This ratio dropped to 3-to-1 by 1980 and is expected to drop further to 2-to-1 by the year 2020 (Fig. 7–14). These changes will have a profound effect on the Social Security System. Some economists predict that the Social Security tax will have to be increased drastically. Others project that benefits will have to be reduced, or that the system will fail entirely.

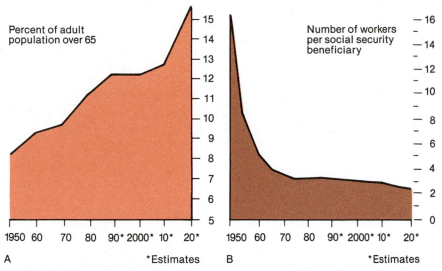

Percent of adult population over 65

15
14
13
12
11
10
9
8
7
6
5

1950 60   70   80   90* 2000* 10*   20*

A   *Estimates

Number of workers per social security beneficiary

— 16
— 14
— 12
— 10
— 8
— 6
— 4
— 2
— 0

1950 60   70   80   90* 2000* 10*   20*

B   *Estimates

Figure 7–14
Changes in the age distribution in the United States will place a growing burden on the active workers to support an increasing number of retired people. (*A,* from U.S. Bureau of the Census; *B,* from U.S. Social Security Administration)

7.7
Predicting the Future Population of the Earth

Predictions of future populations are always uncertain. Dramatic upsets such as major wars, cataclysmic geological changes, and global climatic shifts are, by their very nature, unforeseeable. But even in a relatively stable global environment, fertility and mortality rates may change quite rapidly in response to social and political trends.

If the Earth were infinitely large, the human population might possibly continue to increase indefinitely. But our planet and our resources are certainly finite; therefore, the continued increase in population must eventually stop, that is, **zero population growth** must be achieved. Perhaps the two most important questions in demography are: 1. When will zero population growth be realized? 2. What will the population be at that time?

As one limit, imagine what would happen if by some miracle, birth rates were reduced to the replacement level today. As previously explained, even if this nearly impossible event were to occur, the human population would continue to increase, because, in most countries, especially the less-developed ones, there is a disproportionately large

number of women in the reproductive and prereproductive age groups. For example, in 1985 nearly 40 percent of the females in India were in the prereproductive age groups, and an even larger number of women were between 15 and 39. Even if women began to bear children at the replacement level immediately, the population would rise until it is 1.6 times as great as it is now.

Of course this discouraging analysis is only a beginning, for no one expects birth rates to drop to the replacement level overnight. In order to extrapolate trends accurately, it is necessary to return to an analysis of birth rates and death rates. A summary of vital rates for the developed and the less-developed countries is given in Table 7–3.

Less-Developed Countries   As shown in Table 7–3, the death rates in the less-developed countries have dropped by almost one third during this century. Since 1960, birth rates have also been dropping, but at a much slower rate. As the death rates in the less-developed countries approach those of the developed areas, the decline will necessarily level off. If birth rates continue to decline as expected, the rate of natural increase will diminish. However, population growth rates are still extremely high, and there is a long way to go before zero population growth is reached.

Table 7–3
Vital Rates for the Less-Developed and the Developed Nations 1900–1985

Period	Less-Developed Nations			Developed Nations		
	Birth Rate (%)	Death Rate (%)	Rate of Natural Increase (%)	Birth Rate (%)	Death Rate (%)	Rate of Natural Increase (%)
1900–1950	4.1	3.2	0.9	2.6	1.8	0.8
1951–1960	4.3	2.2	2.1	2.2	1.0	1.2
1961–1970	4.1	1.7	2.4	2.0	0.9	1.1
1971–1980	3.7	1.5	2.2	1.9	0.9	1.0
1981–1985	3.1	1.1	2.0	1.6	1.0	0.6

There are marked differences in the TFR and the natural rate of increase within the less-developed countries (Fig. 7–15 and Table 7–4). The TFR is declining rapidly in China, parts of Southeast Asia, and a few countries in South America. Significant but less dramatic changes have occurred in India, Egypt, Mexico, Chile, Argentina, and Paraguay. However, the TFR is constant or even rising throughout most of Africa, Southwest Asia, and parts of Latin America, although many of the people in these regions are already experiencing debilitating poverty, inadequate diets, and abysmal living conditions. It is difficult to predict when birth rates in these regions will drop.

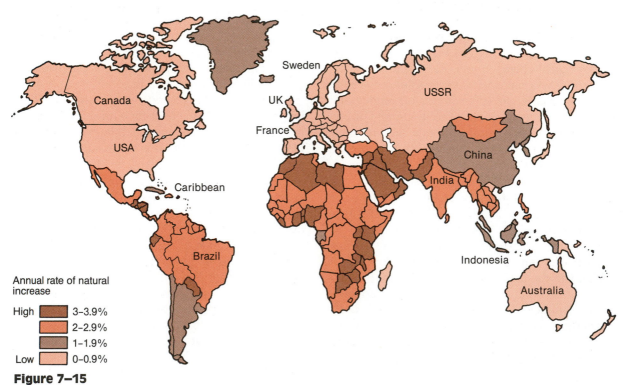

Figure 7–15
The annual rate of natural increase for the countries of the world. (Source: *U.N. Demographic Yearbook*, 1984).

Table 7–4
Total Fertility Rate by Region (1986)*

Africa	6.3
Latin America	4.1
Asia	3.7
Oceania	2.7
USSR	2.4
North America	1.8
Europe	1.8

*Population Reference Bureau

Developed Countries   The TFR in many developed countries is already well below the replacement level. In a few regions, population growth has all but stopped, and, in many more, rates of growth are expected to stabilize by the turn of the century. Many demographers predict a rapid approach to zero population growth.

Population Predictions   In 1986, the world population was about 5 billion people. Although the rates of growth are expected to decrease in all areas of the world except Africa and Latin America, the actual population almost certainly will continue to increase. In the mid 1980s, approximately three quarters of the people in the world (3.75 billion) live in the less-developed countries, and only one fourth (1.25 billion) live in the developed regions. Because rates of growth are higher in the less-developed countries and there are more people to begin with, demographers expect that most of the increase in population in the next century will occur in the poorer regions of the world (Fig. 7–16).

Readers should be aware that Figure 7–16 is a prediction that may or may not prove to be correct. Figure 7–17 illustrates other predictions. Almost all projections assume that the population will eventually stabilize in a smooth and orderly manner. However, such a transition is not guaranteed. There is always the possibility of a disaster. In such a scenario, the population will continue to increase rapidly until the carrying capacity of the Earth is greatly exceeded, and then starvation and strife will combine to bring about a rapid drop in population. Such a pessimistic and cataclysmic outcome is illustrated by the colored line in Figure 7–17.

7.8
Consequences of Population Density

What would life on our planet be like if there were two or even three times as many people in the world as there are today? As the population density in a given area increases, each person's propor-

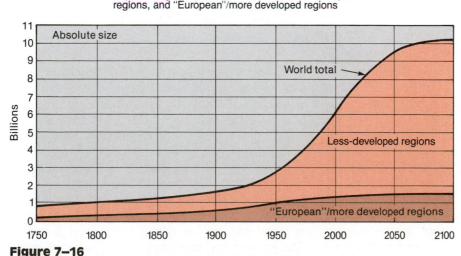

Figure 7–16
Projected population growth to the year 2100. Note that by far the greatest increase in population is expected to occur in the less-developed regions.

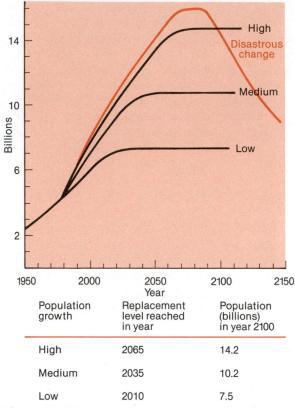

Population growth	Replacement level reached in year	Population (billions) in year 2100
High	2065	14.2
Medium	2035	10.2
Low	2010	7.5

Figure 7–17
Four different predictions for world population growth.

tionate share of the available supplies of land, water, fuels, wood, metals, and other resources must necessarily decrease. (Since the distribution is never proportional, the poor often become much worse off.) In the past, people in many parts of the world have raised their standard of living despite a rising population by developing new resources or by using available resources with increased efficiency. But millions of others have recently fallen into dismal poverty, leading to hunger and starvation.

No one knows what the ultimate carrying capacity of the Earth is. Some suggest that, given a stable political climate (in particular, a sharp drop in today's excessive global military expenditures) and some key advances in technology, the planet could comfortably support a human population of 13 or 14 billion. According to one argument, population growth should even be encouraged because people generate new ideas and staff the laboratories and factories that can provide techno-

logical solutions and machinery to solve the problems of the world. Others claim that we have already exceeded the carrying capacity of global ecosystems and are sustaining ourselves artificially on nonrenewable resources. This argument predicts that the human race is rushing headlong toward an unprecedented calamity that may lead to the deaths of billions of people.

In a sense, much of the rest of this book is an examination of the limits of human population growth and the consequences of population density. Appropriate chapters will address such key questions as: How many people can be fed on a sustained basis by global agricultural systems? Will useful energy be exhausted in the near future? How much metal, fertilizer, and water will be available? How does pollution affect our lives?

If the future of humans is to be a gloomy one, the quality of life on Earth will steadily deteriorate as the population increases. Many forests and wild places will disappear and be replaced by cities and indoor environments. Under ideal conditions, a city can be a pleasant environment for many. Given money, mobility, and freedom from oppressive pollution, a wealthy urbanite can enjoy excellent career opportunities, the best medical attention, theaters, art, fine restaurants, and an intellectually stimulating society. But this reality is a privilege for only a fortunate minority. In less-developed countries, unskilled workers often cannot find jobs in the countryside. As a result, millions of jobless poor have been moving into the cities. Yet the cities are often unable to provide relief for these people, and many live in unbelievably squalid slums. This topic, too, will be examined in greater detail in later chapters.

Social Consequences of Population Density Some people have claimed that a high population density naturally leads to violence, disunity, and political upheavals. This opinion has been supported by a series of experiments with strains of domestic rats. In one such study, cages were supplied with enough food and water for many more rats than the space would normally hold. A few animals were placed in each cage and allowed to breed. The population and the density grew quickly, and the animals began to act bizarrely. The females lost their ability to build proper nests or to care for their infants. Some of the males became sexually aggressive; most retreated from

A street scene in Hong Kong. Even though this is the most densely populated city in the world, crime rates are relatively low, showing that crime and density are not necessarily related. (Stuart Franklin, Sygma)

communication with others. In short, the normal processes of socialization were destroyed.

However, all mammals do not necessarily respond in the same manner as rats. For example, when a group of chimpanzees was crowded into a small cage in a zoo in Holland, behavior patterns were very different from those that had been observed in the communities of rats. The chimpanzees established a social hierarchy. Chimps of a lower social status exhibited a behavior known as "submissive greeting" toward the more dominant animals, and members of the community spent long periods of time grooming one another.

Research into the relationship between human population density and social problems has yielded a morass of conflicting conclusions. No consistent patterns emerge when national population densities are defined as population size divided by total national area. Such densities are grossly misleading, because they do not measure population densities in populated areas. For example, the Netherlands, one of the most densely populated areas of the world, had 350 persons per square kilometer in 1986. By contrast, the population density in India was only 180 persons per square kilometer and, in Algeria, only 7 persons

per square kilometer. However, almost all of the Netherlands is inhabitable, whereas much of India is jungle, and most of Algeria is desert. Therefore, the *average* population density of the Netherlands is not so high as some *local* population densities in India and Algeria. Thus, the stability of Dutch society does not by itself disprove a hypothesis that high population densities are socially detrimental. These examples are not isolated instances, because the 62 percent of the Earth's surface that is semiarid, taiga, tropical jungle, arctic tundra, or desert holds only 1 percent of its population.

The social consequences of population density on arable land are also confusing. Japan, which supports 1700 persons per square kilometer of arable land, is an example of a very densely populated country that maintains a prosperous and relatively crime-free society.

Some psychologists and sociologists claim that density by itself is not relevant to the feeling of being crowded. A more important factor, they say, is the amount of space available in the individual's dwelling unit. Even here, the evidence is ambiguous. Hong Kong has probably the highest residential density ever known in the world. Nearly 40 percent of the residents of Hong Kong share their

A typical living unit in Hong Kong. Hong Kong is the most densely inhabited city in the world and 40 percent of the residents must share their dwellings with nonrelatives. (Stuart Franklin, Sygma)

dwelling unit with nonrelatives; almost 30 percent sleep three or more to a bed, and 13 percent sleep four or more to a bed. Most of the population lives in a dwelling unit of a single room, and most dwelling units are homes to more than nine persons and to two or more unrelated families. Even under these conditions of extreme crowding, there is little or no proof that antisocial behavior is attributable to the crowding itself.

On the other hand, when one picks up a newspaper and reads about continued warfare in Central America and strife and starvation in Africa, it is easy to think Malthusian misery and vice have already overtaken us. Again, the facts do not support any direct correlation between population density and warfare or political instability. Despite the misery of the poor throughout Mexico and the dismal conditions in Mexico City itself, the Mexican government has survived 50 years without a revolution. This record of stability is better than that in many countries with a much lower population density. In Central America, the population density in Costa Rica is approximately 2.5 times as great as that in neighboring Nicaragua. Yet Nicaragua has experienced bloody civil warfare in the late 1970s and the mid 1980s, whereas Costa Rica has been internally peaceful for decades. Similarly, India, which is large, heavily populated, and poor, has experienced relatively stable conditions for decades.

Thus, there is no conclusive proof that density itself breeds antisocial behavior. One difficulty in studying the effects of population density on humans is that spatial requirements may, in part, be culturally determined. Much sociological research is needed to gain an understanding of the factors that cause members of different societies to feel crowded.

7.9
Case History: Population and Public Policy in the People's Republic of China

Approximately 1 billion individuals—one fifth of the world's population—live in the People's Republic of China. Between 1950 and 1980, the population of that country increased by about 400 million people; this increase is nearly twice the size of the population of the United States in 1980. In 1957, one of China's most prominent economists, Ma Yinghu, published a paper claiming that the rapid population rise was interfering with economic development and threatening to nullify important gains in agriculture and industry. At that time, the official government policy stated that more people meant more production; therefore, population expansion should be encouraged. For his boldness in contradicting established policy, Mr. Yinghu was

Figure 7–18
Billboard in Beijing, capital of China. The picture shows a couple with a young girl to show families that it is not necessary to continue to have children until a son is born. (Photo courtesy of Jack Tackle)

removed from his post at the Beijing University and publicly denounced.

During the 1960s and 1970s, continued modernization in China led to further increases in agricultural and industrial output. However, the standard of living of the average person remained constant during that time because the additional goods and services were needed to support the growing population. In 1978, official policy changed, and the government announced its intentions to reduce population growth.

In order to realize this goal, birth control devices and medical abortions became available, free, for all citizens. In addition, a countrywide information campaign promoted the idea "Later Longer Fewer," which meant to marry late, space their births at long intervals, and to have few children (Fig. 7–18).

Advice and free contraceptive devices were only the first step. In the late 1970s and mid-1980s, the Chinese government began to promote a set of rewards for couples who chose to have only one child and punishments for those who have larger families. Although the exact rules are established by local authorities and vary from region to region, a typical system is as follows: A newly married couple is asked to sign an agreement to have only one child. If the agreement is signed, the first child will receive free medical care, free education, and preferential treatment in obtaining jobs. The couple is rewarded by receiving special consideration for better housing and 13 months pay every year. Newlyweds who refuse to sign the agreement receive no benefits and must pay for the health and education of their children. Those who sign the agreement and then elect to have two or more children are punished with official reprisals, pay cuts, loss of seniority in the workplace, and low priority in finding adequate housing.

This incredibly austere program has had immediate results. As shown in Figure 7–19A and B, the birth rate and the TFR in China have declined drastically in recent years, leading to a rapid decline in the rate of natural increase. In 1985, the TFR was just about equal to the replacement level.

In initiating this program, the Chinese government made a conscious choice between two different sets of problems. If the fertility rate had been

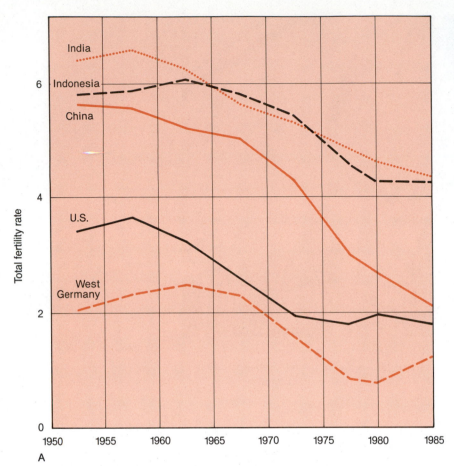

A

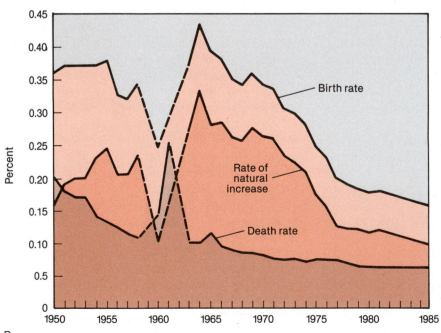

B

Figure 7–19

A, The TFR for some representative countries. Note that the TFR in China is dropping faster than in any other region. *B,* Changes in vital rates in China from 1950 to 1985. Note that a rapidly falling birth rate has led to a rapid decline in the rate of natural increase.

allowed to grow unchecked, the rapidly rising population would have placed a heavy burden on the land. On the other hand, as explained earlier, when fertility rates decline rapidly, fewer babies are born and the percentage of old people in the population increases. Therefore, a social problem results in which a large group of old people must be supported by a relatively small group of young workers. This is a problem that must be faced by the Chinese people in the years ahead.

Even though birth rates have dropped below the TFR, the Chinese population will continue to increase. This demographic momentum is the result of the large number of people now in the reproductive and prereproductive age groups. Demographers estimate that if current trends in fertility and mortality continue, the population will reach 1.2 billion by the year 2000 and then level off at 1.5 billion by the year 2075. If a high percentage of the women in the population continue to have only one child, the population will eventually decline.

A program such as that initiated by the Chinese is only possible in a totalitarian government. It would not be acceptable in a free society. In most regions, people do not believe that the government has the right to legislate family size. People also ask, "Why should a second, third, or fourth child, who didn't ask to be born, be punished?" The example of China, therefore, represents the recognition of the problems of population growth along with the use of extremely severe measures to control it.

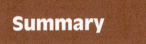

Summary

Since the onset of the industrial revolution, the human population has been increasing at a rapid rate. Prediction of future population size should be performed on the basis of a variety of different vital rates. **Birth and death rates** are the number of births or deaths as a percentage of the population as a whole. The **rate of natural increase** is the birth rate minus the death rate. The shape of an **age–sex distribution** reflects past history and provides insights into future growth. The **total fertility rate** (TFR) is the total number of children a woman can be expected to bear during the course of her life if birth rates remain constant for at least one generation. The rate of **infant mortality** is the death rate of newborn infants.

The rate of growth of the global population has been declining, but the rate remains positive, so the population continues to grow. Growth rates in the developed countries are much less than those in the less-developed countries.

Societies that have inadequate medical services are characterized by both high birth and high death rates and very little overall population change. Modern medicine leads to a rapid decrease in mortality among children but does not affect birth rates appreciably. Therefore, the population rises rapidly. Slowly, in response to economic trends, the birth rate falls, and the population size stabilizes once more. This pattern of changing vital rates is called the **demographic transition.**

Mortality has remained relatively constant in the United States but fertility has been variable. There is a wide difference in opinion concerning future growth patterns in the United States. The prediction for the year 2000 and beyond is for an increasingly elderly population.

Birth rates are falling in many countries of the world, but an increase in the present world population is virtually certain. In 1986 the global population was about 5 billion. Demographers expect the population to stabilize somewhere between 7.5 and 14 billion, with most of the increase occurring in the less-developed countries.

Dense populations strain the available resources, and the worst possible circumstances may lead to dismal living conditions or mass starvation. However, it is very difficult to assess the social effects of human crowding. Experiments with animals suggest that crowding produces antisocial behavior, but the relevance of these findings to the human condition is unclear.

Questions

Demography

1. Explain how the agricultural revolution and the industrial revolution affected the growth of the human population.

2. How would you expect each of the following to affect population growth? Consider which age groups are most likely to be affected by each event and how the event affects population change: (a) famine; (b) war; (c) lowering of marital age; (d) development of an effective method of birth control; (e) outbreak of a cholera epidemic; (f) severe and chronic air pollution; (g) lowering of infant mortality; (h) institution of a social security system; (i) economic depression; (j) economic boom; (k) institution of child labor laws; (l) expansion of employment opportunities for women.

3. Explain the difference between the birth rate and the TFR. How would a small rise in the TFR affect the birth rate in West Germany? Would the effect be any different if the TFR rose in India? Explain. (Hint: Study Figure 7–6 before attempting to answer this question.)

4. Explain the difference between the death rate and the infant mortality rate. Why is the infant mortality rate an important demographic indicator?

5. Predict the age–sex distribution for India, France, and West Germany in 15 years if current trends continue. Redraw a curve for 15 years from now for: (a) India if the TFR dropped to the replacement level; (b) West Germany if the TFR rose to 4.0; (c) France if the TFR dropped to 1.0.

6. What is the replacement level? If women in the United States bear children at the replacement level, will zero population growth be realized immediately? Why or why not? Explain.

7. Would it be practical to stop population growth in India immediately with an active family planning program? Discuss.

8. Explain the difference between a declining population level and a declining rate of growth.

9. Draw a graph showing how the population changes when rate of population growth: (a) is high, then decreases but remains positive; (b) is negative and then becomes positive; (c) is positive and then becomes negative; (d) changes from a large negative value to a smaller negative value.

The Demographic Transition

10. What is a demographic transition? How does it arise? Compare birth rates and death rates before, during, and after a demographic transition.

11. Discuss several factors that have been responsible for reducing death rates in developed nations. How have these factors affected the less-developed nations differently from developed nations? Discuss.

12. Explain why populations in many less-developed countries have increased rapidly in recent years.

13. In general, the death rates in the developed countries are lower than those in the less-developed countries, yet the population is growing faster in the less-developed countries. Explain.

14. Explain how improved medical care, which lowers infant mortality, could actually lead to a decrease in the rate of growth of a population.

15. Rapid introduction of medical care in poorer countries has led to rapid population growth. In many cases, this population growth has, in turn, led to starvation and misery. Do you believe that people should stop sending medical aid to developing nations? Or should they send more aid? Defend your choice.

16. List and discuss briefly an economic, a political, and a social factor that is important in determining birth rates.

17. Is it likely that birth rates in the less-developed nations will decrease to the replacement level within the next 5 years? Discuss.

Demographic Changes in Developed Countries

18. Explain why a sudden decrease in the TFR will lead to a population with a high percentage of old people.

19. Discuss the relationship between changing social patterns and the TFR in the United States.

20. Explain why economic factors encourage a couple to have several children in India, whereas economic factors favor fewer children in the United States.

21. How large was the family that your grandparents grew up in? Your parents? How many children are there in your family? How many children do you think an average family in a country such as the United States should have? Compare your answers with the answers of your classmates. Discuss in terms of changes in population growth rates.

Social Policy

22. In the United States, the income-tax deduction for each child in constant U.S. dollars has decreased in the past 25 years. How do you think this change in the tax law could affect family size?

23. If you had the responsibility of discouraging population growth, would you consider reducing income tax deductions if a family has more than four children? Reducing health benefits? Whom would such policies harm?

24. Discuss the effects of population growth in your community. How do these problems compare with the problems of population growth in the less-developed nations?

Suggested Readings

The population data for this chapter were taken from the following sources:

Population Reference Bureau: *World Population Data Sheet.* Washington D.C., 1986.

Population Reference Bureau: *Planet Earth 1984–2034: A Demographic Vision.* Washington D.C., 1984.

Population Reference Bureau: *World Population in Transition.* Washington D.C., 1986.

U.N. Statistical Office: *Demographic Yearbook 1984.* New York, 1984.

U.N. Statistical Office: *Population and Vital Statistics Report.* New York, Supplement update to January, 1985.

U. S. Bureau of Census: *Estimates of the Population of the United States by Age, Sex, and Race: 1980 to 1985.* 1986.

For a discussion of the effects of crowding on rats, see:

John B. Calhoun: *Scientific American, 206:*139, February 1962.

Several periodical articles of interest are:

Lester R. Brown and Edward C. Wolf: Global prospects. *Not Man Apart,* March-April, 1985.

Ansley J. Coale: Recent trends in fertility in less developed countries. *Science, 221*:828, August 1983.

Paul R. Ehrlich and Anne H. Ehrlich: World population crisis. *Bulletin of the Atomic Scientist, 42*:4, April 1986.

Stanley A. Freed and Ruth S Freed: One son is no sons. *Natural History,* January 1985.

Davidson R Gwatkin and Sarah K. Brandel: Life expectancy and population growth in the third world. *Scientific American, 246*:5, May 1982.

Nathan Keyfitz: The population of China. *Scientific American, 250*:2, February 1984.

Anne Firth Murray: A global accounting. *Environment, 27*:6, 1985.

Jeannie Peterson: Global population projections through the 21st century. *Ambio, 13*:3, 1984.

John Tierney: Fanisi's choice. *Science, 86*: January/February, p. 26, 1986.

8

Soil and Agriculture

8.1
Introduction

As the population of the Earth soars past the 5 billion mark and seems destined to climb even higher, people are seriously asking how many people our planet can actually support. This concern is not new. Recall from Chapter 1 that in 1789, the Reverend Thomas Malthus postulated that food production increased arithmetically, whereas population increased exponentially. Therefore, he concluded that starvation was inevitable, and, with starvation, the human race was doomed to a future of "misery and vice." In fact, in modern times, starvation is a serious problem in many regions of the world. On the other hand, if we look at global averages, not at regional problems, Malthus' predictions have been proved to be incorrect. Over the course of the past 200 years, worldwide food production has generally kept pace with the exponential rise in the human population (Fig. 8–1). The rapid increase in global food production has been brought about by very large increases both in the productivity of existing farmland and in the amount of land that is being farmed. In addition, increased availability and efficiency of transportation have enabled people to ship food from one area or continent to another and, therefore, to alleviate problems arising from local drought or pestilence. Yet, the Malthusian doctrine cannot be ignored, because a global carrying capacity does exist and our planet cannot support an infinite number of people. In this and the following three chapters, we will examine agriculture and land use, study past trends, and attempt to look into the future.

8.2
Plant Nutrients

Plants are autotrophs and therefore produce their own food from inorganic substances. The major elements required by all living organisms, plant and animal, are carbon, oxygen, and hydrogen. Plants obtain carbon and oxygen from carbon dioxide and oxygen in the air, and hydrogen and oxygen from water. In addition, plants need many different mineral nutrients, most of which they obtain from the soil. Some minerals, collectively called the **macronutrients,** are used in relatively large quantities. The important macronutrients are nitrogen, phosphorus, potassium, calcium, magnesium,

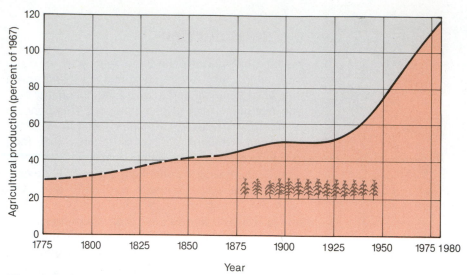

Figure 8–1

Total agricultural productivity in the United States from 1775 to 1980. Note that the greatest increases did not occur in the 1700s and 1800s as the country was being settled. It was the industrial and chemical revolutions of the 1900s that brought the most rapid change in productivity. Note also that the increase in production has been accelerating and is not linear as Malthus had predicted.

and sulfur. Those needed in the largest amounts are nitrogen, phosphorus, and potassium. Commercial fertilizers are rated by the percentages of these elements that they contain, for example, 5-10-5 fertilizer contains 5 percent nitrogen, 10 percent phosphorus, and 5 percent potassium by weight.*

In addition to macronutrients, plants require tiny quantities of several different **micronutrients,** often called trace nutrients or trace minerals. For instance, whereas crops use several hundred kilograms of nitrogen per hectare per year, the treatment for molybdenum-deficient soils in Australia is 140 g of molybdenum oxide per hectare, applied once every 10 years. Despite the tiny quantities involved, plants with an inadequate supply of molybdenum grow slowly and exhibit a characteristic paleness. In contrast to these general symptoms, some minerals are used in only part of a plant's development, and their deficiency symptoms may be quite specific. Zinc, for example, is needed to produce certain plant hormones (called auxins) that cause growing stem cells to elongate. If a plant lacks zinc, its stem cells remain so stunted that

there is little space between adjacent leaves and the plant assumes a rosette shape.

Some plants have special adaptations that demand particular nutrients. For example, legumes (plants in the pea family) are unusual in needing cobalt, a component of vitamin B used by the bacteria that live in the roots of these plants. These

**Box 8.1
Area**

The standard unit of land area used in the United States is the acre. One acre is 43,560 sq ft, equal to a square just about 209 feet on a side. Perhaps easier to visualize: A square one quarter mile long on a side contains 40 acres; 1 square mile equals 640 acres. The hectare is the accepted SI, or metric measure, of land area. A hectare is defined as 10,000 square meters, or a square 100 meters on a side. One hectare is approximately equal to two football fields plus two end zones, or 2.5 acres.

*These are all in chemically combined forms, and are not present as free elements. Elemental nitrogen is a gas, phosphorus is a toxic nonmetal, and potassium is a chemically active metal.

Onions grown on soil that does not provide them with enough zinc are severely stunted and have yellow, crooked tops (right). At left, normal onions of the same variety and age. (USDA)

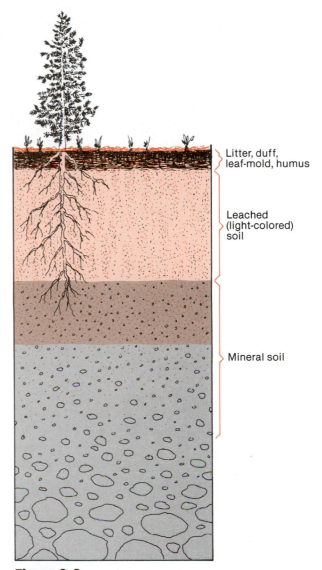

Litter, duff, leaf-mold, humus

Leached (light-colored) soil

Mineral soil

Figure 8–2

Soil profile. Note the rapid decrease in organic matter with depth.

bacteria are very important to agriculture, because they fix nitrogen from the air into a form that plants can use.

8.3
Soil Structure

Healthy soil is an integrated mixture of inorganic mineral matter and decayed organic matter. The inorganic components arise from bits and pieces of rock and minerals that have been chipped away from the Earth's crust. The organic portion of soils is formed from the decaying and decayed bodies of dead organisms. Both components are essential constituents of healthy soil (Fig. 8–2).

Inorganic Components

When bare rock is exposed to the weather, it is broken apart by a variety of processes. Wind, moving water, environmental chemicals, and changes in temperature act together to decompose exposed rock until it is ultimately degraded into very small particles. These particles form the fundamental matrix for all soils.

Most rock is composed of many independent crystals containing many different chemical compounds. Some of these chemicals may eventually be released as plant nutrients. The acidity and the

nutrient content of the resultant soil will depend, in part, on the chemical composition of the parent rock.

Soils are also categorized by several different classification schemes (Fig. 8–3). A textural classification is based on the average size of the particles that make up the body of the soil. Go outside some day and dig up some soil. Pick up a small amount of this in your hands, mix it with a little water, and rub the muddy mixture between your fingers. If the material feels distinctly gritty, it contains large particles and is a **sandy** soil. Soils with

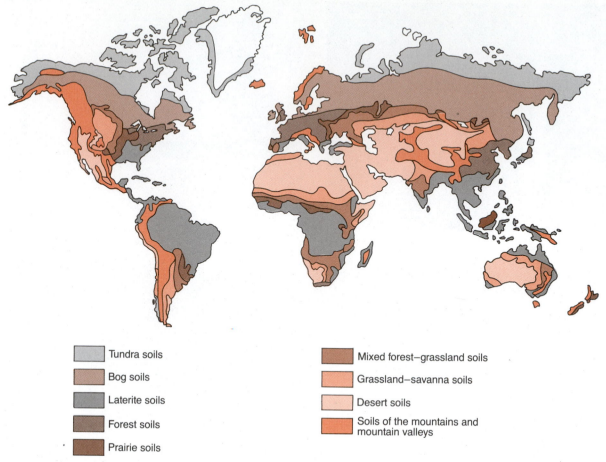

Legend:

Tundra soils

Bog soils

Laterite soils

Forest soils

Prairie soils

Mixed forest–grassland soils

Grassland–savanna soils

Desert soils

Soils of the mountains and mountain valleys

Figure 8–3

Soils of the world. (Soil scientists use a variety of different classification schemes. The terminology used in this figure represents the global soils in a generalized way.) Note how much of the world is tundra, bog, desert, mountainous, or laterite soils. Although agriculture is possible in these soils, considerable inputs are required to realize continued high yields.

smaller particles feel a little smoother and are composed of **silt.** If your sample is slippery and has a "greasy" feeling, it is probably made up of **clay.** Clay particles are so small that they can best be differentiated by looking through an electron microscope. In addition, the particles are bound together by chemical attractions, whereas in silt and sand, the particles are physically and chemically independent of one another.

Particle size influences the capacity of a soil to hold water. The water that is in contact with soil can be held in three different ways. First, some of it forms a film around the soil particles. Second, wedges of water are held between soil particles by capillary attraction. These films and wedges to-

gether make up the capillary water of the soil. Third, water may be chemically bonded to certain soils, especially clays (Fig. 8–4). When soil dries out, capillary water wedges are removed most rapidly, followed by the films around soil particles. In some instances, the bonded water is so tightly held by chemical attraction to the mineral components that plants may suffer water deficiency, even when considerable reserves remain in the soil.

In general, sandy soils have such large particles that water flows through them easily. The rapid movement of water through the layers of sand washes minerals out of the root zone, so that, other factors being equal, sand loses its reservoir of nutrients faster than other types of soil. On the other

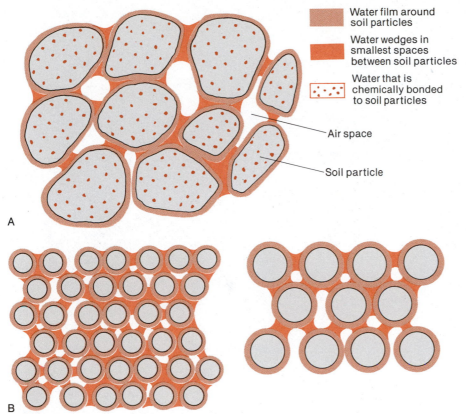

A

Water film around
soil particles

Water wedges in
smallest spaces
between soil particles

Water that is
chemically bonded
to soil particles

Air space

Soil particle

B

Figure 8–4

A, Soil water is held in three ways: (1) as capillary films around individual soil
particles, (2) as capillary wedges in small spaces between soil particles, and
(3) as water that is chemically bound into the structure of some particles, such
as certain clays. *B,* Comparison of water held by small soil particles and water
held by larger particles.

hand, clays tend to be relatively impermeable.
Rainwater falling on clayey soils tends to collect in
puddles on the surface, and the uppermost layers
of the soil become totally saturated with water. The
excess water displaces gaseous oxygen, and, without gaseous oxygen, plant roots and soil microorganisms cannot survive. Therefore, these soils become waterlogged and are not fertile.

The best soils for plant growth are those that
have a mixture of particle sizes. A soil that contains
approximately equal proportions of sand and silt
with a small amount of clay is called **loam.** Loams
are particularly favorable for sustained agriculture.

Organic Components

Soils also contain large quantities of organic matter, including both living organisms and the decomposed bodies of dead ones. The living organ-

isms are essential to the process of decay, and the
accumulated decay products are vital to the chemistry of the soil.

The complexity of root systems and the number of living organisms in fertile soil are staggering.
A single rye plant may spread as much as 650 km
of roots underground. One kilogram of rich soil
contains up to 2 trillion bacteria, 400 million fungi,
50 million algae, and 30 million protozoa, as well
as thousands of different worms, insects, and
mites. Soil organisms decompose organic matter
and convert many nutrients into forms that plants
can absorb. The burrowing of larger organisms
breaks up the soil and allows air to penetrate (Fig.
8–5). Recall from discussion in Chapter 5 that **humus** is a complex mixture of organic matter that is
formed when a given piece of tissue such as a leaf,
a stalk of grass, or a dead bird has decomposed
sufficiently in the soil system so that its origin has

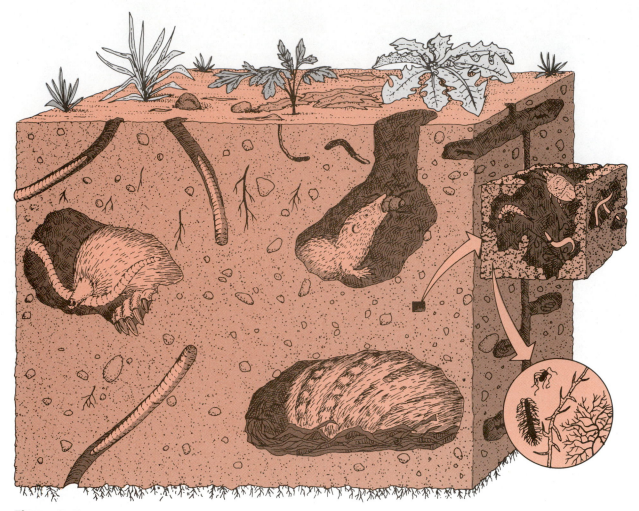

Figure 8–5

A schematic drawing showing life within the soil, from small mammals to microbes. Here we see a shrew eating a beetle, a ground squirrel burrowed safely
in its nest, and a mole eating an earthworm. These animals aerate and mix the
soil and carry nesting materials underground. The leaves and grasses used as
nests eventually rot to increase the humus content of the soil. Smaller animals,
such as earthworms and ants, are so numerous that they move more soil than
do the large animals; a colony of earthworms can circulate many tonnes of
soil in a single season. The first enlargement shows nematodes, mites, and
springtails. These creatures are barely visible to the naked eye, and the drawing is a view through a good hand lens. Nematodes destroy the roots of plants
and are destructive to agriculture. However, there is a balance, because even
under the soil, the herbivore population is controlled by various predators. In
the lower portion of this enlargement, one of the nematodes has just been captured by a thin tendril of a predatory fungus. The second enlargement shows a
view through a microscope where bacteria, fungi, and a variety of other organisms live out their lives.

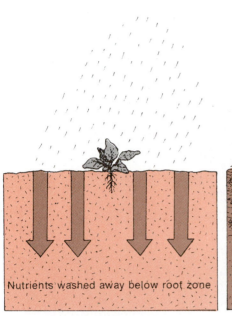
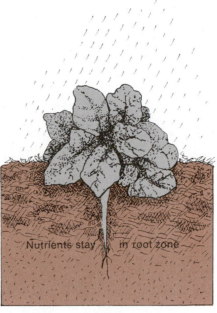

A Soil with low humus content   B Soil with high humus content

Figure 8–6
Humus retains nutrients and moisture in the soil.

become obscure. Humus is an essential component of most fertile soils. If possible, dig up some forest or rich garden soil and hold it in your hand. If it is rich in humus, it will be light and spongy. If you pour a small amount of water into it, most of it will be absorbed and very little will run off between your fingers.

Humus retains moisture both by capillarity and by chemical attraction. It also insulates the soil from excessive heat and cold and reduces evaporation. The organic matter retains so much moisture that it swells after a rain and then gradually shrinks during dry spells. This alternate shrinking and swelling keeps the soil loose, allowing roots to grow through it easily.

Another function of humus is to bind nutrients in the soil and release them in forms that are readily usable by plants (Fig. 8–6). To understand the importance of these functions, consider the fate of minerals in inorganic soils. If a mineral is highly soluble in water, it will dissolve in water droplets and can easily be transported downward through the soil until it is eventually carried into groundwater reservoirs that lie below the root zone. This movement of soluble minerals out of an ecosystem is called **leaching.** On the other hand, if a

mineral is insoluble, it will react with other compounds in the environment to form various types of solids. For example, as stated earlier, calcium ions react with atmospheric carbon dioxide and water to form calcium carbonate, the major component of limestone. This mineralization also removes nutrients from an ecosystem.

Richly humic soils provide chemical reaction pathways for metal ions that are not available in simple inorganic solutions. Certain chemicals in the humus, known as **chelating agents,** react with inorganic ions such as Ca^{2+} to form a special class of compounds known as chelation complexes. Ions bonded in chelation complexes are held tightly under some conditions but are easily released under others. A calcium ion chelated by humus will not react readily to form insoluble calcium carbonate, nor will it dissolve in water easily to be lost by leaching. Rather, it will tend to remain bonded to the chelating agent and thus be retained in the humic matter.

Plants and soil microorganisms have evolved mechanisms whereby they can release chelated ions readily and incorporate them into living tissue, as shown schematically in Figure 8–7. The specific chelation chemistry is different for each soil nu-

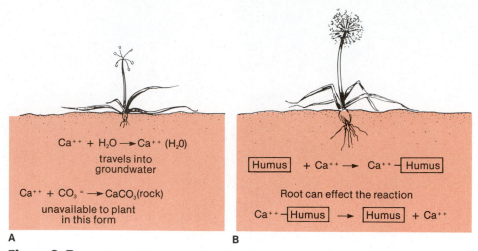

A

B

Figure 8–7

Schematic illustration of pathways for transfer of inorganic nutrients. *A,* Without humus. *B,* With humus.

trient, but, in general, humus maintains a nutrient reservoir and enhances the ease with which nutrients are used by the soil organisms. When humus is not maintained, the ability of soils to store reserves of nutrients is poor. In addition, the efficiency of converting fertilizer to plant tissue is low. As a result, large quantities of nitrogen or mineral nutrients escape from the system or are tied into the soils in chemically unusable forms.

8.4
Soils in the Tropics, the Temperate Region, and the Arctic

Because the structure of the soil varies dramatically from region to region, it is obvious that some areas will be better suited to intensive agriculture than others. Cereal crops—mainly wheat, rice, and corn—are the most important human foods. Cereals are cheap to produce, remain fresh for a long period of time when they are stored, and have high nutritional value. Many of the world's cereals are grown in a wide belt of land that stretches through the temperate zones. These zones cover the middle of North America and the middle of Europe and Asia in the Northern Hemisphere, and Argentina, southern Africa, Australia, and New Zealand in the Southern Hemisphere. The temperate belt is much larger in the Northern than in the Southern Hemisphere (see the map on the inside of the front cover).

The natural ecosystems in this huge farming belt are mainly temperate forest and, even more important, the grassland that makes up the prairies of North America, the steppes of Asia, the pampas of South America, and the veldt of southern Africa. The soil in temperate areas may be very deep. Parts of the North American prairie had soil more than 2 meters deep before it was farmed, and forests may have soil nearly 1 meter deep. This soil lies on top of a layer of subsoil, which contains a small amount of organic matter. In turn, the subsoil lies over solid rock. This rock slowly weathers and decomposes, adding minerals, first to the subsoil and then to the soil above. As explained in Chapter 5, temperate soil is richly fertile, because, in most cases, organic matter accumulates faster than it decomposes. During the winter, the temperature is so low that bacterial and fungal action is slow. A deep layer of partially decomposed organic matter accumulates, forming soil that can support agriculture for hundreds of years, even if very little fertilizer is added.

If decomposition is slow in the temperate zone, it is even slower at higher latitudes, and one might expect that the soil would be correspondingly deeper. Such is not the case, however, because the summer in these areas is so short that plant growth is limited and little organic matter is produced. Decomposition is so slow that much of

Box 8.2
Hydroponics

Plants do not necessarily need soil to grow. All they need is water, mineral nutrients, and air. The cultivation of plants without soil is called **hydroponics.** The plants are usually grown in plastic sacs of water and mineral nutrients. Because their roots are in water and not in soil, plants grown hydroponically require support, either from their plastic containers or from frameworks over the containers.

The advantage of hydroponic culture is that the nutrients supplied to the plants can be regulated precisely. The disadvantage is that it is much more expensive to buy and maintain hydroponic tanks and the required support systems than merely to plant the crops straight into the ground. Large-scale hydroponic agriculture may always remain economically impossible, but the technique is used in isolated cases for specialty crops.

this organic matter remains on the surface for long periods of time before it is converted to humus. Even further north, where permafrost occurs in the tundra, only a few centimeters at the surface of the soil ever thaw out at all during the summer. A layer of ice, frozen subsoil, and rock lie just beneath the surface. The only topsoil present extends in a thin layer on the surface of the ice. This soil has very little mineral content because it lies on ice instead of on rock. There is no rock to decompose and add minerals to the soil as it does in other places.

In the Tropics, precisely the opposite conditions prevail. Conditions are warm and moist, ideal for decomposition throughout the year. Organic matter decomposes rapidly after it falls to the ground, releasing minerals that are quickly absorbed by plant roots. As a consequence, only a narrow layer of partially decomposed organic matter remains. In many regions, when a tropical forest is cut down, the thin layer of soil may support crops for only a few years. In primitive agricultural systems, people native to these areas have traditionally farmed a small area for a short period of time, abandoned it, and moved on to farm a new area. If the abandoned area is small enough, forest will rapidly re-establish itself in the clearing. On the other hand, if a large area of forest is cut down, the heavy rainfall rapidly leaches any remaining minerals out of the thin soil. In some cases, the remaining ground may be stripped down to the bare rock. A common soil in other tropical areas is **laterite,** which contains a large proportion of aluminum and iron oxides and only a thin surface layer of organic matter. When this surface layer is washed away, the remaining clayey soil can bake to a brick-like texture during a subsequent dry period. Such soil is useless for agriculture. In recent years, many billions of dollars were spent in Brazil to develop agricultural land where tropical rainforests had been cleared. However, only about one third of this type of land is capable of supporting agriculture. As a result, large developments have been abandoned, huge amounts of money have been lost, and, in some instances, barren wasteland has replaced lush forests.

One of the reasons why many less-developed countries are so poor is that their soils are poorly suited to agriculture. As a result, it is expensive or, in some cases, impossible to feed the population adequately. Unfortunately, there is no simple remedy for this problem.

8.5
The Basic Techniques of Agriculture

In hunter–gatherer societies, nearly everyone is involved in the process of gathering food. However, agriculture is potentially so much more efficient than hunting and gathering that a relatively small segment of the population can provide food for everyone. As a result, individuals are free to pursue other endeavors such as science, art, and trade. In turn, developments in science and technology have been applied toward improving crop yields, so that agriculture and civilization have developed hand in hand. Neither could have progressed to its present state without the other. In this chapter and in the next we will examine the state of modern agriculture and the prospects for future food supplies. But before we can address these questions directly, we must understand the basic techniques used by farmers everywhere.

Heavy equipment is used to prepare fields on this farm in southern Idaho.

Tillage

One of the oldest agricultural practices is **tilling,** or **plowing.** Soil is often turned over before seeds are planted, and, then, the bare soil between the plants is often tilled again as the seedlings grow. Tilling has three main functions. First, it mixes up the nutrients and loosens soil particles, making it easier for roots to penetrate the soil. Second, it gives crop plants, which are left alone, a competitive advantage over weeds, which are deliberately disturbed to damage their root systems. Third, tilling introduces oxygen into the soil.

Fertilization

Farmers fertilized their crops with manure, straw, or dead fish long before they understood the chemistry of fertilization. Today, mined and manufactured fertilizers are used so extensively that they have become a major component of most agricultural systems.

Plants need nitrogen in large quantities, because it is a major constituent of proteins and nucleic acids. Nitrogen makes up about 78 percent of the atmosphere by volume, and the supply is therefore virtually unlimited, but gaseous nitrogen cannot be used by most plants. Therefore, plants often lack sufficient nitrogen for optimal growth. Nitrogen can be "fixed," that is, converted to usable forms, by bacteria that live on the roots of plants of the legume family (which includes alfalfa, beans, and peas). Thus, soil fertility can be maintained by rotating crops. One typical rotation scheme would

be to grow corn, a plant that depletes soil nitrogen, one year and then cultivate a nitrogen-enriching crop such as alfalfa the following season. Unfortunately, there is a greater market for corn than for alfalfa, and, in many regions, the farmer would realize more profit if corn were planted every year. To offset this problem, chemists have learned to convert atmospheric nitrogen to synthetic plant fertilizers by producing ammonia:

$$N_2 \quad + \quad 3H_2 \quad \longrightarrow \quad 2NH_3$$

nitrogen gas   hydrogen gas   ammonia

Ammonia can be used on soils directly or converted to other usable compounds such as nitrates (NO_3^-). Taking all manufacturing steps into account, the manufacture of nitrogen fertilizers requires large expenditures of energy. Therefore, in modern times, the price and availability of nitrogen fertilizers are tied to the cost and supply of coal and oil.

Large quantities of phosphorus and potassium are also added to commercial farms. Both are mined commercially from mineral deposits. Of these, the world's supply of phosphorus is more limited (see Chapter 16), and the price of this fertilizer is linked to the availability of the deposits.

Irrigation

Since antiquity, people have known that semiarid land can be made to be productive if water is imported for irrigation. Thus, for example, Mesopotamia, one of the richest civilizations of the ancient

Mechanized irrigation system in the United States.

world, was located in a harsh, dry, near-desert zone in southwest Asia, in the valley between the Tigris and Euphrates Rivers (Fig. 8–8). The average rainfall in this region is only 15 cm to 20 cm (about half the rainfall that collects in the wheat-growing "breadbasket" of North America). Summer temperatures are among the hottest recorded in the world, only a few degrees cooler than temperatures in the central portions of the Sahara Desert. Yet, with an extensive irrigation system, the area became

A boy tends an irrigation ditch in a nonmechanized farming system in Peru.

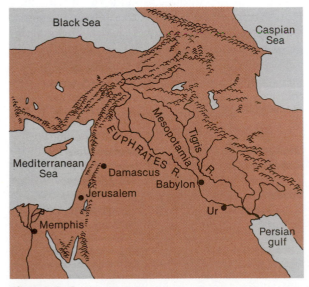

Figure 8–8
The Mesopotamia region in ancient times.

known as the "Fertile Crescent," and enough grain was raised to feed between 17 million and 25 million people.

Today, approximately 20 percent of the total cropland in the world is irrigated. The 20 percent figure is, of course, a global average, and some regions are much more highly dependent on irrigation. For example, in Pakistan, 65 percent of the cultivated land is irrigated. In India, the nation's

Table 8–1
Extent of Irrigated Lands and Their Use for Food Production in Selected Countries

Country	Percent of Cultivated Land Under Irrigation	Percent of Total Food Production From Irrigated Land
India	30	55
Pakistan	65	80
China	50	70
Indonesia	40	50
Chile	35	55
Peru	35	55

grain production increased from 55 million tonnes in 1950 to 140 million tonnes in 1985, and about half of the increase would not have been possible without irrigation (Table 8–1). In the United States, most of the vegetables grown throughout the country depend on irrigation systems, and, in recent years, widespread use of irrigation has also been extended to field crops. For example, in Nebraska, yields of corn can be tripled and profits increased if large mechanized sprinkling systems are installed.

Pest Control

In all agricultural systems, a variety of different types of pests compete with humans for food. Pests may be quite large, such as rhinoceroses or elephants, or they may be small, such as microscopic disease organisms. Small organisms, such as insects, roundworms, fungi, and bacteria, are so numerous that they represent the greatest threat. In traditional agriculture, pest control depended mainly on the maintenance of diverse agricultural systems. A variety of organisms within these systems were predators of the pests, and many crops produced natural chemicals that were effective pesticides. In modern agriculture, these ecological defenses are often replaced by synthetic chemical sprays. These poisons are a serious threat to our environment and will be discussed further in Unit 5, Chemicals in the Environment.

Despite the impressive success of modern agriculture, many people are now asking basic questions about the sustainability of current farming practices. There is ample evidence that many croplands are being destroyed, and there is fear that if current trends continue, the global potential for food production will be jeopardized.

8.6
Soil Erosion

The radius of the Earth is approximately 6378 km. Of this total depth, very little is actually accessible to humans. The deepest experimental drilling project has succeeded in reaching a depth of nearly 15 km, but most wells or mines extend less than a kilometer or two into the ground. Yet, in biological terms, even a kilometer or two underground is a great distance. In mountainous, rocky, or arctic regions, the soil depth is only a few centimeters, whereas in fertile forests or prairies, it may be a meter or two (Fig. 8–9). Yet, nearly all of the terrestrial life on our planet depends on this tiny veneer. In natural ecosystems, new soil is formed by the physical and chemical decomposition of rock and by organic decay. At the same time, some of the soil is carried away by **erosion.** Erosion is the process whereby soil particles are removed from the ecosystem, usually by wind or flowing water. In most ecosystems, the rate of production is equal to or greater than the rate of removal, so soil depth and fertility increase with time.

Plants and their decomposition products are primarily responsible for soil retention. Roots absorb moisture and physically bind soil particles together, and litter and humus provide a protective

In traditional agriculture, large areas of exposed soil lie between rows of certain field crops. However, a better system is to leave residues of previous crops in the field. In this photograph, soybeans are planted in residues from last year's corn crop. The corn stocks serve to hold moisture, reduce erosion, and add organic matter to the soil. (USDA Soil Conservation Service)

Figure 8–9

A view of the ramparts along the McKenzie River. The high, white cliff is made of limestone. The thin dark line beneath the trees is the soil that supports the forest above it. Note how thin the soil zone is. Yet, if such zones are destroyed, life on Earth as we know it could not survive.

cover and a water-absorbing medium. Agriculture is potentially disruptive to this natural order for four major reasons:

1. In many areas, farmers must first destroy forests or woodlands before they can adapt the land for agriculture. The process of removing the trees from a region is called **deforestation.** Today, many timbered areas are also being cut for fuel and fiber. As explained in Section 3.11, rates of erosion increase dramatically when land, especially hilly land, is deforested. This topic will be discussed further in Chapter 11.

2. Generally, farmers till the land before they plant, thus disturbing any remaining natural surface and its protective armor. At this point, the field

is particularly vulnerable to erosion. If a drought occurs, the soil will dry up and be blown away by the wind. On the other hand, if, after plowing, the spring rains are too heavy, the soil can be easily washed away before the seeds have an opportunity to grow.

3. Many crops, such as corn, cotton, or vegetables, are cultivated in distinct rows, and competitive weeds growing between the rows are removed by further tillage or are destroyed by the application of chemical poisons. The net result of these activities is that significant portions of the soil are exposed to the elements throughout the growing season.

4. Natural ecosystems are generally diverse. Consider a prairie, for example. As explained in Section 4.10, a prairie contains many different spe-

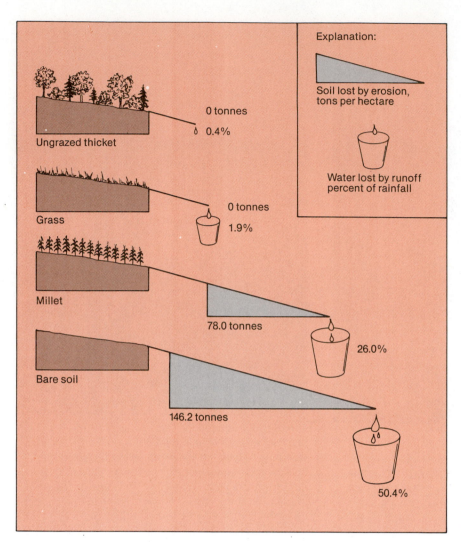

Explanation:

Soil lost by erosion, tons per hectare

Water lost by runoff percent of rainfall

Ungrazed thicket
0 tonnes
0.4%

Grass
0 tonnes
1.9%

Millet
78.0 tonnes
26.0%

Bare soil
146.2 tonnes
50.4%

Comparison of water loss and soil erosion from four different systems.

cies of plants, each with its own unique growth strategy. The net result of this diversity is that if changes occur in the weather or in other environmental conditions, some of the species are likely to survive or even thrive. Even though the character of the system may change, the system, as a whole, is likely to continue. In an agricultural system, however, a field is generally planted with only a single species; therefore, the system becomes vulnerable to unpredictable events such as floods, drought, unseasonable frosts, or pest epidemics. For example, a spring drought could kill an entire cornfield, and the soil would then be vulnerable to erosion from wind or from heavy rains that might occur in the fall.

Despite these potential problems, farmers in many areas of the world have maintained sustain-able agricultural systems for many centuries and have even increased productivity from generation to generation. Soil conservation has been traditionally based on various combinations of three basic technologies, rotation, fallowing, and terracing, all of which were understood by the ancients.

Rotation Soil erosion can be reduced and soil fertility can be maintained by planting two or more different kinds of crops in a single area. This process is known as **rotation.** There are fundamentally two different types of rotation. Earlier in the chapter, we discussed the advantage of planting crops that require nitrogen, such as corn, one year and then planting nitrogen-fixing crops in the same field the next year. This strategy can be called **alternate year rotation.** A different type of

This farm in Maryland uses a variety of different techniques to reduce erosion and to increase soil fertility. Crops are rotated and planted in alternate bands along the contours of the slope. In addition, a band of trees in the middle of the farm serves as a windbreak. (USDA Soil Conservation Service)

rotation scheme involves use of alternate bands of different crops in a single year. Recall that, other factors being equal, soil erosion will be greater when plants are cultivated in rows than when growth is more uniform. Certain crops such as hay, alfalfa, and many cereals are generally grown as **cover crops,** where the seed is dispersed evenly and there are no bare spots. If cover crops are grown in bands between row crops, the flow of water and the force of wind will be broken, and erosion rates will be reduced (Table 8–2).

Another type of band rotation is the establishment of **windbreaks.** A windbreak is a row of trees planted between the fields to deflect the wind and reduce wind erosion. In many regions, especially the less-developed countries where timber and fuel are scarce, the trees can also be used for firewood or construction materials.

Fallowing The Old Testament directed farmers to leave fields unplanted — resting — one year out of every seven. This technique of *not* planting crops in a given field is called **fallowing.** In semiarid lands, crops absorb more moisture from the soil in a given year than is returned by rainfall. If a field is left fallow one year, the moisture content of the soil will accumulate and the land will be productive the following season. Fallowing is also used in tropical regions but for different reasons. Recall that soils in many tropical rainforests are poor and contain few nutrients. Primitive farmers in these regions traditionally

Table 8–2
Cropping Systems and Soil Erosion

Cropping System	Average Annual Loss of Soil
	(tonnes/acre)
Corn, wheat, and clover rotation	2.7
Continuous wheat	10.1
Continuous corn	19.7

Source: *Soil Degradation: Effects on Agricultural Productivity.* Washington, D.C., 1980.

This hillside in Nepal is extensively terraced. Without terracing it would be impossible to farm a slope as steep as the one shown here.

would clear a small segment of the forest, farm it for a few years, and then move elsewhere. In many cases, they would not return for 10 to 20 years, during which time the forest would reclaim the small farm and replenish the nutrient pool.

Terracing Water erosion is more likely to occur in a field perched on a hillside than in one that is nestled in the bottom of a valley. For example, research in Nigeria has shown that if plants are cultivated on a 1 percent slope, an average of 3 tonnes of soil are lost per hectare per year. At this rate, formation of new soil will equal or surpass soil loss. However, on a 5 percent slope, annual soil loss is 87 tonnes per hectare. At this rate, a topsoil layer of 15 cm would disappear entirely in a single generation. If farmers work on a 15 percent slope, erosion increases to 220 tonnes per hectare, which would lead to total removal of the soil in only 10 years. One solution to the problem of hillside erosion is to build terraces so that individual fields are level, even though they are layered along a steep hill or mountain. An alternative procedure on low-angle slopes is to plow along the contours of the land so that each furrow becomes its own small dam or terrace.

Rates of Soil Erosion

In recent years, farmers in many regions have not practiced the best agricultural techniques. As a re-

sult, soil erosion is severe throughout the world. Furthermore, there is serious concern that the rate of soil erosion is increasing so rapidly that the future agricultural productivity of our planet is being seriously threatened. This concern is summarized by a statement made by Lester Brown in a pamphlet entitled *Soil Erosion: Quiet Crisis in the World Economy.*

> Over most of the earth's surface, the thin mantle of topsoil on which agriculture depends is six to eight inches thick. Although the depletion of this thin layer may compromise economic progress and political stability even more than dwindling oil reserves, nowhere has the depletion of topsoil gained the attention paid to the depletion of oil reserves. . . . With only occasional exceptions, national agricultural and population policies have failed to take soil depletion into account. . . . Indeed not until topsoil has largely disappeared and food shortages have developed or famine threatened does this loss become apparent.

In the pamphlet just quoted, erosion problems in the four largest food-producing areas of the world are documented. This information is summarized in the following paragraphs. Remarks on rates of erosion in other regions are listed in Table 8–3.

United States In 1977 and again in 1982, the federal government called for a detailed survey of soils in the United States. According to these re-

Table 8–3
Observations of Soil Erosion in the Third World

Country	Observation	Source
Nepal (Katmandu)	"Local inhabitants . . . all concur that the problem is more severe now than a generation ago."	*Mountain Research and Development,* (Boulder, CO)
Peru	"Erosion is estimated to affect between 50 and 60 percent of the surface of the whole country."	*Mountain Research and Development,* (Boulder, CO)
Indonesia (Java)	"Soil erosion is creating an ecological emergency in Java, a result of overpopulation, which has led to deforestation and misuse of hillside areas by land-hungry farmers. Erosion is laying waste to land at an alarming rate, much faster than present reclamation programs can restore it."	U.S. Embassy, Jakarta
Ethiopia	"There is an environmental nightmare unfolding before our eyes . . . over 1 billion tons of topsoil flow from Ethiopia's highlands each year."	U.S. AID Mission, Addis Ababa
South Africa	"The province of Natal incorporating Kwazulu, is losing 200 million tons of topsoil annually."	John Hanks, Institute of Natural Resources, Natal,
Bolivia	"Recent aerial photographs have shown the rapid extension of desert-like conditions caused by wind erosion."	Hélène Rivière d'Arc, Institut des Hautes Études d'Amérique Latine, Paris
Iran	"The area of abandoned cultivated land has doubled in recent years."	Harold Dregne, Texas Tech University

Source: Lester R. Brown and Edward C. Wolf: *Soil Erosion: Quiet Crisis in the World Economy.* Washington, D.C., Worldwatch Institute, 1984.

ports, approximately one third of the natural topsoil in North America has already been lost since the start of agriculture on the continent. In 1982, erosion was continuing in the United States at an average rate of about 10.5 tonnes per hectare per year. However, in some regions, the rate was considerably higher (Fig. 8–10). Average yearly losses of 31 tonnes per hectare were reported in parts of Tennessee, 25 tonnes per hectare in New Jersey, 33 tonnes per hectare in Texas, and 22 tonnes per hectare in Iowa. A little arithmetic puts these numbers in perspective.

- A metric tonne of soil represents about 0.008 cm of soil over an area of 1 hectare.
- At an erosion rate of 25 tonnes per hectare per year, the net annual loss amounts to (25 tonnes per hectare per year $\times$ 0.008 cm per tonne) = 0.2 cm per hectare per year. (This loss is partially compensated by natural formation of soil, but rates of formation are generally much lower than the values just quoted. Owing to the very approximate nature of these calculations in general, rates of formation will be omitted.)
- In many agricultural areas, topsoil is about 30 cm deep.
- Therefore, a loss of 25 tonnes per hectare per year would lead to complete loss of the topsoil in about 150 years.

On a national average, about 44 percent of cropland in the United States is losing soil faster than it is being formed. Today, an equivalent of 1.2

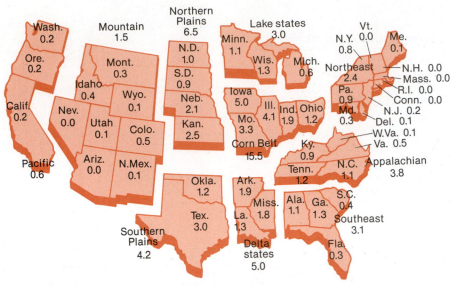

Figure 8–10

The amount of land (in millions of hectares) in the United States in which the rates of soil erosion exceed tolerance levels established by the U.S. Department of Agriculture.

million hectares (3 million acres) of prime farmland are being destroyed every year. (This number was derived by calculating the partial soil loss over all the cropland in the country and mathematically concentrating it to a total loss over a smaller area.) This loss amounts to the destruction of the agricul-

Heavy rains and improper farming practices led to extreme erosion on this farmland. When erosion of this magnitude occurs, agriculture must be abandoned, and many centuries will elapse before the original fertility will be re-established. (American Farmland Trust)

tural capacity of an area the size of the state of Rhode Island every 4 years.

India   The average rate of topsoil loss in India is approximately 20 tonnes per hectare, or about twice that in the United States. Whereas in the United States, erosion is faster than natural replacement on 44 percent of the farmland, the figure is slightly higher in India (Fig. 8–11).

The Soviet Union   Although accurate statistics are not available, Western observers believe that soil erosion in the Soviet Union may be more extensive than in any other region of the world. In one article from a Soviet journal, scientists report that erosion is faster than replacement in 66 percent of the plowed land in the Soviet Union, and erosion rates of 30 to 60 tonnes per hectare are reported in many regions.

China   Studies of the sediment carried by the rivers of China and analysis of agricultural reports indicate that the erosion rate in China may exceed that of India by 30 percent.

You may ask, "Why are modern farmers, with all the information and technology available to them, so destructive to the land?"

Perhaps the main answer lies in the fact that people are often more likely to respond to short-term economic considerations than to factors that

Table 8–4
Effect of Topsoil Thickness on Agricultural Yields

Location	Crop	Yield Reduction Per Inch of Topsoil Lost	
		(Bushels/Acre)	(Percent)
Wooster, Ohio	wheat	1.7	9.5
Oregon	wheat	2.5	5.8
Akron, Colorado	wheat	0.5	2.0
Geary Co., Kansas	corn	3.5	7.5
Fowler, Indiana	corn	3.8	5.5
Wooster, Ohio	corn	4.8	8.0
Bushland, Texas (irrigated)	sorghum	3.0	5.2

Source: Crosson and Stout: *Productivity Effects of Cropland Erosion in the United States.* Washington, D.C., Resources for the Future, 1983. 103 pp.

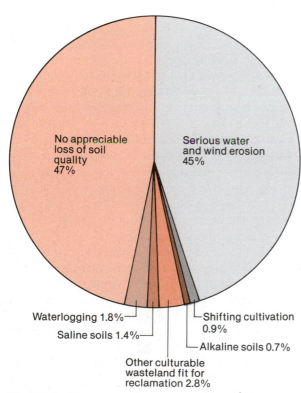

Figure 8–11

Various types of soil degradation in India in 1985. (Waterlogging and salinity will be discussed later in this chapter.)

promote long-range sustainability. For example; imagine that you are a farmer in the midwest region of the United States. The price of corn is expected to be higher this year, whereas there is little market for alfalfa or hay and the price of wheat is low. You have just borrowed money to buy a new tractor and to make some repairs on your barn, and your loan payments are high. You figure that even with additional fertilizer costs, you will realize a higher profit by planting corn exclusively than by using a crop rotation of corn and a cover crop. Assume that you are well aware of the fact that rotation reduces erosion problems. You are also aware that at the current rate, erosion will not really cause a significant decline in productivity in the immediate future. On the other hand, if you don't make your payments this fall, the bank will foreclose on your farm. As a rational individual, what do you do? You plant the corn.

Let's take another example. You are a young Nepali farmer living in a mountain village. You have inherited a small plot of land from your parents but wish to expand your holdings by clearing part of a timbered hillside. As you start the job of felling the trees and building terraces, an opportunity arises to work for a month as a porter carrying loads for a mountain-climbing expedition traveling through your village. If you take the job, you will be guaranteed a salary, which can be put to use to buy food and clothes for your growing family. But,

When hillsides are excessively steep, even terracing cannot hold the soil during heavy monsoon rains. In this photograph, an entire hillside was washed away after it had been logged and then terraced. Local farmers would have fared better if they had left the trees and harvested wood on a sustained basis.

on the other hand, if your terracing is done poorly, the monsoon rains could permanently destroy the field you have been working on. However, if the monsoon is light this year, the temporary terracing will hold, and you can finish your farmwork next year. So you take the chance, leave a hastily built terrace, and accept the job.

In a third example, imagine that you are a peasant living in the jungle of Indonesia. Your grandparents used to farm land for 3 years, then let it lie fallow for 5 years, but, today, there are so many more people that there simply isn't enough land for this seminomadic agriculture. Would you, as an individual, choose to starve and maintain the traditional fallow cycle, or try to farm a marginal area and hope to raise enough to eat this year?

In all three cases, it appears that the rational choice is to forfeit long-term economic considerations for immediate gains. Certainly, every situation is different. In many cases, it is impossible to find simple and satisfying solutions to particular problems. In other situations, however, creative rethinking of priorities can enable farmers to conserve the land *and* realize a short-term profit. For example, many farmers in the United States have found that if they simultaneously lower both production and production costs, their profitability may increase. One example is found in organic farming, to be discussed in the next section.

Another possible solution is that governments can offer incentives for good farming practices. For example, in the United States, the Soil Conservation Service has a variety of programs to reimburse farmers for many projects that promote conservation. One such program involves the payment of subsidies for the construction of dams and holding ponds that reduce spring run-off. Some people propose that incentive programs be expanded. One proposal suggests that the government establish a fund to compensate farmers who abandon profitable row cropping on highly erodible land and instead plant less profitable but more sustainable crops such as hay or timber. Others disagree with these suggestions. An opposing argument contends that government funds are limited and asks why farmers should receive long-range economic support not offered to other types of businesses.

An alternative proposal is for the government to penalize farmers who engage in wasteful practices. In the United States, farmers are aided by a great variety of different programs. One suggestion is to suspend aid from those farmers who do not take adequate soil conservation precautions.

Others suggest that the best solutions involve research or education in innovative ways to adapt agricultural practices so that conservation becomes profitable. Two examples, one from the developed countries and one from the less-developed regions, illustrate this point.

1. Tillage requires a great expenditure of energy and, as previously stated, leaves the soil vulnerable to erosion. An alternative procedure is to leave the surface of the ground intact and to dig a little hole to plant each seed. This practice maintains the integrity of the surface vegetation, which, in turn, reduces the risk of erosion. In addition, soil humus is retained more effectively, because tillage speeds the destruction of humus by accelerating the rate of oxidation. If the humic content of the soil is maintained, the soil retains and stores water more efficiently. In recent years, farmers in the developed countries have become interested in this technique, called **no-till agriculture.** As a result, machinery has been developed to mechanize the process. Many farmers report that no-till agriculture is less expensive than tillage, because the no-till method saves fuel and irrigation water, and reduces the need to fertilize. However, the machinery required is expensive, and conversion to this technique is far from universal.

2. Traditional terracing with stonewall retainers requires considerable labor and, therefore, is not cost-effective in the short-term. In Kenya, local scientists working with Swedish consultants devised a procedure to establish and maintain terraces quickly with a special type of plow that could be built with local materials. Furthermore, a program was started to plant trees along the borders of the terraces. The particular species of trees chosen grows quickly, and, when the plants are mature, the timber can be used for fuel and construction. In addition, the leaves can be used to provide fodder for cattle or, alternatively, can be bundled into a waterproof thatch, which is an excellent building material for roofs.

8.7
Chemical Fertilization and the Loss of Organic Matter in the Soil

Unquestionably, commercial fertilizers have increased global agricultural production and thus have helped feed the expanding human population. For this reason, modern farmers all over the world are using fertilizer in ever increasing amounts whenever they have been affordable. But several problems have arisen. First, chemical fertilizers are expensive and are therefore unavailable to farmers in many less-developed countries. Second, soil chemistry is complex. If too much fertilizer is applied, or if the fertilizer is not chemically compatible with the soil, large quantities of it will leach

In societies where neither tractors nor animal power are available, people often practice no-till agriculture simply because they do not have either the time or the energy to till the soil. For example, no-till farming was used extensively by the American Indians before the Europeans arrived. Today, most native Americans use tractors, but a few remain rooted in the old ways. Navajo farmer George Blue-Eyes works much harder than his neighbors, because he tills his fields entirely by hand. But traditional farming methods limit moisture loss and erosion and bring him consistently higher yields per hectare. (Photo by Janet Bingham)

out into streams and groundwater supplies. Leaching represents not only a financial loss but also a significant source of water pollution.

Perhaps the most serious concern about the use of chemical fertilizers is related to the quality of the soil itself. In a system where land is tilled every year, where crop residues such as straw are removed, and where only chemical fertilizers are used, the soil humus is continuously depleted and is not replaced. Many people fear that even though agricultural yields are high in chemical farming systems today, the loss of humus could lead to a decline in productivity in the future. If the humus is destroyed, water losses will increase, leaching problems will become more severe, trace minerals will be removed, and the agricultural system will become totally dependent on applications of large quantities of fertilizer.

One solution to this downward spiral is to formulate increasingly sophisticated fertilizers that in-

Special Topic A
Wind Erosion: The Dust Bowl in the United States

The early European settlers found millions of hectares of virgin land in America. The eastern coast, where they first arrived, was so heavily forested that even by the mid-eighteenth century, a mariner approaching the shore could detect the fragrance of the pine trees more than 300 km from land. The task of clearing land, pulling stumps, and planting crops was arduous, especially in New England, where long winters and rocky hillsides contributed to the difficulty of farming. It was natural that pioneers should be lured by the West, for here, beyond the Mississippi, lay expanses of prairie farther than the eye could see. Deep, rich topsoil and rockless, treeless expanses promised easy plowing, sowing, and reaping. In 1889, the Oklahoma Territory was opened for homesteading. A few weeks later, the non-Indian population there rose from almost nil to close to 60,000. By 1900, the population was 390,000—people living off the wealth of the soil.

The southwestern plains of the United States are at best a near-arid ecosystem, and periodic droughts have occurred every 20 to 25 years in this region for centuries. For reasons discussed in the text, the natural prairies on which the bison grazed were resistant to these droughts. However, over a period of 20 to 35 years, improper farming practices led to a decline in soil fertility. Incomplete fertilization and loss of soil from wind and water erosion took their toll. Finally, when a prolonged drought struck, the seeds failed to sprout, and disaster struck. In 1934, a summer wind stripped entire counties of their topsoil and even blew some of this dust more than 1500 km eastward into the Atlantic Ocean. Altogether, 3.5 million hectares of farmland were destroyed, and productivity was seriously reduced on an additional 30 million hectares.

Moreover, farmers have not necessarily learned the lessons from the past. Serious wind erosion continues to this day in many parts of the Great Plains, and some agronomists fear that another major Dust Bowl is possible.

During the 1920s and 1930s, wind-blown dust had a devastating effect on agriculture in the United States. This photograph, entitled "Buried machinery," was taken in South Dakota on May 13, 1936. (Reprinted with permission of the National Archives.)

clude synthetic soil conditioners. Another solution involves using agricultural wastes or other organic matter as fertilizers.

Organic Farming

In the twentieth century, most farmers in developed countries make extensive use of fertilizers, herbicides, and pesticides. Others believe that these practices are not only harmful to the environment but don't even make sound economic sense. This argument states that the use of herbicides and pesticides is an expensive and inefficient way to control pests (see Chapter 19) and that the loss of humus related to a program of chemical fertilizers ultimately reduces soil productivity. An **organic farmer** is one who uses only organic fertilizer such as manure, bone meal, and waste plant products and applies no synthetic pesticides or herbicides.

In recent years, some large-scale commercial farmers in the United States have switched to organic techniques, even though organic fertilizers are heavy and therefore expensive to spread and the threat of pest invasions is always a concern. A study of these farms showed that the switch to organic practices led to a decline in energy use by 15 to 50 percent, depending on the crop. In some cases, yields improved with the change, but, in most instances, total yields decreased somewhat. However, in many cases in which yields were diminished, the farmer's profit went up because operating costs decreased. According to a report by the U.S. Department of Agriculture, if all the farms in the United States reverted to organic techniques, great quantities of energy would be saved, and the American people could still be adequately fed, but overall yields would decrease. This decrease would lead to a reduction in the quantity of food available for export. This report supports the conclusion that if only short-term factors are considered, agriculture based on fossil fuel energy is the most productive system available. On the other hand, the problems raised by this system are potentially so severe that many believe that the gain of extraordinarily high yields at present is more than offset by the threat of a serious decline in productivity in the future.

8.8
Agricultural Disruption Caused by Improper Irrigation

Recall from Section 8.5 that in ancient times, the desert region between the Tigris and the Euphrates Rivers of western Asia supported a complex civilization and a large population. The productivity of much of this region was a direct consequence of an extensive irrigation system, one of the great wonders of early civilization (Fig. 8–12). Thousands of kilometers of sophisticated aqueducts

Figure 8–12
Aerial photographs of old irrigation canals along the Tigris River. (Courtesy of the Iraq Tourist Authority)

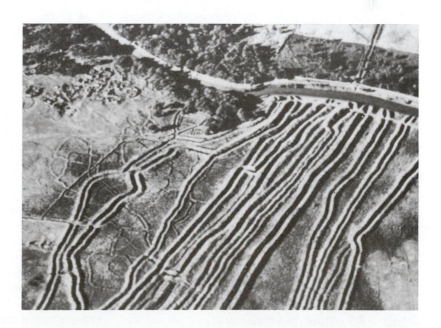

were built to support the agriculture that in turn supported ancient cities such as Babylon and Ur. Today, much of this region is barren semidesert, badly eroded, and desolate. Archaeologists dig up ancient irrigation canals, old hoes, and grinding stones in the middle of the desert. How did this change occur?

All surface water and groundwater reserves contain small concentrations of salts that have dissolved when the water has been in contact with various rock formations and sediment deposits. When irrigation water is applied to a field, particularly in dry areas, much of it evaporates, leaving the salts behind. As these minerals accumulate, the salinity (salt content) of the soil increases. This process is called **salinization.** Because most plants cannot grow in salty soils, the productivity of the land decreases.

A second problem that can be caused by improper irrigation is **waterlogging.** In most farming systems, irrigation water is not carefully controlled, and, in many situations, more water is applied than is needed. In regions where the soil is sandy, the excess water will flow through the ground and escape. However, in clayey soils or in certain regions where an impermeable layer of clay lies beneath the surface, water cannot move efficiently through the soil. If excess water accumulates in the root zone, the soil will become waterlogged and plants will die. Waterlogging and salinization are **synergistic,** that is, when the two problems occur together, the negative effect is greater than would be expected by simply adding the independent effects of each. If irrigation leads to salinization and then this salty water saturates the root zone, many crops simply cannot grow.

Extreme salinization and waterlogging destroyed the agricultural system of ancient Mesopotamia. The salinization occurred as a consequence of centuries of irrigation. Part of the story of the waterlogging starts at the source of the great rivers in the Armenian highlands. The hillside forests were cleared to make way for pastures, vineyards, and wheat fields. But croplands, especially if poorly managed, cannot hold the soil or the moisture as well as natural forests or grasslands can. As a result, large water run-offs such as those from the spring rains or melting mountain snows tended to flow down the hillsides rather than soaking into the ground. These uncontrolled waters became spring floods. The flood waters carried large quantities of clayey silt into the irrigation canals of Mesopota-

mia. At first, these floods caused no major problems. Every spring the canals were dredged, and the recovered soil was spread onto the fields. Since flood-silts are generally fertile, crops flourished. But because clayey soils are relatively impermeable to water, the natural drainage of the fields was disrupted, with the result that the soils eventually became waterlogged. Today, some of the original farmlands of Mesopotamia are barren deserts, whereas on others, agriculture is still practiced but yields are less than they were 4000 years ago.

Irrigation in Modern Times

Agricultural systems supported by irrigation are also being threatened in modern times. One problem lies in the availability of water. In many regions, farmers are drawing water from deep underground reserves faster than these reserves are being replenished by natural processes. Thus, the high yields of foodstuffs that are produced today will be endangered when the supply of water becomes depleted. Water resources and their availability will be discussed further in Chapter 17.

In addition, there is a serious concern that salinization and waterlogging are occurring on a global scale. A few examples illustrate this point.

- In Pakistan, where 65 percent of all croplands are irrigated, a third of the irrigated total is already experiencing severe salt problems, and an additional 16 percent is threatened.
- In India, one third to one half of all irrigated land is threatened by salinization and waterlogging.
- In Egypt, the land bordering the Nile River has been irrigated for at least 6000 years. In this area, the annual flooding of the Nile washed any excess salt out of the soil and the salts did not accumulate. However, in the early 1960s, the Aswan High Dam was built to control flooding, store water for additional irrigation, and provide electrical power. In the mere 20 years since construction of the dam, salinity problems have already become acute, and, today, one third of Egypt's farmland is threatened.

Of the total irrigated acreage throughout the entire world, about half has been developed since 1950, and approximately 20 percent is already suffering serious loss of productivity owing to increased salinization and waterlogging.

The question now arises, "What can be done about the problem?" Possible answers to this question can be approached by studying a particular system in some detail.

The San Joaquin Valley in central California is one of the most important and productive agricultural regions in the world and currently produces $5 billion worth of crops every year. However, before farmers inhabited the area in 1870, the valley was mostly desert, and, today, all croplands in the region are irrigated. In 1987, just a little over 100 years after the start of agriculture in the San Joaquin Valley, about half of the valley was suffering partial loss of productivity owing to salinization and waterlogging. Part of the problem stems from the fact that an impermeable layer of clay lies beneath the soil, and, as explained earlier, this clay reduces drainage and traps the salty water. There are two generic types of solutions to the problems of salinization and waterlogging. One is to continue existing irrigation practices and then solve the resulting problems by some sort of technological fix. The other is to change or adapt existing practices so that problems do not arise as quickly in the first place.

One technological fix is to build a drainage system. Such an approach would involve installation of underground tiles and pipes to collect the salty water from individual fields. However, once this waste water is collected, it must be disposed of in some manner. Therefore, government officials in the San Joaquin Valley have initiated construction of a central drain. This drain is expected to cost $1.25 billion when completed, and, according to the initial plan, it was to collect the water from individual farms and pump it into the sea. However, serious ecological and economic problems have arisen (see Section 8.9).

Another proposal is to route the salty brine into special open-air ponds and simply allow the water to evaporate. The engineering involved in the solution is relatively simple, but, again, the cost is high, because the evaporation ponds preempt between 5 and 10 percent of a farmer's land. Agronomists estimate that the expense of either a drainage system or evaporation ponds will lead to significant increase, perhaps as much as a doubling, in the price of vegetables.

Although such a price increase would certainly affect many Americans, the United States is a rich nation, and most people could afford to eat well, even if the price of certain commodities did,

in fact, double. However, in many less-developed countries, it is very difficult to find the money for even the simplest type of drainage system.

An alternative approach is to eliminate the source of the problem by using less water. The benefits of conservation are twofold: First, if water is conserved, the useful life span of limited groundwater reserves will be extended. Second, if less water is used, fewer salts will be spread over the land and, thus, fewer salts accumulate. There is significant room for improvement; the average efficiency of irrigation systems is estimated to be only 37 percent. Thus, for every 100 liters of water, 37 liters are absorbed by plants, and 63 liters soak into the soil or evaporate into the air.

There are several ways to conserve water used for agriculture. One is simply to line irrigation canals with concrete or plastic to eliminate seepage during transport. Although this solution is technically simple, it is expensive.

Once water is brought to an individual field, the goal is to direct it to the roots of the economically valuable plants. In primitive irrigation systems, water is simply allowed to flow along the furrows between the plants. Some of this flowing water is used by the crops, but much of it soaks into the soil or evaporates, leaving its salts behind. Unfortunately, many farmers today are still using 5000-year-old irrigation technology.

One relatively simple approach is to level individual fields. If a field is not level, water collects

Drip irrigation in a cotton field in California. In this system, water is conserved because it is delivered directly to the root zone and less is lost to evaporation. (USDA Soil Conservation Service)

Special Topic B
Case History: Wheat Farming in the Northern Great Plains

The indigenous prairie of North America consisted of a varied mixture of grasses growing on a base of rich topsoil. In many regions, especially in the northern prairies, the subsoil beneath the surface consists of **glacial till.** Glacial till is a mixture of rock, soil, and sand that was left behind when the last great continental ice cap retreated about 10,000 years ago. Beneath this till is a vast layer of impermeable clays and shales. The prairie ecosystem was traditionally subject to seasonal cycles. In the springtime, melting snows and heavy rains saturated the soil. In some years, excess water leached downward into the glacial till. As water leached through the till, it dissolved many of the natural salts found there. This salty water then collected on the impermeable layer of clay and shale. Eventually it flowed along this underground layer until it collected in natural depressions on the plains, as shown in Figure 8–13. This process is called **saline seep.** During the hot dry summers, the water in the salty pools eventually evaporated, leaving behind concentrated salt deposits that killed all the grasses in the area. These small dead areas were first reported by Lewis and Clark when they explored the Northwestern plains in 1804.

As explained earlier, the natural prairie had been a diverse system containing many different species of annual and perennial plants. When this natural system is plowed under and replaced with a single plant species such as wheat, problems arise. Wheat is an annual grass. If there is not enough moisture in the soil, the wheat will die and the surface of the land will become barren. One solution to this problem is an agricultural practice called **summer fallowing.** In this technique, a field is plowed over early in the spring, thereby killing all the grasses, and then left barren all summer. Since there are no plants to absorb moisture and allow it to transpire, the soil acts like a sponge, collecting and storing the water that enters the system. When enough moisture has accumulated, the farmer can plant a new crop, either in the fall or in the following spring. This system leaves the land idle for periods of time but gives greater assurance that a crop, once planted, will succeed.

If summer fallowing operates exactly as planned, the new crop is planted just when the soil moisture has reached optimal levels. In practice, the amount of rainfall hardly ever exactly matches the farmer's needs. Usually, there is more or less than the optimum. If there is too little moisture, the farmer may elect to plant the crop and take a chance or to wait another season until the soil stores more water. On the other hand, if rainfall is too heavy, the soil becomes saturated, because there are no plants to absorb the excess moisture, and the excess water seeps down into the glacial till. Here it picks up salts, collects on the impermeable layer of shale, and then runs off into natural depressions on the prairie. The important point to emphasize is that in a summer fallow system, this salty run-off is much greater than it is in a natural prairie.

The problem is further aggravated by the use

in pools in low points and eventually harms crops rather than helps them. In developed countries, leveling can be performed precisely by laser-guided plows pulled by powerful tractors. On the other hand, in less-developed regions, the process must be performed by hand.

Another type of conservation technology is the use of **drip irrigation.** For fruits, vegetables, or orchard crops, inexpensive perforated pipes can be used to carry water directly to individual plants. In this way, only the soil immediately around the root system is moistened. Overall, drip systems use about half the water used by conventional irrigation.

In the United States, a complex series of laws and subsidies actually combine to discourage conservation in many instances. When irrigation systems were first developed in the early part of the twentieth century, the government financed the construction of a large number of dams to store

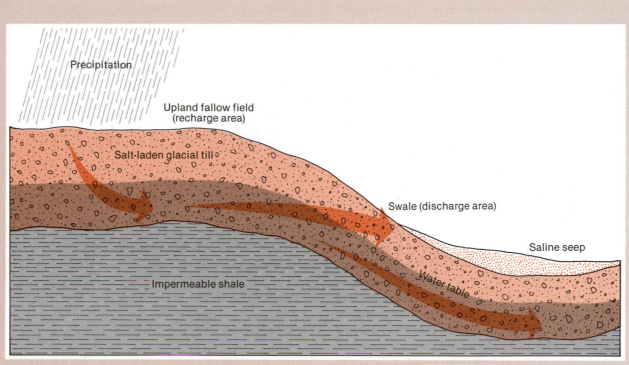

Figure 8–13
Saline seep formation.

of chemical fertilizers. Chemical fertilizers per se arenot harmful, but the practice of using chemicals instead of organic matter causes a gradual loss of humus. As a result, the water-holding capacity of the soil decreases, and saline seep increases.

In the natural prairie, a few thousand hectares of grassland had been destroyed by saline seep. Today, 80 million hectares of farmland have been ruined, and 8 million additional hectares are being lost every year. In some communities, the salt water has crept into wells, making the domestic water supply unfit to drink.

water and a complex network of canals to dispense it. Then each field or farmland was allotted a certain quantity of water annually. In some regions, the law states that if a farmer does not use the entire deeded allotment, some or all of it will be permanently revoked. One proposal is to establish a system whereby a farmer who conserved water, for example, by installing drip irrigation, could sell part of his allotment to someone else. Then the farmer would gain, not lose, by conservation, be-

cause the proceeds of the sale would offset the cost of the more expensive irrigation system.

Development of Salt-Resistant Crops

Another approach is to allow the land to become salinated and then breed special varieties of grains and vegetables that can grow in salty soils. The advantage of this approach is obvious; there is no need for expensive reclamation or conservation measures. However, development of a salt-resistant variety is only a temporary solution, because, if salinization continues, the soil will become even more salty, and, new, even more highly resistant varieties will be needed. Eventually, a limit will be reached, because extremely high salt concentrations represent a particularly harsh environment.

8.9
Case History: Selenium in the San Joaquin Valley

Throughout this chapter, we have discussed how agricultural practices affect farms, farmers, and food productivity. However, a related issue is the effect of agricultural pollution on nonagricultural ecosystems. When soils are eroded from farmlands, not only is the farm affected, but the air may also be filled with dust, and silt may collect in streambeds. In addition, pesticides and fertilizers pour into streams and leach into groundwater supplies. In many agricultural regions, well water contains such a high concentration of nitrate that it is unfit to drink. To illustrate this general problem, we will examine a specific case history.

Recall from the previous section that many farmers have placed subsurface drains in some agricultural areas where salinization problems are acute. But the drains merely remove the salts from the farms, not from the environment. The next problem is how to dispose of this water that is not only brackish but also, in many cases, is polluted with fertilizer and pesticide residues. The cheapest (although not necessarily the most ecologically sound) dumping place is the ocean. Consequently, in 1975, the U.S. Bureau of Reclamation formulated plans to build a system, called the San Luis Drain, to carry drainage water from the San Joaquin valley farms and disperse it into San Francisco Bay.

However, funding for the project was curtailed before it was completed, leaving engineers with a system of pipes and canals that led essentially nowhere. By coincidence, the end of the half-completed project was close to the Kesterson National Wildlife Refuge, a wintering ground for migratory waterfowl on the Pacific flyway. Therefore, for convenience, the drain was diverted into the refuge (Fig. 8–14).

In 1982, a large fish kill occurred in the Kesterson Reservoir, and, a year later, many dead and deformed birds were discovered by Fish and Wildlife biologists. Analysis of the dead animals showed a very high concentration of the element selenium. Selenium is an element that is essential to plants and animals in trace amounts but becomes toxic when it is more concentrated. The soil of the San Joaquin valley contains naturally high but nontoxic quantities of selenium. However, the concentration of selenium in the brackish water pouring into the San Luis Drain is several orders of magnitude greater than it is in the natural system.

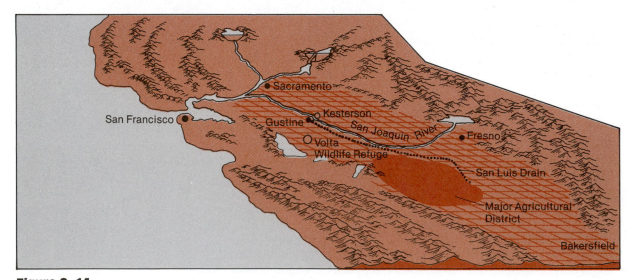

Figure 8–14
The location of the San Luis drain and the Kesterson wildlife refuge.

In 1984, a local rancher filed a cease-and-desist order, claiming that the Interior Department was in violation of the Migratory Bird Treaty Act, which forbids the killing of migratory birds. This action prompted an announcement by the U.S. Department of Interior Secretary Donald Hodel, ordering immediate closure of San Luis Drain. Furthermore, he ordered that if the farmers continued to dump drainage water into the refuge, the government would immediately terminate all deliveries of irrigation water to the 42,000 acres of land using the drain.

The farmers of the area countered that this sudden and drastic directive was unduly harsh. Therefore, a compromise agreement was reached, whereby the drain discharge was stopped by 1986. The 2-year grace period was allowed to give the farmers an opportunity to implement solutions such as use of on-farm and regional evaporation ponds and to install more efficient irrigation systems.

At the present time, studies are under way to assess the economic feasibility and environmental implications of completing the drain and discharging the polluted water into the Pacific Ocean.

8.10
Desertification

Just over one hundred years ago, the United States government commissioned John Wesley Powell to explore the land in the western United States and analyze its potential for development. Part of his study was summarized in a pamphlet entitled "Report on the Land of the Arid Region of the United States." Basically, Powell observed that most of the West received less than 50 cm (20 inches) of rainfall. In its natural state, much of this region was open prairie, and Powell concluded that these rangelands would be unable to support highly productive agriculture and large human populations. He wrote:

> There . . . remain vast area of valuable pasturage land bearing nutritious but scanty grass.
> Within the Arid Region only a small portion of the country is irrigable. The irrigable tracts are lowlands lying along the streams.
> The limit of successful agriculture without irrigation has been set at 20 inches [annual rainfall]. . . . Many droughts will occur; many seasons in a long series will be fruitless; and it may be doubted whether [dryland] agriculture will prove renumerative.
> This land will maintain but a scanty population.

In many ways, Powell's predictions have been incorrect. In the 1880s, only 1.5 million people lived in the arid West, whereas today, there are more than 30 million people in the area. In 1985, more than $17 billion worth of crops and livestock were raised in the region. Some of this unforeseen development has been made possible by major advances in irrigation technology. The development of gasoline and electric motors has led to the use of pumps that today can draw water from deep underground. The construction of major dams—unimaginable in Powell's time—has led to massive storage systems for spring run-off, and the improvements in the technology of building pipes and canals has increased the ease with which water can be transported.

The experience in the American West has been mirrored in many other regions around the world. Nearly one third of the Earth's surface is arid. In prehistoric times, these lands supported small numbers of nomadic hunters or herders, but, in recent years, in Africa, in Asia, in Oceania, and in the Americas, the nonmigratory human population living in arid lands has increased dramatically.

However, the core of Powell's argument cannot be ignored; arid lands do have a lower carrying capacity than do moist areas. Therefore, large populations have placed unprecedented pressures on arid lands. Some of the consequences that can result when field crops are raised in dry regions have already been documented. If land is irrigated improperly, a farmer runs the risk of salinization or waterlogging. On the other hand, if fields are not irrigated, there is a constant threat that drought will destroy a crop, leaving the soil bare and vulnerable to erosion.

Now imagine what can happen when a semiarid rangeland is farmed improperly and the soil becomes salinated or eroded. If the disruption is severe enough, even the natural grasses and shrubs cannot re-establish themselves. Without plants, the natural rainfall that does fall is not retained and, instead, flows rapidly over the surface or escapes into the ground. When both soil quality and moisture content decline, a productive semiarid region can be converted into an unproductive desert. This process is called **desertification.**

Starving cattle in the Sahel. The area has been devastated by low rainfall and overgrazing during the past few decades. (Wide World Photos)

Desertification can also be caused by improper grazing. When cattle feed on a natural range, they select the most nutritious grasses and ignore noxious weeds or inedible shrubs. If an area is lightly grazed, the grasses remain healthy and are able to compete successfully with weeds and shrubs for water, nutrients, and space. Thus, a natural balance is maintained. However, if the grasses are overgrazed, their growth will be so seriously disrupted that they cannot reseed themselves. In turn, this loss of the grasses leads to several subsequent problems. One problem is that the less edible plants will become dominant, and the value of the range will be destroyed. In addition, the loss of the grasses leaves the soil susceptible to erosion during heavy rains. When the water runs off the land instead of seeping in, the water table is lowered. Because the deep-rooted bushes depend on the underground water levels, depletion of the water table ultimately leads to death for all plants. The whole process is further accelerated as the grazing cattle pack the earth down with their hooves, blocking the natural seepage of air and water through the soil. When the plant cover and the soil moisture are lost, the range has become desertified.

Overgrazing and the resultant desertification have occurred extensively in North Africa. One hundred years ago, most of the semiarid range lands bordering the Sahara Desert were populated by nomadic herders. For centuries, these people survived by adapting to their harsh environment. They moved across the continent with little regard for national boundaries, traveling with the seasons and abandoning an area after it had been grazed for a short period of time. This constant movement allowed rejuvenation of affected areas and prevented overgrazing. In addition, population levels of these nomadic tribes were stable and relatively low. In recent years, however, their lifestyle has changed. The demographic transition has been accompanied by decreased infant mortality and a rapidly rising population. In addition, enforcement of national borders and frequent hostilities in some areas have curtailed nomadism. As people have become settled and populations have grown, land has been overgrazed, plant systems that normally conserve the sparse rainfall have been destroyed, and the desert has grown.

Since 1958 the Sahara Desert has been growing outward in all directions, toward the north, south, west, and east. For example, between 1958 and 1985 it expanded about 125 km eastward, and, today, it continues to grow at a rate of up to several km per year. This process has also been repeated in many other regions of the world (Fig. 8–15).

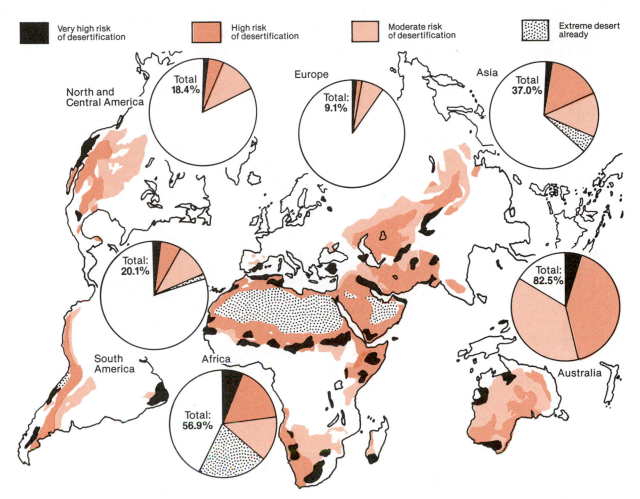

Figure 8–15

The Earth's spreading deserts. The map shows existing deserts and areas into which deserts may spread. The "desertification" hazard is based on a calculation of rainfall and evaporation in a given place. Where rainfall is low and evaporation is high, the risk of desertification is great. Circles show percentage of total land area on each continent that is, or that may become, desert.

Globally, about 70,000 sq km (27,000 sq miles) of land are turning into desert every year. To appreciate the scale of global desertification, if the annual newly formed desert were concentrated in a single square, each side would be 265 km long. A fast hiker can cover about 40 km per day. Traveling at this rate, it would take almost a month to walk around the perimeter of the land ruined by desertification every year.

In countries where desertification is particularly severe, notably Algeria, Iraq, Jordan, Lebanon, Mali, Niger, and Ethiopia, per capita food production declined by an alarming 40 percent between 1950 and 1985. Millions of people are literally starving, and it is very difficult for a government to order people with hungry babies at home to reduce their herds or to save a range for future generations. Yet, the destruction of the land today may lead to a downward spiral of increasing starvation followed by even more overgrazing and acute desertification the following season.

Even in the United States, overgrazing and desertification are a problem. In a wealthy nation such as the United States, it is feasible to initiate a program to halt the spread of deserts on public lands. In 1976, the Federal Land Policies and Man-

Special Topic C
How Permanent is the Process of Desertification?

If land is desertified by improper farming, can it be reclaimed in a reasonable amount of time? There is no universal answer to this question, because different ecosystems have different regenerative powers. In some areas, rainfall is sufficient to allow grasslands to re-establish themselves. In other areas, when the plant cover is destroyed, the water content of the soil drops so low that the land loses its ability to support life.

In recent years, scientists have been asking a broader question: Is there a relationship between plant cover and climate, and, if there is, could the destruction of an ecosystem lead to a permanent shift in regional weather patterns? When water is present in the environment, large quantities evaporate either from the soil or through the leaves of plants. This evaporation cools the air, and, in turn, a cooling process tends to cause atmospheric moisture to condense into rain. Therefore, weather, which is often considered to be controlled only by abiotic factors, is also influenced by living organisms. If an ecosystem is destroyed and the land loses its ability to retain moisture, the evaporative cooling is disrupted. In addition, land without vegetation reflects more sunlight than does a forest or grassland. (Which is hotter on your bare feet in the summertime, a dry sandy beach or a grassy lawn?) This change in reflectivity also causes the air above a desertified region to remain hot and promotes a dry climate.

Now look at Figure 8–16. The center line is the average rainfall in North Africa from 1900 to 1984. Notice that there have always been wet years and dry years. But notice that from 1968 to 1984, rainfall was below normal *every single year,* and severe droughts were a regular occurrence. Is this extreme drought cycle a random fluctuation of nature, or, alternatively, is it an unnatural disaster caused by the effects of overgrazing and desertification? Experts disagree on the answer to this question. Therefore, no definitive answer is available, but we must consider the possibility that destruction of semiarid ecosystems leads to a long-term change of climate.

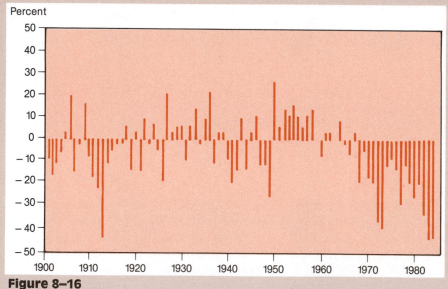

Figure 8–16
Rainfall fluctuations in the Sahel and Sudan expressed as a percent departure from the long-term mean, 1901–1984. (Source: Sharon Nicholson, Florida State University)

agement Act was passed, mandating the Bureau of Land Management to care for the land and ensure that grazing rights are not overextended. Some argue that the Bureau of Land Management is still favoring short-term profits for ranchers rather than long-term stability of the range, but the region is subject to at least some control and regulation. In many less developed countries, the situation is far more desperate.

Summary

Nitrogen, phosphorus, potassium, calcium, magnesium, and sulfur are used by plants in relatively large quantities and are called **macronutrients. Micronutrients** are those elements that are essential to growth but are used only in trace amounts.

Healthy soil is made up of a mixture of inorganic mineral matter and decayed organic matter. Soils that contain the largest inorganic particles are **sandy. Silt** soils contain smaller particles, and clay particles are microscopic. Water readily passes through sandy soils but is retained by clays. Organic matter provides a reservoir of nutrients, a physical matrix that retains moisture, and chelating agents that regulate nutrient retention and release.

The temperate regions contain the richest natural soils because growth and decomposition are balanced. Growth and decay are slow in the Arctic, resulting in poor soils. Decay is so rapid in the Tropics that there is little organic matter in the soil.

The basic techniques of agriculture are: **tillage, fertilization, irrigation,** and **pest control.**

A major concern today, particularly in fertile temperate agricultural areas, is the loss of soil as a result of erosion by wind and water. Such erosion can eventually destroy the soil completely or reduce its depth to the point where agricultural productivity is reduced. Some common conservation measures include **rotation, fallowing,** and **terracing**. Often conservation is not practiced because farmers forfeit long-term economic considerations for immediate gains.

If chemical fertilization is used exclusively for long periods of time, the quantity of organic matter in the soil will diminish, with consequent loss of soil quality. **Organic farming** produces a slightly lower yield per hectare than farming with conventional fertilizers and pesticides. However, because production costs are often lower, the economics of the two systems are often comparable.

Irrigation has brought vast areas of arid land into cultivation. Sustained agriculture is often interrupted, however, because irrigation increases the salt content of the soil and often leads to waterlogging. This problem can be alleviated by the use of drainage systems, by conservation of water, or by the development of salt-resistant crops.

Improper agricultural practices can lead to pollution of ecosystems that are adjacent to farms. One example is the selenium poisoning that occurred when drainage water from the San Joaquin valley was dumped into a wildlife preserve.

The world's deserts are expanding as a result of overgrazing or salinization of semiarid regions.

Questions

Soil

1. Explain why plants could become nutrient deficient even when adequate supplies of nitrogen, phosphorus, and potassium were available.

2. Explain why soils with very large or very small particle sizes are not optimal for the growth of plants.

3. The mineral composition of rocks collected from the surface of the Moon is similar to that of many rocks found on Earth, but there is no life on the Moon. How would lunar soils differ from those found on Earth?

4. Give an example of a chemical, a physical, a living, and a nonliving, but organic component of soils. Show how the various components are interconnected.

5. Explain how organic matter alters both the physical and the chemical nature of soils.

6. If you had a garden area that contained clayey soils, what types of treatments would improve the productivity of the plot? What would you do if the garden was sandy?

7. Explain why areas with very rapid or very slow rates of decomposition contain poor soils. Give examples.

Agriculture

8. What are the four major techniques of agriculture? Discuss briefly how each technique was used in ancient times and is used in modern times. Discuss the similarities and differences between the two approaches.

9. Explain why farmers in some regions let their fields lie fallow for a season or a year, whereas in other regions, fields are fallowed for as much as 20 years.

10. List three reasons why tillage promotes the growth of crops, and three reasons why tillage can lead to soil erosion.

11. What are the advantages of organic over inorganic fertilizers? Is it correct to say that organic fertilizers are more nutritious for plants than inorganic fertilizers? Defend your answer.

12. Explain why a natural prairie is inherently more stable than an agricultural region. Explain how croplands can be stabilized by mimicking some of the qualities of the natural systems.

Soil Erosion and Salinization

13. In the developed countries, the use of large tractors reduced the amount of labor required to raise a given quantity of product. Explain how the use of large machinery could reduce a farmer's willingness to adapt the best measures to conserve the soil. Give examples of situations in which the use of heavy equipment could simplify and reduce the cost of some conservation measures.

14. In Chapter 2, a distinction was made between social and technical solutions to environmental problems. Discuss the interplay between these two approaches in searching for ways to reduce soil erosion and salinization.

15. Some people have suggested that in the developed countries, if people grew vegetables in their back yards rather than lawns and flowers, many of the agricultural problems in those regions would be reduced. Write a short paragraph in which you imagine how a massive home gardening effort would affect agriculture in the United States. Would salinization problems in the San Joaquin Valley or soil erosion in Tennessee be reduced? Compare your opinions with those of your classmates.

16. Discuss the tradeoff between short-term profit and long-range stability in agriculture. In many regions, farming is marginally profitable at best, so farmers must maximize their return in a particular year. Do you believe that it is in a nation's best interest to provide economic support for soil conservation by subsidizing farmers? Discuss.

17. In some regions where local land prices for residential or commercial development are high, it is profitable to buy agricultural land, farm it for a few years with little regard to preserving soil quality, and then sell the fields after the soil is depleted. What type of economic externalities are ignored in this type of accounting? Who pays for these external costs?

18. Discuss the statement: American farming, as practiced today, is essentially mining a nonrenewable resource rather than exploiting a renewable one.

19. Discuss the relationship between population growth and rates of soil erosion and desertification in the less-developed countries.

20. Explain how salinization and waterlogging can be synergistic.

21. Explain how salinization problems can be reduced by: (a) drip irrigation; (b) organic farming; (c) leveling a field; (d) fallowing.

Desertification

22. Explain how a semiarid region can be converted into desert, even if the patterns of rainfall are constant.

23. Explain how overgrazed pastures are likely to be overgrown with inedible bushes such as sage.

24. Explain how nationalism in North Africa has led, indirectly, to increased desertification from overgrazing.

Suggested Readings

Information on soils and soil fertility is available in several standard texts:

R. Akeny: *Conservation Tillage: Problems and Potentials.* Iowa Soil Conservation of America, 1977. 75 pp.

Heinrich Bohn, Brian McNeal, and George O'Connor: *Soil Chemistry.* New York, John Wiley & Sons, 1979. 329 pp.

A. D. Bradshaw and M. J. Chadwick: *The Reforestation of Land: The Ecology and Reclamation of Derelict and Degraded Land.* Boston, Blackwell Scientific Publications, 1980. 317 pp.

Charles B. Heiser, Jr.: *Of Plants and People.* Norman, Oklahoma, University of Oklahoma Press, 1985. 272 pp.

Hans Jenny: *The Soil Resource.* New York, Springer Verlag, 1979. 377 pp.

Richard Lowrance (ed.): *Agricultural Ecosystems, Unifying Concepts.* Somerset, NJ, John Wiley & Sons, 1984. 233 pp.

Soil erosion is documented in the following sources:

Nelson L. Bills and Ralph E. Heimlich: *Assessing Erosion on U.S. Cropland.* Washington D.C., USDA, 1984. 19 pp.

Lester R. Brown and Edward C. Wolf: *Soil Erosion: A Quiet Crisis in the World Economy.* Worldwatch Paper 60; Washington, D.C., Worldwatch Institute, 1984. 49 pp.

Ann Crittenden: Soil erosion threatens U.S. farms' output. *The New York Times,* October 26, 1980. p. 1.

Pierre R. Crosson and Anthony T. Stout: *Productivity Effects of Cropland Erosion in the United States.* Washington, D.C., Resources for the Future, 1983. 103 pp.

Gordon K. Douglass (ed.): *Agricultural Sustainability in a Changing World Order.* Boulder, CO, Westview Press, 1984. 282 pp.

W. E. Larson, F. J. Pierce, and R. H. Dowdy: The threat of soil erosion to long-term crop production. *Science, 29:*458, 1983.

United States Department of Agriculture: *Analysis of Policies to Conserve Soil and Reduce Surplus Crop Production.* Washington D.C., USDA Agricultural Economic Report No. 534, 1985. 21 pp.

Information on irrigation and desertification can be found in:

Harold E. Dregne: Aridity and land degradation. *Environment, 27:*8, 1985.

H. F. Lamprey and Hussein Yussuf: Pastoralism and desert encroachment in northern Kenya. *Ambio, 10:*2–3, 1981.

Janet Raloff: Salt of the earth. *Science News, 126:* 1984.

Janet Raloff: Surviving salt. *Science News, 126:* 1984.

David Sheridan: *Desertification of the United States.* Washington, D.C., Council on Environmental Quality, 1981. 142 pp.

Mohamed Skouri: Regional development and desertfication in arid zones around the Sahara. *Nature and Resources, 20:*1, 1984.

J. Walls: *Land, Man, and Sands.* New York, MacMillan, 1980. 336 pp.

Agricultural problems in the United States are discussed in:

Sandra S. Batie and Robert G. Healy: *The Future of American Agriculture as a Strategic Resource.* Washington, D.C., The Conservation Foundation, 1980. 291 pp.

W. Wendell Fletcher and Charles E. Little: *The American Cropland Crisis.* Bethesda, MD, American Land Forum, 1982. 191 pp.

Wes Jackson, Wendell Berry, and Bruce Colman (eds.): *Meeting the Expectations of the Land.* San Francisco, North Point Press, 1984. 250 pp.

United States Department of Agriculture: *Report and Recommendations on Organic Farming.* Washington D.C., USDA, 1980. 94 pp.

The effects of agricultural practices on nonfarm systems are discussed in:

Edwin H. Clark II, Jennifer A. Haverkamp, and William Chapman: *Eroding Soils, The Off-Farm Impacts.* Washington, D.C., The Conservation Foundation, 1985. 252 pp.

Kenneth Tanji, Andre Lauchli, and Jewell Meyer: Selenium in the San Joaquin Valley. *Environment 28* (6), July/August 1986.

9

Food Production and World Hunger

9.1
Introduction

Well-watered, fertile farmland can be quite productive. An intensively cultivated garden that is only 0.07 hectares (1/6 acre) can supply a family of four with plentiful amounts of green vegetables for a year. Yet for many people in the world, green vegetables are a rare luxury; in fact, even the basic grains necessary for the barest existence are often not available.

It is difficult for people in the developed countries to appreciate the despair of not having enough to eat. Yet according to a study by the World Bank, about 16 percent of the total global population, some 800 million people, are so severely undernourished that they cannot lead a normal working life, and perhaps as many as 30 percent of the people in the world are chronically hungry. A reporter in a refugee camp in East Africa recently wrote,

> Once seen, it can never be forgotten: more than 70,000 people, 90% of them women and children, clustered together on a barren hillside, their only shelter small huts made of thornbush branches, animal skins, and pieces of cloth. No one in the camp had received food rations in two days, and it was uncertain when the next food supply truck would arrive. . . .

That reporter was observing only one refugee camp of many in Africa, and people are hungry in many other parts of the world as well. In this chapter, the problem of world hunger will be examined and possible solutions considered.

9.2
Human Nutritional Needs

Humans, as well as other animals, need food to serve three functions:

1. Food provides energy for maintaining body temperature, for performing essential biological processes, and for doing work. The amount of energy needed depends on the outside temperature and the rate at which the individual works. On the average, an adult needs about 2500 to 3000 kilocalories of food energy every day. (Remember, 1 Calorie, when spelled with a capital C, equals 1 kilocalorie.)

2. Food provides essential materials for growth, for replacement of body tissues that are lost as wastes or in injury, for development of the fetus in a pregnant woman, and for production of milk for breast-feeding.

3. Food provides materials that are needed for the regulation of life processes such as transport of oxygen in the blood and maintenance of the nervous and digestive systems.

The first requirement, energy, is met mainly by intake of carbohydrates and fats. These nutrients contain only carbon, hydrogen, and oxygen. Carbohydrates are sugars and starches and occur mainly in fruits, cereals, vegetables, nuts, and milk products. Fats (which include oils) are widely distributed in both plant and animal foods. In addition to supplying energy, fats are stored in the body as a reserve supply of energy and are also essential constituents of nerves and of cell membranes.

The second requirement, the need for material for growth and repair of body tissues, is supplied mainly by proteins. Proteins are very large molecules made up of combinations of smaller units called **amino acids.** There are about 20 natural amino acids, 8 of which cannot be synthesized by the human body and must therefore be obtained from the diet. Two more are produced only meagerly by adults and hardly at all by children and should also be obtained from food. The 8 (or 10) amino acids that are essential to the human diet are called **essential amino acids.** Proteins occur in both plant and animal foods but in widely varying concentrations. Proteins also differ in their *quality,* which means that they differ in their content of essential amino acids. An **incomplete protein** is one that does not contain all the essential amino acids; a **complete protein** is one that does. Gelatin is an example of an incomplete protein; if gelatin were the only protein in a human diet, it could not support life. An ideal protein contains all the essential amino acids in the proportions needed by the body. A mother's milk provides ideal protein for her infant. Eggs provide protein of very high quality. However, different incomplete proteins can be combined to make a complete protein meal. Examples are found in various traditional ethnic food combinations, usually containing beans combined with either nuts, rice, or bread.

The third requirement, the need for materials for regulation of life processes, is supplied by a large number of nutrients that are needed in small, sometimes even trace, quantities. These nutrients include vitamins and minerals, which are distributed very unevenly in a wide variety of foods. A good diet should therefore be a varied one and should include foods of different types (proteins, grains, dairy foods, vegetables, and fruits) as well as foods from different geographical areas in which the soils have different mineral contents.

The opposite extreme of a plentiful, nutritious diet is **starvation,** which means death from lack of food. However, many people who are inadequately fed do not actually die for lack of calories to sustain life. Instead, they are malnourished, because the food is deficient in essential amino acids and vitamins, and death occurs because they have little resistance to diseases that would not be fatal if a healthy diet were available.

In general, young children who are growing and developing require a more nutritious diet than adults. Therefore, in regions where food is scarce, children often suffer most severely. Two common and devastating diseases resulting from malnutrition in children are **marasmus** and **kwashiorkor.**

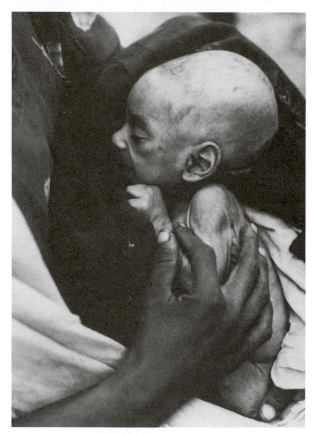

A starving baby in Ethiopia is cradled by a relief worker. (Bill Granger, US AID)

Marasmus is a protein and calorie deficiency that occurs when infants are deprived of mother's milk and are not fed an adequate substitute. It can occur if the mother dies or is so weakened by hunger that she can no longer lactate (produce milk). In some regions, young mothers are persuaded to switch from breast-feeding to bottle-feeding. But, if the parents lack the money to purchase enough milk formula or if distribution systems are interrupted, malnutrition will result. The symptoms of marasmus include general growth failure, development of weakened limbs, anemia, and diarrhea. In many cases in which parents rely on powdered formulas, the powder is dissolved in unsanitary water. The microorganisms in the water may then infect the infants with a wide variety of debilitating or fatal diseases.

Kwashiorkor is a disease that occurs among young children who do not receive enough protein. Although some infants show symptoms of marasmus and kwashiorkor simultaneously, kwashiorkor is most common among children who are already eating solid food. Children who suffer from this disease develop characteristic bloated bellies, thin arms and legs, wide eyes, and shriveled skin. Perhaps even more sinister is the fact that severe malnutrition in young people leads to early and irreversible brain damage. This results in a negative feedback cycle, because if undernourished and retarded children do survive to become adults, they will have decreased learning ability. Therefore,

when they grow up, they will be likely to have a hard time finding work, and, if work is found, it is often of the kind that pays the least money. When these impoverished adults in turn have children, their young are also likely to be undernourished, thereby perpetuating the tragic cycle.

Other diseases caused by nutritional deficiency are common throughout the world. By one estimate, a quarter of a million children become permanently blind every year because their diets are deficient in vitamin A. An additional uncounted number of persons die of infectious diseases because their bodies and immune systems have been weakened by hunger and lack of proper nutrients. All told, approximately 15 million people starve to death or die indirectly from malnutrition every year.

9.3
World Food Supply—An Overview

As shown in Figure 9–1, the total food production of the Earth has increased dramatically in recent years. But the population has been increasing as well, so a more useful indicator of the availability of food is the per capita production, or the food production per person. According to Table 9–1, the global grain output increased by an average of 3.1 percent between 1950 and 1973. During the same period, the population grew by only 1.9 percent, so the grain output per capita increased by 1.2 per-

Figure 9–1
World food production from 1950 to 1985. (Worldwatch Institute)

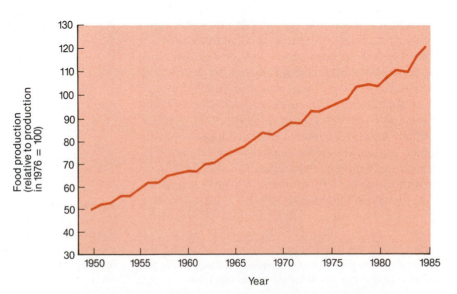

Table 9–1
Annual Growth in World Grain Production, Total and Per Capita, 1950–1973 and 1973–1985

Period	Grain Output	Population	Grain Output Per Capita
	← (growth percent) →		
1950–1973	3.1	1.9	1.2
1974–1985	2.2	1.8	0.4

cent.* However, the rate of increase of grain production decreased to 2.2 percent per year between 1973 and 1985, leading to a very small increase in per capita output.

On the one hand, these data are alarming. If current trends continue, per capita grain production will continue to decline, and there will be less food available than there is today. On the other hand, Table 9–1 tells us that per capita grain production increased continuously between 1950 and 1985, so, you may ask, why are so many people starving today?

The data offered so far represent global averages and tell us very little about production from region to region. Figure 9–2 shows a comparison of the per capita grain production in Western Europe versus that in Africa. Note the vast difference between the two curves. In Europe, where the population is stabilizing and agricultural production is increasing rapidly, the per capita grain production has more than doubled in the past 25 years. However, in Africa, the population is increasing faster than the rate of food production, and, today, millions are starving. The increasing separation between the rich and the poor is shown in Table 9–2. Note that in the 1930s, *all* the major regions of the world, with the exception of Western Europe, exported grain. Now observe the changes over the years. Africa, Asia, and eastern Europe have become increasingly dependent on the developed world and especially on exports from North America. What a vulnerable system! Think of what

would happen to people all over the world if a drought crippled the wheat crop in North America for even 1 year.

Two major factors account for the difference in per capita food production between the rich nations and the poor. First, as documented in Chapter 7, the population is growing much faster in the less-developed countries than in the developed countries. Therefore, if the total agricultural production increased at the same rates in the two regions, the less-developed countries would realize a much smaller increase, or even a decrease, in per capita food production.

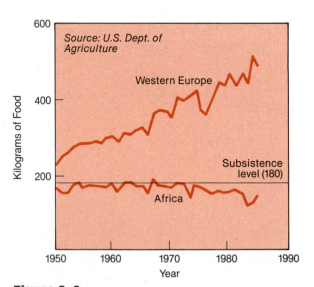

Figure 9–2
Comparison of food production in Africa with that in Western Europe from 1950 to 1985. Note that during most of the 35-year period, food production in Africa has been below the subsistence level of 180 kg per person per year.

*Note that the graph in Figure 9–1 shows total food production, whereas Table 9–1 lists total grain production. Since grains constitute about 90 percent of the total food production, the two different indices are similar enough to be compared.

Table 9–2
The Changing Pattern of World Grain Trade

Region	1934 to 1938	1948 to 1952	1960	1970	1980	1985
North America	+5	+23	+39	+56	+131	+103
Latin America	+9	+1	0	+4	−10	+1
Western Europe	−24	−22	−25	−30	−16	+11
Eastern Europe and Soviet Union	+5	0	0	0	−46	−35
Africa	+1	0	−2	−5	−15	−29
Asia	+2	−6	−17	−37	−63	−72
Australia and New Zealand	+3	+3	+6	+12	+19	+21

The results are expressed as millions of tonnes of grain; plus signs indicate net exports; minus signs, net imports.

Second, there is an ever increasing relationship between wealth and agricultural production. As will be discussed further in the following section, high-yield agriculture depends on the use of the best varieties of seeds as well as on efficient fertilization and pest control. In the developed regions, farmers can afford these inputs, and, therefore, they can produce higher yields. This is not the case, however, for farmers in the poorer nations, and, therefore, agricultural yields suffer.

The incredible difference in the problems faced by the farmers in different regions of the world is summarized in the following quotation.

> The state of the world's food and agricultural systems in the mid-1980s can best be described as an almost intractable paradox. While humankind has demonstrated once and again the planet's awesome ability to produce ever more food and fiber, television sets around the world were revealing pitiful scenes of mass starvation in Africa and record books were disclosing grim statistics that more people than ever—about half a billion—were living in a serious state of malnutrition.*

9.4
Food Production, Weather, and Climate

Farmers have always been at the mercy of the weather. If the temperature and rainfall are favorable, food will often be plentiful, but frost, flood,

*Lester Brown et al: *State of the World 1986*. (See bibliography.)

or drought may lead to crop failures. In one sense, people today are less vulnerable to changes in the weather than they were 100 years ago. Rapid communication and transportation systems make it possible to transport food large distances across the globe. Thus, for example, a poor harvest in the U.S.S.R. can be counterbalanced by a bumper crop in North America, simply by shipping food from one continent to the other. In this way, trade can minimize the effect of local disasters.

In another and perhaps larger sense, however, people are much more vulnerable than they ever were before. In the past, famine was often alleviated by migration. As long as the human population was low, farmers could often offset crop failures by moving to a new area and clearing previously virgin land. Today, this option is rapidly drawing to a close.

From the beginning of agriculture until the early 1900s, most increases in worldwide food production resulted from an expansion of the total area of farmland under cultivation. Today, however, the most highly productive farming areas in the world have already been cleared, plowed, and planted. Therefore, most of the new farms that are being started are located in the far north, in recently cleared rain forests, in deserts, and in alpine environments. Although these farms can be highly productive in good years, they are potentially vulnerable in bad years. For example, if the temperature in Kansas falls by a degree or two, the wheat crop will probably not be seriously affected. But a small drop in temperature on a barley farm near

Many new farms are being started in areas that were once considered too harsh to farm. These can be productive in good years but are extremely vulnerable to slight changes in weather and climate. The photograph on the left shows a gladioli plantation that is being grown on land reclaimed from the Negev Desert in Israel (courtesy of Israel Government Tourist Office). The picture on the right shows a man plowing a steep mountainside in the Andes in Peru.

Box 9.1
Global Climate Patterns

The fragility of global climate and weather patterns can be illustrated by the following example. Africa and Asia are subjected to cycles of monsoon storms. Summer monsoons arise because continents generally warm up faster in the spring than do oceans. When the air over the land is heated, it rises, drawing moisture-laden sea air inland. This sea breeze carries moisture, which eventually falls as rain. During the 1970s, the temperature across the planet fell slightly. A temperature drop of a degree or so is insignificant by itself, but, in this case, it extended the range of cold arctic air. In turn, this cold air moved southward and displaced monsoon clouds by a few hundred kilometers. The result was a series of increasingly severe droughts in the northern parts of the grain-producing areas of Africa and Asia, which contributed to the food shortages of 1972 to 1974.

Fairbanks, Alaska, may mean that the last spring frost arrives 2 weeks later than usual and the first killing frost in the fall is early enough to stunt the growth of the crop severely. Similarly, a 10 percent decrease in rainfall won't spell disaster for a pea farmer on the rainy northwest coast of the state of Washington, but it could lead to starvation in the Sahel region of North Africa, which is near-desert even in the best of times.

The problem that causes great concern is this: Historical records show that the period between 1950 and 1985 were years of unusually plentiful rainfall and mild climate. During that time period, both food production and population increased rapidly. If the climate were to change adversely, farms in many regions of the world could fail. In turn, massive agricultural failure could lead to unprecedented famine. Therefore, it is natural to ask whether the climate will change and, if so, whether it will change for the better or for the worse. Of course, no one knows the answer. It is difficult enough to predict what the weather will be next week, let alone project temperature and rainfall patterns 5, 10, or 25 years from now. Scientists do know that climates have changed radically during the geological history of the Earth. For example, within the past 100 million years, the area that now includes the fertile wheatfields of Colorado has been alternately covered by swamps, thick glaciers, and dry deserts. This historical information reminds us that global climates do change, but it doesn't provide information useful for forecasting future trends. In the late 1970s, many climatologists believed that the Earth was cooling. In the early 1980s, there was increased speculation that a warming trend would occur within a decade. This prediction is based on the fact that carbon dioxide released when fossil fuels are burned absorbs infrared radiation and warms the air (see Chapter 21).

9.5
Energy and Agriculture

A wild oat plant in an unfarmed prairie and a domestic oat plant in a farmer's field live in very different environments. To survive, the wild oat must compete successfully with its neighbors for sunlight, moisture, and soil nutrients (Fig. 9–3). A plant that is tall, that sprouts early, or that has an effective root system has a competitive advantage. The energy that a wild plant needs to grow a tall stalk or a deep root comes only from the Sun. On the other hand, a cultivated oat is supplied with external aid to help it survive. The farmer waters it when necessary, removes competitive plants (weeds), and loosens the soil to stimulate the growth of root systems. Since all the seeds in the field are planted at the same time and are of the same variety and since unwanted weeds are removed, competition is minimal. The plant does not need as tall a stalk or as specialized and fast-growing a root system as a wild plant, and there is less competition for available nutrients. These advantages are not free. A farmer adds auxiliary sources of energy to till the land, to irrigate it, to apply fertilizer, and to combat weeds, insects, and other pests.

The differences in energy utilization and food production between natural systems and agricultural systems are illustrated by the following comparison of two types of meat production.

In a natural system, grazing animals wander around a prairie eating indigenous plants. Recall from Chapter 3 (Fig. 3–6), for every 1000 Calories of energy a plant receives from the Sun in such a

Figure 9–3
Plants compete for space, light, water, and nutrients in a natural grassland.

natural system, 990 Calories are lost; only 10 Calories are converted into plant tissue. Of these 10 Calories, 9 Calories are left uneaten; of the 1 Calorie that is eaten, herbivores convert only 0.1 Calorie to body tissue.

Modern mechanized production of meat operates very differently, because the solar energy is supplemented with considerable quantities of energy derived from fossil fuels. Only selected plants are grown, and the growth of these crops is often encouraged by irrigation and the addition of fertilizers and pesticides. These plants are then fed to steers in a feedlot (Fig. 9–4). An animal in a modern feedlot need not move but may stand in front of a feedbin, eating the hay or grain that the farmer, with the help of a tractor, baled or threshed and brought in from the field. In addition, food additives and growth hormones, synthesized in factories powered by coal or oil, help to increase growth. Therefore, meat production can be 10 times as great as it is in a natural prairie (Fig. 9–5). Although a feedlot system is more efficient in using sunlight to produce meat than is a natural system, the feedlot requires large quantities of fossil fuels.

As a national average, in the United States, 3 Calories of fossil energy are used on the farm to

Figure 9–4
Cattle in a feedlot.

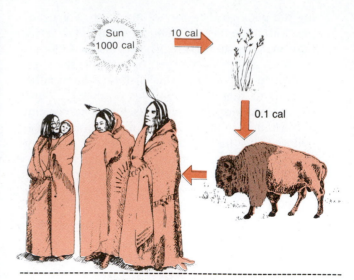

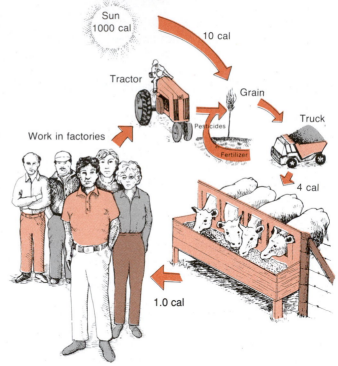

produce food with an energy content of 1 Calorie. If the energy used in processing, transportation, and preparation is also included, nearly 10 Calories of fossil energy are consumed to place every Calorie's worth of food on our tables. In the less-developed countries, less than 1 Calorie obtained from fuels is used to raise, transport, and prepare a Calorie's worth of food.

Mechanized food production is based on a technological cycle. High crop yields are needed to feed urban workers, who, in turn, provide the technology required to maintain the high food production. The individual components of the cycle are interdependent. Large populations of humans depend on high agricultural yields, while, at the same time, these high yields depend on high industrial outputs.

Chemical Inputs

Chemical fertilizers and pesticides are widely used in modern mechanized agriculture. There is very little unfarmed but potentially prime agricultural land left on the Earth today. The unfarmed land that exists is mostly marginally productive. On the

Figure 9–5
Comparison between meat production on the range and in a feedlot. The feedlot system produces more meat for humans but consumes fossil fuel energy.

other hand, most existing farmland is being either depleted by erosion or eliminated entirely by urbanization. Therefore, in recent years, the major solution to the problem of feeding the world's people has been to increase productivity on existing farmland. These gains have been realized largely

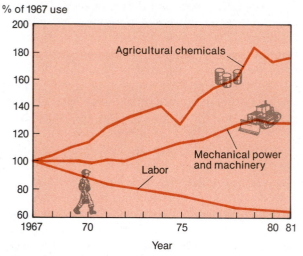

Figure 9–6
Use of chemicals, mechanical power, and labor on farms in the United States between 1967 and 1981. Note the rapid rise in chemical use and the decline in labor.

through addition of fertilizers (Fig. 9–6). Thus, humans have, in effect, traded fossil fuels for food.

What will happen when the oil runs out? The worst case imaginable is one in which there is very little fuel of any kind available. Then potential fertilizers for next year's crop, such as manure or crop residues, will be used as fuel to cook this year's food. Today, hundreds of millions of people are caught in this type of downward spiral, which results in increasingly severe soil depletion, leading to deeper poverty and to continued exhaustion of the soil. For example, in Nepal, the dung used for fuel every year represents a nutrient loss severe enough to reduce grain output by 25 percent by the year 2000. In a more hopeful scenario, alternative energy sources may be used to manufacture fertilizers or to cook food and to heat homes so that agricultural wastes can be used to improve the quality of the soil.

Pesticides and herbicides are another form of chemical input, and these, too, require energy to manufacture and disperse. Efficient biological pest control would reduce this energy requirement, but, at the present time, chemical sprays are widely used.

Mechanization

High agricultural yields require specific varieties of seeds, an active fertilizer program, and pest control. In many regions, irrigation is also essential to high yields. In most less-developed countries, irrigation systems are designed so that water flows downhill from a river into the fields. However, in developed countries, water from deep wells is often used in agriculture and considerable energy is required for pumping. On the other hand, the use of tractors does not improve the yield per hectare. In fact, yields are often *less* in mechanized agriculture than they are in high-intensity, nonmechanized systems. The reasons for this reduction in production are twofold. First, in many cases, crops must be planted further apart if machinery is to be driven between the rows than if the field is worked by hand. Thus, crop density will be less and, consequently, the potential yields will be smaller. Sec-

Mechanization in agriculture. *Left,* combine; *Right,* tomato picker. (Photo courtesy of Rorer-Amchem, Inc., Ambler, PA)

Using animal power to harvest wheat in India. Animals do not use fossil fuels, but some farmland must be set aside to raise food to feed them. (Courtesy of Agency for International Development)

The advantages and disadvantages of mechanization can be illustrated by comparing farming practices in North America with those in Japan. In North America, where tractors are used extensively, consumers spend a smaller proportion of their incomes on food, on the average, than any other people in the world. In addition, large quantities of grains are raised for export. Although this abundance is caused by many different factors acting in concert, the inexpensive availability of machinery certainly contributes. In contrast, in Japan, many farmers own small, two-wheeled rotary tillers, but very few own four-wheeled tractors, and heavy farm machinery is virtually unknown. Even though the use of heavy equipment is minimal, large quantities of fertilizer and much manual labor are used. Crop density is high, fields are cared for intensively, and, as a result, the average yield in Japanese agriculture is higher than that in North America.

Energy Use in Food Processing and Transportation

In its simplest form, energy for food processing involves cooking a pot of rice over a stone fireplace. In many less-developed countries, even the small quantity of fuel needed for this task is not always available. Table 9–3 shows the energy used in food

ond, machinery is not capable of handling food as precisely as can a laborer. This difference is especially critical for fruits and vegetables that are easily damaged. For example, a mechanical tomato picker moves through a field once, picks the fruit before it is ripe, and destroys the plants. (Ripe red tomatoes would be bruised by the machine; the green tomatoes are later ripened with ethylene gas.) If the crop is harvested manually, laborers can move through the field several times, picking only the fruit that is ready at the moment. The plants are thus allowed to keep producing for a longer time, and more tomatoes can be harvested. Or, as another example, there are machines that shake apples from trees onto collecting frames, but more apples are bruised with this method than when picking is done by hand.

Despite these disadvantages, almost all commercial farmers in the developed countries rely heavily on the use of machinery. The reason for this choice is that in regions in which fuel and equipment are inexpensive relative to the price of labor, the use of machinery saves money. In addition, farmers using tractors can cultivate or harvest large tracts of land quickly and thereby take advantage of short periods of favorable weather.

> **Box 9.2**
> **How to Reduce Energy Consumption in Agriculture**
>
> 1. Use less mechanization, more manual labor.
> 2. Use fewer commercial fertilizers, more recycled waste.
> 3. Use fewer pesticides and herbicides, more integrated management.
> 4. Use less packaging.
> 5. Locate farms closer to urban areas.
> 6. Improve the dietary efficiency of people, reducing overconsumption.
>
> Note: These suggestions are easy to propose; to implement them would require a significant readjustment of many segments of society.

Table 9–3
Use of Energy from Farm to Table in the United States

Use	Energy Consumed (trillions of kcal)	
On farm		
Fuel for tractors	232	
Electricity	64	
Energy to manufacture fertilizers	94	
Energy to manufacture farm machinery	101	
Irrigation	35	
	526	Subtotal
Processing industry		
Food processing industry	314	
Packaging industry	207	
Transportation	321	
	842	Subtotal
Commercial and home		
Refrigeration and cooking	804	
Grand total	2172	

processing from farm to table in the United States. Note some interesting facts. More than twice as much energy is used to package food products as is used to manufacture fertilizers. Such a large allocation of resources for packaging is unique in the history of human food production and presents an attractive target for energy conservation.

Another large allocation is the energy used to transport food from the farm to the market, which is more than the energy needed to fuel the tractors used directly on the farm. This circumstance is a result of various economic factors. Since the 1950s, there was an increasing trend in the United States toward centralization of farming practices. For example, economy of scale has made it more profitable to raise milk on a large corporate farm in Wisconsin and ship it to Massachusetts than to operate a small dairy farm in a Massachusetts community. As a result, many local farmers have sold their farms, and the land has been developed for residential or commercial use. In the early 1980s, food traveled an average of 2000 km before it was eaten.

What is our agricultural future? In 1987, there were about 5 billion people in the world. Some sci-entists have suggested that if modern agricultural techniques were widely available and food distribution were more equitable, our planet could easily support 10 billion or even 15 billion inhabitants. But others disagree. They say that when fuel supplies become limited, agricultural productivity will decrease. According to this analysis, the real carrying capacity of the Earth is closer to 2.5 billion, only one half the number that are alive today.

9.6
Increases in Crop Yields and the Green Revolution

Next time you are walking in the country, look closely at the wild grasses growing in meadows and fields. Notice that each plant has a slender stalk, a few leaves, and a small cluster of seeds at the top. These seeds are rich in starch, protein, and vitamins, but they are so small that they are not harvested and processed for human consumption. Ancient farmers living in the Stone Age probably started cultivating grains that were only slightly more productive than these modern "weeds." As

Special Topic A
Energy Consumption for Food Production

An example of extreme energy consumption for food production is processed cereal or snack foods made from rice grown in the San Joaquin Valley in California.

The rice paddies are first prepared using heavy tractors and grading equipment. Maximal efficiency is realized if the field is absolutely flat. Therefore, the most mechanized farms use a laser-computer leveling system. A rotating laser transmitter is first established in the center of the field. This device beams an electronic reference elevation. A tractor then drags a leveling plow with a laser receiver mounted above it. A small computer on the tractor determines whether the elevation of the field at any point is above or below the required reference level. The computer then operates a motor that raises or lowers the leveling blades behind the tractor. Fertilizer is applied heavily. Water, piped in from hundreds of kilometers away, is used to flood the fields. Rice seeds, previously treated with chemicals to control seedling diseases, are spread by airplane. Further aerial spraying of pesticides and herbicides protects the crop, which is finally harvested by large combines.

Growing and harvesting is only a first step. The rice is cleaned, milled to remove the nutritious outer hull, refortified with vitamins to replace some of the removed nutrients, and finally puffed, blown, cooked, packaged, and transported to produce cold cereal products or snack foods available at a supermarket. The efficiency of the entire process depends on how you look at it. In terms of total yield (kilogram of grain per hectare of land), U.S. rice culture is nearly twice as efficient as the world average. But, in terms of energy input to energy output, the system is woefully inefficient.

various farmers replanted only the seeds of the largest, healthiest plants, modern strains of wheat, rice, and other grains were developed gradually over the centuries (Fig. 9–7). These grains were generally well adapted to local growing conditions. They were genetically adjusted to peculiarities in soil conditions, water supply, length of growing season, and seasonal temperatures, and they were at least partially resistant to local diseases and pest infestations. However, as population increased in the nineteenth and twentieth centuries, it became apparent that traditional farming practices were not

Figure 9–7
The wheat stalk on the right supports much larger quantities of grain than the native grass shown on the left.

Special Topic B
Appropriate Technology in Agriculture

Modern technology is often associated with grandiose schemes such as nuclear power plants, gigantic hydroelectric facilities, and sophisticated machinery. But the electricity produced by advanced technologies is not distributed to the poorest farming communities in the less-developed countries, and poor farmers certainly cannot afford heavy equipment or laser-guided plowing systems. Yet, villagers could benefit greatly from modern science and engineering if it were applied directly to their needs. Such direct application of modern expertise is called **appropriate technology.**

As an example, throughout the world, approximately 400 million draft animals—horses, oxen, donkeys, mules, cows, water buffaloes, camels, yaks, llamas, and elephants—work for people. In many cases, harnesses and plow yokes are poorly designed. For example, the traditional wooden yoke weighs about 45 kg and burdens the animal unnecessarily. In addition, the strap under the neck tightens around the animal's windpipe, choking it as it pulls. Although a well-designed, anatomically efficient yoke would improve agricultural efficiency around the world, yoke design is not a popular engineering field. As N.S. Ramaswamy, Director of the Indian Institute of Management, said, "India has put a satellite in space and harnessed the atom, but our yokes are 5000 years old because professors are scared they may not get promoted if they work on finding better ones."

In many cases, technology imported from developed countries upsets traditional agricultural ecosystems and actually disrupts previously stable systems. For example, in Sri Lanka, farmers have traditionally plowed their fields with the help of water buffaloes. But the buffaloes provide more than simple pulling power. The animals produce protein-rich milk to drink and manure that can be used as a fertilizer or a fuel. Buffaloes also need ponds, called **wallows,** to lie in and cool themselves during the heat of the summer. These wallows have become part of traditional agricultural ecosystems. Fish survive the dry season by retreating to the wallows. In the springtime when the rice fields are flooded, these fish migrate outward and feed on the larva of malarial mosquitoes. In turn, the fish provide essential protein for the villagers. In addition, the thickets around the wallows shelter nonpoisonous snakes and lizards that control the population of agricultural pests such as rodents and land crabs.

The introduction of tractors in Sri Lanka has increased rice production; land that was set aside as pasture for buffaloes can now be used for growing grain. But tractors are expensive, and, in addition, when the animals and their wallows are gone, farmers must buy fertilizers and pesticides for their fields and milk, fish, and meat for their tables.

Water buffaloes in a wallow in Sri Lanka (Christine Seashore).

adequate to feed the world's people. Therefore, agriculturalists searched for ways to increase crop yields. It was obvious that heavy doses of fertilizer could augment food production, but there appeared to be a limit to the quantity of fertilizer that could be used. When a native grain plant is fertilized heavily, the leaves grow broader and larger, thereby shading nearby plants, and the stalk grows to be long and thin. The heavy grain causes the elongated stalk to break and bend, and the grain falls to the ground and rots.

In the mid-1960s, an interdisciplinary team of scientists working in Mexico and the Philippines developed new varieties of wheat and rice that were adaptable to tropical climates and were capable of producing higher yields than any native grains. These varieties have short, upright leaves, so that plants can be grown close together without shading each other. In addition, their stalks are short and thick so that they will not bend and break when the plant is heavily fertilized. The potential yields of these new varieties are so spectacular that many people heralded their introduction as the **Green Revolution.** For example in Mexico, in the 1940s, the yield from wheat fields averaged 750 kg per hectare, whereas the yields from the new strains of seeds in the 1970s averaged 3200 kg per hectare. In India and Pakistan, massive shipments of Green Revolution wheat in the late 1960s raised the wheat harvest between 50 and 60 percent during a period of two growing seasons. In Colombia,

rice production increased by a factor of 2 1/2, despite the fact that the area of cultivation remained nearly constant (Fig. 9–8). Such increased food production across the globe has reduced famine and increased the well-being of millions.

Despite the phenomenal success of the Green Revolution, it is important to appreciate its drawbacks and potential problems. First, a "wonder seed," by itself, does not produce large quantities of food. The seed only carries the genetic potential for high-grade production. If this production is to be realized, the plant must be fertilized heavily, watered, and protected from disease and insects. The new grain varieties planted in an impoverished soil and dependent on variable rainfall for growth produce equal or smaller yields than the native grains, which have been cultivated in such poor areas for centuries. In addition, the new grain varieties are less resistant to insect pests and fungal diseases than the traditional plants. As a result, farmers who invest in the seed, the fertilizer, and the advanced irrigation systems must also invest in pesticides.

If a farmer has the money to buy the new vigorous seeds as well as to provide the necessary fuel, fertilizer, pesticides, and irrigation facilities and knows how to manage a modern integrated farming program, high yields and an eventual profit can be realized. Otherwise, the Green Revolution may provide no help.

Many people have actually been harmed by the introduction of the new high-yield varieties of

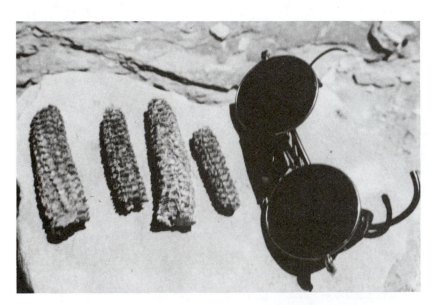

Corn cobs found in a prehistoric Native American dwelling in the southwest United States. Note how small they are compared with the sunglasses on the right. Plant breeders have increased cob size and seed weight through conventional breeding techniques, and modern corn is much larger.

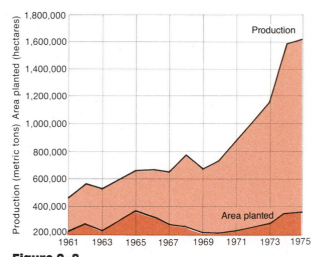

Figure 9–8

Rice production in Colombia following introduction of improved "Green Revolution" seeds in 1969.

grain. If more grain is grown by wealthy farmers, the price of food will drop. The poor, who cannot afford to plant the new seeds, grow the same amount of food as they did in past years, but receive less money for their harvest when it is time to sell.

Paradoxically, the very success of the Green Revolution raises problems of its own. In many areas, the new seeds have become so profitable that farmers have abandoned the traditional practices of planting many different types of crops in an area and have planted one or two high-yield varieties exclusively. The use of a single crop is called **monoculture.** Monoculture may be economically attractive, but it is ecologically unstable. In many regions, farmers have abandoned less profitable but more nutritious foods such as soybeans in favor of Green Revolution grains. Thus, food quality is sacrificed in favor of total yield. In addition, if only one type of plant is grown in a region, a very favorable environment for pests is provided. Furthermore, when a pest epidemic does break out in a monoculture system, a farmer can lose everything. The threat of pest invasions forces farmers to become increasingly dependent on pesticides. Alternatively, in a diverse agricultural system, pest invasions are less likely in the first place, and, when they do occur, the chances are good that some of the crop varieties will be resistant to the particular pest.

Despite the drawbacks, the Green Revolution has increased food production throughout the

In this rice field in Nepal, the farmer used too much fertilizer. The grain grew to be so heavy that it could not be supported by the thin stalk, and the plants have fallen over or become lodged. Green Revolution seeds are less likely to lodge as compared with conventional seeds.

Special Topic C
Exploitation of Exotic Species

Of the millions of different species on Earth, people use only a few dozen for food. Of course, most species are not suitable as food sources, but, recently, some agronomists have pointed out that in our search for new varieties of popular crops, we have been overlooking valuable wild species. According to this argument, the human race is dependent on a small number of different types of plants, and these species have been highly inbred in recent years. Therefore, the genetic pool that we are dependent on is dangerously shallow. In general, wild species are more resistant to disease, drought, and frost compared with domestic varieties. One solution to this problem is to crossbreed domestic hybrids with wild varieties of the same species. For example, if high-yield domestic corn is crossed with hardy wild corn, it might be possible to develop a hardy, high-yield hybrid. Alternatively, another so-lution is to exploit wild species that have not been previously cultivated. For example, the wild grain, quinoa, contains twice as much protein as wheat or rice and a better balance of amino acids. Agronomists are currently developing a strain of quinoa suitable for agriculture, and the food is being marketed in local areas. Or, as another example, the buffalo gourd is a member of the genus that includes squash and pumpkins. The roots of the buffalo gourd are rich in starch and can be eaten like potatoes or cassava, the fruits and seeds are edible and nutritious, and the stems and leaves provide excellent food for cattle. Moreover, yields per hectare are high, and the plant is frost- and drought-resistant.

The relationship between wild plants and agriculture will be discussed further in Chapter 12 in relation to the extinction of species.

world. Without these gains, hunger and starvation would be much more severe than they are today. Yet, even with these encouraging improvements, the sad reality is that most of the less-developed countries that have been "revolutionized" by new varieties of grains are importing food today. Increases in yields have not been sufficient to surmount the twin hurdles of population growth and increasing scarcity of cheap energy.

Let us focus for a moment on the relationship between energy and Green Revolution agriculture. As previously explained, energy is needed to manufacture the pesticides and fertilizers needed by the new seeds. We thus return to the question, "What will happen when fossil fuel supplies are depleted?" Predictions of future events are always uncertain. Recall from discussions in earlier chapters that one technique is to extrapolate current trends.

Harvesting wheat on a large farm in Kansas. Monoculture is economically advantageous, but such a system is ecologically unstable. (USDA Soil Conservation Service)

Figure 9–9
Traditional crossbreeding techniques that were available before the development of genetic engineering.

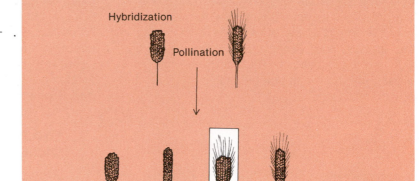

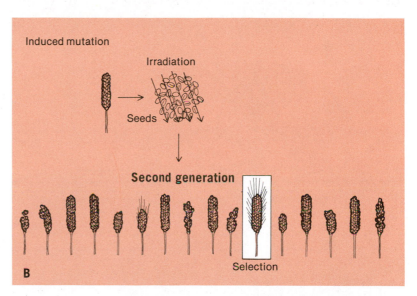

This type of analysis would lead to the argument that since agriculture is becoming increasingly dependent on energy and since energy supplies are limited (see Chapter 13), global agriculture is, indeed, in grave danger. The alternative argument is that we can expect even newer technologies to provide increased yields with lower fuel requirements.

The search for this seemingly magical solution is an active area of research today. To understand the techniques involved, let us start by first examining the basic concepts of breeding. Individual wheat plants in a given field are not exactly alike. They differ from each other in various characteristics, just as do individuals in a human population. These differences occur because different individuals, even those of the same species, have

different genetic compositions. Traditionally, farmers have replanted seeds only from those plants that produce the most grain. In this manner, the farmer selects certain genes over others, and the yields of grain crops have increased slowly throughout history. During the development of seeds from the first Green Revolution, scientists accelerated these processes by two techniques, **crossbreeding** and **artificial mutation.** Suppose that one wheat plant has a heavy cluster of grain but a thin stalk, whereas another has a thick stalk and less grain. A scientist will cross the two with the hope that a plant in the next generation will have a thick stalk and a heavy grain cluster (Fig. 9–9). Another possibility is to change the plant's characteristics by irradiating it with ultraviolet light or x-rays. Radiation randomly alters the genes of any organism, leading to mutation. A mutated plant may contain characteristics never before seen in the species, and, occasionally, these characteristics may be beneficial. These experimental techniques are slow and unpredictable because they rely on chance.

9.7
The Second Green Revolution

In recent years, a new field of biology, called **genetic engineering,** has been developed. The fundamental goal of genetic engineering is to alter genetic information of an organism artificially in order to produce new organisms with unique characteristics that are favorable to humans. This tech-

nique is finding application in a variety of different fields such as medicine and synthetic chemistry. Although genetic engineering has as yet had little impact on agriculture, the potential of the new technology is so great that biologists are already heralding the dawn of a new era, called the **Second Green Revolution.**

Two Techniques of Genetic Engineering

Somaclonal Variation
One of the amazing characteristics of all complex multicellular organisms is that even though each cell in an organism carries the same genetic information, the organism as a whole signals different cells to specialize in different ways. Thus, a tomato

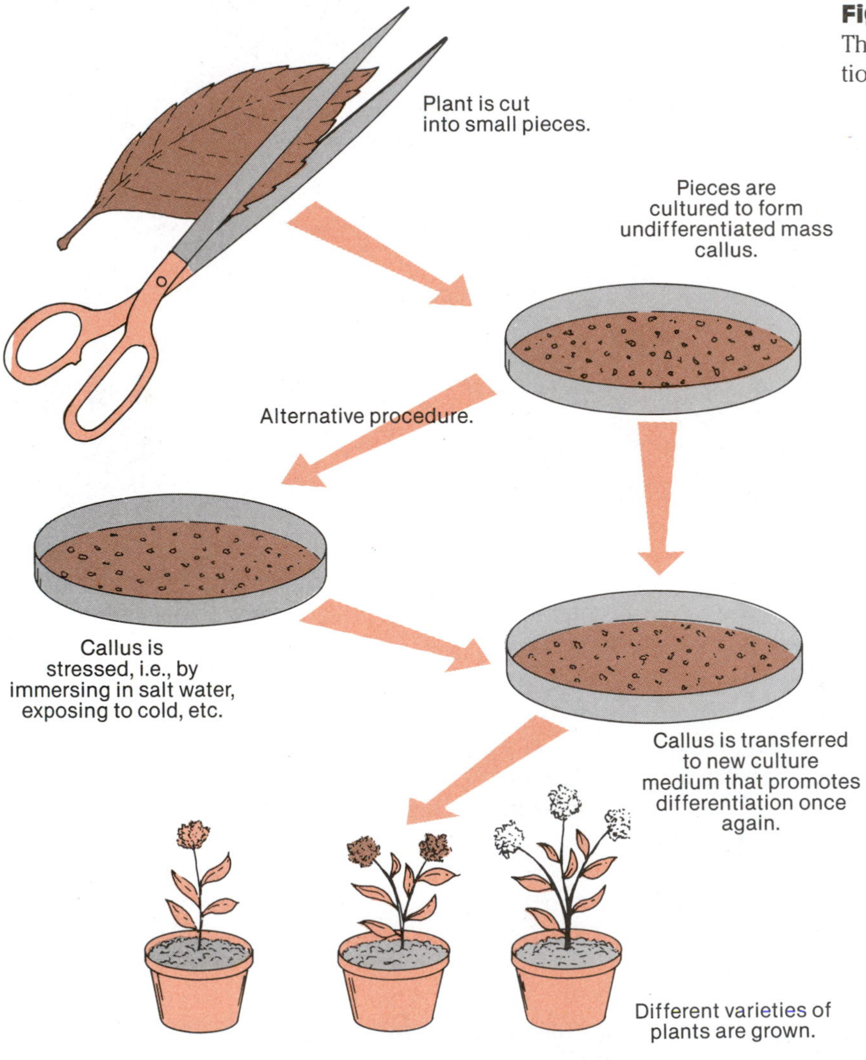

Figure 9–10
The techniques of somaclonal variation.

Plant is cut into small pieces.

Pieces are cultured to form undifferentiated mass callus.

Alternative procedure.

Callus is stressed, i.e., by immersing in salt water, exposing to cold, etc.

Callus is transferred to new culture medium that promotes differentiation once again.

Different varieties of plants are grown.

plant has roots, stems, leaves, and fruit, and the cells of each of these tissues are vastly different from the cells of other tissues. However, biologists have learned how to treat a plant with specific chemicals that neutralize the internal signals that regulate this differentiation. If a plant is chopped up and placed in a solution of these chemicals, the cells will grow into an unorganized mass without any specific function. This mass of cells without differentiation is called a **callus** (Fig. 9–10). After the callus is allowed to grow for a while, it is sep arated into small bits. These bits are then transferred into a number of jars that now contain chemicals that will signal the cells to differentiate once again. The net result of this series of steps is to create a number of plants from a single parent. When this experiment was first performed, biologists expected that the new plants would be physically and genetically identical to the original. However, for reasons that are not clearly understood,

the new plants are often strikingly *dissimilar* from each other and from the original parent. Somehow, mutations develop during the growth of the unorganized mass of cells, and these mutations result in a rapid production of a large number of new plant varieties. This technique has already produced a number of new varieties of commercial crops. For example, two new kinds of tomatoes have been developed. One has more pulp and less juice than normal tomatoes and is ideal for production of tomato paste and sauce, whereas the other is especially sweet and juicy, and therefore desirable for the table.

Gene Transfer

A more sophisticated technique is called **gene transfer.** In this approach, scientists start their research with bacteria, not with higher plants. The process can be separated into individual steps, as shown in Figure 9–11:

Figure 9–11

Schematic representation of gene transfer techniques.

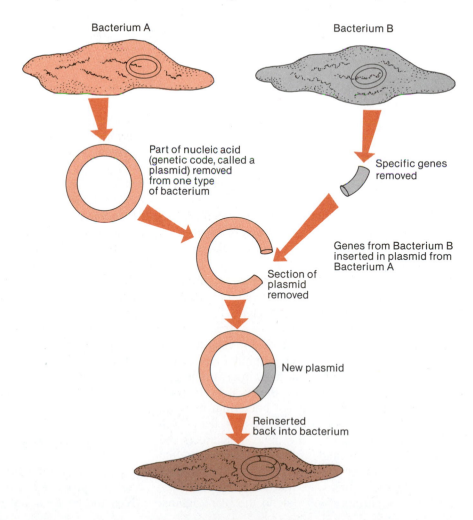

Bacterium A

Bacterium B

Part of nucleic acid (genetic code, called a plasmid) removed from one type of bacterium

Specific genes removed

Genes from Bacterium B inserted in plasmid from Bacterium A

Section of plasmid removed

New plasmid

Reinserted back into bacterium

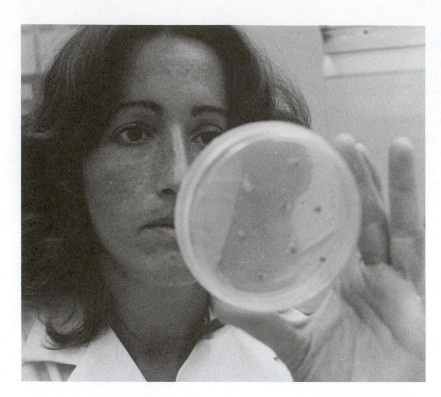

Genetic engineering offers the hope that new plant varieties will be developed that produce high yields and at the same time are resistant to pests or possess other desirable characteristics. (International Plant Research Institute)

1. A part of a DNA strand, called a **plasmid,** is isolated from one variety of bacteria.

2. The individual genes that direct certain cell functions are identified and located.

3. Specific genes are artificially removed.

4. These genes are replaced by similar genes from another species of bacteria. Thus, the original genetic code has been altered.

5. The newly recombined genetic material is inserted back into the original species of bacteria.

6. If the genes are accepted, a new species will be produced.

You may ask, "What does this research on bacteria have to do with higher plants?" The answer is twofold: First, many bacteria live on the leaves, stems, and roots of plants. If these can be altered in some way, the bacteria can alter the way that the plant adapts to its environment. For example, a certain bacterium that lives freely in the soil produces a natural pesticide that is toxic to rootworms. A different species of bacterium lives on root surfaces but does not produce a pesticide. Scientists have transported the gene that directs the production of pesticide from the bacterium that lives freely in the soil to the one that lives on the root surfaces. In this way, the bacterium that lives on the root surfaces will defend the plant against

rootworms. Or, as another example, legumes, such as alfalfa, harbor bacteria on their roots that can "fix" atmospheric nitrogen, thus providing nitrogen fertilizer for the plant. If this capability could be genetically engineered into a rice or wheat plant, a farmer would no longer need to apply expensive nitrogen fertilizer to these grains.

The second link between experiments on bacteria and agricultural crops involves the transfer of genetically engineered genes into the plant itself. Certain bacteria have the ability to invade a plant and actually alter its genetic makeup. In nature, these organisms are generally harmful to plants and sometimes can cause unregulated growth, something like a cancer. However, biologists are attempting to disarm these bacteria by separating the genes that make them able to invade the DNA of a plant from those that cause harm. Then, it is hoped that the invasive ability can be fused with genes that can alter the plant in such a way as to make it more beneficial to humans.

Genetic Engineering—The Hope

As previously explained, genetic engineering has already produced new varieties of certain vegetables and bacteria that provide resistance to various pests. Biologists hope to learn how to insert a great number of additional changes into plants. Some of these changes are mentioned below. But remember, this is a "shopping list for the future," not a list of goals that have already been achieved.

- Plants could be made to be resistant to many diseases and insect pests.
- New varieties could be developed that can live in salty soils or resist drought.
- As previously mentioned, it seems feasible to engineer staple food crops such as corn, wheat, and rice that manufacture their own nitrogen fertilizer.
- Some scientists believe that it might be possible to increase yields by improving the way that plants use the Sun's energy during photosynthesis.
- Looking into the future, we can even imagine a drought-resistant, nitrogen-producing plant that has the roots of a potato plant, the leaves of spinach, and the fruit of a tomato.

Genetic Engineering—The Danger

On the other hand, think of a worst-case scenario that could occur with a genetic engineering experiment. Imagine that scientists were working with a bacterium that has the ability to invade the DNA of a plant. Imagine further that an experiment went awry and that—by mistake—the bacterium was somehow engineered to be lethal rather than helpful to agricultural crops. Then think of what would happen if this new organism were accidentally released into the environment. A nightmare can be envisioned in which the new species would proliferate and decimate an essential cereal crop such as wheat or rice. This could result in unprecedented crop failure and global famine. This fear has prompted some people to oppose both experiments with genetic engineering and field tests of organisms that it has produced.

Unfortunately, it is very difficult to assess the threat accurately. To appreciate this, let us apply the principles of risk assessment that were introduced in Chapter 2. Imagine that someone asks you to estimate the probability that you will be involved in an auto accident if you drive to a nearby city. Many, many people have already driven billions and billions of miles, and there are records of the number of accidents that have occurred. Thus, a risk assessment can be made on the basis of past experience. But, with genetic engineering,

there is very little past experience, because the entire science is new. Therefore, an analysis of the risk is difficult and uncertain. So, we are left with opinions.

Supporters of genetic engineering argue that with proper care, the dangers of genetic engineering are small. Moreover, if the projects are successful, the human race will gain immeasurably. Not only will famine or the threat of famine be reduced, but other environmental problems may also be solved. For example, if pest-resistant crops are engineered, the proliferation of poisonous chemicals will be reduced.

Critics disagree. They argue that new technologies always produce unforeseen environmental problems. For example, nuclear energy was once heralded as safe and inexpensive. Today, both the safety and cost of nuclear energy are being questioned. The argument continues that the unknown dangers may be so great that the prudent choice is simply not to let the genie out of the bottle.

9.8
Social and Political Barriers to an Adequate Diet

Refer back to Figure 9–1 and Table 9–2. Notice that in 1985, both global food production and per capita food production were still increasing. True, the per capita food production was increasing less than it was a decade before, but it was rising nevertheless. In 1987, world grain production amounted to about 1.0 kg per person per day. If distributed evenly, this would provide every person in the world with an adequate caloric intake. In addition, uncounted numbers of cattle, sheep, and goats were grown on marginal range lands, and millions of tonnes of vegetables and fruits were produced as well. Faced with these statistics, one must ask, why does so much hunger and starvation still exist?

The question is easy to answer, but the problem is extremely difficult to solve. There is an unequal distribution of resources. Some examples follow:

- Periodically over the past few decades, floods have destroyed many rice fields in Bangladesh. Millions of poor farming families have starved. Yet floods only affect certain regions, and bumper crops may occur in other parts of the country. During one famine, approximately 4 million tonnes of rice were stockpiled in the central cities. The rice did not reach the hungry because they were "too poor to buy it."

- Even though the price of fuels declined in the first half of the 1980s, many poor farmers could not afford to buy enough fertilizer to enrich their soil. Wealthy people buy fertilizers for their ornamental lawns and gardens, but, in the less-developed countries, many poor farmers cannot purchase the fertilizer they need to provide food for their families. By one estimate, the fertilizers used for ornamental purposes in the United States could have increased crop production in the less-developed countries by enough to feed 65 million people.

- In many places around the world, large corporations own extensive plantations devoted to raising nonfood items such as coffee, tea, and tobacco. These products are exported while starving farmers living nearby do not have enough land to grow food for their families. In other situations, food crops such as bananas or cattle are grown and the products are then exported to foreign countries while, once again, local peasants have little to eat. It is not easy to change present economic and political patterns. But such changes would reduce suffering considerably.

- In the early 1980s, disastrous famines struck North Africa. Pictures of starving children in Ethiopia and Somalia appeared on television screens throughout the world. In response, a great relief effort was mounted both by governments and private charities, and millions of tonnes of grain were shipped to the famine areas. However, a significant proportion of this food never reached the intended victims. Many ships loaded with wheat and rice were detained by customs agents. In other instances, the food was unloaded but was not distributed, and, during the height of the famine, warehouses alongside the docks were full of food. Government officials denied allegations that they were interfering with shipping and complained that they did not have adequate transportation facilities. However, many people suspect that dictatorial regimes were actually fostering the famine to punish or destroy segments of the population that were considered to be a political threat.

Part of the problem of uneven distribution of resources arises from overconsumption. Many people in wealthy societies are overweight and would be healthier if they ate less. Even more food could be conserved if people whose diet consists largely of meat would eat more grain instead.

In Chapter 3, it was explained that an omnivore uses its food resources most efficiently if it eats vegetable proteins rather than meat. In the example described in that chapter, a given quantity of soybeans and corn could feed 22 vegetarians or one person who eats nothing but meat. The average person in North America uses 900 kg of grain every year. Only 90 kg are consumed directly as rice, bread, or cereals. The other 810 kg are used as animal feed to produce meat, milk, and eggs. In India, by contrast, the average person uses only 180 kg of grains per year, almost all of which is eaten directly. These figures do not mean that everyone should become a vegetarian. Animal products are rich in the essential amino acids, and some vitamins needed by humans can be obtained only by eating other animals or their products, such as milk and eggs. Young people, especially, need the protein found in animal products. In addition, many areas of land such as steep hillsides or semiarid prairies cannot support conventional grain agriculture but do serve as range for various grazing animals. Therefore, this land is used most efficiently for meat production. In many wealthy nations, however, especially in North America, cattle are housed in feedlots and fed prime grains. It is estimated that the feedlot grains used yearly in the United States could feed 400 million vegetarians. If North Americans reduced their feedlot meat consumption to the level of the people in Sweden and if the grain saved were distributed equitably, 200 million starving people would have plenty to eat (in total calorie content, if not in protein).

Related to the general problem of overconsumption is the issue of food for pets. Domestic dogs and cats provide comfort for many, but, in North America, they consume enough grain to feed 20 million people. The following statistic emphasizes the point still further: The average farmer in Central America eats less beef than is fed to the average pet cat in the United States. One of us (A.T.), while traveling in a less-developed part of the world, remarked to a companion that the area seemed quite poor, as evidenced by the presence of many half-starved dogs. His companion replied,

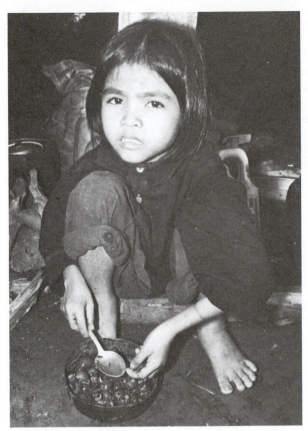

Before intense warfare spread throughout this region, southeast Asia was self-sufficient in food production. However, during the decades of warfare in the 1960s and 1970s, millions of people starved to death; today, rice must be imported. This photograph shows a girl eating a meal at a Thai military-run camp near the Cambodian border. The girl said she fled from an area near the control of soldiers of the fallen Phnom Penh regime (1979). (World Wide Photos)

"No. If it were as poor as you think, there wouldn't be any dogs at all."

Warfare and Food Supplies Civilian populations suffer whenever a war is fought. Families are uprooted from their homes, crops are destroyed or confiscated, and, in many instances, relief convoys are hijacked. Many of the most serious famines in recent times, for example, those in Cambodia in Southeast Asia and Somalia in East Africa, affected refugees that had been displaced from their self-sufficient lifestyles by the horrors of war.

Even in the absence of direct hostilities, the threat of war continues to take a terrible economic toll. In 1985, the global expenditure for military uses amounted to $940 billion. This sum, nearly one trillion dollars, exceeded the combined gross national products of China, India, and all the African countries south of the Sahara. In every nation in the world, fuel, machinery, technical expertise, and human effort are diverted from feeding people to supplying armaments. Given enough fertilizer, fuel, and machinery, the crop yields in the Ganges River delta in India could be increased sixfold. The impoverished Sudan in northeast Africa could be a bread-and-cereal basket for the continent. The rice paddies of Southeast Asia could feed the hungry in that region. But great quantities of fuel and machinery are used for weapons, and there is not enough left over for farming. This viewpoint is summarized by the following quotation by Lester Brown.

> Since World War II, the concept of national security has acquired an overwhelmingly military character, rooted in the assumption that the principal threat to security comes from other nations. . . . Consideration of military threats have become so dominant that new threats to the security of nations, threats with which military forces cannot cope, are being ignored.
>
> The new sources of danger arise from oil depletion, soil erosion, land degradation, shrinking forests, deterioration of grasslands, and climate alteration. These developments, affecting the natural resources and systems on which the economy depends, threaten not only national economic and political security, but the stability of the international economy itself.

9.9
Food from the Sea

People have often regarded the sea as a boundless source of food, especially protein. After all, more than 70 percent of the planet is ocean. Moreover, the ocean has traditionally been an unregulated commons, open to any individual or nation caring to exploit it. Shortly after World War II, with the seas again free of wars and warships and the first pinch of global food shortages being felt, global fishing industries boomed. From 1950 to 1970, the world fish catch more than tripled, and, in 1970, fish supplied more protein for human consumption than all the herds of land-based cattle combined. Despite an ever increasing effort, fish harvests barely rose from 1970 to 1985, and, as shown in

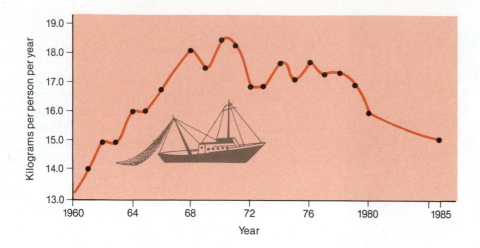

Figure 9–12
World per capita fish harvest, 1960 to 1980.

Figure 9–12, per capita production of fish declined significantly in those years. What has happened?

Most of the central oceans are biological deserts. The highly productive parts of the oceans are concentrated along the coasts and continental shelves. Yet today, the productivity of these areas has been reduced by overfishing and by pollution.

Overfishing   Garrett Hardin's essay on the Tragedy of the Commons (Chapter 1) explains that a single individual stands to gain in the short term by grazing as many cows as possible on a common pasture. The oceans are a type of commons, and unregulated fishing, like unregulated grazing, is profitable in any given year. International maritime laws have always been very complex and they are often rather ineffectual, opening the way for wholesale exploitation of many ocean fisheries. As a result, fish stocks have declined, and the potential food production of many of these areas has diminished.

In response to this threat, individual nations have recently claimed jurisdiction over an increasingly large area of coastal water. Traditionally, a nation's border was considered to extend to 3 miles (4.8 km) beyond its shore. This practical limit was defined by the range of cannons on the warships of the time. As artillery became more efficient, it seemed reasonable to demand that potentially hostile warships should remain further off shore, so a new coastal border of 12 miles (19 km) was defined. In recent times, maritime nations have realized the economic value of their fisheries and have decided that their territories extend 200 miles (320 km) out to sea. This extended limit allows individual governments to regulate fishing

and prevent overexploitation. In some areas, regulation has been poor and fish populations continue to decline, but, in other areas, fish harvests have been carefully controlled and are increasing.

Pollution   Protected coastal areas are prime breeding grounds for fish, but they are also ideal sites for industrial development. The disputes have usually been resolved in favor of heavy industrialization of the coastlines and the seemingly inevitable disposal of sewage, oil, pesticides, and other chemicals into the sea. The result has often been the poisoning of marine organisms. For example, Chesapeake Bay on the east coast of the United States was once one of the world's richest estuaries, but it lies right in the heartland of a huge commercial zone with easy deep-water shipping access to Europe. In recent times, the bay has become polluted, and, although fishing has been regulated to control overexploitation, the traditional catch of oysters, shad, and bass has declined precipitously. This topic will be discussed further in Chapter 11.

Ecologically, the destruction of an estuarine marsh is disastrous, because estuaries are nursery grounds for many fish that spend their adult lives in deeper waters. It has been estimated that one hectare of estuary produces enough young per day to grow into 270 kg of marketable fish.

Commercial Fish Farms

People have been raising domestic cattle for centuries because herders can harvest more meat on a given area of land than can hunter–gatherers. Why not apply the same principles to food from the sea

Shrimp fishing near Galveston, Texas. (National Oceanic and Atmospheric Administration).

and raise fish in artificial ponds? This process, known as **aquaculture** or **mariculture**, is being practiced throughout the world.

One technique is to raise fish like feedlot cattle by feeding them in artificial enclosures. Although this process is efficient in terms of numbers of fish that can be raised in a given area, the food for the fish must be raised on land. Therefore, if the entire system is considered, grains are converted to animal protein and considerable quantities of energy are lost, just as in a land-based feedlot.

An alternative process is to breed fish in an enclosed area but to allow a large quantity of nutrient-rich water to flow through the feeding ponds. Then the organisms in the ponds eat food that grows in the aquatic environment. For example, mussels and oysters obtain nourishment by filtering small plankton and algae out of the water. If these shellfish are raised in estuaries, the movement of the tides will continuously renew the available food supply and remove wastes. Thus, high-quality protein can be raised with very little expenditure of energy.

In many less-developed countries, fish are raised in irrigation canals. They survive on a natural food chain and provide an important source of protein for families unable to afford meat. Unfortunately, when heavy doses of pesticides are used to improve yields on land, there is risk that chemical residues will leach into the waterways and poison or contaminate the fish. This sequence illustrates the importance of an accurate cost/benefit analysis

when a new technology is introduced into an established system. In many cases, people tend to view only one segment of a complicated problem. Thus, many farmers balance the cost of pesticide only with increased rice yields. However, a larger question to ask is, "Would the added profits be sufficient to purchase quality protein that is lost when fish are killed or made unfit to eat?"

9.10
Other Methods of Increasing Food Production
Processed and Manufactured Foods

Food chemists have pursued different concepts in developing new foods. Three of these approaches are discussed in the following paragraphs.

Alteration of Natural Foods

Perhaps the most familiar example of alteration of natural foods is the conversion of vegetable oils into the butter substitute, oleomargarine. Food conversion is becoming increasingly important in both the developed and the less-developed nations. In some areas, such high-quality protein sources as soybeans, lentils, and other legumes, although readily available, are unpopular. One solution is to use concentrated vegetable protein as a base for manufactured foods that taste like something else. Thus, soy protein "hamburger," soy "milk," soy "bacon," and other simulated products are available in retail stores in many parts of the world. In

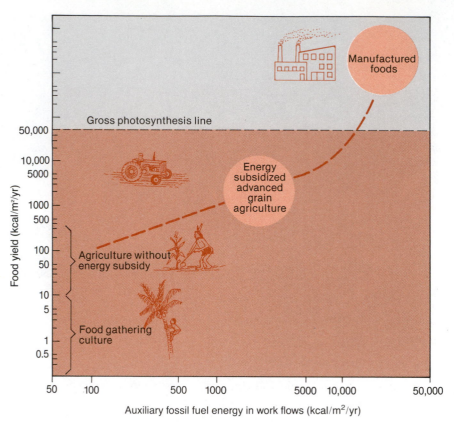

Figure 9–13
The relation between food production and auxiliary energy.

some areas, undernourished people spend their money on soft drinks rather than on protein-rich foods. Recently, soy protein has been used as an ingredient in soft drinks, and various sweetened, carbonated, soy beverages are now sold in Asia, South America, and Africa.

Conversion of Agricultural Wastes

When cooking oils are extracted from peanuts, soybeans, coconuts, cottonseeds, corn, or any other vegetable seed, the residue is a waste mash high in vegetable protein. At present, most of these residues are fed to cattle or discarded. However, it is relatively easy to incorporate the proteins into processed foods.

Sawdust, straw, old newspapers, and other inedible plant parts also represent a major source of waste materials. The major chemical component of sawdust and straw is cellulose. Paper is also a cellulose product, but the chemicals of the printing ink must be removed first. Cellulose consists of very large molecules that, when heated with dilute

acid, decompose into a sugar solution. Yeasts can thrive on this sugar mixture if other nutrients such as urea (a source of nitrogen) and mineral salts are added to the culture medium. In turn, yeasts are sources of high-quality protein and can be eaten directly. Alternatively, yeast protein extract can be fed to cattle or used as an additive in manufactured or processed foods.

Chemical Synthesis

Chemists can manufacture many basic foods from coal and petroleum, but the problem is, once again, that large quantities of energy are required. However, chemical synthesis is used to produce materials such as vitamins that are consumed in small amounts but nevertheless enrich our diets considerably.

As novel as these ideas sound, they are unlikely to provide a magic way out of the problem of world hunger, because large quantities of auxiliary energy are required to manufacture foods or to alter existing protein sources. Once again, the limiting factor appears not to be technological know-how or imaginative potential, but the availability and cost of energy (Fig. 9–13).

9.11
World Food Outlook—A Look into the Future

The analysis of the world food outlook leaves ample room for either pessimism or optimism, depending on which facts you choose to emphasize. If you look at the rapidly rising population, eroding soils, uneven distribution of food, and prospect of depletion of our fossil fuel supply, it is easy to predict unprecedented famine as part of the future for humankind. However, if you have hope in the rapid advances in genetic engineering, technological ingenuity in general, and in basic human goodness in distributing resources, one might predict a better world tomorrow.

As a summary of this chapter, the following list outlines the major components of the problem of feeding the world's people and some solutions. But remember, a list by itself doesn't feed hungry people. Therefore, the deceptively short, easy "solutions" that follow are not necessarily answers for tomorrow. Rather, you may think of them as a set of goals that would mandate drastic, sweeping global changes in society if they were implemented.

World Hunger—An Overview

Reasons Why There Is Not Enough Food	Solutions
Overpopulation (Chapter 7)	Limit population growth
Soil depletion through erosion (Chapter 8)	Educate farmers and encourage them to conserve their soils
Uneven distribution of food	Reduce overconsumption and excess meat consumption in developed nations and improve international mechanisms for food distribution
Loss of food-growing potential through war	Initiate international disarmament
High cost of energy for fertilizers and pesticides	Use recycled organic fertilizer; use renewable energy sources such as solar energy for many tasks, thereby saving fossil fuels for situations where needed
High cost of energy for farm machinery, transportation, and packaging	Use more labor-intensive agriculture; encourage decentralized agriculture; eliminate waste in packaging and processing
Agricultural land preempted for industrial development (Chapter 11)	Better land use planning to save farmland
Agricultural land preempted by mining (Chapters 15 and 16)	Reclamation of land after mine is abandoned
Loss of food to pests (Chapter 19)	Improve pest management; use integrated techniques

Special Topic D
Agriculture in Specific Regions Around the Globe

The United States and Canada In terms of total production, North America is the most successful agricultural region in the world. As you can see from Table 9–2, much of the world depends on food exports from this region. However, North American agriculture is facing an extremely serious economic imbalance. Today, high productivity is maintained through expensive and sophisticated mechanization and heavy application of fertilizers and pesticides. Both the capital outlays and the daily operating expenses are enormous. By the mid 1980s, profits had declined to the point where many farmers were facing bankruptcy despite the existence of substantial government subsidies. In 1983, for example, government subsidies actually exceeded on-farm income! Yet most farmers are actually increasing production costs—and their debt—because the prevailing attitude is to increase production, not to cut costs and conserve resources.

China and the Soviet Union China and the Soviet Union are the world's largest food-producing regions after North America. Notice from Table 9–2 that between 1950 and 1970, the Soviet Union was self-sufficient with regard to food, but production did not keep pace with population growth in the first half of the 1980s. The decline in productivity is also shown in Figure 9–14. In contrast, productivity has increased dramatically in China. How can we account for these differences? In the period between 1950 and 1978, both countries based their agriculture on communal farms that were owned and con-

trolled by the government. In 1978, the Chinese observed that the federal bureaucracy was unable to implement efficient day-to-day decisions such as determining when or what to plant and how to manage sudden changes in weather, pest populations, and other factors that affect the farmer. Therefore, farmers were allowed to manage their own fields with a greater degree of autonomy. Furthermore, the Chinese decided that it was more important to feed its people than to maintain an aggressive military. Therefore, the military budget has been reduced from nearly 15 percent of the gross national product in 1969 to 7.5 percent in 1985. In contrast, the Soviet Union has increased its economic investment in the military and has maintained such an inefficient agricultural bureaucracy that total food production has dropped from a high of 229 million tonnes in 1978 to 190 million tonnes in 1985.

Africa Unquestionably, the people of Africa have experienced the most precipitous decline in living standards of any region in the world. Twenty-five years ago, the region was self-sufficient, but today, even with massive food supports, millions of people are starving. Not only is this vast and agrarian continent losing its ability to feed itself, but the population is growing at an alarming rate. At the present time, no one has outlined and initiated a practical program that is capable of reversing the trend. Systems that were ecologically stable in 1950 when the population was 219 million are breaking down as the African population approaches 600 million. Un-

Summary

People need both quantity (calories) and quality (proteins, vitamins, and minerals) in their daily food intake.

Between 1950 and 1985, global food production and global per capita food production have increased, but the *rate of increase* in per capita food production has declined. There has been an increasing separation between rich nations and poor ones, leading to a centralization of food production and pockets of extreme poverty.

Agricultural systems have extended to marginal croplands in many areas of the globe, and a small change in climate would be disastrous in these regions.

Energy is used in agriculture for fertilizers, pesticides, machinery, processing, and transportation. Some energy inputs, such as those for

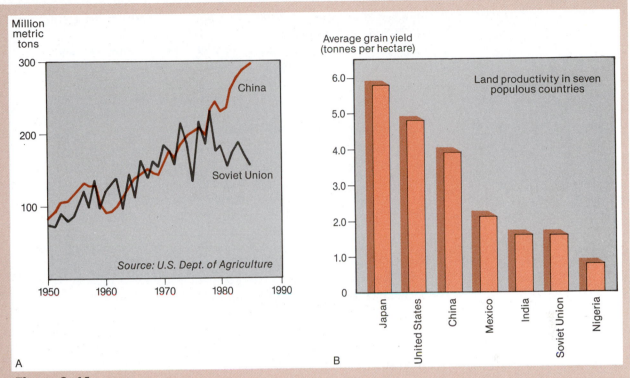

Figure 9–14

A, Comparison of agriculture in China and the Soviet Union between 1950 and 1985. B, Agricultural productivity in seven populous countries.

der the intense pressure to feed all these people, overgrazing has become all too common, and fallow cycles have been shortened, with the result that erosion and desertification have become endemic. Moreover, the poor often cannot afford the fertilizers, the pesticides, and the improved seed varieties that have led to dramatic improvements in other parts of the world.

fertilizers, actually increase productivity, while others reduce labor costs or increase consumer convenience.

In the mid-1960s new grain varieties were developed, leading to the **Green Revolution.** Green Revolution seeds lead to higher yields only if sufficient water, fertilizer, and pesticides are applied. The **Second Green Revolution,** if it is actually realized, will rely on advances in genetic engineering techniques such as **somaclonal variation** and **gene transfers.** The goal of the most recent research is to improve yields and at the same time decrease reliance on fossil fuels.

If food were divided equally, there would be enough for everyone to eat, but overconsumption, unequal distribution of resources, and war lead to pockets of extreme poverty.

Global fisheries provide valuable protein, but fish stocks are threatened by overexploitation and pollution, and the per capita production of fish has declined in recent years.

Food can be produced by a variety of processing techniques, but large quantities of energy are required.

Human Nutritional Needs

1. (a) What three functions are served by the human diet?

(b) Which is the main function provided by (i) potatoes; (ii) a vitamin tablet; (iii) egg whites; (iv) iodized salt?

(c) What *combination* of the three functions is served by a meal of (i) beans, nuts, enriched or brown rice, and orange juice; (ii) a jelly doughnut, multivitamin pill, and black coffee?

2. Explain how a person whose diet supplies enough calories to support life can still die from the effects of an inadequate diet.

3. What age segment of the population is usually most severely affected by famine? Discuss the implications of your answer.

World Food Outlook

4. Explain why a small shift in climate could seriously affect world food supplies.

5. Discuss some problems inherent in farming deserts; jungles; temperate forest hillsides; the Arctic.

6. Prepare a class debate. One side argues that it would be possible to feed 10 billion people by the year 2100, and the other side holds that only 2 billion people could be supported.

7. Discuss the following statement (you can defend it or argue against it): Even though per capita food production has increased over the past 35 years, the global food supply is more vulnerable now than it was in 1950.

Energy in Agriculture

8. Outline a system of growing and preparing food that uses no fossil fuels. Are there any energy inputs in such a system? If there are, explain what types of energy are used.

9. The text describes three major categories of energy use in agricultural systems: chemical inputs, mechanization, and processing and transportation.

(a) Which of these represent energy used on the farm, and which represent off-farm uses?

(b) Which types of energy inputs increase crop yields, and which ones save labor?

(c) If you were searching for social solutions to the problem of energy use in food production, what suggestions would you make?

(d) List two technical advances that could save energy used in food production.

10. One hundred years ago, most farmers used horses or oxen to plow fields and harvest crops. Today, tractors are commonly used.

Imagine that the fossil fuel crisis became so severe that farmers were forced to rely on animal power again. Would the total food production increase, decrease, or remain constant? Defend your answer.

11. In general, manure is heavier and therefore more expensive to spread than chemical fertilizers. However, the use of manure saves energy used in agriculture. Explain this apparent contradiction.

The Green Revolution

12. Discuss the advantages and disadvantages of Green Revolution seeds.

13. Briefly discuss the relative importance of each of the following characteristics to a plant species existing (a) in a natural prairie; (b) in a primitive agricultural system; (c) in an industrial agricultural system—(i) resistance to insects, (ii) a tall stalk, (iii) frost resistance, (iv) winged seeds, (v) thorns, (vi) biological clocks to regulate seed sprouting, (vii) succulent flowers, (viii) large, heavy clusters of fruit at maturity, (ix) ability to withstand droughts.

14. What is monoculture? Explain why mechanization and green revolution seeds encourage monoculture. Discuss some advantages and disadvantages of monoculture.

15. Explain why the Green Revolution has not helped the very poorest farmers.

The Second Green Revolution

16. Explain the similarities and differences between genetic engineering and traditional breeding techniques such as crossbreeding and artificial mutation.

17. Describe the similarities and differences between somaclonal variation techniques and gene transfer techniques.

18. Discuss the current developments and future hopes for genetically engineered varieties of plants.

19. Prepare a class debate: Have one side argue that genetic engineering experiments should be encouraged, while the other side argues that they should be prohibited.

Social and Economic Factors in Agriculture

20. Many authors have pointed out that if all the fertilizer used in the United States for lawns and ornamental gardens were shipped to farmers in less-developed nations, many millions of people could grow more food to feed their starving families. Imagine that you would normally fertilize your lawn, but this year you chose not to do so that there would be more fertilizer for the poor. Would the fertilizer that you chose not to buy actually get shipped to people in less-developed nations? Would your action do any good? What policy, private or public, would you recommend? Defend your position.

21. Many current events may affect the food supply of groups of people, even though food per se is not a topic of the news headlines. Select an article from the daily newspaper and discuss the impact of the news on local or global food supplies.

22. It has been said that internal threats to national security may be greater than international threats. Discuss this hypothesis and argue for or against it.

23. What types of agriculture, if any, are currently practiced within a 50-km radius of your school or home? What types of agriculture were common in the region 25 years ago? What changes, if any, have occurred? If agricultural productivity has declined, where is the food in your area now coming from? If productivity has increased, where is the food being sold? How have these changes affected centralization and energy consumption in agriculture?

24. Interview a farmer in your region. Ask the following questions. Is farming profitable? Why does he or she choose to be a farmer? Would it be more profitable to sell the land and retire? What can be expected to happen to the land in a generation or two? Report on your results.

Suggested Readings

General references that outline the current global food supply are:

Lester Brown et al: *State of the World 1986.* Washington, D.C., Worldwatch Institute, 1986. 263 pp.

Lester R. Brown: Putting food on the world's table. *Environment, 26:*(4), 1984.

Jessica Mathews (ed.): *World Resources 1986. A report by the World Resources Institute.* New York, Basic Books, 1986. 353 pp.

A specific case history of energy and agriculture is given in:

J. Neil Rutger and D. Marlin Brandon: California rice culture. *Scientific American,* February 1981, p 42.

A discussion of the role of biological diversity of crops in primitive agriculture and the significance of the loss in modern systems may be found in:

O.H. Grankel and Michael E. Soule: *Conservation and Evolution.* New York, Cambridge University Press, 1981. 328 pp.

The Green Revolution occurred in the late 1960s and early 1970s. Two books, published at that time, and a more recent pamphlet discuss its impact and problems:

Lester R. Brown: *By Bread Alone.* New York, Praeger Publishers, 1974. 272 pp.

Francine R. Frankel: *India's Green Revolution.* Princeton, NJ, Princeton University Press, 1972. 232 pp.

Edward C. Wolf: *Beyond the Green Revolution: New Approaches for Third World Agriculture.* Washington, D.C., Worldwatch Institute, 1986. 46 pp.

The Second Green Revolution is discussed in:

Lawrence Busch and William B. Lacey: *Science, Agriculture, and the Politics of Research.* Boulder, CO, Westview Press, 1983. 303 pp.

Robert Cooke: Engineering a new agriculture. *Technology Review,* May/June, 1982.

Jack Doyle: *Altered Harvests.* New York, NY, Viking Penguin Inc., 1985. 502 pp.

Ricki Lewis: Building a better tomato. *High Technology,* May, 1986.

Eliot Marshal: Engineering crops to resist weed killers. *Science, 231,* 1986.

Steve Olson: *Biotechnology: An Industry Comes of Age.* Washington, D.C., National Academy Press, 1986. 120 pp.

The specific problem of famine in Africa is discussed in:

Lester R. Brown and Edward C. Wolf: *Worldwatch Paper 65: Reversing Africa's Decline.* Washington, D.C., Worldwatch Institute, 1985. 81 pp.

The Food and Agriculture Organization of the United Nations (Special Report): *Food Situations in African Countries Affected by Emergencies.* New York, United Nations, 1985. 63 pp.

The Office of Technology Assessment: *Africa Tomorrow: Issues in Technology, Agriculture, and U. S. Foreign Aid.* Washington, D.C., Office of Technology Assessment, December, 1984. 145 pp.

Tore Rose (ed.): *Crisis and Recovery In Sub-Saharan Africa.* Paris, France, Organization for Economic Co-operation and Development, 1985. 335 pp.

Lloyd Timberlake: *Africa In Crisis.* Philadelphia, PA, New Society Publishers, 1986. 232 pp.

An interesting article on food production in China is:

Vaclav Smil: China's food. *Scientific American*, *253*:116–124, Dec. 1985.

Social and political problems of food supply and distribution are given in:

Francis M. Lappe and Joseph Collins: Food First. Boston, Houghton Mifflin Co., 1977. 466 pp. *(Even though this book is dated, the general concepts are still valid.)*

The Independent Commission on International Humanitarian Issues: *Famine: A Man Made Disaster?* New York, Vintage Books, 1985. 160 pp.

Joel Solkoff: *The Politics of Food.* San Francisco, CA, Sierra Club Books, 1985.

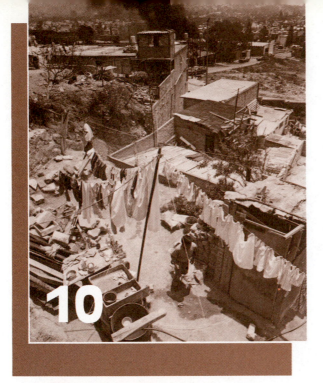

10

The Urban Environment

10.1
Land Use Planning: The Ideal— Design with Purpose

If you were traveling by canoe along the northern coast of Canada or through the Barren Lands that lie immediately to the south, you might paddle for several weeks before you would see another human. On the other hand, during rush hour in New York City, a pedestrian is likely to be bumped and jostled by the crowds, and, on the subways, people have actually had their ribs broken by the compression of the mass of humanity. Unquestionably, the human population is distributed very unevenly across the Earth. Regions that are favorable for industry and commerce are densely populated while hardly anyone lives in deserts, the arctic regions, or the interiors of tropical rainforests. On a global scale, there is no central authority that has the right or the power to regulate where people live, but, as the Earth becomes more and more densely populated, the placement of people, buildings, and roadways has become an important factor in determining human lifestyles. In a larger sense, careless use of the land could eventually lead to a variety of environmental problems. These topics will be discussed in this chapter and in Chapter 11.

If there is a vacant lot or untended field near your house, visit it and look at it closely. Most probably there are various trails or paths cutting through the property. These trails were not planned by an architect or a city engineer; they were formed as people walked from one place to another. The very fact that people will create a trail rather than walk randomly across the land indicates that natural factors favor some routes over others. Some of these factors include the topography, the vegetation, the location of nearby buildings, and the most efficient routes between them.

At its best, land use planning incorporates the most efficient placement of buildings, farms, roadways, and other facilities to preserve the beauty of the land as much as possible while, at the same time, minimizing human effort. At its worst, development of the land can be terribly ugly and can create a system that encourages wasted energy, resources, and time.

Today most land use planning must evolve around existing cities and towns, but, in a few places, entirely new towns are built. Imagine that you were hired to construct a new community in a

In northern Canada, canoeists can travel for days without meeting other people.

previously vacant area of land. The first step of environmentally sound planning considers the immediate and direct needs of any community.

1. Food
2. Water
3. Waste disposal
4. Living spaces
5. Industrial and commercial zones
6. Electrical energy
7. Recreational zones
8. Transportation system
9. Raw materials (fuels, minerals, timber, and so on)

It is obvious from this list that all the needs of any given community cannot possibly be met within a local area. No place on Earth contains natural sources of fuels, minerals, timber, water, and all the other necessities of modern life. Therefore, no city or town can be completely self-sufficient. But, at the same time, it is inefficient to import more goods and services than are necessary. Assume for the sake of argument that no minerals, fuels, or timber resources are available in the area and that the plan must incorporate only the first eight items on the list.

If you were asked to design a new community, your job would be to divide the land in order to leave space for each of these eight requirements and at the same time to maximize the efficiency of the entire system and the beauty of the land.

During the rush hour in New York City commuters have actually had ribs broken by the compression of the mass of humanity.

The first rule of land use planning is to incorporate the natural character of the area with the design of buildings and facilities. Most land is not a flat, planar surface, like a sheet of paper, but includes hills, valleys, forests, rivers, marshes, or coastlines. Maximal efficiency is not achieved by overpowering nature but by designing with it. Design with nature involves an understanding of the type of land that is most suited for a specific need.

1. Food   The most productive farmland is generally found on level plains or in river valleys. In arid or semiarid zones, farmland should be located near a source of irrigation water.

2. Water   Rainwater collects in natural basins and then filters through the earth to concentrate in rivers, ponds, or lakes. To ensure a permanent supply of water, the surface topography and subsurface structure of soil and rock in a watershed either should not be altered at all, or if alteration is necessary, it should be done only with great care. Key watersheds might become recreational areas where no major construction or earth-moving projects are allowed.

3. Waste Disposal   In a well-planned community, wastes are recycled. Products such as scrap newspapers, metals, and glass can be recycled by industrial processes. Sewage and food scraps make excellent fertilizer. Therefore, waste disposal systems should be located near both industrial and agricultural zones.

4. Living Spaces   Maximal efficiency can be realized if living spaces are (a) located both near places of work and recreation to minimize the need for transportation, and (b) positioned favorably to receive maximal sunlight for solar heating.

5. Industrial and Commercial Zones   These areas should be located near enough to living spaces to minimize transportation needs but not so close that noise and pollution become bothersome. Industrial and commercial zones should also be located near water, intercity or international transportation systems, and sources of electricity.

6. Electrical Energy   Power plants must be located near a source of cooling water. If plants are

What factors would you consider if you were asked to build a new, model community on a previously undeveloped piece of land?

located near industrial zones, waste heat can be sold to industries, thereby conserving energy (see Section 15.8).

7. Recreational Zones   Parks, woodlands, waterways, and mountains should be as accessible as possible.

8. Transportation Systems   If the rest of the community is well designed, transportation links connecting the individual components will be short and centralized. If population centers and industrial centers are both clustered, mass transit becomes practical. If the two zones are sprawled out, however, people prefer to travel privately.

These general guidelines may sound simple enough, but many inherent conflicts arise. For example, the banks of a river provide the ideal location for industry, commerce, highways, and electrical energy production because the river offers intercity transportation systems and provides water for cooling, production of steam, and waste disposal. But the same area is generally the most fertile agricultural land. The riverside is also an ideal site for a park. Another problem arises over the choice of living space. People would like to have individual family homes in beautiful natural settings, but, if the most beautiful settings are cut into subdivisions, open spaces are destroyed and little room remains for recreation. Many planners suggest that people should live in central apartment complexes surrounded by green belts and parks. These areas would be a type of commons that everyone could enjoy and might, in the long run, be more pleasurable than thousands of tiny fenced-in backyards.

Even in an ideal situation, these problems are difficult to solve, but, in the real world, land use planning is even more complicated. Planners seldom have the luxury of starting a new community; most often, they must work with a city or town that already exists. Think of something simple such as planning the width of a city street. Most cities were first settled decades or even centuries ago. In many regions that were urbanized many years ago buildings were constructed before automobiles were available. Therefore, streets were built for pedestrians or horses; today, they are woefully narrow for cars and trucks (Fig. 10–1). In order to widen them it is necessary to tear buildings down and redevelop the area. This development is not only horribly expensive, but, in many instances, people are displaced from familiar neighborhoods, and lifestyles are disrupted.

10.2
Urbanization and Urban Land Use

The first cities arose along the Tigris and Euphrates rivers roughly 6000 years ago. Since then, great cities have grown and fallen in many areas of the world. Most people, however, have traditionally lived in rural areas. In Europe, which is the most urbanized continent today, only 1.6 percent of the population lived in cities of more than 100,000 in 1600; the figure rose to only 1.9 percent by 1700 and 2.2 percent by 1800. In fact, before 1800, no country was predominantly urban. Between the time of the fall of the Roman Empire and the beginning of the nineteenth century, no European city had 1 million inhabitants. Thus, on the eve of the Industrial Revolution, Europe was essentially an agrarian continent. Archaeological evidence suggests that the first city population to exceed 1 million persons may have been the capital of the Khmer Republic, Cambodia (Fig. 10–2). Tokyo and Shanghai may have had populations of more than 1 million by 1800. Moreover, by 1800, many parts

Figure 10–1
A street in Cuzco, Peru. This city was designed mainly for travel by pedestrians, donkeys, and llamas, and conversion to multiple-lane automotive traffic would involve a complete and expensive redevelopment plan.

of East Asia boasted very large central cities surrounded by highly productive agricultural areas.

In the hundred years from 1800 to 1900, cities grew rapidly. In 1900, only 12 (or maybe 13) cities had populations of more than 1 million—London, Paris, Berlin, Vienna, Moscow, St. Petersburg (now Leningrad), New York, Chicago, Philadelphia, Tokyo, Wuhan (in China), Calcutta, and perhaps Istanbul. By 1985, there were nine cities with populations greater than 10 million, 17 cities with more than 5 million, and a total of 230 cities with a million or more inhabitants. At that time, more than 40 percent of the inhabitants of the world lived in urban areas. By the year 2000, more than 50 percent of the world's population will probably live in urban places, and there will probably be more than 250 cities with more than 1 million inhabitants (Fig. 10–3).

Cities—The Attraction and the Problems

Obviously, cities must be attractive if so many people choose to live in them. Perhaps the main benefits of cities are economic. With the rise of the Industrial Revolution, manufacturing became centralized, and this centralization provided jobs in urban areas. People moved into the urban regions to find good wages and a "better life." For those who

Figure 10–2
A view of Ankhor Wat, ancient capital of the Khmer Republic.
(Courtesy Picon A.P.)

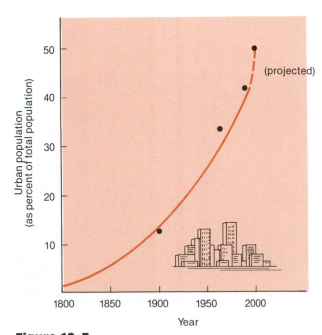

Figure 10–3
The observed and the projected growth of the global urban population between the years 1800 and 2000.

have been economically successful, cities do, in fact, provide an attractive lifestyle. The most modern manufactured goods and the best medical attention are readily available, and urban regions have become centers for art, culture, music, and social activities of all kinds.

But now consider the urban poor. Cities are inherently more expensive to live in than are rural regions. This condition arises because it is more difficult to supply people with the essentials of life when they live in crowded areas than when they are dispersed.

Food and Water   Food and water are not naturally available in urban areas and must be imported from the surrounding countryside. Even if all other factors are equal, the cost of transportation increases the price of these essentials.

Waste Disposal   In very rural societies, the production of wastes is balanced by the capacity of natural ecosystems to recycle and decompose these materials. For example, sewers are not avail-

apartment buildings rather than single-story, single family dwellings. But the engineering and the materials used in a multi-story building are necessarily more expensive than those used in a small building. In addition, when an apartment building is constructed, considerable interior space is preempted by hallways, elevator shafts, and centralized heating and air conditioning corridors. Therefore, it costs more to provide basic living spaces in the cities than it does in the country.

Recreation In the country, people can relax by walking into the woods or wandering down to a nearby stream to go fishing. On the other hand, these opportunities are much less available in cities. Parks preempt costly land and require daily maintenance. Movies, theater, and other cultural activities are available, but there is almost always a

able in rural regions, and, in some cases, human wastes are simply deposited in outhouses. The environment is not polluted by this process because the wastes are decomposed by a variety of organisms. Similarly, even though smoke and soot from rural fireplaces are usually vented directly into the air, the total quantity of pollutants is so low that the particles are dispersed rapidly and eventually removed from the atmosphere by natural processes. In the cities, however, wastes are produced in a concentrated manner; therefore, pollution control becomes essential. These control measures are expensive and add to the cost of urban living.

Living Spaces In densely populated areas where the number of people per unit area is large, the demand for land is great and therefore the price of land is high. When land is expensive, it becomes economically attractive to build multi-story

Housing is expensive in urban regions. Therefore, many poor people in New Delhi, India, live in small tents on the sidewalks.

For wealthy people in developed countries, cities are desirable places to live where residents have easy access to art, music, and rewarding careers.

price of admission. Finally, city dwellers can vacation in the country, but they must pay for transportation and living accommodations.

For the lucky people who find quality employment in urban areas, salaries are high enough so that the urban environment can be an attractive place in which to live. But for those who are underemployed or unemployed, the cost of living can become oppressive and cities can indeed be dismal.

Cities in the Developed and in the Less-Developed Countries

Two types of cities should be distinguished. In the more developed, industrialized countries, a large proportion of the urban population holds lucrative jobs. In recent years, a significant number of these people have moved from the central cities to less densely populated suburban areas. On the other hand, many unskilled, uneducated, and largely unemployable people also live in the cities of even the most wealthy countries. Therefore, the typical city in the developed world has a densely populated core containing both luxury and slum housing, as well as commercial and manufacturing areas. Surrounding the central city is a rapidly expanding peripheral suburban region, growing both in population and in area.

Cities are also expanding in the less-developed world. Indeed, urbanization is proceeding at a faster rate in less-developed countries than it is in the industrialized nations, although the less-developed countries are still much less urbanized than is Europe, North America, Australia, New Zealand, and East Asia. The land area of a city in less-developed countries grows slowly in relation to the increase in the population. There are several reasons for this. First, because jobs are often not available, people do not earn enough money to pay for adequate housing. Second, systems of transportation are not developed, so the inhabitants must live close to the center of the city. As a result, these cities become overurbanized, that is, there are too many people for the economic base. As a result, the city suffers from poor sanitation and increasing social problems. The fringes of cities in the less-developed countries are often characterized by dismal living conditions.

Figure 10–4 shows a comparison between urbanization in the developed and in the less-developed countries. Note a few important facts. In the developed countries, about 72 percent of the population lived in cities in 1985, whereas in the less-developed countries, less than half that percentage lived in cities. However, because the population in less-developed countries is so much greater than it is in the wealthier nations, the total number of peo-

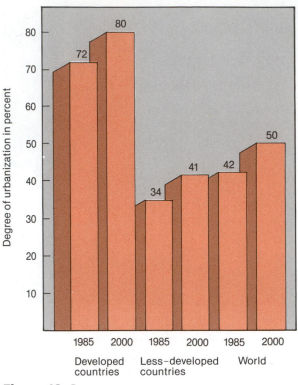
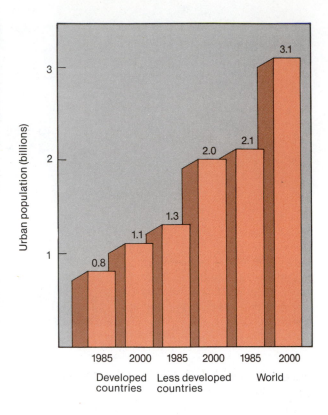

Figure 10–4

A, The degree of urbanization in 1985 and projections to the year 2000 in the developed countries, the less-developed countries, and the world total. In this graph, the numbers are expressed as a percentage of the total population. *B,* In this graph, urbanization is expressed in terms of the total number of people. Note that although the less-developed countries are less highly urbanized in terms of percentage of the population, because there are more people in these regions, the total number of urban inhabitants is greater.

ple living in cities in the less-developed countries is greater than it is in the developed regions.

10.3
Urbanization in the Developed World—The United States
Historical Trends

When North America was first settled, it was predominantly nonindustrial, and the majority of the people worked on farms to raise enough food to feed the entire population. Therefore, the population was predominantly rural. As technology advanced, however, workers migrated from the farm to the city. Today, industrial workers supply farmers with an intricate support system that includes machinery, chemicals, and scientific knowledge.

As a result, relatively few agricultural workers are needed. For example, in the United States, only 3 percent of the population work directly on farms, but these 3 percent not only raise enough food for everyone in the United States to eat but also supply large surpluses. In addition, as the character of our society has evolved, cities have become centers for commerce, art, education, exchange of ideas, and many other manifestations of civilization.

In the early stages of the Industrial Revolution, urban regions were concentrated into dense, central cores (Fig. 10–5*A*). These cores contained factories and transportation networks. Workers and their families lived close to places of work. Secondary businesses such as retail outlets, law firms, and engineering services were also situated within the core. In the 1950s and 1960s, automobiles and fuel became inexpensive relative to the price of labor.

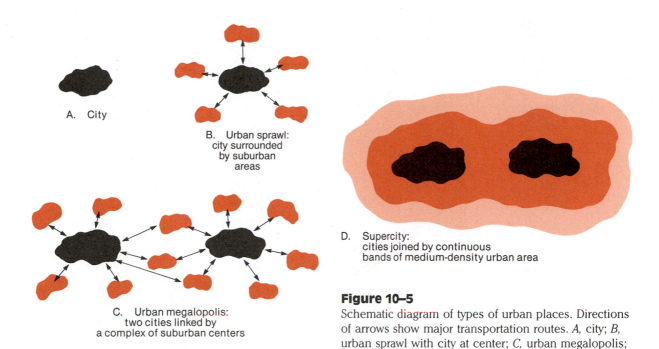

A.   City

B.   Urban sprawl:
     city surrounded
     by suburban
     areas

C.   Urban megalopolis:
     two cities linked by
     a complex of suburban centers

D.   Supercity:
     cities joined by continuous
     bands of medium-density urban area

Figure 10–5
Schematic diagram of types of urban places. Directions of arrows show major transportation routes. *A,* city; *B,* urban sprawl with city at center; *C,* urban megalopolis; *D,* supercity.

Mobility intensified as a way of life, and many people moved outward into suburban areas to live in one-family homes surrounded by small lawns and gardens. Frequently, suburbanites still worked in the urban cores, and elaborate highway systems were built to accommodate an ever increasing number of commuters. The establishment of suburban regions and highway systems linking them to the cities led to what was called **urban sprawl** (Fig. 10–5*B*). During the next decade, from 1960 to 1970, many people moved even further away from the central cities, into the outer suburbs. Eventually, suburban centers were established approximately midway between neighboring cities. As a result, cities became linked by smaller towns and residential areas. These sprawling urban complexes became known as **megalopolises** (Fig. 10–5 *C*) Even though residential areas were being established in the outlying regions during this time, most of the commercial activity remained in the cities, and many people commuted long distances to work.

During the next 15-year period, from about 1970 to 1985, the character of American commerce changed and, as a result, the character of cities also changed (Fig. 10–6). Previously, the backbone of economic activity was the manufacture of heavy durable goods. Large factories such as steel mills must be located along rail lines or major waterways to facilitate the shipping of large quantities of raw materials and finished products. In recent years, however, manufacturing has shifted toward the production of lighter, more sophisticated "high-tech" products. In addition, service industries have assumed an increased importance in the economy. To understand the importance of these changes, consider a comparison between a steel mill and a factory that produces electronic calculators. As mentioned previously, the steel mill receives and ships a tremendous tonnage of material every day and must be located near centralized transportation systems. On the other hand, a few truckloads of electronic components can supply a factory with enough material to make *many* pocket calculators. Therefore, the calculator company does not need to be located in the urban core. In fact, it is often desirable to build factories of this type in the countryside, where rent is cheap and where the limited number of employees can find inexpensive and desirable housing.

Service industries are even less dependent on traditional patterns and pathways of commerce. This independence is illustrated by the following example. Several years ago, one of us (JT) attended

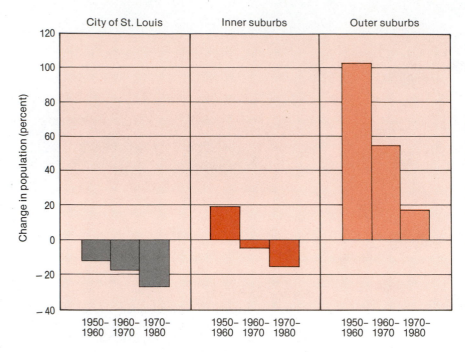

Figure 10–6

Changes in patterns of urbanization in St. Louis between 1850 and 1980. Notice that the population of the central city has been declining during the entire 30-year period. Between 1950 and 1960, the population of the inner suburbs rose, but then a decline occurred during the following decades. The population of the outer suburbs has risen continuously, but the rate of rise has been declining steadily.

This aerial photograph shows suburban housing reaching out into prime farmland outside of Denver, Colorado. (Dakers Gowans)

a planning meeting for the town of Telluride, Colorado. At that time, there were only about 1500 people in the town, which is located in a very rural mountainous region 8 hours drive, in good weather, from the nearest urban center. The economics of Telluride was based almost exclusively on tourism; a world-class ski area attracts people in winter, and excellent hiking and sightseeing opportunities attract summer visitors. One large real estate developer suggested that the town should purchase its own stationary communications satellite. He pointed out that the satellite would cost no more than a single ski lift, but, with instant communication with the outside world, the region could attract a variety of new types of businesses. For example, a credit card billing company handles only information and mail; no durable products at all are produced. If the information could be transmitted by the satellite, and the mail shipped by truck, a profitable business would thrive in this previously isolated setting. Although the satellite has not yet been launched, this example emphasizes the possibilities that exist in a commercial era that is dominated by communications and electronics.

As the character of American commerce has changed, patterns of commerce and living have also changed. Between 1970 and 1985, many businesses have moved away from the city to the coun-

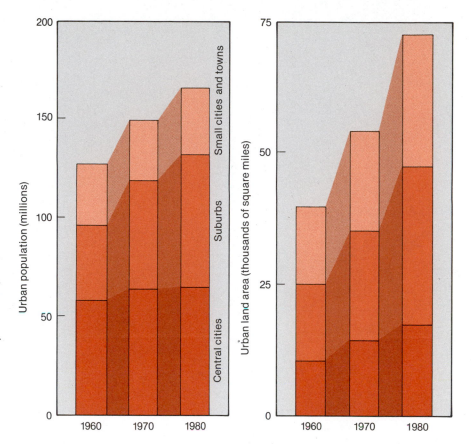

Figure 10–7
The rise of the urban popula-tion and the urban land area in the United States. Note that the land area preempted by urban settlements is rising much faster than is the urban popula-tion. (The darkest shade indi-cates changes in the central cities, the lighter shade repre-sents suburban areas, and the lightest shade shows changes in small cities and towns.)

tryside. As a result, many rural areas have become urbanized, but the population density in these new urban areas is much less than the density in tradi-tional cities (Fig. 10–7). The large expanses of land that are not as densely populated as traditional cities but are much more densely populated than the truly rural environments are called **supercities** (Fig. 10–5*D*).

10.4
Consequences of Urbanization in the United States
Urbanization and Agriculture

A garden that is only 0.02 hectares can produce enough vegetables to last a person for an entire year. In contrast, the average urban North American requires over six times as much land (0.13 hec-tares) for nonagricultural purposes—for homes, lawns, roadways, parking lots, shopping centers, and factories. Moreover, as discussed in the pre-

vious section, a predominant demographic trend in the United States is a rapid expansion of urbaniza-tion into the countryside. Therefore the amount of land that is preempted by urban development is growing faster than the urban population. Much of this urban development has occurred in regions that were once prime farming areas. Thus, the loss of farmland to urban development has become a serious concern in recent years.

In the United States, about 37,000 sq km (14,000 sq mi) of farmland was converted to urban uses between 1960 and 1970, and an additional 49,000 sq km (19,000 sq mi) was converted in the decade of the 1970s. (In comparison, the state of Maryland covers 27,000 sq km, and Massachusetts covers 21,000 sq km). By 1986, a total of 192,000 sq km, approximately 2 percent of all land in the United States, was covered with concrete, asphalt, or housing (Fig. 10–8). (This is a little more than the entire state of Missouri, which has a land area of 180,000 sq km.) Unfortunately, the loss is con-centrated in many of the most productive agricul-

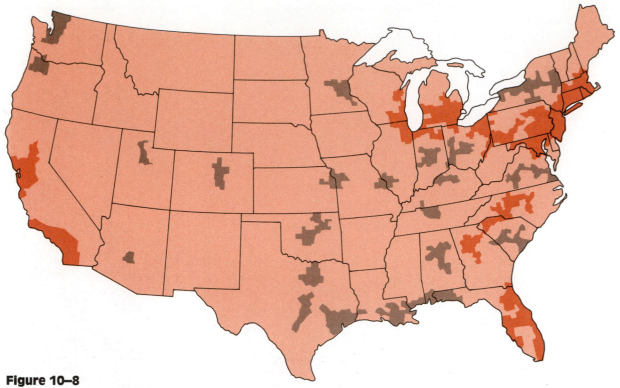

Figure 10–8

Urban areas in the United States. (Dark orange shade indicates the most heavily urbanized areas, light gray shade indicates less densely populated urban areas, and the light orange background represents more rural regions.)

tural areas. In addition, as relatively wealthy nonagricultural workers have moved into the countryside, many developers have purchased productive farms and subdivided them into smaller plots. In turn, these residential "minifarms" are usually set aside for raising horses or some other nonfood-producing activity. Thus, although the land is not actually paved, it is removed from production.

If current trends continue, about 20 percent of the most fertile farmland in the United States will be urbanized by the year 2000. For example, unless our priorities change, all of Florida's citrus groves, 16 percent of the vegetable-producing regions of Southern California, and 24 percent of the prime agricultural land in Virginia will all be removed from production.

Urbanization and Energy Consumption

In a central city, most people walk or use buses or subways for their daily transportation. However, as more and more people have moved to the suburbs, these patterns have changed. This development has led to many problems. The growth of suburban regions gained momentum in an era when fuel was cheap and seemingly plentiful. For millions of people, commuting became an attractive alternative to life in the city. Today, commuting is expensive, slow, and frustrating; traffic jams are common, parking is difficult, and, in the event of fuel shortages, entire communities can become paralyzed. During the "energy crises" of the 1970s, many commuters had to wait long hours in gas lines and others were simply unable to get to work.

Moreover, there are no easy solutions. When populations are dispersed, walking and even cycling become impractical because the distances are too great. Public transportation systems are harder to operate because people must be funneled together from a wide area. In the suburbs, the population density is often so much lower than it is in a central city that mass transit routes become expensive and complex. In an urban megalopolis or a supercity, the situation is even more complicated, because the population is even more diffuse. In these regions, close neighbors or even two people in the same house may travel in opposite directions to work. Even car-pooling is difficult; in many cases, each person in the community drives alone in an automobile to work and back. Not only are fossil and human energies wasted, but large land areas are preempted for transportation systems.

Many other problems have arisen with urban sprawl. For example, when houses and businesses are dispersed, electrical transmission lines must be longer, and efficiency is lost. As local agricultural areas are paved and developed, farming has been pushed far away from urban areas, and, as a result, increased quantities of energy are required to transport food.

Urbanization and the Character of Rural Regions

As discussed in the last section, many nonagricultural workers are moving out to the countryside. This movement has occurred, in part, because people enjoy peace and quiet and the recreational opportunities of the rural environment. However, as

The South Platte River basin is potentially one of the richest agricultural regions in Colorado, yet much of the farmland has been preempted by commercial interests.

In this rural region of Idaho, large parcels of agricultural land have been purchased and converted into suburban "minifarms." Many residents raise horses, but essentially no food is grown.

more and more people migrate into the rural landscape, the very qualities that were being sought after are being destroyed. The topic of rural land use will be discussed further in Chapter 11.

10.5
Urban Land Use Planning

Is there any way to regulate the use of land in order to preserve agricultural and recreational areas and, at the same time, conserve fuels and encourage economic growth? Before we answer this question, let us examine how land use decisions are made in the absence of regulation or legislation. For example, if there are no land use laws, what happens when a prime site for a new harbor is also the mouth of a river in which fish come to spawn? Or, suppose that a valuable seam of coal lies under a wheat field? Should a vegetable farm be converted to a more profitable shopping center? In the last example cited, if a developer offers the vegetable farmer enough money, the farmer may sell. The developer will then bulldoze the topsoil away and cover the land with concrete and asphalt. If this process is repeated over and over again, many prime agricultural areas will be converted to non-

agricultural uses. This loss can be considered to be another form of the tragedy of the commons. In this case, even though agricultural land is owned by an individual, it can be considered to be a common resource, because the population as a whole depends on agricultural production for survival. When an individual farmer makes a rational, personal, economic decision to sell a piece of land, the commons is damaged. Therefore, governments have initiated several different types of actions to preserve the quality of existing landscapes.

Zoning Laws   Zoning is a type of legislation that regulates the kinds of activities and buildings that are allowed in certain regions. For example, many residents do not like to have factories in their neighborhoods, so many towns and cities have established laws that set aside residential areas where commercial activities are prohibited. Other zoning laws might limit the allowed heights of buildings in a given area or specify the maximal number of living units allowed on a given area of land. Zoning is a powerful tool in land use management, but these laws are used mainly to regulate areas that are already partially urbanized. In most instances it has been difficult to maintain a truly rural or agricultural quality in an area purely by the use of zoning.

Traditionally, planners have thought that the rural character is best maintained by zoning for single-story buildings with a relatively low density. However, not all land use experts agree with this approach. One-family suburban dwellings and sprawling single-story stores and malls require a lot of space. If these were replaced with multistory apartments and department stores, considerable areas of land could be saved and set aside for parks and other recreational areas (Fig. 10–9) while other regions would remain agricultural. However, many people like to live in private homes, and it would be a drastic infringement of personal liberty to ban construction of single-family dwellings.

Establishment of Parks and Greenbelts
People have long recognized the value of recreational land in urban areas. Consequently, many town and city governments have purchased land that is then set aside as open spaces. For example, the city of New York has maintained Central Park, a 340-hectare region lying just north of the down-

Box 10.2
Land Use and Economics

The following quotation is taken from a regular column in *Newsweek* magazine that offers economic and investment advice.

To follow your next investment you're going to need Wellingtons—because Wall Street is trekking back to the land. . . .

The new law abolishes the special, low capital-gains tax and, with it, the handcuffs of passive investing. Today's partnerships intend to buy property, subdivide it, bring in water and electricity, put in roads, negotiate building permits with the planning board—in short, turn a piece of farmland into a ready-to-go residential, industrial or commercial building site. That's where the the big bucks really lie.

From Jane Bryant Quinn: The next land boom. *Newsweek,* March 1987.

Joggers in Central Park in New York City.

Figure 10–9
Two possible types of settlements. In *A*, people live in a suburban type setting, but there is little land left over for parks or open spaces. In *B*, populations and businesses are concentrated, leaving vacant land for recreation.

town business district. Even though the park is crisscrossed by several multilane road systems, and even though parts of it are unsafe at night, the rolling grassy hills, the jogging trails, and the playgrounds receive heavy use. In other areas, a protective belt of undeveloped land is maintained around a city. For example, many cities such as Boulder, Colorado and Anchorage, Alaska, have purchased massive tracts of land between the city and the mountains.

Regulation of Population Size Many municipalities have considered attempts to regulate the population within the city limits. Usually this is done by limiting the number of building permits that will be issued or by curtailing construction of roads, sewers, or other services. Although many people applaud these approaches to braking the spread of urbanization, others believe that legislation of this type limits the economic development of a region. Intense political battles often occur between the people who want to encourage business and development and those who want to preserve a more rural quality of life.

Changes in the Tax Laws In many regions of the United States, land is taxed according to its market value. If the land is valuable, the taxes are high. Imagine, then, what happens in some agricultural communities. One farmer sells fields to a manufacturing corporation, and a factory is built. When jobs are available, more people move into the area, and the price of land rises. Rising land prices lead to rising taxes. The high taxes then become a great burden to neighboring farmers. As profits from farming decline and the market value of farmland skyrockets, many more farmers sell their land. The spiral continues (Fig. 10–10). Even-

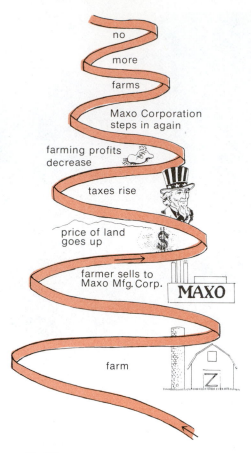

Compared with mass transit systems, freeways represent an inefficient use of land surfaces. (Wide World Photos)

Figure 10–10
Schematic representation of a price–tax spiral that leads to destruction of agricultural land.

tually, an agricultural region is converted into an industrial region. In order to reverse this trend, some municipalities tax land according to the type of use rather than its intrinsic market value. For example, the rural character of an area can be preserved by taxing farmland at a lower rate than is applied to land used for commercial or urban development. In Japan, this concept is carried one step further. Agricultural land is taxed at a very low rate, but if the land is sold for commercial use, any profits from the sale are subject to a high rate of taxation.

Purchase of Rights of Development   Other laws protecting farmland are even more far-reaching. In several regions, governments have begun to subsidize the maintenance of agricultural land. If a farm is worth $200,000 to a developer but only $100,000 if it remains farmland, the state will pay

the farmer the difference if the land is set aside permanently for agricultural purposes.

Construction of Mass Transit Systems Instead of Highways   A two-track local subway uses a roadbed 11 meters wide and can carry 80,000 passengers per hour. On the other hand, an eight-lane superhighway is 38 meters wide and carries only 20,000 people per hour under normal traffic conditions. A superhighway capable of carrying 80,000 people per hour would have to be 152 meters wide (approximately 1 1/2 times as wide as the *length* of a football field). Therefore, a shift to mass transit would conserve land surfaces. However, once again, it is easier to propose a solution than to implement it. Mass transit systems are extremely expensive, and, often, people don't want to change habits or patterns of living. This topic will be discussed further in Chapter 15.

Despite the difficulties in reversing the trend toward increased urbanization, remember that once a piece of land is developed, the change is, for all practical purposes, permanent. Once a system is set in concrete, it becomes almost impossibly expensive to tear down buildings, dig up superhighways, or move factories.

10.6
Cities in the Less-Developed Countries—Mexico City

Before Europeans arrived in the New World, Mexico City, the capital of the Aztec Empire, had housed approximately 200,000 people. In 1975, Mexico City had 11 million people. That total rose to 14 million by 1980, to 17 million by 1986, and is expected to increase further to between 27 and 28 million by the year 2000, which is more than three times the present population of New York City. Today, problems relating to health care, employment, housing, and pollution are extreme, and no one knows what will really happen when another 10 million people are added to this mass of humanity. The Latin novelist Carlos Fuentes calls the region "the great flat-snouted and suffocating city, the city forever spreading like a creeping blot." In less poetical, but more practical, terms, some of the problems are outlined in the following paragraphs:

Population   Of the 17 million people in Mexico City, half of them are younger than 18 years of age, so even if birth rates were to drop today, the population would continue to rise for another generation. In addition, about 400,000 people migrate from the country into the city every year.

Housing   City officials conservatively estimate that half the population of Mexico City lives in substandard housing. What this means in practice is that many people live in squatter communities made up of shanties and shacks or in abandoned or condemned buildings. The poorest people live in cardboard windbreaks, old concrete pipes, in tents under bridges, or even in caves dug out of old garbage in the city dump. Approximately 30 percent of all families live in a single room, and, on the average, there are five people to a family.

Employment   Twenty to 40 percent of the work force in the region is underemployed or unemployed.

Water   Mexico City lies in a valley situated high in the mountains. There are no natural rivers in the immediate vicinity. In the past, wells supplied the region with fresh water, but these are no longer adequate. Today, water from distant locations must be pumped over the mountains and into

In Mexico City many people live in tents along the roadside with inadequate access to clean water, sewage, or waste disposal facilities. (Tonio Turok)

the city. By United States standards, the city water is unsafe to drink. By the year 2000, water will have to be transported an average distance of 350 km, and 20 percent of the nation's total electrical generating capacity will be needed to drive the pumps.

Sewage and Waste Disposal   There are no sewers in the poorest communities. Where sewage systems exist, the wastes are disposed of by pumping them over the mountains and into nearby valleys. This process requires expensive piping and consumes additional supplies of energy. Only 60 percent of the garbage in Mexico City is ever collected. The remainder is burned in the open air or collects in unhealthy, unsanitary, clandestine dumps.

Air Pollution   Mexico City is located in a high mountain valley ringed on all sides by higher

Slum housing in Mexico city. The plume of black smoke in the background is rising from an uncontrolled fire in an open garbage dump. (Tonio Turok)

Natural Disasters Mexico City is built on an old saltwater marsh. Over the years, as the weight of buildings and roadways has increased, and as some of the brackish water has been pumped away, the city has slowly been settling. Many millions of dollars have been spent to maintain a complex city on an unstable base.

In addition, the entire valley lies within an active earthquake zone. A total of seven quakes struck the city between 1979 and 1986, and some of these caused extensive loss of life and property.

10.7
Cities in the Less-Developed Countries—The Despair and the Hope

The picture of Mexico City is indeed bleak. In fact, you might ask, "Why do people live in places like Mexico City?" In a broader sense, "Why do people continue to migrate into cities in the less-developed countries?"

The answer seems to be that extreme poverty is also commonplace in the countryside. Therefore, as difficult as it is for people in a developed society to imagine, many poor families actually improve their living standards by moving to the cities. Furthermore, for those who unfortunately are worse off in the cities than they were in the countryside, there is always the hope that they can eventually find high-paying jobs that will lead to a more comfortable and satisfying life.

What does the future hold? Naturally there are differences of opinion. Some observers are predicting some sort of catastrophic collapse of urban centers in the less-developed countries. They emphasize that there is simply not enough money to maintain these impoverished, gargantuan complexes. According to this viewpoint, city services cannot possibly keep up with population growth, and living conditions will decline even further. As a result, disease will spread, or social unrest will prevail, leading to an era of turmoil and increased misery. Furthermore, fuel shortages are likely to occur in the near future, and, when this happens, the cost of living in a city will increase even more drastically. Thus, the outlook for large impoverished cities is indeed bleak.

Not everyone agrees with this prediction. Some economists believe that cities in the less-developed countries are suffering growing pains, but

peaks. As a result, the natural movement of air is often obstructed, and pollutants tend to be concentrated over the region. The problem is augmented by the fact that there are 300,000 factories and 3 million private cars in the city. Air pollution control laws are not particularly strict. Many factories spew noxious gases into the air and release a variety of contaminants. In addition, many automobiles are old and in a such a poor state of repair that they release relatively high concentrations of air pollutants. Average carbon monoxide concentrations in certain neighborhoods in Mexico City have been measured to be approximately 20 parts per million (ppm), and rush-hour peaks of 35 to 40 ppm have been recorded. (See Appendix A for a definition of ppm.) According to the United States Environmental Protection Agency, an 8-hour exposure to 20-ppm carbon monoxide is described as "very unhealthful."

that a more pleasant equilibrium will be reached. According to this viewpoint, as the central cities become expensive and unpleasant, factories and businesses will move outward into the countryside, just as they have in the more developed countries. At this point, the growth of cities in the less-developed countries will level off, and order will be maintained.

Summary

Demands on land use are varied and often conflicting. They include needs for food, water, waste disposal, living space, industrial and commercial zones, electrical energy, recreation, transportation, and raw materials.

It is inherently more expensive to live in urban areas than in the country. For the majority of people in the developed nations, jobs are available, and the affluent can enjoy the advantages that are offered by the cities. Urbanization in the developed countries has led to urban sprawl, and the growth of **supercities.** This type of development has led to the destruction of large tracts of agricultural land. Actions that can be used to preserve the quality of existing landscapes include zoning laws, establishment of parks and greenbelts, regulation of population size in specific areas, changes of tax laws to favor agricultural use of land, direct purchase of rights of development, and construction of mass transit systems instead of highways.

Urbanization in the less-developed countries is proceeding at a rapid rate. In recent years, urban populations have increased rapidly, and many of the urban poor live in inadequate housing, are unemployed, do not have access to sanitary water or waste disposal facilities, and must breathe air that is heavily polluted. Some people project that these conditions will foster social unrest, while others predict that stable societies will develop.

Questions

Uses of Land

1. Classify the environment that you live in as urban, rural, or suburban. Obtain a map of your region and use different colored pencils to shade areas occupied by: (1) factories and warehouses, (2) retail businesses, (3) low-density housing, (4) high-density housing, (5) agricultural areas, and (6) open spaces. Try to design a more efficient system of land use. How would you alter the present system to make your region more efficient or more pleasant? Discuss.

2. Review the list of the nine needs of any community that were given in the text. Outline how these needs are met within your community.

3. Obtain a copy of your local zoning ordinance. Do the zoning laws promote efficient or inefficient land use? Do they promote pleasant living areas? Would it be possible to improve the efficiency of land use in your neighborhood? Discuss with government officials any proposals you might have and report on their reaction.

Urbanization

4. Briefly review the history of urban development. Discuss major differences in urbanization in the developed countries and in the less-developed countries.

5. Why is it inherently more expensive to live in a city than it is to live in the country? Why have cities grown nevertheless?

6. Discuss the similarities and the differences in the problems that would arise in a city, a suburban area, and in the countryside in the event of a fuel shortage.

7. What economic factors encourage constructions of multistory buildings? Obtain a map of your county. Divide the map into sections rated according to the average building height in the area. What trends can be observed?

Urbanization in the United States

8. Outline the major differences among the following types of settlements: a city, a megalopolis, a supercity, and a rural region.

9. Obtain a telephone book for a rural region in your state. Study the yellow pages and estimate the number of business that: (a) are directly related to agriculture; (b) are peripherally related to agriculture (for example a clothing shop sells clothes to farmers as well as nonfarmers); and (c) are unrelated to agriculture. Show how your list reflects the character of the town.

10. In 1985, General Motors announced that the site for their new Saturn assembly plant would be located in a previously rural region in Tennessee. Discuss the factors that you would consider if you were responsible for choosing a site for this plant. Discuss some tradeoffs involved in choosing between a rural and an urban area.

11. Discuss how the assembly plant, mentioned above, would affect the existing community.

12. In the western United States, many farms are being subdivided into smaller lots, ranging from about 2 to 10 hectares. Owners of these lots frequently raise horses and a small garden. Would you classify this land as agricultural or suburban? Defend your answer.

13. Explain why careless urbanization can be considered to be part of the tragedy of the commons.

14. In Section 10.5, six approaches to urban land use planning were outlined. (a) Compare these specific suggestions with the broad outlines for legal approaches to environmental problems given in Chapter 2. (b) Do the legal techniques for preserving land quality also infringe on certain human rights? Discuss the tradeoffs involved.

15. Explain how tax laws can influence decisions in land management.

16. Prepare a class debate: Have one side argue that the government should subsidize a landowner who preserves agricultural land, while the other side supports the opinion that the sale of land is a private matter between individuals, and the government should not interfere with free enterprise.

17. Explain how recent trends in the United States are causing land to become urbanized at a faster rate than the urban population is growing.

Urbanization in the Less-Developed Countries

18. Explain why urban problems are more severe in the less-developed countries than they are in the wealthier nations.

19. Prepare a class debate: Have one side argue that the future for cities in the less-developed countries is bleak, while the other side argues that a more hopeful future can be anticipated.

Suggested Readings

Urban land use is the subject of the following references:

Donald A. Krueckenberg (ed.): *Introduction to Planning History in the United States.* Piscataway, NJ, Center for Urban Policy Research, 1982. 235 pp.

W. Patrick Beaton (ed.): *Municipal Expenditures, Revenues, and Services.* Piscataway, NJ, Center for Urban Policy Research, 1982. 166 pp.

David Listoken (ed.): *Housing Rehabilitation: Economic, Social and Policy Perspectives.* Piscataway, NJ, Center for Urban Policy Research, 1982. 312 pp.

William Whyte: Design as if people mattered. *Technology Review,* p. 37, July, 1982.

An interesting sociological study of urban development in the United States is given in:

Kenneth Kusmer: *A Ghetto Takes Shape.* Chicago, University of Illinois Press, 1978. 299 pp.

A classic but still pertinent book on the theory of land-use planning is:

Ian McHarg: *Design with Nature.* New York, NY, Doubleday and Co., 1969. 187 pp.

Changing patterns of urbanization in the United States are discussed in:

John Herbers: *The New Heartland, America's Flight Beyond the Suburbs and How it's Changing Our Future.* New York, New York Times Books, 1986. 228 pp.

Larry Long and Diana DeAre: The slowing of urbanization in the U.S. *Scientific American, 249,* (1):33, 1983.

Daniel Vinning, Jr.: Migration between the core and the periphery. *Scientific American, 247,* (6):45, 1982.

Sharon Zukin: *Loft Living, Culture and Capital in Urban Change.* Baltimore, MD, Johns Hopkins University Press, 1982. 224 pp.

Development of agricultural land is documented in:

Lester R. Brown: *Building a Sustainable Society.* New York, W.W. Norton and Company, 1981. 443 pp.

Lester R. Brown: Vanishing croplands. *Environment, 20* (10): 1978.

Douglas M. Costle: Growth, land, and the future. *EPA Journal,* July/Aug 1980. pp 2ff.

Robert G. Healy and James L. Short: The changing rural landscape. *Environment, 23* (10):7, 1981.

Robert Howard: *The Vanishing Land.* New York, Villard Books, 1985. 318 pp.

Archibald M. Woodruff (ed.): *The Farm and the City—Rivals or Allies.* Englewood Cliffs, NJ, Prentice-Hall, Inc., 1980. 184 pp.

A study of urban development in the less-developed countries is given in:

Allen Kelley and Jeffrey Williamson: *What Drives Third World City Growth.* Princeton, NJ, Princetown University Press, 1984. 273 pp.

11

Rural Land Use

The Value of Rural Lands

So far in this book, we have discussed the value of rural lands as an agricultural resource. When we studied agriculture and the world food supply, we asked questions such as, "If we cut down this forest would the soil be suitable for sustainable grain production? If we irrigated this prairie or drained this swamp, could we raise more food for the human population?" Now let us look at rural land from another perspective. Is there any intrinsic value in undeveloped, wild lands? What would the human race gain if a particular forest, prairie, or wetland were left alone, unfarmed, and untouched by the plow or the bulldozer?

Rural Lands and the Human Spirit

In his book, *Arctic Dreams,* the author, Barry Lopez, writes:

> And I would think as I walked of what I had read of a creature of legend in China, an animal similar in its habits to the unicorn.* It is called the *ki-lin*. The *ki-lin* has the compassion of the unicorn but also the air of a spiritual warrior, or monk . . . Unlike the western unicorn, the *ki-lin* has never had commercial value; no drug is made of any part of its body; he exists for his own sake and not for the medication, enrichment, entertainment, or even edification of mankind. He embodied all that was admirable and ideal. . . .
>
> In the simple appreciation of a world not our own to define, we might find some solace in discovering the *ki-lin* hidden within ourselves, like a shaft of light.

In this passage, Mr. Lopez is saying that we shouldn't have to count the value of wild lands or wild creatures in terms of financial return. Instead we should listen to that voice deep within ourselves that finds a spiritual peace and a feeling of well-being when we come in contact with the natural environment. This sentiment is shared by a great many people and is expressed in a variety of ways in literature, in art, and in music.

Other people do not feel this compelling unity between wildness and the human spirit. They

---

*The unicorn is a mythical, horse-like animal with one horn growing out of its forehead. The animal and its horn were alleged to have magical properties.

An eskimo woman rows home through the arctic ice.

argue that humans should use the environment for their own physical gain and enrichment.

For the sake of argument, let us set aside the spiritual value of the natural environment for a moment and focus only on economic issues. Imagine that there were a piece of undeveloped land near your home. This parcel could either be preserved as a park or wilderness area, or, alternatively, it could be opened for commercial or agricultural development. What are the economic tradeoffs between the two approaches? The gains that can be realized by development are obvious. Farms are created or land is made available for factories and stores. But on the other side of the coin, what are the external costs of development? To answer these questions, we must appreciate the material value of untouched land.

Rural Lands and Water Balance

The rate of flow of water across the land is vitally important to all terrestrial organisms. Consider a simple experiment in which two different materials, a sheet of metal and a sponge, were propped up at an angle to form two imaginary hillsides. Pour a measured amount of water over each. The water would run off the metal quite rapidly, whereas it would be retained and stored in the sponge. In the real world, an asphalt parking lot can be compared to the sheet of metal; rainwater flows rapidly across

the surface. At the other extreme, a forest or natural wetland is more like the sponge. For example, recall that the floor of a temperate forest is covered by a thick layer of partially decomposed litter. Beneath this litter, the soil is interlaced with roots and is richly endowed with humus. The soil and the litter are both effective in retaining and absorbing rainwater. As a result, the water from heavy rains or melting snow does not run rapidly off the land but percolates through the soil and drains slowly downslope. This slowly moving water recharges creeks, streams, and groundwater supplies during the dry season.

Thus, if forests are left intact, they help to regulate the flow of rivers. This regulation is especially important in areas such as the Himalayan foothills, where distinct rainy seasons are followed by dry periods. In Nepal and India, hillside forests have been cut for fuel or for agricultural expansion. As a result, devastating floods have occurred with increasing regularity in recent years. In addition, when water runs off the land during the wet seasons, less is available for natural plant growth or for irrigation during the summer months.

Rural Lands and Erosion

When water runs rapidly across the surface of the land, soil resources are destroyed by erosion. This loss of topsoil is a multifaceted problem:

Erosion is a serious problem that is leading to severe loss of farmland throughout the world. This photograph was taken in Nepal.

1. As documented in Chapter 8, when soil is removed from an area, productivity decreases, and the land is less fit either for agriculture or the regeneration of natural ecosystems.

2. When particles of soil are deposited in the bottoms of rivers, the sediment fills the tiny spaces between rocks that provide homes for insects, crustaceans, and other small animals. Sediment also smothers shellfish and covers the leaves of aquatic plants, thereby blocking out the light needed for photosynthesis. Thus, erosion can disrupt the entire aquatic food web.

3. Additionally, sediment raises the level of the river bed. In turn, when the river bed is raised, the water level rises and floods become more likely. Silt also fills reservoirs and shortens the useful life of expensive dams.

4. Finally, in many areas characterized by especially steep hillsides, erosion has been so severe that massive landslides occur. In many deforested regions in Nepal and India, entire hillsides are washed away during the monsoon seasons. Roads and transportation networks are cut, and farms,

both on the hillsides and in the valleys, are ruined. In some cases, villages are buried and people are killed.

Rural Lands and the Regulation of Climate

Many ecologists believe that natural ecosystems play an important role in the regulation of climate. For example, recall from Chapter 5 that tropical rainforests receive as much as 400 cm of rainfall per year. Of this total, more than half is continuously recycled within the forest itself. Plants absorb moisture, and much of this is immediately returned back into the atmosphere through leaf tissues. This process, called **evapotranspiration,** not only recycles the moisture back into the air but also cools the atmosphere. This cooling promotes condensation and additional precipitation. Therefore, a rainforest can be considered to be a self-perpetuating system, for it helps to generate the rainfall that it needs for survival.

In addition, climate is affected by the reflectivity of land surfaces, called the **albedo.** A flat, barren plain such as a sandy beach or an exposed snowfield reflects much of the incident sunlight and is said to have a high albedo. Alternatively, a forest, with its multitude of trees and leafy floor, absorbs sunlight and has a low albedo. When a forest is cut, the albedo will increase, and, as more heat is radiated outward, the atmosphere becomes warmer. This warming tends to decrease the probability of rainfall.

For these reasons, there is fear that if a continental-sized region such as the Amazon rainforest is destroyed, climatic patterns will change. If a small segment of a tropical forest is cut, the temperature of the clearing will fluctuate from extreme highs during the day to cool temperatures (by tropical standards) during the night. In large areas that have been deforested, local weather patterns have been altered. For example, in Panama, rainfall in areas that were deforested 50 years ago has decreased by 1 cm every year for a total of 50 cm, compared with nearby unlogged regions. There is still no convincing evidence, however, either to support or contradict the prediction of global climate change. (Recall from Special Topic C in Chapter 8 that a similar scenario was outlined for arid regions.)

Another environmental benefit we receive from natural ecosystems is that they play an important role in the recycling and storage of carbon. Recall from Chapter 6 that some scientists believe that the composition of our atmosphere is controlled and maintained by biological processes. If this theory is correct, the destruction of these systems might eventually affect the entire life-support system of the biosphere. In addition, when a forest is cut and the branches and other debris are burned or allowed to rot, carbon dioxide is released to the atmosphere, just as it is in the burning of fossil fuels. It is feared that a buildup of the carbon dioxide concentration in our atmosphere will cause global warming and a drier climate in some areas, as will be discussed further in Chapter 21.

Rural Lands and Pollution Control

Many biodegradable pollutants such as human sewage can be readily consumed by a variety of different organisms, both plant and animal. Once consumed, the pollutants are eventually converted by biological processes to nontoxic products such as carbon dioxide, water, or simple nitrogen compounds. This process occurs naturally in all ecosystems, but some ecosystems cleanse themselves more rapidly than others. Bogs and marshes are areas of naturally rapid growth. When biodegradable pollutants enter these areas, they fertilize many different organisms, populations expand quickly, and the pollutants are consumed and thereby removed. For example, in the mid-1970s, a study of the upstream portions of the Alcovy River in Georgia showed that the waterway was heavily polluted with human sewage and chicken offal. The river then passed through approximately 4.4 km of swampy forest. This region purified the water so that the river downstream from the swamp was clean enough to support species of fish that could not survive in the polluted zone upstream.

Rural Lands as a Home and a Source of Livelihood

Primitive people have traditionally lived in a sustainable union with the natural environment. In such a relationship, food and resources are consumed and wastes are discarded, but the rates of

A satellite photograph of road-building projects in the Amazon Basin. (Wide World Photos)

consumption and disposal generally lie within the ability of an ecosystem to regenerate itself. Although estimates vary, perhaps as many as 250 million people still live in and make their living from relatively undisturbed places. Most of these people are found along the fringes of the tropical rainforests. In many cases, when major development occurs in these areas, a previously stable and relatively comfortable lifestyle is destroyed. Although 250 million people represent only 5 percent of the global population, in human terms, the displacement of families and the disruption of lifestyles become a serious ethical problem.

Destruction of Habitat and the Extinction of Species

Many types of organisms adapt well to ecosystems that have been disturbed by humans. For example, several species of cockroaches are thriving so well in urban environments that their range is actually expanding. However, many other species—millions and millions of them—can survive only in the natural habitats in which they have evolved. As natural habitats are being destroyed, especially as tropical rainforests are being destroyed, uncounted numbers of species are being driven to extinction. This important and complex topic and the consequences of species extinction will be discussed in Chapter 12.

Rural Land Use and Recreation

This section was started with a discussion of rural land and the human spirit. Now we introduce the topic of rural land use and recreation. In one sense any discussion of recreation brings us full circle, and we return to the spiritual value of wilderness. Every year millions of people vacation "in the country" and thereby gain an intangible reward that can be called relaxation, enjoyment, or peace of mind. However, for those who believe that rewards must be balanced on an economic tally sheet, the tourist industry is a major source of revenue for many Americans. In addition, as outdoor recreation has become big business, companies that manufacture camping supplies, canoes, skis, and other forms of recreational equipment have prospered.

The Economic Balance Sheet

Now let us return to the question posed at the beginning of this section, "What are the costs and the benefits incurred when a piece of previously undeveloped land is opened for commercialization?" It is relatively easy to calculate the number of jobs that new industry will bring to an area and the increase in the tax base that inevitably follows when land becomes commercialized. These are the benefits of development.

But how do you add up the costs? You can calculate the number of families displaced from a previously stable rural economy and the number of jobs lost when a tourist industry is disrupted. You can calculate the value of a watershed in terms of reservoir capacity and potential to supply water for irrigation. On the other hand, how do you include spiritual, long-range, or global effects in the tally? As asked in Chapter 2, "Is it possible to place a dollar value on a feeling of happiness or of well-being?" Or, as another example, if erosion depletes soil resources, silts a river, or fills the reservoir be-

hind a dam, the full economic impact may not become acute for a number of years. It is easy to ignore these long-term effects and difficult to calculate them accurately. Consider yet another problem. No one is sure that the destruction of ecosystems will cause climatic change, and, even if such a relationship does exist and could be proved, the negative effects might not occur for decades. With all these uncertainties, it becomes very difficult to use cost/benefit analysis to weigh the consequences of the destruction of ecosystems. Therefore, some people argue that answers to important environmental issues cannot be approached solely in economic terms.

11.2
Tropical Rainforest

In modern times, people are using many of the planet's resources faster than these resources are being replenished. Forests are no exception. Four thousand years ago, a mere blink in geological time, much of the Earth was covered with forests. As civilization developed, most of the woodlands in Europe and large portions of those originally found in central Asia, the Middle East, and India were cleared. Later, the same thing happened in North America, where in some regions in the midwest, 99.9 percent of the virgin timber has been cut.

Today, most of the remaining woodlands in the developed countries are being replanted and reforested at the same rates at which they are being logged. But extensive deforestation is occurring in most tropical, less-developed countries. Before humans became numerous and efficient enough to alter significant portions of the Earth's biosphere, tropical rainforest covered approximately 16 million sq km, or about 11 percent of the land area of the planet. It is difficult to make an accurate counting of how much has been destroyed already and how much is now being destroyed every year, for several reasons. First, many nations do not maintain accurate statistics on patterns of land use. Second, even when data are available, there are several different criteria that can be used to define destruction. To some people, a forest is destroyed only if every tree is cut down, whereas to others, a forest is destroyed when enough plants are removed to cause a significant change in the character of the ecosystem. Nevertheless, rough estimates are available. According to the World

Box 11.1
Tropical Rainforests and Songbirds in North America

In 1962, Rachael Carson wrote the book *Silent Spring,* in which she claimed that widespread pesticide use was killing nontarget organisms. She warned that if the existing practices continued, populations of songbirds would be destroyed, and we would be greeted with a "silent spring." This problem will be discussed in Chapter 19. It is mentioned here because songbirds are now faced with a new menace. Many of them migrate to Central or South America to winter every year in the rainforests. If these forests are destroyed, the loss of habitat could be at least as disastrous as poisonous sprays.

Figure 11–1
A road-building and clearcutting project in Brazil. After the initial road is established, adjacent areas are opened to loggers, who can then cut vast expanses of forest. (Wide World Photos)

Resources Institute, approximately one third of the original tropical rainforest has already been cleared, and destruction continues at a rate of about 7 million hectares per year (or about 0.6 percent of the total rainforest). This rate amounts to about 13 hectares per minute, day and night throughout the year.

As discussed in the previous section, conservation of a natural ecosystem such as a tropical rainforest maintains long-term, sustainable values that are often difficult to quantify. Some types of logging, cultivation of certain types of plantations, and limited farming can also be sustained on a long-term basis. However, conservation and careful use of resources often realize less *immediate* profit than wholesale exploitation. Therefore, a conflict frequently arises between conservation and development.

Logging   Wood is a valuable commodity, and the hardwoods that thrive in the tropical rainforest are in high demand in the global marketplace. There are two fundamentally different ways that an area can be logged. When a region is chosen for **selective cutting,** loggers harvest only those mature trees that produce the most valuable timber and they leave the rest of the forest untouched. This approach minimizes ecological disruption, because it leaves the forest ecosystem intact. If loggers move into an area and cut selec-

tively every 20 years or so, the most valuable commercial timber can be removed, and at the same time, the quality of the natural system can be conserved. However, in many cases, this technique is more expensive than an alternative approach called **clearcutting** (Fig. 11–1). In a clearcutting operation, all the trees in an area are cut. Small logs are used to manufacture paper, and large logs are sawn into boards. The region is reduced to rubble, and the ecosystem is destroyed. If soil resources are conserved and if seedlings are replanted to replace the trees that were cut, the forest will, in time, regrow. On the other hand, if the soil is lost to erosion, if it reacts to form a rock-like layer of laterite, or if the cleared land is then used for farming or industrial development, the forest is lost.

Consider, then, what happens in many less-developed countries. Often, the governments are

Special Topic A   The Condition of Tropical Rainforests Around the World

Table 11-1
Annual Losses of Tropical Forests

Country	Hectares cut/year	Comments
Brazil	1,480,000	The Amazon basin, the Earth's largest rainforest, lies mainly in Brazil. Despite the rapid commercialization in the region, large portions of the central basic remain intact.
Colombia	820,000	About one third of the country was originally forested. Rainforest destruction has recently slowed.
Indonesia	600,000	Contains the largest rainforest in Asia, but much of it has already been destroyed. Log production multiplied sixfold between 1970 and 1980, and farming has expanded greatly in the area.
Nigeria	300,000	Dense population and a century of logging have already destroyed most of the rainforests in this country.
Ivory Coast	290,000	More than 70 percent of the original forest has been cleared, and the rest may be gone by 1995.
Malaysia	250,000	About two thirds of the original forests have already been cut; many have been converted to commercial plantations.
India	150,000	India had only patches of forest at the turn of the century, and most of these are going rapidly.
Nicaragua	120,000	Two thirds of the original forests in Central America have already been removed by heavy population pressures and extensive ranching.
Guatemala	90,000	
Costa Rica	65,000	
Belize	22,000	

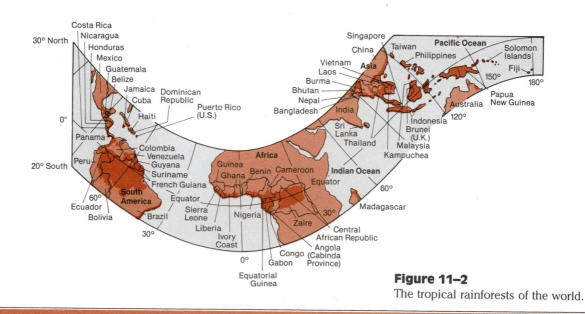

Figure 11–2
The tropical rainforests of the world.

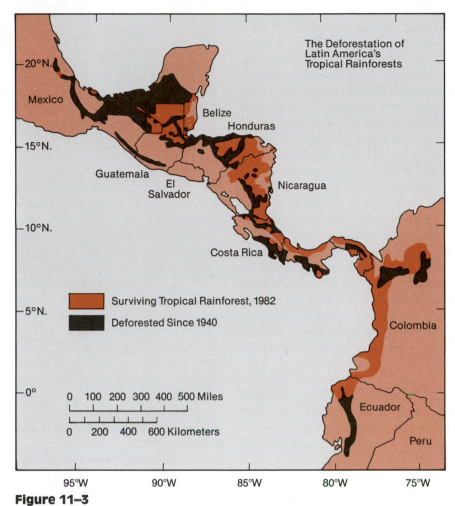

Figure 11–3
The deforestation of the tropical rainforests in Latin America.

impoverished, a large number of people are hungry and out of work, and there are very few ways to obtain valuable foreign exchange. It is understandable that the rainforests are cut and the wood is sold to foreign buyers. On a global scale, wood exports bring approximately $8.7 billion a year to less-developed countries. Unfortunately, this gain is balanced by a number of losses. For one, there are relatively few mills in the less-developed countries that are capable of processing logs into lumber, plywood, or paper. Therefore, in many instances, the unprocessed logs are exported, and finished products are imported at a higher price. As a result, most of the foreign exchange that is gained by the initial sales is spent in purchasing forest products.

At present, very little attempt has been made to reforest the logged regions. On the contrary, the first step in a logging operation is to build roads into previously unsettled areas. These roads provide access into the wilderness, and, in every less-developed country in the world, logging has inevitably been followed by a potentially more disruptive activity—farming.

Farming As you will recall from earlier chapters, the soils of tropical rainforests are often incapable of supporting sustainable agriculture. In some cases, depleted soils can be enriched and made productive by heavy (and expensive) application of fertilizer. However, as discussed previously, laterite soils harden irreversibly after a few years and cannot be rejuvenated. In 1987, it was estimated that more than 200 million people were farming the edges of the world's tropical rainforests. As the population continues to increase, there is no longer enough land to leave croplands fallow until the full, natural fertility can be re-established. This problem is aggravated by shifts in population as well as numerical growth. Land-poor people in Asia, Africa, and Latin America are being relocated to undeveloped forest regions by governments that are unwilling to implement land reform or unable to cope with the problems of rapidly increasing populations. Many of these relocated farmers do not understand the importance of leaving the land fallow. Therefore, large expanses of land are destroyed, so more and more forest must be cleared each year.

Cattle Ranching In southeastern Mexico, modern descendants of the Mayan Indians have tra-

A government official inspects crops at a recently opened farm settlement in the Amazon Basin. Although soils vary from region to region in the Amazon area, many of the new farms are established on soils that cannot support sustained agriculture. (Wide World Photos)

ditionally practiced a fallow-type agricultural system. Farmers plant corn and vegetables in alternate rows and produce about 10,000 kg of food per hectare per year. In this area, which is richer than most tropical rainforest systems, a farm can be maintained for 5 to 7 years before it must be left fallow for a cycle of 5 to 10 years. However, rather than allow the land to remain unproductive during the fallow period, farmers in the region plant citrus, rubber, cacao, avocado, and papaya trees. These trees conserve the rainforest biome, regenerate the soil, *and* produce cash crops.

At the present time, large parcels of land in this region are owned by wealthy individuals or foreign companies. A short-term profit can be made by clearing the land, planting it to pasture, and raising beef for export. In the first year, one hectare of pasture produces about 100 kg of meat. Compare this quantity with the 10,000 kg of grains and vegetables that are produced in traditional agriculture! However, even this low rate of food production is not sustainable. Within a few years, the soil fertility declines, and the nutritional grasses become invaded by toxic weeds. In addition, the soil becomes impacted and hardened by the heavy rainfall. Within 5 to 10 years, the meat production drops to 10 kg per hectare per year. However, even though cattle ranching destroys the soil in a relatively short period of time, large landowners have learned that a short-term profit can be realized by raising beef for export. The range-fed beef from Central and South America is of lower quality than the grain-fed beef produced in the United States, but it is cheaper and is adequate for use in fast foods and pet foods. In fact, it is estimated that our imports of cheap beef from Latin American countries lower the price of hamburgers sold at fast food restaurants by about $.05 per burger.

Cattle ranching is threatening tropical rainforest systems throughout South and Central America. For example, in 1950, cattle ranches covered only one eighth of the land area of Costa Rica. By 1986 more than one third of the country had been converted to pasture land, and most of this new grazing land was originally tropical rainforest. On a larger scale, throughout Latin America, approximately 20,000 sq km of forest land are cleared every year to be converted to cattle ranching oper-

ations. Two thirds of the beef produced on these pastures is exported to the more developed countries, providing Latin American countries with valuable foreign exchange. However, much of this money remains in the hands of the rich. In many Latin American countries, governments have actually encouraged this process by offering tax and other financial incentives to leisure-class ranchers to graze cattle on cleared forest land. In the meantime, many poor peasants do not have enough to eat.

Gathering Wood for Fuel Recall that primitive agriculture coexisted with forest systems over long periods of time. In the same manner, forests have been able to supply local populations with adequate supplies of wood for heating and cooking. Consider how such a sustainable wood harvest operates. Tropical rainforests are incredibly dense and consist of a great diversity of different species of trees. If the human population is low, people can take fallen branches and harvest different species so that there are always enough trees left to maintain the system. However, if the population is too high, the demand for wood becomes greater than the rate at which timber is replaced by natural growth. In this case, the forest resource will be depleted. In 1983, roughly 3.1 billion cubic meters of wood were felled throughout the world, and more than 50 percent of this was burned to provide heat and power (Fig. 11–4).

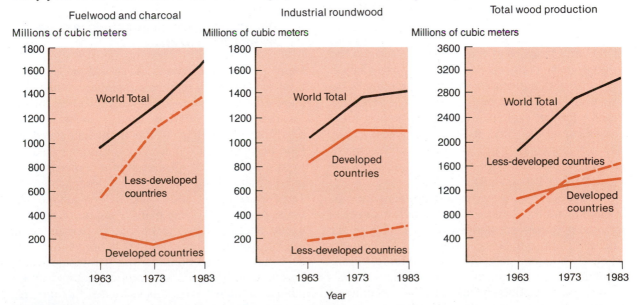

Figure 11–4
Wood consumption in the developed and the less-developed countries.

In many instances, fuel wood gatherers compete with loggers for a limited resource, and the combined pressure of both interests aggravates the destruction of the forest. For example, in one region in India, neighborhood woodlands were traditionally administered by the village governments. Cutting was limited, the most valuable tree species were conserved, and grazing was carefully controlled. In the 1970s, the federal government assumed responsibility for management of many of these forests. In order to promote logging as an industry, teak and eucalyptus plantations were established in place of the natural ecosystems. In this new system, the forest was no longer considered to be a community resource. Local farmers knew that some day the trees would be cut and the logs would be sold, and, most probably, a contractor from outside the village would realize the profit. Therefore, the villagers saw no particular reason to work together to conserve the resource. Although laws were established making it illegal to collect fuel wood in the plantations, these laws proved difficult to enforce and people managed to sneak into the tree farms and steal firewood. Under the combined pressure of logging and uncontrolled firewood gathering, many of these forests are being severely depleted.

Hydroelectric Development The Amazon River, which runs through the central part of Brazil, carries more water than any other river in the world. There are more than 1000 major tributaries of the Amazon, several of which are larger than the Mississippi River. Dams can be built across many of the tributaries, and the energy of water falling through these dams can be converted into electricity. In turn, this electrical energy is important, because, at the present time, a very large portion of Brazil's foreign exchange is spent to import fuels. For example, the Tucurui Dam, the largest in Brazil, can generate 8000 megawatts of electricity, equal to the power output of six nuclear plants the size of Three Mile Island.

However, many ecological problems are associated with the dams. For one, large expanses of tropical rainforest are flooded. The lake behind the Tucurui Dam will cover more than 2000 sq km when it is completely filled. In addition, during construction of a dam, roads are built into the wilderness, and small towns and cities are established to support the workers. When the dam is finished,

many of these people move on to new projects, but many others remain to settle in the new area. These settlers invariably clear additional forested areas. Finally, there is some question as to how long the dams and their electrical turbines will last. Tropical regions support lush growth of a wide variety of organisms. When forests are flooded, the submerged vegetation rots, and the decay process releases large quantities of organic acids. In turn, the acidic water has corroded mechanical systems of several dams that have recently been built in the Amazon. The warm water in these artificial lakes, combined with the nutrients released from the decomposing trees, has also provided a favorable habitat for many harmful species of plants and animals. Incredible quantities of aquatic plants have bloomed, and, when the lake water flows through the turbines to produce electricity, these plants jam the mechanisms and damage the equipment. In addition, disease organisms abound in the lakes, spreading misery and death to many local inhabitants. In many cases, the water pouring over the dam is so foul and polluted that massive fish kills occur in the water below the dam. Finally, the rapid decomposition of such large amounts of vegetation produces an offensive stench.

Perhaps there are technical solutions to these problems, although the cost will be significant. Meanwhile, the fundamental question, "What are the overall consequences of the destruction of tropical rainforests?" remains unanswered.

Saving the Tropical Rainforest—A Novel Approach

Many people throughout the world believe that tropical rainforests represent a global heritage that should be preserved. Yet for many others in the less-developed countries, this argument is not nearly as compelling as the immediate need for food and foreign exchange. One possible solution to this dilemma was proposed at a conference entitled "Plan of Action for Wise Management of Tropical Forests," sponsored by the United Nations. According to this plan, a system of reserves would be established to protect 10 percent of all rainforests worldwide. Although the program would be voluntary, the countries that participate would be compensated for lost revenues incurred by establishing the reserves. It is estimated that the plan would cost $3 billion a year (approximately what the world spends every 36 hours on armaments). This sum could be raised by imposing a levy on all countries with per capita income of more than $1,500 per year. This kind of proposal recognizes that environmental problems that occur within the borders of an individual country really represent a global concern. Although this plan is being considered, it has not yet been implemented.

11.3
Forestry in the Developed Countries

In contrast to the rapid loss of forest lands in the tropical regions, forested areas are stable or are even increasing in many temperate regions, where most of the developed countries are located (Fig. 11–5). This stabilization can be attributed to several factors. First, most of the forests in the temperate regions were already cut before the start of the twentieth century. On a more positive note, most of the governments of the developed countries have recognized the importance of woodlands and have initiated management programs to maintain sustainable timber harvests.

Although the area of forested land in the developed countries is not changing appreciably, questions are nevertheless being raised about changes in the quality of temperate forest ecosystems. One important issue is the impact of air pollution on the vitality of forests. By one estimate, in 1986, about 14 percent of all the forests in Europe were seriously damaged by air pollution. This topic will be discussed further in Chapter 21.

Other questions arise over the sustainability of modern logging practices. For example, in the United States timber crews often clearcut patches of about 16 hectares (40 acres), leaving alternate patches of timber. In most instances, young seedlings are then planted in the clearcut areas. Clearcut patches are not particularly disruptive to wildlife; in fact, many animals thrive on the lush new growth that sprouts up after the trees are cut. However, there is a serious debate over how much soil depletion is caused when the vegetation is removed and logging roads are built. Some foresters claim that when areas are logged, rates of erosion become so high that streams are silted, and much of the ability of the land to retain water is lost. Moreover, the overall soil depletion is so great that the land will no longer be able to sustain forests

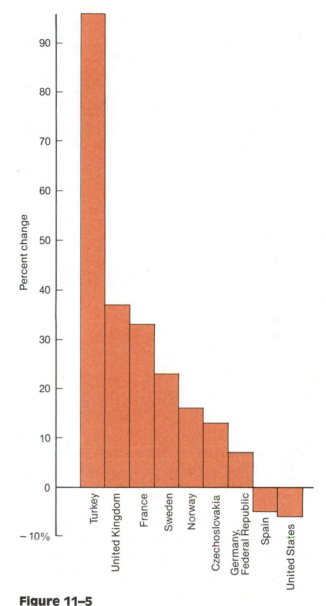

Figure 11–5
Changes in forested area in some selected countries between 1954 and 1984. Note that in seven of the countries chosen, the area of forest lands has actually increased. Forest lands decreased slightly in the United States and Spain.

after a few generations of cutting and regrowth. Others argue that, except when logging occurs on steep hillsides, grasses and brush grow back quickly, reduce erosion, and replenish lost nutrients after a year or two. Undoubtedly, the impact of clearcutting will vary considerably with local climate, type of soil, and many other factors.

Clearcutting operations. *A*, Broad view of a clearcut logging operation in Wilamette National Forest. *B*, Area in the foreground is a 15-year-old Douglas Fir plantation that is well established. In the background is a recent clearcut, with mature timber on both sides. (*A, B,* Courtesy of U.S.D.A. and the Forest Service)

Statistics on the amount of land that is covered by forests tell very little about the size and the ages of the trees on that land. There is concern today that as the old, large trees are being cut, the quality of the remaining timber is declining. Figure 11–6 shows the volume of wood produced by a tree as a function of time. When a tree is young, it grows slowly and produces only a small amount of wood every year. Then, in its adolescence, the tree grows quite rapidly. Finally, in old age, growth rates diminish again. In a planned forest, the maximal dollar yield per year is realized by cutting the tree just at the end of its period of maximal growth.

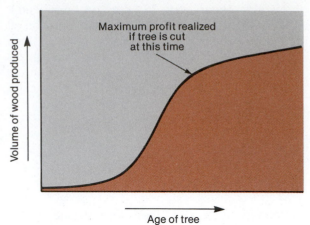

Figure 11–6
Lumber production as a function of the age of a tree. Note that the tree grows most rapidly during adolescence, and maximal profit can be realized by cutting it before it matures fully.

In many commercial logging operations, trees are cut just after adolescence. Figure 11–6 gives no information, however, on lumber quality or, in a larger sense, on the "quality" of a forest. As a tree ages, the wood becomes harder, denser, and stronger. Thus, lumber from a mature tree is superior to that from an adolescent tree. To make up for this lack of quality, people have learned to substitute steel, concrete, synthetics, or glue-laminated beams made of small boards bonded together for applications that once required premium lumber.

When we talk about the "quality" of a forest we are once again returning to nebulous aspects that are difficult to define and evaluate in dollars. A noted environmentalist, Garrett Hardin, once asked the question, "How much is a redwood tree worth?" Suppose a person bought a seedling for $1 and planted it. It would take approximately 2000 years for the tree to grow to maturity. If the tree were then cut and sold for lumber, the investor would realize a profit of about 0.5 percent interest per year. That isn't very much, considering that government savings bonds offer 5 to 10 percent interest per year. Should this calculation be used to argue that redwood trees have no value? Of course not! Since the beginning of time, people have recognized that places or things can have a value that cannot be expressed monetarily. People will lose a great part of their heritage if the beautiful places on this Earth are altered.

Figure 11–7
Undisturbed estuaries are prime breeding grounds for fish. However, industrial development and pollution can destroy these delicate habitats. This photograph shows garbage scows being unloaded in Long Island. (Gamma/Liaison)

If you hike through a quiet stand of climax timber and then continue into a clearcut, stumbling over the rubble and the tire ruts, you can feel that something significant has been altered. In return, relatively inexpensive houses, newspapers, books, and packaging materials are made available. Jobs are created, and our economic well-being is enhanced.

11.4
Coastlines and Marine Estuaries

Although coastal zones make up only a small portion of the world's land surface, environmental pressures on these regions are particularly intense. In the United States, for example, over 50 percent of the population, 40 percent of the manufacturing plants, and 65 percent of the electrical power generators are located within 80 km of the oceans or the Great Lakes. These waterways provide many resources, including international transportation systems, water for industrial cooling and waste disposal, food in the form of fisheries, and recreation. Unfortunately, a given section of coast cannot be used for all these purposes simultaneously, and conflicts arise. The most serious problems are encountered because industrial development is often incompatible with coastal food production and recreation. Estuaries provide nursery grounds for deep-water fish and therefore represent a signifi-

cant food-producing region. On the other hand, many manufacturers see an estuary as an ideal dumping ground for wastes, and, to many developers, a protected bay or inlet would provide an ideal harbor or industrial zone (Fig. 11–7).

Pollution of Estuaries: Chesapeake Bay

Chesapeake Bay is not only the largest estuary system in the United States, but it was once the most productive. The shores of the bay itself lie primarily within the states of Maryland and Virginia, but the 8 major rivers and 150 creeks that empty into the bay drain a much larger area of the eastern seaboard (Fig. 11–8).

When cities were first settled along the eastern seaboard, sewage was dumped directly into the rivers and coastal waters. As a result, by the 1850s, the Potomac River, one of the tributaries of Chesapeake Bay, was reported to be unhealthy and malodorous. The first sewage treatment plant in Washington D.C. was established in 1889, and in 1897 the city of Baltimore followed suit. These early efforts at pollution control were successful and the condition of the waterways improved, but in the 1900s, as population increased, and as industry grew both in size and complexity, new pressures on natural ecosystems were introduced. A significant date that might be used to mark the modern history of pollution in the Chesapeake Bay

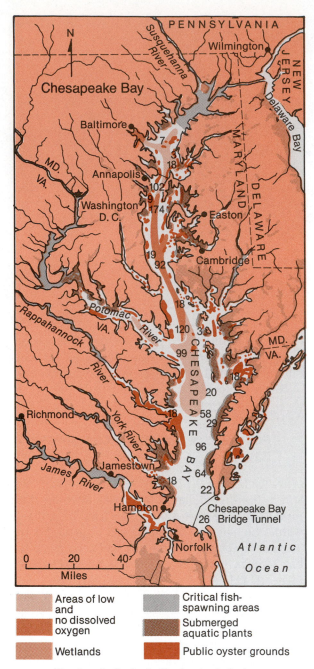

Figure 11–8

Chesapeake Bay and its surrounding area. Rivers from a six-state area drain into the bay. Therefore, any cleanup efforts will be successful only if there is significant interstate cooperation.

region would be 1952, when a bridge was built across the water to connect the previously isolated eastern peninsula with the more heavily industrialized western shore. Soon after the bridge was built, development bloomed and the population on the eastern side of the bay increased dramatically. Of course, much larger factors are involved here than the construction of a single bridge. Chesapeake Bay lies right in the heart of one of the major political, commercial, and industrial regions of the United States. The saltwater estuary and the rivers that drain into it cover more than 150,000 sq km and include the major cities of Washington D.C., Baltimore, Maryland, and Harrisburg, Pennsylvania, to name a few. Between 1950 and 1985, the population of the entire drainage basin increased by about 50 percent, and the land area devoted to urban uses tripled.

As the number of people and factories increased, so did the quantities of a variety of pollutants. Sources of pollution can be divided into two generic categories. **Point-source pollution** occurs when a specific source such as a factory or treatment plant discharges chemical or organic wastes. **Non-point pollution** results when runoff from a broad area disperses pollutants into the environment. As an example of the latter category, when forests are converted into farms and farms are converted into urban settlements, rates of erosion increase. The silt that is carried into waterways kills many species that form the foundation of the food chain, such as sea grass and small crustaceans. In addition, fertilizers and phosphate detergents that are dispersed into aquatic ecosystems encourage the rapid growth of unappetizing forms of life. (See Chapter 20.) The full impact of the pollution is documented in part by records of commercial seafood harvests. In 1960, 2.7 million kg of striped bass were harvested in Chesapeake Bay; by 1985, the catch dwindled to 270,000 kg (a 90 percent reduction), and harvests of other species of fish, crabs, and oysters have also dropped.

A variety of laws regulate the disposal of wastes into aquatic environments. For example, The Clean Water Act (to be discussed further in Chapter 20) sets limits on the quantity of toxic substances that can be dumped into rivers and estuaries. The Fisheries Conservation and Management Act, passed in 1976, requires federal agencies to propose management plans to ensure optimal yield and guaranteed perpetuation of all commercial species of coastal fish. In practice, however, a law is only as effective as its enforcement, and the fact remains that the quality of the environment of Chesapeake Bay has deteriorated despite environmental legislation.

On the other hand, there has been significant public concern about the fate of Chesapeake Bay in recent years, and specific actions have been initiated to restore some of its original vitality. In 1976, the EPA initiated a study of the bay and its ecosystems. The study required 7 years to complete and confirmed what was already known informally—that the bay is suffering badly from pollution. In 1984, in an unusual solidarity of interstate cooperation, the governments of Maryland, Virginia, Pennsylvania, and the District of Columbia agreed to work together to save the estuary. As a first step, all the states tightened regulations on municipal sewage treatment facilities. In 1985, Maryland banned phosphate from detergents, and in 1987, Virginia followed suit. However, these control measures did not significantly reduce the flow of industrial pollutants. Many people thought that the EPA was not particularly aggressive in enforcing the Clean Water Act. Consequently, in 1984, two private-citizens' action groups, the Chesapeake Bay Foundation and the Natural Resources Defense Council, initiated private action. A lawsuit was filed against the Bethlehem Steel Corporation for illegally dumping wastes into the estuary. According to the suit, Bethlehem Steel had discharged excessive quantities of pollutants in the bay on more than 300 different occasions, and the EPA had failed to enforce compliance with the law. The environmental groups won their suit in 1985, and Bethlehem Steel was fined over a million dollars. According to an attorney for the Natural Resources Defense Council:

> Our victory in this case is a turning point for citizen enforcement of environmental laws. Bethlehem Steel claimed we could never beat them in a courtroom. Their defeat has to be a shock to the thousands of other major water polluters who have been following this case closely. They know the free ride is over. They can obey the Clean Water law or they can face citizens in court.

However, the cleanup has barely begun. The total cost to bring Chesapeake Bay back to life could range from one to three billion dollars, and it will be decades before the project is complete.

Physical Disruption of Coastlines: The South Shore of Long Island

When waves strike a beach, grains of sand and small pieces of rock are dislodged from the shoreline and carried along the coast, where they are later redeposited. This continuous movement of material creates many distinct land forms and ecological habitats. Along the southern coast of Long Island, movement of sediment has formed a series of thin, low-lying **barrier islands** (Fig. 11–9). Between the barrier islands and the mainland lies a series of quiet, protected salt marshes. These marshes represent an estuary system that provides home and shelter for many forms of aquatic life, including the young of many species of deep-water fish. The predominant movement of water along this coastline is from east to west, as shown in Figure 11–9. On the eastern end of Long Island, near Montauk Point, there is a region of tall cliffs composed of sand and gravel originally deposited by the glaciers of the great ice ages. At the present time, the ocean waters are eroding the sediment from these cliffs and carrying the material westward toward Rockaway Beach and New Jersey. If we studied a beach midway along the island, say Fire Island (shown on the map), we would find that the existing beach sand is constantly being eroded and carried westward, only to be replaced by sand from the eastern end of the island. The beach, in dynamic equilibrium, remains stable.

Superimposed on this east-west movement are variations caused by seasonal changes and severe storms. In the wintertime, series of steep, sharply undercut waves remove large quantities of beach sand, carry the sediment out to sea, and deposit it in a formation known as a sand bar, which lies parallel to the shore. Thus, in winter, the beach erodes and grows smaller. This erosion is only temporary, however, because the gentler waves of summer carry sand from the bar inland and rebuild the beach. In this manner, long-term stability is maintained despite seasonal fluctuations.

In any coastal system, severe storms periodically strike the shore. In a natural barrier system such as the one in southern Long Island, storms completely overrun the low-lying outer islands, but

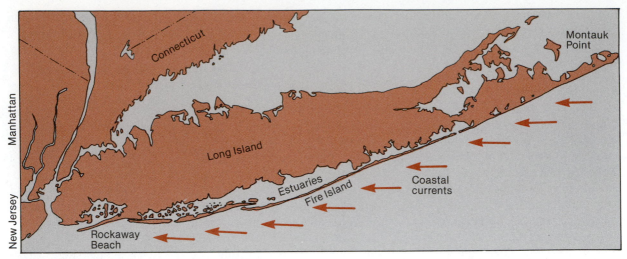

Figure 11–9
Map of Long Island showing predominant movement of coastal currents.

the system is not permanently damaged by these periodic inundations. The high waves that wash across the beach and roll inland over the dunes and salt marshes flatten some dunes, build others higher, and move sand and rock here and there. When the storm is over, there is little significant long-lasting erosion. Beaches remain intact, salt marshes rejuvenate quickly, and the dune grasses that had evolved in such a system grow back within a few months.

We do not mean to imply that geological forces have no effect on coastlines, because they do. But the change is generally slow. When the sand deposits near Montauk Point become depleted and no new inflow of sand can travel westward, the island will be reshaped, and beaches will erode. But such changes are generally measured in centuries or millennia rather than in months or years.

The biological-geological balance that exists on Long Island has given rise to a fertile estuary system. However, the ebb and flow of beach sand and the rise and fall of storms are not always compatible with human activity. A shore–sand-dune system is dynamic—always changing. It is also prime waterfront real estate. So people build houses, resorts, and hotels on the shifting sands. Then, in winter, the beach starts to recede. Although this recession is entirely natural, many property owners have tried to save their personal stretch of beach from these cycles of the ocean. This can be done (temporarily) by building a

groin, commonly called a **breakwater.** As mentioned previously, sand steadily moves from east to west along this particular stretch of coast. If a large stone barrier is built just west of a person's property (Fig. 11–10A), it will trap sand moving from the east and keep that particular beach from receding in winter. But now the overall flow of sand has been impeded (Fig. 11–10B). The property just west of the breakwater receives no sand, but the currents that move the sand originate from further out to sea and are not impeded. So behind the breakwater, the beach is eroded as usual, but not replenished. The beach then recedes, as shown in the figure.

This unnatural recession aided by the upstream breakwater is much more extensive than the natural ebb and flow of the beach, and erosion could remove the entire beach and any beach house behind it in a short period of time. So now, the person living behind the breakwater may decide to build another one, west of his or her land, and pass the problem on downstream (Fig. 11–10 C). The situation can perpetuate itself indefinitely, with the net result that millions of dollars must be spent to attempt to stabilize a system that was originally stable in its own dynamic manner.

Storms pose another dilemma. Periodic storms have flooded the dune lands every decade or so for millennia. A developer building a luxury home or an elite resort hotel cannot allow the buildings to be flooded or washed away every 10 or 15 years. Therefore, large sea walls are con-

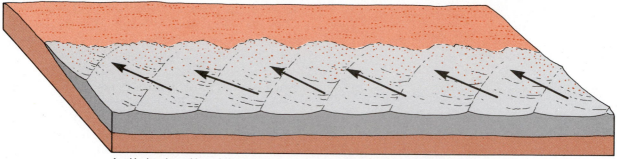

A   Undeveloped beach; ocean currents (arrows) carry sand along the shore, simultaneously eroding and building the beach

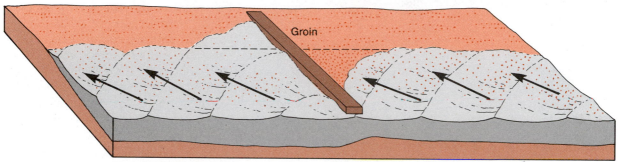

B   A single groin or breakwater. Sand accumulates on upstream side and is eroded downstream

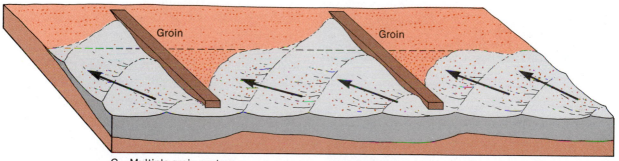

C   Multiple groin system

Figure 11–10
Effect of breakwaters on a beach. *A,* Undeveloped beach; ocean currents (arrows) carry sand along the shore, simultaneously eroding and building the beach. *B,* A single groin or breakwater. Sand accumulates on the upstream side and is eroded downstream. *C,* Multiple groin system.

structed just inland of the beach itself. When a storm wave rolls over a low-lying dune, it dissipates its force gradually over the hills and pushes the beach sand inland. But if a sea wall interrupts this orderly flow, the waves will crash violently against the barrier. The steep breaking waves establish a circular turbulence that carries sand out to sea and erodes the beach.

An example of the futility of these human interferences is the case of Hurricane Ginger, which struck Long Island on September 30, 1971. Undeveloped islands were nearly completely flooded, and dunes were flattened, but within 10 months, the beach had restabilized and was actually larger than it had been before the storm. By contrast, other beaches, which had been "protected" by sea walls, were severely eroded. In the spring of 1972, one community spent $500,000 to replenish the beach, but a storm later that year destroyed it again. In 1973, the National Park Service an-

A

B

C

A breakwater system on Long Island. *A,* A beach house on Atlantic Beach, Long Island. The photograph was taken in February; note that natural rocks are exposed, and there is no sandy beach. *B,* This photograph, taken from inside the house, shows a newly constructed breakwater. *C,* The same house the following winter has a sandy beach. However, the sand had to come from somewhere, perhaps from elsewhere along the coast.

nounced that "after spending $21,000,000 since the 1930s to effect and maintain artificial barriers against waves and storms, the agency concluded that such work does more harm than good."

The social and political issues involved in beach erosion neatly illustrate some of the complications that develop when people try to occupy naturally delicate ecosystems. Perhaps a dynamic system such as a dune land should not be open to development at all. After all, the community as a whole benefits from unspoiled recreational areas, and the economic value of the estuaries as a breeding ground for commercial fish represents a valuable national asset. Furthermore, when an individual or a corporation owns a section of beach, poor people are generally excluded. Since breakwaters and sea walls traditionally have been built with government support, this type of activity is a means whereby the poor pay taxes for the benefit of the rich. Therefore, many believe that shore reconstruction should be abandoned.

The counter argument is that significant development along the beach has, in fact, already occurred and that the tourist business is an economic boon to local communities. In any event, the next hurricane must not be allowed to wash innumerable houses, businesses, and roadways to the sea. Therefore, new and better sea walls and breakwaters should be built. Since breakwaters must be built along the entire stretch of coast to be effective, the government should support such projects.

11.5
Freshwater Wetlands

In its original, undeveloped condition, there were somewhere between one half million and one million square kilometers of wetlands in the lower 48 states. Over the years, as part of a wholesale change in the face of a continent, the wetlands have been converted into sites for factories, housing developments, shopping malls, croplands, golf courses, city dumps, and sewage treatment plants. By 1950, one third of the original wetlands had been destroyed, and, by 1985, that loss had risen to half. Think of it. A quarter to half a million square kilometers of swamps have been dredged, drained, bulldozed, or filled in.

Many people consider swamps and marshes to be areas of wasted, useless land. After all, you can't grow wheat or tomatoes or build a house in

A marsh is an important asset to natural systems, providing water storage and regulation, pollution control, recreation, and a habitat for many species of plants and animals. (Photo by Daniel Turk)

a bog; they are a nuisance to hike through and are often choked with mosquitos, gnats, and even alligators. In a recent survey, 28 percent of the people in Florida thought that wetlands had no redeeming qualities and should be drained or buried with fill. But recall from Section 11.1 that any undeveloped land has a certain value if left untouched. Two qualities of wetlands that deserve specific emphasis are (1) the regulation and control of water and (2) the maintenance of crucial wildlife habitats.

Maintenance of the Water Balance

As explained earlier, natural ecosystems control run-off and reduce flood potential during the wet season of the year and serve as a reservoir for water during the dry months. Wetlands perform these functions particularly well.

In many areas, swamps and bogs have been drained, and engineers have replaced them with artificial systems of reservoirs, dams, and flood control systems. Such projects are a type of technological fix. If well designed, the artificial system does work, and it has been the method of choice in many cases, but it is expensive. In 1972, the Army Corps of Engineers was asked to build a flood control system for the Charles River watershed in Mas-

sachusetts. Rather than build an expensive structure, the engineers decided to acquire about 3500 hectares of wetlands and simply leave them alone. The final report concluded:

> Nature has already provided the least-cost solution to future flooding in the form of extensive wetlands which moderate extreme highs and lows in stream flow. Rather than attempt to improve on this natural protection mechanism, it is both prudent and economical to leave the hydrologic regime established over the millennia undisturbed. In the opinion of the study team, construction of any of the most likely alternatives, a 55,000 acre-foot reservoir, or extensive walls and dikes, can add nothing.

The land acquisition provided recreational areas and wildlife habitats and saves the government $1.2 million every year.

Wetlands and Wildlife Habitat

The first effective wildlife conservation movement in the United States centered around the preservation of egrets and other wading birds that live and feed in wetland areas. In the 1800s, many of these birds were hunted nearly to extinction for their valuable feathers. The first step in saving the birds was to place a ban on hunting. However, as people began to study the problem in more detail, they came to realize that the control of hunting and poaching is merely a first step. No organism can survive if its habitat is destroyed. Therefore, the maintenance of wetlands is an essential part of the campaign to preserve the organisms that live in them. In recent years, wetland preservation has been seen as a crucial step in saving various endangered species, such as whooping cranes and Everglade kites. This important topic will be discussed further in Chapter 12.

Many aquatic birds such as ducks, geese, and cranes migrate between summer nesting grounds in the far north and winter homes in the south. In North America, many of the northern zones in Canada are relatively free of industrialization, and large areas of swampland still exist in the south. But in-between lies the industrial heartland of North America. In many areas, especially along the east coast, wetlands are disappearing at an alarming rate. Loss of just a few hectares of strategically located swamps or lakes may mean removal of an ecosystem that is an essential resting zone for birds during their spring and fall migrations. The water-fowl may occupy the stopover points for only a few weeks of the year, but, without them, the birds could not survive.

11.6
Case History—The Everglades

The **Everglades** is a broad, swampy region of southern Florida (Figs. 11–11 and 11–12). The Seminole Indians called it **Pay-hay-okee,** the river of grass. Indeed, it is a large, shallow, slow-moving river that starts from the shores of Lake Okeechobee and flows approximately 160 km (100 mi) into the ocean. The waters do not travel between well-defined river banks. Rather, they flow through a series of swamps that are nearly 60 km wide in places and slowly wind their way to the sea. One region of this swamp is covered mostly by low-lying plant matter called sawgrass.* Here and there

*Actually, the sawgrass is not a true grass, but a type of sedge. Sedges look like grasses, but the structure of their stems is different.

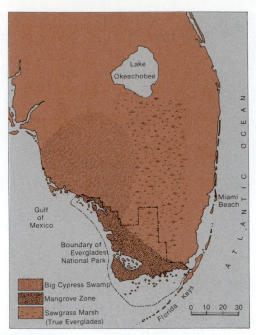

Figure 11–11
Southern Florida and the Everglades.

Figure 11–12
The Everglades. This river of grass, or Pay-hay-Okee, as the Seminoles call it, is a strange mix of temperate and tropical zones. Forest and jungle, fresh- and salt-water ecosystems survive together in the 2000 sq mi that constitute the national park. The 'glades are home to rare species of wildlife, such as crocodile, manatee, and wood stork, which are found nowhere else in the United States. (Courtesy of National Park Service)

in the sawgrass plain, there are tree islands where dense stands of trees and bushes grow. These tree islands serve as nesting grounds and shelter for many species of birds, mammals, and reptiles. South Florida has both a rainy and a dry season. During the rainy season, the "river" level is high and the entire sawgrass plain is covered with about a meter of water. During the season of drought, some water flows through sloughs (miry channels), but the sawgrass plain is dry.

Animals and plants have adapted uniquely to the Everglade system. During the wet season, plant growth is quite rapid. The sawgrass grows in abundance. If this growing season were to continue year round, the Everglade marsh would probably fill in with plant matter and evolve into a forest system. Instead, the water level starts to fall in the winter, and the grasses dry up. Almost every year, fires started by either lightning or people race across the plain. The timing of these fires appears to be crucial to the Everglade cycle. The sawgrass becomes dry and yellow during the start of the drought, even when there still may be a few centimeters of water left on the ground. If the grasses burn at this time, the fire does little permanent damage to the swamp. The roots of the plants are covered with water and do not burn. The tree islands are usually safe from early winter fires. At this time, there is still enough water so that the plants are damp and resistant to fire. The grass fires move rapidly across the plain and burn around the tree islands but do not consume them.*

As the yearly drought continues, the waters recede still further. If not for another peculiar ecological adaptation, the swamp would dry up, and most of the animals in it would die. It is the alligators that save the swamp. These animals scoop out large depressions in the marsh with their tails. Water collects in these "gator holes." When the plain dries up, the fish seek the deep water of the holes to survive the drought. In fact, much of the aquatic life of the region becomes concentrated within the gator holes to survive until the next rainy season. Fish live and breed here. They also serve as food for the alligators as well as for predator birds and mammals.

The plants and animals of the Everglades have adapted to a complex cycle of seasonal

Female alligator and young resting in a pool in the Everglades. (Courtesy of National Park Service; photo by Richard Frear)

growth, fire, and drought. Alligators alter their own physical environment. In doing so, they have also ensured the continuation of other forms of animal life. The existence of all species is interconnected.

At the present time, civilization threatens this delicate cycle. Dairy farms, sugar cane fields, and orange groves lie just north of the Everglades. When farmers fertilize their crops, some of the fertilizers spill into local streams and eventually enter the sawgrass marsh. Sewage run-off from the cities also flows into the Everglades and fertilizes it. Fertilizer promotes more rapid growth in the marsh. If the grasses and other plants grow too rapidly, the delicate relationships among plants and animals may be disturbed. Excess plant matter might choke the gator holes and fill the marsh with litter, algae, and weeds. Then the alligators, fish, and birds might die during the dry season. The plant–animal balance could be altered, and the 'glades could be changed forever. Pesticides also leak into the Everglades, killing plankton, fish, reptiles, and birds.

---

*Occasionally, large fires do destroy the tree islands.

Perhaps the most serious threat to the marsh comes from water and flood control projects. The Everglades is dependent on a seasonal cycle of flood and drought. If the land did not flood during the wet season, the grasses and trees would not grow. If there were no drought, there would be no fire, and the marsh would slowly fill and die. But if the drought were too severe, the gator holes would dry up, and the animals would die. At the present time, large quantities of water are pumped from Lake Okeechobee for irrigation and domestic use in the fields and cities of south Florida. Some of this water never returns to the Everglades. The United States Army Corps of Engineers has built a series of canals, levees, and water control gates in the marsh. They can reduce or even stop the flow of water to the southern Everglades. In fact, when a drought struck Florida from 1961 to 1965, most of the available water was pumped to nearby cities and farms, and millions of animals died. A public outcry forced the Water Control Bureau to reflood the 'glades. The threat, however, still exists: In 1971 and again in 1981, seasonal rains were below normal, and the 'glades became parched.

The effects of the pollution and urbanization of the Everglades is reflected in the vitality of the wildlife population. For example, in 1935, there were 2.5 million wading birds in the region; in 1986, there were 250,000. The Florida panther and the American crocodile once flourished in south Florida; now they are on the list of endangered species.

Just as public awareness has led to a movement to save Chesapeake Bay, a grass roots' appeal has encouraged efforts to save the Everglades. New water control strategies that recognize the peculiar needs of natural swamps have been implemented. The Army Corps of Engineers has abandoned some of its canals and has returned the water to the original stream beds. The state of Florida is attempting to purchase approximately 125,000 hectares of swamplands outside the Everglades National Park and add this land to existing refuges.

The Everglades is a unique and fragile ecosystem. It is a product of millennia of coevolution of plants and animals with their physical environment. If excess pollution or improper control destroys the swamp, it will most probably be gone forever. It would be very unlikely that it could ever be re-created.

11.7
Government Lands and the Conservation Movement in the United States

Before European settlers immigrated to this continent, the forests and prairies were loosely apportioned among a variety of native tribes, many of whom were nomadic and often warred with each other over adjacent hunting grounds. When Columbus landed in the new world, he planted the Spanish flag and claimed the lands for the King and Queen. In true colonial fashion, other explorers followed suit. Thus, when the English settled the eastern seaboard of North America, there was no private ownership of land; everything belonged to the King of England. According to this arrangement, the king provided protection and leased the land in exchange for taxes. When the Thirteen Colonies were awarded independence by the British in 1783, individuals assumed title to land that they had settled and were living on. However, the fate of unsettled land remained in dispute. Some states claimed jurisdiction over vast areas of unsettled forests in the western regions of the new country, but the smaller coastal states such as Rhode Island objected. Finally, a compromise was reached whereby the states would retain control of their immediate territories, but all land between the Appalachian Mountains and the Mississippi River would be owned by the federal government. The power and the right of the federal government to regulate public lands is written clearly in the Constitution, which states (Article IV Section 3).

> The Congress shall have power to dispose of and make all needful rules and regulations respecting the territory or other property belonging to the United States; and nothing in this Constitution shall be so construed as to prejudice any claims of the United States. . . .

During the remainder of the 1700s and the first half of the 1800s, the United States grew at a rapid rate through the acquisition of new territory, as shown in Figure 11–13. These western lands were attractive to trappers and later to settlers who moved westward where virgin soil, mineral resources, and timber could provide wealth for individuals and for the growing nation. In 1796, Congress passed a bill known as the Land Act, which

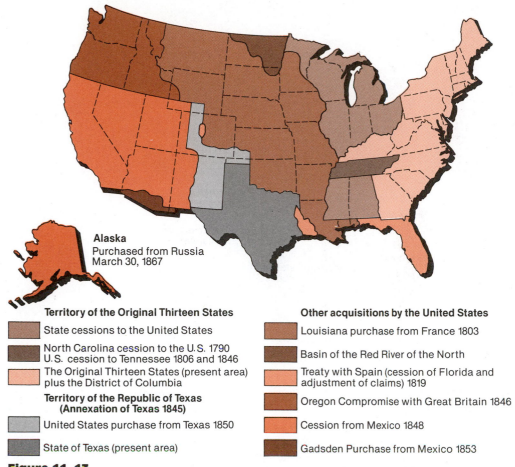

Alaska
Purchased from Russia
March 30, 1867

Territory of the Original Thirteen States

State cessions to the United States

North Carolina cession to the U.S. 1790
U.S. cession to Tennessee 1806 and 1846

The Original Thirteen States (present area)
plus the District of Columbia

**Territory of the Republic of Texas
(Annexation of Texas 1845)**

United States purchase from Texas 1850

State of Texas (present area)

Other acquisitions by the United States

Louisiana purchase from France 1803

Basin of the Red River of the North

Treaty with Spain (cession of Florida and
adjustment of claims) 1819

Oregon Compromise with Great Britain 1846

Cession from Mexico 1848

Gadsden Purchase from Mexico 1853

Figure 11–13
The acquisition of territory during the growth of the United States.

provided for a survey of western lands and public auction sales with a minimum price of $1 to $2 per acre, payable within a year.

In the 1800s and early 1900s, a variety of other land acts were enacted and a total of nearly 500 million hectares of federal lands were sold or given away, but more than 175 million hectares remained under government jurisdiction (Fig. 11–14). The original holdings were administered under what was called the Land Office, which was later to be known as the Bureau of Land Management, (BLM), under the auspices of the Department of the Interior.

Although the frontier mentality emphasized development over conservation, even in the early days, a glimmer of a land ethic started to grow. People began to feel that special areas should be set aside as a public—not a private—resource. As a result, the government deeded one section (640 acres, or 280 hectares) of land in every new township to the local government for the school system. Some of this land was sold to provide revenue for construction of the school buildings, but other parcels were held as public parks.

In the late 1800s, an entirely new concept in land management was initiated. There was a belief that certain areas are so special that they should remain permanently within the control of the federal government. In 1872, the system of National Parks was initiated with the establishment of Yellowstone Park.

Parks represent only a small portion of federal lands. As shown in Figure 11–15, federal lands are controlled by a variety of different agencies. The agency that administers the most land is the BLM (Bureau of Land Management). Second is the

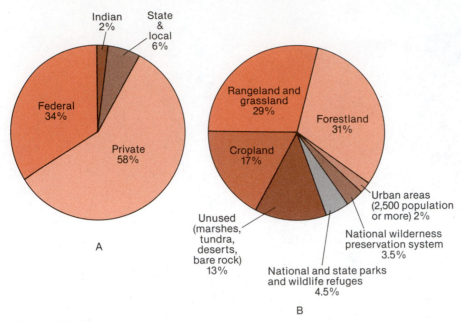

Figure 11–14
Land use in the United States. *A,* Ownership of land in the United States. *B,*
Use of land in the United States.

National Forest Service, which was established in 1891 as part of the Department of Agriculture. Most of the land that is presently owned by the government was retained because it was considered to be so useless that it couldn't even be given away. At the time, no one knew that valuable deposits of coal, petroleum and uranium lay under the ground, that transportation systems would be built to provide access to previously isolated stands of timber, and that with improvements in irrigation technology, arid lands could be converted into fertile farms. However, as industrial development expanded into the West, the situation changed. The value of public lands was recognized and in many cases these resources were sold or leased to private individuals. Speculators learned that they could gain control over key resources for very little money and then turn around and sell them for enormous profits. This exploitation set the stage for a classic controversy with modern overtones. Under the administration of Theodore Roosevelt, certain parcels of land that were valuable sites for hy-

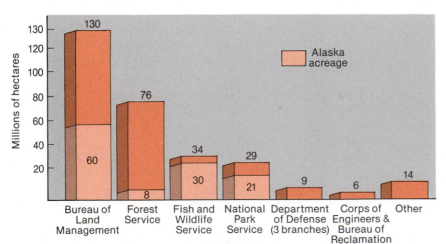

Figure 11–15
Federal lands. The agencies responsible for management of federal lands.

droelectric projects were retained by the government and were not sold to private individuals. However, when William Taft rose to office, this withdrawal was reversed and the land was sold. Conservationists were outraged. In 1909, Gifford Pinchot, chief of the U.S. Forest Service, publicly accused the Taft administration of injuring the conservation program in order to aid corporate interests. Pinchot was fired and the sale was upheld.

Other conflicts arose as well. For example, ranchers had traditionally allowed their cattle to graze on the public domain. By the early 1930s, the common range was becoming so degraded that Congress passed protective legislation entitled the Taylor Grazing Act of 1934. This law put grazing on federal lands under the control of the Department of the Interior. Yet even to this day, many environmentalists feel that federal lands are being overgrazed and a few individuals are profiting at the expense of the general public.

During the decade between 1950 and 1960, demands and uses of public land increased dramatically. The logging industry requested an increasing number of permits to cut old growth timber on National Forests. Thus, the volume of timber cut from National Forests rose from less than 4 billion board feet per year in 1950 to more than 9 billion by 1960; the number of outdoor recreation visits increased from fewer than 30 million user days to more than 90 million user days in the same period. In addition, the number of oil and gas leases rose from fewer than 30,000 to nearly 140,000 and the number of actively producing oil and gas wells more than doubled. Mineral leases also increased severalfold.

The problems involved in managing a major resource base have led to seemingly unavoidable conflicts among various segments of society. Consider, as another example, the administration of the national forests. The management strategy is outlined in the Multiple Use–Sustained Yield Act, which was passed in 1960. Multiple use is established with the understanding that different people wish to use a forest in different ways. Some people like to hike or ski cross-country in solitude, others like to drive through the area in cars, motorcycles, or snowmobiles. Many would like to exploit the land for logging, mining, grazing, or commercial development of recreation such as downhill skiing. Local residents often view a national forest as a potential site for gathering firewood or Christmas

Box 11.2
Forests

"Next to earth itself the forest is the most useful servant of man. Not only does it sustain and regulate the streams, moderate the winds, and beautify the land, but it also supplies wood, the most widely used of all materials. Its uses are numberless, and the demands which are made upon it by mankind are numberless also. It is essential to the well-being of mankind that these demands should be met. They must be met steadily, fully, and at the right time if the forest is to give its best service. The object of practical forestry is precisely to make the forest render its best service to man in such a way as to increase rather than to diminish its usefulness in the future. Forest management and conservative lumbering are other names for practical forestry. Under whatever name it may be known, practical forestry means both the use and the preservation of the forest."

Source: Gifford Pinchot: *A Primer of Forestry, Part II Practical Forestry.* Washington, D.C., U. S. Government Printing Office, 1905. 88 pp.

trees. The Forest Service has been given the nearly impossible task of managing the forests for use by all the various special interest groups simultaneously. Thus, the Forest Service sells timber, issues grazing permits, leases land for ski areas, cuts and maintains hiking trails, and even contracts for the construction of dams to conserve water and the building of roads to ensure access.

Almost no one is totally pleased with the management of national forests. Some claim that resource development is being hampered by the government and that too much land is set aside for recreation. According to this argument, logging and mining should be further encouraged to provide jobs and accelerate economic growth. Others criticize the government for "selling out" to special interest groups. For example, the Forest Service sells standing timber to logging companies. But in order to provide access to the sale areas, the government finances the construction of new roads into the for-

Special Topic B
Major Land Use Legislation in the United States

Law	Purpose of the Law
Taylor Grazing Act 1934 Sustained Yield Act 1960	Preserve range land by regulating grazing on federal lands. Established a set of guidelines for multiple use of National Forest lands, ". . . the combination (of uses) that will best meet the needs of the American people; making the most judicious use of the land without impairment of the productivity of the land . . . and not necessarily the combination of uses that will give the greatest dollar return or greatest unit output."
Wilderness Act 1964	Established the National Wilderness Preservation System.
National Wild and Scenic Rivers Act 1968	To designate certain rivers to be protected from development based on primitive natural characteristics.
Alaska Lands Act 1980	Designated about 23 million hectares of land in Alaska as wilderness. This quadrupled the amount of land in the wilderness system.
Classification and Multiple Use Act 1964	Mandated the Bureau of Land Management (BLM) to classify its land holdings and manage them with multiple use as an objective.
Forest and Rangeland Renewable Resource and Planning Act (FRRRPA)	Required that an assessment of all renewable resources be made every 10 years, and a plan for use of National forests be made every 5 years, allowing participation by the public.
National Forest Management 1976	Amended the FRRRPA of 1974, placing more emphasis on economic management of national forests.
Federal Land Policy and Management Act 1976	Requires planning similar to FRRRPA on BLM-administered lands.

ests. In many instances, the cost of building roads is greater than the revenues received from the sale of timber; therefore, the government loses money in the deal. In 1980, the Forest Service realized a gross income of $655 million. But management and construction costs were $1.7 billion, resulting in a net loss of more than one billion dollars.

By the early 1960s, the conflict between recreational uses of national land and commercial development became acute. Very simply, it was obvious that logging, mining, and the passage of motor vehicles disrupted wildlife, destroyed climax ecosystems, and detracted from the peace and solitude that characterize wilderness recreation. Therefore, environmentalists proposed that special areas be set aside where roads, buildings, motorized vehicles of any kind, and commercial activities would be prohibited, and anyone who wanted to visit them must do so by foot, canoe, or horseback. The establishment of these wilderness areas was emotionally applauded and bitterly opposed. Proponents argued that the establishment of protected areas recognizes that undisturbed lands represent a real and valuable resource that belongs to

Special Topic C
The Sagebrush Rebellion

Federal lands are not equally distributed among the states. The land area of several western states such as Nevada and Arizona is almost entirely owned by the federal government, while there are comparatively few federal lands in the midwest, the south, or along the eastern seaboard. In the 1970s, a group of people in the western states believed that conservation regulations imposed on government lands were discouraging commercial development in their regions. In 1970, the state governments in Nevada and Arizona tried to persuade the federal government to donate 2.4 million hectares of federal land to each state. This proposal was rejected. Considerable conflict resulted, and, in 1978, the state of Nevada passed a law laying claim to BLM and Forest Service land within the state borders. This movement was called the **Sagebrush Rebellion.**

The Sagebrush Rebellion gained considerable support and publicity in the early 1980s. Proponents claimed that the western states should have control of their lands to manage or to sell as they wished. As justification for this claim, they stated that they could manage the land more effectively than the federal government does. Opponents of the Sagebrush Rebellion countered that it was clearly unconstitutional for states to appropriate federal land. When the land issue was originally debated in the Constitutional Convention, the decision was made that land resources belonged equally to everyone, regardless of where they lived.

By 1986 the Sagebrush Rebellion had fizzled owing to lack of public support. A majority of the people in the country upheld the constitutional mandate. Furthermore, people believed that if the states obtained possession of the land, the resources might easily be exploited by a privileged few, and the people of the country, as a whole, would lose.

be exploited. As a compromise, the Wilderness Act, passed in 1964, set aside 54 special areas. As of 1987, several other roadless areas were still under consideration for wilderness designation. In 1980, the total wilderness area was quadrupled by the Alaskan Lands Act, which established large tracts of wilderness in Alaska. According to the legislation, wilderness areas are permanently closed to road-building, motorized vehicles, logging, and commercial recreational facilities such as ski areas, hotels, and restaurants. However, the Act declared that mining would be allowed in the wilderness areas on any claims filed before the end of 1983. As a result, exploration and preliminary development were intense in 1981 and 1982, and many mining companies filed large claims that can be developed in the future.

11.8
National Parks

In its purest concept, a national park is a piece of land that is set aside in its natural, "untouched" state, to be enjoyed by all forever. However, an inherent conflict exists between the concepts "untouched" state and "enjoyed by all." On one level, every individual, no matter how careful, makes an impact on an ecosystem. Footprints destroy pristine alpine meadows, and even the most careful campers trample grasses and forest mosses. Thus, the sheer popularity of the parks is becoming part of their downfall (Fig. 11–16).

However, a larger problem is commercial development in park areas. One argument contends that if people are to visit the parks and vacation in them, roads, gas stations, picnic grounds, hotels, and restaurants are needed (Fig. 11–17). Others believe that these structures detract from the beauty of natural areas. Today, traffic jams are common in the most popular parks, and many visitors peer over rows of "recreational vehicles" to view the wonders of Yosemite or Yellowstone.

The conflict between use and the conservation of natural ecosystems has led people to ask fundamental questions about the real purpose of our National Parks system. Are these areas being preserved primarily as mechanized, sanitary vacationlands with all the comforts of home, or are they genuine preserves to conserve unique ecosystems and habitats? Recently this author, Jon, was visiting Teton National Park. A severe windstorm swept our

the American people. Critics argued that strategically valuable metals or fuels may exist in these areas and our national interests demand that these

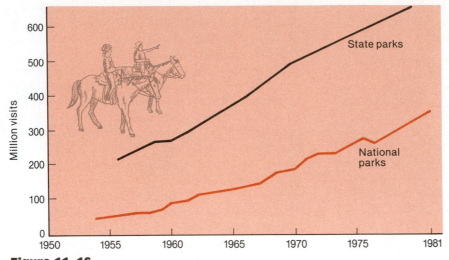

Figure 11–16

The increasing use of parks in the United States.

Special Topic D
Careers in Land Management: The United States Forest Service

The United States Forest Service manages 155 national forests, 19 national grasslands, and 17 land utilization projects on 76 million hectares in 44 states. In 1987, 33,000 permanent and 10,000 seasonal employees were on the payroll. Some of the major job classifications are listed briefly below:

Foresters are responsible for managing woodlands according to the multiple use concept. Thus management involves both conservation and sale of timber resources. This difficult task involves conducting inventories of existing timber, evaluating rates of growth, and assessing the impact of various types of logging practices.

Recreational managers work closely with foresters to determine the recreational potential of an area. They are also responsible for the construction and maintenance of trails and campgrounds and the negotiation of leases for special uses such as ski areas.

Range biologists are responsible for prairies and ranges in much the same way that foresters are responsible for woodlands. Grazing leases are sold, but at the same time the vitality and ecological integrity of the land must be maintained.

Wildlife biologists study the needs of wildlife and work in close cooperation with foresters and range managers to insure that development projects in National Forest lands do not destroy wildlife resources or endanger specific species.

The upper level managers spend a large portion of their time in offices, and a relatively small portion of their working hours in the field. For example, a regional forester does not personally conduct timber surveys, but analyzes data collected by others. On the other hand, many other jobs involve primarily outdoor work. In the timber example cited above, people are hired to actually walk through a forest and evaluate the number of trees and the volume of wood available.

Other field jobs include: tree planters, thinning and brush disposal crews, fire lookouts and firefighters, trail and campground construction and maintenance personnel, and avalanche forecasters.

Figure 11–17
A view of Yellowstone National Park. Even in winter, certain roads, restaurants, and hotels are maintained to simplify access. These facilities enable many to visit the park, but they also detract from the wilderness quality. (Donny Black)

campground one evening, and a tree blew down and crushed my bicycle. A park ranger visited our site and informed me that if I wished to sue the government for the accident I would have to fill out such and such a form. I was surprised that this kind of lawsuit was a common occurrence, and asked him whether people actually sued the government for allowing trees to blow down in a forest. "Oh, yes," he explained, "and that is not all. When some people are injured by wild animals, they sue the Park Service for allowing the animals to run loose."

In order to protect vacationers, Park Service employees remove dead timber from campsite areas. In addition, if a dangerous animal such as a grizzly bear becomes a nuisance by raiding garbage dumps or threatening campers, the animal is trapped and flown to a remote part of the park. If an animal actually injures or kills someone, it is hunted down and shot. Those who favor this type of management argue that first and foremost, the parks are for people, and, therefore, they must be rendered safe. But others argue that the parks are really nature preserves. Therefore, dead trees should be left alone because they provide habitats for a variety of insects and birds. Furthermore, grizzly bears are an endangered species in the lower 48 states and should receive more protection than they are currently given. According to this

viewpoint, it is indeed unfortunate if people are occasionally injured in the parks, but, if we are to conserve our natural heritage, the twentieth century concept of comfort, and sometimes even safety, will have to be compromised.

11.9
Park Management in the Developed and the Less-Developed Countries—Two Case Histories

Grand Canyon in the United States Imagine yourself floating down the Colorado River through the Grand Canyon. For the moment, the current is smooth and placid, but, around the bend, you hear the roar of white water. Soon you are committed to the rapids and dwarfed by standing waves that tower over your head. Today, many thousands of white-water enthusiasts run the river every year. Some ride 40-foot motorized rafts, whereas others seek challenge in tiny kayaks that can barely be seen amid the waves (Fig. 11–18). In many places, the rocks of the canyon walls drop precipitously to the water's edge. In others, smooth sandy beaches offer comfortable camping sites. By the early 1970s, it became obvious that most of the prime beaches were becoming polluted. Blackened fire sites and collections of human waste were despoiling the canyon. The National Park Service realized that something had to be done. There were simply too many people on the river. The Park Service placed severe restrictions on the handling of wastes and fires. They limited traffic through the canyon to 89,000 user days per year. They also stipulated that 92 percent of the traffic should be carried by commercial guide services and that 8 percent of the permits could be used by private groups.

The problem is that private river runners feel cheated. Noncommercial groups are allowed only 8 percent of the user days, but there are many more people who would like to float the canyon on their own. Therefore a waiting list has been established. Individuals who wish to float down the Grand Canyon place their names on this list, and then must wait about 7 years for their turns.

Private boaters claim that the present system discriminates in favor of the rich. Just about any-

A

B

C

Figure 11-18
Grand Canyon National Park. *A,* The Grand Canyon of the Colorado. *B,* A large commercial outfitter preparing rafts for the journey downstream. *C,* An independent kayaker in the rapids of the Colorado. (*B, C,* Courtesy of Hunt Worth)

one who cares to spend the money and travel with a guide can make the journey. But enthusiasts who wish to row or paddle their own boats and travel cheaply must wait for long periods of time. Some environmentalists fear that a trend may develop. In the future, is it possible that hiking, backpacking, canoeing, scuba diving, rock climbing, and horseback riding will be similarly regulated? The problem is that some type of rules and regulations must be enforced when population pressures threaten an ecosystem. Yet it is difficult to write laws that are universally just. Moreover, political lobbyists and commercial interests often sway legislative decisions. The challenge is to preserve natural ecosystems without discriminating unfairly against anyone.

In recent years the National Forest Service has built many roads to permit logging in national forests. In many instances the cost of these roads is greater than the proceeds received from the sale of timber. At the same time, many trails for recreational use have been abandoned. For example, in Montana, between 1957 and 1985 road mileage in national forests increased by 268 percent, and trail mileage decreased by 25 percent. Although the total number of miles of trails is declining, trail use has increased, with each mile of trail receiving 4.5 times the use it did in 1965.

Chitwan National Park in Nepal   Nepal is a country of contrast. The Himalayan ranges stretch across the central and northern regions, while the southern plains are low and tropical. Before 1950, most of south central Nepal was tropical forest and was the home of a wide variety of species, including the tiger and the Asian rhinoceros. Few people ventured into the region, and fewer still decided to live there because malaria was endemic. However, when pesticides became widely available, people sprayed the ponds and swamps where the mosquitos bred, and the incidence of malaria was greatly reduced. Farmers migrated south and started to clear the land and plant rice. Within a few decades, large expanses of forest had been cleared, unique habitats were being destroyed at a rapid rate, and several key species were being threatened with extinction. International concern was generated, and the remaining wild places were set aside as a reserve, which was named Chitwan National Park.

The establishment of Chitwan Park has been regarded as a major victory for conservationists interested in the preservation of species. But parks are not totally wild places; they are reserves located in the center of human civilization. In the Chitwan area, rhinos frequently swim across the river to graze in farmer's fields, and, occasionally, tigers cross the park boundaries to feast on easy prey such as domestic cattle. Because the people who live adjacent to the park are poor, the loss of crops or livestock represents an extremely serious problem. At night, local farmers often sleep in small shelters perched on stilts in the center of their fields. When wild animals invade, they try to scare them away with gongs and burning torches. Sometimes they are successful, but, occasionally, a rhino or tiger will charge. Many ask, should poor Nepali peasants risk the loss of their sustenance or even their lives so that wild species can be preserved?

Several types of management plans have been proposed. Some people think that the parks could be simultaneously managed for wildlife preservation and for profit. The per capita income in Nepal is $125 per year. The plush resort, Tiger Tops, charges wealthy tourists $100 per night for lodging and guide service. This resort already provides jobs and income for many local people. Perhaps a small tax could be levied against the visitors, and the proceeds could be used to compensate local people who suffer from the wildlife. An alternative might be a hunting fee. Biologists have observed that the population of certain animals such as the rhinos has increased dramatically within the protected boundaries of the park. Limited hunting would control the size of the herds, and many hunters would be willing to pay $10,000 or more for a chance to shoot exotic game.

A second proposal recognizes that a preserve such as Chitwan is a global heritage, not just a na-

A rhinoceros in Chitwan National Park in Nepal.

tional one. Therefore, some people argue that it should be supported by those people who can most easily afford the expense. Thus, the wealthiest nations should contribute to a fund for the Chitwan Preserve and for crucial preserves in other impoverished countries. The fund would be used to improve the management of the parks, build fences, and compensate farmers for damage caused by marauding wildlife.

Summary

For many people, rural lands provide a spiritual sense of well-being. In addition, undisturbed ecosystems maintain water balance, reduce erosion, regulate climate, degrade certain types of wastes, provide a home and a source of livelihood for certain people, provide habitat for nondomestic plants and animals, and establish lucrative tourist industries.

Tropical rainforests are being depleted at an alarming rate. Commercial pressures include timber harvests, farming and ranching, fuel wood gathering, and hydroelectric development. Unfortunately, most tropical rainforest soils cannot support sustained agriculture.

The forested area in the developed countries has remained relatively constant in recent years, but pollution and logging activities are changing the character of the forests.

Estuaries represent a small land area but are highly productive marine ecosystems. Unfortunately, they are often profitable locations for development. Productive estuaries, such as Chesapeake Bay, that lie in highly industrialized zones are particularly vulnerable. When coastlines are developed, the natural movement of beaches is often interrupted.

Freshwater wetlands are valuable because they maintain groundwater levels, control flooding, purify natural waterways, and provide a habitat for many species of animals including migratory waterfowl.

According to the Constitution, the federal government originally owned all lands that were unclaimed when the country was formed, and all lands that were acquired in subsequent years. Much of this land was sold or given away, but large tracts are still retained. National lands are administered by a variety of different agencies. Some important classifications include: forests that are designated as multiple use areas; parks where roads and tourist facilities are permitted but no industrial development is allowed; and wilderness areas where all commercial activities are prohibited except for mining on claims made before 1983. Management of parks and forests is difficult because there are many different groups of people with conflicting interests, and, in many cases, human interests conflict with the character of wild areas.

Questions

The Value of Rural Lands

1. List six benefits that we derive from rural lands. Explain why some of these are difficult to quantify in economic terms.

2. Do you believe that preservation of the Alaskan wilderness is worthwhile for people who live on the eastern seaboard and never intend to travel to Alaska? Do you think that it is worthwhile for people who live in Alaska or for those who plan to visit that state?

3. Study an undeveloped forest, river, valley, estuary, or swamp in your area (if one exists). Discuss the present human impact on the area and the future threat of increased pressure. What is the value of the area in its present state? Discuss the tradeoffs involved in future development.

4. Explain how the maintenance of a natural ecosystem on a hillside can maintain the stability of natural, agricultural, and commercial areas along the valley floor.

5. Relate the material in Section 11.1, Rural Lands and Regulation of Climate, with the development of the concept of atmospheric stability introduced in Chapter 6.

Tropical Rainforests

6. In tropical rainforests, the tops of trees are intertangled, and vines tie the branches of neighboring trees together. How would this biological reality affect a logger's decision whether to cut selectively or to clearcut? Discuss the implications of your answer.

7. Many of the rich food-producing areas of the United States were once forested. Is it hypocritical for U.S. ecologists to recommend that people in tropical countries preserve their forests when North Americans have gotten rich destroying theirs? Defend your answer.

8. Explain how logging would affect an area even if trees were replanted so that the forest would re-establish itself.

9. Compare and contrast the following three uses of a tropical region after the rainforest has been removed: (a) sustainable agricultural system, (b) nonsustainable grain production, and (c) ranching. Discuss the techniques used in each system and the reasons why people would choose one over the other.

10. Explain how conservation can often be encouraged by selfish motives. Give one example from the book and another from your own experience. Would a nomadic society or a stationary society be more apt to realize a gain by practicing conservation? Discuss.

11. Prepare a class debate: Have one side argue that wealthy nations should contribute toward saving tropical rainforests, and the other side oppose this contention.

Forestry in the Developed Nations

12. Make a brief inventory of the woodlands in your area. Answer the following questions: (a) What is the climax vegetation that would establish itself in the absence of human intervention? (b) What is the present vegetation in the area? (c) Is there a commercial logging industry? (d) If the answer to part c is yes, is most of the logging done on public or on private lands?

Coastlines and Estuaries

13. Discuss the impact that a bridge can have on coastal ecosystems.

14. In the text, records of commercial fish catches were used as an indicator of the vitality of an aquatic ecosystem. List advantages and disadvantages of this type of indicator. Suggest three other categories of data that could be used to illustrate the present condition of an estuary.

15. Many rivers rise significantly in the springtime when the winter snows melt and floods are a relatively common occurrence. In a natural ecosystem, minor flooding dissipates the energy of the spring run-off, and causes little permanent damage. However, people who live along the edges of rivers often build concrete retaining walls to control flooding. These walls channel the stream, causing it to speed up. This channelized, fast-moving water causes severe erosion and, eventually, extreme flooding downstream. Compare this situation with that of the construction of groins along coastlines.

16. Explain how flood control could destroy the Everglades.

National Lands

17. Briefly trace the history of federal lands.

18. Obtain a list of state and national lands closest to your home. Are these parks, wilderness areas, or forests managed for multiple use? Describe the management of these areas.

19. Compare and contrast management problems in national parks in the developed and the less-developed countries.

20. Prepare a class debate: Have one side argue that dead trees should be removed from campground areas in national parks and the other side argue the opposite viewpoint. Now argue whether or not troublesome bears should be removed.

Suggested Readings

The quotation on the first page of the chapter was taken from the following discussion of Arctic ecosystems:

Barry Lopez: *Arctic Dreams.* New York, Charles Scribner's Sons, 1986. 464 pp.

General land use theory is discussed in:

Craig W. Allin: *The Politics of Wilderness Preservation.* Westport, CT, Greenwood, 1982. 304 pp.

Robert W. Burchell and Edward E. Duensing (eds.): *Land Use Issues of the 1980s.* Piscataway, NJ, Center for Urban Policy Research, 1982. 220 pp.

Several references on the tropical rainforests are:

Catherine Caufield: *In the Rainforest.* New York, Alfred A. Knopf Inc., 1984. 266 pp.

Norman Myers: *The Primary Source.* New York, W. W. Norton and Company, 1985. 387 pp.

Richard P. Tucker and J. F. Richards (eds.): *Global Deforestation and the Nineteenth-Century World Economy.* Durham, NC, Duke University Press, 1983. 210 pp.

Hugh H. Iltis: Tropical forests: What will be their fate?. *Environment, 25:*10, 55, 1983.

Peter Jackson: The tragedy of our tropical rainforests. *Ambio, 12:*5, 252, 1983.

James D. Nations and Daniel Komer: Rainforest and the hamburger society. *Environment, 25:*3, 12, 1983.

Material on Chesapeake Bay was taken in part from:

The Conservation Foundation: Has the time come to rescue Chesapeake Bay? Conservation Foundation Letter, March-April 1984.

Robert C. Cowen: Bailing out Chesapeake Bay. *Technology Review,* May/June 1984.

Christopher F. D'Elia: Too much of a good thing, Nutrient enrichment of the Chesapeake Bay. *Environment, 29:*2, 3, 1987.

Six references that deal with coastlines are:

Dennis W. Ducsik: *Shoreline for the Public.* Cambridge, MA, Massachusetts Institute of Technology Press, 1974. 257 pp.

Joseph M. Heikoff: *Politics of Shore Erosion: Westhampton Beach.* Ann Arbor, MI, Ann Arbor Science Publishers, Inc., 1976. 173 pp.

Thomas C. Jackson and Diana Riesche (eds.): *Coast Alert, Scientists Speak Out.* San Francisco, The Coast Alliance, 1981. 181 pp.

Bostwick H. Ketchum: *The Water's Edge, Critical Problems of the Coastal Zone.* Cambridge, MA, Massachusetts Institute of Technology Press, 1972. 393 pp.

Petrillo and Grenell, eds: *The Urban Edge: Where the City meets the Sea.* Los Altos, CA, William Kaufmann, Inc., 1985. 108 pp.

Elizabeth A. Wilman: *External Costs of Coastal Beach Pollution: An Hedonic Approach.* Washington D.C., Resources for the Future Books, 1984. 208 pp.

Additional reading on wetlands can be found in:

William J. Mitsch and James G. Gosselink: *Wetlands.* New York, Van Nostrand Reinhold, 1986. 536 pp.

Ralph W. Tiner, Jr.: *Wetlands of the United States: Current Status and Recent Changes.* Washington D.C., United States Government Printing Office, 1984.

United States Congress Office of Technology Assessment: *Wetlands: Their Use and Regulation.* Washington D.C., United States Government Printing Office, 1984.

Wilderness Society: A world in the shallows: The American wetlands. *Wilderness,* Winter 1985.

The Everglades marsh system is discussed in:

Jean Craighead George: *Everglades Wild Guide.* U.S. Department of the Interior, National Park Service, 1972. 105 pp.

Jeffery Kahn: Restoring the Everglades. *Sierra,* September/October 1986.

An interesting book on the exploration and settlement of the arid West is:

Wallace Stegner: *Beyond the Hundredth Meridian.* Boston, MA, Houghton Mifflin Co., 1953. 438 pp.

Further information on Public Lands in the United States is found in:

Marion Clawson: *The Federal Lands Revisited.* Washington D.C., Johns Hopkins University Press, 1983. 302 pp.

Marion Clawson: Debating the federal lands issue. *Environment, 25:*8, 6, 1983.

The Conservation Foundation: Program to sell federal lands sets off alarms. *Conservation Foundation Letter,* April 1982.

Gary D. Libecap: *Locking Up the Range, Federal Land Controls and Grazing.* San Francisco, Pacific Institute for Public Policy Research Press, 1986. 128 pp.

Olen Paul Matthews, Amy Haak, and Kathryn Toffnetti: Mining and wilderness: Incompatible uses or justifiable compromise? *Environment, 27:*3, 13, 1985.

Glen O. Robinson: *The Forest Service: A Study in Public Land Management.* Washington D.C., Resources for the Future Books, 1975. 356 pp.

Roger A. Sedjo: *The Comparative Economics of Plantation Forestry: A Global Assessment.* Washington D.C., Resources for the Future Books, 1983. 168 pp.

Richard L. Stroup and John A. Baden: *Natural Resources, Bureaucratic Myths and Environmental Management.* San Francisco, Pacific Institute for Public Policy Research, 1983. 148 pp.

Wilderness Society: Of trees and hope in the National Forests. *Wilderness,* Summer 1983.

A few selected references that deal with issues concerning the National Parks are:

Dennis Brownridge: Filling the parks with noise. *Sierra,* July–August 1986.

Alston Chase: *Playing God in Yellowstone, The Destruction of America's First National Park.* New York, Atlantic Monthly Press, 1986. 446 pp.

Gundars Rudzitis and Jeffrey Schwartz: The plight of the parklands. *Environment, 24:*6, 8, 1982.

Wilderness Society: Problems and prospects in the National Parks. *Wilderness,* Spring 1983.

12

Extinction and Genetic Resources

12.1
The Extinction of Species

Since life first appeared on Earth, species of organisms have originated and existed for a time, and then many have become **extinct,** which means that all members of the species have died. Extinction is a natural event, part of the normal process of evolution and change. One of the most familiar examples of extinction is the demise of the dinosaurs approximately 65 million years ago. However, many other waves of extinction have occurred throughout the period of life on Earth. Altogether, probably 99 percent of all species that have ever existed are now extinct.

Studies of the fossil record indicate that throughout the history of the Earth, the average rate of formation of new species through evolution has been slightly greater than the rate of extinction. Therefore, the number of species on Earth has increased gradually over time. No one knows exactly how many different species exist on the Earth today. Approximately 1.5 million have been *identified*, but many more are believed to exist. Estimates vary, but the most generally accepted total is between 5 and 10 million. Insects are by far the most successful class and outnumber any other type of organism.

Historically, most extinctions have been caused either by a change in environmental conditions or competition between species. Environmental conditions change as a result of (1) geological forces that cause the surface of the Earth to rise and fall, and (2) atmospheric phenomena that cause climates to change. For example, the southwest desert of North America was once a humid swamp, and, before that, it was covered by a shallow sea. Some cataclysmic changes are also believed to have occurred. According to one theory, a giant meteorite struck the Earth about 65 million years ago. The theory states that the force of the impact scattered dust into the upper levels of the atmosphere. In turn, this dust reflected enough sunlight to cause a dramatic cooling of the Earth. Some scientists believe that this cooling led to the demise of the dinosaurs.

When environmental conditions change, the ecological balance changes and certain species are replaced by others. Recall from Chapter 4 that when two organisms compete for a resource that both of them need to survive, whether it is food,

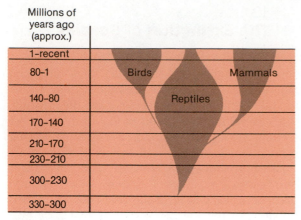

Millions of years ago (approx.)

1–recent	
80–1	Birds / Mammals
140–80	Reptiles
170–140	
210–170	
230–210	
300–230	
330–300	

Figure 12–1

Diagram to show when birds and mammals replaced reptiles. The width of each area shows the number of species of each group that lived at any one time.

light, or shelter, the organism that is more effective at capturing the resource will survive, and the other organism must either change its niche requirements, emigrate, or die. The fossil record shows that particular groups of organisms, such as fish, reptiles, or birds, have replaced each other over long periods of time. Figure 12–1 shows that approximately 300 million years ago there were very few species of reptiles. The number of species of reptiles then increased, peaking about 110 million years ago, when tens of thousands of species of reptiles existed. After this, the number of reptile species decreased steadily, until today only about 6000 species remain. The reptiles were replaced by mammals and birds. As shown in Figure 12–1, a small number of birds and mammals had existed for about 100 million years, but these organisms increased dramatically as the reptiles declined.

Why this constant replacement of one group by another? Organisms are constantly evolving new adaptations to changing conditions, and one might expect that once major habitats were filled, the existing species would be able to evolve fast enough to keep up with changing physical conditions and to outcompete any new species that came along. Clearly, this does not occur. Existing species are not necessarily more effective at making a living from the habitats they occupy than new species that may invade the area. Mammals, for example, are simply more effective at exploiting the resources of most terrestrial habitats than were the ancient reptiles, although there are exceptions to

this generalization. In some warm, moist tropical habitats, mammals have not displaced reptiles.

Today, conditions on Earth are significantly different from conditions at any other time in its history. The major difference arises from the phenomenal success of humans and the development of a technological society. Within the past 50 to 100 years, which amounts to merely the tiniest blink in geological time, technological advances have been so rapid that significant changes have occurred across the face of the globe. These social changes have occurred many times faster than the normal process of evolution, and, as a result, a great number of species have been unable to adapt. As a result, the rate of extinction is thought to be greater today than at any other time in the history of the world.

At the present time, 300 to 400 species of mammals and 400 to 500 species of birds are listed as endangered. However, these numbers are dwarfed by the numbers of endangered plants and smaller animals such as insects, mites, and worms. Altogether, if present rates continue, a staggering total of one million species could become extinct by the year 2000. This amounts to the loss of 100 species *per day* for the remainder of this century. The total will never be known with certainty, because many tropical species are becoming extinct even before they have been classified!

In the modern world, the five major factors leading to the extinction of species are (1) destruction of habitat, (2) introduction of foreign species into an existing ecosystem, (3) commercial hunting, (4) human control of predators, and (5) pollution.

12.2
Destruction of Habitat

No organism can survive if its habitat is destroyed. A population of salmon will die out if a dam blocks the path of migration to the headwaters of the stream where the fish must return to lay their eggs; a woodpecker cannot live if there are no decaying bug-infested trees; and many tropical plants and insects cannot find the food or shelter needed for survival if the forest canopy is cut and burned.

With the increase in human populations, the amount of land used for agriculture, logging, mining, roads, and towns has steadily increased. This development has destroyed the habitats that many

The populations of many different species are being reduced in modern society, so it is sometimes subjective to decide when a reduced population has become endangered. Conservationists categorize a species as threatened when the organisms are still relatively abundant in their range but a variety of factors are contributing to a severe reduction of their range. For example, grizzly bears once roamed over vast segments of North America. Today, a few isolated populations exist in Wyoming and Montana and perhaps in Idaho. Larger numbers are found in Canada and Alaska. Although they are safe now, if current trends continue, they will not be. Therefore, they are characterized as **threatened.**

On the other hand, an **endangered species** is one whose numbers have been reduced so far that there is a present danger of extinction.

Ivory-billed woodpecker. This photograph was taken in the 1930s when the birds were common; today they are believed to be extinct. (James T. Tanner, National Audubon Society)

animals and plants need to survive. Although some organisms, such as pigeons, house sparrows, rodents (particularly rats and mice), and deer, flourish in the modified habitats provided by human activity, many others do not.

More than three quarters of the species that are in danger of extinction today are threatened because their forest habitats are being destroyed. A majority of these species are from the Tropics, where human population growth has been most explosive and habitats have been destroyed most rapidly. As discussed in previous chapters, tropical rainforests cover a mere 7 percent of the Earth's surface, yet they house about three quarters of its species. Today, these forests are being destroyed at an alarming rate, and, if the ecosystems are obliterated, hundreds of thousands of species will be lost.

Other examples of habitat destruction involve surprisingly little land. For example, several years ago, a hillside in Mexico was being plowed when a few alert scientists discovered that a previously unknown species of wild corn *(Zea diploperennis)* grew on that hill and was found nowhere else. These corn plants are perennials, whereas domestic varieties of corn are annuals. Moreover, the wild corn is resistant to many diseases that infest domestic varieties. The species was saved and is now being used to breed a new domestic variety.

The destruction of habitat may be quite subtle, and small changes in the environment may have surprisingly deleterious effects. For instance, even though millions of hectares of forest remain in the southeastern United States, the character of these ecosystems has changed dramatically. Almost every hectare of forest in this region has already been lumbered. When a forest is harvested for timber, trees are cut and removed before they die of old age and decay. The disruption of the decay cycle, in turn, disrupts the entire food web. For example, the insects that feed on the rotting trees are a food source for other species in the system, such as the woodpecker. The ivory-billed woodpecker, once a common species in the southeastern United States, is now believed to be extinct, a victim of current methods of timber management.

At the other extreme are species whose needs are so unspecialized that they thrive despite habitat disruption. The cockroach *(Blattus* sp.*)* can eat almost anything organic and survives in temperate regions as well as the tropics. Some species of blue-green algae that live in almost all parts of the world appear to have survived essentially unchanged for more than a billion years. Their fossils are among the oldest that have ever been found.

12.3
Introduction of Foreign Species

When Charles Darwin explored the Galapagos Islands off the west coast of South America, he discovered several species that are unique to these islands. One of these species is a giant tortoise that lived on Abingdon Island. In 1962, an expedition was sent to the island to check on the status of this historic animal. A search showed that the tortoise was extinct, although the expedition found the remains of tortoises that could not have been dead for more than a year or two. The reason for the extinction was clear. In 1957, some fishermen had introduced goats onto the islands. Because there were no predators, the population of goats multiplied rapidly and ate all the food that the tortoises had depended on for survival.

The rapid destruction of the food previously eaten by the tortoises illustrates a general fact about extinction: A competitor, predator, or disease organism that invades or is introduced into an area may have a much more devastating effect on local populations than organisms that have coexisted for long periods of time. When predator and prey, parasite and host, or competing organisms with similar food sources exist together for any length of time, they reach an equilibrium. Competing organisms coexist by evolving subtle differences in their niche requirements. Similarly, a predator does not wipe out its prey, because then it has no food. Selection ensures that those predators and parasites that survive are those that permit the host species to survive as well. At the same time, there will be selection for the prey or host to evolve defenses that protect it against indigenous enemies. When organisms are introduced into an area for the first time, however, the mechanisms that lead

Figure 12–2

American chestnuts infected with chestnut blight. (From E. P. Odum: *Fundamentals of Ecology.* 3rd ed. Philadelphia, W. B. Saunders Co., 1971)

to a balanced ecosystem do not exist, and one or more species may become extinct.

There are many examples of this type of disturbance. The American chestnut tree *(Catanea dentata)* was once common in the United States, but most of the trees were killed by a parasitic fungus imported from China at the beginning of the twentieth century (Fig. 12–2). Both Chinese and American trees had evolved resistance to the parasites that grew in their own habitats but not to foreign parasites. All the large chestnuts in the United States are now gone. Many chestnuts, however, survive because their roots are not destroyed by the fungus. They put up new shoots from the roots, and some of these shoots form fruit before they are killed by the fungus. The fact that some chestnuts reproduce offers hope that the species may slowly evolve resistance to the fungus and reappear in our forests.

Another example of the effect of introduced predators is evident in the case of domestic cats *(Felis catus)*, which were introduced into New Zealand several hundred years ago. Many of the cats escaped from domesticity and established feral populations. (A feral animal is one that was domestic and has returned to the wild.) Predation by

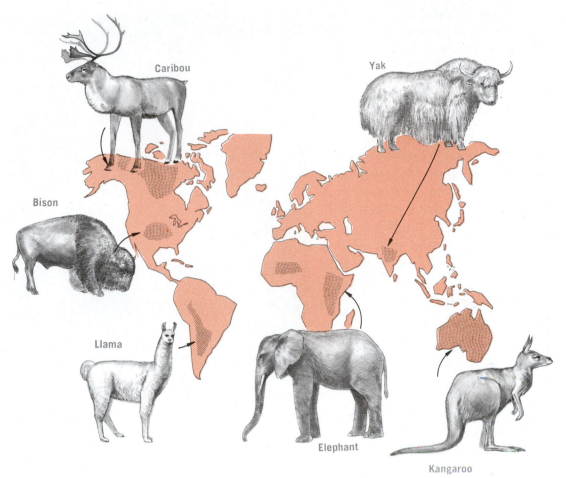

Some important grazers that have evolved on different continents. Notice how different these animals are, even though their biological function is similar. Although none of the animals pictured here is endangered, there is a real fear that if dominant species are allowed to invade new territories, many native species will be driven to extinction and the biological diversity of our planet will suffer.

the cats has caused the extinction of at least five species of birds that were found in New Zealand and nowhere else.

Even where they do not cause extinction, invading species can cause economic problems. In fact, more than half of the most serious agricultural pests in the United States have moved here from somewhere else. The Japanese beetle, imported from the Orient, feeds on many crops such as soybeans, clover, apples, and peaches; the boll weevil, which migrated north from Mexico, has caused billions of dollars of damage; and the Mediterranean fruit fly (Medfly), originating in West Africa,

caused extensive damage to fruits and vegetables in California in the early 1980s.

It is a curious fact that species invading from a continent or large island usually outcompete the species present on small islands. The reason for this is not entirely clear, but it is obvious that species evolving on continents have an advantage. The number of species on an island is invariably smaller than the number on an adjacent continent. As a result, species evolving on a continent have to cope with more competition and, if they survive this pressure, are likely to be superior competitors. In general, the larger the land mass, the more successful the species. For instance, most dominant vertebrate groups, including humans, have arisen in the Tropics of the Old World (Africa and Asia). Members of these groups have spread from this center of origin and have migrated successfully in all directions, predominating over other animals they encountered and forming many new species on the way.

Although predators, parasites, and diseases have migrated from one environment to another since life began, human activities have sharply accelerated the process. Humans are mobile and transport organisms all over the world in their trucks, boats, airplanes, and clothing. In turn, this transportation has led to numerous extinctions.

12.4
Commercial Harvest
Wildlife Management

Recall from our discussion of ecology that most populations in most ecosystems remain relatively stable, even though all organisms have an innate capacity to produce an increasing number of individuals in each succeeding generation. The mechanisms that regulate population size include predation, competition for shelter or for food supply, and other ecological pressures. Biologists have found that if humans harvest a limited number of plants or animals, the size of the resident population will hardly be changed. To understand this observation, imagine that one million sockeye salmon migrate upstream to spawn in a tundra lake. Since the lake has only a limited number of prime nest sites, some females will lay their eggs in unprotected regions where the eggs can be easily found and consumed by predators. When the surviving eggs hatch, many of the young will be unable to find adequate food or shelter, and, as a result, mortality will be high. If the ecosystem is stable, a few million fingerlings will survive and migrate to the ocean. Some of these will perish during their life at sea, and about one million salmon will return to spawn again. Now, suppose that a fishing fleet harvests half of the salmon as they return to spawn. Even though the spawning population is reduced by half, the number of nesting sites remains constant. Therefore, a high percentage of the females will find protected places to lay their eggs, and survivorship of the eggs will be high. Similarly, the

A snowy egret. These birds were almost hunted to extinction in the late 1800s because their feathers were in high demand for fashionable hats and other apparel. (Allan D. Cruickshank, National Audubon Society)

hatchlings will face less competition and will also also fare better. Therefore, when their life cycle is complete, one can expect almost as many salmon to return and spawn as in the system in which there was no fishing at all.

Wildlife management operates on the principle that selected species can be harvested on a sustained basis without depleting the breeding stock or disrupting the biological balance. This principle applies to a wide variety of species, from fish to terrestrial game animals such as deer and elk.

Extinction Caused by Commercial Harvest

Whereas controlled, managed harvests of wildlife resources do not disrupt biological systems, wanton destruction may be harmful and may even lead to extinction.

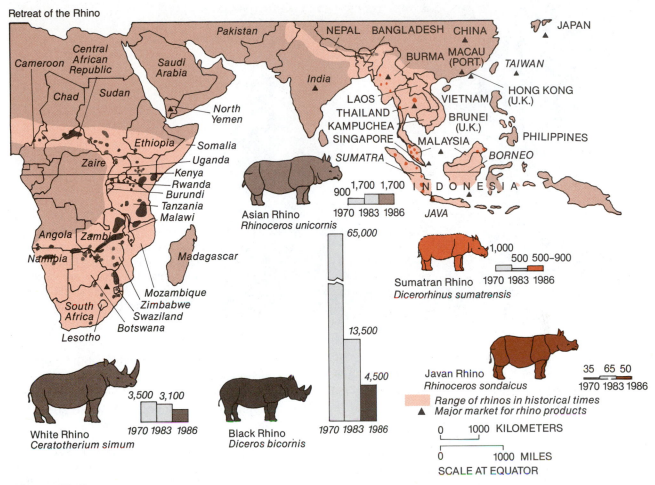

Retreat of the Rhino

Asian Rhino
Rhinoceros unicornis

900 1,700 1,700
1970 1983 1986

Sumatran Rhino
Dicerorhinus sumatrensis

1,000
500 500–900
1970 1983 1986

65,000

13,500

4,500

1970 1983 1986

Javan Rhino
Rhinoceros sondaicus

35 65 50
1970 1983 1986

■ Range of rhinos in historical times
▲ Major market for rhino products

White Rhino
Ceratotherium simum

3,500 3,100
1970 1983 1986

Black Rhino
Diceros bicornis

0   1000   KILOMETERS

0   1000 MILES
SCALE AT EQUATOR

Figure 12–3
The family of *Rhinocerotidae* originated in Europe approximately 60 million years ago, soon after the demise of the dinosaurs. Although more than 30 species are found in the fossil record, today there are only 5. As shown on this map, the range of all 5 species has drastically been reduced in recent years. Although the populations of the Indian and the Javan rhinos have increased slightly in recent years, all the species are considered to be threatened or endangered.

One of the early initiatives to preserve species in the United States concerned the fate of the snowy egret, a bird with spectacular plumage. In the 1880s, egret feathers sold for $50 an ounce, and, to supply fashion lovers with a single ounce of feathers, hunters had to kill six courting males. As the birds became endangered, laws were passed to protect them, but these measures were largely ignored. Finally, in 1900, Congress passed the Lacey Act, which banned interstate transportation of any wildlife products that had been killed illegally. This initiative virtually eliminated the slaughter, and the population of egrets has since increased.

In many countries, especially in the poorer regions of Africa and Asia, enforcement of wildlife management programs has not been effective in recent years. In 1970, there were about 65,000 black rhinoceroses *(Diceros bicornis)* in Africa; in 1983, there were 13,500. In 1986, the total dropped to 4500 (Fig. 12–3). What had happened? Black rhinos are characterized by two prominent horns on their forehead. These horns, made of twisted, matted hair, are considered to be very valuable in

An elephant that was killed by local residents using poisoned spears. Despite laws protecting their safety, thousands of elephants are killed every year for their meat and their valuable tusks. (Patrick Bordes/ Sygma)

many parts of the world. For example, in the desert country of Yemen, a rhino horn knife handle is highly prized. Throughout Asia, powdered rhino horn is sold as a medicine for a variety of ailments and as an aphrodisiac. To appreciate the real value of this commodity, consider the following: In 1986, rhino horn wholesaled for $650 per kilo, and a single horn averaged about 2.5 kilos. At the same time, the average yearly income in many regions in Africa ranged between $100 and $300 per year. Therefore, a single rhino horn may be equivalent to the salary someone would earn in 7 to 8 years!

Rhinos are protected throughout Africa, but, nevertheless, they are relentlessly pursued by poachers. For example, there were about 750 rhinos in Zimbabwe Valley in January of 1985. During that year, about 100 were slaughtered. Game wardens announced that they would shoot poachers on sight and backed up their threats by killing 13 of the hunters. In discussing this action, the chief game warden said, "It's a sensitive subject—killing a man for killing an animal, but as far as I'm concerned, killing an animal is no different than robbing a bank." Nevertheless, poaching continues, and the continuity of the species is in question.

When Europeans started to explore and colonize Central Africa in the 1800s, they sought to extract whatever wealth they could from this vast continent. Most of the wildlife found in Africa was of little value on foreign markets, but elephant tusks—ivory—were a marketable resource. Novelist Joseph Conrad, who himself worked for a trading company on the Congo River, wrote about the ivory trade in his book *Heart of Darkness.*

> Ivory? I should think so. Heaps of it. Stacks of it. The old mud shanty was bursting with it. You would think there was not a single tusk left either above or below the ground in the whole country.

Although the African elephant population has been decimated in the past century or so, 750,000 to one million of them remain, and, at the present time, the species is not in immediate danger of extinction. However, poaching continues at an alarming rate. One African wildlife expert recently wrote, "We're talking about the danger of a 95 percent reduction of the elephant population. This is not speculation: it has already happened in places." In 1985, an estimated 60,000 elephants were slaughtered for their tusks.

Environmental problems are not always segmented into neat categories. At the same time that poaching is taking a large toll on the elephant population, the animals are also suffering from loss of habitat. As human populations grow and as large, previously uninhabited areas are being converted to farmlands, the wild creatures are being excluded from their traditional range and barred from water-

The sable antelope, an African ungulate that has been hunted almost to extinction by trophy hunters avid for its beautiful horns. (Courtesy of Richard D. Estes)

Several years ago, the trailing arbutus was on the endangered list, owing to loss of habitat and pressure by people who collected the delicate flower for houseplants. In recent years, laws have been enacted to protect it, and the arbutus is now thriving in selected areas. (Photo by Alvin E. Steffan from National Audubon Society)

holes that they need for survival. In many cases, hungry elephants raid farmers' fields and then are shot for the intrusion.

Another form of commercial destruction occurs when live plants and animals are removed from their natural habitats to be used as pets or houseplants or as subjects in scientific research. In 1985, an estimated 5.5 million wild birds were captured and sold as pets, and, as a result, at least nine species are on the endangered list. On a similar note, there is an active trade in potted cactus plants, and, today, nearly one third of the species of cactus native to the United States are believed to be endangered. In other regions of the world, several rare species of primates are being hunted to supply scientists with subjects for research.

12.5
Predator Control

Another persistent conflict between humans and animals has been with other predators, particularly the large carnivores. From earliest times, humans have competed with predators such as wolves, lions, tigers, and bears for food (Fig. 12–4). In addition, some of the large carnivores are capable of killing humans and have been feared and killed for this reason. In general, as civilization has covered the face of the globe, the large carnivores have been pushed into the remaining uninhabited areas, which grow smaller and smaller as time passes.

Farmers almost invariably believe that the benefits of killing predators outweigh the disadvantages. They see that the predators kill sheep or young cattle and may not realize that they also kill many pests, such as rabbits or mice, which compete with sheep and cattle for grass. In the western United States, farmers and the government spend millions of dollars each year killing coyotes and other carnivores. As the populations of the predators are reduced, the populations of many rodents have multiplied, and many more millions of dollars are spent trying to eliminate this problem.

Pollution   Finally, as pollution has grown to be a global problem, many ecosystems have been altered chemically, even though the land surfaces have not been destroyed. This important and complex topic will be discussed in Unit 5, Chemicals in the Environment.

Figure 12–4
A mountain lion, or cougar *(Felis concolor)*, cornered by bounty hunters in Colorado. (Photo by Carl Iwasaki, *Life* magazine)

12.6
Characteristics of Endangered Species

As discussed in the previous sections, many different factors, operating independently of each other or in concert, are responsible for the destruction of species in modern times. These pressures act on entire ecosystems, yet certain species are more susceptible than others. For example, hunting and destruction of habitat have all but exterminated the bison from North America, but many species of deer have flourished, and their populations have actually increased over the past century. The general characteristics of a species that make it especially vulnerable to extinction pressures are summarized in Table 12–1.

12.7
How Species Become Extinct

Environmental pressures reduce the populations of a number of species, but rarely does a single pressure eliminate the last few surviving individuals. What factors lead to the final extinction of a species, or, in other words, how does an endangered species become an extinct species?

Let us consider the case of the passenger pigeon. In the late 1880s, approximately two billion birds flew over the North American continent in flocks that darkened the skies. Commercial hunters, shooting indiscriminately into the flocks, killed millions for food and many more for fun, because the species was thought to be indestructible. As hunting pressures increased, the pigeon populations naturally suffered, and, by the early 1900s, market hunting was no longer profitable. Yet thousands of pigeons survived. Then suddenly they all vanished. Ducks, geese, doves, and swans had all

A peregrine falcon's nest. The egg shells were weak because the mother had ingested DDT. The eggs are cracked, and the chicks, which were near to hatching, are dead. (Peregrine Fund)

Table 12–1
Characteristics of Endangered Species

Characteristics That Cause Some Species To Be Susceptible to Extinction	Reason Why Characteristics Tend to Cause Extinction	Examples
Island species	Unable to compete with invasion from continental species	More than half of the 2000 plant species in Hawaii are endangered
Species with limited habitats	Some species are found in only a few ecosystems	Woodland caribou, Everglades crocodile, millions of species in the tropical rainforest
Species that require large territories to survive	Large-scale habitat destruction in the modern world	California condor, blue whale, bengal tiger
Species with specialized niches	The niche can be destroyed even if the ecosystem remains more or less intact	Ivory-billed woodpecker, whooping crane, orangutan
Species with low reproductive rates	Many species evolved low reproductive rates because predation was low, but in modern times, people have become very effective predators against some of these species	Blue whale, California condor, polar bear, rhinoceros
Species that are economically valuable or hunted for sport	Hunting pressures by humans	Snow leopard, blue whale, elephant, rhinoceros
Predators	Often killed to reduce predation of domestic stock	Grizzly bear, timber wolf, bengal tiger
Species that are susceptible to pollution	Some species are more susceptible than others to industrial pollution	Bald eagle (susceptible to certain pesticides)
Incompatibility with civilization	Some species are simply unable to adapt	Red-headed woodpeckers often fly in front of cars, a habit that other species have learned to avoid

been hunted, and they survived in reduced numbers. Why did the passenger pigeons succumb?

Although no one can give a definite answer, biologists say that the pigeon population was reduced below its **critical minimum size** and, thus, could not survive, even though many mating pairs remained alive. The critical minimum size is the minimum number of individuals in a population that must be maintained in order for the population to survive. In order to understand this concept and why it differs from species to species, the following aspects must be considered:

1. When animals face certain types of stress, many of them fail to reproduce normally. This phenomenon is fairly common in the animal kingdom. Female rabbits reabsorb unborn fetuses in the bloodstream during drought, and many animals such as the Javanese rhinoceros have never bred successfully in captivity. It even extends to people. For example, an abnormally high percentage of

The passenger pigeon—a lesson learned too late.

potential of the remaining stock. A sudden decrease in the reproductive rates in the face of mounting pressures would certainly lead to rapid population decline.

2. Often the pressures that act on one species of an ecosystem do not affect the entire ecosystem equally, and severe imbalance can result that might lead to extinction. The original North American population of a few billion passenger pigeons must have supported a large and varied population of predators. When commercial hunters slaughtered a significant number of pigeons, they did not shoot a proportional number of predators, and it is possible that the pigeon was exterminated because the ratio of predator to prey was so unfavorable.

3. The population density may decline to a point at which members of the opposite sex have a hard time finding each other.

4. When the population of a species becomes low, that population is particularly subject to bad luck, and a few unfortunate events can lead to extinction. The situation is analogous to that of a gambler who is playing a game that is rigged so that the odds are in his favor. If he has a large cash reserve and can play for a long time, he will win, but, if he starts off with a small stake, a few unlucky hands in the beginning can end the game. So it is with species. Any large population living in its own natural surroundings would be expected to survive. However, if only a small breeding stock exists, chance occurrences can be disastrous.

An unlucky example is the Steller's albatross. Despite decimation by hunters, a few viable flocks survived and bred. Then, in 1933, as one flock was nesting peacefully on an offshore island, a volcano erupted, killing most of the adults and all of the young. Again, in 1941, another volcano erupted and destroyed a second nesting population. The species survived for another 20 years, and reproduction had just begun to accelerate when the last sizeable flock was caught in a typhoon and destroyed. The future of the species is in question.

5. Inbreeding poses another danger to the existence of reduced population. Geneticists have shown that, in general, unions between brother and sister or cousin and cousin have a high probability of producing weakened offspring. In a small population, such mating must necessarily occur quite frequently. This inbreeding increases the probability that a species will become genetically weak and perhaps extinct.

American males became impotent during the Great Depression of the 1930s. We just don't know enough about behavior to predict how a certain stress will affect fertility of a given animal, but we do know that, in certain cases, destruction of range and harassment by hunters alter the reproductive

One animal that is suffering from the effects of inbreeding is the cheetah. Cheetahs are the fastest terrestrial animals. When in full chase, they can sprint at speeds of 110 km/hour (70 miles per hour) and, over a short distance, can outrun any prey species. Yet cheetah populations are declining quickly, and biologists fear that they may become extinct. In some populations, infant mortality is as high as 70 percent. Scientists who have studied these animals have learned that the genetic composition of all cheetahs is almost identical. According to current theory, the population of cheetahs was reduced to a very small number several generations ago by some unknown set of factors. When the population increased again, very little genetic variation remained. Today, with such a small gene pool, deleterious traits become predominant, and there is little potential to develop new and innovative adaptations.

12.8
The Nature of the Loss

Does extinction caused by human activities really matter? What will happen to the biosphere if species continue to become extinct as rapidly as they have in recent years? Ecosystems and food webs may become simplified, but the pattern of primary, secondary, and tertiary consumption will continue. If deer replace bison as the largest grazers and the coyote replaces bears and mountain lions as the largest nonhuman predator, grazing and predation will continue, so why worry about extinction?

There are several reasons to worry. In some ways, the most compelling reason is the aesthetic and religious argument. Different individuals may express their feelings in different ways. To some, species and the wilderness should be preserved simply because they exist. Others might reformulate this by saying that humans have no right to exterminate what God has created. Still others may believe that an unobtrusive passage through an untouched wilderness area is a source of enormous aesthetic gratification, as valid and moving an experience as a great play or a string quartet. As many of the greatest and noblest creatures of the Earth fall prey to the thoughtless acts of people, the richness, variety, and fascination of life on this planet diminish with their passing.

A second reason to conserve species is strictly economic. The world's ecosystems harbor

Cheetahs are an endangered species. Biologists have discovered that the genetic variability within the cheetah population is very low; they believe that the animals are suffering from the negative effects of severe inbreeding. (Leonard Lee Rue, National Audubon Society)

an incredible number of different organisms, and these can be beneficial to humans in a wide variety of ways.

- *Direct use as a source of food.* Throughout history, people have used about 7000 different kinds of plants for food, but, today, farmers are concentrating the greatest portion of their effort on about a dozen varieties of grains, such as wheat, rice, and maize as well as tubers such as potatoes and cassava. However, biologists estimate that there are at least 75,000 edible species of plants and that many of these are actually superior to varieties that are commonly cultivated. For example, the winged bean *(Psophocarpus tetragonolous)*, a plant found in the jungle of New Guinea, grows to a height of 4 to 5 meters in a few weeks. All the parts of the plant—tubers, seed, stems, leaves, and flowers—are edible

**Special Topic A
Preservation of Species**

A number of authors have expressed a variety of arguments for the preservation of species. The following quote is taken from George Schaller: *Stones of Silence* (New York, Bantam Books, 1982. 288 pp.).

The high altitudes are a special world. Born of the Pleistocene, at home among pulsating glaciers and wind-flayed rocks, the animals have survived and thrived, the harshness of the environment breeding a strength and resilience which the lowland animals often lack. At these heights, in this remote universe of stone and sky, the fauna and flora of the Pleistocene have endured while many species of lower realms have vanished in the uproar of the elements. Just as we become aware of this hidden splendor of the past, we are in danger of denying it to the future. As we reach for the stars we neglect the flowers at our feet. But the great age of mammals in the Himalaya need not be over unless we permit it to be. For epochs to come the peaks will still pierce the lonely vistas, but when the last snow leopard has stalked among the crags and the last markhor has stood on a promontory, his ruff waving in the breeze, a spark of life will have gone, turning the mountains into stones of silence.

. . . To me the most startling discovery was the extent to which the mountains have been devastated by man. Forests have become timber and firewood, slopes have turned into fields, grass has vanished into livestock and wildlife into the bellies of hunters. The future of some animals and plants is now in jeopardy. However, the earth is remarkably resilient, and habitats can recover if species have not been exterminated. Some day man may want to rebuild what he has squandered, and to do that he must save all species, he must maintain the genetic stock. This can best be done in reserves where the fauna and flora can prosper with little or no interference from man. In the not too distant future much of the world's biological endowment may well be found in reserves, in islands of habitat surrounded by biologically depleted environments. However, species cannot always be maintained in a reserve: it has been found that the natural extinction rate in small, isolated habitats is remarkably high, that a Noah's Ark in which species are saved two by two is not possible, for chance alone would eliminate some. Large reserves are needed, especially for such animals such as markhor, which migrate seasonally, and for snow leopard, which roam widely in search of prey.

and have a high protein and vitamin content. Moreover, this species is highly resistant to a wide variety of tropical diseases and insect pests. If plants such as the winged bean are driven to extinction, humankind will suffer a real and irretrievable loss.

- *Existence of genetic information to improve traditional food crops.* Recall from Chapter 9 that agronomists have continuously improved existing crops by the process of interbreeding. This technique is still being used today. For example, earlier in the chapter, we mentioned that a rare strain of wild corn was recently discovered in Mexico. This strain is resistant to a variety of different types of diseases. When this wild corn was crossbred with domestic varieties, a disease-resistant, high-yield type of corn was developed. As a result, farmers in the United States have realized an annual saving of $300 million per year. In the modern science of genetic engineering, segments of genetic codes are actually removed from one species and transplanted into another. Obviously, if species are driven into extinction and the global pool of genetic information is reduced, the potential for innovative breeding will be reduced.

- *Wild species have provided humankind with a large assortment of chemicals that have been used for a wide variety of applications.*

Box 12.2
Reasons to Preserve Wild Herbivores

Herbivores that compete with domesticated animals for grazing land have often been killed by farmers. The Europeans who settled Africa believed that the wild ungulates in the area competed with their cattle. The settlers therefore undertook a program of systematic destruction. The blue buck *(Hippotragus leucophaeus)* was brought to extinction by 1800, and the last of the quagga *(Equus quagga),* once a common zebra, died in 1878. A major disadvantage of destroying native ungulates is that these animals are often better adapted to the area than are the cattle imported from foreign lands. The wild species often use the feed more efficiently and are more resistant to disease.

Before the advent of modern medicine, primitive people used herbs to cure many diseases. Modern scientists recognize that many of these herbs contain potent pharmaceuticals. For example, within the past few decades, Mexican scientists have conducted a careful survey of herbal remedies that were used by the Aztec Indians. During this study, drugs that are effective in the control of diabetes, various parasites, and certain cardiovascular problems were identified and isolated. Throughout the world, scientists have extracted a large array of biologically active medicinal compounds from plants and marine organisms. In fact, in the mid 1980s, 25 percent of the prescription drugs sold in the United States contained chemicals that are either found directly in plants or are produced from compounds found in plant tissues. According to Edward Wilson, a biologist from Harvard University, one in every 10 plant species contains compounds that have some anticancer activity. Now consider the fact that of 250,000 species of flowering plants around the world, only 10 percent have been scientifically examined for chemical content, and only 1 to 2 percent have been subject to an intensive study of their medicinal potential. If

current trends continue, 25,000 species of plants could become extinct by the turn of the century, and, if that happens, a great and unstudied chemical richness will be lost forever.

- *Wild species are used in scientific research.* When Thomas Hunt Morgan initiated his famous studies of genetics, he needed an animal that was easy to breed in large numbers and had few, large, and accessible chromosomes. He chose the fruit fly, *Drosophila,* not because the lifestyle of these insects was of particular interest in itself, but because the animals were easy to study and the lessons learned from them could be generalized to studies of other creatures. In more recent years, a rare and endangered species of Hawaiian fruit fly has been chosen as a research subject. In other studies, many scientists use various species of primates because of their genetic similarity to humans. If species are driven to extinction, scientists will lose the ability to perform certain types of experiments.

The final reason for preserving species, and perhaps the most compelling of all, concerns the richness and variety of life on this planet. The Earth is constantly changing. Climates change, environments change, products and foodstuffs change. Traditionally, species of plants and animals have always evolved along with their changing environment. If a mountain range uplifted, certain organisms evolved to live at a higher altitude; if a species of small, slow-moving horses developed into large, fast-moving horses, quicker, smarter, stronger predators evolved to pursue these horses. Our world is now developing and changing rapidly, but evolution is slow. If species are allowed to become extinct now or in a few years, the total global potential for adaptation and change will be greatly diminished, and the diversity of future ecosystems may be endangered.

12.9
Actions to Save Endangered Species

Several types of actions are needed to preserve endangered species:

1. Research and Documentation As a first step, lists of endangered species are established by

Giraffes flourish and breed in the Serengeti Park in Tanzania where tourists can photograph them with ease. The giraffes browse on these small scrubby acacias and larger trees.

various national and international agencies. Another important action used to save an endangered species is the compilation of information about it. What is the current size of the population, and what is the critical minimum size of the species? What does the species need in the way of breeding area, food, and climate in order to survive? Why has the population been reduced to the danger point?

2. Habitat Preservation and Development of Wildlife Refuges The most effective way to preserve many species is to maintain natural habitats by establishing wildlife preserves, parks, or refuges. Sometimes a small preserve can be extremely effective. For example, preservation of a few wetlands along the routes of migratory birds can ensure the completion of the migration and survival of the species. In other cases, large areas of land are needed.

Many of the world's largest and most impressive mammals are indigenous to parts of Africa, which boasts a number of magnificent game parks. The first such park was the 12,000 sq km Kruger

Park, established in South Africa in 1895. It was followed by the Etosha Game Preserve in Southwest Africa—the largest wildlife sanctuary in the world—and the Serengeti Park in Tanzania. All these large parks have existed long enough to prove that they serve their function well. The Kruger Park preserves nearly 500 species of birds and 114 species of mammals. Not a single species has been lost from this park since it was established.

Almost every country in the world has established a system of national parks and wildlife refuges. The problems involved in the establishment of these parks and the benefits that can be derived from them were discussed in Chapter 11.

3. Providing Critical Resources Another way to improve the habitat of an endangered species is to determine which resource is limiting the population size and to provide more of that resource. Construction of nestboxes for wood ducks has increased the wood duck population in parts of America. The white-naped crane *(Grus vipio)* winters in Japan, but the one area where these large, beautiful birds used to feed has now been built over. In 1958, only 45 birds appeared in all of Japan. The Japanese, therefore, started feeding the birds at just one location in Kyusu, and more than 700 birds now winter in the area each year.

4. Legal Actions for the Preservation of Species Several legal approaches have been used to preserve species. One is to enact laws regulating the killing of members of certain species, with severe penalties for breaking the law. These laws may be very effective. For instance, in the United States, the hunting of deer is controlled by allowing hunting only during a specific time of year and by issuing tags to each person who applies for a hunting license. Fines await those caught with a dead deer that does not carry a tag or one that was killed out of season. This system permits wildlife agencies to control deer populations very precisely. In many countries, it is illegal to kill any member of an endangered species.

Even strict penalties do not eliminate poaching if the products can be sold for a high price (Fig. 12–5). An alternative approach is to ban trade or transport of plants or animals that may have been killed illegally. In 1969, the hides of 113,069 ocelots, 7,934 leopards, and 1,885 cheetahs were imported into the United States. Many more hides were shipped to Paris, London, and Tokyo. Conser-

Figure 12–5

Leopard skins and other hides on sale in a street market in Srinagar, India. This author (Jon) asked the head of game management in Srinagar if it was legal to trap leopards and sell their skins. He informed me that the animals are endangered and carefully protected. I then asked about the hides for sale in the street. He told me that sometimes the law is difficult to enforce.

Figure 12–6

The Tellico Dam when it was partially completed. (Courtesy of the Tennessee Valley Authority)

vationists realized that legal action was necessary. In 1975, 81 nations signed the Convention on International Trade in Endangered Species (CITES), which prohibits all trade of endangered species or their products. But a law on paper must be enforced if it is to save animals' lives. At John F. Kennedy Airport in New York City, custom officials confiscate about $300,000 worth of products of endangered species every year, and the World Wildlife Fund estimates that illegal trade in plants and animals amounts to $2 to $5 billion annually. The contraband products include leopard skin coats, hunting trophies, crocodile shoes, and many other items.

In the United States, two important pieces of legislation, the Marine Mammal Protection Act of 1972 and the Endangered Species Act of 1973, have been passed to protect species in the marine and terrestrial environments. The Endangered Species Act states that it is illegal to import or transport endangered species or products of endangered species. Furthermore, it is illegal to destroy the habitat of any endangered species. Several other nations have also passed similar legislation.

The power and controversy of the Endangered Species Act are illustrated by the following example. In 1967, the construction of a large dam, called the Tellico Dam, was started in Tennessee (Fig. 12–6). Six years later, when the Endangered Species Act was passed, the dam was nearly complete. Construction had already cost $103 million. The dam was to provide enough electricity for about 20,000 homes in the region.

In August 1973, a zoologist studying the rivers in the area discovered a small species of snail-eating fish that he called the snail darter (Fig. 12–7). Early reports claimed that the snail darter was found only in the water behind the Tellico Dam, and, if the construction was completed, the habitat of the darter would be destroyed and the species would become extinct. A United States District Court ruled that since the Endangered Species Act states that it is illegal to destroy the habitat of an endangered species, the completion of the dam must be halted. The Tennessee Valley Authority (TVA), builders of the dam, took the case to the Supreme Court. In June 1978, the Supreme Court upheld the decision of the lower court. Further construction of the dam was forbidden. The majority opinion of the court stated that, "The plain intent of Congress in enacting this statute was to halt and reverse the trend toward species extinction, whatever the cost." But the case was not closed.

Special Topic B
The California Condor

The California condor is the largest wild bird in North America (Fig. 12–8). Condors are scavengers and feed on the meat of dead animals. Although many scavenging birds, such as vultures and magpies, have thrived in the twentieth century, condors have not. A century ago, their range included a wide area throughout the western United States, but, by the 1970s, they were found only in a small mountainous region in southern California. It is difficult to explain exactly why one species can adapt to encroaching civilization while another cannot. However, a number of factors contribute to the condor's lack of success. First, they are large and therefore need a substantial food supply, which implies that they must hunt over a wide territory. As wild lands are disappearing at a rapid rate, an animal with a large territory is often the first to feel the effects of loss of habitat.

Second, the condors have a very low rate of reproduction. A pair mates for life and produces a single egg every 2 years. The offspring must be 6 years old before they can reproduce.

Third, many condors appear to have succumbed to an unusual form of chemical contamination. Deer hunting is permitted in the condor range, and unfortunately, hunters often shoot an animal and then allow it to escape. In turn, many condors have died from lead poisoning as a result of feeding on deer carcasses that had been mortally wounded by hunters using lead shot.

Finally, and this factor is admittedly subjective, the birds are shy and tend to avoid proximity to humans and human settlements. This factor has further reduced their effective habitats.

As early as the 1950s, conservationists recognized that condor populations were declining. By 1964, it was estimated that the population was reduced to only 40 birds. In 1977, serious concern about extinction prompted the state of California, the U.S. Fish and Wildlife Service, and the National Audubon Society to work together to start a Condor Recovery Project. The strategy of this $27 million program was to capture and breed condors in captivity and, at the same time, maintain a small population in the wild. The leaders of the project hoped that eventually captive birds could be released back into their natural environment where they might learn survival techniques from the wild population.

Several conservation groups opposed this program because they thought that it placed too much emphasis on captive breeding and neglected efforts to protect the bird's remaining habitat. In 1980, when a condor chick was accidentally killed during a study of nesting, public sentiment against the program grew. However, the project continued, and, by early 1984, biologists were optimistic that condor recovery would be as successful as the effort to save whooping cranes from extinction. This opti-

Figure 12–7
The snail darter.

In 1978, Congress amended the act to allow exceptions in federal disaster areas, in cases involving national defense, and in cases permitted by a special review committee. After a continued legal and legislative struggle, snail darters were relocated in nearby streams, and, in 1979, permission was granted to complete the dam. Later, other natural populations of snail darters were found some miles from the dam, so continued existence of the species seems more secure.

After the lengthy battle over the Tellico Dam and the snail darter, many people claimed that the Endangered Species Act was excessively strict, and some even suggested that it be scuttled entirely. However, in June 1982, the Act was renewed with some changes. On one hand, the revised law con-

Figure 12–8

A California condor *(Gymnogyps californianus)*. These birds are endangered in part because they need a large area if they are to find enough food. Human activities have destroyed much of their habitat. (Photo by Carl Koford, from National Audubon Society)

mism was shortlived; between November 1984 and April 1985, 6 of the remaining 15 wild condors suddenly disappeared. The loss of the 6 condors was a serious blow, because it left only one breeding pair intact. The Fish and Wildlife Services applied for permission to capture all the remaining wild condors and raise them in captivity, but this initiative was opposed by the Audubon Society. Audubon officials argued that it would be politically difficult to preserve condor habitat if there were none left in the wild and that it was important to have some wild birds to guide the captive birds when they were eventually released. The issue was taken to court, and a restraining order was issued to prevent the capture of the wild birds. However, by September 1986, an additional 6 of the wild condors disappeared, leaving 3 males alive in the wild. A federal court reversed the decision of the lower court and granted permission to capture these birds. In April of 1987 the last known wild California condor was captured and transported to join the 27 remaining birds in the captive breeding program. Concessions were made to ensure that a ranch that included key habitat would be purchased in the event that birds would eventually be released. By the spring of 1987, there were no successful matings of California condors in captivity, although biologists in charge of the program were optimistic that matings would soon occur.

tains procedures that would allow future projects such as the Tellico Dam to proceed with only minor delays. At the same time, the general operating procedures were streamlined to strengthen the protection of many biologically important species of plants and animals.

Laws are flexible and are continually subject to change or revision. Many people object to spending the millions of dollars needed to study and categorize organisms in order to determine whether or not they are in need of protection. Others object when commercial projects such as the Tellico Dam or diversion of water for irrigation systems are halted to save a type of bird, fish, or flowering plant. Thus, the Endangered Species Act is under constant criticism and potential attack.

5. Breeding in Captivity When a species has become rare, biologists sometimes capture some of the few remaining animals and attempt to breed them in captivity. The idea is that if they can increase the population size, the animals can be released again into the wild. Breeding in captivity may involve artificial insemination, farming out juveniles or eggs to females of other species to act as foster mothers, and various other devices for increasing the number of offspring produced. Some captive breeding programs have been successful, but others have not (Special Topic B). Supporters of the programs argue that it is better to maintain a small population in captivity than to allow a species to slide into extinction. Critics argue that first, it is very difficult and expensive to induce many animals to breed in captivity. Second, even if breeding is successful, animals bred in captivity of-

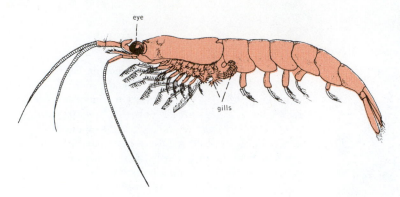

Figure 12–9
Krill *(Euphausia superba)*.

ten cannot cope with life in the wild when they are released. Third, it is doubtful whether any except the most experienced biologists should be encouraged to attempt to breed endangered animals. Many amateur breeders exist, paying enormous sums for animals captured in the wild. The often illegal trade in wild animals that this hobby encourages has killed millions of endangered animals.

12.10
Case History: The Blue Whale

Antarctica is a cold, frozen continent covered with ice and nearly devoid of vegetation. By contrast, the southern oceans that surround this continent are rich, fertile, and teeming with life. In fact, life is more abundant in the Antarctic Ocean than in many central tropical oceans, because deep-sea currents carrying valuable nutrients rise in the lower latitudes and fertilize the surface layers. The nutrient-rich waters support large populations of phytoplankton, the primary producers in the ocean. In turn, there are a great many zooplankton that feed on the tiny plant species. The zooplankton population consists in part of various species of small, shrimp-like crustacea, known collectively as **krill** (Fig. 12–9). An individual krill organism is only about 1 cm or 2 cm long, but these animals congregate in schools that can be 10 m thick and cover a surface area of several square kilometers. These schools contain enough biomass to feed the largest animal that has ever lived on this planet—the blue whale *(Sibbaldus musculus)* (Fig. 12–10). A blue whale is about 30 m (100 ft) long and weighs 90,000 kg (100 tons). It has no true teeth, but rather a set of elastic, horny plates called **baleen** that forms a sieve-like region in the whale's

mouth (Fig. 12–11). A blue whale feeds by swimming through a school of krill with its mouth open, allowing the krill to pass through the baleen but excluding any larger objects.

Blue whales are mammals; they are born alive and breast-feed for some time after birth. Scientists believe that a young animal becomes sexually mature when it is about 6 years old and that a mature cow gives birth to a single infant every 2 or 3 years. Thus, the low reproductive rate of these animals has ensured that they do not overpopulate their range.

At about the turn of the century, it was estimated that the blue whale population numbered about 200,000 individuals. In 1920, more than 29,000 whales were killed. The blubber was boiled down to oil to be used directly as a lighting fluid or as a raw material for the manufacture of cosmetics, medicinals, lubricants, shoe polish, paint, and other products. Some of the meat was eaten by humans, some was thrown away, and, in later years, some was ground into food for dogs and domestic mink. The whales, having evolved in a predator-free environment, could not adapt to the new predatory pressure; thus, the population started to decline precipitously. In the mid-1950s, marine biologists warned the whaling communities that if current practices continued, blue whales would be threatened with extinction. Furthermore, the indiscriminate slaughter of whales was economically unsound in the long run. If whalers could practice reasonable conservation methods and allow a large breeding population to survive, they would be able to harvest several thousand individuals annually on a prolonged and sustained basis. On the other hand, if the wholesale slaughter were to continue, and the breeding population destroyed, in a very short time there would be no whales. Both whales

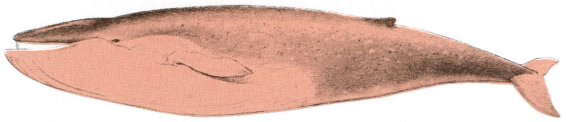

Figure 12–10
A blue whale.

and whalers would suffer. At that time, the open ocean was subject to virtually no national or international control. Owners of whaling ships must meet interest and loan payments and cover maintenance and docking fees whether or not whales are caught. Since few companies are willing to accept immediate losses in exchange for long-term stability, especially when others continue to exploit the resource, the slaughter continued.

The International Whaling Committee (IWC) was established in 1946 to regulate whaling practices. Initially, the Committee ignored the recommendations of marine biologists and set limits that greatly exceeded the sustainable catch levels. The whalers ignored even these generous guidelines and killed more whales than the IWC recom-

mended. Predictably, the whale population declined and total catch decreased. In 1964–1965, only 20 whales were harvested, and in 1974–1975 the catch dropped still further. With the blue whale population nearly extinct, whalers turned to hunting other smaller species—fin, sei, and brydes whales.

In 1982, the IWC realized that many species of whales were seriously endangered and ordered that all commercial whaling be terminated by January 1, 1986. This decision was applauded by many environmental groups. However, problems remained. The IWC has no legal jurisdiction over sovereign nations, and its rulings cannot be enforced directly. Japan, Norway, and the USSR objected to the ruling and refused to cooperate fully. Although

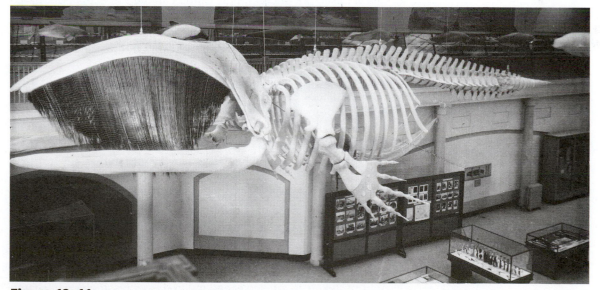

Figure 12–11
Skeleton of an Atlantic right whale *(Eubalaena)*. Note the numerous sievelike baleen in the whale's mouth. Blue whales have the same feeding mechanism. (American Museum of Natural History)

hunting of blue whales was curtailed, exploitation of other endangered species, such as the sperm whale, continued. Other nations, such as Portugal, do not belong to the IWC and are not subject to its rulings.

Even though the IWC has no real power, there are mechanisms whereby one government can pressure another to abide by various international agreements. For example, Japanese fishermen are allowed to operate in United States territorial waters under a special permit system. In the mid-1980s, the United States government threatened to reduce these permits if Japan continued its wildcat whaling. Agreements were reached and breached, lawsuits were filed, and, finally, the Japanese agreed to stop whaling by 1988, 2 years after the IWC deadline.

At the present time, the blue whale population is estimated at a few thousand. Some experts believe that the critical minimum size may have already been reached and that the blue whale, largest of all animals ever to live on this planet, is destined for extinction. At the same time, the total yield, whether we count that yield in number of animals killed, in kilograms of food harvested, or in dollars, rubles, or yen, has declined well below the theoretical productivity of the southern ocean. As a result, the world community has directly suffered from the slaughter of the whales.

Summary

During evolutionary history, organisms continually become extinct, usually because they are replaced by other species that capture a limited resource more efficiently.

The most important way in which human activities cause extinction is by destroying or altering habitats. Today, organisms that live in tropical forests are particularly endangered by habitat destruction.

Diseases and predators that have recently invaded or been imported into an area may drastically reduce the populations of their prey. In many cases the introduction of foreign species has become a primary cause for extinction.

If hunting and fishing are regulated, animals can be harvested on a sustained basis, but uncontrolled killing can lead to extinction. In the modern world, many predators are threatened. Pollution kills plants and animals alike and alters ecosystems.

Species that are most susceptible to extinction are those that live on islands, are highly specialized, require large territories to survive, have low reproductive rates, are economically valuable or hunted for sport, are predators, are susceptible to pollution, or are generally incompatible with civilization.

If a population is reduced below its critical minimum size, the species may become extinct, even if the pressures are removed.

When a species becomes extinct, everyone suffers an aesthetic loss. In addition, there are a variety of economic incentives for preserving species. Wild plants and animals: (a) can be used directly for food, (b) contain genetic information that can be used to improve traditional food crops, (c) contain a wealth of chemicals that are used for a variety of applications such as medicines, (d) are useful in scientific research. Finally, it is important to preserve species to preserve the pool of genetic information available on the Earth.

Actions taken to preserve endangered species include research and documentation, habitat preservation and the establishment of wildlife refuges, providing resources needed by endangered species, legal protection of endangered species, and captive breeding.

Questions

The Extinction of Species

1. List the two major factors leading to the extinction of species in prehistoric times. List the five major factors leading to extinction in modern times. Compare and contrast the two patterns.

2. Explain why habitat destruction is the primary cause of species extinction today.

3. Elk normally feed in the high mountains in summer and travel to lower valleys during the winter months. Imagine that a developer was planning to build a housing complex in a mountain valley in Montana. The developer claims that since only 10 percent of the elk's annual range is being preempted, the herd will not be seriously affected. Do you agree or disagree with this argument? Defend your position.

4. When ships pass from ocean to ocean through the Panama Canal, they are raised through a series of locks, sail across a freshwater lake, and then are lowered through a second series of locks. Passage through the canal would be facilitated if a deep trench were dug to connect the Atlantic and Pacific Oceans directly. Would such a canal affect the survival of aquatic species? Discuss.

5. Explain why a species that has been imported into an ecosystem is more likely to cause ecological disruptions than a native species.

6. In the text, the factors leading to the extinction of species were separated into five categories. Explain how these categories can be interlinked, and how different types of pressures can operate together to affect a given species.

7. There are several different types of hunting. People pursue animals for sport, for food, and for economic gain. Discuss moral and ethical issues raised when each of these types of hunting is restricted to preserve endangered species.

8. As mentioned in the text, game wardens in Zimbabwe are shooting and killing poachers. In your opinion, is this a morally defensible policy? Defend your opinion.

9. In recent years, grizzly bears have attacked campers in Yellowstone and Glacier National Parks on several occasions. Several people have been injured, and a few have been killed. Three different policies concerning the grizzly bears have been proposed: (a) Eliminate the bears to make the parks safe for people; (b) prohibit hiking and camping in the parks, or in certain sections of the parks, so that the bears can survive in their natural environment; (c) continue the current policy of removing the most troublesome bears, and allowing people to travel freely, even if some may be mauled in the future. Discuss the relative merits of the various proposals and offer your opinion on the best policy.

Characteristics of Endangered Species

10. Give some reasons why the bison herd in North America has been virtually eliminated whereas the white-tailed deer population has actually increased during the past century.

11. Consider the following fictitious species and comment on the survival potential of each in the twentieth century: (a) A mouse-sized rodent that gives birth to 40 young per year and cares for them well. This creature burrows deeply and eats the roots of mature hickory trees as its staple food. (b) An omnivore about the size of a pinhead. Females lay 100,000 eggs per year. This animal had evolved in a certain tropical area and can survive only in air temperatures ranging from 80°F to 100°F. (27°C to 38°C.) (c) A herbivore about twice the size of a cow adapted to northern temperate climates. This animal can either graze in open fields or browse in forests. It is a powerful jumper and can clear a 15-foot fence. Females give birth to twins every spring.

Preservation of Endangered Species

12. What arguments would you use if your task were to persuade the residents of the county where you live that it would be a good idea to convert part of the county into a wildlife refuge?

13. What criteria should be used to decide whether or not a new species should be introduced into an area?

14. Some people contend that species preservation is a global problem, and, therefore, the developed countries should assist the poorer nations in their efforts to protect endangered plants and animals. Express your views on this controversial topic.

15. Defend or criticize the following argument: Species have become extinct throughout evolutionary times. Therefore, there is no real reason to be concerned with species extinction in modern times.

16. Usually, public support for endangered species is most easily solicited when efforts are made to save large, "noble" animals such as mountain lions, eagles, or snow leopards. Discuss reasons for preserving other types of organisms such as insects or different types of plant species.

17. Some people have argued that condors are not very competitive in the twentieth century and their populations may have declined even if they had not been pressured by civilization. Discuss the nature of this argument. Would you use this premise to argue that conservationists should remove support for the birds?

18. Why are laws restricting the trade of endangered species often more effective than those that restrict hunting?

Suggested Readings

Good introductions to the topic of wildlife preservation are:

M. Soule and Bruce Wilcox (eds.): *Conservation Biology.* Sunderland, MA, Sinauer Associates., 1980.

R. F. Dasmann: *Wildlife Biology.* 2nd ed. New York, John Wiley & Sons, 1981.

O. O. Owen: *Natural Resource Conservation: An Ecological Approach.* 3rd ed. New York, Macmillan, 1980.

Important books on extinct and endangered species are:

David E. Brown: *The Grizzly in the Southwest, Documentary of an Extinction.* Norman, OK, University of Oklahoma Press, 1985. 280 pp.

C. Cadieux: *These are the Endangered.* Washington, D.C., Stone Wall Press, 1981.

P. R. Erlich and A. E. Erlich: *Extinction: The Causes and Consequences of the Disappearance of Species.* New York, Random House, 1982.

Friends of the Earth (FOE) and the Whale Coalition: *The Whaling Question.* 1982. 344 pp.

Les Kaufman and Kenneth Mallory (eds.): *The Last Extinction.* Cambridge, MA, MIT Press, 1986. 208 pp.

Norman Myers: *A Wealth of Wild Species.* Boulder, CO, Westview Press, 1983.

Matthew H. Nitecki (ed.): *Extinctions.* Chicago, University of Chicago Press, 1984. 354 pp.

George B. Schaller: *Stones of Silence.* New York, Viking Press, 1979, 292 pp.

*A classic discussion of the effect of introducing new species
into an area can be found in:*

C. Roots: *Animal Invaders.* New York, Universe Books, 1976.

*A new and provocative theory on the extinction of the
dinosaurs is discussed in:*

Donald Goldsmith: *Nemesis, The Death-Star and Other Theories of Mass Extinction.* New York, Walker and Company, 1985. 166 pp.

David M. Raup: *The Nemesis Affair: A Story of the Death of Dinosaurs and the Ways of Science.* New York, Norton, 1985.

*Several recent periodical articles on selected topics
discussed in this chapter are:*

Manuel F. Baladrin, James A. Klocke, Eve Syrkin Wurtele, and Wm. Hugh Bollinger: Natural plant chemicals: Sources of industrial and medicinal materials. *Science, 228:*1154, 1985.

The Conservation Foundation: Medicinal plants need extensive safeguarding. *Conservation Foundation Letter,* November 1982.

The Conservation Foundation: The endangered species program needs rejuvenation. *Conservation Foundation Letter,* January-February 1985.

T. L. Erwin: Tropical forest canopies, the last biotic frontier. *Bulletin of the Entomological Society of America,* No. 1, 14, 1983.

Peter Jackson: The future of elephants and rhinos in Africa. *Ambio, 11*(4), 1982.

Julian Josephson: Why maintain biological diversity? *Environmental Science and Technology, 16*(2), 1982.

Norman Myers: Genetic resources in jeopardy. *Ambio, 13*(3), 1984.

Stephen J. O'Brien, David E. Wildt, and Mitchell Bush: The cheetah in genetic peril. *Scientific American,* May 1986.

D. L. Plucknett, N. J. H. Smith, J. T. Williams, and N. Murthi Anishetty: Crop germplasm conservation and developing countries. *Science, 220:*163, 1983.

Royal Swedish Academy of Science: Marine mammals. *Ambio, 15*(3), 1986.

Edward O. Wilson: Million-year histories species diversity as an ethical goal. *Wilderness,* Summer 1984.

Unit 4
Resources

13

Sources of Energy

13.1
Modern Energy Use

When most North Americans think about sources and uses of energy, they may think about automobile traffic on a busy freeway, heating systems in large apartment buildings, or mountains of coal stored near a steel mill. Use of energy in other parts of the world is quite different. Several years ago, one of us (Jon) was riding in a truck in the Himalayan mountain region of Ladakh in northern India, traveling through high back-country farmland at an elevation approximately equal to that of the highest peaks in the North American Rockies. The truck was carrying a load of sticks wrapped in bundles. If that wood were used as fuel in the United States, it could supply perhaps one rural household in the northern Rockies for a winter. But here in India, it represented the main source of fuel for an entire town. Once delivered, the fuel would be much too precious to burn for heat; it would be used solely for cooking. As a substitute for a cozy fire during the cold snowy winter, people simply herded their sheep into an anteroom of the main house. The heat released from the bodies of these animals provided a small amount of warmth for the house. The entire population of the town was waiting for the arrival of the truck. There were some rapid negotiations, and the bundles of sticks were thrown onto the ground. I have never seen a pile of wood disappear so quickly; men, women, and children grabbed what they could carry and ran home. Within a few minutes, every small scrap had been

In this village in the mountains in northern India, fuel is much too valuable to be used for heat and is used only for cooking.

taken and only a few small children, too young to run very quickly, were still scurrying home with handfuls of twigs.

This story is told to personalize the concept of energy consumption in less-developed countries. Statistics of global energy generation and consumption are certainly useful and are presented in this book, but, at the same time, it helps to remember that these numbers relate to people and to human lifestyles.

In 1985, the United States, with about 5 percent of the world's population, consumed 25 percent of the available commercial energy in the world. In contrast, India contains 15 percent of the global population and used only 1.5 percent of the global energy supply. Another statistic to think about: In 1986, the 241 million people in the United States used almost as much fossil fuel energy for air conditioning alone as the one billion people in China used for all their needs!

As yet another example, consider a comparison of the per capita energy use in the United States with that in two other nations, Bangladesh, one of the poorest countries in the world, and Sweden, one of the most developed. The average North American uses about 50 times as much energy as the average person in Bangladesh. In Figure 13–1 *A*, notice that 34 percent of the total consumption in Bangladesh is used directly in the form of food.

Agricultural products, food, crop residue, and manure account for 88 percent of this consumption; fossil fuels and wood make up the remaining 12 percent. In contrast, look at the chart for energy consumption in the United States (Fig. 13–1 *B)*. Notice that Figures 13–1 *A* and *B* don't even look as though they are representing the same subject. The use of agricultural goods and firewood, which constitute 91 percent of the energy consumed in Bangladesh, is squeezed into 4.5 percent in the United States. Food energy is not even on the chart in North America because it is so small compared with other forms of consumption. Thus, on the one hand, energy is used for bare survival, whereas, on the other hand, energy is a resource exploited for luxury and convenience.

Many people object to comparisons between the United States and Bangladesh. They argue, and rightly so, that no one would choose to live on the very edge of abject poverty. Everyone hopes for a comfortable world with an enjoyable life. Perhaps a comparison between the United States and Sweden would be more meaningful.

Both the United States and Sweden have well-developed economic systems. In both countries, the majority of the population is well fed; excellent medical care is available; infant deaths are low; educational levels are high. Most families have a car, telephone, television, refrigerator, and vacuum

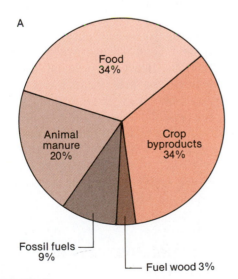

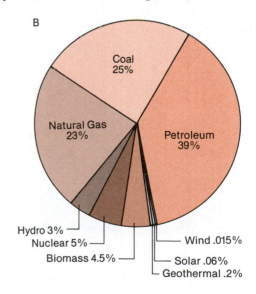

Figure 13–1

A, Sources of energy used in Bangladesh. Note that 91 percent of the energy is taken from renewable plant or animal matter. *B*, Sources of energy used in the United States in 1985. Note that only 7.5 percent of the energy supply comes from renewable sources.

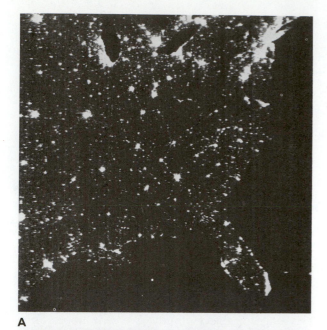

A

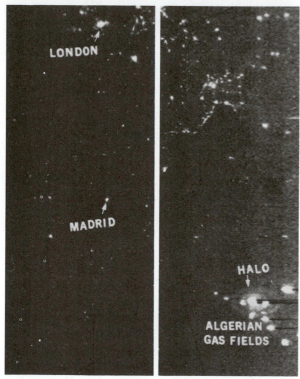

B

A dramatic example of the differences in energy consumption between the United States and Europe can be seen in these two photographs. At midnight, when most people are asleep, vast regions of the United States are lit up, as can be seen from this satellite photograph *(A)*. On the other hand, most of Europe is dark, and much less electricity is needed *(B)*. (*A,* U.S. Air Force photo: *B,* U.S. Defense Meteorological Satellite Program photo)

cleaner. Yet the average person in Sweden uses less than two thirds the energy that an American uses. Perhaps North Americans should look to people of other nations to see how consumption can be reduced.

(a) Transportation   Overall, Swedes use approximately one-fourth the energy for transportation that Americans use. Some of this fuel-saving results because Sweden is much smaller than the United States and the average distance between cities is considerably less. However, this difference alone does not account for the wide discrepancy in energy consumption. Other reasons are: (1) people in Sweden frequently walk or use bicycles for short trips; (2) mass transit is used more frequently; (3) on the average, Swedish cars consume considerably less fuel per kilometer than do American cars.

(b) Space Heating   Winters are considerably longer and more severe in Sweden than in most of the United States. Yet energy consumption per person for heating is less. Swedish houses are generally better insulated and more efficient than their American counterparts.

(c) Industrial Consumption   Swedish industries are generally highly efficient because newer, innovative technology is in use. Thus, less energy is used to produce and refine a kilogram of steel, oil, paper, cement, or chemicals in Sweden than in the United States.

There are several reasons why Swedish consumption is low. Heavy government taxes have raised fuel prices so that, for example, gasoline costs considerably more than it does in North America. But price alone is not the only factor. The government in Sweden has taken vigorous steps to promote energy conservation. The Swedish example teaches people in the United States that it is possible to use considerably less energy without lowering the quality of life.

13.2
Fossil Fuel Sources and Availability

One of the most important questions of our times and one of the most difficult to answer with any real confidence concerns how long our fossil fuel supplies will last. For a realistic estimate of the number of years remaining before all the Earth's

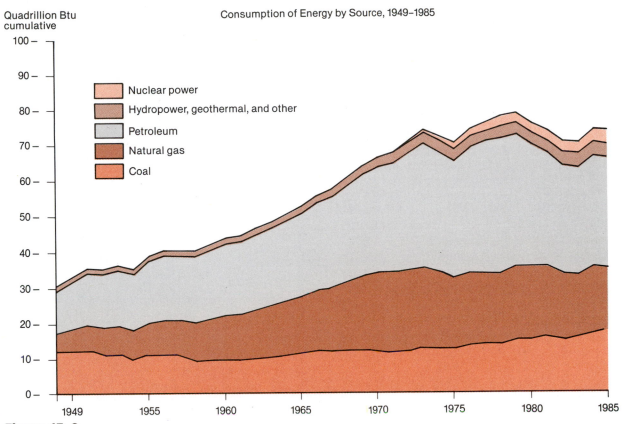

Quadrillion Btu cumulative

Consumption of Energy by Source, 1949–1985

Nuclear power
Hydropower, geothermal, and other
Petroleum
Natural gas
Coal

Figure 13–2
Energy consumption in the United States from 1948 to 1985. Energy demand grew steadily from 1948 to 1973 but oscillated during the following 12 years. These data were taken from information issued by the Department of Energy. Note that use of renewable resources reported in this graph is lower than is shown in Figure 13–1*B*. This discrepancy arises because the Department of Energy does not include biomass sources in its calculations. (Source: *Annual Energy Review 1985*, Energy Information Administration)

fossil fuels are gone, the reserves of fuel must be estimated, human population growth must be forecast, and the future rates of consumption must be predicted. All such forecasts are subject to large errors.

A **reserve** of any natural resource is the amount of that material that can be extracted at a reasonable cost. A thin seam of coal that lies 2000 meters (more than a mile) below the surface of the Earth is not considered to be a reserve, because more energy would be required to extract it than would be gained. Reserves are divided into three categories:

1. *Proven reserves* are deposits that have been located, sampled, and surveyed so that their quality and quantity are known with some certainty.

2. *Indicated reserves* are deposits that are confidently believed to exist based on limited geologic sampling.

3. *Inferred reserves* are deposits that are thought to exist based on general field studies and maps of geological formations. Obviously, the quantities of fuel found in the latter two categories are uncertain, and opinions made by several experts may vary greatly.

The most reasonable method of estimating the energy requirements from the 1980s into the early twenty-first century is to graph past energy consumption and then try to guess how the curve will continue in the future. Figure 13–2 shows the consumption of energy in the United States from 1948 to 1985. Notice that the curves are far from

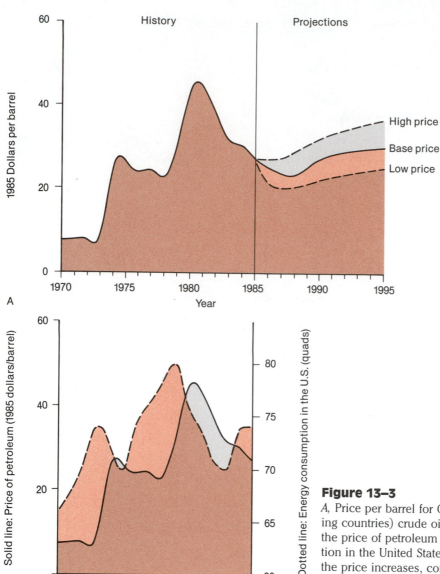

Figure 13–3
A, Price per barrel for OPEC (oil-producing and export-
ing countries) crude oil. *B,* The relationship between
the price of petroleum *(solid line)* and energy consumption in the United States *(dotted line).* Note that when
the price increases, consumption drops, and when the
price drops or remains constant, use increases once
again. (Source: *Annual Energy Review 1985,* Energy Information Administration)

smooth. Total consumption increased steadily from
1948 to 1973. In fact, from 1948 to 1970, energy use
doubled. It is obvious that the United States, or the
world in general, cannot double its consumption of
a depletable resource every 22 years for a long period of time, because each doubling corresponds
to an increasingly large growth.

However, the rapid rate of growth observed
between 1948 and 1970 was not sustained. In the
mid-1970s, countries that owned the fossil fuel reserves began to realize just how valuable their fuels

were, so they raised the prices (Fig. 13–3). As the
prices went up, consumers started to use less fuel.
People drove fewer miles and purchased smaller,
more fuel-efficient automobiles. They added additional insulation to buildings and saved in many
other ways. These conservation measures resulted
in a decline of energy use between 1973 and 1975.
In the years between 1975 and 1988, the cost of
energy and energy consumption have fluctuated.
Simply, when the price has increased, energy use
has declined; when the price has decreased or sta-

When gasoline shortages occurred in 1973 and again in 1978–1979, many commuters had to wait hours to fill their tanks. Emergency measures were enacted in some states that only allowed drivers to buy gas on alternate days. (Alain Dejean/Sygma)

bilized, consumption has inched upward again (Fig. 13–3 *B*).

What will happen in the future? When one attempts to make predictions for the years ahead, it is important to differentiate short-term fluctuations from long-range trends. A variety of economic and political factors influence the immediate cost and availability of energy, and we can confidently expect these factors to continue to oscillate. However, looking beyond the next few years, one inexorable fact remains. Fossil fuels are limited, and consumption rates are high. Therefore, we are certain that the age of cheap and accessible fossil fuels cannot last long. We are talking about a time frame of decades for petroleum and a few centuries for coal.

Perhaps you will argue that a few hundred years is really a long time. But remember, humans have lived on this Earth for over a million years. Matched against this time frame, a few hundred years is minuscule. Our fossil fuel age is destined to be a tiny burst of time in the history of our species.

Petroleum

Petroleum is perhaps the most versatile fossil fuel. Crude oil, as it is pumped from the ground, is a heavy, gooey, viscous, dark liquid. The oil is refined to produce many different materials such as propane, gasoline, jet fuel, heating oil, motor oil, and road tar. Some of the chemicals in the oil are extracted and used for the manufacture of plastics, medicines, and many other products. It is difficult to imagine what would happen to our civilization if the supply of liquid fuels ran out. Automobiles, airplanes, most home furnaces, and many appliances could not operate. Many industries would have to redesign their factories.

In the mid-1970s, as petroleum prices skyrocketed and people had to wait in long lines for gasoline, many sobering predictions were made about the future prospects for our oil-based economy. One of these is shown in Figure 13–4. This graph, first published in 1975, predicted that oil production would continue to meet demand until about 1997. At that time, according to this predic-

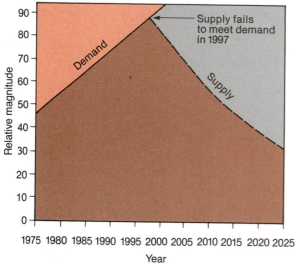

Figure 13—4
One projected estimate of the supply and demand for petroleum through the year 2025. (Adapted from M. King Hubbert)

tion, many of the richest fields will be depleted, and production will slow down. Yet the need for oil will continue to increase. People will want more oil than is available. Therefore, a real and permanent shortage will result. As shown by the graph, oil will still be available, but there won't be enough to supply people's wants.

How accurate is Figure 13–4? First, the demand for oil between 1975 and 1986 was less than was predicted. Thus, conservation is expected to provide more time before the oil runs out. Second, since 1975, several large oil deposits have been discovered. Major strikes have occurred in Mexico and the North Sea, and promising prospects in China, parts of the continental shelf in North America, and elsewhere are being studied. The combined effects of reduced consumption and increased reserves are likely to push our oil reserves into the early years of the next century. However, it is important to understand that we are talking about a few years one way or another, or perhaps a decade or two. It is likely that students who are in their twenties in the latter part of the 1980s will see a massive restructuring of our society owing to permanent fuel shortages within their lifetimes.

Natural Gas

Natural gas is composed mainly of methane (CH_4), the simplest hydrocarbon. Methane is found in underground rock layers, both by itself and lying

Special Topic B
Petroleum Outlook in the United States

In 1986, petroleum production in the United States accounted for about one half of domestic consumption (Fig. 13–5A). What are the prospects for the future? Geologists estimate that the total petroleum reserves in the United States amount to almost 200 billion barrels. This total includes the amount that has already been extracted, as well as the proven and estimated reserves. By 1985, about half of this total had been extracted and burned, about 20 billion barrels existed in proven reserves, and about 80 billion barrels were in estimated reserves. Although experts disagree on the exact figures and although the numbers quoted above are approximate at best, most analysts believe that we are past the peak and that production will drop in the years ahead (Fig. 13–5 B). One indication of the declining reserves in the United States is the productivity of new wells. In 1970, 13,000 new oil wells were drilled, and enough petroleum was extracted to provide 20 quads of energy. In 1985, 38,000 wells were drilled, and only 19 quads of energy were produced. The situation is summarized by the following quotation:

About 80 percent of the 2.6 million oil wells ever drilled in the world have been in the United States, and most large oil pools here have been found. For every foot of drilling, we now find half as much oil as in the 1950s. Unless there are huge discoveries in Alaska, we are inevitably dependent on imports. (Robert J. Samuelson: *Newsweek,* April 1987.)

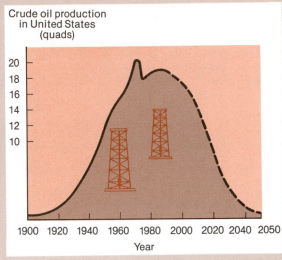

Crude oil production in United States (quads)

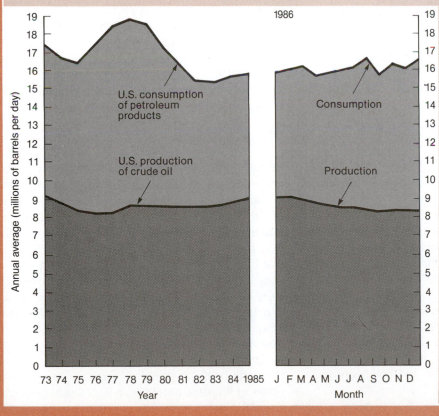

Figure 13–5
A, Petroleum production and consumption from 1973 to 1986. Note that during 1986 production declined and consumption rose. (Source, New York Times) *B,* Crude oil production in the United States from 1900 to 1985, with projections to the year 2050. Note that peak production was realized in 1970. Most experts believe that more than half of our original supply of petroleum has already been consumed, and they expect production to decline in the years ahead. (Source: *Annual Energy Review 1985,* Energy Information Administration)

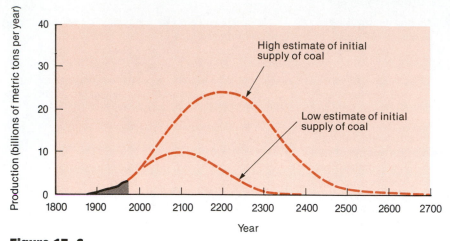

Figure 13–6

Past and predicted world coal production based on two different estimates of
initial supply. (Adapted from M. King Hubbert)

above natural deposits of petroleum. In the mid-
1980s, global consumption of natural gas totaled
about 50 trillion cubic feet (tcf)* per year, and
proven reserves amounted to about 2000 tcf. Therefore, if rates of consumption were to remain constant, proven reserves would last for 40 years. But,
in addition, there are perhaps 6000 tcf of inferred
reserves. Natural gas is a desirable fuel, and global
consumption is increasing. Taking all factors into
account, we can expect this fuel to last about 75
years or until 2060, more or less.

Coal

Large reserves of coal exist in many parts of the
world. As shown in Figure 13–6, widespread availability of this fuel can be expected at least until the
year 2200. However, there are problems with coal.
When coal is mined, large areas of land surface are
disturbed. More air pollutants are released from
burning coal than from burning oil or gas. These
issues are discussed further in Chapter 15.

Another difficulty arises because coal cannot
be used directly in conventional automobiles, in
most home furnaces, or in many industries. One
solution to the problem is to convert coal to liquid
or gaseous fuels. The theory of converting solid to
liquid fuels is well understood and has been prac-

*This volume refers to the gas at room temperature and normal
atmospheric pressure. One cubic foot equals about 28 liters.

ticed both in the laboratory and in industry. In fact,
conversion of coal was common in the 1920s. During World War II, the Germans converted coal to
gasoline for military use. Today, large-scale conversion of coal is not being practiced simply because
the process is costly and is therefore not competitive with petroleum, which is extracted directly
from the ground. However, we can reasonably assume that when petroleum becomes scarce and expensive, conversion of coal to liquid fuel will become competitive.

Heavy Oil

Conventional oil wells do not tap huge underground lakes or pools of oil. There are layers of
porous rock under the surface of the Earth, and the
pores of these rocks are filled with petroleum,
much as a sponge is filled with water. An oil well
is a hole drilled into a formation of porous rock
that is saturated with oil. The petroleum in the rock
near the hole drips down through the pores, collects in a small pool at the bottom of the well, and
can then be pumped out to storage tanks above
ground. In many places in the Earth, underground
deposits of oil are available, but the petroleum is
too thick to flow. This situation develops either
when the oil is particularly viscous or when the
pores in the rock are too small, or both. Petroleum
deposits that cannot be pumped in the conventional manner are called **heavy oils.** Three main

Special Topic C
The Formation of Natural Gas Reserves—A Novel Theory

According to conventional geological thought, methane deposits were formed from the fossilized remains of ancient organisms. These natural gas reserves originated from biological processes and, as discussed in the text, the total reserves are limited. However, a new and revolutionary theory, proposed by Dr. Thomas Gold of Cornell University, states that during the original formation of the Earth, even larger quantities of methane were trapped by a series of geological events. About 4 billion years ago, shortly after the evolution of the primordial Solar System, an intense rain of meteorites struck the Earth over a period of several million years. Dr. Gold believes that many of these meteorites contained simple organic molecules such as methane. These compounds gradually accumulated and were eventually trapped inside the Earth's crust when volcanic eruptions or other geological processes formed a cap over the deposits. If Dr. Gold is correct, then the world's fuel reserves would be vastly greater than they are presently believed to be.

In order to test the validity of this theory, scientists started drilling a test well at the bottom of a meteorite crater in Sweden. This region contained no fossils and geologists did not expect to find fuels of biological origin in the particular type of rock found in the area. In the spring of 1987, just after the drill bit had penetrated over 6 km beneath the surface of the Earth, an unexpected series of events occurred. First, drilling became appreciably easier. Shortly after drilling accelerated, the lubricant that keeps the drill bit spinning freely disappeared, as if it had fallen into a giant cavern deep with the Earth's crust. Without lubricant, the drill bit jammed and became frozen in place. Dr. Gold believes that the lubricant fell into a reservoir of methane, but, at the time this book was written, no one knew for sure, and most geologists remain skeptical.

---

types of heavy oils are discussed in the following paragraphs.

Oils from Conventional Wells   Sometimes less than one tenth and, on the average, less than one half of the petroleum in a conventional underground deposit is fluid enough to flow and thus to be extracted by conventional pumping techniques. The remainder is left in the ground after the oil well has gone "dry." In the United States alone, there are more than 300 billion barrels of oil of this type trapped in known deposits in known oil fields. This represents approximately one hundred times as much oil as was produced in the United States in 1985 and almost as much oil as has been found to date in the Middle Eastern oil fields. Obviously, people are interested in recovering this wealth. Several different methods are currently being investigated. One method is to force superheated steam into old well holes at high pressure. The steam heats the remaining underground oil and makes it fluid enough to flow. Of course, a great deal of energy is needed to heat the steam, so this type of extraction is not always efficient. Another process involves pumping detergent into the rock and "washing" the petroleum out. The petroleum can then be salvaged, and the detergent can be recycled. Still other procedures involve mining the rock and then heating it to extract the oil. No oil geologists believe that all of the 300 billion barrels can be recovered, but, if the price of fuels rises, a size-

Mining tar sands in Alberta, Canada. (Courtesy of Suncor, Inc.)

able portion of it will probably become economical to retrieve.

Tar Sands Oil-saturated sandstone deposits lying near the surface of the Earth are called **tar sands.** Sandstone fields laden with oil have been discovered in Africa, the United States, Canada, and the USSR. In 1980, a Canadian operation produced 45,000 barrels of synthetic crude oil per day from their tar sands deposits. At the time, this was the largest heavy oil development project in the world. Production has varied with the price of oil, but it is still operating profitably.

Oil Shales The largest quantities of heavy oil are locked into shale deposits in the western United States. If all the petroleum in the United States oil shales could be recovered, there would be enough oil to supply the United States for 100 years at the level of petroleum consumption in 1985. However, the shale must first be mined in some fashion and then heated to extract the petroleum. In the poorest deposits, more energy would be used to mine and extract the fuel than would be gained, and some of these deposits will probably never be used. The richest deposits, containing 100 liters or more per tonne of rock, represent approximately one third of the total. Taken all together, a realistic estimate is that all the potentially recoverable heavy oil sources in North America could supply that continent for an additional 75 years or so if consumption remained at current levels. Worldwide deposits, however, are not so rich; therefore, the global situation is not so promising. However, these figures by themselves do not address the economics or the environmental problems of extracting and refining heavy oils. In the early 1980s, several companies invested heavily in oil shale development in the United States and pilot projects were initiated. However, when the price of imported oil fell, the expensive extraction of petroleum from shale was no longer attractive, and the

Oil shale country in western Colorado. (Courtesy of Atlantic Richfield Co.)

oil companies shut down their operations. This topic will be discussed further in Chapter 15.

13.3
The Generation of Electricity

Electricity is not a primary source of energy such as a fuel; rather, it is a link in the chain from the source to final consumption. However, it is such a fundamental part of modern life and it plays such a significant role in the energy scenario that it is important to understand how it is produced. Electricity is generated whenever a wire is forced to move across a magnetic field or when a magnet is forced across an electric field. Most practical generators are operated by spinning a coil of wire within a circular arrangement of magnets. Any conceivable form of work can be used to spin the wire. Old-fashioned portable radio transmitters obtained their electricity from generators driven by human muscle power. The energy inherent in a spinning waterwheel or windmill can also be used.

Most of our electricity is now produced in **steam turbines.** The operating principle here is uncomplicated. Some power source, such as coal, gas, oil, or nuclear fuel, heats water in a boiler to produce hot, high-pressure steam. This steam expands against the blades of a turbine. A turbine is a device that spins when air or water is forced against it. You can think of it as a kind of enclosed windmill. The hot, expanding steam forces the turbine to spin. The spinning turbine then operates a generator that produces electricity. After the steam has passed through the turbine, it is cooled, liquefied, and returned to the boiler to be reused. Normally, the steam is cooled with river, lake, or ocean water (Fig. 13–7). The cooling cycle and the environmental consequences of electric generation are discussed in Chapter 15.

What will happen when the fossil fuel reserves are depleted? Will people be driving horses to town? Will civilization as we know it collapse? Is there any way out?

Nuclear energy may be at least part of the answer. Proponents of a nuclear future claim that this source should be exploited extensively. But, in actuality, the nuclear power industry has stagnated in

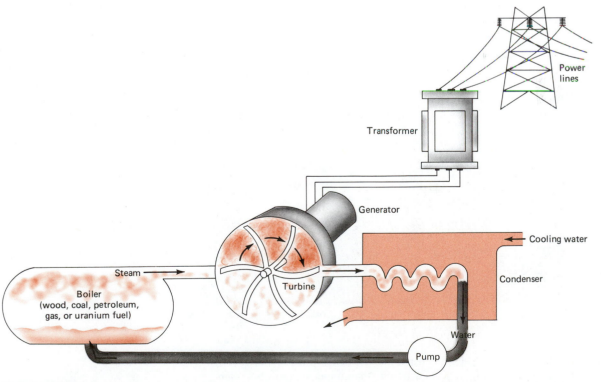

Figure 13–7
Schematic diagram of a steam-driven electric generator.

Will people be driving horses to town when the oil runs out? (Courtesy of National Archives)

some countries in recent years (Fig. 13–8). The nuclear future is therefore uncertain. This subject is discussed in further detail in Chapter 14.

Others suggest that we should use naturally renewable sources such as the Sun, the wind, fuels from plants, the energy of moving water, and the heat of the Earth. The potential for renewable energy sources will be discussed in the following sections.

13.4
Energy from the Sun

Every 29 seconds, the solar energy that falls on our planet is equivalent to human energy needs for a day at the 1986 consumption level. In the *least* sunny portions of the United States (excluding Alaska), an area of only 80 sq m (a square approximately 9 m, or 29 ft, on a side) receives enough sunlight to supply the total energy demands of the average American family. However, not all of this energy can be harnessed.

Passive Solar Design

The simplest way to use solar energy is to design and orient a house so that the structure itself collects and stores heat from the Sun. This concept is not a new or complicated technological trick. When the Anasazi Indians built their cliff dwellings in the American Southwest, they chose south-facing cliffsides. As shown in Figure 13–9, the winter sunlight shines directly into the buildings, providing heat. In the summer, when the Sun is higher in the sky, the edge of the cliff serves as a visor, or awning, to provide cooling shade, as shown in the figure. In contrast, many people in the Southwest today live in rectangular houses oriented and constructed so that large quantities of fossil fuel are needed to heat them in winter and provide the energy for air conditioning in summer.

Many ancient civilizations used passive solar design in home construction. It was standard in ancient Greece and Rome. The Greek playwright Aeschylus (524? to 456 B.C.) believed that only uncivilized barbarian societies didn't understand the concept of solar design. In discussing people who

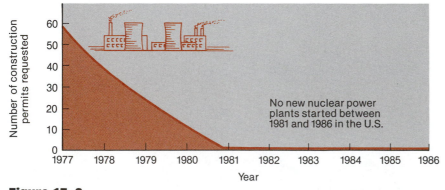

Figure 13–8
Number of construction permits requested by the nuclear power industry in recent years. The rapid decline reflects a smaller than predicted growth in electric consumption and the fact that nuclear power plants are not good business. They are no cheaper than coal-fired plants and involve complex environmental issues. (Source: *Annual Energy Review 1985,* Energy Information Administration)

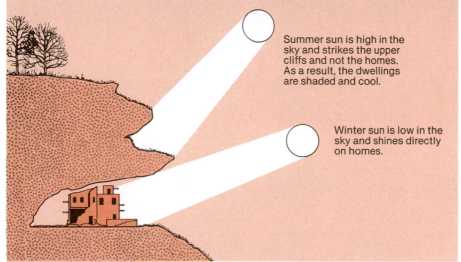

Figure 13–9

The Anasazi cliff dwellings in Mesa Verde, Colorado. *A,* Photograph of the dwellings as they stand today. This picture was taken in the summer. Note that the dwellings are comfortably shaded. In the winter, when the Sun is lower in the sky, sunshine strikes the buildings directly, thereby warming them. (Photo by Mel Davis, courtesy of U.S. Bureau of Reclamation) *B,* Schematic view of the way in which the rock and the Sun combine to provide a warm environment in the winter and a cool one in the summer.

did not use passive solar heating systems, he wrote:

> Though they had eyes to see, they saw to no avail; they had ears, but understood not. But like shapes in dreams, throughout their time, without purpose they wrought all things in confusion. They lacked knowledge of houses turned to face the sun, dwelling beneath the ground like swarming ants in sunless caves.

In a more subdued tone, the Roman architect Vitruvius (first century B.C.) wrote a treatise on building solar bathhouses:

> The site for the baths must be as warm as possible and turned away from the north. They should look toward the winter sunset because when the setting sun faces us with all its splendor, it radiates heat, rendering this aspect warmer in the late afternoon.

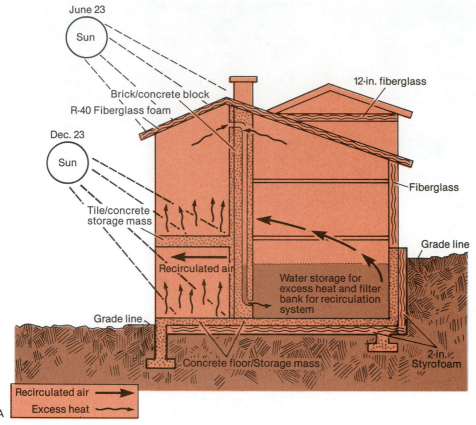

June 23
Sun

Brick/concrete block
R-40 Fiberglass foam

Dec. 23
Sun

12-in. fiberglass

Tile/concrete
storage mass

Fiberglass

Grade line

Recirculated air

Water storage for
excess heat and filter
bank for recirculation
system

Grade line

2-in.
Styrofoam

Concrete floor/Storage mass

Recirculated air ⟶
Excess heat ⟶

A

Figure 13–10
A passive solar house. Living space is directly heated by sunlight through an
expanse of south-facing glass. Masses of concrete and water are strategically
located for heat absorption and storage. Air circulates through the house by
natural convection and forced circulation to carry excess thermal gain to thermal storage masses, such as the central column and a water storage area in
the basement.

The design of a practical passive solar home
is quite straightforward. An ordinary window ad-
mits sunlight. When the sun shines directly on a
window facing south, the radiant energy enters the
room and warms it. Because the heat is trapped
within the room, the house can become much
warmer than the outside air. But heat from inside
also escapes outside through the glass. During the
night, heat escapes and no sunlight enters.

Most homes existing today are poorly
planned. They are heated with a furnace and then
typically lose 20 percent of their heat through their
windows. This trend can be reversed through
proper planning. If houses were built with large,
double-pane, south-facing windows and only small

windows on the north side, the Sun would warm
the house during the daylight hours (Fig. 13–10).
An efficient passive design requires some sort of
heat storage system built into the structure of the
house to conserve the heat overnight. A massive
masonry wall inside the building is one example of
a storage system. During the day, the room heats
up, and some of the heat is absorbed by the masonry. In this way, heat is removed from the living
space, and the house is prevented from becoming
too warm. At night, when the Sun is no longer shin-
ing, the brick or concrete wall radiates the stored
heat and keeps the house warm. In addition, since
heat is lost and none is gained through windows
during the night, heat can be conserved by install-

Ontario Hydro's head office in Toronto, Canada. There is no furnace or heating plant within this building, yet internal temperatures are comfortable throughout both the harsh Canadian winter and the hot summer months. Energy conservation is realized through use of south-facing, double-glazed reflective glass and a system that stores and circulates the heat from lights, people, and machinery to supply heating needs. (Courtesy of Ontario Hydro)

ing drapes or insulated shutters for use after the Sun goes down.

Many homes, even in such cold climates as the Rocky Mountains, have been designed so that windows alone provide 50 percent or more of the heat needed in the winter.

Considerable energy savings can also be realized in commercial buildings. One example of a particularly innovative design is the 20-story office complex built in Toronto, Canada, for Ontario Hydro. This structure uses no fuel at all for space heating during the harsh Canadian winter. Instead, heat from lights, from machinery, and from people's bodies is conserved, stored, and circulated throughout the structure. In addition, double-glazed glass on the southern wall serves as a passive solar collection system. The energy saved every year is enough to supply all the power used by 2500 average homes.

Solar Collectors

Solar heat can be trapped even more efficiently by the use of various types of **solar collectors.** One type of collector consists of a coil of copper pipe brazed to a blackened metal base. The whole assembly is covered by a transparent layer of glass or plastic. The operating principle is uncomplicated.

Sunlight travels through the glass and is absorbed by the blackened surface. Metal conducts heat readily, so the water in the pipe gets hot. The glass traps the heat within the collector so that it does not easily escape back into the atmosphere (Fig. 13–11).

Hot water produced in this fashion can be pumped through radiators to heat a building. A heating system of this type is called **active solar** heat because hot water is actively pumped and regulated by motors and thermostats. Of course, sunshine is not available at night or on cloudy days. Hot water can conveniently be stored overnight, but it is expensive to build a system large enough to heat and store enough hot water to last during several days of cloudy weather. Therefore, most active solar systems are installed together with a conventional furnace. The solar collector is used on sunny days, and the conventional heater is used when it is cloudy. Naturally, such a dual system is initially more expensive than a simple fossil fuel system, but large amounts of fuel are saved every year.

It is difficult to assess the economics of active systems accurately. A system that will save money in Colorado may not be economical in Michigan. Overall, active solar heating is not the cheapest heating system in many areas. Therefore, the concept of solar energy has been looked upon unfa-

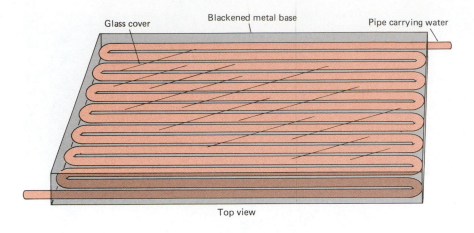

Glass cover

Blackened metal base

Pipe carrying water

Top view

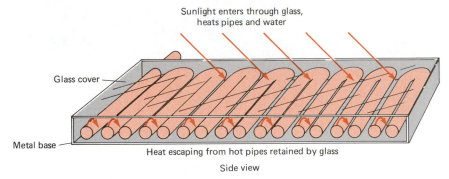

Sunlight enters through glass, heats pipes and water

Glass cover

Metal base

Heat escaping from hot pipes retained by glass

Side view

Figure 13–11
Schematic view of a solar collector. The most efficient collectors of this type can actually boil water, but most practical units heat water to about 80°C.

Solar collectors on a residential home. (Courtesy of Energy Systems Division of the Grumman Corporation, manufacturers of Sunstream Solar Collectors)

Box 13.1
Solar Energy for Home Heating

Advantages

Limitless supply
Produces no air pollution
Produces no water pollution
Produces no noise
Produces no thermal pollution
Produces no harmful wastes
No possibility of a large-scale explosion
 or disaster
Conserves the Earth's resources
Technology available for immediate
 widespread use

Disadvantages

Some active systems are more expensive
 than oil heat in some parts of the
 country. (But passive systems are economical in most applications.)

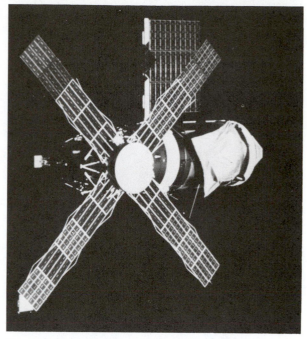

The Skylab space station, powered by a group of photo-electric cells mounted on "windmill" arms. (Courtesy of NASA)

vorably in some instances. This is unfortunate, be-cause, even when active systems do not pay, passive solar architecture is often cheaper, in the long run, than conventional construction. There is no place in the world where it is economical to build an inefficient structure and make up the dif-ference with fossil-fueled heating and air condition-ing.

Solar collectors are most practical for the pro-duction of hot water for washing or bathing. One reason for this is that active heating systems are used for only roughly half the year. During the re-mainder of the time, the expensive capital invest-ment lies idle. But domestic hot water is used all year, summer and winter. The first active solar wa-ter heat was patented in 1891 in the United States. It consisted simply of a bare metal tank, painted black, and tilted facing the Sun. At a time when natural gas sold for more than 10 times the 1985 cost (calculated in equivalent dollars), these early heaters were a commercial success. At the present time, the use of solar collectors for heating water

is economical in most places in the world. Solar water heaters are required by law in all new homes in northern Australia and in San Diego, California. Millions of units have been installed in Japan and in Israel. Despite the fact that they are economi-cally attractive, solar hot water units are not partic-ularly popular in the United States. But the trend is changing slowly. In 1985, the average solar hot wa-ter system was expected to pay for itself in 4 to 7 years. After that time, it would save a homeowner money. In that year, 100,000 units were installed in this country. If passive solar design and solar hot water units were incorporated in every house in the United States, overall national energy consumption would be greatly reduced.

Solar Generation of Electricity

When a beam of light is directed onto certain ma-terials, electrons can be energized. In 1954, a re-search team at Bell Laboratories discovered that the energy from these light-activated electrons can be converted directly to electricity. A device that produces electricity directly from sunlight is called a **solar cell.** Although the invention of solar cells

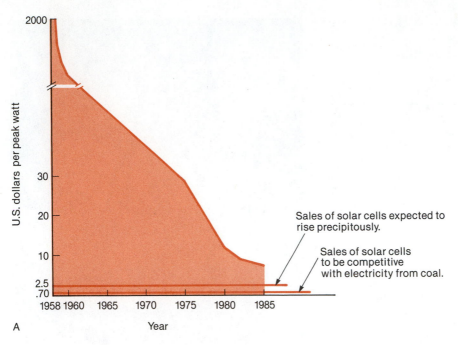

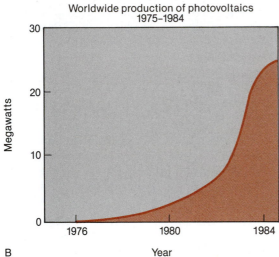

Worldwide production of photovoltaics 1975–1984

Source: Photovoltaic Energy Systems, Inc.

Figure 13–12

A, The average cost of photovoltaic cells from 1958 to 1985. Notice that if the price drops to $2.50 per watt, sales of these units are expected to increase rapidly, and if the price drops to $.70 per watt, solar electricity will be competitive with electricity generated from coal. *B,* Worldwide production of photovoltaic cells. (Source: Photovoltaic Energy Systems, Inc.)

was indeed exciting, the first devices were prohibitively expensive. Scientists estimated that if produced commercially, cell production would cost approximately $2000 per watt of output. Thus, it would require a capital investment of $200,000 to produce a generating capacity sufficient to light up *one* 100-watt bulb. Nevertheless, the technology was used in exotic applications such as spacecraft, where power requirements were low and cost was relatively unimportant. The first commercial use of solar cells was to power the second United States satellite, Vanguard I, launched in 1958.

The first solar cells were made from crystals of silicon and were similar in many ways to transistors. Over the past 25 years, dramatic improvements have been made in the technology for producing these devices. As a result, prices plummeted (Fig. 13–12). In 1986, solar cells were available for $7 to $8 per watt. If the cost of installation and maintenance were included, electricity could be generated in this manner for about $0.85/kWh (kilowatt hour). By comparison, electrical energy is generated in coal-fired power plants and delivered to the average home for about

The use of solar cells has increased dramatically in recent years, especially in out-of-the way places that have no access to commercial power lines. This solar array is used to supply electricity for the visitor center at Natural Bridges National Park, located in the desert in Utah.

$0.10/kWh. Clearly, solar cells were still more expensive than conventional sources of electricity by a factor of almost 10. However, solar cells generate electricity at the location where the power is needed, and there is no need for transmission lines. Furthermore, the cells need no maintenance. Therefore, they become economical in a variety of applications where electricity is needed in remote places. In 1986, more than $300 million worth of solar cells were produced in the United States. They were used to power light buoys anchored at sea, telephones and other communication systems located far from electric lines, and electric fences in the Southwestern desert. More than 6000 buildings were powered exclusively by solar cells. Solar cells are also used routinely in calculators, watches, and other portable devices with small power requirements. The technology has also blossomed in many other countries. About 60 percent of the population of the world has no access to commercial electricity. Portable generators are expensive, require maintenance that is often unavailable, and burn diesel fuel that is also expensive. Therefore, specialized machinery such as solar-powered irrigation pumps is becoming increasingly popular. In one report, health officials in India claimed that millions of solar-powered refrigerators were urgently needed to store heat-sensitive medicines and vaccines.

An extremely important question to ask in considering global energy futures is, "Will solar cell technology improve to the point where sunlight can be used to generate electricity at a rate competitive with traditional coal-fired generators?" If the answer is yes, we can envision a new energy age, in which people would obtain electric power simply by nailing solar panels on their rooftops, and centralized solar power plants would be built in desert regions. Of course, no one knows whether or not such a prospect is realistic. In 1986, several different inventors announced that they had discovered ways to produce solar cells out of non-crystalline silicon at a cost of $2 to $3 per watt, or at about $0.30 to $0.40 per kWh. However, at the time that this book was being written, commercial production of these cheap cells had not yet been realized. On the one hand, some experts are highly optimistic and predict that by the turn of the century, commercial production of solar electricity will be competitive with power from coal- or nuclear-fired plants. Others disagree and support the premise that solar technology has come as far as it can, that it will remain useful in special applications, but it will never become a major replacement for fossil or nuclear fuels.

Of course, solar-generating stations alone could not entirely replace conventional fuels, because the Sun does not shine all the time. There

Solar Challenger was designed and built by a team headed by Dr. Paul Mac-Cready, from Pasadena, California. This airplane is completely powered by an array of solar cells mounted on the wings and contains no batteries or other energy storage devices. (Courtesy of Randa Bishop, Wide World Photos)

are several ways to store solar energy. Perhaps the most practical is to use solar electricity to produce hydrogen fuel according to the equation

$$\text{Water} + \text{Electrical energy} \longrightarrow \text{Hydrogen} + \text{Oxygen}$$

Hydrogen is a versatile and useful fuel that can burn in air and be used as a replacement for gasoline and other liquid fuels. It is a particularly clean fuel, because water is the only byproduct released when it is burned.

$$\text{Hydrogen} + \text{Oxygen} \longrightarrow \text{Water} + \text{Heat energy}$$

Production of High-Temperature Steam

If you take an ordinary magnifying glass and focus sunlight onto a piece of paper, you can easily burn a hole in the paper. The lens concentrates the solar energy from a large area to a small one, so that high temperatures can be realized. Sunlight can also be concentrated through the use of specially designed mirrors. If an array of mirrors is used to focus the sunlight from a large area onto a small space, the energy can be used to boil water, create steam, and produce electricity in a conventional turbine. To date, the largest facility of this type is a project called Solar One which has been built in the Mojave Desert in southern California. This power plant uses more than 1800 mirrors to focus

sunlight onto a 30-story tower. Solar One generates 10 megawatts, enough electricity to satisfy the needs of about 5000 people. This initial project was supported by federal grants, because the research and development costs were high, but, officials believe that when new solar plants are built, they will be competitive with conventional methods of generating electricity.

Solar Ponds

In 1902, a Russian scientist was studying the peculiar properties of a unique lake in eastern Europe. The bottom sediments of this lake contained a vast bed of salt, and the surface layers were washed continuously by a stream of fresh water. The surface of the lake was cool, as was expected, but temperatures a few meters below the surface of the lake reached 85°C (185°F). To understand how water exposed to sunlight can became this hot, first think about the temperature regulation of a normal lake or pond. Sunlight heats the surface directly, but it also penetrates and heats the subsurface water. This heated water, being less dense than cool water, rises to the surface where it loses its heat to the atmosphere through evaporation and direct contact with the air. Now consider a pond with a salty zone at the bottom and fresh water on top. Salt water is denser than fresh water. When the salt water is heated, it rises; but even the warm salt

The power tower in Barstow, California. The circular array of mirrors focuses sunlight on the central tower. This heat is used to convert water to steam, which, in turn, is used to produce electricity. The complex uses a total of 1810 mirrors and, on a good day, produces 10 megawatts of electricity.

water is denser than cool fresh water. Therefore, the heated saltwater bumps against the ceiling of fresh water and cannot rise to the surface (Fig. 13–13). Although the salt water loses some heat to the surface layers during contact, there is no rapid evaporative loss, and the temperature of the salt layer rises.

Scientists have built and maintained artificial salt ponds as a device to trap and store solar energy. The hot, salty water can then be used directly to heat homes, or, alternatively, it can be used to vaporize a liquid that has a sufficiently low boiling point. The vapor can then be used to drive a turbine and produce electricity. The most ambitious solar pond projects are being developed in Israel, where planners hope to produce 2000 megawatts of electricity, about 75 percent of the nation's needs, by the year 2000.

13.5
Energy from Plants

Most people in the world still get most of their energy either directly from the Sun or indirectly by

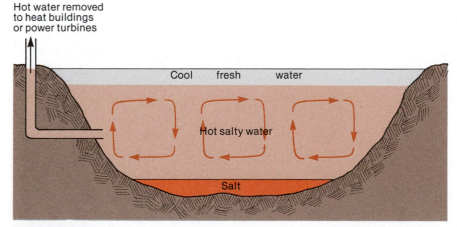

Figure 13–13

The principle of a solar pond. When the subsurface salty water is heated by the sun, it expands and rises. However, it is denser than the cool fresh water and cannot reach the surface. Instead, it cycles in subsurface convection currents, and the temperature rises. In order for the system to continue, operators must maintain the two-layer system.

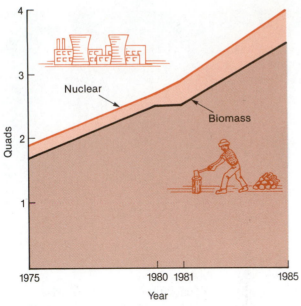

Figure 13–14
A comparison of the use of biomass and nuclear energy in the United States. (Source: *Chemical and Engineering News*)

Splitting firewood on a wintry day. Homeowners save money and conserve fuel by burning firewood, but fireplaces are almost always smoky and polluting.

using the products of plants or the pulling power of animals. Such energy is derived from grains, vegetables, fruits, and meat for food or from wood and dung for fuel. In recent years, energy from plants has aroused interest in more developed societies.

Wood

One hundred and fifty years ago, the major resource for energy in North America was wood. Today, again, there is a renewed interest in this fuel. According to the Department of Energy, in 1984, approximately 20 percent of all private households in the United States used wood for some or all of their heat. In some regions, more heating is done with wood than with oil, coal, and electricity combined. In 1985, more homes nationally were heated with wood than with electricity derived from nuclear energy, and the overall contribution of wood and biomass fuels almost equaled the production of power from nuclear sources (Fig. 13–14). The reason is simple. In many cases, wood is the cheapest source of heat available. Many people are finding that a few weekends' work of cutting and splitting logs can lower their winter heat bills by 75 percent or more.

In many cases, this gain is balanced by various economic externalities. For one, uncontrolled

wood fires in individual homes are likely to be smoky, and air pollution levels in certain regions have risen as a result. Consider the situation in Missoula, Montana. Missoula is a city of only 33,000 people located in a sparsely populated region in the Rocky Mountains in southwest Montana. It has one large pulp mill, which contributes appreciable pollution, but this level of industrial activity, by itself, cannot account for the fact that air pollution levels in Missoula are often greater than those found in Los Angeles, New York, or Chicago. According to the EPA, more than half of the small particles that contribute to Missoula's air pollution come from wood-burning stoves. Although no definite relationship has been established linking this pollution to a health problem, many of the compounds identified in wood smoke are known cancer-causing agents.

The city government is aware of the problem and has enacted legislation that requires citizens to refrain from using their stoves during periods of severe air pollution. Stricter laws have also been considered. One proposal is to make wood-burning stoves totally illegal. A less drastic option is to require that all stoves meet certain standards of efficiency. The debate that has resulted over these proposals can be summarized by the following two quotations. "Wood burning is an old Western

American tradition. It's a way of life a lot of people truly enjoy." To which an opponent replied, "Controlling a stove is no different than controlling sewage. We're subsidizing lower fuel bills with our health."

As more and more families burn wood, timber in many regions is being depleted. In the United States, homeowners burn 50 million cords of firewood a year (1 cord is a pile 4 ft × 4 ft × 8 ft). If 50 million cords were stacked in a pile, the pile would be 1100 ft by 1100 ft at the base and a mile high. Many experts believe that continued large-scale use of wood fuels is not sustainable and that we are mining our forests just as we mine our fossil fuels.

Most people who burn wood in the developed countries do so out of choice; other fuels are available at an affordable price, but wood is chosen because people believe that the immediate benefits outweigh the disadvantages. In many regions in the less-developed countries, however, there is no choice. For most of the world's poor, fossil fuels are simply too expensive, and wood or cow dung are the only reasonable alternatives. The severe deforestation that has occurred in many regions of the world has been described in previous chapters. Recall the discussions of problems such as erosion, landslides, flooding, loss of water, and desertification. There is yet another more immediate problem. In many rural areas, wood is so scarce that people spend a large portion of their time simply finding the fuel needed to cook their meals. In Africa, women and children often travel 50 km a day on their hunts for sticks and leaves; in Asia, it is common for families to spend either one fourth of their income or one fourth of their time obtaining firewood; and, in the Andes of South America, many families must support an extra donkey just to collect and haul firewood. When dung is used instead of wood, the burning and consumption of manure represents the loss of a potential source of fertilizer. Therefore, a conflict arises; when the dung is burned to cook today's dinner, there is less fertilizer available to grow food for the following season. In the very poorest portions of the world, there is no fuel whatsoever to cook the meager food that is available. In some parts of Africa, people eat raw flour and water and then starve, because the body cannot digest and absorb enough nutrients from raw grains.

Patties of cow manure drying on a wall in India. After the material is dried, it is used as fuel for cooking. However, when the dung is burned to cook dinner in one season there is less fertilizer available to grow food for the following year. (Christine Seashore)

Energy Plantations

Some experts suggest that trees grow too slowly to be used as a renewable energy source. Instead, they suggest that traditional crops such as sugar cane, pineapple, corn, soybeans, peanuts, or sunflowers be grown for the energy content in their sugars, stalks, or oils. Nontraditional crops have also been examined. For example, the sap of a Brazilian tree species *Cobaifera langsdorfii* is a good substitute for diesel oil. Tests have shown that each of these trees produces approximately 3 liters of sap every month; the sap can be placed directly in the fuel tank of a diesel-powered car.

The economic and environmental problems related to energy plantations are complex. Consider energy production from corn. If ordinary corn is cooked and then fermented, a watery solution of ethyl alcohol (ethanol) is produced. If this solution is distilled, the alcohol can be separated from the water until it is 95 percent pure. Of course, there is nothing new about this process; it is the same process as that traditionally used for the production of corn whiskey. But the next step is different: If 10 percent ethanol is mixed with 90 percent gasoline, a motor fuel called **gasohol** is produced. In the late 1970s, gasohol manufacture was considered in the United States as a means to reduce dependence on expensive foreign oil. In the 1980s, the price of imported fuel dropped, but ethanol fuel became attractive for another reason. Air pollution regulations triggered a concentrated effort to phase out the use of lead as an additive in gasoline. But lead raises the octane level in ordinary gas, and the conversion to no-lead gasoline requires more expensive refining. On the other hand, if ethanol is used as an additive, the octane level can be boosted without the harmful side effects of lead. For this reason, the production of ethanol for fuel has increased dramatically in recent years. Today, the largest producer of ethanol fuels is Brazil, which distilled about 5 billion liters of this fuel in 1986 (Fig. 13–15). Proponents of an ethanol fuel cycle argue that biomass fuels are renewable and represent a means of conserving limited supplies of fossil fuels. Critics counter on several grounds. In the United States, large quantities of fossil fuels are used to plant, harvest, and transport the corn that is used to produce the alcohol. Additional supplies of conventional fuels are required to manufacture fertilizers and pesticides. Once the corn is

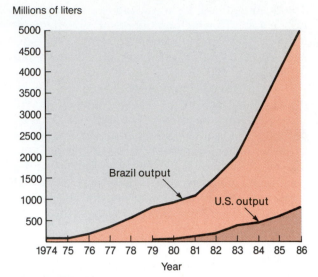

Millions of liters

Figure 13–15
Production of ethanol for fuel in Brazil and the United States. (Source: *Chemical and Engineering News*)

harvested, even more fuel is needed to cook the grain, warm the sugar as it ferments, and then distill the mixture to obtain the pure alcohol (Fig. 13–16). Therefore, when the whole process is taken into account, there is very little, if any, real conservation of fossil fuels. In the mid-1980s, ethanol production in the United States was supported by a variety of tax incentives. Critics of the program argue that this fuel is really not competitive economically and, if the tax laws were changed, production would dwindle.

In less-industrialized countries, such as Brazil, farmers use more manual labor and less fuel to raise crops, so the energy balance in ethanol production is more favorable. However, other critics argue that analysis of energy balance may not be the main point. According to one author, the use of high-quality grains for automotive fuel represents a poor set of priorities in the modern world.

The demand by motorists for fuel from energy crops represents a major new variable in the food/population equation. The stage is set for direct competition between the affluent minority, who own the world's 315 million automobiles, and the poorest segments of humanity, for whom getting enough food to stay alive is already a struggle. As the price of gasoline rises, so, too, will the profitability of energy crops. Over time, an expanding agricultural fuel market will mean that more and

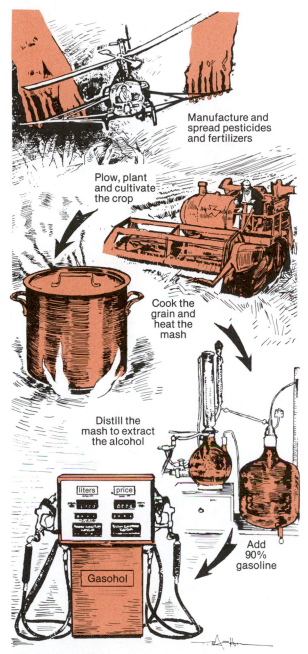

Manufacture and spread pesticides and fertilizers

Plow, plant and cultivate the crop

Cook the grain and heat the mash

Distill the mash to extract the alcohol

Add 90% gasoline

Figure 13–16
Energy inputs required to produce gasohol.

more farmers will have the choice of producing food for people or fuel for automobiles. They are likely to produce whichever is more profitable.*

*Source: Lester R. Brown: Food or Fuel: New competition for the world's cropland. *Worldwatch Paper 35,* March 1980.

Energy from Waste

Many societies in the developed world are incredibly wasteful. More than half of the household trash in the United States and Canada is paper. Huge piles of bark, wood scraps, and logging wastes rot slowly near many sawmills. If people collected these wastes and used them as fuel, considerable quantities of energy could be salvaged. Today, there are almost 300 plants throughout the world that burn municipal garbage to generate electricity or to produce steam to heat houses or commercial buildings. The largest facility in the world is located in Rotterdam, where a 550 megawatt generating plant (about half the electrical output of a large nuclear reactor) operates entirely on refuse. The city of Munich, Germany, obtains 12 percent of its electricity by burning its garbage. In North America, trash represents a considerable, and largely unexploited, resource. However, it is important to remember that technological fixes often create problems of their own. Recall from Section 1.2 that many citizens have objected to proposed municipal incinerators in New York City because they feared that noxious and potentially carcinogenic pollutants would be released even from the most carefully controlled furnaces.

Fuel can also be produced from other waste products. When organic wastes such as sewage, garbage, manure, or crop residues decompose in the absence of air, methane gas is released. The methane produced in this manner is called **biogas.** Despite the difference in names, however, methane produced from wastes is identical to methane extracted from an underground gas deposit. In an ideal sequence, a farmer would collect cow manure and deposit it in a specially designed concrete container, with a steel cap to hold the gas generated. The manure would be allowed to rot naturally, and the gas would be collected and used. The decomposed manure remaining in the concrete tank would then be removed and spread on the fields as a high-quality fertilizer. Studies in China have shown that a small biogas digester using human wastes and manure from a few cows can supply enough fuel to cook three meals and boil 15 liters of water a day for one family. Construction costs are returned in 1 to 3 years in the form of fuel savings. Tens of thousands of these units have been built in China and elsewhere throughout Asia.

Table 13–1
Annual Per Capita Grain and Cropland Requirements for Food Compared with Grain Required to Produce Ethanol for Automotive Fuel

	Grain (kg)	Cropland (hectares)
Subsistence diet	180	0.1
Affluent diet	730	0.4
Typical compact automobile (16,000 km/yr at 10 km/L)	4100	2.3
Typical full-size automobile (16,000 km/yr at 6.3 km/L)	6600	3.7

There has also been limited interest in biogas in the developed world. For example, in Modesto, California, methane from the sewage treatment plant has been collected and used in city vehicles. The cost to the city in 1980 was equivalent to buying gasoline at 30 cents per gallon! Similarly, the Brooklyn Union Gas Company has drilled more than 100 gas wells into the core of an extensive garbage dump outside the city. About 3.5 million cubic feet of methane are collected *every day* from the decomposing garbage. The city realized a profit of $600,000 in the first year of operation of the wells, and 25,000 homes were supplied with gas that otherwise would have been wasted. It is incredible that in this age of depletion of our fossil fuel reserves, there are only a few places in North America where there is commercial interest in this fuel.

13.6
Energy from Wind, Water, and the Earth

Hydroelectric Energy

Many early settlers in North America used the power of falling water to drive their mills and factories. Today, many large rivers are dammed. The energy of water dropping downward through the dam is used to produce electricity. Energy produced in this way is called **hydroelectric energy.** The principle here is uncomplicated. Water falling through a pipe in the dam flows past the blades of a turbine (Fig. 13–17). The blades are forced to rotate, thereby driving an electric generator. No fossil fuels are used, and the power supply is renewable continuously as water evaporates from the ocean

Figure 13–17
A large turbine for generating electric power. The turbine spins when water falls past its blades. Note its size compared to the height of the workers in the background. (Courtesy of Tennessee Valley Authority)

Benefits and Problems of Large-Scale Hydroelectric Development

Benefits	Problems
Cheap, pollution-free, renewable energy is made available.	Silt from soil erosion upriver can fill in the lakes behind large dams, reducing their utility within a few decades. Then the expensive dam projects become useless.
Water stored behind dams can be used for irrigation, thus increasing productivity of local agriculture.	Dams flood valuable farmland, reducing food production in many areas.
Cheap electricity provided by dams can be used to manufacture fertilizer.	In a free-flowing river, soil nutrients released from regions upstream are carried to the valleys below. During flood time, some of these nutrients are spread out on lowland farms, renewing the fertility of the soil. When the river cycle is disrupted by the dam, the flow of nutrients is cut off, reducing soil fertility near the river mouth.
Dams establish lakes that provide a habitat for fish, which in turn can be used for a food supply.	The traditional flow of nutrients to the sea also fertilizes ocean estuaries, providing food for saltwater fish. When this flow is reduced, populations of ocean fish have been disturbed. For example, the sardine catch on the mouth of the Nile River declined by 18,000 tonnes annually when the Aswan Dam was built. In some cases, dams disrupt migration of spawning fish such as salmon. Also, water taken from considerble depths below the surface of the dammed lake is often much colder than surface water and therefore changes the biota of the stream below the dam.
Lakes produced by dams are prime recreational sites.	Great aesthetic loss occurs when beautiful natural canyons are obliterated.
In many areas, a dependable water supply created by dams has increased public hygiene.	In many areas, disease organisms breed in dam-produced lakes or irrigation canals, leading to sickness and death.
Hydroelectric energy reduces the need for fossil fuel, which produces carbon dioxide and may thus disrupt world climate. In this way, world climate is protected.	There is a fear that major dams planned for the future might disrupt the flow off warm water into the Arctic, thereby disrupting world climate.

and falls to the Earth to collect in the high mountains.

Today, about 5 percent of the total world consumption of energy is supplied by hydroelectric generators. However, there are large regional differences in the use of this resource. In the United States, 3 percent of the total energy is supplied by falling water, whereas this total is 50 percent in Norway and about 75 percent in parts of China. Figure 13–18 shows that only a small percentage of the total worldwide potential for hydropower has been exploited. On the one hand, huge projects are being considered or initiated, such as damming the Amazon in Brazil, the Yangtze in China, and many of the rivers flowing into the Arctic such as the Yukon, the Mackenzie, the Ob, and the Lena. On the other hand, environmentalists have raised many serious questions about large-scale hydroelectric projects. Some of the pros and cons of the use of this energy source are listed in the chart above. (See also Chapters 15 and 17.)

In view of the environmental problems outlined here, many people believe that a better answer might be the construction of many small-scale

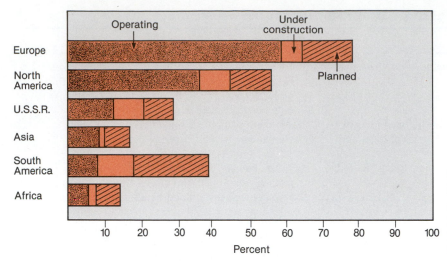

Figure 13–18
Hydropower use in various regions. The numbers represent the percentage of the total hydropower potential in the specific region.

hydroelectric facilities rather than a few large dams. Small-scale hydroelectric power was popular in the United States in the late 1800s, and it is slowly gaining popularity once again because it is cheaper than the construction of large dams. For example, large dams cost about $1,000 per kilowatt of power available. This price includes the construction of both the dams and the installation of the generators. However, small-scale dams and hydroelectric generators can be built for about $500 per kilowatt. Many small dams along a river would produce more electricity at a lower price with less environmental impact than a few large centralized facilities.

An interesting commentary on the energy strategies in the United States is that at the present time, there are more than 50,000 dams that have already been built for flood control, irrigation, and recreation that do not have turbines installed to produce electricity. If the potential energy of these facilities were harnessed, 1 quad of energy, or about 1.3 percent of the total United States consumption, could be generated.

Small-scale hydroelectricity has become popular in the less-developed countries, and, in China, one third of the nation's electrical output is derived from nearly 100,000 small turbines. However, the poorest nations cannot afford even the modest capital investment required to build small dams and spillways. Nepal has the greatest potential for hydroelectric power in the world, as thousands of streams and rivers fall from the heights of the Himalayas to the southern lowlands, which are only a few hundred meters above sea level. However, very little of this potential has been harnessed, and, today, only a few cities and almost none of the villages are electrified. The country can purchase used turbines and even discarded wire from the developed nations at an affordable price. But there are no roads in the mountains where the cascading streams are found. Trails are narrow and bridges are often treacherous. Therefore, the cement needed to build the small dams must be carried into the mountains on peoples' backs, and this arduous type of transportation is too expensive in an impoverished land.

Figure 13–19
Schematic view of a tidal dam and turbine.

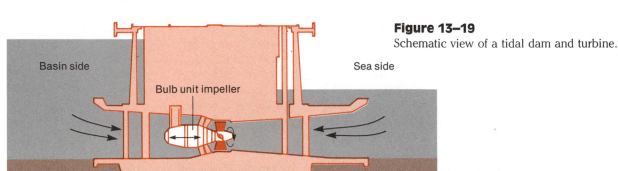

A large hydroelectric dam. (Courtesy of Bureau of Reclamation; photo by E. E. Herzog)

Tidal Power

In many coastal regions, the flow of the tides naturally funnels through narrow entrances into bays and estuaries, and strong currents are established. Twice a day, the water flows inland, and twice a day it rushes outward with the ebb tide. Some of the energy from this movement of currents can be harnessed if a tidal dam is built and a turbine is installed (Fig. 13–19).

During the 1800s, tidal power was popular in the United States. At that time, it was an attractive alternative to bulky steam engines that consumed large quantities of wood. However, when fossil fuels became cheap in the 1900s, these facilities were abandoned. Today, there are very few tidal electric plants in the world. One reason that tidal electricity is not popular is that there are only a few dozen places in the world where tidal differences are great enough to produce large quantities of electricity. Secondly, the economics of existing tidal dams has not proven to be attractive. For example, a 250-megawatt tidal power station was built in France in 1968. Although technically successful, this facility cost 2.5 times more than a conventional hydroelectric project that was built nearby. In addition to cost considerations, tidal power projects raise a host of environmental problems. Tidal bays are often rich estuaries where fish come to breed, and they are also popular places for recreation. If these areas are industrialized, some of the natural qualities and resources will be lost.

Power from Ocean Waves

Since 1876, approximately 150 patents have been issued in the United States alone for devices to harness the energy in waves. One of these devices is shown in Figure 13–20. However, as of 1988, there are no large-scale wave energy generators in use.

The major problem is simply one of economics. Although the wave energy along an entire coastline is enormous, the potential in any one limited area is small. Therefore, in order to harness appreciable quantities of energy, large structures would have to be built, and, at the present time, these are simply too expensive to be practical.

Ocean Thermal Power

It is also possible to use the heat of the ocean to produce electricity. The Second Law of Thermodynamics tells us that a heat engine can be built to do work whenever there is a temperature difference between two bodies. For example, a coal-fired generator runs because the temperature of the steam on one side of the turbine is hotter than the temperature of the exhaust. In certain tropical regions,

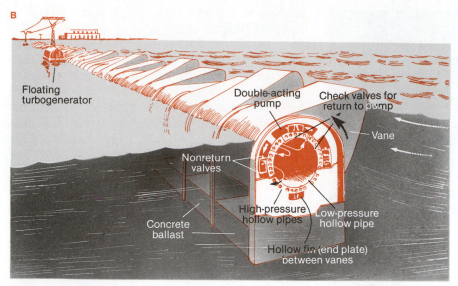

Figure 13–20
A device used to harness energy from waves. The system consists of a series of segmented cam lobes that are rocked on a large spine by waves, which are shown coming from the right. Pumps connected to the lobes send high-pressure water through small pipes to drive a generator. (From *Popular Science,* reprinted with permission)

the surface of the ocean is approximately 20°C warmer than the subsurface layers. The warm water is hot enough to vaporize a pressurized liquid such as ammonia. The gaseous ammonia can drive a turbine just as hot steam drives a turbine in a coal-fired plant. In an ocean thermal generator, the gaseous ammonia is cooled by the subsurface water and reused, as shown in Figure 13–21. The theoretical thermodynamic efficiency of an engine that operates between 5°C and 25°C is only 7 percent (see Appendix A). In practice, engines always operate at less than theoretical efficiency, so the practical efficiency is somewhere around 3 percent. Proponents of the plan to use ocean thermal power plants argue that even if the efficiency is low, there is so much water in the oceans that a large amount

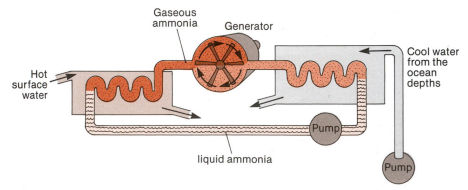

Figure 13–21
Schematic of an ocean thermal power plant. Pressurized ammonia is boiled by the warm surface waters of tropical oceans. The ammonia gas expands against the blades of a turbine, and the spinning turbine drives a generator to produce electricity. The gases are cooled and condensed by colder subsurface waters that are pumped into the power plant.

of energy is available. Opponents argue that the capital costs of the power plants are so high that it will be decades at least before ocean thermal power is economically feasible.

Energy from the Wind

The power of wind has been used since antiquity to drive ships, pump water, and grind grain. What is its potential in modern society? In a report of wind potential in the United States, it was estimated that wind generation could harness one trillion kWh of electricity per year, which amounts to 40 percent of the country's present needs. Furthermore, the technology needed to build the required generators is relatively simple and commercially available. The major problem is one of economics. In the United States, wind power is clearly economical in very rural areas where electricity is expensive or where power lines are unavailable. In urban settings, the situation is more complicated. In 1986, wind energy cost between \$.12/kWh and \$.23/kWh to produce and transmit, depending on how much wind is available. Recall that, in comparison, electric power generated by fossil fuels cost about \$.10/kWh. Therefore, it appears that wind energy is uneconomical. However, in the late 1970s and early 1980s, state and federal governments offered substantial tax incentives for development of wind energy. As a result, development became profitable. In 1985 alone, 5000 wind turbines were installed in California, and, by the end of that year, the total wind generating capacity in that state reached 1100 megawatts, about equal to

A windmill mounted on top of a floating house located in a small bay in a very rural area of Alaska. The electricity produced is sufficient to operate a few conveniences such as a radio, a cassette player, and a few light bulbs. It would be prohibitively expensive to build miles of power lines through the forest to connect this house to conventional sources of electricity.

A "wind farm" in California. Supported by tax incentives, these windmills produce electricity that will be sold commercially. (Gamma Liaison Photo Agency)

Figure 13–22

This oil tanker, built by Nippon KoKan Company of Japan, uses sails to assist the conventional diesel engines. The sails are set and furled by remote control from the bridge and reduce fuel consumption. (Courtesy NKK, American, Inc.)

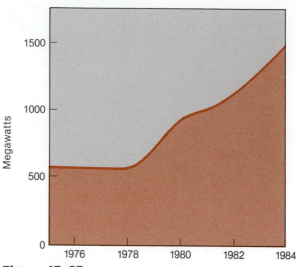

Figure 13–23

Geothermal capacity in the United States, 1975 to 1984. (Source: Geothermal Resources Council)

that of one large coal or nuclear power plant. However, the following year, many of the tax breaks were reduced or eliminated, and it appeared likely that construction of new facilities would be sharply reduced. Of course, economic balance sheets are always changing. If the price of fuels were to rise significantly, wind power could become popular on a wide scale.

In recent years, commercial interests have been examining the economics of sailing ships once again. At the present time, some traditional sailing ships are used in the fishing industry or in local island areas such as the South Pacific or the Caribbean. In addition, designers are interested in the construction of large, technically advanced sailing vessels for commercial trade between major industrial ports. One test vessel is the Japanese-built oil tanker shown in Figure 13–22. The sails on this tanker are operated hydraulically and can be controlled by a single pilot on the bridge. Using sails combined with conventional engines and using advanced hull designs, sailing freighters operating between major industrial cities could save 50 percent of the fuel currently used by commercial ships.

Geothermal Energy

Energy derived from the heat of the Earth's crust is called **geothermal energy.** In various places on the globe, such as in the hot springs and geysers of Yellowstone National Park in Wyoming, hot water is produced near the surface. Although no one suggests harnessing Old Faithful for generating electricity, there are several places where hot underground steam is available. The power company must simply dig a well and pipe the free steam into a turbine. Geothermal energy is economical in certain regions, and its popularity has grown (Fig. 13–23). The Pacific Gas and Electric Company produces 1,250 megawatts of electricity from a generator connected to wells in central California; an Italian facility at Larderello has been in operation since 1913; and parts of new Zealand and Iceland have been supplying all their electricity from geothermal plants for many years.

At the present time, only 0.2 percent of the energy used in the United States is met by geothermal sources. Optimistic supporters of the program expect production to increase to about 6000 megawatts by the year 2000. That is either a large amount or a small amount, depending on your viewpoint. On the one hand, 6000 megawatts can supply almost 3 million people with all their electricity and will replace six coal- or nuclear-fired power plants. On the other hand, it represents only about 1 percent of the total power requirements of the United States.

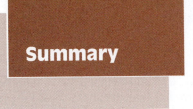

Summary

Energy consumption in the developed countries is considerably greater than in the less-developed countries. The United States uses considerably more energy per capita than do other developed countries.

The best estimates predict that oil and gas shortages will occur in the early twenty-first century, natural gas will be available until about 2050, and coal reserves will be plentiful for 200 years or more. Additional supplies of fuels are available from heavy oils.

Electricity is generated when a moving gas or fluid forces the blades of a turbine to rotate. In turn, the rotating turbine drives a generator.

Solar energy in the form of passive solar design or solar collectors can be used to heat air or water for domestic use. Solar cells can be used for the direct generation of electricity although they are not competitive with traditional sources of electricity in conventional applications. Solar energy can also be harnessed through the use of concentrating mirrors or solar ponds.

Plant energy can be used in the form of wood or other fuels. Some plants or plant products can be converted to alcohol or methane. In addition, domestic garbage, which consists largely of paper, can be burned to generate useful energy. If it is allowed to rot, methane is produced.

Additional energy is available from hydroelectric sources, the tides and waves, temperature differences in the ocean, the wind, and geothermal sources.

Problems

Modern Energy Use

1. Discuss the qualitative and quantitative differences in energy consumption among people in the United States, Sweden, and Bangladesh. Can you explain how these differences may ultimately affect global politics?

Fossil Fuel Reserves

2. Explain the difference between a resource and a reserve.

3. Discuss problems inherent in predicting the future availability of fossil fuel reserves. What is the value of the predictions?

4. Discuss the prospects for the availability of petroleum in the next 10, 20, and 40 years. What types of uncertainties are inherent in these predictions?

5. Discuss the prospects for the availability of coal in the next 10, 40, 100, and 200 years. What types of uncertainties are inherent in these predictions?

6. It was stated in Special Topic B that experts believe that half of the original supply of petroleum in the United States has already been extracted. How are such projections made? Discuss the reliability of this statement.

Solar Energy

7. List five different techniques for harnessing the energy in sunlight. Compare them with respect to availability of the necessary technology, cost, convenience, and environmental side effects.

8. Discuss the utility and limits of using solar collectors and passive solar design to reduce the energy consumption in the United States.

9. Suggest some practical cost-effective improvements that could be added to your school, dormitory, or home that would use solar energy effectively.

10. Discuss the advantages and disadvantages related to use of solar cell–operated generating stations to produce electricity. What could be done to supply energy at night?

11. Explain how wind, waves, ocean currents, plant, and hydroelectric energy resources are all indirect forms of solar energy.

Energy from Plant Matter

12. Increased use of wood heat has led to significant air pollution problems in many small towns. Discuss some of the environmental tradeoffs inherent in the use of wood heat.

13. Loggers in New England have traditionally sold low- or medium-quality logs to pulp mills for the production of paper. During the early 1980s, it was often more profitable to sell logs as firewood. Using these facts as a background, suggest how the cost of energy can affect the price of various agricultural products.

14. Some people have suggested that agricultural wastes such as sugar cane stalks should be used to produce ethanol fuels. What environmental problems would be reduced if such a plan were implemented? Can you think of any environmental problems that would arise?

15. Discuss the environmental impact of burning garbage as a fuel.

16. Speak to a local municipal politician about the feasibility of collecting methane from the city sewage treatment plant. Report the results of your discussion to your classmates.

17. Go to your local supermarket and determine the number of cardboard boxes discarded daily. What is done with this cardboard? Can you suggest other uses for it?

18. Manure can be used to produce methane, CH_4, before the residue is used as a fertilizer. Does the prior removal of methane reduce the fertilizer value of the manure? Defend your answer.

Energy from Water

19. How does the design and operation of a hydroelectric power generator differ from that of a fossil fuel–powered generator? Compare the two with respect to availability of energy supply and environmental impact.

20. Discuss the potential advantages and disadvantages of hydroelectric energy. Refer back to Chapter 11 on rural land use and discuss problems associated with the damming of tropical rivers.

21. Compare the problems inherent in the development of hydroelectric sites with those that would arise if large-scale tidal energy sites were developed.

22. The strength of tidal currents fluctuates on a 6-hour basis. Tidal currents are strongest midway between high and low tides and stop altogether just at high and low tides. How would these fluctuations affect the use of tidal power for the generation of electricity? Suggest some possible solutions to the problem.

23. Explain why ocean thermal power plants are inherently inefficient. Why are they being considered nevertheless?

Renewable Energy Sources

24. Imagine that you are a Peace Corps advisor to a small village in the mountains in India. What energy sources would you encourage the people to develop? Remember, capital for modern machinery would be extremely limited.

25. Analyze the potential for non–fossil fuel energy resources in your home town. What energy sources could you use that would eventually be cheaper than fossil fuels?

Suggested Readings

The following general references provide an overview of the energy issues:

Darmstadter, et al: *Energy Today and Tomorrow: Living with Uncertainty.* Englewood Cliffs, NJ, Prentice-Hall, 1983. 240 pp.

Richard Eden, Michael Posner, Richard Bending, Edmund Crouch, and Joe Stanislaw: *Energy Economics: Growth, Resources, and Policies.* Cambridge, Cambridge University Press, 1981. 442 pp.

OECD: *Energy Technology Policy.* Washington, D.C., OECD Publications, 1985. 124 pp.

S. S. Penner and L. Icerman: *Energy II NonRenewable Technologies.* 2nd ed. Elmsford, NY, Pergamon Press, 1984. 856 pp.

Paul C. Stern (study director): *Energy Use: The Human Dimension.* New York, W.H. Freeman, 1984, 256 pp.

Thomas J. Sargent (ed): *Energy, Foresight, and Strategy.* Washington, D.C., Resources for the Future Books, 1985. 220 pp.

Energy problems in the less-developed countries are discussed in:

Joy Dunkerley, W. Ramsay, L. Gordon, and E. Cecilski: *Energy Strategies for Developing Nations.* Baltimore, Johns Hopkins University Press, 1981. 265 pp.

Fossil fuel sources, availability and consumption are discussed in:

David Glasner: *Politics, Prices and Petroleum, The Political Economy of Energy.* San Francisco, Pacific Institute for Public Policy Research Press, 1985. 284 pp.

OECD: Coal Information: 1985. Washington, D.C., OECD Publications, 1985. 438 pp.

Steven A. Schneider: *The Oil Price Revolution.* Baltimore, MD, Johns Hopkins University Press, 1983. 624 pp.

U.S. Department of Energy, Energy Information Administration: *Annual Energy Review 1985*. Washington, D.C., U.S. Government Printing Office, 1985.

U.S. Department of Energy, Energy Information Administration: *International Energy Outlook 1985*. Washington, D.C., U.S. Government Printing Office, 1985.

Solar technology is discussed in:

Mehdi N. Bahadori: Passive cooling systems in Iranian architecture. *Scientific American,* February, 1978. p. 144.

Ken Butti and John Perlin: *A Golden Thread—2500 Years of Solar Architecture and Technology.* Palo Alto, CA, Cheshire Books, 1980. 283 pp.

Yoshihiro Hamakawa: Photovoltaic power. *Scientific American, 256*(4): April 1987.

Good articles on gasohol production and energy plantations are:

Lester R. Brown: Food or fuel: New competition for the world's cropland. *Worldwatch Paper 35,* March 1980.

Lester R. Brown: Food versus fuel. *Environment, 22*(4):32, 1980.

R.S. Chambers, et al.: Gasohol: Does it or doesn't it produce positive new energy? *Science, 206*:789, 1979.

Gasohol: Does it save energy? *Environmental Science and Technology, 14* (2):1402, 1980.

An excellent article on biogas is:

Edgar J. Dasilda: Biogas: Fuel of the future? *Ambio, 9*(1): 1982.

Renewable energy resources are discussed in:

Daniel Deudney: An old technology for a new era. *Environment, 23*(7):17, 1981.

He Dexin: Wind energy development in China. *Wind Power Digest,* No. 26, 1984.

John D. Isaacs and Walter R. Schmitt: Ocean energy: Forms and prospects. *Science, 207*(4428):265, 1980.

Gerald W. Koeppl: *Putnam's Power From the Wind.* New York, Van Nostrand Reinhold Co., 1982. 470 pp.

14

Nuclear Energy and the Environment

14.1
Nuclear Energy — Past and Future

Nuclear energy burst onto the public consciousness in 1945, when two fission bombs were used against Japan. The reaction everywhere was that a new kind of energy had been unleashed. The public understood that the "new energy" could be used for human betterment as well as for war. There was much hope for the "peaceful use of atomic energy," meaning that nuclear energy could be used in power plants rather than in bombs. Many people believed that an era of practically free and unlimited energy was at hand. Scientists engaged in nuclear research wrote statements such as, "We can look forward to universal comfort, practically free transportation, and unlimited supplies of materials." Some optimists even predicted that electricity from nuclear energy would be "too cheap to meter."

The nuclear energy program was launched with widespread public approval and support. However, the facts that radioactive materials could be deadly, that fission fuels could also become explosives, and that the development of nuclear weapons had not stopped with the end of the war led to a gradually widening sense of unease. Furthermore, a few accidents in which some radioactivity was released to the environment started to happen as early as the 1950s.

By the 1960s, as people became more aware of the biological dangers of radiation, the nuclear debate became a recognized public issue. Concern about nuclear safety increased, while the development of nuclear energy and the plans for its further rapid expansion continued.

Despite these developments, neither the public nor the "experts" were prepared for the more frightening events of the 1970s and 1980s; specifically, those at the Browns Ferry Nuclear Power Plant (Alabama), at Three Mile Island (Pennsylvania) and at Chernobyl (the Ukraine, U.S.S.R.). For the first time, the debates about the advisability of continuing the nuclear program, or even the possibility of scrapping it altogether, reached significant political levels.

In the early 1980s, the nuclear industry in the United States actually stopped growing (Fig. 14–1)—for an unexpected reason. It seemed that it was no longer profitable to generate electricity by

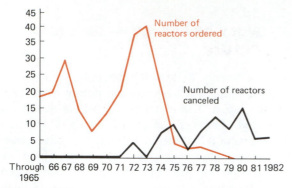

Figure 14–1

The number of new nuclear reactors ordered and cancelled in the United States. This trend is not observed in other countries, where the number of reactors doubled and the total generating capacity tripled between 1976 and 1982.

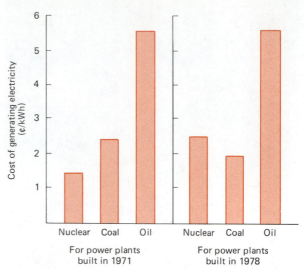

Figure 14–2

The cost of producing electricity from power plants completed in 1971 and 1978. Note that in 1971, electricity from nuclear power plants was cheaper than that derived from coal. However, increased costs reversed that trend by 1978, and the nuclear power industry stagnated so that by the early 1980s, there were no new orders for nuclear power plants in the United States. Therefore, no data based on actual experience are available for the 1980s. (Source: *Environmental Science and Technology, 16*:373A, 1982)

nuclear energy. The costs of building nuclear plants grew until, in some instances, they were 10 times the original estimates. These increases were related in large part to unanticipated difficulties in construction and operation of the new plants and in some measure to the influences of inflation and higher interest rates. In any event, the resulting cost overruns meant that by the end of the 1970s, nuclear energy had little, if any, economic advantage over energy from coal (Fig. 14–2). Costs of electricity from nuclear plants in the 1990s must be based on predictions, because no new plants are being built in the United States. Various estimates indicate that costs would differ in different parts of the country, being lower than costs of electricity from coal in some areas and higher in others. Future costs of fuels and of waste disposal are also difficult to estimate. Furthermore, the demand for energy has not grown as rapidly as expected. The rate of growth of electrical consumption in the United States, which was about 7 percent per year in the early 1970s, had fallen to about 3 percent by 1982.

Industrial countries that cannot depend on their own resources of coal, oil, or gas may view nuclear energy as a necessity rather than an option. For this reason, nuclear plants are still being built in other parts of the world. France, Belgium, Finland, Sweden, Switzerland, and Japan are among the countries that depend more on nuclear plants to generate electric power than does the United States.

Serious discussions about the future of the nuclear industry continue. Some scientists and politicians argue that new technical developments will make nuclear power safe enough to reassure the public; therefore, they favor a nuclear future; others wish to abandon the industry entirely. How, then, can you make your own decisions about such questions? Surely you should at least start with a background of reliable information. This chapter will describe, in principle, where nuclear energy comes from and how it can be used to generate electricity. The potential dangers of the nuclear energy program will also be considered.

14.2
Elements and Atoms

Chemical elements are considered to be the stuff of which all other substances are composed. There are about 105 known elements. Some common elements are hydrogen, carbon, nitrogen, iron, and uranium.

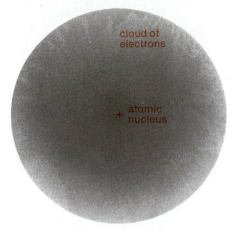

cloud of
electrons

+ atomic
nucleus

Figure 14–3
An atom consists of a positive nucleus surrounded by
an electron cloud.

Atoms are the fundamental units of elements. An atom consists of a small, dense, positively charged center called a **nucleus** surrounded by a diffuse cloud of negatively charged **electrons** (Fig. 14–3). The unit of positive charge in the atom is the **proton,** and the **atomic number** is the number of protons, or unit positive charges, in the nucleus. It is also the number of electrons in the neutral atom. A hydrogen atom, atomic number 1, consists of a proton with a charge of $+1$ as its nucleus, surrounded by one electron with a charge of -1. An atom of carbon, atomic number 6, contains six protons and six electrons.

However, the protons account for only about half the mass of the carbon atom. The remainder is attributed to neutral particles, called **neutrons,**

Table 14–1
Particles in the Atom

Particle	Electrical Charge	Mass Number
Electron	-1	0
Proton	$+1$	1
Neutron	0	1

in the nucleus. The neutron has about the same mass as the proton. The **mass number** of an atom is the total number of protons and neutrons in its nucleus.

The properties of the three fundamental atomic particles are shown in Table 14–1. The atomic number and the mass number of an element are often written with its symbol, as shown below for carbon.

$$12 \longleftarrow \text{mass number}$$
$$C \longleftarrow \text{symbol for carbon}$$
$$6 \longleftarrow \text{atomic number}$$

Table 14–2 gives the nuclear compositions, atomic numbers, and mass numbers of atoms of carbon and uranium. Note that a given element may have more than one mass number. Atoms of the same element (i.e., atoms with the same atomic number) that have different mass numbers are called **isotopes.** Thus, carbon-12 and carbon-14 are carbon atoms because they both have six nuclear protons, and they are isotopes because they have different mass numbers. This difference results from the fact that there are different num-

Table 14–2
Nuclear Compositions of Some Isotopes of Carbon and Uranium

Name and Symbol		Nuclear Composition		Atomic Number (Protons)	Mass Number (Protons + Neutrons)
		Protons	Neutrons		
Carbon-12	$^{12}_{6}C$	6	6	6	12
Carbon-14	$^{14}_{6}C$	6	8	6	14
Uranium-235	$^{235}_{92}U$	92	143	92	235
Uranium-238	$^{238}_{92}U$	92	146	92	238
Uranium-239	$^{239}_{92}U$	92	147	92	239

bers of neutrons in the two nuclei. Isotopes of an element are chemically equivalent (or very nearly so); they have the same ability to combine with other atoms. If the carbon is converted to some other compound, such as carbon dioxide, the isotopes themselves are not altered but retain their separate identities in the carbon dioxide molecules.

The general formula that relates these terms is

mass number = protons + neutrons

or,

mass number = atomic number + neutrons

14.3
Radioactivity

In 1896, the French physicist Henri Becquerel discovered that uranium minerals spontaneously emit energy in the form of radiation. Thus, if a piece of photographic film is held near a uranium mineral in the dark, the film becomes exposed, just as it would if it were held near a light. This emission of radiation from an element is called **radioactivity** (see Box 14.1). The study of radioactivity led to several important findings:

1. The radioactivity of substances such as uranium oxide, uranium chloride, and pure uranium metal depends only on the amount of uranium in the sample, not on whether the uranium is the pure element or combined as a compound. Therefore, the radioactivity of uranium is a property of its *atoms* and is not related to its chemical bonding. This conclusion may be generalized: *Radioactivity is an atomic property.*

2. The emissions from a radioactive element consist of particles and radiant energy (photons). The particles come off at high speed and thus carry energy of motion. Therefore, *all radioactivity is a source of energy.* This fact was recognized from the very beginning. (After all, it takes energy to darken photographic film.) However, naturally radioactive materials give off energy at very low rates. Radioactive substances are also very thinly distributed in the Earth's crust. Therefore, it was evident that natural radioactivity could never be a *practical* source of energy for human needs.

3. *Some elements exist both as nonradioactive (stable) isotopes and as radioactive (unstable)*

Box 14.1
The Origin of Radioactivity

The potential energy in a lump of coal was originally derived from the Sun, which caused green plants to grow. In turn, the plants were converted into coal. If there is potential energy in a nucleus, where did it come from? The answer is that unstable nuclei were formed when dying stars exploded. These explosions generate tremendous amounts of energy, and unstable nuclei are created.

---

isotopes, called **radioisotopes.** For example, carbon-12, the ordinary form of carbon, is stable, but carbon-14, a less abundant isotope, is radioactive. Both substances, however, are the element carbon, with the same chemical properties.

4. *When a radioisotope decomposes, its nucleus changes, and an isotope of a new element is formed.* Some radioisotopes produce new isotopes that are also radioactive; others produce stable isotopes. The production of one radioisotope from another may go cn for several "generations" of new elements, until the sequence ends with the formation of a stable isotope.

Marie and Pierre Curie took up the studies started by Becquerel, and, after a series of careful, tedious separations (Fig. 14–4), they discovered new radioactive elements in the uranium minerals. The first such element was radium. Another was polonium, named after Marie Curie's native country, Poland.

14.4
Nuclear Reactions

Radioactivity and other nuclear changes can be represented by simple equations. An example is

$$^{226}_{88}\text{Ra} \longrightarrow {}^{4}_{2}\text{He} + {}^{222}_{86}\text{Rn}$$

radium   helium   radon
           nucleus

This equation tells us that a $^{226}_{88}\text{Ra}$ nucleus decomposes to give one $^{4}_{2}\text{He}$ and one $^{222}_{86}\text{Rn}$ nucleus. (See Box 14.2.) (A $^{4}_{2}\text{He}$ nucleus is called an **alpha particle.**) Also, note that both the mass numbers

Figure 14–4
Madame Curie's laboratory. (From Weeks and Leicester: *Discovery of the Elements.* 7th ed. Easton, PA, Journal of Chemical Education, 1968)

$(226 = 4 + 222)$ and the atomic numbers $(88 = 2 + 86)$ are balanced.

The first artificial nuclear reaction was carried out by Ernest Rutherford and co-workers in 1919, when they bombarded ordinary nitrogen with helium nuclei to produce oxygen-17, which is nonradioactive:

$$^{14}_{7}N + ^{4}_{2}He \longrightarrow ^{17}_{8}O + ^{1}_{1}H$$

Fifteen years later, in 1934, Irene and Frédéric Joliot-Curie, Mme. Curie's daughter and son-in-law, converted boron-10, which is stable, to nitrogen-13, which is radioactive. This was the first artificially produced radioisotope.

$$\underset{\text{(stable)}}{^{10}_{5}B} + ^{4}_{2}He \longrightarrow \underset{\text{(radioactive)}}{^{13}_{7}N} + ^{1}_{0}n$$

The symbol $^{1}_{0}n$ represents the neutron. (Its charge is zero and its mass number is 1.)

14.5
Half-Life

If you observed just one atom of radium-226, containing one nucleus, when would it decompose? This question cannot be answered because any particular radium nucleus may or may not decompose at any time. In any given interval of time, some nuclei will decompose and some will not; the event is a matter of chance. The **half-life** is the time that it takes for half the nuclei in a sample to decompose. The half-life of radium-226 is 1600 years. Therefore, if 1 g of radium-226 were placed in a container in 1990, there would be only ½ g left after 1600 years (in the year 3590) and only ¼ g after another 1600 years (in the year 5190), and so on. Each radioisotope has its own characteristic half-life. The concept of half-life does not imply that after 1600 quiet years half of the radium will suddenly decompose. The half-life is an averaged value for all the radium nuclei. This means that there is a chance for some decompositions to occur in *any interval of time*. Since there are a great many atoms in a sample of radium, some will be decomposing every second, and any nearby Geiger counter (a device that responds to radiation) will be clicking all the time.

The rate at which the radiation is emitted from a sample of radium-226 depends on its quantity. Since each atom of radium-226 that decomposes is converted into another element (radon-222), the quantity of radium-226 in any sample constantly decreases. However, the radon it produces is also radioactive, and it, too, decomposes to produce another radioisotope. This series of radioactive disintegrations goes on through a number of "generations" until finally a stable isotope, lead-206, is produced. These radioisotopes have various half-lives, ranging from fractions of a second to about 20 years. Therefore, the total radioactivity produced by a sample of radium together with its radioactive waste products is more than that produced by the radium alone.

If nuclei of radioactive elements are unstable, why are there any left on Earth? The answer is that these survivors are descendants of radioisotopes with very long half-lives. The half-life of natural uranium-238, for example, is 4.5 billion years. The radiations from such materials plus the effect of radiation that comes to the Earth from outer space is called the **background radiation.**

The shorter the half-life, the more rapid the release of energy. Thus, for example, iodine-137, with a half life of 24 seconds, decays and releases its energy very rapidly. Uranium-238, on the other hand, with its very long half-life, decays and releases its energy very slowly. As an analogy, think of two logs of wood, one burning and the other rotting (both reactions are oxidations). The burning log is hot during its short lifetime; the rotting log decomposes over a long period but always remains cool.

We cannot invent anything to stop radioactivity. It slows down by radioactive decay at a rate determined by the half-lives of the radioisotopes involved.

14.6
$E = mc^2$

Let us return to the radioactive decay of radium-226, which emits an alpha particle. This emission, on an atomic scale, is not a gentle event; the alpha particle carries kinetic energy as it comes shooting out of the radium nucleus. There is another aspect of this decomposition that can be shown by rewriting the equation and including the accurate atomic weights, rather than the mass numbers which are only whole number approximations:

$$^{226.0254}_{88}Ra \longrightarrow ^{4.0026}_{2}He + ^{222.0175}_{86}Rn$$

The strange result is that the sum of the atomic weights of the products, 4.0026 + 222.0175 is 226.0201, which is *less* than 226.0254, the atomic weight of the starting material. This loss of 226.0254 − 226.0201, or 0.0053 units of atomic weight, seems to contradict the Law of Conservation of Mass. In 1905, Albert Einstein resolved this problem by showing that *mass and energy are different forms of the same property*. This equivalence is stated in the now-famous equation,

$$E = mc^2$$

where E is energy, m is the mass of the object, and c is the speed of light.

Thus, mass can be converted into energy, or energy into mass. The decrease of mass that accompanies the emission of an alpha particle from a nucleus of radium-226 is therefore not considered as a loss, but rather as a conversion of mass into energy.

The energy changes that accompany nuclear reactions are much greater than those involving chemical reactions—often about a million times greater. For example, the total energy evolved from the alpha emissions from 1 g of radium-226 is about the same as the energy generated by the burning of 44 thousand grams (63 liters, or about 17 gal) of gasoline. Even though radium decomposes slowly, it releases heat at a rate fast enough to maintain its temperature measurably above that of its surroundings. This fact dumbfounded scientists in the United States when Marie Curie first brought over a sample of her radium.

14.7
Nuclear Fission

Soon after the discovery of radioactivity, scientists began to wonder whether it would ever be possible to "unlock" the energy of the atom. It seemed hopeless, because there was no known particle that could be used to penetrate the nucleus. This barrier was removed when the neutron was discovered, in 1932. The idea that neutrons might be used to bombard and alter atomic nuclei was very exciting, because a neutron, which does not bear any charge, is not repelled by atomic nuclei and can therefore travel in a straight line until it hits one. If the neutron is absorbed by the nucleus, the ratio of neutrons to protons is changed, and so the stability of the nucleus is also changed.

In 1939 (the year that World War II started), three scientists, Otto Hahn, Fritz Strassman, and Lise Meitner, discovered that when a neutron hits and is captured by a uranium nucleus, the nucleus splits into two roughly equal fragments. This splitting is called **atomic fission** or **nuclear fission.** Further studies showed that the isotope undergoing fission is uranium-235, which makes up less than 1 percent of natural uranium. The abundant form, uranium-238, is not easily fissioned.*

---

*A uranium-238 nucleus can be split only by very energetic neutrons. For all practical purposes, uranium-238 does not undergo fission in nuclear reactors.

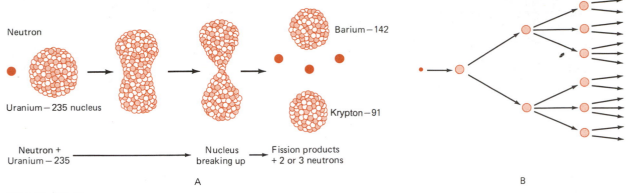

Figure 14–5

Nuclear fission. *A,* Schematic close-up view of the fission of a single uranium-235 nucleus. *B,* The principle of a chain reaction. Each fission reaction requires one neutron but releases two or three neutrons. If each released neutron strikes another fissionable nucleus, the reaction will accelerate rapidly. This is the principle of the atomic bomb. In a nuclear reactor, conditions are carefully controlled so that some neutrons escape or are absorbed without causing fission. Thus, the reaction proceeds at a steady, controlled rate.

It was also learned that extra neutrons were released in the fission reaction of uranium-235. If the reaction is *started* by neutrons and then also *releases* neutrons, a new possibility arises that is very different from natural radioactivity. It is the opportunity for a **chain reaction.** This discovery changed nuclear science from a study of purely theoretical interest to an issue of utmost importance to everyone.

A chain reaction is a series of steps that occur one after the other, in sequence, each step being added to the preceding step like the links in a chain. An example of a chemical chain reaction is a forest fire. The heat from one tree may initiate the reaction (burning) of a second tree, which, in turn, ignites a third, and so on. The fire will then go on at a steady rate. But if one burning tree ignites two other trees, and each of these two ignite two more trees, for a total of four trees, and so on, the rate of burning will speed up. Such an accelerating chain reaction is called a **branching chain reaction.** A chemical chain reaction that continues to branch can produce an explosion. The condition under which a chain reaction just continues at a steady rate, neither accelerating nor slowing down, is called the **critical condition.**

The production of the atomic (fission) bomb and the operation of nuclear reactors depends on branching nuclear chain reactions (Fig. 14–5). The process is initiated when one neutron strikes a uranium-235 nucleus and can proceed in a number of similar ways. For example, as shown in Figure 14–5, uranium-235 plus a neutron can produce barium-142 and krypton-91, while releasing three neutrons. In equation form:

$$^{235}_{92}U + {}^{1}_{0}n \longrightarrow {}^{142}_{56}Ba + {}^{91}_{36}Kr + 3\,{}^{1}_{0}n$$

Note the following important points about this equation:

1. The reaction is started by one neutron but produces three neutrons. These neutrons can initiate three new reactions, which, in turn, produce more neutrons, and so forth. This is, therefore, a branching chain reaction.

2. The uranium-235 nucleus is split roughly in half by these reactions and is therefore undergoing nuclear fission. The total mass of all the fission products is slightly less than the mass of the original uranium-238 atom. This loss of mass is converted to energy in accordance with the $E = mc^2$ relationship, as explained in Section 14.6. The energy is manifested mostly in the form of the kinetic energy of the fission products as they fly apart. These flying fragments then slow down as they hit other atoms and thus transfer their energy to the other atoms in random patterns. This is the way in which nuclear fission releases heat. As has been pointed out, the energies involved in nuclear transformations are much greater than those in chemical reactions. If the branching chain reaction continues very rapidly, energy is released at an accelerating rate, resulting in an atomic explosion.

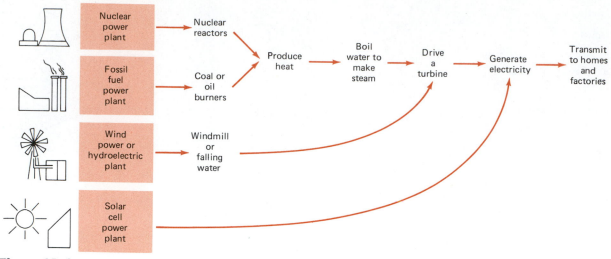

Figure 14–6
Different types of power plants use different systems to generate electricity.

If the chain branching is carefully controlled, energy can be released slowly for useful purposes.

3. Fission reactions produce radioactive wastes. Barium-142 and krypton-91, the products shown in the preceding equation, are both radioactive. Furthermore, the reaction represented by this equation is only one of many that occur in atomic fission. Many different radioisotopes are produced by atomic fission.

14.8
Nuclear Power Plants

Recall that the function of a central power plant is to generate electricity. Different kinds of power plants depend on different sources of the energy. A wind power or hydroelectric plant uses the mechanical energy of wind or falling water. A solar power plant generates electricity directly from solar cells. In a coal-fired plant, the energy is released from the chemical combustion of the coal. This energy is used to heat water and produce steam. The steam then drives a turbine, which, in turn, drives an electric generator. A nuclear power plant is similar to a coal-fired one in that heat is used to produce steam to drive a turbine (Fig. 14–6). The difference lies in the fact that in a nuclear plant, it is atomic fission, not chemical combustion, that provides the heat.

Nuclear fission reactors require fuel, and the fuel must be a substance whose nuclei can undergo fission. Such substances are said to be **fissionable,** or **fissile.** There are two significant nuclear fuels, uranium-235 and plutonium-239. These are not the only known fissile isotopes, but they are the ones on which the current nuclear reactors in the United States are based.

Uranium-235 occurs in nature, but it constitutes only 0.7 percent of natural uranium. The remaining 99.3 percent is the heavier isotope, uranium-238, only very little of which undergoes fission in a reactor.

The second fuel, plutonium-239, does not occur in nature; it is produced by the reaction of uranium-238 with neutrons. Thus, the two important naturally occurring sources of fission energy are uranium-235 (fissile, but not abundant) and uranium-238 (not fissile, but abundant, and convertible to plutonium-239).

Nuclear reactors require another essential ingredient in addition to fuel, namely, neutrons. In fact, the chain reaction is initiated by a source of neutrons. There are four possible events that can happen to a neutron in a reactor. The design and operation of reactors, as well as their safety, depend on how the neutrons are managed and controlled. The four possibilities are:

1. A neutron can be captured by a uranium-235 nucleus, which then undegoes fission. The reaction releases fast neutrons. However, fission is favored by slow neutrons. The fast neutrons can be slowed down by colliding with some other parti-

Figure 14–7

Schematic illustration of a nuclear plant powered by a pressurized water reactor.

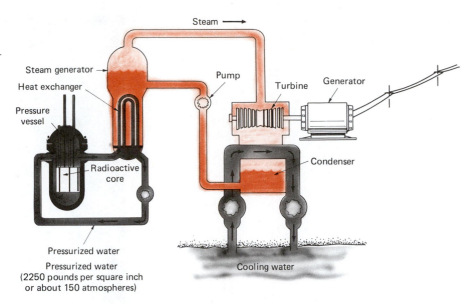

Steam →

Steam generator

Heat exchanger

Pressure vessel

Radioactive core

Pump

Turbine   Generator

Condenser

Pressurized water

Pressurized water
(2250 pounds per square inch
or about 150 atmospheres)

Cooling water

cles with which they can exchange energy of motion. The most effective particles are those with about the same mass as a neutron. As an analogy, a moving billiard ball is best slowed down by colliding with another billiard ball, not by hitting a dust particle, which will hardly affect it, or by hitting a boulder, from which it will bounce back. The particles closest in mass to neutrons are hydrogen nuclei, which is why water, H_2O, the most convenient source of hydrogen, is a good choice. A medium that slows down neutrons is called a neutron **moderator.**

2. A fast neutron can be captured by a uranium-238 nucleus. This capture is followed by the emission of two beta particles (electrons). The overall result is the production of plutonium-239, as represented by the following equation:

$$^{238}_{92}U + ^{1}_{0}n \longrightarrow ^{239}_{94}Pu + 2 ^{0}_{-1}electrons$$

Plutonium-239, in turn, can undergo fission. Thus, the production of plutonium is, in effect, a "breeding" of new fuel and is therefore attractive as a means of utilizing uranium resources more completely. The choice of whether or not to favor the breeding of plutonium determines, in large part, the design of the reactor.

3. A neutron can be captured by the nuclei of other elements. This causes loss of neutrons and slowing down, or "dampening" of the chain. The most direct method is to insert a neutron-absorbing element such as cadmium or boron directly into the spaces near the nuclear fuels. These neutron

absorbers are fabricated in the form of solid bars known as **control rods.**

4. A neutron, traveling as it does in a straight line, may simply miss the other nuclei in the reactor and *escape.* If reactors were very small, too many neutrons could escape and the chain reaction would not be sustained. This circumstance imposes lower limits on reactor size: There will never be pocket-sized fission generators, nor even fission engines for motorcycles. This escaping tendency also demands adequate shielding to prevent neutron leakage.

How, then, can a reactor be constructed to satisfy all these requirements? The first decision to be made is whether the reactor is to be designed only to generate energy from uranium-235 (a "non-breeder") or whether it is also to "breed" plutonium-239.

Non-Breeders

The heart of a nuclear plant is the reactor core, in which the essential components are (1) the nuclear fuel, (2) the moderator, (3) the coolant, and (4) the control rods (Figs. 14–7 to 14–9).

1. The *nuclear energy source* is the uranium-235 isotope, but, in pure form, it could serve as a nuclear explosive, not as a practical fuel. The uranium actually used is natural uranium, enriched up to 3 percent with fissionable uranium-235. Furthermore, the material used is not metallic uranium, but rather uranium dioxide. This compound is fab-

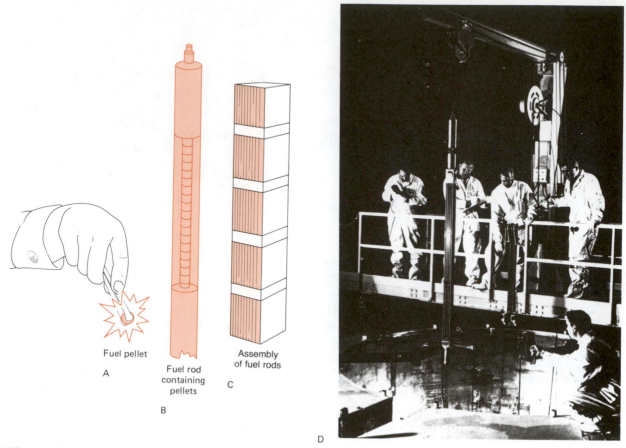

Figure 14–8

A, Fuel pellet; *B,* fuel rod; *C,* assembly of fuel rods; and *D,* fuel assembly being lowered into place in a reactor.

ricated in a ceramic form that is much better than the pure metal in its ability to retain most fission products, even when overheated. The fuel is inserted in the form of pellets into long, thin tubes, called the "fuel cladding," made of stainless steel or other alloys. These "fuel rods" are then bundled into assemblies that are inserted into the reactor core (Fig. 14–8).

2. The *moderator* serves to slow down the neutrons. As mentioned previously, fission is more efficient with slow neutrons, but the fission reaction releases fast neutrons, which must be slowed down to maintain an effective chain reaction. Water is very convenient for this purpose because it can also serve as the coolant. In the United States, almost all commercial reactors use ordinary, or "light," water, H_2O, in which the hydrogen atoms are the $_1^1H$ isotope. This is cheap but not ideal, because H_2O molecules do capture neutrons to some extent. The result of such capture is that natural uranium, which contains only 0.7 percent of uranium-235, cannot be used in light-water reactors. Instead, the concentration of uranium-235 must be enriched to about 3 percent to make up for the neutron loss to the coolant water.

3. When water is the moderator, it is also the *coolant.* In some designs, the coolant water actually boils, and the steam it produces drives the turbogenerators. (You may think it strange for boiling water to be a coolant, but heat always flows spontaneously from a higher to a lower temperature, and even boiling water is much cooler than a fire or a nuclear reactor core. The heat therefore flows from the reactor core to the boiling water.) In

Figure 14–9
Control-rod driving mechanism of a pressured water reactor, partially disassembled.

most of the commercial reactors in the United States, the water is kept under high pressure, as in a pressure cooker, and very little actual boiling occurs. This is the design shown in Figure 14–7. Note that the pressurized water flows through a heat exchanger, where it transfers its heat to a secondary loop of water that actually boils and delivers steam to the turbine.

4. Interspersed into the matrix of fuel, moderator, and coolant are the *control rods* (Fig. 14–9), which serve to regulate the flow of neutrons. A nuclear reactor that generates power at a constant rate must operate at a critical condition, with as many neutrons being produced as are lost by capture or escape. Since no design is that perfect, the control rods provide a means of fine-tuning the operation. But the control rods serve other important functions. Recall that the fission reaction produces impurities that absorb neutrons. Therefore, in the absence of any neutron regulation, the neutron flow would gradually slow down, and the fission reaction would die out before much fuel is exhausted. For this reason, there must be a provision to increase the neutron flow gradually during the life of the fuel to make up for the loss caused by the impurities. The way to do this is to design for an extra large neutron flow at the outset but to limit the actual flow by the control rods. As fuel is consumed, the control rods are gradually withdrawn to compensate for the accumulation of neutron-absorbing impurities. This amounts to a neat balancing of impurities to maintain steady power production. The other purpose of the control rods is to serve as an emergency shut-off system. If an emergency occurs and the fission reaction must be quenched, the rods are pushed rapidly all the way into the core.

Breeders

Recall that neutron capture by abundant uranium-238 can produce fissionable plutonium-239. This reaction makes it possible for one reactor to provide fuel for another. (Hence the reactors "breed.")

The design is determined by the following factors: The breeder reactor uses neutrons to maintain the fission reaction as well as for the breeding reaction; therefore, the breeder reactor needs more neutrons than the non-breeder reactor. A high yield of neutrons is realized when plutonium-239 captures *fast* neutrons—almost 3 neutrons (plus fission products) are produced for every one captured. But recall that fission is initiated more efficiently with *slow* neutrons, which means that a slow neutron has a better chance of being captured than a fast neutron. The neutron "game" with plutonium-239 can thus be represented as follows:

	Fast neutrons (no moderator)	Slow neutrons (moderator)
Yield when 1 neutron is captured	About 3 neutrons	About 2 neutrons
Chance of capturing a neutron	Poorer	Better

What choice can provide both a good chance of capturing a neutron and a good yield of neutrons from fission? The answer is to use a high concen-

tration of plutonium-239 and no moderator. The high concentration (about 15 percent instead of 3 percent) makes up for the poorer capture probability. The absence of a moderator keeps the neutrons fast and allows the plutonium to produce enough neutrons for breeding. The reactor core, then, is compact because no space is needed by a moderator. The other 85 percent of the core is uranium-238, which absorbs most of the excess neutrons to breed more plutonium. The neutrons that escape from this core are absorbed by a blanket of uranium-238. Thus, the overall concentrations of both the fertile and fissile materials in the breeder core are much greater than they are in a non-breeder.

The compactness of the breeder core demands a very rapid removal of heat. Water is disadvantageous because it is a neutron moderator, which must be avoided. Furthermore, water boils at relatively low temperatures, even under high pressures, and steam is a poor heat conductor. The coolant of choice is liquid sodium. Sodium is a silvery, soft, chemically active metal. Its drawbacks are that it reacts with water to produce hydrogen gas; if air is present, the heat of the reaction can trigger an explosion. Also, the sodium becomes highly radioactive when it is exposed to the reactor core. Its saving virtue is its ability to carry heat away from the reactor core rapidly, since it is an excellent heat conductor, and it remains in the liquid state over a very wide temperature range, from 98°C to 890°C at normal atmospheric pressure. The heat exchanger in which steam is produced to drive the turbine must be shielded from the radioactive sodium. This is accomplished by an intermediate loop of nonradioactive sodium. The entire arrangement is shown schematically in Figure 14–10. A more detailed illustration of a breeder reactor is given in Figure 14–11.

Are breeder reactors, then, an attractive energy source for the near future, the distant future, or never? The issue involves uncertainties in both cost and safety. When breeder reactors were first considered, the known uranium resources in the United States were small and the anticipated demand for nuclear energy was high. (Remember that only about 0.7 percent of natural uranium is fissile.) Accordingly, it was assumed that breeders would be necessary and that their development would lead to an abundant supply of energy far into the future. However, the world's uranium resources at the end of the 1980s are now thought to

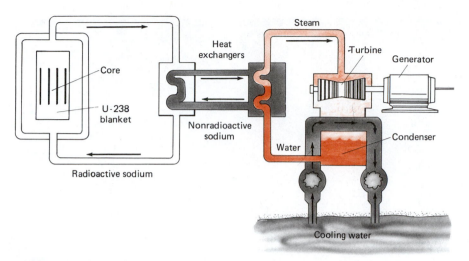

Figure 14–10
Schematic diagram of a fast breeder reactor.

be about 6 million tonnes, which is about a thousand times greater than the earlier estimates. Under these circumstances, the present rate of generation of nuclear power could be maintained for about 100 years without resorting to breeder reactors. With breeders, which use the abundant uranium-238 and could justify its extraction from much lower grade ores (such as ordinary granite rock), nuclear energy would be available into the far distant future.

The cost of building a breeder reactor, even if all goes well, is significantly greater than that for a non-breeder, and the greater complexity of the breeder leads to higher costs. It can be argued that the eventual independence of imported fuels is attractive for countries such as Japan and France, but this is not the case for the United States, with its abundant supply of coal.

We now turn our attention to the issues of health and safety.

14.9
Safety and Hazards in Nuclear Plants

Questions about safety and hazards are at the heart of the nuclear controversy. It will be helpful, in approaching this very complex issue, to itemize the five basic principles of safe practice that apply to any industry. The applications of these principles in nuclear plants will then be described in more detail.

1. *Safe operation must be part of the original design.*

2. *There should be back-up or duplicating systems that will take over in cases of failure.* This approach is usually called **redundancy.**

3. *There should be a system for warning* of possible accident if something starts to go wrong.

4. *A schedule of inspection and maintenance by trained operators* should be provided.

5. Finally, if all these systems fail and an accident does occur, the design should *provide features that prevent or minimize injury to people.* These are called "fail-safe" features.

Safe Design   Recall that in a non-breeder reactor the uranium-238 is only modestly enriched with the fissile uranium-235, so that the fuel cannot explode like an atomic bomb. If the electric power fails or if the reactor starts overheating, the control rods are automatically forced into the core by means of spring action, hydraulic pressure, or gravity. The chain reaction then stops. Ordinary water is both a coolant and a moderator. If excess heat boils away the water, the loss of moderator would also stop the chain reaction. Design specifications require that the materials of construction be of the highest engineering quality and be fully tested before use. The breeder reactor is inherently more dangerous, but this means only that safe design is, if anything, even more critical.

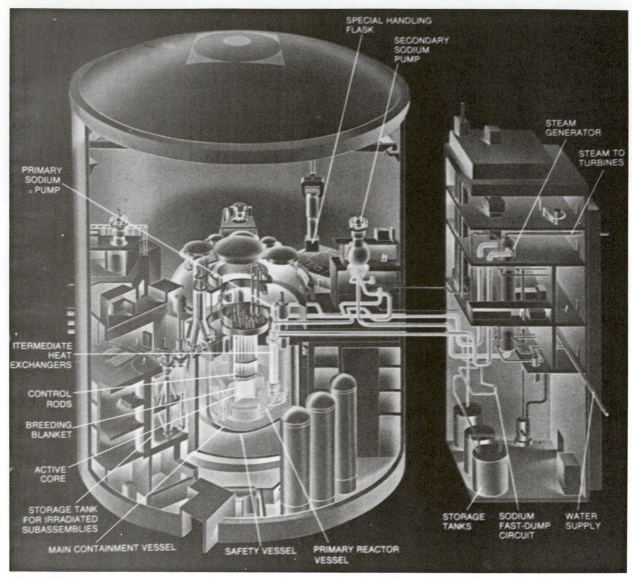

Figure 14–11

A vertical section of the French Superphenix reactor building and one of the four identical steam-generating buildings show the main operating components of the plant. Superphenix is classified as a pool-type breeder reactor, which means that the active core, the primary sodium pumps, and the intermediate heat exchangers are all located within a single large vessel. In this particular design, the main steel containment vessel, which is hung from a steel-and-concrete upper slab, is 21 m across and is filled with 3300 tons of molten sodium. A cylindrical structure welded to the main vessel supports the control-rod mechanisms and the fuel subassemblies, which constitute the active core of the reactor. The four primary pumps convey the sodium upward through the core. The primary reactor vessel separates the "cold" sodium, which enters at the bottom of the subassemblies at a temperature of 395°C, from the "hot" sodium, which leaves at the top at 545°C. The hot sodium then flows downward through the eight intermediate heat exchangers, which form part of a secondary circuit of nonradioactive sodium, inserted for reasons of safety between the primary sodium circuit and the water-steam circuit. Each of four secondary loops consists of two intermediate heat exchangers, a secondary pump installed inside a spherical expansion tank, and a steam generator in the adjacent building. (From George A. Vendryes: Superphenix: A full-scale breeder reactor. *Scientific American*, March, 1977, p. 28. Copyright 1977 by Scientific American, Inc. All rights reserved. Drawing by George V. Kelvin)

Figure 14–12
Control room of a nuclear power plant.

Redundancy   The system for which a back-up is most important is the one that cools the reactor core. If that fails, there are generally at least two other independent cooling systems. If the power system on which the emergency measures depend fails, an off-site source of power can be used. If that fails, on-site diesel generators or gas turbines can take over. Secondary systems of this type are quite complex and are interrelated in such a way that their responses are specifically appropriate to the nature of the emergency. Furthermore, these responses are fully automatic; they do not have to be initiated by a human operator.

Warning   The control room of a nuclear plant displays a panorama of gauges, dials, lights, and buzzers (Fig. 14–12). Individual workers are supplied with badges that are sensitive to radiation and that monitor the degree to which the wearer has been exposed. Detection devices are distributed throughout the plant and are also set outdoors at various distances from the plant.

Inspection and Maintenance   Reactor operators must go through strict licensing procedures with periodic renewal. The plants themselves are inspected several times each year, penalties are applied to violators of regulations, and listings are kept of any defects or failures.

Protection in the Event of Accident   The reactor vessel, made of thick steel, is itself surrounded by an anti-radiation shield several feet thick. As a final barrier, the entire system is surrounded by a vapor-proof, steel-lined, reinforced concrete **containment structure** (Fig. 14–13). This barrier is designed to withstand earthquakes and hurricanes and to contain all matter that might be released inside, even if the biggest primary piping system in the reactor were to shatter instantaneously. Not all containments are alike, however; some of the older ones are less elaborate than the most advanced designs. Nuclear plants in the Soviet Union and some other countries do not always have this last barrier, which is a fact that nuclear

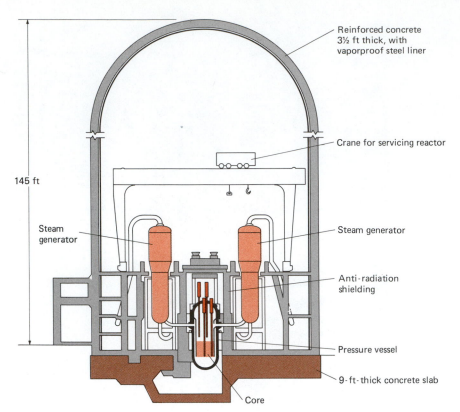

145 ft

Reinforced concrete
3½ ft thick, with
vaporproof steel liner

Crane for servicing reactor

Steam
generator

Steam generator

Anti-radiation
shielding

Pressure vessel

9-ft-thick concrete slab

Core

Figure 14–13
Containment structure for a nuclear power plant.

proponents have cited to emphasize the high priority given to safety in the United States.

All these safety features are necessary and proper but are not a guarantee against accidents.

Six sets of questions must be discussed in assessing the environmental hazards associated with nuclear fission plants: (1) What are the chances and consequences of a serious accident? (2) What are the extent and the environmental effects of the routine emissions of radioactive materials under normal conditions of operation? (3) What are the dangers of terrorism and sabotage? (4) What are the environmental effects of the waste heat released from the nuclear plants? (5) What are the problems associated with the disposal of radioactive wastes? (6) What is to be done with old nuclear power plants at the end of their useful lifetimes?

The effect of waste heat (thermal pollution) will be taken up in Chapter 15 and therefore will not be discussed in this section.

14.10
The Chance of a Serious Accident

The nightmare of the nuclear safety engineer is the possible overheating of the reactor core. If this were to happen, the reactor vessel could melt, and the molten mixture of fuel and fission products might spread out and possibly escape to the environment. Such a disaster would be the result of a series of accidents, each of which has its own probability of occurring. To analyze the overall danger, therefore, it is necessary to consider each event in the series separately and to judge how these events might influence each other.

Imagine, first, that a pipe carrying cooling water to the reactor bursts. Since the water is also the neutron moderator, the fission reactions in the core would slow down. However, there is another source of heat in the reactor that cannot be controlled—the energy released by the radioactivity of

Special Topic A
Atomic Bombs

An explosion develops a sudden pressure on its surroundings by the rapid production of gas and by the further expansion of the gas as the explosive energy heats it. Chemical explosives produce gases very rapidly by the decomposition of their molecules. This effect is called a **blast.** If a stick of dynamite explodes several hundred feet from you, the blast effect feels like a thump on your chest.

The main chemical high explosives of modern warfare have been TNT (trinitrotoluene), picric acid, and cyclonite (the explosive ingredient of "plastic explosive"). Nitroglycerin is the major explosive ingredient of dynamite, used mainly for blasting in construction and mining. The heaviest chemical bombs dropped by aircraft in World War II (the "blockbusters") contained about a tonne (1000 kg) of high explosive.

The nuclear explosive in an atomic (fission) bomb is pure or highly concentrated fissile material: uranium-235 or plutonium-239. Such a material leaves only two significant fates for neutrons—fission capture or escape. The factor that determines which of these two fates will predominate is size, or mass, of the fissile material. If a chunk of, say, plutonium is too small, most of the neutrons will escape and the reaction will not sustain itself. The minimum mass required to support a self-sustaining chain reaction is called the **critical mass.** To set off an atomic bomb, therefore, subcritical masses of uranium-235 or plutonium-239 are slammed together, with a neutron source at the center, by precisely shaped chemical high explosives to make a supercritical mass. The chain reaction instantly branches, and the mass explodes.

A hydrogen (fusion) bomb derives the major portion of its energy from a nuclear fusion reaction (see Section 14.12). The most powerful bombs ever exploded have been hydrogen bombs in tests, not in warfare.

The explosive effect of a fission or fusion bomb is rated in terms of its TNT equivalent. Thus, a "1-megaton" bomb is a nuclear bomb that is equivalent to 1 megaton (1 million tonnes, which is 10^9 kg or about 2.2 billion lb) of TNT. This equivalence, however, refers only to the blast effect. Nuclear bombs have other consequences that are not produced by chemical high explosives. These other nuclear effects include extremely high temperatures that start fires at considerable distances, prompt radiation, radioactive fallout with delayed radiation, electromagnetic pulses that can knock out electronic systems, and climatic changes. (See discussion of "nuclear winter" in Section 21.7.)

The question is sometimes asked, "Can a nuclear reactor explode like an atomic bomb?" The answer is no, it cannot, because the fuel in a nuclear reactor does not contain concentrations of fissile isotopes that approach the levels of bomb-grade material. The explosion at Chernobyl was a hydrogen-oxygen chemical explosion, not a nuclear one.

---

the accumulated fission products. It has been predicted that if all cooling systems failed, parts of the reactor would heat up to 1480°C in about 45 seconds, at which temperature water would react with the metal surrounding the fuel to release hydrogen gas, which can explode in air.

To prevent such an occurrence, an **emergency core cooling system** automatically introduces another stream of water. Even if this works as expected, large quantities of water and steam carrying radioactivity will still spray out of the reactor at high pressure. The containment structure is designed to prevent any of this material from escaping to the outside. However, if the emergency cooling system fails to operate—or if it fails to hold the reactor below the 1480°C danger point—the fuel rods may buckle or even break and thus block the passage of water. In such an event, the temperature would continue to rise until, in about half an hour, the fuel would melt. Within a few hours, the hot liquid fuel would melt other materials in contact with it and thus continue to melt its way right into the ground. (This scenario is sometime jokingly called the **China Syndrome,** meaning that the molten mass is moving toward the other side of the globe.) Large quantities of radioactive matter might be released from the ground to the air, to subsurface water, or, if the containment structure itself failed, directly from the reactor core to the atmosphere.

What, then, are the chances that such a series of accidents, leading to a disaster, could occur? It is possible to survey places where industrial pipes have been in service for many years and to find out how many *have* burst. Furthermore, radiation can make metals more brittle and hence more liable to failure. Such information may then be used as a basis for calculating the chance of a loss-of-cooling accident in a nuclear plant. Remember, however, that such an accident triggers the emergency core cooling system, and that, too, would have to fail before a catastrophe could occur. Again, one can obtain a history of failures of pipes, valves, motors, and monitoring instruments (they are all susceptible) and, in like manner, apply the results to the nuclear reactor. Finally, if a radioactive cloud did escape, where would it go? Local weather records can be used to calculate the chances that the wind would blow the cloud toward populated areas, or that the cloud would be washed down by rain, and so on.

If you were to represent such possible sequences by a chart, you might start with a notation such as "pipe carrying cooling water bursts." You could then draw two lines from this notation, one leading to the statement, "Emergency cooling system works," the other to the statement "Emergency cooling system fails." You could continue with more branches leading to the various possibilities in the sequence, and, as your chart continued to grow, its appearance would explain why such an exercise is called a "fault-tree analysis." Every line leading from one possible event to another might carry a number showing the estimated probability that the second event could follow from the first. The probability of going from one portion of the "tree" to another is then calculated by multiplying all the probabilities between them.

Many estimates of nuclear safety have been based on just such an approach. One set of estimates, released by the Nuclear Regulatory Commission (NRC) in 1975, led to the conclusion that the risks of serious nuclear accidents are extremely small, so small, in fact, that no such accident could realistically be expected to happen. Opponents of nuclear power rejected this conclusion on two main grounds: (1) "Fault-tree" analysis assumes that the various possible events are independent of each other. This assumption is the basis for *multiplying* the various probabilities and is the reason why the probability of a *sequence* of events turns out to be very small. (The probabilities are always less than 1, and, as they continue to be multiplied, the product continues to become smaller and smaller.) Different events, however, are not always independent. On the contrary, two or more accidents may result from the same cause, as would happen if a flying object under a car made the brake fluid leak out and also severed the emergency brake cable. Also, accidents may trigger each other, as when a collision between two cars leads to a pile-up of many cars that follow. (2) An analyst may think of many possible accidents and take them all into account in a calculation, but no analyst can think of them *all*. Many unanticipated events may be very improbable, but their number is unlimited. We all know that weird, unimagined, events happen frequently. They have certainly happened in nuclear plants.

14.11
"Routine" Radioactive Emissions

Even with the best design and with accident-free operation, a small amount of radioactivity is routinely released to the air and water outside the plant. In the boiling-water reactor, for example, the water passes directly through the reactor core and thus circulates around the fuel elements. Some of the fuel claddings, which are very thin (about 0.05 cm), inevitably develop small leaks, which permit direct transfer of radioactive fission products to the water. Even in the absence of leaks, however, some neutrons get through to the water and generate some radioactivity, and this effect, too, is a source of "routine" emissions to the watercourses that serve as the ultimate coolants for the power plant.

Radioactive material can also be gaseous. Krypton-85, for example, is a radioactive fission product (half-life, 11 years) that is insoluble in water and escapes to the atmosphere through a tall stack. These emissions, taken together, are so small that their effect may be compared with the background radiation from cosmic rays and from naturally radioactive materials in the Earth's crust to which all life is subject. Supporters of the nuclear industry point out that the practical alternative to nuclear power is coal-fired generation of electricity and that coal contains small amounts of radioactive matter. When coal is burned, these radioactive materials are released. In fact, higher lev-

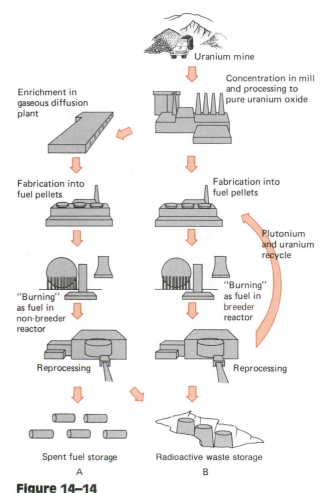

Enrichment in gaseous diffusion plant

Uranium mine

Concentration in mill and processing to pure uranium oxide

Fabrication into fuel pellets

Fabrication into fuel pellets

Plutonium and uranium recycle

"Burning" as fuel in non-breeder reactor

"Burning" as fuel in breeder reactor

Reprocessing

Reprocessing

Spent fuel storage
A

Radioactive waste storage
B

Figure 14–14

Nuclear fuel cycles. *Left,* once-through uranium cycle; *right,* plutonium cycle.

els of radioactivity can be found in the emissions from the stacks of some coal-fired plants than from nuclear plants. This finding is often cited to support the contention that the routine radioactive emissions from nuclear plants are trivial.

14.12
Terrorism and Sabotage

Uranium and plutonium inventories are not always fully accounted for. There are documented cases of substantial quantities of missing materials. Such discrepancies may not be real but may be only the results of errors in bookkeeping. Nevertheless, the question remains, "Can fissionable materials be stolen, and, if so, can amateurs convert them into

bombs?" A related question is, "Can saboteurs damage nuclear power plants so that radioactive matter is released to the environment?" Some writers have speculated on this question; some physics majors have written term papers on how to make a bomb (but they didn't make one); and some terrorist acts have actually been threatened and attempted. All these circumstances have led to increased security measures around nuclear installations. Since our past experience, fortunately, is so limited, we can only guess at the possibilities.

14.13
The Disposal of Radioactive Wastes

The movement of radioactive matter from the mine through various processes to ultimate disposal could follow either of two different sequences, sometimes called the "nuclear fuel cycles." The first sequence applies to non-breeder reactors and can also be characterized as a "once-through" process rather than a cycle (although the wastes do eventually return to the Earth). The second sequence applies to breeder reactors, which may or may not represent the nuclear economy of the future. At the present time (1988), however, there is no commercial U.S. breeder program and, therefore, no commercial plutonium recovery. Both cycles are illustrated in Figure 14–14, and the uranium cycle is further described below.

The "Once-Through" Uranium Cycle

Uranium ore is mined in various areas of the Earth as a black deposit containing perhaps 0.3 percent uranium. It is concentrated and then converted to a brilliant orange oxide, UO_3. (Some American homes contain old orange-colored kitchen pottery prepared from this uranium oxide pigment. Get them out of your kitchen and donate them to the nearest university!)

The next step is **enrichment,** which increases the concentration of the fissionable uranium-235 isotope. The enrichment process is very complex and costly to operate, and few countries have the technology and resources to do it. The enriched material is reconverted to an oxide and fabricated into the fuel pellets used by the power plant.

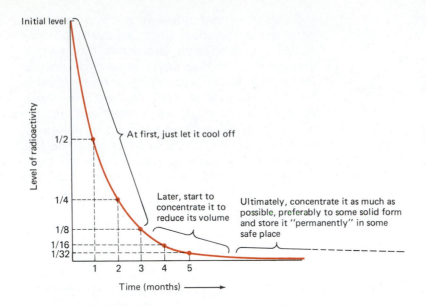

At first, just let it cool off

Later, start to concentrate it to reduce its volume

Ultimately, concentrate it as much as possible, preferably to some solid form and store it "permanently" in some safe place

Figure 14–15
Disposal procedures for a hypothetical radioactive waste product with a 1-month half-life.

Overall Strategy for Handling Wastes

After a year or more in a reactor, an appreciable portion of the uranium-235 is consumed, and fission products have accumulated. When the fuel is no longer useful in the reactor, the entire assembly, containing unused uranium, newly formed plutonium, and waste products, is removed. At this time, the waste products are in their most intensely radioactive state, since many of them have short half-lives. The decay curve of a hypothetical isotope with a half-life of 1 month is shown in Figure 14–15.

The handling of radioactive wastes involves a sequence of three steps: First, the spent rods are held underwater in cooling ponds for several months to allow the initial, very intense, radioactivity to die down. Second, the wastes must be "reprocessed" to convert them into a form suitable for the final step. Third and (it is hoped) last, the reprocessed wastes must be "permanently" stored somewhere. Reprocessing and final storage are discussed below.

Reprocessing The spent fuel rods are first dissolved in strong acid. The resulting solution is hot, radioactive (the radioactivity keeps the temperature up), and corrosive. Figure 14–16 illustrates storage tanks for such liquids used for the nuclear weapons program.

The dissolved wastes must next be chemically separated. Remember that some uranium and plutonium remain in the spent fuel. These elements could be recovered and reused. The uranium, from which much of the uranium-235 isotope has been used up, would have to be recycled for enrichment, but, at present, this process is more expensive than simply mining new uranium ores. Some of the radioisotopes that have special applications in science, medicine, or industry could also be extracted and set aside for such uses. Consider, for example, a 1000-megawatt nuclear plant using uranium fuel enriched to 3.3 percent uranium-235. Such a plant will use about 28 tonnes of fuel per year and will produce 28 tonnes of waste fuel, as shown in Figure 14–17. A crucial aspect of the problem involves the decision whether to recover the uranium and plutonium or to dispose of them. Plutonium presents a particular danger because it is intensely carcinogenic, and because, if stolen, it can be used to make illicit fission bombs. If the process were completed, plutonium could be separated for possible future use in reactors.

The technical aspects of reprocessing are not theoretically difficult, but the commercial experience in the United States has not been good. The first such reprocessing plant, near Buffalo, New York, opened in 1963 but was closed in 1972 when reprocessing was determined to be economically unfeasible. However, reprocessing plants are operating in France, England, Japan, and India, and pilot plants have been built in West Germany, Italy, and Belgium.

Figure 14–16
Three one-million-gallon capacity, double-shell tanks (shown during construction) were completed in the spring of 1977 and tied into Hanford waste management operations. After completion, the tanks were covered with a minimum of 6 to 7 ft of soil. The tanks use the latest monitoring and leak detection equipment and are linked by computer to the integrated tank surveillance system. Despite the precautions, however, leaks have occurred at the Hanford storage facility.

Final Disposal   The final step concerns safe, "permanent" storage. How long is permanent? It has been suggested, as a reasonable target, that the wastes should be reduced to the same radioactivity level as that of a natural uranium mine. (Not everyone would consider that sufficient; uranium mining is a contributing cause of lung cancer.) If that target is accepted, the time needed for "permanent" storage depends on whether reprocessing is done. If the uranium and plutonium are removed, only the fission products need to be permanently stored. These wastes decay more rapidly and would reach the radioactivity level of a uranium mine in about

500 years. If unreprocessed spent fuel is to be stored, it is estimated that about 7000 years would be necessary. There have been various suggestions for storage places: deep in the sediments under the ocean floor, under the Antarctic ice cap, or even in outer space. All major current effort, however, is devoted to developing underground, geologically stable, waste sites. At present, several different types of rock formation have been proposed, including salt mines (Fig. 14–18), desert sandstones, and granite or basalt formations. Various types of impervious containers have been designed. After the container is sealed in the rock, it continues to

Figure 14–17
Conversion of uranium fuel in a 1000-megawatt reactor operating at 62 percent capacity, in tonnes per year. (Data from B. J. Skinner and C. A. Walker: *American Scientist, 70*:180, 1982)

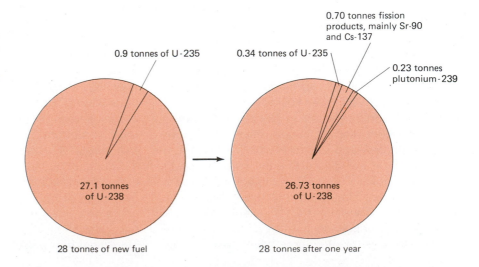

0.9 tonnes of U-235

27.1 tonnes of U-238

28 tonnes of new fuel

0.70 tonnes fission products, mainly Sr-90 and Cs-137

0.34 tonnes of U-235

0.23 tonnes plutonium-239

26.73 tonnes of U-238

28 tonnes after one year

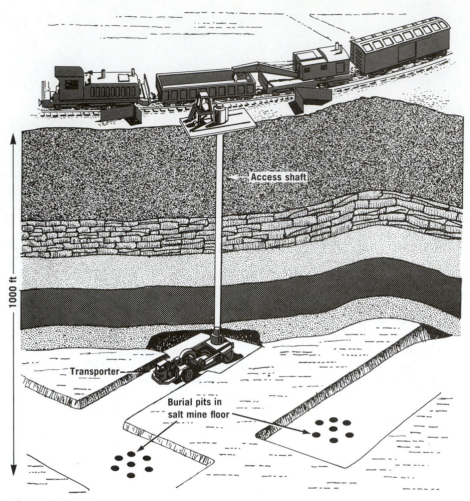

Figure 14–18
Final disposal of radioactive wastes in a salt mine.

give off heat from its radioactivity. Its temperature, and that of the surrounding rock, remain elevated for about a thousand years. There are two ways in which the radioactive waste could get out: It could be physically exposed (by geological or human activities), or it could be carried out by groundwater. The risks of damage to the host rock by the evolved heat, of erosion by streams or glaciers, of transport by groundwater, and of human intervention have all been studied, and scientists who work on these problems have concluded that the risks are small and acceptable. Critics of the nuclear program have disagreed. They point out that political systems, on which we depend for reliable continuity of any public policy, do not last as long as radioactive isotopes. Furthermore, the assumptions

about the permanent segregation of the radioactive containers in salt caverns or rock formations are not proved; they are only predictions.

One other matter regarding the ultimate disposal of reprocessed high-level wastes is the total quantity involved. By comparison with various other wastes, the volume is not large. For example, accumulations of wastes from mining ("mine spoil") and from domestic garbage look like mountain ranges. By contrast, it has been estimated that the volume of high-level radioactive wastes produced by all commercial nuclear power plants in the United States by the year 2000, if concentrated and reprocessed into glassy solids, would make a pile only about 4 m high on one football field. Translated to a personal basis, that would mean a cube about 4.5 cm on each side, a convenient size for a paperweight, for every man, woman, and child in the United States. (But you wouldn't want your cube!) These figures do not mean that the problems described here are trivial. Rather, they are presented to show that it is not the ultimate volume of the wastes, but rather their radioactivity, that is the problem.

Also, a large variety (and large volume) of low-level radioactive waste is generated by activities related to nuclear medicine from physicians, hospitals, and pharmaceutical manufacturers. These wastes must be disposed of somewhere, but many communities want to make sure that it is somewhere else. As of 1987, there were only three such low-level disposal sites in the United States (Barnwell, South Carolina; Hanford, Washington; and Beatty, Nevada), but additional sites are expected to be approved in the near future.

Decommissioning

A nuclear power plant itself has only a finite lifetime. After about 30 or 40 years, unavoidable deterioration progresses to a point at which the facility can no longer be used. This aging results in part from the buildup of radioactivity in the plant to dangerous levels. Some of this radiation comes from the effect of escaping neutrons that are captured by various atoms in the steel and concrete surrounding the reactor core. The atoms may thus be converted to radioactive isotopes—a process called **neutron activation.** In addition, various materials may become embrittled or otherwise weakened by such processes. Workers who confront a closed nuclear plant are faced with a maze of contaminated piping and equipment, as well as with radioactive matter coating many of the concrete surfaces. The first step in decommissioning such a plant involves removing the spent fuel rods, draining out all the coolants and other liquids, and flushing out the pipes to rinse out any residues. All of this material must be disposed of safely, so it is important to control the volumes of rinsewater. Those steps are only the beginning, however. Now comes the difficult part—doing something with the entire plant. There are three possible approaches: (1) Continue to decontaminate the plant as much as possible by mechanical and chemical scrubbing methods, then disassemble and cut up all the parts and ship them to a burial ground. (2) "Mothball"

the plant, that is, do nothing but monitor the radioactivity levels. Then disassemble it when most of the short-lived radioisotopes have decayed, which will be about 50 years from now. (3) Convert it to a tomb by covering it with concrete and erecting barriers to keep people out.

The entombment option is considered to be a poor one, because the concrete would deteriorate before the radioistopes would decay. (However, entombment was used in Chernobyl.) Mothballing for later removal is the most likely choice, because it is the least expensive at the outset. However, the major economic and political burdens will fall unfairly on others.

14.14
Case Histories: Accidents at Nuclear Power Plants

The introduction to this chapter referred to accidents at the Browns Ferry Nuclear Power Plant, at Three Mile Island, and at Chernobyl. The first incident has been largely forgotten by the general public, and even the second is beginning to recede from memory. Since the estimates of risks from nuclear power are based to a great extent on untested assumptions (called "guesses" in plain English), it is at least interesting to review real rather than imaginary malfunctions.

1975—The Incident at Browns Ferry

The Browns Ferry Nuclear Power Plant was constructed by the Tennessee Valley Authority (TVA) as a prototype for future U.S. power production. Browns Ferry is a complex of three nuclear reactors, located on the red clay banks of the Tennessee River near Decatur, Alabama. It went into operation on August 1, 1974, and was eventually to supply electricity for the needs of about 2 million people.

At noon on March 22, 1975, Reactors 1 and 2 were operating at full power, delivering 2200 megawatts of electricity. Just below the control room, an electrician and his engineering aide were engaged in some post-construction modifications of the plant. They were in a space called the "cable spreading room," which is where electrical cables come together from various parts of the plant and are then separated, or spread, and routed through different tunnels to the reactors. The mission of the men was simple enough—to plug air leaks where the cables passed through a wall into the reactor building. It is not very difficult to detect air movements; ventilating and air-conditioning workers do it all the time. Since air is invisible, the method is simply to introduce something visible into the air stream, such as a puff of smoke. At Browns Ferry, the two men were using candles! One of the cable pass-throughs was a bit too high for the electrician to reach. His 20-year-old aide, Larry Hargett, who had long arms, volunteered. This was a technical violation, because Hargett was new and untrained and his official function was merely to check that the electrician tested each pass-through. What happened next is described in Hargett's own words:

> We found a 2 × 4 inch opening in a penetration window in a tray with three of four cables going through it. The candle flame was pulled out horizontal, showing a strong draft. [The electrician] tore off two pieces of foam sheet for packing into the hole. I rechecked the hole with the candle. The draft sucked the flame into the hole and ignited the foam, which started to smolder and glow. [The electrician] handed me his flashlight with which I tried to knock out the fire. This did not work, and then I tried to smother the fire with rags stuffed in the hole. This also did not work, and we removed the rags. Someone passed me a CO_2 extinguisher with a horn which blew right through the hole without putting out the fire, which had gotten back into the wall. I then used a dry chemical extinguisher, and then another, neither of which put out the fire.

The fire continued to spread for several hours and was eventually put out by the local fire department. Although the control systems behaved erratically, there was no meltdown, and the shutdown of the two reactors was completed by the next morning. The important lesson from this incident was that events that are too weird to be considered in calculations of the probabilities of accidents happen anyway.

1979—Three Mile Island

The Three Mile Island nuclear plant in Middletown, Pennsylvania, is a subsidiary of the General Utilities Corporation. Starting at 4 A.M. on March 28, 1979, a series of mishaps occurred. The sequence is enormously complicated; approximately 40 different events have been identified during the subsequent investigations.

The operation that seems to have started the trouble was a routine one, the change of a batch of water purifier in a piping system. For a nuclear plant, this job is considered to be as routine as, say, changing the oil filter in an automobile. But a problem developed; some air got into the pipe, causing an interruption in the flow of water. Of course, the back-up systems in a nuclear plant are designed to respond automatically to such an event, but, in this instance, several other things went wrong:

- Two spare feedwater pumps were supposed to be ready to operate at all times. However, the valves that control the water from these pumps were out of service for routine maintenance; therefore, the spare pumps could not deliver water. The controls for these valves were provided with tags to indicate that they were being repaired. The tags hung down over red indicator lights that go on when the spare pumps are not feeding water. Since the lights were obscured by the tags, the operators did not see that they were lit and did not realize that no water was flowing.
- As a result, pressure built up in the reactor core. A relief valve in the primary coolant loop then opened automatically (as it should have) to let out superheated steam. But the relief valve failed to close, causing a dangerous drop in pressure. This malfunction is considered to be the crucial failure of equipment in the entire sequence.
- When the emergency core cooling system came on automatically, the pressure gauges in the control room gave a false reading, leading operators to think that the water level was still above the fuel rods. It wasn't. Instead, bubbles of gas from below were pushing the water up, leaving part of the core exposed.
- The primary and emergency cooling pumps, which should have been left on, were turned off twice by operators misled by the faulty pressure gauges.

The net result of this confusing series of mishaps or errors was that the nuclear core overheated. The temperatures inside the reactor vessel climbed off the recorder charts. For 13½ hours, the situation was very unclear.

The "void" or "bubble" that caused the problem was something entirely unexpected—it was a 28,000 liter (1000 cu ft) volume of steam and hydrogen gas. The plant management as well as the federal regulators were utterly unprepared for this possibility. Where did the hydrogen come from? There were two possibilities, both of which probably played a part. One was radiolysis, which is a chemical change produced by radiation. In other words, the radioactivity in the core chemically decomposed the water and produced hydrogen (as well as oxygen). The other possibility was the chemical reaction of water with metals, which also produces hydrogen (but not oxygen). The metal tubes holding the uranium fuel are made of zirconium, which reacts with water when the temperature gets high enough.

The net result of this confusion, in the words of Roger J. Mattson, director of the Division of Systems Safety, was that "We saw failure modes the likes of which have never been analyzed."

The situation was finally brought under control. The fuel rods had cracked, and the pieces had fallen onto the floor of the pressure vessel, but there was no meltdown. The complete cleanup, however, has been a major and continuing problem.

1986—Chernobyl

On Monday morning, April 28, 1986, a worker at a nuclear power plant in Sweden walked past a radiation detector and set off its alarm. Radioactive dust was found on his shoes, but there was nothing wrong at the Swedish plant. Monitoring stations in other parts of the country were also showing abnormally high radiation levels. Analysis of the radioactive fallout showed that it contained isotopes of krypton, iodine, cesium, and other elements that are common among fission products from a nuclear reactor. The wind indicated that the source was in the Soviet Union, and that night a Russian news broadcast acknowledged that an accident had occurred at the Chernobyl Nuclear Power Plant.

The Chernobyl reactor uses graphite (a form of carbon) as a moderator and boiling water as a coolant. The graphite consists of massive blocks honeycombed with three sets of holes: one for the fuel rods, another for the control rods, and a third for the boiling water. The response of a graphite-moderated plant to a loss of coolant water is different from that of the light-water plants such as those in North America and Western Europe, in the following way:

- In the light-water plants, water serves as both coolant and moderator. Remember that the function of the moderator is to slow down the neutrons so that the fission reaction proceeds more efficiently. If most of the water boils off, there is less moderator and the fission reaction becomes less efficient and slows down.
- In the graphite plant, the water is not needed as a moderator, so its loss does not slow down the fission reaction. But water does absorb some neutrons, so when it boils away these extra neutrons acutally *increase* the fission reaction.

Here, then, is what happened:

- 1 A.M., April 25, 1986: The operators at the Chernobyl plant began to reduce the reactor power. This was to have been a routine safety test of a type that had been carried out before.
- 2 P.M., same day: The emergency core cooling system was disconnected to keep it from interfering with the test. However, the city of Chernobyl needed power that evening, so the test was put on hold, with the emergency cooling system still off.
- 11:10 P.M., that night: Power reduction was resumed. The object was to reduce the power from its maximal level of 3200 megawatts down to about 850 megawatts. However, the reactor was difficult to control, and the power went all the way down to 30 megawatts. To get the power back up, the operators started to withdraw the control rods.
- 1:22 A.M., April 26: Effectively, about 204 of the 211 control rods had been withdrawn. The power level was ready for the test, but the reactor was in a very unstable condition.
- 1:23 A.M.: The test was started, but it lasted only 40 seconds. The power surged out of control. The fuel was shattered into red-hot fragments, which flashed the water into steam, which reacted with the metal fuel cladding to produce hydrogen and at the same time blasted a hole through the concrete above the reactor. The hole let air in, and, in about 3 seconds, the hydrogen mixed with the air and exploded. The explosion showered the surroundings with blazing core material, starting about 30 fires. The graphite,

too, started to burn and continued to burn for some time. The radioactive matter carried up by the blasts and the fires entered the atmosphere and went where the winds carried it.

The Chernobyl debris included many long-lived isotopes, which will be dangerously radioactive for decades. The local area and many materials, including foodstuffs, were heavily contaminated. About 135,000 people were evacuated from the area within 30 km from the plant, and no one is expected to return for about 4 years. Two people died in the initial explosion; 29 more had succumbed to radiation illness within a few months. Predictions of the total number of cancers worldwide that will result from the Chernobyl accident vary from a few thousand to more than a million, which shows how much scientists disagree about the long-term effects of exposure to low doses. There have already been many illnesses. (For a general discussion of the biological effects of radiation, see Section 14.17.)

What is to be concluded from these nuclear accidents? No one was injured at Browns Ferry, and, although radiation was released to the environment from Three Mile Island, the dose received by the public is estimated to have been so low that the additional cancers, if any, will be statistically unverifiable. Some people even felt reassured by the fact that there were no evident injuries despite the serious malfunctions that occurred in these two incidents. Chernobyl, on the other hand, will be responsible for many injuries and deaths. Nonetheless, Western policymakers who favor a nuclear future are still convinced that nuclear power is safe, because our plants are designed differently. Soviet scientists, too, favor continued expansion of nuclear power, because they believe that the Chernobyl accident was largely caused by operator errors and that both operator training and reactor design will be improved. The future effects of political and economic pressures, however, cannot readily be controlled by decree.

14.15
Nuclear Fusion

Fission reactions occur when heavy nuclei split apart. On the other hand, **nuclear fusion** reactions occur when nuclei of light elements, particularly hydrogen, are joined together. The energy derived from middle-aged stars such as the Sun

Special Topic B

Careers in Nuclear Energy The President's Commission on the Accident at Three Mile Island faulted the nuclear power industry and the Nuclear Regulatory Commission for complacency. The Commission recommended that improvements be made in the design of power plants, that regulatory personnel should be more diligent, and that control room operators should receive more education and training. Thus, if you decide to chose a career in the nuclear power industry, you will be required to perform well in public school, continue your education in college, and perhaps pursue advanced degrees or special training programs provided by the nuclear industry. The important areas of study include physics and chemistry, as well as chemical, electrical, and mechanical engineering. In addition, skilled mechanics and technicians are needed at all levels.

If you consider the possibility of such a career, you may wonder about the personal hazards from low-level exposure to radiation or from accidents. Look at all sides. Various nuclear plants conduct public tours or their representatives will answer your questions about working conditions and employee safety. Such viewpoints are expected to be favorable. If you can, talk to employees. Other views are available from the Union of Concerned Scientists in Cambridge, Massachusetts, an anti-nuclear group. Also, you must compare risks in any one industry with those in other areas that might interest you. In general, get all the information you can, think about it, and the final decision is yours.

comes from hydrogen fusion reactions. Controlled nuclear fusion is a potential source of energy that, on a human time scale, is limitless. However, no useful fusion reactor has yet been developed.

Unlike the fission reaction, fusion cannot be triggered by neutrons. Instead, the nuclei to be fused must be brought into contact with each other. Positive nuclei repel each other at normal interatomic distances, but, if they are very close (within about the radius of the nucleus itself), a different type of attraction, known as the "strong

Table 14–3
Isotopes of Hydrogen

Isotope	Names	Radioactive?	Natural Abundance (%)
^1_1H	"Ordinary" hydrogen "Light" hydrogen Hydrogen Protium	No	99.985
^2_1H or ^2_1D	"Heavy" hydrogen Deuterium	No	0.015
^3_1H or ^3_1T	Tritium	Yes (12-year half-life)	Almost none

force," predominates and binds them together. In order to overcome the electrical repulsion and bring the nuclei close enough together for the strong force to take over, the nuclei must be moving very rapidly, or, in other words, they must be elevated to very high temperatures. The resulting fusion is therefore called a **thermonuclear reaction.** If a large mass of hydrogen isotopes fuses in a very short period of time, the reaction cannot be contained and it goes out of control; this is the explosion of the "hydrogen bomb." On the other hand, useful energy could be extracted from fusion if it were possible to devise a controlled thermonuclear reaction.

Any fusion reactor would use hydrogen nuclei. There are three isotopes of hydrogen: **protium, deuterium,** and **tritium.** Some information is given about them in Table 14–3. Fusion reactions can occur between any two hydrogen isotopes. The lighter isotopes are more abundant but require much higher temperatures to initiate fusion.

For example, to start the reaction between two deuterium nuclei, the temperature would have to be raised to about 400 million degrees Celsius. The problems imposed by this requirement are so severe that it is not even being attempted. Instead, all efforts to control fusion are being directed to a cooler reaction ("only" 40 million degrees Celsius), namely, the fusion of deuterium with tritium to give helium-4 plus a neutron:

$$^2_1H + {}^3_1H \longrightarrow {}^4_2He + {}^1_0n$$

This process requires a source of tritium, which is not naturally available on Earth. Tritium is produced artificially by neutron bombardment of lithium. Even though this process is expensive, it is the only feasible fusion reaction and is the one now being studied.

Think for a moment about high temperatures. An iron bar turns red hot at about 600°C, white hot at about 1100°C, melts at about 1500°C, and the molten iron boils, actually boils, at 2885°C. Other solids survive to higher temperatures—carbon and tungsten, for example, to about 3500°C—but no solids, liquids, or even any chemical bonds survive much above 5000°C. At these temperatures, everything is a gas consisting of lone atoms that are much too energetic to combine chemically with each other. At the temperatures involved in nuclear fusion reactions, measured in millions of degrees, not even atoms survive, because electrons are extensively stripped away from the nuclei. Such an extremely hot mixture of independently moving electrons and nuclei is called a **plasma.** Obviously, then, no rigid container exists that can survive long enough to confine a plasma for the useful production of thermonuclear energy. Instead, what is envisaged is a sort of "magnetic bottle," which does not consist of a physical substance at all, but rather is a magnetic field so designed that it will confine the charged particles of the plasma in which the thermonuclear reaction is going on. Research efforts have shown promise, in a modest way. On November 3, 1984, scientists at the Massachusetts Institute of Technology maintained a controlled nuclear fusion for 50 milliseconds (about the blink of an eye), and the brief process

Figure 14–19
A, Nuclear fusion reactor *(cut-away view).*
B, Schematic drawing of a thermonuclear power plant.

A

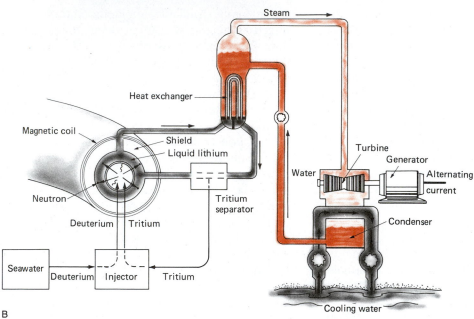

B

actually yielded as much energy as was put into it. A practical reactor, however, would have to be able to operate on a continuous basis.

The useful energy, once liberated, will have to be extracted in the form of the kinetic energy of the evolved neutrons. Since the neutrons carry no charge, they will pass through the magnetic field and escape from the plasma. The energy of the speeding neutrons can then be extracted by a moderator, just as in a fission reactor. If the moderator were water, the energy would create steam that could drive a turbine. The entire fusion reactor would be encased in a sheath or blanket in which molten lithium would be continuously circulated. The lithium would absorb the neutrons, supply the tritium, and then release its heat to water in a heat exchanger (Fig. 14–19).

Other efforts have been directed to an alternative approach, **laser fusion.** The object of this method is to create miniature thermonuclear explosions by hitting frozen pellets of fuel with converging laser pulses of enormous power. The combined laser pulses compress the hydrogen pellet and heat it to the point of thermonuclear fusion.

Figure 14–20
A hydrogen bomb explosion. Note that the giant battleships are dwarfed by the cloud. (Photograph by H. Armstrong Roberts)

Recent progress in laser fusion that uses more energetic lasers of shorter wavelengths has been encouraging. However, estimates of the time that it will take to develop a practical fusion reactor of either type—magnetic bottle or laser—are still uncertain.

Could a fusion reactor get out of control and go off like a hydrogen bomb (Fig. 14–20)? Nuclear scientists are entirely confident that the answer is no, an explosion could not occur. The reason is that the hydrogen isotopes are continuously fed into the reactor and continuously consumed; they do not accumulate. The total quantity of fuel in the plasma at any one time would be very small—far below the critical mass required for a runaway reaction. If the temperature dropped or the plasma somehow dispersed itself, the reaction would stop; in effect, the fusion would turn itself off. The situation is rather analogous to that of a burning candle; if something goes wrong, the flame goes out; the candle does not explode.

Would there be a problem of environmental radioactivity? The answer here is yes, because both tritium and neutrons could be released. Tritium is radioactive (half-life, 12 years) and can combine with oxygen to form radioactive water. However, the beta particles emitted by tritium have so little penetrating power that tritium is virtually harmless to living organisms as long as its source is outside the body. The neutrons released from the reactor can be absorbed by atomic nuclei, and the new isotopes thus produced may be radioactive. As a result, there could be substantial quantities of radioactive matter to be disposed of. We are so far from a practical fusion reactor that we have hardly begun to study the problems of handling its wastes.

14.16
Biological Effects of Radiation
Effects of Radiation on Living Cells

Photons (electromagnetic radiation) in some energy ranges can knock electrons away from their atoms or molecules. An atom or molecule from which one or more electrons is missing is an **ion,** and radiation that is energetic enough to do this is called **ionizing radiation.** X-rays or gamma rays, which are released from nuclear reactions, are in this category. If certain key molecules in a living cell are ionized, cellular function may be disrupted and the cell may die. Radiation may also alter or break chemical bonds, and the affected molecule may be essential to the cell. One such molecule is deoxyribonucleic acid, DNA, which contains all the genetic information that is required for the growth and maintenance of the cell. DNA is a sensitive target for radiation; when a cell is irradiated, the DNA

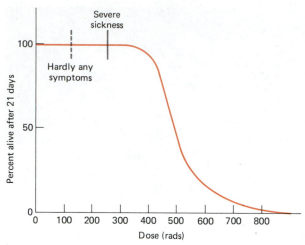

Figure 14–21

Curve showing the approximate relationship between the dose of radiation administered to a whole animal (such as a mouse or a human) and the percentage of the treated population that survives 3 weeks afterward. Mice have been intensively studied in the laboratory; accidents in industry and the nuclear explosions in Japan have provided the approximate data for humans. (From *American Scientist, 57*:206, 1969. Copyright 1969 by Sigma Xi National Science Honorary)

strands tend to break into fragments. If the rate of delivery of the radiation is low, the cell's repair mechanisms can seal the breaks in the strands, but, above a certain dose rate, the repair process cannot keep up, and the DNA fragmentation becomes irreversible.

Early Somatic Effects: Radiation Sickness

On several occasions in this century, groups of people have been exposed to large doses of ionizing radiation over periods of time ranging from a few seconds to a few minutes or longer. The victims of atomic bombs at Hiroshima and Nagasaki and of accidents at nuclear installations, as well as the observers of atomic bomb tests, have provided much information about what radiation can do when a lot of it is administered to the entire body over a short period of time. Let us first consider the simplest and most drastic measure of radiation effect, death. Figure 14–21 shows the relation between the dose administered to a population of animals and the percent of the population remaining alive 3 weeks or more after the exposure. Up to a

dose of about 250 rads (see Table 14–4 for definition of a rad), virtually everyone survives. When the dose is increased above this level, survival begins to drop sharply, and above a dose of 800 rads, everyone dies.

Does this mean that below doses of 250 rads there is no observable effect? Not at all. Even if the exposed persons do not die, they may become quite ill. At doses between 100 and 250 rads, most people will develop fatigue, nausea, vomiting, diarrhea, and some loss of hair within a few days of the exposure; the vast majority, however, will recover completely from the acute illness. For doses of about 400 to 500 rads, however, the outlook is not so positive. During the first few days, the illness is similar to that of the previous group. The symptoms may then go away almost completely for a time, but beginning about 3 weeks after the exposure, they will return. In addition, because the radiation has impaired bone marrow function, the number of white cells and platelets in the blood will decrease. This is of great significance, since without white cells, the body cannot fight infection, and, without platelets, the blood will not clot. Figure 14–21 shows that about 50 percent of those exposed in this dosage range will die, most as a result of either infection or bleeding.

If, instead, the dose administered is about 2000 rads, the first week of the illness will be the same as for those in the previous groups, but rather than waiting 3 weeks for symptoms to return, these people become very ill in the second week, with severe diarrhea, dehydration, and infection leading to death. At these dosage levels, the cells of the gastrointestinal tract are affected before the bone marrow toxicity has a chance to become severe, and these patients may die even before their blood counts have dropped to life-threatening levels.

At doses above 10,000 rads, animal experiments have shown that death, which may occur within hours of administration of the dose, is due to injury of the brain and heart.

Delayed Somatic Effects

Among the late somatic effects of radiation (i.e., those occurring months or years following the exposure), none is better studied or of greater concern than the increased incidence of cancer. Although the molecular mechanisms at work here are still largely obscure, the evidence that radiation

Table 14–4
Units Related to Radioactivity

Unit and Abbreviation	Definition and Explanation
disintegrations per second, dps	A rate of radioactivity in which one nucleus disintegrates every second. The natural radiation for a human body is about 2 to 3 dps.
curie, Ci	37 billion (3.7×10^{10}) dps.
microcurie, μCi	A millionth of a curie, or 37,000 dps.
roentgen, R	A unit of the energy received from a radioactive dose. One R delivers 8.4×10^{-3} J of energy to 1 kg of air.
rad	Another measure of radiation dosage, equivalent to the absorption of 0.01 J/kg of biological tissue. Rad is an acronym for *radiation absorbed dose*.
rem	A measure of the effect on the human body of exposure to radiation. The damage potential is based on the following set of biological damage factors:
	X-rays, gamma rays, electrons: 1
	neutrons, protons, alpha particles: 10
	high-speed heavy nuclei: 20
	The rem is then defined by the relationship:
	rems = rads $\times$ biological damage factor
	For example:
	0.01 J/kg (x-rays) = 1 rad $\times$ 1 = 1 rem
	0.01 J/kg (neutrons) = 1 rad $\times$ 10 = 10 rems
	Rem is an acronym for *roentgen equivalent man*.
millirem, mrem	A thousandth of a rem.

does increase the incidence of cancer in exposed populations is overwhelming. Before the dangers of radiation were appreciated, early workers were careless in their handling of radioactive materials and suffered a greatly increased incidence of skin cancer. The famous case of the radium dial workers in the 1920s also deserves mention. These women were responsible for painting the dials of watches with the phosphorescent radium paint in use at that time; they routinely tipped the end of the brush in their mouths before applying the paint to the dial faces. In later years, this group experi-

enced a very high incidence of bone tumors. (Ingested radium, like strontium, is preferentially incorporated into bone.)

The atomic attacks at Hiroshima and Nagasaki occurred in 1945, and it is estimated that the survivors had absorbed an average of 15 to 20 rads each within a decade of the attacks. Many survivors received 100 rads, and a few endured as much as about 500 rads. (Most of those who were exposed to radiation at these upper levels were not survivors.) By comparison, the average person exposed to radioactivity from natural sources receives about one tenth or two tenths of a rad per year. The first major delayed effect, starting about 2 years after the bombs, was a highly elevated level of leukemia, although these rates droppped off by the mid-1960s. Later, the survivors showed a higher incidence of various cancers than one would have expected from a group of this size. Young children, especially those younger than 6 years of age at the time of the bombing, grew up to be, on the average, an inch or two shorter than their contemporaries. About 4000 pregnant women survived and bore children who have now passed their 40th birthdays. Many of these babies were born mentally retarded, some severely so.

Also significant, although not always discussed, is the social stigma that affects victims of radiation, regardless of whether any adverse health effect is evident. As the children grow up, they may find that others are reluctant to marry them. The victims become suspicious of themselves. If they tire easily, get nosebleeds, lose hair, or catch colds easily, they do not view such events in the way that most others do. Instead, they remember the radiation they were exposed to, and they wonder about it. Even if they live almost as long as others, they may enjoy life less.

Effects of Low Doses of Radiation

Even if there were no x-ray machines or nuclear power plants, people would be exposed to measurable amounts of high-energy radiation in the form of gamma rays originating from outer space and various forms of radiation from natural substances such as uranium found in common rocks and soils (Fig. 14–22). Attempts have been made to quantify the health effects of small doses of high-energy radiation. These estimates may be tabulated as follows:

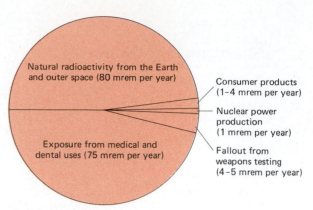

Figure 14–22
Estimates of radiation dose per capita from all sources of exposure. (Data from Merril Eisenbud: *Environment, 26*:6, 1984)

What are the risks of a fatal cancer from such exposures? A maximum permissible exposure from environmental and medical sources of 500 mrem per year has been suggested by the N.R.C. For an 80-year lifetime, this would be 500×80, or 40,000 mrem, which is 40 rem. The lifetime risk of a fatal cancer from natural and consumer sources (about 6 or 7 rem) may be too small to estimate, and, if the risk is doubled by exposure to medical and dental x-rays, for a total of 13 rem, it is still very small.

Exposures in the workplace, however, may be much more severe. For example, if a worker is exposed to 5 rems per year for 20 years, the total exposure would be 100 rems. In that case, one estimate of the risk of fatal cancers is 520 per 10,000 people, as shown in Figure 14–23 (add up the numbers). The ratio of 520/10,000 translates to a lifetime risk of about 5 percent that a person would get a fatal cancer from such exposure.

Source	Approximate 80-yr lifetime dose
Natural	80 mrem/yr for 80 yrs = 6400 mrem = 6.4 rem
Natural + consumer products and nuclear	80 + 8 = 88 mrem for 80 yrs = 7000 mrem = 7 rem
Above + x-rays	88 + 75 = 163 mrem for 80 yrs = 13,000 mrem = 13 rem

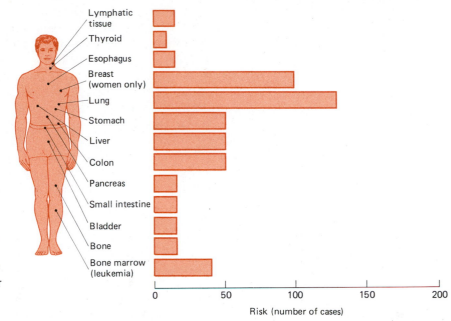

Figure 14–23
Lifetime risk of various types of cancer from low-level radiation to a population exposed to 100 rems. The risk is expressed in number of cases of fatal cancer per 10,000 people. (From Arthur Upton: *Scientific American, 246*:45, 1981)

How accurate is Figure 14–23? Some authorities claim that it exaggerates the risks; others claim that it underestimates them. In brief, no one really knows how serious the effects of low doses of high-energy radiation may be.

Genetic Effects

We must also consider those effects of radiation that do not manifest themselves in the irradiated individual but result in mutations in the genetic material of the germ cells (the sperm cells of the testis and the egg cells of the ovary) that are passed on to succeeding generations. In every experimental system studied in the laboratory, in organisms as diverse as viruses, bacteria, fruit flies, and mice, radiation has been shown to be a potent inducer of mutations. As far as humans are concerned, the evidence thus far is incomplete. However, recessive genetic traits caused by radiation could be passed to later generations. Furthermore, there is no theoretical reason to believe that humans should behave differently in this respect from every other well-studied species; thus, scientists and policymakers must assume that radiation is also mutagenic in humans.

Summary

The nuclear energy program, which started with bomb production in World War II, is seen as a substitute for the diminishing supplies of fossil fuels but has also been plagued by concern about safety and recent accidents.

Atoms consist of nuclei containing electically neutral **neutrons** and positively charged **protons,** surrounded by negative **electrons.** The **atomic number** is the number of protons, and the **mass number** is the total number of protons and neutrons in the nucleus. Nuclei with the same atomic number but different mass numbers are **isotopes.**

Isotopes with unstable nuclei are said to be **radioactive.** Such nuclei emit particles such as electrons or alpha particles, as well as radiation in the form of gamma rays. Radioactivity and other nuclear reactions can be represented by equations in which mass numbers and atomic numbers are balanced. The electron is assigned an atomic number of -1. The **half-life** of a radioactive isotope is the time required for half of the nuclei in a sample to decompose.

In nuclear reactions that release energy, such as radioactivity and fission, the products have less mass than the starting materials. The relationship between the released energy and the decreased mass is given by the Einstein equation $E = mc^2$.

In **nuclear fission,** an isotope of a heavy element is split into lighter elements, releasing a large amount of energy. The important naturally occurring fissionable, or fissile, isotope is uranium-235. The fission is triggered by a neutron, and each uranium-235 nucleus releases 2 or 3 neutrons. The result can be a **chain reaction,** in which a series of steps occurs in sequence.

Natural uranium is mostly uranium-238, which is not fissile. However, it can be converted to plutonium-239, which is fissile. The natural abundance of uranium-235 is less than 1 percent.

Nuclear fission can be used in an atomic bomb or in a nuclear power plant. The difference between the two applications depends on the neutrons. There are four things that can happen to a neutron:

1. Fission capture by uranium-235 to yield energy and fast neutrons. But the reaction is favored by slow neutrons. Therefore, a *moderator,* which is a substance that slows down neutrons, can be used.

2. Non-fission capture by uranium-238, thereby producing plutonium-239, which can undergo fission.

3. Non-fission capture by impurities, which causes loss of neutrons. This action can be used to control the fission process.

4. Escape, in which a neutron might miss everything and get lost.

In a **non-breeder reactor,** cartridges of uranium-238 containing 3 or 4 times the natural abundance of uranium-235 are surrounded by a moderator such as water. The heat of the reaction produces steam, which drives a turbine to generate electricity.

In a **breeder reactor,** the fuel contains uranium-238 mixed with a higher percentage of uranium-235 and plutonium-239 but no moderator. The fast neutrons are captured by the uranium-238 to produce fissionable plutonium-239. The heat is removed by a flow of liquid sodium, which eventually transfers its heat to water to make steam.

In a **bomb,** a large enough quantity of pure or nearly pure fissile material supports a rapidly branching chain reaction.

Safety in a nuclear plant depends on (1) safe design of the entire system, (2) back-up or **redundant** safety systems, (3) warning devices, (4) inspection and maintenance procedures by trained operators, and (5) final protection in case an accident does happen.

The environmental hazards from fission reactors include (1) the possibility of a serious accident that releases a large amount of radioactivity, (2) the hazard of even the usual small radioactive emissions with normal operations, (3) the dangers of terrorism and sabotage, (4) the thermal pollution resulting from the waste heat of the nuclear plant, (5) the problem of disposal of radioactive wastes, and (6) the isolation of old nuclear plants after their useful life is over.

The strategy for waste management depends on the type of reactor used. The non-breeder reactor requires a **once-through uranium**

fuel cycle, in which the mined uranium ore is processed, enriched in the uranium-235 isotope, used in the reactor, and then stored as spent fuel. The breeder reactor uses the **plutonium fuel cycle,** in which the uranium, instead of being enriched in uranium-235, is mixed with plutonium-239, which is produced from uranium-238 in the reactor. The uranium is thus in effect recycled. The preferred repositories for final disposal of high-level wastes are geologically stable underground sites.

Frightening accidents at nuclear plants include those at Browns Ferry (1975) and Three Mile Island (1979), which were brought under control before a meltdown occurred, and Chernobyl (1986), where a meltdown and release of radioactive matter caused injuries and deaths.

In controlled nuclear fusion, the nuclei of the isotopes deuterium and tritium would combine to produce helium and release energy. Because of the extremely high temperature required for the reaction, it has not yet been possible to design a practical fusion reactor.

Radiation can disrupt living cells and produce both acute and delayed somatic effects as well as genetic effects such as mutations.

Questions

Nuclear Reactions

1. Complete the following nuclear equations:
   (a) $^{29}_{13}\text{Al} + ^4_2\text{He} \rightarrow ^1_0\text{n} + \,?$
   (b) $^{43}_{21}\text{Sc} \rightarrow ^{42}_{20}\text{Ca} + \,?$
   (c) $^{95}_{42}\text{Mo} + ^1_0\text{n} \rightarrow ^1_1\text{H} + \,?$

Radioactivity

2. (a) A geiger counter registers 256 counts per second (cps) from a sample of polonium-210; 414 days later, the counter registers 32 cps. What is the half-life of polonium-210? What will the counter register after another 414 days? (b) Polonium-210 decays in one step to lead-206, which is not radioactive. If you are asked to give a rough estimate of the length of storage time needed to reduce the radioactivity of polonium-210 to a safe level, would you say it is a matter of months, years, decades, or centuries? Would you be concerned about any radioactive products that might be produced?

3. Iodine-131 is a radioactive nuclear waste product with a half-life of 8 days. How long would it take for 2000 mg of iodine-131 to decay to 62.5 mg? Would it be correct to say that iodine-131 is no environmental hazard because its half-life is so short? Defend your answer.

4. A 24 mg sample of tritium (^3_1H) decays to 1.5 mg in 49 years. What is the half-life of tritium?

5. Strontium-90, produced in nuclear explosions and present in radioactive fallout, has a half-life of 29 years. If the activity of a "bomb-test" strontium-90 sample collected in 1957 was about 80 disintegrations per second (dps), how many years would it take to reduce the activity to the natural background count of 2.5 dps? (Note that the dps count is registered as clicks on a Geiger counter and is proportional to the amount of strontium-90 present in the sample.) In what year would that count be reached?

6. All the uranium from a sample of uranium ore is extracted and purified. The uranium is less radioactive than the ore from which it came. Explain.

7. Radon-222 has a half-life of 3.8 days. Radon gas is emitted from some rocks and soils. Since the half-life of radon is so short, why is there any left on Earth?

Nuclear Fission

8. The following reaction occurs with one uranium-235 atom in a sample of pure uranium 235:

^{235}U + 1 neutron → fission products + 3 neutrons

How many neutrons must escape (a) to maintain a critical condition; (b) to initiate a branching chain reaction; (c) to terminate the reaction?

Nuclear Reactors

9. What are essential features of a nuclear fission reactor? Explain the function of each feature.

10. List the possible fates of neutrons in a fission reactor. Which of these events should be favored, and which should be inhibited in order to (a) shut down a reactor, (b) breed new fissionable fuel, (c) produce more energy?

11. Explain how breeder reactors differ from non-breeders in fuel, moderator, coolant, and any other features.

12. Could a nuclear reactor ever be miniaturized to provide long-term power for your wristwatch? Your camera? Your pocket radio? (Assume that the proper shielding against radioactivity could be provided.) Defend your answer.

13. If no emergency ever occurred, and if a nuclear reactor always operated at steady power production, would control rods still be needed? Defend your answer.

14. Construct a "fault-tree" according to the procedure described in Section 14.10 to illustrate the following possibilities for an automobile accident: Statement 1: Person driving an automobile. Branch 1A, probability (P) = 0.99, leading to Statement 2A: Car operates normally. Branch 1B, P = 0.01, leading to Statement 2B: Brake fluid leaks out. Continue with various probabilities (shown on branches) and statements about events such as collisions, skidding, wearing or neglecting seat belts, and so on. One branch ends in death of the driver; other branches end in injury or survival at the end of the trip. From your fault-tree, calculate the probabilities of death, injury, or survival at the end of the trip. (Remember, the sum of the probabilities must be 1.)

15. Explain why fast neutrons are needed in breeder reactors.

Nuclear Fuel Cycles

16. Outline the steps in the once-through uranium fuel cycle. Do you think it is appropriate to use the word "cycle" in this context? Defend your answer.

Nuclear Safety

17. (a) What are the five principles of industrial safe practice? (b) How are they applied to the construction and use of automobiles? Of the place where you live? Of a nuclear plant?

18. Outline the general concept and approach to safety used in nuclear power plants.

19. Do you think it would be reasonable to set safety limits in nuclear power plants that would prohibit *any* release of radioactive matter? Defend your answer. If your answer is no, what criteria would you use to set the limits?

20. Explain why a critical mass of pure fissionable material must be attained if an explosion is to occur. Why is it that a nuclear reactor could not explode like a fission bomb? What type of explosion did occur at Chernobyl?

Radioactive Wastes

21. Describe the three steps involved in the handling of radioactive wastes.

22. Is the storage time for radioactive wastes that contain uranium and plutonium measured in years, hundreds of years, or thousands of years? If the wastes are reprocessed by removing the uranium and plutonium, is the required storage time increased, decreased, or unchanged? Explain.

23. Sand-like radioactive leftovers from uranium ore processing mills, called "mill tailings," have been used to make cement in the construction of houses in Colorado, Arizona, New Mexico, Utah, Wyoming, Texas, South Dakota, and Washington. These tailings contain radium (half-life 1600 years) and its daughter, radon (a gas, half-life 3.8 days), as well as radioactive forms of polonium, bismuth, and lead. Radon gas seeps through concrete but is chemically inert. Are the following statements true or false? Defend your answer in each case:
(a) Since radon has such a short half-life, the hazard will disappear quickly; old tailings, therefore, do not pose any health problems.
(b) Even if the radon gas is present, it cannot be a health problem because it does not enter into any chemical reactions in the body.
(c) Continuous ventilation that would blow the radon gas outdoors would decrease the health hazard inside such a house.

24. List the various proposals for "permanent" storage of radioactive wastes. Suggest some advantages and some problems or uncertainties associated with each.

Fusion

25. Suppose that someone claims to have found a material that can serve as a rigid container for a thermonuclear reactor. Would such a claim merit examination, or should it be ignored as a "crackpot" idea not worth the time to investigate? Defend your answer.

Health Effects

26. Outline the types of damage to the body that can result from exposure to high-energy radiation. Can there ever be any benefits? Explain.

27. Relate the effects of radiation in bone marrow to the symptoms of early somatic radiation sickness.

28. What effects of nuclear power plants can you imagine that might *increase* the general level of health?

29. Give two reasons why a 70-year-old person does not face so serious a health problem from exposure to radiation as a 17-year-old.

30. Since a 6-year-old girl is too young to bear children, there is no need to shield her body from radiation produced by dental x-rays. True or false? Explain.

31. The formula for thyroxin, an essential chemical growth regulator, is $C_{15}H_{11}I_4NO_4$. Explain why the nuclear waste product CH_3I containing I-131 is a particular threat to the thyroid gland. When an area is threatened with exposure to a radioactive cloud from a nuclear accident, it is recommended that the people, especially children, be given special doses of potassium iodide, KI. What is the reason for this treatment? Should the KI be radioactive or not? Explain.

Suggested Readings

A history of nuclear policy is described in:

Robert C. Williams and Philip L. Cantelon (eds.): *The American Atom: A Documentary History of Nuclear Policies.* Philadelphia, Univ. of Pennsylvania Press, 1984. 333 pp. Paperback.

For a general overview of nuclear reactors, written at a level that is not too technical, the best choice is:

Anthony V. Nero, Jr.: *A Guidebook to Nuclear Reactors.* Berkeley, University of California Press, 1979. 289 pp. Paperback.

Another general overview is:

Walter C. Patterson: *Nuclear Power.* London, Penguin Books, 1976. 304 pp.

The pro-nuclear viewpoint is presented in:

Samuel McCracken: *The War Against the Atom.* New York, Basic Books, 1982. 206 pp.

Bernard L. Cohen: *Nuclear Science and Society.* Garden City, NY, Anchor Press/Doubleday, 1974. 268 pp.

Antinuclear viewpoints are given in:

John J. Berger: *Nuclear Power—The Unviable Option.* Palo Alto, CA, Ramparts Press, 1976. 384 pp.

Union of Concerned Scientists: *The Nuclear Fuel Cycle.* Revised ed. Cambridge, MA, 1974. 291 pp.

Robert D. Pollard (ed.): *The Nuggett File.* Cambridge, MA, Union of Concerned Scientists, 1979. 95 pp.

Essays with divergent views are given in:

Michio Kaku and Jennifer Trainer: *Nuclear Power: Both Sides.* New York, W.W. Norton, 1982. 280 pp.

Books that integrate social and technical aspects of nuclear energy include:

Nuclear Energy Policy Study Group: *Nuclear Power Issues and Choices.* Cambridge, MA, Ballinger, 1977.

David Rittenhouse Inglis: *Nuclear Energy: Its Physics and Its Social Challenge.* Reading, MA, Addison-Wesley Publishing Co., 1973. 395 pp.

Specific discussion of nuclear hazards may be found in:

Geoffrey G. Eicholz: *Environmental Aspects of Nuclear Power.* Ann Arbor, MI, Ann Arbor Science Publishers, 1976. 681 pp.

Problems of sabotage and terrorism are considered in:

Mason Willrich and Theodore B. Taylor: *Nuclear Theft: Risks and Safeguards.* Cambridge, MA, Ballinger, 1974. 252 pp.

Nuclear and other accidents are described in:

Thomas H. Moss and David L. Sills (eds.): *The Three Mile Island Nuclear Accident: Lessons and Implications.* New York, NY Academy of Sciences, 1981. 343 pp. Paperback.

David R. Marples: *Chernobyl and Nuclear Power in the USSR.* New York, St. Martin's Press, 1986. 228 pp. Paperback.

Christopher Flavin: *Reassessing Nuclear Power: The Fallout from Chernobyl.* Washington, D.C., Worldwatch Institute, 1987. 91 pp.

Arguments about the dangers of radioactive wastes are presented in:

Donald L. Barlett and James B. Steele: *Forevermore: Nuclear Waste in America.* New York, W.W. Norton, 1985. 352 pp. Paperback.

Fred C. Shapiro: *Radwaste.* New York, Random House, 1981. 320 pp.

Discussions of the options for handling of radioactive wastes appear in:

American Scientist, Vol. 70, March–April, 1982.

Discussions of the health effects of radiation can be found in:

Thomas M. Koval (ed.): *Environmental Radioactivity.* Bethesda, MD, National Council on Radiation Protection and Measurement, 1983. 284 pp. Paperback.

Merril Eisenbud: *Environmental Radioactivity.* 2nd ed. New York, Academic Press, 1973.

W. J. Baire and R. C. Thompson: Plutonium: Biomedical Research. *Science, 183*:715, 1974.

D. J. Crawford and R. W. Leggett: Assessing the risk of exposure to radioactivity. *American Scientist, 68*:524, 1980.

Constance Holden: Low-level radiation: A high-level concern. *Science, 204*:155, 1979.

Itsuzo Shigematsu and Abraham Kagan (eds.): *Cancer in Atomic Bomb Survivors.* New York, Plenum Press, 1986. 196 pp.

Finally, the excellent periodical Bulletin of the Atomic Scientists *carries many articles on the general problems of nuclear energy and nuclear weapons. The August/ September, 1986 issue (Vol. 43, No. 1) is devoted largely to the Chernobyl nuclear accident. A large selection of articles from* Bulletin *sources appears in:*

Len Ackland and Steven McGuire (eds.): *Assessing the Nuclear Age.* Chicago, IL, University of Chicago Press, 1986. 382 pp. Paperback.

15

Use of Energy and Its Consequences

15.1
Introduction

Primitive people lived within constraints posed by natural ecosystems. They collected fruits and vegetables and hunted game. Before the use of fire, each person needed approximately 2000 kcal per day, all in the form of food energy. In later times, farmers domesticated animals, raised grains and vegetables, and used fuels for cooking and heating. Energy requirements per person rose to about 12,000 kcal per day (Fig. 15–1). The fuels burned for cooking were largely wood and animal dung, the same fuels characteristic of less-developed societies even today.

Gradually, over a period of many centuries, manufacturing and trade became important in human societies. At first, trade systems were powered by animals, which were used to pull wagons or to carry loads, and by wind, which drove ships. But manufacturing was another matter. Heat was needed to produce metals such as iron, copper, and tin from their ores and to fuse sand into glass. For many years, wood and charcoal (made from burning wood slowly) were the only fuels used for manufacturing. As populations expanded and manufacturing became more widespread, timber resources began to be depleted. By the Middle Ages, it was clear that, in many regions, trees were being cut faster than they were being replaced by natural growth. In Europe, the British Isles felt the lack of wood sooner than did the countries on the continent. During the period from 1550 to 1640, the price of wood in England skyrocketed, leading to rapid inflation and economic hardships. Deforestation became so severe that military leaders feared there would be no wood left for shipbuilding.

Then, when the situation looked particularly bleak, people discovered that coal could be substituted for wood. Mining operations flourished, and the age of fossil fuels began. These manufacturing processes completely changed the face of society and introduced what has been called the "industrial revolution." By the mid-1800s, manufacturing boomed, steam engines had been invented, and the per capita fuel consumption in London was about 70,000 kcal per day. As technology developed, machines became so efficient that people's lives became easier and healthier. In the United States in 1986, per capita energy consumption was approximately 210,000 kcal per day. Most of this

A

1. Man without fire
(2000 kcal/day)

B

2. Primitive agriculture
(12,000 kcal/day)

C

3. ca. 1860
(70,000 kcal/day)

D

4. ca. 1985
(210,000 kcal/day)

Figure 15–1
Human energy consumption has risen from the 2000 kcal per day needed by Stone Age people in the form of food to 210,000 kcal per day used by North Americans.

energy was derived from the use of fossil fuels. This enormous rate is unique in the history of the world. At no other time and in no other place have people used energy faster than North Americans do today.

On the one hand, energy—especially in the developed world—has made peoples' lives incredibly easier than life was a century or two ago. On the other hand, many of the environmental problems that we face today originate from the transformations and utilizations of energy. Problems related to nuclear energy were discussed in Chapter 14. The environmental consequences of fossil and renewable energy uses are explained below.

15.2
Environmental Problems Caused by Mining and Drilling

Oil   Oil drilling on temperate farmlands or deserts does little environmental damage. An oil well requires the use of only a few hundred square meters of surface land. In many instances, wells are located in farmers' fields or even in people's backyards with minimal environmental problems. In recent years, however, oil companies have begun to search for petroleum in more hostile environments, such as in the Arctic or under the ocean floors.

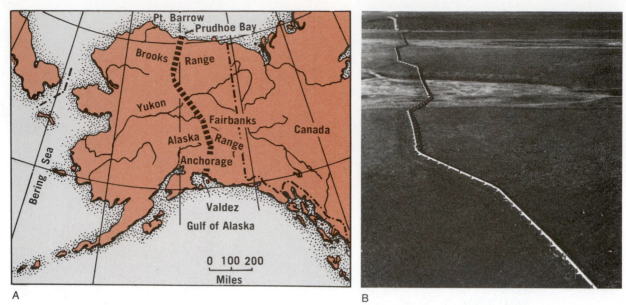

A

B

Figure 15–2

The Alaska Pipeline. *A,* Route of the Pipeline across Alaska. *B,* Pipeline zigzags over the tundra so that the pipe will resist fracture if the earth moves. Despite these precautions, the pipe fractured twice between 1977 and 1986. (World Wide Photos)

An oil well in a temperate ecosystem, such as this one near Bakersfield, California, does little environmental damage.

In Alaska, major problems arose in transporting the oil from a region far above the Arctic circle to large cities farther south. After a lengthy court battle, oil companies were given permission to build a pipeline across Alaska (Fig. 15–2). The completed pipe crosses previously untracked wilderness, delicate icy tundra, mountains, rivers, and active earthquake zones. In winter, outside temperatures drop to −50°C (−58°F). In the summer, they soar to +35°C (+95°F).

Environmentalists have argued that remote wilderness areas have been altered. Roads were built where none existed before, leading to improved access for hunters and tourists. Tundra and caribou migration routes have been disturbed.

During the first 9 years of operation, from 1977 to 1986, the pipeline ruptured twice, spilling oil over the landscape. The most serious rupture released more than 5000 barrels of petroleum onto the tundra and into local rivers. Overall, the oil spill was less ecologically damaging than some people had feared. One of the reasons for this is that the contaminated rivers were not economically important salmon spawning grounds. If a break had occurred along the Yukon or the Copper Riv-

Offshore oil drilling operations are planned and built with great care, but nevertheless oil spills have occurred in all major drilling areas.

Aerial view of a strip-mine in southeastern Montana. To the left, piles of rubble are being reclaimed and blended into the terrain. (Courtesy of Bureau of Reclamation, photo by Lyle Axthelm)

ers, the disruption could have been much more severe.

In many places around the world, valuable oil fields are located under the sea. To obtain this oil, engineers must first build fixed platforms in the ocean. Drilling rigs are then mounted on these steel islands. Despite great care, accidents occur in all types of drilling operations. Broken pipes, excess pressure, or difficulty in capping a new well have repeatedly led to blowouts, spills, and oil fires. When these accidents occur on shore, small areas of farmland are destroyed, but entire ecosystems are not affected. When accidents occur at sea, millions of barrels of oil can be dispersed throughout the waters. Fish and other marine life are poisoned, and ocean ecosystems are disrupted. Significant oil spills have occurred in virtually all underwater drilling areas—in the waters of southern California, Louisiana, and Mexico and in the North Sea in Europe.

Another problem arises when oil is transported over the ocean. Large supertankers carry oil around the globe. Many accidents have occurred in recent years, and large amounts of oil have been spilled. Additional quantities of oil have been released when irresponsible ship captains pump residues from their tanks directly into the ocean. The ecological damage of these activities will be discussed in further detail in Chapter 20.

Coal   Coal can be mined either in underground tunnels or in exposed open strips. **Tunnel mines** do not directly disturb the surface of the land, but the earth and rock dug out to make the tunnel must go somewhere. This material, called **mine spoil,** is often seen as ugly surface pollution of land near mining operations. Sometimes the land above the tunnel collapses, leaving gaping holes on the surface. Perhaps most significantly, underground mining is dangerous and unhealthy for the workers. Fires, explosions, and cave-ins claim many lives. In addition, fine coal dust suspended in the air enters the miners' lungs. This dust gives rise to a series of serious and often fatal ailments known as **black lung disease.**

Tunnel mines alter the flow of groundwater and also pollute it. In many situations, they are

Decker Coal Mine in Montana. (Courtesy of Bureau of Reclamation, photo by Lyle Axthelm)

new cut is started. If the land is not reclaimed, strip mines leave behind vast holes and huge piles of rubble. Neither arguments nor figures are needed to convince anyone that open, rootless dirt piles are uglier and less useful than a natural forest, a prairie, or a wheat field. The ugliness is a loss to all of us. The dirt piles erode, clogging streams and killing fish. As shown in Figure 15–3, a mine may also disrupt the flow of groundwater. This in turn upsets river flows and disturbs drinking water supplies in nearby areas. Furthermore, sulfur deposits are often associated with coal seams. This sulfur reacts with water in the presence of air to produce sulfuric acid, which pollutes the streams and kills fish.

Additional problems arise because millions of hectares of coal lie under farmland in many parts of the world. For example, large deposits exist under the fertile wheat fields of the Great Plains in North America. Is the land more valuable as a wheat field or as a coal mine? A wheat field can provide needed food for many years to come. Coal is used only once and then it is gone.

Perhaps people can have both wheat and coal if old mines are reclaimed. After the coal is removed, the holes can be refilled with subsoil and covered with topsoil. If the land is then fertilized, it

also more expensive and less efficient than open **strip mines.** To dig a strip mine, the surface layers of topsoil and rock are first scooped off (stripped) by huge power shovels. This exposes the underlying coal seam. The coal is then removed, and a

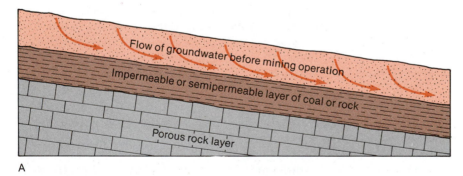

A

B

Figure 15–3
One possible sequence whereby strip mining can disrupt the traditional flow of groundwater. Groundwater flow *(A)* before and *(B)* after the mining operation.

is possible to plant wheat and corn over the mines after about 5 years. However, the soil is not generally as rich as it was originally.

In the absence of environmental regulations, a mining company could buy a farm that lies over a coal seam, mine the coal, destroy the land, leave it, and still realize a large profit. But the government has realized that farmland is a national resource, a type of commons. The economic externalities of destroying this resource include pollution of waterways, the specter of rising food prices, and perhaps eventual food shortages. Therefore, laws have been enacted that require coal companies to reclaim the land. In the United States, the Surface Mining Control and Reclamation Act was passed in 1977. It required that:

1. Mining companies must prove that they can reclaim the land before a mining permit will be issued.

2. After a mining operation is finished, the land must be restored so that it is useful for the same purposes for which it was used before the mining operation was started.

3. Strip-mining is not allowed in certain regions containing particularly prime agricultural land.

4. Mining companies must use the best available technology to minimize water pollution and disruption of streams, lakes, and the flow of groundwater.

5. A tax of 35 cents per tonne of strip-mined coal and 15 cents per tonne of coal mined in underground tunnels is levied. This money will be used to reclaim land that was mined and destroyed before the law was put into effect.

In the 1980s, the federal government initiated proceedings to soften regulations on strip mine reclamation. Claims were made that the $7500 to $25,000 per hectare ($3000 to $10,000 per acre) that it costs to restore land was hurting the mining companies and upsetting the economy. The argument over strip mine regulations is a classic environmental controversy. According to the view of frontier economics, when a resource is exploited for the lowest possible cost, commodities will be cheap, and society will gain. Therefore, the government should not require mining companies to undertake expensive reclamation projects. On the other hand, environmentalists point out that severe economic externalities would result if all the untouched coal fields in the United States were reduced to bare, muddy piles of dirt alternating with long rows of deep trenches (Fig. 15–4). According to this view, these economic externalities cost society more than the cost of reclamation. Furthermore, if we are to build a sustainable society for future generations, reclamation and pollution control are absolutely essential.

15.3
Environmental Problems Caused by Production of Synfuels

Environmental problems do not end after a fuel is extracted from the ground; mining and drilling are only the first steps. Then the fuels must be processed, transported, and eventually burned. Each step represents a potential threat to the environment. For example, crude petroleum is a gooey, tarry fluid that must be refined to produce conventional fuels. The refining process consumes energy and produces significant air pollution. Fuels such as heating oil, gasoline, kerosene, and coal also produce air pollution when they are burned.

However, the pollution problems that occur when conventional fuels are refined are small compared with the problems that are expected to occur when heavy oils are extracted and refined. As explained in Chapter 13, liquid fuels can be produced from oil shale, tar sands, and coal. Fuels produced in this manner are called synthetic fuels, or **synfuels.**

Liquid Fuels from Oil Shale   Oil shale can be mined either in open pits or in underground tunnels or caverns. In either case, environmental disruptions such as those related to coal mining are routinely encountered. But there are additional problems specific to shale development. Shale deposits are made of dense, heavily compacted rock. If the shale is dug up, broken apart, and treated to extract the oil, the volume of rock actually increases even though oil is removed from it. If you find it difficult to visualize this, take a potato, slice it into thin strips, and make potato chips out of them. Now place the potato chips in a pile. Which occupies more volume, the pile of potato chips or the original potato? Some people suggest that this mine spoil could be simply used to fill in some of the scenic canyons in western Colorado and central Utah. What a price to pay for gasoline!

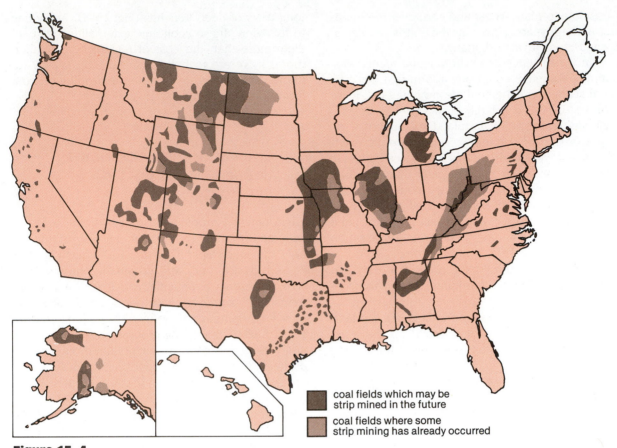

coal fields which may be
strip mined in the future

coal fields where some
strip mining has already occurred

Figure 15–4
Areas in the United States where economically attractive coal deposits are
found. Lightly shaded areas indicate coal fields where some strip-mining has
already occurred. Dark shading indicates coal fields that may be strip-mined in
the future.

Another problem inherent in shale development is water consumption. Approximately two
barrels of water are needed to produce each barrel
of oil from shale. The western states where shale
is found are semiarid. Today, water is used for agriculture and industry in the area. Proponents of
energy development claim that new dams can be
built to conserve water and that industries can
move elsewhere. Moreover, some of the farmers in
the area use water inefficiently because much of
the land is marginally productive anyway. Therefore, according to this argument, it would be in the
national interest to use that water for other purposes. Even if all these sources of water were exploited, shale development would still be limited.
Beyond that, one wonders, should rural ranchers
and local business people be forced to forfeit their
lifestyles in the interests of national efficiency? The
case history in Section 15.4 dramatizes this issue.

Liquid Fuels from Coal As discussed in
Chapter 13, coal can be readily converted to liquid
or gaseous fuels, but, in the mid-1980s, petroleum
was so cheap that conversion of coal was not economical in most places in the world. Nevertheless,
when petroleum reserves become depleted, the
price of this desirable fuel is certain to rise, and, at
some point, conversion of coal is likely to become
economical. At that time people will have to address the environmental consequences that will
arise.

The only commercial coal conversion plant in
production today is in South Africa. This facility is
a source of considerable air and water pollution.

According to one reporter, "Indeed, smoke often hangs like a gray curtain for days over Sasolburg (where the plant is located)—people are now prepared to accept the air pollution . . ." Many of the byproducts of coal conversion are carcinogenic, and radioactive trace elements are also released. It is certainly possible to build a modern plant that emits less pollution than the South African model, but significant problems would always remain.

Coal is composed mainly of carbon, whereas natural gas or gasoline consists of compounds of carbon and hydrogen. In order to convert coal to liquid or gaseous fuels, hydrogen must be added, and the cheapest source of hydrogen is water, H_2O. However, the same problem that affects shale development also affects synfuels derived from coal—water is scarce in many regions where coal is being mined. Representatives of industry claim that in the southwestern part of the United States, there is enough water for production of 500,000 barrels per day of synfuels. However, some environmental experts disagree and claim that beyond 250,000 barrels per day severe problems would be encountered. In 1985, the United States imported approximately 4.6 million barrels per day of petroleum. If more than 5 to 10 percent of this import level were to be replaced with synthetic fuels, water priorities would have to be adjusted drastically.

Hundreds of thousands of hectares of valuable farm land and scenic regions would be disrupted by a coal mining industry of the scale required for a significant synfuel program. Much of the insult can be reduced by extensive reclamation programs, but, even if utmost care is taken, many years would be required for the Earth to recover fully.

None of the problems just outlined is totally insurmountable, but it is important to understand that a synfuel program would entail heavy economic and social costs.

15.4
Case History: Water and Coal in the Southwest United States

A few years ago, one of us (Jon Turk) was driving through northeastern Arizona. This region is semi-arid, and small herds of cattle and sheep graze amid sparse grasses and sage. Just outside of Kayenta, my car broke down, and I was forced to hitch-

The SASOL (South Africa Coal, Oil, and Gas Corporation, Ltd.) refinery in South Africa. The plant produces commercial quantities of gasoline, diesel, and heating fuels and many different types of chemicals, using coal as the raw ingredient. (Courtesy of South Africa Consulate General)

hike to town to get help. An old, 1950 vintage flatbed truck slowed down but did not stop. The driver shouted, "Jump in, I don't have any first gear and can't stop!" I ran along and hopped onto the moving vehicle. The engine groaned, the bearings rattled, but we slowly accelerated onto the highway. The driver, a Navajo rancher, was hauling a load of hay south from Green River, Utah. In other areas with wetter climates, late summer is the time to gather in the hay. But there is too little rainfall in this region to grow much hay. Therefore, the Navajo and Hopi ranchers must drive north to buy feed for their animals. The man who was driving the truck explained to me that it is very difficult to make a living as a rancher if you cannot grow your own hay. Calves and lambs are born in the springtime, and the animals are raised on grass until fall. Every fall he sells many of his animals. Most of the money is used to buy hay to feed the rest of his herd during the winter. None of the farmers of the region makes much money. He was hoping that his animals would bring a high price at the auction this year so that he could afford a rebuilt transmission for his truck.

Later I spoke with Keith Smith, the Navajo Chapter President in Kayenta, about the water prob-

"A man can ride under the power lines and feel the energy traveling through them. But the electricity is going to Phoenix, Tucson, Las Vegas, and Los Angeles. We can't tap into that power and many farms have no electricity. I have to drive eight miles in the pickup truck to get water because I don't have a pump and the water table is going down."—Ernest Yellowhorse, Cove, Arizona.

lems in the region. He told me, "The last few years the water table has been going down. During June and July, people's wells have gone dry. Ranchers have to drive to town to haul water in pick-up trucks so the cattle won't die." After a silence he continued, "A rancher can hardly break even if he has to haul water in a pick-up."

There is a large coal mine a few kilometers south of Kayenta. Some of the coal from the mine is shipped by rail to a power plant nearby. Most of the rest is sold to the Mohave Power Project nearly 480 km (300 miles) away (Fig. 15–5). There the fuel is burned to produce electricity for Las Vegas and Southern California. In order to ship the coal, it is first ground into a fine powder and then mixed with water. The whole mixture, called a **slurry,** is pumped through a large pipe. This process is advantageous for the company because shipment by pipeline is cheaper than shipment by rail. The problem is that it uses water. Water for the project is taken from several large wells near Kayenta. The pipeline uses approximately 7500 liters (1900 gallons) of water *per minute* and operates 24 hours per day, 7 days a week.

As the water is removed, the water table for the entire region has dropped, and many of the shallower wells in the area have gone dry. If the coal for the Mohave Power project were shipped by rail instead of by pipeline, the price of fuel would rise slightly. However, the ranchers in the region would have enough water to maintain their stock.

If coal liquefaction and gasification ever become practical, the coal companies will need even more water than they use now. As explained in the previous section, water is an absolutely essential chemical ingredient in the conversion. Where will the power companies find the water? Even now, the farmers near Kayenta cannot get what they need. Experts believe that even if other consumers were rationed more severely than they are currently, there still might not be enough water to manufacture the needed fuel. In some regions, water, not energy, is becoming the limiting resource. (See Chapter 17 for a further discussion of the utilization of water resources.)

15.5
Environmental Consequences of Using Renewable Resources

There are no magic solutions to the problem of harnessing energy for human consumption. Even production of energy from renewable energy sources has environmental consequences. During the production of solar cells, small quantities of poisonous arsenic compounds (used in the production of gallium arsenide) find their way into toxic waste dumps. Solar concentrators such as Solar One preempt large areas of land. Ethanol production uses corn that could be fed to hungry people, and, when wood is burned as a fuel, timberlands are affected and air is polluted. Hydroelectric and tidal dams disrupt scenic areas and natural breeding grounds for fish. Windmills are noisy. The list can go on and on. For this reason, comparisons are needed to assess the relative merits of various energy systems. The important question is not "What are the environmental consequences of one individual system?" but "What are

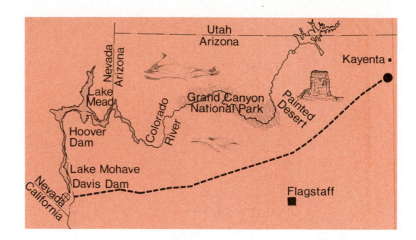

Figure 15–5
Dotted line shows the route of the coal slurry pipeline.

the relative consequences of all the various alternatives?" The only truly benign solution to the energy problem is conservation.

15.6
Electricity and Thermal Pollution

As explained in Chapter 13, most of our electricity is now produced in **steam turbines.** A steam turbine is a type of heat engine; thermal energy from the fuel is ultimately converted to the work required to spin the shaft of the generator. Recall from Chapter 2 that the Second Law of Thermodynamics states that during the operation of a heat engine, it is impossible to convert all the energy of a fuel into work. However, the efficiency can be improved if the exhaust gases are cooled. Therefore, the **cooling cycle** of a power plant is essential to the entire process.

Even the best electric generators operate at only about 40 percent efficiency, but, if old power plants are considered, the average efficiency in North America is closer to 38 percent. This means that for every 100 units of potential energy in the form of fuel, only 38 units of electrical energy can be produced. The other 62 units of heat energy are lost to the environment in the form of heat. Additional energy is lost when electricity is transmitted through long distance power lines, so that energy delivered to the home represents only about 34 percent of the original potential in a fuel. Although modern electrical production is only 34 percent efficient, it is more efficient than other common heat engines. An automobile is also a heat engine, but,

because of various engineering difficulties related in part to size and weight limitations, automobile engines are only 25 percent efficient. Therefore, electricity is an efficient way to perform work. Less fuel is needed to operate electric cars or other small engines such as saws or lawn mowers than to operate gas-powered machines.

Electric Heat   In modern society, electricity is often used to provide heat. Advertisements advise people to "live better electrically" and buy electric stoves, toasters, space heaters, and water heaters. But the use of heat engines to generate electricity for electric heaters is thermodynamically inefficient. Sixty percent of the heat is discarded at the power plant. On the other hand, a gas-fired stove can be nearly 100 percent efficient, and home furnaces are 60 to 80 percent efficient. Electricity is essential for many functions, but it is wasteful when used to produce heat. Much energy could be conserved if electricity were used only where it is needed and if fuel were used directly when heat is needed (Fig. 15–6).

Thermal Pollution   The amount of heat that must be removed from an electrical generating facility is quite large. A 1000-megawatt power plant running at 40 percent efficiency heats 10 million liters of water 35°C (63°F) every hour. It is not surprising that such large quantities of heat, added to aquatic systems, cause ecological disruptions. The term **thermal pollution** has been used to describe these heat effects.

What happens when the outflow from a large generating station warms a river or lake? Fish are

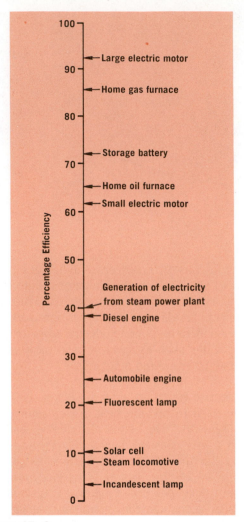

Figure 15–6

Maximal efficiencies of some common engines, devices, and processes. The values for electrical devices do not include the energy losses at the generating station.

cold-blooded animals. This means that their body temperature increases or decreases with the temperature of the water. When the temperature is raised, all the body processes of a fish (its metabolism) speed up. As a result, the animal needs more oxygen, just as you need to breathe harder when you speed up your metabolism by running. But hot water holds less dissolved oxygen than cold water. Therefore, fish accustomed to cold water may suffocate in warm water. In addition, warm water can cause outright death through failure of the nervous system. In general, not only fish but also the entire aquatic ecosystems are rather sen-

sitively affected by changes from the temperatures for which they are adapted. For example, many animals lay their eggs in the springtime when the water naturally becomes warm. If a power plant heats the water in mid-winter, some organisms may start reproducing, but, if the eggs are hatched at this time, the young may not find the food needed to survive.

Not all power plants discharge waste heat directly into natural environments. Many use artificial lakes called **cooling ponds.** Hot water is pumped into the ponds, where evaporation as well as direct contact with the air cools it, and the cool water is drawn into the condenser from some point distant from the discharge pipe. Water from outside sources must be added periodically to replenish evaporative losses. Cooling ponds are practical where land is cheap, but a 1000-megawatt plant needs 400 to 800 hectares of surface, and land costs can be prohibitive.

An alternative solution is a **cooling tower,** which is a large structure, typically about 180 m in diameter at the base and 150 m high (Fig. 15–7). Hot water is pumped into the tower near the top and sprayed onto a wooden mesh. Air is pulled into the tower either by large fans or convection currents and flows through the water mist. Evaporative cooling occurs, and the cool water is collected at the bottom. No hot water is introduced into aquatic ecosystems, but a large cooling tower loses more than 3.8 million liters of water per day to evaporation. Thus, fogs and mists are common in the vicinity of these units, reducing the sunshine in nearby areas. Reaction of the water vapor with sulfur dioxide emissions from coal-fired plants can cause the resultant air to carry sulfuric acid aerosols, as described in Chapter 21.

15.7
The Politics and Economics of an Energy Transition

People in the United States used 74 quads of energy in 1985. If all that energy were supplied by petroleum, we would burn more than 12 billion barrels of oil a year, or 34 million barrels a day. Thirty-four million barrels would fill a square pool 1 meter deep and about 2.3 kilometers on each side. Remember, that is the fuel needed every day! Obviously, a tremendous mechanical and physical network is needed to produce this energy and

Table 15–1
Comparison of Various Energy Sources in the United States

Energy Source	Current Use	Future Availability of Energy Supply	Current Cost	Pollution Problems
Oil	39%	Shortages by year 2000	Relatively inexpensive	Pollution of the ocean from oil spills; air pollution when fuel is burned; global climate change possible from release of carbon dioxide
Natural gas	23%	Shortages by year 2050	About the same as oil	Cleanest fossil fuel
Coal	24%	200- to 300-year supply	Less expensive than oil	Land disruption from mining; air pollution from burning; global climate change possible from release of carbon dioxide
Hydroelectric	3%	Possible doubling of current supply (renewable)	Less expensive than oil	Disruption of farmland and scenic and recreational areas
Heavy oils and synfuels	<1%	As long as coal	More expensive than conventional fossil fuels	Large disruption of land surfaces; depletion of water resources; other pollution problems associated with burning of coal and oil
Nuclear	5%	Supply of fuel abundant	More expensive than fossil fuels	Hazards from nuclear wastes and fears of potential radioactive contamination
Wood and plant matter	4.5%	Uncertain	The least expensive fuel in certain regions	Disruption of forests; preempts land that could be used for food production; air pollution
Garbage	<1%	2.5% (renewable)	Variable	Air pollution problems but conserves resources and eliminates a solid waste problem
Solar	<1%	Excellent and renewable	Cheaper than fossil fuels in some applications, more expensive in others	Minimal
Wind	<1%	Excellent and renewable	More expensive than fossil fuel	Noise from windmills; use of land
Waves and tides	<1%	Excellent and renewable	Some tidal generators are competitive today—others are not	Disruption of coastal habitats for fish and recreation
Geothermal	<1%	Small expansion	Inexpensive where available	Some pollution from released steam
Hydrogen fusion	0	Excellent and virtually limitless if reactors can be built	Technology not yet available	Serious thermal pollution

Figure 15–7
Cooling towers. *A,* Schematic view of the operating principle of a cooling tower. *B,* This large cooling tower dwarfs the nuclear reactor at a reactor site in southern Washington.

transport it to individual users. Electric power lines and gas stations are seen in all urban environments. Mines, oil wells, hydroelectric dams, refineries, power plants, pipelines, supertanker terminals, and the facilities needed to build and maintain this superstructure are less visible, but, nevertheless, they are an integral part of our society.

We have documented the fact that fossil fuel reserves are limited and that we will face some sort of major transition, probably within the next generation. We have also discussed the potential for

A gas station in the early 1900s.
(National Archives)

the development of renewable and other alternative energy sources. However, we have not discussed how difficult, expensive, and time-consuming it will be to restructure the entire nature of society in order to adapt to change.

In 1973 and again in 1978–1979, gasoline shortages occurred practically overnight. Cities were disrupted as commuters could not find the fuel needed to drive to work and industries were forced to reduce production. True, plenty of solutions were available. The cars used at that time were mainly heavy "gas-guzzlers," and a shift to smaller more efficient cars would have saved enough fuel to avert the crisis. In addition, mass transit systems can move people quickly from place to place with a fraction of the fuel consumption of private automobiles. Other solutions would have involved the development of alternative energy sources. But a few years are needed before a new type of automobile can be designed, built, and marketed. Similarly, buses cannot be purchased overnight, and new rail lines cannot be built by Monday morning. In fact, approximately 5 to 10 years are needed to design and build a subway system. New energy sources also take time and money to develop. A new oil well can take from 5 to 8 years to be put into production; a nuclear power plant requires a decade or more from drawing board to start-up. Synfuel programs may require more than that. Best estimates indicate that in the United States, it would cost about $50 to $75 billion (in 1985 dollars) to construct enough conversion plants to cut the U.S. oil import level by 25 percent. The engineering difficulties involved are also enormous. As one expert wrote during the last gas crisis,*

> Synfuel plants are very large enterprises—a 50,000 barrel per day coal (liquefaction or gasification) plant would cost, at a minimum, over 2 billion dollars and use several times as much coal as the largest electric generating plant. And no one has ever built even one at this scale. And we are talking about building 20 to 30 of them in the next ten years. . . . The managers, engineers, and laborers will have to be trained or diverted from other activities, (and) new plants will have to be built to produce the equipment going into the synthetic fuels plants. . . . Some of these steps . . . can be compressed, but, taken together, the prospects for anything like 2.5 million barrels per day

by 1990 (note: 1990 was 10 years from the time this article was written) seem to me slim unless as a nation we decide nothing much else is important.

During the mid 1980s, when energy was plentiful, there was a general air of complacency about preparations for our future. Yet many people were warning the nation of hard times to come. In June of 1985, the president of Mobil Oil Corporation wrote:

> Whenever I warn people that another energy crisis is on the way, I draw raised eyebrows and skeptical sneers.
>
> "We thought we were through with those things," my friends hoot. "Don't we have oil and gas running out of our ears? And plenty of electricity?"
>
> My answer is, "Yes, for the moment," but I also add this warning: energy plenty is not going to last.
>
> In the three years before the 1973-74 energy crisis, we began warning of impending shortages, urging more reliance on mass transit, more domestic petroleum development and the creation of a national-energy policy. But no one wanted to hear it.
>
> The trouble is, Congress—like all of us—tends to be complacent until a crisis fires the adrenaline. Unfortunately, government's worst decisions in energy have been those responding to crisis. Sound energy decisions that avert crisis usually come in quiet times like these.
>
> So let me say it once again:
>
> We're headed for another round of energy shortages. Certainly by the end of this century. Possibly well before that.

So far, fairly predictable limits and problems related to energy supply and use have been discussed. If reasonable estimates can be made of current supplies and drilling potential and of how rapidly a fuel is being used, it is not difficult to predict the near future. However, all these predictions assume that the resources will be exploited in an orderly, uninterrupted fashion. Such order is not guaranteed. In 1985, energy was relatively available worldwide and economic conditions were favorable. At the same time, the global political climate was underlaid with tension. Some Middle Eastern oil-producing nations were already involved in warfare, and all the others were armed and ready for war (Fig. 15–8). As economist Robert J. Samuelson wrote:*

*Science, 205:978, Sept. 7, 1979.

*Robert J. Samuelson in *Newsweek,* April 6, 1987

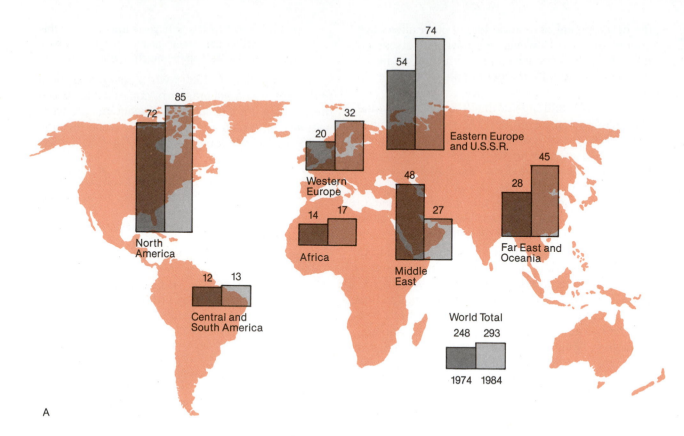

A

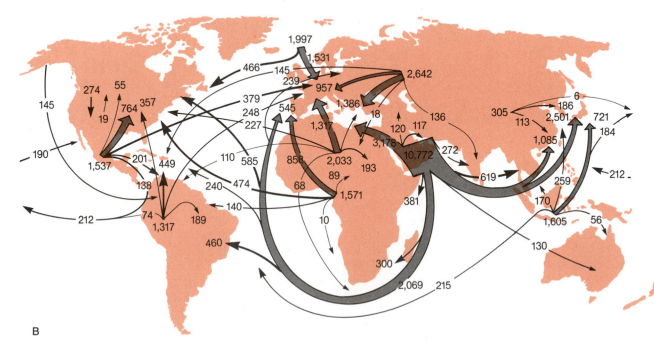

B

Figure 15–8

A, International primary energy production by area, 1974 and 1984. *B,* International trade in crude oil. Numbers are given in thousands of barrels per day. (Source *Annual Energy Review,* 1985, Energy Information Administration)

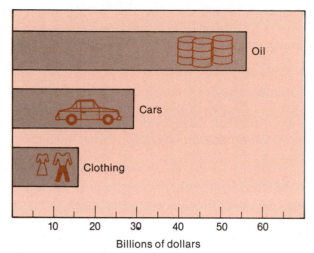

Figure 15–9
The three costliest imports into the United States.
(Source: U.S. Dept. of Commerce)

The Persian Gulf is the late 20th century's tinder box. As long as it contains two-thirds of noncommunist oil reserves, energy security hangs on hope . . . A region that has given us the six-year Iran-Iraq war and Lebanon's national suicide is surely a candidate for even greater chaos.

Even in the absence of a major crisis, the cost of energy has a serious effect on the economy of most nations. A country has a zero **balance of trade** when the total value of all imports equals the total value of all exports. A positive balance of trade means that there is a net flow of wealth into a nation and is naturally desirable for that country. On the other hand, a negative balance means that more resources are leaving the country than are entering it. In 1985, the United States spent approximately $50 billion on imported fuels, almost $1 billion per week! This expenditure was nearly one third of the entire trade deficit (Fig. 15–9). What would have happened if that $50 billion spent on foreign fuel had been kept within the country? International economics is complex, experts disagree on cause and effect, and predictions based on conventional theories do not always come to pass. Therefore, the effect of this tremendous trade deficit is difficult to quantify. One traditional view is that one effect of a negative balance of trade is that the country's money loses value in world markets, leading to inflation. The high inflation of the 1970s was believed to be linked to rising oil prices and a rapid outflow of money to oil-producing nations.

Special Topic A
Government Subsidies and Energy Development

The United States government subsidizes a wide variety of industries that are perceived to be beneficial to the country. Subsidies may take the form of outright grants, support of relevant research, tax advantages, or a variety of other forms of aid. The energy industry is one of the beneficiaries. For many years, mining and drilling companies have been allowed what is called **depletion allowances,** which are tax exemptions offered when a resource is extracted and sold. The nuclear industry has received billions of dollars in government support from numerous programs. Similarly, development of renewable energy has been boosted by special tax incentives.

Supporters of these various types of subsidies claim that they encourage national energy production and therefore reduce the dependence on foreign fuels. Opponents argue that government subsidies to different industries are never equivalent. Some industries always receive more than others, and the result is unfair competition. For example, nuclear power receives an inordinately large share of subsidies. Thus, nuclear energy is cheaper than it would be in a free market. According to this argument, if subsidies were removed, renewable energy sources would become more competitive.

However, in the mid-1980s, inflation in the United States declined dramatically despite the even larger negative balance of trade. Another possible effect is that when money is leaving the country, there is less capital available in the nation for loans, for capital investment, and for modernizing industry. On the average, it takes about $50,000 per year to create and support one job; therefore the money spent on foreign oil represented about 1 million jobs.

Certainly, a sudden fuel shortage would cause widespread unemployment. Factories would be forced to shut down, gas station attendants and automobile mechanics would be out of work, shippers and truckers would become unemployed. On the other hand, a gradual conservation program would *increase* jobs. Suppose, for example, that people in the United States gradually shifted toward increased use of mass transit. Automobile factories would slow production, but the automobile workers would not necessarily lose their jobs. They could be employed to manufacture buses and trains. Workers who now specialize in road construction could build and repair rail systems. If cars and appliances were maintained longer and thrown away less frequently, more repair specialists would be needed. Plumbers and carpenters could be hired to install solar collectors and to add extra insulation to homes.

Conservationists argue that if energy consumption remains high, and if we continue to be dependent on fossil fuels, then when oil or coal shortages develop, the economy will collapse disastrously. After a crisis situation is reached, many years will elapse before patterns of energy supply and demand can be altered. On the other hand, if people start now to build a low-energy society, changes can be made gradually. The economy need not suffer; in fact it could prosper.

15.8
Energy Conservation

Although virtually all energy analysts believe that a transition will occur in the near future, different experts disagree on what steps will, or should, be taken. Some argue that we must rely on electricity derived from nuclear or coal-fired electrical generators, whereas others believe that we are very close to a major breakthrough in the deployment of renewable resources. Yet everyone must agree that if we use less energy today, we will delay the eventual depletion of fossil fuels and extend the time available for an orderly transition in the future.

The savings that have been realized from conservation and the potential savings that can be realized are enormous. For example, during the 1950s and 1960s, consumption of electricity increased at a rate of 8 percent per year. In 1960 the total electrical generating capacity in the United States was 250,000 megawatts. If the existing rate of increase had continued, the required generating capacity would have skyrocketed to 2 million megawatts by 1990. The increase of 1.75 million megawatts would have required a total of 1750 new 1,000-megawatt power plants. The Atomic Energy Commission predicted that 800 to 1200 new nuclear reactors would be needed. New hydroelectric dams and coal fired plants were also planned.

This prediction did not come to pass. In fact between 1973 and 1985, in an era that was supposed to mark the height of the period of construction of new power plants, only 173 large plants were completed. As documented in the last chapter, no new nuclear power plants were ordered between 1978 and 1986.

What has happened? Throughout all sectors of our society, people are simply using less electricity to perform the same tasks that they performed a decade or two ago. If the projections made in 1970 are used as a baseline, then in the year 1986 alone, energy conservation saved the people of the United States $150 *billion* in fuel costs. In contrast, the use of all alternative energy sources saved only $200 *million* in avoided fuel costs.

As another example of the effects of conservation, between 1980 and 1985, the populations of both Texas and California increased by the same amount, just over 2 million people. In California, there are a number of laws encouraging or mandating conservation; in Texas there are virtually none. During the first half of the 1980s, 11 new 1,000-megawatt power plants were built in Texas, whereas only 3 were needed in California.

According to one expert on energy conservation,

If we had done nothing about energy conservation since 1973, we would now be using the equivalent of almost one whole OPEC's worth of additional energy. Instead of spending 11 percent of the GNP on energy we could be spending 20 percent. For the next twenty years, if we did everything right—which we won't—I think we could get by without any new power plants.*

In general, social solutions offer the quickest and most cost effective methods of conservation. For example, no capital outlays or technological advances are required to turn off unused lights, drive to work in carpools, or turn the thermostat down and put on a sweater.

Technical conservation measures require some investment in terms of new equipment such

*Dr. Arthur Rosenfeld as quoted in the article: Marc Reisner: The rise and fall and rise of energy conservation. *Amicus Journal*, Vol 9, No 2, 1987.

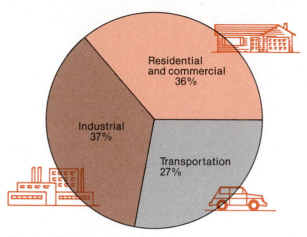

Figure 15–10

Uses of energy in the United States in 1985. (Source: *Annual Energy Review*, 1985, Energy Information Administration)

as energy-efficient cars, additional insulation, or new industrial processes. However, society must balance these costs against the cost of building new power plants or oil refineries. In many instances, conservation is simply cheaper than sup-

plying more energy. In California, electric utilities are offering commercial customers $300 cash rebates for every kilowatt of peak-hour electricity they conserve. Why? It would cost the utilities $1500 per kilowatt to build a new generator to supply that electricity.

Figure 15–10 shows how energy is used in the United States, and Figure 15–11 shows the flow of energy production and consumption. We will refer to both figures during our discussion of energy conservation.

Energy Use in Transportation

The two least efficient modes of transportation, the automobile and the airplane, are the two major transportation industries in the United States (Fig. 15–12). The automobile in particular has modified our lives. Houses are far from places of work and from shopping centers. Many people live in the suburbs and must commute long distances daily. What can be done in the immediate future? No one can reorganize the cities overnight. The system is set in concrete.

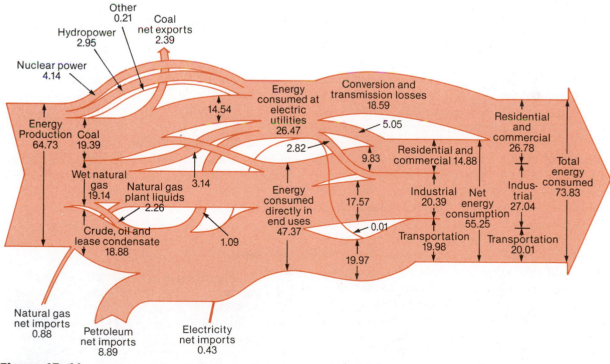

Figure 15–11

Total energy flow in the United States in 1985. (Source: *Annual Energy Review*, 1985, Energy Information Administration)

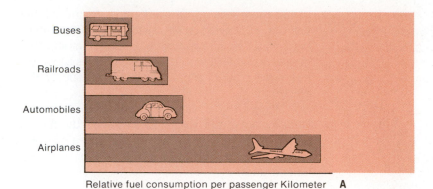

Relative fuel consumption per passenger Kilometer **A**

Airplanes use 60 x as much fuel as railroads per ton of freight

Relative fuel consumption per ton Kilometer **B**

Figure 15–12
Relative fuel consumption of various means of transportation. In each case, estimated average load capacities were used to compute efficiencies. *A,* Intercity passenger carriers. *B,* Freight carriers.

People can't easily move existing buildings, but they can and are changing transportation patterns. As mentioned previously, carpooling is an ideal and effective short-term solution. It isn't necessary to buy new automobiles; move houses, stores, or factories; or build new mass transit systems. If people shared rides, they could reduce fuel consumption by 50 percent or more overnight. Consider another factor. In the United States, most automobile trips are for distances of less than 8 km. People drive to the corner market to pick up a newspaper and a container of milk or to mail a letter. These trips are costly. Large amounts of gasoline are needed to start a cold automobile. As a rough approximation, a car that is capable of operating at 10 km/liter on long trips operates at 2 km/liter on short trips.*

If people reduced the number of short trips, walked, or rode bicycles, large quantities of fuel would be saved.

Other changes cannot be implemented so quickly, but, in future decades, they will become increasingly important. For example, the average

car sold in 1985 drove nearly twice as far on a gallon of gasoline as the average car sold in 1970. Looking into the future, prototype cars have been built that can travel 60 miles per gallon at highway speeds with 5 people, and experimental one- to two-person commuter cars achieve an efficiency of 100 miles per gallon.

Surface Mass Transit Surface mass transit—buses, trains, and trolleys—can provide clean, efficient transportation. At the present time, only 3

*To change km/liter to miles/gal, multiply by 2.35.

Box 15.1
MPG

In 1979, a contest was held in England to determine the maximal mileage possible with a motorized vehicle. The winner was a tiny, torpedo-shaped "car" using a 50-ml engine and three bicycle wheels. It averaged 597 km/liter (1403 miles/gal) over an oval-shaped racetrack.

A   B

The bicycle is an energy-efficient means of transportation. *Left,* Two women ride double. (From D. Plowder: *Farewell to Steam.* Brattleboro, Vermont, Stephen Greene Press, 1966) *Right,* in this village in Mexico, three-wheeled freight bicycles are more numerous than cars and are used for a variety of transportation needs.

percent of urban transport and 4 percent of intercity traffic is carried by public ground transportation systems; the remainder is carried by automobiles and airplanes. The most recent trend is an overall reduction of urban mass transit, rather than an increase. Although bus and subway systems are relatively popular in the largest cities in North America, the automobile still reigns supreme in most small- or intermediate-sized urban centers. As a result, a dangerous situation has evolved. If fuel shortages were to develop quickly, the existing mass transit system could not possibly handle transportation needs. Millions of commuters would be stranded and unable to get to work. Cities would be paralyzed.

Most mass transit systems in the United States and Canada are far behind their European counterparts. Intercity rail services have been reduced in the United States while the federal expenditure for new highways has escalated. In many cities, a person may have to wait up to 20 minutes for a local bus, whereas bus service in most European cities is available every 5 minutes during rush hours. At the present time, traffic is often stalled for long periods of time during rush hours and travel is slow; accidents are common. Moreover, parking spaces

are often difficult to find; rarely can people drive directly to their destination and park nearby. If quiet, efficient, comfortable mass transit systems were built in most cities, mass transit might become an efficient, economical, and therefore popular alternative to the automobile.

The BART rapid transit system in the San Francisco Bay area.

Special Topic B
Amtrak—America's Railroad

In the early 1900s, before commercial air travel was a reality, and during an era when roads were poor and automobile travel was slow and arduous, railroads were the premier way to travel. However, as times changed, more and more Americans opted for the convenience and flexibility of the automobile or the speed of the airplane. As a result, passenger trains kept losing popularity until they eventually became uneconomical to operate. Rather than witness the demise of passenger service, the government took control of the ailing passenger railroad system and consolidated it to form Amtrak.

Train travel is broadly divided into two separate categories—short-haul lines between closely linked cities, and long distance lines. The short-haul lines carry the bulk of Amtrak's passengers. For example, 54 percent of the railroad passengers in the country ride on the northeast corridor between Washington, Philadelphia, New York, and Boston. In contrast, the long distance lines across the western states carry relatively few people. Amtrak loses money on virtually all of its runs and is solvent only because it receives about $700 million in subsidies from the government every year. The Office of Management and Budget estimates that federal subsidies amount to about $94 per ticket for long distance runs, $27.50 per ticket on all short-haul lines, and $17.50 per ticket on the northeast corridor.

There is significant public debate on future funding for Amtrak. Opponents of the railroad argue that if the system cannot operate profitably, it should simply be abandoned. They argue that the expensive long distance routes, in particular, are a drain on the budget. According to this view, there is no reason why people who do not ride the trains should pay for those who do. On the other hand, those who support Amtrak argue that mass transit systems encourage commerce, reduce dependency on foreign oil, and are therefore an asset to the economic well-being of the country. Furthermore, the unprofitable long distance lines carry large numbers of elderly people who cannot, or choose not to, travel by any other means. No passenger rail system in the world operates without government support, and proponents of subsidies argue that it would run counter to the national interests to eliminate the network in the United States.

A small, but politically unpopular, group of people believe that mass transit is so vital to the national interests that it should not only be supported, but that automobile use should be discouraged at the same time. These people suggest that gasoline taxes should be raised, new highway construction should be curtailed, tolls on bridges and tunnels should be increased, taxes should be levied on downtown parking areas, and private automobiles should be entirely prohibited from some streets or highway lanes. Those who propose such draconian measures argue that if we make a gradual transition to more efficient transportation systems today, we will save ourselves from a more painful crisis transition in the future.

Energy Use in Residential and Commercial Buildings

Perhaps in no other sector of our society can more energy be saved with less need for social change than in the area of heating and cooling homes and commercial buildings. The easiest solution is simply to change the thermostat setting. The decision to make such a change involves a sacrifice; people must adjust to living under what are considered to be less than optimally comfortable conditions. The sacrifice is really not that great, however, and can be largely overcome by changes in dress habits. For example, according to research carried out by the American Society of Heating and Ventilating Engineers in 1932, the preferred room temperature during the winter for a majority of subjects was 18.9°C. Similar research at later dates showed that the comfort range had risen to 19.3°C in 1941 and up to 20°C by 1945. In 1987, many homes were heated to 21°C to 22°C. The increase in preferred indoor temperature is due in part to changes in fashion. Fifty years ago, people naturally wore sweaters and long underwear indoors. (If one lives through several winters at 18°C, then 21°C seems uncomfortably warm.) Today, men wear jackets, ties, and long pants in business offices in summer and then feel the need to turn the air conditioners

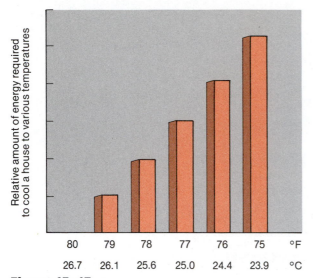

Figure 15–13

Relative extra fuel consumption for air conditioning to cool an average home to various temperatures below 80°F (26.7°C). For example, it takes three times as much extra fuel to cool the average home from 80°F (26.7°C) to 77°F (25°C) as it does to go from 80°F to 79°F (26.2°C).

Box 15.2
Saving Energy

In some areas of northern Japan, temperatures often fall well below freezing on winter evenings. Yet local residents use very little fuel for heating. After dark, family social life is centered around the dinner table. Tables are low to the floor, and people sit on cushions rather than on chairs. A large, heavy tablecloth extends beyond the table and rests on people's laps to serve as a common blanket. The primary source of heat in the dining room comes from a small electric heater located under the table. The heat produced is retained by the tablecloth, so the air around people's lower bodies is warm. The remainder of the house is cool, and the people simply wear heavy sweaters to keep their upper bodies comfortable. After dinner and tea, they go to bed and snuggle down under warm quilts.

on to "high." In the winter, many women wear dresses and skirts and turn the heaters up. If business fashion changed so that men wore short pants and light shirts during the hot weather, and women wore wool pants in the winter, less fuel would be needed for heating and air conditioning (Fig. 15–13).

The recent rise in the use of energy for air conditioning is another measure of social demand. In 1952, only 1.3 percent of the houses in the United States had air conditioning; by 1985, 60 percent of all homes were air-conditioned. The United States, with a mere 5 percent of the world's population, uses 50 percent of the energy consumed in the world for air conditioning. Houses, cars, shopping malls, and even entire sports arenas are cooled. In the hottest regions of the country, air conditioning does indeed make life more pleasant. However, in many areas, a room can be made comfortable at a fraction of the energy consumption simply by opening the window and turning on a fan. If a wet towel is hung in front of the fan, even more cooling is achieved.

Social solutions to conservation in home heating, powerful as they are, are really only a first step. Greater savings can be realized by more efficient construction. Most houses in North America are not built with sufficient concern for energy conservation. Large amounts of heat are lost through the insulation layer. Additional quantities are lost by leakage of air around windows and doors and through joints between floor and wall or wall and ceiling. If a house is built with about twice as much insulation as is used conventionally and if air leaks are meticulously sealed, large energy savings can be realized. However, if a house is totally sealed, indoor air pollution from cooking, cigarette smoke, or simple body odors can become oppressive. To combat this problem, fresh air from the outside is brought in through an air-to-air heat exchanger (Fig. 15–14). In the heat exchanger, warm polluted air flows outward past the cold fresh air moving into the house. The two are separated by baffles. The cold incoming air absorbs heat, so that by the time it enters the house, it is warm. If a house is built in this manner, heating costs can be reduced by as much as 90 percent in comparison with conventional housing, and the additional cost of the careful construction will be returned to the homeowner in the form of fuel savings within a few years.

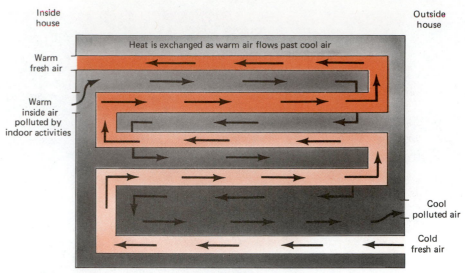

Figure 15–14
Schematic diagram of an air-to-air heat exchanger.

In a recent study, it was shown that the most economical housing can be achieved by choosing different construction styles in different parts of the country (Fig. 15–15). In most of the northern United States, superinsulation, as previously ex-

plained, is the method of choice. Passive solar is more efficient along a central band. Farther south, fuel bills are lowered if houses are dug into a hillside or covered with a thick layer of soil. The soil retains enough heat and provides adequate insula-

Figure 15–15
The most efficient type of house construction varies with location.

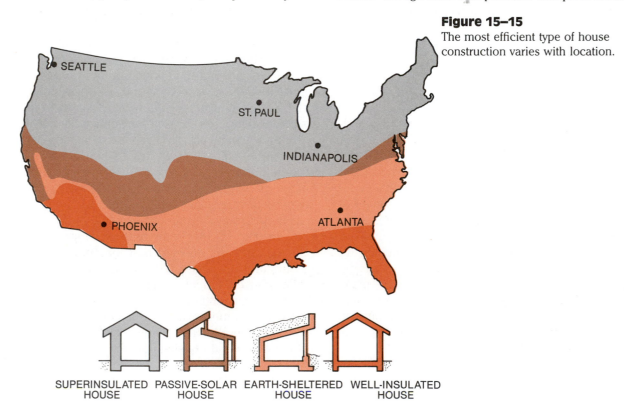

Special Topic C

How You Can Save Energy

How You Can Save Fuel In Transportation

Method	Fuel Savings Compared To Wasteful Practices
Walk or use a bicycle, stay at home	Saves 100%
Use mass transit	Saves 50% (or more)
Carpool	Saves 50% (or more)
Keep car well tuned	Saves 20%
Drive smoothly (no jerks, fast starts and stops)	Saves 15%
Purchase car without an air conditioner	Saves 10%
Keep tires inflated to proper pressure	Saves 5%

How You Can Save Fuel In Home Heating

Method	Heat Savings Compared to Energy-Inefficient House
Have your furnace maintained, cleaned, and tuned properly	Saves 10%–20%
Add extra insulation in ceilings and walls	Saves 30%–50%
Add storm windows	Saves 10%
Caulk leaky windows and doors	Saves 5%–15%
Cover windows with drapes and shades at night	Saves 5%–15%
Close off and do not heat un-used rooms	Variable
Turn thermostat down	Saves 3% per °F, or 1⅗% per °C

Energy-Saving Methods That Don't Cost Money

1. After taking a bath, open the bathroom door and let the water stand in the tub until it cools to room temperature. The heat from the water is enough to heat a small house for an hour.
2. Similarly, after doing the dishes, don't let the kitchen sink water drain out until it cools.
3. Use kitchen and bathroom exhaust fans sparingly, as they blow away a houseful of warm air in 1 hour.
4. Wear sweaters and long underwear in winter, and light clothes in summer. Then adjust the thermostat accordingly.
5. Close off unused rooms, walk-in closets, and stairways, and save the fuel that would otherwise be needed to heat them.

How You Can Save Fuel For Home Appliances

Method	Savings (Dollars/Year)*
Place extra insulation around hot water heater	Saves $19/year
Place insulation around hot water pipes	Saves $20/year
Hang clothes on line in summer rather than use dryer	Saves $25/year
Disconnect drying cycle from dishwater	Saves $25/year
Put covers on pans when cooking	Saves $5/year
Use wool or down blankets rather than electric blankets	Saves $8/year
Use proper size light bulbs, turn lights off when not in use	Variable
Turn off pilot lights on gas stove	Saves $10/year

*Energy savings here have been calculated using a value of $.05 per kilowatt hour.

Figure 15–16
Energy loss from a poorly insulated two-story home with an open fireplace.

tion for the mild climate. In the warmest parts of the country, the cheapest technique is simply to build a conventional but well-insulated home.

What about the houses that have already been built? Significant savings can be realized through simple and inexpensive conservation practices (Fig. 15–16). If an old, uninsulated house were insulated, if storm doors and windows were added, and if leaky seams were caulked, fuel consumption could be cut in half. Further savings can be realized by fitting solar design features onto existing structures. Two suggestions are shown in Figure 15–17.

Another approach to saving fuel in residential and commercial buildings is to install more efficient heating systems. In order to understand some possible technologies, one must consider the entire pathway of fuel use from its beginning in the

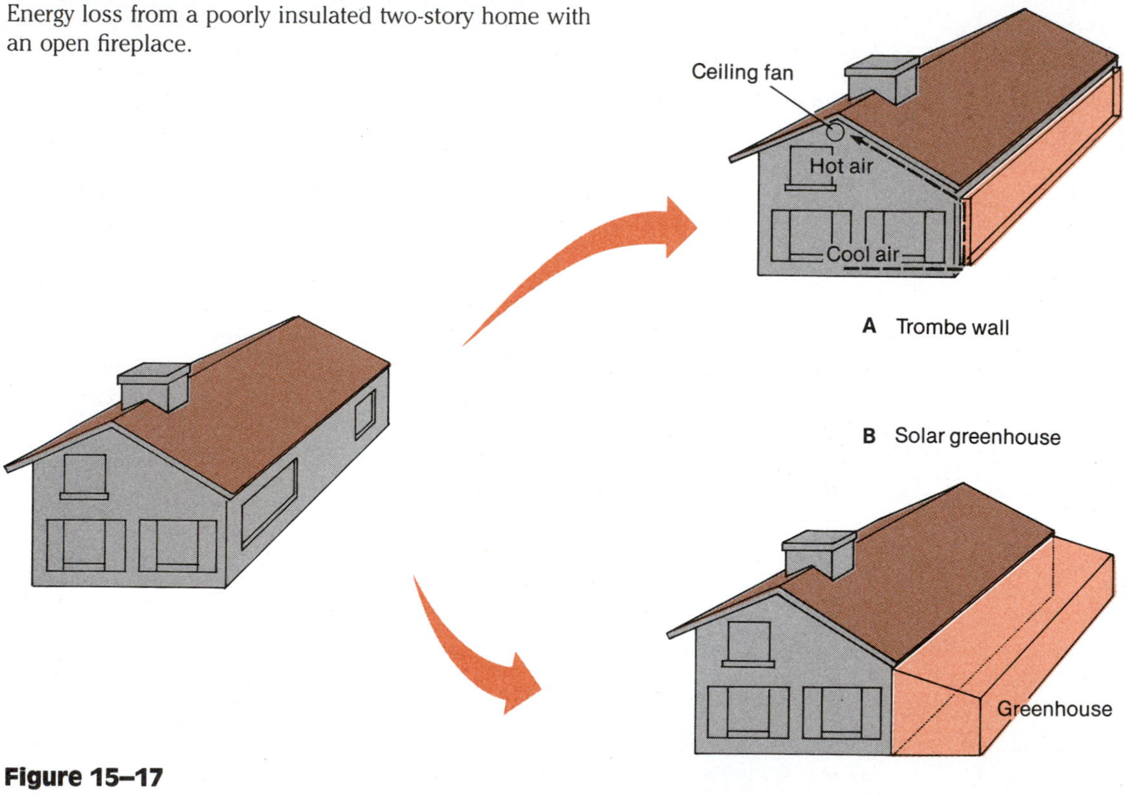

Figure 15–17
Two ways to fit passive solar design onto an existing structure. *A,* Trombe wall. A layer of glass is set 3 to 5 cm in front of the existing south wall, and holes are cut in the inside wall for the passage of air. The newly formed air space becomes a solar collection system. *B,* Solar greenhouse. A solar greenhouse is a passive solar collection system. The air in this space heats up, and hot air can be conducted into the main house. Plants can also be grown here; thus, the greenhouse can provide a household food source.

Special Topic D
Energy Efficiency of Refrigerators Used in the United States

Before World War II, electric refrigerators were about 90 percent efficient and used about 300 kWh/year. By 1975, the efficiency of equivalent-sized models had been reduced so that the average refrigerator consumed 1800 kWh/year—six times the consumption of prewar models. One major difference was that the older models had the motor mounted on the top of the frame so that the heat generated by the motor escaped into the room. On the other hand, in modern units, the motor is mounted at the bottom of the appliance, and as a result the waste heat warms the air directly under the food compartment. In addition, starting in the 1970s, most of the models were "frost-free." In a frost-free unit, warm air is periodically blown along the inside walls to prevent accumulation of frost. Finally, over the years, manufacturers gradually reduced the amount of insulation in the frame.

Currently, refrigerators consume about 6 percent of the nation's electricity. In 1981, it was reported that if all the refrigerators in the country were made as efficient as the units sold in the 1930s, the energy savings would equal the total output of about 30 nuclear power plants. In the early 1980s, the state of California enacted legislation that set standards for energy efficiency of appliances. All new refrigerators must be 50 percent more efficient than the units sold in the late 1970s, and air conditioners must be 20 percent more efficient. In March 1987, Congress passed the National Appliance Energy Conservation Act requiring appliance manufacturers to meet similar standards of efficiency over the next 3 to 5 years (Fig. 15–18).

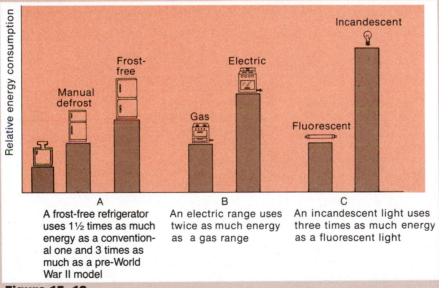

A frost-free refrigerator uses 1½ times as much energy as a conventional one and 3 times as much as a pre-World War II model

An electric range uses twice as much energy as a gas range

An incandescent light uses three times as much energy as a fluorescent light

Figure 15–18
Fuel consumption in the home could be reduced without any loss of comfort if more efficient appliances were used.

ground to its eventual consumption. Figure 15–19 shows different ways that petroleum can be used to heat buildings. Note, however, that for the fuel to be eventually used, the petroleum must first be extracted, refined, and transported. These processes, especially refining, use tremendous quantities of fuel. Approximately 20 percent of every liter of crude oil extracted is used up before any of it is available at the retail level, leaving only 80 percent for consumption. Of course, drilling and transportation are absolutely essential. Although it would be possible to burn unrefined crude in a home fur-

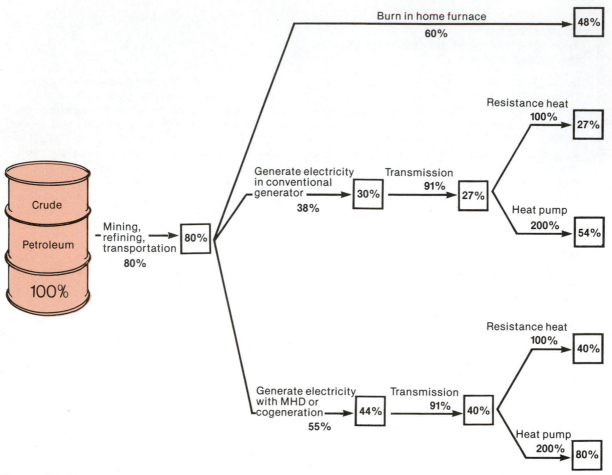

Figure 15–19

Energy efficiency of various ways of heating a building using petroleum as a fuel. In each case, the number under the arrow indicates the efficiency of the individual process, and the number in the box indicates the percentage of the original fuel remaining after the sequence of steps. (The number 80 percent for mining, refining, and transportation represents a rough average of widely divergent figures. Published values for the efficiency of refining vary from a low of 2 percent to a high of slightly over 100 percent. The difference is not necessarily an index of efficiency, but reflects the different chemical compositions of different fuels and the different endproducts desired. The values 10 percent loss in mining and transportation and another 10 percent loss in refining were chosen as a world average on the basis of a private communication with a representative from the Gulf Oil Corporation.)

nace or in an electric generating plant, the engineering problems involved in handling the thick goo and the pollution that would be released have discouraged direct consumption.

Once the fuel is available, the most direct form of usage is to burn it in a household furnace. Typically, a small furnace operates at about 60 percent efficiency. Thus, 40 percent of the remaining fuel is wasted as heat that escapes out the chimney. The result, as shown in Figure 15–19, is that 48 percent of the original energy in a barrel of petroleum is converted to useful heat; the remaining 52 percent is lost and dispersed into the environment.

This may seem shockingly inefficient, but other systems are worse. As explained in Section 15.6, electrical generation and transmission are only about 34 percent efficient. If losses in fuel extraction, transportation, and refining are also added, electricity, as delivered to a home, represents only 27 percent of the original energy in the petroleum. A conventional electric heater, called a **resistance heater,** is simply a wire or filament that resists the movement of electrons. As an electric current is forced through the wire, the electrons collide with the atoms in the wire, making them vibrate more energetically. This movement of the atoms causes the temperature in the filament to rise. Electric ranges, toasters, hot water heaters, baseboard heaters, and a wide variety of other electrical appliances operate on this principle. There is no loss of energy in a resistance heater; the process is 100 percent efficient. Therefore, the overall efficiency of resistance heaters, as shown in Figure 15–19, is 27 percent.

Despite the fact that resistance heating is 100 percent efficient, it does not represent the best use of electricity for supplying heat. To understand how it is possible to obtain greater than 100 percent efficiency, consider the workings of an ordinary refrigerator. A refrigerator is actually a type of **heat pump;** heat is pumped from inside the appliance into the room. Thus, the refrigerator heats the room while it cools the food. An air conditioner is another form of heat pump except that it is designed to cool a room, not heat it. Of course the energy is not lost, so heat removed from the room is exhausted outdoors. Thus, the air conditioner heats the outdoors while it cools the inside of a building. If you took a conventional air conditioner unit and simply turned it around, it would heat a room and cool the outside environment. This is exactly the principle of the heat pump. As it turns out, an air-conditioner turned backward is not always an efficient heating unit. Think about a house in Montana in January. Outdoor temperatures might typically be $-10°C$, and indoor temperatures are, say, $+20°C$. A lot of energy is needed to pump heat across a difference of 30°C, and considerable amounts of electricity are required. As an alternative system, suppose that a hole is dug under the house about 5 m into the earth. The subterranean soil and rocks, insulated from the air above, are surprisingly warm, approximately $+10°C$. If a heat pump is used to pump heat from this warm earth into the house, the machine is only required to operate across a temperature difference of 10°C, not 30°C. This is, in a sense, a form of geothermal heating, because the heat from the earth is used to warm a house. Because the earth's heat supply is free, the overall fuel efficiency of a heat pump can be 200 percent. Thus, as shown in Figure 15–19, a system of this type uses petroleum with an overall efficiency of 54 percent, twice that of resistance heating and slightly better than a common oil furnace.

Heat pump technology is well developed, and, in most cases, these units are the cheapest form of heat over the life of a house. However, heat pumps are not widely used. At the present time, the problem is twofold. First, most people are not familiar with this technology and its advantages. Second, today, most homes and apartments are built

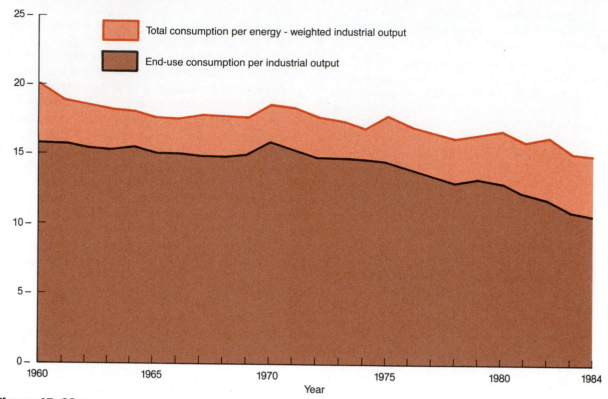

Figure 15–20

Industrial energy consumption per constant dollar of industrial output. (Source: *Annual Energy Review,* 1985, Energy Information Administration)

by a construction firm and then sold or rented to someone else. Builders try to offer housing at the lowest possible price; they are not the people who must pay the heat bills for decades to come. The cheapest heating systems to build are baseboard electric resistance heaters, so they are what is commonly used, even though they are the least efficient and in many cases the most expensive in the long run. The consumer saves a few thousand dollars initially, or has a lower rent, but then must pay twice as much for fuel. This is a classic example of short-sighted economics.

Energy Use in Industry

In general, industrial energy users are more likely to analyze the entire economic picture than are homeowners. This difference arises because if a factory is to stay in business, it must be competitive, and, to remain competitive, the total cost per unit of product must be considered. Therefore, manufacturers have a strong incentive to alter their physical plants or their operating procedures in such a way as to save energy. The nature of these conservation practices is specific to the industry involved.

As a result, energy consumption per dollar of industrial output has fallen steadily in recent years (Fig. 15–20). Between 1960 and 1984, industrial energy consumption per quantity of product has dropped a full 25 percent, and the trend is expected to continue.

Conservation of Energy Used to Produce Electricity

The recommendations proposed above apply to conservation of energy at the site where it is being used. However, as shown in Figure 15–11, more than 18 quads of energy, approximately 25 percent of the total energy consumption in the United States, is lost during the generation of electric power.

Figure 15–21

In a typical cogeneration system, fuel is burned in a boiler (1). The steam that is produced drives a turbine (2) that is connected to an electric generator (3). The generator produces electricity (4). The exhaust steam from the turbine can be used for heating, food preparation, or industrial processes (5). If needed, excess steam is cooled in a condenser (6), and the water is returned to the boiler.

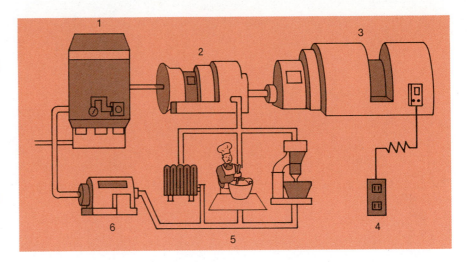

Cogeneration

The Second Law of Thermodynamics assures us that it is impossible to convert heat to work without the production of waste heat as a byproduct. In the United States, nearly all of this waste heat is released into the environment. At the same time, homes and other industries need large quantities of hot water for processes such as heating, canning food, or refining petroleum. Thus, a system exists in which hot water is thrown away at one place, and fuel is burned to heat water a few kilometers way. A better approach is to sell hot water from an electric generator to those who need it. Such a tandem operation is called **cogeneration.**

In a typical power plant, electricity can be produced at an efficiency of about 40 percent. If the efficiency of the electric production is lowered slightly and the steam is used by a neighboring industry, the efficiency of the two plant operations can reach as high as 80 percent, although only 50 to 60 percent is achieved in most applications (Fig. 15–21).

Cogeneration, largely overlooked for many years in the United States, has recently become increasingly popular. The reason for its popularity is simple economics. The cost of energy from a new coal-fired cogeneration system is about half the cost of energy from a new nuclear power plant. According to the United States Department of Energy, the nation could derive 44,000 megawatts of cogenerated power by the year 2000. This conservation measure alone would eliminate the need for 44 large, new coal- or nuclear-fired power plants.

Small-scale cogeneration systems are also gaining popularity. A typical unit consists of a small diesel- or gasoline-powered electric generator. Waste heat from the engine is used directly in a heating system. For example, a YMCA in Freehold, New Jersey, purchased a cogeneration system for $130,000. It generates 70 percent of the electricity used at the facility and produces all the heat needed for its rooms, showers, and swimming pool. The net savings amounts to $50,000 per year; therefore, the unit can pay for itself in 2½ years.

MHD

Another promising design that increases the efficiency of electric generation is based on the principle of **magnetohydrodynamics (MHD).** In this system, air is heated directly and is seeded with metals such as potassium or sodium, which lose electrons at high temperatures:

$$K + heat \longrightarrow K^+ + e^-$$

potassium   potassium   negative
atom   ion   electron

This hot, electrified air stream is allowed to travel through a large pipe ringed with magnets (Fig. 15–22). The movements of these charged particles through a magnetic field generate electricity. Furthermore, the exhausted hot air can operate a conventional turbine, thus producing additional electricity. The advantages of this system are twofold. First, the overall efficiency of the system is expected to reach 55 percent, and, second, most of the waste heat is dissipated directly into the air

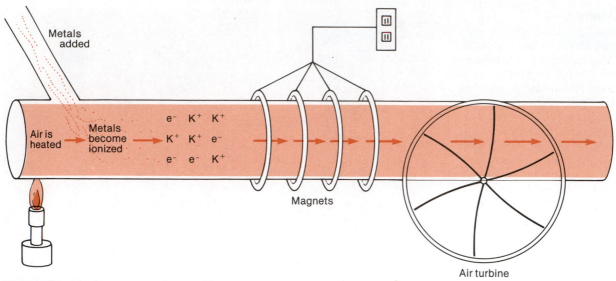

Figure 15—22
A schematic view of an MHD generator. Hot air is used to ionize certain metals such as potassium. When ions pass through a magnetic field, electricity is produced, just as when a coil of wire is rotated in a magnetic field. The exhaust gases will then drive an air turbine to generate even more electricity.

rather than into aquatic ecosystems. In the United States, most of the funding for MHD research was cut during the first half of the 1980s, and, as a result, development stagnated.

Return to Figure 15–19 for a final comparison. The bottom line illustrates an overall heating system that uses electricity derived from a cogenerator or an MHD generator to drive a heat pump. This system results in 80 percent efficiency—3 times as much as ordinary resistance heating. In other words, by using the best available technology, the petroleum used for heating can be stretched by a factor of three without mandating any sacrifice or inconvenience.

15.9
Predicting an Energy Future for North America

Conservation can delay the ultimate depletion of our fossil fuels but cannot conserve them forever. Therefore, we must consider what will happen when the mines are exhausted and the wells run dry. As mentioned earlier, coal reserves are expected to remain abundant for a few hundred years, and, because it is virtually impossible to look that far into the future with any degree of certainty, we will not consider the end of the age of coal. However, permanent oil shortages are expected within the next few decades, and we can and must consider that eventuality.

- After liquid petroleum resources are depleted, large reserves of heavy oils remain, but the cost of gasoline from these sources is certain to rise (Fig. 15–23).

- There is a great potential for the development of renewable energy. At the present time, many renewable sources such as wind or solar are more expensive than energy derived from conventional fuels, but as technological developments drive the price of renewable energy down and depletion drives the price of fossil fuels upward, the two curves are eventually expected to cross.

- The renewable energy technologies, with the exception of biogas and ethanol production, are most easily adapted to the production of **electricity.** But electricity can also be generated by the use of nuclear fuels or coal, which are abundant. There is no simple, inexpensive way to produce liquid fuels from most of the renewable technologies already discussed. True, hydrogen can be produced if electricity and water are available, and coal can be liquefied or gasified. Moreover, efficient coal-driven locomotives and electric

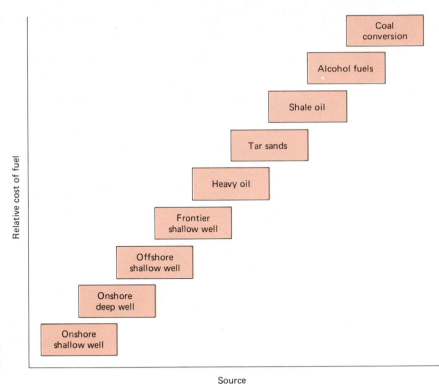

Figure 15–23
The cost of petroleum is sure to rise when readily accessible reserves are depleted.

cars and trains can be built. However, if these alternatives are chosen, massive changes in our industrial output are required, and it takes time and money to retool an entire society.

Therefore, it seems inevitable that modern society will face some sort of painful adjustment in the future. Just how serious this period of change will be is open to question. When wood was replaced with coal as a primary energy source in England at the start of the Industrial Revolution, there was a period of difficult times, but the transition was made in an orderly manner. However, there are no guarantees for the future, and we simply don't know what will happen.

Summary

Environmental problems associated with oil drilling are particularly severe for wells in the Arctic or under the seas. Coal can be mined either in tunnels or in **strip mines.** Strip mines deface the land, but reclamation programs reduce the impact.

Production of **synfuels** produces a wide variety of serious environmental problems, including destruction of land surfaces, depletion of water resources, and air pollution. The processes are also expensive.

Environmental problems also occur when energy is harnessed from renewable sources.

Production of electricity is about 40 percent efficient at best; therefore, electric heating systems are inefficient. **Thermal pollution** occurs when waste heat from an electric power plant is discharged into natural waterways. **Cooling ponds** and **cooling towers** are an alternative to direct discharge into aquatic ecosystems.

In most countries, fuel costs strain the national economy, and supplies are vulnerable to war and political instability. In the immediate future, conservation is the most effective energy strategy. Some examples of conservation strategies are:

• In transportation—use of carpools, more efficient vehicles, and mass transit.

• In residential and commercial buildings—social solutions such as changing fashions and thermostat settings, and technical solutions such as improved construction techniques and use of efficient heating systems and appliances.

• In industrial applications—use of new technology to reduce energy consumption.

In addition, electricity can be generated more efficiently by co-generation or use of MHD systems.

Looking into the start of the next century, several trends become apparent:

1. After liquid petroleum resources are depleted, large reserves of heavy oils remain, but the cost of gasoline from these sources is certain to rise.

2. There is a great potential for the development of renewable energy sources.

3. The industrial superstructure of our society is complex, and the transition to new energy sources will involve massive changes.

Questions

Extraction of Fossil Fuels

1. Explain why the environmental impact of mining and drilling for fossil fuels is likely to *increase* as fuel reserves are gradually exhausted.

2. Compare the environmental impact of tunnel- and strip-mining.

3. Who pays for the cost of reclaiming strip mines? What are the external costs that result from strip mines if they are not reclaimed, and who pays for these expenses? Which costs are more immediately apparent for the average citizen? Discuss the relative merits of mine reclamation.

4. Recent reports indicate that many carcinogenic compounds are produced when liquid fuels are synthesized from coal. In addition, more than one third of the fuel content of the coal is consumed during the conversion. Using this information and the material in the text, list the categories of direct costs and external environmental costs required to produce liquid fuel from coal.

Renewable Energy

5. People who live near large wind farms complain that the generators are noisy and that they preempt land that could otherwise be used for recreation. Discuss relative pros and cons of electricity generated from wind.

Electricity

6. Explain why thermal pollution is an unavoidable result of the Second Law of Thermodynamics.

7. In each of the following examples, list the systems in order of increasing energy efficiency: (a) a gas-operated clothes dryer, an electric clothes dryer, a clothesline; (b) an electric saw, a gasoline-operated saw; (c) an electric refrigerator, a propane-operated refrigerator. Defend your answers.

8. In North America, many homes are built by developers and are then sold immediately. Thus, the builder never lives in the house. In general, electric baseboard heating is cheaper to install than any other type of heating system and is therefore the system of choice in a large number of developer-built homes. Do you think that it would be a legitimate role of government to dictate the types of heating systems used in new construction? Defend your answer.

Energy Politics and Economics

9. In 1985, the United States spent approximately $50 billion on imported fuels. Discuss some problems involved with replacing half of the imported oil with synfuels. Compare some of the social costs of synfuel production to the costs of energy imports.

10. Some people have suggested that a tax be placed on all imported oil. Would you approve or disapprove of such a tax? Defend your answer.

11. Many people suggest that the government should provide low-cost loans for solar collectors. Others disagree. They argue that solar energy would benefit only those living in suburbs or in the country. They argue further that if solar energy were such a good idea, it would be profitable enough to work without government support. Discuss these arguments.

12. Gasoline taxes have traditionally been used for the construction of new roads. This practice has been considered fair because the roads are paid for by those who use them most. Increasingly, economists and social philosophers believe that many of our traditional concepts of fairness must be re-evaluated in the light of environmental problems. Do you think that there should be a re-evaluation of road tax use? If so, how would you allocate funds? If not, defend your position.

Conservation

13. Explain how an energy crisis could cause people to lose their jobs. Explain how a gradual energy conservation program could increase jobs.

14. List 5 actions that could be taken on a municipal level and 5 actions that could operate on a national level to conserve energy. How difficult would it be to implement these measures?

15. List five ways to improve the heating efficiency in your home or apartment. If you live in a private home, estimate the cost of implementing these changes. If you live in an apartment house, do you think that such changes would be a worthwhile investment for the owner?

16. Which of the following conservation procedures involve primarily technical solutions; which would involve social readjustment; and which involve a combination of both: (a) carpooling; (b) use of small cars; (c) addition of storm windows on houses; (d) turning the thermostat down to 65°F in winter; (e) use of gas stoves rather than electric ranges; (f) use of rooftop solar cells for household electricity?

17. Give some reasons why it is often difficult to alter patterns of surface transportation.

18. It takes only a few hours to fly across the United States. A comparable journey by train takes several days. Yet the cost to the passenger is more by train. Discuss the impact of the economic structure on world fuel reserves.

19. As stated in the text, only 3 to 4 percent of the transportation mileage in the United States is carried by public ground transportation systems. Thus, even if mass transit systems were to double the number of passengers they carry, there would be relatively little impact on overall fuel consumption rates. Should these figures be used in an argument against building new mass transit systems? Defend your answer.

20. Compare the relative fuel consumption of: (a) a single person driving in a heavy, luxury car; (b) four people riding in a heavy, luxury car; (c) one person driving in a small subcompact car; (d) four people riding in a small subcompact car; (e) travel by bus; (f) travel by bicycle.

21. How do clothing styles affect energy consumption in the United States?

22. Name the three appliances in your home or apartment that consume the most electricity. Can you think of ways to conserve some of the energy used by these devices? Do your suggestions involve personal sacrifice or technological improvements?

Energy Futures

23. Prepare a class debate. Have one side argue that we are quickly approaching an energy crisis that will debilitate our society, while the other side argues that society will adjust to changes in energy supply without massive disruption.

Suggested Readings

The general references listed for Chapter 13 also provide background material for this chapter. Additional materials that refer to specific sections are listed below.

Environmental problems caused by extraction of fossil fuels:

J. L. Anastasi: SASOL: South Africa's oil from coal story—background for environmental assessment. EPA Report 600/8-80-002. Washington, D.C., U.S. Government Printing Office, January 1980. 36 pp.

E. J. Hoffman: *Synfuels: The Problems and the Promise.* Laramie, WY, The Energon Co., 1982. 547 pp.

R. F. Probstein and R. Edwin Hicks: *Synthetic Fuels.* New York, McGraw-Hill, 1982. 490 pp.

Carroll L. Wilson: *Coal—Bridge to the Future.* Cambridge, MA, Ballinger Publishing Company, 1980. 247 pp.

Environmental consequences of using renewable resources:

John P. Holdren: Energy Hazards: What to measure, what to compare. *Technology Review,* April 1982.

William N. Rom and Jeffrey Lee: Energy alternatives: What are their possible health effects? *Environmental Science and Technology, 17:*3, 1983.

The politics and economics of energy supply are reviewed in:

Irvine H. Anderson: *Aramco, the United States, and Saudi Arabia.* Princeton, Princeton University Press, 1980. 259 pp.

William U. Chandler: *Energy Productivity: Key to Environmental Protection and Economic Progress.* Washington, D.C., Worldwatch Institute, 1985. 62 pp.

Wilson Clark and Jake Page: *Energy, Vulnerability, and War.* New York, W.W. Norton and Company, 1980. 251 pp.

Cutler J. Cleveland, Robert Costanza, Charles A. S. Hall, and Robert Kaufmann: Energy and the U.S. economy: A biophysical perspective. *Science, 225:*890, 1984.

David A. Deese and Joseph S. Nye (eds.): *Energy and Security.* Cambridge, MA, Ballinger Publishing Company, 1980. 489 pp.

J. Goldemberg et al: An end-use oriented global energy strategy. *Annual Review of Energy,* 1985.

Don E. Kash and Robert W. Rycroft: *U.S. Energy Policy: Crisis and Complacency.* Norman, OK, University of Oklahoma Press, 1984. 334 pp.

Amory Lovins and Hunter Lovins: *Brittle Power: Energy Strategy for National Security.* Andover, MA, Brick House Publishing, 1982. 486 pp.

Bruce Nussbaum: *The World After Oil: The Shifting Axis of Power and Wealth.* New York, Simon and Schuster, 1985. 319 pp.

Marc Reisner: The rise and fall of energy conservation. *The Amicus Journal, 9:*2, 1987.

Daniel Yergin and Martin Hillenbrand (eds.): *Global Insecurity. A Strategy for Energy and Economic Renewal.* Boston, Houghton Mifflin, 1982. 427 pp.

References on energy conservation include:

Thomas Johansson, Peter Steen, Erik Borgen, and Roger Fredriksson: Sweden beyond oil: The efficient use of energy. *Science, 219:*355, 1983.

Robert C. Marlay: Trends in industrial use of energy. *Science, 226:*1277, 1984.

Alan Meier, Janice Wright, and A. H. Rosenfeld: *Supplying Energy Through Greater Efficiency.* Berkeley, CA, University of California Press, 1983. 196 pp.

James W. Morris: *The Complete Energy Saving Handbook for Home Owners.* New York, Harper and Row, 1980.

Paul C. Stern and Elliot Aronson (eds.): *Energy Use: the Human Dimension.* New York, W. H. Freeman, 1984. 237 pp.

U.S. Department of Agriculture: *Cutting Energy Costs.* U.S. Government Printing Office, Superintendent of Documents, 1980.

Betty Warren: *The Energy and Environment Checklist.* San Francisco, Friends of the Earth, 1980. 222 pp.

Excellent references on the energy future are:

D. Allen Bromley: *A Desirable Energy Future.* Philadelphia, Franklin Institute Press, 1982. 255 pp.

Manas Chatterji (ed.): *Energy and Environment in the Developing Countries.* Somerset, NJ, John Wiley, 1982. 352 pp.

Jae Edmonds and John M. Reilly: *Global Energy in the 21st Century.* New York, Oxford University Press, 1985. 336 pp.

John M. Fowler: Energy policy: Toward the year 2000. *Environment, 25:*7, 1983.

John Gever and others: *Beyond Oil.* Cambridge, MA, Ballinger Publishing Co., 1986. 304 pp.

John H. Gibbons and William U. Chandler: *Energy, the Conservation Revolution.* New York, Plenum Press, 1980. 258 pp.

SERI-Solar/Conservation Study: *A New Prosperity: Building a Sustainable Energy Future.* Andover, MA, Brick House Publishing Company, 1980. 454 pp.

Jon Van Til: *Living with Energy Shortfall.* Boulder, CO, Westview Press, 1982. 209 pp.

Miscellaneous references on specific topics are:

Jim Harding and the International Project of Soft Energy Paths: *Tools for the Soft Path.* San Francisco, Friends of the Earth Publishing, 1982.

Glen H. Lovin: Cogeneration the Precursor to Cogen Power? *ASHRAE Journal,* February 1987.

Simon Rosenblum: *The Non-Nuclear Way: Creative Energy Alternative for Canada.* Regina, Saskatchewan, Regina Group for a Non-Nuclear Society, 1981. 112 pp.

Robert P. Taylor: *Rural Energy Development in China.* Washington, D.C., Resources for the Future, Inc., 1981. 274 pp.

16

Nonrenewable Mineral Resources

16.1
Introduction

Living organisms use a source of energy (ultimately, the Sun) to convert materials from the environment (nutrients) into body tissues. The time scale of these conversions is the time scale of the spans of life—months for plant fibers such as cotton, years for animal materials such as bone and hide, and decades for wood. On the time scale of human lives, therefore, these materials are **renewable;** if we do not use them up faster than they are produced, they need never be exhausted.

Geological processes, like those of life, can also organize and concentrate materials, but here the time spans extend to many millions, or even a few billion years. Because humans cannot wait that long, mineral resources are said to be **nonrenewable.**

16.2
The Formation of Mineral Deposits

Scientists believe that the Earth and, in fact, our entire Solar System was originally formed out of a vast cloud of gas and specks of dust and frozen crystals that were floating about within the galaxy. One can imagine that this primordial cloud was relatively homogeneous, which is to say that the chemical composition was constant throughout. By far, the most abundant elements were hydrogen and helium, which together constituted more than 99 percent of the cloud. Slowly, over the millennia, the dispersed particles were drawn together by their mutual gravitation. Most of the mass of the original cloud fell inward toward the center, and eventually formed the Sun, while smaller amounts separated and coalesced to form the nine planets, their moons, and other assorted objects found within our Solar System. Today. the Sun is still composed mainly of hydrogen and helium. However, on small planets such as the Earth, the gravitational field is so weak that most of these light elements gradually escaped into the vastness of space, leaving behind a sphere composed predominantly of heavier elements.

We can imagine that in its earliest form, the solid Earth was relatively homogeneous. If the Earth had remained in this state, modern civilization could never have developed, because the con-

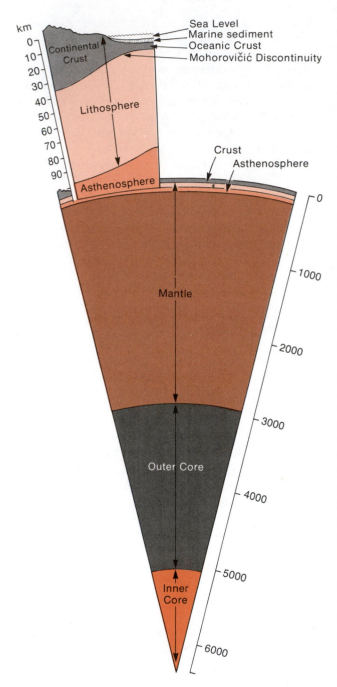

Figure 16–1

Cutaway view of the interior structure of the Earth. Note that the core is subdivided into an inner and outer core. The upper levels of the mantle also contain distinct layers as shown in the drawing.

centrated deposits of metals necessary to the modern age did not exist. But the Earth has always been a dynamic system, and changes have been occurring continuously since its formation. Slightly more than 4 billion years ago, the interior of the Earth was melted by the heat of radioactive decay, and the surface was melted by an intense rain of meteors. Thus, the entire planet was liquefied. Most of the dense elements such as iron and nickel gravitated toward the center, which we now call the **core.** These elements became surrounded by a **mantle** of lighter rock and a surface **crust** of comparatively low density. The present structure of the Earth is shown in Figure 16–1.

The boundaries between the layers of rock inside the Earth are not rigid and impenetrable. Rather, rock flows upward and downward in slow but continuous and dynamic exchange. Thus, the Earth is believed to have cooled sufficiently to form a hard solid crust about 3.5 to 4 billion years ago, but virtually none of that original crust remains. Almost all the original rock has been pushed downward into the mantle, reabsorbed, and replaced by material coming from deep within the globe.

The mantle itself is not homogeneous but is separated into layers and regions, each with its own unique physical and chemical characteristics. Certain regions are relatively fluid. This fluid, called **magma,** consists of melted rock mixed with various gases such as steam and hydrogen sulfide. When magma flows quickly to the surface of the Earth, a volcanic eruption occurs, and the outpouring magma is called **lava.** If magma protrudes into the crust slowly through a crack or fissure in the rock but does not travel all the way to the surface, it will cool gradually deep within the crust (Fig. 16–2).

Other regions of the mantle are not free-flowing liquids but are viscous and semifluid, somewhat like a heavy putty. Various forces within the mantle create large stresses, pushing this viscous mixture in one direction or another.

For most practical purposes, it may safely be assumed that the Earth's crust is a rigid mass of rock covering the surface of our planet. Thus, we expect that the distance between any two cities in the world will remain constant from year to year and that the continents will always lie in the same relationship to each other as they do now. However, as explained in Chapter 3, the continents are

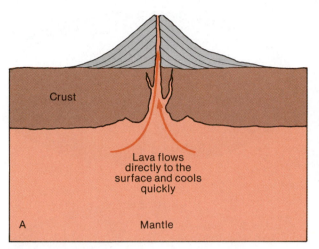
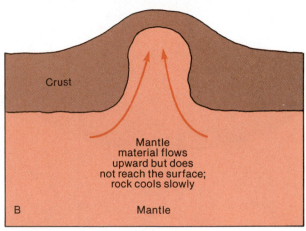

Figure 16–2

A, In some instances, molten material from the mantle flows directly to the surface of the Earth through fissures in the crust. Such flows are called *volcanoes. B,* In many other cases, fluids from the mantle push upward into the crust but do not reach the surface. These fluids then cool slowly because they are insulated by a thick layer of crustal rocks.

not immobile and rigidly fixed in position. Rather the Earth's crust is segmented into several distinct pieces called **continental plates.** These plates float on the denser mantle fluid, much as tightly packed icebergs might float on water. Figure 16–3 shows how, over a period of a few hundred million years, the continents have fused, broken apart, and then slowly drifted away from each other to their present positions. This idea is called the theory of **continental drift.** Of course, as continents move, they carry their mineral deposits with them.

Thus, we see that the Earth's elements are in a constant state of motion. Fluids or semifluids flow within the interior, and sometimes these materials push upward into the crust or onto the surface. In addition, the surface itself is in motion, and, in certain regions, surface rocks are pushed back into the mantle. Other processes shape and transport surface rocks. For example, winds and flowing water erode mountains and deposit sediments in the valleys and ocean basins. All these different types of movement act together to separate minerals from one another and to create the concentrated deposits that our civilization depends on. A few specific processes that concentrate minerals are discussed in Special Topic A.

16.3
Minerals—Their Value to Civilization
Metals

Civilization has always been associated with metals. Ancient civilizations arose as the Stone Age was transformed to the Bronze Age and, in turn, bronze was replaced with iron. The Industrial Revolution and the rise of modern technological society was intimately linked with advances in metallurgy and the development of new alloys such as steel.

Most metals are not found in their metallic state in nature but, instead, exist in the form of compounds such as oxides or sulfides. The metals must be extracted from these ores by processes that had to be invented, that require energy, and that generate pollution. On the other hand, there has always been a natural abundance of stone, clay, wood, bone, and fiber. So why are metals important? There are several reasons, three of which are listed here.

1. Metals are extremely strong compared with traditional building materials such as wood or

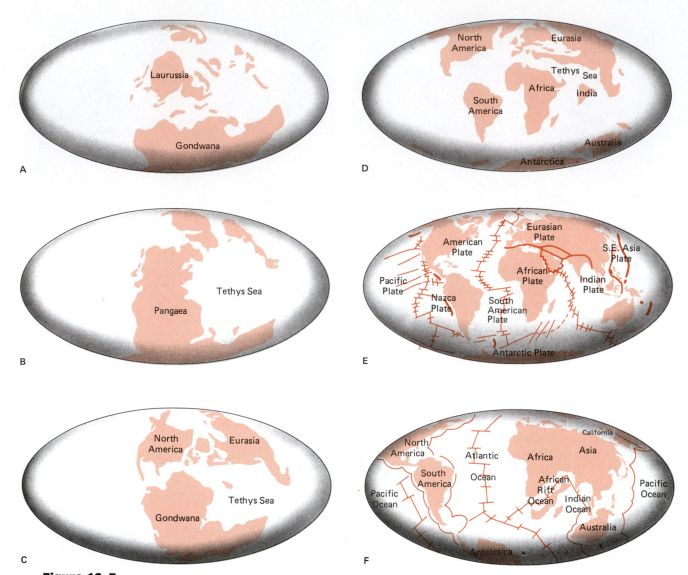

Figure 16–3

A, About 320 million years ago, the precursors of today's continents converged. *B*, About 250 million years ago, most of the land surface on Earth was fused into one single continent, called Pangaea, meaning "all lands." *C*, About 180 million years ago, this supercontinent started to break up, and the individual pieces started to drift apart. This map shows the world as it was 135 million years ago. *D*, The Earth 45 million years ago. India was separated from Eurasia and traveling northward, and Australia had recently separated from Antarctica. *E*, The Earth as it is today, showing the plates and the present plate movement. *F*, If the plate movement continues as predicted, the map of the Earth will look like this 100 million years from now. Note that the Atlantic Ocean will be larger than it is today, and the Pacific Ocean will be smaller. Africa is believed to be splitting apart today, and, in the future, it will be separated by a new seaway. At the same time, the bulk of the African continent is plowing into Eurasia, and the new mountain ranges will be formed.

stone (Table 16–1). Furthermore, metals are not brittle, whereas stone is. Heroic structures, such as the pyramids (Fig. 16–4), can be built of stone, which resists compression. Long spans, however, such as those of modern bridges (Fig. 16–5), require the tensile strength that metals can provide.

Figure 16–4
One of the pyramids of Gizeh, near Cairo, Egypt.

Table 16–1
Approximate Tensile Strengths of Materials

Material	Maximum Tensile Strength (kg/cm²)
Carbon fiber composite	40,000
High-grade steel*	11,000
Commercial-grade steel	4500
Brass	3000–4000
Aluminum	900
Oak (load applied parallel to grain)	100–115
Granite	30
Concrete	25–30

*Steel is iron alloyed with carbon and other metals to impart strength and resistance to corrosion. There are many different types of steel, depending on the materials used in the alloy. Each alloy has its own unique characteristics.

Figure 16–5
Steel is much stronger than stone. *Left,* The Pont-du-Gard aqueduct, erected in the last quarter of the first century B. C. as part of a canal that brought water to Nimes. Although this is an impressive structure, note that massive masonry is needed to support small spans. *Right,* The New River Gorge Bridge, world's longest arch (520 m), under construction. The delicate steel arch is designed to support a roadway above it.

Special Topic A
Some Geological Processes That Have Led to the Formation of Concentrated Deposits of Commercially Important Minerals

Separation by Gravity Suppose that two minerals were mixed together within a molten lava. If the magma is agitated and pushed upward to the surface by a volcanic eruption and then frozen quickly, the minerals will be more or less uniformly dispersed in the newly formed rock. But suppose, instead, that the magma had started to move up slowly through a fissure in the crust and cooled gradually while still kilometers under the surface. Say, for example, that one of the minerals solidified when cooled to 1200°C while the other solidified at 1000°C (Fig. 16–6). As the total mixture cooled, the mineral with the 1200°C melting point would start to solidify while the rest of the magma remained liquid. But now remember that the cooling process occurs slowly, sometimes requiring many thousands of years. During this time, all the tiny crystals of solid minerals would settle downward through the lighter liquid until there existed a concentration of one mineral at the bottom of the uplifting magma. This deposit may lie deep in the crust, unreachable by modern mining techniques. However, it may be pushed upward through a crack or fissure in the surface rock and then be exposed by weathering and erosion.

Separation by Differential Solubility Minerals may also become concentrated inside the Earth by differential solubility. To understand how this process works, take a little bit of salt and mix it up with a lot of sand. It would be physically difficult to pick out the grains of salt from the grains of sand. But suppose you put the entire mixture in a glass of water and stirred it up. The salt would dissolve in the water, and the sand would settle to the bottom. You could then pour off the water and collect the sand. The salt, which remains in the water, could be retrieved by evaporating the water and collecting the residue that remained.

Similar processes can occur at the Earth's surface. Many valuable mineral deposits in Utah were formed by differential solution of rock in water. Rainwater traveling across rock and soil dissolves minerals such as salt ($NaCl$) and potash (K_2CO_3), whereas other minerals, such as quartz (SiO_2) are largely unaffected. In most natural ecosystems, these dissolved salts are either reabsorbed by plant roots or carried into the ocean. But, occasionally, large land-locked lakes develop that have no outlet into open sea. Water flows into these lakes through streams and rivers but can escape only by evaporation. When salt water evaporates, the water escapes as vapor and the salt remains behind. As time passes, the mineral concentration of land-locked lakes increases. There was once a large land-locked sea in North America, covering much of northwest Utah. The salinity of this sea increased from age to age. Over the years, the waters receded due to a combination of geological and climatological factors. As the lake grew smaller, mineral deposits were left on dry land, and these are now mined commercially.

Placer Deposits Gold exists in its natural state as a pure metal and is denser than any rock. Therefore, if a mixture of gold dust, sand, and soil is swirled in a glass of water and the solids are allowed to settle

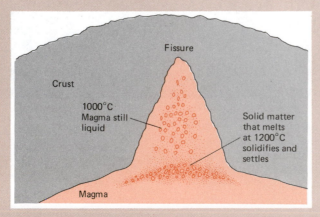

Crust

Fissure

1000°C
Magma still liquid

Solid matter that melts at 1200°C solidifies and settles

Magma

Figure 16–6
Minerals can separate by gravity from magma that cools very slowly.

out, the gold will fall to the bottom first. Differential settling may occur by natural processes. Suppose, for example, that small amounts of gold from a mountainside are carried downstream by a river. Chances are that the concentration of gold in the river water and surface sediment will be too small to mine economically. But now imagine that the river is partially blocked downstream by a beaver dam. As the water reaches the pond behind the dam, it slows down but does not stop and continues over the dam and on toward the sea. When rains fall and snows melt in the early spring, the stream may carry a lot of soil—mostly fine sediment with an occasional speck of gold. When the water reaches the beaver pond and slows down, the sediment will settle. Gold, being much denser than rock, will settle first. If the stream flows at just the right speed, the water will carry most of the lighter sediments downstream. As the years go by, more and more gold specks collect in one location until a small concentration, called a **placer deposit,** is formed.

Minerals Under the Sea   As continental plates separate and travel away from each other, new mineral matter from the mantle flows up through the gap and solidifies. When this occurs under the sea, large ridges rise up from the sea floor. Very deep cracks and crevices have been observed along these boundaries. Sea water seeps downward through the cracks and comes in contact with fresh, rising magma. Such valuable minerals as iron, manganese, copper, lead, and zinc may be dissolved or suspended in this water. As the water rises back up to the ocean floor, it mixes with the oxygen-rich waters above, and many metallic minerals can react with the oxygen to form oxides. These metal oxides are insoluble, and they fall to the sea floor near the ocean ridges in rich layers (Fig. 16–7). As a result, valuable minerals are found near the mid-ocean ridges. Some deposits that were formed in this manner have been uplifted by geological processes to become part of the continental land masses. The rich iron, copper, lead, and zinc deposits that contributed greatly to the wealth and power of the early Roman empire were formed in this manner. Other valuable deposits lie relatively inaccessible under several kilometers of sea water.

Another type of mineral deposit found under the sea exists in the form of small rocks, called **nodules.** These are formed by precipitation of chemicals present in seawater. A given nodule grows extremely slowly, about 1 mm every million years, but owing to the size of the ocean floor and the long expanses of geological time, sizable quantities of minerals have accumulated.

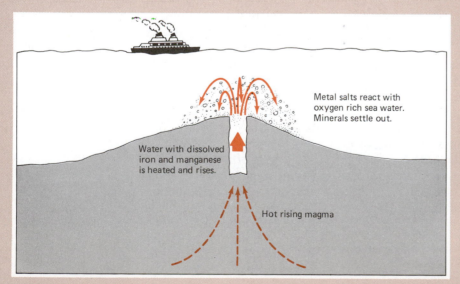

Metal salts react with oxygen rich sea water. Minerals settle out.

Water with dissolved iron and manganese is heated and rises.

Hot rising magma

Figure 16–7
Formation of undersea mineral deposits.

Figure 16–8
The crankshaft, camshaft, timing chain, and pistons of an automobile engine. Metals are valuable because they are strong, resistant to high temperatures, and can be machined precisely.

2. Metals can be melted and cast into any shape that a mold can provide. Metals can also be machined to precise dimensions (Fig. 16–8). Wood does not melt; it decomposes first. Some stones, such as limestone and marble, also decompose when heated. For stones that do melt, the high temperatures required and the brittleness of the product make casting in molds impractical.

3. Metals conduct electricity very well. No other materials even come close. A society that needs electricity needs metals.*

Table 16–2 summarizes the sources, uses, availability, and pollution problems associated with a few key metals.

Two Key Nonmetals

Metals are not the only elements that are extracted from our environment and used in modern society. Two key nonmetals are discussed briefly below:

Helium

Helium (He) is the second lightest (after hydrogen) of all gases. It is chemically inert—it does not react with anything. It does not even become radioactive with neutron bombardment. (The nucleus of the helium atom is an alpha particle, which is *ex-*

*Scientists are now experimenting with various synthetic organic materials that conduct electricity well, but, to date, nothing is commercially available that can compete with metal wires and electrical connections.

tremely stable; it is the *product* of nuclear fusion in the Sun and in the hydrogen bomb.) Helium has the lowest boiling point (−269°C) of any substance. When it does cool to a liquid, it remains liquid almost down to absolute zero. Liquid helium (which is available commercially) is therefore the ultimate cooling agent.

Because of these unique properties, helium has uses for which there are no substitutes:

1. For lifting, with safety. Its lifting ability in balloons is almost as good as hydrogen, but helium cannot burn.

2. To create an absolutely inert atmosphere, for welding and other processes, by excluding air.

3. For use as a cooling agent in some nuclear reactors and supercomputers.

4. To test for potential leaks in anything. If helium doesn't leak, nothing else will.

5. For use as a substitute for nitrogen in divers' breathing gas. (The presence of nitrogen causes the painful "bends" when the pressure on the diver is reduced.)

Phosphorus

Recall from Section 3.10 that phosphorus (P) is one of the important nutrients needed by living organisms. However, this element is not abundant in the Earth's crust. (At 0.13 percent, it ranks tenth among the elements.) Therefore, it is not easily replaceable in an ecosystem from which it is leached out or removed in the tissues of organisms. Many agricultural systems are dependent on the addition

Table 16—2
Sources, Uses, and Environmental Problems of Some Important Metals

Metal	Properties and Uses	Sources and Reserves	Environmental Problems
Iron (Fe)	Major metal for all structures and machinery. Demand for iron exceeds that for all other metals combined by severalfold.	Hematite (Fe_2O_3) and magnetite (Fe_3O_4). The highest grade hematite ores are largely exhausted. Magnetite is found in taconite rock; reserves are still vast and extraction technology has improved. Current resources are more than sufficient through the year 2100, and low-grade ores should last centuries more.	Air, water, and land pollution occur both at the mine and in the chemical production of iron from the ore. Taconite deposits also contain asbestos.
Aluminum (Al)	Aluminum is the second most widely used metal. It is only 1/3 as dense as iron, resists corrosion, and is a good electrical conductor. Used in aircraft, wires, automobiles, beverage cans, and many structural applications.	Bauxite, an impure form of Al_2O_3. Reserves are inexhaustible for centuries to come.	Much electrical energy used in production (about 67,000 kilowatt hours per tonne of Al). Also some fluorine-containing gases and dusts are produced in manufacture.
Copper (Cu)	Excellent conductor of heat and electricity. Used for electric wire, water, and steam pipes, and cooking utensils.	Elemental copper, mined since ancient times, is largely exhausted. Major sources are now copper sulfides, CuS and Cu_2S. Conventional resources expected to be exhausted in 60 to 70 years, but lower grade reserves expected to last until 2100.	Acid mine drainage. Smelters that process the sulfides produce large amounts of SO_2.
Lead (Pb)	Soft, dense metal that is fairly resistant to corrosion and has fairly low melting point (327°C). Used for pipes, solder, electrodes in batteries, and pigments in paint. Its use as an antiknock agent in gasoline is declining.	Major source is galena, PbS. Reserves are concentrated but not abundant. Low-grade ores will extend lead reserves until the year 2100.	Acid mine drainage. SO_2 is produced in lead smelters. Lead compounds are cumulative poisons.

Table 16–2 *(Cont)*

Metal	Properties and Uses	Sources and Reserves	Environmental Problems
Gallium (Ga)	Used in solar cells to convert solar energy to electricity. If the solar energy program expands, Ga reserves will be critical.	Found as an impurity in ores of zinc and aluminum but in small amounts. As long as Al is mined in quantity, Ga will be available.	No special problems.
Mercury (Hg)	The only metal that is liquid at ordinary terrestrial temperatures. Used in electrical switches, in thermometers, and for many special chemical and medical uses.	Sometimes occurs as the native element in small amounts, but the important ore is cinnabar, HgS. Reserves are very limited. If current rates of use were to continue, demand for Hg would be 8 times the available supply by the year 2100.	Mercury compounds are toxic.
Platinum (Pt)	Unsurpassed as a catalyst for oxidation reactions, for which it is used in catalytic converters to reduce pollution from automobile exhaust. Pt is also used as a catalyst in industry.	Occurs as the native element in widely scattered ores. Current reserves are abundant, but are concentrated in politically vulnerable areas such as Zimbabwe and South Africa.	No special problems.

Helium is lighter than air and does not burn; therefore, it is used in commercial and recreational balloons. (Gamma Liaison Photo Agency)

of imported phosphorus fertilizers. Fortunately, phosphorus is concentrated in the form of phosphate rock in various parts of the Earth, and these phosphates are mined and used as fertilizers that are essential to modern agriculture. Phosphate reserves are estimated to be sufficient for several hundred and perhaps even a thousand years, but that is not forever. It is not at all clear how global agriculture will be maintained when high-grade phosphate ores are depleted.

16.4
Mineral Sources and Availability

Minerals exist all around us throughout the environment. If you walked outside and picked up any rock at random and sent it to a laboratory for analysis, chances are very high that the report would show that the rock contained measurable quanti-

Table 16-3
Comparison of Concentration of Specific Minerals in Earth's Crust to Concentration Needed to Operate a Commercial Mine

Element	Natural Concentration in Crust (% by weight)	Concentration Required to Operate a Commercial Mine (% by weight)
Aluminum	8	24–32
Iron	5.8	40
Copper	0.0058	0.46–0.58
Nickel	0.0072	1.08
Zinc	0.0082	2.46
Uranium	0.00016	0.19
Lead	0.00010	0.2
Gold	0.0000002	0.0008
Mercury	0.000002	0.2

ties of iron, gold, silver, aluminum, and a variety of other valuable metallic elements. The problem is that the concentrations of these materials would be so low that it would be absolutely uneconomical to mine them. The absurdity of extracting metals from ordinary rock can be illustrated in the following example. Tungsten is used to harden the drill bits and crushing machinery used in mining. If you tried to open a tungsten mine in your back yard, you would use more of this metal to replace worn machinery than you would collect by operating the mine.

An **ore** is considered to be a rock mixture that contains enough valuable minerals to be mined profitably with currently available technology. As shown in Table 16-3, the mineral content in an ore body may be 10,000 times more concentrated than that found in ordinary rock. The **mineral reserves** of a region are defined as the estimated supply of ore in the ground. Reserves are depleted when they are dug up, but our reserve supply may be augmented by either of two processes. First, new deposits may be discovered. In addition, there are many known deposits that are relatively rich but are still uneconomical to mine. For example, a deposit containing 30 percent iron is not considered an ore, because it is so expensive to extract the metal from the rock that it would not be profitable under current market conditions. If technology improves so that the materials can be refined more cheaply, or if the market price of iron

increases, the deposit will suddenly become an ore reserve.

It is important to evaluate the present level of mineral reserves and to predict the future availability of essential raw materials. Some people have proffered a "gloom and doom" scenario whereby mineral reserves will soon be depleted and civilization as we know it will suffer severe hardships, whereas others have put forth carefree predictions of limitless supply and declining prices. In order to make a reasonably accurate analysis of the situation, we must evaluate the following factors:

1. Estimate the amount of minerals available in the ground.
2. Determine the cost of extraction of these minerals in terms of capital investment, processing requirements, and environmental impact.
3. Predict future demand.

The Romans discovered veins of almost pure copper lying under a thin layer of soil. These deposits have been exploited and are gone. In more modern times, many of the very high-grade, concentrated, and easily accessible ores, such as the 50 percent iron deposit of the Mesabi Range in the north central United States, are being used up rapidly and either have been depleted or will soon be depleted. These mines are essentially nonrenewable; once they are gone, our civilization will have suffered an irreplaceable loss. But our technological life will not end with the exhaustion of these rich reserves, because less-concentrated deposits are still available.

As an example of how erroneous predictions can be made, in 1966, it was estimated* that the global reserve of iron was about 5 billion tonnes. At that time, the global annual consumption rate was about 280 million tonnes. If these figures were correct and if consumption continued at a constant rate, the iron reserve of the Earth would have been consumed in 18 years,† bringing the end of iron reserves to 1966 + 18 years, or 1984. There must be something wrong with such calculations. Remember that a reserve is not a constant factor but can change markedly with exploration and with the development of methods suitable for processing ores of lower grade. In the case of iron, the big change was the development of improved methods of processing lower grade ores. Thus, deposits that were uneconomical to mine in 1966 and were not considered to be ores have become valuable reserves in more recent times. In fact, as shown in Figure 16–9, the reserves of many minerals have actually *increased* dramatically in recent years. Furthermore, many regions, especially in the less-developed countries, have not been explored systematically, so that it is reasonable to expect that new deposits will be discovered.

The optimism generated by the expectation of increasing reserves is further augmented by the likelihood that demand for key minerals will taper off. In the 1970s, the rate of doubling for the demand of an average metal was approximately once every 14 years. However, the rapid increase is expected to level off in the future. This prediction is based on three major assumptions: (1) Most demographers believe that the rapid rise of global population will level off and eventually stabilize. (2) It seems probable that, at least in the near future, the people in the less-developed countries will not attain the affluence now enjoyed by people in the developed countries. (If every family in Asia were to purchase two cars, a refrigerator, a television, and other luxuries, the global demand for resources would be astronomical.) (3) Consumption of materials will stabilize in the developed countries as the major economic base shifts from heavy industry to service and communications and as im-

---

*B. Mason: *Principles of Geochemistry.* 3rd ed. Appendix III. New York, John Wiley & Sons, 1966.

†5 billion tonnes/280 million tonnes per year = 18 years.

Special Topic B
Careers in Mineral Extraction

There are essentially three major stages in mineral extraction: exploration, mining, and finally mine reclamation. One hundred years ago, most exploration was conducted by solitary prospectors who often endured incredible hardships with the hope that they would be one of the lucky few to strike it rich. Some independent prospectors exist even today, but most of the mineral exploration is conducted by teams of professionals who are hired by large companies. In a typical example, one or more geologists will make an initial survey of an area. Before going out into the field, the geologists will study satellite photographs, reports of previous geological surveys, and results from other mining operations in the vicinity. Once a particular region is selected for closer study, a helicopter is generally hired to fly the researchers from site to site. If promising mineralization is found, drillers are called in to sample cores of underground rock. An exploration camp might be established with a full complement of mechanics, welders, cooks, and construction personnel to support the geologists, pilots and drillers. None of these workers will become rich if ore is found, but they are paid a wage even if they discover nothing.

If the results from the exploration are encouraging, then mining engineers will study the site and draw plans for starting a mine. The engineers are followed by the miners who operate equipment, do the blasting, and extract the ore. Once again, mechanics are needed to maintain equipment, carpenters are hired to erect buildings, and if the site is far from civilization, cooks, nurses, storekeepers, and office workers all become part of the small town that will be developed.

In modern times, mining operations must conform to a great variety of environmental regulations. The object of these laws is to restore the land to its original condition when the mining operation is complete. In order to realize this goal, biologists, ecologists, and soil scientists study the ecosystems in their undisturbed states, and then work together with engineers to direct the actual reclamation, which is performed by heavy equipment operators and their helpers.

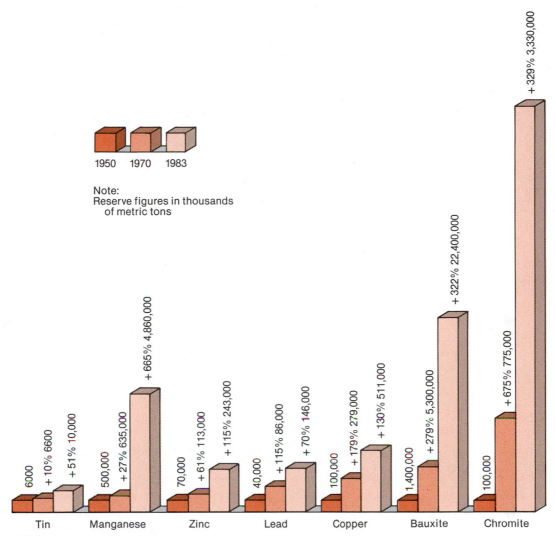

Figure 16–9
The change in the reserves of selected ores from 1950 to 1983.

provements in engineering reduce the amount of materials needed to produce a given item such as a car or a television.

In a recent article in *Science* magazine, the authors predicted that if the previously outlined trends continue, 33 of the 65 commercially important elements would still be in abundant supply by the year 2100. As shown in Table 16–4, 19 metals, including iron, aluminum, chromium, and nickel are on this list.

For various other commercially important elements, however, the picture is not nearly so rosy.

Several factors combine to project a pessimistic future for many materials that are vital to our civilization.

The Structure of Mineral Deposits

When the rich 50 percent iron reserves were exhausted, geologists found even greater quantities of 45 percent iron, and when these were exploited, still larger quantities of iron remained in 40 percent deposits. If the geology of a mineral follows this general pattern, small improvements in mining

Table 16–4
Predictions of Future Supplies of Elements Used in Industry

Metals	Nonmetals
Limitless Supply Sodium, magnesium, calcium	Nitrogen, oxygen, neon, argon, xenon, krypton, chlorine, bromine, silicon
Abundant Supply Aluminum, gallium, iron, potassium	Sulfur, hydrogen, carbon
Should Be Abundant if Research Continues to Improve Extraction Lithium, strontium, rubidium, chromium, nickel, cobalt, platinum, palladium, rhodium, ruthenium, iridium, osmium	Boron, iodine
Elements That Might Be in Short Supply by the Year 2100 Gold, silver, mercury, copper, zinc, lead, arsenic, tin, molybdenum, plus 22 other less familiar metals	Helium, phosphorus, fluorine

technology or small increases in prices can ensure a continued flow of materials. Unfortunately, this trend does not hold true for all minerals. To the contrary, in some cases, once the richest deposits are exploited, there is a sharp decline in both concentration of ore bodies and total quantity of ore available. For example, take the case of silver. Rich sources occur in sharply defined veins that branch out between shallow rock layers like a tree. If you discovered a vein like the famous Comstock lode, you would be boundlessly rich. This source yielded bonanzas of silver from 1860 to 1880 (Fig. 16–10). When the richest veins of such a lode are exhausted, production falls off, but, later, as prices rise, it pays to mine lower grade ore in the same lode. When these, in turn, are exhausted, the mine is abandoned. The miners do not return until either the price rises to very much higher levels or an entirely new processing technology is developed. Note from Figure 16–10, however, that the *overall* production trend is down; the latter peaks do not reach the heights of the earlier ones. The result of such a condition is that the availability of the metal decreases over time and eventually there are shortages. A similar situation is true for gold, mercury, copper, and several other metals.

Availability of Energy

It is important to understand that except for radioisotopes, elements are never used up or destroyed. When we talk about the depletion of a mineral resource, we simply mean that concentrated deposits are extracted and dispersed. The problem of concentration is really just another manifestation of the Second Law of Thermodynamics. Recall from earlier discussions that natural systems tend toward disorder. Thus, a drop of ink in a glass of water will spontaneously disperse until the water is uniformly lightly colored. The ink can be concentrated once again but *only* if some form of energy is expended. Similarly, if an ore is dug up, used, and dispersed, no atoms are lost, but large amounts of energy would be required to collect the material once again.

Within the Earth, energy from natural sources drove geochemical processes that in turn led to the concentration of minerals. However, these processes were never complete, and even the richest ores contain many materials of no commercial value mixed with the valuable minerals. To extract a metal from an ore, the dirt and rock must be dug up and crushed, the ore itself must be separated

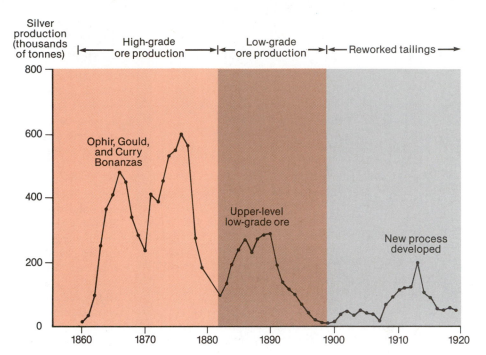

Figure 16–10
The depletion of the Comstock silver lode in Nevada. The first discoveries were very rich in silver. Later periods of mining followed, but the quantity of silver produced in each period was less than that in the previous period. This pattern has been followed in many other mining districts. The graph reminds us that mineral depletion is a real problem and that once rich mines are exhausted, a permanent loss has occurred.

and chemically reduced to the metal, and the metal must finally be refined to purify it. Each step, especially the chemical reduction, requires energy. Moreover, without exception, low-grade ores require much more energy to process than do high-grade ores. For example, if you are mining ore containing 29 percent phosphorus, more material must be dug, transported, and crushed to obtain a given yield of product than if you are mining ore containing 32 percent phosphorus.

Figure 16–11 shows the energy consumption required to extract and refine 1 tonne of copper or 1 tonne of aluminum as a function of the concentration of the ore. Note that if the ore contains very high concentrations of metal, relatively little energy is needed. However, as the mineral concentration in an ore body drops below a certain point, the energy consumption needed to produce a tonne of product rises very rapidly.

Some low-grade ores differ from high-grade ores not only in concentration but also in chemical composition. Some chemicals are easier to purify than others. For example, it is energetically advantageous to extract lead from its sulfide ore (PbS) according to the generalized reaction:

$$PbS + O_2 \longrightarrow Pb + SO_2$$
lead sulfide + oxygen $\longrightarrow$ lead + sulfur dioxide

Box 16.1
Minerals and Civilization

When metals were first exploited, ores had to be dug out of the ground with primitive tools. It was possible to do this because rich, concentrated, surface deposits were available. Today, most of these readily accessible deposits have been exhausted, but machinery is available to extract ores from deep underground and from harsh environments. As a hypothetical question, we ask, "What would happen if some catastrophe occurred, such as a nuclear war, that destroyed the structure of modern civilization?" Assuming that the human race, itself, survived, how quickly could an industrialized society be rebuilt? Of course no one knows the answer, but it is at least possible that if the technological cycle were broken, it would be very difficult to start a mechanized civilization over again. If there were no machines to dig up the iron, there would be no iron to make the machines. People would have to resort to mining old dumps, and society would become organized on a more simple basis.

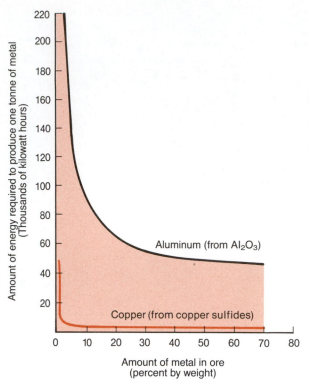

Figure 16–11

The energy required to mine and refine aluminum and copper ores as a function of the metal concentration in the ore. Note that there is very little change in energy requirements for very concentrated ores, but then, as the metal concentration drops off, the energy requirements rise very rapidly. Note also that there are no mines that contain 70 percent aluminum or 20 percent copper. Most mining is already being done in the steep section of the curve, so considerably more energy will be needed as lower-grade ores are exploited.

Lead also occurs in ores of other chemical compositions, but the overall energy requirements for processing them are much greater.

Pollution and Land Use

Most mining processes cause significant pollution of land, water, and air. The environmental problems associated with mining fall into three major categories.

1. Chemical Pollution Sulfur is found in large quantities in many ore deposits. This sulfur, bound in forms such as metallic sulfides, reacts with wa-

ter in the presence of air to produce sulfuric acid (H_2SO_4), which runs off into the streams below the mine. This pollution, known as **acid mine drainage,** kills fish and disrupts normal aquatic life cycles. When sulfur accompanies other chemicals through manufacturing processes, it is often converted to gaseous air pollutants such as hydrogen sulfide and sulfur dioxide. Sulfur, of course, is not the only polluting chemical from mining operations. Many other mine pollutants cause serious air and water pollution. Just as more energy is required to handle low-grade ores than high-grade ones, more pollution generally results from processing these impure materials. The pollution can be controlled with highly specialized pollution-abatement equipment, but such measures are expensive and add to the total cost of refining ore.

2. Solid Wastes As explained previously, metals are always mixed with rock that has no commercial value. When the metals are extracted, the rock must be disposed of somewhere, and a solid waste problem is generated. As lower grade ores are exploited, more wastes are produced per tonne of metal. The piles of rock and rubble are not only ugly, but they are also prone to erosion, and the muddy runoff silts streams and destroys aquatic habitats. In addition many environmental poisons are leached into natural and agricultural ecosystems. This problem will be discussed in detail in Chapter 18.

3. Land Use The world is running short of food, energy, and recreational areas as well as of high-grade mineral deposits. What should our policy be if a valuable ore or fuel lies under fertile farmland or a beautiful mountain? Which resource takes precedence? At present, this question is being raised principally with respect to exploitation of fuel reserves, for vast coal seams lie under the fertile wheat fields of Montana and the Dakotas in the United States and southern Saskatchewan in Canada. If large areas of low-grade ore must be exploited, the problem will also extend to metal reserves.

Political Barriers to Resource Availability

In Chapter 15, we discussed the relationship between global politics and potential disruptions in the availability or the price of energy. Similar relationships apply to certain minerals. For example, half of the world's cobalt is produced in the African nation of Zaire. Cobalt is an essential component of certain alloys used in the construction of jet engines and other specialized machinery. In January of 1978, the government of Zaire sought to follow the lead of OPEC nations and reduce cobalt production in an effort to force the price to rise. Later that year, a genuine disruption occurred as a result of a civil war that ravaged the mining district. Prices rose rapidly from $11/kg to $25/kg, and then skyrocketed briefly to $120/kg.

As shown in Figure 16–12, the industrial nations are highly dependent on imports for many essential metals. Some of these metals are purchased from politically stable countries, and the supply seems secure. On the other hand, the supply of others, such as cobalt, is relatively tenuous and vulnerable to disruption.

The reserves of some metals, such as iron and aluminum, are abundant. Therefore, if energy is available and problems of environmental pollution can be answered satisfactorily, we can expect a continued supply far into the future. On the other hand, there are 32 critical elements that are either in short supply or are available, but the supplies are vulnerable to political disruption. There is high probability that the reserves of some of these 32 elements will increase in the future or that we will learn in some way to live without them, but our society is so complex and its needs are so finely interwoven that a shortage of even a single element can cause severe repercussions throughout a broad spectrum of our economic structure.

16.5
Solutions to the Problem of the Scarcity of Minerals

As long as we continue to live in a civilized society, metals will continue to be valuable. Moreover, there are various trends that lead to ever increasing demand. For one, at least in the near future, the human population will continue to rise, and as more people come into the world, more materials are consumed. Secondly, most people wish to raise their standard of living. Increased wealth leads to additional purchasing power, which means that people collect more possessions, many of which are made of metals. Finally, every year some metals are more or less permanently bound up in buildings, bridges, dams, and roadways. However, despite this inexorable consumption, there are several ways that our existing metal reserves can be extended.

Exploiting Exotic Sources

One approach is to look for entirely new areas to explore. What about the sea floor, or the moon, or the planets? Various explorations have indicated that the mineral deposits on the sea floor are vast. Much of this material is concentrated in the form of round, flat, or odd-shaped pieces, typically weighing about a kilogram or so, that are rich in manganese. They are called **manganese nodules,** but they also contain copper, iron, nickel, alumi-

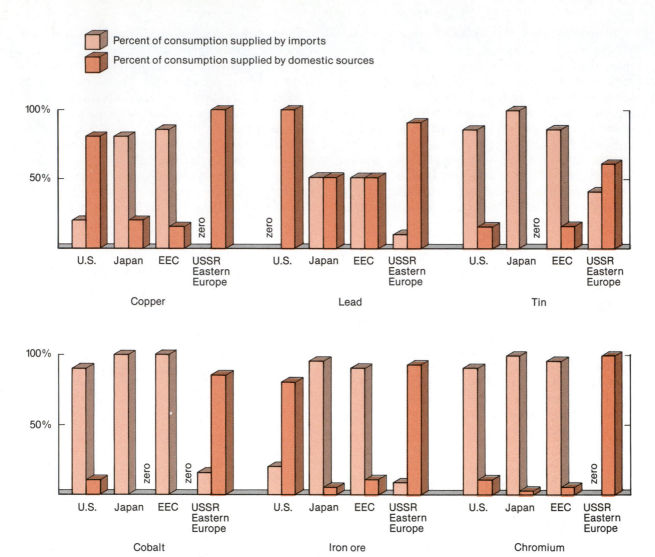

Figure 16–12
The percentages of six strategic metals that are imported and produced internally in the industrial regions of the world. (EEC is an abbreviation for European Economic Community, often called the Common Market.)

num, cobalt, and about 30 or 40 other metals. It is estimated that there are a trillion or more tonnes of these nodules on the sea floor. The sea floor does not have to be drilled or blasted, and explorations can be done with undersea TV cameras. Furthermore, no one "owns" the sea floor, but the question of just how the mining rights are to be allocated is still unclear. Nonetheless, the technology of collection is complicated, and costs are expected to be high. The sea is not the easiest environment in which to operate complex machinery.

Possible methods of collection include scoops, dredges, and vacuum devices (Fig. 16–13). Various groups of corporations are already involved in exploration and planning.

In the early years of the space age, some enthusiasts wrote optimistic speculations about minerals from the Moon and the planets. These voices are hardly ever heard anymore.

So far, we have discussed ways in which mineral reserves can be increased and high-level consumption can be maintained. Another option, how-

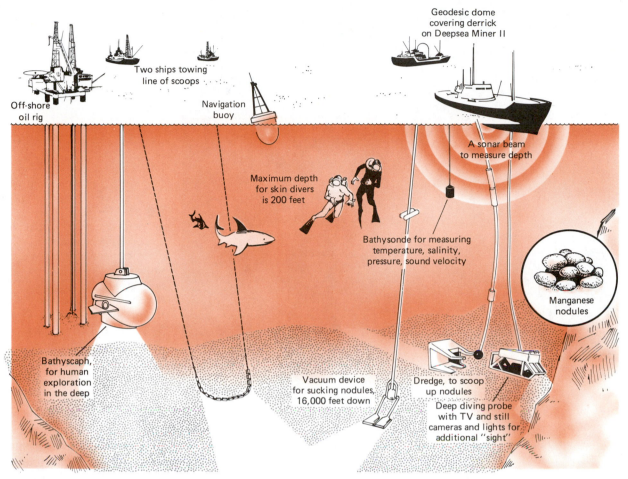

Figure 16–13
Mining the sea floor for manganese nodules.

ever, is to conserve existing reserves by using less. There are many different ways to reduce the consumption of mineral resources.

Substitution

In many cases, a scarce resource can be conserved by using a more plentiful one as a substitute. There are many examples of substitution in our society. In some cases, engineers have gone backward—in a sense—to more simple styles of using wood, stone, and concrete instead of using steel, whereas in other cases, they have advanced toward the use of high-tech plastics, glasses, ceramics, and composites to replace a variety of metals. A few examples are listed below:

- Masonry, by itself, cannot be used to build beams; therefore, the bridges and buildings constructed before the Industrial Revolution were limited in scope. In modern times, however, a structural material called **reinforced concrete** is made by pouring concrete over a relatively light matrix of steel rod. As shown in Figure 16–14, strong but delicate forms can be built in this manner, and comparatively little steel is used.

- Everyone is familiar with the use of plastics for a wide range of products such as toys, packaging materials, and furniture. If plastics and various types of fibers are bonded together with selected adhesives, it is possible to construct materials that are far lighter and

Figure 16–14
Although concrete, by itself, is a poor structural material, reinforced concrete is quite strong and can be used to build strong, but delicate, shapes. This photograph shows the interior of the TWA flight center at John F. Kennedy International Airport. (Courtesy of TWA)

stronger than even the most advanced metal alloys (Fig. 16–15). For example, in late 1986, an airplane called the Voyager succeeded in flying around the world nonstop without refueling. When the builder, Burt Rutan, was first designing the plane, he calculated that if the frame were built of even the lightest metal, it would have to be the size of an aircraft carrier to carry enough fuel to complete the journey. Instead, he built a honeycombed core of plastic that was then bonded to a shell of carbon-graphite fibers. The resulting substance was strong and light enough to do the job and may be the precursor to plastic airplanes of the future. In other applications, experimental automobile engines have been built out of plastics or ceramics, and some have proved to be highly efficient.

- As stated earlier, metals are essential to modern society because they conduct electricity far better than do other materials. There are generally two different categories of electrical

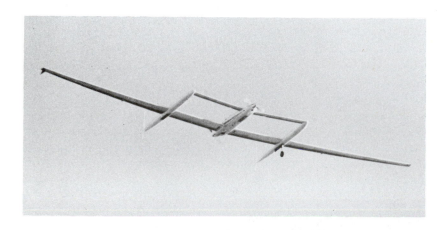

The Voyager, the first airplane to fly around the world nonstop without refueling. The wings and fuselage of this craft were made of sophisticated composite materials that have higher strength-to-weight ratios than metals. (Ron Siddle/Sygma)

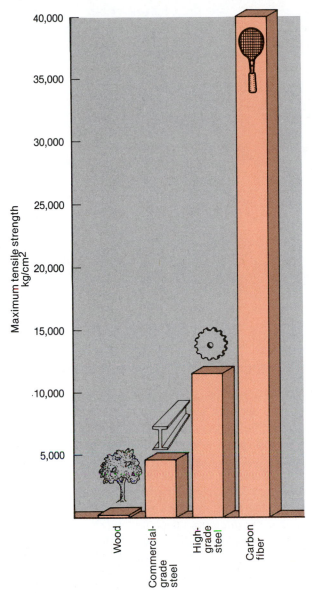

Figure 16–15
Tensile strengths of wood, steel, and carbon fiber, a synthetic composite. Note that although carbon fiber is 10 times as strong as commercial-grade steel, it is so much more expensive that it is used only in specialty applications.

transmission. One is the transmission of energy to perform work or to transfer heat. The large power lines carried by massive steel towers and the smaller "electric lines" that carry electrical energy into your house serve this purpose. The second category involves the transmission of information such as tele-

---

Special Topic C
Some Materials for Which There Are No Adequate Substitutes

Structural steel—It is possible to built strong supports from a variety of different materials, and composites such as carbon fibers are 10 times stronger than structural steel. However, these high-tech materials don't come even close to steel in terms of the ratio of strength to price. Thus, unless technologies improve greatly, there is no practical substitute for steel girders, beams, and rods.

Phosphorus—Phosphorus is as essential nutrient for plants—nothing else will do, and there can be no substitutes.

Manganese—About 70 percent of the manganese used in the world today is consumed as a chemical agent necessary during the production of steel. After centuries of research, no better material of equally low cost has been found, so, at present, there is no substitute.

Copper—Substitutes have been found for copper pipe (plastic pipe), copper wire (aluminum wire or glass fibers), and many other traditional uses of this metal. However, no other metal can compete with copper for wiring motors and generators.

phone conversations or communications between computers. The only practical way to transport electrical energy is through metal wires, usually made of copper or aluminum. When the communications age first dawned, messages were also transmitted through metal wires. Although electrical cables are still used in communications systems today, new technologies are replacing wire in many other applications. For example, many telephone signals are transmitted through the air by microwaves. Alternatively, signals can be transmitted by directing a pulsed laser beam through a glass fiber. This technique, called **fiber optics,** permits the substitution of abundant reserves of silicon (the raw material from which glass is made) for copper, which is less abundant.

Substitution, powerful as it is, is not a panacea for all our problems. Some properties of some

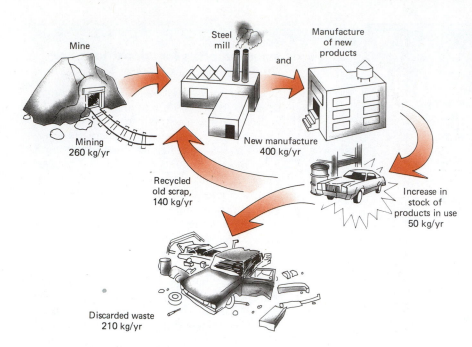

Figure 16–16
Estimated annual manufacture and flow of iron and steel in the United States, in kilograms per capita.

elements are so unique that scientists cannot imagine how alternative materials can be used as replacements. In addition, we must also examine the environmental impacts of the substitute. Sand and gravel are mined in unsightly open pits. Plastics are made from chemicals derived from limited reserves of petroleum and coal. Large amounts of energy are needed to manufacture glass. A variety of environmental problems are associated with the harvesting of timber.

Recycling

An alternative approach is to reuse or recycle materials. As shown in Figure 16–16, in the United States, 400 kg of iron and steel are manufactured per person per year. Of this total, 50 kg, or 12.5 percent, is converted into durable goods such as bridges, buildings, and roadways. Approximately 35 percent, or 140 kg, is recycled, and the remaining 52.5 percent is simply thrown away to be put in dumps and landfills. If all this discarded material were recycled, mining could be reduced to 50 kg per person per year and our iron reserves would last five times as long as they would under current rates of consumption. The same type of analysis can also be made for other minerals. This important topic will be discussed further in Chapter 22.

Miniaturization and Durability

Materials can also be conserved if manufactured items were built to be smaller and lighter. For example, during the decade from 1975 to 1985, manufacturers reduced the overall weight of an average automobile by 25 percent, which led to a tremendous reduction in the consumption of a variety of resources. Another example is the modern pocket calculator, which weighs a few ounces and has replaced the old slow, mechanical, office calculating machine, which weighed about 20 or 25 kg.

In addition, the practical life of our resources would be extended if goods were machined or constructed more carefully so that they would last longer. Cheap, flimsy products not only are uneconomical to the consumer, but also represent an indirect insult to our environment. Savings could be extended even further if people repaired worn goods. For example, energy and materials are conserved if an old, worn car engine is remachined and rebuilt rather than shredded and scrapped and a new automobile manufactured to take its place.

Conservation

In the previous chapter, we stated that conservation is the easiest and in many ways the most effective method of extending fossil fuel supplies.

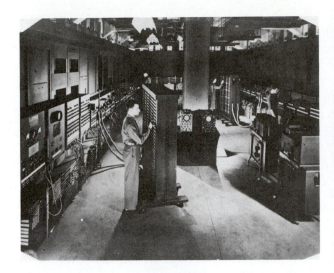

Left, A photograph of ENIAC, a vacuum tube computer used in the 1940s. Even though ENIAC filled an entire room, its memory and computing capabilities were several thousand times less than the 1-million-bit super chip shown in the man's hand on the right. (ENIAC Courtesy of University of Pennsylvania News Bureau; chip courtesy of IBM)

Conservation can also extend reserves of key elements. Even modest measures that can be realized in the home, in commerce, and in industry can have a cumulative effect that benefits the entire society. Finally, most categories of wasted materials are small in comparison with the allocation of resources to the world's military establishments. And, of course, war itself is the greatest waste of all.

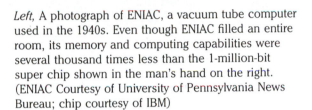
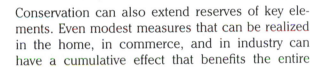

Summary

The Earth was formed from a homogeneous cloud of dust and gas, but geological processes led to a separation of elements. Today, our planet consists of a core of iron and nickel surrounded by a mantle of lighter rock and surface crust, on which we live. Various forces within the mantle create large stresses, which produce motion. The entire crust is composed of several continent-sized plates of rock floating on a semifluid layer of mantle. The slow movement of these plates is called **continental drift.**

Crustal rock is far from homogeneous in composition; in fact, there are many sharp discontinuities. Discontinuities in crustal composition result from geological processes such as the invasion of older rock by upflowing **magma,** differential weathering and erosion, and a variety of other processes.

Metals are valuable to civilization because they (1) are strong, (2) can be cast and machined, and (3) conduct electricity. Helium and phosphorus are two key nonmetals. Helium is a light, inert gas. Phosphorus is an essential element in agricultural fertilizers.

An **ore** is a rock mixture that contains enough valuable minerals to be mined profitably with currently available technology. **Mineral reserves** are the estimated supplies of ore in the ground. This estimate can change with the discovery of new deposits, with improvements in extraction and refining, and with changes in the value of raw materials.

For some elements, there are much larger deposits of low-grade ores than of high-grade ores. In this situation, small advancements in mining technology or small increases in price can increase the mineral reserves. However, for other minerals, such as silver, there seems to be a threshold, and the quantity of metal that is available drops precipitously once the high-grade ores are extracted.

The availability of energy, problems related to pollution and land use, and political barriers to trade also affect the availability of minerals.

Solutions to the problem of the scarcity of minerals include exploiting exotic sources, substitution, recycling, miniaturization, construction of more durable goods, and conservation.

Questions

The Structure of the Earth

1. Imagine that you dug a hole to the center of the Earth. Starting with the surface on which you live, identify the layers in the order that you would reach them. Which layer would be the thinnest?

Formation of Mineral Deposits

2. It is common for a single mine to contain fairly high concentrations of two or more minerals. Discuss how geological processes might favor the deposition of two similar minerals in a single location.

3. If one compound is to be separated from a complex mixture, it must somehow be transported away from the rest of the material. How are ores moved out of a mixture in each of the following processes— (a) separation by gravity, (b) separation by differential solubility, (c) formation of placer deposits.

Mineral Reserves

4. What are mineral reserves? Mention three factors that can cause a change in the estimation of mineral reserves.

5. Explain why minerals on the sea floor are concentrated near mid-ocean ridges.

6. If minerals are widely distributed in ordinary rocks, why should we worry about ever running short?

7. Explain why iron is likely to be available for a long time to come, although the price may rise gradually, whereas the price of silver might rise precipitously after a certain threshold is reached.

8. Explain why it is important to recycle aluminum.

9. What factors can make our metal reserves last longer? What factors can deplete them rapidly?

10. Name one synthetic and two natural classes of materials that can be used as substitutes for metals. Which property of metals *cannot* be furnished by substitutes?

11. Compare the depletion of mineral reserves with the depletion of fossil fuels. How are the two problems similar; how are they different?

12. Relate the Second Law of Thermodynamics and the Law of Conservation of Matter to the problems of depletion of fossil fuel and metal reserves.

13. Imagine that you were planning to write a novel about a society that lived on the Earth sometime in the future. Imagine further that in your story a nuclear war had occurred and major industries had been destroyed. Write a brief description of the types of materials that would be available to your characters and explain how they would extract and process them.

Metals

14. Name three properties of metals that make them important in modern civilization.

15. List five classes of objects that you own that were constructed from metals a decade or two ago but are now made of synthetic materials.

16. Discuss some environmental benefits of substituting plastics for metals. Discuss some environmental problems involved in substituting plastics for metals.

17. List 10 objects that you own. What materials are they made of? How long will each of the objects be used before it is discarded? Will the materials eventually be recycled, or deposited in the trash? Discuss ways of conserving materials in your personal life.

Suggested Readings

The geology of the Earth and the formation of mineral deposits can be reviewed by reading any standard geology textbook. One recommended source is:

Harold L. Levin: *Essentials of Earth Science.* Philadelphia, Saunders College Publishing, 1985. 574 pp.

Several different views on the future availability of minerals are expressed in:

Phillip H. Abelson: Future supplies of energy and minerals. *Science, 231:*657, 1986.

H. E. Goeller and A. Zucker: Infinite resources: The ultimate strategy. *Science, 223:*456, 1984.

Peter J. Kakela: Iron ore: Energy, labor, and capital changes with technology. *Science, 202:*1151, 1978.

Julian L. Simon: *The Ultimate Resource.* Princeton, NJ, Princeton University Press, 1981. 363 pp.

John E. Tilton (ed): *Material Substitution, Lesson from Tin-Using Industries.* Washington D.C., Resources for the Future Books, 1984. 136 pp.

The helium controversy is described in:

Earl Cook: The helium question. *Science, 206:*1141, 1979.

Edward Hammel, Milton Krupka, and K. D. Williamson: The continuing U. S. helium saga. *Science, 223:*792, 1984.

Statistics on the mineral industry in the United States are available from:

Robert C. Horton (director): *Mineral Industry Surveys.* U. S. Department of the Interior, Bureau of Mines.

The question of phosphorus reserves is reviewed in:

Richard P. Sheldon: Phosphate rock. *Scientific American, 246:*6, 1982.

The possibility of mining the ocean floor has stimulated much recent interest:

F. T. Manheim: Marine cobalt resources. *Science, 232:*600, 1986.
David Sleeper: *Nations eye deepsea minerals.* Washington, D.C., Conservation Foundation, April, 1981.

Economic and public policy aspects are emphasized in:

Lois Ember: Strategic minerals policy. *Chemical and Engineering News,* May 11, 1981.
Emery N. Castle and Kent A. Price (eds): *U.S. Interests and Global Natural Resources, Energy, Minerals and Food.* Washington D.C., Resources for the Future Books, 1984. 242 pp.
Dennis L. Little, Robert E. Dils, and John Gray (eds.): *Renewable Natural Resources.* Boulder, CO, Westview Press, 1982. 316 pp.
John A. Butlin: *The Economics of Environmental and Natural Resources Policy.* Boulder, CO, Westview Press, 1982. 206 pp.

17

Water Resources

Water is the most abundant substance on the Earth's surface. The oceans cover approximately 71 percent of the planet; glaciers and ice caps cover additional areas; and water is also found in lakes and streams, in soils and underground reservoirs, in the atmosphere, and in the bodies of all living organisms. Thus, water, in all its forms—ice, liquid water, and water vapor—is very familiar to us. Compared with other substances, however, water has unique properties. Ice floats on liquid water; much energy is consumed when ice melts or when water evaporates; and water is an excellent solvent for many different kinds of substances. All these properties of water affect its role in the biosphere. The movement of water on Earth (the hydrologic cycle) is closely related to the energy changes that take place when water changes its form between solid, liquid, and vapor.

Humans use water in the home, in industry, in agriculture, and for recreation. These applications differ widely in the quantities and quality of the water that they require. In one way or another, we use all available sources—inland waters, groundwater, and even ocean water. We pollute it, repurify it, and reuse it over and over again.

In this chapter, we examine the practices and policies in regard to our water resources, with special attention to environmental effects and long-term consequences.

17.1
The Properties of Water

Chemical substances are generally classified into groups of compounds with similar properties, such as salts, alcohols, or sugars. Water, however, is unique; there is nothing else like it. Thus, corn oil is more like cottonseed oil, kerosene is more like gasoline, grain alcohol is more like wood alcohol, and silver is more like gold, than *anything* is like water.

To understand the properties of water, it is best to start with its molecules, which consist of two hydrogen atoms bonded to an oxygen atom. This composition is expressed by the familiar chemical formula, H_2O. The molecule has a bent shape—the angle between the bonds is 105° (Fig. 17–1A). The negative charges (electrons) in the H_2O molecule are crowded somewhat toward the oxygen atom. As a result, the oxygen end of the molecule has a partial negative charge. The other

A

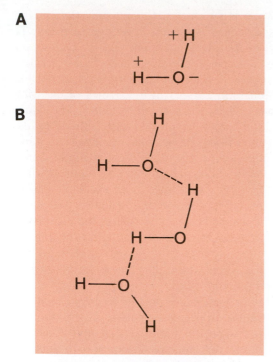

B

C

Figure 17–1
A, Structural formula for water, showing partial electrical charges. *B,* Water molecules bonded to each other *(dashed lines). C,* A drop of water hanging from a leaf. The forces that bond water molecules to each other pull the drop into a spherical shape.

side of the molecule, where the hydrogen atoms are, is somewhat electron-deficient and therefore has a partial positive charge. The important consequence of all this electrical separation is that the oppositely charged sides of different water mole-

cules attract each other strongly, as shown in Figure 17–1B.

The shapes of water molecules and the strong bonding between them lead to some important and remarkable properties. As a result, water, more than any other substance, influences the physical environment of the biosphere:

1. Ice has a high melting point, and water has a high boiling point. It is true that melting ice feels cold to the touch, but think of it this way: A molecule of water is about the same size as a molecule of ammonia (NH_3) or a molecule of methane (natural gas, CH_4). The melting point of ice is 0°C. The melting point of solid methane is −183°C, and that of solid ammonia is −78°C (which is why they are seldom seen as solids). It is the strong bonding between the H_2O molecules that keeps ice solid up to 0°C. Similarly, the boiling point of water (100°C) is very high for a molecule as small as H_2O. Furthermore, it takes a lot of energy (80 cal/g) to melt ice—almost twice as much as it takes to melt a gram of, say, beef fat.

2. When ice does melt, the results, though familiar, are remarkable. Melting is a process in which the regularity of a crystal structure (Fig. 17–2) breaks apart, and the partially liberated molecules (liquid) move about more freely. For most substances, this freer movement causes expansion. As a result, most solids, being denser, sink in the liquids into which they melt. The behavior of water is just the opposite. When the crystal structure of ice breaks apart (melts), the partially liberated molecules attract each other so strongly that they pack together even closer than in the ice crystal. Consequently, ice is *less* dense than water and floats on it. If it did not, a body of water would freeze from the bottom up instead of from the top down, and aquatic life as we know it would not exist on Earth.

3. Large amounts of energy are needed to melt ice or to vaporize water. When water vaporizes and becomes steam, or water vapor, the molecules are completely liberated from each other, that is, all the bonds between water molecules are broken. This requires about seven times as much energy as it does to melt ice. It also takes about seven times as much energy to vaporize water as it does to vaporize gasoline. When these processes (melting or vaporization) are reversed, the energy flow is also reversed. Thus, when a gram of water freezes, 80 calories are released, and, when a gram of water vapor liquefies, about seven times that energy, or 540 calories, are released. Since much of the sur-

Figure 17–2
Snowflake crystal.

face of the globe is water, the Earth's climate is intimately related to the energy that is stored and released as the Earth's waters change from one form to another. Water is the essential fluid of all living organisms; it is the solvent of the blood and lymph of animals and of the sap of plants. Could any form of life exist without water? Not so far as we know; certainly it would not be life in any form that we can now visualize.

17.2
The Hydrologic Cycle (Water Cycle)

If you travel widely on land, by sea, and in the air and look at the Earth's waters, three observations will be apparent. First, much of the water is *stored* in places that look rather permanent. The largest quantities, of course, are in the oceans. But there are also the Arctic and Antarctic ice masses, as well as many lakes and glaciers. Second, some of the Earth's water is in motion: Snow and rain fall, clouds drift, and rivers flow toward the sea. Third, the water on land is very unevenly distributed. As you wander through tropical jungles, everything is wet, and water often drips on you throughout the day. But you had better not try to trek across Australia, Libya, or even southern California, without taking all your water with you. These regions get very little rainfall; most of the year they get none.

The movement of water on Earth (the **hydrologic cycle**) is rather complex, involving various interrelated loops (Fig. 17–3A). However, it is convenient to break down the different transports of water into three simple categories—evaporation, precipitation, and run-off.

Evaporation or **vaporization** is the formation of vapor. Dissolved solids such as salts remain behind when water evaporates. Most water vapor is produced by evaporation of liquid water from the surface of the oceans. Water can also vaporize *through* the tissues of plants, especially from leaf surfaces. This process is called **evapotranspiration.** Ice can also vaporize without melting first. This process (which is called **sublimation**) is slower than vaporization of liquid water.

Precipitation means falling from a height. Referring to water, precipitation includes all forms in which atmospheric moisture descends to earth—rain, snow, hail, and sleet. The water that enters the atmosphere by vaporization must first condense into liquid (clouds and rain) or solid (snow, hail, and sleet) before it can fall. Recall that vaporization absorbs energy. (Water that evaporates from your skin absorbs heat, making you feel cold.) This energy is released in the form of heat when the water vapor condenses.

Run-off is the flow back to the oceans of the precipitation that falls on land. In this way, the land returns the water that was carried to it by clouds that drifted in from the ocean. Run-off occurs both from the land surface (rivers) and from underground water.

Assuming that the water in the oceans and ice caps is fairly constant when averaged over a period of years, the water balance of the Earth's surface can be expressed by the simple relationship:

Water lost = Water gained

The oceans lose water by evaporation and gain water by precipitation and by run-off from the continents. The continents lose water by run-off and evaporation and gain water by precipitation. Therefore,

● *For the oceans:*

$$\underbrace{\text{Evaporation}}_{\text{loss}} = \underbrace{\text{precipitation} + \text{run-off}}_{\text{gain}}$$
$$\underbrace{E}_{\text{loss}} = \underbrace{P \quad + \quad R}_{\text{gain}}$$

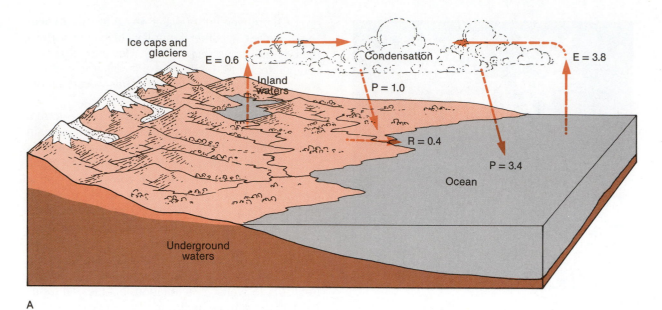

A

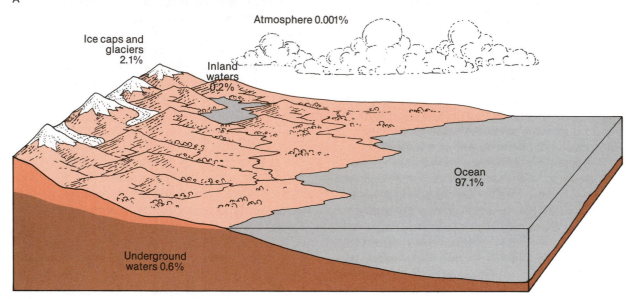

B

Figure 17–3

A, The hydrologic cycle. E = evaporation; P = precipitation; R = run-off. Numbers are in geograms (10^{20} g) of water transferred per year. One geogram is about 100,000 cu km. *B*, Percentages of total global water in different portions of the Earth.

- *For the continents:*

  Evaporation + run-off = precipitation

  $$\underbrace{E \quad + \quad R}_{\text{loss}} = \underbrace{P}_{\text{gain}}$$

With these relationships in mind, look at Figure

17–3A. The numbers (in geograms/year) for the oceans are:

3.8 = 3.4 + 0.4

and for the continents:

0.6 + 0.4 = 1.0

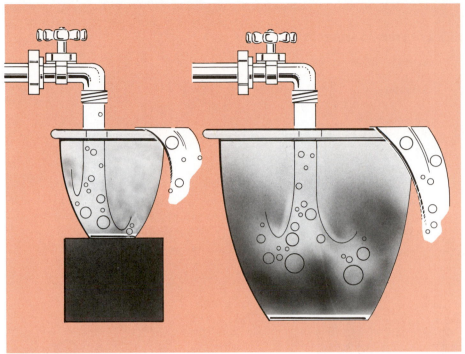

Figure 17–4
The same rate of water flow rinses pollutants out of a small basin faster than
out of a large basin.

Now refer to Figure 17–3B, which is the same diagram with different numbers. Here the numbers tell you where the waters of the Earth *are* at any given time, not where they are going. The numbers are given in percentages of the total quantity of global water, which is about 1.35 billion cu km.

Note that of this vast amount, only 0.8 percent is in the form of inland and underground waters and that most of this amount (0.6 percent) is underground. The remaining 0.2 percent is the inland surface water such as lakes and streams. The least amount of water is in the atmosphere (0.001 percent). Since all this water is in motion (Fig. 17–3 A), it follows that all the waters of the Earth renew themselves—that is, they come and go.

An important question is, "How long does it take for water in a given part of the Earth to renew itself?" Consider, for example, two flows of pure water, one that goes into a small basin, the other into a large basin (Fig. 17–4). Both basins are well stirred, so that the water in each is always uniform throughout. If the water in both basins is polluted, the time it takes for the fresh water to rinse out the pollutant depends on the flow rate of the water and

the volume of the basin. The greater the flow rate and the smaller the basin, the faster the rinsing action. Under such circumstances, the *average* time that a water molecule spends in the basin is called the **residence time.** Some molecules, however, will remain for a longer or shorter time than the average. Any particular water molecule in a natural basin such as Lake Erie may be lost by evaporation or run-off the very next day, or it may still be there 1 year or 100 years from now. Table 17–1 gives average residence times for water in various parts of the hydrologic cycle.

Note that water spends the least time in the atmosphere and the longest time in the deepest ocean layers. Changes in global energy patterns can therefore readily affect atmospheric moisture and, hence, rainfall and agricultural productivity.

The fresh water available for human use is the run-off from rivers and underground sources. Rivers renew themselves rapidly (in weeks), but groundwater is much slower (hundreds of years). Pollution of waters with long residence times is not easily reversed. Figure 17–5 shows the overall water budget for the "lower 48" United States.

Table 17-1
Average Residence Times of Water Resources

Location	Average Residence Time
Atmosphere	9–10 days
Ocean	
Shallow layers	100–150 years
Deepest layers	30,000–40,000 years
World ocean average	3000 years
Continents	
Rivers	2–3 weeks
Lakes	10–100 years
Ice caps and glaciers	10,000–15,000 years
Shallow groundwater	up to 100s of years
Deep groundwater	up to 1000s of years

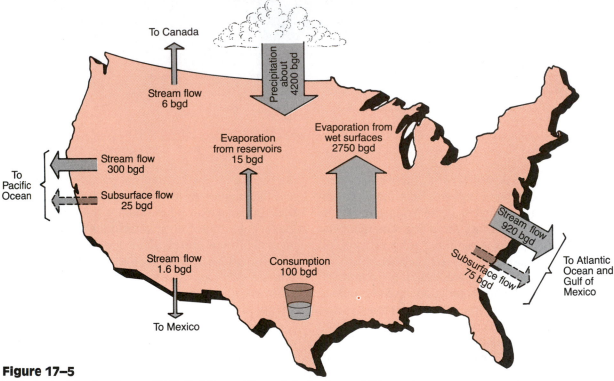

Figure 17–5
Water budget for the "lower 48" United States. The unit bgd refers to billions of gallons per day. To convert to billions of liters per day, multiply by 3.785. (Data from U. S. Geological Survey)

17.3
Human Use of Water

Water is used in the home and office, in industry, in agriculture, and for recreation. Both the quantities used and the quality needed differ widely, depending on the application. The strictest requirements for quality apply to drinking water for humans. The least strict requirements probably apply to water used for cooling, where the prime concern is its temperature. Sea water is therefore adequate. For some industrial applications, the most important consideration is whether the water will corrode the equipment; control of acidity is often the only requirement in such cases. For most human needs, however, including the large amounts used in agriculture and industry, water must be fresh, not salty.

In the average American home, each person uses about 8 liters of water a day for cooking and drinking. In comparison, one flush of a toilet consumes 20 liters, or enough water to satisfy the drinking and cooking requirements of a person for 2 1/2 days. The water used for one load in a clothes washer would be enough for almost 1 month. Even this consumption is often dwarfed by consumption for watering ornamental lawns and gardens. The amounts used in industry and agriculture are, in turn, far greater than those needed for personal use. For example, the water used in industry to refine a tonne of petroleum would be enough to do about 200 loads in a clothes washer. When crops are irrigated, it takes much more water to grow a tonne of grain than it does to manufacture a tonne of most industrial materials, such as metals or plastics.

The use of water is measured in terms of **withdrawal** and **consumption.** Withdrawal of water refers to its removal from surface or underground sources and its transfer to home, business, industry, farm, or other point of use. "Consumed" water is that part of the withdrawn water that is not returned to the source of supply. Thus, for example, the water used to flush a toilet in one city may be piped through a sewer that empties into the river from which it came; this is water that has been withdrawn but not consumed. On the other hand, the tap water that you add to your potted plants and that eventually enters the atmosphere by transpiration through its leaves is withdrawn *and* consumed, because it is not directly returned to its source. Irrigation consumes the highest percentage of its withdrawn water (an average of about 55 percent), because so much of it evaporates or is transpired through plant matter. The loss varies widely, however, because it depends on the manner in which the irrigation water is applied, as discussed in Section 8.8. The choice of crop makes a big difference, too. For example, all the water needed by a crop of barley during its growing season would cover the land to a depth of about 0.5 meter. A crop of alfalfa, on the other hand, would need about three times as much—1.5 meters. Cooling

Older brownstone buildings on a street in Manhattan, all with a basement level plus four stories. The water pressure from the flow into the city is great enough to lift the water to the top floors. Water for the higher modern buildings shown in the background must be pumped up to storage tanks at the roof level.

for steam-powered electrical utilities consumes the least water (about 2 percent), because the water is confined in pipes and there is little chance for evaporation. The overall U.S. proportion is about 22 percent consumption of withdrawn water.

Water from any source can also be fed into the ground by pumping it through **recharge wells** (Fig. 17–6). The amount available from such sources is limited, because the water is sometimes chemically contaminated or is not available at the best locations for recharge. Another option is to channel natural stream water into recharge wells during wet periods when the flow is high, thus augmenting the natural percolation through soil and rock. The problem of pollution of groundwater re-

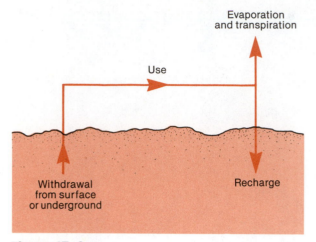

Figure 17–6
Recharging.

sulting from contamination during recharge will be discussed in Chapter 20.

Figure 17–7 shows the pattern of use of fresh water in the United States. Note that the highest water use does not occur in the most densely populated areas. In general, rates of water use reflect the needs of agriculture much more than those of the home, of commerce, or of industry. One conclusion from this difference is that efforts to conserve water in the home, while locally helpful, cannot make a significant contribution to the demands of agriculture. A comparison of Figure 17–8 with Figure 17–7 shows that some of the areas where the surface water supply is often depleted are also the areas where the largest quantities of fresh water are needed. Therefore, if the only fresh water available were the water on the Earth's surface, in lakes and rivers, it would hardly be enough. Even in years of average rainfall, much of the Midwest and Southwest of the United States depletes most of its surface waters. Two approaches to the problem of water supply have been the use of groundwater reserves and the diversion of water from one region to another.

17.4
Groundwater

When rain falls on the land, two forces act on it. One force is the Earth's gravity, which pulls the water downward through any open path. The second force is the electrical attraction between water and other materials to which water tends to stick. (That is why water makes things wet. Not everything, however. Water doesn't stick to oil, which is why ducks, whose feathers are oily, do not get wet and sink.) Thus, drops of rainwater will stick to the vertical side of a window. Water can also be pulled into tiny holes. If a corner of a paper towel is placed in a dish of water, the liquid travels upward, against the force of gravity. In this case, the electrical force attracting water molecules to paper molecules is stronger than the gravitational force pulling the water downward. The movement of water upward through small holes is called **capillary action.**

Now consider what happens when rain falls on dry soil. The first raindrops will simply wet the soil; they will not flow down or away. As the rain continues after all the land surface is wet, gravity will pull the excess water down through the spaces in the rock, sand, or gravel below. The larger the underground spaces, the faster the water will flow down. Eventually, the downward flow is stopped when the water meets rock or clay that has no porosity. Since the water can go no further, it backs up, filling all the pores in the rock above the barrier. This completely wet section is called the **zone of saturation** (Fig. 17–9). The upper boundary of the zone of saturation is called the **water table.** Below the water table, the rock is saturated; above it, the rock may be moist but is not saturated. If rainfall recharges water faster than it is lost by flowing out to a lake or stream or by being pumped out, the water table rises. If the recharge is slower than the loss, the water table falls. A well dug below the water table will have water; a well that is not that deep will be dry.

When the rain stops, the water content of the soil decreases in three ways: (1) Water drains downward by gravity—most of this action is complete in a day or two. (2) Water evaporates from the surface. (3) Water is absorbed by plants and is then lost to the atmosphere by transpiration. To offset these losses, water can be drawn up toward the surface by capillary action, but only within a narrow layer, called the **soil-moisture belt.**

These natural processes of gains and losses of water establish the essential features of the land's water balance—the moisture content of the soil and the level of the water table. If more groundwater is removed for irrigation, mining, or manufacturing than is replenished by rainfall and

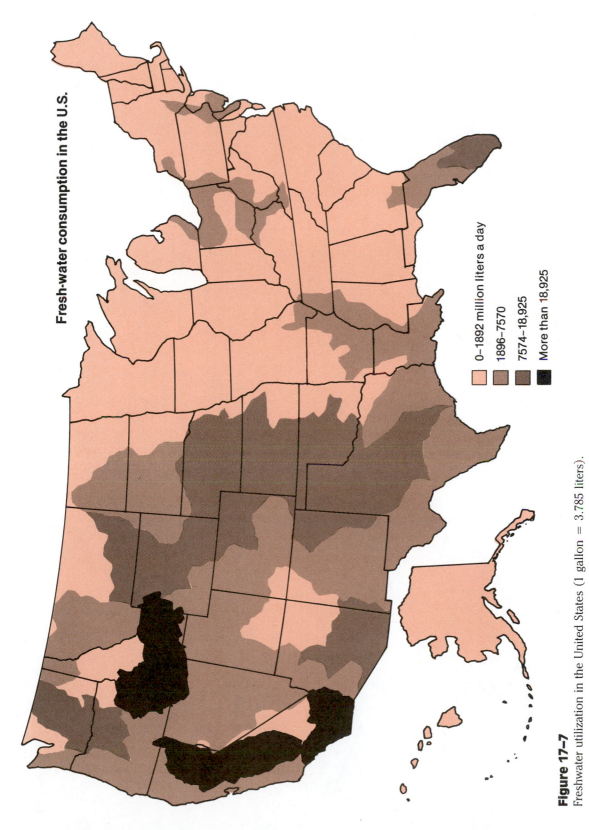

Fresh-water consumption in the U.S.

0–1892 million liters a day

1896–7570

7574–18,925

More than 18,925

Figure 17–7

Freshwater utilization in the United States (1 gallon = 3.785 liters).

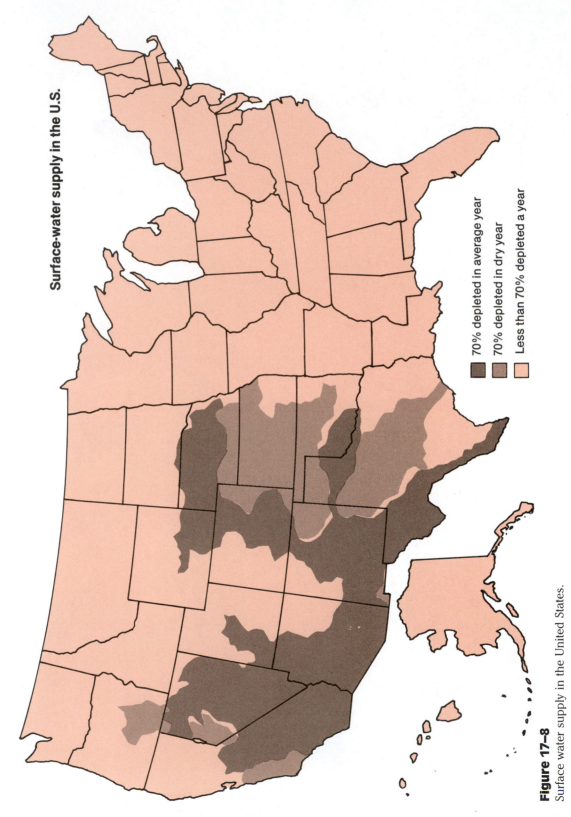

Surface-water supply in the U.S.

70% depleted in average year

70% depleted in dry year

Less than 70% depleted a year

Figure 17–8

Surface water supply in the United States.

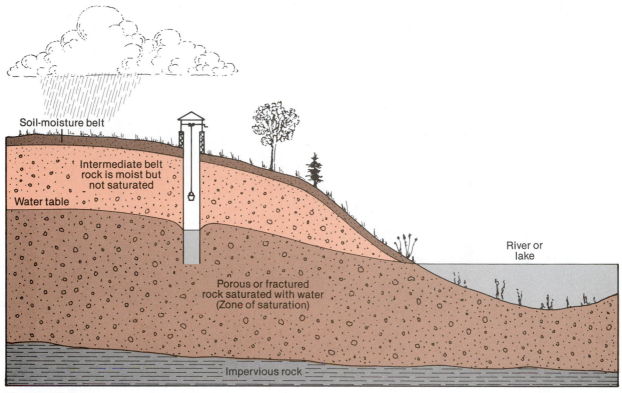

Figure 17–9
Distribution of groundwater.

run-off, the water table will drop. This problem exists in areas that are attractive because of their favorable climate and abundant natural resources but have low rainfall. The southwestern regions of the United States known as the "Sunbelt" constitute such an area.

When porous and impervious beds of rock alternate, there can be more than one layer of groundwater. Figure 17–10 shows inclined strata in which seepage introduces water into a lower layer of porous rock. Such a reservoir of groundwater is called an **aquifer.** The lower portion of an aquifer may be under considerable pressure from the weight of water above it. Under such circumstances, a deep well may allow the water to flow up without having to be drawn or pumped. A well of this kind is called an **artesian well.**

The total quantity of water in aquifers is very large. In fact, about half of all groundwater occurs in these deep layers. Note, however, from Table 17–1, that these waters are replaced *very* slowly (up to thousands of years). Much of the water in some aquifers was accumulated many centuries

ago in wetter climates than the present one. Under such conditions, deep groundwater may be considered to be, for all practical purposes, nonrenewable. Just as coal and petroleum are called fossil fuels, so is deep groundwater sometimes called "fossil" water. The removal of deep groundwater is therefore analogous to mining.

The Ogallala aquifer, which is one of the world's largest reservoirs of fresh groundwater, is a major source of water for farmers in Kansas, Nebraska, Oklahoma, the Texas panhandle (the northern, almost square, portion), and parts of neighboring states. Recall from Chapter 8 that farmers in many regions around the globe irrigate their crops. When the needed water is withdrawn from surface sources such as lakes and rivers, the supply is replenished and the system is sustainable. However, if groundwater is used as the source for intensive irrigation, its slow replenishment cannot keep up with the rate of withdrawal, and the reserves can be depleted rapidly. For example, the average annual rainfall in the Ogallala region ranges from about 25 to 100 cm per year, in contrast to the

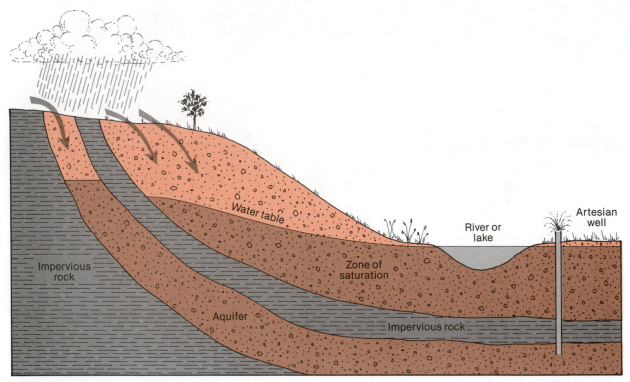

Figure 17–10
Sloped layers of porous and impervious rock that give rise to artesian flow.

more abundant 100 to 150 cm per year typical of the Eastern United States. In the early days of Western agriculture in semiarid areas, farmers had to learn to accommodate to the scant rainfall, and so they practiced what is called "dryland farming." The great change to modern methods resulted from three developments: (1) the finding that there is a large supply of underground water (it seemed limitless); (2) the invention of the centrifugal pump,* which made it possible to get the groundwater to the surface; and (3) the availability of energy on the farm from electrification or from gasoline engines, to power the pumps.

It is estimated that some of the aquifer water tables in the United States are being lowered at rates of several centimeters to about half a meter a year. At such rates, serious depletion of the aqui-

*The centrifugal pump is a turbine. You may think of a turbine as a device whose blades are pushed by a forceful stream of fluid such as water or steam and which thus provides power. Now think of it running the other way and *requiring* power so that it can push a stream of water, and you have a centrifugal pump.

fers can occur early in the next century (Fig. 17–11). It is important to understand that the viability of an agricultural–industrial–urbanized society that depends on fossil water can be at risk when that source is "seriously depleted."

Two problems other than depletion can arise as a result of the excessive removal of groundwater. One of these problems is **subsidence,** or settling, of the ground as deep groundwater is removed. This removal allows the rock particles to shift somewhat closer to each other, filling some of the space left by the departed water. As a result, the volume of the entire rock layer decreases, and the surface of the ground subsides. (Removal of oil from wells has the same effect.) Subsidence rates can reach 5 to 10 cm per year, depending on the rate of water removal. These effects have been observed in such areas as the San Joaquin Valley of California, Houston (Texas), and Mexico City. Unfortunately, subsidence is not a readily reversible process. As a result, the water-holding capacity of a depleted groundwater resource may be permanently reduced so that it cannot be completely re-

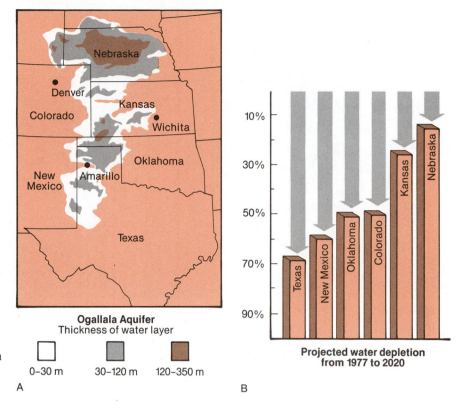

Figure 17–11

A, Location of the Ogallala aquifer. *B,* Projected water depletion in various sections from 1977 to 2020. (Numbers given in percent of original supply.)

Ogallala Aquifer
Thickness of water layer

0–30 m   30–120 m   120–350 m

A

Projected water depletion from 1977 to 2020

B

charged, even when water becomes abundant again.

The other problem is **saltwater intrusion** (Fig. 17–12). As groundwater is removed from a coastal area, the zone of freshwater saturation is reduced both from above and below. From above, the water table declines. From below, salt water seeps in. As a result, salt water may be drawn into wells, making the water unfit for drinking.

17.5
Human Control of Water

We cannot significantly affect the total quantity of water on Earth, but we can store it, change its flow patterns, and purify it. The choices that people make among such options depend heavily on the amount of water available, on sources of energy, on technological skills, and on prevailing patterns of living. In many arid less-developed areas, for example, water must be carried over distances of several kilometers from its source to where it is needed. Such tasks not only place a heavy burden on the carriers (generally women and children) but

also create other problems. The precious water is used only for essentials, particularly for drinking and cooking. Unless it rains, there is not enough water for sanitary uses. As a result, many people, especially children, suffer from eye infections and other diseases that could have been prevented by frequent washing. An interesting choice arises when a limited amount of capital becomes available that can be used either for a pumping and distribution system or for a water purification system but not for both. One of us (A.T.) discussed these problems with a group of environmental engineers from the Cooperative for American Relief Everywhere (CARE) in a rural area of Kenya. The engineers pointed out that even though the water supply under consideration (a pond formed by damming a small river) was somewhat polluted by animal wastes, much of the water consumed by people was first boiled, either in cooking or as tea. Furthermore, if the water were purified (by chlorination, see Chapter 20), its taste would be changed and people might drink less of it, which would be undesirable. Finally, purification without distribution would not ease the burden of the water carriers. Therefore, the choice was for distribution

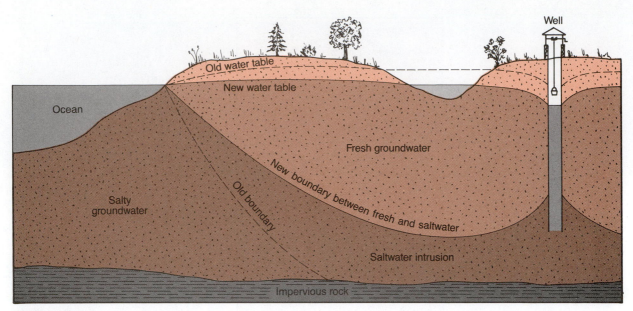

Figure 17–12
Saltwater intrusion.

over purification, so the pump and pipes were installed, but the water was not chlorinated.

In the following section, we will examine and evaluate the various options available for controlling water supplies. The reader should bear in mind, however, that the choices are often made on a cultural as well as on a technical basis.

17.6
Dams

As is apparent from the residence times listed in Table 17–1, water stays in lakes much longer than it does in rivers. Dams make lakes, which are used as reservoirs. In fact, dams have been erected on many rivers, large and small, all over the world, from ancient times until the present. Consider the physical events that start to happen when a river is dammed. First, the downstream flow is interrupted as the lake behind the dam begins to fill. The time needed for this step may be only a few weeks for a small lake fed by a fast-flowing stream, or it can take years. For example, construction of Glen Canyon Dam in Arizona was started in the 1950s. Lake Powell, which is the reservoir created by the dam, was finally filled in 1980.

Once the lake is filled, water spills over the dam, and the normal flow is re-established. Several benefits can now be realized from the dam and the lake that it has created.

1. Hydroelectric Energy. The potential energy of the water has been increased by the rise in its level. The water can be made to fall through a turbine and generate electricity (see Chapter 13). Otherwise, all the energy of the falling water would have been released as heat by friction in the old stream bed.

2. Control of Water Flow. Dams are provided with pipes and valves so that water can be drained from below. Thus, water can be released when it is needed. In the western United States, for example, snow falls in the mountains mostly during the months of November through April. Almost all of it melts during May and June, but the peak irrigation months are July and August. Therefore, the storage capacity that dams provide for the interim period is very important for obtaining maximum agricultural yields. In a dry period, water stored during previous seasons can be made available. During heavy rains or rapid melting of snow, the valves are closed and the reservoir is allowed to fill up, thus providing protection against flooding.

3. Recreation. The lake behind the dam can be used for fishing or for water sports. (But the flooding of canyons and white-water sporting areas is a recreational and esthetic loss.)

Kayaking in white water on the Yampa River, the last undammed tributary of the Colorado River. When dams are built, this recreational quality is lost.

There are also environmental problems associated with dams. These may be grouped into the following categories:

1. Loss of Water. The reservoir provides more surface for evaporation and more area for seepage from below compared with the stream that preceded it. For example, evaporation from Lake Powell removes about 270,000 cubic meters of water per year, enough to serve the water needs of a city with a population of half a million. Since salt does not evaporate, the remaining water becomes more saline and its use for irrigation hastens the rate of salinization of the soil.

2. Silting. Consider the physical events that take place during the life of the dam and its reservoir. The water in the reservoir is calm and slow moving compared with the stream that it flooded. A rapid stream always carries some soil particles in it, just as a high wind blows dust into the air. In still water, a grain of sand might settle at a rate of about 2 cm/second (see Fig. 20–1), which is a bit less than 1 km/hour. Water in a turbulent stream moves up and down faster than that; so some of the particles are always suspended and move downstream. But in a lake, there is little upward motion to keep the particles in suspension. Most of the sediment that enters the reservoir from the run-off that feeds it, therefore, settles to the bottom before it can get a chance to spill over the dam. Thus, the reservoir gradually fills up. Rates of buildup can reach 10 cm, or 0.1 m, per year. At such a rate,

the lakes behind high dams can last up to hundreds of years, but that is not forever.

3. Erosion. The water that flows over the dam is quite free of sediment. Even water that is discharged from outlets below the surface carries less sediment than would have been present before the dam was built. As the water now moves more rapidly in the stream below, it starts to scour out the stream bed, because it has an unused *capacity* for carrying sediment. The water level below the dam is thus lowered. In addition, a deeper main canyon promotes more soil erosion in the side canyons.

4. Risk of Disaster. Areas near rivers (their flood plains) are attractive for farming, industry, and commerce, especially when flood control promises to make the region safe. But unusually heavy rainfall can fill and overflow a reservoir, which then can no longer limit the flow. Furthermore, dams have been known to break. Under such circumstances, the population in the flood path is vulnerable to disaster.

5. Ecological Disruptions. Disturbances of ecological factors are listed in Chapters 11 and 15.

17.7
Diversion of Water Over Long Distances

It seems reasonable to divert water from an abundant source to a dry region where the soil would be fertile if irrigated. Likewise, fresh water can be

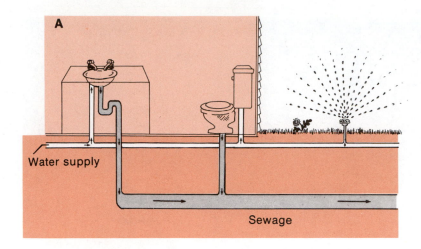

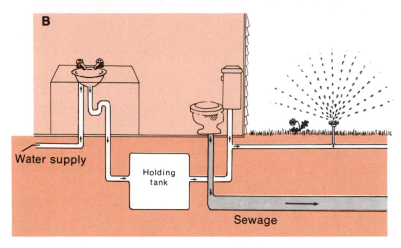

Water use. *A,* Present, wasteful system—pure water is used for sinks, toilets, and lawns. *B,* More conservative system—wastewater from sinks is stored and used for toilets and lawn irrigation.

taken from the countryside to a densely populated city that needs it. (Sometimes, however, it works the other way: A small city manages to get an abundant supply of water, and *then* it becomes densely populated.) Southern California offers examples of both types of water diversion. The All American Canal channels water from the Colorado River to the farms and cattle ranches of the Imperial Valley (east of San Diego), and the great Los Angeles Aqueduct, completed in 1913, brings water south from Owens Valley to Los Angeles.

Such large water diversion projects can create problems at both ends—at the source, and at the area to which the water is supplied:

1. Dams. An abundant source should also be a dependable one, which means that a diversion project generally starts with the construction of a dam. Therefore, all the problems asscociated with dams that were discussed in the preceding section must be considered.

2. Encouragement of Waste. Planners often underestimate the ability and willingness of people to conserve when it is necessary to do so. (The unexpected decline in energy use in the early 1980s is one such example.) Most people use water wastefully when they know that it is abundant, but, when it is scarce, conservation is not seen as a serious burden. Thus, it is convenient to leave the water running while you are washing your hands or brushing your teeth. But, if you must, you can use only about one tenth as much water in a stopped sink to accomplish the same purpose in about the same time. There are many other ways to conserve water in the home, on the farm, and in water distribution systems. In many cases, these measures would be an adequate or at least a partial substitution for water diversion projects.

3. Salinity. The problems caused by buildup of salts from irrigation water were discussed in Chapter 8.

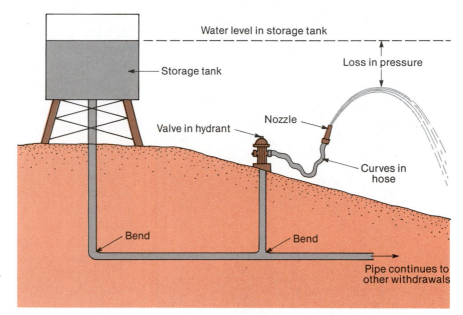

Figure 17–13
Reduction of pressure of flowing water caused by friction. Most of the frictional losses occur at bends, valves, and constricted nozzles.

4. Deterioration of Water Quality at the Source. When water is diverted from an area, the *quality* of the remaining water can be affected, even if the amount is adequate. Fresh water from a stream or river becomes progressively saltier as it enters and mixes with ocean water. A fast-flowing river carries its fresh water well out to sea. A slow-flowing tidal basin (such as the Hudson River valley) is saline well inland. In a large water diversion project, the low natural flow in late summer may be further aggravated by peak demand for air conditioning and irrigation. Under such conditions, saline water can back up into regions of a river delta that serve nearby farms. This phenomenon, called "reverse flow," can reduce agricultural production in delta areas. Changes in water flow can also disrupt the life cycles of fish and wildlife in the area.

5. Energy Consumption. A cubic meter of water weighs 1000 kg, and it takes about 10 kW of power to lift this amount 1 m every second. Of course, work is done *by* the water that flows downhill, and this benefit offsets the work needed to lift the water. But the rise and fall of water during transport are not the only processes that involve exchanges of energy. Another important factor is friction. As water molecules hit the inside surfaces of the pipes that carry them (especially around curves), they transfer some of their energy to the atoms in the pipe. Thus, the pipe and its surroundings get warmer and the water slows down, with the result that its pressure decreases (Figure 17–13). The net expenditure of energy involved in the transport of water is therefore the work done to overcome friction plus the work needed to lift the water from its initial to its final elevation. If the net change in elevation is a drop rather than a rise, a gain in energy is realized, and, if this gain is greater than the frictional losses, no net work need be done. This benefit was realized by the great aqueducts of ancient Rome (see Fig. 16–7), which were sloped downward. New York City's water, too, flows down from the hilly regions to the north. Its pressure is great enough to lift the water in Manhattan to a height of about 30 to 35 m, which is why many of the older buildings there are no higher than five stories (see photograph on p. 489). Farmland on the floodplain of a river can be irrigated by pumping water to a height of only a few feet (Fig. 17–14).

Modern water diversion projects, carrying water over hilly terrain, suffer considerable frictional losses. Moreover, such projects often involve *large* quantities of water (hundreds of cubic meters per second) and therefore need much energy. One estimate for an expanded California State Water Project, for example, foresees a use of 10 billion kWh of electricity in the year 2000—about as much power as is used in two million homes.

A

B

Figure 17–14
Waters from the Nile even today are pumped up to farmland *(A)* by human power, using a hand pump credited to Archimedes, or *(B)* by animal power.

17.8
Desalination

The lament of the Ancient Mariner—"Water, water everywhere, nor any drop to drink"—expresses what we all know about seawater: There is plenty of it, but you cannot use it for drinking or for irrigation of crops. The reason you cannot drink it is that salt in seawater is more concentrated than the salts in your blood. **Osmosis** is the process by which a solvent (usually water) flows through a semipermeable membrane from a less concentrated to a more concentrated solution. (A semipermeable membrane does not allow dissolved matter to pass through.) Therefore, if you drink seawater, your cells will not gain water but will lose it by osmosis through the cell membranes. It would be better not to drink anything at all. For the same reason, saltwater kills terrestrial plants; it does not water them.

Osmosis can be reversed. The pressure created by the flow of water during osmosis is called **osmotic pressure.** If enough back pressure (greater than the osmotic pressure) is applied, pure water may be forced out through a membrane, leaving the salts behind. This process, called **reverse osmosis,** is further described in Chapter 20. Another method of desalination is **distillation,** in which water is boiled, leaving the salts behind, and the resulting steam is then condensed to produce distilled water. Both reverse osmosis and distillation require energy and equipment, and the costs are high. Perhaps the best application would be in hot dry areas near the sea, such as the Middle East, where solar energy could be used to boil the water.

17.9
Cloud Seeding

Water *vapor* is water in gaseous form; it is not visible. The moisture content of clear air is in the form of water vapor. A cloud consists of tiny droplets of water, or tiny crystals of ice, whose diameters may range from about 2 to 40 μm. In still air, such particles settle very slowly (mostly slower than 1 cm/second; see Fig. 21–2) and are therefore kept aloft by the slightest air currents. This is the reason why clouds do not fall down. Thin clouds appear white as the sunlight is scattered going through them. Thick clouds look dark from below, because they shade most of the sunlight; viewed from above, as from an airplane, they look white. For rain or snow to form, the water droplets or ice particles must become large—from about 0.5 mm (a drizzle) to about 5 or 6 mm (large raindrops). Often the precipitation starts as snow in the cloud, and then melts to form rain on its way down.

The freezing point of water is 0°C. However, this statement does *not* mean that water will freeze when it is cooled to 0°C. The statement means only that when water and ice are in contact with each

Icebergs that break off ("calve") from continental glaciers were formed from compacted snow. Therefore, when they melt, they yield fresh water. If saltwater is carefully stirred and partially frozen under controlled laboratory conditions, the salt remains in the liquid water, not in the ice. The ice is then pure H_2O, and can be melted to yield fresh water. This situation is approached in "old" ice in the Arctic Ocean near the North Pole, which has been partly thawed and refrozen again and again for thousands of years. Such ice is pure enough so that it can be melted to yield water that is fit to drink. However, ice that is formed in the ocean during a single winter contains pockets of saltwater that were trapped during the freezing process, and when these pockets freeze, the salt has no way to get out. The water made from melting such ice is too salty to drink.

Figure 17–15
Tabular Antarctic iceberg. (Official U. S. Coast Guard Photo)

tempted from time to time, but it has been difficult to determine how much precipitation is gained. What can be done is to shift rainfall from one location to another, with the object of watering an otherwise dry area such as the "rain shadow" (the dry side) of a mountain range. Precipitation can be spread out to a wider zone in an effort to reduce local intensive concentrations, such as the heavy winter snowfalls in the Buffalo, New York, area. One region's gain is then another region's loss. Furthermore, the control over the redistribution of rain is not always precise. As a result, conflicts of interest and political problems may arise.

17.10
Water from Icebergs

It has been proposed that Antarctic icebergs, which are very large and rather flat, could be towed to dry southern coastal areas where they could be melted to provide fresh water (Box 17.1). The potential supply is very large: A table-like Antarctic iceberg may be 500 m thick and cover an area of 260 sq km or more (Fig. 17–15). The technology and economics, however, are uncertain. Some tests have been carried out with smaller icebergs, but the towing and handling of the Antarctic monsters may be impractical.

17.11
Epilogue: Small Projects, Large Projects: The Future of Water Resources

Marc Reisner, in his book, *Cadillac Desert* (see bibliography), describes the transformation of the American (U.S.) West from its natural semidesert condition to its modern agricultural wealth. How-

other, they come to a stable state, or equilibrium, at 0°C. Pure water can readily be cooled below 0°C if no ice is present; in fact, water droplets in clouds are often as cold as -10 or -12°C. Such water is said to be **supercooled.** If a crystal of ice (here called a **seed**) is added to supercooled water, freezing occurs rapidly as the cold water *warms up* to 0°. The rapid formation of ice tends to produce large particles that can precipitate.

In the 1940s, the scientists Vincent Schaefer and Irving Langmuir thought that they might be able to seed clouds artificially to make rain. They tried it first in large freezers, and it worked. Next, they did it from an airplane, pouring pellets of dry ice (frozen carbon dioxide, -78°C) into supercooled clouds. Sure enough, it worked again—ice particles grew rapidly. Later, it was learned that the seed crystal need not be cold; it need only have a *shape* similar to that of an ice crystal. The most effective crystal was found to be silver iodide. Unfortunately, silver iodide is a poison and, in sufficient quantities, may produce toxic effects on plant and animal life.

Cloud seeding on a practical scale is at-ever, he argues, the downfalls of ancient desert civilizations predict that this one cannot be sustained indefinitely. The end will be caused by the problems of salinization and of depletion of groundwater, as discussed in this chapter and in Chapter 8. Reisner also maintains that the payout, or the benefit/cost ratio, of many large-scale water projects including dams, water diversions, irrigation, and hydropower, is poor.

Of course, not everyone agrees with Reisner. The arguments fall into familiar categories: The technological fix versus social and cultural adjustments. Here we will use two examples to illustrate how these factors operate in issues involving water resources.

Mono Lake, A Small Project

Los Angeles, which was little more than a village at the start of the 1849 California Gold Rush, grew to a megalopolis in the years after World War II. The area did not have nearly enough natural supply of fresh water to support such growth and, therefore, required diversions from other areas. One of these sources was the waters of the Mono Basin, which flowed down the eastern slope of the Sierra Nevada at Yosemite into Mono Lake. Since the lake has no outlet, it is a saline evaporation sink, like the Great Salt Lake or the Dead Sea. Under natural conditions, the gain by inflow approximately balances the evaporative loss, so the level does not change much. All this changed after the 1950s, when the Los Angeles Department of Water and Power (LADWP) began to take water from four of the five streams that feed into Mono. Deprived of most of its natural inflow, the lake shrank sharply, its surface dropping by about 36 feet. In most years Rush Creek, the largest of the feeder streams, became a dry bed from the point at which the water was withdrawn. So far, there was nothing extraordinary about these circumstances; many streams are entirely depleted by such diversions. However, the years starting with the winter of 1981–1982 were wet enough that the run-off exceeded the capacity of the LADWP pumping and piping system. The excess water then returned to the old stream bed and started to raise the level of Mono Lake, reversing its former decline. Some trout accompanied this renewed flow and began to reproduce, and it has been estimated that by 1984, approximately 30,000

brown and rainbow trout inhabited this 10-mile section of Rush Creek. However, it was clear that dry years would return, and that the continued diversion of Rush Creek would once again dry up the river and kill most of the fish.

California law prohibits any activity that would endanger an existing fishery, implying that the renewed diversion would be clearly illegal. This environmental dispute, like most others, involves various complexities. For example: (1) The LADWP offered to net some of the fish and transfer them to other streams. The counterargument is that only a small proportion, about 10 percent, would be saved and that this does not preserve the fishery. (2) Another argument in favor of the diversion is the cost to Los Angeles of replacing the water lost from Rush Creek (about $14,000 per day), which would exceed the value of the trout being preserved. Such figures, however, are estimates (sometimes called "guesstimates") and are generally disputed as being biased, or based on incorrect assumptions or calculations. (3) The LADWP people point out that the loss of Rush Creek had already been compensated for by the construction of a fish hatchery elsewhere. The conservationists countered that the hatchery was built to avoid the necessity for constructing fish ladders elsewhere and, therefore, would not compensate for the loss of the fish in Rush Creek. (4) When Rush Creek and other streams were diverted and the water level at Mono Lake dropped by evaporation, its salinity rose rapidly. Freshwater shrimp died, which depleted a food source for migratory birds.

The legal actions in this issue have been going on for some years. In 1983, the California Supreme Court handed down a decision in a case brought by the National Audubon Society, on behalf of the conservationists, against the LADWP. The central issue was the conflict between the environmental values protected by the public trust and the city's need for water. The plaintiffs (Audubon) claimed that the public trust takes precedence over all rights to appropriate water. The LADWP argued that the regulations permitting the withdrawal of water had displaced the public trust doctrine and that the water could be withdrawn indefinitely without concern for the environmental consequences. The court said, "We are unable to accept either position." Therefore, there should be an accommodation between the two viewpoints. If the environmentalist stand on withdrawal of water were broadly and totally upheld, the harm to the population and economy of California would be unacceptable. However, the State has a duty to "protect public trust uses wherever feasible." The Court recognized that no such consideration to environmental consequences had ever been given. Therefore, according to the Court, "Some responsible body ought to reconsider the allocation of the waters of Mono basin." This decision was obviously not a clear win for either side, and the issue has since been bogged down in the courts. As of 1988, other cases on this matter are still pending.

This dispute is described here not because the Rush Creek and Mono Lake issue is crucial to the environmental quality of all North America or to its water resources, but rather to highlight some of the complexities that can arise in disputes over water. You can think of others, not all of which might be brought up in a court of law. For example, one may assume that city dwellers could make adjustments in lifestyles that would conserve water. From that viewpoint, the water in Rush Creek need not be diverted. On the other hand, those who fish for food and recreation could find other things to eat and other sports to enjoy. So, which group should be asked to sacrifice? As another example, how important is the esthetic value of having a running stream with jumping fish in place of a dry stream bed? In the case of a small project such as this one, such questions are very important for those persons affected but are not usually even brought to the attention of the general population. Keep these issues in mind, however, as we consider the possible consequences of much larger projects in the example that follows.

Water from Canada, A Large Project

If it is true that the agricultural productivity of the American West cannot last indefinitely, what are we to do? Should we start a drastic program of water conservation, backed up by efforts to curtail and even reverse the growth of population? Or can we continue and extend the technology that has brought so much productivity to lands that were once semidesert?

There is abundant water in western North America; it is in Canada. Canada's westernmost province, British Columbia, is blessed with great rivers* and an annual rainfall of about 5 m. It has been estimated that the available fresh water in this province alone is somewhere between 5 and 10 percent of the *world's* supply. If this rich source could be treated like, say, the Colorado—dammed and pumped and piped to where it could be used for irrigation and for the convenience and growth of cities, and its hydropower likewise electrified and distributed over a vast energy grid—the United States could stop worrying about water in the West for at least a few centuries. Remember, hydropower creates no acid rain or greenhouse effect. The lands already impoverished by salinization could be washed clean with the great flow of fresh water from the north.

Are such ideas to be considered seriously, or are they more in the category of science fiction? Think of it this way: If your great-great-grandparents had moved West after the Civil War and started to farm in, say, Nebraska, they would have had a hard time surviving with the bare necessities of life on a homestead of 160 acres (65 hectares). If such pioneers could be brought back to life to see how people live in the same areas today with plumbing, electricity, automobiles, refrigeration, school buses, and medical care, all with the help of abundant water, it would seem like a miracle. Would the transition that might be brought about by a heroic project using Canadian water be any more miraculous than what has already taken place? Consider the other side, however. The American West is now very different from the land we still preserve in myth and imagination. Gone is the great abundance of wildlife—the herds of bison, the grizzly bears, the cougars, the antelope, the bald eagle feasting on spawning salmon.†

What would it mean to bring about another alteration of even larger magnitude—to flood great valleys, to cause far-reaching changes and probably extinctions among the species of our continent, to displace whole populations? If the small Mono Lake project became a complex problem, how involved would such a mammoth project be, with its international political aspects?

---

*The Fraser is the longest river in Canada and carries almost twice as much water as all the run-off of California.

†Read the novel *Seven Rivers West,* by Edward Hoagland, Summit Books, New York, 1986, for a vivid picture of those times.

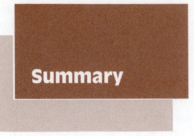

Summary

Molecules of water, H$_2$O, attract each other strongly; therefore, water has high melting and boiling points compared with other substances of similar molecular size. It also takes a lot of energy to melt ice or to boil water.

The movement of water on Earth (the **hydrologic cycle**) involves evaporation, precipitation, and run-off. The oceans lose water by evaporation and gain it by precipitation and run-off. The continents gain water by precipitation and lose it by evaporation and run-off. The Earth's waters spend the longest times (tens of thousands of years) in the oceans, icecaps, and glaciers and the shortest times (days) in the atmosphere.

Water for human use is withdrawn from surface and underground sources and transferred to homes, offices, factories, and farms. The portion of withdrawn water that is not returned to its source of supply is said to be **consumed.** Irrigation consumes the highest percentage of its withdrawn water. Water can be fed into the ground through **recharge wells.**

Of the water that falls on land, some percolates down until it is stopped by impervious rock or clay. The overlying porous layers become saturated up to a level called the **water table.** Water is drawn into narrow pores by **capillary attraction,** which is the result of the wetting action of water. The moist layer at the surface that is available for plant growth is called the **soil-moisture belt.**

Alternating strata of porous and impervious rock can provide lower layers of groundwater known as **aquifers.** These waters are replaced very slowly, and their rapid removal may be regarded as the mining of a nonrenewable resource. Other possible effects of removal of groundwater are **subsidence** of the land and **saltwater intrusion.**

Water can be stored by means of dams, which create reservoirs behind them. The resulting benefits include hydroelectric energy, control of water flow, and the recreational use of the reservoir. Disadvantages include silting of the reservoir, increased loss of water by evaporation and seepage, erosion of the stream bed below the dam, the risk of disaster if a dam breaks or when heavy rains overflow the dam onto heavily populated areas, and ecological disruption related to changes of habitats and redistribution of nutrients. Other methods of recycling or redistributing water for human use include diversion of fresh water by aqueducts or canals, recharging groundwater, desalination of seawater, cloud seeding to induce rain, and towing icebergs to areas that need water.

Questions

Properties of Water

1. Speculate on what the Earth and its biosphere (if any) might be like if (a) ice were denser than water; (b) at normal atmospheric pressure, heat added to ice at 0°C caused it to evaporate directly to water vapor rather than to melt (just as "dry ice," which is solid CO$_2$, does), and liquid water could exist only under high pressure, such as under layers of rock; (c) the amount of energy needed to melt ice and to vaporize water were reduced by 90 percent, but no other properties of water in any of its forms were changed.

The Hydrologic Cycle

2. In which physical state (solid, liquid, or vapor) does most of the Earth's H_2O exist? Which physical state contains the least?

3. Does the average residence time of water in a given source depend on the total volume of the water, the rate of flow of water into and out of the source, or both? Explain. Which effects increase the residence time? Which decrease it?

4. Describe the various ways in which (a) a rise and (b) a fall in the average global temperature could affect the hydrologic cycle.

5. (a) Under what conditions is the equation

evaporation + run-off = precipitation

true for the movement of water on the continents?
(b) Write a more general equation that would hold true under *all* conditions for the continents. (c) Write a similar general equation for the oceans.

Human Use of Water

6. Assume that you had water available from the following five sources: (1) Rainwater drained from your roof; (2) good well water or tap water; (3) water from the wash cycle of your dishwater or clothes washer; (4) water from the rinse cycle of your dishwasher or clothes washer; (5) water drained from your bath or shower. List all the applications in your home, in your garden, for your pets, or for other purposes for which each of these water supplies could be used. Using this information as a guide, suggest a water conservation strategy for your home.

7. List the following requirements for water in the increasing order or the quantity needed (least quantity first): (a) washing a load of clothes in a washing machine; (b) irrigation to grow a tonne of wheat; (c) drinking and cooking food for one person for a day; (d) one flush of a toilet; (e) one watering of the lawn of a suburban house.

8. (a) Explain the difference between withdrawn and consumed water. (b) In which of the following withdrawals is the water considered to be consumed? (i) The portion of your drinking water that is eventually exhaled through your breath; (ii) your bath or shower water; (iii) the tap water that you use to wash your car and that then returns to the river from which it came; (iv) the same water that drains directly to the ocean; (v) industrial cooling water that is pumped into a recharge well.

9. True or false: Most water is used where there are most people. Defend your answer.

10. List as many uses as you can think of for water in industry, in agriculture, and for recreation.

Groundwater

11. (a) Describe what happens to rainwater that starts to fall onto a very dry area and then continues heavily for several days. (b) Describe what happens to this water when there is no more rain for a month.

12. (a) List the following in the increasing order of their levels (lowest level first): soil-moisture belt, zone of saturation, water table. (b) Explain each of the preceding terms.

13. What is an aquifer, and how does water reach it? Under what conditions can a well that reaches an aquifer provide artesian flow?

14. What three developments greatly increased the agricultural productivity of the American West? Could the same result have been achieved with only two of the three? If so, which two? If not, why not?

15. Describe three problems that can arise from excessive use of groundwater.

16. Explain why land subsides when groundwater is depleted. If the removal of groundwater is stopped, will the land necessarily rise again to its original level? Defend your answer.

Human Control of Water

17. If you were faced with the same choice between distribution and purification of water described in Section 17.5, what decision would you make? How would the cultural and climatic environment affect your decision?

Dams and Diversions

18. The following three statements refer to the costs and benefits to different groups of people that result from the building of a dam. For each statement, identify the different groups of people: (a) People in some locations are benefited; people in other locations are disadvantaged. (b) People in some years are benefited; people in other years are disadvantaged. (c) People with some occupations or hobbies are benefited; people with other occupations or hobbies are disadvantaged.

19. List the advantages and disadvantages of dams as (a) a means of providing electrical energy, (b) a source of water for irrigation, (c) a method of flood control.

20. Is the silting of a reservoir a case of ecological succession? (See Chapter 6.) If so, would you classify it as primary succession or secondary succession? Defend your answer.

21. List the problems associated with diversions of water over long distances. Which problems occur mainly at the source? Which are felt at the destination?

Water Resources

22. Fresh water can be obtained by seeding clouds, desalinating seawater, or melting icebergs. Which method (a) is most promising for use in hot climates; (b) may transfer water from one source to another without making any more available; (c) is most energy intensive; (d) is least energy intensive?

23. Outline a program to conserve water in the home. Do your suggestions involve social or technical approaches or both?

24. Imagine that you are the chief executive of a country that has been depleting its groundwater reserves. You call in your experts. One says, "Conserve and recharge our waste water!" The second says, "Desalinate our seawater!" The third says, "Seed the clouds!" The fourth says, "Tow icebergs!" Your response is to ask them all for information to back up their advice. Make a list of the questions that you want each expert to answer for you.

25. Imagine that you live in an area with abundant water and it is proposed that some of the excess water be diverted to another region that needs it. List the questions that an environmental impact study should consider before construction is started.

Suggested Readings

Some of the material in this chapter can be supplemented by the references given for Chapter 20 on water pollution. Additional references are given below.

Water resources are discussed in:

Marc Reisner: *Cadillac Desert. The American West and its Disappearing Water.* New York, Viking Penguin, 1986. 582 pp.

Kenneth D. Frederick and James C. Hanson: *Water for Western Agriculture.* Washington, D.C., Resources for the Future Books, 1982. 241 pp.

David A. Francko and Robert G. Wetzel: *To Quench our Thirst. The Present and Future Status of Freshwater Resources in the United States.* Ann Arbor, MI, University of Michigan Press, 1983. 148 pp.

Anon: *America's Water. Current Trends and Emerging Issues.* Washington, DC, The Conservation Foundation, 1984. 114 pp.

Yacov Y. Haimes (ed.): *Risk/Benefit Analysis in Water Resources Planning and Management.* New York, Plenum Publishing Corp., 1981. 304 pp.

William E. Martin, Helen M. Ingram, Nancy K. Laney, and Adrian H. Griffin: *Saving Water in a Desert City.* Washington D.C., Resources for the Future Books, 1984. 128 pp.

E. J. Hofkes (ed.): *Small Community Water Supplies, Technology of Small Water Supply Systems in Developing Countries.* Somerset, NJ, John Wiley & Sons, 1984. 488 pp.

Geoffrey E. Petts: *Impounded Rivers, Perspectives for Ecological Management.* Somerset, NJ, John Wiley & Sons, 1985. 328 pp.

Donald Worster: *Rivers of Empire: Water, Aridity, and the Growth of the American West.* New York, Pantheon Books, 1985. 402 pp.

Thomas Dunne and Luna B. Leopold: *Water in Environmental Planning.* New York, W.H. Freeman, 1978. 818 pp.

Books specifically devoted to groundwater include:

Wendy Gordon: *A Citizen's Handbook on Groundwater Protection.* New York, National Resources Defense Council, 1984. 208 pp.

Charles W. Fetter: *Applied Hydrogeology.* Columbus, OH, Merrill, 1980, 448 pp.

Allan Freeze and John A. Cherry: *Groundwater.* Englewood Cliffs, NJ, Prentice-Hall, 1979.

The problem of salinity is taken up in:

Taylor O. Miller, Gary D. Weatherford, and John E. Thorson: *The Salty Colorado.* Washington, D.C., The Conservation Foundation, and Napa, CA, John Muir Institute, 1986. 102 pp.

For the politics of water in the West, see:

Harry Dennis: *Water and Power.* San Francisco, Friends of the Earth Books, 1981. 167 pp.

Terry L. Anderson (ed.): *Water Rights: Scarce Resource Allocation, Bureaucracy, and the Environment.* San Francisco, Pacific Institute for Public Policy Research Press, 1985. 374 pp.

Unit 5
Chemicals in the Environment

The river that burned. The Cuyahoga River was so polluted that in November 1952 it caught fire. Incidents of this type brought pollution problems to the public attention. The environmental laws written in the following few decades arose out of this awareness. (Cleveland Plain Dealer)

18

The Environment and Human Health

In places where food and medical attention are readily available, the average span of human life is longer than it has ever been. Modern medical science has drastically reduced death from infectious diseases, surgeons can repair or replace many damaged organs and joints, and even those who suffer from cancer are often cured or given years of relief. Yet, at the same time, there is increasing concern that the environment that we live in today—the air we breathe, the water we drink, the food we eat, even the sounds that assail us—endanger our health and our general well-being. In this chapter, we explore some of the issues of human health in our modern world.

18.1
Environmental Hazards to Health

The human body has many separate organs such as blood, bones, brain, heart, stomach, liver, and kidneys, all of which must function properly if the individual is to survive. Scientists recognize that the development of these organs in the embryo and the maintenance of their functions in an adult are controlled by genes, which in turn are composed of molecules of DNA. In a discussion of heredity and regulation of body functions, biologists distinguish between **germ cells** and **somatic cells.** Germ cells are involved in reproduction—the sperm of the male and the eggs of the female. Somatic cells comprise the other parts of the body. The complete hereditary information, carried by DNA, is found in the cell nuclei.

Somatic cells from many tissues and organs are being replaced all the time. When you get a sunburn, the burned skin peels and falls off, and a new layer of skin takes its place. DNA is responsible for directing the development and the replacement of our tissues so that skin cells produce more skin cells, bone marrow produces new blood cells, and so on. Sometimes, however, the internal regulatory processes break down. Then cells may start to reproduce in an unorganized, uncontrolled way. They spread beyond their normal limits and invade other areas of the body. This abnormal growth is called **cancer,** and a clump of such cells is called a **tumor.**

No one knows precisely how cancer develops. Recent research indicates that viruses may be involved in some instances. Two types of environmental agents, high energy radiation and certain chemicals, have been shown to cause cancer. The link between chemicals and cancer was first recognized more than 200 years ago in 1775 by a British scientist, Sir Percival Pott. He observed that chimney sweeps suffered an abnormally high incidence of cancer of the scrotum and correctly deduced that chemicals in soot must be responsible.

Since that time, many other materials have been shown to increase the incidence of various cancers in a population. These correlations are so convincing that scientists are certain that exposure to certain chemicals leads to a higher probability that an individual will develop cancer. Such statistical relationships warn us that some materials are indeed dangerous to health.

If chemicals can disrupt DNA in somatic cells, it should not be surprising that they can also alter the DNA in germ cells. If the DNA molecules in germ cells are altered, the effect may be passed on to the following generation. Such changes in the genetic material in either parent are called **mutations,** and substances that cause mutation are called **mutagens.** Although a carcinogenic chemical is not necessarily a mutagen, nor is every mutagen a carcinogen, evidence indicates that the two effects are correlated. Thus, populations that suffer a high exposure to environmental carcinogens also experience a high incidence of birth defects.

Mutations occur naturally and are the source of the genetic variation that, together with natural selection, account for the evolution of species. Why, then, are people concerned because environmental factors produce additional variation? Concern arises because most mutations bring a potential or actual disadvantage to the affected individual; only rarely does a mutation confer an advantage. This outcome is simply a matter of chance: There are always more ways for something to go wrong than to go right (the Second Law of Thermodynamics again).

Radiation has also been implicated as a cause of cancer and mutations. This subject was discussed in Section 14.17.

18.2
What Is a Poison? What Is a Toxic Substance?

In popular terms, a **poison** is a substance that can destroy life rapidly, even when taken in small amounts. However, our concern covers a wider range of health effects, not merely death. Effects that are slow or delayed, such as cancer, or mutations that are not observed until later generations, also represent serious problems. In this chapter we will refer to the wider category of **toxic substances,** which include any substance whose physiological action is harmful to health. Human health effects include lung and heart disease, kidney damage, skin rashes, cancer, birth defects, reproductive malfunction (such as sterility), and nerve and behavioral disorders, as well as acute poisoning. There may also be more subtle effects that are difficult to detect, such as mental depression or lowering of intelligence.

Still, substances cannot be divided sharply into two categories, "toxic" and "nontoxic." The difficulty is that "toxic" is a relative term, which depends on several factors:

It Depends on the Route of Entry   There are four ways for a substance to invade your body: (1) It can be inhaled; (2) it can be ingested (eaten or drunk); (3) it can be absorbed through the skin; or (4) it can be forced into the bloodstream, as with a snake bite or a puncture wound. The toxicity of a substance is generally strongly dependent on its route of entry. For example, although it would hardly be a good idea to swallow a drop of mercury from a broken thermometer, it would be *much* more harmful to heat the mercury on a stove and inhale all its vapors. Some substances are harmful no matter how they invade the body. Benzene, for example, will poison you if you drink it or if you breathe its vapor, and, if the liquid touches you, it can pass right through your intact skin.

It Depends on the Dose   Obviously, the more poison you absorb or ingest, the more serious are the effects. The amount of toxic material that enters your body is called the **dose.** The relationship between the dose and the health effects can be plotted on a graph (Fig. 18–1). However, it is no simple matter to acquire the information from which such a graph can be plotted. The next section explains how such data are obtained. Here, the meaning of the graph will be considered. First, note the vertical axis labeled "Effect on health." Since there can be different kinds of effects, the values can be taken from different sets of data, such as number of deaths in a given population,

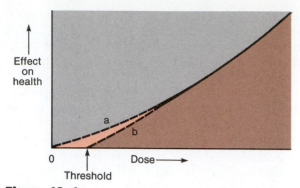

Figure 18–1

Generalized function showing the relationship between the dose of a toxic substance and its harmful effect on health.

number of individuals that develop a tumor, and so on. Now look at the horizontal axis labeled "Dose." You have just learned that there are different routes of entry to the body. Therefore, the route of entry must be specified. The shape of the graph depends on all these factors as well as on the nature of the toxic substance. For example, the effects of some poisons become sharply worse as the dose increases; the graph would then curve sharply upward.

The most uncertain (and controversial) parts of the graph are the two dashed lines, *a* and *b*. Both of these lines represent the health effects *when the dose is low.* Here is where it is most difficult to get reliable information. For instance, a graph may show data on the carcinogenic effects of dimethylnitrosamine (DMN), a chemical found in salami, bacon, and frankfurters (up to 440 parts per billion [ppb]) as well as in many varieties of fish (up to 40 ppb) and dairy foods (up to 10 ppb).

Experiments with animals reveal that DMN can cause liver cancer. But the experiments use high doses of DMN. Common sense and ordinary experience tell us that if we eat a frankfurter or salami sandwich today, we are not likely to get liver cancer tomorrow. Isn't it possible that the body can handle small amounts of DMN without any danger at all and that only an *excessive* amount of DMN is a threat? Yes, it is possible, and that possibility is represented by the dashed line *b*. This curve shows that below a certain dose, there is no effect at all on human health. The dose at which the danger starts is called the **threshold.** Above the threshold, the hazard increases as the dose increases.

But there is another possibility, represented by the dashed line *a*. In this case, even the tiniest amount of the substance could have an adverse effect on health. What if even one molecule of DMN could change a normal cell into a cancer cell? The chance would be small, but not zero. For the danger to be zero, the dose would have to be zero, and that would mean that there is no such thing as a threshold dose.

Scientists know that a threshold does exist for many chemicals. In fact, some substances that are essential to life in small amounts are toxic in excess. But for other chemicals, the threshold versus no threshold question is a difficult one and is often subject to much controversy. You can see why. If a threshold exists, a "toxic" chemical is no danger to anyone if the dose is small enough. Therefore, it would be wasteful to try to remove all of it from our food, air, or water. Sometimes the argument is expressed the other way: It can be said that *everything* is a poison if you get too much of it—salt, sugar, even water. So why worry as long as you don't overdo it? Such reasoning leads to the conclusion that the best way to remove the danger of a toxic chemical is to disperse it so widely in the environment that the "dose" anywhere is below the threshold. This doctrine is summarized in the often cited short sentence, "Dilution is the solution to pollution." But, on the other hand, if there is no threshold, this argument is invalid, and any trace of an environmental contaminant poses a threat to health.

It Depends on the Susceptibility of the Individual Individuals are different from one another, not only in personality and appearance but also in the chemistry of their bodies. For any specific poison, some people are more resistant than others. For a given dose, some may get sick, some may die, others may not be harmed.

It Depends on Other Factors Two different toxic substances may produce worse effects when they are combined. For example, the toxic effects resulting from inhalation of trichloroethylene (a dry-cleaning solvent) are increased if the individual also drinks alcohol. It has been shown that alcohol interferes with the ability of the body to get rid of the trichloroethylene. This enhancement is called **synergism,** which is a way of saying that the combined effect of the two chemicals is greater than

Box 18.1
Synergism

Synergism (from the Greek for "working together") originally referred to the doctrine that the human will cooperates with God's grace in the redemption of sinners. Later, the word was used in medicine to describe the cooperation between a drug and a bodily organ, or between two bodily organs, in carrying out some organic function. In modern scientific usage, synergism refers to any combination of actions in which the result is more than that which would be attained if the actions were entirely independent of each other. In other words, in a synergistic process, the whole is greater than the sum of its parts.

the sum of the effects of the two components taken individually. Another example of synergism is the combination of smoking and exposure to asbestos fibers, which results in a greatly increased probability of lung cancer compared with the risk of either smoking or asbestos exposure alone (Box 18.1).

18.3
How Are Toxic Substances Tested?

In practice, it is often quite difficult to determine the toxicity of a particular substance. Acute poisoning is relatively easy to document, but it is much more difficult to determine the effects of low doses. After all, there are hundreds of thousands of different chemical compounds present in our environment. How can the effect of a small dose of one of them be identified?

Epidemiology **Epidemiology** is the study of the distribution and determination of health and its disorders. A frequent objective of epidemiology is to establish cause-and-effect relationships. For example, one way to test a suspected toxic substance is to separate a population into two groups: one that is exposed to the chemical, and one that

is not. A classic example of this type of study is the analysis of the effects of cigarette smoke. Since there is a reasonably clear distinction between people who smoke cigarettes and those who do not, it is relatively easy to examine the medical records (especially the death certificates) of large numbers of people in these two distinctly different groups. The knowledge that cigarette smoking is harmful comes from many studies of this kind, involving records from hundreds of thousands of subjects (Fig. 18–2).

Now suppose that the effects of a certain widely used pesticide are being studied. If this material is dispersed throughout the global environment, it would be impossible to find a group of people who have had zero exposure to it. In such a case, it is impossible to compare health records of those who are exposed to the pesticide with those who are not; therefore, epidemiological studies are much more difficult to interpret and the conclusions are more tentative. One approach to this problem is to compare people with high levels of exposure with those who have lower levels of exposure. Workers in various industries are in contact with higher concentrations of certain materials than is the general public. In a classic example of an industrial study, one quarter of the male employees who worked in a coal tar dye factory in the United States between 1912 and 1962 contracted bladder cancer. This study led to the conclusion that several of the chemicals in the coal tar dyes were carcinogenic. Unfortunately, not all companies are willing to release such data, because the information may lead to lawsuits or may generate adverse publicity. Another problem with this approach is that the number of workers affected is often small, and the results, therefore, may be statistically ambiguous.

Another approach is to survey the geographical incidence of a certain disease. Figure 18–3 shows the probability of dying of cancer of the large intestine in relation to place of residence in the United States. This graph shows that a person living in the Northeast has a higher risk of dying of intestinal cancer than does someone living in the Southwest. These data suggest that regional pollutants may be associated with cancer, but the suggestion does not constitute proof. Several other factors must also be considered. Perhaps people in the Northeast smoke more cigarettes or get less exercise than people in other parts of the country.

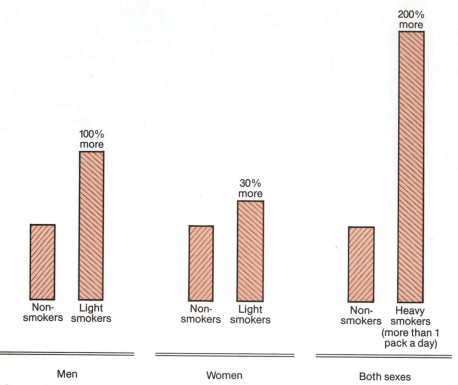

Figure 18–2

The relationship between cigarette smoking and risk of death by cancer.

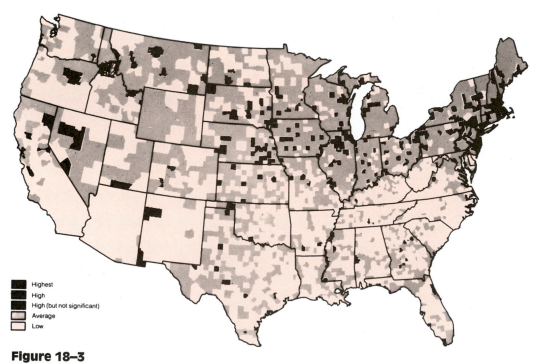

Figure 18–3

Deaths from cancer of the large intestine in the United States. (Courtesy of Dr. William Blot and *The Sciences*)

Perhaps they eat a different diet. Moreover, the ethnic distribution in the United States differs by location, and different ethnic groups have been shown to have different susceptibilities to cancer. Thus, no unequivocal conclusions can be drawn.

Another reason why it is difficult to prove a direct relationship between an environmental substance and cancer is that cancer may not appear for 10 to 20 years after exposure to a harmful chemical. For example, a high percentage of people who are exposed to asbestos fibers eventually die of lung cancer, but acute symptoms do not usually occur until at least 20 years after contact with this substance. Yet, when a new substance is released into the environment, people want information concerning its toxicity immediately, not a generation later after deaths have occurred.

Laboratory Studies Because of the inherent problems of epidemiological studies, laboratory studies of toxicity are often performed as an alternative approach. In a few instances, laboratory studies using people are carried out, but only with small doses that may produce only slight effects, such as the onset of discomfort or irritation. Of course, acute toxicity studies with humans are immoral. But even if such wrongful acts were contemplated, the results would not be helpful in cancer studies, since the onset of cancer may be delayed by a decade or two.

The most expedient alternative is to experiment on animals. The usual choices are small animals (mice, rats, guinea pigs, cats, dogs, and small monkeys). Scientists can't wait 20 years to see whether a rat that eats a synthetic chemical will get cancer. For one thing, the rat doesn't live that long. So scientists do to the rat what they would never do to a human—they feed the rat a concentrated diet of the suspected chemical. If the rat gets cancer, the chemical is considered a carcinogen for rats and a suspected carcinogen for humans (Box 18.2).

The arguments in favor of such tests are: (1) The laboratory animals will dine quite happily on the food that people eat and can be poisoned by chemicals that are harmful to people; (2) several known human carcinogens were predicted from animal studies; and (3) no animal carcinogen has ever been *shown* to be noncarcinogenic in humans.

The argument against such tests is that they are too exaggerated. No one eats concentrated

Box 18.2
The Ames Test

A laboratory test of the possible carcinogenicity of a substance using mice or rats takes about 3 years and costs more than $200,000. It has therefore been recognized that a faster, less costly screening test is needed. A very useful procedure was developed in the 1970s by Bruce Ames and his co-workers at the University of California (Berkeley) that can be done in 3 days for a very modest cost. The method utilizes a particular strain of bacteria that is very sensitive to mutation. These bacteria are exposed to the chemical to be evaluated, and the number of mutated bacterial colonies is then counted. The Ames test detects mutagens, not carcinogens, but about 9 of 10 carcinogens are mutagenic. Therefore, a chemical that is shown by the Ames test to be mutagenic can be classified as a suspected carcinogen and can then be studied more thoroughly.

amounts of synthetic chemicals, so how do the rat experiments apply to humans? The answer to this objection takes the following form: Suppose that the possible carcinogenicity of an additive used in a soft drink—perhaps a synthetic color, flavor, or sweetener—is being tested. Imagine that the additive is fed to the rats in such concentrated form that a human would have to drink 10,000 cans of soda per day to get the same equivalent dose. In this experiment, one rat out of every five rats develops a cancerous tumor (Fig. 18–4). Then the dose is reduced to the equivalent of 1000 cans of soda per day for a person, and, on this dose, one rat in every 50 develops a tumor. At a dose equivalent to 100 cans of soda per day per person, one rat in 500 gets a tumor. Now the research is becoming more difficult. The experiment is using too many rats, and the dose is still too high—no one drinks 100 cans of soda per day. Ultimately, the important question is whether it is dangerous to drink *one* can of soda per day. The data obtained thus far are plotted in Figure 18–4. As plotted, the three points lie in a straight line. If the straight line is continued down to the one can per day equivalent dose, there

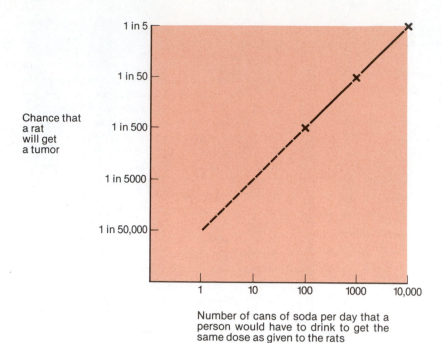

Chance that
a rat
will get
a tumor

1 in 5
1 in 50
1 in 500
1 in 5000
1 in 50,000

1   10   100   1000   10,000

Number of cans of soda per day that a
person would have to drink to get the
same dose as given to the rats

Figure 18–4
An attempt to extrapolate a laboratory study on rats to the probability that a food additive will cause cancer.

would be a 1 in 50,000 chance that a rat would develop a tumor. What does this number mean? Let us make two assumptions: (1) It is valid to continue the straight line as shown. This assumption is called "linear low-dose extrapolation." (2) After correction for differences in body weight, the chances of a tumor in rats and in people are equal. Both of these assumptions are really guesses. They may or may not be true. If they are true, we can calculate the effect of this additive on a population. There are approximately 240 million people in the United States. If everyone drank one can of soda per day and the probability of developing a cancerous tumor from this dose was 1 chance in 50,000 for each person, the results would be 240,000,000/50,000, or 4,800 human cancers in each generation from this exposure.

No one really knows whether such arithmetic makes sense. This uncertainty brings up questions of acceptable risks, which were discussed in Section 2.6. The questions involve both personal choices and public policy. Inconsistencies are common at both levels. Some persons will avoid all suspected carcinogens while they smoke cigarettes, whose carcinogenicity to humans has been demonstrated by extensive studies (see Section 21.8). Public policy with regard to the banning of suspected carcinogens is subject to economic and political pressures, which are difficult to counteract with uncertain evidence.

18.4
Sources of Hazardous Chemicals

The sources of hazardous chemicals may be grouped into three categories: (1) Those that exist in nature or are produced by natural processes; (2) those that are manufactured intentionally; and (3) those that are produced unintentionally.

Hazardous Chemicals in Nature An untouched wilderness is not a Garden of Eden. There may be poisonous minerals lying about and almost certainly many varieties of toxic plants. Volcanoes may emit noxious gases, and animals that sting or bite can inject their venoms directly into your bloodstream. These hazards may be thought of as a kind of "background toxicity," just as cosmic rays and the emissions from some rocks make up the background radiation to which all life is exposed. These natural hazards are often cited to make the point that an additional toxic chemical (or additional radiation) may be disregarded because it is no greater than the background effect; it is sometimes said to be "lost in the background." The counter argument is that an added hazard has a real effect even if it cannot be measured by the available statistical methods. This is the argument that was brought to bear by Linus Pauling in his successful effort to stop atmospheric tests of nuclear bombs, for which he won the Nobel Peace Prize in 1963.

Hazardous Chemicals Manufactured Intentionally These chemicals make up a large category that includes pesticides, industrial explosives, fuels, and, unfortunately, chemicals used in warfare. Such chemicals are intended to be confined to specific applications or used against specific targets, not to be dispersed indiscriminately in the environment. However, what if a little of the chemical vaporizes into the atmosphere or leaks onto the ground or into a lake or stream? If this happens at the plant, it may be cheaper just to manufacture more than to recover such small losses if economic externalities are not taken into account. It is even less cost-effective to recover dispersed chemicals at the points of use.

There is another very large group of chemicals that are never intended to be used outside of a manufacturing plant. These chemicals are intermediates in processes that require a number of steps from starting materials to final product. If they are transported, it is only intended to be from one plant to another, often by special means such as railroad tank cars, tank trucks, compressed gas cylinders, or pipelines. For example, the pesticide Sevin* is synthesized by a series of steps in which the intermediates include phosgene (a World War I poison gas), monomethylamine (an obnoxious fishy-smelling gas), hydrogen chloride (a strong acid), methylisocyanate (a deadly poison), and naphthol (a carcinogen). None of these intermediates should ever go anywhere but to the next step in the synthesis, but they can and do get out in the form of small, uncontrolled losses or, occasionally, in large quantities released by an accident (see Section 18.6 on the Bhopal accident).

Pesticides are toxic products that are synthesized through toxic intermediates. On the other hand, many products used by the consumer are chemically inert; in fact, they may have to be inert to be durable. Thus, synthetic plastics are used as containers for foods and as textiles for clothing; therefore, we do not consider them to be hazardous environmental chemicals. But an inert product is not synthesized from inert intermediates. On the contrary, materials used in chemical synthesis are

necessarily reactive, not inert. Moreover, they are generally not natural to the biosphere and are therefore almost all toxic—some very much so.

Hazardous Materials Produced Unintentionally Introductory chemistry classes present chemical reactions in the form of tidy, balanced equations. A student asked to describe the chemical change for the burning of coal in air might write the equation:

$$C + O_2 \rightarrow CO_2$$

According to this formulation, coal is represented as carbon, C; the atmospheric gas that reacts is oxygen, O_2; and the product is carbon dioxide, CO_2, an odorless, colorless gas. Not one of these statements describes a whole truth. The fact that burning coal produces foul-smelling smoke shows that more than carbon dioxide is produced. Atmospheric nitrogen is not entirely inert in a flame, so oxygen is not the only gas involved. And coal contains many elements other than carbon, notably sulfur and various metals.

But even if pure carbon were burned in pure oxygen, CO_2 would not be the only product—some carbon monoxide, CO, is also likely to be formed, depending on the manner in which the reaction is carried out.

Thus, two reasons why various chemicals are produced unintentionally are: (1) The starting materials contain impurities, and (2) chemical pathways are complex, and the wanted route is usually accompanied by side reactions that yield unwanted products. Some of these byproducts are harmless, others are toxic, and still others are unknown and untested.

The chemical manufacturing industry produces and sells thousands of chemicals, and, undoubtedly, small concentrations of millions of byproducts are also formed. Anyone who cooks food, burns leaves, drives a car, or smokes cigarettes adds to this total. In fact, most uncontrolled fires leave sooty residues. These byproducts contain many compounds that are carcinogenic. This is the reason that smoked foods and the burnt fringes of your charcoal-grilled steak are suspected carcinogens. Cigarette smoke is full of such compounds; they are in the "tar" referred to on the package. These products are environmental hazards, because they are stable enough to be produced in chemical reactions, even at high temperatures, but they are not biologically inert.

*Sevin is a trademark of the Union Carbide Corporation. See Appendix D for its formula.

Special Topic A
Notes on Six Environmental Contaminants

Tobacco Smoke The relationship between tobacco smoke and cancer has been established beyond any reasonable question. The effects of smoking are described in Section 21.8. Tobacco smoke is a mixture of gases, liquid droplets, and solid particles, all of which contain complex mixtures of a great many different chemicals. No one knows exactly which combinations of chemicals are responsible for which specific diseases. Cigarette filters do not remove gases, such as carbon monoxide and nitrogen dioxide, and they only partially remove droplets and solid particles. There is a relationship between tar and cancer, so that a low-tar cigarette is preferable to a high-tar one, although not enough is known to be able to say how much better it is. However, smokers of low-tar cigarettes (which are also lower in nicotine) often smoke them down to a shorter butt in an unconscious effort to make up for their nicotine deprivation. Since the tar accumulates at the butt end, such smokers inhale a larger proportion of the tar content of their cigarettes.

Asbestos About 5 to 10 percent of all workers employed in asbestos manufacturing or mining operations die of mesothelioma, an otherwise rare form of cancer of the membranes lining the chest and abdominal cavities. There are about 1100 new cases of mesothelioma each year. Of course, asbestos workers also die of other forms of cancer, and, if they are smokers, their risk of cancer is much higher than would be expected from a simple combination of the two exposures. The risks also extend to the families of these workers, presumably because of asbestos dust carried on clothes and in workers' hair.

Nitrosamines Nitrosamines were referred to in Section 18.2 in the discussion of threshold effects. These carcinogenic chemicals appear in food as a result of a series of chemical reactions that start with common, naturally occurring substances. One reaction starts with nitrates, such as sodium nitrate, which are common chemicals in soil and plants. Nitrates are also used for curing meats such as salami and hot dogs, or for smoking fish. Nitrates are reduced to nitrites by various microorganisms; therefore, nitrites also occur naturally in many foods. A second reaction starts with amines, which are another class of nitrogen compounds related to ammonia. Amines also occur naturally in many foods, including fish, dairy products, various fruits and vegetables, cereals, wine, beer, and tea. Some amines react with nitrites to produce nitrosamines, which are carcinogenic. What is one to do? One cannot cut out all the foods involved in sequences of reactions leading to nitrosamines. As noted in Section 18.2, however, cured meats such as frankfurters contain up to 440 ppb of dimethylnitrosamine (DMN); foods not cured by nitrites contain much less. A reasonable personal choice, then, would be to eat mostly fresh or fresh-frozen fish and meat, rather than that which has been cured.

Diethylstilbestrol (DES) DES is a synthetic hormone that, when fed to cattle, increases their rate of growth. As a result, in the 1960s, DES was fed to about three fourths of all the cattle raised in the United States. DES was also prescribed for pregnant women to reduce the chances of miscarriage. However, DES was shown to be carcinogenic in mice and is also linked to vaginal and cervical cancers in women. (Women born in the years from 1950 to 1966 whose mothers took DES during their pregnancies are at increased risk of developing a vaginal growth. Any such family history should be reported to a physician.) DES was therefore banned by the FDA in 1971. However, the federal courts reversed this ban on the grounds that DES was fed to cattle, not added directly to foods. The FDA countered that measurable quantities remain in meat after the cattle are slaughtered, and the ban was reinstated. Today, the entire issue of legislation of growth additives used in meat production is still not completely resolved.

Dioxin Dioxin has been a subject of epidemiological controversy since the Vietnam war, in which it was part of Agent Orange, the herbicide spray used by U.S. forces to defoliate the rainforest. Dioxin has been said by some to be the most toxic known chemical substance and a powerful carcinogen, while others argue that there is no overwhelming evidence for such assertions. There is no doubt that exposure to dioxin causes chloracne, a persistent, severe form of acne, and there are strong indications of other adverse health effects. Other populations have been exposed to dioxin as the result of herbicide applications and, in two cases, from accidents at chemical plants (in Nitro, West Virginia and in Seveso, Italy), and birth defects have been linked to these episodes. Furthermore, there is concern in some communities that proposed garbage incinerators would pollute the community with dioxin released from the smokestacks.

Here we will consider the question of where dioxin comes from, since no one tries to make it. You cannot buy dioxin at your local garden or hardware store, or pharmacist, nor is it readily available from chemical supply houses, so how can it show up in the smoke from your burning garbage? To answer these questions, we return to the herbicide Agent Orange, which is a 50–50 mixture of two common herbicides: 2,4–D and 2,4,5–T. The chemical formulas of these compounds are shown in Appendix D; the important parts of the formulas to note are the hexagonal rings of carbon atoms (benzene rings) and the chlorine atoms attached to them. The formula of dioxin is also given in the Appendix, and is repeated here:

This formula represents one of a family of compounds; the differences are only in the number and positions of the Cl atoms and need not concern us here. Benzene rings are stable structures that survive even when other parts of the molecule are broken down. Cl atoms attached to a benzene ring make it even more stable. The herbicides in Agent Orange are synthesized from starting materials that already have benzene rings with attached Cl atoms. In spite of the efforts of the manufacturing chemists to make the reactions produce only the intended herbicides, some of the molecular fragments take a different path—one that leads to dioxin. What's more, if human error or other malfunction allows the reacting mixture to get too hot, the molecular fragments go their own way and produce even more dioxin.

Now, what about dioxin in the effluent from garbage incinerators? Domestic garbage doesn't contain much benzene or its derivatives, but it is likely to include substances that contain Cl atoms, such as polyvinyl chloride (PVC) plastics. Molecules that are partially oxidized at incineration temperatures can rearrange themselves to *form* benzene rings. If chlorine atoms are also present, dioxin can be produced.

Many scientists believe that the amounts of dioxin released to the atmosphere from garbage incinerators are much too small to constitute a public health hazard, and there is certainly no epidemiological evidence of any such hazard. The opposing argument is that experiments with laboratory animals indicate that dioxin is an extremely toxic substance, that epidemiological studies of humans are necessarily very uncertain because the target population is not easily identified, and that we should not wait for the onset of human illnesses before restricting chemicals that are known to be toxic to animals.

Polychlorinated Biphenyls (PCBs) PCBs are organochloride chemicals that are structurally similar to the pesticide DDT (see Appendix D). Their unique electrical insulating properties make them useful in the manufacture of transformers and other electrical components. They have also been used in the production of plastic food containers, epoxy resins, caulking compounds, and various types of wall and upholstery coverings and as ingredients in soap, cosmetic creams, paint, glue, self-duplicating ("no-carbon") paper, waxes, brake linings, and many other products. In the late 1960s, scientists began to realize that PCBs were also serious environmental poisons. In 1968 the accidental contamination by PCBs of some cooking oil in Japan caused several thousand people to suffer from enlarged livers, disorders of the intestinal and lymphatic systems, and loss of hair. In New York City, workers in an electrical factory that used PCBs complained of similar ailments. Laboratory studies have shown that PCBs interfere with reproduction in rodents, fish, and many species of birds and monkeys. PCBs are soluble in the fat of animals and are stored in living tissue. They are also suspected of being carcinogenic, but conclusive evidence is lacking.

In the early 1970s, PCBs were found in cows' milk, many inland and deep sea fish, most meats, and in people's bodies. As evidence of the harmful effects of PCBs mounted, chemical manufacturers voluntarily curtailed their production and use, so that by 1972, applications of PCBs were restricted to the manufacture of electrical components. By 1977, all further production was banned under the Toxic Substances Control Act.

About 540 million kilograms (1.2 billion lb) of PCBs were manufactured in the United States between 1929 and 1977. Where did that all go? It is estimated that about half of that amount is in products that are still in use. Most of the other half was dispersed into the environment, and, because PCBs are not easily biodegradable, much is still there. Their persistence means that the contamination will continue far into the future. Even when PCBs do decompose, problems will continue, because evidence indicates that the decomposition products are even more poisonous than the original material. It will require decades for all these compounds to be removed from the natural environment.

18.5

Disposal of Toxic Chemicals: Love Canal and the Superfund

Another serious problem arises from the disposal of chemical wastes. Chemical wastes are produced in many industrial processes. As previously explained, chemical change rarely produces only the desired product. In some cases there is no way to avoid some unwanted materials, or byproducts. Sometimes an entire batch goes wrong because it overheats or was not mixed correctly.

The resulting wastes may be solids, liquids, or gummy, gooey mixtures that are messy to handle. They may contain compounds of chlorine, bromine, or sulfur, which would generate air pollutants if they were burned. Many of the wastes are very toxic; some are deadly. They cannot (or should not) be mixed with ordinary domestic or commercial garbage. They certainly must not be emptied into any river or lake, nor into the ocean. They can be destroyed or converted to harmless products by incineration. However, the contaminants in the incinerator exhaust would have to be removed by air pollution control devices. Alternatively, toxic wastes can be isolated from the environment in repositories that are confined by impermeable barriers of rock, or other material, and monitored to ensure against possible leakage. But the easiest and cheapest way to dispose of them is to pack them into 55-gallon steel drums (the "garbage cans" of the chemical industry) and just store or dump them somewhere. As these drums accumulate, often in hundreds or thousands, a "toxic waste site" is born.

The story of the discovery of one of these sites is an interesting one. The Hooker Chemical Company is a manufacturer of chemicals, with its main plant located in Niagara Falls, New York. Early in the 1940s Hooker purchased an old, abandoned canal called Love Canal. Employees loaded many of the chemical wastes into 55-gallon steel drums and dumped approximately 19,000 tonnes of these wastes into the canal. In 1953, the company covered one of the dumpsites with dirt and sold the land to the Board of Education of Niagara Falls for $1. The deed of sale stated that the site was filled with "waste products resulting from the manufacturing of chemicals." The deed also specified that Hooker would no longer be responsible for the condition of the land. The site was then used for an elementary school and a playground. But steel drums, exposed to moist soil from the outside and often strong acids or bases from the inside, cannot remain intact indefinitely. They rust from the outside, corrode from the inside, and eventually leak. The chemicals then seep into the soil and may travel through groundwater systems into rivers, streams, lakes, and reservoirs.

In the spring of 1977, heavy rains raised the level of the groundwater and turned the region into a muddy swamp. But this was no ordinary swamp. Mixed with the water and dirt were thousands of poisonous chemicals. The chemical goo floated about the playgrounds, flowed into people's basements, and settled over flower gardens and lawns (Fig. 18–5). Many of the children who attended the school and many of the adults who lived nearby suffered serious illnesses. Epilepsy, liver malfunctions, miscarriages, skin sores, rectal bleeding, severe headaches, and birth defects were reported.

Investigators learned that the drums, buried decades before, were leaking. A study revealed that several other similar dumps were scattered about the city. Practically overnight, a new and serious environmental concern was brought to the attention of the public. Some scientists said that the Love Canal issue was being blown out of proportion because it was impossible to prove that the illnesses in the Niagara Falls area were directly caused by chemical poisoning. Others disagreed and expressed the view that the diseases caused by the chemical spills were severe and that even greater disasters could follow. In 1978, the state of New York spent $37 million to relocate the families who lived closest to the Love Canal dump. Two years later, President Carter declared the region a federal disaster area and released an additional $30 million to aid families in the area.

The concern aroused by Love Canal and the fear that there might be many other such episodes was great enough so that in December, 1980, the United States Congress passed the Comprehensive Environmental Response, Compensation, and Liability Act, commonly known as the Superfund. This law provided for a $1.6 billion emergency fund over a 5-year period to deal with the problem of hazardous wastes. Before the Superfund law was enacted, if a hazardous site was discovered, it could take months or years to find the responsible parties and force them to remove the dangerous chemicals.

Figure 18–5

A, Steel drums full of poisonous chemicals were buried near the city of Niagara Falls, New York. The landfill was then covered and leveled, and the property was sold to the city as a site for a school playground. However, the drums rusted, and many of the liquids leached to the surface. Many children contracted strange and serious diseases. This photograph shows a pool of rainwater polluted with industrial chemicals from the dump beneath the surface. (Wide World Photos) *B,* A school child's opinion of the problems in Niagara Falls, New York. (Wide World Photos)

Under the new law, the presumed responsible parties are contacted and given the opportunity to investigate the pathways and effects of the contamination, then to conduct a cost/benefit study of cleanup measures, and finally to do the cleanup and to keep the site clean. If the responsible parties refuse, the EPA can use Superfund money to do the cleanup and sue them for *three times* the costs incurred.

How is a cleanup actually carried out? Since the atoms in the wastes cannot be destroyed, the only alternatives are to isolate the wastes so that they do not contaminate the environment, or to convert the wastes to nonhazardous products. In either case, a decision must be made as to whether the operation should be carried out at the waste site or whether the wastes should be transported elsewhere. A further difficulty is that wastes are usually complex mixtures of many components; their compositions are often unknown because records were lost or never kept; and, in any event, the wastes are often altered by chemical reactions that occur over time. Also, different sites contain different toxic substances.

Therefore, effort in the first years of the Superfund was devoted largely to organization, preparing a list of the most hazardous sites, establishing standards and priorities for cleanup, and developing technology. By the spring of 1982, only 10 actual cleanup operations had been undertaken.

By September 30, 1985, when the original Superfund expired, the Environmental Protection Agency (EPA) had identified 20,766 potential hazardous waste sites in the United States. Action on the rapid removal of the most dangerous of these had begun at 507 sites and was substantially completed at 458 of them. The program limped along into 1986 on projects that were already funded. On October 17, 1986, President Reagan signed into law the Superfund Amendments and Reauthorization Act, which increased Superfund revenues to $8.5 billion and strengthened EPA's authority to conduct cleanup and enforcement actions.

18.6
Chemical Accidents in Industry—Case History: Bhopal, India

Starting shortly after midnight on December 3, 1984, and continuing for about 2 hours, approximately 80,000 pounds (about 36 tonnes) of methyl isocyanate (MIC) escaped in a cloud of mist and vapor from a storage tank at a Union Carbide plant in Bhopal, India. Acute exposure to MIC severely damages the lungs and burns the corneas of the

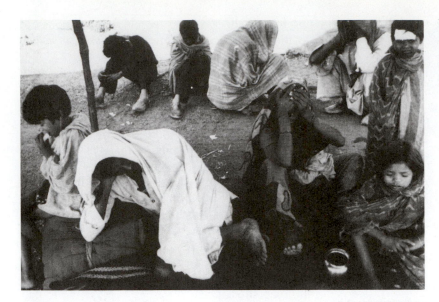

Victims of methyl isocyanate poisoning from the accident at Bhopal, India, on December 3, 1984. Symptoms include eye injury and shortness of breath. (Wide World Photos)

eyes. Immediate deaths result from respiratory failure. Survivors suffer damage to the central nervous system and to the body's immune mechanism for fighting disease, and these effects can be responsible for subsequent deaths.

The area around the plant was a poor, densely populated neighborhood; many people lived in shacks. The MIC cloud caught people in their sleep, killing many and awakening others to choking pain, terror, and panic. Many tried to outrun the cloud but could not see which way to go because of the darkness and the blinding effect of the MIC and were rapidly overcome. The Indian government puts the number of dead at about 2300, but other estimates are as high as 10,000. The lower figure comes from records at hospitals and burial grounds, the higher one from data such as the number of death shrouds sold in Bhopal in the days after the accident. The number of injured is put at more than 200,000. Many survivors suffer from permanent respiratory illness and impairment of vision. About 500,000 claims for damage were filed against Union Carbide by the victims and their families. The Bhopal event was thus the worst industrial accident in history.

How could such a tragedy happen? A larger question is, "Are such accidents to be expected from time to time in the chemical industry, and is such risk part of the price we must pay for the products that chemistry brings to us?" We will first describe the details of the Bhopal incident, then return to the general question.

MIC is used in the synthesis of Sevin, a pesticide. MIC itself is made by the reaction of phosgene (a poisonous gas) with methyl amine (a fishy-smelling gas). Hydrogen chloride is produced as a byproduct. You need not memorize the chemistry, but if you are interested, the equation is:

$$COCl_2 + CH_3NH_2 \rightarrow CH_3NCO + 2HCl$$
phosgene   methylamine   MIC   hydrogen chloride

Chloroform is used as a solvent throughout the process.

The MIC was stored in two horizontal stainless steel tanks, each with a capacity of 15,000 gallons and covered by an earth mound topped by concrete. The MIC tank, if set on rails, would be a typical size for a railroad tank car. Or, if the MIC tank held your gasoline and you filled your car once a week, it would last you about 20 years. MIC is a reactive chemical (recall the fact that chemical intermediates are generally more reactive than the final products) that decomposes if subjected to heat and/or moisture. Chemical decomposition at elevated temperatures typically produces gases, and, if hot gases are confined, their pressure rises and they may burst their container. It is for this reason that runaway industrial chemical decompositions may cause explosions or uncontrolled releases of toxic gases. The MIC tanks were to be protected against such an accident by means of a refrigerating system to keep the temperature down to 0°C, a rigorous exclusion of moisture, a safety system to release pressure that might get too high,

Special Topic B
Emotional Effects of Environmental Catastrophes by Nancy D. Kayne, M.D., Department of Psychiatry, Yale University School of Medicine, New Haven, CT

Environmental catastrophes include wars, earthquakes, floods, volcanic eruptions, explosions, and accidental releases of radioactive matter or chemical poisons. The injury, loss of life, and destruction of property that result from such events command our attention when they occur and for a while afterward, but, in time, they are largely forgotten, or rarely thought about, by the general public. For the victims, however, the emotional impact of such traumatic events can be severe and long-lasting. There have been extensive clinical discussion and research in the mental health field to study the effects of trauma. More recently, with the Vietnam war experience, a new diagnostic category has been elaborated in the mental health field, that of Post-Traumatic Stress Disorder (PTSD). Although it was largely generated as a consequence of treating patients suffering from war-related trauma and has specific "symptom requirements," the diagnosis of PTSD may be applied to victims of any other type of environmental catastrophe.

In general, survivors of trauma, regardless of the cause, may experience similar symptoms of varying duration and intensities with or without accompanying physical injury. When the event is sudden and unexpected, as is often true for environmental disasters, the lack of time to prepare defenses may increase the severity of the symptoms. Loss of family, friends, and source of income add to the trauma. Finally, if survivors have reason to believe that human error, negligence, or greed was involved, they are likely to feel increased anger, and this factor, too, can lead to more severe effects.

Onset of symptoms of PTSD varies from hours to days to months after the incident. Commonly, people experience increased anxiety and nervousness, hyperarousal, and vigilance. Many experience depression or a form of grieving response to personal loss, often along with a feeling of guilt that they have survived while loved ones did not. Survivors often experience recurrent nightmares or flashbacks of the event, and many find themselves avoiding any experience that recalls such memories, as this may lead to increased symptom severity. Memory and intellectual functioning may be altered as a result of poor concentration. These and other associated symptoms are likely to last many years after the event. Survivors may turn to alcohol or drugs to "numb the pain," but this only complicates recovery.

Thus, the short and long-term emotional effects of environmental disasters are serious and debilitating, often handicapping an individual irreversibly. An example is given by the following quotation from Vitaly Korotich, a poet and physician living in Kiev, Russia, describing the effects of World War II on his father:

> He was big microbiologist and was dean in Kiev Institute. Till now, he live, but he cannot be alone in closed room. After Gestapo. He must know he can open the door. He cannot travel in trains because the door is closed. He cannot travel in planes. He has this complex from war.*

*Studs Terkel, *The Good War: An Oral History of World War II.* Ballantine Books, New York, 1984.

and a chemical scrubber (see Chapter 21) to wash out any MIC that escaped through the safety release. Alternative protections included a flare (a flame for burning off pollutants) that could substitute for the scrubber and a spare tank into which excess material could be pumped. Despite all these precautions, a catastrophe occurred. The sequence of events was:

- On Sunday night, December 2, MIC tank # 610 was about 70 percent full, and its pressure was 2 psi.* The work shift changed at 10:45 P.M., and at 11:00 P.M. the control room operator noted that the pressure was 10 psi.

*Psi stands for "pounds per square inch." These units are not part of the metric system, but are still used by engineers in English speaking countries. A pressure of 2 psi in your auto or bike tire would be a flat; most auto tires take between 24 and 30 psi, and bicycle tires take about 80 psi. All these values refer to the pressure in excess of normal atmospheric pressure, sometimes designated as "pounds per square inch gauge," or psig. (If you want to go metric, one psi is 6.89 kilopascals.)

This was not considered unusual because the normal range in the tank was from 2 to 25 psi.

- Monday, 12:15 A.M. An operator in the process area (where the MIC is being produced) reported an MIC release. The control room operator looked at the tank pressure again. The reading was 30 psi and rising rapidly. In a few moments, the pressure was beyond 55 psi (the top of the scale on the gauge). He called his supervisor and ran outside to the tank. He heard rumbling sounds and a screeching noise from the safety valve, and felt heat radiating. The screech meant that the safety valve had opened and vapors were shooting out. As the frightened operator ran back to the control room, he heard the cracking of the concrete over the tank. He tried to turn on the scrubber but neglected to activate the circulating pump. The flare could not be used because it had been removed from service for maintenance work.
- About 80,000 pounds of mist and vapor, comprising most of the contents of the tank, were discharged to the atmosphere within a period of about 2 hours. During this time, the tank pressure probably reached about 180 psi, and the temperature rose above 200°C.
- Sometime after 2:00 A.M., the pressure dropped below 40 psi, the safety valve reseated, and the emission stopped.

Now we return to the questions, "How could such a tragedy happen?" "Are such accidents to be expected in the chemical industry, just as automobile accidents are to be expected on the highway?" With regard to the Bhopal episode, a Union Carbide investigating team came to the following conclusions:

- The accident started when a large amount of water (100 to 200 gallons) was introduced into the tank. The water reacted with the MIC, releasing heat and raising the temperature rapidly until the situation was out of control. The iron from the corrosion of the tank walls acted as a catalyst to speed up other chemical reactions that added to the temperature rise.
- The introduction of water into the tank was a deliberate act of sabotage by a disgruntled worker.

The Indian Government denies the Carbide allegation and states, instead, that the accident was caused by poor management and bad plant design and that Carbide had failed to maintain high safety standards at the Bhopal plant and to share information about the toxicity of MIC with the government.

Such disputes are settled by negotiations or in courts of law, not in textbooks. However, the general question about accidents from the chemical industry deserves attention here. Some manufacturing chemists point out that accidents are part of our experience in all types of activities and that when toxic chemicals are involved, accidents can be deadly. But, they add, human life would suffer much more from a lack of the medicinals, agricultural chemicals, refrigerants, plastics, and other materials that chemistry brings to us. They also note that industrial accidents tend to happen during the night shifts when workers are tired, especially during the first night shift after a weekend, as in the Bhopal episode.

Such an answer will not satisfy everyone. It is reasonable to ask whether it is possible to raise safety standards in the chemical industry to a much higher level, through the use of redundant systems, more "fail-safe" devices, and the like, as described in Chapter 14 on nuclear energy. The history of accidents in the nuclear industry, however, does not encourage confidence that such measures will solve the problem. We are thus led to a final question: "Can we reduce human error?"

Human errors in the management of emergencies result from incorrect decisions. It will therefore be helpful, in analyzing this important problem, to think about how decisions are made in such situations, and how they can go wrong. Think of how you might behave in a possible emergency. You are alone in a building and just barely smell smoke, but you don't see any fire. Do you call the fire department, or try to find the fire yourself, or assume it's just something from outdoors that can be ignored? As a second example, you are the pilot of a passenger plane whose wings have been accumulating ice on the runway for about 29 minutes and the rule is not to take off without de-icing after a half-hour accumulation. Do you take off or do you delay the flight? As a third example, you are an operator in a chemical plant where a pressure gauge on a tank shows a higher reading than you have ever seen before. The gauge has been erratic before (but not this erratic!) and nothing has gone wrong. Do you dump the contents of the tank (at great loss to the company) or assume it's just the gauge acting up again and save the chemicals?

What is common to all these examples is two sets of questions:

1. Does an emergency *really* exist?

2. Do you *decide* that an emergency exists?

The answer to each question can be yes or no. These possibilities lead to four combinations of questions and answers, which can be set out in what is called a "payoff matrix" as follows:

Does an emergency really exist?

		Yes	No
Do you decide that an emergency exists?	Yes	Correct recognition	False alarm
	No	Miss	Correct rejection

Thus, there are two ways to be right and two ways to be wrong. In the example of your smelling a bit of smoke, if there was a real fire and you called the fire department, that was a correct recognition, but, if you did not, then you missed. If it was just a smell from outdoors and you did nothing, that was a correct rejection, but if you called the fire department, that was a false alarm.

So how do you make your decisions? There is one constraint that cannot be escaped: *You can't always be right.* It is possible for you never to miss a real emergency by assuming that every signal is a real one. But, in reality, there are false signals—a wisp of smoke that is not a fire emergency, or a faulty gauge that does not mean the batch will explode. So if you always decide that an emergency exists, you will ring many false alarms. On the other hand, you can avoid all false alarms by never sounding any, but then you will miss real emergencies.

Therefore, you must strike a balance, which will be determined by rewards for correct judgments and punishments for wrong ones, by your expectations of what such rewards and punishments might be and by your own moral judgments of right and wrong. Let us see how these factors operate in the context of industrial accidents for each of the four possibilities shown in the "payoff matrix."

1. One might think that *correct recognitions* would be greatly rewarded, because they prevent damage. In many cases, however, they are not rewarded at all, or they may even be punished. Think about the Bhopal situation: Imagine that a responsible individual at Union Carbide had decided that the large quantity of MIC stored near that populated area and the absence of additional safety features and procedures constituted an emergency condition. For these reasons, all production should be stopped until the necessary changes were made. Such a decision would have saved many lives and avoided many illnesses (not to mention the corporate damage to Union Carbide), but no one would have known anything about an accident that did not happen, so the only tangible result would have been more expense and less profit to the company. The individual who made that decision might have been ignored or even fired.

2. *False alarms* are incorrect judgments that are clearly costly.

3. A *miss* is a very costly incorrect judgment, but it does not happen very often in the life of a given individual. After all, most houses do not burn down, most airplanes do not crash, and most chemical plants do not blow up. Therefore, an operator who perceives something unusual, such as a whiff of smoke, or a gauge with an unusual reading, must make a risk assessment that is usually based on insufficient experience. (Refer back to the discussion of risk assessment in Chapter 2.)

4. *A correct rejection* is a decision that clearly saves effort and money. The fire department saves a trip, the flight is not delayed, and the chemical production does not have to be slowed down or interrupted.

This analysis shows why, when the question arises, it is often more rewarding to assume that an emergency does *not* exist. To reduce the incidence of accidents such as that at Bhopal, we must do more than provide additional safety devices. We must also tilt our evaluations of right and wrong decisions to favor those that can prevent tragedies, even though such benefits are not easily proved in the short term.

18.7
Case History: The Clark Fork River—Contamination by Toxic Metals

As you drive into the city of Butte, Montana, a sign reads, "WELCOME TO BUTTE—THE RICHEST HILL ON EARTH." The hill referred to by the sign still contains the remnants of a massive copper deposit, but today it is recognized by the yellow/orange scars of abandoned mines and mining dumps. Some mining activity still occurs, but boarded up stores and bankrupt businesses in the city center tell a story of recent economic decline.

The mining era in Butte began with the first gold strike at Silver Bow Creek in 1864. By 1883, the gold and silver bonanza had collapsed, but the world's largest known deposit of copper had been discovered, and the big boom was on. It is difficult to appreciate how isolated the city of Butte must have been. In 1882, when the first millions were being made, bison still roamed the plains. (General Custer was defeated a few hundred miles to the southeast in the year 1876.) Because transportation was slow, dangerous, and expensive it was natural to locate mills and smelters in the Butte area to concentrate the copper ore and reduce it to the metal. Thus, only the most valuable materials, the actual metals, were actually shipped across the plains to the eastern cities.

There were no environmental regulations imposed on the early smelters, and the pollution must have been awful. A grey pall hung over the city, and the sun seldom shone through, yet Butte was considered to be a desirable place to live. Much wealth was being created, and there was money for opera halls, race tracks, and art exhibits, making Butte a fashionable center in the Rockies. What's more, pale faces were considered to be stylish, so the fact that smoky clouds blocked out the sun throughout the year became an added advantage. However, as time passed, the pollution was severe enough to become uncomfortable and unhealthy. (There were no accurate epidemological studies to chronicle the illnesses or deaths that occurred.) As a result, most of the smelter operations were moved to a site about 40 miles to the west. This site was chosen because water was available and because a steady wind helped to disperse the smoke plumes. A smelter was built, and the town that grew around it was named Anaconda after the dominant company in the area. The facility continued to operate for some 70 years until it was closed down in 1980 for a variety of reasons.

With the demise of major industrial activity in the area, air quality improved immediately, but a major hazardous waste problem remained. In order to understand the root of this problem, it is essential first to remember that an ore is not a source of a single metal, but rather a mixture of metals or their compounds combined with various kinds of rock. Some of the raw ore from the mines in Butte contained as little as 0.3 percent copper, with smaller concentrations of manganese, zinc, arsenic, lead, cadmium, and a variety of other metals. In the early days, the extraction of the copper was inefficient, so copper residues still remain. Furthermore, copper ore often contains traces of gold, which the early miners attempted to extract by dissolving it in mercury, so mercury, too, is still present. The discarded mixture of crushed rock combined with small amounts of all these mineral contaminants, called **tailings,** was first pumped directly into the river and then was built up into large mounds. Today, the volume of the tailings is enormous. There are about 25 sq km (about 10 sq miles) of piles with an average height of 15 m (about 50 ft), or about as high as a five-story building. Other smaller tailings that were deposited by the original smelters are found in Butte.

These tailings have posed, and continue to pose, a serious environmental concern because the metals found in them are low-level poisons. Many studies have established a connection between environmental metal contamination and a variety of diseases. For example, in one study, it was shown that workers in a cadmium recovery plant suffered a higher incidence of lung cancer than the public at large. In another study, it was shown that skin cancer was prevalent among a group of people who drank well water contaminated with arsenic. Metal contamination is also harmful to the environment, causing a reduction in the growth rate of plants, of animals that eat the plants, and of microorganisms in the soil.*

If the metals from the smelter operation remained localized in well-defined tailings piles, only a relatively small area would be severely disrupted, and the effect on the wider environment would be negligible. In order for a poison to contaminate an ecosystem, it must first be dispersed. There are

*The references to these three articles are, in the order that they were mentioned:

Michael J. Thun, et al.: Mortality among a cohort of U.S. cadmium production workers—an update. *Journal of the National Cancer Institute, 74*(2):325, 1985.

W. P. Tseng, et al.: Prevalence of skin cancer in an endemic area of chronic arsenicism in Taiwan. *Journal of the National Cancer Institute, 40*(3):453, 1968.

Germund Tyler: The impact of heavy metal pollution on forests. *Ambio, 13*(1):18, 1985.

several ways that the contaminants can be transported.

Wind Metallic compounds are present not only in the tailings but also in the ash emitted from the smokestack of a smelter. Both dust and ash are transported by winds, and, over the past 75 years, this material has been deposited throughout the valley surrounding Anaconda.

Erosion by Rainwater If rainwater falls on a bare, unvegetated tailings pile, the water physically carries small particles downslope. This process is known as erosion. Most of the soil particles transported by moving water are eventually deposited in rivers and flood plains. As years go by, these sediments are carried slowly downstream.

Leaching As explained in Box 18.3, a metallic element such as iron can exist either as a metal or as a compound such as iron oxide (commonly called rust). Some metallic compounds, such as sodium chloride (table salt, NaCl), are very soluble in water. If there are grains of salt in the soil and rainwater percolates through it, the salt will dissolve and will be carried downslope. Other metallic compounds, such as iron oxide, are insoluble. Still others are slightly soluble. Obviously, soluble compounds will be transported more easily than insoluble compounds. Leaching rates are complicated by the fact that solubilities vary with the presence or absence of other chemicals in the water. Most minerals are more soluble in water that is acidic than in neutral or basic solutions.

With this background, let us briefly trace the events that have occurred in the Butte–Anaconda environment over the past 70 to 100 years.

Windblown contaminants from the mining operations have been dispersed throughout the valley. For example, although the town of Mill Creek lies upstream of the smelter, the topsoil throughout the region now contains high levels of arsenic and other metals. In turn, these materials are transported to the human population by a variety of mechanisms. Children play in the dirt and inadvertently swallow small amounts and inhale some of the dust. Or, alternatively, adults plant gardens, the minerals are absorbed by the roots of the plants, and are then ingested by the people. Altogether, studies have shown that school children in Mill Creek have levels of arsenic in their urine approxi-

> **Box 18.3**
> **Resource Conservation and Recovery Act (RCRA)**
>
> This law, passed in 1976 and amended in 1980, addresses the problem of wastes. The approach calls for reducing the amounts generated, for maximizing recovery, and for establishing procedures for the safe disposal of hazardous wastes. The regulations therefore must specify what makes a waste hazardous. The issue is more than a simple one of toxicity. Can the waste be leached into groundwater? Can the waste, when mixed with some other chemical, produce a toxic gas? For example, many metallic sulfides are highly insoluble in water, and therefore in this chemical composition they are relatively harmless. However, on contact with acid they generate deadly hydrogen sulfide gas; such materials are therefore classified as hazardous. The technical and enforcement problems are complex, and progress in achieving the objectives of the law has been slow. Improvements have been made, but much hazardous waste still gets through.

mately seven times the levels recorded in children living in similar-sized towns in Montana located far from the smelter site.

The plight of downstream communities is even worse. High concentrations of metals are recorded downstream of both Butte and Anaconda. Silver Bow Creek, running out of Butte, is truly a dead stream. There are no fish of any kind living there. The water is not only unfit to drink, it is unfit to touch. Children playing by the banks have been burned by pools of highly acidic water leaching out of some of the old tailings. In one instance, a young boy uncovered a lump of phosphorus lying under the water. When he lifted it out and exposed it to the air, it caught fire and burned his hands severely.

Below Anaconda, the situation is not so severe as it is in Silver Bow Creek. The tailings piles have been partially stabilized in recent years, and the creek is diluted by clean-flowing streams from the mountains. Today, remedial action to clean the streams has been partially successful, and trout

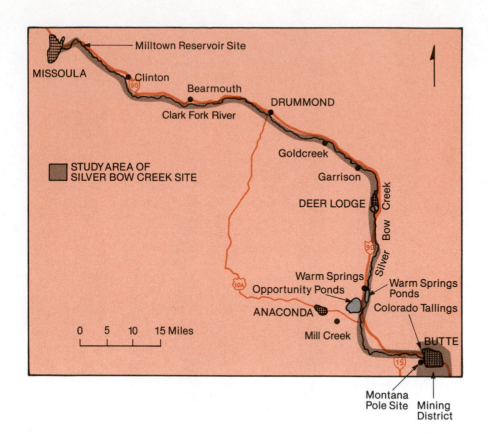

MISSOULA

Milltown Reservoir Site

Clinton

Bearmouth

Clark Fork River

DRUMMOND

Goldcreek

Garrison

STUDY AREA OF
SILVER BOW CREEK SITE

Silver Bow Creek

DEER LODGE

Warm Springs
Opportunity Ponds

Warm Springs
Ponds

Colorado Tallings

ANACONDA

Mill Creek

BUTTE

0   5   10   15 Miles

Montana
Pole Site   Mining
District

Silver Bow Creek.

can be caught below the treatment ponds at Warm Springs. However, the stream is far from healthy compared with other streams in nearby regions.

Two additional problems deserve special attention. Montana has a harsh environment with cold winters. In most years, streams freeze in the winter. During spring thaw and breakup, ice jams dam the river, channels flood, and new river channels are formed. This process has been going on for millennia. Since the onset of mining, the streams have carried high loads of contaminated sediments. During flood cycles, these sediments have been dispersed throughout the entire valley.

Yet another problem has occurred at a site about 100 miles (about 160 km) downstream from Anaconda. In 1907, the Milltown Dam was built just upstream from the city of Missoula. The dam was originally constructed of large wooden boxes nailed and pegged together and filled with rocks. Electrical generators were built, and the installation has been a source of electrical power ever since. This dam was not constructed in conjunction with the mining operations, and, originally, there was no connection between the two facilities. However, over the years, approximately 6.5 million tonnes of

polluted sediments from the Anaconda and Butte operations have been deposited behind the dam. The metals dispersed in these sediments include arsenic, lead, zinc, chromium, copper, and cadmium, all in the form of toxic compounds.

The sediment-filled pond at Milltown poses a twofold problem. First, water leaching through the sediments becomes polluted, and the contaminated solutions have seeped into groundwater reserves in the neighborhood, rendering the water in most of the old wells in Milltown unfit to drink.

The second concern revolves around the physical stability of the dam itself. The 80-year-old timbers are rotting, and parts of the surface are eroding. Measurements have shown that the entire dam is settling at a rate of 1 cm per year and has been creeping slowly downstream at a rate of 1.5 mm per year. At a hearing conducted in April of 1986, an engineer for the power company testified that if spring run-off water levels rose to 150 percent of normal, there was a "high probability" that the dam would breach. Records show that the likelihood of such an abnormal height in any one season is about 15 percent. Dam failure would lead to flooding, with consequent dispersal of millions of tonnes of contaminated sediment over the valley just upstream of the city of Missoula.

The mining boom in southwestern Montana is mostly past, but the legacy remains: Many linear kilometers of contaminated creeks, 25 sq km of tailings piles, metal pollution throughout the flood plain, and 6.5 million tonnes of sediment behind a rotting wooden dam.

We ask three questions: (1) What has been done to alleviate the problem? (2) What is the cost both in terms of dollars and of nonquantifiable effects such as damage to human health? (3) What can be done about it?

1. What Has Been Done to Alleviate the Problem? Three large Superfund sites have been designated in the area. One is Silver Bow Creek, including the entire Butte area; the second is the tailings piles in Anaconda; and the third covers the dam, the pond, and the polluted groundwater in Milltown. Within these areas, several types of solutions are possible. Metals are elements that cannot be destroyed; a tonne of arsenic will always be a tonne of arsenic. However, they can be isolated from the food chain in some way. Despite the fact that the tailings piles represent a large volume of material, they are relatively localized and therefore fairly easy to isolate. Recall that metallic compounds generally dissolve much faster in acidic solutions than in neutral or basic ones. The goal of isolation is to convert the minerals into insoluble forms. Therefore the tailings piles have been covered with a thick layer of lime (the cheapest available base) and then covered with soil. Finally, grasses are planted to stabilize the entire system.

The next problem is to detoxify the pollutants in the creeks and rivers. The preliminary strategy has been to forfeit the most heavily polluted upstream portions and to intercept contaminants before they move on downstream. To realize this goal, dams have been constructed to act as a physical barrier to the movement of sediments. A physical barrier is effective in stopping soil particles but cannot intercept dissolved minerals. To control the dissolved materials, large quantities of lime are added to the ponds behind the dams. The lime neutralizes the acids and precipitates dissolved metals. The effectiveness of this process is evidenced by the fact that a healthy population of trout lives below the ponds.

The third activity has been remedial action to protect the inhabitants of Milltown, adjacent to the dam. As stated earlier, contaminated water has traveled from the ponds into the groundwater. The contaminated water was used for many years before the problem was recognized. This neglect led to an accumulation of toxic materials in the pipes, the hot water heaters, and the faucets in most of the homes in Milltown. Therefore, the first step in the cleanup process was an emergency order condemning most of the wells and plumbing in the area. New, deeper wells were drilled, and new pipes were installed. The total cost of this remedial action has been about $1.3 million.

2. What Is the External Cost of the Current Level of Pollution? The Montana Governor's office estimates that the high levels of pollution in the area have resulted in an annual loss of about $15 million in tourism and recreational business. In addition, about 1500 hectares (3700 acres) of prime farmland have been totally destroyed by contaminated sediments, and agricultural production has been reduced on 10,000 hectares (25,000 acres), leading to a total agricultural loss of about $2.5 million annually.

What about health effects? When the smelter was in operation, the death rate for the middle-aged segment of the population in Anaconda was about seven times the national average. However, this statistic includes all types of mortality—accidents at the smelter, automobile accidents, and so on. It doesn't isolate or even directly address the question of premature death due to low level toxicity. The smelter closed in 1980, only a few years ago. The number of people living in the area is small. Therefore, any significant epidemiological study would be difficult, and none has been completed. In short, we don't know what the cost in terms of human health really is.

3. What Can Be Done, and How Much Will it Cost? In researching this case history, one of us (J.T.) drove to the Montana state capitol in Helena, met with the EPA officials in charge of the project, and asked them this very question. The two men in the room both smiled, shrugged their shoulders, and looked at each other, each waiting a moment for the other to speak first. The best answer that they could give was that many avenues are being explored, but no one knows what the final cost will be. It will take several years to develop an accurate cost projection plan, and this plan must precede the actual cleanup.

The general approach is expected to be the following: The polluted banks and sediments of Silver Bow Creek will be covered with clay and/or concrete and therefore isolated from the environment. This process is called **armoring.** More settling ponds will be built to clean the river still further. The most heavily polluted portions of farmlands will also be armored. The pond behind the dam at Milltown will be drained, and the sediments, too, can be armored. The soil contamination throughout the valley is more difficult to deal with. It is unrealistic to spread concrete over the whole region and turn it into a huge parking lot! If nothing is done, scientists estimate that the pollutants will slowly leach out so that the concentration of arsenic in the groundwater will reach acceptable levels in 350 years. But 350 years is too long to wait. Some experts have suggested that in heavily contaminated areas such as Mill Creek, the topsoil could be dug up and removed, the subsoil covered with plastic, and new layers of topsoil could be imported. An alternative approach would be to buy the town and all the houses in it, level everything with a bulldozer, cover it with clay, and leave it. There are no acceptable solutions to the low-level contamination of farms throughout the region. All in all, it is obvious that there are no cheap, simple, or entirely satisfactory methods of detoxifying the valley.

What about the cost? Officials at Atlantic Richfield (the company that bought Anaconda Minerals) estimate that the total cleanup will cost about $20 million. However, government officials disagree and one told me, "We figure the cost at $200 million to $400 million and that is probably conservative."

There is an important environmental lesson to be learned from the disaster in the Butte–Anaconda area. When toxic wastes are produced by any industrial activity, they are initially concentrated in the immediate area of operation. Thus, for example, the metals that are now spread about an entire valley were once located in a relatively small pile within the immediate perimeter of the smelter site. It is often expensive to address a pollution problem at the time that the pollutants are produced, but this cost is small compared with the cost of reconcentrating the pollutants once they are dispersed throughout the environment (the Second Law again). Thus, in many cases, strict environmental legislation is economically justifiable.

18.8
Chemicals in Foods

Most of us have relatively little choice over the water we drink and even less over the air we breathe. In this section, we examine the opportunities and limitations we have in selecting the foods we eat.

Almost every food available in modern supermarkets contains small amounts of chemicals that are not natural to the food itself (Fig. 18–6). Fruits and vegetables contain pesticide residues. (Pesticide pollution will be discussed in Chapter 19.) Cattle are fed artificial growth compounds before they are slaughtered, and some of these chemicals remain in the meat when it is sold. Almost all pre-prepared "convenience foods" contain a variety of additives, often identified by complex and strange chemical names. Many people ask why so many chemicals are needed and whether they pose a hazard to health.

Figure 18–6
Most packaged foods contain a variety of additives.

To reassure the public, representatives of the chemical industry remind us that the words "chemical" and "chemical substance" refer to *any* kind of matter. "Chemicals" therefore include the chlorophyll in a leaf of spinach, the protein in a lamb chop, and the salt in the sea. Everything is a chemical. Since this is true, why worry about chemicals in food? You might answer that you are concerned about environmental problems caused by *synthetic* chemicals. In response, the industrial chemist could point out that the properties of a chemical have nothing to do with where it came from— whether from natural or from manufactured sources. Vanillin, for example, is the chemical that imparts a vanilla flavor to food. Vanillin can be extracted from vanilla beans, or it can be synthesized. It is the same substance either way. Vanillin is vanillin, so why distinguish between natural and synthetic vanillin? Furthermore, the chemist continues, not all natural substances are good, and not all synthetic ones are bad. Cobra venom and the aflatoxin found on moldy peanuts are both natural substances. But the venom is a deadly poison and the aflatoxin is a potent carcinogen.

Many natural foods are believed to cause specific diseases. For example, saturated fats may contribute to hardening of the arteries and consequent heart failure, sugar leads to obesity and dental caries, and too much alcohol can cause cirrhosis of the liver. Studies have also indicated that spinach, cabbage, and charcoal-broiled meats contain measurable quantities of some carcinogenic chemicals that are also found in automobile exhaust and in tobacco smoke.

These arguments are well presented, yet they leave many with a sense of unease. How trustworthy are the industrial reassurances? The issue is complex, because there are several different categories of food additives, as listed below:

1. Preservatives are used to prevent spoilage.

2. Vitamins and minerals enhance the nutritional value of foods.

3. Artificial colors, flavors, and sweeteners alter the taste or appearance of various products.

4. Other additives, such as emulsifiers, are used to blend foods. For example, the oil in natural peanut butter separates and floats to the top of the jar. Emulsifiers are added to peanut butter so that the oil will not separate out.

5. Many chemicals are added to animal feed to encourage the production of meat, milk, or eggs.

Similarly, use of pesticides and herbicides leads to chemical contamination of plant products.

The use of all of these chemicals has risen in response to modern ways of life (Table 18-1). Homemakers no longer bake bread every morning; instead, many shop once a week. Since bread without preservatives may go moldy in a week, chemical preservatives are added to reduce the possibility of spoilage. Similarly, many people do not have time to cook an elaborate breakfast before work. So they pour some cereal out of a box, add milk, and eat an instant meal. The vitamins and minerals in the packaged foods add to these people's dietary intake. Hormones added to animal feed speed growth and reduce the cost of many foods. Other additives do not improve the quality of the food. For example, natural peach ice cream is a dull pink. However, with the simple addition of some coloring, a bright, almost "day-glo" color can be achieved. The color does not improve the taste, flavor, or nutritional value of the ice cream. But the advertising companies have conditioned us to expect highly colored foods and to buy their clients' products.

There are two levels of decisions to be made about food additives. The first is a political one, the second is on a personal level. One legitimate role of government is to protect the health of its citizens. As a result, most nations have established various agencies to monitor the quality of foods. In the United States, the Food and Drug Administration (FDA) was first established in 1906 to set guidelines for the safety of various foods and drugs. In the beginnning, the law was not focused primarily on chemical additives. In fact, before 1958, a new chemical could be released on the market *before* it was tested for toxicity. The law was then changed to require extensive tests on each new chemical additive or drug before it is released on the market. But what about those products in use before 1958? Are they safe? It costs upward of $1 million and several years' work to test a single product completely, and the cost and time required to test all the products traditionally used in food preparation seemed prohibitive. As a result, in 1958, FDA officials made up a list of all the chemicals that were at that time added to foods and sent the list to a panel of several hundred experts. Each expert was asked to choose, on the basis of professional opinion (not direct research), which chemicals were safe and which were sus-

Table 18–1
Some Commonly Used Classes of Food Additives

Additive	Purpose	Common Compounds Used
Preservatives	Retard spoilage caused by bacterial decay and growth of molds	Benzoic acid, calcium propionate, citric acid, potassium sorbate, salt, sodium benzoate, sodium nitrate, sodium nitrite, sorbic acid, sulfur dioxide
Antioxidants	Maintain freshness by retarding chemical oxidation	Butylated hydroxyanisole (BHA), butylated hydroxytoluene (BHT), propyl gallate
Nutritional supplements	Add nutrients or replace those lost in food processing	Minerals, vitamins, and certain amino acids
Coloring agents	Alter the color of foods to make them more appealing and also identify products for advertising purposes	Many compounds, natural and synthetic
Flavoring agents	Enhance flavor or identify a product for advertising purposes	More than 1500 different chemicals, both natural and synthetic. Two of the most common synthetic ones are monosodium glutamate and saccharin
Emulsifiers	Disperse droplets of one liquid in another liquid (used for example, to disperse oil in water)	Lecithin, polysorbates, mono- and diglycerides, propylene glycol
Stabilizers and thickeners	Change texture, produce smooth consistency	Dextrin, gelatin, seaweed extracts, vegetable gum

pect. After analyzing the reports, the FDA made up a list, called the *GRAS* list, of those compounds that were "Generally Recognized as Safe."

Another important piece of legislation relating to food additives is called the Delaney Clause, after its author, Representative James Delaney. This regulation states that the FDA is required to ban any food additive that has been shown to cause cancer in animals or in humans. The Delaney Clause has been both praised and condemned. Supporters claim that it protects our health and well-being. Critics claim that a product that causes cancer in large doses in rats may be perfectly safe in small doses in people, and, therefore, the law is unnecessarily harsh.

Using the Delaney Clause, the FDA has banned various chemicals that were originally on the GRAS list, including cyclamate sweeteners, certain vegetable oils, and several food dyes, includ-

ing the controversial Red Dye No. 2. Other additives undergo scrutiny from time to time. In 1978, the FDA discovered that an alternative artificial sweetener, saccharin, caused cancer in laboratory animals. However, under heavy pressure from the food industry, Congress suspended the ban on this additive pending the establishment of a more definite link between laboratory tests and human health.

When experts disagree, how can you as an individual know how to act? Well, you can't know for sure, so you have to make certain value judgments. You could think about it in the following way. Suppose you were seriously ill, near death, and your doctor prescribed a medicine to cure you. Imagine that the medicine worked 99 percent of the time, but there was a 1 percent chance that there might be some bad side effects. You would probably take the medicine, because the benefit (99 per-

Special Topic C

Diet and Cancer The Commission on Life Sciences of the National Academy of Sciences issued a 496-page report on *Diet, Nutrition, and Cancer* in June, 1982. According to the report, there is strong evidence that what we eat affects our chances of get-

ting cancer, especially particular kinds of cancer. It is not yet possible to predict *how much* cancer is linked to diet. The report does recommend some dietary changes, however, as summarized below.

Recommendation	Expected Benefit
1. Reduce your consumption of both saturated and unsaturated fats. (The present average U.S. level of dietary fat is 40% of the total calories. A suggested decrease is one fourth of this intake, down to a level of 30%.)	Lowered incidence of certain cancers, particularly of the breast and the colon.
2. Include fruits, vegetables, and whole-grain cereal products in your daily diet. Especially include citrus fruits and vegetables from the family of cabbage, broccoli, and brussels sprouts.	These foods contain vitamins A and C. They also contain some coumpounds that, although non-nutritive, appear to inhibit chemically induced cancers. Therefore, dietary supplements such as vitamin pills are not a substitute for these foods.
3. Limit your consumption of salt-cured, salt-pickled, and smoked foods, such as bacon, frankfurters, and smoked fish.	Reduced incidence of cancers of the stomach and esophagus.
4. Try to limit your intake of food additives.	The evidence here is not firm. The data are insufficient to show that any individual food additive is a *major* contributor to the risk of cancer. The combination of these chemicals, however, may pose significant risks.
5. Alcoholic beverages should be consumed only in moderation, if at all. The combination of alcohol and smoking should be avoided.	Reduced incidence of cancers of gastrointestinal and respiratory tracts.

cent chance of cure) would be well worth the 1 percent risk. In the case of a soft drink, the risk is much less—for the sake of this example, let us retain the earlier assumption that a person who drank one glass per day would risk a 1 in 50,000 chance of developing a tumor eventually. But the benefit would also be much less—after all, you could drink water or orange juice. So what should you do? If you were offered a glass of soda, should you drink it? One argument may be, well, it's only one glass, not a glass every day. Besides, the 1 in 50,000 chance might be an incorrect assumption—

it might be much less, or even nothing. It would certainly be much more dangerous to ride in an automobile, or even cross the street. So you accept the soda. Some people would look at it in another way. Why risk any chances of an adverse health effect if you didn't have to? Or still another viewpoint: Someone else is putting me at risk with an artificial color that is not for my benefit, or with an artificial flavor that is cheaper than a natural one—why should I go along with that? If that were how you felt, you wouldn't drink the soda (Special Topic C).

18.9
Noise

Sound is not a chemical; it is simply a wave motion in air. As such, it does not accumulate in the environment. Ring a bell or whisper a few words to your friend and in about a thousandth of a second, the sound is gone. But sounds, especially loud ones, do affect humans, and these effects do not disappear so easily (Fig. 18–7).

The human ear is sensitive to a wide range of sound intensities. The loudest sounds that we can

Motorcycle noise.

Traffic noise.

Jack hammer noise.

Grinding noise.

Figure 18–7
Various noises common in our society.

hear, such as a rocket taking off or the noise of battle, are billions of times more powerful than the softest sounds, such as the patter of raindrops on soft earth or a child's whisper. Sound intensity is measured on a scale of values called a **decibel** (abbreviated as dB) **scale.** The decibel scale is set up as follows: (a) The softest sound that can be heard by humans is called 0 dB. (b) Each *tenfold increase* in sound intensity is represented by an *additional* 10 dB. Thus, a 10-dB sound is 10 times as intense as the faintest audible sound. (That still isn't very much.) The sound level in a quiet library is about 1000 times as intense as the faintest audible sound. Therefore, the sound level in the library is 10 + 10 + 10, or 30 dB. Typical sources of sound from 0 to 180 dB are shown in Table 18–2.

Noise can be defined simply as unwanted sound. Noise can interfere with our communication, diminish our hearing, and affect our health and our behavior. An occasional loud noise interferes with sounds that we wish to hear, but we recover when quiet is restored. However, if a person is exposed to loud noises for long periods of time, there may be significant permanent loss of hearing.

The general level of city noise, for example, is high enough to deafen us gradually as we grow older. In the absence of such noise, hearing ability need not deteriorate with advancing age. Thus, inhabitants of quiet societies hear as well in their seventies as New Yorkers do in their twenties. It is important to understand that most instances of loss of hearing that result from environmental noise are not immediately noticeable. Victims are often unaware that they are slowly losing their ability to hear well. Occupational noise such as that produced by bulldozers, jackhammers, diesel trucks, and aircraft is deafening many millions of workers. There has been recent concern that rock-and-roll music in nightclubs is often indeed very loud. Sound levels of 125 dB have been recorded in some discotheques. Such noise is at the edge of pain and is unquestionably deafening. Noise levels as high as 135 dB should never be experienced, even for a brief period of time, because the effects can be instantaneously damaging. If the noise level exceeds about 150 or 160 dB, the eardrum might be ruptured beyond repair.

Many investigators believe that loss of hearing is not the most serious consequence of excess noise. The first effects are anxiety and stress or, in extreme cases, fright. These reactions produce body changes such as increased rate of heartbeat, constriction of blood vessels, digestive spasms, and dilation of the pupils of the eyes. The long-term effects of such overstimulation are difficult to assess, but we do know that in animals, it damages the heart, brain, and liver and produces emotional

A street sign in the city of Taiywan, Shan-Xi Province, China, that displays decibel readings. The dBA scale is a decibel scale that is adjusted for the different sensitivities of human hearing at different sound frequencies.

Table 18–2
Sound Levels and Human Responses

Sound Intensity Factor	Sound Level, dB	Sound Sources	Perceived Loudness	Damage to Hearing	Community Reaction to Outdoor Noise
1,000,000,000,000,000,000	180	Rocket engine			
100,000,000,000,000,000	170		Painful		
10,000,000,000,000,000	160			Traumatic injury	
1,000,000,000,000,000	150	Jet plane at takeoff			
100,000,000,000,000	140			Injurious range: irreversible damage	
10,000,000,000,000	130	Maximum recorded rock music			
1,000,000,000,000	120	Thunderclap / Textile loom / Auto horn, 1 m away	Uncomfortably loud		
100,000,000,000	110	Riveter			
		Jet fly-over at 300 m		Danger zone; progressive loss of hearing	
10,000,000,000	100	Newspaper press			
1,000,000,000	90	Motorcycle, 8 m away / Food blender / Diesel truck, 80 km/hr, 15 m away	Very loud		Vigorous action
100,000,000	80	Garbage disposal		Damage begins after long exposure	Threats
10,000,000	70	Vacuum cleaner			
1,000,000	60	Ordinary conversation / Air conditioning unit, 6 m away	Moderately loud		Widespread complaints
100,000	50	Light traffic noise, 30 m away			Occasional complaints

Table 18–2 *(Continued)*
Sound Levels and Human Responses

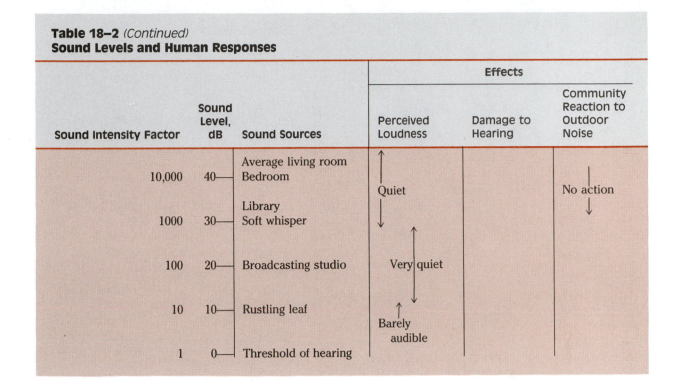

Sound Intensity Factor	Sound Level, dB	Sound Sources	Effects		
			Perceived Loudness	Damage to Hearing	Community Reaction to Outdoor Noise
10,000	40	Average living room Bedroom	Quiet		No action
1000	30	Library Soft whisper			
100	20	Broadcasting studio	Very quiet		
10	10	Rustling leaf	Barely audible		
1	0	Threshold of hearing			

disturbances. The emotional effects on people are difficult to measure, but psychologists have learned that work efficiency goes down as the noise level goes up.

There are three techniques that can be used to control noise.

1. Reduce the Source Machinery should be designed so that parts do not needlessly hit or rub against each other. It is possible to design machines that work quietly. For example, rotary saws can be used to break up street pavement. They do the job perfectly well and are much quieter than jackhammers. Another approach is to change operating procedures. If a suburban sidewalk must be broken up by jackhammers, it would be better not to start early in the morning, when many people are asleep. Also, aircraft take-offs can be routed over less densely inhabited areas. All too often, machines are built to perform a task most efficiently without consideration of how much noise is produced. If machines were originally designed properly, noise levels could be substantially reduced.

2. Interrupt the Path of Transmission Sound waves travel through air. They also travel through other media, including solids such as wood. However, some materials, especially soft or porous ones, absorb sound. Such sound-absorbing media are called **acoustical materials.** Acoustical tiles and wallboard can be used in house construction to reduce noise levels. The muffler used in automobile exhaust systems is another example of a sound-absorbing device.

3. Protect the Receiver The final line of defense is strictly personal. We protect ourselves instinctively when we hold our hands over our ears. Alternatively, we can use ear plugs or earmuffs, as shown in Figure 18–8. (Stuffing in a bit of cotton does very little good.) A combination of ear plugs and earmuffs can reduce noise by 40 or 50 dB, which could make a jet plane sound no louder than a vacuum cleaner. Such protection could prevent the deafness caused by combat training (Fig. 18–9) and should also be worn for recreational shooting.

Figure 18–8
Man wearing acoustical earmuffs while using chainsaw.

Figure 18–9
Combat noise has partially deafened many soldiers.
(Photo courtesy of the U.S. Army)

18.10
Epilogue

It is easy to become alarmed by the potential dangers of chemicals in the environment. Yet, as mentioned at the opening of this chapter, the average span of human life has increased in many seg-

Special Topic D

Careers in Environmental Health   Careers in any of the health professions may be directed to environmental aspects. If medicine is not your choice, you may consider industrial hygiene, which deals with the health aspects of the workplace. Industrial hygiene usually requires a two-year master's program after a bachelor's degree in biological, chemical, or engineering studies. Some universities offer financial support obtained from training grants, so that there is little burden to the student.

The disposal of hazardous wastes has developed into an entire industry since the passage of the Resource Conservation and Recovery Act (RCRA) in 1976.

Over the past ten years, hazardous waste management has been among the fastest growing and most lucrative industries in America. . . . Since 1972, the industry's revenues have increased more than 2000 percent to well over $2.6 million. Thousands of firms specializing in waste transportation, treatment, storage, disposal or cleanup have sprouted over the past two decades to help get rid of the 266 million metric tons of hazardous waste generated annually.*

Thus the hazardous waste problem has provided jobs and economic opportunities for many with a wide range of skills and levels of training. There is a need for research in the chemistry of hazardous waste and in the engineering of its disposal. There are business opportunities for those who wish to become involved in sales or services required by recent environmental legislation. In turn, these firms must hire managers, office workers, and technicians to install equipment, operate disposal facilities, and handle the wastes.

*National Wildlife Federation: *Conservation Exchange*, Vol. 4, No. 2, 1986.

ments of the population. Although about 3 of every 100 human babies in the United States are born with major birth defects, this ratio has not changed significantly since the 1960s, when such records began to be kept. European studies dating from the

1890s support this conclusion.

These facts are encouraging, but comparisons with the past may be misleading. In recent years there have been vast improvements in medicine and nutrition in the developed societies, and to some extent, the beginnings of a decrease in smoking. These changes would offset the adverse effects caused by chemicals in the environment.

Therefore it is difficult to isolate and identify the trends that promote health and those that impair it. Many environmental hazards in the home, workplace, and elsewhere have not yet been adequately addressed, and it is hoped that further environmental improvement will continue to better the potential for human well-being and will alleviate the sufferings of the least fortunate.

Summary

Cancer is an unregulated growth of cells. A **mutation** is an alteration in the DNA molecules of the germ cells, and a substance that causes such a change is a **mutagen.** In some cases, environmental chemicals may cause cancer or mutations.

A **poison** is a substance that can destroy life rapidly. A **toxic substance** is any substance whose physiological action is harmful to health. Toxicity depends on the route of entry, the dose, the susceptibility of an individual, and the possible synergistic effects. Some compounds may have threshold levels below which the substance does not affect human health. The effects of toxic substances are evaluated by epidemiological studies and by laboratory tests.

Hazardous chemicals occur in nature or are produced synthetically. Those toxic materials produced by the chemical industry are intended for specific targets or are intermediates in the synthesis of other chemicals. Nevertheless, some may escape to the environment in small leaks or large spills. Other hazardous chemicals are produced unintentionally because many chemical reactions yield unwanted byproducts.

Many poisonous chemical wastes are buried in dumps or landfills, such as the site at Love Canal, near Niagara Falls, New York. In 1980, the Superfund Legislation was passed in the United States to speed the cleanup of dump sites of hazardous wastes. After a slow start, some progress was made by 1985, when the law expired. Additional funds have since been provided, and many more years of effort will be needed.

Instances of dispersal of toxic chemicals to the environmental include the release of methyl isocyanate to the air at Bhopal, India, and the contamination of the area near Anaconda, Montana, by toxic metals from mining operations.

Food additives are used as preservatives, nutritional supplements, colorants, and flavorants, as well as for control of physical properties such as texture. The Delaney Clause is legislation that requires the banning of any food additive that has been shown to cause cancer in humans or animals.

The GRAS list is a compilation of food additives released before 1958 that are "*G*enerally *R*ecognized *a*s *S*afe" by a panel of experts. Occasionally, a product on the GRAS list is removed after tests show it to be toxic. The Delaney Clause states that any product that has been shown to cause cancer in animals or humans may not be marketed.

Noise, defined as unwanted sound, can cause loss of hearing or lead to anxiety, stress, or fright, with consequent adverse physiological effects. Noise can be reduced by more careful design of machinery, by installation of acoustical materials, or by the use of ear plugs.

Questions

Health Effects from Environmental Chemicals

1. Exposure to a certain substance in the environment is said to be hazardous to human health. Which of the following reasons would you find convincing, which would lead you to conclude that more study is needed, and which would not convince you at all? Defend your answers. (a) A large percentage of the people who are exposed to this substance in the course of their employment develop an unusual type of cancer. However, the total number of exposed persons is small. (b) Mice exposed to the substance in very high concentrations develop tumors. (c) In areas where this substance is found, children have a higher than normal incidence of birth defects.

2. In each of the following cases, specify the route(s) of entry of the toxic substance to the body: (a) A child living in an old house in which the paint is peeling is found to have an elevated level of lead in his blood. (b) A worker in a retail dry-cleaning establishment who specializes in removing stains by rubbing them with special solvents develops liver disease, diagnosed to be caused by chlorinated hydrocarbons. (c) A hiker becomes violently ill after being bitten by a rattlesnake.

3. If a dose-versus-effect curve were plotted in each of the following cases, which one(s) would show a threshold level at a dose greater than zero?

Dose	Effect
Electric current passed through your body	Electric shock
Number of bullets entering body	Injury from a gunshot
Concentration of odorous gas	Odor
Height of fall	Injury from a fall
The amount of sugar in your tea	Sweet taste

4. Under what conditions is the statement "Dilution is the solution to pollution" correct? Under what conditions is it wrong? Are there any conditions under which a diluted pollutant can do more harm than a concentrated pollutant?

5. Imagine that an accident at a chemical plant released a large quantity of a previously unknown chemical into the local source of drinking water, but that no increased illnesses in the community were noted for 5 years. Would you be reassured that the accident was harmless? Explain. What more, if anything, would you want to know?

6. A public official, discussing the problem of public policy regarding chemicals that threaten to have adverse environmental effects, asserted that "we cannot afford to give chemicals the same constitutional rights that we enjoy under the law" and that "chemicals are not innocent until proven guilty." Argue for or against this position.

Hazardous Wastes

7. List the major natural sources of hazardous chemicals, if any, that you would expect to find in (a) a tropical rainforest, (b) a temperate woodland, (c) a subtropical desert, (d) a tundra.

8. Explain why intermediates in chemical manufacturing are generally more hazardous than final products. Give an example of a product where the opposite is true.

9. List two ways in which unwanted chemicals are produced in industrial processes. Which way can best be prevented by human actions?

Decisions about Hazards

10. Methane, the major component of natural gas, is practically odorless. Utility companies inject sulfur compounds into natural gas so that the smell serves as a warning of a gas leak. (a) What would be the effect of using high concentrations of a warning agent so that people with a poor sense of smell will still detect the odor? (b) What would be the effect of reducing the concentrations so that harmless leaks do not create an offensive odor? (c) Is it possible to find the correct amount of warning agent so that any dangerous leak will be detected but that a small harmless leak will be ignored?

Contamination by Metals

11. What are the pathways by which heavy metals in mine tailings become dispersed in the environment? Which pathways lead to the atmospheric environment, which to the water, and which to the land? Do some pathways lead to more than one destination?

12. What natural processes operate to block the environmental dispersal of heavy metals from mine tailings? What can people do to stop the spread?

Chemicals in Food

13. Which substances among the various categories of food additives can be advantageous to health? Which are for the convenience of the consumer? Which are mainly for the benefit of the manufacturer?

14. Too much salt in a person's diet may promote hypertension, whereas some salt is an absolute necessity for survival. Discuss the concept of a threshold level for toxicity from salt.

15. Figure 18–10 (p. 542) shows a graph of cancer of the large intestine plotted as a function of meat consumption in several countries. Do these data prove that meat causes intestinal cancer? What other possible conclusions can be suggested by the data?

16. Large doses of the artificial sweetener saccharin have been shown to cause cancer in laboratory animals. Yet this additive was available on the market during the early 1980s. Prepare a class debate. Have one side argue in favor of banning saccharin and the other side argue against the ban.

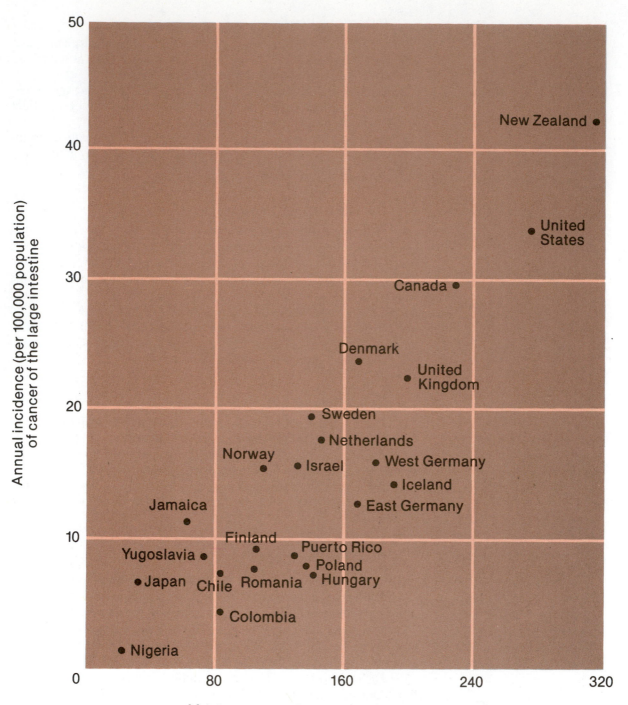

Figure 18–10
Statistical correlation between meat consumption and cancer of the large intestine in several countries.

Noise

17. Make a list of the five most distressing noises you hear in a specific day. How could each one be reduced or eliminated?

18. It has often been stated that some damage to hearing may be "inevitable" to people living in a developed society. Do you agree? If so, defend your answer. If not, describe some ways of living that would prevent damage to hearing over a lifetime.

Suggested Readings

Several books on chemicals and public health are:

Benjamin A. Goldman, James A. Hulme, and Cameron Johnson: *Hazardous Waste Management: Reducing the Risk.* Washington, D.C., Island Press, 1986. 336 pp.

Michael Gough: *Dioxin, Agent Orange: The Facts.* New York, Plenum Press, 1986.

Paul Brodeur: *Outrageous Misconduct: The Asbestos Industry on Trial.* New York, Pantheon Books, 1985. 374 pp.

William Lowrance (ed.): *The Public Health Risks of the Dioxins.* Los Altos, CA, William Kaufmann, Inc., 1984. 390 pp.

Anthony S. Wohl: *Endangered Lives, Public Health in Victorian England.* Cambridge, MA, Harvard University Press, 1983. 440 pp.

Howard H. Fawcett: *Hazardous and Toxic Materials, Safe Handling and Disposal.* Somerset, NJ, John Wiley & Sons, 1984. 269 pp.

John H. Gibbons (dir.): *Environmental Contaminants in Food.* Washington, D.C., U.S. Office of Technological Assessment, U.S. Government Printing Office, 1978. 227 pp.

Books that cover the general subject of environmental health include:

Edward J. Calabrese: *Nutrition and Environmental Health.* Somerset, NJ, John Wiley & Sons, Volume I, 1980, 585 pp; Volume II, 1980, 468 pp.

Herman Koren: *Handbook of Environmental Health and Safety,* Vols. 1 and 2. New York, Pergamon Press, 1980. 697 pp.

A. R. Rees and H. J. Percell (eds.): *Disease and the Environment.* Somerset, NJ, John Wiley & Sons, 1982. 206 pp.

The entire issue of *Chemical & Engineering News* for June, 1983 (Vol. 61, No. 23) is devoted to dioxin.

A book on Bhopal is:

Ward Morehouse and M. Arun Subramaniam: *The Bhopal Tragedy.* New York, Council on International and Public Affairs, 1986. 189 pp.

Two books on the Love Canal disaster are:

Michael Brown: *Laying Waste: The Poisoning of America by Toxic Wastes.* New York, Pantheon Books, 1979.

Adeline Gordon Levine: *Love Canal: Science, Politics and People.* Lexington, MA, Heath, 1982. 266 pp.

Books that deal with the effects of noise include:

William Burns: *Noise and Man.* 2nd ed. Philadelphia, J.B. Lippincott, 1973. 459 pp.

Donald E. Anthrop: *Noise Pollution.* San Francisco, CA, 1973. 176 pp.

Rupert Taylor: *Noise.* Baltimore, Penguin Books, 1970. 268 pp.

19

Control of Pests and Weeds

19.1
Introduction

Ecosystems are complex. Thousands or hundreds of thousands of different species and trillions of different individuals may live within a small area. Each individual has inherited complex survival mechanisms and every species has the reproductive potential to overpopulate the globe within a relatively short period of time. Yet, in most cases, no one species predominates. Competition, predation, and other biological mechanisms combine with physical pressures to regulate the population of any particular species and to protect the viability of the ecosystem. Despite this internal regulation, all ecosystems undergo disturbances. The population of one species may bloom for a period of time and decimate the populations of other species. Attacks by predators or disease, hard times, and famine have been encountered by all species throughout the history of the planet.

Humans are unique among the organisms of the Earth because they can control their environment significantly through cultural, technological, and scientific means. Certainly, one of the greatest technological advancements of the human race was the development of agriculture, a discovery that gave people an advantage over other organisms by providing a concentrated food supply and by reducing competition from other species. However, a farmer's field, efficient as it is, is still a ecosystem and is thus subject to the same types of checks and balances that affect all ecosystems. Herbivores, both large and small, eat the plants, and, in turn, a variety of natural mechanisms act together to control the populations of these herbivores. Natural controls, by themselves, are not always effective enough to ensure high yields for the farmers, so people have devised a variety of means to kill or repel competing species. It is relatively easy for a farmer to develop defenses against large herbivores. Very simply, if a cow wanders into a field to eat the corn, the farmer can either chase her away or build a fence. But, an insect, a field mouse, the spore of a fungus, or a tiny root-eating worm is more difficult to deal with. Since these small organisms reproduce rapidly, their total eating capacity is very great. Over the course of history, an incredible amount of suffering has been caused by agricultural pests. There were 1800 recorded periods of famine in China between 100 B.C.

A locust invasion in Morocco. Local infestations of this type can completely destroy crops. (Courtesy of Food and Agricultural Organization of the United Nations, Photo by Studios du Souissi)

and 1910 A.D., and many of these were caused by pest outbreaks. The Bible relates an account of famine following an invasion of locusts. In more recent times, 1 million people died during the potato blight in Ireland in the 1840s, and 3 million deaths are at least partially attributed to a pest bloom in China in 1943. Small pests may also be carriers of disease. Malaria and yellow fever, spread by mosquitoes, and the bubonic plague, carried by fleas, have killed more people than have all wars.

Today, in an age when the human population is so large that tremendous quantities of food are needed, the threat of famine continues to pose a problem to humankind. Surely, everyone must agree that one desirable goal of modern society is to control the pests that can potentially destroy crops and carry vectors of disease. However, there is a significant debate concerning the best approach toward realizing this goal. The nature of the debate is the subject of this chapter.

19.2
Insecticides—A Great Debate

When a plant is attacked by a predator, it can neither flee nor defend itself actively. Why, then, have plants survived? Why haven't herbivores completely

Special Topic A
Insects, Fungi, and Microorganisms that Are Beneficial to Humans

Not all insects, fungi, or microorganisms are harmful to humans. Most are benign, and many are directly helpful. For example, as discussed in the text, many predator insects eat pest species, and bees are essential to the process of pollination. Decay organisms are essential to the recycling of nutrients in natural systems. Penicillin and many other antibiotics are produced by fungi. A variety of foods and drinks such as cheese and alcoholic beverages are produced by microbial action, and yeasts produce the gases that force bread to rise. In recent years, genetic engineers have developed microbes that produce human proteins for medicinal use such as insulin and several growth hormones. The list could go on and on; it is important to understand that the goal of modern science is not to destroy insects and microbes, but to selectively destroy the few that are harmful to humans and their food supply.

Many insects are predators. Here a praying mantis is eating a Satyrid butterfly. (Courtesy of Emeritus Professor Alexander B. Klots, Biology Department, the City College of the City University of New York)

destroyed their prey? In natural ecosystems, the populations of herbivores are controlled by two separate types of mechanisms. First, plants produce a wide variety of different chemical substances that repel their predators. The exact compositions of these substances and the mechanisms by which they function are complex. Some plants manufacture compounds that repel insects but do not kill them; others produce lethal toxins. Tomato plants produce chemicals that inhibit digestion in certain caterpillars, and, as a result, the caterpillars become malnourished and die. A particularly novel defense mechanism has evolved in wild potato plants. The aphids that dine on potato leaves communicate with each other by excreting chemical agents called pheromones. One alarm pheromone is released when an aphid senses the approach of a predator such as a ladybug. However, a similar compound is released by the potato plant. Thus, the aphid pests are tricked into being alerted to a predator attack and they flee.

Second, insect pests are controlled by a wide variety of predators and disease microorganisms. Herbivorous insects are eaten by carnivorous insects such as ladybugs and praying mantises as well as by larger animals such as snakes, rodents, and birds. In addition, viruses, protozoa, bacteria, and fungi attack specific hosts, and thereby control their populations.

Yet, as mentioned previously, natural controls are not always effective, and severe crop losses have occurred throughout history. Therefore, scientists have devised alternative control measures. The modern pesticide era started in about 1940 when a chemical called **DDT** was found to be a potent insecticide. DDT (See Appendix D for the chemical formula) was much cheaper and more effective against almost all insects than the previously known control measures. The use of DDT led to dramatic early successes. It squelched a threatened typhus epidemic among the Allied army in Italy during World War II. Antimosquito programs saved millions from death from malaria and yellow fever. Pest control, leading to increased crop yields all over the world, saved millions more from death by starvation.

Enthusiastic supporters of DDT predicted that chemicals would liberate people from the uncertainties of a changing environment and lead to the complete destruction of all pest insects within the foreseeable future. Paul Muller, the chemist who discovered its insecticidal properties, received a Nobel Prize. Encouraged by the success of DDT, chemical companies developed a wide range of additional poisons. Some of these are chemically similar to DDT and are called **organochlorides,** because they contain chlorine atoms bonded to the organic molecules. Others are not at all similar to

Table 19–1
Three Common Classes of Chemical Insecticides

Compound Class	Examples	Persistence in the Environment
Organochlorides (also called chlorinated hydrocarbons)	Aldrin Chlordane DDD DDT Dieldrin Endosulfan Endrin Heptachlor Kepone Lindane Mirex Toxaphene	High—5–15 years
Organophosphates	Azodrin Diazinon Malathion Parathion Phosdrin	Intermediate—1 week to several months
Carbamates	Carbaryl (Sevin) Matacil Temik Zectran Zineb	Low—2 weeks or less

Chemical formulas of various pesticides are shown in Appendix D.

DDT and belong to different chemical classes as shown in Table 19–1. Millions of tonnes of these substances were sprayed onto fields and forests throughout the world. But within 30 years, the promise of insect-free abundance had been broken. The "miracle" chemical that started the pesticide era had fallen from grace. On January 1, 1973, all interstate sale and transport of DDT in the United States was banned except for use in emergency situations. Nor was DDT the only victim: Aldrin and dieldrin were banned between 1972 and 1974, chlordane and heptachlor in 1975, and others in more recent times.

What had happened? First, people became aware that pesticides are harmful to the environment in general and, in addition, pose a direct threat to human health. Second, for reasons that will be explained, many chemical pesticides have become less and less effective over the years. According to one estimate, insects ate 20 percent of the food crops in the United States in 1900. At that time, very few pesticides were being used and the pest populations were controlled by natural mechanisms. In 1985, after decades of intensive use of pesticides, crop losses remained the same—20 percent.

Today, a number of people point to such data and suggest that traditional types of pesticides should be banned altogether and, instead, farmers should actively encourage natural control mechanisms. However, not everyone agrees. The counter-argument runs as follows: In 1900, farms were relatively small, and many different crops were raised in a given area. Today, fields are much larger, and hundreds or even thousands of hectares of a single species of plant may be grown in one region. This type of monoculture provides a favorable environment for pest insects, because their food supply is much more concentrated than it would be in a series of small farms or in a natural environment. Some plant scientists and most growers claim that modern agricultural practices must be accepted if the people of the world are to be fed, and, therefore, pesticides are a necessity. Without such controls, insect populations would flourish and consume a large percentage of the world's food supply.

19.3
Four Problems with Chemical Pesticides
Broad-Spectrum Pesticides Kill Insect Predators

Chemical insecticides were initially received with great enthusiasm because they are inexpensive, easy to use, fast-acting, and effective against a wide range of pests. Their promise engendered an uncritical optimism. It was imagined, for example, that farmers faced with a mid-season invasion of some insects would not have to identify the pest. They would simply call in an aerial spray company and expect 90 percent destruction of the pests in the next day or two. A simple problem, a simple solution—or so it seemed.

Yet, if the problem is examined more closely, complexities emerge. As previously explained, a field under attack by some insect is not merely a two-species system. The plants and pests are only two members of a large agricultural ecosystem of many different species including predator insects, bacteria, parasites, and many types of soil dwellers, as well as carnivorous, herbivorous, and omnivorous birds and other migratory animals. Therefore, despite the undeniable fact that innumerable successes of spray programs have been recorded during the past 30 years, it is important to look more closely into the intricacies of the problem.

The use of nonselective sprays has often led to the destruction of the natural controls on population sizes. As an example, when DDT and two other chlorinated hydrocarbons were used extensively to control pests in a valley in Peru, the initial success gave way to a delayed disaster. In only 4 years, cotton production rose from 490 to 730 kg/hectare. However, 1 year later, the yield dropped precipitously to 390 kg/hectare, 100 kg/hectare less than before the insecticides were introduced. Studies indicated that the insecticide had destroyed predator insects and birds as well as the insect pests. Then, with natural controls eliminated, the pest population thrived better than ever before.

A second example illustrates the same point. In the San Joaquin Valley in California, chemical manufacturers sold the organophosphate Azodrin for use against the cotton bollworm, a pest of cotton plants. After several heavy spray dosages, it was discovered that the predator populations were killed more effectively than the pest species. Losses to the bollworm grew more severe. Sales representatives recommended that more pesticide be used. An independent research team at the University of California determined that if *no* pesticides were used *at all*, bollworms would consume approximately 5 percent of the crops. After three spray applications, so many predators had been killed that 20 percent of the crop was destroyed.

Another effect of broad-range pesticides is that destruction of one species sometimes leads to a bloom of another pest that hadn't been a problem in the first place. Consider the story of the spider mite in the forests of the western United States. The spider mite feeds on green leaves and evergreen needles. Because, in a normal forest ecosystem, predators and competition have kept the number of mites low, mites have never been a serious problem. However, when the U.S. Forest Service sprayed with DDT in a campaign to kill another pest, the spruce budworm, complications arose. The budworms were effectively killed, but the insecticide also poisoned such natural enemies of spider mites as ladybugs, gall midges, and various predator mites. The next year, the forests were plagued with a spider mite invasion. Although spraying had temporarily controlled the spruce budworm, the new infestation of spider mites proved to be more disastrous.

Spruce budworm larva and adult.

Genetic Resistance

How do pests stage such a successful comeback? Why don't the predators stage an equal comeback? Why can't the farmers combat the pest resurgence with more spraying?

One of the major problems with chemical insecticides is that many insects have become genetically resistant to the poisons. In other words, a given insecticide at a given concentration often becomes less effective after some years of use. It appears as though the chemical has diminished in potency, although its chemical composition has, of course, remained unchanged. To understand the reason for this phenomenon, recall that in any environment, whether chemicals are present or not, the genetic information of individual plants and animals changes from time to time as a result of random mutations of the hereditary material in their reproductive cells. Some mutations endow individuals with genetic resistance to specific poisons. If poisons are present in the environment, those organisms that are resistant to them will survive, and this mutation will be favored by natural selection. This mechanism of genetic change has allowed insects to adapt to their environment for millions of years. When plants have evolved particularly powerful chemical defenses against their insect enemies, insects have responded by evolving chemical defenses that either detoxify the poisons or develop some sort of immunity to its effects. Insects have adapted the same kinds of defenses against synthetic pesticides. In areas where spraying is heavy, strains of insects have evolved that are genetically resistant to a particular chemical. Genetic resistance to insecticides is an extremely serious problem. By 1945, at least a dozen species of insects had developed some resistance to DDT. By 1970, the number had increased to more than 200 species, and, by 1985, there were 428 species of harmful insects that were resistant to one or more pesticides (Fig. 19–1). An additional 150 kinds of fungi and bacteria are immune to specific chemicals, and 50 species of weeds are resistant to the herbicides that were used to control them. Since resistant parents tend to pass this characteristic on to succeeding generations, the old pesticides are rendered ineffective. This process was directly demonstrated in an experiment in which DDT-resistant bedbugs were placed on cloth impregnated with DDT. They thrived, and mated, and the females laid

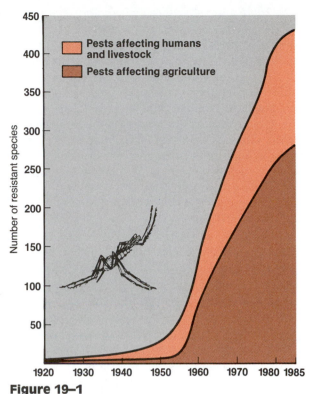

Figure 19–1

The number of insect species that have become resistant to one or more pesticides between 1920 and 1985.

eggs normally. The young, born on a coating of DDT, grew up and were healthy. Attempts to change pesticides have, in many cases, simply produced strains of insects that are resistant to more than one chemical.

The problem of resistance of insects to poisons can be compounded if the pest becomes resistant and various predators do not. If this happens, the pests have a new biological advantage and can thrive in greatly increased numbers. This is favored by three factors:

1. Insect pests are often smaller and reproduce at a greater rate than their predators. More frequent reproduction promotes more frequent mutation and thus improves the chances that resistant strains will arise. Furthermore, once a resistant population of insect pests appears, it can repopulate its ecological niche much faster than can a larger, more slowly reproducing species. In effect, the pest species develops resistance faster than the predator.

2. *There are always fewer predators than herbivores (including pests) in an ecosystem.* A small population runs the risk of local extinction, because it is more likely that a small group containing only a few individuals will be wiped out by some disaster than it is for a large group to be eliminated. Therefore, the species of herbivores (the pests), which are more numerous, have a greater chance of survival than the species of predators. In addition, in a large pest population, there is a statistically greater chance that some individuals will develop resistant mutations compared with the same probability in a smaller predator population.

3. *Predators generally eat a diet richer in insecticides than that of the original pests.* Because chemical poisons are not immediately excreted by herbivorous insects (or any other organism for that matter), the concentration of the chemical in their bodies becomes greater as more contact is made with the poison either directly or through the ingestion of sprayed leaf tissue. Since death may be delayed for some time after poisoning, many poisoned but living insects will be eaten by their natural enemies. In this way, predators eat a diet that is more concentrated in poison than the diet of the herbivores, the original pests.

The series of events that has occurred in many agricultural systems can now be reconstructed. Although the pesticide causes a rapid decrease in the pest population at first, resistant mutants soon displace the susceptible individuals. The situation then becomes worse than it was originally because natural predators do not achieve immunity as well as do the pests. As a result, the controls on the pest population actually diminish, and the pests grow and multiply faster than ever.

Effects on Other Nontarget Species

Chemical pesticides not only are poisonous to insects and disease microorganisms, but many are also toxic to higher animals. Wild animals and even livestock have been affected. For example, when several communities in eastern Illinois were sprayed aerially in an effort to stop the westward movement of the Japanese beetle, ground squirrels and many species of birds were almost completely eradicated, 90 percent of all farm cats died, some sheep were killed, and muskrats, rabbits, and pheasants were poisoned. These unwanted side effects might have been considered a necessary price to pay for pesticidal success, but the cost did not yield the desired benefit; the Japanese beetle population continued its westward advance. As will be documented in the next section, the use of organochloride pesticides has led to the decline of many species of predatory birds such as eagles and falcons.

The deaths of large animals such as cats and eagles attract considerable attention, whereas the effects of pesticides on other organisms are often overlooked. Even 1 kg of fertile soil may contain a few trillion different decomposer organisms. These organisms are vital for continued fertility of the soil. They fix nitrogen, they break down rock and thus make minerals available to the plants, they retain moisture, they aerate the soil, and they bring about the essential process of decay. Without these organisms, the plants above ground usually die out. The effect on these organisms of an increasing concentration of poison in the soil is largely unknown. In many heavily sprayed areas of the world, farmers are harvesting more food per acre than ever before. Yet some facts are coming to light that may presage future disaster. Studies in Florida have shown that some pesticides seriously inhibit nitrification by soil bacteria. Termites have not been able to survive in soils that were sprayed with toxaphene 10 years previously. Similarly, endrin present in as low a concentration as 1 part per million (ppm) caused significant changes in the population of soil organisms and, consequently, in the relative concentrations and availability of important soil minerals. As a result, beans and corn grown in soils treated with endrin had different nutrient values than the same crops grown in untreated soil—some minerals were increased, others decreased. The net result, however, was a decrease in the total plant growth. In another instance, aldrin routinely sprayed on a golf course decreased the number of earthworms.

As is the case for many types of environmental disruptions, the long-term effects of insecticides in soils are not known. Perhaps many soil organisms are or will become resistant to the pesticide accumulations. But the stakes in the gamble are high, because, if life in the soil is disrupted, the rates of decay, nutrient recycling, and formation of humus will also be disrupted. If this happens, farmers will have to counteract the loss by installing more irrigation systems and applying increased quantities of expensive fertilizers.

In a natural ecosystem, bees pollinate many plant species as they travel from flower to flower. But bees are also killed by pesticides. When the bee population is decimated, crop losses occur from lack of pollination. In some cases, these losses have been more damaging than the insect attack itself.

Pesticides and Human Health

It should come as no surprise that if a substance is biologically active enough to kill many different species of insects, as well as birds, fish, cats, dogs, and a variety of other animals, that substance would also be toxic to humans. In fact, most pesticides are poisonous, although the effects and the lethal doses vary from compound to compound. This topic will be explored in more detail in Section 19.5.

19.4
Why Was DDT Banned?

Most of the insecticides manufactured today are broad-spectrum poisons. They all kill nonpest species and have led to disruption of ecosystems. Why, then, have DDT and other organochloride pesticides been banned while other types of pesticides are still used freely?

Persistence When parathion, an organophosphate pesticide, is sprayed onto loamy soil, more than 98 percent will decompose after 4 months. Materials that decompose rapidly in the environment are said to be **biodegradable.** The organochlorides are not biodegradable. They persist for long periods of time. For example, in some soils, DDT and aldrin have been detected 15 years after a single spray application. Such persistence leads to a series of severe environmental problems.

For example, if a field is sprayed once, predators are subject to continuous exposure to poisons for many years. If a field is sprayed many times, the insecticide accumulates in the environment. Therefore, all the problems outlined in the previous section may persist and actually increase for many years.

Physical Dispersal of Insecticides A chemical pollutant that is nonbiodegradable persists not only in the immediate environment but also in transport as it is being mechanically and biologically distributed throughout the biosphere. The physical dispersal of organochlorides has been particularly well studied. To understand the mobility of insecticides, some of their physical characteristics must first be reviewed. Organochlorides are relatively insoluble in water, evaporate slowly, have a strong tendency to adhere to tiny particles of dust, dirt, or salts, and are soluble in the fatty tissues of living organisms.

Now consider the fate of an application of DDT or one of its sister compounds sprayed from an airplane onto a crop. Not all of the spray will hit the target. The accuracy of dispersal is dependent on such factors as the skill of the pilot, the number and position of electrical wires and trees that must be dodged, and the wind direction, velocity, and turbulence. Some of the insecticide that misses the desired target lands on nearby houses, roads, streams, lakes, and woodlots, while some is carried into the air either as a gas or as a "hitchhiker" on particles of dust or on water droplets. Of the pesticide that reaches its target, only a small portion is actually ingested by pests. By far, the largest quantity remains as a residue on plant parts. Some of this material is consumed by people or farm animals, and the remainder is dispersed during processing or transportation.

Although the use of DDT in the United States was banned in 1973, it was still being manufactured in this country in the mid-1980s and exported for use in other nations. In fact, many of the fruits and vegetables imported into the United States have been sprayed with some type of organochloride pesticide. Thus, long-term global contamination continues. As a consequence, all major rivers in the United States still contain measurable insecticide concentrations in the parts per billion (ppb) range. In river water at 7.2°C (45°F), which is normal temperature for trout, 1.4 ppb of endrin will kill half of a population of rainbow trout in 3 days. Similarly, many other species of fish cannot survive insecticides in concentrations greater than about 1 to 10 ppb. Trout in the United States today live in the more mountainous regions, which are not so polluted, but populations that used to thrive in waterways such as the Great Lakes or the lower Missouri

This airplane is spreading pesticides on a field. Note the agricultural worker in the foreground. His job is to direct the plane; inadvertently he is exposed to high levels of pesticide contamination. (EPA)

River have either been decimated or exterminated. Under severe conditions, such as occurred during 1950 in parts of the South when heavy rains followed heavy spray applications, agricultural run-off was so high that the residual pesticide concentrations were raised 1000-fold. Nearly all the fish in many watersheds were killed.

Inevitably, if insecticides are present in major rivers, they must also be present in the ocean, and the concentrations must be highest in estuary systems, that is, at river mouths and in coastal bays. One of the most serious problems in estuary systems is that insecticides reduce photosynthesis carried out by plankton. DDT at a concentration of 1 ppb can reduce phytoplankton activity by 10 percent and at 100 ppb by 40 percent, compared with plankton grown in unpolluted waters.

Is there any place that is entirely free of pesticide contamination? Apparently not. Measurable residues have been found in the central ocean, in the fat of penguins in Antarctica, and in people's bodies just about everywhere.

Concentration in Biological Systems

Plants and animals are able to wash many poisons out of their systems. Most wastes are removed from the body in water solutions of urine, sweat, or pus. But organochlorides do not dissolve in water. Instead, they dissolve in fat. Therefore, they tend to remain in the body for very long periods of time. If an organochloride pesticide is sprayed onto a hay field and a cow eats the hay, the cow consumes small concentrations of poison every day. The pesticide then remains in the cow's body; each daily intake is stored. Therefore, the pesticide residues slowly accumulate in the animal (Fig. 19–2). A person who then eats the cow's meat will consume the large concentrations of this accumulated chemical. In most cases, pesticide concentrations in meat do not cause acute illness, and the consumer might not even be aware of the problem. Yet there is concern that the long-term effects of these compounds may be detrimental to human health (see Section 19.5).

Clear Lake in north-central California is a popular recreational area. But the shallow, calm waters have been a breeding place for annoying colonies of mosquitoes and gnats. In the 1950s, government workers sprayed Clear Lake with the organochloride DDD to control the insect pests. After the project was completed, the water contained 0.02 ppm of DDD. Plankton that live in Clear Lake concentrated and stored some of the pesticide until there was 5 ppm in their tissues. Plant-eating fish ate the plankton and further concentrated the poison. As a result, their bodies contained 40 to 300 ppm of DDD. Some predatory fish and birds had as much as 2000 ppm of DDD in their tissues (Fig. 19–3). Thus, the original concentration of the pesticide in the water seemed innocently low, but, higher in the food chain, fish and birds were poisoned. The

Figure 19–2

Physical dispersal of insecticides with some average values for DDT levels, as recorded in 1970, before the ban on DDT.

problem persisted for a long time. A year after the spray application, no pesticide could be detected in the water at all. Yet the poison still existed in the plants and animals. This increase in pesticide concentration within a food chain is called **biomagnification** (Fig. 19–4).

The effects of high levels of insecticides on carnivorous fish, mammals, and birds have been particularly severe. In many cases, the animals die soon after being poisoned. In other situations, small doses may not kill the animals directly, but they may upset the normal activities of the body and cause delayed death. In some cases, the adults may survive but the infants will die. For example, when mink were fed fish that were contaminated with DDT, the adults remained healthy, but 80 percent of the newborn infants died within a few days.

The evidence seems undeniable that DDT poisoning was responsible for the sharp decline in

Figure 19–3

"Biological magnification" of DDD (Clear Lake, California).

444 ppm
in Robin

41 ppm
in earthworm

Soil 9.9 ppm

Figure 19–4
"Biological magnification" of DDT after spray
application for Dutch elm disease.

populations of many predatory birds. Birds that
have ingested DDT cannot use calcium properly.
This has led to the production of thin-shelled eggs.
Often, these weakened eggs crack and break in the
nest, resulting in death of the unborn chicks. Before several of the organochloride pesticides were
banned in the United States, the populations of several species of birds—among them, the peregrine
falcon, the pelican, and some eagles—were declining so rapidly that many conservationists feared
that they were on the verge of extinction.

Pesticides can be fatal to animals that store
food energy in fat for use during winter months.
Trout build up a layer of fat during the summer
months, when food is plentiful. In areas where
spraying has been done, this fat contains high concentrations of DDT. During winter, the fat is used
as a source of energy. The DDT released into the

bloodstream upon fat breakdown has been known
to kill the fish. The eggs of fish also contain a considerable amount of fat, which is used as food by
the unborn fish. In one case, 700,000 hatching salmon were poisoned by the DDT in their own eggs.

19.5
Insecticides and Human Health

In 1985, about 500,000 tonnes of insecticides and
fungicides were sprayed onto farmlands in the
United States (Fig. 19–5). Included in this sum
were hundreds of different compounds that were
mixed into thousands of different formulations. Although the sprays permitted today are generally
less persistent and more specific than DDT and
other products that are now banned, most are still
toxic to many different nontarget species. Almost
all produce sold in the United States contains residues of a variety of pesticides, and 1.5 percent of
the food tested in a recent study contained residues in excess of federal tolerances. In addition,
many of the pesticides have found their way into
drinking water supplies. For example, groundwater
in 23 states is contaminated. In regions where agriculture is most intense, such as the Central Valley
of California, the water in many wells has been
condemned as unfit to drink. (See Chapter 20 for a
more complete discussion of groundwater pollution.) But our problems do not end with contamination within the United States. Twenty-five percent
of all fruit, 6 percent of all vegetables, and 98 percent of all coffee consumed by Americans is imported from other countries. Most of these countries permit use of a wide variety of pesticides that
are banned in the United States, including DDT and
its sister products. In a recent survey by the National Resources Defense Council, 22 percent of
the vegetables for sale in supermarkets in San Francisco contained residues of pesticides that are considered to be too dangerous to be used on farms
in the United States. When a random sample of
Americans was tested in 1983, all of the subjects
carried small but measurable quantities of DDT in
their fatty tissues, and most carried several other
contaminants as well (Table 19–2).

It is easy to measure levels of chemical contamination, but as explained in the previous chapter, it is much more difficult to determine how this
contamination actually affects human health. Scientists are certain that high concentrations of most

Table 19–2
Organochlorine Residues in Human Fatty Tissue

Residue	Possible Origin	Frequency of Detection, %
Total DDT	DDT and its analogs	100
trans-Nonachlor	Chlordane/heptachlor	97
Heptachlor epoxide	Chlordane/heptachlor	96
Oxychlordane	Chlordane/heptachlor	95
Dieldrin	Aldrin/dieldrin	95
β-Benzene hexachloride	BHC	94
Hexachlorobenzene	Chlorinated benzene manufacture	93
Polychlorinated biphenyls	PCBs	23
γ-Benzene hexachloride	Lindane	2
Other BHC isomers	BHC	<1
Mirex	Mirex	<1

Limits of detection: 10 to 20 parts per billion (or 10–20 μg/liter)

pesticides are acutely toxic to humans. In many instances, factory workers who manufacture these materials or farm workers who handle them have been sickened or killed by excessive exposure. Symptoms of pesticide poisoning include loss of muscular control, nervous disorders, loss of mental awareness, and eventual death. In 1985 the Farmworkers Health Board in California recorded 2499 accidental poisonings in that state, but officials claim that a great many additional cases were not reported either because workers were afraid that they would lose their jobs if they called in sick or because they had migrated into this country illegally. Nationwide an estimated 100,000 to 250,000 people are poisoned every year from excessive exposure to pesticides.

On the other hand, it is difficult to obtain unequivocal proof concerning the long-term, chronic

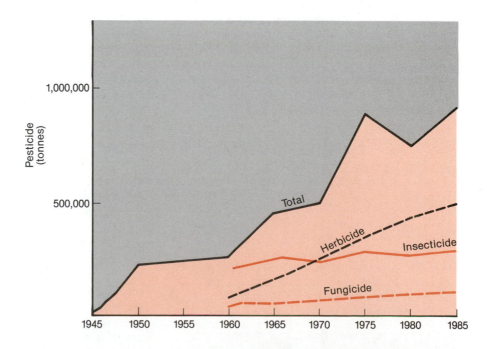

Figure 19–5
Use of pesticides and herbicides in the United States from 1945 to 1985.

Special Topic B
Pesticides and Groundwater Pollution: A Short Case History

Temik is a carbamate pesticide that was developed in 1962. Several factors made Temik the chemical of choice in a wide variety of applications. (1) It is extremely toxic to a wide variety of insects and soil pests such as nematodes. (2) Early tests showed no evidence of carcinogenic or mutagenic effects on mammals. (3) It is water soluble and is therefore easily eliminated from mammals through their urine. (4) One application of Temik is effective against a wide variety of pests. When it is worked into the soil, it kills nematodes. Because it is water soluble, some of it will also be absorbed slowly through the root system of plants and transported to the leaf tissue, where it kills pests that chew on the leaves.

On the other hand, Temik residues in the soil are easily leached into the groundwater. For example, this pesticide was used widely in Long Island to combat various pests of potatoes. Much of the soil in Long Island is sandy, and therefore porous, and rainwater filtering through the potato fields has carried Temik into the drinking water supplies in the region. Of 17,000 wells that were tested in eastern Long Island, 2300 exceeded the EPA's health advisory level for Temik. One of the geologists working on the project reported that owing to the nature of the soil, "Any pesticide they put down will get into the water supply. People must realize that using chemicals on the surface of Long Island is a game of high risk in which you are playing with your community's drinking water." Temik has also been discovered in the groundwater of other agricultural states such as Florida, California, and Missouri.

As previously stated, Temik was developed in 1962. Residues of this pesticide were first detected in drinking water supplies in 1979. Five years later, in 1984, the EPA initiated a special review of Temik. One of the scientists working on the project has called it a "tweenie" chemical, in between the clearly dangerous and the clearly benign. There is no question that groundwater contamination has occurred, but the health effects of such contamination are uncertain. Therefore, the regulatory process has been slow, and officials estimate that a decision won't be reached before the 1989 growing season.

effects of pesticides. Suppose there were two large groups of people with similar cultural and socioeconomic backgrounds. If one group ate contaminated food and lived in a contaminated environment while the second group ate pesticide-free food and lived in a pesticide-free environment, and if these groups were studied for 20 or 30 years, then the long-term effects of pesticides could be measured. However, it is morally unjustifiable and impossible in practice to control the diets and living conditions of large groups of people over many years. Therefore, scientists must rely on studies of laboratory animals, and on statistical correlations based on geographical or occupational differences. Such studies are valuable but they also contain an element of uncertainty.

Experiments have shown that various pesticides induce cancer in laboratory animals. As explained in Chapter 18, these experiments suggest, but do not prove, that the same pesticides may induce cancer in humans.

Statistical studies on humans involve an examination of "clusters," or unusually high concentrations of a particular type of cancer in a local area. For example, McFarland and Fowler are two small towns in adjacent counties in the San Joaquin Valley in California. McFarland has a population of 6000 and Fowler has a population of 3000. Based on national averages, one would expect 0.02 cases of childhood leukemia per 1,000 residents, per year. Therefore, the two towns taken together would have been expected to have about 1 case of childhood leukemia between 1980 and 1985 (0.02 cases/1000 residents/year × 9000 residents × 5 years = 0.9, or about 1 case). In the first half of the 1980s, there were 6 cases of childhood leukemia in the two towns as well as 8 other childhood cancers of various types. Therefore, officials began to search for a possible environmental contaminant that caused the cancers. Eventually a suspect was isolated. High concentrations of the soil fumigant DBCP (1,2-dibromo-3-chloropropane) were found in the drinking water in the region. A prior report had shown that childhood leukemia increased four-fold as the DBCP level in the drinking water rose from 0.05 ppb to 1 ppb. All these data, taken together, implicate DBCP as the cause of the cancers reported in McFarland and Fowler. Yet, as previously stated, this statistical correlation does not constitute proof. Consider the following objections.

1. Despite the small probability of such an event occurring by chance, there are 17,000 townships in

Migrant farm workers near Salinas, California. These people are not told of past spray applications and are sometimes exposed to high concentrations of pesticides.

the United States, and two of them might have just encountered bad luck. However, epidemiologists estimate that the likelihood that these 6 cases of childhood leukemia were just a random occurrence was only 1 in 50,000.

2. It is possible that the cancers were caused by some environmental contaminant other than DBCP. After all, no one has studied the toxicology of all the chemicals in the environment.

Despite the objections to statistical correlations, and despite the absence of an unequivocal link between DBCP and childhood leukemia in these two small California towns, people in the area remain uneasy.

On a national level, the results of a large number of different types of experiments are disturbing enough to raise public concern about the long-range health effects of human exposure to low levels of pesticides. As a result, the government has enacted legislation to regulate pesticide manufacture and use. Although chemical pesticides have been regulated to some extent since the Insecticide Act of 1910, the first comprehensive law on the subject was the Federal Insecticide, Fungicide, and Rodenticide Act (FIFRA), originally written in 1947. It is important for the modern reader to understand that in 1947, most people welcomed the benefits of chemistry enthusiastically, and there was little public concern about the harmful side effects of these substances. Therefore, in its original form, FIFRA mainly required that manufacturers

register pesticides that were used in interstate commerce. The government was given almost no power to test these materials for toxicity or to ban them if they were deemed harmful. This law was significantly rewritten in 1972.

Under the new law, after a new pesticide is developed, the manufacturer must conduct detailed tests of its toxicity to humans and its effects on the environment in general. The results of these tests are then submitted to the Environmental Protection Agency (EPA), and, in turn, the EPA reviews the data and decides whether or not the substance is safe enough to be sold and distributed. The entire regulatory process is complex.

According to FIFRA, the government will approve sale and distribution of a compound only if "When used in accordance with widespread and commonly recognized practice it (the pesticide) will not generally cause unreasonable adverse effects on the environment." As explained in Chapter 2, it is the duty of the EPA to interpret these ambiguous phrases and establish specific guidelines for action. The general procedure is as follows: EPA officials recognize that if a pesticide is commonly used, some residues will escape into the environment and some will eventually be found on produce that is delivered to the supermarkets. They then estimate the effects of these residues. Consider, for example, chemical contamination of food. The estimated residues are multiplied by a **food factor,** an estimate of the quantity of the treated commodity that will be eaten daily by the average consumer. This multiplication gives the total quantity of the pesticide that the average consumer will ingest. This quantity is then compared with the results of the toxicity tests. If the perceived harm is small and the expected benefits of the pesticide are great, it is approved. If the estimated harm is greater than the estimated benefits, approval is denied.

This entire regulatory process has been both praised as far-sighted and criticized as short-sighted. Supporters of the program argue that the review process is thorough and protective. True, the food we eat contains pesticide residues, but there is no proof that these low level residues are harmful to human health. Furthermore, they claim that, given modern farming practices, pesticides are absolutely essential. Without them, agricultural productivity would decline, many farmers would go bankrupt, and food would become prohibitively expensive. For many people in the less-developed regions of the world, bans on pesticides could lead to starvation.

On the other hand, many others believe that the EPA is dangerously lax and that the regulatory system does not provide sufficient protection for the consumer. They argue that any substances that are as biologically active, persistent, and foreign to natural food webs as many insecticides can be *presumed* to be harmful to human health. They point out that cigarette smoke and asbestos dust cause cancer several decades after exposure. Perhaps it would be slightly better to be cautious now than to risk a large-scale epidemic of cancer in the next decade or two. Furthermore, critics of the EPA claim that many of the estimates and assumptions used in reaching the final decision are flawed. For example, the EPA estimates a person's daily intake of specific fruits and vegetables. Many people eat a diet that is very rich in certain types of produce. For example, some ethnic groups use large quantities of a particular type of vegetable, and vegetarians eat more produce than the national average. These people will be exposed to greater than the maximal allowable exposure of various pesticides. Another problem arises because, in making the estimates, the EPA assumes that "commonly recognized practices" will be used. What if a farmer is careless? Should a chemical be approved if it is safe when applied by trained and responsible personnel, but dangerous when applied carelessly by

untrained workers? Some chemicals are environmentally safe if sprayed on dry fields, but are potentially dangerous when dispersed just after or during a rainstorm. Should these compounds be recognized as safe or banned as dangerous? Finally, opponents of current policy argue that chemicals are not the best way to control pests anyway. Many insects are genetically resistant to the poisons, and natural control measures are more effective.

Another concern of the 1972 law is what should be done about the pesticides that were already in use before the law was written. At that time, there were 600 active ingredients that were combined into more than 50,000 different mixtures and formulations. According to FIFRA, the EPA was ordered to test all these compounds and to remove any that were deemed unsafe. Between 1972 and 1985, a total of five pesticides were banned and the use of 23 others was restricted. By 1985, however, over half of the pesticides used in the United States had not even been minimally tested for their toxicity. To understand the time scale required to reverse existing practices, consider the case of a class of fungicides known as EBDCs (ethylene bis-dithiocarbamates). EBDCs were first approved in the 1950s under the old law and were not even considered for testing at all until the 1972 law was put into effect. In the 1970s, these compounds were used on 30 percent of American tomatoes, tobacco, spinach, and apples as well as on 50 percent of the potato crop, 65 percent of the mushroom crop, and virtually 100 percent of all imported bananas. When EBDCs were finally tested, scientists learned that, in high concentrations, they are extremely toxic to laboratory animals and presumably to humans and, in lower doses, are believed to cause cancer, birth defects, genetic mutations, and thyroid malfunctions. These compounds were deemed dangerous enough to be placed under "special review" in 1977, 5 years after the amended FIFRA was signed into law (Fig. 19–6). However, manufacture and use was not restricted during the review period. Following a lawsuit initiated by the Natural Resources Defense Council and the AFL-CIO, the EPA agreed to reassess its decision by December 31, 1986, 9 years after the situation was originally placed under review. Just before the December deadline, the EPA claimed that some necessary data were not available and without this information a final decision

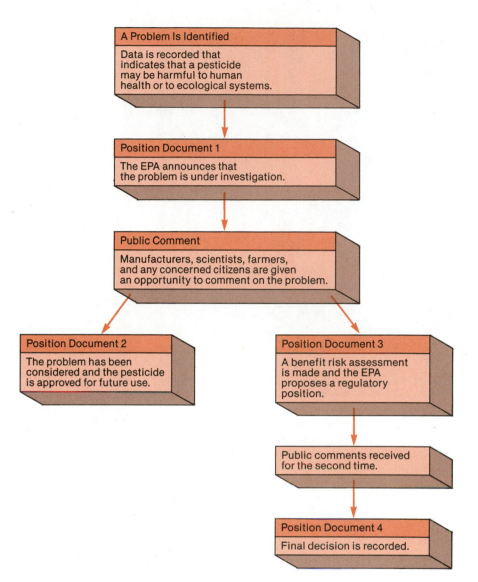

A Problem Is Identified

Data is recorded that indicates that a pesticide may be harmful to human health or to ecological systems.

Position Document 1

The EPA announces that the problem is under investigation.

Public Comment

Manufacturers, scientists, farmers, and any concerned citizens are given an opportunity to comment on the problem.

Position Document 2

The problem has been considered and the pesticide is approved for future use.

Position Document 3

A benefit risk assessment is made and the EPA proposes a regulatory position.

Public comments received for the second time.

Position Document 4

Final decision is recorded.

Figure 19–6
A flow sheet showing the process that the EPA uses to review a pesticide that was approved before the 1972 revision of FIFRA. Note that after the first public comment, EPA officials make a choice whether to grant approval of the chemical or to consider the case further. The entire review process can take anywhere from two to five years, and during that time the pesticide can still be sold and used.

could not be made. Therefore, a 3½ year extension was requested. The Natural Resources Defense Council objected, claiming that the delay was too long. By the summer of 1987, no resolution had been reached.

19.6
Other Methods of Pest Control

Broad-spectrum pesticides have been effective in many situations, but they also have serious flaws. They destroy populations of predators, upset ecosystems, and poison people and animals. In addition, pesticides may possibly cause cancer, birth defects, and other illnesses. What are the alternatives?

Use of Natural Enemies

Pesticides have caused problems where they have poisoned natural predators. Why not use the opposite treatment and, instead of poisoning predators, import them? This type of approach has been quite successful in many cases.

In the late 1880s, the newly formed citrus industry in California faced disaster. A pest known as the cottony cushion scale had migrated from Australia and was threatening to destroy crops of or-

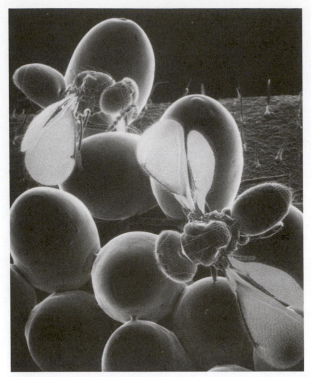

The small South American wasp, *Edovum puttleri,* bores into the eggs of the Colorado potato beetle, a serious agricultural pest. The gnat-sized wasp will kill the beetle embryo by piercing the egg as many as 50 times with its microscopic syringe-like egg layer, stopping occasionally to dine on the egg's contents. During this process, the female wasp inserts a single egg of its own into the host egg. A mature wasp then emerges within two to three weeks. In turn the new wasp will kill even more beetles during its reproductive process. (Robert Schroder, USDA)

anges, lemons, and grapefruit. However, biologists learned that the cottony cushion scale did not pose a serious threat to citrus groves in Australia. Scientists studying the problem learned that in its native habitat, the Australian Ladybird beetle preyed on the scale and kept pest populations under control. For a total cost of about $5000, these predators were imported in the United States. They thrived and saved a multimillion dollar industry.

Today, 100 years later, as people have become aware of the harmful effects of sprays and as many insects have become resistant to chemical controls, the technique of encouraging predator populations is receiving renewed enthusiasm. However, problems have arisen, because once a predation enhancement strategy is initiated, it is

Box 19.1
Biocontrol at Home

Homeowners can implement their own mini-biological control programs against many common house and garden plant pests. "Biological Pest Management for Interior Plant-scapes" (available for $2.00 from The Entomology Section, Alberta Environmental Centre, Vegreville, Alberta, TOB 4L0, Canada) describes how to control certain whiteflies, aphids, mealybugs, scales, and mites by releasing beneficial insects such as green lacewing larvae and ladybird bettles. "Biological Control and Insect Pest Management, /4096," discusses the basic concepts of biological control and other pest management strategies (send $3 to Agricultural Sciences Publications, University of California, 1422 Harbour Way, Richmond, California 94804). Also available (free) from Agricultural Sciences Publications is Leaflet 21105, "Some Commercial Sources of Biological Control Agents in California," which allows you to order beneficial insects by mail.

imperative to reduce chemical sprays in the area. For example, in more recent times, another insect, the woolly whitefly, migrated into California from Mexico and again threatened the citrus industry in that state. A parasite of the woolly whitefly was identified and imported, and the situation was brought under control. A few years later an infestation of Japanese beetles occurred, and massive amounts of pesticides were used to control this pest. The beetles were in fact brought under control, but the parasites of the woolly whitefly were also killed. The whitefly population bloomed and caused millions of dollars worth of damage.

Insects can also be controlled through the use of certain strains of bacteria and viruses. A virus effective against the cotton bollworm and the corn earworm has been manufactured as a pesticide in the United States. It has been approved by federal regulatory agencies and is now ready for mass production. Viral strains that combat several other species of pests should be commercially available in the near future.

There are many advantages to importing enemies of pests. Because these agents are living or-

Table 19–3
Mathematical Population Decline When a Constant Number of Sterile Males Are Released Among an Indigenous Population of One Million Females and One Million Males

Generation	Number of Virgin Females	Number of Sterile Males Released	Ratio of Sterile to Fertile Males	Number of Fertile Females in the Next Generation
1	1,000,000	2,000,000	2:1	333,333
2	333,333	2,000,000	6:1	47,619
3	47,619	2,000,000	42:1	1107
4	1107	2,000,000	1807:1	less than 1

ganisms, they reproduce naturally, and one application can last for many years. Most insect parasites and disease organisms are very specific and do not interfere with the health of large animals. No harmful or questionable chemicals are introduced into the environment.

Sterilization Techniques

Pests can be controlled without killing them directly if the adults of one generation are sterilized. For example, if males are sterilized, they cannot impregnate females, so the pest population will soon die off.

In theory, the technique is simple and should produce rapid results. For example, as shown in Table 19–3, if there is a population of 2,000,000 insects, the release of an additional 2,000,000 sterile males for four successive generations should completely eliminate the pest. Although this arithmetic seems encouraging, in practice, no pest has been eliminated in this manner. The screwworm fly (Fig. 19–7) is a metallic green insect a bit larger than a housefly. Unlike the housefly, however, its

A

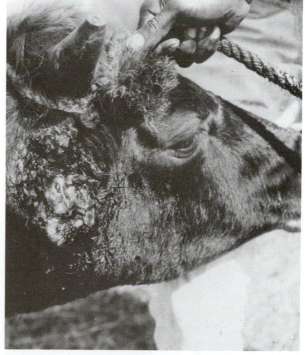

B

Figure 19–7
A, Female screwworm fly—the one that lays the eggs and does all the damage. B, Screwworm larvae infestation in the ear of a steer. An untreated grown animal may be killed in ten days by thousands of maggots feeding in a single wound. (A, B, Courtesy of USDA)

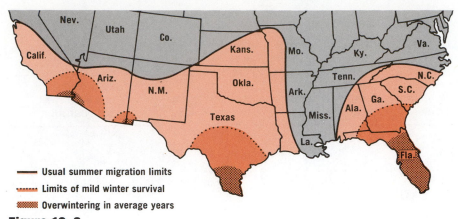

Usual summer migration limits

Limits of mild winter survival

Overwintering in average years

Figure 19–8

Screwworm distribution in the United States.

larvae feed on living tissue. They can kill a mature steer in 10 days. In 1976, they killed an invalid elderly woman in San Antonio who was unable to help herself. Some years ago, the United States Department of Agriculture initiated a program in the southeastern states to raise male screwworm flies, sterilize them by irradiation, and release them in their natural breeding grounds (Fig. 19–8). If a sterile male mates with a normal female, she will lay eggs, but they will not hatch.

For several years, millions of sterilized males were released annually to mate with healthy females living in the area. Initially, the program was a spectacular success, and screwworm infestations were completely eliminated from 1962 to 1971. But, in 1972, the screwworm population increased dramatically and infested nearly 100,000 cattle. During the following 3 years, screwworms continued to cause serious losses of cattle. What had happened?

Researchers reasoned that perhaps the screwworms raised in captivity evolved into a domestic strain that was no longer well adapted to natural conditions. For some reason, these domestic irradiated flies no longer mated successfully with wild females. Perhaps the males could not fly so far or fast, or perhaps they lost resistance to natural predators or disease organisms. In 1977, the program was renewed using a new strain of male flies. In May of that year, pilots dropped 400 million sterilized males each week in Mexico and parts of Texas. The infestations were stopped in the control regions, but, the following year, the screwworm fly opened new fronts in New Mexico, Arizona, and California. Air drops of sterile flies were raised to

500 million a week and extended to New Mexico. At that time, Dr. Carl R. Watson, a staff scientist with the eradication program, said, "This is a war. You may lose a battle here and there, but we won't lose the war."

Dr. H. Q. Sibley, the program director, predicted, "I'd say that we'll eventually eradicate the screwworm fly in the continental U.S.A. and Mexico, and hope we can do it sometime in '81, '82—along in there."

By the fall of 1981, however, the flies continued to survive in many regions. Biological selection had favored those females that were able to recognize sterile males and to reject them in favor of the wild fertile ones. Thus, an extremely expensive program proved only partially successful.

Other attempts at control through sterilization have been even less effective. When sterilized males were released against the codling moth, a serious pest of apple and pear orchards, the initial control was successful, but migration of fertile males from nearby areas spoiled the early gains.

In 1981, an imported pest of fruits and vegetables, the mediterranean fruit fly, nicknamed the **medfly,** appeared in California. Local agricultural experts feared that because there were few natural enemies of the medfly, populations might flourish and destroy billions of dollars worth of produce. As part of the program to control the pests, "sterilized" males were released in several target areas. A few days later, scientists learned that the released males were fertile after all. Therefore, the "control" procedure proved to aggravate the problem rather than to solve it. The story has a happy ending, however, because medflies did not adapt well to the environment in California and populations never expanded to crisis levels.

These examples should not be used an an argument against new techniques, but they do serve as a reminder that insect control is a formidable problem and that quick and permanent solutions are not yet available.

Control by Hormones

Many insects begin their lives in some larval stage and later metamorphose into a mature adult. As an example, a caterpillar is a larva that later matures to become a moth or butterfly. When an insect is in the larval state, it continuously produces a chemical called the **juvenile hormone.** As long as sufficient quantities of juvenile hormone are in the insect's system, it remains a larva. It is only when the flow of that biochemical agent stops, that the insect metamorphoses (Fig. 19–9). If an insect larva is artificially sprayed with the juvenile hormone specific to its species, it will never mature into its adult form. Because insects can neither mate nor survive long as larvae, such a spray application is eventually lethal. Therefore, juvenile hormones can be used as insecticides. It is likely that widespread use of these chemicals or their analogs would produce minimal environmental insult, because they are biodegradable and active only against specific insects. With the aid of careful timing, pests can be destroyed without killing their predators.

The first hormone control chemical to be marketed commercially is an agent that combats three species of floodwater mosquitoes, including *Anopheles albimanus,* the malaria vector in South and Central America. Spray doses of 150 g/hectare (about 2 ounces per acre) have resulted in complete control of this mosquito.

Despite this success, some technical difficulties with hormone control have arisen. One difficulty is that although natural juvenile hormone is stable in the body of a caterpillar, it is not stable in the environment and often breaks down chemically before it can act. This problem has been circumvented by the discovery of organic chemicals that are structurally similar to natural juvenile hormone and are biologically active but more stable. Another difficulty is in choosing the best time for the spray application. Juvenile hormone is an effective

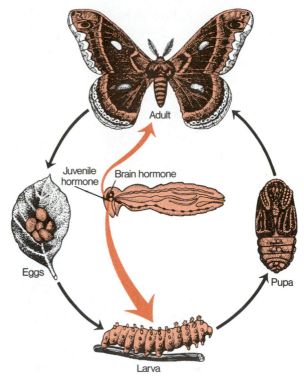

Figure 19–9
The role of hormones in insect metamorphosis. The juvenile hormone, secreted mainly during the larva stage, keeps the caterpillar in this immature state until it is ready to metamorphose into a pupa and adult. The hormones must be secreted in the right amounts at the right time.

insecticide only during the relatively brief period of an insect's life when the *absence* of juvenile hormone is essential to normal insect development. If the chemical is sprayed before the larva is ready to metamorphose, it has no effect. Since the timing of spray applications is so crucial, considerable expertise and precision are necessary for effective control.

In recent years, scientists have been studying a variety of other types of natural compounds that aren't broad-spectrum poisons, but nevertheless kill specific pests by interrupting their life cycles or by interfering with their reproductive cycles. One scientist has found that if a certain chemical is fed to female cockroaches, the muscles used in egg-laying cease to function. Thus, even though the female remains healthy and is fertilized by a healthy male, no eggs are laid. Another chemical sterilizes roaches before they reach breeding age. As a final example, a team of researchers has discovered a chemical that fools insects so that males of one species attempt to copulate with females of another. Such interspecific mating never produces viable offspring and sometimes leads to outright death of the partners.

Sex Attractants

In many species of insects, a female signals her readiness to mate by emitting a small amount of a species-specific chemical sex attractant, called a **pheromone.** The males detect (smell) very minute quantities of pheromone and follow the odor to its source. Attempts have been made to bait traps either with the chemical or, more simply, with live females. In this program, only minute quantities of natural chemicals are released into the air by evaporation, and environmental perturbations are nonexistent. As in the case of the sterile male technique, however, there is a statistical problem in areas of heavy infestation. Very simply, if there are a million males in the area and 1000 traps are set, and if each trap catches 100 males before they find a female, the control project is only 10 percent effective.* Further, the traps and the labor of setting them up are expensive. In parts of Europe, the cost of this program has been reduced by having schoolchildren set the traps as part of an educational program. Still, the trapping technique is probably best suited for special applications, such as for the control of migration where the migratory populations are small, or for control after a single effective spray application.

Some successes have been registered by the confusion technique. In one application, millions of cardboard squares were impregnated with pheromone and dropped from an airplane. With a high ratio of cardboard squares to females, males become confused and were observed to try to copulate with the cardboards. Another approach has been to spray the area with pheromone so that the entire atmosphere smells of females (to the male insect, that is, not to the human nose). Then the males are unable to track down a mate.

Use of Resistant Strains of Crops

As discussed earlier, some plants are naturally resistant to pests, because they synthesize their own

*$\frac{1000 \text{ traps} \times 100 \text{ males/trap}}{1,000,000 \text{ males}} \times 100\% = 10\%$

insecticides. One goal in the development of new plant hybrids is to select for insect-resistant strains. Successful breeders have produced a variety of alfalfa that is resistant to the alfalfa weevil, various strains of cereal crops resistant to rust infections, and many other successful strains. At the present time, biologists are using techniques of genetic engineering to assist in this approach.

The successes achieved have been encouraging, and further research deserves support, but it should be remembered that the technical problems are difficult. The new plant variety must produce high yields as well as maintain the natural resistance to other diseases. Moreover, genetic adaptation is not stagnant; throughout biological time, genetic defense in one species has traditionally been met by genetic changes in the attacking organism to neutralize the defense. Thus, many resistant crops lose their immunity after several years, and new resistant varieties must be developed.

Control by Cultivation

Uniformity is not typical of virgin land masses. The systems created by modern agriculture differ from natural systems, because farms tend to specialize in a very few species of plants, whereas areas untouched by people do not. For instance, in Kansas and Nebraska, thousands of hectares of land are planted almost exclusively in wheat. The result of such specialization is that a mold, fungus, or insect that consumes wheat has a vast food supply and an extremely hospitable environment. Few barriers to spreading exist, so the pest can grow quickly at uncontrolled rates. A fungus that attacks wheat will spread more slowly if half the plants in a field are something other than wheat, because the spores have a reduced chance of landing on a wheat plant. Moreover, if the disease spreads slowly, there is more time for the development of natural enemies of the fungus or of naturally resistant strains of wheat. Therefore, one solution to the problem of pests is to grow plants in small fields, with different species grown in adjacent fields. Unfortunately, the mechanization that is essential to modern agriculture is best suited to large fields of single crops.

Simply planting small fields of different crops is effective in itself, but, by judiciously choosing the companion plants, additional success can be realized. For example, the grape leafhopper, a pest of vineyards, can be controlled by a species of egg parasite that winters in blackberry bushes. Knowledgeable grape growers therefore maintain blackberry thickets. Conversely, one variety of stem rust that attacks North American cereal crops must live part of its life cycle on barberry bushes, and selective destruction of these plants will reduce rust infestations.

Other methods of cultivation that have been successful in controlling pests include (1) crop rotation, so that a given pest species cannot establish a permanent home in one field; (2) specific plowing and planting schedules to favor predators over pests; and (3) planting certain weeds that some omnivorous insects that prey on pests during part of their life cycle need for food during other stages.

Integrated Pest Management

If any lesson was learned during the DDT era, it was that insects are not passive recipients of control measures, and that any approach to pest management is subject to resistant reactions from the insect world. Therefore, many scientists now believe that unilateral attacks are not the answer, but that farmers should use as many control measures as possible in an integrated and well-planned manner. Integrated pest management (IPM) will never be so conceptually or technically simple as straightforward chemical control can be. It will be slower acting, more labor-intensive, and initially more expensive, although experts hope that it will be more effective and cheaper in the long run.

Recall from Section 19.3 how the yields of cotton in a valley in Peru were reduced after several years of insecticide use. Following the crop failure, a new program was initiated. First, predacious and parasitic insects were imported from nearby valleys. Second, all cultivation of marginal soils was banned in an effort to cull out weak plants, which are often breeding centers for disease. Third, the cycles of planting and irrigation were adjusted to interrupt the life cycles of the pests most effectively. Last, all spraying with synthetic organic insecticides was banned except under the permission and supervision of a panel of scientists. The result was that, despite the facts that some land was left fallow and that very little insecticide was used, cotton yields were higher than had ever been recorded in the area.

Special Topic C
Labor-Intensive Methods of Pest Control

Many nonchemical pest control practices used in the less-developed countries are quite effective, but they cannot be used in the developed countries because they are too labor-intensive. Three examples, taken from observations of farms in the People's Republic of China, are given below.

Every day, farmers walk through the fields, looking for plants that are infested with bugs. Then, individual stems are pruned, or specific plants are sprayed by hand. In this way, pest populations are controlled before they have a chance to bloom and infest the entire area.

In one commune, 600 people were employed to herd ducks through the fields. The ducks ate insect pests and then were eaten, in turn, by people.

The Egyptian Nile sparrow is a grain-eating bird that appears at harvest time in huge and destructive flocks. Modern control practices have been frustrated by the fact that one cannot poison the grain just prior to harvesting. However, the Chinese have successfully used an interesting technique against their own sparrows since the beginning of recorded history. They have discovered that the birds take to the air when bothered by noise and, furthermore, that they die of exhaustion if forced to fly for more than 15 minutes at a time. When a sparrow infestation threatens, farmers over a wide area race through fields yelling, beating gongs, or generally making noise in a coordinated effort. The technique is often successful in destroying entire flocks.

19.7
Economics and Social Choices of Pest Control

There are four groups of people involved in the pesticide controversy (Fig. 19–10): (1) Farmers want to grow as much food as possible in order to earn a living. (2) Pesticide manufacturers want to sell pesticides and realize a profit. (3) Government agencies have the responsibility of regulating and

3

1

Figure 19–10

There are four groups of people involved in the pesticide controversy. (1) Farmers want to grow as much food as possible in order to earn a living. (2) Pesticide manufacturers want to sell pesticides and realize a profit. (3) Government agencies have the responsibility of regulating and controlling dangerous chemicals. (Courtesy of USDA Soil Conservation Service) (4) Consumers want a plentiful supply of food at reasonable prices, but they want to avoid pollution that endangers their health.

4

controlling dangerous chemicals. (4) Consumers want a plentiful supply of food at reasonable prices, but they want their food to be free of toxic or questionable chemical residues. Since it is impossible to satisfy all four groups simultaneously, pesticide policy arises out of conflict and compromise.

Think for a minute of an "ideal" pesticide. Perhaps it would be a virus or bacterium that would attack a specific insect pest. These microorganisms would infect only one pest species. They would not attack nontarget species. No foreign chemicals would be introduced into the environment. Moreover, bacteria and viruses reproduce themselves. One spray application would protect a field for years to come. With these encouraging advantages, one may wonder why insect enemies are not used more frequently.

One problem is that this type of control measure acts too slowly. A chemical pesticide kills pests within a few hours. A disease organism requires weeks or even months to act. Although effective pest control may eventually be realized, results cannot be expected immediately.

Another problem is that, in most cases, biological pest management initially requires more labor and expertise than chemical control techniques. At the very least, some knowledgeable person must walk through the fields, study the insect life cycles, and decide when to spread the biological agents. Bad timing may lead to failure. For example, predators that are released when there are few pests in the area may migrate to other areas in search of food. Alternatively, a parasite that thrives only on the larvae of a species may die out if released when the pest is in the adult stage.

Even if a biological pest program is carefully monitored, difficulties may arise. A farmer who does try biological control may find that the expense and effort are lost when chemical sprays from a nearby field blow across the unsprayed area and kill the predator populations.

Many farmers operate with a tight yearly budget. Most are unwilling or unable to risk a high expense in one year on the chance that it will more than pay for itself in the future. This reluctance is actually encouraged by the pesticide industry. An ideal pesticide program would not be likely to be highly profitable to the manufacturer. Many millions of dollars are needed to develop, produce, test, and market a new product. If the product can be used against many pest species, the company can expect large sales. On the other hand, if the insecticide is effective against only one species of pests, sales and profits will be much lower. In addition, recall that parasites and disease organisms reproduce naturally. Therefore, a farmer could buy one application of the pest control organism and enjoy protection for many seasons. Obviously, sales of a truly effective pest program would be much lower than sales of chemicals that must be used every year. Therefore, it is not surprising that industry has traditionally been more interested in broad-spectrum poisons than in biological control. Government support of truly effective pesticide measures would be a valuable environmental goal.

As one final point: Even though consumers naturally want to reduce exposure to pesticide residues, consumer attitudes actually encourage increased use of these compounds. In the United States, shoppers have come to expect blemish-free produce. Yet the hidden cost of "flawless" fruits and vegetables is an increased use of biologically potent chemical poisons. As an example, San Jose scale attacks apples as well as other fruit such as pears, peaches, plums, and apricots. This insect pest produces many pin-sized red dots on the skin of the fruit. An apple blemished in this way is still as edible as any other apple but is unappealing to the consumer. The grower cannot sell such apples, and San Jose scale must therefore be controlled by spraying with a broad-spectrum insecticide at petal fall and then on a 10- to 14-day schedule until harvest. Thus, consumers are trading a visible but harmless blight for pesticide residues that are invisible but potentially harmful.

19.8
Case History: The Boll Weevil

Many of the most serious agricultural pests are immigrants that have moved to a new and hospitable environment relatively free of the predators and pathogens native to their original home. The boll weevil (Fig. 19–11) is a small insect, about 0.65 cm (¼ in) long, that first migrated to the United States from Mexico in about 1880. Weevils feed on the buds and bolls of young cotton plants, thereby destroying the valuable fiber. Since there are few natural enemies of the weevil in the United States, population blooms of these insects are common. If left uncontrolled, a light infestation of 10 weevils per hectare can increase to 10,000 weevils per hectare within a single growing season and can completely consume an entire crop. The weevils' reproductive and eating capacity are so great that these pests are responsible for approximately $300 million worth of crop losses in the United States annually.

In the early 1900s, farmers used cultural controls to combat the weevils. Cotton was planted and harvested as early in the year as possible, and the plant stalks and leaves were burned immediately after harvest. If a large portion of the weevil population could be destroyed by fire, frequently an early crop could be harvested the following year, before the weevils could repopulate. On the other hand, this nip and tuck race with growing weevil populations was often unsuccessful. By the 1920s, about 96 percent of the American cotton crop was infested with weevils, average yield had declined by 30 percent, and many crops were com-

A

B

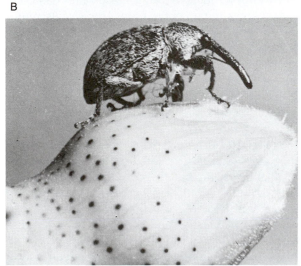

C

pletely destroyed. In the 1930s, a new pesticide, calcium arsenate, was introduced, but it was so highly toxic to nontarget species (including soil microorganisms) that it was largely replaced by DDT in the 1940s. At first DDT, was extremely effective—so effective, in fact, that farmers largely abandoned the cultural controls that had been used earlier. However, by 1960, many DDT-resistant strains of boll weevil had evolved. Disaster threatened. In response, farmers did not return to cultural control techniques but, instead, switched to other chemical pesticides, the organophosphates.

Broad-spectrum pesticides were effective in partially controlling the populations of weevils, but many secondary problems were raised. Weevils are not the only pest of cotton plants, and cotton is not the only crop grown in the South. Tobacco, corn, peanuts, soybeans, and vegetables are also commercially important. When cotton fields were sprayed heavily with broad-spectrum chemicals, many different types of insect predators in the region were killed. As a result, herbivorous insects that had previously been controlled by natural means began to replace the boll weevil as significant pests of cotton. In addition, epidemics of

Figure 19–11
A, Cotton flower. *B,* Open cotton boll. *C,* Boll weevil on a cotton plant. (*A, B, C,* courtesy of USDA)

pests of tobacco and corn became a problem for the first time. During the 1970s, a new concern was raised. What would happen if the boll weevil became resistant to organophosphates just as it had become resistant to DDT?

Obviously a new strategy was necessary. A Special Committee on Boll Weevil Eradication was formed with government support, and a five-pronged attack on this insect pest was outlined. Farmers were asked to (1) spray lightly with chemical pesticides during the growing season; (2) spray again in the fall just before the weevils hibernate for the winter; (3) destroy all plants, leaves, and stalks just after harvest to starve any remaining insects before they go into hibernation; (4) set traps in the early spring baited with a sex pheromone to catch and destroy males emerging from hibernation; and (5) release sterile male weevils to prevent fertile matings of any remaining females.

A pilot project was initiated in 1971 to determine the overall effectiveness of such a program. Some optimistic scientists even predicted that perhaps the boll weevil could be eradicated permanently. The project was effective in controlling weevil populations in the target area, but total annihilation was not realized. Research teams found that 95 percent control was feasible, but it is extremely difficult to destroy every weevil in a region.

In the late 1970s and early 1980s, additional programs were initiated. In some regions, light spraying continued, whereas in others, all chemical poisons were abandoned and a virus that attacks bollworms and budworms was introduced. Throughout the South, cotton production has risen and the quantities of pesticides used have declined. These results are encouraging, but the battle is not over and perhaps never will be.

19.9
Herbicides

Have you ever grown a garden? If you have, you know how much work is involved in hoeing and weeding (Fig. 19–12). Yet, if the weeds are not killed, they will choke out your flowers and vegetables and reduce yields. Farmers have battled weeds for as long as they have battled insect pests. People have known for centuries that certain chemicals may kill plants. The challenge in modern times is to develop chemicals that will kill weeds but not valuable crops. Such formulations are called **herbicides.**

Herbicide development and production has been quite successful in recent years. A laborer spends an average of 10 to 25 hours hoeing the weeds between the rows of 1 hectare of cotton. Today, an airplane can spray hundreds of hectares in a few hours for $5 to $15 per hectare. Agriculture in North America and Europe depends on small inputs of labor and a heavy use of machinery and chemicals. Certainly, herbicides are an important part of such a program. As a result, herbicide use has increased in the United States (see Fig. 19–5).

Figure 19–12
Many workers with hoes are needed to clear a field of weeds, whereas it is much cheaper to spread herbicides. However, chemicals pollute the environment.

Whenever large quantities of synthetic chemicals are spread throughout the environment, serious ecological problems are likely to arise. Although herbicides are not nearly as persistent in the soil as are organochloride insecticides, they pose difficulties nevertheless. Some herbicides kill earthworms and other organisms that contribute to a healthy soil. Others have been known to kill certain insect predators. If the predators are killed, pest populations will rise again. Then, farmers are likely to use more pesticides along with the herbicides, resulting in a spiraling pollution problem.

The herbicide 2,4,5–T has been used for a variety of agricultural applications. It was also an ingredient in Agent Orange, a defoliant used in Southeast Asia during the Vietnam War. After the war, the herbicide was used by the United States Forest Service to kill brush that interferes with the growth of valuable timber. 2,4,5–T is poisonous to humans. Perhaps even more frightening is the fact the commercial preparations of this herbicide are contaminated with minute quantities of dioxin. As explained in Chapter 18, dioxin is a very potent poison. Concentrations in the parts per billion range have been known to kill laboratory animals, and dioxin is suspected as a cause of birth defects and cancer. Vietnam War veterans have claimed that exposure to Agent Orange has led to a variety of adverse effects, including headaches, nausea, muscular weakness, loss of sex drive, numbness, liver damage, loss of sleep, skin rashes, and depression. Some of these claims have been supported by studies of herbicide workers in Sweden and tests on laboratory animals. When the government sprayed forests in Oregon, reports indicated that an abnormally high number of women in the region had miscarriages within a few months after the spray application. No one denies that 2,4,5–T in large doses is an acute poison, but all the other allegations about its chronic low-dose effects have been disputed by the chemical manufacturing industry. Persons who believe that they have been harmed by commercial or military spray applications have been involved in long and bitter battles with the government and herbicide manufacturers. Studies have been made and refuted; lawsuits have been filed and fought. Some scientific data presented on both sides have been discredited as false or misleading. However, some steps have been taken to address the issue. The Veterans Administration has settled some of the soldiers' claims by offering payment for partial disability. In 1979, the EPA issued an emergency order suspending domestic use of 2,4,5–T. This order was challenged, but, in 1985, after spending $10 million in legal fees, Dow Chemical Company, the last domestic manufacturer of 2,4,5–T, dropped its legal action, and the temporary suspension was changed to a permanent ban.

Agricultural scientists are faced with a dilemma. If herbicides are banned, the price of food will rise sharply. Farmers might not be able to find the laborers needed to work long hard hours in the fields picking weeds. Then food production would decrease. Therefore, the use of herbicides continues. However, chemical pollution of the environment is also increasing, and no one knows how this pollution is affecting human health and global ecosystems.

Summary

In natural ecosystems, herbivorous insects are controlled by chemical pesticides that are produced by the plants themselves and by a variety of different species of predators. These controls are usually, but not always, effective.

There are four generic types of problems associated with broad-spectrum pesticides. (1) They kill predators as well as pest species and thus disturb natural controls. (2) In many cases, pest species have evolved to be resistant to the poisons, and various predators have not. Then, the pest populations have bloomed. (3) Many broad-spectrum pesticides are poisonous to birds and mammals as well as to insects, and livestock and wildlife are affected. (3) Many pesticides are poisonous to humans.

DDT and other organochloride insecticides were banned because: (1) They are not biodegradable, (2) they are easily transported throughout the environment, and (3) they are concentrated in biological systems and poison many nontarget species.

After two and a half decades of study, proof for or against the carcinogenicity of pesticides in humans is still lacking, but the very fact that these materials are potent poisons makes caution advisable. FIFRA gives the EPA the power to regulate pesticide use.

Other methods of pest control include (1) natural enemies such as predators, parasites, and disease organisms; (2) sterilization of pests (usually males); (3) control by hormones; (4) use of sex attractants; and (5) resistant strains of crops. The most effective controls use a multifaceted approach called **integrated pest management.**

Species-specific biological control methods are environmentally sound but are not highly profitable to the manufacturer. Farmers are wary of them because their action is slower than that of chemical pesticides.

During the past 10 years, the use of herbicides has become increasingly popular. The compound, 2,4,5–T, an ingredient of Agent Orange, was used as a defoliant in Vietnam in addition to its use in agriculture. Some commonly available herbicides, including 2,4,5–T, are believed to cause birth defects. Others are suspected carcinogens. Weed control is necessary in agriculture, but indiscriminate use of herbicides may lead to ecological imbalance.

Questions

Effects of Chemical Pesticides

1. What are the harmful effects and the benefits that insects bring to people? How did people cope with insect problems before the introduction of modern insecticides?

2. An amateur ecologist studying wildlife populations before and after a heavy spray application determined that since no animals were directly killed by the spray, no harm had resulted. Would you agree? Defend your answer.

3. Do you think that some bird species might become resistant to DDT? Could that resistance save the birds from the harmful effects of the pesticide? Defend your answers.

4. Imagine that there was an impending malaria epidemic in a region and that an aerial spray program using DDT would be likely to kill the mosquitoes and avert the epidemic. Proponents of DDT argue that we know that malaria weakens and kills many people. Furthermore, since the chronic effects of DDT on human populations are not known, it would be wise to protect people against the direct danger and use the pesticide. Opponents of the program, on the other hand, argue that DDT is a potent environmental poison and should not be used under any circumstances. What position would you take on this issue? Defend your answer.

5. Explain how one indiscriminate spraying with DDT could destroy the effectiveness of an integrated control program.

Transport and Dispersal of Pesticides

6. Describe three ways in which DDT is transported through the environment by natural means. Why is an organophosphate less likely to be widely dispersed?

7. Explain why carnivorous fish are generally more susceptible to low levels of pesticides in the water than are herbivorous fish.

8. If no measurable quantities of DDT were found in the water of a pond, would that necessarily mean that the aquatic ecosystem was free of DDT? Explain.

Other Methods of Pest Control

9. Explain why it is important to spray pests with hormones at a precise time. If a spray application were successful on May 1 of one year, would it be safe to assume that farmers could spray successfully on that date every year?

10. Birds often become major pests in vineyards because they eat the grapes. (a) Which of the following control programs would you recommend for bird control: (i) spreading poison; (ii) broadcasting noise from a loudspeaker system to scare them; (iii) shooting; (iv) covering the vineyard with some fencing material? Defend your choices. (b) Do you think that it might be wise to initiate research directed toward: (i) developing a sterilization program against the birds, or (ii) developing new strains of grape that would be unpalatable or poisonous to birds? Explain.

Health Effects of Pesticides

11. Prepare a class debate on one of the two related topics listed below. (a) Have one side argue that a pesticide should not be banned until it is proved to be carcinogenic. The other side should argue that even a suspected carcinogen should be banned. (b) Have one side argue that the current regulatory process protects consumers, growers, and manufacturers in a balanced manner. The other side should take the position that the regulatory process is too slow to provide adequate environmental protection.

12. Argue that the wording of the FIFRA law, as quoted in section 19.5, could be used to ban automobiles. Discuss the difficulties in writing a general law that gives a governmental agency the power to ban a pesticide.

13. Explain how the establishment of a pesticide policy is an exercise in risk assessment. Discuss the probability that a person will be harmed by low-level exposure to pesticides and the severity of the effects.

Herbicides

14. Ragweed is considered to be a major plant pest because its pollen causes misery to hay fever victims. In natural systems, ragweed is characterized as an early successional plant. A few years ago, the state of New Jersey initiated a program to eliminate ragweed. Thousands of acres of roadways and old fields were sprayed with herbicides. Why do you think this program failed?

Economics and Politics of Pesticides

15. Explain how some peoples' jobs (e.g., that of a crop duster pilot, a pesticide sales manager, a government inspector, or a farmer) may affect their opinions on pesticide use.

16. Discuss the statement: "Pest control techniques that are truly effective would be a disaster for the pesticide industry."

17. Sometimes an integrated control program may not become effective until the second season of its application. Moreover, crop losses during the first season may actually be greater than average. Do you think that it would be good policy for the government to subsidize such losses in an effort to improve environmental quality? Defend your answer.

18. A worm that thrives in the core of an apple does not usually eat a large proportion of the apple, but people do not like wormy apples nevertheless. Discuss the social and economic factors that influence the choices between wormy apples and apples that might contain pesticide residues.

Suggested Readings

The book that started much of our current concern about pesticides, and a later sequel to it, are the following: (Even though these books are quite old, many of the concepts discussed remain pertinent.)

Rachel Carson: *Silent Spring.* Boston, Houghton Mifflin Co., 1962. 368 pp.

Frank Graham, Jr.: *Since Silent Spring.* Boston, Houghton Mifflin Co., 1970. 333 pp.

Several general references on pesticides include:

Keith C. Barrons: *Are Pesticides Really Necessary?* Chicago, Regnerry Gateway, Inc., 1981. 245 pp.

K. H. Buchel (ed.): *Chemistry of Pesticides.* Somerset, NJ, John Wiley & Sons, 1983. 618 pp.

David Bull: *A Growing Problem, Pesticides and the Third World.* Oxford, Oxford Print Room, 1982. 192 pp.

Thomas R. Dunlap: *DDT Scientists, Citizens, and Public Policy.* Princeton, NJ, Princeton University Press, 1981. 318 pp.

Frank Graham Jr.: *The Dragon Hunters.* New York, E. P. Dutton Inc., 1984. 334 pp.

William H. Hallenbeck and Kathleen M. Cunningham-Burns: *Pesticides and Human Health.* New York, Springer-Verlag, 1985. 166 pp.

F. L. McEwen and G. R. Stephenson: *The Use and Significance of Pesticides in the Environment.* Somerset, NJ, John Wiley & Sons, 1979. 538 pp.

Lawrie Motta: *Pesticides in Food: What the Public Needs to Know.* San Francisco, Natural Resources Defense Council, Inc., 1984. 123 pp.

John H. Perkins: *Insects, Experts, and the Insecticide Crisis.* New York, Plenum Press, 1982. 304 pp.

Carol Van Strum: *A Bitter Fog: Herbicides and Human Rights.* San Francisco, Sierra Club Books, 1983. 288 pp.

20

Water Pollution

Water purification systems in many regions of the world are either inadequate or nonexistent. Millions of infants die at an early age from drinking polluted water, and even adults suffer from stomach illness. North Americans have long prided themselves on the fine quality of their drinking water, but, in recent years, many people have questioned whether the drinking water is really so excellent. The tap water in several American cities has a strong smell and a bad taste. Local residents have turned to large-scale consumption of bottled spring water. Chemists analyzing water supplies have raised disturbing questions. Articles published in both technical journals and local newspapers have raised fears about water supplies. In this chapter we review some of the problems of water pollution and purification.

20.1
Types of Impurities in Water

Chemically pure water is a collection of H_2O molecules—nothing else. Such a substance is not found in nature—not in wild streams or lakes, not in clouds, rain, or snow, nor even in the polar ice caps. Very pure water can be prepared in the laboratory, but only with specialized equipment. Water accepts and holds foreign matter in various ways:

1. Water is an unusually good solvent. It is especially good at dissolving mineral salts, which typically consist of negative and positive ions. The positive ions are those of metals, including many that are poisonous, such as the ions of copper, cadmium, mercury, and lead. Water is also a good solvent for many organic compounds that contain oxygen, such as alcohols, sugars, and organic acids. Furthermore, many materials that are normally considered insoluble in water are, in fact, very slightly soluble. Thus, hydrocarbons are said to be insoluble in water. ("Oil and water do not mix.") Yet benzene, for example, dissolves in water to the extent of almost 0.1 percent. That may not sound like much, but it would have a terrible taste, and besides, benzene is toxic to humans.

2. Insoluble particles, if they are small enough, may settle so slowly that, for all practical purposes, they remain in water indefinitely (note the data in Fig. 20–1).

3. Some insoluble materials, especially certain metals, react with water to produce soluble products.

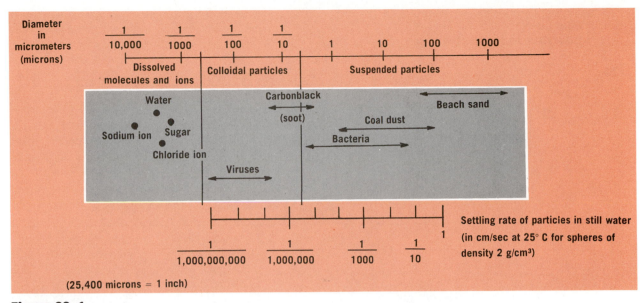

Figure 20–1
Small particles in water.

4. Nutrient matter is metabolized by living organisms in water, and the resulting waste products may be pollutants.

5. Living organisms themselves, if they are carriers of disease, may be considered pollutants.

6. A soluble substance may react with an insoluble contaminant to bring it into solution. For example, acids in water react with many minerals and thus dissolve them.

7. Finally, a contaminant may pollute water simply by floating on it. Water is denser than almost all hydrocarbons; therefore, petroleum floats on water. A floating oil spill is certainly a water pollutant.

It is useful to classify foreign substances in water according to the size of their particles, because this size often determines the effectiveness of various methods of purification. Figure 20–1 shows a spectrum of particles arbitrarily divided into three classes—suspended, colloidal, and dissolved. Let us consider each in turn, referring to the figure.

Suspended particles, which have diameters of more than about 1 μm, are the largest. Rainwater that runs off a dusty road into a storm drain carries suspended particles. They are large enough to settle out of quiet water reasonably quickly and to be retained by many common filters. They are also large enough to absorb light, thus making water containing them look cloudy or murky.

Colloidal particles are so small that their settling rate is insignificant, and they pass through the holes of most filter media; therefore, they cannot be removed from water by settling or by ordinary filtration. Water that contains colloidal particles appears cloudy when observed at right angles to a beam of light. (The same phenomenon occurs in air; colloidal dust particles can best be seen when observed at right angles to a sharply focused light beam in an otherwise dark room.) The colors of natural waters, such as the blues, greens, and reds of lakes or seas, are caused largely by colloidal particles.

Dissolved matter does not settle out, is not retained on filters, and does not make water cloudy, even when viewed at right angles to a beam of light. The particles of which such matter consists are no larger than about one-thousandth micrometer in diameter. If they are electrically neutral, they are called molecules. If they bear an electrical charge, they are called ions. Cane sugar (sucrose), grain alcohol (ethanol), and "permanent antifreeze" (ethylene glycol) are substances that dissolve in water as electrically neutral molecules. Table salt (sodium chloride), on the other hand, dissolves as positive sodium and negative chloride ions.

Natural waters contain substances in all three categories, as shown in Table 20–1. Natural waters range from tastily potable to poisonous; in salti-

Table 20–1
Impurities in Natural Water

Source	Particle Size Classification				
	Suspended	Colloidal	Dissolved		
Atmosphere	←Dusts→		*Molecules* Carbon dioxide, CO_2 Sulfur dioxide, SO_2 Oxygen, O_2 Nitrogen, N_2	*Positive ions* Hydrogen, H^+	*Negative ions* Bicarbonate, HCO_3^- Sulfate, SO_4^{2-}
Mineral soil and rock	←Sand→ ←Clays→ ←Mineral soil particles→		Carbon dioxide, CO_2	Sodium, Na^+ Potassium, K^+ Calcium, Ca^{2+} Magnesium, Mg^{2+} Iron, Fe^{2+} Manganese, Mn^{2+}	Chloride, Cl^- Fluoride, F^- Sulfate, SO_4^{2-} Carbonate, CO_3^{2-} Bicarbonate, HCO_3^- Nitrate, NO_3^- Various phosphates
Living organisms and their decomposition products	Algae Diatoms Bacteria ←Organic soil (topsoil)→ Fish and other organisms	Viruses Organic coloring matter	Carbon dioxide, CO_2 Oxygen, O_2 Nitrogen, N_2 Hydrogen sulfide, H_2S Methane, CH_4 Various organic wastes, some of which produce odor and color	Hydrogen, H^+ Sodium, Na^+ Ammonium, NH_4^+	Chloride, Cl^- Bicarbonate, HCO_3^- Nitrate, NO_3^-

ness, they range from fresh rainwater (not salty) to brackish (partly salty, where river water mixes with seawater), to ocean water, to a saturated solution such as the Dead Sea, where evaporation of water concentrates the salts until no more can dissolve.

20.2
Productivity in Aquatic Systems

The productivity of an ecosystem reflects the rate at which its producers photosynthesize (see Chapter 3). In most ecosystems, such as a farm, a forest, or an oceanic fishing ground, higher productivity is beneficial for humans, because the system sup-

plies useful products such as grains, wood, or fish. In lakes and streams, however, the opposite type of ecosystem is preferred. For example, picture a clear mountain lake full of trout and so pure that a person could drink the water. Such a system, called an **oligotrophic** lake, is characterized by *low* productivity. The water is clear because it contains comparatively few plankton or rooted plants. Ecologists have learned that productivity is low because the growth of producers is limited by a shortage of nutrients. The low productivity of an oligotrophic lake or stream is beneficial for humans.

As time passes, nearby mountains or hillsides erode and sediments are washed into all freshwater systems. These sediments carry nutrients, which

Box 20.1
The Taste of Carbonated Water

Carbonated water, also known as "sparkling water," "club soda," or "seltzer," is saturated with carbon dioxide under pressure. When the container is opened and the pressure is released, bubbles of carbon dioxide come out of solution. Carbonated water has a slightly tart taste because of the acidity contributed by the carbon dioxide. Club soda usually contains added salts; seltzer does not (read the label).

When the same brand of bottled water is available in both carbonated and noncarbonated forms, the noncarbonated water is usually rated higher in taste tests. The poorer taste of the carbonated waters comes from impurities in the carbon dioxide, which may be obtained from fermentation gases or from the burning of oil. The carbon dioxide is purified before it is used to carbonate beverages, but the purification is not always 100 percent effective.

Box 20.2
Eutrophication

Eutrophication originally meant "tending to promote nutrition." In this sense, a vitamin supplement would be a eutrophic medicine. The term was later applied to describe the nourishment of natural waters as a contributor to the process of succession.

Figure 20–2
The effect of phosphorus on the productivity of a lake. This lake in Manitoba was divided in two by plastic sheeting across the narrow neck in the middle of the photograph. Phosphorus was added to half of the lake in the upper part of the photograph. Several weeks later, the phosphorus-fertilized half of the lake was opaque as a result of massive plankton bloom; the lower part of the lake was as clear and oligotrophic as it was before the experiment. (Photograph courtesy of David Schindler)

fertilize the system and increase its productivity. A lake with high productivity, called a **eutrophic** lake, has a dense population of producers, often visible as a green scum on the surface of the murky water. In a natural system, many thousands of years may elapse before an oligotrophic waterway becomes visibly eutrophic. When this slow process is speeded up by human activity, it is called **cultural eutrophication.** For example, water that runs off farmland may contain fertilizer residues, and the waste matter in raw sewage is also a fertilizer. Either of these nutrient sources can lead to cultural eutrophication (Box 20.2).

The inorganic nutrient whose absence most often limits freshwater productivity is phosphate. (Phosphates are a group of ions that contain the elements phosphorus and oxygen, such as PO_4^{3-}, $P_2O_7^{4-}$, and others.) The consequences of increasing the phosphate content of an oligotrophic lake were demonstrated in a dramatic experiment illustrated in Figure 20–2. A small lake in Manitoba, Canada, was divided in two by suspending a plastic sheet across a narrow neck in the middle of the lake. The bottom of the sheet was secured to the lake's rocky bottom. A large amount of phosphate fertilizer was then added to one half of the lake,

leaving the other half as a control. Within a few weeks the fertilized half had become opaque as a result of a massive bloom of plankton.

When phosphorus is added in a single dose, as in this experiment, the effect is short-lived, because phosphorus is continuously removed from the system by deposition into bottom sediments or by stream outflow. On the other hand, if phosphorus is added continuously, as it often is in the form of sewage, phosphate-containing detergents, or fertilizer run-off from agricultural land, the productivity of a lake will remain high, and eutrophication will be hastened, changing the character of the lake, often irrevocably. Such changes have fundamentally altered Lake Erie, which is relatively shallow. Even deep oligotrophic lakes, such as Lake Tahoe on the California-Nevada border, have become noticeably more eutrophic in the last 20 years as a result of pollution.

Geologically young oligotrophic lakes are rare, especially in developed areas, where cultural eutrophication is common. When the American pioneers migrated to the West, they found lakes that were so clear that the fish could be seen deep below the surface. Today, approximately 75 percent of large lakes in the United States are eutrophic. In some, cultural eutrophication is advanced, and the problem is aggravated by the presence of an additional potential supply of nutrients stored in the sediments. Small concentrations of nutrients are essential to aquatic ecosystems, whereas large concentrations of the same materials are pollutants.

Severe eutrophication is sometimes considered to be almost irreversible. The situation is not always hopeless, however. For example, recent experience with Lake Washington (Seattle) has shown that eutrophication caused by excessive fertilization can be reversed if the nutrient inflow is drastically reduced.

The Role of Oxygen

Most organisms require oxygen to metabolize their food and release the energy they need. This process is known as **aerobic respiration** (**aerobic** means "with oxygen"). Aquatic organisms use the oxygen dissolved in water for respiration. Oxygen is not very soluble in water. One liter of water in contact with air at 25°C contains 0.0084 g of oxygen. In contrast, 1 liter of air at 25°C contains 0.27 g of oxygen. Thus, aerated water contains only about one thirtieth as much oxygen as the same volume of air.

There are two natural processes that can replace the oxygen consumed by aquatic organisms.

One process is the introduction of air directly into the water. If the water is stagnant and the air is still, this introduction is very slow; it is much faster in places where turbulence mixes water and air, as it does in the "white water" of shallow rapids. The second process is photosynthesis by aquatic plants, which can occur only at depths penetrated by sunlight. Both of these processes, at best, are very much slower than the replacement of the oxygen in the air we breathe. In fact, such replacement is so rapid that we normally don't think about it. The breath we exhale is continuously swept away by drafts, small air currents, even the mixing caused by slight head and body motions. These are the reasons why insufficient nutrition on land means lack of food, whereas in water, it often means lack of oxygen.

The bottom mud of freshwater streams and lakes where the water does not move rapidly contains very little oxygen. This bottom mud provides the perfect environment for microorganisms that can respire **anaerobically** (without oxygen). These organisms live by releasing energy anaerobically from the dead organic matter, such as the bodies of phytoplankton, that falls from above. Many bacteria can respire either aerobically or anaerobically, depending on conditions. Since anaerobic respiration yields much less energy than aerobic respiration (Table 20–2), these bacteria use oxygen when it is available.

As explained earlier, nutrient levels and productivity are low in a clear, oligotrophic lake. Therefore, dissolved oxygen is consumed slowly, and its concentration is maintained by natural replenishment. However, if slow-moving fresh water is rich in nutrients, the populations of various organisms will increase dramatically. In this situation, oxygen-consumers may use the oxygen in the water faster than it can be replaced by dissolving it from the air or by photosynthesis. Then, most of the oxygen may disappear even from the surface layers of the water. When this occurs, phytoplankton that require oxygen die by the millions and are replaced by organisms, such as the bacteria from the bottom mud, that can survive anaerobic conditions. Many larger organisms such as trout need a lot of oxygen and they also die.

If the greenish scum of a bloom of photosynthetic plankton is unpleasant, a scum of dead plankton and fish, combined with a population explosion of anaerobic bacteria, is even more repulsive. Anaerobic sulfur bacteria, for instance, produce hydrogen sulfide, a gas that smells like rotten eggs.

Biochemical Oxygen Demand

Imagine that a biodegradable material is added to a natural waterway. This substance, by itself, may be harmless; it could be something as innocuous as waste food from a cannery. But once it is spilled into an aquatic ecosystem, it will be eaten and oxidized by a variety of organisms. If the organisms are aerobic, the process will also consume dissolved oxygen. If consumption is great enough, oxygen levels in the water will be depleted, and organisms in the ecosystem will die. Thus, the quality of the waterway is degraded, and pollution has occurred (Fig. 20–3).

The index of pollution by nutrients is called the **biochemical oxygen demand,** or **BOD.**

The BOD is defined as the amount of oxygen that will be consumed when a biodegradable substance is decomposed in an aquatic system.

Some organic materials, such as chlorinated hydrocarbons, that are synthesized by the chemical industry, cannot be used as food by living organisms and therefore do not contribute to the BOD (Box 20.3).

BOD values are expressed in milligrams of oxygen per liter of water. Recall that pure water sat-

Turbulence introduces oxygen into flowing water.

urated with air at 25°C contains 0.0084 g, or 8.4 mg, of oxygen per liter. Compare this with some typical BOD values in the table on p. 580:

Table 20–2
Energy Yields from Aerobic and Anaerobic Processes

Nutrient	Process	Products	Approximate Energy Yield per Gram of Nutrient (calories)
Carbohydrates	Respiration (aerobic)	$CO_2 + H_2O$	4000
	Fermentation (anaerobic)	Alcohol $+ H_2O$	100
	Biogas production (anaerobic)	Methane $+ CO_2$	220
Proteins	Respiration (aerobic)	$CO_2 + H_2O$ + nitrates and sulfates	4000
	Putrefaction (anaerobic)	CO_2 + ammonia, methane, and hydrogen sulfide	370

A

B

Figure 20–3

The choking of waters by weeds. *A*, The dam on the White Nile at Jebel Aulia near Khartoum, Sudan. The area was clean when photographed in October 1958. *B*, The same area in October 1965 shows the accumulation of water hyacinth above the dam. (From Holm: Aquatic Weeds. *Science 166*:699–709, 1969. Copyright 1969 by the American Association for the Advancement of Science)

Type of Water	BOD (mg/L)
Pure water	0
Typical fresh natural water	2 – 5
Domestic sewage	hundreds
Water from food processing	thousands
Sewage after primary and secondary purification (see Section 20.8)	10 – 20

Thus, domestic sewage with a BOD of, say, 200 mg/liter would require 200/8.4, or about 24 times as much oxygen as is available in pure aerated water, and even treated sewage demands about twice as much oxygen as is available.

20.3
Pollution of Inland Waters by Nutrients

Streams and Rivers

When sewage is discharged into a freshwater stream, the stream becomes polluted. This does *not* mean that the oxygen content drops instanta-neously. But the *potential* for oxygen depletion exists wherever there is sewage. The measure of this potential is the BOD, which rises as soon as the sewage goes in. Figure 20–4 shows this sudden increase in BOD in a hypothetical river. Now follow the water downstream from "Pollutionville." Three processes are going on, all at the same time:

- *Process 1.* The bacteria are feasting on the sewage. Because of this action, the amount of sewage in the water is decreasing, so the BOD is going down.
- *Process 2.* As the bacteria consume the sewage, they also use dissolved oxygen, so that component, too, starts to decrease.
- *Process 3.* Some of the lost oxygen is being replenished from the atmosphere and from photosynthesis by the vegetation in the stream.

For the first 50 km or so downstream, as shown in Figure 20–4, the natural ability of the river to recover its oxygen (Process 3) simply cannot keep up with the feasting bacteria (Process 2), so the dissolved oxygen concentration goes down. The fish begin to die (Fig. 20–5), but it is not the sewage that is killing them. (In fact, the sewage provides food.) Instead, the fish die from lack of oxygen, beginning when the dissolved oxygen con-

Figure 20–4
River pollution from hypothetical cities.

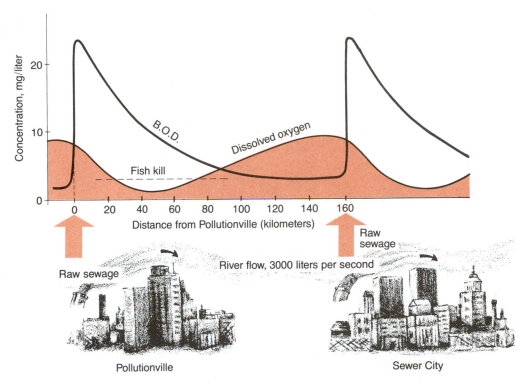

Box 20.3
Measurement of Biochemical Oxygen Demand (BOD)

The rate of biochemical oxidation depends on three factors: (1) temperature, (2) the particular kinds of microorganisms, and (3) the amount and kinds of nutrients present. If the first two factors are controlled, the rate of oxidation depends only on the nutrient content. After 5 days, under typical conditions, almost all the nutrient is gone and almost all the oxygen that is going to be used has been used. This length of time is considered to be a good compromise between completion of the oxidation and not having to wait forever. Therefore, a standard test is carried out by saturating a sample of the polluted water with oxygen at 20°C and determining how much oxygen has been used up after 5 days. The amount of oxygen thus consumed per liter of contaminated water is a practical measure of BOD.

Figure 20–5
A fish kill caused by water pollution.

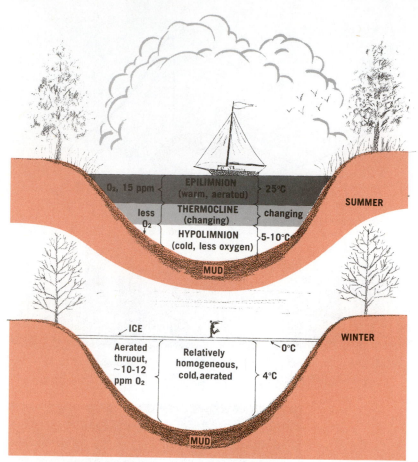

Figure 20–6
Thermal stratification in a small, temperate lake.

centration falls below about 4 mg/liter, depending on the particular species.

Figure 20–4 shows that the fish kills start about 25 km downstream from the introduction of the raw sewage. In time, as the sewage is used up by bacteria, the BOD goes down (Process 1), the consumption of oxygen also slows down, and the natural ability of the river to recover (Process 3) becomes predominant. The river then begins to repurify itself. About 75 km downstream, the fish begin to survive again, and at about 140 km, the oxygen content has increased to its former, unpolluted level.

Of course, if additional sewage is discharged before recovery is complete, as shown in the illustration at 160 km, the river becomes polluted again. When sources of pollution are closely spaced, pollution becomes practically continuous. Rivers in such a condition, which unfortunately can be found near densely populated areas all over the world, support no fish, are high in bacterial content

(usually including pathogenic organisms), appear muddily blue-green from choking algae, and, in extreme cases, stink from putrefaction and fermentation.

Lakes

Water flows more slowly in lakes than in rivers, and, therefore, the residence time of water is much longer in a lake. Figure 20–6 shows typical conditions in winter and summer in a small lake in a temperate climate, such as New England. In the summer, the upper waters, called the **epilimnion** (the "surface lake"), are warmed by the sun. These warmer waters, being less dense than the colder waters below, remain on top and maintain their own circulation and oxygen-rich conditions. The lower lake waters (the **hypolimnion**) are cold and relatively airless. Between the two lies a transition layer, the **thermocline,** in which both temperature and oxygen content fall off rapidly with depth. As winter comes on, the surface layers cool and become denser. When they become as dense as the lower layers, the entire lake water circulates as a unit and becomes oxygenated. This enrichment is, in fact, enhanced by the greater solubility of oxygen in colder waters. Furthermore, the reduced metabolic rates of all organisms at lower temperatures result in a lesser demand for oxygen. When the lake freezes, then, the waters below support the aquatic life throughout the winter.

With the spring warmth, the ice melts, the surface water becomes denser,* and again the lake "turns over," replenishing its oxygen supply.

Now, what are the effects of oxygen-demanding pollutants on these processes? During the summer, increased supplies of organic matter serve as nutrients in the oxygenated upper waters. If the demand is not too great, this oxygen can be replaced as needed by physical contact with the air and from photosynthesis by algae and other water plants. But some organic debris rains down to the lower depths, which are reached neither by air nor by sunlight. Therefore, in an organically rich or eutrophic lake, the bottom suffers first. Fish that live best at low temperatures are therefore the first to disappear from lakes as the cold depths they seek become depleted of oxygen by the increased inflow of nutrients. These fish are frequently the ones most attractive to human diets, such as trout, bass, and sturgeon.

Soap and Detergents

Soap was produced in ancient times by heating animal fat with wood ashes. Soap is biodegradable but does not contain nitrogen or phosphorus. The mineral matter in most groundwater (calcium, magnesium, and iron) makes soap insoluble, leaving a "ring around the collar," or around the bathtub. Such water is said to be "hard." Water with little or no mineral content is said to be "soft."

Starting in the 1940s, the chemical industry developed and marketed a series of synthetic substitutes for soap called **synthetic detergents,** which could be used in hard water. Other ingredients, such as brighteners, fabric softeners, and bleaching agents were also added. These new de-

*Water reaches its maximum density at 4°C, so any approach to this temperature, from above or below, is accompanied by an increasing density.

tergents, however, contained phosphates. Because they are not effectively removed by municipal sewage treatment facilities, phosphates contribute to the cultural eutrophication of the lakes and streams that receive them. In recognition of this problem, several states and cities in the United States have banned or limited phosphates in detergents.

How, then, can people wash their clothing and dishes and yet minimize the effects on the aqueous environment? One possibility is to return to soap if soft water is available. Unpolluted rainwater is indeed soft, but not many households are supplied with rainbarrels. Commercial water softening systems are available. If hard water must be used, a combination of soap and washing soda (also called sal soda), in a ratio of about 5 to 1, is effective. Another possibility is simply to use less detergent. Manufacturers often recommend quantities appropriate (or even excessive) for extreme conditions. Frequently half of the recommended amount of detergent gives very good cleaning action, and as little as one eighth results in fairly good cleaning. As far as personal health is concerned, soap sanitizes clothes very effectively. Therefore, the use of bleaches makes clothes whiter but not more sanitary. As far as "brightening" effects are concerned, you must decide for yourself how important it is to have "dazzling" underwear.

20.4
Industrial Wastes in Water

Several years ago we (J.T. and A.T.) inspected a factory that recovered felt from old fur scraps. The company purchased smelly scraps of animal hides and then boiled them down in a huge vat of dilute sulfuric acid. The acid separated the valuable fur fibers from the bits of skin and flesh. The fur was then collected and used to manufacture felt products such as hats or the insoles of winter boots. The hot sulfuric acid solution of decomposed skin and animal fat was then dumped directly into the river. This small company was eventually forced out of business by pollution control laws and a changing economy. But the pollution of waterways continues to this day. Large quantities of water pollutants are currently released into streams and rivers from paper production, food processing, chemical manufacturing, steel production, petroleum refining, and other operations (Fig. 20–7).

Figure 20–7
Industrial wastes in water.

Some of these wastes are known to be poisonous. The effects of others are unknown. Some have existed in drinking water since ancient times. Many are quite recent, and new types of wastes continue to appear as new technology develops.

Many large American cities obtain their drinking water from nearby rivers. Rivers are also convenient repositories for the discharge of industrial wastewaters. In the United States and most other developed countries, there are legal requirements for cleanup of such wastes before they leave the factory boundaries. Many factories and chemical plants include elaborate water purification systems as part of their manufacturing operations. However, the purification process is never 100 percent complete, and "purified" industrial wastewater cannot be assumed to be fit to drink. As a result, the major rivers of the industrialized countries, such as the Mississippi, the Rhine, and the Volga, contain small concentrations of thousands of industrial chemicals. Cities and towns along the rivers draw this water and purify it again before it is piped to homes for drinking. This purification process, however, is also incomplete; sometimes the major objective is only to kill microorganisms and to make the water look clear. Trace concentrations of heavy metals, pesticides, and industrial organic chemicals, some of them suspected carcinogens, are therefore found in the drinking water of many cities that are located near major rivers.

20.5
Pollution of Groundwater

The accumulation, use, and recharging of groundwater were discussed in Chapter 17. In recent years, the pollution of groundwater in some areas has increased to the point where its quality for drinking is seriously threatened.

All groundwater is derived from rain, snow, or ice that falls to the surface and percolates through the soil or rock. The various additions and subtractions that occur during these transfers determine the final composition of the groundwater. These changes are summarized below:

Additions

1. Rainwater picks up some pollutants from the atmosphere, especially acidic gases, as described in Section 21.6.

2. As surface water percolates into the ground, it dissolves mineral matter out of the soil and rock. If the water is acidic, it is a better solvent for most mineral matter. Therefore, all groundwater contains some dissolved inorganic salts. In rare instances, such dissolved matter may be toxic, as, for example, when the water seeps through areas containing lead or arsenic minerals. Some groundwaters contain natural concentrations of fluorides, which reduce the incidence of dental cavities in children but which, in larger concentrations, mottle the teeth.

3. Mine tailings can be very troublesome, because their leachates* generally introduce more toxic minerals into groundwater than come from ordinary soil or rock. Recall the history of contamination at Clark Fork River described in Section 18.6.

4. Sewage from septic tanks, cesspools, and uncontrolled outflows, as well as leachates from domestic solid wastes, may contaminate groundwater. Viruses, which can multiply in sewage and in landfills, are very difficult to remove from water. Viruses pass through ordinary filters and are resistant to chlorination. Seepage from improperly designed

---

*To **leach** is to cause a liquid, usually water, to percolate through some material and remove its soluble components. Thus, water that percolates through mine tailings leaches out the soluble mineral matter. The **leachate** is the liquid that has leached through the material. The word is commonly used in discussions of water pollution.

landfills (Chapter 22) therefore imposes a danger of groundwater contamination by viruses.

5. Wastewater is often stored in a basin, pit, pond, lagoon, or other such facility. The purpose of such storage is to hold the wastewater prior to treatment or simply to allow oxidation by air to decontaminate it. There are probably between 100,000 and 150,000 such sites in the United States. About 75 percent of them are industrial; the remainder are agricultural and municipal. Many of them are unlined, and the soils beneath them are permeable, so the polluted water can seep down.

6. Bioresistant pesticides, which are sometimes heavily applied (or misapplied) to deal with large infestations of insects, sometimes percolate down to groundwater. Recall the discussion of groundwater contamination by the pesticide Temik in Chapter 19.

7. Liquid chemical wastes are sometimes injected into deep wells below an aquifer. If the wastes are acidic, the pipe may corrode, or, if the pressure is high, the pipe may spring a leak. The wastes may then migrate up into groundwater sources.

Subtractions

1. The soil itself acts as a filter, blocking large particles of pollutants and allowing liquid to pass through. Smaller particles and even molecules of contaminants, although not physically blocked, may adhere to grains of soil and thus be removed.

2. Polluted groundwater may be joined by unpolluted water, so that the pollutant concentrations are reduced (but not thereby eliminated).

3. To the extent that the water pollutants have nutritive value, they can be consumed by organisms in the soil. This mechanism is used in sewage treatment plants, as will be described in Section 20.8.

These subtractions, however, do not adequately counter the effects of major pollutions of groundwaters from sources such as those just summarized. There are two main reasons for this failure:

1. Most groundwater moves quite slowly through its zones (see Table 17–1); a typical rate might be about 30 cm (1 foot) per day. Furthermore, the waters do not mix as much during motion through porous rock as they would, say, in a river (Fig. 20–8). Instead, the flow of water advances more like a column of marchers in a parade, who do not mingle much with each other or with the crowds on either side. Consequently, contaminants introduced into groundwater are diluted only very slowly. Figure 20–8B shows a schematic view of a wastewater pond that leaks into the ground. The contaminated "plume" follows the flow of underground water until it is discharged into a lake or stream. Water taken from above or below this plume (wells A or B) may be uncontaminated, but the unfortunate user of well C will get polluted water.

2. Groundwater does not have the access to air that is available to surface waters. Therefore, the biochemical oxidation that can purify surface waters is less effective and less complete underground, especially so in deep aquifers.

There is no practical technology for cleaning up contaminated groundwater before it is pumped up to the surface. Pollution of groundwater must therefore be prevented.

20.6
Pollution of the Oceans

For many years, people were relatively unconcerned about the pollution of the oceans because the great mass of the sea can dilute a huge volume of foreign matter to the point where it has little effect. This attitude changed in the 1960s and 1970s, as pollutants reached high concentrations in local areas. In addition, the quantity of pollutants dumped into the ocean grew so large that some scientists feared that global effects might become significant. Petroleum has been the major source, but other wastes are also a serious concern.

Oil

Crude oil (petroleum) consists of many thousands of components of widely differing boiling points. It is usually a dark brown, smelly liquid, about as thick as engine oil. It is largely composed of hydrocarbons (compounds of carbon and hydrogen), but there is an appreciable proportion of sulfur compounds, and there are trace concentrations of metals such as vanadium and nickel. Oil finds its way into the oceans from tanker wrecks, drilling operations, "mini-spills," atmospheric deposition, and natural leakages.

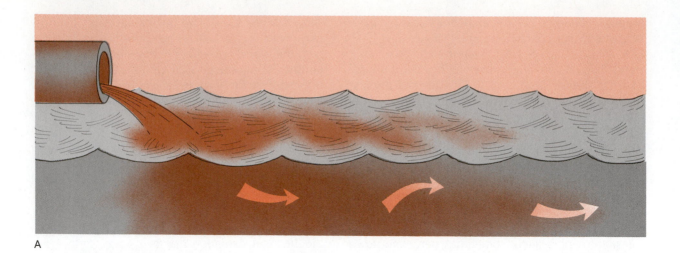

A

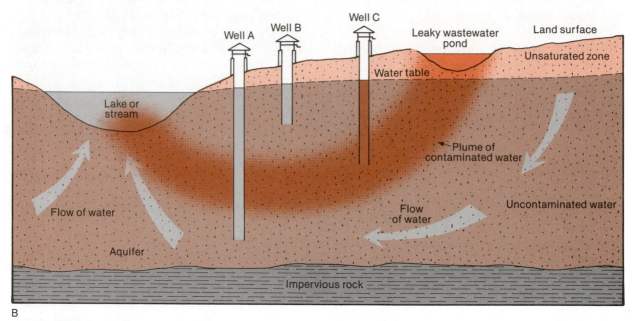

B

Figure 20–8

A, Wastewater is diluted in a turbulent stream. B, Wastewater leaks into the ground from an improperly lined storage basin. The "plume" of contaminated water follows the prevailing groundwater flow but does not mix much with it and is therefore not diluted. Water taken from well A (below the contaminated plume) or from well B (above it) is good, but water from well C is polluted.

An example of a wreck is the accident that occurred in March, 1978, when the oil tanker *Amoco Cadiz* lost her steering off the coast of Brittany in France. High winds blew the ship ashore, and, within the next few days, she broke apart, spilling her entire cargo of 223 thousand tonnes (about 1.6 million barrels) of crude oil onto the beaches and into the water (Fig. 20–9).

The largest spill from drilling started on June 3, 1979, at an offshore oil well owned by Pemex, the national Mexican oil company. Mud, rapidly followed by oil and gas, started to gush through an unsealed drill pipe. The fumes ignited on contact with the pump motors, the drilling tower collapsed, and the spill was out of control. It took 9 months to stop it, by which time 3.1 million barrels

A

B

Figure 20–9

A, Big waves are rolling over the wrecked tanker *Amoco Cadiz* while large amounts of oil are still pouring out. (Wide World Photos) *B*, Location of the wreck.

(440,000 tonnes) of oil—about twice the amount lost by the *Amoco Cadiz*—had been spilled into the Gulf of Mexico.

"Mini-spills" include sludges from automobile crankcases that are dumped into sewers, routine oil-handling losses at seaports, leaks from pipes, and so on. Tanker captains often clean the oily holds of their ships by washing them out with seawater despite the fact that this is strictly illegal in many parts of the world.

Some oil aerosols also settle into the sea from the atmosphere. Finally, undersea sources do release some oil without human help. In fact, the question of how much leakage is natural and how much is caused by undersea drilling is sometimes a matter of dispute about offshore oil pollution.

The fate of all this oil is determined by its physical, chemical, and biological properties. Most hydrocarbons are less dense than water, and, therefore, the major portion of a mixture of hydrocarbons such as crude oil floats. Crude oil also contains some low-boiling compounds that can evaporate in a few days. Hydrocarbons are slightly soluble in water, forming a true solution, and can also become fragmented into colloidal particles, forming a stable emulsion. Some hydrocarbons are dense enough to sink even in seawater, and these materials, together with a portion of the metallic components, settle to the bottom. Oil can also serve as a nutrient for microorganisms (it is a rich energy source) and can be oxidized by atmospheric oxygen with the aid of sunlight. Some of the oxidation products are denser than sea water.

Other Chemical Wastes

There is no known inexpensive and guaranteed safe method of disposing of highly poisonous chemical wastes, such as byproducts from chemical manufacturing, chemical warfare agents, and pesticide residues. It is cheap and therefore tempting to seal such material in a drum and dump it in the sea. But drums rust, and outbound freighters do not always wait to unload until they reach the waters above the sea's depths. As a result, many such drums are found in the fisheries on continental shelves or are even washed ashore. It is estimated that tens of thousands of such drums have been dropped into the sea.

Of course, all rivers carry pollutants to the same sink—the world ocean. The organic nutrients are recycled in the aqueous food web. But the chemical wastes from factories and the seepages from mines are all carried by the streams and rivers of the world into the sea. Many air pollutants, too, such as airborne lead and other metals from automobile exhaust, mercury vapor, and the fine particles of agricultural sprays, ride the winds and fall into the ocean.

How Serious Is the Overall Threat to the World Ocean?

We mentioned at the beginning of this section that the traditional complacency about the condition of the oceans turned to serious concern during the 1960s and 1970s. However, natural systems are sometimes amazingly stable and seem to be barely affected by pollution. In other situations, ecosystems seem to be extremely fragile and are disrupted by small concentrations of pollutants. Scientists are not sure what goes out of adjustment.

Figure 20–10
Cleaning oil-soaked beaches in Northern France after the wreck of the *Amoco Cadiz*. (Wide World Photos)

These concerns, expressed in 1972 at the United Nations Conference on the Human Environment in Stockholm, led to a study released in 1982. The findings of the study were optimistic. The world's oceans actually seemed healthier in 1982 than in 1972. Some of this improvement was a result of environmental laws in the most industrialized countries, which now restrict the production and distribution of many toxic substances such as pesticides and harmful metals. The total quantity of oil spilled into the oceans per year, estimated to be about 6 million tonnes in 1975, was reduced to half that rate by 1985.

In light of these improvements, it is interesting to consider the fate of the oil spilled from the wreck of the *Amoco Cadiz*. The initial effects were severe. Brittany had long been a vacation area, and tourists avoided the area for years after the spill (Fig. 20–10). More than a million sea birds were killed within a few days of the disaster. The oil clogged their feathers and respiratory tracts so that they drowned or died from inhaling the oil. A huge oyster fishery was destroyed. In the decade since the accident, however, the area has recovered. A recent study provides an estimate of the fate of the spilled oil; the results are displayed in Figure 20–11. Since the wave action in Brittany is energetic, removal of onshore oil is expected to continue. Microbial action, too, is helped by the aeration provided by waves. Not all areas are as favorable as Brittany for recovery from oil spills, but, thus far, there has been no case in which oil alone has threatened the survival of a species.

Such encouraging findings may lead to complacency about the health of the ocean. However, it is also possible that the regulations and procedural changes resulting from the alarms of the 1960s and 1970s helped to lessen the threat to the seas. If so, it is important to maintain and strengthen these efforts.

20.7
The Effects of Water Pollution on Human Health

On a worldwide scale, the pollution of water supplies is probably responsible for more human illness than any other environmental influence. The diseases so transmitted are chiefly due to microor-

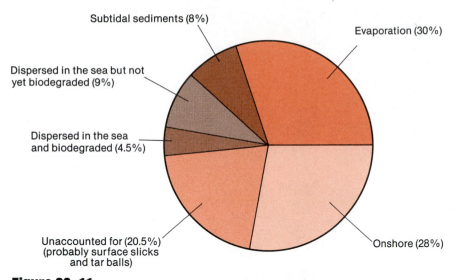

Subtidal sediments (8%)

Dispersed in the sea but not yet biodegraded (9%)

Dispersed in the sea and biodegraded (4.5%)

Evaporation (30%)

Unaccounted for (20.5%) (probably surface slicks and tar balls)

Onshore (28%)

Figure 20–11

Quantitative estimate of fate of oil 1 month after 223,000 tonne spill from *Amoco Cadiz.* (Adapted from *Science, 221*: 128, 1983.)

ganisms and parasites. Two examples will illustrate the dimensions of the problem. Cholera, an illness caused by ingestion of the bacterium *Vibrio cholerae,* is characterized by intense diarrhea, which results rapidly in massive fluid depletion and death in a very large percentage of untreated patients. Its distribution in the past was virtually worldwide. During the twentieth century, however, it has been largely restricted to Asia, particularly the area of the Ganges River in India (Fig. 20–12). During the 9 years from 1898 to 1907, about 370,000 people died from this disease, and thousands of Indians continue to die from it each year.

Most Americans have never heard of schistosomiasis. This is actually a group of diseases caused by infection with one of three related types of worms. (Which worm you get depends on where in the world you live.) Current estimates are that more than 100 million people are infected with schistosomiasis; these cases are distributed throughout the African continent, in parts of Asia, and in areas of Latin America. Estimating the amount of human suffering caused by schistosomiasis is much more difficult than for a disease such as cholera, because, unlike cholera, it is a cause of much chronic as well as acute disease.

In contrast with other waterborne diseases, schistosomiasis is very difficult to control. Its main

mode of transmission is water supplies contaminated with the feces of infected individuals. The infectious agent is a worm, whose eggs must find a certain type of snail to complete its life cycle. Once safely in the snail, the worm develops into a free-living form that leaves the snail and may infect people if ingested in drinking water. Alternatively, it may penetrate human skin on contact and enter the bloodstream. Thus, many people who bathe in contaminated water, or who work barefoot in fields that are irrigated with such water, become infected, even if they have alternative sources of drinking water.

The usual measure of microbiologic purity of a water supply is the so-called coliform count. Coliforms are the class of bacteria present in the intestines of humans and other warm-blooded animals. Therefore, the concentration of coliforms in a water supply is a measure of the amount of fecal contamination, not a direct measure of the disease-causing microorganisms. Water is generally considered safe if it contains fewer than 10 coliforms per liter. Although this method generally serves to safeguard the purity of water, its major pitfall is that some steps in water purification, notably chlorination, may destroy bacteria without killing viruses; hence viral disease may be transmitted by water that satisfies rigid bacteriological standards.

Figure 20–12
In India, wastes are discharged directly into the Ganges and other rivers. People use the same water for washing and cooking. As a result, water-borne diseases are widespread.

As noted earlier, water supplies may become contaminated with a wide variety of chemical substances. Fortunately, there are very few actual accounts of major illnesses resulting from chemically contaminated water in the United States. But the simple fact that acute illness is uncommon does not rule out the possibility of chronic illness, about which there is very little definite information. Over the years, the United States Public Health Service has suggested standards for drinking water in the form of maximal allowable concentrations of various substances, particularly metals and some classes of organic pollutants. Some of these may be acutely toxic; others produce chronic illness.

20.8
Water Purification

Water molecules have no memory; therefore, it is irrelevant to talk about the number of times that the water you drink has been polluted and repurified, as though the molecules gradually wore out. All that is important is how pure the water is when you drink it.

In Section 20.1, impurities in water were classified as suspended, colloidal, or dissolved. Suspended particles are large enough to settle out or to be filtered. Colloidal and dissolved impurities are more difficult to remove. One possibility is somehow to make these small particles join together to become larger ones, which can then be treated as suspended matter. Another possibility is to convert them to a gas that escapes from the water into the atmosphere.

With these principles in mind, consider the procedures used in handling municipal waste waters. The first step is the collection system. Water-borne wastes from sources such as homes, hospitals, and schools contain food residues, human excrement, paper, soap, detergents, dirt, cloth, other miscellaneous debris, and, of course, micro-organisms. This mixture is called **domestic sewage.** Unfortunately, domestic sewage also contains some chemical wastes that do not belong there, such as household paints and solvents, that are illegally flushed into toilets. These waters, which are sometimes joined by wastes from commercial buildings, by industrial wastes, and by the run-off from rain, flow through a network of sewer pipes, as shown in Figure 20–13. The sewer water can

Special Topic A
Legionnaire's Disease

In the summer of 1976, the Pennsylvania Division of the American Legion held its convention in Philadelphia, at the Bellevue-Stratford Hotel. An epidemic of disease broke out among the attendees. The initial symptoms of fever, chills, and chest pains were followed by a type of pneumonia. Similar outbreaks have since occurred in other locations, and examination of old records showed that the same disease had also been noted previously but not identified. About 15 percent of all known cases have been fatal.

The cause was a mystery that took 6 months of intensive, careful study to solve. Finally, an unfamiliar, rod-shaped bacterium, which was named *Legionella pneumophila*, was found to be responsible. The human body is not the natural home of this organism. Therefore, the disease, unlike most pneumonias, is not contagious. Instead, the organism's natural habitat is water. It has been isolated from many lakes and streams, and occasionally from mud. It thrives in warm water, and its concentration can therefore be increased by thermal pollution. As a result, the organism is widely distributed in the aqueous environment.

L. pneumophila is transmitted through the air on water droplets. It enters the human body through the lungs, not through the stomach. The danger therefore comes from contaminated water that is sprayed into the air in fine droplets—from cooling towers, decorative fountains, water-cooled air conditioning systems, and even shower heads. The air conditioning industry has pointed out that transmission of the disease in air conditioning systems can be controlled by rigorous compliance with standard maintenance procedures, which are now followed in only about 50 percent of existing installations.

the following paragraphs. After the water passes through the treatment plant, it, too, is discharged to the river, lake, or ocean.

Primary Treatment

When the sewage reaches the treatment plant (see schematic diagram of Fig. 20–14), it first passes through a series of screens that remove large objects such as rats or grapefruits. The next stage is a series of settling chambers designed to remove first the heavy grit, such as sand that rainwater brings in from road surfaces, and then, more slowly, any other suspended solids—including organic nutrients—that can settle out in an hour or so. Up to this point, the entire process, which is called primary treatment, has been relatively inexpensive but has not accomplished much. If the sewage is now discharged into a stream (as, unfortunately, is sometimes the case), it does not look so bad because it bears no visible solids, but it is still a potent pollutant carrying a heavy load of microorganisms, many of them pathogenic, and considerable quantities of organic nutrients that will demand more oxygen as their decomposition continues.

Secondary Treatment

The organic matter and other impurities remaining after the primary treatment are in solution or in a fine suspension that does not settle and cannot readily be filtered. Any process that involves heat would be prohibitively expensive because of the very large quantities involved. Since the treatment must take place at ambient temperatures, the only practicable choice is some form of accelerated biological action. What is needed for such decomposition is oxygen and organisms and an environment in which both have ready access to the nutrients. One device for accomplishing this objective is the **trickling filter,** shown in Figure 20–15. In this device, long pipes rotate slowly over a bed of stones, distributing the polluted water in continuous sprays. As the water trickles over and around the stones, it offers its nutrients in the presence of air to an abundance of rather unappetizing forms of life. A fast-moving food chain is set in operation. Bacteria consume molecules of protein, fat, and carbohydrates. Protists consume bacteria. Farther

then follow either of two paths: (1) It can be returned to surface waters without purification. This untreated water is called **raw sewage.** (2) It can be piped into a sewage treatment plant, where it is processed in one or more stages, as described in

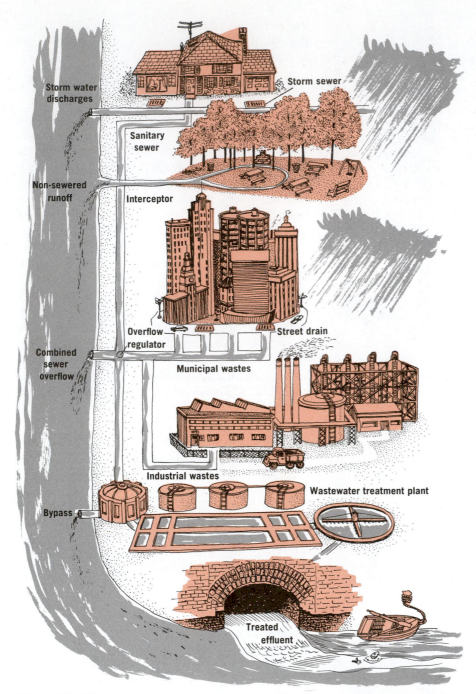

Figure 20–13
Sewer collection system.

up the chain are worms, snails, flies, and spiders. Each form of life plays its part in converting high-energy chemicals to low-energy chemicals. All the oxygen consumed at this stage represents oxygen that will not be needed later when the sewage is discharged to open water. Therefore, this process constitutes a very significant purification.

An alternative technique is the **activated sludge** process, shown schematically in Figure 20–16. Here, the sewage, after primary treatment,

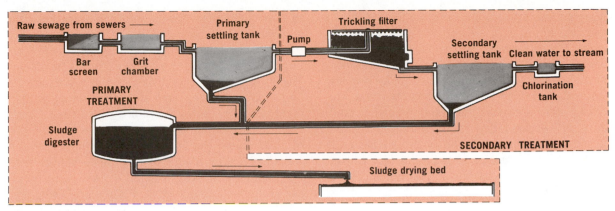

Figure 20–14
Sewage plant schematic, showing facilities for primary and secondary treatment. (From *The Living Water,* U.S. Public Health Service Publication No. 382)

Figure 20–15
A trickling filter with a section removed to show construction details. (From Warren: *Biology and Water Pollution Control.* Philadelphia, W.B. Saunders Co., 1971)

Figure 20–16
Activated sludge process (schematic view).

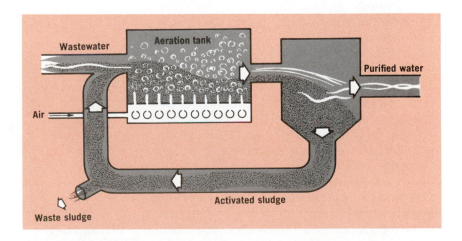

is pumped into an aeration tank, where it is mixed for several hours with air and with bacteria-laden sludge. The biological action is similar to that which occurs in the trickling filter. The sludge bacteria metabolize the organic nutrients; the protists, as secondary consumers, feed on the bacteria. The treated waters then flow to a sedimentation tank, where the bacteria-laden solids settle out and are returned to the aerator. Some of the sludge must be removed to maintain steady-state conditions. The activated sludge process requires less land space than the trickling filters, and, since it exposes less area to the atmosphere, it does not stink so much. Furthermore, since the food chain is largely confined to microorganisms, there are not so many insects flying around. However, the activated sludge process is a bit trickier to operate and can be more easily overwhelmed and lose its effectiveness when faced with a sudden overload.

The effluent from the biological action is still laden with bacteria and is not fit for discharge into open waters, let alone for drinking. Since the microorganisms have done their work, they may now be killed. The final step is therefore a disinfection process, usually chlorination. Chlorine gas, injected into the effluent 15 to 30 minutes before its final discharge, can kill more than 99 percent of the harmful bacteria.

Now let us return to the sludge. Each step in the biological consumption of this waterborne waste, from sewage nutrients to bacteria to protozoa and continuing to consumers of higher orders (such as worms), represents a degradation of energy, a consumption of oxygen, and a reduction in the mass of pollutant matter. Also, and perhaps most important from a practical point of view, the process brings about an increase in the average size of the pollutant particles. Look at Figure 20–1 to see how dramatic this change can be. Sugar is dissolved in water in the form of molecules that never settle out. Partially degraded starch and protein occur as colloidal particles in approximately the same size range as viruses. Bacteria are much larger, growing up to about 10 μm. Protists are gigantic by comparison; some amoeba reach diameters of 500 μm and thus are comparable in size to fine grains of beach sand. Some agglomeration also occurs in the metabolic processes of the protozoa, so that their excreta are usually larger than the particles of food that they ingest. Finally, when the microorganisms die, their bodies stick together

to form aggregates large enough to settle out in a reasonably short period of time. This entire process of making big particles out of little ones is of prime importance in any system of wastewater treatment. The mushy mixture of living and dead organisms and their waste products at the bottom of a treatment tank constitutes the biologically active sludge (Fig. 20–17). Typical sewage contains about 0.6 g of solid matter per liter, or about 0.06 percent by weight, whereas a liter of raw waste sludge contains about 40 to 80 g of solid matter, corresponding to a concentration of 4 to 8 percent. Even after this magnification, however, the raw sludge is still a watery, slimy, malodorous mixture of cellular protoplasm and other offensive residues. The final disposal of the sludge, whether by incineration, landfill (Fig. 20–18), or other means, becomes a problem in the handling of solid wastes (see Chapter 22).

Tertiary or "Advanced" Treatments

Although considerable purification is accomplished by the time that wastewaters have passed through the primary and secondary stages, these treatments are still inadequate to deal with some complex aspects of water pollution. First, many pollutants in domestic sewage are not removed. Inorganic ions, such as nitrates and phosphates, remain in the treated waters. These materials, as we have seen, serve as plant nutrients and are therefore agents of eutrophication. If there is excess chlorine, it may react with industrial wastes such as organic solvents and produce chlorinated prod-

Figure 20–17
Sewage sludge.

Figure 20–18
The Metropolitan Sanitary District of Chicago transporting its sewage and sludge by barge and pipeline (*A*) to a 6000-hectare site in Fulton County, Illinois, where it is spread on agricultural areas that had been left in poor condition by strip-mining (*B*).

ucts that are more objectionable than the original pollutants.

Additionally, many pollutants originating from sources such as factories, mines, agricultural run-offs, and even homes cannot be handled by munic-

ipal sewage treatment plants. Some synthetic organic chemicals from industrial wastes are foreign to natural food webs (that is, they are nonbiodegradable). They not only resist the bacteria of the purification system but may also poison them and thereby nullify the biological oxidation. There are also inorganic pollutants, including acids and metallic salts. The treatment methods available to cope with these troublesome wastes are necessarily specific to the type of pollutant to be removed, and they are generally expensive. Some of these techniques are described in Special Topic B.

20.9
Legal and Economic Strategies in Water Pollution Control

Domestic wastes were once collected in pits called cesspools, from which they were periodically shoveled out and carted away. As cities grew denser, the task became more onerous, and, toward the end of the last century, it became customary to connect series of cesspools with pipes so that they could all be flushed out with water in a single operation. The next obvious step was to eliminate the cesspools and use the piping systems alone with flushing water continuously available. Thus were sewer systems born. According to some environmentalists, this was the point at which sanitary engineers and public health officials took civilization down the wrong road. What we are doing now is diluting our wastes with large amounts of water and then spending billions of dollars to restore the water to a quality that is eventually fit for drinking. The wastefulness of the process is illustrated by the fact that the average toilet flush uses about 20 liters of water to carry away about one quarter of a liter of body wastes and that the average user of a flush toilet flushes it about seven times a day.

In the United States, national goals for pure water are proclaimed in federal legislation. In 1972, Congress passed the Federal Water Pollution Control Act. This legislation was revised several times from 1977 to 1987, and the amended law is now known as the Clean Water Act. The general objective of the legislation is to "restore and maintain the chemical, physical and biological integrity of the nation's waters." To accomplish this goal, the Environmental Protection Agency (EPA) establishes standards for the quality of water that is discharged by industries and provides funds for research. Each

Special Topic B
Some Tertiary Treatments for Water Purification

Coagulation and Sedimentation As mentioned earlier in the discussion of biological treatment, it is advantageous to change little particles into big ones that settle faster. So it is also with inorganic pollutants. Various inorganic colloidal particles are water-loving (hydrophilic) and therefore rather adhesive; in their stickiness, they sweep together many other colloidal particles that would otherwise fail to settle out in a reasonable period of time. This process is called **flocculation.** Lime, alum, and some salts of iron are among these so-called flocculating agents.

Adsorption Adsorption is the process by which molecules of a gas or liquid adhere to the surface of a solid. The process is selective—different kinds of molecules adhere differently to any given solid. To purify water, a solid that has a large surface area and binds preferentially to organic pollutants is needed. The material of choice is activated carbon, which is particularly effective in removing chemi-cals that produce offensive tastes and odors. These include the biologically resistant chlorinated hydrocarbons. (See Chapter 21.)

Other Oxidizing Agents Potassium permanganate, $KMnO_4$, and ozone, O_3, have been used to oxidize waterborne wastes that resist oxidation by air in the presence of microorganisms. Ozone has the important advantage that its only byproduct is oxygen.

$$2O_3 \longrightarrow 3O_2$$

Reverse Osmosis Osmosis is the process by which water passes through a membrane that is impermeable to dissolved ions. In the normal course of osmosis, as illustrated in Figure 20–19A, the system tends toward an equilibrium in which the concentrations on both sides of the membrane are equal. This means that the water flows from the pure side to the concentrated "polluted" side. This is just what we don't want, because it increases the quantity of polluted water. However, if excess pressure is applied on the concentrated side (Fig. 20–19B), the process can be reversed, and the pure water is squeezed through the membrane and thus freed of its dissolved ionic or other soluble pollutants.

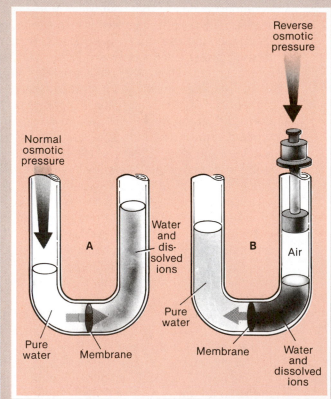

Figure 20–19
Reverse osmosis.

source must disclose the volume of discharged water and the nature and content of its pollutants. The EPA sets limits that must be met to achieve the mandated water quality, but cost and availability of technology are taken into account. Specific limitations may apply to particular toxins such as arsenic, asbestos, benzene, cyanides, pesticides, and heavy metals. The 1987 extension provides for grants of up to $9.6 billion and a revolving loan fund to the states of up to $8.4 billion to finance the construction or upgrading of sewage treatment plants.

In 1974, Congress passed the Safe Drinking Water Act, which was designed to ensure that water supply systems serving the public meet minimum national standards for protection of public health. The Act gave the EPA responsibility for setting minimum national drinking water regulations throughout the United States. Interim regulations in subsequent years set maximum levels permitted for bacteria, cloudiness, and concentrations for a number of organic and inorganic chemicals. The water standards for human health and for satisfactory odor, appearance, and taste required by the Safe Water Drinking Act are more stringent than the "fishable-swimmable" goals of the Clean Water Act. Unfortunately, the quality of some of the drinking waters in the United States has not reached the mandated goals. More effective citizen action may be needed to prod the enforcement agencies.

Box 20.4
First Flush

Think of a popular swimming area at an ocean or lake near the outfall of a wastewater system that combines rainwater with a small amount of domestic sewage. Sometimes the coliform count is low enough so that swimming is judged to be safe; at other times, it is high and swimmers are warned to stay away. One day, there is a heavy storm, and a lot of rainwater comes through the sewer pipes. The next morning is bright and clear but there is still a lot of run-off from the storm. Would this be a good time to assume that the stormwater has diluted the sewage so that the pollution level is down and it is safe to swim? The assumption sounds reasonable, but it is usually incorrect. Instead of a dilution, the mechanical action of the increased water flow scours out a lot of contamination stuck to the bottoms of the pipes, and much of it comes out the next day. So, the day after a cleansing storm is *not* when the water pollution is lowest. It's called "first flush."

Summary

Water can be polluted by impurities that dissolve in it, are suspended in it, live in it, float on it, or enter it as a result of some chemical or biochemical change. Particles that are too small to be filtered out or to settle out but are large enough to make the water look cloudy are called **colloidal particles.** The oxygen dissolved in water can be depleted faster than it is replaced from the atmosphere. Oxygen therefore becomes the limiting factor when organic and inorganic nutrients are plentiful. Under such conditions microorganisms become more numerous while larger organisms, such as fish, decline in population. Excess nutrients thus pollute water. Many bacteria can survive, even when no oxygen is present.

The pollution of a lake by nutrients is **eutrophication.** Phosphorus, which is the usual limiting nutrient in natural lakes, is often introduced from sewage, detergents, or agricultural fertilizers. **Anaerobic** processes yield much less energy than **aerobic** processes and produce foul-smelling pollutants such as hydrogen sulfide. **Biochemical oxygen demand** (BOD) is the measure of water pollution by nutrients.

The BOD of a stream or river increases instantaneously when raw sewage is added to it, but the concentration of dissolved oxygen decreases gradually. As the river continues to flow, it recovers oxygen from the atmosphere and from photosynthesis.

In lakes, the oxygen content and temperature of the various layers— **epilimnion** (surface), **hypolimnion** (lower), and **thermocline** (intermediate)—change with the seasons.

Groundwater can be polluted by contamination from pesticides, mine tailings, viruses, wastewater storage basins, and liquid chemical injection wells. Natural purification of groundwater is very slow because it is not readily diluted and it does not have access to air.

Many water pollutants, such as heavy metals and organic chemicals, come from industrial sources. A major source of pollution in the oceans is petroleum from tankers. The ultimate effect of pollution on aquatic life is uncertain, although the immediate effects can be devastating.

Worldwide water pollution is probably the major environmental cause of human illness. Waterborne diseases are due chiefly to microorganisms and parasites. Reports of chemical poisoning from polluted water are still relatively rare, although the potential may be serious and the possible long-term effects are not well known.

Water purification systems involve three stages. The **primary treatment** consists of mechanical processes such as screening and settling. The **secondary treatment** is a biological process in which

Special Topic C
Careers in Water Quality

Activities related to water quality offer many career opportunities. Two important factors influence the nature of such work. First, the human use of water involves very large quantities; thus, the common unit by which sewage treatment plants are rated is the "mgd," or "millions of gallons per day." Second, the cost of heating or cooling such large quantities is prohibitive, so most operations are carried out at ambient temperatures, which means under conditions that are favorable to the growth of microorganisms. These circumstances lead to two categories of careers. Large quantities are handled by many kinds of large equipment—pumps, electric generators and motors, pipes, filters, blowers, gates, storage tanks, and so on. The technical people in charge of such work have studied sanitary engineering, which is a branch of civil engineering. Other workers include skilled mechanics of all kinds— pipe fitters, electricians, welders, masons, and operators of cranes and other heavy equipment. The

fact that water is a hospitable medium for biological growth means that many careers in the biological and health sciences are relevant, including bacteriology, medicine, biochemistry, and public health.

The analysis and purification of water involves chemistry and chemical engineering. Many sewage treatment plants are equipped or associated with chemical laboratories, and the analyses are carried out by technicians who may have a bachelor's degree in chemistry.

Work in these fields may bring you to the outdoors to take samples from streams and lakes or may keep you in a treatment plant where the air might be rather smelly, but not overwhelmingly so. Workers get used to it, and modern plants have odor control systems. You might also work in a laboratory or at the offices of consulting engineers far from the actual sewage. You will also know that what you do is for the purpose of protecting human health and well-being.

microorganisms, in the presence of an adequate supply of oxygen, consume the organic pollutants. The effluent from this stage is then disinfected, usually by chlorination. The resulting mushy mixture of organisms and waste products, called **sludge,** is disposed of by incineration, landfill, or ocean dumping. **Tertiary,** or **advanced, treatment** may be one of a series of chemical or physical processes, such as adsorption, oxidation, or reverse osmosis, that removes additional pollutants.

Legal requirements for water quality in the United States are mandated by the Clean Water Act (for "fishable-swimmable" waters) and the Safe Water Drinking Act (for human health and pleasant taste, appearance, and odor).

Questions

Water Pollution

1. It was pointed out in Section 20.1 that water can accept and hold foreign matter (i) by dissolving it, (ii) in suspension, (iii) by chemical reaction with water, (iv) as metabolized wastes, (v) in the form of living organisms, (vi) by reaction of an insoluble substance with a contaminant already present in the water, and (vii) by supporting it on the surface of the water. To which of these categories does each of the following water pollutants belong? (a) *Vibrio cholerae,* the bacterium responsible for cholera; (b) very fine particles of clay; (c) kitchen grease dumped into a swimming pool; (d) the products of the same grease after it has been consumed by bacteria; (e) copper sulfate, which exists in water in the form of individual copper ions and sulfate ions; (f) dolomite rock (calcium and magnesium carbonates) that is dissolved by acid rain; (g) caustic solution formed by dropping pure sodium (a very reactive metal) into water.

2. When you are healthy, you live in harmony with bacteria in your digestive system. Why, then, should water that contains digestive bacteria be considered to be polluted?

3. Suppose that a manufacturing plant in your area starts to generate liquid chemical wastes before its wastewater treatment plant, now under construction, is ready for use. Meanwhile, there are three possible ways to handle the wastes: (a) Store them temporarily in a holding basin. (b) Dump them in a local river. (c) Pump them into a deep injection well below the local aquifer level. Describe the conditions, if any, under which you would favor each of these.

4. What are the various ways in which groundwater can become polluted? Which of these can be readily avoided by changes in industrial or agricultural practices?

5. How can polluted groundwater repurify itself? Explain why such purification is slower for groundwaters than for surface waters.

6. What are the major sources of ocean pollution? For each category, discuss the problems involved in preventing the pollution.

7. The contents of our stomachs are acidic, and we drink acidic fruit juices without doing ourselves any harm. Why, then, are acids considered to be pollutants in drinking water?

8. The half-life of carbon-14, which is produced in the atmosphere by cosmic rays, is about 5700 years. As a result, recently produced organic matter has practically its original concentration of carbon-14, whereas "old" organic matter, such as fossil fuels, has practically none. Explain how you could differentiate between sewage and oil pollution in a stream, based on observations of carbon-14 levels.

9. In its article on "Sewerage," the Eleventh Edition of the *Encyclopedia Brittanica,* published in 1910, states, "Nearly every town upon the coast turns its sewage into the sea. That the sea has a purifying effect is obvious. . . . It has been urged by competent authorities that this system is not wasteful, since the organic matter forms the food of lower organisms, which in turn are devoured by fish. Thus the sea is richer, if the land is the poorer, by the adoption of this cleanly method of disposal." Was this statement wrong when it was made? Defend your answer. Comment on its appropriateness today.

Productivity in Aqueous Systems

10. What is eutrophication? Explain how it occurs and why it is hastened by the addition of inorganic matter such as phosphates.

11. In what kinds of areas would you expect to find eutrophic lakes? Where would you go to look for oligotrophic lakes?

12. Imagine that you live in a community of homes on the edge of a small lake. The water is suitable for swimming, but, by midsummer, it looks greenish and there is some growth of weeds. Which one or ones of the following actions would you recommend to slow down or counteract the eutrophication? (a) Restrict the use of septic tanks for homes situated near the lake. (b) Stop all swimming and boating in the lake for a few years. (c) Stop using lawn or garden fertilizer on property adjoining the lake. (d) Do not allow any fishing in the lake for a few years. (e) Treat the lake with a herbicide each spring. (f) Harvest the weeds each summer and dump them in a landfill.

13. Explain how a nontoxic organic substance, such as chicken soup, can be a water pollutant.

14. An apple left exposed on the ground continues to rot until it has no remaining food energy. Yet, when the same apple ferments in a closed container, the resulting mixture of alcohol and other compounds does have calorific value. Why does fermentation stop before all the chemical energy of the apple has been used?

15. You are given a sealed container of pure water: H_2O—nothing else. (a) Could a fish live in it? Would the fish drown? Explain. (b) How could you introduce air into the water rapidly?

16. It has been suggested that the world food shortage could be alleviated if we cultivated algae in sewage and processed the final product in the form of "algae-burgers." (a) Could such production be carried out on a 24-hour basis? Only during the daytime? Only at night? Explain. (b) If the sewage were used as food in a "fish farm," would the product be able to feed more people or fewer people? Explain.

17. Choose the correct answer: Water with a high BOD (a) has a lot of oxygen in it; (b) is deficient in oxygen; (c) has a high content of biodegradable nutrient; (d) has a high content of nonbiodegradable nutrient.

18. The BOD curve of Figure 20–4 shows that the rise and fall occur sharply but not instantaneously. How would the curve look if both the rise and fall did start instantaneously? Which of the following is the more reasonable explanation for the non-instantaneous character of the changes? (1) Some smaller discharges, such as those from individual homes or small farms, occur both before and after the main sewer effluent. (2) The sewage does not react instantaneously with oxygen. Defend your answer.

19. (a) Draw a graph of temperature versus depth of a small lake in winter as follows: Let the horizontal axis be temperature, from $-10°C$ to $+30°C$, and let the vertical axis represent a depth profile, starting with 0 at the top and going down to 10 m at the bottom. Assume the outside temperature is $-10°C$ and the ice is 0.5 m thick. (b) Draw a similar graph representing summer conditions, assuming the outside temperature to be 30°C. Label the different layers of the summer lake.

Health Effects

20. What are the criteria for water considered fit for drinking? Is such water always safe? Is water that does not meet these criteria always harmful? Explain.

Water Purification

21. Imagine that you had a sample of water containing all the impurities listed in Table 20–1 and that you purified it in the following successive stages: (a) Boil it so that dissolved gases are expelled. (b) Distill it so that inorganic compounds are left behind. (c) Filter it through insect screening. (d) Filter it through filter paper that removes suspended but not colloidal particles. List the steps in the increasing order of the energy required. Give examples of substances that would be removed in each step.

22. An alternative method of waste water treatment is the **stabilization** or **oxidation pond,** which is a large shallow basin in which the combined action of sunlight, algae, bacteria, and oxygen purifies the water. It may be said that the stabilization pond trades time, space, esthetics, and flexibility for savings in capital and operating costs. Explain this statement.

23. Biological treatment of waste water reduces the mass of the pollutant. Where does the lost matter go?

24. Distinguish among primary, secondary, and tertiary types of waste water treatment.

25. Is the speed of settling of particles in water directly proportional to their diameters? If the diameter is multiplied by 10, is the settling speed 10 times faster? (Justify your answer with data from Fig. 20–1.) Is a settling pond a good general method of water pollution control? Explain.

Career Opportunities

26. How different would the career opportunities be if water (a) were inhospitable to the survival of microorganisms; (b) had such a low heat of vaporization that it could be vaporized inexpensively by solar energy?

Suggested Readings

The following two companion books are standard engineering texts on water pollution and its control:

Metcalf & Eddy, Inc. (George Tchobanoglous, editor): *Wastewater Engineering: Treatment, Disposal, Reuse.* New York, McGraw-Hill, 1979, 890 pp., and *Wastewater Engineering: Collection and Pumping of Wastewater.* New York, McGraw-Hill, 1981, 432 pp.

An older but less technical book is:

Charles E. Warren: *Biology and Water Pollution Control.* Philadelphia, W.B. Saunders Co., 1971. 434 pp.

The biological aspects of water treatment are described in the following texts:

Larry D. Benefield and Clifford W. Randall: *Biological Process Design for Wastewater Treatment.* Englewood Cliffs, NJ, Prentice-Hall, 1980. 526 pp.
Anthony F. Gaudy, Jr. and Elizabeth T. Gaudy: *Microbiology for Environmental Scientists and Engineers.* New York, McGraw-Hill, 1980. 736 pp.

For discussions of groundwater quality, refer to:

National Research Council: *Groundwater Quality Protection.* Washington, D.C., National Academy Press, 1986. 328 pp.
James J. Geraghty: Techniques for protecting groundwater quality. *American Water Works Association Journal, 49*(5), 1984.
C. H. Ward, W. Giger, and P. L. McCarty: *Ground Water Quality.* Somerset, NJ, John Wiley & Sons, 1985. 500 pp.
Larry W. Canter: *Ground Water Pollution Control.* Chelsea, MI, Lewis Publishers, 1985. 29 pp.
Veronica I. Pye, Ruth Patrick, and John R. Quarles: *Groundwater Contamination in the United States.* Philadelphia, University of Pennsylvania Press, 1983. 352 pp.

Two more advanced books on water chemistry are:

Samuel D. Faust and Osman M. Aly: *Chemistry of Natural Waters.* Woburn, MA, Butterworths, Inc., 1981. 400 pp.
David Jenkins: *Water Chemistry.* New York, John Wiley & Sons, 1980. 463 pp.

Health aspects are the subject of a multivolume series:

National Research Council: *Drinking Water and Health.* Washington, D.C., 1977-1986, National Academy Press, Volumes 1 through 6.

The Amoco Cadiz *wreck is described in:*

Rudolph Chelminski: *Amoco Cadiz: The Shipwreck That Had to Happen.* New York, William Morrow, 1987. 254 pp.

The following two books deal with drinking water. The first tells some pollution horror stories and offers practical information; the second is more technical:

Jonathan King: *Troubled Water. The Poisoning of America's Drinking Water—How Government and Industry Allowed it to Happen, and What You Can Do to Insure a Safe Supply in the Home.* Emmaus, PA, Rodale Press, 1985. 256 pp.
Rip G. Rice: *Safe Drinking Water. The Impact of Chemicals on a Limited Resource.* Chelsea, MI, Lewis Publishers, 1985. 283 pp.

21

Air Pollution

Most of us have had direct and personal experiences with air pollution. Perhaps you were standing behind the smoky exhaust of a car, bus, or truck. Or maybe you were driving from the hilly countryside down into a city and suddenly felt a slight irritation in your eyes or throat as you entered the yellow-brown haze that hung close to the ground. You might have been in an airplane, or on a hilltop, or even on a tall building looking down on that haze and wondering how hazardous it was to the health of the people who lived and worked in it. The city might have been any of a number of commercial-industrial centers. It might have been Denver, Tokyo, Los Angeles, Milan, or Mexico City.

Air pollution is not confined to cities, nor is it produced only by human activity. Volcanic eruptions, naturally occurring forest fires, and dusts stirred up by storm winds can also contaminate the atmosphere.

In this chapter, we discuss the sources of air pollution, its effects, methods for controlling it, and legislative approaches.

21.1
The Atmosphere

The Earth's atmosphere is a mixture of gases, water vapor, and a variety of solid particles and liquid droplets. In some respects, air differs from place to place around the globe. The air in a tropical rainforest is hot and steamy. People travel to the seaside to enjoy the "salt air." Visitors to the Smokey Mountains in Tennessee view the bluish hazy air. On a cold night in the Arctic, the air feels particularly dry and "pure." Dry, filtered air is roughly 78 percent nitrogen, 21 percent oxygen, and 1 percent other gases (Fig. 21–1). A more detailed breakdown is given in Table 21–1. Most samples of natural air also contain some water vapor. In a hot, steamy jungle, air may contain 5 percent water vapor, whereas in a dry desert or a cold polar region, there may be almost none at all.

If you sit in a house on a sunny day, you may see a sunbeam passing through the window. The visible beam is light reflected from tiny specks of dust suspended in air. There are many sources of airborne particles (Fig. 21–2). Sand, dirt, pollen, bits of cloth, hair, and skin are all suspended in air. There are also living particles, such as bacteria and viruses. All these materials are natural components of air.

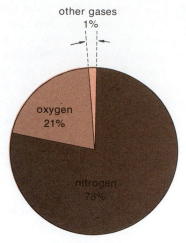

other gases
1%

oxygen
21%

nitrogen
78%

Figure 21–1

Approximate gaseous composition of natural dry air.

Table 21–1 arbitrarily separates natural pollutants from the components of "pure air." However, any significant variation in the compositions shown in the table could also be harmful. For example, air containing, say, 10 percent carbon dioxide would be toxic; therefore, carbon dioxide in high concentrations is a pollutant.

21.2
Sources of Air Pollution

Air pollution from human activity is probably as old as our ability to start a fire. But large-scale air pollution from industry is a relatively recent development. Furthermore, the resulting contaminants, by the nature of the activities that produce them, are likely to be emitted to the air in regions where many people live. Therefore the effects, even if small on a global scale, may be locally very severe. The following paragraphs summarize the major categories of air pollution from human sources.

Table 21–1
Gaseous Composition of Natural Dry Air

	Gas	Concentration (by volume)*	
		ppm	percent
"Pure" air	Nitrogen, N_2	780,900	78.09
	Oxygen, O_2	209,400	20.94
	Inert gases, mostly argon (9300 ppm), with much smaller concentrations of neon (18 ppm), helium (5 ppm), krypton, and xenon (1 ppm each)	9,325	0.93
	Carbon dioxide, CO_2	350	0.03
	Methane, CH_4, a natural part of the carbon cycle of the biosphere; therefore, not a pollutant, although sometimes confused with other hydrocarbons in estimating total pollution	1	
	Hydrogen, H_2	0.5	
Natural pollutants	Oxides of nitrogen, mostly N_2O (0.5 ppm) and NO_2 (0.02 ppm), both produced by solar radiation and by lightning	0.52	
	Carbon monoxide, CO, from oxidation of methane and other natural sources	0.3	
	Ozone, O_3, produced by solar radiation and by lightning	0.02	

*See Appendix A for expressions of concentration. Concentration of gases "by volume" is the same as concentration by number of molecules. Thus, a concentration of nitrogen of 78 percent by volume means that there are 78 molecules of nitrogen in every 100 molecules of air. The initials ppm mean "parts per million." To change percent to ppm, multiply by 10,000.

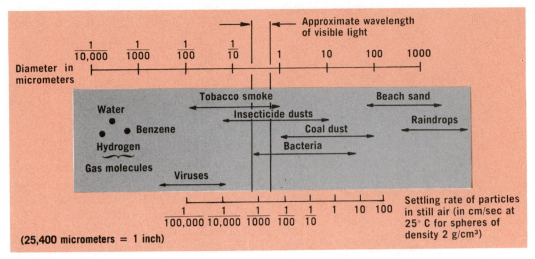

Figure 21-2

Small particles in air. Note that the size scale, shown in micrometers (μm), is not linear but progresses by factors of 10. The largest diameter shown, 1000 μm, is equal to 1 mm; it is the size of large grains of sand or small raindrops. The lower scale tells how rapidly or slowly particles settle in still air. Very small particles can be kept aloft indefinitely by wind currents. The smallest particles are not removed from air by gravitational settling. Usually, these small particles have or acquire some electrical charge, and the consequent electrostatic forces are much greater than gravitational forces. As a result, the particles are attracted to surfaces with an opposite charge or to other particles and stick to them.

Table 21-2
Vocabulary of Particles

Term	Meaning	Examples
Aerosol	General term for particles suspended in air	
Mist	Aerosol consisting of liquid droplets	Sulfuric acid mist
Dust	Aerosol consisting of solid particles that are blown into the air or are produced from larger particles by grinding them down	A dust storm; dust from the grinding of grain or metal and so on
Smoke	Aerosol consisting of solid particles or a mixture of solid and liquid particles produced by chemical reactions such as fires	Cigarette smoke, smoke from burning garbage
Fume	Generally means the same as smoke, but often applies specifically to aerosols produced by condensation of hot vapors, especially of metals	Zinc fumes, lead fumes, smelter fumes
Plume	The geometrical shape or form of the smoke coming out of a chimney	
Fog	Aerosol consisting of water droplets	
Haze	Any aerosol, other than fog, that obscures the view through the atmosphere	Summer haze around a large pine forest
Smog	Popular term originating in England to describe a mixture of smoke and fog. Now usually implies photochemical air pollution.	

Box 21.1
Gases and Smokes

The properties of gases and smokes arise in large measure from the sizes of the particles that comprise them. Gases consist of molecules in constant motion, moving in straight lines between collisions with each other and with the walls of any container. The molecules are so small, so speedy, and so numerous, and their collisions are so frequent, that nothing in our experience (not even, say, a swarm of gnats) can be called upon to help us visualize them in a quantitative way. Most of the space in a volume of gas is empty. At ordinary pressures, the molecules themselves occupy less than one percent of the total volume. Thus "1 liter of gas" consists of many molecules darting about in almost 1 liter of empty space.

Smokes consist of particles. A particle is a very small portion of matter; therefore, a molecule is a particle, and so is an atom or even an electron. But, in air pollution usage, the word "particle" has come to have a more restricted meaning; it refers to portions of matter that, although small, are much larger than molecules, large enough, in fact, to settle out, or at least to reflect or scatter a beam of light that shines on them. (Hence smoke is visible.) Grains of sand are particles, and so are droplets of mist and tiny organisms such as bacteria. Figure 21–2 shows their relative sizes.

Matter consisting of particles is called "particulate matter." This term is often shortened to "particulates," which means, simply, "particles." Just as Eskimos have many words for different kinds of snow, so air pollution engineers have many words for different kinds of airborne particles. All the common words are listed in Table 21–2.

bons (compounds of hydrogen and carbon), which, when they burn completely, form CO_2 and water. However, fossil fuels contain other chemicals, and incomplete combustion yields other products. Coal is always mixed with some of the uncombustible mineral matter of the Earth's crust; when the coal burns, some of this mineral ash flies out the chimney. The smoke that it produces is called **fly ash** (Fig. 21–3).

Sulfur is an essential element of life, and, since coal and oil are derived from living organisms, these fuels always contain some sulfur. When the fuels burn, so does the sulfur, producing a mixture of oxides, mainly **sulfur dioxide,** SO_2, and **sulfur trioxide,** SO_3. High SO_2 concentrations have been associated with major air pollution disasters of the type that have occurred in large cities, such as London, and that were responsible for numerous deaths.

Nitrogen, like sulfur, is common to living tissue and therefore is found in all fossil fuels. This nitrogen, together with a small amount of atmospheric nitrogen, also oxidizes when coal or oil is burned. The products are mostly **nitrogen oxide,** NO, and **nitrogen dioxide,** NO_2. Chemists frequently group NO and NO_2 together under the general formula NO_x. NO_2 is a reddish-brown gas whose pungent odor can be detected at concentrations above about 0.1 ppm, and it therefore contributes to the "browning" and the smell of some polluted urban atmospheres.

Finally, even if no other elements are present, carbon and hydrocarbons produce pollutants, because they usually burn incompletely. Some of these pollutants are gaseous, others are particulate. One such gas is **carbon monoxide,** CO, which is colorless, odorless, and nonirritating, yet very toxic. Particles that consist mostly of carbon are called, collectively, **soot,** which is known to be carcinogenic (see Chapter 18).

Mobile Combustion Sources

With the demise of the steam locomotive, the prime sources of energy for mobile engines are gasoline, diesel fuel, and jet fuel. Because all these fuels are hydrocarbons, the pollutants released when they are burned have features in common with those from stationary combustion sources, but there are important differences. First, these fuels do not have the mineral content of coal; therefore,

Stationary Combustion Sources

Since the Industrial Revolution, the major fuels in the developed areas of the world have been coal and petroleum. Coal is largely carbon, which, when it burns completely, produces **carbon dioxide,** CO_2. Petroleum consists largely of hydrocar-

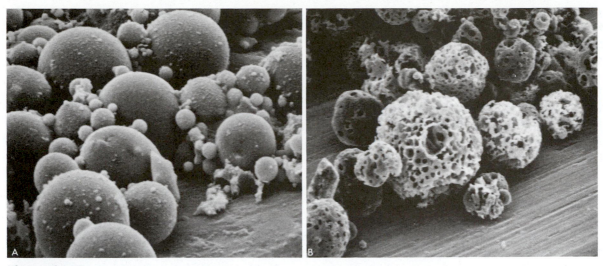

Figure 21-3
Particulate matter sampled from the effluent of (*A*) coal-fired and (*B*) oil-fired power plants. (Illustrations obtained with scanning electron microscope, courtesy of Atmospheric Sciences Research Center of the State University of New York at Albany)

trucks, automobiles, and airplanes are not a significant source of fly ash. Second, fuels used in mobile engines are generally more highly refined than those in stationary engines, and therefore contain and release fewer pollutants. However, they do produce gases, smoke, and smog (see Fig. 21–4 and the Case History of Section 21.7).

Manufacturing Sources

Many thousands of products are manufactured for industry, for commerce, and for domestic use. Some of the manufacturing processes produce unwanted particulate matter or gases that can escape into the atmosphere. Following are three important classes of air polluting processes:

Any Process that Uses Air   Air is used in industry as an oxidizing agent (to support combustion), as a coolant, and as a carrier. The use of air as an oxidizing agent invariably produces some unwanted impurities that find their way into the atmosphere. When air is used as a cooling agent (as in wet cooling towers), any pollutants that can evaporate into the air stream are carried out into the atmosphere. Air is also widely used as a "carrier" gas, especially in drying operations in which

Figure 21–4
Automobile pollution along a freeway in Denver, Colorado. (Photo by Mel Schieltz; courtesy of *Rocky Mountain News*)

hot air carries away moisture or solvents. Air is also used to blow dust particles, as in sand blasting. The air always takes some of the contaminants along with it to the outside atmosphere.

Any Process that Uses High Temperatures Heat promotes evaporation, which produces gases. Metals, too, can evaporate. For example, lead evaporates rapidly at the temperature of an ordinary gas flame. The resulting lead vapor cools in air to produce the aerosol known as a lead fume. Heat also makes compounds break down, or decompose. The decomposition products may be gaseous or particulate matter that escapes into the atmosphere. When air is heated to a high temperature, as in flames, some of its nitrogen and oxygen combine chemically to produce oxides, mostly NO and NO_2, which are pollutants.

Any Mechanical Process that Breaks Down Materials This category includes operations such as blasting, drilling, crushing, or grinding. These mechanical processes are carried out extensively in industries such as mining, agriculture, construction, and metallurgy. In fact, the manufacturing or handling of any product that consists of small particles, such as sand, cement, soil, fertilizer, or flour, can give rise to particulate air pollution.

21.3
The Meteorology of Air Pollution

To assess the extent to which your health is affected by, say, sulfur dioxide, you must be concerned with the quantity or concentration that you inhale. The total quantity of SO_2 in the Earth's atmosphere, or the concentration in the exhaust of some particular copper smelter, does not affect you directly because you do not breathe all the world's air, nor do you stick your head in the smokestack. Therefore, you must consider how pollutants are transported in the atmosphere and how atmospheric conditions affect their concentrations. The

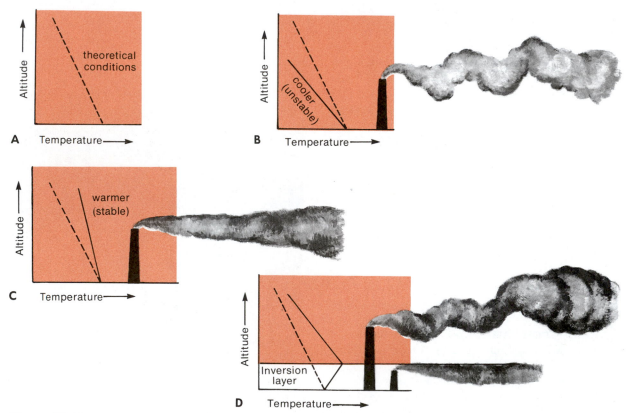

Figure 21–5
Air temperature versus altitude. *A*, Theoretical condition when gains and losses of energy are in balance. *B*, Actual temperatures (*solid line*) are cooler than theoretical conditions. *C*, Actual temperatures (*solid line*) are warmer than theoretical conditions. *D*, Atmospheric inversion layer.

science that deals with atmospheric phenomena is **meteorology.**

If you were to ascend vertically from the Earth in a balloon, under average meteorological conditions, you would find that the air temperature drops steadily with altitude. This cooling, which is shown in Figure 21–5*A*, occurs because the atmospheric pressure decreases with increasing altitude, and gases cool as they expand. Thus, mountaintops are generally colder than valley floors.

Atmospheric conditions do not always conform to this theoretical model. At any particular time, for example, the actual temperature at some elevation above ground level may be cooler than the equilibrium conditions. This situation is unstable, because cool air, being denser than warm air, tends to fall. The result is an unstable, turbulent atmosphere with gusty winds blowing this way and that. If polluted air from a chimney enters such an atmosphere, it mixes well with the turbulent air, and this mixing helps to dilute the pollutants. The resulting smoke pattern would resemble that shown in Figure 21–5*B*.

Now consider the situation in which the air at some given altitude is *warmer* than the equilibrium conditions (Fig. 21–5*C*). Such a warm layer rests in a stable pattern over the cooler, denser air beneath it. This condition is called an **atmospheric inversion** (Fig. 21–6). Such a situation may start to de-

Figure 21–6

A, Three views of downtown Los Angeles. *Top*: A clear day. *Middle*: Pollution trapped beneath an inversion layer at 75 m. *Bottom*: Pollution distribution under an inversion layer at 450 m. (Photos from Los Angeles Air Pollution Control District) *B*, Photograph showing a fog layer held low by an atmospheric inversion; the fog obscures the stacks from a paper mill in Missoula, Montana, whose effluents pierce the inversion layer and are visible as the rising smoke plumes.

Figure 21–7
World's tallest chimney. Built in Ontario, Canada, at a cost of $5.5 million, this chimney stands 380 m high. (Photo courtesy of M.W. Kellogg Company, division of Pullman, Inc.)

velop an hour or two before sunset after a sunny day, when the ground starts to lose heat and the air near the ground also begins to cool rapidly. This inverted condition often continues through the cool night and reaches its maximum intensity and height just before sunrise. When the morning sun warms the ground, the air near the ground also warms up, and it rises. Within an hour or two, the inversion may be broken up by turbulent mixing. Sometimes, however, atmospheric stagnation allows the inversion to persist for several days. Imagine that such an inversion layer existed between the ground and, say, 200 meters but not at higher altitudes (Fig. 21–5D). Even if the lower air were turbulently stirred by warm currents, the total volume available for mixing would be limited by the 200-m ceiling, and any pollutants discharged at lower levels would concentrate beneath the ceiling. The longer the inversion lasted, the greater the

buildup. However, a chimney tall enough to penetrate the 200-m barrier would discharge its effluents into the upper atmospheric layers where they would be diluted in a much larger volume.

The world's tallest chimney (as of 1988), built for the Copper Cliff smelter in the Sudbury District of Ontario, Canada, is as tall as the Empire State Building. It is illustrated in Figure 21–7, together with three smaller chimneys. Such heroic structures can be quite effective in reducing ground-level concentrations of pollutants. For example, during a 10-year period studied by the Central Electric Generating Board in Great Britain, the SO_2 emissions from power stations increased by 35 percent, but, because of the construction of tall stacks, the ground-level concentrations decreased by as much as 30 percent. However, tall chimneys do not collect or destroy anything; therefore, they do not reduce the total quantity of pollutants in the Earth's atmosphere.

Atmospheric inversions have been associated with air pollution disasters that have caused human injury and death. In all such cases, the inversion layer traps the pollutants into a limited volume of air, where their concentrations can build up to harmful levels.

21.4
Effects of Air Pollution on Global Temperatures

The possibility that the Earth's temperature may be drifting away from its previous range of conditions is alarming. A warming trend may cause a melting of glaciers and a flooding of the populous coastal plains. A cooling can mean the beginning of a new ice age.

The major factor that determines global temperature is solar radiation. Figure 21–8 shows what happens to the solar radiation that the Earth receives. Only 21 percent of it strikes the surface of the Earth directly. The other 79 percent is intercepted by the atmosphere—the clouds, gases, and aerosol particles. Some of this intercepted radiation is reflected back to space, some is absorbed as heat, and some is rescattered down to Earth. On a global average, about half the heat energy received from the Sun reaches the surface of the Earth. Some of this heat is reflected back into the atmosphere, while some is absorbed, thereby warming the Earth. Heat energy is then carried

Figure 21–8
Energy balance of the Earth. The sets of numbers in the dashed areas total 100 percent.

back into the atmosphere by several processes, including evaporation and recondensation of water, conduction, and reradiation. The warm atmosphere radiates some heat back to Earth and some to outer space. Thus, a complex set of interactions occurs, in which radiation bounces back and forth between the surface and the atmosphere until it is ultimately lost to space.

Dust in the Atmosphere

Particulate matter can absorb as well as reflect solar radiation. In the stratosphere,* both actions produce a screening effect that interrupts solar radiation and cools the Earth's surface. So far, major volcanic eruptions far outstrip human activities in producing stratospheric dust. The most spectacular eruption in modern times was that of Krakatoa (near Java) in 1883; its dust particles stayed in the

stratosphere for 5 years. Summers seemed to be cooler in the Northern Hemisphere during this period, although the extent of temperature fluctuations makes even this observation somewhat doubtful. More recently, the violent eruptions of Mt. St. Helens in the state of Washington released great quantities of volcanic dust (Fig. 21–9).

Most of the airborne dust generated by human activity is concentrated in the lower atmosphere. The net heat effect of absorption and reflection by industrial and agricultural dusts near the ground is not at all easy to interpret. There is no convincing evidence that pollutant dusts in the lower atmosphere have any important effect on the Earth's temperature. However, the dust that settles to the ground is another matter. Most of us have

---

*The stratosphere is the section of the atmosphere ranging between 15 and 45 km above sea level.

Figure 21–9
The upper portion of Mt. St. Helens, Washington, protruding through the cloud layer during one of its eruptions in 1980. Large quantities of smoke and ash are discharged 15,000 m into the atmosphere. The peak to the right (actually 80 km NE and about 1450 m higher) is Mt. Rainier, a dormant volcano. (Wide World Photos)

seen how snow in the city can become dirty after a few days. If you live in a rural area where snowfall is common, spread a thin layer of ashes on a 1-sq-m section of snow on a warmish sunny winter day in late February or early March. By evening, you will notice that the snow under the ashes has melted faster than the snow nearby. The dark ash absorbs sunlight (lowers the snow's albedo) and causes the snow to melt. If increasingly larger quantities of dust from industry and agriculture were to settle on snow packs over wide areas, a change in global climate might possibly occur.

Absorption of Radiation: The Greenhouse Effect

If there were no atmosphere, the view from the Earth would be much like what the astronauts see from the Moon—a terrain where starkly bright surfaces contrast with deep shadows and a black sky from which the sun glares and the stars shine but do not twinkle. The atmosphere protects us by serving as a light-scattering and heat-mediating blanket. A large portion of the heat emitted from the Earth is reabsorbed by the atmosphere and is, in effect, conserved, with the result that the surface of the Earth is warmer than it otherwise would be.

This warming is called the **greenhouse effect,** by analogy with the ability of a greenhouse to keep its inside warmer than the outside during the daytime. The energy emitted from the Earth is, of course, invisible (the Earth does not shine); it is largely infrared radiation, sometimes called heat rays.

Some molecules in the atmosphere absorb infrared radiation, and others do not. Oxygen and nitrogen, which together constitute almost 99 percent of the total composition of dry air at ground level, do not absorb infrared. On the other hand, molecules of water, carbon dioxide, and ozone do absorb infrared. (The molecules absorb the energy by vibrating, just as a tuning fork absorbs a blow.) In recent years, there has been concern that this absorption is increasing. The concern is centered around the following substances:

Carbon dioxide is particularly significant because its atmospheric concentration is being increased by the accelerated combustion of fossil fuels and by the burning of forests to make way for agricultural and commercial development. It is estimated that the worldwide carbon dioxide concentration has increased from about 280 ppm in 1870 to about 350 ppm in 1988.

Chemicals from bacterial decomposition and fertilizers include the nitrogen-containing gases NH_3 (ammonia), N_2O (nitrous oxide), and NO (nitric oxide). A recent, fairly large-scale addition to this natural atmospheric load of nitrogen compounds comes as a secondary effect of the destruction of tropical rainforests. As was pointed out in Chapter 8, the soil in such forests does not hold many nutrients. It is therefore necessary to make extensive use of nitrogen fertilizers, such as ammonium nitrate, NH_4NO_3. This compound decomposes to produce N_2O.

$$NH_4NO_3 \longrightarrow N_2O + 2H_2O$$

This gas then adds to the other nitrogen oxides produced by stationary and mobile combustion sources.

Exhaust from aircraft, particularly supersonic airplanes, which fly at 18,000 to 20,000 m, can cause stratospheric air pollution. Jet exhaust contains water, CO_2, oxides of nitrogen, and particulate matter. For example, it is estimated that a fleet of 500 supersonic aircraft over a period of years could increase the water content of the stratosphere by 50 to 100 percent, which could result in a rise in average temperature of the surface of the

Earth of perhaps 0.2°C and could cause destruction of some of the stratospheric ozone that protects the Earth from ultraviolet radiation (see discussion of ozone in Section 21.5). On the other hand, the particulate matter would nucleate clouds of ice crystals and would increase stratospheric reflection to some extent. This could lead to a slight cooling of the Earth. One visible effect of such continued high-altitude pollution would be that the skies would gradually become hazier and lose some of their blueness. Because water vapor is predicted to warm the atmosphere and particulate matter may cool it, the net effect of supersonic aircraft is uncertain.

Methane, CH_4, is a normal component of the atmosphere (see Table 21–1), and, like the other gases discussed here, absorbs infrared. Methane is produced by bacterial decomposition of organic matter in oxygen-deficient environments such as swamps. This natural production has been approximately tripled by the methane generated by bacteria in the digestive systems of cattle and in rice paddies—both oxygen-poor environments. Studies of ancient air trapped in polar ice show that atmospheric methane was very constant for thousands of years but began rising around 1600. It is now increasing by about 1 to 2 percent per year (Box 21.2).

The rise in the average global temperature is expected to be somewhere between 1.5 and 4.5°C by the middle of the next century if the CO_2 levels continue their present upward trend. The infrared absorptions by the other gases previously discussed would add to this increase. If the temperature tomorrow were 5° higher than it is today, that would not seem to be a serious problem (unless you were already in the midst of a heat wave!). But, on a global scale, such a change would have profound and possibly catastrophic consequences. In fact, the consequences would begin long before such a large warming were reached. As the average temperature started to rise (some scientists believe that this is happening now), the effect would be far from gradual and not at all uniform. Solar energy accounts for the forces that drive the winds, evaporate surface waters to form clouds that bring rain, and melt the past winter's ice each spring. Slight changes in the distribution of solar energy can shift these processes from one part of the globe to another. A previously productive agricultural area can suffer severe droughts until it no longer pays to

farm there, while the rains fall in locations that were once desert. All the ecological niches could become transformed, and ensuing changes among species of natural plants, agricultural crops, insects, livestock, and microorganisms may not be those that best suit human needs. Since we do not live under a world government, the political consequences of such rearrangements are hardly imaginable. The other major effect of a global warming could be a rise in the sea level. Various measurements indicate that such a rise may have started (Special Topic A). Some long-range planners are beginning to think of gigantic levees to protect coastal cities, and they are visiting Holland to see how the Dutch do it.

21.5
Ozone in the Stratosphere

Ozone, O_3, is very different from oxygen, O_2. Pure ozone is a blue, explosive, poisonous gas. Very few people ever see it, but most have smelled it. The pungent odor from electric sparks, such as from a worn, sparking electric motor, or the slightly pungent odor of the atmosphere after a lightning storm, is the odor of ozone. Small amounts of ozone are produced naturally in the stratosphere by the action of sunlight on oxygen, and the prevailing ozone concentration in the stratosphere from this source is normally about 0.1 ppm.

The chemistry of ozone in the stratosphere attracted considerable public attention after scientists at the University of California at Irvine suggested, in 1974, that some gases newly introduced into the atmosphere threaten the ozone layer. To

Special Topic A
The Effect of Global Temperature on the Sea Level

Since ice melts when it is heated, is it not correct to say that a rise in global temperature will melt polar ice and raise the sea level? Perhaps so, but the mechanism is complex, and the conclusion is not certain. It is true that a large quantity of water is locked up in the form of glaciers and polar ice caps (see Fig. 17–3). Most of this is in Antarctica, which is covered by an ice cap that is about 14 million square km in area and averages more than 2000 m in thickness. Recent reports have speculated that if the global temperature were to rise by even a few degrees, enough of this ice would melt in a relatively short period of time (100 years or so) to raise the sea level 1 to 3 m and flood many coastal regions. But why would the ice melt? The average temperature of much of the Antarctic interior is far below freezing for the entire year. Even in summer, a typical average temperature is −8°C, so a rise in temperature of 2 or 3 degrees would not be enough to reach the melting point, and one might assume that no ice would melt. However, the ice cap is not a static system, but rather a collection of glaciers that flow down off the land toward the sea. When the glacier ice reaches the coast it breaks off and empties in the form of icebergs. In winter the glacial flow is held back by a dam of sea ice, and no icebergs break off. The sea ice differs from the glacier ice in two ways: (1) The sea ice is relatively thin at its outer edges, much thinner than glacier ice. (2) The sea ice, being in contact with the seawater, is much warmer than the glacier ice. If the global temperature warmed slightly, the sea ice barrier could melt and the resistance to the movement of the glaciers would be removed. Large amounts of the interior ice would then flow more rapidly into the sea.

This prediction is reasonable but by no means certain. There could be counterbalancing processes. Most of the interior of Antarctica receives very little precipitation, and these regions are classified as meteorological deserts. If global temperatures were to rise, there could be increased precipitation there, which would have the effect of transferring ocean water to Antarctic snow and ice. This effect could lessen, nullify, or even reverse the rise in sea level caused by the addition of more glacial ice. That result is not viewed as very likely, but global ecosystems are complex, and their actions often surprise us.

What about the expansion of the ocean water as it warms up? This factor, too, is complicated. Imagine a vertical-walled container of water 1 km in depth. If the water warmed from 0°C to 4°C, the level would *fall* 3 cm for every degree. (Water is densest at 4°C.) From 5°C to 10°C, the level would rise 5 cm/°C, and from 10 to 20°C, the rise would be 15 cm/°C. But the ocean basin does not have vertical walls, so its shape would affect the results. Besides, much of the deep ocean is quite cold, so the effect on that water would be small. Furthermore, some of the land in the Northern Hemisphere is still rising as it recovers from the load of the last glaciation, so this factor makes the sea level appear to be falling.

---

understand the nature of the problem, we must consider, first, why the stratospheric ozone is important to the biosphere and, second, how that barrier may be weakened by human activities.

Stratospheric ozone has an important effect on the solar radiation that reaches the Earth. Much of the energy from the sun is transmitted in the form of ultraviolet (UV) radiation. UV radiation is energetic enough to break chemical bonds and cause chemical changes. Infrared radiation is less energetic; it is perceived as heat but does not have ultraviolet's ability to bring about chemical change. Ozone can absorb UV radiation and then emit IR radiation. This change does not violate the Law of Conservation of Energy, nor are such transformations unusual. Think of a fire inside a pot-bellied stove. The radiant energy of the flame is absorbed by the iron, which, in turn, radiates heat out into the room to keep you warm. But the stove is not bright like the flame; its radiation is infrared. In the same way, stratospheric ozone reduces the *energy level* (not the total amount of energy) of the solar radiation that reaches the Earth's surface.

The conversion involves the following steps:

Step 1. Recall that UV radiation is energetic enough to break chemical bonds. In the stratosphere, UV radiation breaks down an ozone molecule, O_3, into ordinary molecular oxygen, O_2, and atomic oxygen, O:

$$O_3 + UV \longrightarrow O_2 + O$$

Step 2. The O_2 and O then recombine, and IR radiation (thermal energy) is released.

$$O_2 + O \longrightarrow O_3 + IR$$

Adding steps 1 and 2 gives:

$$O_3 + UV + O_2 + O \longrightarrow O_2 + O + O_3 + IR$$

Note that all the chemical formulas on the left exactly balance those on the right, so they cancel out. Therefore the net result is:

$$UV \longrightarrow IR$$

In this way, stratospheric ozone provides a chemical pathway for converting some (not all) of the solar ultraviolet radiation into infrared radiation. The ozone itself is regenerated, so there is no net consumption.

> A substance that influences the rate of a chemical transformation but that is not consumed in the process is a *catalyst,*

and therefore ozone is a catalyst in this reaction (Box 21.3).

If this conversion of UV to IR were weakened, more of the solar radiation reaching the Earth's surface would be in the UV wavelengths. The UV content of sunlight can affect human skin in various ways, some good and some bad. The good ways include the attractive tanning of a pale skin and, more important for health, the conversion of ergosterol (a chemical naturally present in skin) to vitamin D. The bad effects may include a painful sunburn and, more seriously, skin cancer. Other organisms, too, plants as well as animals, are affected by UV radiation. The life forms that now exist on Earth have adapted to the present ranges of UV intensities. These intensities, however, differ from place to place and are about seven times greater in the tropics than in the Arctic. People who migrate from high to low latitudes may be damaged by the more intense UV exposure, and it is possible that migrants in the other direction may suffer from a deficiency of UV. These complexities make it difficult to predict accurately what would happen if a depletion of the ozone layer resulted in a general rise of UV intensity on the surface of the Earth. Var-

Box 21.3
Ozone in the Lower Atmosphere

The natural concentration of O_3 in the lower atmosphere is about 0.02 ppm. At one time, you could buy home "air purifiers" that were supposed to make your air fresher by producing ozone. However, ozone is a toxic gas, even though small concentrations of it in air do give a sensation of freshness. Therefore, these devices did not purify the air; they polluted it.

ious reports project increases of 2 to 5 percent in the incidence of skin cancer in humans for every 1 percent decrease in stratospheric ozone concentration. It is difficult to predict the numbers of additional deaths from such increases, because some skin cancers respond to minor surgery, whereas others are much more lethal. If present trends in ozone depletion continue to the end of this century, the annual death rate from skin cancers in the United States may increase by 5000 to 10,000, as a very rough guess. Other possible environmental damages include the retardation of the growth of some food plants, the death of larvae of important seafood organisms such as shrimp and crab, and depletion of microorganisms at the base of the marine food chain.

The thought that human activities might weaken the ozone layer was triggered by findings that chlorofluorocarbons (CFCs)* are widely dispersed in the lower atmosphere. CCl_2F_2 has been used as a coolant in refrigerators since the 1930s, and later as the refrigerant in air conditioners. Its use was welcomed as a nonflammable and nontoxic substitute for the sulfur dioxide or ammonia refrigerants formerly used. CCl_3F has been used as the propellant in aerosol cans and as a foaming agent in the manufacture of polyurethane; here,

*Chlorofluorocarbons are compounds of chlorine, fluorine, and carbon. They are also known as **Freons,** which are Dupont trade names. The two that are environmentally most significant are CCl_2F_2 (dichlorodifluoromethane, also known as Freon-12 or CFC-12) and CCl_3F (trichlorofluoromethane, Freon-11 or CFC-11). Both of these CFCs absorb infrared, and so contribute to the greenhouse effect.

too, its nonflammability is an advantage. The environmental question is, "Where do these compounds go eventually?" The compressors in refrigerators and air conditioners end their lives as scrap; they rust or are destroyed, and their gases enter the atmosphere. The gases in aerosol cans do not wait so long; they are released as they are used. Then what happens? They are not soluble in water, so they are not washed down by rain. They are chemically inert (that's why they don't burn) and do not react with the other components of the lower atmosphere. So they drift around. Eventually, they reach the stratosphere. Here, they encounter more intense solar UV radiation, which is energetic enough to decompose the chlorofluorocarbon molecules. Specifically, the UV radiation breaks the C—Cl bonds, releasing unattached Cl atoms:

$$UV + \underset{\underset{F}{|}}{\overset{\overset{F}{|}}{Cl-C-Cl}} \rightarrow \underset{\underset{F}{|}}{\overset{\overset{F}{|}}{Cl-C-}} + Cl$$

(Fluorine atoms are not released, because the C–F bond is too strong to be broken by the UV radiation.) The chlorine atoms react chemically with ozone and destroy it by converting it to oxygen. What's more, the chlorine atoms are not used up in this conversion, so that one chlorine atom can serve to destroy an indefinite number of ozone molecules. Thus, the chlorine is a catalyst. The mechanism for the catalysis may be written as follows:

$$Cl + O_3 \longrightarrow ClO + O_2$$
$$\underline{ClO + O \longrightarrow Cl + O_2}$$

Net equation: $O_3 + O \longrightarrow 2O_2$

Note that the Cl atoms react but are then regenerated. The net equation shows that ozone reacts with atomic oxygen (which is also formed by the action of UV radiation on O_2) to produce ordinary molecular oxygen, O_2.

How real is the problem? The chemical equations shown above imply that one Cl atom could continue to destroy ozone molecules forever, but those equations do not tell the whole story. The Cl atoms can also be incorporated into less reactive molecules by other chemical changes. It was first estimated that one Cl atom could be responsible for the destruction of tens of thousands of ozone

molecules within a year or so. But we still do not know what quantity of chlorofluorocarbon chemicals will continue to be manufactured and exactly how much of it gets into the stratosphere. Therefore, no one can confidently predict the rate at which the stratospheric ozone will be depleted, the increase in the UV radiation that will reach the surface of the Earth, and the biological effects of the increase.

The attention to CFCs raised the question of whether other chemicals might also contribute to stratospheric ozone depletion. Oxides of nitrogen (mainly NO and NO_2) from high-flying aircraft and nitrous oxide (N_2O) from fertilizers are suspect.

These uncertainties bring up questions of public policy: If it turns out that there is a significant decrease in stratospheric ozone or an increase in solar UV radiation reaching the surface of the Earth, will there be time to take remedial action, or will it then be too late? Environmentalists have taken the position that aerosol sprays containing chlorofluorocarbons should be banned. Manufacturers of the chemicals argued that the ozone depletion process was a hypothesis based on computer models of what would happen in the stratosphere, that there was no real proof of the hypothesis, and that a ban would cause economic hardships to some and inconvenience to many. Therefore, they concluded, the problem should be studied further, and action is unwarranted until the ozone-depletion theory is proved. Think about this argument: Every point is correct or reasonable except the conclusion, which is arguable. But the conclusion is the one on which the issue of public policy hinges. In the years between 1974 and 1985, public concern about the matter waxed and waned. In 1978, the use of CFCs in aerosol cans was banned in the United States, but other uses continued. There were also bans in Canada, Sweden, Norway, and Denmark, but CFCs are still being manufactured elsewhere. Global production dropped by about 20 percent as a result of these curtailments, but then started to rise again, in response to continued demand, to a level of about 650,000 tonnes per year. In 1986, however, it was found that the stratospheric ozone in the Antarctic had become unusually low. It is still not clear whether this ozone "hole" is the beginning of an early global depletion (which would be much earlier than the most pessimistic predictions), or just some aberration that will adjust itself. This sudden and unexpected finding highlights another characteristic of environmental stresses: There is often a large threshold before an effect is apparent. (Recall the concept of threshold from Section 18.2.) For example, your body may tolerate a certain rise of temperature, or increase in acidity, or loss of moisture but then, suddenly, suffer greatly when these stresses pass a certain point. In the same way, an ecosystem may seem to resist increasing stresses without apparent change but then, beyond a given threshold, may be rapidly disrupted. It is for this reason that many environmentalists do not accept the argument that there is no point in preventive action until we begin to see the start of some damage. This position was finally recognized in 1987, when international negotiations, held under the auspices of the United Nations Environmental Program, produced a tentative agreement to freeze production of CFCs at 1986 levels, starting in 1990. Further cuts are projected for the future.

21.6
Acid Rain
Acidity

In recent years, the subject of acid rain (Box 21.4) has received considerable attention. Before we can understand the problem, we must first review the nature of acidity. Acidic solutions in water contain hydrogen ions (protons) attached to water molecules. These ions are represented as H^+ (not showing the water molecule) or, if we include the water molecule, as $H(H_2O)^+$ or H_3O^+. A weak acid is one that releases only a small concentration of hydrogen ions. An example of a weak acid is vitamin C (ascorbic acid); it tastes sour, but you can chew and swallow a tablet of it without harm. Sulfuric acid, H_2SO_4, on the other hand, is a strong acid. When sulfuric acid is dissolved in water, practically all the hydrogen available in the original acid is released as hydrogen ions to the water. A drop of pure sulfuric acid could burn itself into your skin, and even a dilute solution is extremely toxic. Acids can be neutralized by **bases,** which are substances that furnish hydroxide ions, OH^-, to water. In the neutralization reaction, the two ions combine to form water:

$$H^+ + OH^- \rightarrow H_2O$$

The measure of the acidity of a solution in water is its concentration of hydrogen ions. These

Box 21.4
Acid Rain, or What's in a Name

Some writers object to the term "acid rain" as being too limited, because acidic matter can also fall to Earth in the form of solids such as ice, snow, or dust. More inclusive terms are **acid precipitation,** meaning acidic matter that descends from above, or **acid deposition,** meaning acidic matter that is deposited. However, although the word "rain" commonly refers to water, it is also sometimes used in the general sense of any liquid or solid bodies falling in the manner of rain. ("The batteries blazed, Kneading them down with fire and iron rain." Shelley, in *Hellas,* 1821.) For this reason, the expression "acid rain" is generally used in the wider sense of falling acidic matter.

concentrations are expressed as pH values on a scale in which a pH of 7 is neutral. Values below a pH of 7 represent acidic solutions; the lower the pH, the more acidic the solution. Values above 7 represent basic solutions; the higher the pH, the more basic the solution. Table 21–3 shows approximate pH values of some common solutions. For a more complete discussion of acidity and pH, refer to Appendix C.

It is important to recognize that even rain that falls through unpolluted air is slightly acidic. The reason is that water reacts to a slight extent with atmospheric carbon dioxide to produce carbonic acid, a weak acid:

$$CO_2 + H_2O \rightarrow H_2CO_3$$
$$\text{carbonic acid}$$

In addition, a small amount of nitric acid is formed during lightning storms by the oxidation of nitrogen, N_2, in the presence of water:

$$2N_2 + 5O_2 + 2H_2O \rightarrow 4HNO_3$$
$$\text{nitric acid}$$

The combined effects of carbonic acid and nitric acid in unpolluted air account for the fact that the pH of rainwater (or snow) is typically about 5.6 or 5.7.

Table 21–3
Approximate pH Values of Various Substances

pH	Substance
14	←NaOH solution (lye), 4%
13	←Limewater
12	←Household ammonia
	←Washing soda (about 1%)
11	
10	
9	
8	←Bicarbonate of soda (about 1%)
	←Blood
7	←Pure water
	←Cow's milk
6	
	←Unpolluted rainwater
5	←Squash, pumpkin
4	
	←Oranges
3	←Vinegar; soft drinks
2	←Limes
1	←Dilute hydrochloric acid solution, HCl

Basic / Neutral / Acidic

Acidic Episodes

In recent years, however, rain and snow in many parts of the world have become considerably more acidic. Much of this acid precipitation has been between pH 4 and 5, but more severely acidic episodes occur from time to time. For example, a rainstorm in Baltimore in 1981 had a pH of 2.7, which is about as acidic as vinegar, and a fog in southern California in 1986 reached a pH of 1.7, approaching the acidity of some solutions of hydrochloric acid used as toilet bowl cleaners. Most of this excess acidity can be traced to a series of chemical reactions involving air pollutants whose molecules include sulfur or nitrogen atoms. The general sequence is:

$$\text{Fuel containing S or N} \xrightarrow{\text{combustion}} \text{oxides of S or N}$$

$$\xrightarrow{\text{action of moisture and oxygen}} \text{strong acids}$$

Acid Reactions Involving Sulfur

All in all, the total atmospheric acidity that starts with sulfur is greater than that coming from nitrogen. The reason is that sulfur, being essential to life, existed in the organisms from which fossil fuels originated. As the remains of prehistoric plants and animals gradually became transformed to coal and oil, some of the hydrogen and most of the oxygen and nitrogen escaped, but the sulfur stayed put and is still present in these fuels. Coal

Figure 21–10
Acid precipitation.

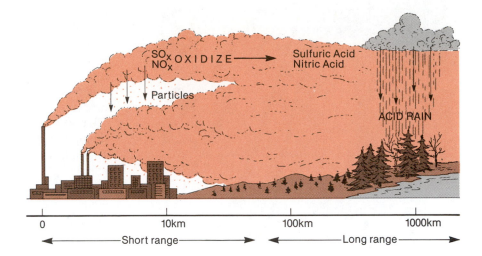

is especially rich in sulfur. As coal is burned, the carbon is oxidized to CO_2, and the sulfur is oxidized to sulfur dioxide, SO_2, which is also a gas:

$$C + O_2 \rightarrow CO_2$$
$$S + O_2 \rightarrow SO_2$$

The oxidation of sulfur to SO_2 occurs directly in the flame; therefore, SO_2 is discharged to the atmosphere from the smokestack. As the SO_2 is swept along by the prevailing winds, it is slowly oxidized at ordinary temperatures to SO_3:

$$2SO_2 + O_2 \rightarrow 2SO_3$$

SO_3 then reacts rapidly with atmospheric moisture to form sulfuric acid, which is a very strong acid:

$$SO_3 + H_2O \rightarrow H_2SO_4$$
$$\text{sulfuric acid}$$

Sulfuric acid is very soluble in water and is therefore washed out by rain. It is for these reasons that acid rain often occurs at considerable distances from the sources at which the sulfur dioxide is introduced into the atmosphere.

Acid Reactions Involving Nitrogen

The small concentrations of nitric acid that are formed by the action of lightning are augmented by the burning of fossil fuels. In the gasoline engine, for example, the electric spark generated by the spark plug serves as a substitute for lightning, and some nitrogen in the air in the cylinder is oxidized to NO:

$$N_2 + O_2 \rightarrow 2NO$$

When the NO leaves the exhaust pipe and comes in contact with the air and moisture of the outside atmosphere, it is further oxidized to nitric acid:

$$4NO + 3O_2 + 2H_2O \rightarrow 4HNO_3$$

Pathways of Damage

Even before the acids are formed in the atmosphere, some of the oxides of nitrogen and sulfur become attached to dust particles and adhere to them as the particles fall to earth. When they come in contact with rivers, lakes, or the moisture in soil, they react to form acidic solutions. These acidic dusts often precipitate closer to the pollution sources than the acid rain and snow, as shown in Figure 21–10.

Acid rain kills trees and fish, reduces the growth of certain agricultural crops, degrades various materials, and can be indirectly responsible for injury to the health of humans, livestock, and wildlife. However, there is no simple relationship between the amount of acid and the resulting environmental damage. Some of the complications follow:

• Most of the acid precipitation that reaches a lake does not fall directly into it but instead falls on the land and then runs off into the water. If the soil is rich in limestone, it can neutralize most of the acid before the rain runs off the land:

$$CaCO_3 + H_2SO_4 \rightarrow CaSO_4 + H_2O + CO_2$$
$$\text{limestone} \quad \text{sulfuric acid} \quad \text{calcium sulfate}$$

Heimo van Ellsberg, chief forester of Sieberg Forest near Bonn, West Germany, points to the tops of fir trees damaged by acid rain. (Wide World Photos)

liquid droplets. Sulfuric acid and nitric acid are highly soluble in water; therefore, they dissolve in fog droplets, where their concentration becomes about 10 times higher than their average concentration in rainwater. This difference is related in part to the fact that fog droplets are much smaller than raindrops. Therefore, the water in a fog droplet does not dilute the acid as much as do the greater amounts of water in raindrops. For this reason, fogs have been called the "vacuum cleaners of the atmosphere." It is these high acid concentrations that cause the greatest damage to trees.

- Another unexpected effect has been the greater damage done to pine trees by nitric acid, even though the atmospheric concentration of nitric acid is much less than that of sulfuric acid. Here the damage may be caused by the nutrient effect of nitrogen, which fertilizes the trees and causes excess growth in the late fall, making them more susceptible to winter injury.

- The damage to masonry is most severe for limestone and marble, both of which are forms of calcium carbonate (see the preceding chemical equation). Many marble structures and sculptures that have survived for centuries are now deteriorating rapidly. Metals, except for some precious ones such as silver, gold, and platinum, dissolve in acid. Paints and other coatings offer only temporary protection. The combination of wind-blown particles, which erode paint, and acid rain, which corrodes the exposed metal, is particularly harmful.

Economic Costs and Remedies

Acid rain was recognized as a potentially serious environmental problem by the mid 1970s, when it became obvious that pH levels in various areas had dropped very sharply (Fig. 21–11). Many studies of economic costs have since been carried out, and others are continuing, but accurate assessments are not easy to attain, and proof that a specific damage comes from a particular source of acid emission is even more difficult.

Overall estimates must include costs from destruction of timber, fish kills, decrease of agricultural productivity, damage to materials, injury to

In some instances the added sulfate even acts as an agricultural fertilizer. When the soil is poor in limestone, however, this mechanism does not work. The lakes in the Adirondacks of New York, for example, are fed by waters that run off soil that lies mostly over granite and contains little limestone. This soil does not neutralize much acid, so the lakes are not protected.

- Observations in West Germany's Black Forest and elsewhere indicated that trees on mountaintops and hilltops suffered a much greater percentage of losses than those at lower levels. This curious phenomenon is related to the prevalence of fogs at these summits. A fog or mist is not a gas but a collection of tiny

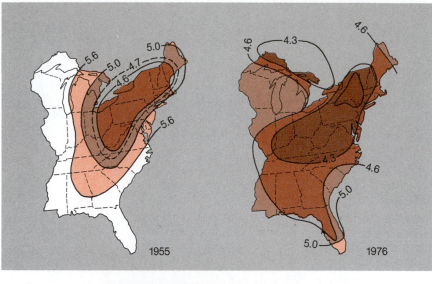

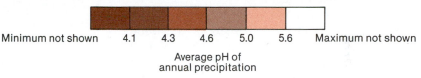

Figure 21–11

Acid precipitation in the eastern United States. (From Council on Environmental Quality)

Minimum not shown   4.1   4.3   4.6   5.0   5.6   Maximum not shown

Average pH of
annual precipitation

livestock, acid leaching of toxic metals from mine tailings and other sources, degradation of recreational areas, and possibly adverse effects on human health (see Section 21.8). It is estimated that the cost in the United States alone approaches $3 billion per year, and the annual cost in Western Europe is in the tens of billions of dollars.

The threatened loss of European and North American forests is frightening. Some of the economic cost is postponed by cutting the dead trees and selling their lumber, but this expedient is nonrenewable. If the damage continues, other losses will mount. As forest barriers are thinned out, more alpine villages may be destroyed by avalanches. Tourism would probably decline. Climatic changes, too, can yield unforeseen economic consequences.

The major technological choices for reducing acid emissions are: (1) Scrub the acid from the gases that are discharged to the atmosphere. (See Section 21.9 for a description of scrubbers and other control devices.) (2) Remove sulfur from the fuel (particularly from coal) before it is burned. There is much controversy over the relative costs and effectiveness of these alternatives. By all reckonings, however, any costs of prevention would be far less than that of the damage caused by acid rain. A major difficulty is that costs and benefits are not easily matched. Areas that suffer from acid rain may be many hundreds of miles from the source and often are not even in the same country. What's more, the source is probably not a single factory, but rather an entire industrial area or set of areas. If the source of acid emissions is from power plants, the costs of control measures may be passed on to its customers, who will be unhappy when their electric bills go up. It is for such reasons that disputes over problems of acid rain are usually dealt with on a political, often international, basis, rather than by legal battles between specific industrial sources and the communities they affect.

21.7
Nuclear Warfare and the Atmosphere

In the preceding sections, we have discussed atmospheric changes that can arise from industrial and agricultural activities. Now we confront a potentially much more serious issue—the atmospheric effects that could result from nuclear warfare. In October, 1983, an international conference of 100 atmospheric physicists and biologists from the United States, Western Europe, and the Soviet Union studied the problem. The conclusions of the study were:

1. Multiple ground-level nuclear blasts would lift phenomenal amounts of very finely pulverized soil particles into the atmosphere. This soil would be accompanied by soot from fires initiated by the blasts. The soil and soot would be concentrated enough to block out 95 percent of the normal solar radiation. Temperatures in the Northern Hemisphere would plummet to $-25°C$ ($-13°F$), even if the war occurred during the summertime. The resulting freeze is called **nuclear winter.** Crops and natural ecosystems would die, and billions of humans as well as an uncountable number of animals would starve to death.

2. The intense heat of the blasts would vaporize a large variety of different materials, which would then be carried aloft by dust clouds. Many of these would include industrial chemicals of all sorts. Many of these are toxic. Others are benign in their present form but can be converted to toxic products by heat or by oxidation. Today, very large quantities of different chemical compounds are integrated throughout our society in the form of products used in industry, commerce, agriculture, and the home. In the event of a nuclear war, many of these would be blasted into the atmosphere and converted to vapors or aerosol particles that would be dispersed over the entire globe in the form of deadly acid and chemical rains.

3. The heat of the blasts would convert large quantities of atmospheric nitrogen to nitrogen oxides. In turn, these compounds would destroy much of the ozone layer, exposing survivors and ecosystems to high levels of ultraviolet radiation, as discussed in Section 21.5.

A summarizing statement* by 20 prominent scientists is:

> The extinction of a large fraction of the Earth's animals, plants, and microorganisms seems possible. The population size of *Homo sapiens* conceivably could be reduced to prehistoric levels or below, and extinction of the human species itself cannot be excluded.

*See R. P. Turco, O. B. Toon, T. P. Ackerman, J. B. Pollack, and Carl Sagan: Nuclear winter: Global consequences of multiple nuclear explosions. *Science*, 222:1283ff, 1983. Also see Paul Erlich et al.: Long-term biological consequences of nuclear war. *Science*, 222:1293ff, 1983.

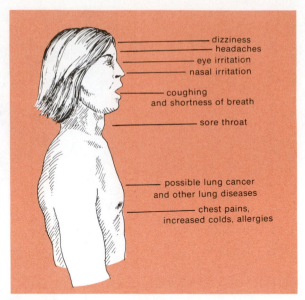

Figure 21–12
Effects of air pollution on the human body.

21.8
Effects of Air Pollution on Human Health
Acute Effects

Much of the earlier public attention to air pollution was focused on episodes in which deaths occurred during periods of pollution and were clearly caused by its toxic effects (Table 21–4). These disasters were generally caused by three conditions, all operating at the same time: (1) a severe atmospheric inversion, (2) the presence of airborne particulate matter such as fog, and (3) the continued generation of pollutants during the inversion. Table 21–4 outlines several such episodes. The combination of particulate and gaseous pollutants can be very harmful because both are inhaled into human lungs together (Fig. 21–12).

The fate of a particle, once it is inhaled, depends largely on its diameter. If it is greater than about 2 μm, it is usually trapped in the nasal passage or in the mucus of the bronchi and is generally coughed up and perhaps swallowed. If the diameter is less than 2 μm, the particle may be carried all the way through the air passages into the air sacs (alveoli) of the lung, where it may be trapped by specialized cells, or alternatively, it may be absorbed into the bloodstream.

Table 21–4
Some Early Examples of Air Pollution Disasters During Atmospheric Inversions

Location and Meteorology	Sources of Pollution	Effects
Meuse Valley, Belgium, 25 km long, with 100-m high hills on either side. Atmospheric inversion, Dec. 1 to 5, 1930	Coke ovens, steel mills, glass factories, zinc smelters, sulfuric acid plants	60 people died. Many illnesses of respiratory tract—chest pains, shortness of breath, and so on. Also deaths of cattle
Donora, Pennsylvania, on inside of a horseshoe bend of the Monongahela River. Steep hills on either side of the valley. Very severe inversion and fog, Oct. 26 to 31, 1948	Steel mills, sulfuric acid plant, zinc production plant, and other industries	20 deaths and about 6000 illnesses. Severe irritations of throat and lungs
Poza Rica, Mexico, low inversion and fog during the night of Nov. 23–24, 1950	A single pollutant, hydrogen sulfide gas, H_2S, released between 4:45 and 5:10 A.M. on Nov. 24	320 people hospitalized; 22 died. H_2S first stinks, then causes loss of sense of smell, then severe respiratory irritation and death
London, fog and atmospheric inversion from Dec. 5 through Dec. 9, 1952	Coal smoke from individual home heating units and fireplaces	Between 3500 and 4000 excess deaths during the month of December, mostly in older age groups

The fate of gases is determined largely by the solubility of the gas in water. Since biological tissues are rich in water, a water-soluble gas such as SO_2 will rapidly dissolve in the soft tissues of the mouth, nose, throat, bronchi, and eyes, where it produces the characteristic dry mouth, scratchy throat, and smarting eyes that most city dwellers have sometimes experienced. In contrast, NO_2, which is relatively insoluble, may bypass this part of the respiratory tract and be carried to the alveoli, where, in very high doses, it may cause gross accumulation of fluid in the air spaces and thus make effective lung function impossible.

The net toxic effect when various pollutants are inhaled together, however, may be much greater than the sum of the effects of these same pollutants if they are inhaled separately. (Recall the discussion of **synergism** in Chapter 18.) It is known, for example, that SO_2 may be adsorbed onto particles; if these particles are smaller than 2 μm, molecules of SO_2 may gain access to the alveoli in greater concentrations than they would otherwise. The retention of carcinogenic hydrocarbons in the human body has been shown to be greatly enhanced if they are first adsorbed onto soot particles. Also, oxygen and water can react with SO_2 to form sulfuric acid and with NO_2 to form nitric acid.

Chronic Effects of Community Air Pollution

Another question of concern to medical scientists for many years has been the issue of whether exposure to mildly polluted air results in a higher rate of illness and death than is experienced by those who breathe relatively clean air. Many illnesses have been examined, but the ones that have prompted the most research have been diseases of the respiratory tract—lung cancer, chronic bronchitis, and emphysema.

Various studies have shown that lung disease is up to four times as prevalent in cities as in rural areas. It is possible that the differences in any disease from city to country may be due to factors other than air pollution. Many of the better studies of this problem take into account some of the dif-

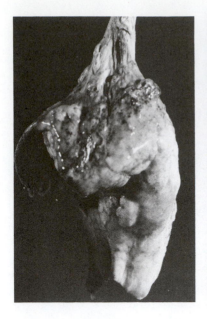

Normal human lung *(left)*. Lung with emphysema *(right)* from cigarette smoker is enlarged and misshapen and has lost elasticity. (Photo by Glen Cuerden, Cuerden Advertising Design)

ferences between city and country living. The preponderance of the evidence indicates that, after most of these factors have been taken into consideration, there still remains an excess incidence of lung disease in urban environments. The most likely element of the "urban factor" seems to be air pollution, athough conclusive proof is lacking.

Those with pre-existing cardiac disease, particularly the type caused by narrowing of the blood vessels to the heart (so-called coronary heart disease), risk serious illness when exposed to very high levels of air pollution. Air polluted by ordinary automobile exhaust can have deleterious effects on the cardiovascular function of people whose heart is already compromised by other disease. One wonders how many people have died (or killed others) on crowded highways from heart attacks triggered by dirty air.

Personal Air Pollution—Cigarettes

The air whose quality is important to your health is the air *you* breathe, not the entire global atmosphere. If the outdoor air in any community resembled the self-polluted air that a smoker inhales, it would be considered a national disaster. Smokers are, on the average, approximately 10 times more likely to develop and die of lung cancer as are nonsmokers. They are also 6 times as likely to die from

pulmonary diseases and nearly twice as likely to die from coronary heart disease. A host of other illnesses are also significantly associated with smoking. The more you smoke, the greater are your chances of getting lung cancer.

Cigarettes and the urban environment seem to have a more than additive effect on the incidence of lung cancer; that is, if one compares urban nonsmokers with rural nonsmokers, the difference in incidence of lung disease is small; but urban smokers have a much greater incidence of the disease than do rural smokers. These studies indicate that the combination of smoking and living in large cities is particularly pernicious.

Recent attention has been devoted to the exposure of nonsmokers to tobacco smoke. (The expressions used are "passive smoking," or "environmental tobacco smoke.") A committee of the National Research Council has found that such exposure increases the risk of respiratory illness in young children and infants (especially when the mother smokes) and that nonsmokers married to smokers have an elevated risk of lung cancer.

Chemical analysis of tobacco and cigarette smoke has revealed the presence of at least seven distinct hydrocarbons that have been shown to be able to produce cancer in animals. Cigarette smoke also contains polonium-210, a radioactive substance that may be carcinogenic.

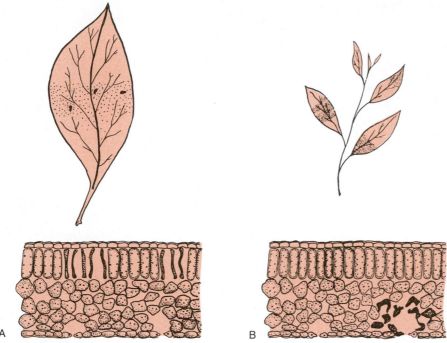

Figure 21–13

Effects of air pollution on plants. *A,* Ozone injury. Note the flecking or stippled effect on the leaf. On sectioning, only the palisade layer of cells is affected. *B,* Smog-type injury. Note the change in position of the effect with the age of the leaf. On sectioning, initial collapse is in the region of a stoma. (From A. Stern: *Air Pollution,* New York, Academic Press, 1962)

21.9
Other Effects of Air Pollution
Injury to Vegetation and Animals

Air pollution has caused widespread damage to trees, fruits, vegetables, and ornamental flowers (Fig. 21–13). The total annual cost of plant damage caused by air pollution in the United States, exclusive of acid rain, has been estimated to be in the range of $1 to $2 billion. Such figures are obtained in part from experiments carried out in chambers into which analyzed concentrations of pollutants are introduced. For example, California navel orange trees exposed to 0.0625 ppm of NO_2 for 290 days yielded 57 percent less fruit than those in filtered air. The results of such tests, combined with analyses of air pollution in the areas of orange groves, permit calculations of the total crop loss and its economic cost. Some plant scientists point out that the figures obtained in this way may be too low, because they do not take various factors into

account, such as losses due to unregulated pollutants, to synergistic effects of pollutant mixtures, and to predisposition to plant diseases caused by pollutants.

The most dramatic early instances of plant damage were seen in the total destruction of vegetation by sulfur dioxide in the areas surrounding smelters, where this acid-forming gas is produced by the "roasting" of sulfide ores. There is a wide variety of patterns of plant damage by air pollutants. For example, all fluorides appear to act as cumulative poisons to plants, causing collapse of the leaf tissue. Photochemical (oxidant) smog bleaches and glazes spinach, letttuce, chard, alfalfa, tobacco, and other leafy plants. Ethylene, a hydrocarbon that occurs in automobile and diesel exhaust, makes carnation petals curl inward and ruins orchids by drying and discoloring their sepals.

Countless numbers of North American livestock have been poisoned by fluorides and by ar-

Figure 21–14
A cow afflicted with fluorosis.

senic. The fluoride effect, which has been the more important, arises from the fallout of various fluorine compounds on forage. The ingestion of these pollutants by cattle causes an abnormal calcification of bones and teeth called **fluorosis,** resulting in loss of weight and lameness (Fig. 21–14). Arsenic poisoning, which is less common, has been transmitted by contaminated gases near smelters and by siltation and flooding of nearby rivers (refer to the case history of the Clark Fork River in Section 18.6).

Deterioration of Materials

As discussed in Section 21.6 on acid rain, acidic pollutants are responsible for many damaging effects, such as the corrosion of metals and the weakening or disintegration of textiles, paper, and marble. Hydrogen sulfide, H_2S, tarnishes silver and blackens leaded house paints. Ozone produces cracks in rubber.

Particulate pollutants driven at high speeds by the wind cause destructive erosion of building surfaces. The desposition of dirt on an office building, as on a piece of apparel, leads to the expense of cleaning and to the wear that results from the cleaning action (Fig. 21–15). An outline of air pollution damage to materials is shown in Table 21–5.

Esthetic Insults

A view of distant mountains through clear, fresh air is esthetically satisfying, and an interfering acrid haze is therefore a detriment. Unpleasant esthetic

Figure 21–15
Old post office building being cleaned in St. Louis, Missouri, 1963. (Photo by H. Neff Jenkins. From A. Stern: *Air Pollution.* 2nd ed. New York, Academic Press, 1969)

effects cannot be neatly separated from the other disruptions caused by air pollution. The acrid haze is sensed not only as an annoyance but also as a prediction of more direct harm, somewhat as the smell of leaking gas signals a possible explosion. Thus, the pollution engenders anxiety, and anxiety may depress our appetites or rob us of sleep, and these effects, in turn, can be directly harmful.

21.10
Control of Air Pollution

It is easy to think of air pollution control as something one does to the source of the pollution—the engine or tailpipe of an automobile or the smoke-

Table 21–5
Air Pollution Damage to Materials

Material	Damage	Responsible Air Pollutants
Metals	Tarnishing, corrosion, structural weakening	Acidic gases,* moisture, salt
Masonry	Surface erosion, soiling	Acidic gases, moisture, particulate matter
Ceramics	Surface erosion, encrusting	Acidic gases, especially hydrogen fluoride
Paints	Surface erosion, discoloration	Acidic gases, H_2S, ozone, particulate matter, moisture
Paper	Embrittlement, discoloration	Acidic gases, moisture
Textiles	Reduced strength, soiling	Acidic gases, moisture
Textile dyes	Fading	Ozone and oxides of N in sunlight
Leather	Weakening	Oxides of sulfur
Rubber	Cracking	Ozone
Photographic film	Blemishes	Oxides of sulfur, moisture

* Unless otherwise noted, "acidic gases" refer to oxides of nitrogen and sulfur that react with moist air to form the strong acids H_2SO_4 (sulfuric acid) and HNO_3 (nitric acid).

stack of a power plant. That is, of course, a valid concept, but it is not the only one. One could also make cultural choices of many kinds that serve to reduce air pollution. Some of these are discussed in the sections of Chapter 15 that deal with energy sources.

The emission from a polluting source such as an industrial smokestack contains many harmless gases such as nitrogen or oxygen, mixed with a much smaller concentration of pollutants. Typically, the volume of polluted matter in a contaminated air stream is in the range of 1/1000 to 1/10,000 of the total volume.

There are two approaches for controlling air pollution:

1. The pollutants can be separated from the harmless gases and disposed of in some way.

2. The pollutants can be somehow converted to harmless products that can then be released to the atmosphere.

Particulate matter can be separated from a moving gas stream in a variety of ways, depending on the physical and chemical properties of the pollutants. Commercial air pollution control devices such as those shown in Figure 21–16 consist of large, semiporous bags that filter dust from a polluted air stream.

There are various mechanical collection devices that depend on the fact that particles are *heavier* than gas molecules. If a gas stream that contains particulate pollutants is whirled around in a vortex (Fig. 21–17), the more massive pollutant particles may be spun out to the outer walls. These particles will then settle toward the bottom, while clean gases will move upward and out the top of the collector. Such a device is called a **cyclone.**

Particles may also be removed from a gas stream by virtue of their behavior in an electrical field. If a balloon is given an electrical charge by rubbing it against your hair, it will stick to a wall.

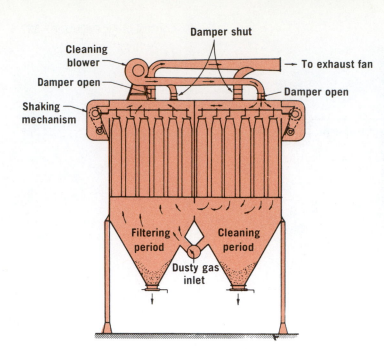

Figure 21–16

Typical bag filter using reverse flow and mechanical shaking for cleaning. The figure shows the dusty gas being blown from the inlet toward the left and up. When the dusty gas reaches the six bags on the left, the gas goes into the bags, while the dust remains on the outside (just like a vacuum cleaner running backward). The cleaned gas then comes out the tops of the bags and is discharged by the exhaust fan to the atmosphere. Meanwhile, the bags on the right, which have collected dust on their outer surfaces from the previous cycle, are being shaken and blown so that their dust falls to the bottom, where it can be removed. When the bags on the right are clean and those on the left are dusty, the air flow pattern is reversed. (From A. Stern: *Air Pollution*. 2nd ed. New York, Academic Press, 1969)

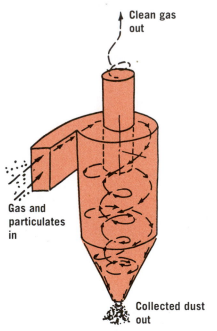

Figure 21–17
Basic cyclone collector. (From Walker: *Operating Principles of Air Pollution Control Equipment*. Bound Brook, NJ, Research-Cottrell, Inc., 1968)

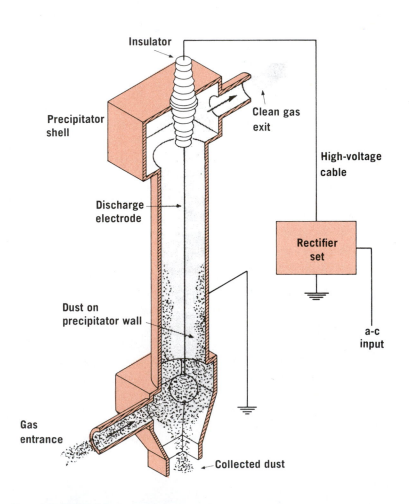

Figure 21–19
Right view shows how fumes would pour from the smokestack of a steel furnace if pollution control devices were not installed. Left view shows operation with an electrostatic precipitator. (Photo courtesy of Bethlehem Steel)

Similarly, if dust particles are charged, they will adhere to a chamber wall or to each other. An **electrostatic precipitator** (Fig. 21–18) operates on just this principle. Electrostatic precipitators operate at efficiencies of 99 percent or higher and can convert a smoky exhaust to a visually clear exhaust (Fig. 21–19). Furthermore, the energy requirements are modest compared with those for other air cleaning devices, because work is done only on the particles to be removed, not on the entire air stream. However, the installations are expensive and require much space. Most electrostatic precipitators are used in power plants and steel mills that burn fossil fuels.

Pollutant gases cannot feasibly be collected by mechanical means, because their molecules are not sufficiently larger or heavier than those of air. However, some pollutant gases may be soluble in a particular liquid (usually water). For example, ammonia, NH_3, is a common gas that is very soluble in water. If an air stream is polluted with ammonia, the mixed gases can simply be bubbled through a water bath or sprayed with a water mist. The ammonia will dissolve and be removed with the water, whereas the air molecules will pass through unaffected. Devices that effect such separation are called **scrubbers** (Fig. 21–20).

Gas molecules adhere to solid surfaces. Even an apparently clean surface, such as that of a bright piece of silver, is covered with a layer of molecules of any gas with which it is in contact. The gas is said to be **adsorbed** on the solid. If a

◀ **Figure 21–18**
Basic elements of an electrostatic precipitator. A dusty gas is blown upward through a tube that contains a fine wire (the discharge electrode) running through the center. A high voltage on the wire transfers an electrical charge to nearby dust particles. This charge forces the dust particles to drift to the outer tube, where they stick to the walls. The accumulated dusty layer then can be removed, while the clean gases exit out the top of the chamber. (From White: *Industrial Electrostatic Precipitation,* Reading, MA, Addison-Wesley Publishing Company, 1963)

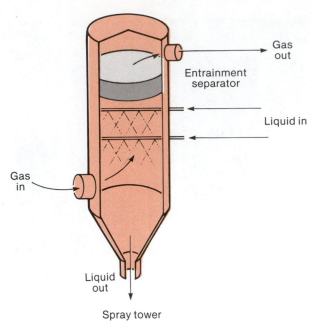

Figure 21–20
Schematic drawing of a spray collector, or scrubber. (After A. Stern: *Air Pollution.* 2nd ed. New York, Academic Press, 1969)

solid is perforated with a network of fine pores, its total surface area (which includes the inner surfaces of the pores) may be increased so much that its capacity for gas collection becomes significant. One such solid is **activated carbon,** which can have many thousands of square meters of surface area per kilogram.

Activated carbon is made from natural carbon-containing sources, such as coconut shells, peach pits, dense woods, or coal, by charring them and then causing them to react with steam at very high temperatures. The resulting material can retain 10 percent or more of its weight of adsorbed matter in many air purification applications. Furthermore, the adsorbed matter can be recovered from the carbon and, if it is valuable, recycled.

The adsorbent bed consists of carbon granules about 3 mm in diameter. It may seem strange that gases, which pass through the finest filter, can be effectively purified by a bed of loose granular material. But gas molecules move very rapidly between collisions. This rapid darting motion, when superimposed on the much slower speed of the entire current of gas, enables the molecules to reach some surface of the granular adsorbent particles in a very short period of time.

Sometimes it is difficult to remove chemical pollutants from a rapidly moving air stream, and it is easier to convert them to some relatively harmless compounds without separating them at all. By far the most important *conversion* of pollutants is by oxidation in air. If a gas stream is passed through an incinerator, the pollutants will burn, and, if the combustion is complete enough, the pollutants will be converted to less objectionable products. When organic substances containing only carbon, hydrogen, and oxygen are completely oxidized, the resulting products are carbon dioxide and water, both innocuous. However, the process is often very expensive because considerable energy must be used to keep the entire gas stream hot enough (about 700°C) for complete oxidation to occur. One way to reduce this energy requirement is with the aid of a catalyst. The application of this method to automobile exhaust is described in the case history in Section 21.13.

Cigarette Filters   Cigarette smoke contains carbon monoxide and other gases, as well as particulate matter. The filters in some brands contain activated carbon for gas removal, but carbon monoxide is as light a gas as air, and it is not removed by activated carbon. Other filter media do not remove any gases. Filters can remove some of the particulate matter that contains the nicotine and other components classified as "tar." However, the particles in cigarette smoke are very small, and a really efficient filter would have to be so densely packed that it would make the cigarette hard to smoke. Besides, if a filter worked really well, only warm air and moisture would come through, so there would be little incentive to smoke.

21.11
Indoor Air

Most people in developed areas of the world spend most of their lives indoors. Many, in fact, spend very little time outdoors—from home to car perhaps, and from car to factory or office. It is therefore important to consider the quality of indoor air. Indoor air carries pollutants from outdoors that are drawn in by fans or blown in by the wind as well as pollutants that are generated indoors. Because of this double burden, indoor air is generally more

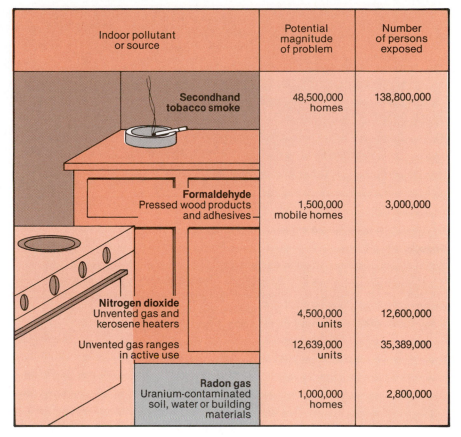

Indoor pollutant or source	Potential magnitude of problem	Number of persons exposed
Secondhand tobacco smoke	48,500,000 homes	138,800,000
Formaldehyde Pressed wood products and adhesives	1,500,000 mobile homes	3,000,000
Nitrogen dioxide Unvented gas and kerosene heaters	4,500,000 units	12,600,000
Unvented gas ranges in active use	12,639,000 units	35,389,000
Radon gas Uranium-contaminated soil, water or building materials	1,000,000 homes	2,800,000

Sources of indoor air pollution. Since an individual may be exposed to more than one pollutant, the sum of the numbers in the last column does not represent the total number of people exposed to indoor air pollution. Also, since 1984, the U.S. Department of Housing and Urban Development has set limits on formaldehyde emissions from pressed wood products used in mobile homes, so the magnitude of the formaldehyde problem is decreasing. (Source: American Lung Association)

polluted than outdoor air (Fig. 21–21). The significant pollutants from indoor sources are:

Carbon monoxide, CO, is released to the indoors from unvented combustion sources such as gas stoves, gas ovens, and tobacco smoking. Kerosene space heaters are often unvented, and these, too, generate CO. Indoor CO levels from gas stoves and ovens may reach levels of about 30 to 40 ppm when all burners are going at the same time. These levels may be compared with the Occupational and Safety and Health Administration (OSHA) standard of 50 ppm for the average 8-hour day limit for industrial workers, and with the 9 ppm (8-hour average) and 35 ppm (1-hour average) U.S. ambient air quality standards (Table 21–6). These comparisons imply that CO from gas cooking is not an acute hazard to health but suggest that ventilation from kitchen to outdoors is prudent. The recirculating ("ductless") hoods commonly used over kitchen stoves provide a metallic filter for grease particles followed by an activated carbon adsorber. Neither of them has any effect on CO, as was pointed out

in the discussion of cigarette filters. Unvented space heaters such as kerosene heaters, and leaks from coal, oil, or wood burners can generate higher concentrations of CO. All such possible sources should be carefully monitored. (If they give off strong odors, they are probably also releasing CO, which is odorless.) Some unvented space heaters are provided with catalytic converters, such as those used in automobiles (Section 21.13). These devices can promote the oxidation of CO to CO_2. One final caution: Charcoal briquettes generate large amounts of CO when they burn. Never bring your "cook-out" indoors; it could be deadly.

Oxides of nitrogen, particularly nitrogen dioxide, NO_2, are also products of combustion, because some atmospheric nitrogen oxidizes in flames. There is some evidence of adverse, but not acute, health effects from NO_2 in homes where gas is used for cooking. To minimize unwanted combustion products in cooking, keep the gas flame entirely under the pot or pan being heated. A large flame that extends out beyond the diameter of the

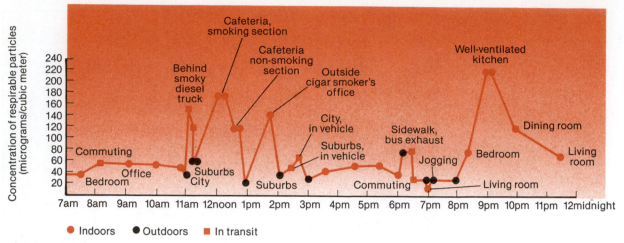

Figure 21–21

When an air pollution monitor was worn by a government official in Washington D.C., large daily variations were noted. This graph shows particulate air pollutant levels to which the subject was actually exposed during a typical working day. Note that the levels found indoors were significantly higher than those found outdoors, even in a busy, congested city.

pot is wasteful and generates more pollutants. Filters do not remove NO_2.

Formaldehyde, H_2CO, is a gas with just about the same density as air. The "formaldehyde" used to preserve biological specimens is a solution of the gas in a mixture of water and methyl alcohol. Formaldehyde is used in large quantities (more than 3 million tonnes per year in the United States) in the manufacture of various plastics, resins, and adhesives. In these syntheses, formaldehyde reacts with another chemical, such as urea or phenol, to yield a solid product. The problems are that some of the products contain excess formaldehyde that has not reacted and that the reaction can go backward, to generate formaldehyde and, say, urea. The urea, being a solid, stays put, but the gaseous formaldehyde escapes. Moisture favors this reverse reaction. The products that give rise to indoor formaldehyde pollution are urea-formaldehyde foam insulation and fiberboard or other wood products as well as various textile fabrics that contain formaldehyde adhesives. A typical worst case is a brand-new, well-sealed mobile home with formaldehyde escaping from its insulation, wall-board, furniture, and fabrics. On a warm, humid day, formaldehyde concentrations in such spaces can reach 100 ppm, which is an unliveable level. Formaldehyde is intensely irritating to mucous membranes and has been listed as a carcinogen by the EPA. Severe instances of indoor formaldehyde pollution, such as that just described, can be remedied only by structural changes, such as replacement of the insulation and wallboard.

Radon is the radioactive decomposition product of radium (see Box 14.1.), which, in turn, is a descendant of the long-lived uranium-238. Many rocks, particularly granite, as well as soils, contain tiny concentrations of uranium. All the other radioactive elements in the series of decompositions from uranium are solids, which remain fixed in the rock. Radon, however, is a gas, so it can diffuse out of the rock or soil and then into the cellar or basement of a house through cracks or openings in the foundation. The radon then mixes with the indoor air, and thus is inhaled and enters the lungs, where it decomposes (half-life about 4 days) to form polonium, a radioactive metal. The metal, being a solid, is not exhaled and continues

Table 21–6
U.S. Primary* Ambient Air Quality Standards (as of 1987)

Air Pollutant	Averaging Time†	Concentration‡	
		$\mu g/m^3$	ppm by Volume
Sulfur oxides	24 hr	365	0.14
	1 yr	80	0.03
Particulate matter	24 hr	260	—
	1 yr	75	—
Carbon monoxide	1 hr	40,000	35
	8 hr	10,000	9
Ozone	1 hr	235	0.12
Hydrocarbons (excluding methane)	3 hr (6 to 9 AM)	160	0.24
Nitrogen dioxide	1 yr	100	0.05
Lead	3 mo	1.5	—

*Ambient air quality standards are *maximum* allowable outdoor concentrations of air pollutants. Primary standards are those necessary to protect the public health. Secondary standards (not shown here) are those necessary to protect against other effects, such as damage to plants or materials. They differ somewhat from the primary standards only for sulfur oxides and particulate matter.

†The 1-hr, 3-hr, and 24-hr standards are not to be exceeded more than once per year.

‡For gases at 25°C and 1 atm pressure, the relationship is $\mu g/m^3$ = ppm × mol. wt/0.0245. Concentration in ppm does not apply to particulate matter.

to emit radiation in the lungs—that is the health hazard. If the concrete in the house contains uranium mine tailings, that, too, is a source of radon. In some locations, radon gas can build up to hazardous concentrations. The most practical remedies are to seal up the cracks in the basement floor, or, if there is a crawl space, to exhaust its air to the outdoors by means of a small fan or blower before it can enter the house. If the source is the masonry itself, the house needs to be well ventilated.

Particulate matter is generated by tobacco smoke. In spaces where the proportion of smokers corresponds to the United States national average (about one smoker for every three persons over the age of 16), the concentration can far exceed the U.S. Ambient Air Quality Standard of 260 $\mu g/m^3$ for a 24-hour average. Tobacco smoke contains gases as well as liquid and solid particles and is difficult to filter. Regulations to limit smoking in public places, and social pressures in private ones, are becoming widespread. Particulate matter also seeps out of wood stoves, which have become very common. Users of wood stoves should learn how to operate them properly to minimize the amount of smoke that they produce.

In general, measures that conserve heat by reducing leaks of air make matters worse by slowing down the escape of indoor air pollutants to the outdoors. Various measures that you, as an individual, can take to protect the quality of your indoor air are shown in Table 21–7. Air conditioning (which is not listed in the table) cools air but is not in itself a method of purification.

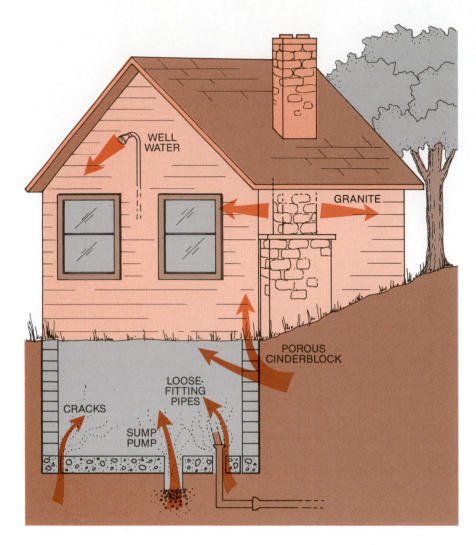

WELL WATER

GRANITE

POROUS CINDERBLOCK

CRACKS

LOOSE-FITTING PIPES

SUMP PUMP

Routes of entry of radon into a house: Temperature fluctuations and the effects of the wind bring about small differences in pressure in various parts of a house. When the indoor air pressure is lower, radon is sucked into the house from the soil through openings in the walls and floors. Some masonry, especially granite, may also be a source of radon.

21.12
Public Policy Aspects of Air Pollution Control
Standards of Outdoor Air Quality

The wind dies down and the air is still, but traffic continues to move, homes are heated, and industry operates. The air becomes hazy, murky, then uncomfortable. How dangerous is it? At what point should factories be shut down and traffic stopped? Clearly, to answer such questions something must be measured. Should it be SO_2, particulate matter, carbon monoxide, or all such pollutants together? After the measurements have been made, what is the most reasonable basis for action? The usual approach is to establish a set of air pollution standards that can serve as guidelines for governmental policies or regulations.

An air pollutant can be measured at the point where it is discharged to the atmosphere, such as at the chimney top, or in the surrounding (ambient) atmosphere where people live. The concentration at the source is not *directly* related to effects on human health, because people do not live in chimneys. Nonetheless, such measurements are valuable aids to the enforcement of air pollution control regulations. When permissible limits are established for such sources, they are called **emission standards.** The ambient concentrations are those in the air that people breathe, and the recommended limits are called **ambient air quality standards.**

Table 21–7
Measures to Protect Your Own Indoor Air Quality

What You Can Do	Advantages	Disadvantages
Don't stop *all* the air leaks—allow for a reasonable amount of ventilation.	Outdoor air replaces some indoor air, forcing pollutants outside.	Either (a) your fuel bills will be higher or (b) you will have to put up with cooler temperatures in winter and less air conditioning in summer.
Do not allow smoking indoors.	Less indoor pollution	Inconvenient for smokers
Insulate only with high-grade material such as fibrous glass.	Does not decompose readily	Cannot be blown behind walls in existing homes
After using paint, lacquers, glues, and so on, ventilate thoroughly until all odors are gone.	Removes large amounts of temporary indoor pollution	Fuel bills will be temporarily higher
After clothes are dry-cleaned, air them outdoors for a day before bringing them inside.	Much of the residual dry-cleaning solvent (trichlorethylene or perchlorethylene) evaporates.	Inconvenient; risk of rain
If you use a wood stove, learn how to operate it so that it produces a minimum amount of smoke.	Reduces indoor pollution by particulate matter	None
If your building is so tightly sealed that some forced ventilation is needed, bring air in through an air-to-air heat exchanger.	Saves heating and air-conditioning costs	None except for initial cost
Use an indoor air purifier.	Saves energy compared with outdoor ventilation	Some electrostatic indoor air purifiers generate ozone, which is toxic. Air cleaners based on adsorbers are effective, but the adsorber must be replaced when it becomes saturated.

Table 21–6 lists air quality standards set up by the U.S. Environmental Protection Agency (EPA). Note that the concentrations refer to levels that must not be exceeded, that is, maximum allowable levels.

To advise the public about levels of air pollution, the EPA and other agencies have developed a Pollution Standards Index (PSI), as shown in Table 21–8. A score of 100 or lower means that the short-term (24-hour or less) ambient air quality standards are met. If the concentrations are higher than the standards, the PSI goes up proportionately. Health effects and warnings to the public are also shown in the table.

Legislative Approaches

In Western society, the significant beginnings of legislative approaches to air pollution control occurred during the early use of coal in Great Britain,

Table 21–8
Pollutant Standards Index—Health Effects Information and Cautionary Statements

PSI	Air Quality	Health Effects	Warnings
0–50	Good		
51–100	Moderate		
101–200	Unhealthful	Mild aggravation of symptoms in susceptible persons, irritation symptoms in healthy population	Persons with existing heart or respiratory ailments should reduce physical exertion, outdoor activity.
201–300	Very unhealthful	**First stage alert** Significant aggravation of symptoms, decreased exercise tolerance in persons with heart or lung disease, widespread symptoms in healthy population	Elderly persons with existing heart or lung disease should stay indoors, reduce physical activity.
301–400	Hazardous	**Second stage alert** Premature onset of certain diseases, significant aggravation of symptoms, decreased exercise tolerance in healthy persons	Elderly persons with existing heart or lung disease should stay indoors, avoid physical exertion; general population should avoid outdoor activity.
401–500	Significant harm	**Third stage alert** Premature death of ill and elderly, healthy people experience adverse symptoms that affect normal activity	All persons should remain indoors, windows and doors closed; all persons should minimize physical exertion, avoid traffic.

starting in the fourteenth century. During the reign of Edward II (1307–1327), for example, a man was put to torture for filling the air with a "pestilential odor" through the burning of coal. Later, less brutal and (one hopes) more effective methods of regulation took the form of taxation, restriction of the movement of coal into congested areas such as the City of London, and application of the common law of nuisance (see Chapter 2).

Polluters are no longer tortured, although it is possible under United States federal law for responsible company executives to be sentenced to prison for violation of air pollution regulations. Some regulations are based on the nature of the localities whose air is polluted. For example, higher concentrations are allowed in areas zoned for industry than in residential areas. There are also some zones of pure air, such as in wilderness areas, where very little pollution is allowed. Such discrimination may be regarded as a form of regulation of land use. Although the legislative protection of pure air no longer depends entirely on statutes declaring air pollution to be a public nuisance, much of the tradition that pollution is only a minor crime remains. In particular, it is still customary to be "flexible" in administering air pollution regulations, particularly when an injunction would close down an otherwise lawful business where the immediate economic well-being of the community is seen to be involved.

In the United States, the first federal legislation exclusively concerned with air pollution was enacted in July, 1955. With a very modest beginning, it authorized the Public Health Service to perform research, gather data, and provide technical assistance to state and local governments. The major air pollution legislation in the United States is now the Clean Air Act of 1963, together with a series of amendments added in later years. This legislation recognized at the start that polluted air crossed state boundaries, and that, in such instances, if individual states did not act to correct the problems, the federal government could do so. The Act further called for the publication of documents on air quality criteria and control techniques. The states were then to develop ambient air quality standards and plans for implementing them.

It turned out that these measures were not sufficient to promote rapid progress in air cleanup, and, in 1970, amendments to the Clean Air Act called for development of national ambient air quality standards. These are the standards displayed in Table 21–6. The law also limits the quantities of air contaminants that may be emitted by any new factory. These standards are distinct from the ambient air quality standards, because they are intended to control directly the pollution given off by a specific source, such as a power plant or foundry.

Furthermore, the legislation is not static. Debates on environmental policy occur in every session of Congress, and new amendments are added from time to time.

In view of all these legislative safeguards, how is it that you can still see and smell air pollution in many places? This deficiency may be blamed, in part, on the usual problems of enforcement—administrative complexities, inadequate staffing, judicial delays. But there is more to it than that. First, recall the traditional reluctance to close down an otherwise lawful business for the "minor" crime of committing an air pollution nuisance. For example, consider a factory that emits air pollutants in violation of regulations. The company may claim that it will take more time to develop, test, and install the control systems needed to reduce their air pollution emissions than the law allows. Representatives of the government may or may not agree. Lengthy negotiations usually follow, and extensions are often granted, especially if a plant is experimenting with "innovative" technology that promises to be more efficient than existing control methods.

Such negotiations are sensitive to economic conditions. In the years before an "energy crisis"

was recognized, some environmentalists took the position that *any* air pollution should be opposed. During times of high energy costs and economic slowdown, however, public policy tends to turn in the opposite direction. The research studies on which air quality standards were based are re-examined, and statistical uncertainties are pointed out. Arguments are made in favor of relaxing the standards. Sometimes the argument takes another form, which might be expressed as follows: "Let us maintain our pollution standards, but we must relax the time schedule for achieving them. The technical and economic problems can be reviewed each year to see how much further progress we can make toward our air quality goals." This viewpoint may be more palatable to the public, but the actual effect of an indefinite delay in reaching a standard is not really different from relaxing the standard.

21.13
Case History: The Automobile Story

By the early 1900s, many industrial cities were heavily polluted. The major sources of pollution were no mystery. The burning of coal was number one. Other specific sources, such as a steel mill or a copper smelter, were readily identifiable. The major air pollutants were mixtures of soot and oxides of sulfur, together with various kinds of mineral matter that make up fly ash. When the pollution was heavy, the air was dark. Black dust collected on window sills and shirt collars, and new-fallen snow did not stay white very long.

Imagine now that your great grandfather had decided to go into the exciting new business of making moving pictures. Old-time photographic film was "slow" and required lots of sunlight, so he would hardly have moved to Pittsburgh. Southern California, with its warm, sunny climate and little need for coal, was more like it. A region of Los Angeles called Hollywood thus became the center of the movie industry. Population boomed, and, after World War II, automobiles became almost as numerous as people. Then the quality of the atmosphere began to deteriorate in a strange way. It was certainly air pollution. But it was somehow different from the smog in London or Pittsburgh. The differences may be summarized as shown on the following page.

Los Angeles (Photochemical) Smog	London Smog
Begins only during daylight	Begins mostly at night
Smells something like ozone; can also irritate the nose	Smells smoky
Looks yellow to brown	Looks gray to black
Damages certain crops such as lettuce and spinach	Damages stone buildings, especially marble
Irritates your eyes, causes blinking; makes rubber crack	

Most puzzling of all, people did not burn coal in Los Angeles! In 1951, A. J. Haagen-Smit, a chemist, reported on his experiments with automobiles. He piped automobile exhaust into a sealed room equipped with sun lamps (UV; Fig. 21–22). The room contained various plants and pieces of rubber. The room was also provided with little mask-like windows that permitted people to stick their faces in and smell the inside air.

Experiment	Condition	Results
1	Auto exhaust piped into room; UV lamps turned on	SMOG! Plants were damaged; rubber cracked. If you stuck your head in the window, your eyes became irritated
2	Auto exhaust piped into room; UV lamps turned off	Smelled like auto exhaust but not like smog; smog effects not evident
3	Auto exhaust piped into room; UV lamps off; ozone added to room	Smog again, just as in Experiment 1

These were the crucial experiments that pointed the accusing finger at the combination of automobile exhaust and sunlight. The results explained why Los Angeles smog begins in the daytime, not at night. The role of ozone was also understood. Ozone is an essential chemical agent in the production of smog, as shown by the result of Experiment 3. In the simplest terms, the chemistry of Los Angeles smog can be expressed in two equations:

(1) oxygen + ultraviolet light → ozone
(2) auto exhaust + ozone → smog

Of course, these equations are an extreme simplification. The detailed chemistry is devastatingly complex, and many separate chemical steps are involved. The rates of these various reactions change during the course of the day as the intensity of the sunlight changes. In fact, the whole story—all the reactions and their rates—is not yet known. One thing, however, is known. If hydrocarbons and other organic compounds were not introduced into the atmosphere, the polluting process would not take place. The remedy, then, is to drive the combustion of gasoline to completion, to produce only CO_2 and H_2O:

hydrocarbon + O_2 → CO_2 and H_2O

Fundamentally, there are two ways to reduce hydrocarbon emissions from automobile exhaust. One is to improve the design of the engine itself so that the gasoline is burned more completely. Such a design approach also improves engine efficiency and results in substantial fuel savings. The other approach is to oxidize unburnt fuel before it is released into the air.

The second objective is achieved by using the catalytic converter (Fig. 21–23). The best catalysts for speeding up the oxidation of organic molecules to CO_2 and H_2O are certain heavy metals, especially platinum and palladium.

However, two major problems arise. For many years, a lead compound, tetraethyl lead,

Figure 21–22
Smog is produced when automobile exhaust is exposed to sunlight.

$Pb(C_2H_5)_4$, was added to gasoline to improve engine performance. But the lead poisons the catalyst, destroying its effectiveness. It is for this reason that automobiles equipped with catalytic converters must use unleaded gasoline. The second problem is that the catalytic oxidation of gasoline hydrocarbons generates heat within the catalytic converter that promotes other, environmentally unfavorable oxidations. Probably the most harmful of these is the increased conversion of N_2 to NO and NO_2. The production of oxides of nitrogen is just what we want to avoid, since these compounds are also involved in the photochemical smog sequence.

The technical development of antipollution systems for automobiles is far from complete, and steps are being directed to the objective of minimizing the production of oxides of nitrogen.* Our

* The N_2 is part of the air drawn in to the cylinder. Since only a little of it reacts there, most of it goes out with the exhaust gases and enters the catalytic converter.

Figure 21–23
Cutaway view of a catalytic converter, showing catalyst pellets.

exhaust from engine

purified exhaust

experience with the problems of atmospheric pollution from automobiles shows that the environmental aspects of this single process are extremely complex. Of course, decisions of public policy are also involved; pollution from the use of gasoline can be effectively reduced by using less gasoline—by driving fewer miles in cars with more efficient gasoline consumption.

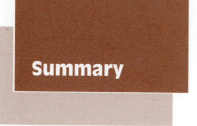

Summary

Dry air is roughly 78 percent nitrogen, 21 percent oxygen, and 1 percent other gases. Natural air also contains water vapor and various suspended particles such as soot, pollen, bacteria, and viruses. An **air pollutant** is any substance that adversely affects air quality.

Air pollution from human activity originates mainly from stationary combustion sources, mobile combustion sources, and manufacturing sources. The latter category includes any process that uses air or heat or that breaks down materials mechanically. Significant pollutants include sulfur oxides, nitrogen oxides, carbon monoxide, and particulate matter.

Under average meteorological conditions, air temperature drops steadily with altitude. However, if the upper air is *warmer* than the air beneath it, the atmosphere becomes very stable, and pollutants are trapped under the warm air. This condition is an **atmospheric inversion.**

Air pollution can affect global temperatures in two directions: (1) dust may reflect solar radiation, resulting in a cooling effect, and (2) increased concentrations of carbon dioxide, methane, and other gases absorb infrared radiation from the Earth and may thus cause a warming known as the **greenhouse effect.** Chlorofluorocarbons that reach the stratosphere may destroy the ozone there by catalyzing its decomposition to oxygen. Since ozone converts some of the solar UV radiation to infrared, this loss may result in increased UV reaching the surface of the Earth, with possible serious increases in human skin cancer and other stresses on the biosphere. Oxides of nitrogen and of sulfur react in the atmosphere to produce strong acids, which precipitate in the form of acid rain, snow, or dust. These acidic deposits have caused extensive destruction of forests and fisheries, as well as damage to masonry, metals, and other materials. The dust raised by nuclear bombs in a full-scale war could obstruct sunlight to a degree that could cause a drastic cooling, called a **nuclear winter.**

Air pollution is also responsible for acute and chronic damage to human health, as well as to various agricultural crops.

Particulate air pollution can be controlled by **bag filters, cyclones,** and **electrostatic precipitators.** Gaseous air pollution can be controlled by **activated carbon adsorbers, scrubbers,** and **incinerators,** with or without the use of catalysts.

Indoor air carries additional burdens from such sources as gas cooking stoves, tobacco smoke, unvented kerosene heaters or leaky wood stoves, formaldehyde from resins and adhesives, and radon from soils and masonry.

The combination of automobile exhaust and sunlight is primarily responsible for photochemical smog. In contrast, smog that is caused primarily by pollutants from the burning of coal does not require sunlight.

Air pollution legislation provides for the support of research, the dissemination of information, and the enforcement of controls. The degree of control to be mandated, however, is often seen as a compromise between the conflicting goals of air quality and those of economic development.

Questions

Air Pollutants and Their Sources

1. Identify each of the following substances as either a gas, smoke, dust, or mist. (a) A gray material stays suspended in the air without settling. A flashlight beam that shines through it is clearly visible, even when viewed from the side. (b) A brown transparent material is in a closed container. When the container is opened, the brown color becomes lighter, first near the top, then throughout the container. Finally, the material disappears entirely from the container. (c) Black particles slowly settle from the air to the ground. The settled material feels gritty. (d) Transparent particles slowly settle from the air to the ground. The settled material feels wet.

2. Table 21–1 refers to 14 gases. List them in descending order of their concentrations in natural dry air. (Be careful—you must separate some gases that are grouped together in the table.) What is the sum of all their concentrations, expressed in ppm? Divide this number by 10,000 to get the sum expressed in percent. Is the total 100 percent? If not, how can you account for the discrepancy?

3. True or false: If coal were burned completely, it would produce no air pollution. Defend your answer.

4. True or false: Coal and diesel oil are both fossil fuels; therefore, the air pollution generated by steam locomotives and diesel engines are both equivalent. Defend your answer.

5. State which of the following processes are potential sources of gaseous air pollutants, particulate air pollutants, both, or neither: (a) Gravel is screened to separate sand, small stones, and large stones into different piles. (b) A factory stores drums of liquid chemicals outdoors. Some of the drums are not tightly closed, and others have rusted and are leaking. The exposed liquids evaporate. (c) A waterfall drives a turbine, which makes electricity. (d) Automobile bodies in an assembly plant are sprayed with a coating consisting of pigments dispersed in a solvent. The automobile bodies then move through an oven that drives off the solvent. (e) A garbage dump catches fire.

6. Is the speed of settling of particles in the air directly proportional to their diameters? (If the diameter is multiplied by 10, is the settling speed 10 times faster?) Justify your answer with data from Figure 21–2. Is a settling chamber a good general method of air pollution control? Explain.

Meteorology

7. Which is the more stable condition, cool air above warm air, or warm air above cool air? Which of these conditions is called an atmospheric inversion?

8. Describe the meteorological conditions most conducive to the rapid dispersal of pollutants. Describe those that are least conducive.

9. Under some conditions, two inversion layers may exist at the same time in the same vertical atmospheric structure. Draw a diagram of temperature versus height that shows one inversion layer between the ground and 200 m, and another aloft, between 1000 and 1200 m, while the temperature variations between them approximate equilibrium conditions.

10. "Since tall chimneys do not collect or destroy anything, all they do is protect the nearby areas at the expense of more distant places, which will eventually get all the pollutants anyway." Argue for or against this statement.

11. Refer to Figure 21–8. (a) What percent of the incident solar energy is received by the Earth? (b) Does the Earth's surface receive any additional energy? If so, from what source? (c) Is the amount of energy emitted by the Earth greater, less, or the same as that which it receives from incident solar radiation? Explain.

12. Imagine that you must determine whether some particular climatic effect, such as increased fog or rainfall in a given area, is caused by human activity. Which of the following experimental method(s) would you rely on? Defend your choices. (a) Compare current data with those of previous years, when population and industrial activity were less. (b) Compare the effects during weekdays, when industrial activity is higher, with those on weekends, when it is low. (c) Compare effects during different seasons of the year. (d) Compare effects just before and after the switch from daylight-saving time to see whether there is a sharp 1-hour shift in the data. (e) Compare effects in different areas where population and industrial activities differ.

Effects of Air Pollution

13. Discuss the probable effects on global temperatures of dusts in the upper atmosphere, in the lower atmosphere, and on the ground.

14. Which ones of the following gases can contribute to the greenhouse effect by absorbing infrared radiation? If the gas is an absorber, identify its possible sources. (a) Carbon dioxide; (b) oxygen; (c) methane; (d) nitrogen; (e) oxides of nitrogen; (f) chlorofluorocarbons.

15. Explain why a small change in average global temperatures can have profound environmental, economic, and political effects.

Ozone

16. Explain how an SST airplane or an aerosol spray might reduce the level of stratospheric ozone.

17. Stratospheric ozone protects us from excessive ultraviolet irradiation. If you were trying to get a skin tan by using UV sunlamps, do you think it would be a good idea to use an ozone-producing device in your room to protect you against a burn from excessive exposure? Defend your answer.

18. The Law of Conservation of Energy tells us that energy cannot be created or destroyed. UV radiation is a form of energy. How, then, can stratospheric ozone reduce the solar UV radiation that reaches the surface of the Earth? What happens to it?

19. Which of the following compounds could threaten the ozone layer if they reached the stratosphere? (a) Carbon tetrachloride, CCl_4, formerly used as a cleaning solvent but now banned because of its high toxicity; (b) benzene, C_6H_6, another toxic solvent; (c) carbon tetrafluoride, CF_4, a refrigerant; (d) methyl bromide, CH_3Br, an agricultural fumigant. (C–Br bonds are weaker than C–Cl bonds.)

Acid Rain

20. What are the sources of the slight acidity of rainwater in unpolluted atmospheres?

21. How can automobile exhaust contribute to the acidity of rainwater? (Assume that the automobile uses sulfur-free gasoline.) What happens in the cylinders? What happens in the outdoor atmosphere?

22. How can sulfur in coal contribute to the acidity of rainwater? What happens in the furnace when the coal is burned? What happens in the outdoor atmosphere?

23. Sulfur dioxide emitted from a stack is responsible for acid dusts and acid rain. Which is more likely to fall to Earth closer to the stack? Explain.

24. Can acid rain ever be a benefit? Explain how.

25. The extent of environmental damage caused by acid rain is not necessarily proportional to the quantity of acid deposited. Describe two circumstances in which there is no such direct relationship.

Health Effects

26. An air pollution disaster can occur when both gaseous and particulate contaminants are released during an atmospheric inversion. Explain why this combination can be deadly. What are the synergistic effects of exposure to both gaseous and particulate pollutants? How does the inversion make matters worse?

27. Cigarettes have been implicated as an extreme menace to the health of smokers and hazardous also to nonsmokers who live or work in smoky areas. (a) Discuss the proposition that all smoking should be banned. (b) What recommendations, if any, would you favor regarding regulation of smoking in schools, in public buildings, in workplaces?

28. Which of the following groups of subjects would you study to learn the separate effects of cigarettes and air pollution on human health? Explain. (a) Urban smokers versus urban nonsmokers; (b) urban smokers versus rural smokers; (c) urban smokers versus rural nonsmokers; (d) urban nonsmokers versus rural smokers; (e) urban nonsmokers versus rural nonsmokers; (f) rural smokers versus rural nonsmokers.

Control Methods

29. Suppose that you keep some animals in a cage in your room and you are disturbed by their odor. Comment on each of the following possible remedies, or some combination of them, for controlling the odor: (a) Spray a disinfectant into the air to kill germs. (b) Install a device that recirculates the room air through a bed of activated carbon. (c) Clean the cage every day. (d) Install an exhaust fan in the window to blow the bad air out. (e) Install a window air conditioning unit that recirculates and cools the room air. (f) Install an ozone-producing device. (g) Spray a pleasant scent into the room to make it smell better. (h) Light a gas burner in the room to incinerate the odors. (i) Keep an open tub of water in the room so that the odors will dissolve in the water.

30. Distinguish between separation methods and conversion methods for source control of air pollution. What is the general principle of each type of method?

31. Explain the air pollution control action of a cyclone; a settling chamber; a scrubber; activated carbon; an electrostatic precipitator; an incinerator.

Legislation and Public Policy

32. A report of air pollutant concentrations shows 24-hour average values of 1.0 ppm for sulfur dioxide, 1000 $\mu g/m^3$ of particulate matter, and 0.5 ppm of nitrogen dioxide. However, this analysis was carried out at the top of a 200-m stack of a power plant, the only factory in town that is a potential source of air pollution. If you were the health officer or mayor, what action, if any, would you recommend? Would you require any additional information? If so, describe the data you would request.

33. Explain the legal concept of a nuisance. What implications does this concept have with regard to air pollution regulations?

34. Describe some of the important features of the Federal Clean Air Act of 1963 and its amendments. (If you or the entire class wish to study this in more detail, get a copy of the Act from your U.S. representative or senator.)

35. Table 21–6 shows that the longer the averaging time for a given pollutant, the lower the permissible concentration. Explain.

36. The hydrocarbon entry in Table 21–6 applies only to morning hours. Explain.

Automobile Exhaust

37. Gasoline vapor plus UV lamps do not produce the same smog symptoms as do automobile exhaust plus UV lamps. What do you think is missing from gasoline vapor that helps to produce smog?

38. Why is it illegal, as well as harmful, to use leaded gasoline in a modern automobile?

Suggested Readings

The basic text on air on air pollution is an eight-volume work that includes supplements through 1986:

Arthur C. Stern: *Air Pollution.* 3rd Ed. Orlando, FL, Academic Press, 1976–1986. Volume I, 715 pp.; Volume II, 656 pp.; Volume III, 799 pp.; Volume IV, 946 pp.; Volume V, 672 pp.; Volume VI, 483 pp.; Volume VII, 523 pp.; Volume VIII, 206 pp.

Three good one-volume texts are:

Arthur C. Stern, Henry C. Wohlers, Richard W. Boubel and William P. Lowry: *Fundamentals of Air Pollution.* New York, Academic Press, 1973, 492 pp.

Samuel J. Williamson: *Fundamentals of Air Pollution.* Reading, MA, Addison-Wesley Publishing Co., 1973. 473 pp.

Samuel S. Butcher and Robert J. Charlson: *An Introduction to Air Chemistry.* New York, Academic Press, 1972. 241 pp.

A textbook specifically devoted to control methods is:

Howard E. Hesketh: *Air Pollution Control.* Ann Arbor, MI, Ann Arbor Science Publishers, 1979. 362 pp.

A less technical introductory textbook is:

Virginia Brodine: *Air Pollution.* New York, Harcourt Brace Jovanovich, 1973.

The following books are devoted to acid rain. The first four are general reviews; the two from the National Research Council are research reports:

Jon R. Luoma: *Troubled Skies, Troubled Waters: The Story of Acid Rain.* New York, Penguin Books, 1985. 192 pp.

Steve Elsworth: *Acid Rain.* Dover, NH, Longwood Publishing Group, 1985. 154 pp.

Thomas Pawlick: *A Killing Rain: The Global Threat of Acid Precipitation.* San Francisco, Sierra Club Books, 1984. 216 pp.

Robert H. Boyle and R. Alexander Boyle: *Acid Rain.* New York, Schocken Books, 1983. 146 pp.

National Research Council: *Acid Deposition: Long-Term Trends.* Washington, D.C., National Academy Press, 1986. 520 pp.

National Research Council: *Acid Deposition: Atmospheric Processes in Eastern North America.* Washington, D.C., National Academy Press, 1983. 375 pp.

A book devoted to indoor air is:

Isaac Turiel: *Indoor Air Quality and Human Health.* Stanford, CA, Stanford University Press, 1985. 173 pp.

Some references on special topics are:

S. K. Tabler: EPA's program for establishing national emission standards for hazardous air pollutants. *Journal of the Air Pollution Control Association, 34*(5): 1984.

T. H. Tietenberg: *Emissions Trading: An Exercise in Reforming Pollution Policy.* Washington D.C., Resources for the Future Books, 1985. 238 pp.

F. Pasquill and F. B. Smith: *Atmospheric Diffusion, Study of the Dispersion of Windborne Material for Industrial and Other Sources.* 3rd ed. Somerset, NJ, John Wiley & Sons, 1983. 473 pp.

Two sources on the atmosphere and climate are:

Jill Jager: *Climate and Energy Systems: A Review of their Interactions.* New York, John Wiley & Sons, 1983. 231 pp.

J. E. Hansen and T. Takahasi (eds.): *Climate Processes and Climate Sensitivity.* Washington, D.C., American Geophysical Union, 1984. 368 pp.

Various introductory pamphlets as well as more technical documents on the effects of specific air pollutants and on methods for controlling them are available from the U.S. Environmental Protection Agency, Washington, D.C., or from its various regional offices.

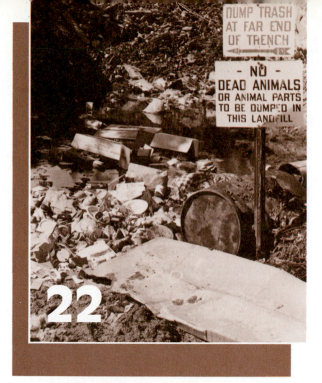

22

Solid Wastes

22.1
Introduction

Every day, Americans use 187,00 tonnes of paper. Made into newsprint, that much paper would cover 3500 sq km, an area the size of Long Island. In a year, enough paper is generated to cover the states of Texas and California combined.

Every day, Americans open about 200 million beverage cans. Stacked one on top of each other, these cans would make a pile 24,000 km high, which is about twice the diameter of the Earth. In a year, 70 billion cans are used. With these, you could make 20 piles from here to the Moon.

Every day, the city of New York alone collects 25,000 tonnes of refuse. If an average truck carries 10 tonnes, that quantity amounts to 2500 truckloads. In a year, nearly 1 million truckloads of trash are collected.

At the very least, one wonders what happens to all this trash. As the years go by, will there be enough space in dumps and landfills to contain it all? Yet the issue of solid wastes goes much deeper than mere disposal. In fact, the solid waste problem provides an overview, in a sense, of many of the environmental issues discussed thus far in this text.

Energy forms the basis for our entire technological society. Fuels are used to produce all manufactured goods. Therefore, it follows logically that whenever goods are discarded, energy, too, is being wasted. For example, every time you throw away an aluminum beverage can, you are wasting as much energy as though you had filled the can half full with gasoline and poured it onto the ground. If you read one of the large urban newspapers and then throw it away, you are discarding the energy equivalent of another half a can of gasoline.

Yet energy consumption represents just one type of the environmental problems that arise when material goods are produced. The loss of goods represents a depletion of resources. For example, 75,000 trees must be cut to supply the paper for one printing of the *New York Times* Sunday edition. In addition, when resources are consumed, other environmental disruptions also occur. Timberlands and wildlife habitats are destroyed when trees are cut to produce paper and building materials. Land surfaces are disturbed and mineral reserves are depleted when ores are mined. Further-

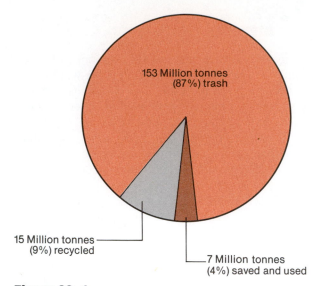

153 Million tonnes
(87%) trash

15 Million tonnes
(9%) recycled

7 Million tonnes
(4%) saved and used

Figure 22–1

The fate of nondurable consumer goods produced in
the United States.

more, some pollutants are always released when
raw materials are extracted and converted to finished products.

Now consider the fate of goods that are produced at such an expense to our environment. In
the United States, about 175 million tonnes of
household and consumer goods were produced in
1985. (Durable goods such as appliances and automobiles are not counted in this figure.) Of this
sum, approximately 153 million tonnes were
thrown in the trash. Only 15 million tonnes were
recycled, and, even less, about 7 million tonnes,
were saved and reused in subsequent years (Figs.
22–1 and 22–2). For this reason, we are sometimes
said to live in a "throwaway society."

Packaging practices have a considerable impact on our national resources. Figure 22–3 shows
the percentage of the total production of some important resources that are currently used for packaging in the United States. An automobile made of
steel and aluminum may be used for 10 years before it is discarded, but a steel or aluminum can is
used only once before it is disposed of. In the
United States, packaging materials amount to be-

Table 22–1
Some Environmental Effects of the Production of Consumer Goods

Process			Typical Environmental Effects
Extraction			Resource depletion occurs whenever materials are extracted
	Mining and oil drilling		Surface land disruption, acid mine drainage, mine tailings, sludge ponds, oil spills, fuel consumption
	Agriculture		Disruption of natural habitats, soil erosion, fertilizer run-off, water consumption, poisonous pesticides
	Forestry		Habitat disruption, soil erosion, pesticides, pollution and disruption of natural streams
Manufacturing			Air pollution, acid rain, water pollution, dust, mine tailings, noise, fuel consumption
Energy conversion and transmission			Depletion of resources, air pollution, water pollution, weather modification, thermal pollution, radioactive wastes, disruption of land for transmission rights of way, oil and chemical spills
Disposal			Litter, land use disruption, air pollution, water pollution, fuel consumption, release of hazardous wastes, disruption of natural waterways, dust, noise

tween 30 and 40 percent of the municipal refuse. The average American discards almost 300 kg of packaging each year, and per capita consumption of packaging has doubled over the past 30 years. One dollar out of ten spent in the grocery store pays for packaging. Americans spent more for food packaging in 1986 than the nation's farmers earned in net income.

Municipal sources contribute only a fraction of the types and amounts of solid wastes discarded in the United States. Agricultural activities, for example, produce more than 1.8 billion tonnes of wastes each year (Fig. 22–4). About three quarters of this is manure. Much of this manure is piled in dumps where it pollutes streams and waterways. Yet, at the same time, farmers across the continent are suffering from worn-out and depleted soils that could be enriched with manure. The other one quarter of agricultural waste includes a variety of items. Some of this waste, such as branches and slash left over from logging, are not particularly harmful to the environment. In fact, if left alone, these logging wastes eventually rot and enrich the soil. Many byproducts of food-processing operations, such as the discarded parts of fruits and vegetables, place a strain on local waste disposal facilities, but they could be shredded and returned to

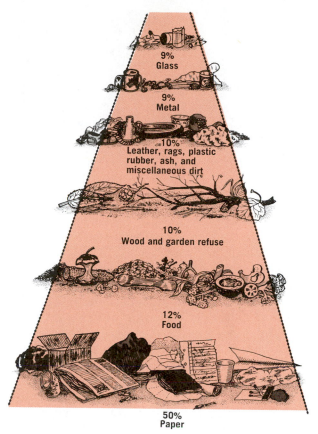

9% Glass

9% Metal

~10% Leather, rags, plastic rubber, ash, and miscellaneous dirt

10% Wood and garden refuse

12% Food

50% Paper

Figure 22–2
Composition of municipal trash in the United States.

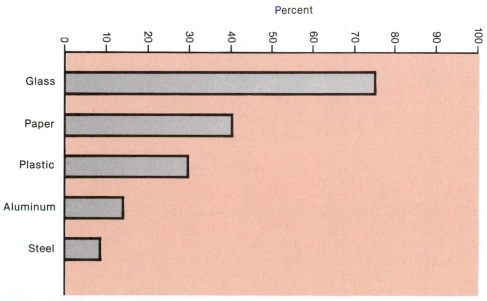

Figure 22–3
Percentage of several resources used in packaging in the United States.

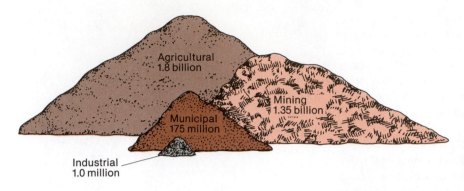

Industrial
1.0 million

Figure 22–4
Sources and quantities of solid wastes in the United States (approximations expressed in tonnes per year).

the land as fertilizers. Animal wastes from slaughterhouses are a more difficult problem and require special processing (see Section 22.6). Pesticide residues are perhaps the most serious of all, because they are usually toxic.

Mining operations produce about 1.35 billion tonnes of debris per year. Most of this material is rock, dirt, sand, and slag that remain behind when metals are extracted from the Earth. These piles do not represent a loss of valuable raw materials, but they are ugly and can lead to pollution as explained in Section 18.7. Industrial wastes are by far the smallest category in terms of total mass, but many of these materials are particularly noxious because they contain toxic chemicals. The entire problem of hazardous wastes is discussed in Chapter 18.

22.2
Disposal on Land and in the Ocean

The least acceptable disposal method is the **open dump** (Fig. 22–5). Waste is collected and, to save space and transportation costs, is compacted. The compacted waste is hauled to an available site and simply dumped on the ground. Organic matter rots or is consumed by insects, birds, or rats or, if permitted, by hogs. In some communities, the pile is set afire in the evening to reduce the total volume and the odor. There are serious environmental problems with the open dump. The dump itself is a potential source of disease. The fires are uncontrolled and therefore are always smoky and polluting. Rain erodes the dump and the polluted water flows into nearby rivers and groundwater reserves. And, of course, the dumps are ugly. In urban regions, open dumping is illegal, but it is practiced in some rural areas.

Figure 22–5
This untended landfill in southern Colorado has gradually turned into an open dump.

Ocean dumping is practiced by many coastal cities. Barges carrying the refuse travel some distance from the harbor and dump their loads into a natural trench or canyon on the ocean floor. In this way, most of the trash is removed from sight, although not from the biosphere. Not surprisingly, ocean dumping upsets the ecological balance of regions of the sea. Many organisms are killed outright. Although certain plankton and fish

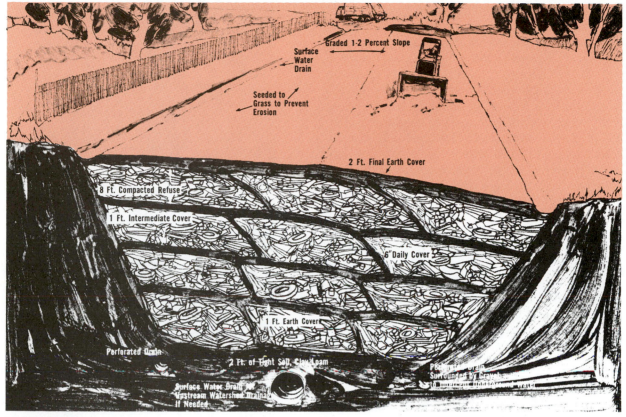

Graded 1-2 Percent Slope

Surface Water Drain

Seeded to Grass to Prevent Erosion

2 Ft. Final Earth Cover

8 Ft. Compacted Refuse

1 Ft. Intermediate Cover

6" Daily Cover

1 Ft. Earth Cover

Perforated Drain

2 Ft. of Tight Soil, Clay Loam

Surface Water Drain for Upstream Watershed Drainage If Needed

Perforated Drain Surrounded by Gravel to Intercept Infiltrated Ground Water

Figure 22–6

Sanitary landfill in a ravine or valley. Where the ravine is deep, refuse should be placed in layers of 6 to 10 feet deep. Cover material may be obtained from the sides of the ravine. To minimize settlement problems, it is desirable to allow the first layer to settle for about a year. This is not always necessary, however, if the refuse has been adequately compacted. Succeeding layers are constructed by trucking refuse over the first one to the head of the ravine. Surface and groundwater pollution can be avoided by intercepting and diverting water away from the fill area through diversion trenches or pipes or by placing a layer of highly impermeable soil beneath the refuse to intercept water before it reaches the groundwater. It is important to maintain the surface of completed layers to prevent ponding and water seepage. (Courtesy of New York State Department of Environmental Conservation)

survive in these areas, they are affected by the unusual environment. For example, flounder caught in the former New York City dump region have had an off-taste. Biologists have found old adhesive bandages and cigarette butts in fish stomachs. Therefore, it is not surprising that the flesh had a foul flavor.

A more serious threat can arise if toxic wastes are found in municipal trash. Some of these enter the refuse through routine disposal of pesticides or other chemicals that are used by homeowners. Others are illegally shunted into municipal dis-

posal systems by law-breaking industrialists. These materials can be harmful to aquatic ecosystems.

The **sanitary landfill** is much less disruptive to the environment than uncontrolled dumping on land or into the ocean. A properly engineered landfill should be located on a site where rainwater will not flow through the trash and pollute nearby ecosystems. After waste is brought to a landfill, it is further compacted with bulldozers or other heavy machinery. Each day, 15 to 30 cm of soil is pushed over the trash to exclude air, rodents, or vermin (Fig. 22–6). In practice, however, the distinction between a sanitary landfill and an open dump is not always sharp. For example, a thin layer of earth may be an ineffective barrier against burrowing rats, flies, or gases evolving from decomposition.

Several serious problems are associated with sanitary landfills. First, when undeveloped land is converted to a landfill, habitats are destroyed. In many cases wetlands are used as landfill sites, but, as we saw in Chapter 11, marshes and swamps house many valuable species of plants and animals. To eliminate them is to destroy valuable ecosystems. Second, many large metropolitan areas have used up their available sites for landfills. They are now being forced to transport their trash farther into the countryside. In these instances, transportation costs are high. Third, and perhaps most serious, such disposal represents a depletion of resources. Food wastes and sewage sludge that could be used as fertilizers are buried deep underground. Paper and wood scraps that could be recycled are lost, and nonrenewable supplies of metals are dissipated.

22.3
Energy from Refuse

Many metropolitan areas burn their garbage rather than dump it. The process, as applied to waste disposal, is more complex than simply setting fire to a mass of garbage in an open dump. In a modern incinerator unit, the trash is burned in a carefully engineered furnace. The heat from the fire is used to boil water and produce steam. Then, the steam is sold for industrial use. Thus, the trash is used as an energy source.

In some incineration plants, the money received from the sale of steam does not pay the operating costs. Economic problems arise because trash is not an ideal fuel. The incineration of certain waste products produces acidic gases that corrode the furnace walls. Particularly notorious is polyvinyl chloride (PVC), a plastic used in the manufacture of rainwear, toys, containers, garden hoses, and records. The burning of PVC produces hydrogen chloride gas. This gas reacts with water to produce hydrochloric acid, a strongly corrosive liquid. Even more threatening is the fact that some of the PVC decomposes before it burns completely. Some decomposition products are known carcinogens, such as vinyl chloride, or suspected ones, such as dioxin. Most of these can be removed from

Much energy could be conserved if glass jars were refilled rather than discarded. In this store, cooking oil is dispensed from drums into reusable jars. (Photo by Marion Mackay)

the exhaust stream if proper air pollution controls are installed, but these measures are expensive and are never 100 percent effective.

At the present time, many industries and municipalities across the globe are burning trash as fuel. As mentioned in Chapter 15, large-scale incineration is practiced in many countries in Europe. In 1985, 75 percent of the wastes in Switzerland were burned to produce energy, 51 percent of the wastes were burned in Sweden, and 34 percent in West Germany. On the other side of the globe, 64 percent of the municipal trash was incinerated in Japan. In contrast, only about 3 percent of the trash in the United States was burned for fuel.

22.4
Conservation

Most refuse contains a wealth of raw materials. Consider, for example, the element aluminum. Large quantities of this metal go into nondurable goods that are discarded soon after they are purchased. "So what," you may say, "aluminum metal

A voluntary recycling center.

does not disappear. Can't the old dumps eventually be mined?" To answer this question, one must consider the total environmental costs of waste recovery. Dumps contain aluminum mixed with many other materials. The aluminum could be extracted, but it is not very concentrated. Therefore, mining old dumps is so expensive and uses so much fuel that it is impractical.

The most efficient way to conserve resources is to use goods for longer periods of time or to reuse them after they have served their original function. If an automobile is old and runs inefficiently, the engine can be rebuilt; it is not necessary to throw the whole car away and buy a new one. That peanut butter jar in your garbage could be used over and over again if there were a large tub of peanut butter at the grocery store. Then you could simply take your jar to the store and refill it. The paper towel that you threw away need never have been purchased, for a cloth towel would have worked just as well. Or what about that chair with rickety legs? A few thin wooden wedges and some good strong glue can make it as good as new again.

22.5
Recycling—An Introduction

Many items cannot be reused in their present state, but the materials can be recycled. When an item is recycled, it is first destroyed; then it is treated in some manner to extract its useful raw materials. For example, discarded metals can be shredded, melted, and recast into new products. Similarly, used tires can be shredded and converted to raw rubber. Old newspapers can be repulped and converted to new paper. Spoiled meat can be rendered and converted to tallow and animal feed.

Recycling is environmentally favorable for a variety of reasons. For one, it conserves material resources. In comparing the fuel consumption of recycling versus that of production from virgin resources, two separate processes must be distinguished. One is the energy used in extraction and refining, and the second is the energy used in collection and transportation. In almost all cases, more energy is needed to extract and refine virgin resources than to process recycled materials. For example, nearly 20 times as much fuel is needed to produce aluminum from virgin ore as from scrap aluminum. More than twice as much energy is needed to manufacture steel from ore as from scrap. It is also twice as costly in energy to make paper from trees as it is to recycle used paper (Table 22–2). On the other hand, recyclable scrap is often widely dispersed, and fuels are required to collect these materials and transport them to central processing plants. It is difficult to estimate the environmental cost of collection and transportation. For example, consider the recycling of aluminum cans. You can calculate the average distance between households and the closest recycling cen-

Table 22–2
Environmental Benefits of Recycling†

	Paper (%)	Aluminum (%)	Iron and Steel (%)	Glass (%)
Energy use reduction	30–55	90–95	60–70	5–25
Spoil and solid waste reduction	130*	100	95	80
Air pollution reduction	75	95	85	20

*More than 100 percent reduction is possible because 1.3 kg of waste paper is required to produce one kg of recycled paper. If all paper were recycled, the waste reduction, of course, would equal only 100 percent.
†Reduction of environmental insults during manufacturing when recycled materials are substituted for materials made from virgin resources.

ter. In addition, estimates have been made of the average number of cans that are brought to the recycling center per trip. Therefore, *if everybody made a special trip to the recycling center to drop off cans,* you could calculate the energy required to transport cans to the recycling center. But people *don't* make special trips just to return their cans; they drop them off when they are running other errands. Therefore, it is necessary to estimate the amount of *extra* gasoline used to transport the cans. However, despite the uncertainties, it is safe to say that when all factors are considered, recycling conserves energy.

In most cases, recycling operations also emit less pollution than the original processes. Significant quantities of pollutants are released when paper is manufactured from wood pulp or when metal is refined from ore. The Environmental Protection Agency (EPA) has estimated that recycling all the metal and papers in municipal trash in the United States would prevent the release of more than 2000 tonnes of air pollutants and 700 tonnes of water pollutants every year.

Box 22.1
Recycling in the Old Days

One evenin' he decided t'go out an' still hunt; try t'kill 'im a bear or somethin'. Sittin' at th' head a'th' swamp an' there's three bear come walkin' out. A small little bear in the front, and they's a big he bear in th' center, an' they's a little cub behind this'um. An' he waited 'til this big bear got betwixt him an' a tree t'shoot it wi' his hog rifle so he could save his bullet—go cut it out of th' tree. And he shot this big bear . . . An' he went home an' took a axe an' cut th' bullet out. He'd take it back an' remold it. Lead was hard t'get, so that's th' way they'd try t'save their bullets. (From Elliot Wigginton (ed.): *The Foxfire Book.* Garden City, NY, Anchor Books, Doubleday & Co., 1972. 380 pp.)

22.6
Recycling Techniques

Many materials such as metal and glass can be **melted,** purified, and reused.

Plastics pose a special problem because the generic term, *plastic,* covers a wide variety of different materials of different chemical composition. It would be difficult to separate different plastics from one another out of a complex mixture such as municipal garbage; therefore, many plastics have traditionally been considered to be nonrecyclable. One solution is to collect a variety of plastics of different origins and grind them all into small particles. These particles can then be treated chemically so that the complex mixture bonds together into a single, impure product. A composite of this sort would not meet rigid performance criteria and could not be used for technical applica-

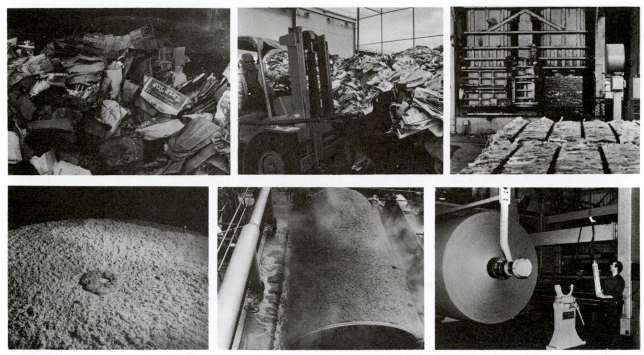

Figure 22–7
Wastepaper cycle: Scrap paper is collected, pressed into bales, pulped into a slurry, and re-formed into new paper. (Courtesy of Container Corporation)

tions, but it is entirely satisfactory for many uses. For example, recycled plastics of this sort could be used for the manufacture of boxes, some types of building materials, or even synthetic railroad ties. Despite the availability of these technical solutions, most plastics in municipal garbage are discarded; very few are actually recycled.

Any material containing natural cellulose fiber such as wood, cloth, paper, sugar cane stalks, and marsh reeds can be beaten, **pulped,** and made into paper. Thus, for example, scrap newspaper can easily be repulped to manufacture recycled paper (Fig. 22–7). Agricultural wastes can also be reused. When sugar is extracted from cane, the remaining fibrous stalks are well suited to paper production. These stalks currently contribute up to 60 million tonnes of solid waste annually and could easily be converted into paper.

If organic wastes are partially decomposed by bacteria, worms, and other living organisms, a valuable fertilizer and soil conditioner can be produced. This process is called **composting.** Almost any plant or animal matter, such as food scraps, old newspaper, straw, sawdust, leaves, or grass clippings, will form a satisfactory base for a composting operation.

Composted sewage sludge represents a valuable soil conditioner that can be used to increase the humus content of soils. Problems arise, however, because most domestic sewage contains small amounts of toxic metals, and, if sludge is used as a fertilizer, these metals enter our food chain. As a result, some food processors will not accept agricultural produce fertilized with sludge.

When sewage sludge and animal manure are composted, large quantities of methane gas are released. As discussed in Chapter 13, methane is an excellent fuel. Some farmers have collected methane from cow manure, used the fuel to drive their tractors, and then recycled the compost as fertilizer.

If animal wastes such as fat, bones, feathers, or blood are cooked **(rendered),** several valuable products can be produced. These include a fatty product called **tallow,** which is the raw material for soap, and a nonfatty product that is high in protein and can be used as an ingredient in animal feed. The raw material for a rendering plant con-

Table 22–3
Various Recycling Routes for Some Common Wastes

Waste	Recycling Possibilities
Paper	Use the backs of business letters for scrap paper or personal stationery; lend magazines and newspapers to friends.
	Repulp to reclaim fiber.
	Compost.
	Incinerate for heat.
Glass	Purchase drinks in deposit bottles and return them; use other bottles as storage vessels in the home.
	Crush and remelt for glass manufacture.
	Crush and use as aggregate for building material or antiskid additive for road surface.
Tire	Recap usable casings.
	Use for swings, crash guards, boat bumpers, etc.
	Shred and use for manufacture of new tires.
	Grind and use as additive in road construction.
Manure	Compost or spread directly on fields.
	Ferment to yield methane; use residue as compost.
	Convert to oil by chemical treatment.
	Treat chemically and reuse in animal feed.
Food scraps	Save for meals of leftovers.
	Sterilize and use as hog food.
	Compost.
	Use as culture for yeast for food production.
Slaughterhouse and butcher-shop wastes	Sterilize and use in animal feed.
	Render.
	Compost.

tains wastes from farms, slaughterhouses, retail butcher shops, fish processing plants, poultry processors, and canneries. If there were no rendering plants, these wastes would impose a heavy burden on sewage treatment plants. They would add pollutants to streams and lakes and nourish disease organisms. At the rendering plant, the waste materials are sterilized and converted to useful products. But the rendering process generates odors. Although these odors can be controlled most of the time, they do get away now and then.

22.7
The Economics of Recycling in the United States

The technology of recycling is relatively well established. Recall from Section 22.1, however, that in the United States, less than 10 percent of house-hold and consumer goods is ever reused. Why is there such a large gap between available techniques and actual practice?

In the late 1960s and early 1970s, the ethic of environmental conservation became a significant public issue. Across the country, groups of concerned citizens set out to do their small part to initiate programs that would conserve fuels and protect the land. As a result of this aroused consciousness, recycling centers were established in many cities and towns. In one sense, these centers have achieved remarkable success. Over the past decade and a half, tens of millions of tonnes of refuse have been collected, sorted, and recycled. However, the majority of Americans have not joined these voluntary efforts, and, as explained previously, only a small fraction of consumer goods is actually recycled. Unfortunately, direct economic or legal incentives are often required before environmental conservation becomes widely practiced.

The economics of recycling is closely associated with the economics of energy. One hundred years ago, coal was dug out of the ground primarily by men with picks and shovels, aided by animals such as horses and oxen. As a result, a large number of man-hours were required to produce a tonne of coal, and *fuels were expensive relative to the price of labor.* Today, this situation is reversed. In the United States, mining and oil drilling are highly mechanized, and large quantities of fuels are extracted with a minimal amount of human effort. Therefore, today, *fuels are cheap relative to the price of labor.* Thus, for example, if you wish to dig a foundation for a house, it is much less expensive to hire a bulldozer, which burns diesel fuel, than to hire a crew of laborers to move dirt with picks and shovels. This relationship is shown in Figure 22–8.

Now let us return to the production of material goods. In a forest or a mine, the resources are concentrated in one place. Therefore, they can be collected with a minimal amount of human effort. On the other hand, if goods are recycled, they must first be collected from individual homes and then brought to a municipal center where they are handled again and shipped to a central processing plant. Each of these steps is labor-intensive.

Therefore, when comparing recycling with production from virgin resources, it is important to remember the following generalizations:

Recycling	Production from Virgin Resources
Uses comparatively large amounts of labor	Uses comparatively little labor
Uses comparatively little energy	Uses comparatively large amounts of energy

Obviously then, if *only the costs of energy and labor are considered,* recycling was the economic choice 100 years ago when fuels were expensive relative to the price of labor. Today, in instances in which fuels are cheap relative to labor, recycling is not economic.

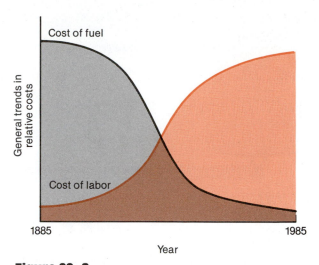

Figure 22–8
A highly schematic representation of the shift in the relative cost of labor versus fuels between 1885 and 1985.

However, energy and labor are not the only components of the economic tally. External factors include the inherent value of resources and the cost of pollution control and waste disposal. Figure 22–9 shows, in a schematic way, how these components are stacked on a pictorial economic balance.

Pollution   As shown in Table 22–2, production of goods from virgin sources produces more pollution than production from recycled materials. Therefore, the cost of pollution control must be added to the cost of goods produced from virgin resources. Remember, however, that pollution control is not an on or off affair. Strict regulations require the removal of most pollutants from a manufacturing operation, making pollution control expensive. If laws are lax, pollution control is less expensive, but the population must pay the economic externalities of living in a polluted environment. However, since manufacturers do not pay external costs, these expenses are often ignored in short-sighted economic tallies.

Value of Resources   How much is a resource really worth? Is it basically free, because it was produced—without cost—by geological and biological processes? Or is a resource a valuable part of the material wealth of a nation or of our planet? In a practical sense, the answer to this question is a matter of public policy. If a society

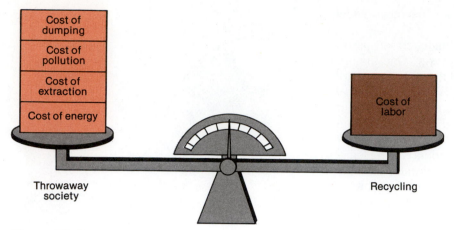

Figure 22–9

A comparison of the costs of a throwaway society versus those incurred if products are recycled. Note that the scale indicates only net amounts. Thus, energy is used both during recycling and during production from virgin materials. However, since a throwaway society uses more energy, the cost of energy is placed only on the left side of the scale.

espouses a frontier mentality, resources not only are considered to be free but the government actually encourages their exploitation. Thus, even today, a miner who finds gold on public lands in the United States can file a claim and be given the land without charge. In this way, both the land and the resources pass from the public domain into private ownership, and the owner decides how and when the gold is to be extracted. Other examples illustrate the same point. In the mid-1980s, the United States Forest Service was selling timber to logging companies at a loss, and many tax laws have been written to favor extraction of petroleum. In addition, railroads charge more to transport scrap materials than logs and virgin ores. The federally approved rate schedules are such that it is cheaper to ship a tonne of iron ore than a tonne of recycled iron, and cheaper to ship a tonne of logs than a tonne of wastepaper. Railroads not only charge more, they also realize a higher profit from transportation of recycled goods.

Think for a moment of what would happen if the government took an alternative stance and declared that extraction of resources was, in a sense, like taking money out of the bank. According to this view, whenever a resource is extracted, the "bank account" diminishes, and the nation becomes a little bit poorer. If this philosophy became public policy, rates of extraction could be regulated or materials produced from virgin resources

could be taxed. As an example of this type of law, the State of Montana has imposed a **coal severance tax** on every tonne of coal mined in the state. The money that is collected is then used for conservation programs, public education, and other programs that will benefit the people of the state. Despite examples such as the Montana law, however, most environmentalists believe that public policy in the United States still favors exploitation rather than conservation.

Cost of Disposal If goods are used once and then thrown away, the cost of disposal must be paid by someone. Therefore, this expense must be added to the price of goods used in a throwaway society.

If the total cost of living in a throwaway society is less than the cost of recycling (see Fig 22–9), most people will be wasteful. On the other hand, if people save money by recycling, then recycling will become popular. As you can see, the scale can be tipped by a change in any of the relevant factors. For example, if the government were to impose strict pollution standards or to place taxes on mineral extraction, materials produced from virgin resources might become more expensive than goods produced from recycled products.

As explained previously, 50 or 100 years ago, recycling was profitable in the United States be-

Special Topic A
Aluminum Beverage Containers

Seven hundred watt-hours of electricity, enough to light a 100-watt bulb for 7 hours, are needed to manufacture *one* 12-ounce aluminum beverage can. In 1986, about 70 billion aluminum beverage cans were produced in the United States. If they were all made from raw materials, approximately 49 billion kilowatt-hours of electricity would be required to manufacture them. This amount of energy could provide 2,500,000 people with all their electricity and consumes the entire output of 5 large power plants. Electricity is produced with 33 percent efficiency, so 84 million barrels of oil are needed to supply the energy to manufacture this number of beverage cans.

Fortunately, recycling of aluminum cans has grown significantly in the United States in recent years. Figure 22–10 shows the growth of aluminum recycling in this country. In 1986, approximately half of all aluminum beverage cans sold were recycled. As stated in the text, once cans arrive at the factory, recycling uses only 5 percent of the energy needed to process raw ore. It is difficult to calculate the fuel used to collect and transport all the aluminum cans, and estimates by different experts vary considerably. However, a few facts are clear. The potential energy savings from recycling aluminum cans is great. Significant progress has already been made. Even greater progress could be realized (1) if people brought even more cans to the recycling centers, and (2) if collection centers were located conveniently in shopping centers and other commonly frequented places, so that people could drop off their cans without driving extra miles.

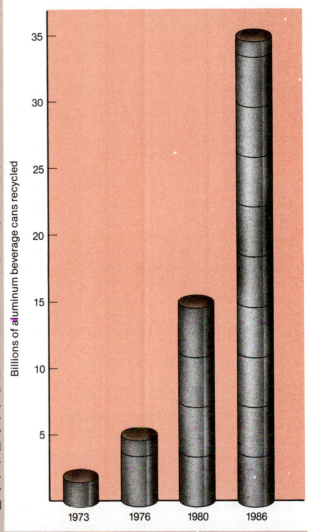

Figure 22–10
More and more Americans are collecting used aluminum cans. In 1986 alone, 35 billion cans were turned in for recycling. That's more than twice as many cans as were collected in 1980, and more than 10 times the number of cans collected in 1973. (Courtesy of Aluminum Corporation of America)

cause energy was expensive relative to the price of labor. By the 1950s, the tide had turned in favor of a throwaway society. As stricter pollution control laws were written in the 1960s and 1970s, many factories and industries began to recycle their scrap, but municipal garbage was, for the most part, discarded. In the mid-1980s, an interesting change occurred. In some regions, especially along the densely populated eastern seaboard, many of the available landfills became filled to capacity. For example, in New Jersey, there were 100 operating landfills in 1980; at the end of 1986, there were only 10 remaining. Overall, more than half of the cities in the United States are expected to exhaust their current landfill sites by 1990. Furthermore, it is difficult to open new dumpsites because there is little undeveloped land available near urban centers and real estate prices are very high. As a result, dumping fees have risen sharply from $9 per tonne in 1980 to as much as $98 per tonne 5 years later. Furthermore, as the last remaining dumps are rapidly being filled, the cost of disposal could rise even further. In 1984, the city of Philadelphia closed its last large landfill. The next closest dump was in Harrisburg, which requires a 210-mile round trip.

This steep rise in the cost of dumping trash has suddenly made the throwaway society so expensive that alternative choices are being sought. For example, in Philadelphia, it costs about $30 a tonne to operate a curbside collection program to pick up newsprint and bring it to the recycling center. A tonne of recyclable paper is worth only $20 to $25, so a recycling business would operate at a net loss of $5 to $10 a tonne. However, it costs nearly $100 a tonne to throw the trash away. If the city would pay recyclers a disposal fee of $50 a tonne, both sides would come out ahead, and the environment would benefit.

Current Trends in the Handling of Municipal Refuse in the United States

Legislation that Favors Recycling   In recent years, a variety of states and municipalities have enacted laws that encourage recycling. Traditionally, the most common legal approach has been to place a mandatory deposit on aluminum cans and glass bottles used for soft drinks and beer. These deposits are redeemed when the containers are returned. In 1987, nine states* had container laws in effect. In these states, between 90 and 96 percent of aluminum cans were recycled compared with a national average of 50 percent. In addition, more than 90 percent of all bottles were recycled compared with a national average of less than 10 percent.

Many new jobs are generated by the bottle bills. For example, in Michigan, 4600 people are employed in the collection and recycling industry. The United States General Accounting Office estimates that a total of 100,000 jobs would be gener-

*Connecticut, Delaware, Iowa, Maine, Massachusetts, Michigan, New York, Oregon, and Vermont

ated if container deposit laws were enacted nationwide.

However, container deposit laws do not address other solid waste problems such as paper, plastics, or other packaging materials. Recently, several municipalities in the United States have enacted mandatory recycling laws that require citizens to separate their trash into specific categories and to leave the items on the curbside for collection. For example, in 1985, more than half of the 567 cities in New Jersey offered curbside recycling programs, and 159 of these were mandatory.

Establishment of a Municipal Refuse Handling Industry   It is also possible to separate municipal garbage automatically in large recycling plants. In recent years, several different types of garbage separating factories have been designed (Figure 22–11). Some of these factories are devoted exclusively to recycling, whereas others recycle glass and metals and incinerate the remaining materials.

22.8
Solid Waste Management Outside the United States

We have shown that in the United States economics and need—not altruism and environmental consciousness—have provided the massive boost to initiate large-scale recycling and refuse incineration. The situation in other developed countries is complex, and, of course, varies from region to region. Certainly, economics contribute to differences in solid waste production and disposal, but other cultural factors are important as well.

Consider, first of all, the production of solid waste. As stated in Section 22.1, North Americans use tremendous amounts of materials for packaging, and the average resident of New York City generates 1.8 kg of garbage per person per day. In contrast, Europeans consume much less and discard much less, even though their standard of living is quite high. The average resident of Hamburg, Germany generates only 0.85 kg of trash per day, and the daily per capita disposal rate in Rome is only 0.7 kg. When many cities in the developed world are compared, no obvious relationship exists between waste disposal and wealth; one can only conclude that tradition and habits are important factors.

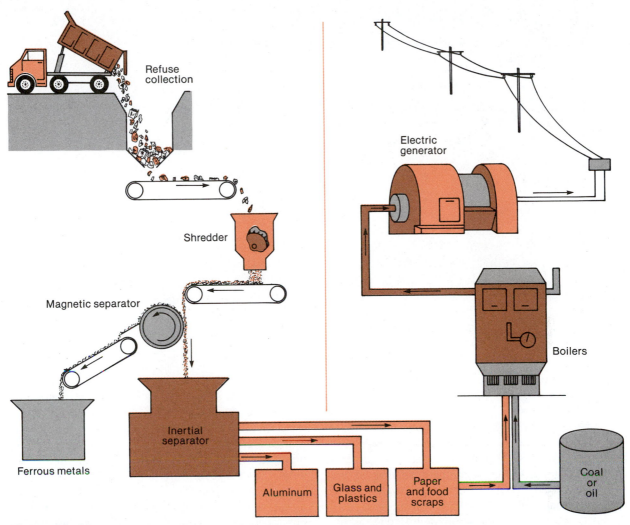

Figure 22–11
A schematic view of one possible type of municipal refuse center. Note that in this case paper and food scraps are fed into an incinerator. Other pathways are possible. For example, paper could be repulped, and food wastes could be composted.

Both cultural and economic factors are also apparent when disposal patterns are compared. As explained earlier, voluntary recycling has engendered only limited participation in the United States. However, voluntary programs have been much more successful in other countries. In Tokyo, when people were asked to separate their trash for curbside collection and recycling, participation was nearly universal. Yet many attempts to operate voluntary programs in the United States have failed simply because residents have been unwilling to cooperate. In Japan, more than half of the paper is recycled, despite the fact that much of the paper produced is exported as packaging for manufactured goods. As shown in Table 22–4, only 27 percent of the paper is recycled in the United States. If the rate of recycling were increased to 50 percent in the United States, approximately 100 million trees would be saved, and the energy saved would be enough to supply 750,000 homes with electricity. As another example, in West Germany, there are no laws that require people to return glass beverage containers and there is not even a deposit system that rewards shoppers for recycling. Yet 39

Table 22–4
Recovery Rates for Aluminum, Paper, and Glass in Selected Countries, 1985*

Country	Aluminum %	Paper %	Glass %
Netherlands	40	46	53
Italy	36	30	25
West Germany	34	40	39
Japan	32	51	17
United States	28	27	10
France	25	34	26
United Kingdom	23	29	12
Austria	22	44	38
Switzerland	21	43	46
Sweden	18	42	20

*These data include all uses of the given materials. In Europe, most glass beverage containers are refilled, not recycled. Therefore, conservation is greater than is indicated by the table.

percent of the glass in West Germany is recycled, compared with only 10 percent in the United States.

In the less-developed countries, most people are too poor to buy many things and therefore trash production is low. In addition, wages are so low that fuels are generally expensive relative to the price of labor, so recycling is profitable. Many items are even recovered after they are thrown away. In Mexico City, an estimated 10,000 people make their living by scavenging recyclable or reusable products from the city dumps. In Manila, each garbage collector is accompanied by an unpaid partner who scavenges before the trash is thrown in the truck.

22.9
Municipal Recycling—A Success Story

As discussed earlier, during the increased environmental consciousness of the early 1970s, voluntary municipal recycling centers were started across the country. Many of these concentrated their efforts on aluminum, because this metal has a high scrap value and can be handled economically. However, in terms of bulk, the heart of the municipal solid waste problem is paper, not aluminum. Paper,

largely newsprint, accounts for 50 percent of a city's trash. In a city the size of Boulder, Colorado, approximately 12,000 tonnes of paper are buried in the landfill every month. (This amounts to 400 tonnes per day.) Nationwide, 75 percent of our newsprint is imported, leading to an annual trade deficit of $2 billion.

Although paper is definitely recyclable, it isn't as valuable a product as aluminum; therefore, it is challenging to recycle this product profitably. Nevertheless, when a recycling center called ECO-CYCLE was started in Boulder in the mid-1970s, the founders decided to concentrate on the paper issue. ECO-CYCLE started with a generous grant from the city of Boulder. The city government offered a 5-year free lease on land and a donation of 50 percent of the cost of the building needed to house the operation. The founders of ECO-CYCLE realized that in order to realize any profit, it could not afford to pay anything at all for scrap. They also understood that large numbers of people would not bundle their newspapers and drive them out to the recycling center if there were no economic incentive to do so. In light of these problems, the strategy was to purchase a fleet of vehicles (old school-buses) and pick up sorted trash directly from people's homes on weekend collection drives. Although aluminum, glass, paper, and used motor oil

A

B

C

The ECO-CYCLE operation involves three steps: *A,* Collection; *B,* sorting: *C,* compacting into bales for shipment.

were also handled, the success of the operation mainly depended on the paper drive. A central core of ECO-CYCLE personnel were paid regular salaries. The pick-up drivers were assisted by members of local organizations such as the Boy Scouts or athletic teams. These groups, too, were paid for their labors.

By 1979, the project had stagnated; it was losing money and was not considered a success. The problem: Only 15 percent of the people in Boulder were willing to separate their trash. As a result, the total volume of recyclable material was too low, and operating expenses were greater than the value of scrap sold. An extensive advertising campaign

was considered and rejected. Consultants from the University of Colorado argued that selling the concept of recycling isn't like selling a product such as toothpaste. Most people already use toothpaste and other products, and advertisers merely try to convince people to use their specific brand. On the other hand, an effort to convince people to recycle asks for a fundamental change in the behavior of a population. The consultants argued that advertising isn't powerful enough to alter behavior patterns. An alternative approach was needed. Somehow, people needed to be convinced that recycling is a socially responsible act. The city was divided into several hundred small communities, or blocks. A volunteer block leader was recruited from each region. These leaders were given the task of visiting all the neighbors personally and placing peer pressure on them to bundle their papers and cans and leave them on the sidewalk on the appropriate weekends.

This approach was a success. Over a period of 3 years, the total participation throughout the city rose from 15 to 33 percent. By 1983, ECO-CYCLE was recycling 900 tonnes of materials each month. Money that had previously left the community to purchase new products such as paper and aluminum was spent within the city, providing 32 full-time and 14 part-time jobs. By the end of that year, the company had posted a profit—the first in its history. In the following 2 years, however, the value of scrap paper fell while the cost of collection and shipping remained constant. Therefore, ECO-CYCLE went into the red, losing about $15,000 a month in 1986. However, the recycling effort has saved the city considerable sums by reducing the amount of trash that is carted into the landfill. As a result, the city has reciprocated by absorbing ECO-CYCLE's debt.

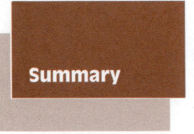

Summary

Municipal refuse is composed largely of unnecessary packaging materials and items that have been discarded because they weren't built to last in the first place. Depletion of resources and environmental disruptions are caused when these goods are produced.

Much of the solid waste in the United States is deposited in unsightly, uncontrolled, smelly, polluting **open dumps.** Some wastes are dumped untreated into the ocean. A **sanitary landfill** is an area where trash is deposited, compacted, and covered with soil daily to reduce pollution.

Many metropolitan areas **incinerate** their garbage and use the heat to produce steam. In recent years, the fuel content of trash, the value of the steam, and the operating costs of alternative methods of disposal have all increased; thus, incineration has become more desirable.

If an item cannot be reused or repaired, it may be practical to recycle the materials of which it is made. In general, recycling conserves material resources and fuel reserves and produces less pollution than manufacturing from virgin sources.

Some recycling techniques include melting, repulping, composting, and rendering.

Recycling has stagnated in our society mainly because the cost of labor is high relative to the cost of energy. In addition, the economic externalities of manufacturing, waste disposal, and depletion of resources are generally ignored. However, a shift in any relevant factor can change the balance. For example, along the eastern seaboard, the cost of disposal is rising, and, as a result, there is strong incentive toward recycling or incineration.

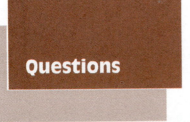

Questions

Solid Wastes

1. Plastics, made from coal and oil, have a high heat content. If garbage incinerators were commonly used in the United States and the resulting heat of combustion were used industrially, would you feel that plastic packaging would be an advantageous way to use fossil fuels twice? Defend your answer.

2. An old-timer complains that years ago, a man could store canned milk in a creek for 3 years before the can would rust through, but now a can will only last 1 year in the creek. Would you agree with the old-timer that cans should be made to be more durable? What about automobiles? Explain any differences.

Recycling

3. Broken or obsolete items can be repaired, broken down for the extraction of materials, or discarded. Which route is more conservative of raw materials and energy for each of the following items? (1) A 1948-model passenger car that doesn't run; (2) a 1983-model passenger car that doesn't run; (3) an ocean liner grounded on a sandbar and broken in two; (4) an ocean liner sunk in the central ocean; (5) last year's telephone directory; (6) an automobile battery that won't produce current because the owner of the car left the lights on overnight?

4. Sand and bauxite, which are the raw materials for glass and aluminum, respectively, are plentiful in the Earth's crust. Since we are in no danger of depleting these resources in the near future, why should we concern ourselves with recycling glass bottles and aluminum cans?

5. List the most efficient recycling technique and the resultant products for each of the following: (1) steer manure; (2) old clothes; (3) scrap lumber; (4) aluminum foil used to wrap your lunch; (5) a broken piece of pottery; (6) old bottle caps; (7) stale beer; (8) old eggshells; (9) a burnt-out power saw; (10) worn-out furniture; (11) old garden tools; (12) tin cans; (13) disposable diapers. How does your choice of technique depend on your community?

6. At the present time, recycling of paper is a marginally profitable business, and many repulping mills have gone bankrupt in recent years. List some of the economic externalities associated with the production of paper from raw materials. Who bears these costs? How could the burden be shifted to encourage paper recycling?

7. A family lives in a sparsely populated canyon in the northern Rocky Mountains. Their household trash is disposed of in the following manner: Papers are used to start the morning fire in the potbelly stove; food wastes are either fed to livestock or composted; ashes are incorporated into the compost mixture; metal cans are cleaned, cut open, and used to line storage bins to make them rodent-resistant; glass bottles are saved to store food; miscellaneous refuse is hauled to a sanitary landfill. Comment on this system. Can you think of situations in which this system would be undesirable? Do you think that it is likely that many people will adopt this system?

8. Rendering plants recycle various slaughterhouse and cannery wastes. Despite careful controls, these factories sometimes emit foul odors. Comment on the overall environmental impact of a rendering plant.

9. Environmental organizations have been active in establishing collection centers for old newspapers, cans, and so on. Can you think of other activities that these groups might initiate that would produce increased recycling?

10. As stated in the text, 50 percent of all aluminum beverage cans sold in the United States are recycled, whereas in states where a bottle bill is in force, the recycling rate is 90 percent or greater. (a) If you live in a state that does *not* have a bottle bill, walk along a street or roadway for 15 minutes and pick up all the cans you can find. At $.05 per can, how much could you make an hour picking up cans? Would your return be high enough to justify the work? If you sell the cans for scrap, your return is closer to $.01 per can. At that rate is it worth it to pick up cans? If cans were worth $.05 each, do you think that you would find as many lying around? (b) If you live in a state with a bottle bill, estimate the amount of time you spend per week collecting and returning bottles. Interview the manager of a local supermarket and record his or her views on the bill.

11. In 1976, voters in Colorado were asked to decide whether or not to levy a mandatory tax on nonreturnable cans and bottles. The beverage industry strongly opposed the law. In one brochure published by a major beer manufacturer it was stated:

> Claim: Amendment #8 [the proposed bottle law] would conserve energy and resources.
>
> Fact: Any savings in coal consumption resulting from the law would be offset by an increase in the consumption of gasoline, natural gas, and water.
>
> Returnable bottles are heavier than nonreturnable cans. Manufacturing their heavy, durable carrying cases would require an increase in energy consumption.
>
> Bottles would also require twice as much space as cans. Trucks would have to make at least twice as many trips to haul refillable containers, to say nothing of the extra trips to pick up empties, resulting in increased gasoline consumption.
>
> Washing re-usable bottles requires five times more water than cans. Heating the water for sterilization and removing the detergents that are used means increased energy consumption.

Examine these statements critically. Have all the facts been presented fully and accurately, or do you think that the brochure states the case incompletely? Is it reasonable or misleading? Defend your position.

12. In arguing against a mandatory bottle deposit bill, the president of a supermarket chain instead recommended a bill for "total litter control." Such a law would provide public funds to pay jobless youths at minimum wage to remove all litter (not just beverage containers) from streets and highways and to establish community recycling centers and a public education campaign. Prepare a class debate in which one side favors the bottle deposit bill, while the other side favors the "total litter control" approach.

13. As stated in the text, the energy required to manufacture one aluminum can is approximately equal to the energy content of half a can of gasoline. Assume that the deposit on the can is $.05 and its volume is 12 fluid ounces. How many aluminum cans would be equivalent to the energy content of 10 gal of gasoline? How much money would you receive if you recycled those cans? How much would 10 gal of gasoline cost? Are the two values equal? Explain any discrepancies.

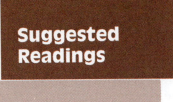

Suggested Readings

General references on solid wastes and information on recycling can be found in:

Nicholas Basta: A renaissance in recycling. *High Technology,* October, 1985.

Peter Bohm: *Deposit-Refund Systems, Theory and Applications in Environmental, Conservation, and Consumer Policy.* Washington, D.C., Resources for the Future Books, 1981. 192 pp.

William U. Chandler: Materials recycling: The virtue of necessity. *World Watch Institute Paper* 56, October, 1983.

Bruce Hannon and James R. Broderick: Steel recycling and energy conservation. *Science, 216,* 1982.

Donald Huisingh, Larry Martin, Helene Hilger, and Neil Seldman: *Proven Profits from Pollution Prevention.* Washington, D.C., Institute for Local Self-Reliance, 1986. 316 pp.

Cynthia Pollock: Mining urban wastes: The potential for recycling. *World Watch Paper, 76,* 1987.

Arthur H. Purcell: *The Waste Watchers: A Citizen's Handbook for Conserving Energy and Resources.* New York, Anchor Press/Doubleday, 1980.

Allan M. Springer: *Industrial Environmental Control, Pulp and Paper Industry.* Somerset, NJ, John Wiley & Sons, 1985. 432 pp.

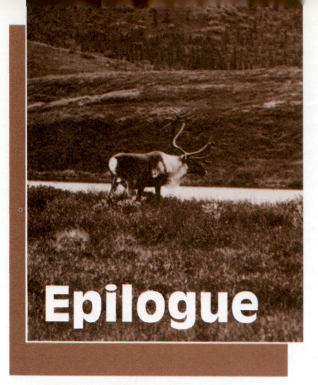

Epilogue

Thresholds of Change

It is natural for people to want to improve their lot in life. The very poor desire enough food to eat; the middle class or the rich would like to add more conveniences or luxuries to their existence. By many indicators, technology has been very successful at raising the standard of living of much of the human population. Despite large pockets of extreme poverty and starvation, the average global per capita income has increased dramatically during the course of this century. In 1900, the average global per capita income was $400 (in 1986 dollars). In 50 years, this value tripled to $1200, and, in the next 36 years, between 1950 and 1986, it more than doubled to $2600 per person per year. In human terms, this means that many of the world's people have attained a life of ease and well-being. Even many poor people in the developing and the less-developed countries have access to tools, education, and medical attention that were simply not available one hundred years ago.

Nearly everyone will agree that one goal of modern society is to continue to improve the human condition. The question is how to meet this goal. Whenever someone takes an action to increase the economic well-being of some portion of the population, environmental side effects are generated. In most cases, these side effects are detrimental in some way. Therefore, there is a balance of gains and losses. If the gains are greater than the losses, the human condition is indeed improved. If the losses outweigh the gains, however, we are sliding backward. This concept is easy enough to understand, but, in actual practice, the essential issues are not always clear. Problems arise because gains and losses are not always located in the same place, do not always affect the same people, and do not always occur at the same time.

One issue of great importance is the balance between short-term gain and long-term loss. If the gain is immediate and the loss may occur sometime in the future, it is tempting to ignore the loss. Or, if the loss is not ignored, it is tempting to predict that it will be small. In actual fact, many environmental effects are *more* severe than would have been predicted from a simple extrapolation of past events.

In order to understand why this is true, it is important to review the concept of thresholds. Recall from Sections 18.2 and 21.5 that a **threshold** is a point near the edge of a very rapid change. To understand how environmental thresholds function, consider the following two examples:

Ice melts at 0°C. Imagine that during the summer, the average temperature in an area that contains massive glaciers is −2°C. If the temperature increases by 1.5°C, nothing much happens because the temperature rises to −0.5°C, and the glaciers remain solid. If you didn't know the melting point of ice, and observed that a temperature rise of 1.5°C caused little effect, you might make the extrapolation that another 1.5°C temperature rise would also cause little change. However, this prediction would be wrong, because it ignores the fact that the first temperature rise placed the environment on the edge of a threshold. If the warming trend continued, only a small additional rise in temperature would cause the ice to melt. Then the sea level might rise, coastal cities might be flooded, and climates might change (see Special Topic A in Chapter 21).

As another example, recall the riddle posed in Chapter 1 (Box 1.4). Assume that the area covered by lily plants in a lake doubles in size every day. If allowed to grow freely, the plants would cover the entire surface of the pond in 30 days. On what day will the pond be half covered, and how much time will you have to avert disaster? The answer: The pond will be half covered in 29 days and you have only 1 day to act. The mathematics behind this riddle applies equally well to the growth of a population or to the consumption of a resource. In the real world, however, the problem is compounded, because we often don't know how big the lily pond is, that is, we don't always know the carrying capacity of populations in ecosystems or the total quantity of many resources.

Anyone who tries to extrapolate future environmental problems must ask, "Are we already poised at the edge of a threshold?" In a recent publication by the Worldwatch Institute, the authors warn:*

> With many of the natural systems now at risk, however, thresholds are not well defined, systemic responses to threshold crossings are not well understood, and the consequences of those crossings are largely incalculable. . . .
> Any system pushed out of equilibrium behaves in unpredictable ways. Small external pressures may be sufficient to cause dramatic changes.

*Lester Brown et al.: *State of the World 1987*. New York, W.W. Norton and Co, 1987. 268 pp.

Stresses may become self-reinforcing, rapidly increasing the system's instability.

In the reference just cited, the authors discuss six areas where global environments may be approaching environmental thresholds.

Population In 1800, there were 1 billion people on the Earth. The population doubled to 2 billion by 1930, and doubled again to 4 billion by 1975. Sometime in 1986, the human population topped the 5 billion mark. Over the next generation, 3 billion young people will enter the reproductive years. Since each future doubling adds an ever-increasing number of persons, there is a real risk that, like the population of lilies in the pond, the human population may someday reach a threshold at which there is little time left to act.

Soil and Agriculture Before 1950, most of the increases in world grain production resulted from an increase in the total land under cultivation. By 1950, however, most of the potentially prime agricultural land in the world was already being farmed, and, between 1950 and 1987, increases in grain production were realized mainly by increasing productivity per hectare. These increases have largely been possible by increased use of fossil fuels. Between 1950 and 1985, the global fleet of tractors quadrupled, irrigation systems have increased threefold, and fertilizer use has increased ninefold. During that period, the total fossil fuel energy needed to produce a tonne of grain has increased by a factor of 2.6. Thus, world food production has become highly dependent on production of fuels. If fuels become expensive or unavailable, food production will suffer a sudden decline and prices will rise rapidly.

In any ecosystem, soil is both produced and removed by natural processes. In most natural ecosystems, the rate of production is greater than the rate of removal, and soil quantity and fertility increase with time. In recent years, however, the rate of soil erosion in many agricultural systems has become greater than the rate of production. Up to a point, productivity can remain high, even as soil is being lost. For example, if the topsoil is 100 cm deep and 50 cm are lost, crops can still be grown, and, especially if fertilizers are available, productivity will remain high. However, when the second 50 cm are lost, there is nothing left. A threshold has been crossed.

Species Many organisms can survive only in specific habitats. As ecosystems are being destroyed across the face of the globe, the populations of many species are dwindling rapidly. The critical minimum size of a population (discussed in Chapter 12) is a threshold quantity, and, when a species is reduced to this level, it will slide into extinction, even if many of the original pressures are removed. Although it is impossible to predict the critical minimum size of any given species, many extinctions have already occurred, and biologists are convinced that we are heading toward a much more massive wave of extinctions in the near future.

Fuels and Other Resources In 1987, fuels and other resources such as timber, minerals, and fresh water were available in most parts of the world. However, depletion rates for many of these materials were high relative to the total quantity of reserves. In the United States, proven oil reserves were enough to supply domestic needs for less than 8 years without the use of imported fuels. India, with 20 percent of the global population (1 billion people) has less than 1 percent of the world's oil reserves. Many people in the world use wood as a primary source of fuel, yet timber reserves, too, are declining. Between 1977 and 1984, the price of fuelwood in India increased by 42 percent as a result of declining reserves. The price and availability of other commodities fluctuates, but we cannot ignore the central fact that any resource will eventually be depleted if consumption is faster than regeneration.

Chemicals in the Environment To understand how thresholds operate in the field of chemical contamination, consider the following example. Solutions containing a chemical in both its acidic and basic forms, such as carbonic acid (acidic) and sodium bicarbonate (basic) are said to be **buffered**. If a small amount of a strong acid is added to a buffered solution, the base in the solution will neutralize most of this acid, and the pH will change only slightly. Similarly, if a small amount of a strong base is added, the equilibrium will shift to counteract this addition. In natural ecosystems, most soils are buffered in this manner. Therefore, if a small amount of acid rain falls in a temperate forest, the soil acidity will change very little—much less than would happen if the soil

were not buffered. However, if acids are added continuously, eventually the buffering mechanism becomes overwhelmed. When this happens, the pH of the soil suddenly changes radically with an addition of a small amount of acid. This rapid change, after a long period of relative constancy, is the essence of a threshold effect and is being observed in forest soils in Europe and North America.

Climate The problem of ozone in the stratosphere, discussed in Section 21.5, is an important example of an environmental problem that may be very close to passing a threshold. Some scientists even believe that the threshold has already been crossed. Similarly scientists have posted warnings that excess atmospheric carbon dioxide will cause global warming (see Section 21.4). Yet, for many years, no such warming trend was recorded. Then, in the mid-1980s, global warming was documented. Here, too, climatologists are asking whether or not thresholds have already been crossed.

A warning is different from a prediction. A prediction is a statement that some event will occur. A warning is a statement that if nothing is done, some event will occur. A warning is a call to action. If future economic advances are to improve rather than detract from the human condition, these advances must be guided toward the development of a sustainable society. In a sustainable society, we do not take from the Earth, rather we enter into a cycle that removes and returns. The net result of such a cycle is that resources are not permanently depleted. Six major steps toward a sustainable society are listed below:

- Stabilize world population.
- Protect cropland.
- Reforest the Earth and protect endangered species.
- Conserve the fossil fuels that we have now, and develop renewable energy sources for the future.
- Move beyond the throwaway society.
- Protect natural ecosystems and global climates by reducing emission of pollutants.

The transition to a sustainable society will challenge the capacity of countries everywhere to change and adapt. Some adjustments will occur in response to market forces, some in response to public policy changes, and still others as a result of voluntary changes in lifestyles. In order to take the necessary steps, all nations will have to make major financial commitments as soon as possible. . . .

Taking part in the creation of a sustainable society will be an extraordinarily challenging and satisfying experience, enriched by a sense of excitement that our immediate forebearers who built fossil-fuel–based societies did not have. The excitement comes from both the vast scale of the undertaking and the full knowledge of the consequences of failure.*

*Lester R. Brown and Pamela Shaw: *Six Steps to a Sustainable Society.* Worldwatch Paper 48, Washington, D.C., Worldwatch Institute, March, 1982. 63 pp.

Physical Concepts and Units of Measurement

FACTOR	PREFIX	SYMBOL	EXAMPLE
10^{20}	geo*		geogram = 10^{20} grams
10^{9}	giga	G	gigajoule, GJ = 1 billion joules
10^{6}	mega	M	megawatt, MW = 1 million watts
10^{3}	kilo	k	kilogram, kg = 1000 grams
10^{2}	hecto	h	hectare, ha = 100 ares (measure of area)
10^{-1}	deci	d	decibel, dB = $\frac{1}{10}$ bel (measure of sound)
10^{-2}	centi	c	centimeter, cm = $\frac{1}{100}$ meter
10^{-3}	milli	m	millimeter, mm = $\frac{1}{1000}$ meter
10^{-6}	micro	μ	micrometer, μm = a millionth of a meter

*Not an official SI prefix.

The International System of Units (SI) defines various units of measurement as well as prefixes for multiplying or dividing the units by decimal factors. The prefixes used in this book are as shown in the table above.

The SI rules specify that its symbols are not followed by periods, nor are they changed in the plural. Thus, it is correct to write "The tree is 10 m high," not "10 m. high" or "10 ms high."

• **Time**   The SI unit is the **second,** s or sec, which used to be based on the rotation of the Earth but is now related to the vibration of atoms of cesium-133. SI prefixes are used for fractions of a second (such as milliseconds or microseconds), but the common words **minutes, hours,** and **days** are still used to express multiples of seconds.

• **Length**   The SI unit is the **meter,** m, which used to be based on a standard platinum bar but is now defined in terms of wavelengths of light. The closest English equivalent is the **yard** (0.914 m). A **mile** is 1.61 kilometers (km). An inch is exactly 2.54 centimeters (cm).* A **nautical mile** is 1.15 miles, or 1.85 km. A **knot** is the speed of a nautical mile per hour, or 1.15 miles per hour.

*All relationships between units of the same system are exact. Those between different systems are approximate, except when otherwise noted.

• **Area** is length squared, as in **square meter, square foot,** and so on. The SI unit of area is the **are,** a, which is 100 square m. More commonly used is the **hectare,** ha, which is 100 ares, or a square that is 100 m on each side. (The length of a U.S. football field plus one end zone is just about 100 m.) A hectare is 2.47 acres. An **acre** is 43,560 square feet, which is a plot of, say, 220 ft by 198 ft.

• **Volume** is length cubed, as in **cubic centimeter,** cm^3, **cubic foot,** ft^3, and so on. The SI unit is the **liter,** L, which is 1000 cm^3. A **quart** is 0.946 L; a U.S. liquid **gallon** (gal) is 3.785 L. A **barrel** of petroleum (U.S.) is 42 gal, or 159 L. A **drum** (not a standard unit of volume) of the type generally used by the chemical industry and often found in chemical waste dumps is 55 gal, or 208 L.

• **Mass** is the amount of matter in an object. **Weight** is the force of gravity on an object. To illustrate the difference, an astronaut in space has no weight but still has mass. On Earth, the two terms are directly proportional and often used interchangeably. The SI unit of mass is the **kilogram,** kg, which is based on a standard platinum mass. A **pound** (avdp), lb, is a unit of weight. On the surface of the Earth, 1 lb is equal to 0.454 kg. A **metric ton,** also written as **tonne,** is 1000 kg, or about 2205 lb. In the English system, a **short ton** is 2000 lb and a **long ton** is 2240 lb. A tonne is therefore between the two English tons but closer to the long ton. This book always uses the term "tonne" because it is the metric unit.

• **Temperature** The SI unit is the **kelvin** (K). In measuring differences in temperature, such as the rise in temperature from the melting point of ice to the boiling point of water, one kelvin is the same as 1 degree Celsius (°C). However, Celsius temperature (not temperature difference) is related to kelvin temperature as follows:

Celsius temperature (°C) = kelvin temperature (K) − 273 K

Freezing point of water	Boiling point of water
0°C or 273 K	100°C or 373 K

difference = 100°C or 100 K

In describing very high temperatures, such as the millions of degrees in stars or nuclear reactions, the 273-degree difference between the two scales is too small to matter, so either the kelvin or the Celsius scale can be used. Fahrenheit temperature (°F) is not used in scientific writing, although it is still popular in English-speaking countries.

• **Concentration** is the quantity of a substance in a given volume of space or in a given quantity of some other substance. "Quantity" can be expressed in units of mass or volume, or even in molecules.

percent = parts per 100 parts
ppm = parts per million parts
ppb = parts per billion parts

Concentration is therefore always a ratio:

$$\frac{\text{quantity of substance X}}{\text{volume of space}}, \text{ or } \frac{\text{quantity of substance X}}{\text{quantity of substance in which X is dispersed}}$$

For example, 1 kg of ocean water contains about 65 mg of the element bromine. The concentration of bromine in the ocean is therefore

$$\frac{65 \text{ mg bromine}}{1 \text{ kg of ocean water}}$$

But a kilogram is 1 million milligrams, so we can write

$$\text{concentration} = \frac{65 \text{ mg bromine}}{1 \text{ million mg ocean water}}$$

When both quantities are expressed in the same units, the units can be dropped (they cancel out), and we can say simply that the concentration of bromine is 65 parts per million (ppm) by weight (or mass).

Quantities of gases are usually expressed in units of volume. For example, the concentration of carbon dioxide, CO_2, in air is 350 ppm by volume. Because the volume of a gas is proportional to the number of molecules it contains, the concentration of a gas "by volume" really means "by number of molecules." Thus, there are 350 molecules of CO_2 per million molecules of air. The concentration of dusts in air cannot be expressed in volume units, however, because dusts are not gases. The concentration of particulate matter in air is expressed in mass per unit volume. For example, the maximum exposure to the pesticide 2,4-D allowed by OSHA for an 8-hour work shift is 10 mg per cubic meter (10 mg/m^3) of air.

Concentrations expressed in parts per million or per billion by volume or mass seem quite small. In terms of molecules, however, such concentrations are very large. For example, if there is 10 ppb by weight of the pesticide DDD in water, each gram of water contains 20×10^{12}, or 20 trillion molecules of DDD. That concentration is high enough to kill some species of trout.

• **Energy** is a measure of work or heat, which were once thought to be different quantities. Hence, two different sets of units were adopted and still persist, although we now know that work and heat are both forms of energy.

The SI unit of energy is the **joule,** J, the work required to exert a force of one newton through a distance of 1 m. In turn, a newton is the force that gives a mass of 1 kg an acceleration of 1 m/sec^2. In human terms, a joule is not much—it is about the amount of work required to lift a 100-g weight to a height of 1 m. Therefore, joule units are too small for discussions of machines, power plants, or energy policy. Larger units are

megajoule, MJ = 10^6 J (a day's work by one person)
gigajoule, GJ = 10^9 J (energy in half a tank of gasoline)

Another unit of energy, used for electrical work, is the **watt hour,** Wh, which is 3600 J. A **kilowatt hour,** kWh, is 3.6 MJ.

The energy unit used for heat is the **calorie,** cal, which is exactly 4.184 J. One calorie is just enough energy to warm 1 g of water 1°C. The more common unit used in measuring food energy is the **kilocalorie,** kcal, which is 1000 cal. When **Calorie** is spelled with a capital C, it means kcal. If a cookbook says that a jelly doughnut has 185 calories, that is an error—it should say 185 Calories (capital C), or 185 kcal. A value of 185 calories (small c) would be the energy in about one quarter of a thin slice of cucumber.

The unit of energy in the British system is the **British thermal unit,** Btu, which is the energy needed to warm 1 lb of water 1°F.

1 Btu = 1054 J = 1.054 kJ = 252 cal

The unit often referred to in discussions of national energy policies is the **quad,** which is a quadrillion Btu, or 10^{15} Btu.

Some approximate energy values are

1 barrel (42 gal) of petroleum = 5900 MJ
1 tonne of coal = 29,000 MJ
1 quad = 170 million barrels of oil, or 34 million tonnes of coal

• Efficiency of energy use

Imagine that you want to heat 1 kg of water from, say, 10°C to 90°C by using the heat from a fuel such as gasoline. The heat that must be absorbed by the water to reach the required temperature is 80 kcal, but let us say that you actually have to use 100 kcal to do the job. Since energy cannot be destroyed, where did the other 20 kcal go? Not into the water, obviously. The pot that contained the water absorbed some heat and so did the air in the room. The efficiency of your operation, therefore, was

$$\text{Efficiency} \atop (\text{1st law}) = \frac{\text{energy absorbed by the desired process}}{\text{total energy actually supplied}} \times 100\%$$

$$= \frac{80 \text{ kcal}}{100 \text{ kcal}} \times 100\% = 80\%$$

The assumption that the energy not absorbed by the water was merely wasted, but not destroyed, is really a statement of the first law of thermodynamics. This is the reason why the efficiency described by the above equation is called the **first law efficiency.**

Now imagine that you take the same amount of energy (100 kcal) and use it to run a heat engine, such as a gasoline engine, to make the engine work. The engine extracts the heat from the fuel and converts it to work. But heat can be extracted from a body only by flowing from a higher temperature to a lower temperature. (That is a statement of the second law of thermodynamics.) If the engine ran in an environment in which the outside temperature was absolute zero (zero kelvin, or −273°C), the engine theoretically could convert all the heat into work. But suppose, to pick convenient numbers, that the engine operated at 1000 K and the outside temperature was 500 K. The outside temperature would then be only halfway down from the operating temperature (1000 K) to absolute zero, and the engine could convert only half of its heat to work, yielding only 50 kcal of work. Anything better than that would be impossible; anything less would be inefficient. Therefore, the measure of efficiency is

$$\text{Efficiency (2nd law)} = \frac{\text{the minimum amount of useful energy (work) needed at a given temperature to do a desired task}}{\text{the amount of useful energy or work actually supplied}} \times 100\%$$

The efficiency calculated in this way is called the **second law efficiency.**

• **Power**   is a measure of energy per unit time. The SI unit is the **watt,** W, which is a joule per second. Other common units are the **kilowatt,** kW, which is 1000 watts, and the **megawatt,** MW, which is 1 million watts. The older English unit is the **horsepower,** which is about three quarters of a kilowatt. The watt rating of a light bulb is its power rating. A 100-watt bulb generates 100 watts of power when it is lit. Your electric bill is a charge for energy, not power—you pay for the wattage multiplied by the time. If the bulb is lit for a day, you pay for 100 watts × 24 hours, which is 2400 watt hours or 2.4 kilowatt hours. A factory that generates electricity is called a power plant, not an energy plant, because it is rated according to the power it can produce (usually expressed in megawatts).

Chemical Symbols, Formulas, and Equations

Atoms or elements are denoted by symbols of one or two letters, such as H, U, W, Ba, and Zn.

Compounds or molecules are represented by formulas that consist of symbols and subscripts, sometimes with parentheses. The subscript denotes the number of atoms of the element represented by the symbol to which it is attached. Thus, H_2SO_4 is a formula that represents a molecule of sulfuric acid, or the substance sulfuric acid. The molecule consists of two atoms of hydrogen, one atom of sulfur, and four atoms of oxygen. The substance consists of matter that is an aggregate of such molecules. The formula for oxygen gas is O_2; this tells us that the molecules consist of two atoms each.

Chemical transformations are represented by chemical equations, which tell us the molecules or substances that react and the ones that are produced, and the molecular ratios of these reactants. The equation for the burning of methane in oxygen to produce carbon dioxide and water is

$$CH_4 + 2O_2 \rightarrow CO_2 + 2H_2O$$

Each coefficient applies to the entire formula that follows it. Thus, $2H_2O$ means $2(H_2O)$.

The atoms in a molecule are held together by chemical bonds. Chemical bonds can be characterized by their length, the angles they make with other bonds, and their strength (that is, how much energy would be needed to break them apart).

In general, substances whose molecules have strong chemical bonds are stable, because it is energetically unprofitable to break strong bonds apart and rearrange the atoms to form other, weaker bonds. Therefore, stable substances may be regarded as chemically self-satisfied; they have little energy to offer and are said to be energy-poor. Thus, water, with its strong H–O bonds, is not a fuel or a food. The bonds between carbon and oxygen in carbon dioxide, CO_2, are also strong (about 1.5 times as strong as the H–O bonds of water), and CO_2 is therefore also an energy-poor substance.

In contrast, the C–H bonds in methane, CH_4, are weaker than the H–O bonds of water. It is energetically profitable to break these bonds and produce the more stable ones in H_2O and CO_2. Methane is therefore an energy-rich substance and can be burned to heat houses and drive engines.

Acidity and the pH Scale

Hydrogen ions render water acidic. The original meaning of acid is "sour," referring to the taste of substances such as vinegar, lemon juice, unripe apples, and old milk. It has long been observed that all sour or acidic substances have some properties in common, notably their ability to corrode (rust, or oxidize) metals. When the attack on a metal by an acidic solution is vigorous, hydrogen gas (H_2) is evolved in the form of visible bubbles. Acidic solutions also conduct electricity, with evolution of hydrogen gas at the negative electrode (cathode). These circumstances imply that acid solutions are characterized by the presence of positive ions bearing hydrogen. A hydrogen ion, or proton, designated H^+, cannot exist as an independent entity in water, because it is strongly attracted (in fact, chemically bonded) to the oxygen atom of the water molecule. The resulting hydrated proton is formulated as $H(H_2O)^+$, or H_3O^+. The simpler designation H^+ may therefore be regarded as an abbreviation.

Some slight transfer of protons occurs even in pure water.

$$H_2O + H_2O \leftrightarrows H_3O^+ + OH^-$$

Hydroxyl ions, OH^-, can neutralize H_3O^+ ions by reacting with them to produce water, as indicated by the arrow pointing left. The concentration of H_3O^+ and of OH^- in pure water at 25°C is 1.0×10^{-7} moles/liter.* This solution is said to be *neutral,* because the concentrations of the two ions are equal. When the hydrogen ion concentration is greater than 1.0×10^{-7} moles/liter at 25°C, the solution is *acidic.* Hydrogen ion concentrations are usually expressed logarithmically as pH values, where pH $= - \log_{10}$ (hydrogen ion concentration).

Recall that the logarithm of a number "to the base 10" is simply the *number of times 10 is multiplied by itself* to give the number. When the number is a multiple of 10, its log is simply the number of zeros it contains. When the number is 1 divided by a multiple of 10, its log is *minus* the number of zeros in the denominator. Therefore, when the number expresses hydrogen ion concentration, the pH is *plus* the number of zeros in the denominator:

---

*One mole of hydrogen atoms is the amount that weighs one gram.

Concentration of H$^+$ (Moles/Liter)	pH
1/10	1 (acidic)
1/10,000,000	7 (neutral)
1/1,000,000,000	9 (basic)

Any pH less than 7 connotes acidity. The lower the pH of a body of water, the more prone it is to be corrosive and, thereby, to become polluted with metallic compounds. Any pH greater than 7 is basic.

Chemical Formulas of Various Substances

Organochlorides
Dichlorodiphenyltrichloroethane
(DDT)

Dichlorodiphenyldichloroethane
(DDD)

Aldrin

Organochlorides
Dioxin

Lindane
(Containing
99% γ-Isomer)

2,4-Dichlorophenoxyacetic Acid
(2,4-D)

2,4,5-Trichlorophenoxyacetic Acid
(2,4,5-T)

Organophosphate Pesticides
Malathion

Polychlorinated Biphenyls
(PCBS)

And Other Isomers

Organophosphate Pesticides
Parathion

A Carbamate Pesticide
Sevin®
(1-Naphthyl-N-Methylcarbamate)

Growth Rates and Doubling Time

A **geometric** (or **exponential**) **growth rate** is calculated as follows: If there are x individuals in the zeroth generation and ax individuals in the first generation (where a is greater than 1), there will be $a(ax)$ or a^2x in the second generation, a^3x in the third, and so on to a^nx in the nth generation.

Generation, n	Number of individuals ($x = 10$)	
	$a = 2$ (doubling)	$a = 3$ (tripling)
0	10	10
1	20	30
2	40	90
⋮		
5	$2^5 \times 10 = 320$	$3^5 \times 10 = 2430$
⋮		
$\dot{n}$	$2^n \times 10$	$3^n \times 10$

In an **arithmetic** (or **linear**) **growth rate,** each generation increases by a constant amount, and there will be $x + na$ individuals in the nth generation.

Generation, n	Number of individuals ($x = 10$; $a = 2$)
0	10
1	12
2	14
⋮	
$\dot{n}$	$10 + 2n$

Geometric growth is always eventually much faster than arithmetic growth.

To compute doubling time from rate of growth, think of an analogy with compound interest at the bank. If a rate of growth (interest rate) is applied once a year to a population of size P_o (capital in the bank), the population (capital) at the end of one year is

$$P_1 = P_o + P_o r = P_o (1 + r)$$

More generally, if population growth is compounded n times each year, the population in year t is

$$P_t = P_o(1 + r/n)^{nt}$$

It is reasonable to suppose that populations grow continuously or that $n \to \infty$. From elementary calculus,

$$\lim_{n \to \infty}(1 + r/n)^{nt} = e^{rt}$$

The doubling time, t_d, is then the solution of the equation

$$2P_o = P_o e^{rt_d}$$

Or, taking logarithms on both sides of the equation,

$$t_d = 0.693/r.$$

Appendix F   The Decibel Scale

Physicists have created a unit that defines a tenfold increase in sound intensity and named it a **bel,** after Alexander Graham Bell. If the sound of a garbage disposal unit is 10 times as intense as that of a vacuum cleaner, it is one bel more intense. A rocket whose sound is a million, or 10^6, times as intense as the vacuum cleaner is therefore 6 bels more intense. The bel is a rather large unit, so it is convenient to divide it into tenths, or **decibels,** dB. A decibel is one tenth of a bel. These definitions lead to the following relationship:

$$\text{Difference in intensity between two sounds, } X \text{ and } Y, \text{ expressed in decibels, dB} = 10 \log_{10}\left(\frac{\text{sound intensity of X}}{\text{sound intensity of Y}}\right)$$

Finally, it is convenient to start a scale somewhere that can be designated as zero. The most convenient zero decibel level is the softest sound level that is audible to the human ear. Then,

$$\text{Intensity in decibels of any given sound} = 10 \log_{10}\left(\frac{\text{intensity of the given sound}}{\text{intensity of a barely audible sound}}\right)$$

Example: The sound of a vacuum cleaner in a room has 10 million times the intensity of the faintest audible sound. What is the intensity of the sound in decibels?

Answer:

$$\left(\frac{\text{sound intensity of vacuum cleaner}}{\text{faintest audible sound}}\right) = 10{,}000{,}000$$

$$\log 10{,}000{,}000 = 7$$

$$\begin{aligned}
\text{Sound intensity} &= 10 \times \log 10{,}000{,}000 \\
&= 10 \times 7 \\
&= 70 \text{ decibels}
\end{aligned}$$

Appendix G
Table of Atomic Weights* (Based on Carbon-12)

	Symbol	Atomic No.	Atomic Weight		Symbol	Atomic No.	Atomic Weight
Actinium	Ac	89	227.0278	Europium	Eu	63	151.96
Aluminum	Al	13	26.98154	Fermium	Fm	100	[257]
Americium	Am	95	[243]†	Fluorine	F	9	18.998403
Antimony	Sb	51	121.75	Francium	Fr	87	[223]
Argon	Ar	18	39.948	Gadolinium	Gd	64	157.25
Arsenic	As	33	74.9216	Gallium	Ga	31	69.72
Astatine	At	85	[210]	Germanium	Ge	32	72.59
Barium	Ba	56	137.33	Gold	Au	79	196.9665
Berkelium	Bk	97	[247]	Hafnium	Hf	72	178.49
Beryllium	Be	4	9.01218	Helium	He	2	4.00260
Bismuth	Bi	83	208.9804	Holmium	Ho	67	164.9304
Boron	B	5	10.81	Hydrogen	H	1	1.0079
Bromine	Br	35	79.904	Indium	In	49	114.82
Cadmium	Cd	48	112.41	Iodine	I	53	126.9045
Calcium	Ca	20	40.08	Iridium	Ir	77	192.22
Californium	Cf	98	[251]	Iron	Fe	26	55.847
Carbon	C	6	12.011	Krypton	Kr	36	83.80
Cerium	Ce	58	140.12	Lanthanum	La	57	138.9055
Cesium	Cs	55	132.9054	Lawrencium	Lr	103	[260]
Chlorine	Cl	17	35.453	Lead	Pb	82	207.2
Chromium	Cr	24	51.996	Lithium	Li	3	6.941
Cobalt	Co	27	58.9332	Lutetium	Lu	71	174.967
Copper	Cu	29	63.546	Magnesium	Mg	12	24.305
Curium	Cm	96	[247]	Manganese	Mn	25	54.9380
Dysprosium	Dy	66	162.50	Mendelevium	Md	101	[258]
Einsteinium	Es	99	[252]	Mercury	Hg	80	200.59
Erbium	Er	68	167.26	Molybdenum	Mo	42	95.94

Table continued on next page.

	Symbol	Atomic No.	Atomic Weight		Symbol	Atomic No.	Atomic Weight
Neodymium	Nd	60	144.24	Scandium	Sc	21	44.9559
Neon	Ne	10	20.179	Selenium	Se	34	78.96
Neptunium	Np	93	237.0482	Silicon	Si	14	28.0855
Nickel	Ni	28	58.70	Silver	Ag	47	107.868
Niobium	Nb	41	92.9064	Sodium	Na	11	22.98977
Nitrogen	N	7	14.0067	Strontium	Sr	38	87.62
Nobelium	No	102	[259]	Sulfur	S	16	32.06
Osmium	Os	76	190.2	Tantalum	Ta	73	180.9479
Oxygen	O	8	15.9994	Technetium	Tc	43	[98]
Palladium	Pd	46	106.4	Tellurium	Te	52	127.60
Phosphorus	P	15	30.97376	Terbium	Tb	65	158.9254
Platinum	Pt	78	195.09	Thallium	Tl	81	204.37
Plutonium	Pu	94	[244]	Thorium	Th	90	232.0381
Polonium	Po	84	[209]	Thulium	Tm	69	168.9342
Potassium	K	19	39.0983	Tin	Sn	50	118.69
Praseodymium	Pr	59	140.9077	Titanium	Ti	22	47.90
Promethium	Pm	61	[145]	Tungsten	W	74	183.85
Protactinium	Pa	91	231.0359	Uranium	U	92	238.029
Radium	Ra	88	226.0254	Vanadium	V	23	50.9415
Radon	Rn	86	[222]	Xenon	Xe	54	131.30
Rhenium	Re	75	186.207	Ytterbium	Yb	70	173.04
Rhodium	Rh	45	102.9055	Yttrium	Y	39	88.9059
Rubidium	Rb	37	85.4678	Zinc	Zn	30	65.38
Ruthenium	Ru	44	101.07	Zirconium	Zr	40	91.22
Samarium	Sm	62	150.4				

*Atomic weights given here are 1977 IUPAC values.
†A value given in brackets denotes the mass number of the longest-lived or best-known isotope.

Glossary

acid deposition   See *acid precipitation*.

acid mine drainage   Mineral acids that may leach from mining operations to pollute ground and surface water supplies.

acid precipitation (Also: acid deposition; acid rain)   A condition in which natural precipitation becomes acidic after reacting chemically with pollutants in the air.

acid rain   See *acid precipitation*.

activated sludge   See *sludge*.

adaptation   The process of accommodation to change; the process by which the characteristics of an organism become suited to the environment in which the organism lives.

adsorption   The process by which molecules from a liquid or gaseous phase become concentrated on the surface of a solid.

aerobiosis (*adj.*, aerobic)   Bacterial decomposition in the presence of air.

aerosol   A substance consisting of small particles, typically having diameters that range from 1/100 μm to 1 μm. See also *fume; smoke*.

age–sex distribution   the number or percentage of persons of each age group and each sex in a population.

air pollution   The deterioration of the quality of air that results from the addition of impurities.

air quality standards   Maximum allowable concentrations of air pollutants. Concentrations that exceed these limits are judged to be harmful. *Primary standards* are those needed to protect the public health. *Secondary standards* protect against other effects, such as damage to materials.

albedo   A measure of the reflectivity of a surface, measured as the ratio of light reflected to light received. A mirror or bright snowy surface has a high albedo, whereas a rough flat road surface has a low albedo.

altruism   Devotion to the interests of others.

anaerobiosis   (*adj.*, anaerobic)   The biological utilization of nutrients in the absence of air.

aquaculture   The science and practice of raising fish in artificially controlled ponds or pools.

aquifer   An underground layer of rock that is porous and permeable enough to store significant quantities of water.

arithmetic growth   In population studies, growth characterized by the addition of a constant number of individuals during a unit interval of time. For instance, if there are x individuals in year 0 and x + a in year 1, arithmetic growth implies x + na in year n.

artesian well   A well in which the groundwater has sufficient pressure to rise above the level of its aquifer.

atom   The fundamental unit of the element.

atomic nucleus   The small positive central portion of the atom that contains its protons and neutrons.

atomic number The number of protons in an atomic nucleus.

autotroph An organism that obtains its energy from the Sun, as opposed to a *heterotroph,* which is an organism that obtains its energy from the tissue of other organisms. Most plants are autotrophs. See also *trophic level.*

background radiation The level of radiation on Earth from natural sources.

bel ten decibels.

benthic organism A plant or animal that lives at or near the bottom of a body of water.

biochemical oxygen demand (B.O.D.) A measure of pollution of water by organic nutrients that recognizes the rate at which the nutrient matter uses up oxygen, as well as the total quantity that can be consumed.

biodegradable Refers to substances that can readily be decomposed by living organisms.

biogas Gas produced by fermentation of organic waste, consisting mostly of methane. The methane in biogas is chemically identical to methane produced by any other process.

biomass The total weight of all the living organisms in a given system.

biome A group of ecosystems characterized by similar vegetation and climate and that are collectively recognizable as a single large community unit. Examples include the arctic tundra, the North American prairie, and the tropical rainforest.

biosphere That part of the Earth and its atmosphere that can support life.

birth cohort A group of individuals born in a given period of time, such as in a particular year.

birthrate The number of individuals born during some time period, usually a year, divided by an appropriate population. For example, the crude birthrate in human populations is the number of live children born during a given year divided by the midyear population of that year.

black lung disease A series of debilitating and often fatal diseases that affect the lungs of miners who work in underground coal mines.

bloom A rapid and often unpredictable growth of a single species in an ecosystem.

boreal forest See *taiga.*

branching chain reaction A chain reaction in which each step produces more than one succeeding step.

breakwater See *groin.*

breeder reactor A nuclear reactor that produces more fissionable material than it consumes.

callus A mass of cells growing without differentiation used in a genetic engineering technique known as *somaclonal variation.*

calorie A unit of energy. When calorie is spelled with a small c, it refers to the thermal energy required to warm 1 g of water 1°C. When Calorie is spelled with a capital C, it means 1000 small calories, or 1 kilocalorie (kcal), the quantity of energy required to heat 1000 g (1 kg) of water 1°C. Food energies in nutrition are always expressed in Calories. The exact conversions to SI units are:

$$1 \text{ cal} = 4.184 \text{ joules}$$
$$1 \text{ kcal} = 4184 \text{ joules}$$

cancer An abnormal, unorganized, and unregulated growth of cells in an organism.

capillary action   The movement of water upward against the force of gravity, through small openings. The liquid is pulled upward by electrical attractions between the water molecules and the sides of the holes.

carnivore   An animal that eats the flesh of other animals.

carrying capacity   The maximum number of individuals of a given species that can be supported by a particular environment.

census   A count of a population.

chain reaction   A reaction that proceeds in a series of steps, each step being made possible by the preceding one. See also *branching chain reaction.*

chaparral   A biome characterized by a dry climate with little or no summer rain. Vegetation is dominated by shrubs that have adapted to regrow rapidly after fires that occur frequently during the dry season.

chelating agent   A substance whose molecules can offer two or more different chemical bonding sites to hold a metal ion in a clawlike linkage. The bonds between chelating agent and metal ion can be broken and re-established reversibly.

chemical bond   A linkage that holds atoms together to form molecules.

chemical change   A transfer that results from making or breaking of chemical bonds.

chemical energy   The energy absorbed when chemical bonds are broken or released when they are formed.

China Syndrome   A facetious expression referring to a nuclear meltdown in which the hot radioactive mass melts its way into the ground. Although a meltdown through the Earth to China is, of course, impossible, an accident in a nuclear power plant may potentially lead to a situation in which a hot radioactive mass melts its way through the containment structure into the earth, contaminating neighboring environments and groundwater supplies.

clearcutting   The practice of cutting all the trees in a designated area. Clearcutting leaves behind barren, open regions but is sometimes the cheapest way to harvest timber if only short-term economic evaluation is used. See also *selective cutting.*

climate   The composite pattern of weather conditions that can be expected in a given region. Climate refers to yearly cycles of temperature, wind, rainfall, and so on, not to daily variations.

climax community   A natural system that represents the end, or apex, of an ecological succession.

cogeneration   A tandem operation in which waste heat from one industrial process such as the generation of electricity is used in another process such as oil refining. In general, such a system uses fuel more efficiently than two separate facilities.

colloid   Material composed of minute particles, generally within a size range too small for gravitational settling but large enough to scatter light.

commensalism   A relationship in which one species benefits from an unaffected host.

competition   An interaction in which two or more organisms try to gain control of a limited resource. *Contest competition* occurs when one organism harms another in an effort to gain control over a resource. *Scramble competition* occurs when a number of organisms share a limited resource in such a way that no individuals have a particular advantage, and, therefore, all the individuals suffer.

composting   The controlled, accelerated biodegradation of moist organic matter to form a humus-like product that can be used as a fertilizer or soil conditioner.

conservation of energy (law of) See *thermodynamics.*

conservation of matter (law of) A law that states that in ordinary physical or chemical changes, matter cannot be created or destroyed.

containment structure A large vapor-proof, steel-lined, reinforced concrete structure built around a nuclear reactor and designed to contain all matter released inside, even in the event of a major accident.

continental drift The theory stating that continent-sized masses of the Earth's crust are slowly moving relative to one another.

control rod A neutron-absorbing medium that controls the rate of fissions in a nuclear reactor.

cooling pond A lake or pond used to cool water from an electric generating station or any other industrial facility.

cooling tower A large tower-like structure used to cool water from an electric generating station or any other industrial facility.

cost/benefit analysis A system of analysis that attempts to weigh the cost of some policy, such as pollution control, directly against the economic gain.

critical condition In general, the state of a system in which some property changes very abruptly in response to a small change in some other property. In nuclear science, it is the condition that exists when a chain reaction continues at a steady rate, neither accelerating nor slowing down.

critical mass (in a nuclear reaction) The quantity of fissile material just sufficient to maintain a nuclear chain reaction.

critical minimum size In ecology, the size of a population whose numbers are so few that it is in acute danger of extinction.

crude rate A vital rate with the entire population of some area as the denominator.

crust (of the Earth) The solid outer layer of the Earth; the portion on which we live. See also *mantle.*

cyclone (for air pollution control) An air cleaning device that removes dust particles by throwing them out of an air stream in a cyclonic motion.

death rate The number of individuals dying during some time period, usually a year, divided by an appropriate population. For example, the crude death rate in human populations is the number of deaths during a given year divided by the midyear population of that year.

decibel (dB) A unit of sound intensity equal to 1/10 of a bel. The decibel scale is a logarithmic scale used in measuring sound intensities relative to the intensity of the faintest audible sound.

defendant A person sued or accused in a court action.

demographic transition The pattern of change in vital rates typical of a developing society that passes through the following stages: (a) Very high birth- and death rates in its preindustrial condition, with consequently very slow population growth; (b) introduction or development of modern medicine causing a decline in death rates and hence a rapid increase in population growth; (c) finally, a fall in birth rates and the re-establishment of a slow growth of population.

demography The branch of sociology or anthropology that deals with the statistical characteristics of human populations, with reference to total size, density, number of deaths, births, migrations, marriages, prevalence of disease, and so forth.

deoxyribonucleic acid See *DNA.*

desert A climax system in which rainfall is less than 25 cm per year. These systems are barren and support relatively little plant or animal life.

desertification   The process whereby arid lands are converted to deserts, often by improper farming practices.

developed countries   Industrialized countries characterized by a population that has realized a high standard of living, good health, and long life expectancy.

developing countries   Countries that have started to industrialize but still contain large segments of the population that live under pre-industrial conditions.

doldrums   A region of the Earth near the Equator in which hot, humid air is moving vertically upward, forming a vast low-pressure region. Local squalls and rainstorms are common, and steady winds are rare.

DNA   A substance consisting of large molecules that determine the synthesis of proteins. DNA carries genetic information from parents to their progeny and therefore accounts for the continuity of species.

doubling time   The time that a population takes to double in size, or the time it would take to double if its annual growth rate were to remain constant.

dust   An airborne substance that consists of solid particles typically having diameters greater than about 1 μm.

ecological niche   The description of the unique functions and habitats of an organism in an ecosystem.

ecological succession   See *succession.*

ecology   The study of the interrelationships among plants and animals and the interaction between living organisms and their physical environment.

economic externality   The portion of the cost of a product that is not accounted for by the manufacturer but is borne by some other sector of society. An example is the cost of environmental degradation that results from a manufacturing operation.

ecosystem   A group of plants and animals occurring together plus that part of the physical environment with which they interact. An ecosystem is defined to be nearly self-contained, so that the matter flowing into and out of it is small compared to the quantities that are internally recycled in a continuous exchange of the essentials of life.

ecosystem homeostasis   The control mechanisms within an ecosystem that act to maintain constancy by the opposition of internal forces.

ecotone   a transitional zone between two biomes or between two different types of ecosystems.

electron   The fundamental atomic unit of negative electricity.

electrostatic precipitator   A device that electrically charges particulate air pollutants so that they drift to an electrically grounded wall from which they can be removed easily.

element   A substance all of whose atoms have the same atomic number.

emission standards   Legal limits on the quantities of air pollutants permitted to be emitted from the exhaust of a source of air pollution.

energy   The capacity to perform work. See also specific types of energy.

entropy   A thermodynamic measure of disorder. It has been observed that the entropy of an undisturbed system always increases during any spontaneous process; that is, the degree of disorder always increases.

environmental resistance   The sum of various pressures, such as predation, competition, and adverse weather, that collectively inhibit the potential growth of every species.

epidemiology   The study of the distribution and determination of health and its disorders.

epilimnion   Upper waters of a lake.

estuary   A partially enclosed shallow body of water with access to the open sea and usually a supply of fresh water from the land. Estuaries are less salty than the open ocean but are affected by tides and, to a lesser extent, by wave action of the sea.

euphotic zone   The surface volume of water in the ocean or a deep lake that receives sufficient light to support photosynthesis.

eutrophication   The enrichment of a body of water with nutrients, with the consequent deterioration of its quality for human purposes.

evapotranspiration   See *transpiration.*

evolution, theory of   A theory that states that species are not unchangeable but arise by descent and modification from pre-existing species.

exponential growth   See *geometric growth.*

externality   See *economic externality.*

extrapolation   The prediction of points on a graph outside the range of observation.

fermentation   An anaerobic process by which certain microorganisms consume sugars, starches, or cellulose to produce various organic byproducts, particularly alcohols. In this manner, some low-quality organic wastes can be converted to useful fuels or animal feeds.

fire climax   A condition in which the continuance of a given ecosystem is maintained by fire.

First Law of Thermodynamics   See *thermodynamics.*

fission (of atomic nuclei)   The splitting of atomic nuclei into approximately equal fragments.

flocculation   The process by which colloidal particles are bound into larger aggregates by chemical agents.

food chain   An idealized pattern of flow of energy in a natural ecosystem. In the classical food chain, plants are eaten only by primary consumers, primary consumers are eaten only by secondary consumers, secondary consumers only by tertiary consumers, and so forth. See also *food web.*

food web   The actual pattern of food consumption in a natural ecosystem. A given organism may obtain nourishment from many different trophic levels and thus give rise to a complex, interwoven series of energy transfers.

fusion (of atomic nuclei)   The combination of nuclei of light elements (particularly hydrogen) to form heavier nuclei.

Gaia   The ancient Greek goddess of the Earth. This word has recently been used to describe the biosphere and to emphasize the interdependence of the Earth's ecosystems by likening the entire biosphere to a single living organism.

gas   A state of matter consisting of molecules that are moving independently of each other in random patterns.

gaseous diffusion   The movement of a gas in space by the random motions of its molecules. Lighter gases diffuse faster than heavier gases.

gasohol   A motor fuel consisting of approximately 90 percent gasoline and 10 percent ethyl alcohol.

gene pool   The aggregate of all genes in an interbreeding community.

gene transfer   The artificial transfer of genetic information from one organism to another that is performed to create new organisms with desirable characteristics.

genetic engineering   The process of artificially altering the genes from one organism to create new organisms with desirable characteristics.

genetic resistance   The development of resistance to a foreign agent (often to a pesticide) by natural mutations.

geometric growth   In population studies, growth such that in each unit of time, the population increases by a constant proportion. Also called *exponential growth.*

geothermal energy   Energy derived from the heat of the Earth's interior.

germ cells   Cells involved in reproduction. See also *somatic cells.*

GRAS list   A list compiled by the FDA of those food additives that are *G*enerally *R*ecognized *A*s *S*afe.

green revolution   The realization of increased crop yields in many areas owing to the development of new high-yielding strains of wheat, rice, and other grains in the 1960s. The *second green revolution* is the use of the techniques of genetic engineering to improve agricultural yields.

greenhouse effect   The effect produced by certain gases, such as carbon dioxide or water vapor, that cause a warming of the Earth's atmosphere by absorption of infrared radiation. The term is an inappropriate analogy to greenhouses, which were once thought to keep themselves warm by admitting sunlight but retaining infrared radiation. However, it has been shown that most of the heat retention in greenhouses results from the conservation of warm air. The atmosphere, of course, is open, so the mechanism is not the same.

gross national product (GNP)   The total value of all goods and services produced by the economy in a given year.

half-life (of a radiactive substance)   The time required for half of a sample of radioactive matter to decompose.

heat engine   A mechanical device that converts heat to work.

heat pump   A mechanical device that uses an outside source of energy to force a separation of heat into a cool reservoir and a warmer one.

heavy oil   Natural petroleum deposits that are too thick to be extracted by conventional pumping techniques. Heavy oils are found in "dry" conventional wells as well as in oil shales and tar sands.

hectare   A metric measure of surface area. One hectare is equal to 10,000 sq m or 2.47 acres.

herbicide   A chemical used to control unwanted plants.

herbivore   An animal that eats only plant matter.

heterotroph   An organism that obtains its energy by consuming the tissue of other organisms.

home range   The area in which an animal generally travels and gathers its foods.

hormone inhibitors   A class of compounds that block the action of juvenile hormones. These compounds can be used as insecticides, because, if sprayed properly, they will disrupt the life cycles of specific insect larvae and kill them.

humus   The complex mixture of decayed organic matter that is an integral part of healthy soil.

hydroelectric power   Power derived from the energy of falling water.

hydrological cycle (water cycle)   The cycling of water, in all its forms, on the Earth.

hypolimnion   The lower levels of water in a lake or pond that remain at a constant temperature during the summer months.

imbibition   A process by which water is tightly bound to soil particles by chemical attractions.

industrial melanism   The shift in color from light to dark of moths inhabiting areas in which the surfaces of trees and other objects have been darkened by industrial pollution.

injunction   A legal order requiring a defendant to stop doing a wrongful act.

innate capacity for increase The maximum rate of growth of a population as determined by the reproductive capacity of the organism.

intertidal zone The region along the seacoast that lies between the high and low tide marks.

inversion A meteorological condition in which the lower layers of air are cooler than those at higher altitudes. This cool air remains relatively stagnant and causes a concentration of air pollutants and unhealthy conditions in congested urban regions.

ion An electrically charged atom or group of atoms.

isotopes Atoms of the same element that have different mass numbers.

joule A fundamental unit of energy. 4.184 joules = 1 calorie.

juvenile hormone A chemical naturally secreted by an insect while it is a larva. When the flow of juvenile hormone stops, the insect metamorphoses to become an adult. These compounds can be used as insecticides, because, if sprayed at critical times, they will interrupt the natural metamorphoses and eventually kill specific insect pests.

kinetic energy Energy of motion.

laterite A soil type found in certain humid tropical regions that contains a large proportion of aluminum and iron oxides and only a small concentration of organic matter. Laterite soils cannot support sustained agriculture.

lava The material produced when magma pours onto the surface of the Earth rapidly through fissures in the crust. A site where lava appears is called a volcano.

leachate The solution obtained by leaching.

leaching The extraction, usually by water, of the soluble components of a mass of material. In soil chemistry, leaching refers to the loss of surface nutrients by their percolation downward below the root zone.

legal standing The set of requirements that must be met before a plaintiff can pursue a case in court.

legume Any plant of the family *Leguminosae*, such as peas, beans, or alfalfa. Bacteria living on the roots of legumes change atmospheric nitrogen, N_2, to nitrogen-containing salts that can be readily assimilated by most plants.

less-developed countries Countries characterized by low levels of industrialization, poor health care, and low life expectancy.

limiting factors (law of) A biological law that states that the growth of an organism (or a population of organisms) is limited by the resource that is least available in the ecosystem.

litter The intact and partially decayed organic matter lying on top of the soil.

magma A fluid material lying in the upper layers of the Earth's mantle, consisting of melted rock mixed with various gases such as steam and hydrogen sulfide.

magnetohydrodynamic generator (MHD) A type of electrical generator that operates by passing ions through a magnetic field. MHD systems are more efficient than conventional mechanical generators because there are fewer moving parts and hence less frictional loss.

mantle The semiplastic portion of the Earth that surrounds the central core and lies under the crustal surface.

mass number The sum of the number of protons and neutrons in an atomic nucleus.

megalopolis   An agglomeration of several smaller cities and towns into a single, expanded, urban area.

meteorology   The science of the Earth's atmosphere.

metric system   See *Système International d'Unités.*

MHD generator   See *magnetohydrodynamic generator.*

mine spoil   The earth and rock removed from a mine and discarded because the mineral or fuel content is too low to warrant extraction.

mineral reserves   The estimated supply of ore in the ground.

mist   An airborne substance that consists of liquid droplets typically having diameters greater than about 1 μm.

moderator   A medium used in a nuclear reactor to slow down neutrons.

molecule   The fundamental particle that characterizes a compound. It consists of a group of atoms held together by chemical bonds.

mortality factors   Factors that lead to mortality of a population. *Density-dependent mortality factors* are those that kill a larger proportion of individuals as the population density increases. *Density-independent mortality factors* are those that kill a constant proportion of the population, regardless of its density.

mutagen   A substance that causes mutations.

mutation   An inheritable change in the genetic material of an individual.

mutualism   An interaction beneficial and necessary to both interacting species.

natural selection   A series of events occurring in natural ecosystems that eliminates some members of a population and spares those individuals endowed with certain characteristics that are favorable for reproduction.

negligence   In legal applications, an act that is performed carelessly or omitted when it should have been performed.

nekton   The collective name for larger aquatic animals that are powerful enough to swim independently of water currents. Fish and marine mammals are types of nekton.

neritic zone   The coastal waters in the ocean, below the low tide mark but shallow enough to support plants rooted to the seafloor.

neutron   A fundamental particle of the atom that is electrically neutral.

niche   See *ecological niche.*

nodules   Small pieces of rock, typically having a mass of about 1 kg, that are found on the floor of the ocean. These nodules are rich in manganese and also contain several other minerals such as copper, iron, aluminum, and cobalt.

noise   Unwanted sound.

nuclear reactor   A device that uses nuclear reactions to produce useful energy.

nuisance   In law, the substantial, unreasonable interference with the reasonable use and enjoyment of property.

nucleus   See *atomic nucleus.*

ocean thermal power   Electrical power generated from the temperature difference between the surface of the ocean and the cooler lower layers.

oligotrophic   Pertaining to a body of fresh water that contains few nutrients and few living organisms.

omnivore   An organism that eats both plant and animal tissue. Common omnivores include bears, pigs, rats, chickens, and humans.

open dump   A site where solid waste is deposited on a land surface with little or no treatment.

ore   A rock mixture that contains enough valuable minerals to be mined profitably with currently available technology.

organic farming   A set of farming practices that uses no synthetic fertilizers or chemicals.

organochlorides   A class of organic chemicals that contain chlorine bonded within the molecule. Some organochlorides, such as DDT, are effective pesticides. They are generally broad-spectrum and long-lived in the environment.

organophosphates   A class of organic compounds that contain phosphorus and oxygen bonded within the molecule. Some organophosphates used as pesticides are broad-spectrum and extremely poisonous, although they are not long-lasting in the environment.

osmosis   The process by which water passes through a membrane that is impermeable to dissolved matter. The water goes from the less concentrated to the more concentrated solution. See also *reverse osmosis.*

overpopulation   The presence in a given area of more people than can be supported adequately by the resources available in that area.

oxidant   An oxidizing agent. Oxidants in polluted air typically contain O–O chemical linkages.

oxidation   The addition of oxygen to a substance. More generally, oxidation is a loss of electrons.

ozone   Triatomic oxygen, O_3.

parasitism   A special case of predation in which the predator is much smaller than the victim and obtains its nourishment by consuming the tissue or food supply of a larger organism.

PCB   See *polychlorinated biphenyl.*

permafrost   A layer of permanent ice or frozen soil lying beneath the surface of the land in arctic or tundra biomes.

perpetual motion machine   A machine that will run forever and perform work without the use of an external energy supply. It is impossible to build such a machine.

pheromone   A substance secreted to the environment by one individual and received by a second individual of the same species. Reception triggers specific behavioral reactions such as alarm, sex attraction, and trailing. When pheromones are discharged artificially into the environment, they lead to inappropriate behavior in the organisms that respond to them.

photosynthesis   The process by which chlorophyll-bearing plants use energy from the Sun to convert carbon dioxide and water to sugars.

phytoplankton   Any microscopic, or nearly microscopic, free-floating autotrophic plants in a body of water. There are many different species that exist in a community of phytoplankton; these plants occur in large numbers and account for most of the primary production in the oceans.

plaintiff   A party that initiates a legal proceeding.

plankton   Any small, free-floating organisms living in a body of water. See also *phytoplankton* and *zooplankton.*

plasma   A gas at such a high temperature that the electrons have been stripped from their atoms, resulting in a mixture of nuclei surrounded by rapidly moving electrons.

pollution   The impairment of the quality of some portion of the environment by the addition of harmful impurities.

pollution tax   A tax on a polluter determined by the quantity of pollutants emitted. Also called residual charge.

polychlorinated biphenyls (PCB)   A class of organochloride chemicals structurally related to DDT. They were used widely in the plastics and electrical industries until they were found to be potent environmental poisons.

population The breeding group to which an organism belongs in practice. A population is generally very much smaller than an entire species, because all the members of a species are seldom in close proximity to each other.

population bloom See *bloom*.

population distribution The composition of a population categorized by several variables, often age and sex.

population ecology The branch of ecology dealing with the size, growth, and distribution of populations of organisms.

potential energy The energy possessed by an object that can be released sometime in the future. Gravitational potential is available when an object at some height has the potential to fall down to a lower level.

power The amount of energy delivered in a given time interval. Power = energy/time.

predation An interaction in which some individuals eat others.

predator An animal that attacks, kills, and eats other animals; more broadly, an organism that eats other organisms.

pressure Force per unit area.

primary consumer An animal that eats plants.

primary treatment (of sewage) The first stage of removal of impurities from water, generally by simple physical methods such as screening and settling.

productivity The rate at which energy is stored as organic matter by photosynthesis. *Gross primary productivity* is the total organic matter fixed during photosynthesis. *Net primary productivity* is the plant matter produced that is not used during the plant's own respiration. *Secondary productivity* is the rate of formation of new organic matter by heterotrophs.

proton A fundamental particle of the atom that bears a unit positive charge.

putrefaction The anaerobic decomposition of proteins.

rad A unit of radiation dosage, equivalent to the absorption of 100 ergs of energy per gram of biological tissue.

radiation Propagation of energy through space in the form of moving particles or electromagnetic energy. *Ionizing radiation* is radiation that is sufficiently energetic to strip electrons from atoms or molecules.

radioactivity The emission of radiation by atomic nuclei.

radioisotope A radioactive isotope.

rate of natural increase The difference between the crude birth and crude death rates. Also called the crude reproductive rate.

rate of population growth The increase in population over a given time period divided by the initial population.

recycling The process whereby waste materials are reused for the manufacture of new materials and goods.

reduction The removal of oxygen from a substance. More generally, reduction is a gain of electrons.

redundancy In the context of safety systems, the provision of a series of devices that duplicate each other's functions and that are programmed to go into operation in sequence if a preceding device in the series fails.

rendering The cooking of animal wastes such as fat, bones, feathers, and blood to yield tallow (used in the manufacture of soap) and high-protein animal feed.

replacement level The level of the total fertility rate, which, if continued unchanged for at least a generation, would result in an eventual population growth of zero.

reserve   The remaining amount of any resource that can be extracted at a reasonable cost.

resource   Any source of raw materials or means of producing raw materials.

respiration   The process by which plants and animals release energy by the stepwise oxidation of organic molecules.

reverse osmosis   The application of pressure to direct the flow of water through a membrane from the more concentrated to the less concentrated phase, which is the opposite of the normal osmotic flow.

saline seep   A process by which excess water leaches through the subsurface layers of soil, carrying dissolved salts. When this solution collects in a local depression in the land, the water may evaporate, and the accumulated salts destroy the fertility of the soil.

salinization   When irrigation water is applied to farmlands, much of it evaporates, leaving the salts behind. Salinization is the process whereby these minerals accumulate until the fertility of the soil is severely impaired.

saltwater intrusion   The movement of salt water from the ocean to terrestrial groundwater supplies that occurs when the water table in coastal areas is lowered.

sanitary landfill   A site where solid waste is deposited on a land surface, compacted, and covered with dirt to reduce odors and prevent disease and fire.

saprophyte   An organism that consumes the tissue of dead plants or animals.

savanna   A type of tropical or subtropical prairie that is subject to seasonal patterns of rainfall. Savannas are common in central Africa.

scrubber (in air pollution engineering)   A device that removes air pollutants by bubbling the polluted exhaust through a suitable solvent (usually water with or without added chemicals).

Second Law of Thermodynamics   See *thermodynamics*.

secondary consumer   A predator that eats an animal that eats plants.

secondary treatment (of sewage)   The removal of impurities from water by the digestive action of various small organisms in the presence of air or oxygen.

selective cutting   The process of cutting selected trees in a stand of timber. See also *clearcutting*.

SI   See *Système International d'Unités*.

sigmoid curve   A mathematical function that is roughly S-shaped, characterized by an initially slow rate of increase, followed by a rapid growth, and then by a second stage of slow, near zero rate of increase.

sludge   Wet residues removed from sewage. When the sludge is laden with microorganisms that promote rapid decomposition, it is said to be activated.

somaclonal variation   A technique used in genetic engineering whereby plant tissues are first treated so that they grow in an unorganized mass, which is then separated, and the separate components are recultured to differentiate once again. The entire process creates new and often valuable strains.

somatic cells   All the cells in the body that are not involved in reproduction.

smog   Smoky fog. The word is used loosely to describe visible air pollution.

smog precursor   An air pollutant that can undergo chemical reaction in the presence of sunlight to produce smog.

smoke   An aerosol that is usually produced by combustion or decomposition processes.

soil-moisture belt The layer of soil from which water can be drawn to the surface by capillary action.

solar cell A semiconductor device that converts sunlight directly into electrical energy.

solar collector A device designed to concentrate solar energy for a useful purpose.

solar design *Active systems*—Heating systems that use a controlled flow of some substance, usually air or water, to collect, store, and transmit heat from the Sun. *Passive systems*—Construction systems that use the structure of a building itself to collect, store, and transmit heat from the Sun.

solar energy Energy derived from the Sun.

speciation The process by which new species are formed. *Branched speciation*—The process by which a single species branches to form two or more new species. *Gradualism*—The process by which a species changes gradually over time. *Punctuated equilibria*—The theory that evolution occurs in a series of rapid steps broken by long periods of little or no change.

species A group of organisms that interbreed with other members of the group, but not with individuals outside the group.

strip mining A mining operation that operates by removing long strips of the surface layers of soil and rock, thereby exposing the deposits of ore to be removed.

subsidence The settling of the surface of the ground as deep groundwater is removed.

subsidies Economic incentives, sometimes used to persuade polluters not to despoil the environment.

succession The sequence of changes through which an ecosystem passes during the course of time. *Primary succession* is a sequence that occurs when the terrain is initially lifeless, or almost so. *Secondary succession* is the series of community changes that takes place in disturbed areas that have not been totally stripped of their soil and vegetation.

survivorship curve A function showing the patterns of mortality for a birth cohort of a given species.

synergism A condition in which a whole effect is greater than the sum of its parts.

synfuels An abbreviation for synthetic fuels, liquid fuels produced from oil shales, tar sands, or coal.

synthetic chemicals Compounds produced by chemical reactions carried on in a laboratory or factory as opposed to compounds formed naturally.

Système International d'Unités (SI) Commonly called the metric system. A system of measurement used in all scientific circles and by lay people in most nations of the world. The standard units in the SI are: meter (length); kilogram (mass); second (time); ampere (electric current); kelvin or degree Celsius (temperature); candela (luminous intensity); and mole (amount of substance).

taiga The northern forest of coniferous trees that lies just south of the arctic tundra.

tailings Residues from a mining operation. Tailings often contain heavy metals or other environmental contaminants.

technological fix An approach to solving an environmental problem by technical or engineering methods.

temperate forest A biome that occurs in temperate regions with abundant rainfall.

tertiary, or "advanced," treatment (of sewage) Any of a variety of special methods of water purification, such as adsorption or reverse osmosis, which are more effective than simple physical or biological processes for special pollutants.

thermal pollution A change in the quality of an environment (usually an aquatic environment) caused by raising its temperature.

thermocline Middle waters of a lake, where temperature and oxygen content fall off rapidly with depth.

thermodynamics The science concerned with heat and work and the relationships between them. *First Law of Thermodynamics*—Energy cannot be created or destroyed. *Second Law of Thermodynamics*—It is impossible to derive mechanical work from any portion of matter by cooling it below the temperature of the coldest surrounding object.

thermonuclear reaction A nuclear reaction, specifically fusion, initiated by a very high temperature.

threshold level The minimal dose of a toxic substance that causes harmful effects.

tidal energy Energy derived from the movement of the tides.

tort A noncriminal action that results in personal injury or damage to property.

total dependency ratio The ratio of the elderly plus the young to the total number of working-age people.

total fertility rate (TFR) The total number of infants a woman can be expected to bear during the course of her life if birthrates remain constant for at least one generation.

toxic substance Any substance whose physiological action is harmful to health.

transpiration The passage of water through the tissues of plants, especially through leaf surfaces. *Evapotranspiration* is the conversion of liquid water to water vapor by transpiration followed by evaporation from the leaf surface.

trespass An illegal intrusion or invasion of other people's property.

trophic level Level of nourishment. A plant that obtains its energy directly from the Sun occupies the *first trophic level* and is called an *autotroph*. An organism that consumes the tissue of an autotroph occupies the *second trophic level*, and an organism that eats the organism that had eaten autotrophs occupies the *third trophic level*.

tropical rainforest A biome that exists when high, fairly constant rainfall and temperature permit plants to grow rapidly throughout the year.

tumor An abnormal growth of unregulated cells.

tundra Arctic or mountainous areas that are too cold to support trees and that are characterized by low mosses and grasses.

turbine A mechanical device consisting of fanlike blades mounted on a shaft. When water, steam, or air rushes past the blades, the shaft turns, and, thus, mechanical energy can be used to generate electricity.

upwelling An ocean current that moves vertically upward, bringing nutrients to the surface and producing highly productive deep-water ocean systems.

urban sprawl The growth of suburban areas and the expansion of cities to preempt increasingly large areas of land.

urbanization A demographic process characterized by movement of people from rural to urban settlements.

vital event In demography, a birth, a death, a marriage, a termination of marriage, or a migration.

vital rate   The number of vital events occurring in a population during a specified period of time divided by the size of the population.

water cycle   See *hydrological cycle.*

water pollution   The deterioration of the quality of water that results from the addition of impurities.

water table   The upper level of water in the zone of saturated subsurface soil and rock.

work   The transfer of energy that results when a force is exerted over a distance.

zero population growth   A condition in which the birth and death rates in a population are equal. Therefore, the size of the population remains constant.

zooplankton   Microscopic or nearly microscopic free-floating aquatic animals that feed on other forms of plankton. Some zooplankton are larvae of larger animals, whereas others remain as zooplankton during their entire life cycle.

INDEX

Note: page numbers in *italic* type refer to illustrations; page numbers followed by t refer to tables; page numbers followed by bx refer to Boxes; page numbers followed by spt refer to Special Topics.

The world's population is most densely concentrated in three main parts — Europe, southern Asia, and eastern Asia. There are also smaller pockets of high density in the United States and Japan. But the wide-open spaces of Africa and Latin America conceal the population growth now taking place in both those continents. The pattern of settlement also shows the human preference for coastal areas. Two-thirds of the world's people live within 500 km (310 miles) of the sea. (Courtesy of Rand McNally & Company, Chicago)